THE LAW OF
Social Security

Fifth edition

N J Wikeley MA
of Gray's Inn, Barrister;
John Wilson Chair in Law, University of Southampton
Deputy Social Security Commissioner
Deputy District Chairman, Appeals Service

Consultant Editor

A I Ogus CBE BCL MA
Professor of Law, University of Manchester
Research Professor, University of Maastricht
Member, Social Security Advisory Committee

Butterworths
LexisNexis™

Members of the LexisNexis Group worldwide

United Kingdom	Butterworths Tolley, a Division of Reed Elsevier (UK) Ltd, Halsbury House, 35 Chancery Lane, LONDON, WC2A 1EL, and 4 Hill Street, EDINBURGH EH2 3JZ
Argentina	Abeledo Perrot, Jurisprudencia Argentina and Depalma, BUENOS AIRES
Australia	Butterworths, a Division of Reed International Books Australia Pty Ltd, CHATSWOOD, New South Wales
Austria	ARD Betriebsdienst and Verlag Orac, VIENNA
Canada	Butterworths Canada Ltd, MARKHAM, Ontario
Chile	Publitecsa and Conosur Ltda, SANTIAGO DE CHILE
Czech Republic	Orac sro, PRAGUE
France	Editions du Juris-Classeur SA, PARIS
Hong Kong	Butterworths Asia (Hong Kong), HONG KONG
Hungary	Hvg Orac, BUDAPEST
India	Butterworths India, NEW DELHI
Ireland	Butterworths (Ireland) Ltd, DUBLIN
Italy	Giuffré, MILAN
Malaysia	Malayan Law Journal Sdn Bhd, KUALA LUMPUR
New Zealand	NexisLexis Butterworths, WELLINGTON
Poland	Wydawnictwa Prawnicze PWN, WARSAW
Singapore	Butterworths Asia, SINGAPORE
South Africa	Butterworths Publishers (Pty) Ltd, DURBAN
Switzerland	Stämpfli Verlag AG, BERNE
USA	LexisNexis, DAYTON, Ohio

© Reed Elsevier (UK) Ltd 2002

A CIP Catalogue record for this book is available from the British Library.

ISBN 0 406 98585 5

Typeset by Doyle & Co, Colchester
Printed and bound in Great Britain by The Cromwell Press, Trowbridge, Wilts

Visit Butterworths LexisNexis *direct* at www.butterworths.com

Preface to the fifth edition

Seven years between editions of legal textbooks is a lengthy period at the best of times. In the fast-moving world of social security law, it is an eternity. So I will start with an apology to those who have been waiting patiently for the fifth edition of this book, not least the editorial staff at Butterworths, but I will not bore the reader with the various (entirely legitimate) excuses. It may be more helpful to highlight the main changes in this edition.

The face of social security has changed dramatically since the first edition of this work was published in 1978, including radical changes since the last edition appeared in 1995. I have therefore taken the opportunity to restructure the book in addition to the inevitable rewriting and revisions occasioned by the many significant developments in both the legislation and case law relating to social security. Previous editions have been based on the Beveridge model of social protection, dealing at the outset with National Insurance contributions, unemployment and other contributory benefits. Later chapters considered the various non-contributory benefits and finally means-tested benefits, administration and adjudication and international issues. The new edition takes a different approach. It is divided into four Parts.

The first Part brings together various overarching issues in social security law. The major innovation here is the new chapter on human rights and social security law, which examines European (both EU and ECHR) and international norms in social security before focusing on the impact of the Human Rights Act 1998. Part I also includes chapters which analyse European Union social security law on migrant workers as well as the administration of the benefits and tax credits systems and decision making and appeals. There has been considerable change in the latter areas as a result of the Social Security Act 1998 and subsequent legislation which has transferred many of the functions of the former Department of Social Security (now the Department for Work and Pensions) to the Inland Revenue. The treatment of National Insurance contributions and the general provisions relating to various social security benefits also belongs here.

Part II examines the various means-tested benefits and tax credits. This includes a new and extensive treatment of income-based jobseeker's allowance. The discussion of tax credits requires a few words by way of explanation. This book seeks to reflect the law as it stands on 1 June 2002, and so concentrates on working families' tax credit and disabled person's tax credit. These benefits will be superseded in April 2003 by the new generation of tax credits (the working tax credit and the child tax credit), which will also have important implications for other means-tested benefits, especially from April 2004. At the time of writing, however, the final form of what will undoubtedly become the Tax Credits Act 2002 had not been finalised, let alone the subsidiary regulations. The only viable approach has been to explain the current state of the law, whilst highlighting the broad thrust of the changes to come.

Part III analyses the contributory benefits, starting in chapter 14 with contribution-based jobseeker's allowance (JSA). The Jobseekers Act 1995, which replaced unemployment benefit with contribution-based JSA and created income-based JSA as the main means of support for unemployed people, posed a major challenge for writers on social security law (evidenced by CPAG's uncertainty over the years as to quite how to handle the benefit in its annual handbooks). In legal terms it is clear that JSA is a single benefit, albeit one of two (very uneven) halves. From the point of view of the overall structure of this book, on the other hand, it made more sense to divide the treatment of JSA between Parts II and III in the manner indicated above. Whether the sixth edition of this book will feature a chapter on contribution-based JSA at all is a moot point. Chapter 15 is another new chapter, dealing with incapacity benefit, which was only dealt with in outline in the last edition. The opportunity has thus been taken to sub-divide the old chapter 4 from the previous edition, dealing with sickness and disability benefits; the non-contributory benefits now appear in Part IV. There have also been substantial changes to the chapters on benefits for birth and death and retirement pensions respectively as a consequence of a steady stream of new legislation since 1995 (principally the Pensions Act 1995, the Welfare Reform and Pensions Act 1999 and the Child Support, Pensions and Social Security Act 2000). The pensions chapter includes an outline of the new system of pension credits under the State Pension Credit Act 2002, due to be implemented in October 2003.

Lastly, Part IV discusses non-contributory benefits (child benefit, disability benefits, industrial injuries benefits and war pensions). There is a nice question as to whether war pensions should remain in this book, as their administration has now been transferred to the Ministry of Defence, but on balance the arguments for their inclusion remain sound.

There are a number of further points which should be made about the new edition. As explained above, the intention has been to state the law as it stands on 1 June 2002. I have sought, however, to highlight (and in some cases even to anticipate the implementation of) a number of future developments. The overviews of the new systems of pension and tax credits have already been mentioned. Other examples include the changes to the national insurance scheme announced in the 2002 Budget, the renaming of invalid care allowance as carer's allowance and reforms contained in the Employment Act 2002. I should also add that this edition, for better or worse, is 'all my own work', whereas the last edition was written by a team of contributors. This is no reflection on their impressive work last time around. Rightly or wrongly, I took the view at the outset of planning this edition that the degree of restructuring involved made it essential for one individual to be responsible for the entire work. However, Anthony Ogus has taken on the chore of reading every chapter in draft and has provided invaluable advice at all stages of this project. The responsibility for any errors, naturally, remains firmly with me. As I hold part-time judicial office as a Deputy Social Security Commissioner and also as an appeal tribunal chairman, I should make it clear that the opinions expressed in this book are personal and should not be associated with either the Office of the Social Security Commissioners or the Appeals Service. I hope, however, that this judicial experience has informed the process of writing this book.

I have, inevitably, a number of further acknowledgements to make. First and foremost I must express my gratitude to Mr Chisholm and his team in the Eye Unit at Southampton General Hospital. A trauma-induced cataract of uncertain aetiology, thus defeating my hope of lodging a claim for industrial disablement benefit in respect of a building site accident 25 years ago, meant that I had no effective vision in my left eye for the greater part of 2001. The expertise of Mr Chisholm and his colleagues rectified that after two complex operations and reflect the finest traditions of the NHS. I should also like to thank Professor Terry Carney for facilitating my prolonged stay at the University of Sydney in 2000, which gave me the space and time to kick-start the process of writing this edition. Over the last few years I have also benefited immensely from discussions on the finer (and also some of the less appealing) aspects of social security law with, amongst others, David Bonner, Godfrey Cole, John Eames, Neville Harris, John Mesher, Richard Poynter and Penny Wood. Ed Bates, Takis Tridimas and David Williams were each kind enough to comment on an individual section or chapter in draft. Phil Larkin and Emma Laurie provided invaluable research assistance at various stages. Joy Caisley, Wendy White and Dick Young of the Hartley Library at the University of Southampton always had the answer to my obscure questions. The Law Faculty at Southampton has provided an invigorating and congenial research environment whilst Aloma Hack and Alison Lampard have rescued me from a series of self-induced computing calamities. The editorial staff at Butterworths, along with their associated production team, have turned the manuscript around efficiently and speedily.

Finally, a number of colleagues have said that writing this book must be like painting the Forth Rail Bridge. As soon as one finishes, one has to start again at the other end. It is actually worse than that. Writing *The Law of Social Security* is like painting the Forth Rail Bridge whilst the bridge is simultaneously being dismantled and rebuilt around you. I hope, nonetheless, that the existing structure will serve for a while yet.

N.J.W.
Southampton
June 2002

Foreword to the first edition

by the Rt. Hon. Lord Scarman, OBE, Lord of Appeal in Ordinary

Social security is now the subject of rights and duties. Inevitably, therefore, it is a legal subject. Anthony Ogus and Eric Barendt by this work have committed themselves, without compromise or condition, to this basic proposition: and I commend their work to all who understand the need of a legal approach to a legal subject. But they do not — nor I for that matter —under-rate the value of the contributions other disciplines make to the development of a coherent and well-grounded national system of social security; and, of course, no lawyer can understand, or help forward, the law unless he is capable of an inter-disciplinary approach.

I expect this book to become one of the indispensable textbooks of the law. Certainly an authoritative, and independent, work is needed. At present, tribunals and practitioners have to rely heavily on the material produced, but not invariably published, by the Department of Health and Social Security. The department does a fine job: but it is not, and never has been, the office of a government department to declare or interpret the law. If law is to be administered justly, the independence, as well as the skills, of the lawyer must be mobilised. Ogus and Barendt will become, I hope, a name as familiar to the lawyer as Chitty, Salmond, Buckley, and Simon.

Finally, this work gives us an opportunity of measuring the extent to which our social security law satisfies the obligations accepted by the United Kingdom as a signatory of the European Social Charter 1961 and the International Covenant on Economic, Social, and Cultural Rights 1966. If any doubt should continue to be entertained that social security has to be part and parcel of English law, our international obligations are the answer.

I commend this book to lawyers primarily — but also to members of the other disciplines concerned with the behaviour of man in society; to politicians; and to all who are concerned to ensure that humanity and compassion are secured by law as well as by generosity.

Scarman

Extract from preface to the first edition

The growth of interest in social security law, both of teachers and practitioners, has been rapid in the last few years. The process has not been free from controversy: opinions differ both as to the academic merit of the subject and to the preferred method of presentation. Some contend that the social security system has not sufficient intellectual weight for the serious student of law; others view the educational objective more in terms of fostering the arithmetic ability to calculate the entitlement of a given individual to benefit rather than of providing any analysis of the principles of the system as a whole. A third approach stresses the desirability of covering, within one university course, broad and diverse areas of the welfare system including not only social security but also housing, education and legal services. We do not adopt these perspectives. The book has been written from a conviction that social security should take its place alongside other, more traditional, legal subjects as fully worthy of critical study, and its unity and technical character make it, in our view, more suitable for this purpose than the necessary vague outlines of 'welfare' or 'poverty' law.

Legal education has tended in the past to concentrate on law as a method of determining relationships between individuals. While public law — the relationship between the state and the individual — has not been neglected, attention has been focussed for the most part on the formal or constitutional nature of the relationship rather than its substance. The emphasis has been on the individual's ability to invoke judical controls over unlawful executive activity rather than on the content of the rights conferred on the individual by the state within the proper exercise of its powers. While social security law raises problems of the constitutional limits of executive powers, it also lays down in considerable detail rules which materially affect the lives of all members of the community. As a body of law, it consists of a complex network of primary and subordinate legislation and case law (notably Commissioners' decisions, though in some areas judicial rulings are not unimportant), the scrutiny of which provides an excellent training in the handling of a variety of legal instruments. As a reflection of competing social and economic policies, it reveals the way in which a very important branch of state activity has evolved, and how general objectives and strategies are translated into particular principles and rules of law.

In contrast to their counterparts in most other countries, the British universities have accepted 'social administration' as an intellectual discipline in its own right, though necessarily it has relied on other disciplines such as economics, history and sociology for its tools of analysis. Social security, in the context of general social policy, has featured prominently in its publications. This work does not attempt to compete with such studies. Quite apart from the limits to our own competence, we have not the space here both to expound a complex area of law and to subject the policies on which it is based to rigorous interdisciplinary analysis. At the same time, we have sought to explain the law in terms of its policy background and the insights offered by other disciplines, as we believe that the functioning of a social security system cannot be understood without reference to the objectives and values which it incorporates.

This goal has, with other factors, created the problem of preserving a satisfactory balance between historical and policy background, general principle and technical rules. In writing this book we have had in mind not only law students but also practitioners and other professional groups with an interest in this area. To accomplish these various objectives, we have adopted a compromise solution. We have inset not only, as is customary in legal texts, quotations and case summaries, but also technical rules which do not raise issues of legal principle.

A.I.O.
E.M.B.

Oxford
April 1978

Contents

Chapter 1

Social security and social policy   1

Chapter 2

International social security, equal treatment and human rights   37

Chapter 3

EU social security law   62

Chapter 4

Contributions   89

Chapter 5

Administration of benefits   130

Chapter 6

Decision making and appeals   177

Chapter 7

General provisions 214

Chapter 8

Income support   269

Chapter 9

Income-based jobseeker's allowance   336

Chapter 10

Working families' tax credit and disabled person's tax credit   382

Chapter 11

Housing benefit and council tax benefit   405

Chapter 12

Common provisions for means-tested benefits and tax credits   442

Chapter 13

The social fund   465

Chapter 14

Contribution-based jobseeker's allowance   495

Chapter 15

Statutory sick pay and incapacity benefit 518

Chapter 16

Benefits for birth and death 556

Chapter 17

Retirement pensions   587

Chapter 18

Child benefit   652

Chapter 19

Benefits for severely disabled people and carers   675

Chapter 20

Industrial injury   713

Chapter 21

War pensions   767

Chronological table of statutes

References in this Table to *Statutes* are to Halsbury's Statutes of England (Fourth Edition) showing the volume and page at which the annotated text of an Act will be found.

Chronological table of statutory instruments

PAGE

Table of EC legislation

Table of international legislation

lxxxiii

List of United Kingdom cases

List of other cases

Alphabetical table of EC cases

J

K

L

M

N

O

P

R

S

T

U

V

W

Z

Numerical table of EC cases

PAGE

PAGE

PAGE

List of ECHR decisions

Note on citation of Social Security Commissioner decisions

Reported decisions of the Social Security (formerly National Insurance) Commissioners provide a most important source of social security law. To preserve the confidentiality of claimants, a special citation system is used. Before 1951 a reported case was referred to simply by its number and series initial, with the addition of the suffix 'K' or 'KL'. For both unpublished decisions, and reported decisions until the end of 1950, the letter 'S' or 'W' was added after the 'C' to denote a Scottish or Welsh case. Thus *CSU 14/48 (KL)* refers to the fourteenth Scottish case on unemployment benefit in 1948 – and a reported case.

The method for citing Commissioners' decisions altered in 1951. Since then the standard prefix 'R' has been used to indicate that the case is reported. There then follows in parenthesis the series initial, denoting the particular social security benefit involved in the case. Including those that are now discontinued, there are 19 series:

(A)   Attendance allowance
(CR) Compensation recovery
(CS) Child support
(DLA) Disability living allowance
(DWA) Disability working allowance
(F)   Child benefit, and formerly family allowances
(FC) Family credit
(FIS) Family income supplement
(G)   General – miscellaneous benefits (maternity allowance and statutory maternity pay, guardian's allowance, bereavement benefits and carer's allowance, and formerly child's special allowance and the maternity and death grants)
(I)   Industrial injuries benefits
(IB) Incapacity Benefit
(IS) Income support
(JSA) Jobseeker's allowance
(M)   Mobility allowance
(P)   Retirement pensions
(S)   Sickness and invalidity benefits, and severe disablement allowance
(SB) Supplementary benefit
(SSP) Statutory sick pay
(U)   Unemployment benefit

After the series initial, the number and (after an oblique stroke) the year of the case follow. For example, *R(P) 9/55* refers to the ninth reported retirement pensions case in 1955, and *R(I) 12/75* refers to the twelfth reported decision on industrial injuries benefits in 1975. The heading of reported decisions indicates if they are decisions of a Tribunal of three Commissioners (see p 201); in this book such decisions are indicated by the initial 'T' in parenthesis after the number and year of the case: for example, *R(U) 4/88 (T)*. The decisions are published individually by HMSO, and used to be bound every few years. (Until 1976 industrial injuries cases were bound in separate volumes.)

The system of reporting Commissioners' decisions became notoriously slow in the 1990s, attracting criticism from the House of Commons Social Security Committee (see p 204). This galvanised the relevant authorities into action. Reported decisions from 1991 to the present day are now available in looseleaf format and also on the website of the Department for Work and Pensions at the following URL:

http://www.dwp.gov.uk/advisers/index.htm#commdecs

In addition, the Office of the Social Security Commissioners has established its own website. As well as reported decisions, this site includes other significant decisions (some of which may in due course be reported) and a search facility:

http://www.osscsc.gov.uk/

Unreported decisions may be obtained for a small fee from the Commissioners' offices. A few of these decisions are discussed in this book. They are identified by reference to two letters ('C' standing for Commissioner, and the relevant series letter), followed by the appropriate number and year. Thus, *CG 17/69* refers to the seventeenth numbered case in 1969 concerning one of the miscellaneous benefits, eg guardian's allowance or widow's benefit. Scottish (but not Welsh) cases are still reflected in the heading for unreported decisions by the insertion of a 'S' after the initial 'C': thus *CSCS 05/02* would be the fifth numbered case in 2002 from Scotland on child support.

Some reference is made in this book to decisions of the Northern Ireland Commissioners. Their decisions are cited in much the same way as British cases, though the number and year precede the series initial. These initials also differ in certain respects from those used in Britain; eg (ICA) is used for invalid care allowance and (UB) was used for unemployment benefit. Thus, *R 10/60 (UB)* refers to the tenth reported Northern Ireland decision during 1960 on unemployment benefit. Before 1960 the letter 'R' was omitted.

Table of decisions

Decisions of the Social Security Commissioner

Decisions of the Northern Ireland Commissioner

Table of Social Fund Directions

Chapter 1

Social security and social policy

Part 1 Introduction

Social security is a massive public enterprise. In 2002–03 the planned budget was £115 billion, 28 per cent of all public expenditure and equivalent to the National Health Service and education budgets together.[1] There are very few individuals who do not, at some stage of their lives, exercise their legal right to benefit of some kind, and the vast majority also pay social security contributions. At any one time, approximately three-quarters of the households in Great Britain derive some of their income from the system.[2] As will be seen, it is governed by a mass of complex statutory principles and regulations, the application of which generates a considerable number of disputes. In 2000, over 260,000 appeals by claimants were registered with appeal tribunals.[3]

To gain a proper understanding of the system as a whole, it is necessary first to address the many theoretical issues to which social security gives rise. After a brief account of its evolution in Britain (Part 2), we then explore possible objectives for the system in the light of social, political and economic values (Part 3). In the final part of the chapter, we consider the different strategies available to meet these objectives.

Part 2 Evolution of social security in Britain[4]

A The family and the poor law

In the period of emergent industrialism and capitalism, welfare was to be achieved through personal effort complemented by family interdependence. There was thought

---

1 H M Treasury *Budget 2002* (2001–02, HC 592) para 1.45. As a result of National Insurance changes coming into force in 2003, expenditure on the NHS is due to increase significantly, rising to £105 billion in 2007–08.
2 Bradshaw in Bean, Ferris and Whynes (eds) *In Defence of Welfare* (1985) p 228.
3 Department for Work and Pensions (DWP) *Work and Pension Statistics 2001* (2001) p 219.
4 See generally Gilbert *The Evolution of National Insurance in Great Britain* (1966); Gilbert *British Social Policy 1914–1939* (1970); Bruce *The Rise of the Welfare State* (1973); Fraser *The Evolution of the British Welfare State* (2nd edn, 1984); Vincent *Poor Citizens* (1991); Hills, Ditch and Glennerster (eds) *Beveridge and Social Security 50 Years On* (1994); Lowe *The Welfare State in Britain since 1945* (2nd edn, 1999); McKay and Rowlingson *Social Security in Britain* (1999); Timmins *The Five Giants: A Biography of the Welfare State* (rev edn, 2001).

to be work available for anyone who wanted it, and destitution was therefore seen as resulting not from social or economic forces but rather from personal failings, a view bolstered by the Puritan work ethic.[5] Moreover, poverty constituted not only a deviation from moral discipline, but also a threat to civil order, as it was typically associated with crime and political unrest.[6] In this context relief of the poor was necessarily repressive and punitive: a generous system of welfare would have encouraged more idleness and therefore more social chaos. The poor law perfectly reflected this ideology: relief was granted to able-bodied persons only if they were willing to subject themselves to the rigours of the workhouse, where life was intentionally made harsh and repellent.[7] The guiding principle was the so-called doctrine of 'less eligibility'.[8] In the words of the Poor Law Commissioners:

> the first and most essential of all conditions is that the situation of the individual relieved shall not be made really or apparently so eligible as the situation of the independent labourer of the lowest class.[9]

Some mitigation of the doctrine was granted only where it was patent that the individual's plight arose from accident rather than from personal inaptitude, eg for the blind, the crippled and the aged.[10]

B   Voluntary devices for dealing with poverty

Victorian society reaffirmed faith in self-help and personal thrift: protection against the hazards of illness, old age and death was to be achieved through voluntary saving, for which purpose friendly societies, trade unions and insurance companies provided the institutional arrangements.[11] At the same time, humanitarian ideals gave rise to a huge philanthropic movement.[12] But the poor law remained as the only state interventionist measure concerned with poverty as such; legislative responses to hardships created by industrialisation concentrated on improvements to health and environmental conditions.[13]

C   National Insurance and means-tested assistance

The 1911 legislation which established National Insurance in Britain was the culmination of complex social and political developments.[14] The condition of the poor had been

---

5   Tawney *Religion and the Rise of Capitalism* (1921) pp 218–249.
6   *Fraser* n 4, above, pp 31–34.
7   The classic study is Webb and Webb *History of English Local Government* (1972) vol 7. See also Rose *The English Poor Law 1780–1930* (1971); and Marshall *The Old Poor Law 1795–1834* (1985).
8   *Webb and Webb* n 7, above, pp 215–264.
9   Report of Royal Commission on Poor Law (1834) para 228.
10   The so-called system of 'out-relief': see *Bruce* n 4, above, pp 117–128.
11   Gosden *Self-Help: Voluntary Associations in 19th Century Britain* (1973). See generally Gladstone (ed) *Before Beveridge: Welfare Before the Welfare State* (1999).
12   Harrison (1965) 9 Victorian Studies 360.
13   Gauldie *Cruel Habitations: A History of Working-Class Housing* (1974) chs 21–25; Burnett *A Social History of Housing 1815–1985* (2nd edn, 1986) chs 2, 3 and 6.
14   Briggs (1961) II Archiv Eur Sociol 221; Hay *The Origins of the Liberal Welfare Reforms 1906–1914* (1983); Ogus in Köhler and Zacher (eds) *A Century of Social Insurance* (1982) pp 156–187; Hennock *British Social Reform and German Precedents* (1987); Gilbert *David Lloyd George* (1987) ch 7.

investigated by the new social sciences[15] which had challenged the traditional assumption that poverty resulted from moral failings. In particular, most forms of unemployment were seen to have economic causes,[16] a finding of the utmost importance to the movement for unemployment insurance which the market could not provide on a general basis. Protection against the consequences of sickness was more widespread but, outside the poor law, medical care was 'organised' on a haphazard basis, particularly in poorer neighbourhoods where much depended on charitable efforts. In all only one-half of the working population were insured (usually with friendly societies) against earnings loss.[17] The most important measure directly concerned with income was the introduction in 1908 of a means-tested pension for those aged over 70. While the conditions of entitlement were somewhat narrowly drawn and included a test of character – 'it was a pension for the very poor, the very respectable and the very old'[18] – nevertheless it constituted the first system of financial aid for a social hazard funded from general resources, administered centrally and independent of the poor law.

Means-tested welfare was not, however, to be the general solution. Lloyd George, who visited Germany to study its system of social insurance,[19] became convinced that this was the best method of making 'provisions against the accidents of life which bring so much undeserved poverty to hundreds of thousands of homes, accidents which are quite inevitable such as the death of a breadwinner or his premature breakdown in health'.[20] Insurance was an attractive solution since it would engender the traditional virtue of individual responsibility and investment of personal resources, and would not be far removed from the typical market economy device of the 'exchange' transaction.[21] The notion that such risks were something which the community as a whole should bear received partial recognition by the sharing of insurance costs between the employer (who would pass it on in the form of increased prices) and the employee; but in order that individual initiative should not be stifled and to discourage idleness, benefit would be paid at only a survival level. This was the scheme adopted for unemployment and sickness under the National Insurance Act 1911. It was also applied by analogy in 1925 to those risks against which individuals might be expected to provide – old age or premature death – but which, in the case of low-earners, typically went unprotected.

There was left a hard core of poverty cases outside these two categories, either because the individual's contribution record was inadequate, or because the duration of the interruption of employment was excessive. The cases might be undeserving and in 1909 the Majority of the Royal Commission on the Poor Law could still argue that it was necessary to treat them as a distinct group of society whose predicament was, in some way, attributable to defects in moral character.[22] But humanitarian sentiments prevailed; eg a means-tested financial benefit had already been introduced in 1908 to protect the aged from the poor law. A similar device, in the form of unemployment assistance, was adopted for the vast numbers of unemployed who during the inter-war period had exhausted their right to insurance benefit.

15 Rowntree *Poverty: A Study of Town Life* (1901); Booth *Life and Labour of the People in London* (1902); O'Day and Englander *Mr Charles Booth's Inquiry* (1993).
16 Beveridge *Unemployment, A Problem of Industry* (1909).
17 *Bruce*, n 4, above, p 214.
18 Thane *Foundations of the Welfare State* (2nd edn, 1996) p 77.
19 *Hennock* n 14, above, pp 149–150.
20 Quoted in *Fraser* n 4, above, p 161.
21 Pinker *Social Theory and Social Policy* (1971) pp 135–144.
22 (1909, Cd 4499) p 643.

D   Beveridge and comprehensive social security

By the end of the 1930s a clear pattern of state provision had been established – social insurance covering the major causes of income loss and conferring benefit at a flat-rate survival level, combined with a scheme of residual means-tested assistance for those remaining. This approach was in essence left unaltered by the programme instituted in 1946-47 and inspired by the Beveridge Report.[23] His primary aims were to make the insurance scheme universal and more comprehensive, to substitute 'subsistence' for 'survival' as the minimum level and to unify its administration. The significance of the Report for the history of British social security lay not so much in these specific aims but rather in the comprehensive review which he undertook of social risks and the methods of meeting them. The primacy of social insurance was reaffirmed: 'benefit in return for contributions, rather than free allowances from the State, is what the people of Britain desire',[24] but it was not to undermine individual responsibility and freedom:

> Social security must be achieved by cooperation between the State and the individual. ...
> The State in organising security should not stifle incentive, opportunity, responsibility; in
> establishing a national minimum, it should leave room and encouragement for voluntary
> action by each individual to provide more than that minimum for himself and his family.[25]

Hence the British approach, flat-rate benefits for flat-rate contributions, was to remain distinct from the traditional continental model of earnings-related social insurance.[26]

Equally important, though sometimes overlooked, is the fact that Beveridge was confident that the comprehensive system of National Insurance and means-tested assistance would ensure 'freedom from want' only if it was combined with three policies external to the system: full employment, family endowment and a national health service.[27] The government adopted the necessary policies: a commitment to 'the maintenance of a high and stable level of employment';[28] the introduction of family allowances; and the replacement of medical benefits under national health insurance by the National Health Service (NHS).

E   Modifications to the Beveridge model

Government complacency engendered by the popularity of the post-war welfare measures was not to last.[29] Empirical studies undertaken by the newly developed discipline of 'social administration', under the inspired leadership of Richard Titmuss,[30]

---

23   Beveridge Report *Social Insurance and Allied Services* (1942, Cmd 6404). See further *Hills, Ditch and Glennerster* (eds) n 4, above.
24   *Beveridge Report* n 23, above, para 21.
25   *Beveridge Report* n 23, above, para 9.
26   Ogus in Zacher (ed) *Bedingungen für die Entstehung und Entwicklung von Sozialversicherung* (1979) pp 337–348. For further comparative studies see Baldwin *The Politics of Social Solidarity* (1990); Esping-Andersen *The Three Worlds of Welfare Capitalism* (1990); and Goodin, Headey, Muffels and Dirven *The Real Worlds of Welfare Capitalism* (1999).
27   *Beveridge Report* n 23, above, para 301.
28   White Paper *Employment Policy* (1944, Cmd 6527) para 3.
29   See generally Hill *Social Security Policy in Britain* (1990); and Lowe *The Welfare State in Britain since 1945* (2nd edn, 1999) ch 6.
30   Reisman *Richard Titmuss: Welfare and Society* (1977).

claimed to have 'rediscovered poverty',[31] especially among the aged.[32] National Insurance benefits did not provide the level of minimum subsistence which had been promised. The principle of flat-rate contributions meant that the latter had to be set at a level which the lowest paid could afford and the government felt that more subsidy from the Exchequer would undermine the insurance basis of the scheme. Beveridge's assumption that individuals would boost National Insurance benefits with private and occupational schemes proved to be well-founded only for the more affluent workers. Provision under superannuation schemes meant that they could look forward to a relatively small drop in living standards when no longer in active employment, whereas the typical manual worker, without such protection, had to fall back on a combination of the flat-rate but inadequate National Insurance pension and means-tested national assistance.

In the 1960s and early 1970s attention was focused on two other disadvantaged groups. Family poverty resulted, in part, from a failure of successive governments to maintain the value of family allowance and, in part, from the rapid growth in the number of lone-parent families,[33] a phenomenon which had not been anticipated. National Insurance provided less than adequate coverage for the severely disabled both because their needs were often greater than those of other beneficiaries and because many had not been able to participate in the labour market sufficiently to establish a title to benefit.[34]

There was a sustained effort in the mid-1970s to deal with these problems. More resources were allocated to child benefit, which replaced the family allowance. A number of non-contributory, but also non-means-tested, allowances were introduced for the disabled. Perhaps most significantly, a new earnings-related pension scheme was introduced and contributions to the National Insurance fund, even for the flat-rate benefits, also became earnings-related – British social security thus began to resemble the European systems.[35]

F The Welfare State and the New Right

By an unhappy coincidence, the reforms described in the paragraph above occurred at the time of international economic crisis.[36] The late 1970s and 1980s were marked by reversals in social security policy, both in Britain and abroad.[37] The rapid growth of unemployment placed a double strain on the financing of the systems: not only from the costs of income maintenance of the unemployed, but also from the fact that the latter were not contributing to the National Insurance fund. Moreover, there was concern that future generations of earners would be unable to meet the obligations of pension schemes to the ever increasing aged population. The economic and political philosophy of the New Right[38] began to exert a profound influence: monetarist policy demanded reductions in public expenditure; social security programmes should guard against the creation of work disincentives and barriers to labour mobility; resources should be

31 Abel-Smith and Townsend *The Poor and the Poorest* (1965).
32 Townsend *The Family Life of Old People* (1957).
33 *Report of the Committee on One-Parent Families* (1974, Cmnd 5629).
34 OPCS *Survey of Handicapped and Impaired Persons in Great Britain* (1971–72).
35 *Ogus* n 26, above.
36 Cf OECD *The Welfare State in Crisis* (1981); Moran (1988) 18 Br J Pol Sci 397.
37 Oyen *Comparing Welfare States and their Futures* (1986).
38 For an influential American work, see Murray *Losing Ground: American Social Policy 1950–1980* (1984); and the critique by Marmor, Mashaw and Harvey *America's Misunderstood Welfare State* (1990). See also Lister (ed) *Charles Murray and the Underclass* (1996) and Green *Benefit Dependency* (1998).

targeted on those whose need is greatest; individual responsibility for, and choice of, welfare provision should be maintained.[39]

After 1979 the impact of these policies was evident in the reforms carried out by the first Thatcher administration – reductions were made to the value of many benefits and responsibility for income maintenance during short periods of sickness was transferred from the state to the employer. This trend became more explicit in the Green and White Papers of 1985 (the Fowler Reviews) which followed what was claimed to be the most important and comprehensive review of the social security system to be undertaken since Beveridge.[40] There were, however, two important omissions in the scope of the Fowler Reviews. First, they avoided any consideration of disability benefits, as the government was awaiting the results of research by the Office of Population Census and Surveys into the circumstances of people with disabilities.[41] Secondly, the Reviews excluded examination of the role of taxation and National Insurance, which were the Treasury's responsibility, and so failed to consider their interrelationship with benefits.[42] Legislation in 1986 implemented most of the proposals:[43] reduction to future entitlement under the state earnings-related pension scheme; the encouragement of personal and occupational pensions as alternatives to the state scheme; transfer to the employer of responsibility for maternity payments; and restructuring of the means-tested benefits (henceforth to be known as 'income-related benefits') including, most controversially, replacement of rights to single and urgent needs payments by a social fund, administered on a discretionary basis and subject to cash limits.

Two of the key goals of Thatcherism were to 'roll back the frontiers of the state' and to end the 'culture of dependency'. The public image in the 1980s was thus one of a government committed to cutting back on social security spending. In fact the economic policies adopted by government during this period made the fulfilment of these objectives unattainable.[44] Social security expenditure actually rose in real terms throughout this decade,[45] and so benefit programmes were kept under almost constant review. The fall of Mrs Thatcher in 1990 had little immediate effect in policy terms.[46] A major review of benefit provision for disabled people, which was already under way, led to the merger of the non-contributory attendance and mobility allowances into disability living allowance in 1992.[47] Disability living allowance provided wider coverage than the benefits it replaced, but this was partly at the cost of cuts in invalidity benefit and in the industrial injuries scheme.[48]

The Major government's concern at the increasing cost of social security was reflected in a series of ministerial speeches and departmental reports. Three areas were identified

39   Seldon *Wither the welfare state* IEA Occasional Paper 60 (1981); and for critical commentary see Plant in Bean, Ferris and Whynes (eds) *In Defence of Welfare* (1985) ch 1; and Harris *Justifying State Welfare* (1987) ch 1. See further the debate in Schmidtz and Goodin *Social Welfare and Individual Responsibility* (1998).
40   Green Paper *Reform of Social Security* (1985, Cmnd 9517) vol 1, esp chs 1–6 and 13; White Paper *Reform of Social Security* (1985, Cmnd 9691), esp ch 1. For critiques, see Deakin *The Politics of Welfare* (1987) ch 5; and Harris *Social Security Law in Context* (2000) ch 5.
41   P 677, below.
42   Fowler *Ministers Decide* (1991) pp 209 and 214; Gilmour *Dancing with Dogma* (1992) p 137.
43   Social Security Act 1986 (SSA 1986).
44   Digby *British Welfare Policy: Workhouse to Workfare* (1989) p 103.
45   Evans in Glennerster and Hills (eds) *The State of Welfare* (2nd edn, 1998) ch 7; and Lowe *The Welfare State in Britain since 1945* (2nd edn, 1999) p 320.
46   The Major government's commitment to up-rate child benefit being a notable exception: p 658, below.
47   Disability Living Allowance and Disability Working Allowance Act 1991, since consolidated in the Social Security Contributions and Benefits Act 1992, ss 71–76.
48   P 678, below.

in which increased welfare expenditure was particularly prominent: invalidity benefit, income support for lone parents and housing benefit.[49] The replacement of sickness and invalidity benefit by incapacity benefit in 1995 was clearly motivated in part by a conviction that this level of spending could not be sustained indefinitely.[50] The integration of unemployment benefit and income support for unemployed people into jobseeker's allowance in the following year was a reflection of the same pressures. Similarly, the Child Support Act 1991 was designed to reduce the dependence of lone parents on benefit.[51] Further restrictions on the scope of the housing benefit scheme, most notably the introduction of the single room rent rule, capping benefit for young adults, were also implemented.[52] Not all commentators, however, shared either the government's analysis of future trends in social security expenditure or the implications to be drawn from these changes.[53] Moreover, the Labour Party, through its independent Commission on Social Justice, sought to establish its own vision of a welfare state fit for the twenty-first century.[54]

G The Welfare State and New Labour[55]

While in opposition Labour's most innovative thinker on welfare reform was Frank Field MP who argued for the construction of a system of stakeholder welfare, building on the contributory principle.[56] Field was made Minister for Welfare Reform in the new government, charged with 'thinking the unthinkable', while Harriet Harman MP was appointed Secretary of State. It was evident from the 1997 Labour Party manifesto that 'welfare to work' was to constitute the centrepiece of the new administration's social policy,[57] most notably in the pledge to establish a New Deal scheme. Beyond that, little was clear as to the intentions of the new government in terms of the details of social security reform.[58] The 1998 Green Paper[59] included few new initiatives, reflecting the tension between Field's vision and the approach of the new Chancellor, Gordon Brown MP. Field advocated a universalist stakeholder philosophy, rebuilding the social insurance system in the private sector, and opposed means-testing. Brown, in contrast, emphasised the use of means-tested in-work benefits, relaunched as tax credits, in order to demonstrate the rewards of work. The Chancellor's ascendancy in social policy making was confirmed by Field's 'resignation' and the replacement of Harman as Secretary of State by Alistair Darling MP in July 1998.[60]

49 DSS *The Growth of Social Security* (1993).
50 P 524, below.
51 P 317, below.
52 P 422, below.
53 Social Security Advisory Committee (SSAC) *Ninth Report 1993* (1993) ch 6; Hills *The Future of Welfare* (1993).
54 Commission on Social Justice *The Justice Gap* (1993) and *Social Justice in a Changing World* (1993).
55 For reviews of the Blair government's first term, see Toynbee and Walker *Did Things Get Better?* (2001) ch 2; Seldon (ed) *The Blair Effect* (2001); and *Timmins* n 4, above, ch 21.
56 Field *Making Welfare Work: Reconstructing Welfare for the Millennium* (1995), *Stakeholder Welfare* (1996) and (1998) 69 Political Q 252.
57 On the US influence, see Deacon (ed) *From Welfare to Work: Lessons from America* (1997); and Deacon (2000) 28 Policy & Politics 5. See further Solow *Work and Welfare* (1998); and Peck and Theodore (2000) 24 Camb J Economics 119.
58 Glennerster in *Seldon* n 55, above, p 385.
59 DSS *New ambitions for our country: A new contract for welfare* (1998, Cm 3805).
60 See generally *Timmins* n 4, above, pp 560–570, citing unattributable views of Field that 'he did think the unthinkable, but it was unworkable'. For Field's own critique of the tax credits strategy, see Field *The State of Dependency* (2000) pp 144–148.

The emphasis on paid work as the primary route out of poverty was summarised in a 'sound-bite': 'Work for those who can and security for those who cannot'.[61] As several commentators have observed, the boundary between those who 'can' and those who 'cannot' may be problematic, particularly in the context of disability and gender.[62] Yet the Treasury-led reforms to the benefits and tax systems, including the transformation of family credit into working families' tax credit by TCA 1999,[63] along with the introduction of a national minimum wage, 'signalled a structural and cultural shift in the operation of the welfare state'.[64] These initiatives reflected the new government's emphasis on reciprocity or 'welfare contractualism' as the basis for a reformed welfare state. In particular, this ideology holds that, as a condition of eligibility for benefit, the state may legitimately enforce the citizen's responsibilities, most notably the responsibility to work or at least to engage in active job search and training.[65]

The new Labour government's commitment to match its Conservative predecessor's public expenditure plans for its first two years of office resulted in opposition from within its own ranks, not least over the decision to implement cuts in lone parent benefits.[66] In March 1999, however, the Prime Minister pledged to end child poverty within 20 years.[67] Although there were further cuts to contributory benefits in the Welfare Reform and Pensions Act 1999 – in relation to incapacity benefit and bereavement benefits – the government's redistributive agenda was also evident in the substantial increases in the rates of the personal allowances for children in the means-tested benefits schemes. The Child Support, Pensions and Social Security Act 2000, however, was principally concerned with reforms of the child support scheme and the replacement of the state earnings related scheme (SERPS) by a distributionally more progressive state second pension (S2P).

Following its re-election in 2001, the Labour government confirmed its intention to implement a more radical restructuring of the tax and benefit systems in TCA 2002. This measure transferred responsibility for child benefit to the Inland Revenue and introduced, as from April 2003, an integrated child tax credit, drawing together the various forms of support for children in existing benefits and tax credits.[68] This measure, described as based on the principle of 'progressive universalism',[69] and taken together with the State Pension Credit Act 2002, marked a significant further shift away from the traditional social insurance model of social security.

---

61   DSS *A new contract for welfare: principles into practice* (1998, Cm 4101) p iii. See further Deacon (1998) 69 Political Q 306; and Hyde, Dixon and Joyner (1999) 52 I Soc Sec Rev 69.
62   See eg Lewis in *Seldon* n 55, above, ch 22.
63   In parallel the Treasury and Inland Revenue took over contributions policy and operational responsibilities from the DSS under the Social Security Contributions (Transfer of Functions, etc) Act 1999.
64   Stephens in *Seldon* n 55, above, p 187.
65   See White (2000) 30 Br J Pol Sci 507. This approach derives from the work of eg Mead *Beyond Entitlement: The Social Obligations of Citizenship* (1987); Layard *What Labour Can Do* (1997); and Giddens *The third way: The renewal of social democracy* (1998). On the influence of US policy initiatives, see further King and Wickham-Jones (1999) 70 Political Q 62.
66   P 297, below.
67   Rt Hon T Blair, Beveridge Lecture, March 1999. See further Bradshaw (2000) 34 Sociology 53. On the search for an appropriate measure of poverty, see DWP *Measuring child poverty: a consultation document* (2002).
68   See p 387, below.
69   HM Treasury *The Modernisation of Britain's Tax and Benefit Systems No 10: The Child and Working Tax Credits* (2002) p 4.

Part 3   Objectives

A   Private and public systems of welfare

Society has always been, and for the indefinite future will remain, afflicted by the problem of scarce resources. To deal with the problem of scarcity, and to avoid anarchy, systems of resource allocation must be developed. Clearly, social security is one such system: the state, by means of legislation, allocates some of the scarce resources to those who satisfy certain conditions, typically assumed, or demonstrated, of need. But equally clearly, in capitalist and mixed economies, it competes with, and is complementary to, a system which preceded it historically: the market. To understand the existence and content of the social security system, it is, therefore, necessary to analyse the market method of dealing with resources and the shortcomings to which it gives rise.

i   The market model of welfare

The basic features of the market model are easily grasped.[70] Individuals, motivated by profit, supply goods and services for which other individuals are prepared to pay. Price plays a key role in the process: it enables potential buyers to communicate the intensity of their demand for a particular good or service; and it allows potential suppliers to compare what they would earn from putting their resources to that use, as opposed to other uses – in the language of economics, supply is determined by opportunity cost. Subject to the substantial proviso that there is competition, the process is said to generate 'efficiency': competition between buyers ensures that resources move to their most highly valued uses; and competition between suppliers ensures that the goods or services are produced at the lowest cost. Enshrined in the process are the values of liberty – individuals are treated as autonomous and responsible for securing the welfare of themselves and their families – and decentralisation – the state does not determine the production or distribution of resources; its role is limited to preserving law and order and upholding property and contract rights.

   The notion of welfare incorporated in this model means not only that individuals are expected to choose how best to exploit resources (typically labour) at their disposal and thus to maximise their income but also that they should make rational decisions on how to cope with contingencies affecting their earning potential, notably sickness, invalidity, unemployment, old age and death. This will involve some sacrifice of current consumption to 'save for the rainy day' and the market will respond to the demand to maximise the value of such savings by means of pension and insurance schemes.

ii   Limitations of the market model

What we have described above is, of course, an idealised model and, while it can be used to explain the early history of social policy, particularly in the nineteenth century, it is difficult to reconcile with social reality, at least as it is perceived in modern times.[71]

---

70   See Creedy and Disney *Social Insurance in Transition* (1985) ch 1.
71   See Glennerster *Paying for welfare: towards 2000* (3rd edn, 1997) ch 2; and Barr *The Welfare State as Piggy Bank* (2001); see also *Bean et al* n 2, above, chs 5–6; and Spicker *The Welfare State: a general theory* (2000).

First, it assumes that individuals have the information available and the capacity to make rational, wise decisions concerning current and future welfare; unhappily, that is not always a realistic assumption. The growth of social security may, then, be attributed either to the greater knowledge possessed by bureaucracies on the risks to an individual's livelihood or to a paternalist policy pursued by governments on the basis that they know better than individuals what is good for them.[72]

Secondly, the insistence on individual decision making fails to take account of the fact that such decisions may affect other people, beneficially or detrimentally. The problem lies not so much in relation to the obvious and immediate effects on the individual's family, because the model assumes an identity of interest within the family unit.[73] The concern is rather with more widespread and longer-term effects: society needs a healthy and well-educated workforce to produce goods; poverty is linked to crime and ill-health; and the existence of deprivation may adversely affect the welfare of others, because a sight of it is 'distasteful' to them, or because they genuinely care about the plight of the less fortunate.[74] Of course, there is nothing to stop those affected in this way from themselves taking steps to alleviate deprivation in a manner not inconsistent with the market model. Charitable gifts and the like may be rationalised on this basis, but, quite apart from the fact that the recipients may find this form of transfer stigmatising, this solution, in its turn, gives rise to what is generally referred to as the 'free rider' problem.[75] Potential donors should appreciate that they will derive benefit from the alleviation of poverty when others make the necessary gifts and they provide nothing. They may, then, make a contribution only if it is matched by contributions from others. In the absence of legislative compulsion, this is difficult to organise; hence the case for forced transfers, financed by taxes or social security contributions.

Thirdly, there may be technical problems in the market meeting the demand for protection against risks to income. Private, voluntary insurance has to cope with the problem of 'adverse selection'.[76] An insurance company may begin by assessing a given risk, eg sickness across a group of individuals defined by (say) age, sex and occupation, and calculating the premiums payable for each within the group on the basis of the average risk for the group as a whole. Those for whom the risk is of higher probability than the average will have an incentive to be insured at this level of premium, while individuals with lower than average risks may find the premium excessive for their needs.[77] A spiralling effect may well ensue: as more low-risk individuals forego insurance, the density of high-risk individuals in the group increases, necessitating a higher premium which may now prove unattractive to those with risks nearer the average. To counter the problem, the insurance company has to engage in some degree of individual risk-rating, so that individuals pay premiums proportionate to their own risk. In itself, this is a costly exercise which will be reflected in the premiums; it also means that high-risk individuals will be charged premiums that they may not be able to afford. Social insurance, because it is compulsory, can obtain an appropriate balance between high-risk and low-risk individuals. Private insurance companies are, moreover, loath to offer any coverage for some important risks to livelihood, notably

---

72 Sugden *Who Cares?* IEA Occasional Paper 67 (1983).
73 And so ignores gender issues: Pascall *Social Policy: A New Feminist Analysis* (1997).
74 Culyer *The Political Economy of Social Policy* (1980).
75 Friedman *Capitalism and Freedom* (1962) pp 190–191.
76 *Bean et al* n 2, above, pp 130–131.
77 It should be noted, however, that the demand for protection will vary according to the individual's degree of 'risk aversion', which is independent of the objectively determined risk itself: Bowles *Law and the Economy* (1982) pp 45–46.

unemployment.[78] It is, actuarially, extremely difficult to assess the risk of unemployment because it is primarily a consequence of general economic circumstances which do not follow consistent patterns or trends; and it is also difficult to verify the validity of claims that individuals are not gainfully employed. The fact that social insurance schemes can be financed on a 'pay as you go' basis enables them to solve the actuarial problem and the existence of broad investigatory powers, to deal with the verification problem, is less controversial if associated with state machinery. Finally, private or public insurance, because they deal with future and uncertain risks, cannot deal with adverse conditions which have already arisen.[79] Some individuals may have been prevented, by eg congenital disablement, from ever having been able to enter the labour market. Non-contributory benefits must be made available if they are to be protected.

This last example is in fact indicative of the fourth and most fundamental problem, concerned with distributional justice: are the processes and the outcomes which they generate *fair*? The welfare obtained by individuals by means of the market depends crucially on the property and other resources, including natural endowments such as skill and intelligence, at their disposal before the process of exchange begins. If, according to some criterion, the initial distribution of resources is regarded as unjust then the process of exchange will tend to reinforce and even aggravate the injustice. Affluence enables individuals legitimately to purchase the means – eg education or expertise – to add to their affluence, and illegitimate means, such as barriers to entry and other restrictive practices, may be used to entrench advantages secured in the labour market.[80]

iii Theories of distributional justice

It is one thing to recognise the importance of the distributional justice problem and that social security programmes may be used to pursue distributional goals; it is quite another to reach agreements on what is a just distribution. A variety of theories have been advanced, each with important implications for the design of welfare systems.[81] The extreme position on the Right taken by libertarians is that distributions are just so long as the process by which the resources were acquired was just and this includes, notably, inheritance and purchase.[82] Interventions by the state to reorganise distributions constitute an infringement of personal liberty; in particular, income tax is equivalent to forced labour and a tax on capital to an unwarranted seizure of goods.[83] Other libertarians accept the need for a purely residual welfare state while opposing any redistributive goals.[84]

---

78 *Barr* n 71, above. See also SSAC *State Benefits and Private Provision* (1995).
79 Though public insurance schemes can adapt to the problem by eg crediting contributions (p 123, below) and the use of deeming provisions, as with the state second pension (p 621, below).
80 On the segmentation of the labour market and the cycle of deprivation, see Reich et al in Atkinson *Wealth, Income and Inequality* (2nd edn, 1980) pp 381–389.
81 George and Wilding *Ideology and Social Welfare* (rev edn, 1985); Barr *The Economics of the Welfare State* (3rd edn, 1998) ch 3; *Harris* n 39, above.
82 Nozick *Anarchy, State and Utopia* (1974). The original acquisition of a resource through an application of an individual's labour is justified by the property right residing in the individual's person: cf Locke *Second Treatise of Civil Government* (Everyman edn, 1943) s 43.
83 *Nozick* n 82, above, pp 169–172. Some libertarians are, however, prepared to admit that a minimum degree of material support for disadvantaged persons may be necessary if they are to be able to exercise their political rights, which are highly valued: Buchanan in Dworkin, Bermont and Brown *Markets and Morals* (1977) ch 6.
84 Hayek *The Constitution of Liberty* (1960) p 257.

Exponents of liberal theories are prepared to temper acceptance of the market order and respect for individual liberty with some concern for distributional consequences. Typical is the well-known proposition advanced by Rawls that individuals, if prevented by a veil of ignorance from knowing their station in society, would agree that social and economic inequalities are justified only if they improve the position of everyone, especially the least advantaged.[85] The state should redress unjustified inequalities by interventionist measures[86] but the vagueness of the criterion makes it difficult to spell out what degree of redistribution is called for.

More explicit, in this respect, are theories based on notions of citizenship; the goal is to:

> ensure that everyone is able to enjoy a standard of living much like that of the rest of the community, and thus is able to feel a sense of participation in and belonging to the community.[87]

This leads to a notion of citizenship rights conferred as an act of social policy on those whose resources are inadequate for full participation in the community and existing alongside the more traditional rights, such as property, associated with the market model.[88] As will be seen, approaches of this kind raise difficult questions of how to measure need.

Egalitarian theories involve a more direct attack on the market method of allocating resources.[89] They go beyond advocating equality of opportunity but typically fall short of advocating equality of income,[90] primarily because they recognise that effort and responsibility should be rewarded. Social policy should be directed towards *reducing* inequalities and opinions obviously differ on how far this process should be taken. Indeed, Marxists argue that the very existence of market relationships is incompatible with notions of just distribution and needs to be replaced by another system of economic organisation which will enable resources to move 'from each according to his ability to each according to his need'.[91]

iv Economic constraints

Policymakers, convinced of the unfairness of the market model and intent on devising social security measures to redistribute resources in the light of one or more of the theories described above, may nevertheless be concerned with the general economic consequences of such measures. On the face of it, social security benefits are simply

---

85   Rawls *A Theory of Justice* (rev edn, 1999), esp chs 11–14. It should be noted, however, that the principle ranks second in priority below that of equal liberty.
86   *Rawls* n 85, above, ch 43. See further Rawls *Justice as Fairness: A Restatement* (2001).
87   Report of the Royal Commission of Inquiry *Social Security in New Zealand* (1972) p 65. For a contemporary Australasian perspective, see Reference Group on Welfare Reform *Participation Support for a More Equitable Society* Department of Family and Community Services, Australia (July 2000).
88   Marshall *Sociology at the Crossroads* (1963) ch 4; Parker *Social Policy and Citizenship* (1975) ch 9; Barbalet *Citizenship: Rights, Struggle and Class Inequality* (1988); Gutmann (ed) *Democracy and the Welfare State* (1988).
89   *George and Wilding* n 81, above, ch 4; *Harris* n 39, above, ch 5.
90   *George and Wilding* n 81, above, p 65.
91   Marx 'Criticism of the Gotha Programme' in Feuer (ed) *Marx and Engels: Basic Writings on Politics and Philosophy* (1969) p 160; and generally, ch 5. See also Piven and Cloward *Regulating the Poor* (1971); O'Connor *The Fiscal Crisis of the State* (1973); Lee and Raban *Welfare Theory and Social Policy* (1988) chs 3–6.

'transfer payments'[92] from one group to another and the aggregate wealth of society is not affected. Indeed, it can be argued that, in terms of utility, redistribution from the rich to the poor makes society 'better off' since £1 in the hands of poor transferees is worth more to them than it was in the hands of richer transferors.[93] However, welfare transfers may involve sacrifices to general economic welfare in three different ways:[94] first, high levels of benefit may create work disincentives and thus productivity losses; secondly, the marginal tax rates necessary to finance progressive redistribution may have the same effect and may also reduce the amount available for investment, thus depleting the capital stocks of society; and, thirdly, the administration of the transfers is itself costly, employing resources which could be put to more productive use. Past Conservative governments have also emphasised the moral dangers inherent in the creation of a so-called 'culture of dependency' if welfare spending is left unchecked.[95] The debilitating nature of life on benefit and its costs in terms of social consequences has also been a central theme of New Labour thinking on welfare reform.[96]

B Political factors

The attribution of stages in the evolution of the social security system to the theories of distribution outlined above would appear to be plausible: nineteenth-century approaches match libertarian ideologies; the combination of National Insurance and means-tested assistance endorses the liberal approach (which is made explicit in the Beveridge Report); the notion of citizenship can be located in eg the non-contributory benefits for the disabled; and egalitarian ideals may lie behind family allowances and child benefit. To explain policy developments by reference to goals is, however, necessarily simplistic because it ignores the political dimension – how policy is implemented.[97]

Political scientists and others have developed several competing theories to explain changes in welfare legislation.[98] On a broad 'macro' level, there are theories which regard such changes as inseparably linked to wider socio-economic factors, such as the degree of industrialisation.[99] Analogously, Marxists argue that social welfare measures are typically a response by capitalists to the threat to stability and order posed by the class struggle.[100]

Less ambitious theories offer, perhaps, more promising hypotheses. One focuses on intellectual activity and perceives policy change to proceed from the way new information is collected and new ideas formulated by professionals and academics and then communicated to the policymaker.[101] The difficulty with this view it is that it takes no account of political structures and institutions and explanations of change in terms of the latter command the widest support among theorists. Some purport to find the key in the party structure: the envisaged reform must be consistent with the traditional set

---

92 Cf McClements *The Economics of Social Security* (1978) ch 7.
93 Cf *Culyer* n 74, above, ch 4. However, interpersonal comparisons of this kind are subject to many theoretical difficulties: *Culyer* p 23.
94 *McClements* n 92, above, ch 4.
95 See eg Rt Hon P Lilley MP, Mais Lecture *Benefits and Costs – Securing the Future of Social Security* (1993).
96 See eg Field *Making Welfare Work: Reconstructing Welfare for the Millennium* (1995).
97 See generally Hill *The policy process in the modern state* (3rd edn, 1997).
98 See, esp, Banting *Poverty, Politics and Policy* (1979).
99 Wilensky *The Welfare State and Equality* (1975).
100 Kincaid *Poverty and Equality in Britain* (rev edn, 1975).
101 Lindblom *The Intelligence of Democracy* (1965).

of values held by the party with dominant power at the time.[102] Others take more seriously the democratic basis of the legislative process: policy is seen as a product of competition to win electoral support.[103] A third view stresses the role of bureaucrats: the real power, it is alleged, is held by those within the departments of government who can force their opinion on politicians, often because of greater expertise and superior information.[104] The latter two approaches are combined in the public choice school of political theory, which ascribes the growth in welfare spending to imperfections in the democratic process and the institutional incentives for bureaucrats to expand their organisations.[105] Finally, on the fourth approach, policy is viewed as the outcome of conflict between different interest groups: it balances the power between these groups, with bureaucrats providing the technical expertise to fashion the appropriate compromise.[106]

As will be seen from a comparison of the three most recent periods of social security reform, it is not easy to reach general conclusions on these rival theories. The modifications to the Beveridge model enacted in the period between 1965 and 1975 would seem to reflect the cumulative importance of different influences on social policy.[107] The reforms had their origin in intellectual activity – the rediscovery of poverty by the academics – but required the efforts of pressure groups to give the campaign momentum. Thereafter, bureaucrats played the decisive role in the way they formulated alternative strategies for their political masters.[108] Party politics and electoral considerations became involved only at a relatively late stage and, arguably, had little influence on the eventual outcome.[109]

The story of the Thatcher reforms was very different.[110] As regards intellectual inspiration, Conservative ministers were somewhat contemptuous of traditional sociological research and preferred to commission studies of the social security system from within government.[111] The primary role of bureaucrats in formulating policy options was maintained but the emphasis changed: the parameters within which reform was perceived as possible were determined by politicians rather than administrators. The impact of most of the interest groups was substantially reduced. While proposals were published for public consultation, seemingly the Thatcher and Major governments were only prepared to make compromises when pressure was exerted from amongst their own supporters.[112]

There is both continuity and change when the Blair reforms are compared with the Thatcher era.[113] As before, politicians, rather than civil servants, have driven the agenda for the New Labour welfare reforms, with the Treasury's role in social policy now

102   Beer *Modern British Politics* (1982).
103   Downs *An Economic Theory of Democracy* (1957).
104   Rose *The Problem of Party Government* (1974); and see Baldwin *The Politics of Social Solidarity* (1990) pp 44–47.
105   Downs *Inside Bureaucracy* (1967); Niskanen *Bureaucracy and Representative Government* (1971); see Dunleavy *Democracy, Bureaucracy and Public Choice* (1991) ch 6.
106   Wootten *Pressure Politics in Contemporary Britain* (1978).
107   Ogus 1034 Acta Universitatis Wratislaviensis 49.
108   Hall, Land, Parker and Webb *Change, Choice and Conflict in Social Policy* (1975) pp 69–72.
109   *Banting* n 98, above, pp 87–100.
110   Taylor-Gooby in Klein and O'Higgins (eds) *The Future of Welfare* (1985) ch 5; *Ogus* n 107, above, pp 61–64.
111   Notably, the Fowler Reviews, summarised in *Green Paper 1985* n 40, above, vols 2–4.
112   Eg abandoning the proposal to abolish the earnings-related pension scheme between the publications of the Green and White Papers in 1985. On the background to this, see Lawson *The View From No 11* (1992) ch 47.
113   See Hills *Thatcherism, New Labour and the Welfare State* CASE paper 13 (1998).

becoming dominant.[114] Pressure groups under New Labour appear to have at best a marginal influence, doubtless reflecting in part their difficulties in attracting sufficient funds and volunteers as well as the size of the parliamentary majorities of the first two Blair governments. Yet since 1997 the government has demonstrated a greater willingness to consult on some social policy issues.[115]

C Other values

i Demographic aims

In some countries, especially France, the level of family endowment is thought to have a significant impact on the birth rate and in this sense social security has been regarded as an instrument of demographic policy.[116] Undeniably it played an important role in the introduction of family allowances in Britain.[117] Yet in the recent discussions about the future of child benefit demographic issues have been almost entirely neglected. However, concerns about demographic trends amongst the elderly lay behind the reform of SERPS in the mid-1980s.

A second demographic goal, that of labour mobility, has featured more prominently in social policy in Britain, particularly under the Thatcher governments.[118] On the one hand, the social security system provides positive incentives notably through maintaining an individual's contribution record and preserving the right to benefit during periods of retraining or rehabilitation,[119] and by insisting on the portability of occupational pension rights.[120] Much of the EU law in this field is designed to encourage the mobility of labour between countries.[121] On the other hand, there are negative sanctions involving the withdrawal of benefit where individuals fail to avail themselves of work opportunities.[122]

ii The family

On a superficial analysis it may appear as if the social security system serves to undermine the integrity of the family unit. In an historical sense, it is true that originally support by other family members was the first and sometimes the only refuge from destitution,[123] and that this function has to a considerable extent been superseded by state financial provision. But while dependence on remoter family relationships may, to some extent, have diminished in importance, the legal interdependence of the inner

---

114 Stephens in *Seldon* n 55, above, p 187. See also Glennerster in the same volume, p 385; and *Timmins* n 4, above, p 563.
115 Eg it would have been difficult to envisage the DSS, prior to 1997, jointly convening a workshop with the Centre for Analysis of Social Exclusion (CASE) on how to monitor progress on tackling poverty and social exclusion: DSS *Indicators of progress* CASE report 13 (2001).
116 Pedersen *Family, dependence, and the origins of the welfare state: Britain and France, 1914–1945* (1993); and Messu (1992) 45 I Soc Sec Rev 71.
117 *Hall et al* n 108, above, pp 170–174.
118 See *White Paper 1985* n 40, above, para 1.1 and *Employment for the 1990s* (1988, Cm 540).
119 Pp 126–127, below.
120 Pp 634–635, below.
121 Ch 3, below.
122 Pp 369–373, below.
123 Eekelaar *Family Law and Social Policy* (2nd edn, 1984) pp 17–21.

family unit has in fact increased and is in no way overridden by the social security system which intervenes to replace maintenance obligations only when they remain unfulfilled.[124] Moreover, social security can have a positive effect on family relationships by materially enabling individuals to care for their weaker relatives.

Another argument turns on the extent of support for natural, as opposed to legal, family relationships. It has been said that recognition of de facto relationships acts as an incentive to marital breakdown.[125] It must be conceded that for some, but by no means all, purposes, social security has regard to the consequences of such a relationship rather than the legal family as the basic unit. But there is little evidence to suggest that such state support as exists for de facto families acts as an incentive to marriage breakdown.[126] Even if it does, the consequent evil has to be weighed against the competing desire to protect the welfare of children by not forcing couples to continue to cohabit when a marriage has already disintegrated, and by recognising new obligations that may arise from alternative relationships. This accounts in part for the controversy surrounding the Child Support Act 1991, which gives priority to an absent parent's obligations to children of a first rather than any subsequent relationship.[127] Whether for the purposes of social security the 'family' is that recognised by the law generally or a broader concept, it is indisputable that its economic welfare constitutes one of the primary objectives of the system. This is evident from the way in which, in sharp contrast to that of some other countries, British law has traditionally concentrated its income maintenance programme on family needs rather than earnings replacement.

iii Sex equality

There have always been significant differences in social security systems between the treatment of men and women.[128] Although this area of law was deliberately excluded from the sex discrimination legislation, nevertheless as a result of membership of the EU[129] successive governments have made steady, if at times grudging, progress towards greater sex equality. As regards single women, the pre-war discrimination based on the assumption that they were 'poor risks' was abolished in 1945[130] and the only difference remaining is that the pensionable age for women is currently five years earlier than that for men. However, the state pension age for men and women will be equalised at 65 following a transitional period between 2010 and 2020.[131]

The different treatment of married women stemmed in part from the practice of regarding the family as a single financial unit. The model which traditionally dominated social policy thinking was that of the wife doing the housework and rearing the children while the husband was the breadwinner. The structure of National Insurance was based on the assumption that a married woman's earnings were subsidiary and, in the words

---

124   See pp 316–328, below.
125   The argument is stated and repudiated in Friedmann *Law in a Changing Society* (2nd edn, 1972) pp 287–289.
126   McKay and Rowlingson *Social Security in Britain* (1999) pp 177–180.
127   Pp 318–324, below. See Davis, Wikeley and Young *Child Support in Action* (1998).
128   See generally Pascall *Social Policy: A New Feminist Analysis* (1997); and McLaughlin in Ditch (ed) *Introduction to Social Security* (1999) ch 8; and, for earlier sources, the 4th edition of this book, p 15, n 10.
129   Esp the Council Directive on Equal Treatment in Social Security Benefits: Council Directive (EEC) 79/7, OJ 1979 L 6/24, on which see ch 2, below.
130   Cf *Beveridge Report* n 23, above, para 123.
131   Pensions Act 1995, s 126 and Sch 4; see pp 599–601, below.

of Beveridge, her earnings were 'a means not of subsistence but of a standard of living above subsistence', and thus in the case of unemployment or sickness she could fall back on her husband's support.[132] A complex set of rules was formulated to reflect this lower status, including notably the ability to opt out of the insurance scheme. With changing social attitudes, and the increasing participation of married women in the labour market, this option was abolished for those marrying after April 1977.[133] There followed a series of further reforms to other social security provisions. Since 1983, either member of a couple may claim a means-tested benefit and not, as was typically the case before, only the husband or male partner.[134] Until 1986 married women were excluded from the invalid care allowance (now carer's allowance). This was reformed, but only as a result of a decision of the European Court of Justice that the legislation infringed the Council Directive on Equal Treatment.[135] The principles governing the entitlement of husbands and wives to increases to a contributory benefit for a dependent spouse were also harmonised.[136] Additionally, the decision of the European Court of Justice in *Barber v Guardian Royal Exchange Assurance Group*[137] has had important repercussions in relation to equal treatment and occupational pensions.

The logic of these reforms was not pursued in the case of survivor benefits until the Welfare Reform and Pensions Act 1999 replaced widow's benefits with bereavement benefits with effect from 2001, but at the cost of some levelling down of provision. On this occasion litigation before the European Court of Human Rights was a key factor in prompting reform.[138] The Employment Act 2002 introduced statutory paternity pay, but for a much shorter period than statutory maternity pay.[139] The more radical proposals, made by feminists and others, for state benefits for child-carers or 'housewives'[140] have not been taken forward. They emanate from a concern that the principle of aggregating a couple's resources for the purposes of means-tested benefits and the consequent need to formulate and enforce rules on cohabitation[141] in practice discriminate against women and reinforce notions of dependency.[142]

The steps that have been taken in respect of equal treatment in terms of gender have not, to date, been matched with parallel developments in the realm of discrimination on grounds of sexual orientation. In particular, the social security system remains wedded to the heterosexual model of cohabitation. In the context of means-tested benefits, where the resources of partners are aggregated, this has the effect of treating claimants in a same-sex relationship more favourably than either a married or unmarried

---

132 *Beveridge Report* n 23, above, para 108.
133 Beveridge relied on the fact that before the Second World War only about 12.5 per cent of married women of working age were gainfully employed (*Beveridge Report* n 23, above, para 108); by 1978 the figure was 62 per cent: *General Household Survey 1978* (1978) Table 5.1.
134 P 291, below. Indeed, since 2001 certain unemployed childless couples must apply for joint-claim jobseeker's allowance, rather than one partner claiming ordinary income-based jobseeker's allowance for himself and his partner: p 357, below.
135 Pp 523 and 708, below. Married women also had to satisfy special conditions for the non-contributory invalidity pension, the forerunner of severe disablement allowance (now abolished): p 523, below.
136 P 248, below.
137 C-262/88, [1991] 1 QB 344; see pp 642–645, below.
138 Pp 570–571, below.
139 In Germany the take-up rate of parental leave benefits among men is just 1.5 per cent: Bieback (1992) 2 J Eur Soc Pol 239.
140 Bennett in Segal (ed) *What is to be done about the family?* (1983) ch 8; Esam, Good and Middleton *Who's to Benefit?* (1985) ch 4. For an analysis of options for reform, see Duncan, Giles and Webb *Social security reform and women's independent incomes* (1994).
141 Pp 220–223, below.
142 Morris (2000) 7 JSSL 228.

heterosexual couple. By the same token, however, no account is taken of same-sex partners when assessing entitlement to eg retirement or bereavement benefits. Thus the surviving partner in a gay or lesbian relationship (as with a surviving *unmarried* heterosexual cohabitant) would have no right to a bereavement allowance, whereas he or she may be able to inherit a tenancy regulated by the Rent Acts as a member of their partner's family.[143]

Part 4   Strategies

A   Introduction

In Part 2 we considered the range of objectives that a social security system might adopt. In this part we discuss the different strategies available to meet these objectives. In section B, we consider how recipients of cash benefits may be selected and classified according to their needs. Section C is concerned with the principles for assessing benefits, and section D with the methods of financing them. Finally, in section E we contrast the cash benefit system with two other types of social welfare: benefits in kind, and fiscal relief.

B   Selection and classification of need

i   General

The primary question arising under a system of cash benefits relates to the circumstances in which and the persons to whom benefits are paid. To postulate that a social security system must be 'selective' is merely to state the obvious. The same benefits cannot be enjoyed to the same degree by all members of society. Even the most 'universal' of schemes, such as the social dividend proposal (described later in this chapter[144]) which purports to grant benefit to all, nevertheless effectively takes it back from many through the medium of taxation. The debate on 'universality versus selectivity'[145] is thus concerned not with a choice between two extreme alternatives but rather on the nature and extent of the selectivity process. At a very broad level, two fundamentally different approaches should be distinguished. In the first, generally referred to as the means test method, the target is poverty as such, and the primary condition of entitlement is a level of resources below a stipulated amount. The second attempts to focus on presumed needs (often but not exclusively involving income deprivation) arising from certain circumstances, eg unemployment, disability, old age, the maintenance of children. The one approach is not necessarily coterminous with the other – it is possible that entitlement to a particular benefit may depend on conditions both of non-financial circumstances and of income – but the relative weight to be given to each strategy raises an important issue of social policy.

---

143   *Fitzpatrick v Sterling Housing Association* [1999] 4 All ER 705, HL.
144   P 34, below.
145   See Titmuss *Commitment to Welfare* (2nd edn, 1976) ch 10; Davies *Universality, Selectivity and Effectiveness in Social Policy* (1978) ch 7; Garfinkel (ed) *Income-Tested Transfer Programs: The Case For and Against* (1982); Wilson and Wilson *The Political Economy of the Welfare State* (1982) ch 4; Deacon and Bradshaw *Reserved for the Poor* (1983) ch 4.

ii Means-tested benefits

The primary assumption behind the means test approach is that deprivation of income and other resources constitutes the greatest need on which the social security system should concentrate. It is typically combined with concern that welfare expenditure (which involves a substantial degree of redistribution) should be limited to cases of *demonstrated* need and that the conditions for receipt should be kept within carefully observed limits.[146] The process has, however, been attacked by a battery of arguments.[147] Means tests are regarded as socially divisive not the least because those who are subject to them are conscious of the continuity of a tradition dating back to the poor law. They imply strong control functions by governments and bureaucrats whose attitudes may be coloured by their own moral judgments of poverty.[148] This leads to a conclusion that 'there is a general discouragement to use means-tested services which is built into their operating rules and administration by a society which sets great store by self-help and thrift'.[149] Perhaps the most frequently voiced objection is that means tests are stigmatising[150] and for that, and for other reasons, result in a lower than desirable take-up rate.[151] They are, therefore, of only limited effectiveness in alleviating poverty.[152] Moreover, means-testing, as a means of selecting beneficiaries, is expensive to administer,[153] and the additional costs borne by claimants (waiting, frustration, travelling) must also be taken into account. Finally, means-testing only consolidates dependency and discourages thrift.[154]

General considerations of the merits of means tests leave open the question as to the form such tests might take.[155] The McCarthy Royal Commission in New Zealand was quick to assert what appeared to it to be a fundamental distinction between 'means tests' and 'income tests': the former but not the latter take into account the claimant's capital resources.[156] The income test was less stigmatising as the claimant's total circumstances need not be opened to public scrutiny; it also avoided any incentive to dissipate capital resources to gain entitlement. In Britain, while the level of capital resources disregarded under the present income-related schemes is reasonably generous, especially for the elderly,[157] the tradition has always been to take them into account. This is not only because someone with substantial capital is assumed not to be in need but also because to disregard such resources creates inequities between claimants. This same problem is inherent in the difficult choice between simplicity and comprehensiveness:[158] to do justice to each recipient involves a rigorous scrutiny of all

146 Dilnot, Kay and Morris *The Reform of Social Security* (1984) pp 113–118; *Green Paper 1985* n 40, above, vol 1, para 6.3.
147 See the references cited in n 145, above.
148 Squires *Anti-Social Policy* (1990); Dean *Social Security and Social Control* (1991).
149 Townsend *Poverty in the United Kingdom* (1979) p 880.
150 The evidence and arguments are reviewed in Spicker *Stigma and Social Welfare* (1984).
151 See Corden in Ditch (ed) *Introduction to Social Security* (1999) ch 6.
152 Behrendt (2000) 10 J Eur Soc Pol 23.
153 Eg in 1998–99 the administration of income-based jobseeker's allowance cost 10.7 per cent of benefit expenditure, compared with 0.9 per cent for retirement pensions. The comparable figure for the social fund was 19.3 per cent (as a proportion of expenditure and loan recoveries together): DSS *Social Security Departmental Report* (2000, Cm 4614) p 88.
154 Field *Making Welfare Work: Reconstructing Welfare for the Millennium* (1995). See also Murray *Losing Ground: American Social Policy, 1950–1980* (1984).
155 See further *Barr* n 81, above, ch 10.
156 *Report of the Royal Commission of Inquiry* n 87, above, p 139.
157 See pp 459–460, below.
158 DHSS *Social Assistance* (1978) ch 3; Wilding in Adler and Bradley (eds) *Justice, Discretion and Poverty* (1976) ch 4; Titmuss (1971) 42 Political Q 113.

that person's circumstances which is both expensive and disagreeable. If the objective is to be achieved by rules conferring rights, there is a danger of creating a complex and unwieldy body of law which those directly concerned would be unlikely fully to understand. If the more flexible alternative of a wide discretion is preferred, this creates the risk of bureaucratic power and apparent arbitrariness.

There has been no consistent development in British social policy in relation to means-tested benefits.[159] The early forms of welfare were, of course, almost wholly dependent on this method. As we have seen, between the two World Wars unemployment assistance became a necessary complement to National Insurance; and, though Beveridge's aim was to reduce reliance on means-tested welfare to a minimum, the very opposite occurred. Today, it is accepted as an inevitable and major feature of the social security system. But policies have varied on the form and structure of the schemes.[160] In the early 1980s, the emphasis was on detailed rights and regulation. The Thatcher governments modified this trend, as they sought to restrain the costs and the complexities by subjecting important areas of need to discretionary decision making. At the same time, an effort was made to co-ordinate the different schemes, and fiscal control continues to be exerted through amendments to both primary and secondary legislation. The Blair government's emphasis on tax credits necessarily involves greater use of means-testing, albeit outside the traditional social security scheme. Although described as 'progressive universalism',[161] the rhetoric cannot disguise the fact that TCA 2002 represents a substantial extension of such means-testing, exposing increasing numbers of individuals to the negative disincentives inherent in such a process.

iii   Criterion of assumed needs

The alternative strategy of selecting circumstances or individuals whose present or future needs are assumed rather than demonstrated is more widely favoured. Inevitably, it raises the fundamental question of what is comprehended by 'needs' and of whether their satisfaction is properly the subject of state intervention as opposed to individual initiative.[162] A fundamental goal of all social security systems is to make provision for economic insecurity and thus it is a question of identifying the typical causes of such insecurity.[163] The variety of circumstances causing financial hardship is infinite. While some are regarded uncontroversially as properly the subject of individual initiative, eg property loss through fire, theft or vandalism,[164] and others are endemic in a society of mixed cultures and values, eg lack of ambition, idleness, personal extravagance,[165] there is a broad category of hazards which in most industrially developed societies are regarded as appropriate for state intervention. They may be divided into three groups.

A   EARNINGS LOSS

Social security systems have always centred on providing some compensation for the interruption or deprivation of earnings resulting from one or more of the standard risks:

159   *Deacon and Bradshaw* n 145, above.
160   Pp 275–278, 384–386 and 407–410, below.
161   HM Treasury *The Modernisation of Britain's Tax and Benefit System – Child and Working Tax Credits* Report No 10 (2002) p 4.
162   *Harris* n 39, above, ch 7.
163   Cf *Beveridge Report* n 23, above, paras 311–312.
164   *Beveridge Report* n 23, above, para 312.
165   Rejda *Social Insurance and Economic Security* (1976) pp 8–9.

unemployment, sickness, invalidity, maternity and old age. Income maintenance in these circumstances is provided primarily by the contributory (formerly National Insurance) benefits. These benefits are based on a labour market model of traditionally male full-time work which has become out-of-date as the proportion of insecure and part-time jobs and female employees in the economy increases.[166]

B   LOSS OF MAINTENANCE

Impairment of the breadwinner's income can inevitably have adverse consequences on dependants and additions are available to some of the contributory benefits for this purpose. The only cause of loss of maintenance which, under the British system, gives rise to substantial protection is the death of the breadwinner, in the form of bereavement benefits and the guardian's allowance. The breakdown of marriage, while a major source of deprivation, has never been treated as equivalent to death. Moreover, the assistance provided by way of an increased rate of child benefit for lone parents was withdrawn in 1998.[167] Indeed, the scheme introduced by the Child Support Act 1991 reaffirms that this is essentially a private law issue, albeit one where obligations are assessed and enforced through a state agency.

C   SPECIAL EXPENSES

Priority has been conferred on the partial indemnification of two categories of expenditure: the costs of rearing children and those incurred by seriously disabled persons. Maternity and funeral expenses used to be the subject of universal grants but assistance with these expenses is now means-tested, as is help with housing costs. There are, however, non-means tested winter fuel payments to pensioners.[168]

C   Levels of cash benefit

i   Flat-rate or earnings-related

Having determined the circumstances in which a cash benefit will be payable, the social security system must then decide on what principle that benefit will be calculated. Where it is intended as some replacement for the interruption or loss of earnings, the fundamental issue arises as to whether the benefit should be flat-rate or earnings-related. The latter approach is a central feature of the Bismarckian social insurance schemes common in other major Western European states, reflecting the notion that benefit is merely a 'deferred wage' and therefore should reflect the collective bargaining process which determined the amount of that wage.[169] The argument is a compelling one in a wholly state-controlled economy where the state is both the employer and the provider of benefits, on the assumption that the initial wage level accords with the distributional dictates of its conception of social justice.[170] For this very reason it is opposed by those

---

166   McLaughlin (1991) 20 J Soc Pol 485.
167   P 658, below.
168   P 493, below.
169   Burns *Social Security and Public Policy* (1956) p 41.
170   *Report of the Royal Commission of Inquiry* n 87, above, p 173.

who argue that an earnings-related scheme reinforces differentials, on the whole dictated by market forces, and which may therefore be inequitable.[171] This viewpoint is linked to the principle that the social welfare system should operate as a mechanism for redistribution rather than merely as a compensation for losses incurred through social risks.

The UK social security scheme has never fully embraced the earnings-related principle. Beveridge regarded protection of resources above the subsistence level as a matter for individual initiative but the principle of flat-rate benefits led to a glaring disparity between those who were able and willing to augment state provision by occupational schemes and those who were not. The Conservative government's solution, a modest graduated pension scheme, proved to be inadequate and the Labour Party drew up plans for a national superannuation programme of earnings-related provision which nevertheless was slow to be implemented. Earnings-related supplements to the short-term benefits for sickness and unemployment were introduced in 1966 but the state earnings-related pension scheme (SERPS) was not enacted until 1975. The concern of the Thatcher administration to encourage expansion of private provision and to broaden choice naturally led to a reversal of this trend. The earnings-related supplements to the short-term benefits were abolished in 1982 and, though the Conservative government abandoned its original intention of abolishing SERPS, the 1986 legislation reduced entitlements under the scheme. Incapacity benefit, which was introduced in April 1995, has no earnings-related component, unlike its predecessor, invalidity benefit. SERPS itself was superseded from April 2002 by the state second pension (S2P), which deliberately eschews any earnings-related element in the traditional sense. In fact, the S2P scheme provides more help for those on the *lowest* incomes.[172] Thus the substantial demand, at least from middle and higher socio-economic groups, for benefits, particularly pensions, to reflect market differentials is a matter for the market in the UK.[173]

ii   Determination of benefits according to need

Thus all benefits payable under the current system – with the exception of those accrued under SERPS – are *not* related to earnings. These include not only the flat-rate components in the standard income-replacement benefits for sickness, unemployment and retirement, but also those designed to accommodate special expenses or needs and those which are means-tested. For all within this category, decisions must be taken on the appropriate level of financial support. There has been a considerable amount of literature devoted to this question, much of it concerned with theoretical problems of assessing need and defining poverty. Less well treated are the political and other pressures which in practice operate on governmental decision-makers in this area.

A   ASSESSING NEEDS

The Beveridge objective, it will be recalled, was that of a minimum level of 'subsistence' on the basis of 'normal needs'. How were such needs to be assessed? Already earlier in the century some scientific measurement had been attempted, notably by Rowntree. He drew up a list of 'consumption necessities', eg food, clothing and housing

171   Esam, Good and Middleton *Who's to Benefit?* (1985) pp 37–38.
172   Pp 620–625, below.
173   Cf Silburn (ed) *The Future of Social Security* (1985) pp 68–69.

expenditure.[174] The method was adopted by Beveridge as a guide;[175] he applied a variable of age and also added a margin for inefficiency in spending. In another respect, however, his criteria were more stringent than those proposed by Rowntree who had allowed a small amount for 'personal sundries', eg trade union subscriptions, newspapers, radio, beer, tobacco.[176] Of course, as determinants for individual needs, these models were deficient, in that they had to be based on perceived averages.[177] Any shortfall was therefore to be remedied by supplementary schemes based on detailed means tests. This difficulty was only one of a number of aspects which were vigorously criticised by commentators in the 1950s and 1960s. The most comprehensive and widely publicised was that of Townsend.[178] He rejected any absolute objective notion of poverty based on subsistence requirements: he regarded it instead as a relative concept to be measured only by reference to the living standards of a particular society at a particular time. Others have stressed that poverty is a psychological state dependent on an individual's own expectations:[179] this may be conditioned by that person's previous level of earnings or standard of living (or those of his or her neighbour). Finally, there is the perspective which has regard to the effect of deprivation on the lives of individuals within the community – a state of 'virtual non-participation'. In his major survey of poverty, Townsend sought to incorporate these broader dimensions by focusing not only on objective standards as reflected in data on the distribution of resources but also on individuals' perceptions of what constitutes poverty, the effect of environmental factors, and the relevance to deprivation of categorisation into one of the social minorities (eg lone parents, ethnic minorities, unemployed people).[180] Townsend's approach has been highly influential in subsequent studies of poverty in contemporary society.[181]

B FIXING SCALES OF BENEFIT

Undoubtedly the data available on the needs of particular disadvantaged groups influence to a certain extent governmental decisions on the level of benefits, but it is important to appreciate that there are other factors which may play an equal if not primary role.[182] Regard has typically been had not only to the level of prices but also to the general level of earnings: a system in which benefits are significantly above the incomes of the lower paid is likely to be politically unacceptable, if for no other reason than it is thought to have an effect on work incentives.[183] Further, fixing the amount of some flat-rate benefits, such as retirement pensions, may be influenced by the fact that many

---

174 Rowntree *Poverty – A Study of Town Life* (1901), *Human Needs of Labour* (1937).
175 *Beveridge Report* n 23, above, paras 217–232; cf Harris *William Beveridge* (rev edn, 1997) pp 386–389.
176 Rowntree *Human Needs of Labour* (1937) p 61.
177 Cf DHSS *Social Assistance* (1978) para 5.5. Beveridge felt the problem of variations in rent to be particularly acute but, after some hesitation, decided that to make a separate award for household needs would be impracticable: *Beveridge Report* n 23, above, paras 193–216.
178 Townsend (1954) Br J Sociology 330 and (1962) Br J Sociology 210. See also Townsend (ed) *The Concept of Poverty* (1970) and Townsend *The International Analysis of Poverty* (1993).
179 Eg Runciman *Relative Deprivation and Social Justice* (1966).
180 Townsend *Poverty in the United Kingdom* (1979).
181 See eg Mack and Lansley *Poor Britain* (1985); Gordon and Pantazis (eds) *Breadline Britain in the 1990s* (1997); and Bradshaw and Sainsbury (eds) *Researching Poverty* (2000), esp chs 2–4. For accessible introductions to the issues, see Bradshaw in Ditch (ed) *Introduction to Social Security* (1999) ch 1; and Howard et al *Poverty: the facts* (4th edn, 2001). For an alternative neo-liberal perspective, see Dennis *The Invention of Permanent Poverty* (1997).
182 Atkinson in Wilson and Wilson *The State and Social Welfare* (1991) ch 7.
183 But there is little empirical evidence to support the proposition that generous out of work benefits increase unemployment levels: Barr (1999) 1 Australian Social Policy 7 at 15–18.

beneficiaries also receive an earnings-related component. Conversely, account may be taken of equity considerations when determining the relationship between different categories of social security benefit, eg between contributory and non-contributory benefits. The level of social security payments is also necessarily dependent on the general economic policy pursued by government. The restraints imposed on public expenditure by the Thatcher governments in the 1980s, which resulted in reductions in the real value of benefits, were considered to be crucial to the control of inflation and the revitalisation of the economy.[184] However controversial this policy might have been, it was at least consistent with general strategy and in this sense was 'rational'. As such it is to be contrasted with the way in which some decisions as to social welfare spending have been reached on purely political grounds.[185] A remarkable feature of the past three or four decades has been the growth of pressure groups identified with particular categories of beneficiaries or disadvantaged people.[186] They have had a significant influence on decision-making, especially in the area of family and disability benefits.[187]

C   THE PROBLEM OF INFLATION

Of course, the level of a particular benefit depends not only on the policy (or politics) prevailing at the time the benefit was introduced but also on whether governments are prepared to maintain its value relative to changes in prices and earnings.[188] Indeed, inflation can be used to alter policy on particular benefits without direct legislative reform. For example, successive governments allowed the real value of the death and maternity grants to erode so substantially in the 40 years following the Second World War that they no longer served their original purpose. Politically, it then became easier to argue for their abolition as universal benefits, since the cost of administering payment was very high relative to their value.[189] Nevertheless, as regards the major income maintenance programmes, social security would be a misnomer if beneficiaries could not rely on some degree of protection against inflation, particularly when the rate is high.[190] There has been a widespread consensus that legislative duties to up-rate benefits, in some form, should be imposed on governments but, as will be discussed in a later chapter,[191] the provisions have been modified several times since their original enactment in 1973. Perhaps most significant was the repeal in 1980 of the obligation to link pensions to rises in earnings, a decision which generated very substantial savings in social security expenditure.[192] The Blair government has maintained the policy of up-rating the state

---

184   See eg the White Paper *The Government's Expenditure Plans 1980–81* (1979, Cmnd 7746) and the criticisms of the Commons' Social Services Committee, 3rd Report 1979–80, HC 702.
185   Eg the decision to introduce winter fuel payments: see p 493, below.
186   Donnison *The Politics of Poverty* (1982) pp 126–134; McCarthy *Campaigning for the Poor* (1986); Whiteley and Winyard *Pressure for the Poor* (1987).
187   See eg Banting *Poverty, Politics and Policy* (1979).
188   See generally Wilson (ed) *Pensions, Inflation and Growth* (1974); and Hirsch and Goldthorpe (eds) *The Political Economy of Inflation* (1978) ch 4.
189   The universal benefits were replaced by means-tested grants from the social fund from April 1987: p 557, below. It had cost £12 million per year to administer £17 million per year of death grant awards: Fowler *Ministers Decide* (1991) p 205.
190   As was the case in the 1970s: Trinder in Willmott (ed) *Sharing Inflation* (1976) chs 2–4.
191   Pp 265–267, below.
192   Such constraints on public expenditure were considered by the Thatcher administration to be the most effective means of controlling inflation.

retirement pension in line with prices, while linking increases in income support rates for pensioners (the 'minimum income guarantee') to earnings.[193]

iii Determination of earnings-related benefits

As we have seen, the British social security system has never placed as much reliance on earnings-related benefits as its continental neighbours. Indeed, now the only remaining earnings-related benefit is SERPS, although no new rights have been able to accrue to that scheme since April 2002, when it was replaced by S2P. There are, in any event, both practical and policy problems inherent in relating benefits to a claimant's previous earnings.[194] In other European systems where short-term benefits are earnings-related, regard is generally had to the claimant's wages in the period immediately before that of entitlement;[195] but for long-term benefits, it is thought fairer to take account of that period when the earnings were highest in real terms.[196] Neither of these approaches copes adequately with the case where an individual is unable to build up an employment record owing to caring responsibilities or disability.[197]

D Financing of benefits

There are two main methods of financing social security benefits: by a fund, the contributions to which are earmarked exclusively for the purpose; and by general taxation. The first approach is often, though as will emerge largely misleadingly, referred to as the 'insurance' method. It may itself involve either flat-rate or earnings-related contributions.[198]

i The insurance concept

Contributory benefits have traditionally lain at the heart of the British system. Although the term 'national insurance' disappeared from the statute book in 1973, the concept of insurance is deeply rooted in the history of social security.[199] Private insurance to cover what are today regarded as social risks, eg retirement and premature death, was widespread in the nineteenth century[200] and greatly influenced the German and British developments in social welfare. Under the National Insurance Act 1911 benefit was seen to rest on past economic performance rather than need itself, and bad risks, eg those employed in certain industries, women and children, were excluded. The scheme was popular both with the middle classes, for it seemed to encourage thrift, and with the

---

193 The HC Social Security Committee had concluded that this strategy is 'unlikely to be sustainable in the long run': *Seventh Report* (1999–2000, HC 606) para 77. See also ch 17, below.
194 See further the 4th edition of this book, pp 24–25.
195 However, the rules for calculating the British earnings-related supplement which was abolished in 1982 meant that there was often a substantial gap between the period of reference and the period of benefit: see the 1st edition of this book, p 426.
196 SERPS used to have regard to the claimant's best 20 years of working life; after the 1988 changes, entitlement was based on a working-life average: p 617, below.
197 This was a major factor behind the decision to move from SERPS to S2P: p 620, below.
198 See generally Glennerster *Paying for welfare: towards 2000* (3rd edn, 1997) chs 1 and 14.
199 HC Social Security Committee *Fifth Report* (1999–2000, HC 56) paras 20–32.
200 Gosden *Self-Help: Voluntary Associations in the 19th Century* (1973).

working classes, because it created, for the first time, a framework of legal rights to welfare.[201] As was pointed out by Beveridge,[202] and has since been stated by many others,[203] the analogy between the contributory schemes and private insurance is an inappropriate one. In a private insurance scheme premiums are based on the risk attendant on the particular circumstances of the insured person (age, sex, health, occupation, family commitments). Provided that the risk-rating is sufficiently precise, there can properly be no redistribution between insured individuals except in the very limited sense that those for whom the risk does not materialise will support those who become subject to it. The trend in social security legislation has been almost wholly against relating contributions to the degree of risk. Thus at an early stage unemployment insurance and workmen's compensation were extended to industries particularly sensitive to the hazards in question, without varying the rates of contributions. The separate categorisation of married women was abolished in 1975 so that, apart from minor exceptions,[204] all that remains is the very broad division between the employed, the self-employed and the non-employed.[205] There is, it should be noted, an argument that, at least as regards certain hazards which might be avoided by more careful management, employers' contributions should be 'experience-rated'.[206] But in Britain the incentive or prevention objectives of social welfare have been kept distinct from the financing provisions.[207]

The second important respect in which contributory schemes differ from private insurance relates to the actuarial basis of their administration. The latter must be actuarially sound in the sense that the funds available from contributions and investment yields must be sufficient to finance predicted future benefits. A social security fund, on the other hand, may adopt the 'pay as you go' approach so that benefits payable at a particular time are related not to previous accumulations of contributions but to the finances made available from current contributions.[208] As a result there may be redistribution as between generations of insured persons.

ii   Types of contribution

The first question arising under a contributory scheme is whether both employers and employees should participate. Some would argue that the problem is an unreal one, for whichever group pays, the net effect is, in the long run, the same: an employer paying the contributions will pay less in the form of wages.[209] Most economists, however, regard the problem as a complex one:[210] the proportions in which the cost will be distributed between consumer (through higher prices), investor (through lower profits) and employee (through lower wages) will vary according to such factors as the elasticity of demand for the goods or services in question, the bargaining power of the wage-

---

201   Pinker *Social Theory and Social Policy* (1971) p 90.
202   *Beveridge Report* n 23, above, paras 24–25.
203   Eg *Barr* n 81, above, pp 125–126 and *HC Social Security Committee* n 199, above, paras 108–111.
204   Pp 119–120, below.
205   Cf the position in several other EU member states, where public servants are subject to special schemes: Association des Rencontres Européennes des Fonctions Publiques *La Protection Sociale des Agents Publics en Europe* (1993).
206   Pp 718–719, below. See Cane *Atiyah's Accidents, Compensation and the Law* (6th edn, 1999) pp 372–374.
207   Experience-rating is used in France: Dupeyroux *Droit de la sécurité sociale* (14th edn, 2001) p 838.
208   See generally *Barr* n 81, above, ch 5.
209   Kincaid *Poverty and Equality in Britain* (1973) pp 89–90.
210   Cf *Creedy and Disney* n 70, above, ch 11.

earners and the level of unemployment. To the extent that the burden falls on consumers, the distributional effect is likely to be regressive since lower-income groups spend proportionately more on consumption. Conversely, Beveridge contended that social security provision was one of the costs of production which should be reflected in the price of the product if competition was not to be distorted.[211] The other arguments he deployed for employers' contributions were of a more amorphous character: it is in the interest of employers that their employees' health and welfare should be protected; they should feel 'concerned for the lives of those who work under their control, should think of them not as instruments in production but as human beings';[212] finally, it was desirable that employers should have a basis for participation in the administration and strategies of the scheme. Whatever weight be given to these various factors, there is, it is submitted, one overriding consideration: a tax on employers is an easy source of revenue and one that tends to be politically popular.[213]

Should contributions be flat-rate or related to the ability to pay? The principle of the flat-rate contributions was as central to Beveridge's philosophy as that of flat-rate benefit: taxation according to capacity:

> involves a departure from existing practice, for which there is neither need nor justification and which conflicts with the wishes and feelings of the British democracy. ... Contribution means that in their capacity as possible recipients of benefits the poorer man and the richer man are treated alike.[214]

The rhetoric in this passage should not be allowed to cloud the real issue: the extent of redistribution to be admitted as a central objective of the system. Beveridge's commitment to the 'insurance' principle led him to forswear a substantial degree of redistribution which would have resulted from financing by progressive taxation methods, but the alleged dichotomy between on the one hand an 'insurance fund' and on the other hand earnings-related contributions is a false one. There is no reason, in principle, why the 'fund' or 'earmarked taxes' approach, even if used to finance flat-rate benefits, should not be combined with earnings-related contributions.[215] Beveridge's dogmatic preference for flat-rate contributions was indeed one of the reasons why his plan eventually failed. The burden on the lower paid of contributions sufficient to support an adequate level of benefits was too great.

The shift to earnings-related contributions, accomplished in 1975, was an inevitable corollary to the introduction of a broadly based earnings-related pension scheme – continuance of a flat-rate method would, of course, have resulted in regressive redistribution. Similarity to the predominantly progressive income tax method of raising funds was increased as a result of two other developments: the extension of contributions liability to individuals deriving profits from business activities; and, in 1985, the abolition of an upper limit to the contributions paid by employers.[216] Three remaining differences from income tax should, however, be noted: first, contributions are payable on total earnings, not merely those above the threshold; secondly, liability is non-cumulative, in the sense that it is calculated on the basis of each week's earnings, whatever the amounts earned or not earned in other weeks; finally, contributions are not payable on

211   *Beveridge Report* n 23, above, para 276.
212   *Beveridge Report* n 23, above, para 276.
213   George *Social Security: Beveridge and After* (1968) p 48.
214   *Beveridge Report* n 23, above, para 273.
215   Cf Lister *Social Security: The Case for Reform* Poverty Pamphlet No 22 (1975) pp 39–41.
216   P 110, below.

unearned income.[217] As we have seen, since April 2002, with the replacement of SERPS by S2P, it has not been possible to accrue new rights to earnings-related benefits. There has, however, been no suggestion that this affects the earnings-related basis of the contributions system.

In determining the principles and level of contributions there is clearly a need to maintain equity as between different sections of the community. Within the broad category of employed persons, and in sharp contrast to private insurance methods, it is not regarded as appropriate to differentiate according to susceptibility to risk – healthy individuals in secure employment pay the same rates as those with a record of illness or with an unstable participation in the labour market. Differentials may be applied when a class of contributors can have no recourse to a benefit or group of benefits.[218] Those opting out of SERPS or S2P eg pay a lower rate of contributions and the liability of the self-employed (who have no entitlement to jobseeker's allowance or under SERPS) is calculated on a different basis.[219]

iii   General taxation

Under Beveridge's plan and consistently thereafter, a place in the contributory scheme was allotted to general taxation but it was a small one (between 10 per cent and 20 per cent).[220] It was thought desirable not on redistributional principles but because it was clear that contributions recovered by the flat-rate method would otherwise be insufficient. With the introduction in 1975 of earnings-related contributions, this rationale lapsed and the Thatcher administration substantially reduced the Exchequer contribution to the National Insurance Fund in the 1980s, leading to its abolition in 1989.[221] It was then revived in 1993,[222] principally because of the shortfall in the Fund caused by the number of employees contracting out of SERPS in order to take out personal pension schemes. Non-contributory benefits are, of course, funded by general taxation and the massive growth of these programmes (most obviously the means-tested benefits, but also those payable to people with disabilities) has meant that more than half of current social security expenditure is derived from this source.[223]

There has been much discussion, particularly by economists,[224] on the respective merits of contributory schemes and general taxation as methods for funding social security benefits. The arguments are difficult to unravel because not only do the contributory schemes themselves contain several different strategies (employer or employee, flat-rate or earnings-related), but also because the effect of the methods on industrial growth and level of earnings is still highly controversial. The general consensus of opinion is, however, as one might expect, that the taxation approach is more redistributional, and therefore preferable on grounds of social justice, while the

---

217   Additionally, until April 2003 at least, an *employee* is not liable on earnings above an upper limit: but see further National Insurance Contributions Act 2002.

218   On this basis, married women have in the past been treated as a special category: cf *Beveridge Report* n 23, above, paras 107–117.

219   See also DHSS Discussion Document *The Self-Employed and National Insurance* (1980); and Brown *A Policy Vacuum* (1992). It has recently been argued that the self-employed under-contribute to the National Insurance scheme: p 112, below.

220   *Beveridge Report* n 23, above, para 282.

221   SSA 1989, s 3.

222   SSA 1993, s 2. See p 95, below.

223   DSS *Social Security Departmental Report* (2000, Cm 4614) p 76.

224   Culyer *The Economics of Social Policy* (1975) pp 202–204; *Rejda* n 165, above, pp 162–172; *Creedy and Disney* n 70, above, ch 10. For a social policy perspective, see Alcock (1996) 49 I Soc Sec Rev 31.

contribution approach tends to greater economic efficiency and therefore increased overall welfare. As important as these theoretical studies are, they do not feature much in the discussions within the political arena. Instead, we tend to be confronted with broad vague sentiments based on what the public allegedly wants. Thus Beveridge felt able to report that:

> benefit in return for contributions, rather than free allowances from the State, is what the people of Britain desire,[225]

and the mood was echoed in the government White Paper which followed it.[226] More recently, the House of Commons Social Security Committee concluded in its study of the contributory principle that 'there is a fundamental distinction in origin and purpose between benefits which people have earned on the basis of their contributions to cover identified risks, and benefits paid by the state to people on low incomes'.[227]

Such statements, however vacuous, provide the key to understanding why in the British and other systems the contributory approach remains the primary strategy for social security provision: the popularity of the method rests on its psychological appeal. People are prepared to subscribe more by way of contributions, which they see as offering returns in the form of personal and family security, than they would be willing to pay by taxation, which might be diverted to a wide variety of uses.[228] They are led to believe that because of their contributions to the scheme they are participating in its administration and may thus exercise closer political control over its development.[229] As has been observed, however, the same degree of public scrutiny should operate through the parliamentary supervision of public spending generally, if our political system is functioning properly.[230] Indeed, the Royal Commission in New Zealand regarded as an important reason for preferring the taxation approach the flexibility inherent in a system which does not tie funds down to a particular form of social welfare but rather allows different political administrations to take different views on social priorities.[231] One undeniably genuine and important factor is that of stigma. Sociologists have shown that we have been conditioned to bestow greater esteem on systems built on exchanges (benefits in *return* for contributions) than those incorporating unilateral transfers.[232] Nevertheless, one may question whether this is an attitude which our social system should foster, and whether it is appropriate to perpetuate beliefs in what are, in most respects, unreal differences between general and earmarked taxation. In the words of one commentator, the main effect of our 'contributory system' is 'to create confusion among the contributors/tax payers and fiscal illusion'.[233]

It remains to be seen how far popular commitment to the contributory approach survives into the twenty-first century. Most British governments since the Second World War have paid lip-service to the contributory principle, whilst their policies, together with economic and social changes, have done much to undermine the National Insurance

---

225 *Beveridge Report* n 23, above, para 21.
226 *Social Insurance* (1944, Cmd 6550) Pt I, para 6. To similar effect see the White Paper *National Superannuation and Social Insurance* (1969, Cmnd 3883) para 25. See also *Green Paper 1985* n 40, above, para 6.8. For discussion of the ideology underpinning the contributory principle, see Harris in Marquand and Seldon *The ideas that shaped post-war Britain* (1996) ch 6.
227 HC Social Security Committee *Fifth Report* (1999–2000, HC 56) para 72.
228 *HC Social Security Committee* n 227, above, paras 50–52.
229 *Beveridge Report* n 23, above, para 274.
230 *Culyer* n 74, above, p 203.
231 Report of the Royal Commission of Inquiry *Social Security in New Zealand* (1972) p 158.
232 Pinker *Social Theory and Social Policy* (1971) ch 4.
233 *Culyer* n 74, above, p 204. See also Dilnot, Kay and Morris *The Reform of Social Security* (1984) p 29.

scheme.[234] Adherence to the contributory principle certainly seems to be stronger in those countries (eg Germany) where the insurance system is embedded in the labour market institutional arrangements.[235] The Blair administration has made it clear that, in its view, the contributory principle is a means rather than end in itself. This has been illustrated by the abolition of the contribution condition for maternity allowance, and its replacement by an earnings threshold requirement, and the availability of incapacity benefit to those without insurance records but who are incapacitated in their youth.[236] The emphasis is thus on outcomes, rather than on modes of delivery: 'the future of contributory benefits will depend on whether they serve the emerging needs of the 21st century'.[237]

E   Other forms of welfare provision

The policymaker concerned to confer welfare on different groups within society has three broad strategies available. Provision may be made by way of cash payments (what we refer to as 'social security'), benefits in kind (typically known as 'social services') or by exploiting the possibilities created by the fiscal systems, through eg tax reliefs. In this section we explore the relationship between social security and the other forms of welfare, and discuss some of the issues involved in the choice between the various strategies. As we shall see, the Blair governments, through the introduction of tax credits, have placed particular emphasis on the use of the fiscal system as a means of pursuing welfare policy.

i   Benefits in cash or in kind

Social welfare, as broadly construed, embraces a wide range of benefits in kind, among many others those for health, education and housing. On a simple view, these services may be regarded as complementary to, and independent from, the cash benefits which form the subject-matter of this book: cash benefits, it might be said, are designed for income maintenance, whereas the services are designed to fulfil other objectives of social policy. But since income is necessary, above all, to purchase essential items for living and those items could be provided directly for those in need, the policymaker is clearly faced with a choice between these strategies. Two opposing theories may be considered.[238]

According to the more traditional liberal, individualist view, welfare measures are necessary to redress inequalities of resources. Since beneficiaries know best how to maximise their own utility from the spending of money, cash transfers must generate at least as much utility as benefits in kind and often more. Moreover, they are cheaper to administer, involve a less intrusive role for the state and avoid the distortion of prices which results from large-scale public purchases. Legal enforcement is also easier: an individual deprived of a cash benefit may without undue difficulty appeal against the

234   *HC Social Security Committee* n 227, above, para 32.
235   Clasen *Paying the Jobless* (1994); and Bolderson and Mabbett (1996) 49 I Soc Sec Rev 3.
236   P 535, below.
237   DSS *Reply to the Fifth Report* (2000) para 25.
238   Tobin (1970) 13 J Law Econ 263; ISSA *The Role of Social Services in Social Security* ISSA Studies and Research No 6 (1974); Thurow in Dworkin, Bermont and Brown (eds) *Markets and Morals* (1977) ch 6.

decision. In contrast, a counterpart with a grievance against the social services may find either that the agency concerned was under no duty to provide it, or, if it was, that a court exercising judicial review is confined to considering the *process* rather than the *outcome*.[239] Not surprisingly, economists tend to prefer this form of welfare and indeed argue that some services traditionally provided in kind, such as education, could instead be the subject of choice and purchase through cash vouchers.[240]

These views are challenged by those who adopt a less individualist approach to welfare. It is argued, first, that certain types of good, eg health or education, are not proper subjects for the operation of market forces either because the social costs of mistaken decisions are too great or because, adopting a paternalist stance, it is not to be assumed that in such areas individuals always act as rational maximisers of their own welfare.[241] Secondly, the model ignores the causes of poverty; by the careful use of services to prevent as well as to react to social hazards, the problem of inadequate income, may, in some cases, be avoided.[242] Thirdly, the income redistribution technique is less sensitive to specific needs and less personal in its administration – the individual guidance implicit in the social service model may both respond in a humane way to individual circumstances and at the same time encourage greater social activity and participation.[243]

ii Social security and taxation

The relationship between the social security and taxation systems constitutes an important feature of the policy issues arising under social legislation, and all the more so with the arrival of the new generation of tax credits. There are three independent but related matters which call for discussion: first, the extent to which social security benefits are taxable, and the implications which this has on the degree of redistribution; secondly, the manner in which the tax system may, through its granting of reliefs, itself operate as a direct instrument of income maintenance; thirdly, the desirability or otherwise of integrating taxation with social security.

A TAX LIABILITY OF CLAIMANTS

If a social security benefit is not taxable, its value will vary according to the tax liabilities of the recipient. The consequent possibility of inequity as between different beneficiaries might be thought to be academic since many social security benefits are payable only when the claimant has no earnings. But income tax liability is cumulative over the tax year and so beneficiaries who have sufficient income during the rest of the tax year to take them above the tax threshold will gain if the benefit does not form part of their taxable income. Quite apart from this problem of equity, such a situation may also give rise to significant work disincentives. Indeed, the existence of the progressive system of taxation collected by the PAYE method means that during spells of unemployment or sickness employees may be entitled to weekly refunds of tax paid on their anticipated

---

239 See Clements *Community Care and the Law* (2nd edn, 2000) ch 12.
240 Harris and Seldon *Welfare without the State* (1987).
241 Titmuss *Commitment to Welfare* (1968) pp 147–150; *Culyer* n 74, above, ch 7.
242 Crosland *The Future of Socialism* (1961) pp 145–146; Lebel in *ISSA Studies and Research No 6* n 238, above, pp 126–127.
243 *ISSA Studies and Research No 6* n 238, above, p 125; *Crosland* n 242, above, p 148; *Titmuss* n 241, above, p 150.

annual earnings, thus creating a kind of 'parallel system of ... benefits ... calculated on the mythical basis that the worker, during his unemployment or sickness, had no social security income at all'.[244]

The policy of the Attlee government, which implemented the Beveridge Report, was that all income-maintenance benefits[245] should be taxed. On grounds of impracticability the policy had to be reversed in 1949 with regard to the short-term benefits: beneficiaries could not be incorporated into the PAYE scheme and taxes had thus to be collected retrospectively; the recovery of millions of small debts by the Inland Revenue was uneconomic.[246] Given the circumstances then prevailing, the decision was not unreasonable. In the half-century since 1949, however, the situation changed dramatically. On the one hand, the real value of benefits increased so that the amounts involved are no longer negligible. On the other hand, the administration of tax and social security is more clearly integrated than it was – indeed, the records of taxpayers are now kept under their National Insurance numbers. In 1980 the Conservative government announced its intention of extending taxation to most income-maintenance benefits, although this was not fully implemented.[247] At that time widow's benefits,[248] retirement and invalidity pensions were already taxable. The contributory and means-tested benefits payable to the unemployed were added to the list in 1981,[249] as were statutory sick pay and statutory maternity pay, which in 1983 and 1988 respectively replaced sickness benefit and maternity allowance for most claimants. The main benefits which, at present, are not subject to tax are income support, housing benefit, child benefit, attendance allowance and disability living allowance and, of course, the tax credits themselves.[250]

B   TAX AS AN INSTRUMENT FOR INCOME SUPPORT

Since the introduction of progressive taxation in 1907 there has been what Titmuss has described as 'a remarkable development of social policy operating through the medium of the fiscal system'.[251] Most significantly this has taken the form of family support, through the granting of children's and other dependants' allowances – the amount of income permitted to be accumulated before tax is imposed. Such a system may be regarded as equitable as between those taxpayers who have, and those who do not have, family commitments but within a broader social perspective the position is different. It can benefit only those with resources sufficient to attract tax and, if it is applied consistently throughout the tax structure, the system of reliefs has a regressive effect, for the value of the relief increases as the rate of tax increases. For political reasons, it proved difficult to modify arrangements in the light of these considerations. For example, the introduction of family allowances in 1945 did not affect the tax relief on children then available.[252] In 1968, a compromise solution was reached: by means

244   Walley *Social Security: Another British Failure?* (1972) p 207.
245   Though, anomalously, not industrial injury benefit.
246   See *Report of the Committee on the Taxation of Pensions for Retirement* (1954, Cmd 9063) paras 271–294.
247   Sir G Howe, Chancellor of the Exchequer, 980 HC Official Report (5th series) col 1460.
248   But not those payable under the war pensions scheme.
249   Finance Act 1981, s 29.
250   See now Income and Corporation Taxes Act 1988, ss 150–152 and 617.
251   Titmuss *Essays on the Welfare State* (3rd edn, 1976) p 45.
252   See White Paper *Family Allowances: Memorandum by the Chancellor of the Exchequer* (1942, Cmd 6134) p 5; and *Beveridge Report* n 23, above, para 422.

of the so-called 'clawback', the amount by which family allowances were increased was in effect deducted from the individual's tax relief.[253] The replacement of family allowances by child benefit in 1975 signalled the government's intention also to abolish tax allowances for children and this was finally achieved in 1979.[254] Subsequently, the question of replacing tax relief for dependent spouses with cash benefits was raised.[255] The then Conservative government rejected this approach, primarily on grounds of cost.[256] The subsequent introduction of 'independent taxation' of husband and wife in 1990 left the tax position of most married couples unchanged; those that did benefit were overwhelmingly higher-income families.[257] However, the married person's allowance was finally abolished (for all bar pensioner couples) in 2000, and replaced from 2001 by a children's tax credit.[258] The latter was not available to all taxpayers with children, but phased out for those paying higher rate tax. This reform, taken together with other measures introduced by the first Blair administration, was markedly redistributive.[259] More ambitious still were New Labour's plans for dealing with the interface between the tax and social security systems, discussed in the following section.

C INTEGRATION OF TAX AND SOCIAL SECURITY

(i) Proposals for a negative income tax or basic income
Beveridge, who envisaged that only a minority of claimants would require means-tested benefits, was writing at a time when many working people fell outside the scope of the income tax system. In the following half-century, both the liability to pay income tax and reliance on means-tested benefits became more common, with the effect that the state was simultaneously both giving income to and taking it away from the same individuals.[260] The need to rationalise the relationship between taxation and social security may appear therefore to be self-evident. A number of ambitious schemes have been advocated over the years, most notably the negative income tax and basic income (or social dividend) approaches.[261]

Some proponents of such a reform have argued that an integrated tax-welfare scheme would not only be administratively more efficient, but might also provide the means of abolishing poverty altogether. Under an integrated system, people earning more than the relevant threshold would continue to pay tax while those with incomes below that level would receive a payment (a 'negative income tax') rather than make one. This idea, first canvassed widely in the US,[262] won support on this side of the Atlantic as a means not only of rationalising the cumbersome co-existence of various benefit schemes

---

253 See generally Lynes in Bull (ed) *Family Poverty* (2nd edn, 1972) ch 10.
254 P 655, below.
255 Green Paper *Taxation of Husband and Wife* (1983, Cmnd 8093).
256 Green Paper *Reform of Personal Taxation* (1986, Cmnd 9756) Pt III.
257 Hills *Changing Tax* (1988) chs 8 and 9. The married couple's allowance was a classic example of a badly targeted benefit: *Hills* p 24.
258 Not to be confused with the child tax credit to be introduced by the Tax Credits Act 2002 (TCA 2002).
259 Glennerster in *Seldon* n 55, above, ch 18.
260 A phenomenon sometimes described as 'churning'.
261 The discussion here is indebted to *Hills* n 257, above ch 11 and *The Future of Welfare* (1993) ch 2. See also Hill *Social Security Policy in Britain* (1990) pp 157–173; Commission on Social Justice (CSJ) *Social Justice: Strategies for National Renewal* (1994) pp 258–265; and Clinton, Yates and Kang *Integrating Taxes and Benefits?* CSJ Issue Paper No 8 (1994).
262 Friedman *Capitalism and Freedom* (1962); Green *Negative Taxes and the Poverty Problem* (1967). One such plan was promoted by the Nixon administration but failed to pass through Congress: Moynihan *The Politics of a Guaranteed Income* (1973).

but also of dealing with the problems of stigma and take-up associated with traditional means tests.[263]

Notwithstanding the apparent attractions of proposals for a negative income tax, there remain a number of difficulties with such schemes. First, benefits are typically assessed weekly, whereas tax is calculated on an annual basis, which is fairer for those whose incomes fluctuate during the year. It is difficult to see how an integrated system of computerised assessment could deal adequately with people's immediate needs, and so some form of discretionary aid would have to complement (and complicate) the general scheme. Secondly, a negative income tax would almost certainly disadvantage women in those households in which income is not shared equally. Thirdly, a redesigned PAYE system which included a comprehensive means test might actually be administratively more inefficient.[264]

An associated approach is the 'basic income' strategy.[265] This dates back to 1943 when, as an alternative to the Beveridge plan, Lady Rhys Williams urged the adoption of a 'social dividend', the payment to all members of society of weekly amounts necessary for the ordinary needs of living.[266] Under such a scheme all citizens would receive a flat-rate benefit payment, but all income (except perhaps a small amount of earnings) would be taxable. As such, in essence, if not in administrative arrangements, it is similar to the negative income tax proposals. The principal difficulty with any 'basic income' scheme is that the marginal rate of taxation would have to be very high to make it viable. Estimates range from at least 50 per cent to in excess of 80 per cent.[267] This would raise serious incentive and evasion problems.

The enormous complexity of the issues involved by such proposals, which must respond, in particular, to the variables of family size, employment status and the impact of existing benefit systems, has given rise to an intimidating critical literature,[268] a detailed account of which is beyond the scope of this book. Nevertheless, some general considerations do call for further comment.

The strongest argument for universal schemes is that they generate information on the existence of poverty and, at the same time, enable claims to be made without the problems of stigma and low take-up. More controversial is the fact that most proposals define eligibility for financial assistance by reference solely to economic criteria (primarily levels of income), thus abandoning the conditions of entitlement traditionally associated with contributory schemes (unemployment, sickness, retirement etc). No doubt this enables the system to become at once more comprehensive and simpler; it would also focus on those in greatest need. Yet the elimination of such categories may be neither possible nor desirable. To avoid abuse, it would presumably be necessary for the unemployed to register as available for work or be relieved from this obligation for a specific reason, eg sickness, retirement or family responsibilities, and thus for administrative purposes some categorisation is inevitable. Finally, many of the proposed schemes for an integration of taxes and benefits have assumed that their introduction

---

263   Institute of Economic Affairs *Policy for Poverty* (1970). A slightly less ambitious, but arguably more practical, plan to cover employed persons and National Insurance beneficiaries was suggested but not pursued by the Conservative government in 1972: Green Paper *Proposals for a Tax-Credit System* (Cmnd 5116).

264   But see Dilnot, Kay and Morris *The Reform of Social Security* (1984).

265   See Van Parijs (ed) *Arguing for Basic Income* (1992).

266   Rhys Williams *Something to Look Forward To* (1943).

267   Atkinson *Poverty and Social Security* (1989) ch 16; and Parker *Instead of the Dole* (1989).

268   *Creedy and Disney* n 70, above, chs 9–12; Dilnot and Walker (eds) *The Economics of Social Security* (1989); *Barr* n 81, above, ch 11, and the references there cited. See also the debate on citizen's income in (1996) 67 Political Q 54–70.

would be facilitated by computerisation. The evidence of the last two decades is that while computerisation in the benefits system has brought undoubted advantages, it has also been fraught with problems.[269]

(ii) The new generation of tax credits

New Labour's 1997 manifesto included a commitment to streamline and modernise the tax and benefit systems with the aim of increasing work incentives and reducing poverty and welfare dependency.[270] A government-appointed task force identified four principal advantages for a system of tax credits: a reduction in stigma; their greater acceptability amongst the public at large; the promotion of work incentives; and an alleviation of the poverty trap.[271] Legislative reform swiftly followed. The Social Security Contributions (Transfer of Functions etc) Act 1999 moved the Contributions Agency from the DSS into the Inland Revenue, consolidating the Treasury's role in raising social security revenue. TCA 1999, following paving legislation the previous year,[272] then transferred the Family Credit Unit from the DSS to the Revenue and relaunched family credit as working families' tax credit (WFTC) in October 1999. The policy objective of emphasising the rewards of work was manifested in the decision to require employers (from April 2000) to pay WFTC through the pay packet, but at the cost of increasing their administrative burden.[273] At the same time, the rates of WFTC were made significantly more generous than those that applied under the family credit scheme.

As we will see in chapter 10, TCA 1999 was effectively a rebranding exercise.[274] It was, however, part of a wider package of reforms designed to implement the government's welfare to work agenda. These included the introduction of a national minimum wage and increases in the rate of child benefit, as well as a 10 per cent income tax band and reform of the contributions system for low earners.[275] TCA 2002 was far more ambitious in scope than its 1999 predecessor. First, it transferred responsibility for the payment of child benefit and guardian's allowance from the DWP to the Inland Revenue.[276] Secondly, it introduced – with effect from April 2003 – two new tax credits: an integrated child tax credit and a working tax credit, again administered by the Inland Revenue.[277]

The new child tax credit (CTC) involved rolling up the existing forms of support for children under the tax and benefit systems into one credit, which is withdrawn as income rises. CTC thus replaces the child elements in income support, income-based jobseeker's allowance and WFTC (and its companion disabled person's tax credit (DPTC)) as well as the children's tax credit, itself a temporary form of tax relief introduced in 2001 following the abolition of the married person's allowance the previous year. Eligibility for CTC follows that for child benefit; thus it will be available to households with at least one child under 16 (or under 19 if in full-time advanced education), regardless of

---

269 See eg National Audit Office *DSS: Operational Strategy* (HC 111, 1988–89); House of Commons Social Security Committee *The Organisation and Administration of the DSS* Minutes (HC 550-ii, 1990–91); and Margetts (1991) 69 Public Administration 325. See also the cancellation of the benefits payment card project: House of Commons Public Accounts Committee *Third Report* (2000–01, HC 358); and p 158, below.
270 Labour Party *New Labour Because Britain Deserves Better* (1997) p 13.
271 HM Treasury *The Modernisation of Britain's Tax and Benefit Systems* Report No 2 (1998) para 3.19.
272 Tax Credits (Initial Expenditure) Act 1998.
273 TCA 1999, s 6. Where this is not appropriate, the Inland Revenue is the default payer.
274 See TCA 1999, s 1(1).
275 On the reforms to the contributions system, see pp 107–108, below.
276 TCA 2002, Pt 2.
277 TCA 2002, Pt 1, see further HC Social Security Committee *Second Report* (2000–01, HC 72).

whether any one is in work.[278] The CTC consists of a basic family component with an additional sum for each child or young person. Entitlement to CTC is reduced by a taper, as for WFTC, once household income exceeds a prescribed threshold. The introduction of CTC follows similar developments in other jurisdictions, most notably Australia.[279]

The new working tax credit (WTC) replaces the adult elements in WFTC and DPTC, as well as the special employment credit for those returning to work under the New Deal 50plus scheme. It is designed to provide financial assistance to single adults or couples in low-paid work or who have a disability. The basic structure of WTC is similar to WFTC, but shorn of the child credits (but not the child care credit), which are now incorporated in CTC. As with CTC, entitlement to WTC is reduced once a prescribed threshold income is reached.[280] The principal advantage of WTC over WFTC is that entitlement is not premised on the presence of a child or young person in the claimant's household. For the first time, therefore, there will be means-tested support in the British system (other than housing benefit or council tax benefit) for working low-paid but childless adults.

The new tax credits represent an increased reliance on means-tested support through supply side measures, but in the context of the tax rather than the social security system. One of the major advantages of the Fowler reforms of 1988 was the alignment of most of the rules for income support and family credit. The extent to which the Inland Revenue adopt its own approach to welfare issues remains to be seen, but this raises the possibility of inconsistent treatment for claimants under the social security and tax credits regimes. To date, in a relatively buoyant economy, tax credits appear to be popular with claimants. The true test for the Blair government's reforms of the wider social security system will come in the event of significant economic downturn.

278   TCA 2002, ss 8 and 9.
279   Battle and Mendelson *Benefits for Children: A Four Country Study* (2001).
280   TCA 2002, ss 10–12.

Chapter 2

International social security, equal treatment and human rights

This chapter examines international norms of social security law and especially the human rights dimension.[1] In Part 1 we consider the development of international (including European) standards in relation to social security law, whilst Part 2 examines in more detail the impact on domestic law of the EC Directive on Equal Treatment in Social Security[2] for men and women. In Part 3 the focus shifts to the impact on social security provision in the UK of the incorporation of the European Convention on Human Rights (ECHR) by the Human Rights Act 1998 (HRA 1998).

Part 1   International regulation of state social security schemes

International regulation of state social security systems takes two forms. One form sets standards governing the nature and content of national systems. The other seeks to ensure continuity of social protection for individuals who move across state boundaries. In both respects, so far as the UK is concerned, the most important source of law has traditionally been that emanating from the EU. In Part 2 of this chapter we examine in detail the principle of equal treatment between men and women in relation to social security, whilst chapter 3 concerns the benefit rights of migrant workers within the Community. In more recent years, with the advent of HRA 1998, the significance of the ECHR has increased (considered in Part 3, below). In the first Part of this chapter the discussion is concerned with the wider context of international regulation of social security on both a global and European basis.

A   International standard setting in social security

International (as opposed to purely European) standards in social security are set out in a number of different instruments.[3] For present purposes the most important sources

---

1   There is, of course, an extensive body of moral and political philosophy relating to the notion of a right to welfare; for a recent contribution, see Fabre *Social Rights under the Constitution* (2000).
2   Council Directive (EEC) 79/7.
3   Space does not permit treatment of regional systems outside Europe; on the African perspective, see further Olivier, Okpaluba, Smit and Thompson (eds) *Social Security Law: General Principles* (1999) ch 18.

are the International Labour Organisation (ILO) and the UN (and in particular the International Covenant on Economic, Social and Cultural Rights).[4]

i   International Labour Organisation

The ILO played a key facilitative role in the growth of international co-ordination agreements between West European states. Together with other international organisations such as the UN, the Council of Europe and latterly the EU, the ILO has also been instrumental in promoting international norms in social security law. This form of regulation conspicuously and judiciously avoids attempts to impose uniformity of provision. The standards are formulated in various ways, some being more specific and less idealistic than others, and are proclaimed in international instruments. States signing and ratifying these instruments commit themselves to the standards and ideals expressed therein.

The ILO has promulgated over 180 Conventions in all. The great majority of these are directly related to workers' employment rights in one form or another. This is reflected in the ILO's decision in 1998 to identify four fundamental principles: freedom of association, the elimination of forced labour, the effective abolition of child labour and the elimination of discrimination in respect of employment and occupation.[5] However, the ILO recognises that social welfare rights form an important feature of social protection more generally.[6] Several ILO conventions are exclusively concerned with social security matters, the most significant being ILO Convention No 102 (1956), the Social Security (Minimum Standards) Convention. This prescribes standards in relation to rates of benefit, to the population which must be covered and to the conditions for receipt of benefit. These standards must be met by signatory states in respect of at least three of the nine categories of benefit covered by the Convention. The nine (traditional risk) categories are medical care, illness, invalidity, industrial accidents, unemployment, old age and death (survivors) as well as maternity and family needs. The obligations imposed on ratifying states are more detailed and onerous than those enshrined in the various UN instruments discussed in the next section. However, ILO conventions do not become part of UK law in the absence of domestic legislation implementing these norms. The principal sanction for breach of an ILO convention is an adverse report by an independent committee on the application of ILO conventions and recommendations.[7]

ii   The United Nations

The United Nations Universal Declaration on Human Rights[8] and the UN Convention on the Rights of the Child,[9] although making some provision for standards in relation to social security provision, are framed in characteristically vague terms.[10] The 1948

---

4   For an invaluable survey, see Storey (1995) 2 JSSL 142.
5   Collins, Ewing and McColgan *Labour Law Text and Materials* (2001) pp 32–33.
6   The ILO also has a Social Security Policy and Development Branch, which seeks to provide support to member states in social security matters. See further on the role of the ILO, ILO *Social security: a new consensus* (2001).
7   *Collins, Ewing and McColgan* n 5, above, p 32.
8   UN Doc A/811 (1948).
9   UN Doc A/44/49 (1989).
10   See also art 55(a) of the UN Charter, which states that the UN shall promote 'higher standards of living, full employment, and conditions of economic and social progress and development', without making any provision for monitoring or enforcement: Steiner and Alston *International Human Rights in Context* (2nd edn, 2001) p 243.

Declaration on Human Rights does not create international legal obligations at all. However, it is the seminal instrument in international human rights law and recognises the right of adults to a standard of living adequate to their health and wellbeing and to security in the event of unemployment, sickness, old age, and other lack of livelihood arising from circumstances beyond their control.[11] The 1989 Convention on the Rights of the Child is even less specific in its terms, simply requiring contracting parties to recognise the right of children 'to benefit from social security'.[12] Rather more assistance may be gained from two international instruments agreed by the UN in 1966, the International Covenants on Civil and Political Rights and on Economic, Social and Cultural Rights respectively.

A   THE INTERNATIONAL COVENANT ON CIVIL AND POLITICAL RIGHTS

The International Covenant on Civil and Political Rights (ICCPR) was framed at a time when a clear distinction was drawn in human rights discourse between civil and political rights, which were seen as enforceable, and economic and social rights, which were regarded as aspirational in nature. This reflected the view that the state need only abstain from certain activities in order to respect civil rights, whereas economic and social rights predicate active intervention by the State and therefore the deployment of resources.[13] ICCPR thus omits any express guarantee of a right to social security. However, article 26 of ICCPR establishes a general right to equal treatment and provides for states to protect individuals against discrimination, which allows some scope for challenges to social security provision. Application of ICCPR is supervised by the Human Rights Committee, which monitors implementation of the Covenant and, if the contracting party ratifies a separate Protocol, it can examine complaints brought by individuals.[14] Thus the Netherlands has been found to be in breach of ICCPR in respect of sex discrimination within its social security system.[15]

B   THE INTERNATIONAL COVENANT ON ECONOMIC, SOCIAL AND CULTURAL RIGHTS

The International Covenant on Economic, Social and Cultural Rights (ICESCR) was adopted by the UN in 1966 and came into force in 1976.[16] Article 9 of ICESCR guarantees everyone the right to social security, including social insurance, and article 25 establishes 'the right to security in the event of unemployment, sickness, disability, widowhood, old age or other lack of livelihood in circumstances beyond [a person's] control'. Monitoring of compliance by states with ICESCR is undertaken by the Committee on Economic, Social and Cultural Rights, but the ILO effectively takes the lead in relation to social protection measures.[17] Moreover, whilst ICCPR relies on clear legal guarantees, it at best commits states to the progressive realisation of the rights

---

11   Art 15 UN Declaration on Human Rights.
12   Art 26 UN Convention on the Rights of the Child. See further Harris (2000) 7 JSSL 9.
13   For a critique of this approach, see Eide in Eide, Krause and Rosas (eds) *Economic, Social and Cultural Rights: A Textbook* (1995); and *Fabre* n 1, above, ch 2.
14   The UK, alone amongst the EU member states, has not ratified this optional protocol.
15   See *Storey* n 4, above, at 147. The Dutch Higher Social Security Court has itself invoked art 26 to strike down discriminatory provisions: see Case C-343/92 *De Weerd* [1994] ECR I-571, para 6.
16   The standard work is Craven *The International Covenant on Economic, Social, and Cultural Rights* (1995); there is a helpful summary from a social security perspective in *Storey* n 4, above, at 144–146.
17   *Craven* n 16, above, pp 224 and 357.

enshrined in the covenant.[18] The formal position under international law today is that civil and political rights and economic and social rights are 'universal, indivisible and interdependent and interrelated'.[19] Yet whilst most governments typically express their support for the notion that economic and social rights enjoy equal status, they fail to take steps to entrench those rights in domestic constitutions.[20]

B   European standard setting in social security

i   Council of Europe

The Council of Europe was established in 1949; its objectives include the protection and promotion of democracy, human rights and the rule of law. Its membership has always been more extensive than that of the EU. The Council of Europe's initiatives include three particular measures which have significant implications for social security provision: the ECHR, the European Social Charter and the European Code of Social Security.[21] These are considered in chronological order.

A   EUROPEAN CONVENTION ON HUMAN RIGHTS

The European Convention on Human Rights and Fundamental Freedoms (ECHR) dates from 1950 and arguably represents the most sophisticated international human rights regime in the world. Based at Strasbourg, the European Court of Human Rights has developed an extensive body of jurisprudence across a range of human rights issues. All 42 contracting states accept the court's compulsory jurisdiction and the ability of individuals within their jurisdiction to petition the court. They are required to comply with its judgments and implementation of such rulings is supervised by the Council of Europe's political body, the Committee of Ministers. At the outset, however, it was widely believed that the Convention had no immediate bearing on social security issues. Indeed, this assumption led to the Council of Europe's decision to develop the European Social Charter, discussed below. Since the mid-1980s, however, the potential of the ECHR to establish certain guarantees in relation to social security matters has come to be realised. The application of the Convention has inevitably taken on greater significance with its incorporation into UK domestic law by HRA 1998. Given the importance of this source of norms for social security provision, the implications for the British benefits system are considered further below in Part 3 of this chapter.

B   EUROPEAN SOCIAL CHARTER

The European Social Charter, agreed by the Council of Europe in 1961, sets out various economic and social rights to complement the predominantly civil and political rights enshrined in the ECHR. The Preamble to the Charter declares that ratifying states 'accept as the aim of their policy... the attainment of conditions in which the following rights

---

18   Art 2(1).
19   Vienna Declaration, para 5. See further *Craven* n 16, above, ch 1.
20   *Steiner and Alston* n 10, above, pp 237–238.
21   For a valuable overview of the Council of Europe's role in social security matters, on which this section has relied, see Storey (1994) 1 JSSL 110 at 119–125.

and principles may be effectively realised'. These include the principles that 'all workers and their dependents have the right to social security' and that 'anyone without adequate resources has the right to social and medical assistance'. A revised European Social Charter was agreed in 1996, but has yet to be ratified by the UK.

The Charter consists of a total of 19 guaranteed rights, mostly expressed in aspirational terms. Thus article 12, the right to social security, requires contracting states: (1) to undertake 'to establish or maintain a system of social security'; (2) to maintain it at a satisfactory level at least equal to that required for ratification of ILO Convention No102; (3) 'to endeavour to raise progressively the system of social security to a higher level'; and (4) to provide for equal treatment of nationals and non-nationals via appropriate international instruments. The right to social security is one of a group of seven core provisions of which any ratifying state must undertake to guarantee at least five rights. In total, contracting states must agree to be bound by at least ten articles or 45 numbered paragraphs in the Charter.[22] The UK's declaration omits article 12 from the core obligations, and states that the government regards itself as bound only by the minimalist article 12(1). The declaration, however, does include article 13, which guarantees the right to social and medical assistance.

The consequence of the UK's limited accession to these guarantees has necessarily somewhat blunted the impact of the Charter on domestic social security provision.[23] The Council of Europe has evolved a detailed system of monitoring of the performance of individual states in meeting their obligations under the Charter. Although its conclusions have no binding effect, the Council's European Committee of Social Rights plays a key role in scrutinising the periodic state reports and, where appropriate, making findings that a state has failed to comply with one or more Charter obligations. As Storey argues, whilst these findings lack any direct legal effect, the Council's supervisory mechanism enjoys some distinct advantages over the EU system of guarantees: the scope of the Council's work is not dependent upon the chance of litigation and extends to cover both non-workers and non-EU nationals.[24]

Successive reports by the European Committee of Social Rights have identified breaches of the Charter by the UK. For example, the report of the Fifteenth Cycle of supervision concluded that the UK was not fully compliant with ten of the 24 provisions considered in that round of monitoring.[25] These included a finding that the habitual residence test for means-tested benefits constituted a continuing breach of article 13(1) of the Charter (the right to social and medical assistance).

C EUROPEAN CODE OF SOCIAL SECURITY

The European Code of Social Security[26] was opened for signature by member states of the Council of Europe in 1964 and came into force in March 1968.[27] The adoption of the Code was provided for in the Council of Europe's European Social Charter, which we have seen in turn is complementary to the ECHR. The Code borrows from and expands upon ILO Convention No 102 and is highly specific, running to 83 articles in

---

22 Art 20.
23 *Storey* n 21, above, at 120.
24 *Storey* n 21, above, at 121.
25 Council of Europe, European Committee of Social Rights *Nineteenth Report* Cycle XV-I (1999); see Ewing (2001) 30 ILJ 409.
26 European Treaty Series, No 48.
27 Entry into force required only three ratifications. So far as the UK is concerned, the Code came into force on 13 January 1969.

total. It defines norms for social security coverage and establishes minimum levels of protection which ratifying states must provide in a range of areas, including family benefits, invalidity benefits, old age benefits, sickness benefits and unemployment benefit. A Protocol annexed to the Code prescribes higher standards still;[28] this has not been ratified by the UK and seems unlikely to be so.

ii   The European Union

The Single European Act 1986 and the Treaty of European Union of 1992 began the process of transformation of the EEC into today's enlarged EU, symbolised by the launch of the Euro in 2002 as a common currency for most (if not quite all) member states. Although the original ECSC and EEC were primarily driven by economic goals, some attention was paid to social security provision in so far as it impacted upon the attainment of those objectives. Thus one of the very first legislative acts of the nascent EEC was to establish a framework for the recognition of the social insurance rights of migrant workers. We consider the evolution and operation of these provisions in chapter 3.

The last five decades have seen an increasing emphasis on social protection as a dimension of the EU's role. This has been reflected in the EU's legal framework by the adoption of a number of Directives which have a bearing on social security provision. The most important of these, Council Directive (EEC) 79/7, is considered in Part 2, below. Two other EU measures, albeit of a non-legislative nature, are worthy of note in this context: the 1989 Social Charter and the 2000 Charter of Fundamental Rights.

A   EUROPEAN COMMUNITY CHARTER OF THE FUNDAMENTAL SOCIAL RIGHTS OF WORKERS

The European Community Charter of the Fundamental Social Rights of Workers, was adopted by the Heads of all member states of the EU, except the UK,[29] in December1989. This instrument, unhelpfully known as the Social Charter (not to be confused with the European Social Charter), combines elements both similar to and different from earlier international instruments. Article 10 of the Charter, concerned specifically with social security, is very much in the declaratory rights tradition of its predecessors. It distinguishes two classes of rights for two categories of persons. Thus workers have the right to adequate social protection and to an adequate level of social security benefits, while persons outside the labour market with no means of subsistence have a right to sufficient resources and social assistance.[30]

Two further sets of measures give substance to these vaguely worded ideals and provide specifically for implementation by member states. It is this latter concern with implementation which marks out the Charter as different from other international instruments. The first of these two measures is the Action Programme,[31] drawn up and published at the same time as the Charter itself. This gives details of how the Charter is

---

28   European Treaty Series, No 48A. See eg Shrubsall (1989) 18 ILJ 39.
29   The UK later acceded to the Charter following the change of government in 1997.
30   Art 25 provides, in addition, for social assistance for people reaching retirement age with no other means of subsistence. It may be noted that the preamble to the Charter makes reference both to the ILO Conventions and to the Council of Europe's European Social Charter.
31   COM(89)568. See also on the subsequent Action Plans on social inclusion Atkinson et al *Social Indicators: The EU and Social Inclusion* (2002).

to be implemented. The plan of action includes the adoption by Council of two non-legally binding Recommendations. These constitute the second set of measures to which we have referred. They spell out in detail what needs to be done and achieved in member states' social security systems if the rights declared in the Charter are to be attained. One instrument is concerned with the common elements of a scheme of social protection which member states are urged to adopt in order to bring about convergence of their systems by voluntary means.[32] The other is concerned with specifying common criteria for social assistance and other types of guaranteed minimum income schemes.[33] Both instruments are explicit in declaring their aim to be to promote social integration and solidarity and to constitute a step in the move towards harmonisation.[34]

B   CHARTER OF FUNDAMENTAL RIGHTS OF THE EUROPEAN UNION

The EU's Charter of Fundamental Rights, signed at Nice in 2000, is essentially a document of an aspirational nature. It does not create new law or extend the scope of EU law. According to article 34, the EU:

> recognises and respects the entitlement to social security benefits and social services providing protection in cases such as maternity, illness, industrial accidents, dependency or old age, and in the case of loss of employment, in accordance with the procedures laid down by Community law and national law and practices ...

It therefore has little immediate impact in the realm of social security law. Instead, the significance of the document as a whole 'lies rather in its statement of common values and principles that are shared throughout the European Union'.[35] Thus the Charter may have considerable future potential as over time it permeates the jurisprudence of the European Court of Justice. We turn now to consider the more immediate influence of EU law in the context of UK social security law.

Part 2   The impact of EU law in the domestic context

A   Introduction

The most important EU instrument in terms of its impact upon domestic social security law is Council Directive (EEC) 79/7 on equal treatment for men and women, which is considered below. There is, however, other EU legislation relating to equal treatment which may have a bearing on entitlement to benefit under domestic benefits law, although space does not permit a full treatment of these provisions here. First, Council Directive (EEC) 76/207 provides for the implementation of the principle of equal treatment for men and women as regards access to employment, vocational training, promotion and working conditions.[36] The European Court of Justice has held that this Directive applies

---

32   COM(92)442: OJ L245 26.8.92 p 48.
33   COM(92)441: OJ L245 26.8.92 p 46.
34   Pennings *Introduction to European Social Security Law* (2001) ch 23.
35   *Collins, Ewing and McColgan* n 5, above, p 8.
36   1976 OJ L39/40. See Ellis *EC Sex Equality Law* (2nd edn, 1998) pp 190–260.

to family credit (now working families' tax credit) on a challenge to the former exclusion of child care costs from any allowance under the scheme.[37] The Commissioner subsequently held that the rule in question, although indirectly discriminatory against women, was objectively justified.[38] Secondly, there are important Directives relating to occupational pensions, which are considered in the context of chapter 17 below.[39] Finally, Council Regulation (EEC) 1612/68 provides for equal treatment in relation to job opportunities and conditions of employment for migrant workers within the Community. In particular, migrant workers have the right to the same 'social and tax advantages as national workers'.[40] In the British context this has been held to preclude indirect discrimination against an Irish national in respect of a social fund funeral grant.[41] Council Regulation (EEC) 1612/68 may well cover any social security benefits which are outside the scope of Council Regulation (EEC) 1408/71 (see chapter 3, below).[42]

B   Council Directive (EEC) 79/7[43]

i   Introduction

Council Directive (EEC) 79/7, promulgated in December 1978, is concerned with the principle of equal treatment between men and women in matters of social security.[44] Its origins lie in the Community principle of equal pay for equal work rather than as any part of the commitment to free movement for migrant workers.[45] Article 1 stipulates that the Directive is designed to achieve the progressive implementation of the principle of equal treatment. Member states were required, within six years,[46] to 'take the measures necessary to ensure that any laws, regulations and administrative provisions contrary to the principle of equal treatment are abolished'.[47] Member states were also required to provide those affected with appropriate remedies through their national legal systems.[48]

---

37   Case C-116/94 *Meyers v Chief Adjudication Officer* [1995] ECR I-2131.
38   *R(FC) 2/98.*
39   Council Directives (EEC) 86/378 and (EC) 96/97. See also Council Directive (EC) 98/49 on supplementary pensions, discussed at p 72, below.
40   Council Regulation (EEC) 1612/68, art 7(2).
41   Case C-237/94 *O'Flynn v Adjudication Officer* [1998] ICR 608; see also *R(IS) 4/98.*
42   Case 94/84 *Deak* [1985] ECR 1873.
43   For a full treatment, see *Ellis* n 36, above, ch 4; and McCrudden *Equality of Treatment between Women and Men in Social Security* (1994). See also Sohrab *Sexing the Benefit* (1996) for a feminist and comparative analysis of the Directive's implementation in member states.
44   (1979) OJ L6/24.
45   Equal pay for equal work is enshrined in art 141 (ex 119) EC. The Directive was based on the Council's residual authority under art 235 (now 308) to take 'appropriate measures' in order 'to attain, in the course of the operation of the common market, one of the objectives of the Community' where the Treaty lacks the relevant powers. For the wider issues relating to equal treatment as regards men and women, see Barnard in Alston (ed) *The EU and Human Rights* (1999) ch 8.
46   Ie by December 1984: Council Directive (EEC) 79/7, art 8(1).
47   Council Directive (EEC) 79/7, art 5.
48   Council Directive (EEC) 79/7, art 6. On remedies, see further Case C-66/95 *R v Secretary of State for Social Security, ex p Sutton* [1997] ECR I-2163, [1997] ICR 961; Case C-410/92 *Johnson v Chief Adjudication Officer (No 2)* [1994] ECR I-5483, [1995] ICR 375 (see *Docksey* (1995) 32 CML Rev 1447); and *R v Department of Social Security, ex p Scullion* [1999] 3 CMLR 798.

ii Persons covered

Article 2 of Council Directive (EEC) 79/7 provides that it shall apply to:

> ... the working population – including self-employed persons, workers and self-employed persons whose activity is interrupted by illness, accident or involuntary unemployment and persons seeking employment – and to retired or invalided workers and self-employed persons.

At one level the European Court of Justice (ECJ) has interpreted this provision very broadly. Thus the Directive applies to someone who gives up work to care for a sick relative, even though the worker is not personally affected by illness.[49] It also clearly includes those in part-time or short-term work[50] as well as work-seekers.[51] But the fundamental limitation on the Directive's personal scope is the required nexus with financially remunerated work.[52] Thus a person who has never been in paid work is outwith the scope of the Directive,[53] as are those – typically women – who give up such work in order to look after their (non-disabled) children,[54] as this eventuality is not covered by article 3, discussed below. The emphasis on the male-orientated paradigm of paid employment is also evident in *Züchner*. Here the ECJ ruled that a wife who provided a high level of personal care for her disabled husband – which would otherwise have had to be bought in – was outside the personal scope of the Directive as she had not been working, or looking for work, before providing such services.[55]

iii Material scope

So far as the coverage of specific benefits is concerned, article 3(1) of Council Directive (EEC) 79/7 provides that it shall apply to:

(a) statutory schemes which provide protection against the following risks:
sickness,
invalidity,
old age,
accidents at work and occupational disease,
unemployment;
(b) social assistance in so far as it is intended to supplement or replace the schemes referred to in (a).

Article 3(2), however, excludes survivors' benefits and family benefits from the scope of the Directive, except for those family benefits which are 'granted by way of increases of benefit due in respect of the risks referred to in paragraph 1(a)'.

---

49 Case 150/85 *Drake v Chief Adjudication Officer* [1986] ECR 1995.
50 Case C-317/93 *Nolte v Landesversicherunganstlat Hannover* [1995] ECR I-4625; Case C-444/93 *Megner and Scheffel* [1995] ECR I-4741.
51 Case C-280/94 *Van Damme* [1996] ECR I-179.
52 *Ellis* n 36, above, pp 276–277.
53 Cases 48/88, 106/88 and 107/88 *Acterberg-te Riele* [1989] ECR 1963; see Cousins (1992) 17 EL Rev 55.
54 Case C-31/90 *Johnson v Chief Adjudication Officer* [1991] ECR I-3723.
55 Case C-77/95 *Züchner v Handleskrankenkasse Bremen* [1996] ECR I-5689. It is arguable, however, that the husband, who did fall within art 2, was discriminated against by the refusal to pay a care allowance in respect of his wife: Waddington (1997) 22 EL Rev 587; and Whiteford (1997) JSWFL 361.

In a series of cases the ECJ has examined the criteria for determining whether a particular benefit falls within or outside the terms of article 3(1). In *Drake* the court held that 'a benefit must constitute the whole or part of a statutory scheme providing protection against one of the specified risks or a form of social assistance having the same objective'.[56] Although the court in *Drake* stated that this test should be interpreted 'in a broad sense', subsequent decisions have been more restrictive. Thus in *Smithson*[57] the ECJ specified that the benefit must be 'directly and effectively linked' to protection against one of the specified risks. Thus housing benefit was held to fall outside the scope of the Directive, as it is a general scheme to assist those whose incomes are insufficient to meet their housing costs – even though the component in issue, the higher pensioner premium, was linked to one of the specified risks.[58] Income support, as a general means-tested benefit, is likewise outside the scope of the Directive[59] but income-based jobseeker's allowance is covered, being a form of social assistance 'intended to supplement or replace' the insurance-based statutory scheme for unemployed people.[60]

Although the coverage of the Directive is expressed in article 3(1)(a) in terms of some (but not all) of the traditional Beveridge risks,[61] it applies to all such statutory schemes, irrespective of whether or not they are based on the contributory principle.[62] Thus the original means-tested winter fuel payments scheme fell within the material scope of the Directive as it was aimed at protecting persons against the risk of old age.[63] It follows that the Directive may cover benefits which would not be regarded as a form of social security in the UK (and so fall outside this book), such as free prescriptions under the NHS for pensioners.[64] There must, however, be some 'direct and effective link' with one of the specified risks. Thus concessionary bus fares, available at different ages for men and women, are not covered by the Directive.[65]

iv   The principle of equal treatment

Assuming that the case in question falls within both the personal and material scope of Council Directive (EEC) 79/7 (and is not excluded by virtue of one of the derogations discussed further below), the requirements of the principle of equal treatment itself then fall to be considered. Article 4(1) defines that principle as meaning that:

> there shall be no discrimination whatsoever on ground of sex either directly, or indirectly by reference in particular to marital or family status, in particular as concerns:
> — the scope of the schemes and the conditions of access thereto, the obligation to contribute and the calculation of contributions,
> — the calculation of benefits including increases due in respect of a spouse and for dependants and the conditions governing the duration and retention of entitlement to benefits.

56   Case 150/85 *Drake v Chief Adjudication Officer* [1986] ECR 1995, para 21.
57   Case C-243/90 *R v Secretary of State for Social Security, ex p Smithson* [1992] ECR I-467.
58   The court thus disagreed with the Opinion of Tesauro AG; see also Hervey [1992] JSWFL 461.
59   Joined Cases C-63/91 and C-64/91 *Jackson and Cresswell v Chief Adjudication Officer* [1992] ECR I-4737; see Durston (1994) 57 MLR 641.
60   *Hokenjos v Secretary of State for Social Security* [2001] EWCA Civ 624, [2001] ICR 966.
61   Art 3(1)(a) lists just five such risks, as against the eight enumerated in Council Regulation (EEC) 1408/71, art 4.
62   This is inevitable as some member states (eg Denmark) have a tax-based social security system.
63   Case C-382/98 *R v Secretary of State for Social Security, ex p Taylor* [2000] ICR 843; see p 494, below.
64   Case C-137/94 *R v Secretary of State for Health, ex p Richardson* [1995] ECR I-3407; [1996] ICR 471.
65   Case C-228/94 *Atkins v Wrekin District Council* [1997] ICR 75. However, a challenge to these rules under the ECHR was declared admissible by the European Court of Human Rights: *Matthews v United Kingdom* Application no 40302/98 (28 November 2000); see now the Travel Concessions (Eligibility) Act 2002.

The principle of equal treatment is also declared to be 'without prejudice to the provisions relating to the protection of women on the grounds of maternity'.[66]

An instance of *direct* discrimination in social security provision is the former rule which meant that a married woman living with her husband (but not a married man living with his wife) was precluded from entitlement to invalid care allowance (now carer's allowance).[67] More problematic are cases of *indirect* discrimination, as these require proof that the benefit rules in question result in a considerably smaller proportion of (eg) women than men becoming entitled to the benefit. The member state may, however, be able to demonstrate that any such discrimination is permissible, being 'based on objectively justified factors unrelated to any discrimination on grounds of sex'.[68] In this context the court has held that member states have a broad margin of discretion in terms of their social policy objectives.[69] Overall, the case law displays 'an extreme reluctance on the part of the ECJ to interfere with the subjective legislative decisions of the Member States in the area of social policy'.[70] That said, weighing the social utility of a measure against its discriminatory effect necessarily involves a delicate balancing exercise.[71]

v   Exceptions

Council Directive (EEC) 79/7 permits certain derogations from the principle of equal treatment. These exceptions are mainly set out in article 7.[72] The first of these, article 7(1)(a), has generated a considerable body of jurisprudence.[73] This provision excludes from the scope of the Directive:

> the determination of pensionable age for the purposes of granting old-age and retirement pensions and the possible consequences thereof for other benefits.

Thus it is clearly permissible for the British social security system to retain the current differential pensionable ages for men (65) and women (60).[74] The ECJ has held that this exception also allows the differential treatment of men and women in the contributions system, under which men have to contribute for five years longer in order to qualify for the same basic state retirement pension.[75] More problematic is the relatively open-ended extension to this exception in respect of 'the possible consequences thereof

---

66   Council Directive (EEC) 79/7, art 4(2).
67   Case 150/85 *Drake v Chief Adjudication Officer* [1986] ECR 1995. For another example, see Case C-337/91 *van Gemert-Derks* [1993] ECR I-5435.
68   Case C-229/89 *EC Commission v Belgium* [1991] ECR I-2205, para 13.
69   Case C-229/89 *EC Commission v Belgium* [1991] ECR I-2205, para 19; see also Case C-226/91 *Molenbroek* [1992] ECR I-5943; and Case C-317/93 *Nolte v Landesversicherunganstlat Hannover* [1995] ECR I-4625.
70   *Ellis* n 36, above, p 304.
71   *Ellis* n 36, above.
72   But see also arts 3(2) (survivors' benefits) and 4(2) (maternity protection).
73   As to the other derogations, see *R(P) 1/96* on art 7(1)(c) and Case C-420/92 *Bramhill v Chief Adjudication Officer* [1994] ECR I-3191 on art 7(1)(d).
74   Under the Pensions Act 1995, the pensionable age will be equalised over a 10-year phasing-in period between 2010 and 2020: see p 601, below. As White observes, this stands in stark contrast to the court's decisions on equal treatment with regard to pensionable age in the occupational pensions sector: White *EC Social Security Law* (1999) p 126.
75   Case C-9/91 *R v Secretary of State for Social Security, ex p Equal Opportunities Commission* [1992] ECR I-4297. In addition, men who work until 65 must continue paying contributions, whereas women who elect to work beyond 60 are not required to do so.

for other benefits', which was considered by the court in the *Thomas*[76], *Graham*[77] and *Hepple*[78] cases.

In *Thomas* the claimants were all women who had given up work between 60 and 65, either because of caring responsibilities or ill-health. However, at that time claimants who had reached pensionable age were only entitled to invalid care allowance or severe disablement allowance if they were entitled to the benefit immediately before reaching that age. The court held that such discrimination was permitted only where it was necessarily linked to the difference in the statutory pensionable age.[79] Moreover, such discrimination had to be objectively necessary in order *either* 'to avoid disrupting the complex financial equilibrium of the social security scheme *or* to ensure consistency between retirement pension schemes and other schemes'.[80] Neither criterion applied to the two benefits in question.

In later decisions the ECJ has been more willing to apply the derogation in article 7(1)(a). The previous differential requirements for men and women as regards entitlement to the former invalidity benefit were at issue in *Graham*. Invalidity benefit was paid at a different rate for men and women between the age of 60 and 65 and a component element, the invalidity allowance, had different upper age limits for qualifying. Departing from the opinion of the Advocate General, the court, in a much-criticised decision,[81] held that the rules in question fell within the derogation in article 7(1)(a).[82] The issues in *Hepple* concerned the differential treatment of men and women for the purposes of reduced earnings allowance (REA). Unlike the previous two cases, the claimants included both men and women, who challenged the domestic rule which provided for REA to be replaced by the lower rate retirement allowance in circumstances which could disadvantage either men or women, depending on the facts of each case. The court held that the rules governing REA were necessarily and objectively linked to the difference in pensionable age in that they ensured coherence as between the retirement pension scheme and other benefits.[83] They therefore fell within the exceptions to the equal treatment principle, even though the relevant legislative amendments had been made *after* the Directive came into force.

Part 3   The impact of HRA 1998

A   Introduction

In 1951 the UK government ratified the ECHR, which came into force in 1953, and in 1966 the right of individual petition to the Strasbourg authorities against the actions of public bodies was established. Since 2 October 2000, however, the Convention rights[84]

---

76   Case C-328/91 *Thomas v Secretary of State for Social Security* [1993] ECR I-1247.
77   Case C-92/94 *Secretary of State for Social Security v Graham* [1995] ECR I-2521.
78   Case C-196/98 *Hepple v Adjudication Officer* [2000] 3 CMLR 271.
79   As was found to be the case for an Italian early retirement benefits scheme in Case C-139/95 *Balestra* [1997] ECR I-549.
80   Case C-328/91 *Thomas v Secretary of State for Social Security* [1993] ECR I-1247, para 12.
81   See eg Cousins (1996) 21 EL Rev 233.
82   There were estimated to be some 40,000 'look-alike cases' affected by this test case appeal: Rowland and White *Social Security Legislation 2001* (2001) vol III, para 3.163.
83   Case C-196/98 *Hepple v Adjudication Officer* [2000] 3 CMLR 271, paras 30–35. But see the rather different approach of Saggio AG.
84   As defined by HRA 1998, s 1.

have been incorporated into domestic law as a result of HRA 1998.[85] Any court or tribunal determining a question involving a Convention right must take into account the extensive jurisprudence of the European Court of Human Rights ('the European Court') and its associated organs.[86] Primary and secondary legislation must also 'be read and given effect in a way which is compatible with Convention rights'.[87] In the event that a court finds *primary* legislation to be in breach of the Convention, it may issue a 'declaration of incompatibility'.[88] Such a declaration does not affect the validity of the legislation, but effectively puts the government on notice as to the incompatibility. It is then for the government to take any appropriate remedial action.[89]

In the specific context of social security law, it is important to note that the discretionary power to issue a declaration of this nature is vested solely in a court;[90] neither appeal tribunals nor Social Security Commissioners enjoy this jurisdiction. Thus primary social security legislation can only be the subject of a declaration of incompatibility if an appeal is taken to the Court of Appeal from a Commissioner, or by way of proceedings for judicial review in the Administrative Court. The exclusion of the Commissioners from the power to make such a declaration, given their status and expertise, is unfortunate.[91] However, both the Commissioners and indeed tribunals have the jurisdiction to find *secondary* legislation – typically regulations – incompatible with Convention rights.[92]

Section 6(1) of HRA 1998 stipulates that 'it is unlawful for a public authority to act in a way which is incompatible with a Convention right'. The concept of a 'public authority' is defined so as to include both government departments (and so the various agencies of the Department for Work and Pensions (DWP)) as well as courts and tribunals.[93] Under section 7, any person who claims that a public authority has acted (or proposes to act) in a way prohibited by section 6(1) may bring proceedings against that body or rely on the Convention right(s) concerned in any legal proceedings. This only applies, however, if that person is (or would be) a 'victim' of the unlawful act.[94] According to the Administrative Court, a widower seeking to establish entitlement to one of the former widow's benefits only became a 'victim' once a claim had been submitted in writing.[95] In addition, a claimant cannot rely on HRA 1998 to challenge the act of a public authority taken before 2 October 2000.[96] Exceptionally, the Act's provisions are retrospective where the proceedings have been 'brought by or at the instigation of a public authority';[97] this might be relevant to cases where the DWP seeks to recover an old overpayment of benefit.

If a breach is established, a court or tribunal has a broad discretion to 'grant such relief or remedy, or make such order, within its powers as it considers just and

---

85   See generally Starmer *European Human Rights Law* (1999); and Clayton and Tomlinson *The Law of Human Rights* (2000).

86   HRA 1998, s 2. For a helpful discussion, see *Social Security Legislation 2001* n 82, above, vol III, paras 4.7–4.11.

87   HRA 1998, s 3.

88   HRA 1998, s 4.

89   HRA 1998, s 10 and Sch 2.

90   Defined by HRA 1998, s 4(5), primarily in terms of the High Court, Court of Appeal and House of Lords.

91   See White in Baker (ed) *Human Rights Act 1998: A Practitioner's Guide* (1998) p 368.

92   But note HRA 1998, s 3(c).

93   HRA 1998, s 6(3).

94   HRA 1998, s 7(1).

95   *Hooper v Secretary of State for Work and Pensions* [2002] EWHC Admin 191.

96   *Hooper v Secretary of State for Work and Pensions* [2002] EWHC Admin 191; see also *R v Lambert* [2001] UKHL 37, [2001] 3 All ER 577 and HRA 1998, s 22(4).

97   HRA 1998, ss 7(1)(b) and 22(4).

appropriate'.[98] The requirement that any such relief, remedy or order be within the tribunal's existing powers constitutes a significant restriction. For example, appeal tribunals have no power to make awards of damages or indeed to award interest on the late payment of benefit.[99]

Clearly, the scope of this book does not permit a full treatment of the developing jurisprudence on human rights.[100] In this Part we provide an overview of the four key provisions of the ECHR which are of particular importance in the field of social security. These are articles 6 (the right to a fair trial), 8 (the right to respect for private and family life) and 14 (the prohibition of discrimination), together with article 1 of the First Protocol (the protection of property). The treatment below will follow this order. The final section considers other Convention rights that may potentially have some bearing on social security rights.

B   Right to a fair trial

Article 6 of the ECHR safeguards a person's right to a fair trial in respect of both civil and criminal matters.[101] As regards the former, article 6(1) provides that:

> In the determination of his civil rights and obligations ... everyone is entitled to a fair and public hearing within a reasonable time by an independent and impartial tribunal established by law.

The Convention thus contains a number of express rights (eg the right to a fair and public hearing), which are considered further below. These are guaranteed rights in that where a person is denied such a right it will necessarily follow that there has been a breach of article 6. But it must be noted that the Strasbourg authorities have also regarded the general right to a fair hearing as including a further number of implied rights (eg to equality of arms). These implied rights are not absolute as they are subject to limitations which are not expressed in the text of the Convention. In particular, the fairness of the proceedings as a whole must be considered, which typically may involve balancing the interests of the individual and the state.[102] This inevitably makes it difficult to predict whether particular challenges under article 6 will find favour with the courts.

i   'The determination of his civil rights and obligations'

There are three pre-conditions for the application of article 6(1) ECHR in civil proceedings. First, the rights or obligations must be 'civil' in nature; secondly, those rights or obligations must have a basis in law; and thirdly, there must be some determination of those rights or obligations.[103] Each of these is considered in turn in the context of social security matters.

---

98   HRA 1998, s 8(1); 'court' in this context includes tribunals: s 8(6).
99   Contrast the position under EU law: p 712, below.
100   For invaluable introductions in the context of social security, see *White* n 91, above; and Jones (2000) 7 JSSL 134.
101   Art 6(2) and (3) deal with criminal trials and so are not dealt with here. It would seem that the forfeiture provisions in social security law are civil penalties rather than criminal matters: *Social Security Legislation 2001* n 82, above, vol III, para 4.81.
102   *Clayton and Tomlinson* n 85, above, paras 11.183–11.184.
103   *Starmer* n 85, above, p 327.

A   CIVIL RIGHTS AND OBLIGATIONS

Article 6(1) ECHR applies, according to the Strasbourg jurisprudence, if 'the proceedings in question are *decisive* for *private* rights and obligations'.[104] However, the classification of a particular dispute as being a private or public law matter under national law is not determinative. Rather, the phrase 'civil rights and obligations' has an independent Convention meaning which focuses on the substantive nature of the right in issue.[105] In two cases in 1986 the European Court ruled that article 6(1) applied to social security disputes. In *Feldbrugge v Netherlands*[106] the applicant, who had claimed sickness benefit, challenged the fairness of the procedures under which her appeal against a finding that she was fit for work had been determined. By a majority the court held that, notwithstanding the public nature of the benefits scheme, her claim related to her 'civil rights and obligations' given the predominantly 'private' nature of sickness benefit. A key consideration in this respect was that 'the right in question was a personal, economic and individual right, a factor that brought it close to the civil sphere'.[107] Similarly, in *Deumeland v Germany*[108] the court held that a statutory right to a widow's pension was subject to article 6(1), given the structural link under the German scheme to her late husband's contract of employment.

Both *Feldbrugge* and *Deumeland* were concerned with benefits payable under traditional social insurance schemes. However, subsequent decisions have indicated that article 6(1) is of wider application in the context of social security. Most significantly, in *Salesi v Italy*[109] the court ruled that article 6(1) is not only of general application in the field of social insurance but also applies to social assistance (ie non-contributory and means-tested benefits paid by the state).[110] It seems, therefore, that any dispute as to an individual's social security rights will be covered by article 6(1), with the exception of matters such as purely discretionary hardship payments.[111]

B   BASIS IN LAW

Article 6(1) ECHR can only apply if there is an arguable claim under domestic law to the civil right or obligation in issue. Thus this Convention provision is essentially procedural in nature; it does not, of itself, guarantee any particular content for those civil rights and obligations under the substantive law of contracting states.[112]

---

104   *Starmer* n 85, above, p 333.
105   *Starmer* n 85, above, p 334; and *König v Germany* (1978) 2 EHRR 170.
106   (1986) 8 EHRR 425.
107   (1986) 8 EHRR 425, para 37.
108   (1986) 8 EHRR 448.
109   (1993) 26 EHRR 187.
110   See also *Schüler-Zgraggen v Switzerland* (1993) 16 EHRR 405 and, as regards the payment of contributions rather than benefits, *Schouten and Meldrum v Netherlands* (1994) 19 EHRR 432. It follows that the European Court of Human Rights has not been required to make the same distinction between social insurance and social assistance benefits as has the European Court of Justice: see p 70, below.
111   *Machatova v Slovak Republic* (1997) 24 EHRR CD 44. See also *R (Husain) v Secretary of State for the Home Department* [2001] EWCA Admin 852, para 27. An example under UK law might be discretionary housing payments: see p 431, below.
112   *Starmer* n 85, above, pp 344–345.

There must be a 'determination' of civil rights and obligations for article 6(1) ECHR to come into play. In this respect the French text, referring to 'contestations', is more helpful in that it emphasises that there must be a *dispute.*[113] It follows that article 6(1) evidently applies in the context of an appeal tribunal (and indeed the Commissioners), but has no relevance at the stage of the initial decision making by the Secretary of State.

ii   'A fair and public hearing'

It is important to appreciate that the 'fairness' of a hearing can only be assessed holistically, having considered the procedure as a whole. In broad terms, the tribunal is under a duty:

> To conduct a proper examination of the submissions, arguments and evidence adduced by the parties, without prejudice to its assessment of whether they are relevant to its decision.[114]

In addition, the Strasbourg authorities have developed a number of specific elements of the right to a fair trial, implicit in article 6(1), to guide this assessment. These will be examined in turn,[115] with a particular focus on their application to the resolution of social security appeals.

A   PRESENCE AT AN ADVERSARIAL ORAL HEARING

The Strasbourg jurisprudence demonstrates that the right to be present at an adversarial oral hearing is of particular importance in relation to criminal charges. As is the case with several other features of article 6 ECHR,[116] the right to be present is not accorded such a high priority in the context of civil proceedings. This may well reflect the fact that continental European legal systems have traditionally relied more heavily on written and inquisitorial procedures. However, the notion of a 'fair trial' may involve the right to a hearing in a civil matter where a person's character or conduct is in issue or where their presence is indispensable to a fair resolution of the matter.[117] But this is less likely to be the case in relation to appeals, especially where only points of law are at issue.[118] It is clear that there is no absolute right to an oral hearing; hence a procedure based on the written documentation in the case may comply with the Convention.[119] Therefore it appears that both the use of paper hearings by appeal tribunals and the disposal by the Commissioners of most appeals from tribunals 'on the papers' are permissible in the efficient administration of justice. The requirement for an 'adversarial' hearing does not necessarily mean that both parties have to be present and/or represented;[120] rather,

113   See *Social Security Legislation 2001* n 82, above, vol III, para 4.75.
114   *Kraska v Switzerland* (1993) 18 EHRR 188, para 30.
115   See *Clayton and Tomlinson* n 85, above, paras 11.204–11.218.
116   See *Dombo Beheer BV v Netherlands* (1994) 18 EHRR 213.
117   *Starmer* n 85, above, p 371.
118   *Starmer* n 85, above, p 378.
119   *Schüler-Zgraggen v Switzerland* (1993) 16 EHRR 405.
120   *Jones* n 100, above, at 152.

it refers to the right to full disclosure and the opportunity to comment on all the relevant evidence.[121] It follows that the traditional adherence by the social security appellate authorities in the UK to an inquisitorial approach is not put in question by the Convention.

There is, as yet, no sign that the Strasbourg jurisprudence will follow the approach of the US Supreme Court in applying the constitutional right to due process to welfare benefits. In *Goldberg v Kelly*[122] the Supreme Court ruled that an oral hearing was required *before* (rather than after, as happens in the UK) a decision was taken to terminate benefit entitlement.[123] The Supreme Court later ruled that this right did not extend to non-means-tested benefits, although Congress subsequently codified such a requirement for certain disability benefits.[124]

B EQUALITY OF ARMS

The concept of 'equality of arms'[125] means that an appellant must have a 'reasonable opportunity of presenting his case to the court under conditions which do not place him at a substantial disadvantage vis-à-vis his opponent'.[126] This implies eg the right of access to the relevant documentation and to comment on such papers and to cross-examine witnesses.[127] A party's right to the fair presentation of evidence is necessarily of more fundamental concern in the application of article 6 ECHR to criminal trials. For example, issues relating to cross-examination, agents provocateurs and illegally obtained evidence are rarely of relevance to social security appeals. However, article 6(1) requires the disclosure of relevant documents to the parties in civil proceedings. Thus in *Feldbrugge*[128] there was a breach of the Convention as the appellant was unable to participate effectively in the proceedings before the welfare tribunal, as she had been denied access to (and the opportunity to comment on) reports on her file. The mere fact that old documents relating to the subject matter of the appeal have been destroyed does not necessarily mean that there has been a breach of article 6(1).[129] There are a number of respects in which UK social security appeals procedures may be found not to conform with the requirement for 'equality of arms'. For example, it remains to be seen whether the provision enabling appeal tribunals to withhold disclosure of harmful medical evidence from appellants is consistent with the Convention.[130] In addition, the so-called 'posting rule' operates unevenly: a document sent by the DWP to a claimant is deemed to have been sent on the day of posting, whereas a letter sent by the claimant to the DWP is only effective when it is actually received.[131] In some cases the operation of this rule may be such as to deny the appellant a fair hearing.[132]

---

121 *McMichael v United Kingdom* (1995) 20 EHRR 205.
122 397 US 254 (1970).
123 See Stein (2001) 8 JSSL 146.
124 *Stein* n 123, above, at 152; and *Mathews v Eldridge* 424 US 319 (1976).
125 As *Social Security Legislation 2001* n 82, above, vol III, para 4.76 notes, an inelegant translation from the original French text *égalité des armes*.
126 *De Haes and Gijsels v Belgium* (1997) 25 EHRR 1.
127 *Feldbrugge* (1986) 8 EHRR 425.
128 *Feldbrugge* (1986) 8 EHRR 425; see also *Kerojavi v Finland* [1996] EHRLR 66.
129 *McGinley and Egan v United Kingdom* (1998) 27 EHRR 1 (action by former service personnel before pensions appeal tribunal claiming to have been affected by nuclear tests in 1958; no breach where some relevant reports had been destroyed and applicants had not sought discovery of others).
130 SI 1999/991, reg 42.
131 SI 1999/991, reg 2. This rule is particularly difficult to justify given that the procedural rules governing appeals before the Commissioners adopt the same rule for all parties: SI 1999/1495, reg 8.
132 See *CDLA/5413/99*.

C   THE RIGHT TO LEGAL ASSISTANCE

The right to legal assistance under article 6 ECHR is less extensive in civil cases as compared with criminal matters. There is certainly no absolute right to legal aid in all civil proceedings. However, the European Court has held that legal aid is required where the assistance of a lawyer is 'indispensable for effective access to court' either because legal representation is compulsory or owing to the 'complexity of the procedure or of the case'.[133] The extent to which article 6 requires the provision of legal assistance in social security appeals is a moot point. One argument is that both appeal tribunals and Commissioners operate in an inquisitorial mode, thus making legal representation unnecessary. On the other hand, research suggests that unrepresented appellants face considerable hurdles in effectively presenting their case. In addition, the complexity and seriousness of some matters heard in the social security jurisdiction (eg relating to overpayments) would suggest that legal assistance should be seen as a requirement for a 'fair trial'. This argument, although carrying some weight at the level of appeal tribunals, is particularly strong in the context of the Commissioners' jurisdiction. Under the present arrangements the Lord Chancellor has the power, exceptionally, to provide legal aid for appellants before the Commissioners (but not appeal tribunals).[134] Whether this would be regarded by the European Court as complying with article 6 would depend on the facts of an individual case.[135]

D   THE RIGHT TO A REASONED JUDGMENT

The right to a reasoned decision is inherent in the concept of a fair trial in a democratic society. However, courts and tribunals may exercise a considerable degree of discretion in meeting this requirement. A judgment need not address every issue advanced by the parties, so long as it indicates the basis of the decision with 'sufficient clarity'.[136] Thus in this respect article 6 ECHR probably adds little to the requirements imposed on appeal tribunals by the Social Security Commissioners in terms of the extent to which reasons must be given.[137] Under the current procedures, tribunals issue appellants with a 'short-form decision', summarising the outcome of the appeal, at the end of the hearing. It seems that this complies with article 6, as the appellant has the right, within one month, to apply for a full statement of reasons.[138]

E   THE RIGHT TO A PUBLIC HEARING

The right to a public hearing is one of the fundamental principles enshrined in article 6(1) ECHR,[139] reflecting the maxim that 'justice must not only be done; it must be seen to be done'.[140] However, article 6(1) qualifies this right by permitting the exclusion of the

---

133   *Airey v Ireland* (1979) 2 EHRR 305; see *Starmer* n 85, above, p 365 but see also the cautious interpretation of *Airey* in *Social Security Legislation 2001* n 82, above, vol III, para 4.78.
134   See p 198, n 193, below.
135   See further the discussion in *Social Security Legislation 2001* n 82, above, vol III, para 4.79.
136   *Hadjianastassiou v Greece* (1992) 16 EHRR 219; see also *Van der Hurk v Netherlands* (1994) 18 EHRR 481.
137   See Northern Ireland decision *C28/00–01(IB)(T)*.
138   See p 199, below and *Social Security Legislation 2001* n 82, above, vol III, para 4.76.
139   *Clayton and Tomlinson* n 85, above, paras 11.230–11.234.
140   This principle applies equally to paper hearings: see *Storey v British Gas plc* [2000] 2 All ER 440.

public and press from hearings in certain circumstances, including 'where the interests of juveniles or of the private life of the parties so require'. The statutory presumption is that appeal tribunals hearing social security matters take place in public (in theory at least),[141] and the former provision enabling the appellant to elect for a private hearing has now been repealed.[142]

iii 'Within a reasonable time'

The requirement under article 6(1) ECHR that there be a 'fair and public hearing within a reasonable time' necessarily imports a degree of flexibility in determining whether there has been undue delay. Obviously regard must be had to all the circumstances of the case in question, including the parties' conduct, the issue at stake and particularly its complexity: what may be manifestly a reasonable time to resolve a highly complex case may represent unwarranted delay in a more straightforward matter.[143] Moreover, delay is not necessarily inimical to the interests of due process: indeed, the dictates of natural justice may at times require an adjournment.[144] The Strasbourg jurisprudence suggests that the proper approach is first to determine whether the overall delay is unreasonable, and then to consider whether the state can justify each period of delay.[145] A shortage of resources and a high volume of work do not, of themselves, justify delays in hearing disputes.[146] It is, therefore, difficult to predict with any certainty whether any particular delay would be construed as unreasonable. The Strasbourg case law suggests that the delay must usually be extensive if it is to be regarded as unreasonable: in one Italian case a delay of more than six years in resolving the applicant's pension entitlement constituted a breach of article 6(1).[147] However, where time is of the essence, eg because of the vulnerability or poor state of health of the applicant, a shorter period will be required.[148]

iv 'By an independent and impartial tribunal established by law'

Article 6(1) ECHR stipulates that civil rights and obligations must be determined by 'an independent and impartial tribunal established by law'. The social security appellate bodies in the UK clearly have a statutory basis under the Social Security Act 1998. To accord with the Convention, they must also be both independent and impartial. Housing benefit review boards, comprising councillors of the relevant local authority, were perceived to be vulnerable to challenge under article 6(1), prompting the government to bring forward legislation abolishing the boards and granting appeal rights on housing benefit matters to the ordinary appeal tribunals.[149] Even if an appellate or review body

---

141 In practice attendance by members of the general public is very rare.
142 SI 1999/991, reg 49(6), as substituted by SI 2002/1379, reg 14(a).
143 See further *Deumeland v Germany* (1986) 8 EHRR 448.
144 Harris (1996) 2 JSSL 11.
145 *Clayton and Tomlinson* n 85, above, para 11.221.
146 *Zimmerman and Steiner v Switzerland* (1983) 6 EHRR 17.
147 *Salesi v Italy* (1996) EHRLR 66; *Ausiello v Italy* (1996) 24 EHRR 568.
148 *X v France* (1991) 14 EHRR 483: see further *Starmer* n 85, above, pp 378–381.
149 Child Support, Pensions and Social Security Act 2000, s 68 and Sch 7; see p 181, below. The High Court subsequently held in *R (Bewry) v Norwich City Council* [2001] EWHC Admin 657 (under the common law) and in *R (Bono) v Harlow District Council* [2002] EWHC Admin 423 (under HRA 1998) that review boards were not independent tribunals; but see also, to the contrary on the facts, *R (Bibi) v Rochdale Metropolitan Borough Council Housing Benefit Review Board* [2001] EWHC Admin 967.

is held to lack the requisite independence, the availability of judicial review may be such as to persuade the courts that there is sufficient compliance with article 6(1).[150]

A   INDEPENDENCE

A tribunal must be independent of both the executive and the parties.[151] Strasbourg case law indicates that in making such an assessment one must have regard to the manner of appointment of tribunal members, the existence of guarantees against external pressure and whether the appellate body in question presents an appearance of independence.[152]

At the time of writing this question is due to come before the Court of Session in *Secretary of State v Gillies*, following the decision of a tribunal of three Commissioners in *CSDLA/1019/99*. The appellant complained that a medical member of a disability appeal tribunal was, when not so sitting, regularly employed for most of the rest of her time as an examining doctor for the DWP. The case predated the coming into force of HRA 1998, but the Commissioners held that there had been a breach of the principles of natural justice in the law of Scotland. The tribunal's independence was compromised, as the circumstances were such as to raise a reasonable apprehension of bias in the mind of an informed and objective observer. The precise terms of appointment of part-time judicial personnel will be crucial in such cases.[153]

But even where the *personal* independence of those involved in the judicial process is beyond reproach, the *structural* independence of the appeals system may be open to question. In this context some of the changes to the appeals system wrought by the Social Security Act 1998 may have exposed appeal tribunals to challenge under the Convention.[154] For example, section 26 of the Social Security Act 1998 empowers the Secretary of State – one of the parties to the appeal – to direct a tribunal or Commissioner to determine an appeal relating to a test case in a particular fashion.[155] It is difficult to see how such a provision represents anything other than a flagrant breach of judicial independence.

B   IMPARTIALITY

Impartiality operates at two levels: objective impartiality, in the sense of the lack of the appearance of bias; and subjective impartiality, meaning lack of actual bias in the particular circumstances of the case.[156] The requirement of objective impartiality includes a consideration of whether the structure of the appeals system offers sufficient guarantees against external influence, and so involves similar issues to those that are relevant in determining the independence of the tribunal. The need for subjective impartiality in

---

150   *R (Husain) v Secretary of State for the Home Department* [2001] EWCA Admin 852; but the courts 'should lean against accepting judicial review as a substitute for the independence of tribunals', per Stanley Burnton J at para 79. See further *R (Alconbury Developments Ltd) v Secretary of State for the Environment, Transport and the Regions* [2001] UKHL 23, [2001] 2 All ER 929, HL.

151   *Ringeisen v Austria* (1971) 1 EHRR 455.

152   *Starmer* n 85, above, pp 261–264 and 368, citing *Langborger v Sweden* (1989) 12 EHRR 416. See also *Bryan v United Kingdom* (1995) 21 EHRR 342.

153   See further *R (Husain) v Secretary of State for the Home Department* [2001] EWCA Admin 852, where it was held that asylum support adjudicators fulfil the requirements of independence under article 6(1).

154   See *CI/4421/00* (starred decision 88/01), para 32.

155   This power only arises in so-called 'look-alike' cases associated with test cases: see p 199, below.

156   *Piersack v Belgium* (1982) 5 EHRR 169.

the context of the individual decision-maker is familiar from the traditional domestic common law requirement of natural justice.[157]

C Right to respect for private and family life

Article 8(1) ECHR provides that 'everyone has the right to respect for his private and family life, his home and his correspondence'. This apparently absolute right is then qualified by article 8(2) which precludes public authorities from interfering with the exercise of this right 'except such as is in accordance with the law and is necessary in a democratic society' in keeping with a number of broadly stated exceptions. These include, amongst others, 'the economic well-being of the country' and 'the prevention of disorder or crime'.

Although this article has generated a considerable body of Strasbourg jurisprudence, relatively few decisions have turned on entitlement to social security or similar issues. In *Logan v United Kingdom*[158] the Commission ruled inadmissible a challenge by a non-resident parent to an assessment under the Child Support Act 1991. One of the appellant's arguments was that his right to family life had been breached because he no longer had sufficient funds to visit his children as a result of the assessment. The Commission was not persuaded that the 1991 Act entailed any lack of respect for his rights under article 8(1). In other cases it has not proved necessary to address the compatibility of particular forms of social security provision with article 8, given that a breach of the Convention has been established on other grounds.[159] Thus article 8 has, to date, yet to be successfully invoked to found a claim to any social security entitlement.[160] Overall, 'there are few indications that the Strasbourg organs regard the Convention right here as including an obligation on the State to make payments to families for their support'.[161]

Appellants seeking to challenge provisions in UK social security law on the basis of article 8 enjoyed equally little success in the first cases to come before the domestic courts. For example, the regulations governing the refusal of housing benefit in cases where the tenant is found to have a 'contrived tenancy'[162] have been attacked as being in breach of the right to family life. The courts, however, have regarded these anti-abuse measures as a legitimate and proportionate response to the problem of contrived tenancy agreements.[163] Similarly, a complaint that the housing benefit regulations discriminated against a life detainee recalled to prison in his enjoyment of his home (when compared with the treatment of a prisoner on remand) was dismissed by the Administrative Court. According to the judge, 'in this complex socio-economic area it is justifiable and proportionate to tolerate the differential ... it is in the final analysis a matter of housing finance and not in the front rank of liberty, life and death issues'.[164] In addition, the right to respect for one's private and family life is not contravened

---

157 See Gamble (1998) 5 JSSL 62.
158 (1996) 22 EHRR CD 178.
159 See eg *Gaygusuz v Austria* (1996) 23 EHRR 364, discussed below, where the European Court of Human Rights found a breach of art 14 and art 1 of the First Protocol and so did not need to consider whether the refusal of emergency assistance for an unemployed applicant amounted to a violation of art 8.
160 *White* n 91, above, p 364.
161 *Social Security Legislation 2001* n 82, above, vol III, para 4.86.
162 Typically a tenancy entered into with a view to taking advantage of the housing benefit scheme: see pp 414–415, below.
163 *Tucker v Secretary of State for Social Security* [2001] EWCA Civ 1646; *R v Carmarthenshire County Council Housing Benefit Review Board, ex p Painter* [2001] EWHC Admin 308.
164 *R v London Borough of Hammersmith and Fulham, ex p Waite* [2001] EWHC Admin 672, para 31; on appeal the Court of Appeal held that art 14 ECHR was not even engaged at all: [2002] EWCA Civ 482.

where the DWP puts a claimant to proof as to her widowed status in circumstances where this has already been acknowledged by the immigration authorities.[165]

In *Hooper v Secretary of State for Work and Pensions*[166] the Administrative Court held that the failure to pay widow's benefits to widowers (before the reform of bereavement benefits in April 2001) fell within the ambit of article 8.[167] However, the court also ruled that the government had established objective justification for the past discrimination against widowers. This suggests that, given the margin of appreciation, the courts may often be prepared to defer to 'the judgment of the legislature in the field of social policy and the allocation of resources'.[168] There may yet be other areas of social security law which are ripe for challenge under article 8. One possibility is the remarkable provision in the jobseeker's allowance scheme relating to the requirement that claimants actively seek employment. The regulation in question permits the authorities to disregard such activity where a person's 'appearance' is thought to undermine their job prospects.[169] Although this has the potential to represent an infringement of a person's private life, there is no evidence that the rule is applied in practice. There is at least one further aspect of social security law where there is a very good prospect that a court may find domestic provision in breach of article 8, particularly when taken together with the prohibition on discrimination under article 14. This is the rule precluding payment of a bereavement benefit to a surviving spouse of an actually polygamous marriage.[170]

D Prohibition of discrimination

Article 14 ECHR provides that:

> The enjoyment of the rights and freedoms set forth in this Convention shall be secured without discrimination on any ground such as sex, race, colour, language, religion, political or other opinion, national or social origin, association with a national minority, property, birth or other status.

It is axiomatic that the article does not stand alone.[171] It must be linked in some way to one of the other substantive articles in the Convention, although an actual breach of that other provision need not be established. Thus it is sufficient that the matter in dispute 'fall within the ambit' of one of the substantive Convention rights.[172] If so, it must then be determined whether there is in fact different treatment and, if so, whether there is a legitimate aim in such discrimination. In this context, as we have seen, states enjoy a wide margin of appreciation in matters of social policy,[173] but very strong reasons

---

165 *R (Nahar) v Social Security Comrs* [2001] EWHC Admin 1049, [2002] 1 FLR 670.
166 [2002] EWHC Admin 191.
167 The government conceded a breach of arts 8 and 14 ECHR so far as the non-payment of widowed mother's allowance to widowers was concerned.
168 *Hooper v Secretary of State for Work and Pensions* [2002] EWHC Admin 191, para 104.
169 SI 1996/207, reg 18(4); see p 349, below.
170 P 218, below.
171 In contrast to art 26 of the International Covenant on Civil and Political Rights. See also Protocol 12 to the ECHR, opened for signature in 2001. There is no indication that the UK is likely to ratify this Protocol.
172 *Belgian Linguistics Case (No 2)* (1968) 1 EHRR 252; *Rasmussen v Denmark* (1984) 7 EHRR 371.
173 *R (Reynolds) v Secretary of State for Work and Pensions* [2002] EWHC Admin 426, para 34. See also *R v DPP, ex p Kebilene* [2000] 2 AC 326 at 381, per Lord Hope; *Waite v London Borough of Hammersmith and Fulham* [2002] EWCA Civ 482, para 37, per Laws LJ; and *R (Carson) v Secretary of State for Work and Pensions* [2002] EWHC Admin 978, paras 68–76, per Stanley Burnton J.

will be needed to justify any discrimination on the basis of race or sex.[174] Even if the differential treatment can be justified, it must still be shown that the discriminatory measure is proportionate to the legitimate aim being pursued.

According to one leading commentator, article 14 ECHR 'is likely to be a fruitful source of complaint in social security cases'.[175] The same author observes that cases of alleged sex discrimination, which have been unsuccessfully fought under EU equal treatment law, might be reopened in the course of Convention challenges.[176] Article 14, taken in conjunction with other Convention rights, most notably article 8, may also be invoked in relation to instances of alleged race discrimination. The example has already been cited of the denial of bereavement benefits to the surviving spouses of an actually polygamous marriage. Another illustration may be the restrictive rules for the payment of overseas funeral costs for non-EU nationals under the social fund.[177]

E Protection of property

Under article 1 of the First Protocol to the ECHR:

> Every natural or legal person is entitled to the peaceful enjoyment of his possessions. No one shall be deprived of his possessions except in the public interest and subject to the conditions provided for by law and by the general principles of international law.
>
> The preceding provisions shall not, however, in any way impair the right of a State to enforce such laws as it deems necessary to control the use of property in accordance with the general interest or to secure the payment of taxes or other contributions of penalties.

Thus the starting point under article 1 of the First Protocol is that there is a right to peaceful enjoyment of one's possessions. However, the state has the power both to *deprive* someone of their property and to *control* its use; the former is permissible only in the 'public interest' and subject to the law, whilst the latter need only be in the 'general interest'.

i Possessions and social security benefits

Those responsible for drafting the ECHR clearly envisaged that it would provide a degree of protection for owners of private property. The Strasbourg authorities have since had to consider whether this protection also extends to social security rights. The early case law revolved around pension entitlements. The Commission held that, although there was no right under the Convention to a pension in itself, rights under a compulsory pension scheme, typically based on employment status, could be assimilated to a property right. The key difference (as compared with purely private pension rights) was that such a right was framed in terms of being able to derive a benefit from the pension scheme – not the right to a pension of a particular amount.[178] The Commission

---

174 *Starmer* n 85, above, p 146. However, this burden was discharged in the challenge by widowers to the pre-Welfare Reform and Pensions Act 1999 benefit rules: *Hooper v Secretary of State for Work and Pensions* [2002] EWHC Admin 191.
175 *Social Security Legislation 2001* n 82, above, vol III, para 4.94.
176 *White* n 91, above, p 367.
177 P 489, below.
178 *Muller v Austria* (1975) 3 DR 25; *X v Sweden* (1986) 8 EHRR 252. See further *R (Reynolds) v Secretary of State for Work and Pensions* [2002] EWHC Admin 426.

thus recognised that fiscal and political considerations might result in fluctuations in such pension provision.

The potential for a social security benefit to qualify as a 'possession' was confirmed by the European Court in *Gaygusuz v Austria*:[179]

> G, a Turkish national who lived in Austria, had paid contributions to the Austrian social security scheme whilst working there. Following periods of unemployment and ill-health, G applied for an advance of his retirement pension in the form of 'emergency assistance'. Entitlement to such payments was conditional upon contributions to the relevant insurance fund. G was denied access to such payments on the sole ground that he was not an Austrian national. The European Court of Human Rights held that the right to emergency assistance was a pecuniary right within article 1 of the First Protocol and the clear discrimination against non-nationals could not be justified under article 14.

The full implications of the *Gaygusuz* decision for the British social security system have yet to be determined, not least owing to the 'not untypical Delphic terms' of the court's judgment.[180] It is clear that the state retirement pension is within article 1 of the First Protocol[181] but not all social security benefits will necessarily be regarded as a 'possession' for the purposes of the protection under article 1. A benefit may not necessarily fall under article 1 simply because the conditions of entitlement are prescribed by legislation. Thus on one view the principle in *Gaygusuz* is limited to contributory benefits. The Administrative Court has held that the previous denial of access by widowers to widow's benefits did not infringe article 1, as the widowers had no entitlement and so no 'possession' – precisely because their deceased wives had not paid contributions.[182] Similarly, in *R (Reynolds) v Secretary of State for Work and Pensions*[183] it was held that contribution-based jobseeker's allowance is covered by article 1 whereas income support is not, as the making of contributions is not a pre-condition for its payment. The broader view is that a benefit may be protected by article 1 even if it is not a contributory benefit, providing entitlement depends on the claimant satisfying conditions laid down in legislation.[184] Whichever approach is adopted, it must follow that it is extremely unlikely that purely discretionary benefits, even where established under statute, will be accorded the status of being a possession.[185]

ii Deprivation and control of possessions

The state may deprive persons of their possessions according to law and in the 'public interest', ie for a legitimate purpose and assuming a 'fair balance' has been struck between the competing interests of the individual and the state. On this basis the Commission declared inadmissible a complaint about the UK's practice of suspending

179   (1996) 23 EHRR 365.
180   *R (Carson) v Secretary of State for Work and Pensions* [2002] EWHC Admin 978.
181   *Szrabjer and Clarke v United Kingdom* [1998] EHRLR 230, but see further below. In some cases the Strasbourg authorities have not found it necessary to determine whether a particular benefit constitutes a 'possession'; see eg *Carlin v United Kingdom* [1997] EHRLR 351 (industrial disablement benefit).
182   *Hooper v Secretary of State for Work and Pensions* [2002] EWHC Admin 191, where it was also held that a claim for an extra-statutory payment fell outwith art 1 of the First Protocol.
183   [2002] EWHC Admin 426.
184   *R (Carson) v Secretary of State for Work and Pensions* [2002] EWHC Admin 978, para 46.
185   Eg payments under the discretionary social fund (ch 13, below) or discretionary housing payments (pp 431–432, below).

payments under the state earnings-related pension scheme (SERPS) whilst the beneficiary was imprisoned. Given that prisoners were maintained at public expense, the temporary deprivation of SERPS benefits was justified.[186]

There appear to be no decisions concerning the control of possessions under article 1 of the First Protocol to the ECHR which are directly relevant to social security matters.

F   Other Convention rights

It is axiomatic that the ECHR is a living instrument and must be interpreted accordingly. It follows that other Convention provisions, beyond those explored above, may also conceivably have some bearing on social security matters. Certain of these can only be highly speculative. For example, the right to life, enshrined in article 2, is not a 'vehicle for arguing for a particular allocation of resources by the State' in the form of specific benefit provision.[187] Likewise, the requirement to be available for employment as a condition of benefit entitlement hardly constitutes 'forced or compulsory labour' within article 4.[188] However, the right to education, contained in article 2 of the First Protocol, may be relevant in the context of the limited social security rights of those students in higher education.[189]

Finally, article 3 stipulates that 'No one shall be subjected to torture or to inhuman or degrading treatment or punishment'. On one view, given that the Convention is primarily concerned with civil and political rights, and not social or economic ones, the state's failure to provide benefits or indeed the basic necessities of life should not found a breach of article 3. The difficulty with this approach is that it ignores the fact that 'there is no watertight division' between the two sets of rights.[190] For example, in extreme circumstances a withdrawal of medical treatment may constitute a violation of article 3.[191] In the context of a challenge to the provisions governing support for asylum seekers, Stanley Burnton J held that 'treatment' under article 3 implies some sort of positive act.[192] In that case there was no need to determine whether a *failure* to support destitute asylum seekers constituted a violation of the Convention. However, a *withdrawal* of existing support would amount to a breach, unless other means of support were available.[193] This sets a high threshold for challenges to the rates of various social security benefits under the main scheme. For example, the reduced rate of benefit paid to young adults in the jobseeker's allowance scheme – less than £6 a day in 2000 – is not an infringement of the rights enshrined in article 3, which 'proscribes ill-treatment of a depth which the level of payment to Ms Reynolds wholly fails to meet'.[194]

---

186   *Szrabjer and Clarke v United Kingdom* [1998] EHRLR 230.
187   *Social Security Legislation 2001* n 82, above, vol III, para 4.66. But note *Gosselin v Quebec* (judgment pending), in which the Supreme Court of Canada is being asked to determine whether cuts in social assistance benefits constitute a breach of arts 7 (right to life, liberty and security of the person) and 15 (right of equality) of the Canadian Charter of Rights and Freedoms.
188   *Social Security Legislation 2001* n 82, above, vol III, para 4.70.
189   See *Social Security Legislation 2001* n 82, above, vol III, para 4.102.
190   *Airey v United Kingdom* (1979) 2 EHRR 305 at 316–317.
191   *D v United Kingdom* (1997) 24 EHRR 423; but see the narrow interpretation placed on this authority by the Court of Appeal in *K v Secretary of State for the Home Department* [2001] Imm AR 11. See also *Othman v Secretary of State for Work and Pensions* [2001] EWHC Admin 1022.
192   *R (on the application of Hussain) v Asylum Support Adjudicator* [2001] EWHC Admin 852.
193   *R (on the application of Hussain) v Asylum Support Adjudicator* [2001] EWHC Admin 852, para 53.
194   *R (Reynolds) v Secretary of State for Work and Pensions* [2002] EWHC Admin 426, para 42.

Chapter 3

EU social security law

Chapter 2 examined the impact of international and European norms on the domestic social security law, including the Directive on Equal Treatment, Council Directive (EEC) 79/7. In this chapter we explore the impact of the EU on social security law in the transnational context. Thus we focus here on the legal regime operated by the EU for the purposes of co-ordinating social security provision for people who move *between* member states.[1] The discussion in this chapter is confined to Council Regulation (EEC) 1408/71. There may, however, be circumstances in which migrant workers can claim the benefit of Council Regulation (EEC) 1612/68, which stipulates that they should 'enjoy the same social and tax advantages as national workers'.[2] Throughout the discussion it is also important to bear in mind that the human rights issues explored in chapter 2 may also be significant in this context.[3]

Part 1   The development of co-ordination of social security in the EU

A   The historical context

International regulation of social security systems aimed at ensuring continuity of provision for people who move between states emerged during the early years of the last century in response to two developments. One was the introduction of state social security itself. The other was migration between West European states of people in search of employment. This movement usually occurred on a one-way rather than exchange basis. The 'emigration' of Italians on a large scale to France is an early example of this migratory flow. More complex patterns involving movements of workers between three or more states followed later in the century. A contemporary example of migration on a large scale is the movement in Northern Europe between Ireland and other states, especially the UK.[4]

---

1   See further Watson *Social Security Law of the European Communities* (1980); White *European Social Security Law* (1999); and Pennings *Introduction to European Social Security Law* (3rd edn, 2001).
2   Art 7(2); see p 44, above and eg Case C-185/96 *EC Commission v Greece* [1998] ECR I-6601. See further Craig and de Búrca *EU Law: Text, Cases and Materials* (2nd edn, 1998) pp 697–707.
3   Mikkola (2000) 2 Eur J Soc Sec 259.
4   See Collins (ed) *Irish Social Security Law in a European Context* (2000).

The regulatory form developed by states experiencing these migratory flows consists of bilateral and multilateral agreements, the key elements of which are rules attempting to secure continuity of social protection for the individuals concerned. The rules provide mechanisms for the cross border co-ordination of social security provision. Three specific devices have been constructed through these bilateral and multilateral agreements over the years. The first and oldest is the prohibition of discriminatory treatment in social security on grounds of nationality. This was the key term in the first international agreement on social security concluded between the Italians and the French in 1904. It committed each of the contracting parties to ensuring that their social security systems treated nationals from the other contracting state on the same terms as it treated its own nationals. Because of the one-way flow of workers, this benefited the Italians who on grounds of nationality at least could not be denied access to the French social security system. A technique ensuring that migrant workers did not lose social security rights in the process of being acquired in their country of origin became a feature of the many later agreements concluded by West European states. The most sophisticated of these agreements went even further and provided that rights already acquired by people in their country of origin could not be taken away from them if they moved their residence to another state.

Notwithstanding the development of Council Regulation (EEC) 1408/71, the fact remains that for some decades there has been no substantial migration of labour between member states. On average across the EU, 1.5 per cent of the total population comprises nationals of other member states.[5] In practice the migration of nationals from non-member states to a member state (but not around the Community) is at least as significant.[6]

B The development of Council Regulations (EEC) 1408/71 and 574/72

As we saw in chapter 2, international regulation of social security through the setting of standards remains in its relatively early stages of development. By contrast, co-ordination directed towards protecting the rights of people who move between states in search of employment, described in the section above, is now at a far more advanced stage. Thus these bilateral and multilateral conventions provided the foundations on which the EU co-ordinating rules have been built. These began with the European Convention on Social Security for Migrant Workers signed in 1957 by the then six member states of the European Coal and Steel Community. This was subsequently adopted as Regulations No 3 and 4 by the European Economic Community established under the Treaty of Rome in the same year.

Regulation No 3 and its implementing Regulation No 4 were the subject of a number of innovatory rulings by the European Court of Justice (ECJ) which, as we shall see, adopted from the outset a teleological approach to their interpretation based on articles 48–51 of the Treaty. In the light of these judgments and after protracted negotiations between the then still six member states, Regulation Nos 3 and 4 were superseded in 1971 by Council Regulation (EEC) 1408/71 and in 1972 by the implementing Council Regulation

5   Guild (1999) 24 EL Rev 22. Annual migration within the EU is less than 1 per cent, and much less than geographical mobility in the US: HL Select Committee on European Union *Fifteenth Report* (2001–02, HL 88) para 11.
6   The clearest example is Germany, where 33 per cent of non-national workers are Turkish, 18 per cent former Yugoslavs and 24 per cent from other member states: Christensen and Malmstedt (2000) 2 Eur J Soc Sec 69 at 91.

(EEC) 574/72. Council Regulations (EEC) 1408/71 and 574/72,[7] much amended, remain in force today. They consist of a vast and complex set of rules supplemented by an extensive body of case law of the ECJ. Their status as regulations means they are directly applicable in every member state in the EU. They may also reach outside this territory in the sense of being applicable, in certain circumstances, to the nationals of states covered by the European Economic Area Agreement[8] and to nationals of Turkey by virtue of the 1980 EU-Turkish Co-operation Agreement.[9]

In this context it should be noted that in December 1998 the Commission proposed a new set of co-ordinating provisions designed to replace the current Council Regulation (EEC) 1408/71 in its entirety.[10] The twin goals of the new Regulation are simplification (by reducing the number of articles) and improvement (eg by extending the co-ordinating provisions to some groups currently excluded). This process began at the Edinburgh Summit in 1992 so it remains unclear as to if (and, if so, when) the new Regulation will come into force, not least given that article 42 (ex 51) EC requires unanimity before the new proposal can be implemented.

C   Council Regulation (EEC) 1408/71: its aims and objectives

The subsequent parts of this chapter examine the principal EU co-ordinating instrument, Council Regulation (EEC) 1408/71, in some detail. Here, we look briefly at two competing views of the philosophy underpinning this area of EU law.

The first is derived almost exclusively from the jurisprudence of the ECJ. The purpose of co-ordination from this point of view is to promote freedom of movement between member states by removing the social security disadvantages which migrant workers might otherwise suffer as a consequence of their move. The court identifies this purpose by reference to articles 39 to 42 (ex 48 to 51) of the Treaty.[11] These provisions

---

7   A consolidated version of which was adopted as annexes to Council Regulation (EC) 118/97, OJ 1997 L28/1.

8   The EEA Agreement which came into force in January 1994 extended Council Regulations (EEC) 1408/71 and 574/72 to nationals of the then EFTA States. Austria, Sweden and Finland subsequently acceded to the EU, and so the Regulation has applied to their nationals in their capacity as members of the EU since 1 January 1995. The remaining EFTA states are Norway, Iceland and Liechtenstein: nationals of those states are covered by the Regulation to the same extent as nationals of EU states.

9   This provides a nice example of the early twentieth-century bilateral and multilateral agreements adapted to meet current economic and political practices. The Agreement, agreed as Council Decision (EEC) 3/80 of the EEC-Turkey Co-operation Council of 19 September 1980, largely applies provisions of Council Regulations (EEC) 1408/71 and 574/72 to Turkish nationals who are workers subject to the legislation of one or more member states. Co-operation Agreements with other non-member states such as Morocco, Tunisia, Algeria and states in Central and Eastern Europe do not apply Council Regulation (EEC) 1408/71 but contain more limited provisions of a similar nature. In Case C-18/90 *Office National de l'Emploi Onem v Kziber* [1991] ECR I-199 the court ruled that the non-discrimination provision in the Co-operation Agreement with Morocco was by analogy identical to the non-discrimination provision contained in art 3 of Council Regulation (EEC) 1408/71. See further Peers (1996) 33 CML Rev 7.

10   COM(778)779. For detailed commentary, see Sakslin (2000) 2 Eur J Soc Sec 169; Eichenhofer (2000) 2 Eur J Soc Sec 231; and Pennings (2001) 3 Eur J Soc Sec 45. See also the Opinion of the Economic and Social Committee: OJ 2000 C75 29/33.

11   Adopted pursuant to art 3(c) of the Treaty which provides for objectives of the EU to be achieved through Community action aimed at abolishing obstacles to the free movement of persons, services and capital. Art 3, in turn, provides for the implementation of the purposes spelt out in the preceding art 2 (as amended by the Treaty of European Union). These purposes include 'a raising of the standard of living and quality of life' and 'a high level of social protection'. Interestingly, Council Regulation (EEC) 1408/71, enacted to give effect to art 51 (now 42), also makes reference in its Preamble (fifth recital) to the aim of raising standards of living as well as to the promotion of free movement.

fall in the first chapter of the Treaty which concerns free movement of workers. Article 42 deals specifically with social security and requires the Council of Ministers, acting unanimously, to adopt the measures necessary to provide freedom of movement for such persons. To this end, the Council is required to make arrangements[12] to secure for the workers and their dependants:

(a) aggregation, for the purpose of acquiring and retaining the right to benefit and of calculating the amount of benefit, of all periods taken into account under the laws of the several countries; and

(b) payment of benefits to persons resident in the territories of member states.

In distilling the purpose of the co-ordinating regulations from these Treaty provisions, the court takes a broad approach to what is required in order to achieve free movement. Thus in one of its first rulings on interpretation of Regulation No 3, it emphasised that the goal of achieving 'the greatest possible freedom of movement for workers' involves 'the elimination of legislative obstacles which might be to the disadvantage of migrant workers'.[13] This focus on disadvantage is a consistent feature of its case law as the judgment in *Rönfeldt*[14] illustrates.

In *Rönfeldt*, a German national sought to rely on a bilateral convention rather than on Council Regulation (EEC) 1408/71 since the Convention gave him greater social security rights than the Regulation. The German authorities argued that he could not do so since article 6 of the Regulation specifies that the Regulation shall replace any bilateral or multilateral conventions between two or more member states. The court ruled, however, that since the Regulation was adopted pursuant to article 51 (now 42), it must therefore be construed in the light of the aim of that article which is 'to contribute to the establishment of the greatest possible measure of freedom of movement'[15] and that this aim:

would not be attained if, as a consequence of the exercise of their right to freedom of movement, workers were to lose advantages in the field of social security guaranteed to them in any event by the legislation of a single Member State.[16]

Applying this reasoning, the court went on to hold in favour of the claimant that the application of Community rules could not bring about a reduction in the benefits awarded by virtue of the legislation of a single member state (since this would constitute a disadvantage arising ultimately from workers' exercise of their right to free movement) and that for this purpose benefits under national law included benefits available under international conventions in force between member states and incorporated into their national law.[17]

A competing view of the philosophy underpinning Council Regulation (EEC) 1408/71 takes issue with the court on this need to avoid disadvantage in order to ensure obstacles

12 It should be noted that the words 'in particular', preceding (a) and (b), are missing from the English text of art 51, although they appear in all the other linguistic versions: Cornelissen (1996) 33 CML Rev 439 at 445.

13 Case 92/63 *Nonnenmacher* [1964] ECR 281.

14 Case C-227/89 *Rönfeldt* [1991] ECR I-323.

15 Case C-227/89 *Rönfeldt* [1991] ECR I-323, para 24.

16 Case C-227/89 *Rönfeldt* [1991] ECR I-323, para 26. The ruling is controversial, not least because of the court's previous ruling in Case 82/72 *Walder* [1973] ECR 599 that the Regulation applied even if workers would be better placed to claim under the convention concerned. Subsequently, *Rönfeldt* has been distinguished in Case C-475/93 *Thévenon* [1995] ECR I-3813; see also Case C-113/96 *Rodríguez* [1998] ECR I-2461.

17 Case C-227/89 *Rönfeldt* [1991] ECR I-323, para 27. Bilateral and multilateral agreements between member states, including the UK, still exist and (subject to the *Rönfeldt* ruling) are applicable to persons and matters not covered by Council Regulation (EEC) 1408/71 (but see Case C-32/92 *Grana-Novoa* [1993] ECR I-4505, involving conventions with a member state and a non member state). In the UK, these agreements are given effect in national law by an Order in Council (Social Security Administration Act 1992, s 179).

to free movement are removed. This second view, instead, regards the territorial character of member states' social security systems as the principal obstacle to free movement of workers. Thus EU law seeks to 'abolish the territorial restrictions on the application of national social security schemes' within the Community[18] and to put social security entitlement onto a personal rather than territorial basis.[19] Applied in its most rigorous form, this 'deterritorial' approach precludes the possibility of claimants gaining social security advantages from their movement between member states and, in this respect, the two views on the purpose of Council Regulation (EEC) 1408/71 not only differ, but compete. The vision underscoring this second competing view of the Regulation appears to be the creation of a logically coherent, technically faultless system achieving perfect 'co-ordination' by ensuring that people are neither disadvantaged nor advantaged as a result of having exercised their right of free movement between member states.[20]

It is a nice question as to whether such a system, were it to be realised, would bring in its train a new variant of harmonisation of national social security schemes. For the interim, however, the court has categorically stated (as in *Rönfeldt*[21]) that Council Regulation (EEC) 1408/71 does not set up a common scheme of social security but leaves in being differences between the member states' social security systems and, consequently, the rights of persons working in the member states. It follows that member states retain the sole competence to determine the criteria for the award of benefit (including making such rules stricter) so long as they do not result in overt or disguised discrimination between migrant workers.[22] Thus the many substantive and procedural differences between the social security systems of individual member states[23] are largely unaffected by article 42 (ex 51) and the very elaborate provisions of Council Directive (EEC) 1408/71 which seek to implement it.

These provisions include rules for determining the personal and material scope of the Regulation, rules for establishing the basic co-ordinating mechanisms, rules for applying these mechanisms to different types of benefits operated by member states and rules providing in general terms for situations where benefit provision overlaps. The remainder of this chapter examines these rules in detail in this order.[24]

Part 2   Personal and material scope of Regulation 1408/71

Council Regulation (EEC) 1408/71 is notable for the categories of persons and spheres of social protection it excludes from its scope.[25] Within these parameters, however, its

18   Steiner [1992] JSWFL 33 at 34, citing Case 44/65 *Hessische Knappschaft v Maison Singer et Fils* [1965] ECR 965. See also Cornelissen (1996) 33 CML Rev 439.
19   *Watson* n 1, above, p 86.
20   See Holloway *Social Policy Harmonisation in the European Community* (1981) p 159 for an expansion of this point.
21   Case C-227/89 *Rönfeldt* [1991] ECR I-323, para 12, citing its own decisions in Case 41/84 *Pinna* [1986] ECR 1 and Case 21/87 *Borowitz* [1988] ECR 3715. In *Pinna* the court ruled that while differences between member states' systems are unaffected by art 51 (now art 42), Community rules on social security introduced pursuant to art 51 must refrain from adding to the disparities which already stem from the absence of harmonisation of the national laws.
22   Case C-12/93 *Drake* [1994] ECR I-4337; Case C-88/95 *Losada v INEM* [1997] ICR 1100; Case C-20/96 *Snares v Adjudication Officer* [1997] ECR I-6057.
23   Expenditure on social protection accounts for 28 per cent of GDP across the EU but with national variations that range from 16 per cent to 35 per cent: Guild (1999) 24 EL Rev 22.
24   On the financing issues, see Verschueren (2001) 3 Eur J Soc Sec 7.
25   See Laske (1993) 30 CML Rev 515.

personal and material scope has been liberally interpreted, particularly by the ECJ. The court's decision in *Martinez Sala* also opens up the possibility that citizens of the EU who are outwith the scope of the personal coverage of the Regulation may have access to social security benefits on the principle of non-discrimination.[26]

A Persons covered[27]

Article 2(1) of Council Regulation (EEC) 1408/71 provides that it shall apply to:

> employed and self-employed persons and to students who are or have been subject to the legislation of one or more Member States and who are nationals of one of the Member States or who are stateless persons or refugees residing within the territory of one of the Member States, as well as to members of their families and their survivors.

Students did not fall within this definition until an amendment in 1999,[28] but two categories of persons remain clearly excluded: the non-employed and third-country nationals.[29] It has been argued that the exclusion of third country nationals is not required by article 42 (ex 51) and is not compatible with the European Court of Human Rights decision in *Gaygusuz*.[30] However, under the Commission's proposed new Regulation, all persons covered by a member state's social security system, including third-country nationals, will fall within the co-ordination framework.[31] Meanwhile, the court has confirmed that the Council was competent to include refugees and stateless persons within the personal scope of the Regulation, but that its provisions do not apply to such claimants unless there is a Community dimension. Thus Palestinians and Kurds who had fled from Lebanon to Germany but who had neither lived nor worked in any other member state were unable to rely on the Regulation.[32]

The two major categories of persons covered by the Regulation, are the employed and self-employed.[33] These terms are defined in article 1(a) of the Regulation as people compulsorily insured under a general social security scheme for the employed or self-employed, if those persons can be identified as such by the manner in which the scheme is administered or financed. This criterion of affiliation to a relevant social security scheme is intended to iron out differences in the way the employed and self-employed are categorised under national schemes and to ensure that, within its parameters, as many people as possible are brought within the Regulation's scope. Article 2(1), it may be noted, makes reference to persons who have been subject to the legislation of 'one or more' member states. This wording enables employed or self-employed people who have never moved from their state of origin to another member state to take up

---

26 Case C-85/96 *Martinez Sala v Freistaat Bayern* [1998] ECR I-2691; see Fries and Shaw (1998) Eur Public L 533.
27 See generally *White* n 1, above, pp 19–37; and *Pennings* n 1, above, ch 6.
28 Council Regulation (EC) 307/99.
29 Other than EEA and Turkish nationals: see nn 8 and 9, above. See generally Peers (1996) 33 CML Rev 7.
30 *Gaygusuz v Austria* (1996) 23 EHRR 364; see p 60, above and Verschueren (1997) 34 CML Rev 991.
31 N 10 above, draft art 1; thus the new Regulation is based on art 8a (now 18) EC, as well as art 51 (now 42) and art 235 (now 308). This proposal dates from 1997: COM(97)561.
32 Joined Cases C-95/99, 96-99 and 97-99 *Khalil, Chaaban* and *Osseili* [2001] 3 CMLR 1246.
33 Council Regulation (EEC) 1408/71 was extended to include the self-employed for all but family benefits with effect from July 1982 by Council Regulation (EEC) 1390/81. The exclusion of family benefits was removed in 1989 by Council Regulation (EEC) 3427/89. The concept of self-employed has been construed broadly by the court: see Case 300/84 *van Roosmalen* [1986] ECR 3097, in which a priest whose income was derived from his parishioners, not from his religious order, was held to be self-employed.

employment (and thus have never been subject to the legislation of another member state) to be covered by the Regulation.[34]

The criterion of affiliation under article 1(a) has been broadly construed to include persons even if they are not in fact affiliated to a social security scheme, as long they ought to be.[35] It has also been held to cover those no longer economically active;[36] those who are entitled under the legislation of a member state to benefits covered by the Regulation by virtue of their having paid compulsory contributions, even if when the contingency occurs they are no longer paying such contributions and are not bound to do so;[37] and those who are employed or self-employed in one state, and then move to another state and become incapacitated six months later without having been employed in that state in the interim.[38] Part-time workers, irrespective of the amount of time they devote to their activities, are also covered by the Regulation.[39] So too are people who are nationals at the time of payment of contributions and hence at the time of their acquisition of the relevant rights, even if they are no longer nationals at the date of the claim.[40] However, workers who at the time they pursue their occupation are nationals of states which have not yet joined the EU and who cease to be nationals of those states prior to the states' accession do not meet the nationality requirement imposed by article 2(1).[41]

A final point to be noted is that the court has resiled from the traditional view that the personal scope of the Regulation only applies to members of families and survivors of the employed and self-employed in respect of rights which they 'derive' from the latter members of their family.[42] Thus the court has held that the Regulation applies to the personal rights of family members and survivors, which are not contingent on and limited by their family relationships.[43]

B   Legislation and matters covered[44]

Article 4 of Council Regulation (EEC) 1408/71 defines its material scope through a process of inclusion and exclusion. Paragraphs (1), (2) and (2a) specify the inclusions; paragraph (4), the exclusions.[45]

Article 4(1) includes within the Regulation's scope all national legislation concerning those branches of social security which relate to sickness and maternity, invalidity, old age, death (survivors), industrial injuries and diseases, death grants, unemployment and family benefits. These categories replicate those used in the International Labour

---

34   The need to invoke the Regulation might arise eg on becoming ill during a visit to another member state: see eg Case 75/63 *Hoekstra (neé Unger)* [1964] ECR 177.
35   Eg because they satisfy the statutory criteria: see Case 39/76 *Mouthaan* [1976] ECR 1901.
36   Case 182/78 *Pierik* [1979] ECR 1977.
37   Case 143/79 *Walsh* [1980] ECR 1639.
38   Case C-215/90 *Twomey* [1992] ECR I-1823, [1992] 2 CMLR 571.
39   Case C-2/89 *Kits van Heijningen* [1990] ECR 1753.
40   Case 10/78 *Belbouab* [1978] ECR 1915.
41   Case C-105/89 *Buhari Haji* [1990] ECR I-4211.
42   Case 40/76 *Kermaschek* [1976] ECR 1669; see also Case 147/87 *Zaoui* [1987] ECR 5511 and Case C-243/91 *Belgium v Taghavi* [1992] ECR I-4401.
43   Case C-308/93 *Cabanis-Issarte* [1996] ECR I-2097; Joined Cases C-245, 312/94 *Hoever* [1996] ECR I-4895; see Hopkins [1997] 19 JSWFL 513.
44   See generally *White* n 1, above, pp 37–47; and *Pennings* n 1, above, ch 7.
45   In contrast, the Commission's new Regulation proposes to apply 'to all social security legislations', with various schemes listed 'in particular', including an extension to cover pre-retirement benefit schemes. Social assistance will remain excluded: COM(98)779, draft art 2.

Organisation (ILO) Convention No 102.[46] Article 5 of the Regulation requires each member state to specify in declarations notified to the Council of Ministers all its legislation and schemes (and thus social security benefits) it considers to be covered by the Regulation. In this connection, the court has ruled that specification by a member state is conclusive that a benefit is covered, whereas its failure to do so does not necessarily mean that the benefit falls outside the Regulation's scope.[47] This remains a matter for the court to decide. All of this, of course, is contingent on member states making provision for social security benefits in the first place. This is a matter solely for them to decide. Because the Regulation is not a harmonising measure, it can only co-ordinate benefits within its scope if member states choose to make provision for such benefits. If they make no such provision, or choose either subsequently to withdraw them or, equally importantly, to modify them so as to take them outside the Regulation's scope, the Regulation will be without effect, since there will be nothing for it to co-ordinate.

Article 4(2) states that the Regulation shall apply to all general and special social security schemes, whether contributory or non-contributory. Article 4(2a), inserted in 1992,[48] provides for the Regulation to apply to 'special non-contributory benefits' which are provided under legislation or schemes other than those referred to in paragraph 1 or excluded by paragraph 4, where such benefits are intended to provide supplementary cover against article 4(1) risks[49] or to provide specific protection for the disabled.[50] Again, in accordance with article 5, member states must specify the national benefits falling within this category.[51] It is to be noted that these special non-contributory 'mixed-type' benefits are defined partly in terms of the risks against which they provide direct or supplementary cover. In this respect they are akin to benefits specified under the Regulation as social security. On the other hand, they are explicitly defined in terms of not falling within paragraph 1 of article 4 and thus of not being social security. Some further guidance on the meaning of 'special non-contributory benefits' has been provided by a resolution of the Administrative Commission on Social Security for Migrant Workers.[52] This specifies a number of criteria for identifying such benefits, including that they are 'closely linked to a particular social and economic context in the member state where the beneficiary resides'.[53] Similarly, means-testing 'is an important though not an essential criterion'. An additional important requirement is that to constitute special non-contributory benefits they must not be excluded under article 4(4).

Article 4(4) identifies the benefits excluded from the Regulation's scope. These are: social assistance, medical assistance, special schemes and war victims.[54] The most

---

46   UNTS 131. The scope of art 4(1) is thus wider than that of Council Directive (EEC) 79/7, discussed in ch 2 above.

47   Case 35/77 *Beerens* [1977] ECR 2249; Case C-327/92 *Rheinhold & Mahla NV* [1995] ECR I-1223. It should be borne in mind that member states' declarations are, in any event, often out of date: *White* n 1, above, p 38.

48   By amending Council Regulation (EEC) 1247/92 with effect from 1 June 1992.

49   Art 4(2a)(a).

50   Art 4(2a)(b).

51   See Annex IIa. The UK's declaration lists invalid care allowance, working families' tax credit, attendance allowance, income support, disability living allowance, disabled person's tax credit and income-based jobseeker's allowance. The member state's designation is not conclusive, if the court takes the view that the benefit in question is in fact contributory in character: Case C-215/99 *Jauch* [2001] ECR I-1901.

52   The Administrative Commission, established under Title IV of Council Regulation (EEC) 1408/71, is a specialised body which is charged with the responsibility of facilitating the smooth functioning of the co-ordination rules: see *White* n 1, above, pp 16–17.

53   Resolution of the Administrative Commission of 29 June 2000: OJ 2001 C44/13-14.

54   The exclusion of special schemes for civil servants was removed by Council Regulation (EC) 1606/98, introduced following Case C-443/93 *Vougioukas v Idrima Koinonikon Asphalisseon* [1996] ICR 913, although certain derogations may apply.

important exclusion is that of social assistance. This term is not defined by the legislation. The court has therefore developed criteria for determining which schemes constitute assistance and which constitute social security, the latter being the only other category specified under the Regulation until the introduction of special non-contributory benefits in 1992. The criteria developed by the court have tended to identify social security according to whether the legislation in question confers a legally defined position and whether the benefit conditions are linked to periods of employment and contributions.[55] For social assistance, on the other hand, the determining factors have tended to be whether there is discretion in the manner in which the benefits are provided and whether financial need is an essential condition of entitlement.[56] The difficulty faced by the court in recent years is that certain benefits provided under national legislation have not been amenable to classification according to these two sets of criteria, mainly because they exhibit characteristics relevant to both and are thus not clearly identifiable as one or the other.[57]

In these instances the court has tended to err on the side of inclusion as social security rather than exclusion as social assistance. Thus in one line of cases the court held that allowances designed to supplement a social security benefit providing protection against one of the risks in article 4(1), payable out of a national solidarity fund, and conferring a legally defined status, were social security irrespective of whether or not they were means-tested.[58] This reasoning was applied to accord social security status to the UK's family credit in *Hughes*,[59] the relevant risk in article 4(1) being identified as family needs. In another line of cases, the court has also made clear that legislation which provides a legally protected right to allowances for disabled adults and children, whether or not entitlement is linked to contributions, is to be regarded as social security within the scope of article 4(1).[60] Again, this reasoning was applied in *Newton*[61] so as to bring the UK's mobility allowance within the Regulation's scope.[62] A notable exception to this trend of inclusion rather than exclusion by the court is its treatment in *Hoeckx*[63] of the Belgian means-tested minimex scheme. In *Hoeckx*, the court ruled that minimex constituted social assistance on the ground that it was first and foremost a needs-based benefit.[64]

In one respect, this problem of demarcating the boundary between social security and social assistance has been resolved by the introduction of the category of special

---

55   Case 28/68 *Torrekens* [1969] ECR 125; Case 1/72 *Frilli* [1972] ECR 457; Case 139/82 *Piscitello* [1983] ECR 1427; Case 379/85 *Giletti* [1987] ECR 955; Case C-356/89 *Newton* [1991] ECR I-3017; Case C-78/91 *Hughes* [1992] ECR I-4839.

56   Case 249/83 *Hoeckx* [1985] ECR 973; Case 122/84 *Scrivner* [1985] ECR 1027.

57   See Preamble to amending Council Regulation (EEC) 1247/92, recitals 3 and 4.

58   Case 28/68 *Torrekens* [1969] ECR 125; Case 1/72 *Frilli* [1972] ECR 457; Case 139/82 *Piscitello* [1983] ECR 1427; Case 379/85 *Giletti* [1987] ECR 955; Case 24/74 *Biason* [1974] ECR 999; and Case 147/87 *Zaoui* [1987] ECR 5511.

59   Case C-78/91 *Hughes* [1992] ECR I-4839; [1992] 3 CMLR 490. Family credit is now working families' tax credit.

60   Case 187/73 *Callemeyn* [1974] ECR 553; Case 39/74 *Costa* [1974] ECR 1251; Case 7/75 *Mr and Mrs F* [1975] ECR 679; Case 63/76 *Inzirillo* [1976] ECR 2057.

61   Case C-356/89 *Newton* [1991] ECR I-3017.

62   More specifically, the allowance was held to be an invalidity benefit for the purposes of art 4(1) provided that recipients invoking the Regulation could show they had been subject as employed or self-employed persons to UK legislation. Mobility allowance has since been superseded by the mobility component of disability living allowance.

63   Case 249/83 *Hoeckx* [1985] ECR 973. See also Case 122/84 *Scrivner* [1985] ECR 1027.

64   Benefits held to constitute social assistance and thus outside the scope of Council Regulation (EEC) 1408/71 may none the less be held to be a 'social advantage' for the purposes of art 7(2) of Council Regulation (EEC) 1612/68 and thus be subject to the prohibition on discrimination on grounds of nationality: see Case 249/83 *Hoeckx* [1985] ECR 973.

non-contributory benefits under article 4(2a), discussed above. Indeed, this new category has been designed to accommodate precisely the type of benefits which the court struggled to classify in the two lines of cases referred to above. In a number of other respects, however, the problem of demarcation may well have been exacerbated by the new article 4(2a). In the first place, there are now two lines of demarcation, not one. One lies between social security and the new 'mixed type' benefit, the other between this new category and social assistance. The UK's income support has proven problematic with regard to the latter. This benefit has very similar characteristics to the Belgian minimex benefit and has been held to be outside the material scope of Council Directive (EEC) 79/7.[65] The UK government, however, has specified income support to be a special non-contributory benefit, a view also taken by the court.[66] In the second place, the status of benefits declared by the ECJ to be social security within article 4(1) but now specified by the member states to be mixed-type benefits under article 4(2a) appears uncertain. The two UK benefits, mobility allowance (now the higher rate of the mobility component of disability living allowance) and family credit (now working families' tax credit),[67] are relevant here. It would seem that article 4(2a) has been inserted into the Regulation to alter and thus render certain the status of such benefits.[68] Indeed, the creation of this new category of benefit, which has had the effect of reducing the protection otherwise provided by the co-ordinating mechanisms under Council Regulation (EEC) 1408/71,[69] has been held to be compatible with article 42 (ex 51) of the Treaty.[70]

Before considering the co-ordinating mechanisms, another exclusion from the Regulation's material scope needs to be highlighted. This exclusion, implicit rather than explicit, concerns occupational (sometimes called complementary or supplementary) social security schemes. The exclusion is to be inferred from the requirement in article 4(1) and (2a) that benefits covered by the Regulation be derived from 'legislation'. Legislation is defined in article 1(j) as statutes, regulations and all other implementing measures. It specifically does not include provisions of 'industrial agreements'.[71] This negative approach to industrial agreements was adopted by the drafters of the 1971 Regulation in order to pre-empt a line of argument, then developing, that occupational social security schemes might, in certain circumstances, be brought within the scope of Council Regulation (EEC) 1408/71 and thus be made subject to some or all of its co-ordinating mechanisms.[72] Since the 1971 revision, it seems to have been generally accepted that the exclusion of industrial agreements effectively prevents occupational schemes being covered by the Regulation even if, one might add, those

---

65 Joined Cases C-63/91 *Jackson* and C-64/91 *Cresswell* [1992] ECR I-4737; [1992] 3 CMLR 389; see p 44, above.

66 Case C-90/97 *Swaddling v Adjudication Officer* [1999] ECR I-1075; but see also *Perry v Chief Adjudication Officer* [1999] 2 CMLR 439.

67 Held in Case C-356/89 *Newton* [1991] ECR I-3017 and Case C-78/91 *Hughes* [1992] ECR I-4839 to be social security. Working families' tax credit is clearly also covered by Council Regulation (EEC) 1408/71 (see Council Regulation (EC) 1386/2001).

68 See the Preamble to Council Regulation (EEC) 1247/92, which inserted art 4(2a).

69 Art 10a of Council Regulation (EEC) 1408/71 precludes the possibility of claimants 'exporting' special non-contributory benefits: see p 79, below.

70 Case C-20/96 *Snares v Adjudication Officer* [1997] ECR I-6057.

71 Except that where such provisions put into effect compulsory insurance under the relevant legislation or set up a scheme administered by the institution which administers schemes under that legislation, a member state may notify by declaration that such provisions are within the scope of the Regulation. The purpose of this exception is to enable the French unemployment benefit scheme to fall within the scope of the Regulation, even though it is set up by a collective agreement.

72 Holloway *Social Policy Harmonisation in the European Community* (1981) p 172.

schemes are set up and regulated by a mix of statutory and non-statutory (collectively or individually-bargained) means.[73]

The European Commission regards the absence of co-ordination as a matter of concern since this might deter skilled and professional groups from moving to member states where their occupational skills are in demand. If, on the other hand, these groups do exercise their rights to free movement, their inadequately protected occupational pension rights might be lost. Consequently Council Directive (EC) 98/49[74] seeks to safeguard the supplementary pension rights of employed and self-employed persons moving within the Community. Member states are required to ensure that the vested pension rights of migrant workers in supplementary pensions schemes are preserved once contributions are no longer being made to the same extent as for former contributors who remain in the same member state.[75] Similarly, pensioners living in other member states are entitled to the full benefit of payments under such schemes, subject to any relevant taxes and transaction charges.[76]

Part 3 The techniques of co-ordination under Council Regulation (EEC) 1408/71

The techniques currently used to co-ordinate member states' statutory social security schemes are four in number. Three of these can be traced back to the early bilateral and multilateral agreements signed by West European states experiencing the migration of labour described in Part 2, above. These three techniques are the prohibition of discrimination on grounds of nationality, the aggregation and apportionment of benefit rights, and the removal of territorial restrictions on continued access to benefit, often referred to as the ability of claimants to 'export' benefit rights from one state to another. A fourth must be added to these three to complete the picture. This is the set of rules used to determine which member state's legislation is to be applied in order to settle questions of affiliation, contribution liability or benefit entitlement. This is variously referred to as the choice of law or conflict of law question. Since the 'single state' rule was introduced in 1971, there can be only one applicable legislation.

The set of rules determining the applicable legislation and the non-discrimination rule are uniformly applied, under Council Regulation (EEC) 1408/71, to all branches of member states' social security systems. Aggregation and apportionment of benefit rights and the 'exporting' of acquired benefit rights are used in a more selective way. The uneven application of these last two makes it unwise to regard them as principles even though explicit provision is made for them in article 42 (ex 51) of the Treaty. Their uneven application also makes it appropriate to deal with them in general terms in this part of the chapter, along with the other two techniques, and then to deal with their selective application to different branches of social security in the next section, Part 5. This part of the chapter, then, examines all four techniques in general terms.

---

73 But note COM(98)779, which proposes to cover 'schemes relating to the obligations of an employer': draft art 2(2).

74 OJ 1998 L209/46-49, implemented in the UK by the Pensions Act 1995, s 66, inserted by the Child Support, Pensions and Social Security Act 2000, s 55. For concern that the Directive does not go far enough, see HL Select Committee on European Union *Fifteenth Report* (2001–02, HL 88) para 59.

75 Council Directive (EC) 98/49, art 4.

76 Council Directive (EC) 98/49, art 5.

A   Determination of applicable legislation and the 'single state' rule

This set of rules is contained in Title II of Council Regulation (EEC) 1408/71, articles 13 to 17.[77] These articles are vital elements in the smooth running of the co-ordination machinery. They constitute a set of procedural rules for settling which of a number of possible national legislations apply to claimants who have been, or find themselves potentially liable to be, insured under or associated with several member states' regimes. This is important to claimants who wish to avoid the situation whereby under national legislation they are either not permitted to contribute to a scheme or are required to contribute to more than one.[78] In particular, claimants might wish to avoid the situation where they are legally obliged to contribute to two schemes yet because of eg national provisions preventing overlapping of benefits, they will receive benefits from only one of those schemes in return. Officials administering member states' schemes will also want to be able to establish quickly and easily whether they can legitimately require persons in, or coming from, another member state to contribute to the national scheme and whether, in the event of a claim, it is their own national rules which will determine entitlement to and calculation of the amount of benefit sought. Procedural rules of the kind provided by Title II will also assist employers required to collect contributions on behalf of the state.

The two basic rules for resolving jurisdictional questions are contained in article 13 of Title II. Article 13(1) provides that a person to whom the Regulation applies is subject to the legislation of only one member state.[79] This is the 'single state' rule. Article 13(2) provides the criterion, or connecting factor, for determining which member state's legislation this shall be. The general rule (otherwise known as the lex laboris rule[80]) is that people will be subject to the legislation of the state in which they are employed, even if they are resident in another member state[81] or the enterprise employing them has its place of business in another state.[82]

Articles 14 to 17 contain a number of exceptions to these two basic rules. Only three of these can be dealt with here. The first exception modifies the single state rule so as to allow people to contribute to a member state's voluntary or optional invalidity, old age or death insurance scheme while compulsorily subject to another state's legislation, provided that the former state permits the overlap.[83]

The second exception modifies the lex laboris principle by permitting people posted by their employer to another member state to work for up to 12 months in that state while still remaining subject to the legislation of the first (home) state.[84] This 12-month period can be extended to 24 months in unforeseeable circumstances.[85] In order to take advantage of this provision, the court has held that a business providing temporary

---

77   See further *Pennings* n 1, above, ch 8.
78   A further complication, however, is that there is little co-ordination as between the conflicts rules governing social security and taxation: Verschueren (2001) 3 Eur J Soc Sec 7.
79   And thus is protected from a double levy of social security contributions where resident in one state but working in another: Case C-34/98 *EC Commission v France* [2000] ECR I-995; and C-169/98 *EC Commission v France* [2000] ECR I-1049 (but contrast Case C-68/99 *EC Commission v Germany* [2001] 2 CMLR 808).
80   See further Christensen and Malmstedt (2000) 2 Eur J Soc Sec 69.
81   Art 13(2)(a); see Case C-404/98 *Plum* [2000] ECR I-9379. The choice of lex laboris is justified on grounds of simplicity, fairness and coherence: see the fourth recital of the Preamble to Council Regulation (EEC) 3427/89 (in the context of amendments to art 73, for which see p 85, below).
82   Art 13(2)(b).
83   Art 15(3). In Case C-297/92 *Istituto Nazionale della Previdenza Sociale v Baglieri* [1993] ECR I-5211 the court ruled that a member state may refuse to allow people voluntarily to contribute to its scheme if they are compulsorily insured in another member state.
84   See generally *Pennings* n 1, above, ch 9; and van Zeben and Donders (2001) 3 Eur J Soc Sec 107.
85   Art 14(1).

personnel from one member state to work in a second member state must itself 'normally carry on its activities in the first State'.[86] Moreover, the social security authorities in the second country must abide by the E101 certificate issued by the first member state, which confirms that such workers are subject to its social security system.[87] A parallel provision applies to the self-employed.[88] Thus self-employed British opera singers, contracted to perform in Belgium for a series of short engagements, remained subject to UK legislation, even though under Belgian social security law such artists are treated as employees.[89] The exception has a number of advantages. Workers continue to be compulsorily insured in their home state and thus they and their employers continue to pay contributions into the home scheme. This avoids the administrative inconvenience of changing insurability for short periods. It also means that where the home state scheme is more generous than that operating in the state to which the workers are being posted, the workers can continue to acquire rights under the more generous scheme. Moreover, since it is thought that if the exception were not available workers would not be willing to be posted abroad, its existence removes obstacles to free movement created by the differences in and lack of harmonisation of member states' social security schemes.[90]

A third exception again modifies the lex laboris principle by permitting two or more member states to agree that people who would otherwise be rendered subject to the legislation of one member state remain or become subject to another state's legislation, on condition that such an agreement is in the interests of the people concerned.[91] In *Brusse*,[92] it was held that such agreements may be retrospective and that member states have a wide discretion as to how to construe and apply the limitation that the agreements be in the interests of those concerned. An advantage of these article 17 agreements, as they are called, is that they have the effect of permitting for an indefinite period what is mandatory for the period of only 12 to 24 months in the case of posted workers. They are said to be regarded favourably by employers of professional and skilled workers for this reason. Some member states are less enthusiastic, particularly states of high immigration who stand to lose the contributions which would be payable to them but for the article 17 agreement.

Two further points regarding Title II deserve mention. First, article 13(2)(f) provides that where people to whom the legislation of one member state ceases to be applicable without their becoming subject (in accordance with articles 13 to 17) to the legislation of another member state, then the legislation of the member state in which they reside shall apply. This reverses the ruling in *Ten Holder*[93] that in such circumstances the

---

86 Case C-202/97 *Fitzwilliam Executive Search* [2000] ECR I-883, para 33. Note also that a worker who occasionally pursues his or her activity in a state other than the state of residence and is affiliated to that state's scheme remains subject to its legislation. See Case 35/70 *Sàrl Manpower v Caisse primaire d'assurance maladie, Strasbourg* [1970] ECR 1251; Case 13/73 *Angenieux v Hakenberg* [1973] ECR 935; and Case 8/75 *Caisse Primaire d'Assurance Maladie de Sélestat v Association du Foot-Ball Club d'Andlau* [1975] ECR 739.

87 Case C-202/97 *Fitzwilliam Executive Search* [2000] ECR I-883, paras 46–59.

88 Art 14a(1).

89 Case C-178/97 *Banks v Théâtre Royal De La Monnaie* [2000] 2 CMLR 754. This judgment has major repercussions, given the relatively widespread practice of self-employment in the UK in certain occupations. As Ruiz-Jarabo Colomer AG noted, some 60,000 self-employed British construction workers operate in Germany and the Netherlands under E101 certificates.

90 To overcome resistance to posting abroad where social security rights are threatened, employers appear willing to insure workers voluntarily in the home state. This will be unnecessary, of course, if advantage can be taken of the posted-worker exception.

91 Art 17.

92 Case 101/83 *Brusse* [1984] ECR 2223.

93 Case 302/84 *Ten Holder v Nieuwe Algemene Bedrijfsvereniging* [1986] ECR 1821, subsequently applied in Case C-215/90 *Twomey* [1992] ECR I-1823, [1992] 2 CMLR 571. See also Case C-202/97 *Fitzwilliam Executive Search* [2000] ECR I-883, para 20; and Case C-404/98 *Plum* [2000] ECR I-9379 para 18.

legislation of the member state (whose legislation has otherwise ceased to be applicable) continues to apply.[94] Secondly, article 17(a) provides that recipients of pensions due under the legislation of one or more member states other than that in which they reside may on request be exempted from the legislation of the state of residence provided that they do not pursue an occupation there.

In summary, then, articles 13 to 17 in Title II contain a set of rules for determining which legislation of which single member state is applicable and for resolving jurisdictional disputes in this respect. The court made clear in *Ten Holder*[95] that these articles constitute a complete system of conflict rules depriving member states of the power to determine the scope and conditions for applying national legislation in respect of persons subject to the legislation and the territory within which it has effect.[96] Subsequently, it has become evident that Title II does not in fact make express provision for a worker employed by an undertaking in the Community but who works wholly outside the EU. The court, adopting a teleological approach, has held that such a worker must be liable for only one set of contributions.[97] The court has also repeatedly affirmed, however, that the power to determine conditions creating the right or obligation to become affiliated to a social security system rests solely with the member state concerned except where those conditions discriminate on grounds of nationality.[98]

The result is that EU law determines the state (and so the legislation) to which people are subject for the purposes of invoking the Regulation, whereas a member state's law determines the conditions of access to its national scheme in respect of those held to be subject to that state's legislation, provided that the conditions do not discriminate on nationality grounds. It is possible to be subject to a particular member state's legislation under Title II but to be precluded from participation in or access to that scheme by the national rules concerned. In the UK, for example, persons earning below the lower earnings limit or over pensionable age would not be able to contribute to the social insurance scheme and would not therefore be entitled to contributory and possibly some other benefits. They might none the less be regarded as subject to UK legislation and could invoke the provisions under Title II in order to establish this. This might be to no avail, however, if because of low wages they were unable to establish entitlement to any relevant contributory (or other) UK benefit.

B Non-discrimination on grounds of nationality

The principle of non-discrimination on grounds of nationality was one of the first devices used in international agreements to regulate social security provision for mobile workers. It is also one of the fundamental principles of EU law.[99] The aim of protecting non-

---

94 See the court's restrictive interpretation of art 13(2)(f) in Case C-275/96 *Kuusijärvi* [1998] ECR I-3419, a decision causing 'some astonishment': *Pennings* n 1, above, p 79.

95 Case 302/84 *Ten Holder v Nieuwe Algemene Bedrijfsvereniging* [1986] ECR 1821; and see also Case C-3/87 *R v Ministry of Agriculture, Fisheries and Food, ex p Agegate Ltd* [1989] ECR 4459.

96 This established conclusively that court rulings pre-dating the 1971 Regulation, which suggested that more than one member state's legislation may be applicable and liability to pay more than one set of contributions may arise, as long as such additional contributions gave rise to additional benefits, are no longer good law. See the 3rd edition of this book, p 601.

97 Case C-60/93 *Aldewereld* [1994] ECR I-2991, in which a Dutch national employed by a German firm but posted immediately to Thailand was held to be liable only for contributions under the German scheme.

98 Case 110/79 *Coonan v Insurance Officer* [1980] ECR 1445, in which the UK was held to be entitled to exclude an Irish woman who came to Great Britain over pensionable age from affiliation to its social security scheme. See also the cases cited at n 22, above.

99 Art 12 (ex art 6) and art 39(2) (ex art 48(2)) EC.

nationals from inferior treatment is reflected in the wording of the non-discrimination principle now contained in article 3(1) of Title I of Council Regulation (EEC) 1408/71:

> Subject to the special provisions of this Regulation, persons resident in the territory of one of the Member States to whom this Regulation applies shall be subject to the same obligations and enjoy the same benefits under the legislation of any Member State as the nationals of that State.

This wording seems to preclude the possibility of the provision being used by nationals to challenge their own member state's preferential treatment of non-nationals, and thus to legitimate what some regard as illegitimate, namely, reverse discrimination. The matter came before the ECJ in *Kenny*,[100] a case in which an Irish national claimed benefit in the UK for a period during which he was imprisoned in Ireland. The UK system contained a rule disqualifying people for a period spent in prison in the UK. Interpreted in literal fashion, this rule could not affect the Irish national's claim since his imprisonment had been in Ireland not the UK. The UK authorities argued, however, that the rule should be construed so as to apply to imprisonment outside the UK otherwise it would constitute discrimination against British nationals, the discrimination in this instance arising from the fact that more nationals than non-nationals making claims under UK rules would be likely to have been in prison or to have served prison sentences in the UK. The court's response was ambivalent. It ruled that article 3(1) of the Regulation does not prohibit nor does it require facts occurring in another member state to be treated as equivalent to facts occurring on national territory which constitute a ground for loss of entitlement, provided that the application does not lead to discrimination against nationals of other member states. Despite this reference to nationals of other member states, the court then went on to hold that this applies equally where the worker concerned is a national of the member state in which the institution is situated, from which benefit is being claimed.

Following *Kenny*, doubt remains as to whether article 3(1) effectively proscribes discrimination by member states against its own nationals.[101] There is more certainty, however, regarding other aspects of this rule. It is clear that it prohibits rules differentiating on the basis of nationality and on the basis of residence. Residence conditions have been successfully challenged in a number of cases.[102] It is also clear that discrimination which is indirect or covert in nature is proscribed along with discrimination of a direct or overt kind. Rules linked to nationality which have a disadvantageous effect on the people to whom they are applied are an example of direct or overt discrimination. Rules which are neutral as to nationality and residence but which have the same disadvantageous effect constitute indirect or covert discrimination. The prison disqualification rule in *Kenny* is an example of the type of rule capable of constituting indirect discrimination.

Similarly, the rule in article 73(1) of the Regulation was itself the subject of a successful challenge on this ground in the *Pinna* case.[103] Under the version of article 73(1) then in force, employed persons subject to French legislation were not entitled to receive family allowances provided under French legislation when their dependent children were resident in another member state, whereas employed persons subject to the legislation of any

---

100   Case 1/78 *Kenny* [1978] ECR 1489.
101   Case C-332/90 *Steen v Deutsche Bundespost* [1992] ECR I-341 and Case C-132/93 *Steen v Deutsche Bundespost* [1994] ECR I-2715 have clarified matters a little.
102   Case 1/72 *Frilli v Belgium* [1972] ECR 457; Case 139/82 *Piscitello v Istituto Nazionale della Previdenza Sociale* [1983] ECR 1427.
103   Case 41/84 *Pinna v Caisse d'Allocations Familiales de la Savoie* [1986] ECR 1.

other member state were entitled to receive the family allowances of the state of employment notwithstanding that their dependent children lived in another member state. Invoking articles 48 to 51 of the Treaty, the court held that this provision of the Regulation constituted indirect discrimination against foreign workers in France when compared with the treatment both of French nationals and of foreign workers in other member states.[104] As a result, the article was rendered inapplicable and, as we shall see, was subsequently amended. The case provides a nice example of how the teleological approach of the court can operate in this area so as to invalidate EU legislation and constrain the activities of the Council in the exercise of its law-making powers.[105]

C Aggregation and apportionment

Aggregation is a key co-ordinating mechanism, developed and refined over many years. At its simplest, it involves the addition of periods of insurance in order to overcome preliminary qualifying periods, the completion of which is a condition of entitlement to benefit. Its purpose is to ensure that people about to move from the state in which they have acquired social security rights do not lose those rights in consequence of the move. Aggregation thus compensates for deficiencies in people's insurance record arising from their employment in more than one member state. There is no general provision applying the aggregation procedure to all benefits. Each benefit has its own set of provisions,[106] adapted to the type of benefit involved, the circumstances in which it is likely to be required and the various functions such benefits fulfil, including (but not restricted to) the welfare function. There is none the less a degree of uniformity in the wording of the aggregation provisions. The one relating to sickness and maternity is illustrative. It provides that:

> The competent institution of a Member State whose legislation makes the acquisition, retention, or recovery of the right to benefits conditional upon the completion of periods of insurance, employment and residence shall, to the extent necessary, take account of periods of insurance, employment or residence completed under the legislation of any other Member State as if they were periods completed under the legislation which it administers.[107]

Some of the terms used here require elaboration. The competent institution usually means the institution with whom people are insured at the time they make their claim.[108] It is situated in the competent state.[109] This will tend to be the state of employment.[110] The notion of the competent institution-competent state is thus similar to but not

---

104 For another case concerning indirect discrimination and French family benefits see Case 237/78 *Caisse Régionale d'Assurance Maladie, Lille v Palmero, née Toia* [1979] ECR 2645.
105 Art 3(1) has also been successfully invoked so as to render inapplicable national legislative and contractual conditions governing access to and awards of social security including maternity, invalidity, retirement and means-tested benefits: Case 33/88 *Allué and Coonan v Università degli studi di Venezia* [1989] ECR 1591; Case C-10/90 *Masgio v Bundesknappschaft* [1991] ECR I-1119.
106 Sickness and maternity, art 18; invalidity, art 38; old age, death (survivors) and certain invalidity, art 45(1) to (4); occupational disease, art 57; death grant, art 64; unemployment, art 67(1) and (2); family benefit, art 72. The aggregation procedure does not apply to benefit in respect of industrial accidents.
107 Art 18(1).
108 Art 1(o).
109 Art 1(q).
110 A notable exception relates to unemployment benefit where it is the state of residence under art 71 (but not under art 67). The same applies to sickness and maternity benefit under art 25(2) if the claimant receives benefit under art 71.

coterminous with the concept of applicable legislation provided for under Title II of Council Regulation (EEC) 1408/71. Another phrase worthy of note is 'to the extent necessary'. This means that where it is possible to establish entitlement under national law alone, recourse to aggregation, though possible, is unnecessary. Finally, the terms 'periods of insurance, employment and residence' need to be defined.[111] Periods of insurance means periods of contributions.[112] What constitutes periods of contributions, employment or residence for the purposes of aggregation is determined by the legislation under which the periods were completed or treated as completed. Thus in *Mura*[113] an Italian worker claiming a disability pension in France was unable to rely on a period of unemployment in Italy because Italy did not treat such a period as a period of employment, although it was treated as a period of employment in France.[114]

We have seen that the aggregation procedure is designed to compensate mobile workers for deficiencies in their insurance record in each member state in which they have been insured. A second procedure, called apportionment, is coupled with aggregation in some circumstances. Apportionment relates to the calculation and funding of benefit. It involves apportioning responsibility for payment of a certain amount of total benefit to each of the member states in which people have worked. Their total pension thus comprises a number of separate awards made by the relevant member states. The amount awarded by each state is a proportion of the rate that would have been available had the people concerned spent their entire working life in that state. The proportion is calculated by dividing the persons' working life by the length of time actually worked in the member state concerned. There are three key differences between the simple aggregation procedure and the procedure in which aggregation and apportionment are combined. The first is that with simple aggregation only one member state goes through the process of aggregating insurance periods in different member states and that is normally the state of last employment, the competent state.[115] With the combined procedure, however, each member state carries out a form of aggregation in the process of calculating the pro rata amount as described above. A second point is that the tendency of these procedures to result in duplication of benefit payments is countered in the first instance by the 'only one state shall aggregate' rule and in the second by the process of apportionment, of only paying a pro rata amount.

The final and most important difference is that the two sets of procedures apply to different branches of benefit systems. The division is roughly between short- and long-term benefits, simple aggregation being applied to unemployment, maternity, sickness and some invalidity benefits, the combined procedure being applied to old age, survivors' and other types of invalidity benefit. This division between long-term and short-term benefits holds the key to what may be considered to be the main purpose of the combined aggregation and apportionment procedure, which is to share the cost of funding the more expensive long-term benefits among all those member states with whom the people concerned have been insured during their working life, rather than to place the entire cost

---

111   The possibility of aggregating periods of employment and residence as well as periods of contributions undoubtedly adds to the complexity of the aggregation provisions. Aggregation works better when the relevant systems are all contribution-based. The assimilation of periods of employment and residence to periods of contributions seeks to ensure that those moving between member states with differently based schemes are not disadvantaged by the lack of harmonisation in this respect.

112   Art 1(r), but includes periods of (self-) employment if the legislation where they were completed treats them as such, and other periods, eg of credits, treated as such.

113   Case 22/77 *Mura* [1977] ECR 1699, [1978] 2 CMLR 416.

114   But see Case 126/77 *Frangiamore v Office National de l'Emploi* [1978] ECR 725 and Case 388/87 *Bestuur van de Nieuwe Algemene Bedrijfsvereniging v Warmerdam-Steggerda* [1989] ECR 1203.

115   In relation to sickness and maternity benefit, it must be the competent state: Case 150/82 *Coppola v Insurance Officer* [1983] ECR 43.

on the state with whom the people concerned were last insured, as happens in the case of short-term benefits. Another advantage of apportionment, from the workers' point of view, is that they can reap the benefits of the higher rates (if any) paid by member states with whom they have at some time been insured and are not restricted to the (possibly) less generous provision made by the state with whom they were last insured.

D The 'exporting' of benefits

The requirement that people must be resident in a member state if they are to continue to be entitled to that state's benefits affords the clearest illustration of the territorial character of member states' social security systems. The aim in abolishing restrictions of this (territorial) kind and of permitting people to 'export' benefits, if and when they cease to be resident in the member state in which entitlement has arisen, is to promote free movement of labour. As already noted, however, this 'exporting' facility is only available in relation to certain types of benefits. In particular, it is not available in respect of the special non-contributory benefits and applies only on a restricted basis to unemployment, sickness and maternity benefits. The policy considerations giving rise to this selective treatment are threefold: one is member states' desire to monitor the work efforts of the unemployed and sick; another is their desire to create the most favourable conditions for a speedy return to work; a third is to prevent people maximising benefit entitlement by moving between member states claiming and taking benefits with them as they go (sometimes known as 'benefit tourism').

The benefits which can be 'exported' without qualification are those to which these considerations do not apply. These, mainly long term, benefits are listed in article 10(1) of Council Regulation (EEC) 1408/71, which also spells out the nature and scope of this particular co-ordinating technique:

> Save as otherwise provided in this Regulation, invalidity, old-age or survivors' cash benefits, pension for accidents at work or occupational diseases and death grants acquired under the legislation of one or more Member States shall not be subject to any reduction, modification, suspension, withdrawal or confiscation by reason of the fact that the recipient resides in the territory of a Member State other than that in which the institution responsible for payment is situated.[116]

It is a moot point as to whether article 10(1) removes territorial restrictions solely in relation to benefit rights which have already been acquired[117] or whether it is also concerned, as the court in *Newton*[118] seems to suggest, with the protection of rights in the process of being acquired.[119]

---

116   In relation to UK social security legislation, art 10(1) has the effect of overriding the disqualification of claimants for temporary or permanent absence abroad provided for in the Social Security Contributions and Benefits Act 1992, s 113(5)(a). It is extended to cover temporary absence by Council Regulation (EEC) 1408/71, Annex VI, Point L, para 12.

117   In Case 32/77 *Giuliani v Landesversicherungsanstalt Schwaben* [1977] ECR 1857 the European Court of Justice stated that 'the waiving of residence clauses pursuant to Article 10 has no effect on the acquisition of the right to benefit'.

118   Case C-356/89 *Newton* [1991] ECR I-3017. The court ruled that the claimant in receipt of UK mobility allowance was still entitled to receive it when he moved to another member state notwithstanding the requirement under UK legislation that he satisfy the residence and presence conditions each day. Note now, however, that such benefits classed as special non-contributory benefits may not be exported: see Council Regulation (EEC) 1408/71, art 10a and also Case C-20/96 *Snares v Adjudication Officer* [1997] ECR I-6057 and C-297/96 *Partridge v Adjudication Officer* [1998] ECR I-3467.

119   *White* n 1, above, p 66–67, citing Case 92/81 *Caracriolo* [1982] ECR 2213, adopts the same approach.

Part 4   The co-ordination of social security and special non-contributory benefits

The preceding section describes the techniques adopted by Council Regulation (EEC) 1408/71 in very general terms. This section looks at how they work in the context of specific branches of benefits.[120] The relevant provisions are contained in articles 18 to 78 of Title III of the Regulation. They are exceedingly complex, partly because of the different principles on which entitlement to member states' benefits are based and partly because of the very different social and economic circumstances under which each benefit is likely to be required and under which member states consider it appropriate to make them available. We have already discussed some of these issues in the last section. More will emerge in the following brief discussion of how co-ordination works in relation to particular benefits.

A   Maternity and sickness benefits

Maternity and sickness benefits are co-ordinated by articles 18 to 31 of Council Regulation (EEC) 1408/71. Co-ordination has to allow for the wide range of benefits offered by member states and the fact that they take the form of awards both in cash and in kind. It also has to cater for provision of benefits in a variety of circumstances, including emergencies. For these reasons the provisions are among the most detailed and complex of all those contained in the Regulation. They are treated here in summary form.[121]

Aggregation of periods of insurance, employment and residence in relation to maternity and sickness benefits is provided for under article 18(1)[122] and is to be carried out by the competent state. There is no apportionment. 'Exporting' of these benefits is possible to a certain extent. The conditions for doing so are spelt out in articles 19 to 22. Article 19 provides for benefits to be 'exported' where the contingency giving rise to the need for benefit occurs while the persons concerned are residing in a state other than the competent state. Article 22(1)(b) provides likewise where the persons concerned become entitled in the competent state and move to reside[123] in another member state. Provision here is subject to the condition that authorisation for the award of benefit be obtained from the competent institution, which can only refuse to give it on the ground that the proposed move by the persons concerned would be detrimental to their state of health. People are also able to receive maternity and sickness benefits even if they are merely staying[124] (as opposed to residing) in another member state and either they have been authorised to go there for treatment[125] or, while there, their condition necessitates immediate benefits.[126] If the stay in the state other than the competent state is for any other reason, eg convalescence, it will not be possible to invoke the Regulation in order to ensure continuity of entitlement. Such limitations on

---

120   Other than benefits for industrial accidents and occupational diseases and death grants.
121   See further *Pennings* n 1, above, ch 14; and *White* n 1, above, pp 75–86 for a fuller treatment.
122   Reproduced at p 77, above.
123   Defined as habitual residence: Council Regulation (EEC) 1408/71, art 1(h).
124   Defined as temporary residence: Council Regulation (EEC) 1408/71, art 1(i).
125   Art 22(1)(c). Authorisation may not be refused where beneficiaries cannot be given the appropriate treatment within the time normally necessary in the state of residence taking account of their current state of health and probable prognosis: art 22(2).
126   Ie treatment: art 22(1)(a).

the degree to which maternity and sickness benefits may be 'exported' are said to be aimed at controlling benefit 'abuse'[127] by claimants eager to avoid an early return to work.

For practical reasons, benefits in kind are provided by the authorities of the state of residence even though the recipients of those benefits are affiliated to an institution in another member state. However, the cost of the treatment will normally be borne by the institution to which the recipients are affiliated.

B Unemployment benefit

Co-ordination of unemployment benefits gives rise to a number of problems, more political than practical in nature. This is because member states generally wish to monitor claimants' efforts to find work, to make that search for work as effective as possible and to limit the number and cost of claims made on their own national system. These objectives are not always compatible with the EU objective of promoting free movement of labour and so co-ordination in these circumstances can sometimes prove problematic. The present compromise is to permit aggregation (but not apportionment) under tightly controlled conditions and to allow the 'exporting' of these benefits but only for a limited period.[128]

Article 67(1) and (2) of Council Regulation (EEC) 1408/71 makes provision for the competent institution of a member state, whose legislation makes the acquisition, retention or recovery of the right to benefits subject to completion of periods of insurance (paragraph 1) or employment (paragraph 2), to aggregate periods of insurance or employment completed in another member state as though they had been completed under their own legislation. The third paragraph of article 67 then goes on to state unequivocally that aggregation can only be carried out by the state in which the persons concerned were lastly insured or employed and in accordance with whose legislation their claim to benefit is subsequently made. The aim of article 67, particularly article 67(3), is to prevent the unemployed from moving between member states, claiming unemployment benefit from funds to which they have made no contribution in the past.[129] Although perhaps justifiable on this basis, these provisions none the less militate against people moving to the states in which work of a kind for which they are suited is readily available. They thus conflict with national policies designed to help people in their search for employment.

A similar conflict arises in relation to people whose last employment was undertaken in a state other than that in which they were (and still are) resident. This is because when they become unemployed, and wish to invoke the co-ordinating provisions, article 67 dictates that the state of last employment, not the state in which they reside, must carry out the aggregation procedure and be liable for payment of benefit, if any. The problem here is that the job prospects of the people concerned are possibly far

---

127   Steiner [1992] JSWFL 33 at 41.
128   See *Pennings* n 1, above, ch 17 and Wikeley [1988] JSWL 300 for a detailed account of the operation of Council Regulation (EEC) 1408/71 in relation to unemployment benefits.
129   In this context, it is readily assumed that the unemployed will willingly cross frontiers in order to gain access to unemployment benefit, gravitating in particular towards those member states where the rates of benefit are highest. According to this logic, member states with the most generous systems are the most vulnerable to 'benefit tourism' of this kind. However, all member states are wary of accepting an open-ended commitment to fund the unemployment benefit of those who have in no way contributed to the system in the past. See eg Case C-88/95 *Losada v INEM* [1997] ICR 1100, paras 29–38.

greater in their state of residence than in the state in which they were last employed, yet to benefit from article 67 they must make their claim in the state in which they were last employed. Invariably, then, they will have to satisfy the national authorities that their efforts to obtain work are adequate, a condition which will prove problematic if their search is being conducted in another member state. From the member states' point of view it seems reasonable for them to insist on effective monitoring of claimants' efforts to find work in exchange for payment of benefit, even if this to some extent reduces claimants' prospects of finding work.

Thus it is clear that co-ordinating unemployment benefit raises some difficult problems. It brings into play EU and national policy objectives, not all of which are reconcilable. The compromise adopted by Council Regulation (EEC) 1408/71 involves two elements. The first is to provide for 'exporting' of benefits for a limited period; the second is to make it possible, in certain circumstances, for the state of residence rather than the state of last employment to aggregate insurance periods and to assume liability for payment.

Article 69(1) provides for limited exportability. Thus people entitled to benefit from the competent state (the state of last employment) may continue to receive it even if they go to another member state, subject to a number of stringent conditions. First, they must register and be available for work in the competent state for the first four weeks of unemployment; secondly, they must register as seeking work in each of the member states to which they go in search of work; thirdly, if they fail to find work, entitlement to benefit from the competent state will cease after three months' absence from that state. In respect of the latter, however, if, in accordance with article 69(2), they return to the competent state within the three-month period, they will continue to be entitled to benefit under the legislation of that state.[130] The limitation in article 69(2) on the length of time for which unemployment benefit may be 'exported' was challenged in *Testa*[131] as being contrary to article 51 (now 42) of the Treaty. The court resisted the challenge, holding the provision valid on the ground that it relieved claimants of the need to make themselves available to the employment services of the competent state for three months, and thus created rather than took away rights which claimants had under national law.[132] The limited 'exportability' of unemployment benefit has none the less been a concern of the Commission and member states for some time.[133] In the light of the European Court of Human Rights decision in *Gaygusuz*,[134] there is an argument that article 69(2) could be challenged as discriminatory.[135]

Article 71 of the Regulation is concerned with wholly or partly unemployed people last employed in a state in which they were not resident and provides, in respect of those people who are wholly unemployed, that they receive benefit from the state of residence rather than the state of last employment. A distinction is drawn between frontier workers[136] and non-frontier workers. Under article 71(1)(a)(ii) wholly unemployed frontier workers receive benefits from the state of residence as though

---

130   This time-limit may be waived or extended by the competent institution: art 69(2).

131   Cases 41/79, 121/79, 796/79 [1980] ECR 1979; see also eg Case 272/90 *van Noorden v ASSEDIC* [1991] ECR I-2543 and Case C-62/91 *Gray v Adjudication Officer* [1992] ECR I-2737, [1992] 2 CMLR 584.

132   The court distinguished Case 24/75 *Petroni* [1975] ECR 1149 (p 87, below) on this ground. *Testa* is a rare example of the court declining to adopt the 'disadvantage' approach to interpretation of the co-ordinating provisions: see p 65, above.

133   A Commission proposal to amend the three-month limitation was made in 1980 (see OJ 1980 C169/22) but has not been implemented. The proposed new co-ordinating Regulation, if implemented, will extend the period for exporting unemployment benefit to six months.

134   *Gaygusuz v Austria* (1996) 23 EHRR 364; see p 60, above.

135   Moore (1998) 35 CML Rev 409 at 456–457.

136   Defined in art 1(b) as employed or self-employed persons who pursue their occupation in one member state and reside in another, returning to the latter daily or at least once a week.

they had been subject to its legislation when they were last employed.[137] Under article 71(1)(b)(ii) wholly unemployed non-frontier workers who are available to the employment services of the state of residence receive benefits under its legislation as though subject to it during their last employment.[138] However, the latter does not apply in respect of periods during which unemployment benefit is being exported by the competent state to the non-frontier workers' state of residence. Because article 71 operates in some instances so as to transfer liability for payment from the competent state to the state of residence, the court has ruled that it must be interpreted strictly.[139]

C Old age, invalidity and death benefits

The co-ordination techniques are given far-reaching application in relation to old age, invalidity and death benefits. Death benefits here refer to survivors' benefits and exclude death grants. With only one or two exceptions, these long term benefits are subject to the combined aggregation and apportionment procedure under articles 38 to 51 of Council Regulation (EEC) 1408/71. They are also fully 'exportable' under article 10 of Title I of the Regulation. This claim to expansive coverage is subject to two qualifications. One is that the benefits concerned must be classed as social security and not as special non-contributory benefits. As we shall see, the co-ordination techniques are more restrictively applied in relation to the latter. A second is that while all invalidity benefits are subject to the aggregation procedure, only some of them are subject to apportionment as well. For this purpose the Regulation distinguishes between Type A invalidity benefits, which are subject to simple aggregation, and Type B, which are subject to aggregation and apportionment.[140] The feature common to Type A benefits is that the rate of benefit does not vary with the length of insurance, whereas with benefits classified as Type B it does.

The provision in the Regulation applying the apportionment procedure to old age benefits is article 46(1), (2) and (3). Article 40 applies article 46 to Type B invalidity benefits and article 44 to survivors' benefits. The account of the apportionment procedure, given below, is based on the provisions relating to old age benefits contained in article 46. The procedure requires each member state, to whose legislation people making a claim to old age benefits have been subject, to make two assessments as follows:

1   If there is entitlement under its own national legislation, it calculates the benefit accordingly, disregarding any period of insurance completed in another member state.[141] National rules providing for a reduction in benefit to take account of other (overlapping) benefits in payment must be applied to arrive at the rate derived from national legislation alone.[142]

---

137   See Case C-131/95 *Huijbrechts* [1997] ECR I-1409. Uniform Community criteria must be applied to determine whether a frontier worker is partly or wholly unemployed: Case C-444/98 *de Laat* [2001] ECR I-2229.

138   Case C-454/93 *Van Gestel* [1995] ECR I-1707.

139   Case 76/76 *Di Paolo v Office National de l'Emploi* [1977] ECR 315.

140   Where a beneficiary has been subject to legislative schemes which provide Type A invalidity benefits, benefit is payable, where necessary following aggregation, only by the competent state: art 39(2). Where a beneficiary has been subject to at least one scheme which provides Type B invalidity benefit, all benefits, including Type A, are subject to aggregation and apportionment: art 40(1).

141   Art 46(1); see also Case 342/88 *Rijksdienst voor Pensioenen v Spits* [1990] ECR I-2259; Cases C-45/92 *Lepore* and C-46/92 *Scamuffa* [1993] ECR I-6497; and Case 325/93 *Del Grosso* [1995] ECR I-939.

142   Art 46(3) provides for the payment of the highest amount calculated in accordance with art 46(1) and (2) from the competent institution of each member state without prejudice to any application of the provisions concerning reduction, suspension or withdrawal provided for by the legislation under which this benefit is due. Where that is the case, the comparison to be carried out shall relate to the amounts determined after the application of the said provisions.

2   In the second assessment,[143] the member state must aggregate periods of insurance or residence completed as employed or self-employed persons under the legislation of any other member state as if completed under its own legislation. The next step is to establish the theoretical rate, which is the amount of benefit under its own legislation to which the persons concerned would have been entitled if all the aggregated periods had been completed under its own legislation. Finally, the member state must divide the aggregated period by the periods actually completed under its legislation. The proportionate figure arrived at will then be applied to the theoretical rate to produce an actual rate.

The two rates of benefit produced as a result of these assessments are then compared by each member state. The member state must then pay the claimant the higher of the two.[144] The number of such payments received by claimants will depend on the number of member states' legislations to which they have been subject during their working life.[145]

D Special non-contributory benefits

This class of benefit fits uneasily into a section divided up according to the type of risks covered by benefits, since, potentially at least, it covers all the risks. It is included for consideration at this point, however, on the basis that many of the member states' benefits to which it will apply will be concerned with providing protection against two of the risks discussed in the preceding section, namely, old age and invalidity. What then is the co-ordinated status of this type of benefit?[146]

First, the benefits concerned are subject to the simple aggregation procedure: there is no apportionment. Thus article 10a(2) of Council Regulation (EEC) 1408/71 provides that a member state whose legislation makes entitlement to its own special non-contributory benefits subject to the completion of periods of employment, self-employment or residence shall regard, where necessary, periods of employment, self-employment or residence completed in the territory of another member state as though they were completed in its own. Secondly, under no circumstances can these special non-contributory benefits be 'exported'. Article 10a(1) provides that special non-contributory benefits shall be granted to people 'exclusively in the territory of the Member State in which they reside, in accordance with the legislation of that State'. The veto on the 'exporting' of these benefits operates so as to ensure that people acquiring access to such benefits in the member states to which they move will lose entitlement immediately they cease to be resident in the states concerned. They will not therefore be able to move from state to state accumulating these types of benefits as they go. One reason for the introduction of this special class of benefit was to prevent 'benefit tourism' of this kind taking place. Another reason may have been the desire to insist that only those physically present in the community enjoy benefits paid out of general taxation or other funds of a solidaristic kind.

---

143   Art 46(2); see Case C-406/93 *Reichling* [1994] ECR I-4061.
144   Art 46(3).
145   Periods of insurance of less than 12 months are taken into account for the purposes of aggregation but not for apportionment: art 48.
146   See also art 4(2a).

E   Family benefits

Council Regulation (EEC) 1408/71 differentiates between 'family benefits' and 'family allowances', the former meaning all benefits in cash or in kind under the legislation to which the Regulation applies,[147] the latter being periodical cash benefits granted exclusively by reference to the number and, where appropriate, the age of members of the family.[148] Family benefits (including family allowances) are subject to the simple aggregation procedure and to a form of exportability. Article 72 provides for aggregation by a member state where that state's legislation makes entitlement to family benefits dependent on periods of insurance or employment. There is no apportionment. Article 73 provides for family benefits to be 'exported'.[149] Here, 'exporting' assumes a slightly different meaning. It covers the situation in which workers are employed in one member state and wish to 'export' the family benefits to which they are entitled in that state to another member state in which the members of their family reside. Thus article 73 provides that employed and self-employed persons subject to the legislation of a member state shall be entitled to the family benefits of that state in respect of members of their family residing in another member state as though they were resident in that state.[150] Article 74 applies the same principle to unemployed people in receipt of unemployment benefit[151] under the legislation of a member state.

The tendency for families of mobile workers to be separated by national boundaries gives rise to a form of duplication of payments not encountered with other types of benefits. This is exacerbated by the different principles on which entitlement to these benefits is based. In some member states, for example, they are linked (as in the UK) to residence and in others to employment. As a result one family may be subject to the legislation of two or more member states and thus be entitled to a multiplicity of family benefits. Two sets of provisions are employed to counter overlapping of benefits. One is article 76 of Council Regulation (EEC) 1408/71 which applies where entitlement to family benefits is conditional upon carrying on an occupation; the other is article 10 of Council Regulation (EEC) 574/72 which applies where entitlement is subject to conditions, not of employment, self-employment or insurance, but of residence or presence. The formula applied by both is that where there is overlapping entitlement to family benefits under the legislation of the competent state and the state of residence, benefits from the latter will be suspended up to the rate of the former (thus ensuring in effect that the highest of the rates set by the relevant member states is paid), unless the parent responsible for the children in their state of residence is pursuing a professional or trade activity there, in which case that state, not the non-caring parent's state of employment, must pay the benefit.[152]

We now turn to look at the more general provisions in Council Regulation (EEC) 1408/71 concerned with the overlapping and duplication of benefit provision.

---

147   Art 1(u)(i). This includes advances of maintenance payments paid in respect of a child to a lone parent by a public authority where the other parent has defaulted on his obligations: Case C-255/99 *Humer* [2002] ECR I-000 (n.y.r.).

148   Art 1(u)(ii).

149   Art 73 was retrospectively amended by Council Regulation (EEC) 3427/89 (with effect from 15 January 1989) to give effect, inter alia, to the ruling of the court in Case 41/84 *Pinna v Caisse d'Allocations Familiales de la Savoie* [1986] ECR 1; see p 76, above.

150   See Case C-78/91 *Hughes v Chief Adjudication Officer* [1992] ECR I-4839 and Case C-266/95 *García v Bundesanstalt für Arbeit* [1997] ECR I-3279.

151   Including payments in lieu of notice: Case C-243/94 *Moreno* [1996] ECR I-1887.

152   See Case C-119/91 *McMenamin v Adjudication Officer* [1992] ECR I-6393; [1993] 1 CMLR 509 in which the court briefly reviews the history and operation of these overlapping provisions, in the course of interpreting them (see also Cousins (1994) 45 NILQ 294).

Part 5   The overlapping provisions under Council Regulation (EEC) 1408/71

Duplication of benefit payments can occur within and across member states' systems. It may also arise as a result of the operation of Council Regulation (EEC) 1408/71. People moving between member states are potential beneficiaries of any one (or more) of these situations. However, national schemes often contain rules reducing, suspending or eliminating benefit in such circumstances. Council Regulation (EEC) 1408/71, directly and indirectly, does likewise.

A   Council Regulation (EEC) 1408/71, articles 12(1) and 46(3)

The principle adopted by Council Regulation (EEC) 1408/71 in article 12(1) is that it (the Regulation) should 'neither confer nor maintain the right to several benefits of the same kind for one and the same period of compulsory insurance'. It is further provided, however, that this principle shall not apply to benefits in respect of invalidity, old age, death or occupational disease awarded by the institutions of two or more member states in accordance with the provisions of the Regulation.[153] The principle of non-cumulation none the less does apply to these latter benefits. It is given effect not through application of article 12(1) but through application of the apportionment procedure.[154] It may be noted, in addition, that other provisions in the Regulation prescribe circumstances in which the duplication of specific benefits is prohibited.[155] Article 12(1), however, gives expression to the general principle and in this respect it is important to emphasise that its scope is limited. It can only be applied to prevent duplication of rights arising from EU law; it cannot be applied so as to diminish or abolish rights arising under national law alone.[156]

We have seen in Part 2 of this chapter that this principle of no diminution of benefit rights arising under national law is a crucial element in what we have called the court's 'disadvantage' approach to interpretation of Council Regulation (EEC) 1408/71. The court developed this approach in part through interpretation of the overlapping provisions, in particular through interpretation of article 46(3) of the Regulation. This provision concerns the apportionment of old age and death benefits and has already been referred to a number of times in this chapter. In its present form, it provides simply that the amount of benefit to which people are entitled from each member state shall be the highest amount derived from the two assessments each member state must make in accordance with the preceding two paragraphs in article 46. Article 46(3) originally contained an additional rule limiting the total amount of benefit paid to one person by all relevant member states to the highest theoretical (or notional) amount calculated according to the second paragraph of article 46.[157]

---

153   Ie under the aggregation and apportionment provisions: arts 41, 43(2) and (3), 46, 50, 51(2), 57(5) or 60(1)(b) or (c).

154   The non-applicability of apportionment to Type A invalidity benefits where a beneficiary has been subject only to schemes which provide such benefits has already been noted: see p 83, above.

155   These include arts 19(2), 25(1)(b), 34(2), 39(2) and (5), 68(2), 71(2), 76 (see p 85, above) and 79(3) and also Council Regulation (EEC) 574/72, arts 8–10.

156   See Case 34/69 *Duffy* [1969] ECR 597; Case 27/75 *Bonaffini* [1975] ECR 971; Case 184/73 *Kaufmann* [1974] ECR 517.

157   This was an anti-cumulation rule since its aim was to ensure that the total pension payable to a person by all member states did not exceed the amount that would have been payable if the person's entire working life had been spent in just one of those states.

In the *Petroni* case[158] the court ruled that the application of this extra provision so as to reduce the amount of benefit arising under national law alone was incompatible with articles 48 to 51 of the Treaty. In 1992 article 46(3) was amended so as to remove the limitation linked to the highest theoretical amount.[159]

This simplification of the apportionment procedure under article 46 has almost certainly increased the likelihood of some workers being better off financially as a result of their having been employed in a number of member states. UK pensions legislation illustrates how this accrual of advantage can occur. Under UK rules, persons employed for 90 per cent of the qualifying years of their working life are entitled to the basic state retirement pension at the full rate. If the remaining 10 per cent of their working life is completed in another member state, it is now possible (following *Petroni* and the amendment to article 46(3)) for the persons concerned to receive a pro rata pension (10 per cent of its theoretical rate) from that other member state, in addition to the full UK pension to which they are entitled under national law alone.[160]

B Council Regulation (EEC) 1408/71, article 12(2)

Although article 12(1) of Council Regulation (EEC) 1408/71 cannot operate to reduce the amount of benefit payable under national law alone, article 12(2) still permits domestic legislation to be invoked to prevent overlapping in such circumstances. This is so even where the overlapping benefit is acquired under the legislation of another member state. However, this general rule is again subject to important exceptions[161] spelt out in detail in articles 46a, 46b and 46c.[162] In brief, these provisions impose restrictions on the extent to which member states can invoke national overlapping provisions so as to reduce benefits. What article 12(2) gives with one hand, therefore, articles 46a, 46b and 46c attempt to take back with the other.

These latter provisions draw a distinction between benefits of the same kind and benefits of a different kind. Benefits of the same kind[163] are defined as invalidity, old age and death (survivors') benefits, and benefits of a different kind as all those not included in the 'same kind' category. Article 46a applies to all benefits whether of the same or of a different kind. It provides that member states may only reduce these benefits to take account of an overlap with those of another member state if their national

---

158 Case 24/75 *Petroni* [1975] ECR 1149. In particular, it ruled that the objectives of arts 48–51 of Council Regulation (EEC) 1408/71 could not be attained if, as a consequence of exercising their right to free movement, workers were to lose advantages in the field of social security guaranteed to them in any event by the laws of a single member state: para 13. See Arnull *The General Principles of EEC Law and the Individual* (1990) pp 148–154 for a useful discussion of art 46(3).

159 By Council Regulation (EEC) 1248/92. Art 46(3) does not apply where a worker has worked in two member states *over the same period* and has been required to pay contributions in both states: Case C-31/92 *Larsy v INASTI* [1993] ECR I-4543 (self-employed Belgian nursery gardener living near French border with land on both sides of the frontier).

160 The apportioned rate of UK pension would have been only 90 per cent of the full rate. If the limitation to the highest theoretical amount were still applicable, each payment by each member state (in this instance two) would have to be reduced proportionately to bring the total payment down to the theoretical amount payable by the UK or other member state, whichever is (or would have been) the highest.

161 Art 12(2) begins 'Save as otherwise provided in this Regulation ...', as inserted by amending Council Regulation (EEC) 1248/92. This replaced a qualifying clause in the preceding version of art 12(2) to the effect that national overlapping rules could not be invoked to reduce benefits of the same kind in respect of invalidity, old age, death or occupational disease.

162 Inserted by Council Regulation (EEC) 1248/92 with effect from 1 June 1992.

163 See Case C-98/94 *Schmidt* [1995] ECR I-2559; [1996] ICR 91 on the meaning of this term.

legislation so provides, and any reduction must not exceed the rate of the other state's benefit. Article 46b applies to benefits of the same kind and provides, inter alia, that no reduction may be made in respect of another member state's benefit arising from the apportionment exercise, nor in respect of another state's benefits where the amount depends on the length of insurance. Article 46c applies to benefits of a different kind. An important restriction in relation to these benefits is that if reductions are due from more than one member state they can only be made on a pro rata basis. The purpose of this provision is to ensure claimants do not have their benefit reduced twice or three times over.

C   The overlapping provisions in context

The *Petroni* ruling nicely illustrates how the ECJ's insistence on the 'disadvantage' approach to interpretation of Council Regulation (EEC) 1408/71 can indirectly result in workers being financially advantaged by the fact that they have moved from one member state to another for employment purposes. It might be thought that this gives rise to a 'new' discrimination against those who continue to be employed in the same territory throughout their working life, who are not so advantaged. Another view is that the financial gain resulting from mobility and the operation of member states' social security systems is, in turn, largely a consequence of the differences in (and lack of harmonisation of) the national systems involved. Moreover, the securing of advantage, though not decried by the court, is not a key element in its interpretative approach. Advocates of the 'deterritorial' approach to interpretation of Council Regulation (EEC) 1408/71, on the other hand, would seem to regard such advantage as unjustified and a source of discrimination against non-mobile workers. For this reason, they see the purpose of co-ordination to be the elimination of both disadvantages and advantages arising from workers' movement between member states. They therefore disapprove of the principle, so instrumental in *Petroni*, which protects rights acquired under national law and call upon the court to reconsider it.[164]

---

164   See further *Arnull* n 158, above, p 153, for an interesting discussion of other arguments used by advocates of this interpretative approach.

Chapter 4

Contributions

Part 1   Introduction

In chapter 1 the various methods of financing social security benefits were considered, and it was seen how British policy has retained a major (but diminishing) role for the contributory approach. In this chapter we describe the liability to pay contributions and the general principles governing the fulfilment of contribution conditions.[1] The basic concepts are derived from the insurance schemes existing before the Second World War but their character has since changed in several fundamental respects.

A   Risk-related insurance

As has already been explained,[2] private insurance influenced the development of National Insurance, and this is particularly evident in the early efforts of the state schemes to relate liability to the risks attached to particular categories of individuals or employments. The first unemployment insurance scheme of 1911 covered only those trades in which the employment pattern was thought to be reasonably stable. Moreover, employers of men who by the age of 60 had paid more by way of contribution than they had received by way of benefit were entitled to a refund.[3] This right lasted only until 1920, at which time also insurance coverage was extended to all manual workers engaged under a contract of service, and non-manual workers of a similar description whose income was below a certain level.[4] However, the principle of differentiation was not totally abandoned, for industries with particularly low unemployment might adopt their own special scheme and, with the approval of the minister, opt out of National Insurance,[5] an arrangement permitted for the finance and banking industries until 1946.[6] Unemployment insurance was extended to agriculture only in 1936 and then at special rates of benefit and contribution.[7] Other forms of insurance did not call for the same

1   See also Williams *Social Security Taxation* (1982).
2   P 3, above.
3   National Insurance Act 1911, s 94 (NIA 1911).
4   Unemployment Insurance Act 1920 (UIA 1920).
5   UIA 1920, s 18.
6   See SR & O 1938/589 and 656.
7   Unemployment Insurance (Agriculture) Act 1936.

degree of differentiation but the health scheme was administered by approved societies, who could offer by way of benefit in return for the nationally determined rate of contributions whatever they wished above the national minimum.[8] The state scheme also imitated some sectors of the private insurance industry in terms of gender discrimination. Thus women paid lower rates of contributions and received even lower benefits on the ground that they were 'poor risks'.[9]

B Comprehensive insurance

One of the primary objectives of the Beveridge plan,[10] and the legislation which implemented it, was to abolish such vestiges of the risk-related approach which remained, and to establish a fully comprehensive system in which all would share in supporting the burden of those subjected to the prescribed social risks:

> The term 'social insurance' ... implies both that it is compulsory and that men stand together with their fellows.[11]

The policy gave rise to four important modifications of the pre-war schemes. First, compulsory insurance was extended to those previously above the income limits. Secondly, it included those substantially free from one or more of the social risks (eg civil servants in relation to unemployment) or with sufficient protection under their terms of employment (eg the police in relation to sickness and old age – though members of HM Forces in a somewhat analogous position were allowed to pay a lower rate of contributions[12]). Thirdly, the approved societies were no longer to administer health insurance, and the special arrangements for agriculture, banking and finance were also abolished. Finally, the self-employed were covered for all purposes except unemployment and industrial injury.[13] The special status of women as such was also eradicated; instead, the legislation singled out for special treatment those who were married. They could opt out of insurance in their own right, and, if they elected to stay in, would pay lower contributions and receive lower benefits.[14] Comprehensive coverage was completed by the compulsory insurance of all remaining persons over 16 who were not gainfully employed: in return for their weekly contributions, they qualified for all benefits except those for unemployment, sickness and industrial injury.[15] Contributions could not, of course, be extracted from those on very low incomes and the problem was met by, on the one hand, exempting from liability (and also therefore from entitlement to all benefits) those whose income did not exceed £2 a week,[16] and, on the other hand, excusing from the payment of contributions, but nevertheless crediting for certain purposes, those unemployed or incapable of work or undergoing education or training.[17]

While Beveridge's assumption was that many would participate in occupational schemes to lift their income above the standard subsistence rate of benefit, there was no

8   See p 521, below.
9   Land in Barker and Allen (eds) *Sexual Divisions and Society* (1976) p 109.
10 Beveridge Report *Social Insurance and Allied Services* (1942, Cmd 6404).
11 *Beveridge Report* n 10, above, para 26.
12 This concession was not removed until 1996: see p 119, below.
13 See generally Brown *A Policy Vacuum: Social Security for the Self-employed* (1992).
14 P 118, below.
15 NIA 1946, s 4(2)(c).
16 NIA 1942, s 5(1)(a)(iii).
17 NIA 1942, s 5(1)(a)(i)–(ii).

question of using this as an argument to justify exemption from the national scheme. Different considerations prevailed when earnings-related pensions were introduced as additions to the basic state pension, in the form first of all of the limited graduated scheme of 1959[18] and subsequently the more comprehensive state earnings-related pension scheme (SERPS) of 1975.[19] In both cases provision was made for certain occupational schemes to be 'contracted out', enabling the employers and employees in question to pay reduced contributions to the state. Only 'defined benefit' schemes, which guaranteed their members minimum benefits equivalent to those provided by SERPS, could qualify for contracting-out, and legislation imposed no obligation upon employers to offer such schemes to their employees. The Social Security Act 1986 (SSA 1986) then extended contracting-out to certain 'money purchase' pension schemes based on defined contributions rather than on a guaranteed level of benefits. It also made membership of SERPS completely voluntary by allowing individuals whose employers did not offer a contracted-out occupational scheme to opt out by paying into a personal pension scheme instead. Where a personal scheme is established in this way, the employer and employee in question remain liable to pay social security contributions in full, but the equivalent of the contracted-out contribution rebate in each case is diverted into the individual scheme; the employer is free to make additional contributions but is not required to do so. Between 1988 and 1993 those choosing to leave SERPS for either a personal or newly contracted out occupational pension scheme qualified for an additional 2 per cent rebate on contributions. In 1993 this was reduced to a 1 per cent rebate for contributors over the age of 30, but this arrangement was in turn superseded by a new system of age-related rebates from 1997.[20] There were estimated to be some 5.6 million personal pensions in force by 1999–2000.[21] The Labour government elected in 1997 brought forward further reforms of pension provision, in particular the launch of stakeholder pensions (a new form of private second pensions, designed for those on moderate incomes) and the introduction of the state second pension, aimed specifically at low earners, which replaced SERPS from 2002.

The principle of state provision continues in relation to other contributory benefits, including the basic state pension and contribution-based jobseeker's allowance. However, as a result of the decline of the contributory principle, many recipients of these benefits also depend on means-tested benefits.[22]

C Liability according to capacity

The policy issues raised by the nature of the contributions payable have already been discussed in chapter 1.[23] Here, it is necessary merely to relate how the insurance system gradually evolved towards a principle of liability according to capacity to pay. Under the early schemes, flat-rate contributions of the worker were matched by those of the employer, generally on an equal basis,[24] and the fund was augmented by a grant from the Exchequer. Certain concessions were, however, made for low-wage earners; they

18 Pp 614–615, below.
19 Pp 615–620, below.
20 Pp 628–630, below.
21 Government Actuary *National Insurance Fund – Long-term Financial Estimates* (2000, Cm 4406) para 7.5.
22 See generally HC Social Security Committee *Fifth Report* (1999–2000, HC 56).
23 Pp 26–28, above.
24 Though not under the original national health scheme to which the employer paid 3d a week and the male employee 4d: NIA 1946, Sch 1.

paid a reduced contribution.[25] The principles were maintained under the 1946 reconstruction, except that the liability of the employer was somewhat lower than that of the employee.[26] The flat-rate approach, of which Beveridge was such an enthusiastic advocate, proved insufficient to finance benefits at the desired level and a shift to an earnings-related method became inevitable. Under the graduated pensions scheme, those contributing paid 4.5 per cent of their weekly earnings between £9 and £15, the employer being liable for a similar amount.[27] The resulting hybrid system of flat-rate and graduated contributions was replaced in 1973–75 by a single system of contributions paid on earnings between a much wider band, but, as already noted, with a reduction for those contracting out of the new SERPS. Those with weekly earnings below a lower threshold were completely exempt.[28] This assimilation to an income tax method of financing was taken even further by imposing on the self-employed, in addition to a flat-rate liability, a charge on profits and gains,[29] notwithstanding that the earnings-related supplements for sickness, maternity and widow's benefits continued to be unavailable to this group. From 1985 legislative policy, while remaining consistent with the capacity to pay principle, also aimed to encourage a growth in low-paid employment.[30] To this end the SSAs of 1985 and 1989 reduced the rates of contributions payable by employers and employees on lower earnings and abolished the upper limit on employers' contributions.[31]

A decade later the first Blair government instituted a radical restructuring of the contributions system through a rolling series of reforms enacted in SSA 1998, the Welfare Reform and Pensions Act 1999 (WRPA 1999) and the Child Support, Pensions and Social Security Act 2000.[32] These changes were designed to improve the interaction of the tax and benefit systems so as to improve work incentives and reduce poverty. They involved, in respect of earnings above the lower earnings limit, the abolition of any liability to pay contributions on earnings below that threshold. In addition, the trigger point for actually paying contributions was aligned with the starting point for liability for income tax (the 'primary threshold'). Those low-paid employees earning between the lower earnings limit and the new primary threshold are treated as having paid contributions. The 1999 Act also abolished the contribution condition for state maternity allowance, replacing it with a minimum earnings threshold requirement, and introduced a new non-contributory route by which persons incapacitated in their youth may qualify for incapacity benefit.[33] Although undoubtedly socially inclusive in social policy terms, these changes represent a marked departure from the traditional contributory principle.[34] Indeed, the government has asserted its belief that the contributory principle is a means of delivering policy objectives rather than an end in itself.[35] This approach was exemplified in the National Insurance Contributions Act 2002, which abolished the upper earnings limit for employees with effect from April 2003 and increased the contribution rates for both employees and employers in order to raise substantial extra revenues for the National Health Service (NHS).

25   See eg National Health Insurance Act 1924, Sch 2.
26   The ratio was approximately 55-45: NIA 1946, Sch 1.
27   NIA 1959, s 1(1).
28   P 106, below.
29   P 116, below.
30   Green Paper *Reform of Social Security* (1985, Cmnd 9517) vol 1, ch 11; for discussion see Deakin and Wilkinson (1991) 15 Camb J Econ 125.
31   SSA 1985, s 7; SSA 1989, s 1; p 106, below.
32   Pp 107–108, below.
33   WRPA 1999, ss 53 and 64.
34   See further *HC Social Security Committee* n 22, above.
35   See DSS *Reply* (September 2000, no reference) para 2.

D Unity of administration

Before the co-ordinating legislation of 1946 there were in effect three independent insurance schemes: those for unemployment and for health, both dating from 1911, and that for widows', orphans' and old age pensions established in 1925. But the financing of the health and pensions schemes was amalgamated so that in practice each insured person had to maintain two insurance records, in the form of cards to which stamps representing weekly contributions were affixed. In 1946 the three schemes were replaced by a single National Insurance system, with the weekly contribution stamp serving for all the contributory benefits. The independent industrial injuries scheme superseded the workmen's compensation legislation, which had imposed liability for compensation on the individual employer, but the contributions to this insurance fund were added automatically to those payable for employed persons under the main scheme. In 1973 the separate industrial injuries fund was abolished and henceforth benefits were financed by the National Insurance Fund. The introduction of earnings-related contributions necessarily made their calculation and collection more complicated and under the legislation of 1973–75 administration was simplified by combining the process with that of income tax assessment, notably for employed persons through the PAYE system. After that the affixing of stamps remained only for the flat-rate contributions payable by the self-employed, and even here they could be paid by direct debit from the contributor's bank or by bank giro. The use of stamps was ended completely in 1993 and flat rate contributors must now make quarterly payments in arrears to the Inland Revenue's Contributions Office, which has a computerised billing system for this purpose.[36] In the late 1990s the then Contributions Agency initiated a programme to upgrade the overall National Insurance Recording System. As with several other computerisation projects within the Department of Social Security (DSS), the process was marred by systems failings, leading to delays in dealing with claims for contributory benefits and rebates and a consequential need for compensation payments.[37] The Contributions Agency was transferred from the DSS to the Inland Revenue in 1999 as part of the new Labour government's plans to integrate the tax and benefit systems.[38]

E The system of financing social security benefits

Revenue from social security contributions is earmarked for the National Insurance Fund,[39] out of which payments for the contributory benefits are made.[40] Payments of all other benefits are met from general taxation.[41] Industrial injury benefits, which at one stage were classed as contributory even though they were not dependent on beneficiaries having paid Class 1 National Insurance contributions, have since 1990 been met out of general taxation.[42] It has been suggested that the system of social security contributions is more closely akin to a form of hypothecated taxation than to insurance premia, given that the National Insurance Fund operates on a 'pay as you go' basis.[43]

---

36 SI 2001/1004, reg 89.
37 The so-called NIRS2 project; for a summary of the problems, see NAO *National Insurance Fund Account 1998–99* (1999–2000, HC 146) Part 1.
38 P 135, below.
39 Social Security Administration Act 1992, s 162(1) (SSAA 1992).
40 SSAA 1992, s 163(1)(a).
41 SSAA 1992, s 163(2).
42 SSA 1990, s 16, amending SSA 1975, ss 1, 134 and 135. See now SSAA 1992, s 163(2)(c).
43 P 26, above; and *Williams* n 1, above, para 1.29ff.

Even then, the element of hypothecation – the separation of the National Insurance Fund from the Consolidated Fund into which general tax revenues are paid – is incomplete in a number of respects.

On the one hand, this is because revenues from general taxation are mingled with those from contributions at a number of points. The Exchequer contribution currently takes the form of the Treasury grant which is set by legislation as a maximum of 17 per cent of estimated benefit expenditure to be met by the National Insurance Fund in a given tax year.[44] Nor, on the other hand, do contributions go exclusively to meet the costs of paying contributory benefits: allocations are made to the NHS[45] and for the purposes of certain social security benefits and employment protection payments.[46] The costs of meeting employers' payments of statutory sick pay and statutory maternity pay also fall, in the first instance, on the National Insurance Fund, in the form of rebates on employers' social security contributions.[47] However, from 1990 the income thereby foregone has been made up by a transfer from the Consolidated Fund,[48] so providing a further source of Exchequer contribution. There is a growing trend for the burden of these payments to be removed from the state altogether and devolved to individual employers. The rebate for statutory maternity pay was originally set at 100 per cent[49] but was reduced to 92 per cent with effect from September 1994.[50] The rebate for statutory sick pay was cut in 1991 to 80 per cent of the employer's payments[51] and then abolished completely from April 1994,[52] except for those employers qualifying for 'small employers' relief', who remained entitled to compensation in full.[53] A year later these arrangements were replaced by the current scheme which provides all employers with the possibility of recovering their statutory sick pay payments, but only if such costs exceed 13 per cent of their liability for Class 1 contribution payments in any one month.[54]

The considerable shifts of recent years in the relative burden placed on contribution revenue and general taxation respectively have to be seen in the context of the strains placed upon the National Insurance Fund by the economic cycle and by wider reforms to the social security system. In the early 1980s the tendency was to cut the extent of the Exchequer contribution to the Fund. The Treasury supplement, which was fixed in 1975 at 18 per cent of revenue from contributions devoted to contributory benefits (ie excluding sums payable under the allocations to the NHS and to employment protection payments),[55] was reduced to 13 per cent in 1983 and 5 per cent in 1988,

44   SSA 1993, s 2. 'Estimated benefit expenditure' here refers to expected payments out of the National Insurance Fund under SSAA 1992, s 163(1)(a)–(d) and under the Employment Rights Act 1996, ss 167(1), 182 (ERA 1996) and Pension Schemes Act 1993, s 124(1) (PSA 1993).
45   Social Security Contributions and Benefits Act 1992, s 1(1)(b) (SSCBA 1992); SSAA 1992, s 162, as amended by the Social Security (Contributions) Act 1994, s 2 (SS(C)A 1994).
46   Non-contributory benefits which are funded out of the National Insurance Fund are the guardian's allowance and certain Christmas bonuses: SSAA 1992, s 163(1). Under ERA 1996, s 182ff, certain specified payments may be made from the National Insurance Fund to employees of insolvent employers.
47   The same arrangements apply to statutory paternity pay and statutory adoption pay under the Employment Act 2002.
48   SSA 1990, s 16, amending SSA 1975, ss 1, 134 and 135; see now SSCBA 1992, s 1(5) and SSAA 1992, s 162(3).
49   SSCBA 1992, s 167; SI 1987/91, reg 4.
50   SI 1994/1882, implementing Council Directive (EEC) 92/85. See ch 16, p 559, below. Small employers with an annual National Insurance liability of £40,000 or less receive an additional payment which varies from year to year.
51   Statutory Sick Pay Act 1991, s 1(1)(a) (SSPA 1991).
52   SSPA 1994.
53   SSCBA 1992, s 158(2); on 'small employers' see n 50, above.
54   SI 1995/512. Effectively this means an employer will have to be facing an epidemic of sickness amongst its workforce in order to qualify for a refund.
55   SSA 1975, s 1(5).

before it was abolished completely in 1989.[56] During the same period the contribution rates for both employers and employees went up at a time when income tax rates were falling, while towards the end of the decade the extent of contribution revenue going to the NHS allocation was increased.[57] The effect of these measures was to increase considerably the proportion of total welfare expenditure funded by contributions, reducing the relative burden on general taxation.[58] After 1990, however, the then Conservative government reversed its policy. In the first place the costs of paying industrial injury benefits and then the lost income represented by payments of statutory sick pay and statutory maternity pay were transferred to general taxation. In 1993 the Exchequer contribution was formally revived as the Treasury grant, which may be set at different levels according to the state of the Fund's balance in a particular tax year, subject only to the ceiling set by SSA 1993. In contrast, the amount of the Treasury supplement was fixed by legislation. Two factors appear to have brought about the reversal of policy after 1990: the greater than expected numbers of individuals contracting out of SERPS in favour of personal pensions after 1988[59] and the fall in general contribution revenue caused by the recession and high unemployment of the early 1990s.[60] The current buoyancy of the National Insurance Fund is such that in 2002–03 there was no need for any Treasury grant.[61] So long as contributions are related to earnings and benefits linked to prices, this surplus is likely to continue.[62]

F Outline of the system

Contributions from insured persons and employers are divided into six categories:[63]

Class 1 *primary contributions from 'employed earners' and secondary contributions from 'employers and other persons paying earnings', both being earnings-related;*

Class 1A *contributions payable by employers as a percentage of the cash value of benefits in kind provided to their employees;*

Class 1B *contributions payable by employers on a PAYE settlement agreement, covering liability on various minor benefits and expenses paid to their employees;*

Class 2 *flat-rate contributions from self-employed earners;*

Class 3 *voluntary flat-rate contributions from earners and others; and*

Class 4 *contributions payable on the basis of profits or gains arising from a trade, profession or vocation.*

Part 2 describes the principles of categorisation, the methods of assessing liability and also the grounds on which persons may be exempt from contributions. In Part 3 we consider the position of married women, widows and other special categories of contributions. Finally, Part 4 is concerned with the contribution conditions which must

56 SSA 1989, s 3.
57 SIs 1987/48, 1988/676 and 1989/26; see now SSAA 1992, s 162(5)–(11), as amended by SS(C)A 1994.
58 See *Deakin and Wilkinson* n 30, above, at 130–131.
59 National Audit Office *The Elderly: Information Requirements for Supporting the Elderly and the Implications of Personal Pensions for the National Insurance Fund* (1990–91, HC 55) para 3.19.
60 See Mr P Lilley, Secretary of State for Social Security, 215 HC Official Report (6th series) col 245.
61 Government Actuary *Report on the drafts of the Social Security Benefits Up-rating (No 2) Order 2002 etc* (2002, Cm 5383) para 21.
62 *HC Social Security Committee* n 22, above, para 142.
63 SSCBA 1992, s 1(2).

be satisfied for entitlement to benefit and the rules to assist those otherwise unable to qualify. Although the framework for the system of National Insurance contributions is set out in Part 1 of SSCBA 1992, the details are contained in the Social Security (Contributions) Regulations 2001.[64]

Part 2   Classification of contributions

A   General

This Part is devoted to the principles governing liability to pay contributions of Classes 1, 1A, 1B, 2 and 4 and entitlement to pay those in Classes 2 and 3. Under the pre-1973 legislation insured *persons* were categorised accordingly.[65] Under the current scheme, the classification is of *contributions*. The important reason for this change of terminology is that an insured person may now be liable to pay contributions both as an employed (Class 1), and as a self-employed, person (Classes 2 and 4). The law defining the various categories remains, however, substantially unchanged. In particular, regard must be had to the complex case law distinguishing between employed and self-employed persons. Historically the adjudication of disputes as to classification and the fulfilment of contribution conditions was within the jurisdiction not of the traditional adjudicating authorities, namely, the adjudication officer, social security appeal tribunals and Commissioner, but of the Secretary of State.[66] A question of law arising from any such decision could be referred for final determination to the High Court (or in Scotland the Court of Session) either by the Secretary of State or by a person aggrieved by the decision.[67] Many of the High Court decisions are, of course, published in the ordinary law reports, and for the period 1950–60, HMSO published selected decisions of the minister on classification questions.[68] Under SSA 1998 the Secretary of State retained the decision making function at first instance in such cases, but a right of appeal to the newly constituted appeal tribunals was introduced.[69] Before this provision could be brought into force, the Contributions Agency was transferred from the DSS to the Inland Revenue.[70] Thus classification questions are now the responsibility of officers of the Board with a right of appeal to the tax appeal commissioners.[71] This will presumably lead to a further convergence in decision making in relation to employment status for tax and social security purposes.

---

64   SI 2001/1004, replacing SI 1979/591. The consolidation was long overdue, as the 1979 regulations were followed by 119 sets of amending regulations (SI 2001/1004, Sch 8, Pt I). As the Joint Committee on Statutory Instruments observed: 'The consequential complexity is illustrated by the need to insert a new paragraph (zaa) in regulation 19(1) and a new regulation numbered 22HA, and by the reference to a regulation 19(1)(zh)(ii). It is doubtful whether even the specialist can confidently establish the exact text of legislation in this form': *Thirtieth Report* (1999–2000, HL 116) Appendix 2.
65   NIA 1965, s 1(2).
66   SSAA 1992, s 17. See Partington *Secretary of State's Power of Adjudication in Social Security Law* SAUS Working Paper 96 (1991).
67   SSAA 1992, s 18 (now repealed).
68   The 'M' decisions. It is not clear why publication ceased in 1960.
69   SSA 1998, ss 8(1)(c) and 12(1)(b) and Sch 3.
70   P 135, below.
71   Social Security Contributions (Transfer of Functions, etc) Act 1999, ss 8(1)(a), 11, 26(3) and Sch 10 (SSC(TF)A 1999).

B Primary Class 1 contributions

Class 1 contributions may confer title to any contributory benefit. The primary contributions of this class are payable by 'employed earners'.[72] An 'employed earner' is defined as:

> a person who is gainfully employed in Great Britain either under a contract of service, or in an office (including elective office) with emoluments chargeable to income tax under Schedule E.[73]

The second alternative was added in 1973, the intention being to correlate Class 1 contributors with Schedule E taxpayers and thus to facilitate the collection of contributions through the PAYE system.[74]

i Gainfully employed

For both alternative formulations, the contributor must be 'gainfully employed'. This replaces the phrase 'gainfully occupied' used in the earlier legislation.[75] The significance of the modification is unclear. A body of case law had been built around the interpretation of 'gainfully occupied' for the purposes not only of the classification of contributors but also in relation to retirement pensions[76] and increases for dependants.[77] One possible view is that, in the light of different policy considerations, it was thought desirable to keep distinct the interpretation of the phrase in its various contexts. If so, this would justify the authorities approaching the changed statutory formula de novo. A more likely explanation is that the notion of 'occupation' was thought to be too restrictive when applied to the new category of 'office with emoluments'.[78] If this is correct, it should follow that the interpretation of the concept has remained substantially unchanged. The basic idea is that the contribution:

> receives from his master under the contract of employment something by way of remuneration for the services which he is contractually bound to render to the master under the contract of service.[79]

Under the former legislation, it was important to determine what was to be regarded as 'remuneration'. Under the current system the problem no longer arises because contributions are earnings-related and there is a body of rules, described below,[80] governing the nature and calculation of 'earnings' for this purpose.

---

72 SSCBA 1992, s 1(2)(a)(i).
73 SSCBA 1992, s 2(1)(a). A 'contract of service' is further defined as a 'contract of service or apprenticeship': s 122(1). On apprenticeships see *Wallace v CA Roofing Services Ltd* [1996] IRLR 435; and *Edmunds v Lawson* [2000] IRLR 18.
74 SSA 1973, s 1(7).
75 NIA 1965, s 1(2).
76 NIA 1965, s 30(2), cf pp 595–596, below.
77 NIA 1965, s 43(1)(b).
78 Cf *R(P) 2/76*, para 22, R J A Temple, Chief Comr.
79 Per Slade J *Vandyk v Minister of Pensions and National Insurance* [1955] 1 QB 29 at 38.
80 Pp 108–109, below.

ii   Contract of service

The classification of individuals into employed and self-employed persons, as characterised by the distinction between a 'contract of service' and a 'contract for services', has been a regular legal conundrum and not only in social security law.[81] SSCBA 1992 makes only a marginal effort to alleviate the problems by prescribing that 'contract of service' means:

> any contract of service or apprenticeship, whether written or oral and whether expressed or implied.[82]

Resort must therefore be had to the case law. As implied above, decisions on the matter are not limited to social security law: many other legal consequences flow from the existence of a contract of service, eg the right to a redundancy payment and the imposition of vicarious liability on the employer. The question arises whether courts and tribunals, interpreting the relevant legislative provisions, should reach uniform answers. The view most popular with judges[83] and writers[84] is that since different legal consequences give rise to different policy considerations, it is dangerous to cross legal boundaries. It can be argued that a classification which only affects the reciprocal rights and duties of two persons, the employer and employee, does not involve the public interest, which is clearly relevant in determining liability to pay social security contributions. There are also policy considerations that apply only in the social security context; eg whether the nature of the occupation is such that insurance against unemployment and industrial injuries, exclusive to Class 1 contributors, is regarded as appropriate. On the other hand, confusion and administrative inconvenience ensue if an individual is an 'employee' for some purposes and not for others and there is, therefore, a pragmatic argument for uniform solutions.[85] As a matter of statutory interpretation, Parliament when using the term 'contract of service' might be assumed to have in mind traditional judicial interpretations of the phrase.

The principles governing the distinction between a contract of service and one for services are not easy to state for two reasons: first, because there are differing views on the extent to which the issue is one of law rather than of fact;[86] secondly, because judicial views on the nature of the distinction have changed substantially over the years and there is currently no uniformly accepted criterion which can be applied to all cases.

The classical nineteenth-century test was one of supervision and control: 'a servant is a person subject to the command of his master as to the manner in which he shall do his work.'[87] The first High Court decisions under NIA 1946 placed great reliance on

81   For particularly valuable discussions see McKendrick (1990) 53 MLR 770; Anderman (2000) 29 ILJ 223; and Collins, Ewing and McColgan *Labour Law Text and Materials* (2001) pp 147–183.

82   SSCBA 1992, s 122(1). See also ERA 1996, s 230(2) to the same effect for employment protection purposes.

83   Eg *Tyne and Clydeside Warehouses Ltd v Hamerton* [1978] ICR 661; *President of the Methodist Conference v Parfitt* [1984] QB 368, [1983] 3 All ER 747; *Ironmonger v Movefield Ltd* [1988] IRLR 461.

84   Calvert *Social Security Law* (2nd edn, 1978) p 18; Williams *Social Security Taxation* (1982) para 3-05; *McKendrick* n 81, above.

85   Cf *O'Kelly v Trusthouse Forte plc* [1984] QB 90 at 115, [1983] 3 All ER 456 at 472, per Ackner LJ. The likely consequence of the transfer of decision making functions to the Inland Revenue has already been noted: p 96, above.

86   But see helpful dicta of Lord Hoffman in *Carmichael v National Power plc* [1999] 4 All ER 897 at 902–905.

87   Per Bramwell B *Yewens v Noakes* (1880) 6 QBD 530 at 532–533.

this criterion,[88] but its limitations in the modern commercial and technological world soon provoked a more critical attitude. It was obvious in the first place that there could be little or no direct control over the work of a professional or skilled employee, such as a doctor working in a hospital,[89] a theatrical or circus artist[90] or a political columnist,[91] nor where the employer was a corporate entity and the employee was of a high status, eg a company director.[92] Secondly, it is imprecise. The 'employer' of an independent contractor, eg may reserve to itself the right to direct not only what is to be done, but in broad outlines how it is to be done.[93]

Satisfaction with the control test prompted Denning LJ (as he then was) to formulate a new criterion, whether the alleged employee was 'part and parcel of the organisation',[94] whether he was 'employed as part of the business, and his work is done as an integral part of the business'.[95] This approach, and an analogous test of 'economic reality' emanating from the United States Supreme Court,[96] have attracted some support.[97] They have the advantage of directing attention to the admittedly important issue of whose assets are involved in the undertaking and who stands to profit or lose on its outcome. However, recent case law suggests that the courts are adopting a more restrictive test of 'mutuality of obligation' which identifies the contract of employment with reciprocal commitments to maintain the employment relationship in being over time; such a test tends to exclude casual workers and others, such as home-workers, who are economically dependent upon a particular employer but who have an irregular and discontinuous pattern of working time.[98] In such cases there remains the possibility that employment status may be found to exist for a specific engagement albeit not as part of the overall arrangement between the parties.[99]

It can be objected that, though these are all factors to be taken into account, they are no more decisive than was (or is) the control element. It has indeed become obvious, and is readily acknowledged in almost all cases on the subject,[100] that it is a question of

---

88   *Gould v Minister of National Insurance* [1951] 1 KB 731, [1951] 1 All ER 368; *Stagecraft v Minister of National Insurance* 1952 SC 288.
89   *Cassidy v Minister of Health* [1951] 1 KB 243, [1951] 1 All ER 574.
90   *Whittaker v Minister of Pensions and National Insurance* [1967] 1 QB 156, [1966] 3 All ER 531.
91   *Beloff v Pressdram* [1973] 1 All ER 241.
92   *Lee v Lee's Air Farming* [1961] AC 12, [1960] 3 All ER 531. Such persons would now be Class 1 contributors by virtue of their office: p 103, below.
93   Eg *Addison v London Philharmonic Orchestra Ltd* [1981] ICR 261 (orchestral musician); M25 (tailoring outworker); M48 (BBC interviewer).
94   *Bank voor Handel en Sheepvaart v Slatford* [1953] 1 QB 248 at 295.
95   *Stevenson, Jordan and Harrison v Macdonald and Evans* [1952] 1 TLR 101 at 111.
96   *United States v Silk* 331 US 704 (1946). See also a dictum of Lord Wright in *Montreal Locomotive Works v Montreal and AG* [1947] 1 DLR 161 at 164.
97   Notably in *Market Investigations v Minister of Social Security* [1969] 2 QB 173, [1968] 3 All ER 732; *Young and Woods v West* [1980] IRLR 201; *Midland Sinfonia Concert Society Ltd v Secretary of State for Social Services* [1981] ICR 454; *Warner Holidays Ltd v Secretary of State for Social Services* [1983] ICR 440; *Lee Ting Sang v Chung Chi-Keung* [1990] 2 AC 374; *Lane v Shire Roofing Co (Oxford) Ltd* [1995] IRLR 493.
98   *O'Kelly v Trusthouse Forte plc* [1984] QB 90, [1983] 3 All ER 456; *Nethermere (St Neots) Ltd v Taverna and Gardiner* [1984] IRLR 240; *Clark v Oxfordshire Health Authority* [1998] IRLR 125; *Carmichael v National Power plc* [1999] 4 All ER 897.
99   *McMeechan v Secretary of State for Employment* [1997] ICR 549.
100 Especially *Ready Mixed Concrete South East Ltd v Minister of Pensions and National Insurance* [1968] 2 QB 497, [1968] 1 All ER 433; *Willy Scheidegger Swiss Typewriting School (London) Ltd v Minister of Social Security* (1968) 5 KIR 65; *Argent v Minister of Social Security* [1968] 3 All ER 208, [1968] 1 WLR 7749; *Rennison & Son v Minister of Social Security* (1970) 10 KIR 65; *Ferguson v John Dawson & Partners (Contractors)* [1976] 3 All ER 817, [1976] 1 WLR 346; *Lane v Shire Roofing Co (Oxford) Ltd* [1995] IRLR 493; *Secretary of State for Trade and Industry v Bottrill* [1999] ICR 592.

having regard to a number of factors, any number or combination of which might be relevant in a given case. The mere reference to such factors does not, of course, indicate how they are to be deployed, or what weight is to be given to each. For the most part, judges have refused to be drawn on this issue, contenting themselves with the general proposition that the relative importance of the different factors will vary from case to case.[101]

Some of the more important factors, to which the Secretary of State should attribute such weight as in his or her discretion seems appropriate, may be described as follows.

A   SUPERVISION OF WORK

Though the control test has rightly been repudiated as the sole or decisive criterion, close and regular supervision of the work process clearly remains an important factor, especially for less skilled occupations.[102]

B   POWERS OF APPOINTMENT AND DISMISSAL

This factor is often mentioned,[103] but if it refers to the appointment and dismissal of the person whose classification is in question it is generally helpful only in indicating to which of two 'employers' that person is contractually engaged.[104] More important for the present purpose is whether the 'employee' has the power to employ a substitute to whom his or her duties may be delegated.[105]

C   FORM OF REMUNERATION

The typical contract of service provides for regular remuneration in the form of a salary or wages, while the typical contract for services prescribes a fixed sum for the job. The distinction accords well with the 'economic reality' theory. In the words of Lord Widgery CJ, 'if a man agrees to perform an operation for a fixed sum and thus stands to lose if the work is delayed, and to profit if it is done quickly, that is the man who on the face of it appears to be an independent contractor working under a contract for services'.[106] While the method of payment may thus provide some guideline,[107] it is not a very reliable criterion. There have been cases where an individual paid on the

---

101   Eg Cooke J in *Construction Training Board v Labour Force* [1970] 3 All ER 220 at 224; Bridge J in *Rennison & Son v Minister of Social Security* (1970) 10 KIR 65 at 68. This is a question of fact not law: *O'Kelly v Trusthouse Forte plc* [1984] QB 90 (Ackner LJ dissenting) and *Carmichael v National Power plc* [1999] 4 All ER 897.

102   *Amalgamated Engineering Union v Minister of Pensions and National Insurance* [1963] 1 All ER 864, [1963] 1 WLR 441; *Thames Television Ltd v Wallis* [1979] IRLR 136; *Hitchcock v Post Office* [1980] ICR 100; *Narich Pty v Comr of Pay-Roll Tax* [1984] ICR 286.

103   Eg by Lord Thankerton in one of the first judicial attempts to enumerate the relevant factors: *Short v Henderson* (1946) 62 TLR 427 at 429.

104   Eg *Mersey Docks and Harbour Board v Coggins and Griffith (Liverpool) Ltd* [1947] AC 1, [1946] 2 All ER 345; M5; M14; M35; and see p 110, below.

105   *Ready Mixed Concrete (South East) Ltd v Minister of Pensions and National Insurance* [1968] 2 QB 497; *Express and Echo Publications Ltd v Tanton* [1999] IRLR 367; M23; M25; M34; M48.

106   *Global Plant v Secretary of State for Health and Social Security* [1971] 3 All ER 385 at 391.

107   Eg *Gould v Minister of National Insurance* [1951] 1 KB 731; *Construction Industry Training Board v Labour Force* [1970] 3 All ER 220; *Challinor v Taylor* [1972] ICR 129.

basis of time has been held to be self-employed.[108] Conversely, the courts have not shown great reluctance to find a contract of service where the employee is paid a fixed rate for the job[109] or where both parties have sought artificially to transform the nature of the contract by converting wages into a different form of payment, eg the so-called 'lump'.[110]

D DURATION OF CONTRACT

Again, there is a tendency for the duration of contracts for services to be determined according to a specific undertaking, or a specific (and often short) time period, whereas a contract of service will often be of an indefinite period or at least contain some element of continuity.[111] While this factor has been adverted to in a number of cases and is a key aspect of the important test of mutuality of obligation,[112] there are many occupations where the pattern is reversed[113] and so it may not be relevant in all cases.

E EQUIPMENT

The question whether the worker is bound to use his or her own plant or equipment is also of assistance and is related to the 'economic reality' idea. Where a worker's own resources in the form of equipment are invested in the undertaking there may be a good argument for categorising the relationship as one of self-employment.[114] But the criterion carries force only where such an investment is on a large scale.[115] In many occupations it is customary for employees under a contract of service to provide their own tools.

F PLACE OF WORK

Individuals who work from their own premises are more likely to be regarded as self-employed. If, on the other hand, the occupation is peripatetic (eg a sales representative) the question is usually resolved by the degree of supervision exercised by the employer.[116]

---

108 Eg *Ready Mixed Concrete (South East) Ltd v Minister of Pensions and National Insurance* [1968] 2 QB 497; *Clark v Oxfordshire Health Authority* [1998] IRLR 125; *Express and Echo Publications Ltd v Tanton* [1999] IRLR 367; *Carmichael v National Power plc* [1999] 4 All ER 897.

109 Eg *Market Investigations v Minister of Social Security* [1969] 2 QB 173.

110 Eg *Ferguson v Dawson* [1976] 3 All ER 817; *Lee Ting Sang v Chung Chi-Keung* [1990] 2 AC 374; cf *Lane v Shire Roofing Co (Oxford) Ltd* [1995] IRLR 493.

111 *Cheng Yuen v Royal Hong Kong Golf Club* [1998] ICR 131 (Lord Hoffmann dissenting).

112 *O'Kelly v Trusthouse Forte plc* [1984] QB 90; *Wickens v Champion Employment Agency* [1984] ICR 365.

113 Eg *Stagecraft v Minister of Social Security* 1952 SC 288; *Willy Scheidegger Swiss Typewriting School v Minister of Social Security* (1968) 5 KIR 65.

114 *BSM (1257) Ltd v Secretary of State for Social Services* [1978] ICR 894; *Midland Sinfonia Concert Society v Secretary of State for Social Services* [1981] ICR 454.

115 Eg *Inglefield v Macey* (1967) 2 KIR 146; *Ready Mixed Concrete (South East) Ltd v Minister of Pensions and National Insurance* [1968] 2 QB 497.

116 *Ready Mixed Concrete (South East) Ltd v Minister of Pensions and National Insurance* [1968] 2 QB 497; *Willy Scheidegger Swiss Typewriting School v Minister of Social Security* (1968) 5 KIR 65; *Market Investigations v Minister of Social Security* [1969] 2 QB 173.

G   OBLIGATION TO WORK

Under some contracts, it is left to the person 'employed' to decide how much, if at all, he or she is to work. If so, it is persuasive evidence that the individual concerned is self-employed.[117] The case may be contrasted with that in which the individual is given an option whether or not to work for a specific period (eg a day) and in which, if he or she so agrees, there is an obligation to perform specific tasks during that period. Such a contract may be one of service, but it is still open to a court to find that the necessary 'mutuality of obligation' to provide work and to be available for work respectively is lacking, with the result that the worker will be classified as an independent contractor.[118]

H   DISCRETION ON HOURS OF WORK

A related idea is that the more discretion individuals have as to when they perform their duties, the more likely they are to be classified as self-employed.[119] But there are also instances of contracts of service being held to confer such a broad discretion.[120]

The question remains as to the weight, if any, to be given to any attempts by the parties themselves conclusively to determine the issue by a declaration in the contract. It is a question which has assumed increased importance in the light of efforts, particularly in the construction industry, to avoid the financial burdens of the employment relationship arising from both fiscal and social security legislation.[121] The approach taken by the judiciary has, with one or two notable exceptions,[122] been uniform. While regard must be had to the obligations arising from the explicit terms of the contract to see whether they are more consistent with a contract of service or a contract for services, the exact terminology in fact used may be of no legal significance.[123] Two alternative justifications have been advanced for this approach. Some judges purport to search for the true 'intentions' of the parties which, they argue, are to be found in the obligations arising under the contract rather than from the exact terminology employed. The problem with this argument is that in many cases the terminology will indeed represent the intentions of the parties.[124] To overcome this objection other judges have relied overtly on public policy considerations. 'I think that it would be contrary to the public interest if ... the parties, by their own whim, by the use of a verbal formula, unrelated to the

---

117   *Willy Scheidegger Swiss Typewriting School v Minister of Social Security* (1968) 5 KIR 65; *Addison v London Philharmonic Orchestra Ltd* [1981] ICR 261; *WHPT Housing Association Ltd v Secretary of State for Social Services* [1981] ICR 737.

118   *O'Kelly v Trusthouse Forte plc* [1984] QB 90, [1983] 3 All ER 456; *Clark v Oxfordshire Health Authority* [1998] IRLR 125; *Carmichael v National Power plc* [1999] 4 All ER 897; cf the earlier case of *Market Investigations v Minister of Social Security* [1969] 2 QB 173.

119   *O'Kelly v Trusthouse Forte plc* [1984] QB 90, [1983] 3 All ER 456; M9; M11; M13; M17; M25; M44.

120   *Market Investigations v Minister of Social Security* [1969] 2 QB 173; *Global Plant v Secretary of State for Health and Social Security* [1971] 3 All ER 385; M40; M60.

121   See the *Report of The Committee of Inquiry under Professor Phelps Brown into Certain Matters Concerning Labour* (1968, Cmnd 3714); Davies and Freedland *Labour Law: Text and Materials* (2nd edn, 1984) pp 94–98; and de Clark (1967) 30 MLR 6.

122   See Lawton LJ in *Ferguson v John Dawson & Partners (Contractors) Ltd* [1976] 3 All ER 817 at 827–829; Ralph Gibson LJ in *Calder v H Kitson Vickers & Sons (Engineers) Ltd* [1988] ICR 232 at 250.

123   *Inglefield v Macey* (1967) 2 KIR 146; *Ready Mixed Concrete v Minister of Pensions and National Insurance* [1968] 2 QB 497, [1968] 1 All ER 433; *Construction Industry Training Board v Labour Force* [1970] 3 All ER 220; *Rennison v Minister of Social Security* (1970) 10 KIR 65; *Ferguson v John Dawson* [1976] 3 All ER 817 (majority judgments); *Narich Pty v Comr of Pay-Roll Tax* [1984] ICR 286; *Young and Woods v West* [1980] IRLR 201.

124   See Lawton LJ in *Ferguson v John Dawson* [1976] 3 All ER 817 at 828.

reality of the relationship, could influence the decision ... .'[125] Such considerations may be especially acute in the context of safety at work.[126] If there is such a principle of public policy, it is one which is both obscure in its origins and vague in its scope: in this regard it has been asserted that 'a man is without question free under the law to carry out certain work for another without entering into a contract of service. Public policy has nothing to say either way'.[127]

The efforts of the judiciary to distinguish between genuine and bogus self-employment have been matched by a variety of responses from the legislature. On the one hand, the increased burden of contributions under Classes 2 and 4 resulting from the 1973–75 legislation has made the status of self-employment less attractive.[128] On the other hand, the Inland Revenue has been given power to make regulations for securing that the liability to pay Class 1 contributions is not avoided by 'abnormal practice' in relation to the payment of earnings.[129] Further anti-avoidance measures were introduced by WRPA 1999.[130] These were designed to deal with employers who dismissed their staff but immediately rehired them through intermediaries, so providing scope to minimise both tax and National Insurance liabilities. Since April 2000, contributions have remained payable in relation to an employed earner's employment even where that earner's services are provided to the client via an intermediary, and not pursuant to a contract of employment between the earner and the client. In such circumstances the earner is treated as employed by the intermediary, who is also treated as the secondary contributor for these purposes.[131]

iii Office with emoluments

The second category of primary Class 1 contributions was introduced to ensure that Class 1 was co-extensive with tax liability under Schedule E. The term 'office' has never been rigorously defined but it has been employed in tax legislation for well over a century and has acquired there a special meaning, to distinguish it from 'employment', 'profession' or 'vocation'.[132] In the leading case of *Edwards (Inspector of Taxes) v Clinch*,[133] a majority of the House of Lords reaffirmed that it involves 'a degree of continuance (not necessarily continuity) and of independent existence: it must connote a post to which a person can be appointed, which he can vacate and to which a successor can be appointed'.[134] So, someone appointed to conduct a public inquiry on a temporary, ad hoc and personal basis was not an 'office-holder'. There are, of course, many honorary office-holders, but if emoluments – statutorily defined as including 'salaries, fees, wages, perquisites and profit'[135] – are payable, they are

---

125 Per Megaw LJ in *Ferguson v John Dawson* [1976] 3 All ER 817 at 825.
126 *Lane v Shire Roofing Co (Oxford) Ltd* [1995] IRLR 493.
127 Per Ralph Gibson LJ in *Calder v Kitson Vickers* [1988] ICR 232 at 250.
128 See pp 112–118, below.
129 SSCBA 1992, Sch 1, para 4(c)–(d); power transferred to the Inland Revenue by SSC(TF)A 1999, s 2 and Sch 3, para 34. See further Employment Relations Act 1999, s 23.
130 WRPA 1999, s 75, inserting SSCBA 1992, s 4A. This was mirrored by changes to revenue law: Finance Act 2000, s 60 and Sch 12.
131 SI 2000/727. A challenge to these provisions under EU law was dismissed by the Court of Appeal: *R (Professional Contractors Group Ltd) v IRC* [2001] EWCA Civ 1945, [2002] 1 CMLR 46.
132 See eg Whitehouse *Revenue Law: Principles and Practice* (19th edn, 2001) para 5.21.
133 [1982] AC 845, [1981] 3 All ER 543 (Lords Edmund-Davies and Bridge dissenting).
134 Per Lord Wilberforce [1982] AC 845 at 861.
135 Income and Corporation Taxes Act 1988, s 131 (ICTA 1988), on which see *Hamblett v Godfrey* [1987] 1 All ER 916, [1987] 1 WLR 357; *Mairs v Haughey* [1993] 3 All ER 801.

chargeable to income tax under Schedule E and thus give rise to liability for Class 1 contributions. Examples of those who have been so classified are: company directors (where there is no contract of service),[136] trustees and executors,[137] consultants under the NHS,[138] accountants acting as company auditors[139] and solicitors acting as company registrars.[140]

iv Classification of earners

As has already been indicated, decisions on the classification of individual cases are in the first instance now made by officers of the Inland Revenue. Quite independently of this jurisdiction, the Revenue and the Secretary of State have two further powers, the exercise of which affects the classification of an individual or an occupation. Under the first, intended to counter the practice of 'lump' payments by means of which employers and employees collaborate in an attempt to avoid Class 1 contributions, the Revenue may where it is:

> satisfied as to the existence of any practice in respect of the payment of earnings whereby the incidence of earnings-related contributions is avoided or reduced by means of irregular or unequal payments, give directions for securing that such contributions are payable as if that practice were not followed.[141]

A rather unhappy feature of this provision is that it appears to confer an absolute discretion, there being no right of appeal to the High Court or other authorities. The second, of a more traditional nature, confers the power to shift earners in prescribed occupations from one class to another. Notwithstanding the transfer of most contributions issues by the 1999 legislation, this power remains vested in the Secretary of State.[142] In some cases, the power will be exercised where there is genuine doubt as to the appropriate classification of a given occupation. In others, it will be a conscious act of policy to extend or reduce insurance cover where this is deemed appropriate in the light of the social needs and circumstances of the occupation in question.[143] Perhaps the most important issue is whether an occupation, otherwise to be categorised as Class 1, should be excluded from contribution-based jobseeker's allowance, and, conversely, an occupation, otherwise characterised as Class 2, should be so included. The prevailing Categorisation of Earners Regulations fall into two groups.

---

136   *McMillan v Guest* [1942] AC 561, [1942] 1 All ER 606; and see SI 2001/1004, reg 27.
137   *Dale v IRC* [1954] AC 11, [1953] 2 All ER 671.
138   *Mitchell and Edon v Ross* [1962] AC 813, [1961] 3 All ER 49.
139   *Ellis v Lucas* [1967] Ch 858, [1966] 2 All ER 935.
140   *IRC v Brander and Cruickshank* [1971] 1 All ER 36, [1971] 1 WLR 212.
141   SI 2001/1004, reg 31; power transferred to the Inland Revenue by SSC(TF)A 1999, s 1(2) and Sch 2.
142   SSCBA 1992, s 2(2)(b); it is only the power to make regulations for specific employments to be disregarded for the purposes of contributions liability which has been vested in the Treasury by SSC(TF)A 1999, s 2 and Sch 3, para 2. This latter power can only be exercised with the concurrence of the Secretary of State.
143   The principle was made explicit by the National Insurance Advisory Committee in its various pronouncements on classification issues: see eg its Reports on Share Fishermen (1947–48, HC 137) and on Actors, Artistes and Entertainers (1952, Cmd 8549).

A EMPLOYMENTS TREATED AS CLASS 1[144]

These are: (a) office cleaners; (b) certain part-time lecturers, teachers and instructors;[145] (c) ministers of religion receiving a stipend or salary; (d) employment by a spouse for the purposes of that spouse's employment; (e) workers supplied by agencies, rendering personal services and subject to supervision or control,[146] where the agency is paid by the 'employer'[147] (though excluding home-workers and models); and (f) entertainers.[148]

B EMPLOYMENTS DISREGARDED[149]

The second group comprises employments which are excluded from both Classes 1 and 2, namely, employment by a member of the family in a private home occupied by both the employer and employee which is not employment for the purposes of the trade or business of that employer; self-employment, where this is not the individual's ordinary employment; employment as a returning or counting officer in an election or referendum; employment in this country in connection with the Visiting Forces Act 1952 or the International Headquarters and Defence Organisation Act 1964; and Gurkhas recruited in Nepal.

Other regulations both extend and restrict the concept of employed earner's employment for the purposes of the industrial injury scheme.[150] These are considered in chapter 20, below.[151]

v *Residence or presence*

SSCBA 1992 refers to gainful employment in Great Britain.[152] The more detailed conditions as to residence and presence are contained in the Social Security (Contributions) Regulations.[153]

(1) The major condition is that at the time of employment the earner is resident or present in Great Britain – temporary absences being disregarded – or is then ordinarily resident in Britain.

(2) If, however, the earner is not normally resident or employed in the UK, but, in pursuance of employment which is mainly abroad for an employer whose place of business is also outside the UK, he or she works for a time in Britain, contributions are payable only after continuous residence in Britain for 52 contribution weeks. The same proviso applies also to other non-residents who, on vacation from full-

---

144 SI 1978/1689, Sch 1, Pt I.
145 For details see SI 1978/1689, Sch 1, Pt I, para 4. See also *St John's College School Cambridge v Secretary of State for Social Security* (12 June 2000, unreported).
146 This implies that the employer has the right not only to tell the worker what to do but how to do it: *Staples v Secretary of State for Social Services* (15 March 1985, unreported).
147 This provision is unaffected by the new rules governing intermediaries (p 103, above): SI 2000/727, reg 12.
148 Defined as 'a person who is employed as an actor, singer or musician, or in any similar performing capacity': SI 1978/1689, reg 1(2). The courts have not been required to consider whether this includes eg lap dancers.
149 SI 1978/1689, Sch 1, Pt III.
150 SI 1975/467.
151 Pp 719–721, below.
152 SSCBA 1992, s 2(1).
153 SI 2001/1004, regs 145–146. For 'resident' and 'ordinarily resident', see pp 230–232, below.

time studies abroad, are in Britain on temporary employment in some way connected with their studies and to those working in Britain as apprentices for foreign masters.

(3) Even if employees are working abroad, they may still be liable to contribute if they are ordinarily resident in Britain, were resident there before the commencement of the employment and (most important of all) their employer has a place of business in Britain. The liability exists only for the first 52 contribution weeks of the foreign employment.

vi   Age

To be liable, the earner must be over 16 and under pensionable age (currently 65 for men, 60 for women).[154]

vii   Calculation of contributions

The basis on which the liability to pay contributions is calculated reflects the economic and political priorities of the government of the day. However, the principles governing the assessment of contributions due from those at either end of the wage spectrum have remained constant throughout. Those with very low earnings are exempt from liability to contribute (and so acquire no title to contributory benefits); this threshold has historically taken the form of a statutory lower earnings limit, a figure fixed annually at a level roughly equal to the basic state pension.[155] An upper earnings limit is also set, beyond which employees are currently not liable to pay contributions on their earnings (although employers have to continue paying secondary Class 1 contributions).[156] To this extent the National Insurance scheme remains a regressive form of taxation.[157]

In 1985, in an attempt to encourage the growth of low-paid employment, a system of graduated contribution rates was introduced, according to which different contribution rates were set (5, 7 and 9 per cent respectively) for those with weekly earnings above the lower earnings limit and between three different brackets.[158] This was abandoned in 1989 on the grounds that the graduated contribution rates created a disincentive for employees to seek out more highly paid work (although a similar system of graduated rates remained in force at that time for employers' secondary Class 1 contributions).[159] Under the revised structure, employees with earnings above the lower earnings limit paid an 'initial' contribution rate of 2 per cent on earnings below that limit (the so-called 'entry fee')[160] and a 'main' rate of 10 per cent on earnings between the lower and

---

154   SSCBA 1992, s 6(1),(2). The equal pensionable age of 65 for both men and women is being phased in: see pp 599–601, below.

155   SSCBA 1992, s 5(2).

156   But see the effect of National Insurance Contributions Act 2002 (NICA 2002) as from April 2003, discussed further below.

157   At its height, in 1982, the upper earnings limit was 136% of male full-time average earnings; by 1999 it had fallen to 110% of that average: Government Actuary *National Insurance Fund – Long-term Financial Estimates* (1999, Cm 4406) para 1.17.

158   SSA 1985, s 7, amending SSA 1975, s 4(6)–(6B).

159   See p 110, below.

160   For discussion of the incentive and employment effects of the lower threshold on contributions, see Dilnot and Webb (1988) 9(4) Fiscal Studies 1 and (1989) 10(2) Fiscal Studies 38; Hakim (1989) 18 J Soc Pol 471; Deakin and Wilkinson (1989) 38 Low Pay Review 18.

upper limits.[161] This imposed a greater burden on the low paid and distorted the labour market, not least by encouraging bunching below the lower earnings limit.

The Blair government introduced a phased package of reforms as part of its programme of modernising the tax and benefit systems. In April 1999 the entry fee was abolished; instead employees paid contributions at the rate of 10 per cent on earnings above the lower earnings limit but below the upper threshold.[162] One effect of this was to increase the proportion of Class 1 contributions being paid by employers.[163] From the following year an employee's liability to contribute began at a 'primary threshold', a figure pitched approximately half-way between the then lower earnings limit and the weekly equivalent of the single person's income tax personal allowance. In April 2001 the primary threshold was aligned with the single person's tax allowance, with the effect that the starting point for liability to pay both income tax and contributions now coincides.[164] This has the merit of simplicity but will presumably result in the continuation of the bunching of labour (ie the phenomenon by which many part-time jobs are offered at rates just below the level at which liability for contributions starts), albeit in relation to the new higher threshold. In the absence of any further measures, those earning between the lower earnings limit and the new primary threshold would have lost their entitlement to contributory benefits. Accordingly, legislation now treats employees in this position as if they had notionally paid contributions on their earnings above the lower earnings limit.[165]

Further structural changes are due to take effect in April 2003 under NICA 2002. Implementing proposals announced in the 2002 Budget, the Act both increased contribution rates and removed the cap on employees' primary Class 1 contributions. Thus from April 2003 employees will pay the 'main primary percentage', or standard rate of contributions (increased from 10 to 11 per cent), on earnings between the primary threshold and the upper earnings limit, and an 'additional primary percentage' of 1 per cent on all earnings above that level.[166] Thus a reform which was supposed to have been a factor in Labour losing the 1992 general election was enacted ten years later. These increases in National Insurance liabilities were not needed to support the National Insurance Fund, which is in a sound financial position. Rather, they provided a mechanism for funding a substantial increase in public expenditure on the NHS, which is due to rise from £65 billion in 2001–02 to £105 billion in 2007–08, without raising rates of income tax.[167]

Those opting out of the state earnings-related pension scheme (formerly SERPS, now S2P) pay 1.6 per cent less on earnings between the lower and upper earnings

---

161 SSA 1989, s 1 and SI 1989/1677; see now SSCBA 1992, s 8, as amended by the SS(C)A 1994. The Secretary of State has powers to alter the contribution rates by order (SSAA 1992, ss 143, 145) and to make special regulations for members of the armed forces, mariners and airmen, married women and widows, persons outside Great Britain and those employed on continental shelf operations: SSCBA 1992, ss 116–120; see pp 118–120, below.

162 SSA 1998, s 51, amending SSCBA 1992, ss 5 and 6, and adopting the recommendations in HM Treasury *The Modernisation of Britain's Tax and Benefit System – Work incentives: A Report by Martin Taylor* Report No 2 (1998) ch 2. The 10 per cent rate may be varied: SSCBA 1992, s 8(2) and SSAA 1992, ss 143 and 145.

163 *Government Actuary* n 157, above, ch 9.

164 SSCBA 1992, ss 5, 6 and 8; these (along with s 9 and a new s 6A) were re-enacted by WRPA 1999, s 73 and Sch 9 with the aim of assisting clarity, given the succession of amendments in the preceding years. On the consequences, see *Government Actuary* n 157, above, ch 10.

165 SSCBA 1992, s 6A.

166 SSCBA 1992, s 8, as substituted by NICA 2002, s 1. The standard rate, but not the additional 1 per cent rate, may be changed by regulations: n 161, above.

167 HM Treasury *Budget 2002* (2001–02, HC 592).

limits.[168] Between 1988 and 1993 an additional 2 per cent rebate on contributions between the lower and upper limits was made available to individuals who contracted out of the state earnings-related pension scheme. From April 1993 this was replaced by a 1 per cent additional rebate for Class 1 contributors over the age of 30 who opted out of SERPS in favour of a personal pension scheme.[169] The point of making the additional rebate age-related was to discourage individuals in their 30s from exercising the right to opt back into SERPS when, as a consequence of the flat-rate nature of the rebate, it might otherwise be in their interests to do so.[170] This additional rebate was itself replaced in 1997, following amendments made by the Pensions Act 1995 (PA 1995), by a new system of age-related rebates for those contracting out via appropriate personal pensions and money purchase occupational pension schemes.[171] The new rebates were significantly lower at younger ages than the previous flat-rate rebates, so making personal pensions less financially attractive than was the case before;[172] allied with concerns over pensions mis-selling, this has reduced take-up of personal pensions.

The earnings on which the calculation of the Class 1 contribution is based are the individual's gross remuneration from his or her employment or employments.[173] This is deemed by primary legislation to include statutory sick pay, statutory maternity pay and other sickness payments made by employer to employed earners[174] as well as payments made under the employment protection legislation.[175] Gains made on share options granted to directors and employees are included, as is compensation paid in pursuance of a restrictive undertaking, along with certain other payments made by companies to their directors.[176] The definition of gross remuneration has been steadily expanded as employers and their advisers have developed ever more ingenious schemes to pay bonuses in various non-cash forms in an attempt to circumvent contributions liabilities.[177] However, regulations also provide for certain items that are disregarded. These fall into the following categories:[178]

- payments in kind;[179]
- payments by way of readily convertible assets and specific assets not disregarded as payments in kind;
- certain non-cash vouchers;

168   SSCBA 1992, s 8(1); PSA 1993, s 41(1) and (1A); SI 1996/1054, Art 2.
169   This rebate, unlike its predecessor, was not available to those who contracted out in favour of an employer-based scheme, whether of a defined-benefit or money-purchase nature.
170   See generally the report of the National Audit Office n 59, above.
171   PSA 1993, ss 42A and 45(1); SI 1996/1055; and SI 1996/1056.
172   *Government Actuary* n 157, above, para 7.8 and Appendix D, para 14.13.
173   SSCBA 1992, s 3 and Sch 1, para 1; SI 2001/1004, reg 24. For the rules governing the determination of earnings periods, see SI 2001/1004, regs 2–9. To calculate contributions where the individual is engaged in both contracted-out and non-contracted-out employment, see SSCBA 1992, Sch 1, paras 1(2)–(3).
174   SSCBA 1992, s 4(1)–(3).
175   SSCBA 1992, s 112, ie Trade Union and Labour Relations (Consolidation) Act 1992 and ERA 1996.
176   SSCBA 1992, s 4 (4)–(5) and SI 2001/1004, reg 22. Cash payments on such undertakings were always within the original SSCBA 1992, s 4(4); the scope of liability was extended to cover non-cash payments by amendments contained in SSA 1998, s 50.
177   See SI 2001/1004, reg 24 and Sch 2, defining the method of calculating remuneration paid by way of various beneficial interests in assets (eg certain share options, vouchers etc).
178   SI 2001/1004, reg 26 and Sch 3. The full list is typically amended several times a year and includes a number of somewhat esoteric occupationally-specific payments, eg contractual payments in lieu of coal made to miners and allowances paid to British Council and Commonwealth War Graves Commission staff to compensate for the extra costs of having to live outside the UK to perform their duties.
179   In *R v Department of Social Security, ex p Overdrive Credit Card Ltd* [1991] 1 WLR 635 the Divisional Court held that payments by employers to cover their employees' private motoring costs did not fall under this exception, but the question of liability for the provision of company cars and expenses to cover petrol costs is now the subject of Class 1A contributions: see p 111, below.

- pensions and pension contributions;
- payments in respect of training and similar courses;
- travelling, relocation and other employment-related expenses and allowances;
- share incentives; and
- miscellaneous payments.[180]

If husband and wife are jointly engaged in employment and the earnings therefrom are paid jointly, the amounts of earnings upon which the calculation of contributions is based are the same as those assessed by the Inland Revenue for the purposes of income tax.[181]

C Secondary Class 1 contributions

i Designation of contributors

Secondary Class 1 contributions are payable by 'employers and other persons paying earnings'.[182] The statutory definition of the contributor depends on the status of the earner:[183] if he or she works under a contract of service, the secondary contributor is the employer. If he or she is engaged in an office with emoluments, it is either 'such person as may be prescribed in relation to that office', or if no such person is prescribed 'the government department, public authority or body of persons responsible for paying the emoluments of the office'. There is little to add to the provisions concerning an office-holder. As regards employment under a contract of service, the principles elaborated under that head should assist in determining not only the existence of such a contract, but also the parties to it. Where it is clear that an earner is employed under a contract of service, but unclear with which of two parties the contract was made, the issue should be resolved by answering such questions as: Who supervised the work? Who paid the employee? Who had the right of appointment and dismissal?[184] Cases of doubt, and cases where the party legally categorised as an employer under a contract of service is regarded as an inappropriate secondary contributor, may be regulated by the Treasury's power to transfer liability to another prescribed person.[185] Under current regulations:[186]

(1) An office cleaner is employed by the person for whom the work is done, unless he or she is supplied and paid by an agency, in which case the agency is the employer.
(2) In other cases, where an employee renders personal services under an agreement with an agency, the agency is treated as the employer.
(3) Where a person is employed by their spouse for the purpose of the spouse's employment, the spouse is deemed to be the employer.
(4) Certain part-time lecturers etc are employed by the person providing the education.

---

180 Eg gratuities not paid directly or indirectly by the employer. For discussion, see NIAC *Report on Draft Contribution Amendment Regulations* (1980, Cmnd 8117).
181 SI 2001/1004, reg 20.
182 SSCBA 1992, s 1(2)(a)(ii). Subject to very narrowly defined exceptions, employers and others paying secondary Class 1 contributions cannot recover them from their employees; Sch 1, paras 3A and 3B. See further SI 2001/1004, reg 69 and Sch 5.
183 SSCBA 1992, s 7(1).
184 Atiyah *Vicarious Liability* (1966) pp 160–161; and see Lord Porter in *Mersey Docks and Harbour Board v Coggins and Griffith (Liverpool) Ltd* [1947] AC 1 at 17. Two reported decisions of the minister, M14 and M35, by implication, apply these criteria. See also *Cheng Yuen v Royal Hong Kong Golf Club* [1998] ICR 131 (caddie).
185 SSCBA 1992, s 7(2).
186 SI 1978/1689, Sch 3.

(5) Where the earner is employed in a company which has gone into voluntary liquidation but which carries on business under a liquidator, the person holding the office of liquidator at the time of the employment is treated as the employer.

(6) In respect of Anglican ministers of religion, the secondary contributions are payable by the Church Commissioners; for other ministers, by the administrators of the fund from which the minister's remuneration is paid.

(7) Where a worker is employed by a foreign employer but provides personal service for the business of a British-based employer, the British-based employer is treated as the employer.

(8) Entertainers are treated as being employed by those engaging their services.

(9) A barrister's clerk is treated as being employed by the head of chambers.

(10) An employee of a foreign employer who is seconded to work for an employer in Great Britain is treated as being employed by the British employer.

Where an earner is employed under two or more independent contracts of service, and is paid by each employer an amount equal to or exceeding the lower earnings limit, both will be liable to contribute. However, if the earnings in one or more of the employments are lower than that limit, and the relevant employer carries on business in association with another employer, the earnings may be aggregated to achieve the necessary liability and the contributions are then payable by each of those employers on a proportionate basis.[187]

ii Residence

Liability for secondary contributions arises only where the party otherwise liable is resident or present in Great Britain or has a place of business there.[188] The same regulation optimistically adds that even if these conditions are not met an employer may pay the contributions 'if he so wishes'.

iii Amount

The employer's liability for secondary contributions is wider than that of the employee in two respects: first, it extends to earnings after the latter has reached pensionable age; secondly, the rate levied is currently 11.8 per cent, rather than 10 per cent, on earnings above the single person's tax allowance.[189] This was increased to 12.8 per cent by the 2002 Budget with effect from April 2003.[190] A uniform rate was introduced in 1999 to replace the complex structure of graduated contributions for employers.[191] The current arrangement has the merit of simplicity and was designed to be revenue-neutral, but individual employers with a greater proportion of highly paid staff faced an increased liability. At the same time the secondary threshold (as it has now been renamed) at which employers are required to pay contributions was raised to the same level as the single person's income tax allowance (ie two years earlier than for employees), with no

---

187 SI 2001/1004, reg 15.
188 SI 2001/1004, reg 145(1)(b).
189 A third difference, until April 2003 at least, is that until this date employees had no liability to pay contributions on earnings above the upper earnings limit, unlike employers.
190 NICA 2002, s 2.
191 SSCBA 1992, s 9(1)–(3), as substituted by SSA 1998, s 51(4). Previously the employer paid 3.6, 5.6, 7.6 or 10.2 per cent, depending on the employee's weekly earnings (SI 1994/544, now repealed).

liability to pay contributions below that level. There is a reduction of 3 per cent in the liability to pay secondary Class 1 contributions on earnings between the lower and upper limits for contracted-out employments.[192]

D Class 1A contributions

This category of contributions, introduced by SS(C)A 1991, was originally confined to benefits granted by employers to their employees in respect of cars and fuel made available for private use. It is closely related to employers' liability to pay secondary Class 1 contributions and was created to close what was seen as a loophole in relation to the widespread use of company cars and subsidised petrol as a form of payment in kind. In order to align National Insurance liabilities more closely with tax liabilities, the Child Support, Pensions and Social Security Act 2000 extended the scope of Class 1A to cover all taxable benefits in kind (eg private medical care).[193] The contributions are payable by the person who is liable for secondary Class 1 contributions in respect of that employment (or would have been, in a case where the employee's weekly earnings fall below the lower earnings threshold).[194] Thus since April 2000 an employer has been liable for Class 1A contributions where three conditions are satisfied.[195] First, the relevant earner must be subject to Schedule E income tax on his emolument. Secondly, the relevant employment must be employed earner's employment[196] and the earner must either be a director or earn more than £8,500 a year. Thirdly, at least part of those emoluments must not count as earnings for the purpose of Class 1 contributions. The Class 1A contribution is then levied on the emoluments not brought within Class 1 liability. The Class 1A percentage rate is the same as that for secondary Class 1 contributions (11.8 per cent in 2002–03 and 12.8 per cent in 2003–04).[197]

E Class 1B contributions

This category of contributions, which was introduced by SSA 1998, is also consequential upon a change in the manner in which benefits for employees are taxed. Employers may enter into a 'PAYE settlement agreement'[198] with the Inland Revenue under which they pay a lump sum to discharge their tax liability on various minor benefits and expenses paid to employees (eg the reimbursement of late-night taxi fares to employees working evening shifts). Class 1B contributions represent the National Insurance liability on such settlements and are charged at the same rate as secondary Class 1 and Class 1A contributions.[199]

---

192   PSA 1993, s 41(1B).
193   Following a recommendation of *HM Treasury* n 162, above, para 2.16.
194   SSCBA 1992, s 10(1)–(2). In certain cases, where the benefits in kind are provided by a third party rather than the employer (eg a manufacturer offers incentives to sales staff in a store), the third-party provider is liable to pay the Class 1A liability: ss 10ZA and 10ZB.
195   For exclusions, see SI 2001/1004, reg 40.
196   SSCBA 1992, s 2(1)(a); see pp 98–103, above.
197   SSCBA 1992, s 10(4)–(5).
198   ICTA 1988, s 206A.
199   SSCBA 1992, s 10A, inserted by SSA 1998, s 53. This rate may be varied by SSAA 1992, s 143A, inserted by SSA 1998, s 65.

F Class 2 contributions

Contributions under Class 2 may confer title to any contributory benefit except contribution-based jobseeker's allowance, and the earnings-related additional components in pensions.[200] They are payable by self-employed earners[201] and differ from Class 1 contributions in three important respects: since by definition there is no contract of service, there is for each employment only one contributor; the contribution is payable on a flat-rate basis; and a self-employed person who is not liable to contribute because, eg, of low earnings or failure to satisfy the residence conditions may pay voluntarily. A recommendation for simplification, involving the abolition of the Class 2 charge and an increase in the Class 4 rate (see below) so as to make good the yield lost from Class 2 has not been implemented to date.[202] However, policy appears to be moving in that direction: in 2000–01 the Class 2 flat-rate was reduced from £6.55 a week to just £2 a week, whilst the Class 4 rate was marginally increased from 6 to 7 per cent (these rates also applied in 2002–03). It has been argued that the self-employed substantially under-contribute to the National Insurance Fund, even allowing for their reduced benefit entitlements, which could justify making such reform revenue-raising rather than revenue neutral.[203]

i Persons liable

A self-employed person is defined as:

> a person who is gainfully employed in Great Britain otherwise than in employed earner's employment (whether or not he is also employed in such employment).[204]

A COMBINATIONS OF EMPLOYMENTS

The negative and rather confusing formulation means that if persons are in a gainful employment for which Class 1 contributions are not payable[205] they are necessarily self-employed[206] even though they may concurrently and independently be employed in a Class 1 employment. The liability to pay under both classes (and as we shall see also under Class 4) was a major innovation of SSA 1973. The justification for this approach is not immediately apparent but may readily be inferred from general policy considerations. The acceptance of an earnings-related principle for contributions naturally led to the conclusion that a proportionate part of a self-employed person's profits should be payable whether or not he or she was also employed under a contract of service: hence Class 4. But, as will be seen, it was thought too expensive

200   SSCBA 1992, s 21(2).
201   SSCBA 1992, s 1(2)(c).
202   *HM Treasury* n 162, above, paras 2.25–2.28.
203   *HM Treasury* n 162, above, paras 2.25–2.28.
204   SSCBA 1992, s 2(1)(b).
205   This includes the single case (examiners, moderators and invigilators employed under a contract to be performed in less than 12 months) where the Secretary of State has prescribed that a person employed under a contract of service shall nevertheless be treated as a self-employed earner: SI 1978/1989, Sch 1, Pt II.
206   Unless they are in a disregarded employment: see p 105, above.

administratively to impose such a charge on profits below a certain figure.[207] The flat-rate contribution under Class 2 has therefore traditionally been fixed so that it roughly represented the same percentage of that figure as the Class 4 contribution did of liable income above it.[208] This linkage appears to have been broken with the substantial reduction in the weekly rate in 2000–01.

B   GAINFUL EMPLOYMENT

The shift in terminology from 'gainfully occupied in employment' to 'gainfully employed' has already been the subject of comment in relation to Class 1 contributions.[209] As was suggested there, the authorities on the interpretation of the earlier formulation should be used as guidelines for the term currently employed. In the present context, the matter is of more than academic interest, for while there is no liability to pay where earnings are below a certain level, the self-employed earner if 'gainfully employed' may in such circumstances voluntarily contribute. Thus individuals undertaking a new enterprise will be *entitled* to pay Class 2 contributions as soon as they are 'gainfully employed', notwithstanding that their current failure to make substantial profits exempts them from *liability* to pay. 'Gainfully occupied' under the former legislation was held not necessarily to imply the making of a net profit on an enterprise.[210] Thus in relation to self-employment, it was said that:

> the question is not to be posed at any particular time, has he in fact received some net profit from his activities ... but does he hold himself out as being anxious to become employed for purpose of gain?[211]

The answer to this latter question is a matter of fact for the determining authority.

C   CONTINUING EMPLOYMENT

The boundaries of self-employment are not always easy to determine. To a certain extent, the answer will be supplied by the 'gainfully employed' criterion discussed in the section above. To reinforce the notion that regard should be had to an individual's endeavours over a substantial period rather than to short-term and spasmodic profit/ loss accounting, regulations prescribe that where a person is a self-employed earner (or is treated as such) 'the employment shall ... be treated as continuing unless and until he is no longer ordinarily employed in that employment'.[212]

D   RESIDENCE

Self-employed earners are liable to pay contributions only if they are either ordinarily resident in Great Britain or were resident there for a period of at least 26 of the

---

207   DHSS Discussion Document *The Self-Employed and National Insurance* (1980) paras 8, 39.
208   *DHSS* n 207,above, para 18.
209   P 97, above.
210   *Vandyk v Minister of Pensions and National Insurance* [1955] 1 QB 29.
211   Per Slade J, *Vandyk v Minister of Pensions and National Insurance* [1955] 1 QB 29 at 38.
212   SI 1978/1689, Sch 2.

immediately preceding 52 contribution weeks.[213] Where there is no liability under these rules an earner may nevertheless voluntarily contribute.[214]

E   AGE

The contributor must be over 16 years and under pensionable age (at present 65 for men and 60 for women).[215]

ii *Exceptions*

There are two grounds on which a self-employed person may be excepted from liability to pay contributions: inability to earn and low earnings. As regards the first, it must be shown that throughout the week for which the exception is claimed (excluding Sunday or an equivalent rest day) that person received incapacity benefit, carer's or maternity allowance, or was in prison or detained in legal custody.[216] An exception for low earnings has existed ever since self-employed persons were compulsorily insured in 1946,[217] the justifications being to exclude occasional profit makers and to reduce administrative expenditure. Earnings, for this purpose, means 'net earnings' from the employment,[218] and is effectively such income as is chargeable to income tax under Schedule D:[219] thus from gross earnings may be deducted expenses necessarily incurred in connection with the employment.[220] In furtherance of this policy of integrating contributions and tax liability, the regulations adopt the Inland Revenue rule of allowing assessments to be based on earnings from a preceding tax year. Earnings for a particular year are treated as less than the threshold if, in the preceding year, the individual's earnings were less than that amount and there had since been no material change of circumstances, or if in the year for which exception is claimed the earnings are expected to be less than that amount.[221] The onus is on the self-employed earner to claim exception, and if successful he or she will be granted a certificate of exception. When an exception is granted on either of the two grounds specified in this paragraph, the self-employed person may voluntarily pay contributions (either of Class 2 or of Class 3).[222]

iii *Amount*

Whether contributions are mandatory or voluntary, a weekly flat-rate contribution is payable (£2 in 2002–03). A slightly higher rate is paid by share fishermen and volunteer

---

213   SI 2001/1004, reg 145(1)(d). For 'resident' and 'ordinarily resident', see pp 230–231, below.
214   If, in the week in question, he or she was either resident in Great Britain; or, if abroad, had been resident in Britain and had paid Class 1 or Class 2 contributions for three years immediately preceding his or her departure; or was temporarily in Britain, without being resident, but was gainfully employed outside Britain: SI 2001/1004, reg 147.
215   SSCBA 1992, s 11(2).
216   SI 2001/1004, reg 43.
217   SSCBA 1992, s 7(5); see in general, NIAC *Report on Liability for Contributions of Persons with Small Incomes* (1955, Cmd 9432).
218   SI 2001/1004, reg 45(2).
219   See *Whitehouse* n 132, above, ch 6.
220   ICTA 1988, s 60(1).
221   SI 2001/1004, reg 45(1).
222   SI 2001/1004, regs 43(3) and 46.

development workers overseas who, exceptionally, may be entitled to contribution-based jobseeker's allowance on the basis of Class 2 contributions.[223]

G Class 3 contributions

Beveridge's conception of social insurance was a comprehensive one – all of working age were to be included. Under his scheme, as implemented in the 1946 legislation, there was to be a third class of compulsory contributions, for those who would need provision for medical treatment, retirement and funeral expenses, and who were not in a gainful occupation but were of working age.[224] Typically included were students, unmarried women engaged in unremunerated domestic work, those retiring early under an occupational pension scheme, and persons in receipt of private income. Of course, they must have had resources to pay contributions, and so there were exemptions for those below a minimum income level. This class of contributions, so defined, was abolished by SSA 1973. The present Class 3 allows only for *voluntary* contributions, and these may be paid either by non-employed persons or those contributing in Class 1 or 2, but with deficiencies in their contribution record. The advent of home responsibilities protection has lessened the need for some people in this position to pay Class 3 contributions, which enable a person to qualify only for bereavement benefits and retirement pensions (Categories A and B).[225] A weekly flat-rate is payable (£6.85 in 2002–03).

i Persons entitled to contribute

The contributor must be over 16[226] and under pensionable age (currently 65 for men, 60 for women),[227] and with some exceptions resident in Great Britain during the year for which contribution is made.[228]

ii Making up a reckonable year

SSCBA 1992 prescribes that:

> payment of Class 3 contributions shall be allowed only with a view to enabling the contributor to satisfy contribution conditions of entitlement to benefit by acquiring the relevant earnings factor for the [relevant] purposes ...[229]

As will be seen, for those benefits for which Class 3 payments may count, a year of contributions will only qualify towards entitlement if a minimum number of contributions has been made. At the end of each contribution year a Class 1 contributor is sent a

---

223 SI 2001/1004, regs 125 and 149–154.
224 *Beveridge Report* n 10, above, paras 310 and 317.
225 SSCBA 1992, s 21(2). See, however, p 128, below (partial satisfaction), for an example of a situation in which Class 3 payments may be advisable.
226 SSCBA 1992, s 13(1).
227 SI 2001/1004, reg 49(1)(e).
228 SI 2001/1004, reg 145(1)(e). Those abroad can contribute on the same conditions as are prescribed in relation to Class 2 voluntary contributions: n 214, above.
229 SSCBA 1992, s 13(2).

statement of his or her account indicating any shortage, and how many Class 3 contributions will be necessary to make up a reckonable year. Class 2 contributors with an incomplete record may, as already indicated, voluntarily pay additional contributions of that class, but if they wish to secure entitlement only to the more limited benefits available to Class 3 contributors, they may in the alternative make up the number with additional payments of the latter class. There are rules to prevent an individual making unnecessary contributions, eg where the record is complete for a given year, or where he or she will be credited with contributions for that year.[230] If such payments have nevertheless been made, the contributor is entitled to a refund;[231] alternatively, if preferred, the extra contributions may be appropriated to satisfy conditions for another tax year.[232]

H   Class 4 contributions

It was evident that if the self-employed were to make earnings-related contributions to the National Insurance Fund, this in practice could be achieved only by integrating assessment and administration with the fiscal system.[233] A fourth category of contributions was therefore created which would effectively coincide with tax liability under Schedule D of the Income Tax Acts. Entitlement to benefit, however, is established by reference only to contributions of Classes 1, 2 or 3; Class 4 is simply the most convenient means of securing earnings-related contributions from those paying Class 2 contributions. Class 4 is based, then, on the principle of coincidence with tax liability. According to SSCBA 1992:

> Class 4 contributions shall be payable for any tax year in respect of all annual profits or gains which—
> (a)   are immediately derived from the carrying on or exercise of one or more trades, professions or vocations, and
> (b)   are profits or gains chargeable to income tax under Case I or Case II of Schedule D.[234]

Moreover, Class 4 contributions are payable '(a) in the same manner as any income tax ... and (b) by the person on whom the income tax is (or would be) charged, in accordance with assessments made from time to time under the Income Tax Acts'.[235]

For the nature and extent of this liability, then, reference should be made to the standard texts on taxation.[236] What follows is an account of those aspects of the assessment that are peculiar to Class 4 contributions.

i   Persons liable

The condition of residence in the UK is that applied under the Income Tax Acts,[237] but in contrast to that legislation, liability for contributions does not extend to earners who

---

230   SSCBA 1992, s 14 and SI 2001/1004, reg 49(1).
231   SI 2001/1004, regs 56–57.
232   SSCBA 1992, s 13(3) and SI 2001/1004, reg 58.
233   For the policy considerations relevant to the liability of the self-employed, see p 113, above.
234   SSCBA 1992, s 15(1).
235   SSCBA 1992, s 15(2).
236   Eg *Whitehouse* n 132, above, ch 6.
237   SSCBA 1992, s 17(2)(d) and SI 2001/1004, reg 91.

are under 16 or over pensionable age.[238] Independent taxation of husbands and wives was introduced in 1990, with the consequence that they may no longer aggregate their income for the purposes of Class 4 contributions. Each is now liable separately for contributions based on their own profits and gains.[239] In the case of partnerships, as under tax law, each partner is liable according to his or her share of the profits,[240] but contributions are not payable by those liable to tax as trustees, administrators, executors and other nominal holders of property.[241]

Persons charged for income tax under both Schedule E and Schedule D, because they are both employed under a contract of service and derive profits from a trade or business, for that reason will also be liable to pay contributions of both Classes 1 and 4, provided that in either case their earnings or profits exceed the relevant lower limit. Some difficulty is caused where tax and social security liability do not correspond in this way. Thus while actors, musicians and those working for agencies pay Class 1 contributions, their earnings or profits may nevertheless be chargeable to tax under Schedule D. The solution provided by the regulations is to deduct from the profits and gains chargeable to Schedule D the amount of earnings on the basis of which the Class 1 contributions were assessed, so that liability for Class 4 will be attracted only if the remainder exceeds the threshold.[242] Conversely, a person paying Class 2 contributions but whose earnings are chargeable to tax under Schedule E will be liable for Class 4 at the same rate as other self-employed persons, though in this case liability is deferred until the end of the relevant tax year.[243]

ii Amount of liability

Class 4 contributions involve the payment of a prescribed proportion (7 per cent in 2002–03 and 8 per cent in 2003–04) of profits and gains between a lower and upper level.[244] With effect from April 2003, as part of the Budget 2002 changes, there is also an additional levy of 1 per cent on profits and gains above the upper level.[245] The profits and gains in question are those which are chargeable to income tax under Schedule D. Account must therefore be taken of such deductions and reliefs as are there provided,[246] but the following tax reliefs do not apply for the purposes of Class 4 contributions:[247] personal allowances; payments under annuity contracts and trust schemes; the carrying forward of losses; and the payment of interest. A person liable for both Class 1 and Class 4 contributions will not have to pay, in aggregate, more than the maximum which would have been payable on contributions of a single class.[248] Given the upper earnings limit on primary Class 1 contributions, this means that the Class 4 liability is effectively negated for very high earners.

238 SSCBA 1992, s 17(2)(a)–(b); SI 2001/1004, regs 91(a) and 93.
239 Finance Act 1988, s 32 and Sch 14, Pt VIII, repealing SSA 1975, Sch 2, para 4; and SI 1991/1935, revoking SI 1979/91, reg 79.
240 SSCBA 1992, Sch 2, para 4.
241 SSCBA 1992, para 5.
242 SI 2001/1004, reg 94.
243 SSCBA 1992, s 18 and SI 2001/1004, regs 71 and 76.
244 SSCBA 1992, s 15. For 2002–03 these were £4,615 and £30,420 respectively.
245 NICA 2002, s 3, amending SSCBA 1992, s 15. The standard rate, but not the additional 1 per cent rate, may be changed by regulations: SSAA 1992, ss 143–145.
246 See *Whitehouse* n 132, above, para 6.131ff.
247 SSCBA 1992, Sch 2, para 3(2).
248 SI 2001/1004, reg 100. This also applies to Class 2 and Class 4 contributions.

There is clearly a strong case for abolishing the Class 2 charge and raising the Class 4 rate (which is substantially below the rate for either primary or secondary Class 1 contributions). However, this would require inventing a new contributions test to establish entitlement to benefit by self-employed people (eg a minimum Class 4 payment).[249]

Part 3   Special categories

A   Married women

Under the Beveridge plan of national insurance, married women required special treatment. This was derived from his view of the family as a single economic unit, the wife doing the housework for the husband, who in return maintained her. According to the figures then available,[250] over 80 per cent of married women of working age regarded marriage as their sole occupation. Even if a wife was an earner, she was different from a single woman in that employment was liable to interruption for childbirth, and, more significantly, her earnings were 'a means, not of subsistence but of a standard of living above subsistence'.[251] According to this thinking, it followed that in sickness or unemployment she did not need compensation on the same scale as the primary breadwinner; she could fall back on her husband's income, or his benefit if his earnings were interrupted. It was therefore proposed that a married woman who was an earner could choose either to opt out of the scheme, and thus become wholly dependent on her husband's contributions for retirement pension and maternity grant, or else to contribute in her own right.[252] These proposals were implemented in full by the 1946 legislation, and with some modifications, remained in force until 1975.

By the 1970s, the social and economic climate had changed considerably in that over 60 per cent of married women of working age were in paid employment.[253] The movement against sex discrimination had intensified, and the social security position of married women was a prime target.[254] The Labour government, in consequence, decided to abolish the married woman's option as part of its programme for pension reform. The ability, for the purpose of pension entitlement, to take into consideration years during which a woman was 'precluded from regular employment by responsibilities at home'[255] was regarded as the key provision which would ensure a fair return for her contributions. However, in order that existing family arrangements should not be unduly prejudiced by the decision to abolish the option, those already married or widowed when the new provisions came into force in 1977 were allowed to choose between 'full' and 'reduced' liability.

To benefit from the reduced liability provisions, married women must either have opted out of liability under the previous contributory system or have elected for reduced liability under the transitional provisions.[256] By 2000 there were some 200,000 women

---

249   *HM Treasury* n 162, above, paras 2.25–2.28.
250   Beveridge relied on the 1931 census. He regarded the much higher figures for wartime work (see Thomas *Women at Work: Wartime Social Survey* (1944)) as a temporary phenomenon.
251   *Beveridge Report* n 10, above, para 108.
252   As a non-earner, she might similarly opt between contributions under Class 4 and relying on her husband's contributions.
253   Eg General Household Survey 1978, Table 5.7.
254   See eg Report of the Labour Party Study Group *Towards Equality: Women and Social Security* (1969).
255   See p 604, below.
256   SI 2001/1004, Pt 9, Case D (regs 126–139); and *Williams* n 1, above, ch 10.

who had been continually married or widowed and in the labour market who had retained their right to pay the reduced rate since 1977.[257] The period of reduced liability then runs until pensionable age (currently 60) is reached, but it terminates earlier:

(1) on the date of a dissolution of marriage by divorce or annulment; or
(2) at the end of the tax year in which she ceases to be entitled to the relevant widow's benefit; or
(3) at the end of the tax year in which she revokes her election for reduced liability; or
(4) at the end of any two consecutive tax years subsequent to 5 April 1978 during which she is neither a self-employed earner nor is engaged in employment which attracts Class 1 contributions liability.[258]

Reduced liability confers on a married woman who has so elected exemption from paying Class 2 contributions[259] and disentitles her from paying Class 3 contributions.[260] The obligation to pay those of Class 4 remains unaffected, however. As regards Class 1, the liability is reduced to 3.85 per cent rather than excluded altogether.[261] These payments are more akin to taxes than to contributions for they cannot assist in gaining title to any benefits or to the crediting of contributions during periods of sickness, unemployment or domestic responsibilities.[262]

B Other special cases

Certain categories of occupation are selected for special treatment either because provision is not necessary for some hazards (eg unemployment) or because there are difficulties in fulfilling the normal conditions for contributions.

i HM forces

One of the consequences of the Beveridge principle of universality was to extend insurance to Crown employees, who had previously been excluded from the national schemes. The principle, affirmed in the SSCBA 1992, is that the provisions apply 'to persons employed by or under the Crown in like manner as if they were employed by a private person'.[263] However, members of HM forces are in a special position. For the purposes of satisfying the residence conditions for contributions, serving members of the forces are treated as 'present in Great Britain'.[264] They also used to pay a reduced rate of Class 1 contribution until this concession was revoked in 1996.[265]

---

257 Government Actuary *Report on the drafts of the Social Security Benefits Up-rating Order 2000 etc* (2000, Cm 4587) Appendix 2.
258 SI 2001/1004, reg 128(1). See also reg 130 on continuation of elections on widowhood.
259 SI 2001/1004, reg 127(1)(b).
260 SI 2001/1004, reg 132.
261 SI 2001/1004, reg 131. On the retention of the reduced rate of 3.85 per cent for earnings below the lower limit, see SI 1989/1677. The liability of the employer for secondary Class 1 contributions is unaffected.
262 SSCBA 1992, s 19(6) confers powers to make regulations enabling reduced liability contributions to be counted towards the necessary qualifying conditions but the power has not been exercised in relation to married women and widows.
263 S 115(1).
264 SI 2001/1004, reg 141.
265 SI 1996/663, reg 2(3), revoking SI 1979/591, reg 115.

ii Employment on the Continental Shelf

The problem here is also simply that of satisfying the residence requirements. Regulations therefore prescribe that an employment in an area designated under the Continental Shelf Act 1964 in connection with the exploitation of resources, or the exploration, of the sea bed and subsoil, is deemed to be employment within Great Britain.[266]

iii Airmen

Similar considerations apply to airmen. Provided that the employer has a place of business in Great Britain, if the aircraft is British, or the principal place of business is in Britain, in the case of other aircraft, the airman is treated as present in Great Britain,[267] though if he is neither domiciled nor has a place of residence there, no contributions are payable.[268]

iv Mariners and registered dock workers

For a person employed as a mariner,[269] the normal residence requirements for contributions are replaced by the simple condition that he or she is domiciled or resident in Great Britain.[270] If the mariner's employment is wholly or partly on a 'foreign-going ship', the secondary liability is reduced by 0.5 per cent.[271] There are also special methods of calculating earnings for the purpose of earnings-related contributions.[272]

v Volunteer development workers

The object is to enable those working abroad in volunteer development but ordinarily resident in Great Britain to make contributions. If such work does not render such individuals liable to pay Class 1 contributions, they are exempt from, but may opt to pay, Class 2 contributions at a higher than normal rate which count towards contribution-based jobseeker's allowance.[273]

Part 4   Contribution conditions

Under the system in force before 1975, contributions were predominantly flat-rate. It was therefore convenient to express the conditions of contributions for the various benefits in terms of the number of weekly contributions paid (or credited) during a specified period (often a 'contribution year'). With the adoption of the earnings-related system and the interdependence with tax liability, such concepts were no longer feasible, and so they were

---

266   SI 2001/1004, reg 114.
267   SI 2001/1004, reg 112(1). For the definition of 'airman' and 'British aircraft' see reg 111.
268   SI 2001/1004, reg 112(2).
269   For definition, see SI 2001/1004, reg 115.
270   SI 2001/1004, reg 117.
271   SI 2001/1004, reg 119.
272   SI 2001/1004, regs 120–123.
273   SI 2001/1004, regs 149–154.

replaced by 'earnings factors' (representing the amount of earnings on which liability to contribute is based) and the 'tax year' (6 April–5 April) as the usual contributory period.[274]

A Earnings factors

Contributions to Class 1 are earnings-related, those of Class 2 and Class 3 are flat-rate. In any one tax year, an individual might combine contributions of one class with those of either or both of the other classes. It was therefore necessary to create some common denominator whereby equivalent conditions could be exacted from those paying different types of contributions, hence the 'earnings factor'. For Class 1 contributions, this is simply the earnings on which such contributions are paid or treated as paid.[275] For Class 2 or 3 contributions (which are flat-rate) it is the lower earnings limit for Class 1 contributions multiplied by the number of contributions made in the relevant tax year.[276] Similar principles govern the calculation of the earnings factors derived from credited and contracted-out contributions,[277] though these are calculated separately from factors derived from contributions actually paid in non-contracted-out employment.

One important function of the earnings factors is to determine the amount of any earnings-related pension in the pensions scheme.[278] Because of what is often a substantial gap in time between the payment of the contributions and the receipt of the benefit, it is necessary to 'revalue' the earnings factors to keep pace with inflation. Under SSAA 1992, therefore, the Secretary of State is directed to review in each tax year the general level of earnings obtaining in Great Britain. If it is concluded that the earnings factors for any previous tax year have not maintained their value in relation to the general level of earnings, an order must be made directing that the earnings factors shall be increased by such percentages as the Secretary of State thinks necessary to restore their values.[279]

B Conditions for benefit

In the section of the book devoted to the individual contributory benefits, the contribution conditions of each will be specified. At this stage, it will be convenient to review the general pattern of rules. Historically the aim of these rules has been to preserve a fair balance between the average contributor and the average beneficiary.[280] This objective of equity has given rise to two fundamental principles. The first is that the claimant's record of contributions should be sufficient in terms both of initial establishment in the scheme and of consistency over a period of time. The second is that there should be a difference according to whether the claim relates to a short-term or a long-term benefit. In the case of the latter, where the beneficiary will draw heavily on the fund's resources,

---

274 SSCBA 1992, s 21(5)(c); note also s 21(5A)(a) applying the definition where contributions are treated as having been paid.
275 SSCBA 1992, s 23(3)(a). For the technically precise mode of calculation, see SI 1979/676, Sch 1, Pt I. No earnings factors are derived from the reduced liability contributions made by married women and widows or, for years before 1987–88, for secondary Class 1 contributions: SSCBA 1992, s 22(4).
276 SSCBA 1992, s 23(3)(b) and SI 1979/676, Sch 1, Pt II.
277 SSCBA 1992, Pt I, paras 4–5.
278 Pp 615–620, below.
279 SSAA 1992, s 148. This responsibility was not transferred to the Treasury under SSC(TF)A 1999, so remains with the Department for Work and Pensions.
280 See NIAC *Report on the Question of Contribution Conditions and Credits Provisions* (1956, Cmd 9854) para 36.

it is appropriate that the tests should be more stringent. The conditions for the short-term benefits were traditionally relatively easy to satisfy. The Conservative government in the late 1980s argued that unemployment benefit,[281] in particular, was payable to many claimants whose employment record was only marginal[282] and in 1988 imposed more onerous conditions.[283] A similar argument was adopted by the Labour government in 1999 in relation to tightening the contribution conditions for incapacity benefit. The purported justification for this was the desirability of greater alignment with contribution-based jobseeker's allowance. The difficulty with this argument is that it ignores the fundamental distinction between a short-term and a long-term benefit (for unemployment and incapacity respectively).[284] The contribution rules are expressed in terms of earnings factors, but it should be noted that claimants to long-term benefits may satisfy an alternative set of conditions formulated in terms of pre-1975 contributions.[285]

The state maternity allowance forms a category of its own: as a result of changes instituted by WRPA 1999, entitlement is now no longer dependent upon the payment of contributions.[286] Instead, women who earn at least £30 a week may now qualify for the benefit. It remains to be seen if a similar and more inclusive approach is adopted for other contributory benefits. The House of Commons Social Security Committee has recommended that eligibility for jobseeker's allowance, incapacity benefit and the retirement pension should be extended to people at the same earnings threshold.[287]

i Initial condition

The first test, based on the idea of initial establishment in the scheme, can be satisfied only by contributions actually paid, ie credits do not qualify. In the case of contribution-based jobseeker's allowance, the claimant must have paid contributions, in either of the two last tax years before the year of the claim, the earnings factor from which is at least 25 times the lower earnings limit for that year.[288] For incapacity benefit, it was sufficient until WRPA 1999 that this test was met for *any* year. Now the condition must be met in one of the last three tax years before the benefit year involved.[289] As regards the bereavement payment, the test can still be satisfied for any tax year.[290] For those contributors at the lower end of the income scale (or making flat-rate Class 2 contributions) this will mean approximately six months' contributions. For the long-term benefits (retirement pensions, Categories A and B, and the remaining bereavement benefits) the qualifying earnings factor is 52 times the lower earnings limit (equivalent to one year's contributions at the lowest end of the scale).[291]

---

281   Now contribution-based jobseeker's allowance.
282   Mr J Moore MP, Secretary of State for Social Security, 121 HC Official Report (6th series) col 659.
283   SSA 1988, s 6; SSA 1989, s 11. See Wikeley (1989) 16 JLS 291; *Deakin and Wilkinson* n 30, above.
284   See Wikeley in Harris *Social Security Law in Context* (2000) p 375.
285   See SI 1979/643.
286   WRPA 1999, s 53; p 564, below.
287   *HC Social Security Committee* n 22, above, para 145. The government has rejected this proposal: *DSS* n 35, above, paras 16–19.
288   SSCBA 1992, Sch 3, para 1(2). The change from unemployment benefit to jobseeker's allowance saw no changes to the underlying contribution conditions; equally, only Class 1 contributions will suffice: s 21(2).
289   SSCBA 1992, Sch 3, para (2)(2)(a). These may be Class 1 or Class 2 contributions: s 21(2). The original proposal was for the rule to specify one year in the last two tax years.
290   SSCBA 1992, Sch 3, para 4(1)(a). Note that there is only one contribution condition for the bereavement payment.
291   SSCBA 1992, Sch 3, para 5(2); if the contributor was receiving long-term incapacity benefit in the year of death or of reaching pensionable age, or in the previous year, this condition is deemed to be met: para 5(6). On the meaning of 'qualifying earnings factor', see s 122(1).

ii Continuing condition

For the second qualifying condition, credits are equivalent to paid contributions, but the difference between the short-term and long-term benefits becomes considerable. For the former, the earnings factor derived from contributions paid or credited during each of the two tax years immediately preceding the year during which the entitlement to benefit falls must have been at least 50 times the lower earnings limit.[292] For the latter, the position is more complicated as the contributions determine entitlement not merely to the basic pension in the benefit, but also to any earnings-related additional pension. To qualify for the basic pension, for each of not less than 90 per cent of the tax years of his or her working life (namely, between 16 and pensionable age) the claimant must have paid, or been credited with, contributions the earnings factor of which was 52 times the lower earnings limit.[293] Alternatively, that earnings factor may be achieved for one-half of 90 per cent of the working life (or 20 years, if that is less) if during each of the remaining years of working life the contributor was 'precluded from regular employment by responsibilities at home'.[294] The additional pension is based on the surplus of earnings factors above the minimum qualifying factor for each tax year.[295] It should be observed, however, that entitlement to the additional pension is not conditional on satisfying the contribution requirements for the basic pension; thus someone without title to the basic pension because, for example, their contribution record was not sufficient over the relevant proportion of the working life will still receive the additional pension based on those years when they did achieve a surplus of earnings factors.

C Credits

The system of crediting contributions is designed to assist those who are already established in the scheme but, for reasons beyond their control, have been unable to continue to make the requisite payments, sufficient to satisfy the second condition.[296] To the extent that crediting is permitted, the beneficiaries are being subsidised by other contributors and for this reason it has been said both that there must be 'real and substantial justification' for the granting of the facility,[297] and that the beneficiary must show a significant degree of participation in the scheme during non-credited periods.[298] It is for the latter reason that married women who have elected for reduced liability[299] generally cannot be credited with Class 1 contributions.[300] With this exception, there are the following main categories of contributors entitled to credits: those unemployed or otherwise incapable of work; those receiving certain tax credits; those receiving statutory

---

292 SSCBA 1992, paras 1(3)(b) (jobseeker's allowance), 2(3)(b) (short-term incapacity benefit). For bereavement payment the earnings factor must be equivalent to at least 25 times the lower earnings limit for the relevant year, which may be any tax year before the benefit year: para 4(3).
293 SSCBA 1992, para 5(3).
294 SSCBA 1992, para 5(7). On home responsibilities protection, see pp 603–604, below.
295 SSCBA 1992, ss 44(3)(b), 45(1). See generally pp 615–620, below.
296 SI 1975/556, reg 3. A credited Class 1 contribution is equivalent to a payment at the lower earnings limit then current.
297 NIAC *Report on Credits for Approved Training Courses* (1953, Cmd 8860) paras 17–18. See also *NIAC* n 280, above.
298 Mr S Orme MP, Minister for Social Security, 928 HC Official Report (5th series) cols 1475–1476.
299 See pp 118–119, above.
300 SI 1978/409, reg 2(2); see SI 1975/556, passim.

maternity pay; those caring full-time for disabled people; those approaching retirement; widows and widowers in certain circumstances; those on jury service; victims of miscarriages of justice; new entrants (for very limited purposes); and those engaged in full-time education or training.[301] In each case the credit is in respect of Class 1 contributions, with the exception of new entrants. The important area of home responsibilities protection is considered separately in the context of pensions entitlement.[302]

i Unemployed or incapable of work

A Class 1 credit is available in respect of each week of unemployment or incapacity for work. An unemployed person qualifies for a credit equivalent to a contribution based on earnings at the lower earnings limit for any whole week for which he or she receives jobseeker's allowance.[303] A person also qualifies for an equivalent credit for any complete week in which they were incapable of work (or would have been had they claimed short-term incapacity benefit or maternity allowance in time) or receiving statutory sick pay.[304] However, claimants of short-term incapacity benefit can only take advantage of these credit facilities if they:[305]

(1) actually paid contributions amounting to an earnings factor of at least 25 times the lower earnings limit in one of the last two tax years before the beginning of the relevant benefit year; or

(2) received the higher rate of short-term incapacity benefit, long-term incapacity benefit or carer's allowance at some time in the last year before the relevant benefit year (or would have done but for the operation of the overlapping benefit rules[306]); or

(3) claimed short-term incapacity benefit, disabled person's tax credit, jobseeker's allowance or maternity allowance in that year and would have met the contribution conditions for short-term incapacity benefit at that time; or

(4) they were credited with contributions for approved training; or

(5) they received statutory sick pay but would have qualified for short-term incapacity benefit had they claimed it.

ii Receipt of tax credits

A person in receipt of working families' tax credit or disabled person's tax credit[307] is entitled to receive credits for any week (other than one in which he or she received credits in respect of unemployment or incapacity) in which he or she is employed either as an employed earner with earnings below the lower earnings limit or as a self-employed earner with earnings below the Class 2 contribution threshold.[308]

---

301 See generally SI 1975/556, regs 7–9C. Credits for women returning to work after the termination of their marriage were withdrawn by SI 1989/893 (see the 4th edition of this book, p 69).
302 Pp 603–604, below.
303 SI 1975/556, reg 8A(1) and (2)(a). Special provision is made to enable persons to apply for credits where jobseeker's allowance is not in payment but they meet the criteria for eligibility, subject to certain exceptions: reg 8A(2)(b) and (3). Note also the inclusion in reg 8A(4) and the exceptions in reg 8A(5).
304 SI 1975/556, reg 8B. Credits based on incapacity must be claimed in writing before the end of the benefit year following the one in which the period of incapacity falls: reg 8(4).
305 SI 1975/556, reg 9.
306 See pp 259–261, below.
307 Pp 398–404, below.
308 SI 1975/556, regs 7B and 7C.

iii Receipt of statutory maternity pay

A woman receiving statutory maternity pay is entitled to credits for each week of receipt.[309]

iv Receipt of carer's allowance

As will be seen,[310] carer's allowance is intended for those who care for a disabled person but who otherwise would be in full-time employment. Their position is therefore similar to that of the unemployed or incapable and they are granted credits for each week for which they are paid the allowance.[311]

v Men approaching retirement

Contributions may be credited for the tax year in which a man reaches 60 and for the four subsequent tax years, sufficient to make the year in question a 'reckonable year' for the purposes of entitlement, without the condition of being either incapable of work or having registered for employment.[312] The aim is to encourage early retirement without adding to the number of registered unemployed. There is, however, a condition that the individual be present in Great Britain for six months of the tax year in question.[313]

vi Widows and widowers

A person who has previously received one of the bereavement benefits will be credited, for every year up to and including that in which entitlement ceased, with such earnings as are necessary to satisfy the second contribution condition for short-term incapacity benefit or contribution-based jobseeker's allowance.[314]

vii Jury service

Credits may be granted for any week part of which has been spent on jury service.[315]

---

309 SI 1975/556, reg 9C. In practice this will only be important if statutory maternity pay is paid below the current lower earnings limit.
310 Pp 707–712, below.
311 SI 1975/556, reg 7A. Widows or widowers who would have been paid the allowance but for the overlapping benefit rules are also entitled to the credit.
312 SI 1975/556, reg 9A. Women are neither entitled nor required to pay contributions once they reach 60: for the equal treatment implications, see p 47, above.
313 SI 1975/556, reg 9A(5).
314 SI 1975/556, reg 8C. This assumes benefit has not been stopped because of remarriage or cohabitation. Widows (but not widowers) are deemed to satisfy the first contribution condition for short-term incapacity benefit (SI 1974/2010, reg 3(1)(a)); the equivalent concession for unemployment benefit was lost with the transition to jobseeker's allowance. See further p 581, below, and the 4th edition of this book, p 70.
315 SI 1975/556, reg 9B (excluding self-employed earners). The public interest in serving on juries is recognised elsewhere in the benefits system; see eg SI 1987/1967, Sch 1B, para 19 as regards entitlement to income support.

viii   Victims of miscarriage of justice

Prisoners who have had their convictions quashed by the Crown Court, Court of Appeal or the High Court of Justiciary are entitled to be credited with earnings to ensure they have a full contributions record covering the period of their imprisonment.[316] This concession, granted in 2001, was in response to a campaign by supporters of the Birmingham Six, following the realisation that the released men had inadequate contribution records for long-term insurance benefits.[317]

ix   Starting credits

Individuals begin contributing to the scheme at different ages, according to their circumstances. Some will commence employment on reaching the school-leaving age of 16; others will remain in full-time education for several more years. At whatever time the entry is made, it will rarely coincide with the tax year (the base period of contribution conditions) and unless concessions are made a substantial number of payments will have no insurance significance. The system of credits has traditionally attempted to maintain equity between these various categories of entrants.[318] However, the facility for the purpose of claims to the short-term benefits was withdrawn in 1988[319] and all that remains is a small concession for someone claiming a retirement pension or one of the bereavement benefits. Such a person is entitled to the number of Class 3 credits required to bring the relevant earnings factor up to a reckonable year for the first three years of possible employment, namely the tax year during which he or she reached the age of 16 and the two following tax years.[320]

x   Education and training

The next set of rules makes concessions for those who start contributing late, or interrupt their contribution record, because they are engaged in education or training. It is not, however, thought appropriate that all persons engaged in education or training courses at whatever age and for whatever purpose should be subsidised by the fund.[321]

A   COURSE BEGUN BEFORE AGE 21

In this case, the policy is an ungenerous one: it is simply to grant credits for the year in which full-time education, apprenticeship or a training course approved by the Secretary of State ended. The effect is that the year may be constituted a reckonable year for the purposes of entitlement to contribution-based jobseeker's allowance or short-term incapacity benefit.[322]

---

316   SI 1975/556, reg 9D.
317   The Birmingham Six were wrongfully convicted in 1975 of involvement in the IRA bombing campaign of the previous year. They were finally released in 1991.
318   This provides little support to those who leave school at 16 and remain unemployed for several years.
319   SI 1975/556, reg 5, revoked by SI 1988/1230.
320   SI 1975/556, reg 4(1).
321   See *NIAC* n 297, above.
322   SI 1975/556, reg 8.

B   INTERRUPTIONS FOR APPROVED TRAINING COURSES

Clearly, it is felt desirable to encourage individuals to improve their capacity for a job or equip themselves with the necessary skills for a new one. This form of vocational training, it may be argued, is in the national interest, and therefore justifies some form of subsidy from the National Insurance Fund.[323] Thus the regulations prescribe that a contributor shall be granted credits for each week during any part of which he or she was engaged in a course of full-time training approved by the Secretary of State,[324] provided that all of the following conditions are satisfied:

(1)   the course is either a course of full-time training, or, in the case of a disabled person within the meaning of the Disabled Persons (Employment) Act 1944, a course involving attendance for not less than 15 hours per week, or a course of introductory training for one of the above;[325]

(2)   the course was not intended to last for more than 12 months;[326] and

(3)   the contributor had attained the age of 18 before the beginning of the tax year in which the week in question began.

D   Other assistance in satisfying contribution conditions

i   Aggregation of contributions by new entrants

The credit facilities available to new entrants serve to assist them only in satisfying the second of the two contribution conditions. The fortuitous timing of their entry in relation to the relevant tax years may constitute an obstacle to the fulfilment of the first condition. The legislation makes a further concession for entitlement to bereavement payment (the equivalent facility for claimants to other short-term benefits was abrogated in 1988). This applies where the last complete tax year, before the beginning of the year in which occurred the event for which benefit is claimed, was either the year in which the claimant's late spouse first became liable for contributions of Classes 1 or 2, or the year preceding that year. In such a case the claimant may, for the purposes of satisfying the first contribution condition for bereavement payment, aggregate the contributions actually paid, and that aggregate is then treated as having been paid in the last complete year.[327]

ii   Widows deemed to satisfy first condition

Widows joining, or rejoining, the scheme once their entitlement to widowed mother's allowance has expired are faced with a similar problem, and for the purposes of entitlement to short-term incapacity benefit or maternity allowance, they are deemed to have satisfied the first contribution condition.[328]

---

323   See *NIAC* n 297, above, paras 20–21.
324   SI 1975/556, reg 7.
325   SI 1975/556, reg 7(2)(a). This regulation appears not to have been amended to take account of the Disability Discrimination Act 1995, which repealed the Disabled Persons (Employment) Act 1944, s 1 (which in turn defines a 'disabled person').
326   Although it involved training of a disabled person under the Disabled Persons (Employment) Act 1944, it may be permitted for 'such longer period as is reasonable in the circumstances': SI 1975/556, reg 7(2)(b).
327   SSCBA 1992, Sch 3, para 7(1)–(4).
328   SI 1974/2010, reg 3(1)(a). This concession appears not to have been extended to widowers.

iii   Incapacity pensioners

The first condition for a widowed parent's allowance, a bereavement allowance, or a retirement pension (Categories A and B) is deemed to be satisfied if the relevant contributor was entitled to long-term incapacity benefit at any time during the year in which he or she reached pensionable age or died, or the year preceding that year.[329]

iv   Spouse's contributions and retirement pensions

As will be seen in chapter 17, a woman who is, or has been, married or a widower may rely on the spouse's contributions for the purposes of a Category B retirement pension;[330] where a marriage has been terminated by death or divorce, a similar facility is available for the purposes of a Category A pension.[331]

v   Industrial accidents and diseases

When the short-term benefit for those rendered incapable of work by an industrial accident or disease was abolished in 1983, it was necessary to provide financial support if the individual was not entitled to statutory sick pay or could not satisfy the contribution conditions for sickness benefit.[332] In such a case, the latter conditions were deemed to be satisfied, at least until this provision was repealed with the enactment of the incapacity benefit reforms.[333] However, a similar facility has been retained for the widow of someone who has died as the result of an industrial accident or disease.[334]

E   Partial satisfaction of contribution conditions

Too rigid an application of the contribution conditions, particularly the second, would lead to an 'all or nothing' result. In consequence, the legislation provides for a reduced rate of long-term benefits[335] where the second contribution condition has been only partially satisfied. Thus the basic pension is calculated according to the proportion of qualifying years (ie years in which the qualifying earnings factor has been achieved) to the number of years prescribed for the benefit in question.[336] Increases for adult dependants are subject to the same reduction but increases for child dependants are payable in full. However, if the percentage is less than 25 per cent, neither the basic pension nor the increase for the dependant (adult or child) is payable. For contributors

---

329   SSCBA 1992, Sch 3, para 5(6).
330   Pp 606–609, below.
331   Pp 605–606, below. For assistance granted to widows and widowers in relation to long-term incapacity benefit, see p 581, below.
332   P 535, below.
333   Social Security (Incapacity for Work) Act 1994, s 11(2) and Sch 2 repealed SSCBA 1992, s 102.
334   SSCBA 1992, s 60(2), (3), (8). This was introduced following the abolition of industrial death benefit in 1988.
335   Categories A and B retirement pensions, widowed parent's allowance, bereavement allowance, widowed mother's allowance and widow's pension.
336   SSCBA 1992, s 60, and SI 1979/642, reg 6. Entitlement to any additional, earnings-related pension is unaffected.

who have a ratio of just less than 25 per cent, this may well be a situation in which the payment of voluntary contributions is highly cost effective.[337]

Analogous provisions used to be available for the purposes of entitlement to short-term benefits but these were abolished in 1986.[338] The argument was that the administrative costs were disproportionately high relative to the small sums that were paid out to beneficiaries.[339]

---

337   CPAG *Welfare benefits handbook 2002/2003* (4th edn, 2002) p 794.
338   SSA 1986, s 42.
339   See Mr T Newton MP, Standing Committee B Debates on the 1986 Bill, col 1498.

Chapter 5

Administration of benefits

This chapter deals with some aspects of the administration of social security benefits. The government department principally responsible for policymaking is the Department for Work and Pensions (DWP), although the Treasury necessarily also has a key role in policymaking in this area.[1] The DWP was formed in June 2001 from parts of the former Department of Social Security (DSS), parts of the former Department for Education and Employment (DfEE) and the Employment Service (ES).[2] The administration of benefits under the DWP umbrella is carried out by several executive agencies (the largest being Jobcentre Plus and the Pension Service). Their respective roles and organisation are briefly described in Part 1 of the chapter. Part 2 considers the role of the Treasury and the Inland Revenue. The standing advisory bodies which have always been a feature of the social security schemes, ensuring some degree of non-official participation in policy formulation, are then discussed in Part 3. The largest section of this chapter (Part 4) is concerned with the rules relating to claims for and payment of benefits. Sometimes benefit is overpaid by the Department, perhaps through its own carelessness or perhaps because the claimant (whether deliberately or otherwise) has misrepresented or failed to disclose some pertinent facts. The rules about recovery of overpayments and prosecutions for fraud and other offences are dealt with in Part 5 of the chapter.

Part 1   The Department for Work and Pensions

Since 8 June 2001 the DWP has been responsible for social security benefits. Between 1988 and 2001 this area was the responsibility of the DSS. From 1968 to 1988 the administration of the benefit system was the responsibility of the Secretary of State for Social Services, who presided over the combined Department of Health and Social Security (DHSS). The survey of the Department's history and organisation here is

---

1   This was enhanced by the transfer of the Contributions Agency and responsibility for working families' tax credits to the Inland Revenue in 1999.
2   The Secretary of State for Work and Pensions has been constituted as a corporation sole: SI 2002/1397.

necessarily brief; a fuller treatment will be found in books on the machinery of government and social administration.[3]

A History

Before the reforms of 1946 heralded by the Beveridge Report,[4] the administration of social security benefits was undertaken in a number of different departments. The only ministry with sole responsibility for a benefit was the Ministry of Pensions, which had been set up in 1916, and was responsible for the award of war pensions for death or disability suffered in the First and Second World Wars.[5] Administration of health insurance (the precursor of sickness benefit) and contributory pensions was shared by the Ministry of Health and the Approved Societies.[6] The Ministry of Labour was responsible for contributory unemployment insurance, which was paid at its labour exchanges. The administration of non-contributory old age pensions paid under the Old Age Pensions Act 1908 was rather anomalously in the hands of the Commissioners of Customs and Excise.[7]

Beveridge proposed the creation of a Ministry of Social Security under a minister with a seat in the Cabinet. It would have been responsible for both social insurance and means-tested national assistance previously administered by an Assistance Board.[8] The Report also urged consideration of an eventual merger of the new Ministry and the Ministry of Pensions.[9] The wartime government accepted these proposals only in part. The suggestion of a Ministry of Social Security, responsible for all welfare benefits, was rejected. Insurance and other universal benefits, such as family allowances, were to be the responsibility of a new ministry, but public assistance was to be administered separately by the National Assistance Board. The new Ministry of National Insurance was instituted by the 1944 Act of that name and became responsible for the administration of family allowances, benefits payable under the National Insurance Act 1946, and industrial injuries benefits.[10] However, unemployment benefit was paid at offices of the Ministry of Labour, and, from 1970, of the Department of Employment. A central office was set up in Newcastle to keep insurance records and superintend the administration and payment of long-term benefits and family allowances.[11] In line with the Beveridge proposals, the ministry worked through regional and local offices.[12]

There was no move at this time to take further Beveridge's suggestion that there might be a merger of the new Ministry of National Insurance and the older Ministry of Pensions. Such a step would have been bitterly resented by the servicemen's organisations and would have run counter to the popular sentiment that war pensioners

3 See eg Willson *The Organisation of British Central Government, 1914–1964* (1967) pp 143–174; Brown *The Management of Welfare* (1975), esp chs 3–5.
4 Beveridge Report *Social Insurance and Allied Services* (1942, Cmd 6404).
5 See ch 21, below, for the history of war pensions.
6 See ch 15, below, for the history of sickness benefit. The role of the Approved Societies in the administration of health insurance is discussed by Gilbert *The Evolution of National Insurance in Great Britain* (1966), esp pp 423–428.
7 See ch 17 (History of retirement pensions) p 590, below.
8 Millett *The Unemployment Assistance Board* (1940).
9 *Beveridge Report* n 4 above, paras 385–387.
10 Workmen's compensation had been subject to the general control of the Home Office: see *Willson* n 3 above, p 145.
11 1st Report of the Ministry of National Insurance (1949, Cmd 7955) paras 19 and 64–80.
12 1st Report of the Ministry of National Insurance (1949, Cmd 7955) paras 81–96.

should have separate and privileged treatment. However, by the early 1950s there was a steady decline of war pensions awarded,[13] and despite fierce opposition the two ministries were merged in 1953.[14]

For the next 12 years there were relatively few changes in the structure of the new ministry.[15] The next fundamental reform came in 1966, when at last Beveridge's wish for an integrated Ministry of Social Security was fulfilled. The Ministry of Social Security Act 1966 had the effect of merging the administration of insurance and means-tested benefits and hence abolished the National Assistance Board. It was considered desirable both from the perspective of policy co-ordination and from the claimants' point of view to have an integrated ministry. But within it there was a separate body, the Supplementary Benefits Commission, with responsibilities for the formulation of policy on means-tested benefits. Two years later the government took the further step of integrating the Ministries of Health and of Social Security into the DHSS. The title of Secretary of State for Social Services emphasised the role of the minister responsible for this mega-department as co-ordinator of the whole range of social services.[16]

In 1980 the Supplementary Benefits Commission was abolished and the DHSS assumed total responsibility for policymaking and the administration of means-tested benefits. The Commission had been given a measure of independence by the Labour government; in 1975 it had been asked to submit a separate annual report, in which it could indicate priorities in policy development. With many members experienced in social services work, it was able to criticise government policy from an informed position.[17] The Conservative government, perhaps discomforted by these criticisms, took the view that there was no place for the Commission when the supplementary benefits scheme was radically reformed in 1980; its advisory role is now performed by the Social Security Advisory Committee, discussed in Part 3, below. There was some criticism of the size of the DHSS in the following years, and in 1988 the government separated the departments responsible for health and for social security.[18] Meanwhile, the agency arrangement with the Department of Employment, under which the ES ran the JobCentre network, survived the transformation of unemployment benefit into jobseeker's allowance and the merger of the Departments of Education and Employment to create the DfEE in 1995.[19] In 1999 responsibility for National Insurance contributions and for working families' tax credit and disabled person's tax credit, which replaced family credit and disability working allowance respectively, was transferred from the DSS to the Treasury and the Inland Revenue. This necessitated relatively little structural change, as the relevant DSS offices were effectively transferred wholesale. In 2001, however, a much more ambitious restructuring of the DSS/DWP was initiated. In particular, the Jobcentre Plus agency was established, with a view to integrating the services provided by the Benefits Agency (BA) and the ES to provide a single point of contact for claimants of working age. As part of the same package of institutional changes, the DWP's pensions operations were brought together under the Pension

---

13   28th Report of the Ministry of Pensions (1952–53 HC 271) paras 116–120.

14   517 HC Official Report (5th series) col 267: the Address was only carried by 226-212 votes.

15   For the definitive account of the structure and work of the ministry, see King *The Ministry of Pensions and National Insurance* (1958). (Sir Geoffrey King had been a Permanent Secretary at the ministry.)

16   Mr R Crossman MP, Secretary of State, 770 HC Official Report (5th series) col 1609ff.

17   The work of the Commission is discussed by its chairman from 1975–80, David Donnison, in his book, *The Politics of Poverty* (1982). See also Donnison (1976) 5 J Soc Pol 337.

18   See SI 1988/1843 and Nairne (1983) 54 Political Q 243.

19   See Jones (1996) 24 *Policy and Politics* 137. In 2001 the DfEE became the Department for Education and Skills (DfES) as part of the 2001 restructuring of central government departments. On the history of the ES, see Price *Office of Hope* (2000).

Service with effect from 2002. Meanwhile, in April 2000 the National Asylum Support Service (NASS), part of the Home Office, assumed responsibility for accommodation and support for asylum seekers.

B The structure and organisation of the DWP[20]

i The Next Steps philosophy

In the late 1980s the Conservative government instituted a radical transformation of Britain's civil service. The main feature of the so-called 'Next Steps' initiative[21] has been the transfer of some government functions to agencies, headed by chief executives (often drawn from outside the civil service), which enter into agreements with central government to achieve certain targets. The stated aim of this strategy is to deliver public services more efficiently and effectively by encouraging managerial initiative and greater responsiveness to consumer demand at all levels. These changes have been especially prominent in the field of social security. The great majority of the DWP's executive operations are now performed by three agencies (Jobcentre Plus, the Pension Service and the Child Support Agency) which employ the great majority of departmental staff. The organisation of these agencies will be considered after discussing the remaining core functions of the DWP.[22]

ii Department headquarters

The Secretary of State for Work and Pensions, a Cabinet minister, is assisted at the political level by two Ministers of State, a Minister for Work and a Minister for Pensions, and three Parliamentary Under-Secretaries. At the top of the civil service structure is the Permanent Secretary. Most headquarters' work is concerned with policy formulation or resource allocation and is discharged by about 1,000 staff, a small fraction of the total of 83,000 civil servants engaged in social security work.

iii Jobcentre Plus

Jobcentre Plus was established in some areas in 2001, with a national network following in the next year. The organisation has been created from a merger of those parts of the BA local offices[23] which dealt with people of working age with the ES's JobCentres. The successful integration of these two public services represents a major task, not least given the different cultures prevalent in each organisation previously.[24] Mr J Griffiths, then Minister of National Insurance, said when introducing the 1946 Bill, that local offices should be 'centres where people will not be afraid to go, where they will be welcome,

---

20 See generally DWP *DWP Departmental Report* (2002, Cm 5424) pp 29–64.
21 Efficiency Unit *Improving Management in Government: The Next Steps* (1988). See Greer (1992) 63 Political Q 222.
22 This information may be updated by reference to the government's annual expenditure plans, published on a departmental basis.
23 The BA, launched in April 1991, was by far the largest of the former DSS's agencies, employing 80 per cent of departmental staff to administer social security payments.
24 The Social Security Advisory Committee (SSAC) has observed that the ES is 'outcome-driven' while the BA is 'rules-driven': SSAC *Fourteenth Report* (2001) para 3.7. On local office work in the BA, see Baldwin, Wikeley and Young *Judging Social Security* (1992) ch 2.

and where they will not only get benefits, but advice'.[25] In the 1970s and 1980s there was concern about the difficulties caused by rapid staff turnover in DSS offices. This particularly affected the administration of supplementary benefits, where there was so much personal contact between applicants and the Department's staff, and led to frequent complaints, particularly in London, about the delay in processing claims.[26] A DSS report in 1988[27] recommended that work which did not require face-to-face contact with the public should be relocated from the most hard-pressed London local offices to Benefit Centres outside the capital. As a result, the work of 21 London offices was relocated to Belfast, Glasgow and Ashton-in-Makerfield.

iv   Other agencies

There are three other DWP agencies. The first of these, and the largest, is the Pension Service, with a network of offices being established during 2002 and 2003. This brings together, on a more centralised basis, the pensions operations previously administered by the BA. The second is the Child Support Agency, launched in April 1993, which administers the child support scheme. Thirdly, the Appeals Service Agency, established following the Social Security Act 1998 (SSA 1998), provides the administrative support for appeal tribunals. Two of the original DSS agencies are no longer part of the DWP. The Information Services Technology Agency (ITSA) was established in April 1990 to oversee the execution of the Operational Strategy, the massive programme of computerisation within the DSS.[28] In 2000 its functions were contracted out to the private sector.[29] The War Pensions Agency, which was hived off from the BA in April 1993, was itself subsequently transferred to the Ministry of Defence in 2001.[30]

v   Other agency arrangements

Housing benefit and council tax benefit are administered by local authorities, with a proportion of the cost met by grants from central government. The relocation of some London benefits work to Belfast means that the DHSS (Northern Ireland) also acts as an agent for the DWP.

Part 2   The Treasury and the Inland Revenue

The Treasury has had an important role in the field of social security since the inception of the welfare state.[31] This is inevitable given that the DWP budget is by far the largest

---

25   418 HC Official Report (5th series) col 1754.
26   Cf SSAC *Second Report 1982–83* (1983) pp 64–73 and *Sixth Report 1988* (1988) pp 34–43. See also National Audit Office *DHSS: Quality of Service to the Public at Local Offices* (1987–88, HC 451). These concerns led indirectly to the proceedings for judicial review in *R v Secretary of State of Social Services, ex p Child Poverty Action Group* [1989] 1 All ER 1047: see p 183, below.
27   DSS *The Business of Service* ('the Moodie Report') (1988).
28   See Margetts (1991) 69 Public Administration 325.
29   DSS *Social Security Departmental Report* (2000, Cm 4614) pp 62–66.
30   SI 2001/3506.
31   This much is evident from any number of political biographies; see eg Lawson *The view from no. 11* (1993). The introduction of winter fuel payments is a recent example: p 493, below.

of any single government department. The Inland Revenue's role has traditionally been much narrower, although it has for many years acted as agent for the DSS in collecting National Insurance contributions, typically via PAYE. The profile of the Treasury and the Inland Revenue assumed much greater prominence as a result of two legislative developments in 1999, which reflected the government's ambitions both to modernise government and reconfigure the tax and benefit systems.

A   Social Security Contributions (Transfer of Functions) Act 1999

The Social Security Contributions (Transfer of Functions) Act 1999 (SSC(TF)A 1999) transferred the Contributions Agency from the then DSS to the Inland Revenue.[32] The Contributions Agency, set up within the DSS in April 1991, is responsible for the administration of the National Insurance scheme. About half its 7,000 staff are employed at the Newcastle office, which holds centralised contribution records on all members of the insured population. The remainder work in local offices on collection and enforcement duties. The Agency also has operational responsibility for statutory sick pay, statutory maternity pay and contracting-out of SERPS. The prime rationale for the transfer was that it would 'reduce the burdens on businesses and individuals as they can sort out taxes and contributions through a single organisation'.[33] As well as operational functions,[34] the 1999 Act also transferred policy responsibility for contributions to the Treasury or Inland Revenue as appropriate.[35] Essentially regulation-making powers affecting substantive issues such as the existence or size of contributions liabilities were vested in the Treasury, whilst those concerned with administrative matters were transferred to the Board of the Inland Revenue. The new arrangements place a premium on 'joined up government' as the DWP retains a role in certain areas. Thus where a regulation-making power affects the operation of the contributory benefits system, it remains the responsibility of the DWP.[36] Similarly policy responsibility (and hence the prime powers to promulgate secondary legislation) for statutory sick pay, statutory maternity pay and contracted-out pension schemes remains with the DWP. In such cases provision is made for the regulations to be made by the Inland Revenue or the Treasury with the concurrence of the Secretary of State or vice versa.[37] Although the legislation did not change the structure or yield of contributions in any way, the transfer clearly facilitates the further gradual alignment of the tax and National Insurance contributions rules.

B   Tax Credits Act 1999

The transfer of contributions work from the then DSS to the Inland Revenue can be characterised as an essentially bureaucratic reform designed to increase efficiency. The Tax Credits Act 1999 (TCA 1999) was much more radical in that it moved the Inland Revenue directly into the business of assessing entitlement to and paying out social

---

32   Primary legislation was required as the Inland Revenue is not formally a government department, and so it was not possible to effect a simple transfer by way of an Order in Council under the Ministers of the Crown Act 1975.

33   Per Baroness Hollis of Heigham, 595 HL Official Report (5th Series) col 1038.

34   SSC(TF)A 1999, s 1 and Schs 1 and 2.

35   SSC(TF)A 1999, s 3 and Sch 3.

36   SSC(TF)A 1999, Sch 3, para 19(3).

37   SSC(TF)A 1999, Sch 3, para 2.

security benefits (initially only family credit and disability working allowance).[38] They were thus transformed from cash benefits, paid out by the BA, into tax credits payable by the employer under the auspices of the Inland Revenue. Thus the centralised Family Credit Unit at Preston was transferred from the BA to the Inland Revenue in October 1999. Following the precedent of the transfer of responsibilities for contributions matters, powers relating to the eligibility rules and amounts of the tax credits were transferred to the Treasury whilst the Inland Revenue and its officers took over operational functions, including decision making powers in individual cases.[39] The Tax Credits Act 2002 further increased the involvement of the Treasury and Inland Revenue in the field of social protection. The Inland Revenue assumed responsibility from the DWP for the administration of child benefit, as well as taking on the new child tax credit and working tax credit.

Part 3   Standing advisory bodies[40]

Government departments have often made use of advisory bodies in the administration of the various social security schemes, the first of these committees being set up soon after the end of the First World War for war pensions.[41] Advisory bodies may be either national organisations or local committees. To a large extent their functions will differ according to this categorisation. Central advisory bodies will tend to be employed to give advice on matters of general policy, and to comment on the drafting of regulations made by the Secretary of State in the exercise of powers delegated by statute. They are not suited to handling complaints from claimants, or to dealing with detailed questions concerning the administration of benefits. On the other hand, local bodies, which now exist only for war pensions, would be able to perform these functions, though, of course, they may also be competent to give advice on broader questions.

A second general point concerns the attitude to be adopted by the advisory committees to the government department on the one hand, and to social security claimants on the other. The question is whether these committees regard themselves primarily as experts consulted to give disinterested advice on the formation of policy, or whether they see themselves as mainly concerned to 'represent' the public as consumers of welfare benefits. In the latter case, there will inevitably be some tensions between the Department and its advisory committee. In its Report for 1997 the Social Security Advisory Committee (SSAC) itself stated 'we are emphatically not a mouthpiece of any pressure group. Equally, however, we are not apologists for Government policy'.[42] Perhaps inevitably during a period when successive governments have been anxious not to increase social security expenditure, the Committee has tended to be critical of its proposals, drawing attention to any resulting hardship, and examining them in the context of other changes.[43] Indeed, one member of the SSAC has argued that whilst advisory bodies may be influential in terms of both distributional equity and procedural justice in times of expansion, their role will be significantly reduced as regards the former in periods of restraint.[44]

---

38   See ch 10, below.
39   TCA 1999, s 2 and Sch 2.
40   This discussion does not cover the work of the Royal Commissions and ad hoc departmental committees, which have also obviously played an important part in the development of social security law and policy.
41   War Pensions Act 1921: see pp 142–143, below.
42   SSAC *Eleventh Report 1997* (1997) p 5.
43   See eg SSAC *Ninth Report 1993* (1993) pp 42–58.
44   Ogus (1998) 5 JSSL 156.

In the last quarter of the twentieth century governments generally appeared not to be well-disposed to advisory committees. Not only was the role of the SSAC reduced, as discussed later, but the local social security advisory committees which used to advise DHSS office managers were abolished in 1971.[45] Subsequent suggestions for the institution of local user consultative committees were not taken up by the government.[46] However, the introduction of agencies within the DSS, combined with the launch of the Citizen's Charter, started to raise the profile of service quality, albeit that this was seen very much in terms of the individual.[47] In more recent years there has been a greater readiness by the Department at national level to consult with representative organisations and an Annual Benefits Forum has been established.[48] At a local level, all the Department's offices have a Customer Service Manager and dissatisfied complainants can take their grievance to an Independent Complaints Panel.

A The Social Security Advisory Committee[49]

i Composition of the Social Security Advisory Committee

This Committee was set up in 1980 to assume the functions previously performed by the National Insurance Advisory Committee (NIAC)[50] and (as has already been mentioned) the Supplementary Benefits Commission.[51] The SSAC consists of a chairman, currently Sir Thomas Boyd-Carpenter KBE, and between 10 and 13 other members.[52] One member is to be appointed after consultation with employers' organisations, one after consultation with the TUC and a third after consultation with the head of the Northern Ireland Health and Social Services Department. In addition, the SSAC must include 'at least one person with experience of work among, and of the needs of, the chronically sick and disabled', and in selecting a member regard is to be had to the desirability of having a sick or disabled person on the Committee.[53] It is also customary for two members to be appointed following consultation with the Secretaries of State for Scotland and for Wales respectively.[54] In practice there is also a member from an ethnic minority community.

ii Role and powers of the Social Security Advisory Committee

The Committee's task is to give advice to the Secretary of State on social security matters, but excluding industrial injuries benefits, war pensions and occupational pensions for which there are separate advisory bodies. There are some further specific exceptions; these include up-rating regulations.[55] Thus it is a body which is able to look at the structure of social security benefits and consider the relationship between

---

45 SSA 1971, s 9. See the 2nd edition of this book, pp 551–552.
46 See the 4th edition of this book, p 624.
47 P 143, below.
48 This provides an opportunity for ministers and senior managers to meet 'customer' representatives.
49 See Logie (1989) 23 Soc Pol & Admin 248; Bett (1994) 1 JSSL 105; and Ogus (1998) 5 JSSL 156. The SSAC website address is www.ssac.org.uk.
50 On the work of NIAC, see the 1st edition of this book, pp 580–583.
51 SSA 1980, s 9.
52 Social Security Administration Act 1992, Sch 5 (SSAA 1992).
53 These provisions closely follow those which governed the composition of NIAC.
54 As social security has not been devolved to either the Scottish Parliament or the Welsh Assembly, this practice has continued.
55 SSAA 1992, Sch 7, Pt I.

them. Under this wide rubric, it is possible to identify four more precise functions discharged by the Committee. First, it must advise the Secretary of State on any general questions concerning the working of the relevant social security legislation referred to it;[56] under this provision it has been asked, for example, to review the time-limits for claiming benefits. Secondly, it may give its views on proposals by the Department, whether it is specifically invited to comment on them or not.[57] The third function is perhaps potentially the most interesting and important. The SSAC is empowered to give the government advice on its own initiative, a role never enjoyed by NIAC, but frequently performed by the Supplementary Benefits Commission.[58] A prime example is the SSAC's work in elucidating the appropriate principles underlying the level of transitional protection at times of change in benefit provision.[59] In the broad exercise of this power the SSAC has also commissioned a number of research reports.[60] Whilst valuable in themselves, such reports are published irregularly (reflecting reductions in the Committee's research budget) and do not command a high profile.

The fourth function of the SSAC – and arguably the most time consuming – is its mandatory role in being consulted on regulations, a role it believes to be unique in UK government.[61] Proposals for regulations, 'in the form of draft regulations or otherwise', must be sent to the Committee for it to comment on, unless it appears to the Secretary of State 'that by reason of the urgency of the matter it is inexpedient so to refer' them.[62] Regulations need not be referred where the Committee itself has agreed to this:[63] this might cover technical amendments that raise no issue of principle. SSA 1986 weakened the obligations to consult the SSAC (and the Industrial Injuries Advisory Council and the Occupational Pensions Board) in two respects. First, any regulations made within a period of six months from the commencement date of the relevant enabling provision are exempted from the consultation requirements.[64] Secondly, even after referring draft regulations to the relevant body, the Secretary of State may make the definitive version before receiving its report or advice, if this course appears appropriate because of the urgency of the matter.[65] (But a subsequent report of the SSAC or the Board must be laid before the Houses of Parliament, with a statement of how far the government proposes to give effect to its recommendations.[66]) When the SSAC decides to take a formal reference on regulations, it almost always conducts a public consultation exercise before submitting its report, thereby giving an opportunity for members of the public and pressure groups to contribute to policy development. There is often a tension here between the government's timetable and the period required for adequate consultation.[67] The demands imposed by the sheer volume of this work can also detract from the fulfilment of the SSAC's other roles.[68] The Secretary of State is required to table the

---

56   SSAA 1992, s 170(3).
57   SSAA 1992, s 170(1)(a).
58   SSAA 1992, s 170(1)(a).
59   SSAC *Twelfth Report 1999* (1999) ch 4. See further Ogus (1999) 6 JSSL 111.
60   See eg Zarb (ed) *Social Security and Mental Health: Report on the SSAC Workshop* SSAC Research Paper 7 (1996).
61   SSAC *Eleventh Report 1997* (1997) p 2.
62   SSAA 1992, ss 172(1) and 173(1)(a).
63   SSAA 1992, s 173(1)(b).
64   This 'quarantine' period was 12 months for regulations made under SSA 1986, a rule that the government originally proposed should apply to all regulations. After critical representations by the SSAC, the period was reduced to six months for regulations made under later enactments: see SSAC *Fifth Report 1986/7* (1987) para 3.6.
65   SSAA 1992, s 173(3).
66   SSAA 1992, s 173(4).
67   *SSAC* n 64, above, paras 3.2–3.3. See also *Logie* n 49, above.
68   SSAC *Eleventh Report 1997* (1997) p iv.

SSAC report with the regulations and to explain, when appropriate, why the government has not followed its proposals.[69]

The duty to consult the SSAC and other advisory bodies is probably mandatory, so that a total failure to honour the obligation would mean that the regulations in question are void.[70] In *R v Secretary of State for Social Services, ex p Cotton*,[71] members of the Court of Appeal expressed a variety of views on whether the Secretary of State had discharged his duty when he referred proposals for changes to regulations in general terms, without a detailed draft. Only Sir John Donaldson MR was of the opinion that this was inadequate and that the SSAC was entitled to see precise proposals. In any case the Secretary of State has a broad discretion not to refer in cases of urgency, and it is unlikely that its exercise could be challenged successfully.[72] It is important that the consultation requirements not be weakened further, for the reports of the SSAC and the other advisory bodies are invaluable aids to the construction of the regulations, as Commissioners have frequently affirmed.[73]

The transfer of responsibility from the DSS to the Inland Revenue for National Insurance contributions, working families' tax credit and disabled person's tax credit has left the SSAC without a defined statutory role in these important areas. It is doubtful whether the informal consultation arrangements put in place between the SSAC and the Inland Revenue are an adequate substitute.[74] The House of Commons Social Security Committee recommended that the role of the SSAC should be extended to include child support matters, or a parallel advisory body be established, but this proposal was not taken up by government.[75]

B The Industrial Injuries Advisory Council[76]

The Industrial Injuries Advisory Council (IIAC) was set up by the 1946 legislation to act as an advisory body to the Minister of National Insurance on industrial injuries matters. It has always been a larger body than the NIAC or the Social Security Advisory Committee, and its procedure less formal. It consists of a chairman, currently Professor A Newman Taylor, and an unspecified number of other members to be determined, and appointed by, the Secretary of State.[77] After consultation with various outside

---

69 SSAA 1992, s 174(2).
70 This seems to have been accepted by counsel for the DHSS in *R v Secretary of State for Social Services, ex p Cotton* (1985) Times, 14 December. For another relevant authority, see *R v Secretary of State for Health, ex p United States Tobacco International Inc* [1992] 1 QB 353, [1992] 1 All ER 212. If the SSAC is misled by the Department's explanation of the proposed changes, the relevant amending regulations are not ultra vires: *CIB/4563/1998*.
71 (1985) Times, 14 December, CA.
72 But by analogy with case law concerning the Secretary of State's duty to consult local authority bodies in connection with changes to the housing benefit scheme, it would seem that the minister cannot create urgency by leaving a decision to the last moment: *R v Secretary of State for Social Security, ex p Association of Metropolitan Authorities* (1993) 25 HLR 131.
73 In *R(SB) 6/86*, J G Monroe, Comr, affirmed the view that SSAC reports (but not DHSS leaflets) could be used as an aid to construction. Also see *R(I) 2/85* and *R(I) 2/01* for the use of Industrial Injuries Advisory Council (IIAC) reports and p 748, below.
74 According to SSAC, 'whilst these are still early days these informal procedures have, in our opinion, worked well': *Thirteenth Report* (2000), para 1.24.
75 See HC Social Security Committee *The 1999 Child Support White Paper* (1998–99, HC 798) para 126 and DSS *Reply by the Government to the Tenth Report* (1999, Cm 4536) paras 73–75.
76 See Harrington (1994) 1 JSSL 70. For critiques, see Lewis *Compensation for Industrial Injury* (1987) pp 95–97 and Wikeley *Compensation for Industrial Disease* (1993) pp 85–90.
77 SSAA 1992, Sch 6, para 1.

organisations an equal number of members must be appointed to represent employers and employed earners respectively.[78] The Council must also include at least one person experienced in the needs of the chronically sick and disabled and, as with the SSAC, in choosing this person the desirability of having a disabled person as a member should be taken into account.[79] The difficult medical questions involved in determining whether there is a case for prescribing a disease as an 'industrial disease' under section 108 of the Social Security Contributions and Benefits Act 1992 (SSCBA 1992) are normally referred for examination to the Council's Research Working Group.[80] Its views are considered by the full Council, and then embodied in a report to the Secretary of State.

The Council has two functions under the legislation.[81] First, it considers draft regulations relating to industrial injuries referred to it by the Secretary of State.[82] He or she is under a duty to refer such regulations unless it appears inexpedient to do this because of urgency or the Council has agreed that this need not be done.[83] The Secretary of State is not required, as with reports of the SSAC and the Occupational Pensions Board, to lay before Parliament the Council's report, or to state why it is not proposed to follow its conclusions. IIAC publishes reports on regulations infrequently, and in general it would seem that its contribution in this context has not been particularly important.

The second function of the Council is to advise on general questions relating to industrial injuries benefits. It now has the power to give advice on subjects of its own choosing.[84] In fact the overwhelming majority of IIAC's work has been on the prescription of particular industrial diseases,[85] though it has also submitted general reports on time-limits and reform of compensation for industrial diseases.[86] There are some indications that the Council now plays a more active role, in eg gathering evidence that a disease should be prescribed.[87] None the less, the process of prescription remains painfully slow.[88] The Council began an overall review of the schedule of prescribed diseases in 1997, which was still under way in 2002.

C The Disability Living Allowance Advisory Board[89]

The Disability Living Allowance Advisory Board (DLAAB) was set up in 1991 as part of the programme of reforming disability benefits.[90] It is a purely advisory body, unlike its predecessor, the Attendance Allowance Board,[91] which rather unsatisfactorily

---

78   SSAA 1992, Sch 6, para 1(2). In practice there are four CBI and four TUC nominees, along with medical experts and other independent members.
79   Chronically Sick and Disabled Persons Act 1970, s 12.
80   See ch 20 on industrial injuries, pp 743–746, below.
81   See IIAC's *Annual Report* (2001), available on its website at www.iiac.org.uk.
82   SSAA 1992, s 172(2).
83   SSAA 1992, s 173(1). As with the SSAC, there are some exceptions: SSAA 1992,Sch 7, Pt II.
84   SSAA 1992, s 171(3) and (4).
85   Ie in giving advice to the Secretary of State under SSCBA 1992, s 108, although IIAC is not itself mentioned in that provision.
86   In 1952 (Cmd 8511) and 1981 (Cmnd 8393), discussed in ch 20, below.
87   *Lewis* n 76, above, p 96; and see also IIAC's irregular Periodic Reports.
88   Pp 743–746, below.
89   The Board's website (where its Annual Report is available) is at www.dlaab.org.uk.
90   Disability Living Allowance and Disability Working Allowance Act 1991, s 3; see now SSAA 1992, s 175.
91   See the 3rd edition of this book, pp 538–539.

combined advisory and adjudicatory functions. It consists of a chairman and between 11 and 20 other members appointed by the Secretary of State.[92] The members must include persons with professional knowledge or experience of physiotherapy, occupational therapy, social work, nursing disabled persons and medical practice.[93] A minimum of six members must themselves be persons with disabilities, and at least one member must have experience as a carer.[94]

The Board's three functions are to advise the Secretary of State on matters relating to disability living allowance and attendance allowance, to give advice on specific cases referred to it,[95] and to publish an annual report.[96] In exercising these functions the Board has a broad power to consult persons or bodies who are especially qualified.[97] However, it may only formally advise the Secretary of State 'on such matters as he may refer to them for consideration',[98] whereas both the SSAC and IIAC may take the initiative in offering advice. The Board's early years were not an unqualified success. Its first published discussion paper expressed 'serious misgivings' about the structure and administration of disability benefits, and advocated a greater focus on the needs of the most severely disabled.[99] Evidence given to the Social Security Committee suggested that the principal organisations representing disabled people had little confidence in the Board, leading the Committee to propose that the government consider how the Board could be restructured to make the best use of its expertise.[100]

D The Occupational Pensions Regulatory Authority

The Occupational Pensions Regulatory Authority (OPRA) has had a central role in the regulatory framework for occupational pensions since April 1997. OPRA assumed several of the functions of the former Occupational Pensions Board[101] as well as acquiring new powers in the wake of the Maxwell pension fund fraud. It has a chairman and at least six other members, one of whom must be appointed after consultation with employers' organisations and one after consultation with trades unions. Other members must be knowledgeable about life assurance business and occupational pensions schemes, and have experience in their management and administration.[102] OPRA has extensive powers to prohibit and disqualify trustees of occupational pension schemes, to impose penalties for non-compliance and to wind up schemes.[103] The Secretary of

---

92 SI 1991/1746, reg 3(1).
93 SI 1991/1746, reg 3(1), reg 3(2)(a).
94 SI 1991/1746, reg 3(1), reg 3(2)(b) and (c).
95 These might be cases of particular difficulty or where a test case is involved. The Board also holds workshops for decision makers and gives advice on the contents of the guidance in *The Disability Handbook* (2nd edn, 1998).
96 SI 1991/1746, reg 2(1). The annual reports contain useful case studies on particular disabilities.
97 SI 1991/1746, reg 2(2).
98 SI 1991/1746, reg 2(1)(a). This would not preclude the Board from using its annual report to voice any concerns it feels on wider policy issues.
99 DLAAB 'The future of disability living allowance and attendance allowance' in HC Social Security Committee *Disability Living Allowance* (1997–98, HC 641) Minutes of Evidence, p 1.
100 *DLAAB* n 99 above, paras 74–78; and DSS *Reply by the Government to the Fourth Report* (1998, Cm 4007) paras 82–87.
101 The Board was instituted in 1973: see the 4th edition of this book, p 628. Responsibility for contracting out issues passed to the Contributions Agency in 1997, now part of the Inland Revenue.
102 PA 1995, s 1.
103 PA 1995, ss 3–15.

State consults OPRA on a number of regulations, in particular those made under the Pensions Act 1975 (PA 1975).[104]

The role of OPRA must be distinguished from the work of the Pensions Ombudsman and the Pensions Compensation Board. The Occupational Pension Board's (OPB) report on protecting occupational pensions[105] led the government to establish a Pensions Ombudsman in 1990.[106] The Pensions Ombudsman has jurisdiction to investigate both complaints of injustice caused by maladministration and factual or legal disputes involving occupational pension schemes.[107] The Pensions Compensation Board, another product of the Maxwell scandal, determines whether compensation is payable where the pension scheme's sponsoring employer is insolvent and the value of the scheme's assets has been diminished as a result of dishonesty.[108]

E The Central Advisory Committee on War Pensions[109]

The Central Advisory Committee was set up by the War Pensions Act 1921.[110] Its role is essentially to give advice to the Secretary of State on questions concerning entitlement to, and the administration of, war pensions. Historically the Committee was a large body consisting of about 30 members, with the Secretary of State as chairman. In part this reflects the former statutory requirement that the membership include at least 12 War Pension Committee chairmen (this dated from 1970, when there were 149 such local committees). There are now fewer than 30 such committees. Consequently, amending legislation in 2000 specified that in future there must be at least one local committee chairman on the Central Advisory Committee, which enables both a smaller and more balanced composition to be secured.[111] It is required to meet at least once a year: in practice it meets no more than twice a year.

F War Pensions Committees

These committees, often known as local war pensions committees, were set up by the War Pensions Act 1921 to give advice to pensioners on benefits they might be entitled to and to give general welfare assistance. With the decline in the number of pensioners in the last few years, several committees have been disbanded or amalgamated with others. The constitution and role of the committees is now governed by SSA 1989.[112] Although one of their functions is to advise the Secretary of State on the local

---

104 Social Security Pensions Act 1975, s 61(2) (SSPA 1975). The same principles used to apply to the Board as govern consultation with the SSAC, but these do not apply to OPRA (SSPA 1975, s 61(3) was repealed by PA 1995, Sch 5, para 6(1)).

105 OPB *Protecting Occupational Pensions: Safeguarding Benefits in a Changing Environment* (1989, Cm 573).

106 SSA 1990, s 12 and Sch 3. See now PSA 1993, Pt X. The OPB's original proposal was for a tribunal. See p 650, below.

107 See DSS *Pensions Ombudsman Quinquennial Review 1999/2000* (2000).

108 PA 1995, ss 78–86. See further p 651, below.

109 See King *The Ministry of Pensions and National Insurance* (1958) pp 33–34; George *Social Security: Beveridge and After* (1968) p 92.

110 War Pensions Act 1921, s 3.

111 War Pensions Act 1921, s 3 and Chronically Sick and Disabled Persons Act 1970, s 9(1), both as amended by the Child Support, Pensions and Social Security Act 2000, s 61.

112 SSA 1989, s 25; and see SI 2000/3180.

administration of war pensions,[113] it seems that the committees' principal role is to help the pensioners themselves.[114] This general 'welfare' role is now unique in the social security system, and shows the particularly favourable treatment often accorded to war pensioners.

Part 4   Claims and payments

A The Customer Charter

The launch of the Citizen's Charter in 1991 focused attention on the quality of service provided by the DSS and its executive agencies to members of the public.[115] This was followed by the publication of the BA's Customer Charter,[116] which sets out targets for processing claims; thus income support decisions should be made within 13 working days. These targets are essentially performance indicators for management use and do not confer any rights on claimants. To borrow Ignatieff's phrase, 'the language of consumption has ... effectively displaced the language of citizenship'.[117] The DWP will make an ex gratia payment only in cases of clear departmental error where benefit has been delayed by several months, depending on the benefit in question and if more than £100 in benefit was involved.[118]

Over the last two decades the DWP and its agencies have launched a series of initiatives designed to improve service delivery. This objective first surfaced as the 'whole person concept' in the 1980s, but its realisation will inevitably depend on the availability of sufficient resources.[119] This later transmuted into the 'one-stop programme', which was intended to ensure that claimants could have all their benefits queries handled at one office, and ultimately by one person at one time. Its latest reincarnation has been the ambitious ONE programme, piloted by the Labour government from June 1999. The ONE service involves the BA, ES, local authorities and other welfare providers 'working together to give a seamless and more coherent service for customers of working age who make new or repeat claims for benefit'.[120] This formed the basis for the development of the Jobcentre Plus network.[121] A key component of the ONE strategy is the requirement for claimants to attend a 'work-focused interview' as a condition for receipt of benefit.[122]

These developments have taken place against the background in recent years of a series of ever tighter amendments to the rigid procedural rules governing claims and payments. These procedural changes are typically justified in terms of encouraging personal responsibility (eg the evidence requirement on new claims), rationalising complex benefit rules (eg as regards time limits) and combating fraud (eg the requirement to produce a National Insurance number on a new claim). However, the result of a claimant's failure to comply with a request for verification of eligibility or to arrive for

113   SSA 1989, s 25(2)(a).
114   SSA 1989, s 25(2)(d).
115   See Drewry [1993] Public Law 248.
116   Initially in 1993; see now Jobcentre Plus *Customers' Charter* (2002).
117   Ignatieff (1989) 60 Political Q 63 at 66.
118   See further BA Circular *Financial Redress for Maladministration* (2000).
119   See Bellamy (1996) Public Admin 159 for a valuable analysis of the implications of increased automation within the benefits system.
120   BA *Business Plan 2000–2001* (2000) p 9.
121   P 133, above.
122   P 148, below.

a scheduled appointment can lead to the rapid administrative closure of claims, with the result that claimants find themselves denied benefit until the necessary formalities are completed. Sociologists characterise these processes of 'bureaucratic disentitlement' as a form of social control.[123]

B Take-up of benefits

The technical rules governing the claiming of social security benefits, discussed in the following section, need to be considered in the context of the problems associated with take-up. The take-up of benefits can be measured by caseload and by expenditure. The caseload take-up rate refers to the proportion of eligible claimants who receive benefit over the course of a year. The expenditure take-up rate relates to the percentage of total benefit claimed in a year. Take-up is usually higher using the expenditure measure, if only because non-claimants are more likely to be those with small entitlements. Yet such calculations are necessarily no more than best estimates and so are often presented in terms of a range of take-up. Take-up rates also vary considerably by benefit and by category of claimant. On either basis the take-up of well-known universal benefits such as the retirement pension and child benefit is close to 100 per cent.[124] Means-tested benefits, which are by definition designed to target assistance on those most in need, are subject to markedly lower take-up rates. For example, income support take-up is between 87 and 94 per cent by expenditure and 77 to 87 per cent by caseload, whilst that for income-based jobseeker's allowance is between 74 and 84 per cent by expenditure and 67 and 78 per cent by caseload.[125] Typically take-up rates for means-tested benefits are higher among lone parents and local authority tenants and lowest among pensioners and owner-occupiers.[126] Early research suggested that low take-up was a function of three factors: ignorance; stigma; and administrative complexity.[127] Later studies have developed more sophisticated models to explain the phenomenon of low take-up.[128]

C Claims: general rules

i When a claim is necessary

It is almost always a necessary condition for entitlement to benefit that a claim is made in the manner prescribed under the legislation. This had always been assumed to be the position, but the House of Lords in 1984 held that a valid claim was not a pre-condition of entitlement, as opposed to the right to payment.[129] However, the original position was restored by amendments to the social security legislation, and it is now clear that a timely claim made in the prescribed manner is necessary to ground entitlement unless regulations state otherwise.[130]

---

123   For the classic study, see Piven and Cloward *Regulating the Poor* (1971). See also Lipsky (1984) 58 Social Services Review 3; and Bennett (1995) 104 Yale LJ 2157.
124   Take-up of lesser known contributory or non-contributory benefits (eg guardian's allowance) is thought to be less: Barr and Coulter in Hills *The State of Welfare* (1990) p 301.
125   DWP *Income Related Benefits Estimates of Take-Up in 1999/2000* (2001).
126   Harris in Harris (ed) *Social Security Law in Context* (2000) pp 63–65.
127   Corden in Ditch (ed) *Introduction to Social Security* (1999) p 142.
128   See *Corden* n 127 above; Craig (1991) 20 J Soc Pol 537; and van Oorschot (1991) 1 J Euro Soc Pol 15.
129   *Insurance Officer v McCaffrey* [1985] 1 All ER 5, [1984] 1 WLR 1353.
130   SSAA 1992, s 1. See also s 2 and Sch 1 for analogous provisions relating to earlier periods.

Regulations originally made under SSA 1986 establish common rules for claims to and payment of all social security benefits, as well as making provisions for particular benefits.[131] The regulations cover all the benefits covered in this book with the exception of war pensions, housing benefit and social fund payments.

A claim is not necessary in the following cases:[132]

- a Category A or B retirement pension, where the beneficiary is a woman over 65 on her ceasing to be entitled to various bereavement benefits, or where she is a woman under 65 in receipt of widow's pension on her reaching 65;
- in some circumstances a Category C or D pension;
- age addition;
- jobseeker's allowance where an existing award has been suspended pending inquiries into the claimant's entitlement but later reinstated; and
- lone parent run-on.

An increase of benefit for a dependant and increases to industrial disablement benefit must be the subject of separate claims.[133]

Although the requirement of a valid claim may occasionally work hardship on someone who has omitted to claim (or claim in time), a system of automatic entitlement to social security benefits would generally be unworkable. There are perhaps some exceptions, where the conditions of eligibility are very easy for the DWP to ascertain, such as the retirement pensions mentioned in the previous paragraph, but in the vast majority of cases it is arguably reasonable for the claimant to be responsible for drawing the DWP's attention to the circumstances which make the payment of benefit appropriate.[134]

A claim may be amended or withdrawn at any time before a determination has been made on it, by giving notice at a departmental office.[135] But after a ruling, it is too late to withdraw the claim.[136]

ii A claim must be made in writing on an appropriate form

The common rule for most benefits is that a claim must be submitted in writing on the form approved by the Secretary of State for the purpose of the benefit for which the claim is made, or in any other manner in writing, which he or she is prepared to accept as sufficient in the circumstances.[137] Claim forms must be supplied without charge,[138] and every claim must be delivered or sent to an office of the DWP.[139] If the claim is defective or has not been made on the appropriate form, it may be referred to the applicant. If it is then returned properly completed within a month (or a reasonable longer period), it may be treated as if it had been properly made in the first place.[140] The questions concerning the respective powers of the Secretary of State and the statutory adjudicating authorities in this context largely disappeared with the abolition of

---

131 SI 1987/1968.
132 SI 1987/1968, reg 3.
133 SI 1987/1968, reg 2(3).
134 See *R(I) 6/62(T)*, para 15.
135 SI 1987/1968, reg 5.
136 *R(U) 2/79*, para 10, per D Reith, Comr.
137 SI 1987/1968, reg 4(1). In practice, of course, such decisions are made by staff on behalf of the Secretary of State.
138 SI 1987/1968, reg 4(5).
139 Claims for tax credits are dealt with by the Inland Revenue. In cases covered by the ONE arrangements, local authorities may receive claims: SI 1987/1968, regs 4A and 4B. See further SI 1999/3108.
140 SI 1987/1968, reg 4(7).

adjudication officers under the SSA 1998. These nice points may still arise on appeal. It is for the Secretary of State to determine whether a written claim should be accepted as an alternative to one made on the proper form, but the question whether the documents constitute a valid claim is for the tribunal or Commissioner to determine.[141]

Special rules have applied to claims for income support and jobseeker's allowance since October 1997.[142] The so-called 'evidence requirement' was designed to inculcate a greater sense of personal responsibility by placing the onus firmly on claimants to provide the essential information to support their claim for benefit.[143] The SSAC expressed its concern that the new rules failed to 'strike the correct balance between the genuine difficulties faced by claimants and the administrative needs of the Benefits Agency'.[144] A claim for either of these two benefits *must* be on the approved claim form and should also, unless certain exceptions apply, be made in accordance with the instructions on the form and include 'such information and evidence as the form may require'.[145] The prescribed exceptions are that:
(1) the claimant is unable to comply because he has a physical, learning, mental or communication difficulty and it is not reasonably practicable for him to seek assistance from another;
(2) the information or evidence (i) does not exist, or (ii) can only be obtained at the serious risk of physical or mental harm to the claimant and it is not reasonably practicable to do so by other means, or (iii) can only be obtained from a third party and it is not reasonably practicable to do so;
(3) the Secretary of State is of the opinion that sufficient information or evidence has been supplied to show that the claimant is not entitled to benefit and it would be inappropriate to seek further information or evidence.[146]
Where either (1) or (2) applies, the claimant may notify the appropriate office 'by whatever means'.[147] The decision on whether a person is exempt from the claiming requirements is non-appealable.[148] There are also special rules, discussed below, for income support and jobseeker's allowance as regards the effective date of claim.

iii   Information to be given when claiming

The Social Security Administration (Fraud) Act 1997 (SSA(F)A 1997) imposed a requirement that any claim for a social security benefit be supported by a National Insurance number (NINo).[149] This requirement now applies to all social security claimants with the exceptions of children under 16 claiming disability living allowance[150]

---

141   *R(U) 9/60; R(SB) 5/89.*
142   See further SI 1987/1968, reg 4(7A)–(7B) on the Secretary of State's duty to inform claimants where forms are defective.
143   The proposal first emerged in the DSS Consultation Paper *Improving Decision Making and Appeals in Social Security* (1996, Cm 3328). For the critical SSAC report on the draft regulations, see Cm 3586 (1997).
144   *SSAC* n 143 above, p 13.
145   SI 1987/1968, reg 4(1A).
146   SI 1987/1968, reg 4(1B).
147   SI 1987/1968, reg 4(1C).
148   SI 1999/991, Sch 2, para 5. SSAC's recommendation that there be a right of appeal to an independent tribunal was not accepted by government: n 143, above, p 5.
149   SSAA 1992, s 1(1A), inserted by SSA(F)A 1997, s 19. Alternatively sufficient information or evidence must be supplied to enable the authorities to trace the NINo, or the person must apply for a NINo and provide sufficient information or evidence to allow one to be allocated.
150   SI 1991/2890, reg 1A. The requirement has been gradually phased in as regards other benefits. It presents a particular problem for successful asylum seekers.

and persons claiming statutory sick pay, statutory maternity pay or social fund payments. The NINo requirement applies to the claimant's partner where a means-tested benefit is being claimed as a couple, or an adult dependant's addition is claimed for a non means-tested benefit; children are again exempt.[151]

A claimant is also required to provide within a month (or such longer period as is reasonable) such certificates, documents, information and evidence in connection with the claim as the Secretary of State may require.[152] The Secretary of State may require the partner of a claimant, where the former's circumstances may affect entitlement to or the amount of benefit, to provide documents, information, etc within a month.[153] In so far as these provisions impose requirements as to the evidence, etc to be produced by *particular* claimants, they are of doubtful validity.[154] The Act would appear only to authorise regulations which set out *general* requirements in various types of case; further, it is for decision makers and tribunals to decide whether the claimant has proved entitlement, and what evidence is in the circumstances necessary for that proof. An example of appropriate general regulations are the Medical Evidence Regulations 1976, which lay down the certificates that are required for entitlement to incapacity benefit or state maternity allowance.[155]

A claimant may also be directed by the Secretary of State to attend any office or place for the purpose of providing documents, information, etc.[156] It is doubtful whether this authorises a medical examination.[157]

iv Interchange with claims for other benefits

In certain circumstances a claim for one benefit may be treated alternatively or additionally as a claim for another benefit to which the applicant is entitled.[158] This rule assists persons who have claimed one allowance and then discover they are entitled to another; if the application for the latter was treated as made at the subsequent date (and not when the original claim was made) they might be out of time to claim it. The regulations set out the detailed provisions in a Schedule. Thus, a claim for a retirement pension of any category may be treated as a claim for a pension of another category, and a claim for income support may be treated as a claim for carer's allowance. The decision whether to accept a claim for one benefit as a claim, either additionally or alternatively, for another is a matter for the Secretary of State with no right of appeal.[159] In principle recourse to a tribunal should be available, for (as mentioned earlier) they have jurisdiction to decide whether there is a valid claim.[160]

---

151 See eg SI 1987/1967, reg 2A and SI 1979/642, reg 1A.
152 SI 1987/1968, reg 7(1). Special rules apply to claimants of jobseeker's allowance: SI 1996/207, reg 24.
153 SI 1987/1968, reg 7(2). In the case of tax credits, the Inland Revenue may also seek documents or information from the employer of the claimant or partner: reg 7(3). Information may also be sought from pension fund holders in relation to claimants for income support, jobseeker's allowance and tax credits: reg 7(4)–(6).
154 A former Chief Commissioner in Northern Ireland has raised this point: see *R 1/75(P)*, T A Blair.
155 SI 1976/615: see p 540, above.
156 SI 1987/1968, reg 8(2).
157 But see the view of the Parliamentary Commissioner for Administration, *3rd Report* (1974–75, HC 241) Case No C 156/1.
158 SI 1987/1968, reg 9.
159 SI 1987/1968, reg 9(1) and *R(S) 3/93*; on the lack of a right of appeal, see SI 1999/991, Sch 2, para 5. There is no duty on the Secretary of State to consider in every case whether eligibility for alternative or additional benefits arises: *R v Secretary of State for Social Security, ex p Cullen* (1997) Times, 16 May (considering the predecessor provisions in SSA 1975, s 80 and SI 1979/628, reg 9).
160 The question has a complex history (see the 2nd edition of this book, pp 555–556).

v   The date of claim

The date on which a claim is made is crucial for determining the relevant time-limit.[161] Regulations provide that, as a general rule, a claim is made on the date on which it is received in the appropriate office.[162] Before April 1988, postal claims were generally treated as made on the day of posting; provided claimants could show they had posted a claim, the risk of non-delivery was on the DSS.[163] What is now the standard rule used to apply only for child benefit, supplementary benefit and family income supplement.[164] There was no obvious justification for this change.[165] This rule, like some others in the 1987 regulations, is harsher on the claimant.[166] The statutory provisions determining the date of claim are an excellent example of the increasingly dense and complex fabric of social security law. In April 1988, when the new rules first came into force, there were just four paragraphs to the relevant regulation.[167] By June 2002, the regulation had grown to 37 separate paragraphs.

Special rules apply to tax credits and the principal means-tested benefits. Where applicants notify the Inland Revenue that they wish to claim a tax credit and are supplied with the appropriate form, there is automatically a month within which to complete and return the form. The claim is then effective from the date of the initial notification or, if the one month time limit is not met, from the actual date of return.[168] Similarly an income support claim is effective from the date that a properly completed claim is submitted, in accordance with the increased emphasis on the claimant's responsibility to provide all necessary information. Where a claim is submitted within a month of an initial notification or an earlier defective claim, that earlier date will apply.[169] These rules are modified for the purposes of jobseeker's allowance.[170]

vi   Work-focused interviews

The Welfare Reform and Pensions Act 1999 (WRPA1999) introduced amendments to SSAA 1992 providing for claims or full entitlement to certain benefits to be conditional on work-focused interviews.[171] The government's intention is for these arrangements to become compulsory on a nationwide basis. There are at present three separate sets of regulations governing such arrangements. The first set is only in force in ONE pilot areas.[172] In these districts, claimants who are required to do so must attend and take part in an interview with a personal adviser if they make a new claim to any one of the following benefits:

161   Subject to certain exceptions, claims can be made up to three months in advance: SI 1987/1968, reg 13.
162   SI 1987/1968, reg 6(1)(a).
163   SSA 1975, s 79(6).
164   For the earlier regulations, see the 2nd edition of this book, p 556.
165   Contrast SI 1999/1495, reg 8(3), which provides that for the purposes of the time limits governing appeals to the Commissioners, a 'document sent by prepaid post, fax or email is effective from the date it is sent'.
166   But when the Department closes its offices and arranges for mail not to be delivered on those days, the date of claim is the day on which it would have been delivered but for that arrangement: *R(SB) 8/89*.
167   SI 1987/1968, reg 6, as amended by SI 1988/522.
168   SI 1987/1968, reg 6(1)(aa).
169   SI 1987/1968, reg 6(1A). The SSAC recommendation that this time restriction be abandoned or lengthened to three months was not accepted by government: Cm 3586 (1997) p 5.
170   SI 1987/1968, reg 6(4A)–(4AB). See also reg 6(4ZA–ZD) and 6(4AA)–(4AB) for joint-claim jobseeker's allowance.
171   SSAA 1992, ss 2A–2C.
172   See SI 2000/897, in force from April 2000.

- income support;
- housing benefit;
- council tax benefit;
- bereavement and widow's benefits;
- incapacity benefit;
- severe disablement allowance; and
- carer's allowance.[173]

A work-focused interview means an interview conducted for any of the following purposes: to assess a person's present or future employment prospects; to assist or encourage a person to enhance their job prospects; and to identify both activities to improve such prospects and any employment, training or educational opportunities.[174] A new claimant who is aged under 60 and is not in remunerative work[175] is required to take part in such an interview.[176] Existing claimants of any of the above benefits in the areas in question may in certain circumstances be required to take part in such an interview as a condition of continuing to receive benefit.[177] The regulations make provision for interviews to be waived or deferred in appropriate cases.[178] A person is only to be regarded as having taken part in such an interview if he or she attends at the relevant time and place and provides answers (where asked) to questions on a range of issues related to their employment prospects.[179] A claimant who fails to take part and is unable to show good cause for doing so may face a benefit sanction of a reduction in benefit equal to 20 per cent of the income support personal allowance for an adult aged 25 or over.[180]

Secondly, a parallel scheme of work-focused interviews for lone parents was introduced in certain parts of the country in August 2000.[181] From April 2001 this 'pathfinder' scheme was extended to lone parents across the whole country who were in receipt of income support but whose youngest child was at least 13. A year later the scheme was extended to those lone parents already claiming income support whose youngest child was aged at least five years and three months; for new claimants, the obligation to participate arises as soon as the youngest child is three years old.[182] However, the requirement to attend and take part in an interview does not apply to lone parents with children under the age of three, or to lone parents who are under 18, over 60, or who are subject to the ONE scheme.[183] Finally, the original ONE pilot scheme was extended to many more areas of the country in October 2001 under the title of 'Jobcentre Plus interviews'.[184]

173 SSAA 1992, s 2A(2).
174 SI 2000/897, reg 3.
175 Defined by SI 2000/897, reg 1(1) in terms of the rule for housing benefit in SI 1987/1971, reg 4.
176 SI 2000/897, reg 4(2). For exemptions, see reg 5. See also SI 1968/1987, reg 6A as to the date of claim.
177 SI 2000/897, reg 6.
178 SI 2000/897, regs 7 and 8.
179 SI 2000/897, reg 11(2).
180 SI 2000/897, regs 12–14. There is a right of appeal to a tribunal against such a penalty: reg 15.
181 SI 2000/1926. Some lone parents were already subject to the ONE pilots.
182 SI 2000/1926, reg 1, as amended by SI 2002/670.
183 SI 2000/1926, regs 2–4. There are parallel provisions to the ONE scheme for waiver and deferment of interviews and for sanctions: regs 5–9.
184 SI 2001/3210. See now SI 2002/1703 implementing this scheme on a national basis, with effect from 30 September 2002.

D   The time-limits for particular benefits

i   *Time-limits: the general principles*

The most important aspect of the Social Security (Claims and Payments) Regulations 1987 is the imposition of time-limits for claiming the various benefits. If the claim is not made within the time prescribed for the particular benefit, then the claimant is disqualified from receiving it, either absolutely or in respect of the period specified in the regulations.[185] The reasons which may justify the imposition of time-limits are largely those which support limitation periods in all civil proceedings: the desire to achieve certainty and avoid adjudicating claims on stale evidence. The absence of time-limits would, moreover, make administration more costly and the financing of social security less predictable. These arguments are persuasive with regard to certain benefits, such as those for sickness and unemployment, where it may well be difficult to decide a late claim because of the unreliability of the evidence. On the other hand, it is more difficult to defend the existence of a time-limit for claiming a retirement pension, when applicants would probably have little trouble in substantiating a claim brought months or years after they attained pensionable age and became entitled. Clearly, a balance has to be struck between the need of the DWP to be protected against stale claims and that of the individual to have a reasonable time within which to claim.[186]

In 1987 the SSAC fully reviewed the issues involved.[187] The SSAC favoured liberalisation of the time-limits so far as possible, though it rejected the superficially attractive view that there should be a common time-limit of 12 months for all benefits.[188] The Committee also considered how far an extension of the time-limits should continue to be allowed where claimants showed 'good cause' for their failure to apply within the prescribed period. The provision for 'good cause' enabled justice to be done in an individual case, where eg the applicant was misled by incorrect official advice and so delayed making a claim, but was expensive to administer.[189] Thus the SSAC recommended an extension of the time-limits for some benefits (eg retirement pensions), with the abolition of the 'good cause' provision for those benefits; on the other hand, it proposed its retention for other benefits where the time-limits remained relatively short. These proposals were accepted by the then government and implemented in the Social Security (Claims and Payments) Regulations 1987.

Ten years later, the government brought forward proposals that radically reduced the scope for backdating claims to benefit. The objectives were stated to be the alignment of the various rules across the social security system and the elimination of the administrative complexity generated by the need to consider the many disparate special reasons for late claims.[190] It was estimated that some 400,000 to 450,000 claimants each year would lose benefit, with an average loss of £290.[191] These changes were

---

185   SI 1987/1968, reg 19.
186   Report of NIAC on Time-Limits (1952, Cmd 8483); Report of IIAC on Time-Limits for claiming industrial injury benefits (1952, Cmd 8511); Report of NIAC on Time-Limits (1968, Cmnd 3597) paras 6–7.
187   SSAC *Time limits for claiming benefits* (1987, Cm 100).
188   *SSAC* n 187, above, para 12. The greater difficulty in investigating a late claim for some benefits, eg based on sickness or unemployment, as opposed to others, warranted differences in the relevant time-limits.
189   *SSAC* n 187, above, paras 16–17.
190   SSAC Report (1997, Cm 3586) p 31. Curiously the SSAC Report makes no reference to its 1987 study of the issue in its 1997 report.
191   *SSAC* n 191, above, p 34.

implemented in October 1997, alongside the introduction of the 'evidence requirement' for initial claims, and contrary to the advice of the SSAC. In 1987 the SSAC had concluded that for practical reasons an absolute cut-off was necessary 'to avoid considerable administrative disruption and doubt',[192] except for cases where an official has misled the claimant, when an extra-statutory payment may be made.[193] At that time most claims for benefit could be backdated for up to 12 months where good cause could be shown.[194] Yet the rules now mostly involve a maximum of three months' backdating for some (but by no means all) contributory and non-contributory benefits, assuming that the relevant eligibility criteria are satisfied. There is no provision for good cause as such in this context. As regards the means-tested benefits, there is the possibility of three months backdating for good cause, a term which is now exhaustively defined in the regulations rather than left to the case law. Administrative backdating for a maximum of one month at the discretion of the Secretary of State was retained for the means-tested benefits. In addition, backdating for reviews of existing claims was reduced to one month for all benefits except housing benefit and council tax benefit.

ii Time limits for contributory and non-contributory benefits

A THE GENERAL RULE

Claims for any of the following benefits can be backdated for up to three months:
* bereavement benefit;[195]
* child benefit;
* guardian's allowance;
* graduated retirement benefit;
* incapacity benefit;
* industrial disablement benefit;
* carer's allowance;
* maternity allowance;
* retirement pension (any category); and
* any increase in benefit for an adult or child dependant.[196]

The claimant must specifically request backdating but the award should automatically be made retrospective assuming that the relevant qualifying conditions have been satisfied throughout the period in question. The concept of 'good cause' is now irrelevant in this context. There are, inevitably, a number of exceptional cases. For example, special provision is made for bereavement benefits where the death of the spouse is difficult to establish.[197] Other special cases are considered below in relation to particular benefits. It should be noted that the rules for contribution-based jobseeker's allowance are the same as those for the income-based component, and so are considered in relation to means-tested benefits further below.

---

192 *SSAC* n 187, above, paras 18–19.
193 *SSAC* n 187, above, para 20. See Partington *Claim in Time* (3rd edn, 1994) pp 145–164.
194 SSAA 1992, s 1(2). See *R(P) 4/88*. Until 1969 there was an absolute bar after six months. There is also a special rule for widow's benefits: p 573, below. Annex A to the DSS Memorandum to the SSAC helpfully set out the existing rules: Cm 3586 (1997) p 36.
195 Ie bereavement payment, widowed parent's allowance and bereavement allowance: SSCBA 1992, s 20(1)(ea).
196 SI 1987/1968, reg 19(2), (3) and Sch 4.
197 SSAA 1992, s 3, as substituted by WRPA 1999, Sch 8, para 17.

B   STATUTORY SICK PAY AND INCAPACITY BENEFIT

A special rule applies where incapacity benefit is claimed after notification that the applicant is not entitled to statutory sick pay. Provided the claim is made within three months of such notification, a claim for incapacity benefit is treated as made on the day accepted by the employer as the first day of incapacity.[198] Otherwise the normal rule applies, namely that a claimant has three months in which to make a claim for incapacity benefit.[199] This is one of the few respects in which the 1997 changes actually provided greater scope for backdating than was previously the case. Ironically, the previous time-limit for initial claims was just one month,[200] which was regarded by both the SSAC and its predecessor, the NIAC, as unduly generous given that most people, even those who have never claimed it, are at least familiar with the existence of what was then sickness benefit.[201]

C   DISABILITY LIVING ALLOWANCE AND ATTENDANCE ALLOWANCE

Disability living allowance superseded attendance allowance for those aged under 65 with effect from April 1992.[202] Neither of these benefits can be paid for any period prior to the date of claim. Claim forms for both allowances are not made directly available to the general public;[203] instead, claimants are invited to use the Freefone service or to return a request slip in order to obtain a form. Providing the claim form is returned within six weeks of the original request, that earlier date is taken as the date of claim.[204] There is no provision for an extension for good cause for a late claim.[205] In its 1987 report the SSAC considered the absence of a good cause provision in relation to attendance allowance unjustified in principle, particularly in view of the difficulty which many claimants and their family may have in appreciating their entitlement. Further, it was not impressed by the government's argument that it would often be difficult to determine eligibility at a date earlier than the date of claim, since attendance allowance in any case requires that the need has existed for six months (which may precede the date of claim).[206] But the Committee's inability to make recommendations that would increase costs precluded it from making any definite proposals.[207] Advance claims for disability living allowance may be made where the claimant can show that the necessary conditions for entitlement will be met within the next three months.[208] There is no

---

198   SI 1987/1968, reg 10.
199   SI 1987/1968, Sch 4.
200   A limitation period increased from 21 days by regulations in 1982.
201   Cmnd 2400 (1964) paras 22–23; and Cm 100 (1987) para 62.
202   Ch 19, below.
203   This is for practical reasons; the disability living allowance claim pack runs to some 40 pages.
204   SI 1987/1968, reg 6(8) and (9).
205   SSCBA 1992, s 65(4) (attendance allowance) and s 76(1) (disability living allowance). The previous rule enabling renewal claims to be backdated, providing that they were made within six months of the expiry of an earlier award, was abolished as part of the 1997 changes: only about 100 people out of more than 150,000 renewing their claims each year made use of the provision: SSAC Report (1997, Cm 3586) p 8.
206   Cm 100 (1987) paras 38–43. The qualifying period for disability living allowance is three months: SSCBA 1992, ss 72(2)(a) and 73(9)(a).
207   But see the response of the Secretary of State for Social Services to the SSAC Report, Annex to Cm 100 (1987).
208   SI 1987/1968, reg 13A.

analogous provision for attendance allowance.[209] Renewal claims for disability living allowance may be made up to six months before the expiry of an existing award.[210]

A claim for disablement benefit that is based on occupational deafness or occupational asthma must be brought within five or ten years respectively of working in a prescribed occupation, or it will fail completely. Indeed, the more restrictive rules on backdating introduced in 1997 have particular implications for victims of industrial accidents and diseases. Under the previous regime, backdating for industrial disablement benefit could potentially be indefinite, as the benefit involved some element of compensation for injury and so an absolute bar was thought to be inappropriate.[211] As a result of the 1987 amendments, industrial disablement benefit is subject to the standard maximum of three months' backdating. This works particular injustice in the case of latent industrial diseases, such as those related to exposure to asbestos,[212] where 'establishing the correct diagnosis may take months or even years'.[213] Both the SSAC and the IIAC opposed this change, but to no avail.

E   WAR PENSIONS

There are no prescribed claim forms or procedures, though a document is usually completed and sent to the central office at Blackpool, where claims are handled. There is no time-limit for claiming a war pension, though the burden of proof shifts to the applicant if the claim is made more than seven years after leaving service.[214]

iii   Time limits and other rules for means-tested benefits

A   INCOME SUPPORT AND JOBSEEKER'S ALLOWANCE

(i)   The general rules
Both income support and jobseeker's allowance must normally be claimed on the first day of the period for which the benefit is claimed.[215] In addition, to submitting a written claim, a person applying for jobseeker's allowance (contribution-based and/or income-based) is usually required to attend in person at a JobCentre.[216] At the JobCentre, claimants are interviewed and their claims processed, their contribution record being checked by reference to the central office in Newcastle. Claimants are told that they must return, usually fortnightly, at a particular time on a particular day of the week, to

---

209   SI 1987/1968, reg 13(3).
210   SI 1987/1968, reg 13C.
211   See *CI/037/1995* (1997) 4 JSSL D87, a somewhat extreme case, in which the Commissioner found that a woman had shown good cause for failure to claim in respect of an industrial accident sustained 33 years previously when she was 17.
212   See generally *Wikeley* n 76, above.
213   SSAC Report (1997, Cm 3586) p 21.
214   Pp 778–780, below.
215   SI 1987/1968, Sch 4.
216   SI 1996/207, reg 23. In practice a person seeking to make a fresh claim will be given an appointment by the receptionist to return for interview in a few days' time. On information requirements, see reg 24.

state that they are still unemployed and looking for work – the procedure known as 'signing on'. After the initial claim it is normally enough that subsequent applications are made on the day specified in the notice given to the applicant by the JobCentre. In effect this means that the requirement of an immediate claim applies at the start of any period of unemployment. This strict rule was traditionally justified on the ground that unemployment benefit was paid on a daily basis and that otherwise it might be difficult to determine whether the claimant was really available for work at the particular time. In 1987 the SSAC considered whether the rule might be unduly harsh and indeed would have liked to recommend an initial time-limit of seven days, but its terms of reference precluded it from proposing changes which entailed increased costs.[217]

Indeed, there are now penalties for failing to attend to sign on as required.[218] Two situations must be distinguished. The first concerns the claimant who attends on the right day but at the wrong time and is subsequently informed in writing of the consequences of failing to attend as specified. Such a claimant loses entitlement to jobseeker's allowance if they are late in attending on the next occasion.[219] However, a new claim made on that second occasion is treated as having been made on the following day, meaning that the claimant loses just one day's benefit.[220] If a claimant fails to attend on the correct day, jobseeker's allowance ceases immediately, without any warning letter.[221] The claimant can make a new claim for benefit but entitlement for the intervening period will normally be lost unless he or she can, within five working days, show good cause for the failure to attend.[222] In certain situations a claimant is automatically regarded as having good cause, eg a carer who is given less than 48 hours' notice to attend.[223] The regulations also specify a number of factors that may be taken into account in deciding whether good cause exists in this context:

- any misunderstanding on the part of the claimant owing to his or her language, learning or literacy problems or to misleading information given by an employment officer;
- any medical or dental appointment, which it would have been unreasonable to rearrange;
- any transport difficulties and whether there was any reasonably available alternative;
- the customs and practices of the claimant's religion; any attendance for a job interview.[224]

These are merely illustrations of good cause, and so other factors may be equally relevant (eg a recent bereavement).

(ii)   Administrative backdating

The Secretary of State has a discretion to backdate entitlement to either benefit by up to one month where both it is considered that 'to do so would be consistent with the proper administration of benefit' and any one of the following circumstances applies:[225]

- the relevant office was closed and alternative arrangements were not available;
- the claimant could not attend owing to transport difficulties and there was no reasonable alternative available;

217   SSAC Report (1987, Cm 100) paras 48–51.
218   SI 1996/207, reg 25.
219   SI 1996/207, reg 25(1)(b).
220   SI 1987/1968, reg 6(4C).
221   SI 1996/207, reg 25(1)(a). See reg 26 on the effective date of disentitlement.
222   SI 1996/207, reg 27.
223   SI 1996/207, reg 30.
224   SI 1996/207, reg 28.
225   SI 1996/207, reg 19(6) and (7).

- adverse postal conditions existed;[226]
- the claimant was in receipt of another benefit and notification of expiry had not been sent before entitlement expired;
- the claimant had ceased to be a member of a couple within the previous month; a close relative[227] of the claimant had died within the last month; or
- (in cases of joint-claim jobseeker's allowance only) one member of a couple had failed to attend at the stipulated time and place for their claim.

There is no right of appeal on this point.[228]

(iii) Backdating with good cause

A claim for income support or jobseeker's allowance can be backdated for up to three months if the claimant can show good cause. Before the 1997 reforms, the maximum period for backdating was 12 months and the issue of 'good cause' was governed by an extensive body of case law.[229] Now, however, the only heads of 'good cause' are those permitted under the regulations. The SSAC was not opposed to these circumstances being set out in regulations, so long as decision makers had the power to decide on analogous situations which were not specifically included within that list.[230] Yet the regulations are exhaustive; the only relevant grounds are that:

- the claimant has difficulty communicating because he has learning, language or literacy difficulties or is deaf or blind, and it was not reasonably practicable to obtain assistance from a third party;
- the claimant was ill or caring for another and it was not reasonably practicable to obtain such assistance;
- the claimant had to deal with a domestic emergency and it was not reasonably practicable to obtain such assistance;
- the claimant was given information by a DWP officer, or written advice by a solicitor, doctor or other adviser, leading him to believe that a claim would not succeed;
- the claimant (or partner) was given written advice by an employer, bank or building society leading him to believe that a claim would not succeed; or
- the claimant was prevented by adverse weather conditions from attending the relevant office.[231]

In addition, the claimant must show that, because of one of these circumstances, he or she 'could not reasonably have been expected to make the claim earlier'.[232]

B   HOUSING BENEFIT AND COUNCIL TAX BENEFIT

The procedures for claiming housing benefit and council tax benefit are covered by separate sets of regulations and include greater scope for the exercise of discretion to take into account individual circumstances other than those relating to income support and jobseeker's allowance. A claim must be made in writing on the form approved by the authority (or one which it will accept as sufficient) and delivered to the office it has

226   The term is undefined but would cover both a postal strike and bad weather affecting deliveries.
227   Defined as 'partner, parent, son, daughter, brother or sister': SI 1987/1968, reg 19(7)(g). Contrast the broader definition in reg 2(1).
228   SI 1999/991, Sch 2, para 5.
229   See the 4th edn of this book, pp 641–644; or *Partington* n 193, above.
230   SSAC Report (1997, Cm 3586) p 22.
231   SI 1987/1968, reg 19(5). There is, therefore, no place for an argument based on ignorance of one's rights or the proper procedure to be followed, however reasonable such a mistaken belief might be.
232   SI 1987/1968, reg 19(4).

designated for this purpose.[233] Alternatively it may be delivered to the appropriate DWP office, when the claimant is also claiming income support, and that office must then forward it to the local authority within two days of its receipt or the determination of the income support claim, whichever is the later, 'or as soon as reasonably practicable thereafter'.[234] A claim for a further grant of benefit may be made from 13 weeks before the expiry of a benefit period until four weeks after that period has ended.[235] Further, a late claim will be accepted if the claimant shows there was good cause for the delay.[236] These rules were not affected by the 1997 changes discussed above and so are more generous in two respects. First, the potential maximum period for backdating remains 12 months; secondly, the grounds for 'good cause' are not defined by regulations and so the issue remains at large.[237] A proposal to bring these provisions into line with the less generous provisions for other social security benefits was abandoned in 2000.[238] Other provisions regarding the evidence and information to be produced with a claim, and the scope for amending or withdrawing a claim, are similar to the requirements in the social security regulations.[239]

C   SOCIAL FUND PAYMENTS

Claims for social fund payments for maternity and funeral expenses must be made within three months of the date of confinement or the funeral, as the case may be. A claim for a maternity payment may also be made within the period starting 11 weeks before the expected date of confinement.[240] Before 1997, it had been possible to backdate claims for such payments for up to 12 months, providing good cause was shown. The SSAC opposed this change, arguing that it 'ignores the issues that can give rise to late claims, for example the birth of a severely disabled child'.[241] No claim is necessary (or apparently possible) for a cold weather payment.[242]

Applications for discretionary social fund payments must be made in writing, either on the official form or on some other document that the Secretary of State is prepared to accept as sufficient in the circumstances.[243] As a result of SSA 1998, it is no longer possible to make a claim on the social fund as a whole. A claim must be made on the relevant form for a budgeting loan, community care grant or crisis loan as appropriate.[244] The skeletal regulations on applications for social fund payments are supplemented by guidance in the Social Fund Guide. The date of the application is the date on which it is received at the DWP office.[245] Since under the Secretary of State's directions eligibility

---

233   SI 1987/1971, reg 72(1) and SI 1992/1814, reg 62(1). There is provision for the claimant to make a claim within a four-week period of grace, 'or such longer period as the appropriate authority may consider reasonable', where a claimant requests a claim form or previously submits a form which is defective: SI 1987/1971, reg 72(7), (8) and SI 1992/1814, reg 62(7), (8).

234   SI 1987/1971, reg 72(4) and SI 1992/1814, reg 62(4).

235   SI 1987/1971, reg 72(12) and (13) and SI 1992/1814, reg 62(13) and (14).

236   SI 1987/1971, reg 71(15) and SI 1992/1814, reg 62(16). An express claim for backdating must be made: *R v Aylesbury Vale District Council, ex p England* (1996) 29 HLR 303.

237   See the 4th edn of this book, pp 641–644; and *Partington* n 193, above.

238   SSAC *Fourteenth Report* (2001) p 13 and Annex A.

239   SI 1987/1971, regs 73–74 and SI 1992/1814, regs 63–64. See p 146, above.

240   SI 1987/1968, Sch 4.

241   SSAC Report (1997, Cm 3586) p 22.

242   SI 1991/2238, amending SI 1988/1724.

243   SI 1988/524, reg 2.

244   For criticism see HC Social Security Committee *Third Report* (2000–01, HC 232) paras 77 and 78.

245   SI 1988/524, reg 3.

for budgeting and crisis loans is determined at the date of the award, the precise date of application will not generally be of great importance, and there are no provisions for the acceptance of delayed claims.[246]

iv Time limits for tax credits

A WORKING FAMILIES' TAX CREDIT

The basic rule for working families' tax credit is the same as for income support and jobseeker's allowance, ie that a claim must be made on the first day of the period in question. There is a separate rule where working families' tax credit has previously been claimed and awarded; further benefit should be claimed within the period from 28 days before to 14 days after the final day of the earlier award.[247] There is an administrative discretion to backdate entitlement for up to one month, as with the two main means-tested benefits, although the grounds are modified for working families' tax credit.[248] The same good cause criteria for backdating for up to three months also apply.

B DISABLED PERSON'S TAX CREDIT

The rules for claiming disabled person's tax credit are essentially the same as for working families' tax credit, with the principal exception that renewal claims for this allowance may be made within a period starting 42 days (rather than 28 days) before, and ending 14 days after, the expiry of the existing award.[249]

E Payments

i General

A full exposition of the rules and practices governing payment of social security benefits would be very complicated, and here the emphasis is placed on general principles. Traditionally the principal methods of payment have been by books of serial orders, cashable at post offices, and by girocheque sent to the recipient's home address. Long-term benefits, child benefit and the means-tested benefits have usually been paid by the former method, while payments of the short-term benefits have been made by girocheque. Payment by the traditional methods is susceptible to fraud and administratively expensive,[250] and it may reflect an outdated paternalist view that recipients could not budget properly, particularly where cash payments are made weekly.[251] On the other hand, weekly cash payments are popular with a large number of social security

---

246 See ch 15, pp 471–479, below.
247 SI 1988/524, Sch 4. See also SI 1988/524, reg 16(1A)–(1C).
248 An additional ground is that the person claimed working families' tax credit within one month of entitlement to income support or jobseeker's allowance ending; the fact that the claim was made within a month of the claimant separating from his or her partner is not available for working families' tax credit.
249 SI 1987/1968, Sch 4. See also reg 6(12)–(15) on backdating in special cases.
250 In 1999 payments by girocheque cost 79 pence each, by order book 49 pence each and by bank transfer (ACT) just 1 pence each: National Audit Office *The Cancellation of the Benefits Payment Card Project* (1999–2000, HC 857) p 22.
251 'The current system belongs to the days of ration books' per Baroness Hollis, 613 HL Official Report (5th Series) col 586.

beneficiaries[252] and removal of this business from many sub-post offices might endanger their survival. Therefore, the present position represents a compromise.

The Conservative government in the 1980s encouraged beneficiaries to receive payments by direct transfer to their bank accounts.[253] Thus the regulations already make provision for direct credit transfer of benefit payments, eg to the claimant's bank account, but the system only comes into operation if the beneficiary applies for this method of payment and indicates in writing that its conditions are understood, and the Secretary of State consents.[254] In this event payment is to be made within seven days of the period of entitlement specified in the application, which might be monthly or quarterly. If this option is not taken up, the traditional methods remain operative. That administration's long-term goal was to replace order books with social security payment cards, and hence since 1995 there has been provision in the regulations for the issue of an 'instrument for benefit payment'.[255] However, the project to introduce a benefits 'smart card' was abandoned in 1999 after continued slippage in the face of technical problems.[256] The Labour government then returned to the plan to make all benefit payments by bank transfer. The Social Security (Claims and Payments) Regulations 1987[257] (and other delegated legislation) also make specific provision for particular benefits, as outlined below. Finally, it is not for decision makers or tribunals to determine whether the Secretary of State has met the obligation to pay benefit.[258] In the last resort disputes over lost or missing giros can therefore be resolved only through the small claims court.[259]

ii Long-term benefits

These comprise the following:
- widow's pension;
- widowed parent's allowance;
- bereavement allowance;
- retirement pension of any category;
- disability living allowance and attendance allowance;
- any allowance for industrial injuries; and
- carer's allowance.[260]

With the exception of disability living allowance, which is to be paid at four-weekly intervals, these benefits are to be paid weekly in advance by order books. However, as

---

252   See generally Kempson *Outside the Banking System* SSAC Research Paper 6 (1994).
253   Thus following the recommendations of a DHSS review team working with Sir Derek Rayner. See Annex II to the *Reply to the First Report from the Social Services Committee on Arrangements for Paying Social Security Benefits* (1980, Cmnd 8106). The publication contains a comprehensive description of the traditional methods of payment, and this section of the chapter is much indebted to it.
254   SI 1987/1968, reg 21. This facility is no longer restricted to a list of prescribed benefits. It is important that the beneficiary understands that overpayments may be recovered from his or her account: see p 166, below.
255   SI 1987/1968, reg 21A.
256   *National Audit Office* n 250, above. The cancellation costs, in excess of £1 billion, made this 'rank as one of the biggest IT failures in the public sector': HC Committee of Public Accounts *Third Report* (2001–02, HC 358) para 31.
257   SI 1987/1968.
258   *R(IS) 7/91.*
259   See *Walsh v DSS* (1990) Bromley County Court, unreported, (1990) 96 Welfare Rights Bulletin 9. A claim that benefit has been underpaid must be resolved through the appeals mechanisms under SSAA 1992, or by way of judicial review, and not in the county court: *Danquah v Official Solicitor* (24 October 1996, unreported), CA.
260   SI 1987/1968, reg 22, and see SI 1987/1968, reg 2 for the definition of 'long-term benefits'.

discussed above, payment may be made by other means; under this provision, some retirement pensioners choose to be paid by direct credit transfer on a monthly or quarterly basis. There are specific rules for the day on which each benefit is to be paid: eg a retirement pension is generally paid on Mondays, though if the beneficiary has been in receipt of a bereavement benefit it is paid (as with the bereavement benefit itself) on a Tuesday.[261]

iii Incapacity benefit

Incapacity benefit is usually payable fortnightly in arrears by order book, although those claimants who were previously in receipt of sickness benefit or invalidity benefit are paid weekly in arrears, as are claimants who claim incapacity benefit after previously having been in receipt of income support on the ground of incapacity for work.[262]

iv Child benefit, guardian's allowance and maternity allowance

The government's desire to achieve administrative economies was also implemented in the changes made in 1982 to the payment of child benefit.[263] Previously paid weekly in all cases, the normal method of payment is now monthly in arrears. However, a claimant may move to weekly payments on becoming a lone parent, or if there is entitlement to income support or working families' tax credit.[264] Furthermore, weekly payments may be made if the normal arrangements are leading to hardship.[265] Since 1999 payment of guardian's allowance has been aligned with that of child benefit.[266] Maternity allowance is payable weekly in arrears.[267]

v Income support

Income support is paid in arrears, either by serial orders cashable at post offices or by girocheque, unless direct credit transfer is used.[268] Where claimants are also entitled to another 'relevant social security benefit', income support is paid together with that other benefit, so that they receive one girocheque or cash one order at the post office.[269] Thus income support will be paid in advance when the beneficiary is also in receipt of

261 SI 1987/1968, Sch 6. Similarly, those entitled to a pension before September 1984 are paid on Thursdays.
262 SI 1987/1968, reg 24. Where the weekly entitlement is less than £1, benefit is paid at four-weekly intervals: reg 24(3). Benefit may be paid at intervals of up to one year where the entitlement is less than £5 per week as a result of the abatement rule for pension payments: ibid, reg 24(3A).
263 This change is now found in SI 1987/1968, reg 23. The changes were widely criticised, inter alia, by the SSAC Report (1981, Cmnd 8453).
264 SI 1987/1968, Sch 8.
265 SI 1987/1968, reg 23(3).
266 SI 1999/2358, amending SI 1987/1968.
267 SI 1987/1968, reg 24(4).
268 SI 1987/1968, Sch 7, para 1.
269 SI 1987/1968, Sch 7, para 3. The term 'relevant social security benefit' means incapacity benefit, severe disablement allowance, retirement pension or bereavement benefit. This used to cause considerable problems when supplementary benefit was paid in advance but unemployment benefit in arrears: see the 3rd edition of this book, p 554.

a retirement pension or bereavement benefit. Otherwise entitlement commences normally on the date of claim, and payment is made weekly on the day determined by the Secretary of State.[270]

vi   Jobseeker's allowance

The general rule is that jobseeker's allowance, although calculated as a weekly benefit, is payable fortnightly in arrears.[271] If the weekly entitlement is less than £1, benefit can be paid in intervals of up to 13 weeks at a time. A joint-claim couple may nominate one of them to be the payee; in default of any such nomination, the Secretary of State may select one partner to be payee.[272]

vii   Housing benefit and council tax benefit

A number of rules are set out in the separate regulations governing entitlement to these benefits. Housing benefit must be paid by the authority at such time and in such manner as it thinks appropriate in the light of the times when payments of rent have to be made and the claimant's reasonable needs and convenience.[273] When it takes the form of a rent allowance, it must be paid at intervals of two or four weeks, or every month, or at greater intervals with the claimant's consent. But in some cases, eg where the claimant's rent is due weekly, benefit may be paid at weekly intervals.[274] The authority is entitled to withhold payments in exceptional circumstances, particularly where it is satisfied that recipients are not using them to meet their rent.[275] The authority's obligation to pay council tax benefit is normally discharged simply by reducing an individual's liability for the council tax.[276] Alternatively the authority must make a payment of benefit where such a reduction would not be possible, or would not meet the entitlement to council tax benefit, or where the claimant is jointly and severally liable for the tax and the authority determines that such a reduction would be inappropriate.[277]

viii   Tax credits

Regulations provide that both working families' tax credit and disabled person's tax credit are to be paid by means of an order book cashable on the Tuesday following the week in respect of which the credit is payable.[278] This is, however, subject to the proviso 'unless in any case the Board arrange otherwise'. In practice in most cases payment of these tax credits is arranged via the employer.[279] If the entitlement is less than 50 pence

---

270   SI 1987/1968, Sch 7, para 3.
271   SI 1987/1968, reg 24A.
272   Jobseekers Act 1995, s 3B.
273   SI 1987/1971, reg 88.
274   SI 1987/1971, reg 90.
275   SI 1987/1971, reg 95.
276   SI 1992/1814, reg 77(1)(a).
277   SI 1992/1814, reg 77(1)(b).
278   SI 1987/1968, reg 27(1). Where the weekly rate of benefit is no more than £4, payment can be in the form of a lump sum for the whole period: reg 27(1A).
279   See pp 396–397, below.

a week, that amount is not payable.[280] A regulation also provides that arrangements may be made to pay working families' tax credit to the partner of a person entitled to it on her (or possibly his) behalf.[281]

ix War pensions

As with other social security benefits, payment by credit transfer is encouraged, but there is provision for payment by order book through a post office.

x Extinguishment of right to sums payable by way of benefit

If payment is not obtained within 12 months from the date on which the right is treated as having arisen, then the right is extinguished.[282] The reason for this time-limit on encashment of benefits is said to be that the administrative costs (eg of storing copies of instruments of payment and cash instruments) necessary to check late requests for payment, and so prevent abuse, could be very heavy.[283] The right to payment under the Social Security (Claims and Payments) Regulations 1987[284] is to be treated as having arisen in the following circumstances:
(1) in relation to a sum contained in an instrument of payment sent to the beneficiary, or to an approved place for collection by him or her, whether or not it has been received or collected – *on the date of the instrument*;
(2) where notice has been given or sent that the sum contained in it is available for collection – *on the date of notice*;
(3) where benefit is payable by means of an instrument for benefit payment – *on the first date when payment could be obtained by such means*;
(4) in relation to sums to which the preceding sub-paragraphs do not apply – *on the date determined by the Secretary of State*.[285]
There is a right of appeal to an independent tribunal against the decision of the Secretary of State.[286] It may be noted that the recipient takes the risk of the notification not being delivered in the ordinary course of post. The 12-month period may be extended where there was good cause for not requesting payment within that period.[287]

The extinguishment provisions do not apply to the payment of industrial injuries gratuities (if paid as a single sum and not by instalments) or a sum paid in satisfaction of a right to graduated retirement pension.[288]

---

280   SI 1987/1968, reg 27(2).
281   SI 1987/1968, reg 36 (this rule does not apply to disabled person's tax credit, but does also apply to child benefit).
282   SI 1987/1968, reg 38.
283   NIAC Report (1968, Cmnd 3591) paras 18–26.
284   SI 1987/1968.
285   See *R(I) 1/84*.
286   SI 1999/991, Sch 2, para 5(c). Query whether this also applies to cases under (4). As regards the general principle, this right of appeal follows recommendations of NIAC in 1952 (Cmd 8483) para 54 and of IIAC in the same year (Cmd 8511) para 28.
287   SI 1987/1968, reg 38(2A). This provision, formerly found in the pre-1988 scheme, did not appear in the 1987 regulations (see the 3rd edition of this book, p 556) but was reinstated in 1989: SI 1989/1686, reg 7 and see *R(F) 1/92*, *R(A) 2/93* and *R(P) 3/93*.
288   SI 1987/1968, reg 38(5).

F   Miscellaneous

i   *Persons unable to act*

A regulation covers the case where persons entitled to a benefit, or alleged to be so entitled, are unable for the time being to act for themselves.[289] The rule is that unless a receiver has been appointed by the Court of Protection with power to claim benefit, etc[290] the Secretary of State may, on written application by a person over 18, appoint that person to exercise, on behalf of the person unable to act, all the latter's rights and to receive benefit to which he or she is entitled. There are provisions for the revocation of, or resignation from, this appointment. An appointment by the Secretary of State is retrospective in operation and validates earlier proceedings by the appointee.[291]

ii   *Payments on death*

When a claimant dies, the Secretary of State may appoint a person of his or her choice to proceed with the claim.[292] If written application is then made for the sums payable by way of benefit within 12 months (or such longer period as the Secretary of State may determine), any sum payable may be paid or distributed (at the discretion of the Secretary of State) among persons over 16 claiming as personal representatives, legatees, next of kin or creditors of the deceased. Benefit may be paid to some person on behalf of another under 16. The same rules apply to sums payable to deceased persons before death, but not obtained by them.

iii   *Payment to a third party*

There is a general power to pay any benefit to another person on the beneficiary's behalf, if the Secretary of State considers this necessary for protecting the latter's interests or those of any child or other dependant for whom the benefit is payable.[293] There is a specific power under the regulations to make deductions from payments of income support (whether payable on its own or together with another social security benefit) or jobseeker's allowance to pay mortgage interest payments to qualifying lenders.[294] Similarly, a non-resident parent in receipt of benefit may face deductions from benefit in order to meet child support liabilities.[295] There is also a more general power to make deductions and pay such sums to third parties on the beneficiary's behalf, eg in respect of liability for fuel costs.[296] Similarly, in certain circumstances local authorities either may or, indeed, must pay housing benefit direct to landlords.[297]

---

289   SI 1987/1968, reg 33. See Lavery and Lundy [1994] JSWFL 313.
290   There is a similar rule for Scotland: SI 1987/1968, reg 33(1)(d).
291   *R(SB) 5/90; R(A) 1/92;* cf *R(IS) 5/91.*
292   SI 1987/1968, reg 30; and see *R(A) 1/92.*
293   SI 1987/1968, reg 34.
294   SI 1987/1968, reg 34A and Sch 9A. See pp 334–335, below.
295   SI 1987/1968, reg 35(1) and Sch 9B.
296   SI 1987/1968, reg 35(1) and Sch 9. See pp 334–335, above.
297   SI 1987/1971, regs 93 and 94. See p 436, below.

iv Benefit to be inalienable

It is a standard provision that any assignment or charge on, or agreement to assign or charge, the benefit is void.[298] It does not pass to the trustee, or any other person acting on the creditors' behalf, on the bankruptcy of the person entitled.[299] There are obvious policy reasons why it is undesirable to allow claimants to give up or put at risk benefits designed to ensure a minimum standard of living for themselves and their families.

v Suspension of benefit

The Secretary of State has the power to direct that benefit be suspended in a number of situations.[300] These include cases where a question has arisen about the claimant's entitlement, pending the outcome of a revision of an award of benefit.[301] There is a similar power to suspend benefit where the claimant is successful on appeal. Benefit can also be suspended where the same question is being determined by the courts in a different appeal or by way of judicial review.[302]

Part 5 Overpayments and Fraud

A Recovery of overpaid benefit

i General

It sometimes happens that benefit is paid, or too high an award is made, in circumstances where either the claimant was not entitled at all or was only entitled to a lower award. In some cases this may be attributable to a misrepresentation of some kind by the claimant, or perhaps more commonly by a failure to disclose some relevant facts which affect entitlement, either at the time of claiming or subsequently when circumstances change. The overpayment may equally be the consequence of some error or omission on the part of the DWP, and of course in some cases both the Department and the claimant may have made mistakes. It is not easy to determine when it is right in principle for the DWP to recover overpaid benefit. On the one hand, it would seem right for it to do so, when claimants have deliberately or recklessly misrepresented their position or concealed relevant facts. And a broader right of recovery can be justified on the argument that otherwise public money is awarded to people who have no justifiable claim on these resources; in the context of a limited social security budget, it can be said that not to recover overpaid benefit is unfair to those claimants for whom better provision could be made with more resources. On the other hand, it is harsh to order recovery from a

---

298 SSAA 1992, s 187. But see *Bank Mellat v Kazmi* [1989] QB 541, [1989] 1 All ER 925 on the effect of a Mareva order.
299 See *Mulvey v Secretary of State for Social Security* 1997 SLT 753, holding that the right to income support is inalienable and could not be owed to a trustee in bankruptcy. However, deductions could lawfully be made from income support to repay a social fund debt incurred prior to sequestration.
300 SSA 1998, s 21.
301 SI 1999/991, reg 16. See also SI 1987/1968, Pt V.
302 See pp 199–200, below.

beneficiary who has not been at fault at any stage, and who may be in no position to repay the overpaid benefit.[303]

Until 1987 there were broadly two main rules reflecting the balance between these arguments. In the case of contributory and non-contributory benefits, recovery would be ordered unless claimants (and any person acting on their behalf) could show that throughout they had used 'due care and diligence', a rule which had superseded an earlier test enabling beneficiaries to avoid repayment if they showed that they had acted in good faith.[304] In contrast, the position for the means-tested benefits was stricter, and in general terms enabled the Secretary of State to obtain recovery whenever the claimant had misrepresented or failed to disclose a material fact, whether fraudulently or otherwise.[305] This formulation was the subject of frequent interpretation by the Commissioners, not all of whose rulings seemed consistent. But it was clear that under this test recovery could be ordered from a claimant who had misstated a relevant fact, albeit in all innocence, which would not have been the case under the other rule.

In its 1987 reform of social security the government sensibly decided to adopt a common rule for all benefits (apart from housing benefit), but more controversially chose the stricter supplementary benefit test.[306] It resisted attempts during the passage of the legislation to incorporate the more liberal 'due care and diligence' provision.[307] Further, it should be noted that the rule for housing benefit is particularly strict: any overpayment is recoverable, except one attributable to an official error, where the beneficiary could not reasonably have been expected to realise that there was an overpayment.[308] Given the alignment of the rules relating to backdating of housing benefit with the mainstream social security benefits, and the common appeals system, it seems difficult to justify the continuance of this harsh rule. The common test is not quite as severe as that, but it may be thought somewhat unsatisfactory in view of the uncertainties of its interpretation, now to be discussed.[309]

ii   The present law concerning recovery

The common provision for recovery of overpayments is set out in section 71(1) of SSAA 1992:[310]

> Where it is determined that, whether fraudulently or otherwise, any person has misrepresented, or failed to disclose, any material fact and in consequence of the misrepresentation or failure.

payment has been made of any relevant benefit,[311] the Secretary of State is entitled to recover any payment which would not have been made in the absence of that

---

303   For an admirable discussion of these policy issues, see the Report of the National Association for the Care and Resettlement of Offenders (NACRO) Working Party *Enforcement of the Law Relating to Social Security* (1986) paras 9.1–9.18.

304   See the discussion in the 2nd edition of this book, pp 576–577.

305   Supplementary Benefits Act 1976, s 20.

306   This amendment had retrospective effect: see *Britnell v Secretary of State for Social Security* [1991] 2 All ER 726; and *Secretary of State for Social Security v Tunnicliffe* [1991] 2 All ER 712.

307   98 HC Official Report (6th series) cols 238–249.

308   SI 1987/1971, reg 99. See *R v Liverpool City Council, ex p Griffiths* (1990) 22 HLR 312.

309   For a detailed account, see Stagg *Overpayments and Recovery of Social Security Benefits* (1996).

310   There are parallel provisions relating to the recovery of jobseeker's allowance hardship payments and discretionary social fund payments: SSAA 1992, ss 71A and 71ZA.

311   These are listed in SSAA 1992, s 71(11).

misstatement or failure to disclose. This *power* needs to be distinguished from the quite distinct *right* to recover certain duplicated payments of benefit.[312] Decisions under section 71 are a matter for the Secretary of State; there is a right of appeal on whether a recoverable overpayment has been made and its amount, but not on the actual decision to effect recovery.[313] Generally, a decision to recover can only be taken after the decision under which the payment was made has been reversed on appeal or revised on review.[314] The overpayment decision and the review decision need not be made at the same time.[315]

The claimant need not be personally responsible for recovery to be appropriate, but in all cases the sum overpaid is to be recovered from the person who made the misrepresentation or failed to disclose the fact.[316] In practice the principal legal problem for resolution by decision makers and tribunals is whether the overpayments have resulted from the misrepresentation of, or failure to disclose, a material fact.[317] In either situation, therefore, the Secretary of State must show that the claimant's conduct has caused the overpayment.[318] So far as the former of the two limbs under section 71 of SSAA 1992 is concerned, the Commissioners have interpreted 'misrepresentation' over the years to cover all types of positive misstatement, whether fraudulent,[319] negligent, or purely innocent.[320] There can be a misrepresentation of a material fact even where there has been a prior disclosure of the same fact on an earlier claim.[321] A claimant who makes a specific declaration that his partner's circumstances have not changed when in fact the partner's earnings have increased (unknown to the claimant) is also caught by the rule.[322] The majority of the Court of Appeal in *Jones and Sharples v Chief Adjudication Officer*[323] held that a misrepresentation may occur whenever a claimant signs his or her weekly order book but neglects to report relevant facts to the issuing office. If this is correct, it is difficult to see where the line is drawn between misrepresentation and failure to disclose. However, the majority also held that, when making a general representation, a claimant can only report facts that are known to him or her at the time.[324] In *Chief Adjudication Officer v Sherriff*[325] the Court of Appeal held that a claimant who has the capacity to make a claim necessarily has the capacity to make any representation as to the facts on which payment of benefit is based.

The second limb of recovery has given rise to even more thorny questions of interpretation. A failure to disclose 'necessarily imports the concept of some breach of obligation, moral or legal – ie the non-disclosure must have occurred in circumstances in which, at lowest, disclosure by the person in question was reasonably to be

---

312 SSAA 1992, s 74.
313 SSA 1998, Sch 3, paras 5 and 6; on the division of functions under the previous decision making arrangements, see *R(SB) 44/83*.
314 SSAA 1992, s 71(5) and *R(IS) 7/91*. But SI 1987/491, reg 12 provides that this need not be so, where the facts and circumstances of the misrepresentation etc do not provide a basis for review of the decision.
315 SSAA 1992, s 71(5A).
316 SSAA 1992, s 71(3). See *R(SB) 21/82* and *R(SB) 28/83*.
317 On the meaning of 'material fact' see the discussion in *Stagg* n 309, above. The decision of the Court of Appeal (Evans LJ dissenting) in *Jones and Sharples v Chief Adjudication Officer* [1994] 1 All ER 225 is singularly unilluminating in this respect.
318 See *Duggan v Chief Adjudication Officer*, reported as an Appendix to *R(SB) 13/89*.
319 Fraud may also lay the claimant open to a caution, penalty or prosecution: see further below.
320 *R(SB) 21/82*. See *Page v Chief Adjudication Officer*, reported as *R(SB) 2/92*. An oral statement may qualify a written representation: *R(SB) 18/85*.
321 *R(SB) 3/90*.
322 *R(SB) 9/85*.
323 [1994] 1 All ER 225.
324 See also *Franklin v Chief Adjudication Officer (R(IS) 16/96)*.
325 *R(IS) 14/96*.

expected'.[326] Where the claimant has kept quiet about a fact which the order book clearly states should be communicated to the DWP, there may well be non-disclosure. Moreover, the obligation to disclose is a continuing one; regulations specifically require claimants to notify the DWP in writing of any change of circumstances which they might reasonably be expected to know might affect their entitlement.[327] Problems arise where the claimant's mental state may affect his or her ability to disclose. In an unreported case the Commissioner has held that the test is objective, so account should not be taken of illiteracy.[328]

The greatest difficulties have arisen where it is argued that some branch of the DWP, albeit not the one dealing with the relevant benefit, is already aware of the facts concerning the claimant's entitlement, and so there is no duty to 'disclose' what is already known. The issues have been considered by a Tribunal of Commissioners;[329] it ruled that normally the duty should be fulfilled by disclosure to the local office dealing with the claim, but that it can be satisfied by giving information to another branch of the DWP, if the claimant reasonably believes the information will be passed on to the appropriate local office.[330] The tribunal also emphasised that the claimant must usually personally discharge the onus of disclosure, and cannot rely on casual disclosure of the relevant facts by some person connected with him or her.[331] Clearly, in applying these principles there is some room for the exercise of judgment by appeal tribunals. Finally, it should be borne in mind that it is for the Secretary of State to prove that a recoverable payment has been made, rather than for the claimant to show that the provision is inapplicable.[332]

iii   Methods of recovery

The Secretary of State, or on appeal the tribunal, has the responsibility of calculating the sum which is recoverable.[333] Although in principle the overpayment is the difference between what was paid and what should have been paid, this figure is subject to adjustment in two ways. First, it may be possible to offset unclaimed benefit against the overpayment, but this only applies to cases where benefit is treated as paid on account of subsequent awards of other benefit and to cases of underpaid income support.[334] In the latter situation offsetting is not permissible if additional facts need to be established beyond the information in the original claim.[335] Secondly, the 'diminishing capital rule' applies where an income-related benefit has been overpaid because of the claimant's misrepresentation about or failure to disclose capital assets. This assumes that the claimant's capital is reduced by the amount of overpaid benefit, taken over a quarterly period.[336]

---

326   *R(SB) 21/82*, para 4(2). It is clear that the beneficiary may disclose material facts orally: see *R(SB) 12/84*.
327   SI 1987/1968, reg 32. See *R(SB) 54/83*. But note that the Secretary of State can accept notice otherwise than in writing, and a breach of reg 32 does not automatically trigger recovery under SSAA 1992, s 71.
328   *CF 26/90*, per M Goodman, Comr. But see *R(SB) 28/83* on establishing knowledge of the material fact in cases of mental incapacity.
329   *R(SB) 15/87(T)*. See also *Riches v Secretary of State for Social Security* 1994 SLT 730.
330   *R(SB) 15/87(T)*, para 28. See also the decisions in *R(SB) 54/83*, *R(SB) 36/84*, *R(SB) 10/85* and *R(SB) 2/91*. More recent case law is discussed in Wikeley (2001) 8 JSSL 157.
331   *R(SB) 15/87(T)*, para 29.
332   *R(SB) 34/83* and *R(SB) 10/85*.
333   SSAA 1992, s 71(2). See also *R(SB) 9/85*.
334   SI 1988/664, reg 13.
335   See *Commock v Chief Adjudication Officer*, reported as an Appendix to *R(SB) 6/90*.
336   SI 1988/664, reg 14.

In complex cases it is permissible for an appeal tribunal to refer the issue of calculation back to the Secretary of State, though it should indicate that the matter should be restored to it for final resolution in the event of lack of agreement.[337] But it is for the DWP, subject to various constraints, to decide whether and, if so, how the payments are to be recovered. Under regulations they may be recovered by deductions from social security benefits in payment to the person concerned, though there are limits on the amounts that may be deducted from weekly payments of income support.[338] In practice this method of recovery is by far the most common; according to one report nearly two-thirds of recoveries are effected in this way.[339] Overpayments of income support and income-based jobseeker's allowance may be recovered from the payments of such benefits to either member of a married or unmarried couple.[340] The fact that the claimant has been declared bankrupt does not prevent the recovery of overpayments from benefit.[341]

Recovery may also be enforced by a court order of a county court in England or a sheriff court in Scotland.[342] Special rules apply where the overpayment has been made by crediting the claimant's bank or other account. The overpayment may be recovered but only if the Secretary of State has certified that it was 'materially due' to the arrangements for direct credit transfer and notice of the effect of the recovery arrangements was given to the claimant when he or she agreed to this method of benefit payment.[343]

Subject to these rules it is for the DWP to decide when to seek recovery of an overpayment or whether to waive it. The NACRO report in 1986 suggested that its policy could be more generous in a number of respects.[344] In particular, it should not recover (except in case of fraud) overpayments which occurred more than two years before their discovery, a proposal which has much to commend it, as under the present practice innocent claimants may find themselves called on to repay debts of thousands of pounds. Secondly, the DWP should be more prepared to waive recovery when the beneficiary has little capital or in other ways faces considerable hardship.[345] In practice in recent years there has been increasing emphasis on securing recovery of overpayments of benefits.[346] Much less attention is paid to the problem of *underpayments* of benefit.[347] The DWP has estimated that total overpayments of benefit amount to £750 million (roughly equally due to DWP and customer error respectively) whilst underpayments constitute some £600 million (some three-quarters of which is due to customer error).[348] The net loss caused by overpayments amounts to a small fraction of one per cent of the social security budget.

---

337   *R(SB) 11/86.*
338   SSAA 1992, s 71(8) and SI 1988/664, regs 15 and 16.
339   See *NACRO Working Party*, n 303, above, para 9.4.
340   SSAA 1992, s 71(9) and SI 1988/664, reg 17.
341   Ie the Insolvency Act 1986, s 285 is no bar to recovery: *R v Secretary of State for Social Services, ex p Taylor* [1996] COD 332.
342   SSAA 1992, s 71(10). This power has existed since 1982.
343   SI 1988/664, reg 11.
344   *NACRO Working Party* n 303, above, paras 9.5–9.18.
345   See *Stagg* n 309, above, pp 178–181.
346   The criteria in which waiver is considered (eg overpayments of less than £25, unless fraudulent) are set out in Committee on Public Accounts *Thirty Second Report* (1999–2000, HC 521) Appendix 1, Q73.
347   In 1996–97 overpayments of income support were estimated to amount to £530 million as against £192 million in underpayments: Committee on Public Accounts *Third Report* (1999–2000, HC 103) Minutes of Evidence. The latter figure is confined to underpayments on *actual* claims and so takes no account of non take-up. The total amount of *unclaimed* income support for 1999–2000 was between £720 million and £1,620 million (DWP *Income Related Benefits Estimates of Take-Up in 1999/2000* (2001); see also p 144, above).
348   DSS *Beating Fraud is Everyone's Business: securing the future* (1998, Cm 4012) p 12.

B   Recovery of overpaid tax credits

i   *The law concerning recovery*

Section 71 of SSAA 1992, discussed above, applies equally to the recovery of overpaid tax credits with the necessary modifications.[349] Thus the right of recovery vests in the Board of the Inland Revenue;[350] moreover, where the issue is whether or not the claimant has disclosed a material fact to the relevant office, any such disclosure must have been to the appropriate tax credits office.

ii   *Methods of recovery*

An overpayment of tax credits is deemed by statute to be an underpayment of income tax.[351] Accordingly, the Inland Revenue may recover any such sum by adjusting the claimant's PAYE code or resorting to other methods permissible under the Taxes Management Act 1970, eg through summary proceedings in the magistrates' court, an action in the county court or High Court or even seizure and sale of goods. Tax credits may not be withheld in order to repay overpaid social security benefits[352] but regulations are silent as to whether an overpayment of tax credits can be recouped through deductions from benefit. The better argument is that there is no warrant to do so.[353] In addition, however, an employer who mistakenly pays an employee more by way of tax credits than the amount specified in the notification from the Inland Revenue is entitled to recover the excess from that person's wages.[354]

C   The control of fraud and abuse

i   *General*

Since the 1970s there has been considerable media publicity about suspected widespread abuse of the social security system, and successive governments have responded by increasing the numbers of staff deployed to investigate possible cases of fraud and so reduce its incidence. In 1971 a committee was set up under the chairmanship of Sir Henry Fisher to review the adequacy of the measures taken to counteract abuse and recommend changes in these procedures.[355] The committee concluded that there was not enough information to show the scale of the problem, and more thorough steps should be taken to acquire it.[356] In particular, detailed surveys should be made on sample claims, chosen at random. The government, however, rejected this approach as likely to lead to intrusion into the lives of wholly innocent claimants.

The Conservative governments in the 1980s and 1990s made a series of much-publicised efforts to eradicate social security fraud and abuse, such as employing more specialist staff to investigate suspected abuses. There is always a danger that specialist

---

349   SSAA 1992, s 71(11)(c) and (d).
350   TCA 1999, s 2(1)(c) and Sch 2, para 7(b).
351   TCA 1999, Sch 2, para 10(1) substituting SSAA 1992, s 71(8)–(9) for the purposes of tax credits.
352   SI 1999/3219, reg 6(9).
353   CPAG *Welfare benefits handbook 2002/2003* (2002) p 1050.
354   SI 1999/3219, reg 6(9). Rather alarmingly, there is no limit on the weekly amount of any such recovery.
355   Report of the Committee on Abuse of Social Security Benefits (1973, Cmnd 5228).
356   *Committee on Abuse of Social Security Benefits* n 355, above, paras 487–490.

officers, entirely divorced from the local office work of processing claims, will develop an attitude of hostility towards claimants.[357] An alternative solution might be the more careful initial scrutiny of claims, which would admittedly require the employment of more staff in hard-pressed local offices.[358] The focus of subsequent anti-fraud initiatives (eg the introduction of benefit 'hotlines' to encourage the reporting of suspected social security fraud) was primarily on detection, prosecution and punishment, rather than prevention. This approach was typified by further statutory measures introduced by SSA(F)A 1997.[359] In doing so official pronouncements fuelled the populist rhetoric of tabloid newspapers, sometimes characterised as 'scroungerphobia'.[360] Such initiatives could also have the effect both of distressing honest benefit recipients and deterring valid claims from others eligible for benefit.[361]

The Labour government elected in 1997 was no less strident in its public denunciation of social security fraud. It also introduced further measures designed to improve the detection and prosecution of benefit fraud, including the Social Security Fraud Act 2001 (SSFA 2001). Its approach, however, was different in that the fraud strategy was seen as a central part of its overall plans for welfare reform.[362] In addition, greater emphasis was placed on the prevention of fraud, both by designing benefits in such a way as to minimise the opportunities for fraud in the first place and by more attention to accurate decision making or 'getting it right, keeping it right and putting it right'.[363]

The true extent of social security fraud is necessarily a matter of some conjecture. In 2000 the DSS's 'best estimate' was in the order of £4 billion, or 4 per cent of the social security budget,[364] but this is necessarily subject to a considerable margin of error.[365] Clearly, some benefits are more susceptible to fraud than others: universal benefits with relatively simple eligibility criteria are less prone to abuse as compared with complex means-tested benefits such as income support and income-based jobseeker's allowance.[366] Equally fraud itself takes many different forms, from relatively minor incidents of individual dishonesty to organised theft on a major scale.[367] The main type of fraud in relation to means-tested benefits is thought to be non-disclosure of earnings.[368]

---

357 See chapter by Smith in Ward (ed) *DHSS in Crisis* (1985). Cf Parliamentary Commissioner for Administration *Annual Report 1990* (1990–91, HC 299) paras 30–31.
358 On the issues involved, see *Baldwin, Wikeley and Young* n 24, above, ch 2.
359 See McKeever (1999) 62 MLR 261 and (1999) 21 JSWFL 357.
360 See generally Deacon *In search of the scrounger* (1976).
361 See eg the much-criticised Benefit Integrity Project (BIP) which reviewed awards of disability living allowance: House of Commons Social Security Committee *Fourth Report* (1997–98, HC 641) pp xvii–xxv.
362 DSS *Beating Fraud is Everyone's Business: securing the future* (1998, Cm 4012).
363 DSS *A new contract for welfare: Safeguarding Social Security* (1999, Cm 4276).
364 HC Committee of Public Accounts *Thirty-First Report* (1999–2000, HC 350) para. 37.
365 Two years previously the DSS had given a conservative estimate of fraud amounting to £2 billion, rising to £7 billion 'if all suspicion of fraud were well founded': *DSS* n 362, above p 12. The Comptroller and Auditor General has qualified the DSS's Appropriation and National Insurance Fund Accounts for more than ten years owing to the levels of errors in payments and benefit fraud: DSS *Resource Accounts 2000–2001* (2001–02, HC 491) p 19.
366 These latter benefits present additional risks (eg claimants working and claiming, or living together when claiming separately). Thus DSS estimates suggest that fraud within income support may amount to as much as 10 per cent as against 'up to 0.13%' for retirement pensions: *DSS* n 362, above, p 56.
367 There is a considerable body of sociological literature: see eg MacDonald (1994) 8 Work, Employment & Society 507; and Dean in Taylor-Gooby (ed) *Choice and Public Policy* (1998).
368 HM Treasury *The Informal Economy: A report by Lord Grabiner QC* (2000) pp 2–3.

ii   Information gathering and investigations

SSA(F)A 1997 significantly extended the powers of the DSS (now the DWP) to seek information from a range of public bodies:

(a)   for use in the prevention, detection, investigation or prosecution of offences relating to social security; or

(b)   for use in checking the accuracy of information relating to benefits or national insurance numbers or to any other matter relating to social security and (where appropriate) amending or supplementing such information.[369]

The public bodies concerned are the Inland Revenue, government departments, the registration service and local authorities.[370] Local authorities do not have the same powers but may be granted access to information obtained by the DWP.[371] It is a criminal offence for those involved in the administration of social security to disclose such information without authorisation.[372] Both the DWP and local authorities may require the return of social security post and information about redirection arrangements.[373] The government's drive to 'bear down on fraud' means that further data-sharing seems inevitable, with such powers to seek information also being extended to cover private sector sources.[374]

The powers of DWP inspectors have been subject to frequent amendment, most recently by the Child Support, Pensions and Social Security Act 2000 and SSFA 2001. The 2000 Act both extended inspectors' powers and aligned the provisions relating to the main social security scheme and the housing benefit and council tax benefit schemes respectively.[375] Inspectors, now known as 'authorised officers', may be civil servants (including officers of the Inland Revenue), local authority officials or their contractors. Their powers may be used either in relation to individual claims or potential offences 'whether by particular persons or more generally'.[376] Such officers have the power to request information by written notice, providing the person at whom the notice is directed falls within one of a number of prescribed categories and that the information is relevant to these purposes.[377] Authorised officers also have a power to enter premises in order to obtain information,[378] but have no power to enter premises by force, to search premises forcibly or to detain persons compulsorily for questioning.

The powers of authorised officers were further extended by SSFA 2001. In particular, this enabled DWP and local authority investigators to require specified private and public sector organisations to provide information about named individuals.[379] These powers may only be used where it appears to the authorised officer that there are reasonable grounds for believing that the person about whom information is sought *either* has committed, is committing or intends to commit a benefit offence *or* is a

---

369   See eg SSAA 1992, s 122(2).

370   SSAA 1992, ss 122–122E, 124–125. SSC(TF)A 1999 made further amendments, inserting SSAA 1992, ss 121E–121F to reflect the transfer of contributions work to the Inland Revenue.

371   SSAA 1992, s 122C.

372   SSAA 1992, s 123 and Sch 4.

373   SSAA 1992, ss 182A and 182B.

374   See *HM Treasury* n 368, above, ch 5; and DSS *Safeguarding social security: Getting the information we need* (2000).

375   SSAA 1992, s 109A–110A. These reforms superseded those made by SSA(F)A 1997.

376   SSAA 1992, s 109A(2).

377   SSAA 1992, s 109B. The prescribed categories include employers, employees and the self-employed.

378   SSAA 1992, s 109C.

379   However, 'reverse searches' of telephone directories (ie by number not name) are permissible: SSAA 1992, s 109(2F).

member of such a person's family.[380] Specifically authorised DWP (but *not* local authority) investigators may require bulk information from utility companies about the quantity of services supplied to residential properties, with a view to detecting possible fraud.[381] In addition, the Secretary of State and local authorities (but the latter only with the consent of the former) may require electronic access to information held by third parties.[382] A Code of Practice has been issued in relation to the exercise of such powers.[383] The Secretary of State also has the power to exchange social security information with other countries to tackle cross-border benefit frauds.[384]

iii Criminal offences

Those suspected of social security fraud may be prosecuted under the specific offences created by the social security legislation, although more serious cases will be tried under the ordinary criminal law. Thus an individual who obtains benefit by deliberate deception might be prosecuted for obtaining property by deception under the Theft Act 1968 whilst more of those involved in still larger scale frauds committed by gangs may face conspiracy charges.[385] As a general principle, frauds of more than £5,000 are dealt with under the Theft Act 1968 rather than the social security legislation.[386] Charges under the social security legislation must be brought within three months of the date when the relevant authority believes it has sufficient evidence to prosecute or within 12 months of the commission of the offence, whichever is the later.[387]

A   OBTAINING BENEFIT BY FALSE STATEMENTS, ETC

It is an offence punishable on summary conviction by a fine of £5,000 or imprisonment for three months, or both, if a person:

> for the purpose of obtaining any benefit or other payment under the social security legislation whether for himself or some other person, or for any other purpose connected with that legislation—
> (a) makes a statement or representation which he knows to be false; or
> (b) produces or furnishes, or knowingly causes or knowingly allows to be produced or furnished, any document or information which he knows to be false in a material particular.[388]

---

380 SSAA 1992, s 109B(2A)–(2C). See also SI 2002/817. On the definition of a 'benefit offence', see s 121DA(5).
381 SSAA 1992, s 109B(2D); eg a claimant may be living with a partner at one address but claim to be living in a different property, which is effectively unoccupied. This power does not extend to details of the content of telephone calls: s 109(2E).
382 SSAA 1992, ss 109BA and 110AA.
383 SSFA 2001, s 3; see s 4 concerning arrangements for payment for the supply of such information. See further DWP *Code of Practice on Obtaining Information* (2002).
384 SSAA 1992, s 179A.
385 Theft Act 1968, s 15. See Smith and Hogan *Criminal Law* (9th edn, 1999) pp 552–570.
386 In 1996–97 the DSS prosecuted some 11,000 individuals, of whom 740 were prosecuted under the Theft Act 1968. The police prosecuted a further 494 cases for theft or conspiracy: *DSS* n 363, above, p 22. The success rate is in the order of 98 per cent: *HC Committee on Public Accounts* n 364, above, para 43. The DSS has announced its intention to pursue more prosecutions under the Theft Act 1968 rather than the SSAA 1992: *DSS* n 362, above, p 50.
387 SSAA 1992, s 116(2).
388 SSAA 1992, s 112(1).

It is now clear that for these offences to be committed it is enough that the defendant knowingly made a false statement; it is immaterial that he or she did not intend to obtain the benefit by fraud, but lied for some other reason.[389] A defendant will also be guilty of the offence by making an untrue representation when accepting *payment* of the benefit.[390] It does not matter that the decision to pay it has been taken before the false statement.

As originally drafted, however, this legislation did not penalise a claimant who, after claiming, subsequently adopted a course of action which precluded entitlement to the relevant benefit (eg working on days for which incapacity benefit had been paid).[391] Thus SSA(F)A 1997 made it an offence, punishable with the same penalties, if a person without reasonable excuse failed to notify a change of circumstances required under the regulations or knowingly caused (or allowed) another person to fail to notify such a change of circumstances.[392] This offence was reformulated by SSFA 2001, so that it now penalises those who fail to report changes in circumstances that they know will affect entitlement to benefit.[393] None the less, both extensions of the law are problematic. So far as the individual claimant is concerned, criminalising a failure to notify a change in circumstances blurs the distinction between ignorance or oversight and dishonesty.[394] The precise scope of the new offence of knowingly causing or allowing another person to fail to notify a change of circumstances is also unclear. In principle it should apply only where the third party is in a position to stop the claimant from making proper disclosure.[395] The government has stated that it does not intend that this offence should apply to advisers acting in good faith.[396]

These offences are all triable before the magistrates' courts. As a result of SSA(F)A 1997, a person who commits any of the above offences dishonestly is liable to the more severe penalty of a £5,000 fine or six months' imprisonment in summary proceedings. If tried on indictment in the Crown Court, the fine is unlimited and the maximum term of imprisonment is seven years.[397] The addition of a specific offence of dishonesty in this context appears to have been in response to a Court of Appeal decision which held that a specimen offence under the original social security legislation could not be used to prove ongoing criminal activity (eg relating to housing benefit).[398]

B   OTHER OFFENCES

Other offences under the social security legislation are less important. First, it is an offence under SSAA 1992 to delay or obstruct wilfully an inspector in the exercise of his or her powers, or to refuse either to answer questions or to provide documents and information.[399] Secondly, under SSAA 1992 regulations may be issued creating criminal offences for

389   *Clear v Smith* [1981] 1 WLR 399; *Barrass v Reeve* [1980] 3 All ER 705, [1981] 1 WLR 408, in which the earlier decision in *Moore v Branton* [1974] Crim LR 439 was disapproved on this point. See also *Department of Social Security v Bavi* [1996] COD 260; and *Harrison v Department of Social Security* [1997] COD 220.
390   *Tolfree v Florence* [1971] 1 All ER 125, [1971] 1 WLR 141.
391   On the duty to inform the authorities of a relevant change of circumstances, see SI 1987/1968, reg 32.
392   SSAA 1992, s 112(1A). See further SI 2001/3252.
393   SSFA 2001, s 16.
394   McKeever (1999) 62 MLR 261 at 266.
395   *R v Chainey* [1914] 1 KB 137 at 142, per Isaacs CJ (in the context of sexual offences).
396   HC Standing Committee E, cols 316–317 (21 January 1997).
397   SSAA 1992, s 111A(3).
398   *R v Clark* [1996] 2 Cr App Rep 282; see *McKeever* n 394, above, at 265–266.
399   SSAA 1992, s 111(1).

breach of any requirements imposed under the social security legislation.[400] This provision is unacceptably wide, for it would appear to enable the government to make it a criminal offence, say, not to provide the required information when making a claim. In practice the provision has been little used and directed more towards non-compliance with reporting obligations imposed upon employers (in relation to statutory maternity pay) and landlords and their agents (housing benefit).[401] Finally, there is a criminal offence of fraudulent evasion of National Insurance contributions.[402] SSA 1998 decriminalised less serious breaches of the contributions regulations, so that these are now subject to a system of civil penalties.[403] (Failure to pay Class 4 contributions, recoverable by the Inland Revenue, may be prosecuted under the Taxes Management Act 1970.[404])

C REPEAT OFFENDERS

In 2000 an independent review of the informal economy concluded that there was no case for increasing the statutory level of fines.[405] It did, however, recommend that benefit might be withdrawn from those convicted twice of working whilst claiming benefit.[406] Repeat offenders are now liable to be sanctioned by a reduction or withdrawal of benefit for a period of 13 weeks under the 'loss of benefit' provisions introduced by SSFA 2001.[407] The person concerned must have been convicted of a 'benefit offence' in each of two separate sets of proceedings during a three-year period.[408] Fraud in respect of virtually all social security benefits counts for these purposes (the definition of 'disqualifying benefit' excludes only maternity allowance, statutory sick pay, statutory maternity pay and tax credits).[409] Finally, the offender must in all other respects be eligible for a 'sanctionable benefit', which means most 'disqualifying benefits' with certain exceptions.[410] The basic rule is that the sanctionable benefit is not payable during the 13-week disqualification period.[411] However, if the claimant's benefit entitlement is to income support, benefit is reduced rather than withdrawn completely for the prescribed period.[412] The level of reduction reflects that applied in cases where hardship payments are made (40 per cent of the offender's personal allowance, or 20 per cent for vulnerable cases, eg where a household member is seriously ill). Where there remains an underlying entitlement to income support or jobseeker's allowance, full housing benefit and council tax benefit remain in payment. If the person sanctioned is not entitled to either of those other benefits, their housing benefit or council tax benefit is reduced.[413]

400 SSAA 1992, s 113(1)(b) and (3).
401 See SI 1986/1960, reg 32 and SI 1997/2436, reg 6.
402 SSAA 1992, s 114. The maximum penalty following conviction on indictment is seven years' imprisonment or an unlimited fine; in the magistrates' court the maximum fine is £5,000.
403 SSAA 1992, s 113(1)(a) and (2). SSAA 1992, s 114A, inserted by SSA 1998, s 61, was repealed before it came into force: SSC(TF)A 1999, Sch 5, para 6.
404 Taxes Management Act 1970, ss 93–107, applied by SSCBA 1992, s 16(1).
405 'Most people caught working in the hidden economy do not have the means to pay large penalties': *HM Treasury* n 368, above, p 35.
406 *HM Treasury* n 368, above, pp 37–38.
407 SSFA 2001, ss 7–13 and SI 2001/4022. Special provision is made for joint-claim jobseeker's allowance in SSFA 2001, s 8 and for benefits for members of the offender's family in s 9.
408 SSFA 2001, s 7(1) and SI 2001/4022, reg 2.
409 SSFA 2001, s 7(8).
410 SSFA 2001, s 7(8); attendance allowance, disability living allowance, child benefit and the retirement pension are amongst those benefits excluded; see also SI 2001/4022, reg 19.
411 SSFA 2001, s 7(2).
412 SSFA 2001, s 7(3) and SI 2001/4022, reg 3.
413 SSFA 2001, s 7(5) and SI 2001/4022, regs 17 and 18.

iv   Cautions and penalties

Following the Conservatives' defeat in May 1997, the incoming Labour government extended their predecessors' move towards the use of sanctions for fraud and abuse other than prosecution through the courts. Thus in December 1997 the new administration brought into force powers enabling the DWP to levy a financial penalty as an alternative to prosecution. A penalty can only be applied where an overpayment of benefit is recoverable from the claimant and:

> it appears to the Secretary or State or authority that—
> (a)   the making of the overpayment was attributable to an act or omission on the part of that person; and
> (b)   there are grounds for instituting against him proceedings for an offence (under this Act or any other enactment) relating to the overpayment.[414]

The Secretary of State must issue the claimant with a formal notice setting out how the penalty scheme operates.[415] The penalty itself is fixed by statute at 30 per cent of the value of the recoverable overpayment. In practice penalties are deployed as an alternative to prosecution in less serious cases of fraud, typically in cases where under £1,500 is involved.[416] Formally the penalty cannot be imposed unilaterally; the claimant must agree to pay the penalty (which is recoverable in addition, to the original overpayment) in return for which there is immunity from prosecution in relation to that matter.[417] The statutory language of 'agreement' cannot mask the concern that, even where the DWP has a weak case, claimants may accede to a penalty for fear of prosecution.[418]

SSFA 2001 introduced a parallel provision to deal with employers who are suspected of colluding in social security fraud by their employees. This penalty regime can only be used where the benefit authorities believe that there are grounds for prosecuting an employer in two types of circumstances.[419] The first is for the general offence in connection with impeding an inquiry into the employment of others, the second for facilitating the commission of a specific benefit offence by an employee (whether or not such an offence was actually committed). The 'overpayment plus 30 per cent' approach for social security fraud perpetrated by claimants is clearly inappropriate for dealing with collusion by employers. The penalties are accordingly banded, with £1,000 for general offences in relation to the employment of others, but £1,000 per employee, up to a maximum of £5,000, for facilitating employees' benefit offences.

Since June 1998 the DWP has also operated an extra-statutory system of 'cautioning' claimants for social security offences, modelled on that operated by the police.[420] Cautions are typically used for less serious frauds where the sums involved are low. A caution provides immunity from prosecution but is an admission of guilt and the details

---

414   SSAA 1992, s 115A(1). This applies to overpayments under SSAA 1992, s 71 (most benefits), s 71A (social fund payments), s 75 (housing benefit) and s 76 (community charge benefit).
415   See SI 1997/2813.
416   *DSS* n 363, above, p 25. There are currently more than 25,000 sanctions (including both penalties and cautions) imposed each year: HC Fifth Standing Committee on Delegated Legislation, col 10 (14 March 2002).
417   SSAA 1992, s 115A(2)–(4). There is also provision for withdrawal of agreement: s 115A(5). On the consequences following revision or appeal, see s 115A(6) and (7). The DWP and local authorities may act together to offer an aggregated administrative penalty: s 115A(7A) and (7B).
418   *McKeever* n 394, above, at 266–269.
419   SSAA 1992, s 115B.
420   See *DSS* n 363, above, p 25.

are recorded on a central database and retained for five years. As with the system of penalties, there is the risk that cautioning will be deployed in cases where there is insufficient evidence to prosecute and an innocent claimant may accede to a caution in order to avoid the perceived threat of prosecution.[421]

v   Prosecution policy and sentencing

The determination of successive Conservative governments to stamp out fraud and abuse, discussed above, did not entail an increase in the number of prosecutions. There were an increasing number of proceedings in the late 1970s, but the 1980s saw a change in policy and a reduction in their number.[422] The then DHSS found that a prosecution policy was not cost-effective.[423] The NACRO Working Party, which in 1984-86 considered at length the enforcement of social security law, welcomed this change, and called for a further reduction in the number of offences prosecuted.[424] It is still the case eg that social security fraud is prosecuted much more readily than revenue offences,[425] though the existence of other sanctions for the latter may provide some explanation. Although the Labour government has again undertaken to increase the number of prosecutions in more serious cases, the full impact of the introduction of cautions and penalties in social security matters has yet to be evaluated. This may result in a policy of diversion from the criminal justice process, but equally cases of what are in fact non-fraudulent overpayments may be brought within the new regime.

In the large majority of court cases, where a conviction for social security fraud is obtained, a non-custodial sentence is imposed. Indeed, in recent years 35 per cent of successful prosecutions in the magistrates' courts lead only to a conditional discharge.[426] However, in a small number of instances the offender is imprisoned, and the NACRO Working Party expressed concern that sometimes the sentence seemed severe. It argued that probation or community service orders, and in some cases moderate fines, were more appropriate. It also urged that compensation orders (under the Powers of the Criminal Courts Act 1973) should not be made in social security cases; magistrates' courts were not a suitable forum to decide whether benefit had been overpaid.[427] To some extent these views have since been reflected in the guidelines laid down by the Court of Appeal in 1987 for sentencing in fraud cases.[428] The court stressed that deterrence should not play a significant part in sentencing, and that prison sentences of two-and-a-half years or more were only appropriate for carefully organised frauds on a large scale.[429] If an immediate rather than a suspended sentence is necessary, normally 9 to 12 months would be sufficient. Cases in which a custodial sentence may not be appropriate at all include those where an original (and perfectly legitimate) claim is

---

421   This reflects a concern with the use of cautioning elsewhere in the criminal justice system: see Sanders and Young *Criminal Justice* (2nd edn, 2000) pp 350–352.
422   *NACRO Working Party* n 303, above, para 10.6.
423   Prosecutions in the Crown Court are also substantially more costly than those brought under SSAA 1992: see *McKeever* n 394, above, at 261.
424   *NACRO Working Party* n 303, above, para 10.11.
425   See Uglow [1984] Crim LR 128; Cook *Rich Law, Poor Law* (1989); and Barker, Watchman and Rowan-Robertson (1990) Soc Pol & Admin 104. The Grabiner Report pointed out 'the risk of inconsistency' caused by the Revenue's approach: *HM Treasury* n 368, above, p 34.
426   *DSS* n 362, above, p 6.
427   *NACRO Working Party* n 303, above, paras 10.21–10.22.
428   *R v Stewart* [1987] 2 All ER 383, [1987] 1 WLR 559. See further Thomas *Current Sentencing Practice* (1982) B6-3.3(F).
429   See *R v Perry* (1989) 11 Cr App Rep (S) 58.

affected by a change of circumstances.[430] The court thought that compensation orders were often of value, though they should generally only be imposed when the defendant was in work.[431]

vi   Tax credits fraud

As the Inland Revenue administers the tax credits schemes, the DWP powers discussed above do not apply. Instead the Revenue's normal powers in relation to the investigation and punishment of revenue fraud apply.[432] The tax authorities tend in the main to seek settlements with tax defaulters or to deploy administrative financial penalties, reserving prosecution for the most serious offences. Employers who are subject to such penalties have a right of appeal to the tax appeal commissioners whereas claimants can challenge sanctions before an appeal tribunal.

---

430   *R v Graham* (1988) 10 Cr App Rep (S) 352.
431   Cf *R v Miah* (1989) 11 Cr App Rep (S) 163.
432   TCA 1999, ss 8–10.

Chapter 6

Decision making and appeals

Part 1   General

A   Scope of chapter

The conceptual distinction between 'administration' and 'adjudication', or to use the modern terminology 'decision making and appeals', the subject-matter of the previous and present chapters respectively, is by no means unproblematic.[1] One approach is to regard all decision making on benefit claims by departmental officials as part and parcel of the system of public administration. Yet, as Mashaw observes, adjudication 'encompasses any determination of eligibility or amount of benefits at any stage of a social welfare claims process'.[2] In typically confused style, the British legislation of 1983 conferred the title of 'adjudication officer' (formerly 'insurance officer') on the civil servant who decided claims for benefit, whereas the courts viewed the same officer's functions as administrative rather than judicial in nature.[3] The abolition of the status of adjudication officer by the Social Security Act 1998 (SSA 1998), with the vesting of all first instance decision making in the Secretary of State, reflected the primacy of the bureaucratic over the quasi-judicial models of decision making in the modernised social security system.[4]

However such initial decision making is characterised, an important feature of the modern welfare state has been the recognition that citizens should have some form of redress against adverse decisions. This could either be by way of recourse to the ordinary courts or by appeal to a specially constituted tribunal.[5] In the years following the Franks Report[6] this debate appeared to have been settled in favour of the latter course, the prime complaint being that a plethora of tribunals was being created. This was seen as creating jurisdictional problems and varieties of procedures that baffled both claimants and their representatives.[7] In the mid-1980s, however, the then Conservative government introduced novel review procedures that precluded any right of appeal to an independent tribunal. The most notable examples, both within the social security field, were the

---

1   See the discussion in Partington *Secretary of State's Powers of Adjudication in Social Security Law* SAUS Working Paper No 96 (1991) ch 1.
2   Mashaw (1974) 59 Cornell LR 772 at 774. See further Mashaw *Bureaucratic Justice* (1983).
3   P 183, below.
4   See Wikeley (2000) 63 MLR 475.
5   For an attack on the 'pathology of legalism', see Titmuss (1971) 42 Political Q 113.
6   *Report of the Committee on Administrative Tribunals and Enquiries* (1957, Cmnd 218).
7   Hence the Council on Tribunal's development of *Model Rules of Procedure for Tribunals* (1991, Cm 1434).

internal review mechanisms for housing benefit and the discretionary social fund, which dispensed with the right of access to an oral hearing before an independent tribunal.[8] In the early 1990s a process of internal review was made a mandatory interim stage before an appellant could appeal an adverse decision relating to disability benefits or child support to an independent tribunal.

SSA 1998 initiated a radical overhaul of the adjudication system under the aegis of the Decision Making and Appeals (DMA) programme, designed to ensure that the benefits system provide 'the right amount of benefit to the right person, at the right time, every time'.[9] Most first-tier decisions are now the responsibility of the Secretary of State, and such decisions may be open to revision or supersession, replacing the former concept of review, whether optional or mandatory. These first-tier decision making processes are considered in Part 2 of this chapter. At the second stage a generic appeal tribunal has been constituted, comprised of one, two or three members, depending on the type of case involved. These tribunals also took over responsibility for housing benefit appeals with effect from July 2001. The composition, jurisdiction and procedure of the appeal tribunals are discussed in Part 3. At the apex of the tribunal system stand the Social Security Commissioners, discussed in Part 4, whose reported decisions constitute the main body of case law in this area. Part 5 covers appeals from the Commissioner to the Court of Appeal (and thence to the House of Lords), as well as considering the scope of judicial review. Part 6 discusses references to the European Court of Justice in the context of social security cases. The final two Parts of this chapter concern relatively peripheral topics: Part 7 deals with reviews under the discretionary social fund scheme, whilst Part 8 briefly describes adjudication of war pension claims, which remains entirely separate from the mainstream tribunal system. Further reform to this system of tribunals may follow, depending on the outcome of the government's deliberations on the recommendations of the Leggatt Review.[10]

B History

From the beginning of the modern social security system before the First World War, powers of adjudication have been vested in special tribunals or other bodies.[11] The decision not to confer jurisdiction on the courts was largely attributable to an understandable fear that their procedure would be too formal and expensive. The 1906 Liberal government was also influenced by the successful use in Germany of special tribunals in this area. Thus in the first instance Board of Trade insurance officers decided claims for unemployment insurance under the National Insurance Act 1911 (NIA 1911). Appeal then lay to a court of referees, a three-member tribunal, with a chairman, one member drawn from an 'employer's panel' and the other drawn from a 'workmen's panel'. A further appeal could be made to an Umpire, a lawyer of standing appointed by the Crown.[12] This became the model for the system introduced by NIA 1946.

---

8   P 180, below. For the concerns of the Council on Tribunals, see its *Annual Report for 1990–91* (1991) paras 1.2–1.14. See further the essay by Sainsbury in Finnie, Himsworth and Walker (eds) *Edinburgh Essays in Public Law* (1991).
9   DSS *Improving decision making and appeals in Social Security* (1996, Cm 3328) p 7.
10 *Tribunals for Users: One System, One Service* (March 2001). A government White Paper is anticipated later in 2002.
11 See Wraith and Hutchesson *Administrative Tribunals* (1973) pp 33–38; Robson *Justice and Administrative Law* (3rd edn, 1951) pp 188–198; Fulbrook *Administrative Justice and the Unemployed* (1978) ch 6.
12 For a full discussion of this system, see the Committee on Procedure and Evidence for the Determination of Claims for Unemployment Insurance Benefit (the Morris Committee) (1929, Cmd 3415).

Another pattern of adjudication was established when contributory pensions were introduced in 1925.[13] A claim for an old age or widow's pension would be made in the first place to the minister. If he or she rejected it, an appeal lay to an independent Referee, a senior lawyer, whose decisions, unlike those of the Umpire under the unemployment insurance legislation, were not publicly reported.[14] This system was adopted in 1945 for the adjudication of disputed claims to family allowances.[15] The Beveridge Report recommended a right of appeal to a local tribunal, analogous to the court of referees, and then to the Umpire, whose decisions would be final.[16] This was accepted in principle by the government. NIA 1946 provided that claims should initially be determined by the insurance officer, with a right of appeal to a National Insurance Local Tribunal, and then to the National Insurance Commissioner or one of the Deputy Commissioners.[17] A similar system was instituted under the industrial injuries legislation. An appeal lay to a local appeal tribunal, and from it to the Industrial Injuries Commissioner or a Deputy Commissioner. But certain questions concerning entitlement to, and the assessment of, disablement benefit were entrusted to medical boards, with an appeal to medical appeal tribunals. In addition, some questions, particularly on contributions, were reserved for the minister, with an appeal only on a point of law to the High Court.

The 30 years after the Second World War saw a series of developments in relation to National Insurance and non-contributory benefits which strengthened the position of the Beveridge model.[18] First, following a recommendation of the Franks Report,[19] the adjudication of claims to family allowances (subsequently, child benefit) was transferred in 1959 to insurance officers and on appeal to the local tribunal and the National Insurance Commissioner.[20] Secondly, the 1959 legislation also conferred a right of appeal on a point of law from the medical appeal tribunals to the Commissioner. This development reflected the general confidence in the Commissioners and enhanced their position at the apex of the tribunal system.[21] Thirdly, NIA 1966 merged the systems of adjudication under the National Insurance and the industrial injuries legislation, so that industrial injury cases (apart from those referred to the medical authorities) came to be determined by the ordinary adjudicating authorities.[22] In 1970, in a variant of these arrangements, the Attendance Allowance Board was set up to adjudicate claims to attendance allowance with an appeal from its decisions on a point of law to the Commissioner.

At the same time as these developments, there were changes in the system of tribunals which heard appeals against a refusal of means-tested benefits. The national assistance tribunals (NATs) set up in 1948 had been modelled on earlier bodies which had heard appeals from decisions of the Unemployment Assistance Board.[23] There was no further

13 For the history of pensions, see ch 17, pp 590–591, below.
14 Safford (1954) 17 MLR 197 at 201 (the author was a Deputy Insurance Commissioner).
15 The Referee could state a case on a point of law for the High Court, though this was done very rarely.
16 Beveridge Report *Social Insurance and Allied Services* (1942, Cmd 6404) paras 394–395.
17 See Bonner (2002) 9 JSSL 11. Under NIA 1966, the National Insurance Commissioner was retitled the Chief National Insurance Commissioner, and the Deputy Commissioners became full Commissioners. For the confusion engendered by the original nomenclature, see Micklethwait *The National Insurance Commissioners* Hamlyn Lectures (1976) p 13.
18 For a full discussion, see *Micklethwait* n 17, above, ch 2. The term 'statutory authorities' was frequently used to refer to the insurance officer, local tribunal and the Commissioner, though its origin is shrouded in mystery: see *Micklethwait* n 17, above, p 18, n 4.
19 N 6, above, para 184.
20 Family Allowances and National Insurance Act 1959, s 1 (FANIA 1959).
21 FANIA 1959, s 2: see 596 HC Official Report (5th series) cols 714–715.
22 NIA 1966, s 8.
23 For the history of these tribunals, see Fulbrook *Administrative Justice and the Unemployed* (1978), esp chs 8–10; and Lynes and Bradley in Adler and Bradley (eds) *Justice, Discretion and Poverty* (1976) chs II and III.

appeal from the decision of a NAT, a factor which highlighted their informal character. This feature was indeed recognised by the Franks Committee, which saw the work of this tribunal as that of 'an assessment or case committee, taking a further look at the facts and in some cases arriving at a fresh decision on the extent of need'.[24] When national assistance was replaced by supplementary benefits in 1966, the tribunals' structure was unaffected, though they were renamed supplementary benefit appeal tribunals (SBATs).

An SBAT, like its predecessors, had three members, but in contrast to the National Insurance tribunals, its chairman was not usually a lawyer. There was considerable disquiet with the performance of SBATs, the major criticisms being that they relied too frequently on the advice of the clerk (an official of the Department of Health and Social Security (DHSS)) and that they gave either no or inadequate reasons for their decisions.[25] Despite these failings, their jurisdiction was expanded in 1970 to hear appeals from refusal of family income supplement. In 1979 a first step to strengthen the tribunal system in this area was taken with the appointment of some Senior Chairmen to oversee the working of the tribunals and to assist in the appointment of chairmen. This development heralded the 'presidential system' which is now one of the features of the appeal tribunals.[26] A second change was the institution in 1980 of a right of appeal on a point of law to the Commissioners, whose expanded jurisdiction was marked by their restyling as Social Security Commissioners.[27]

A major reform was brought about in 1984 with the merger of the local insurance tribunals and SBATs into integrated social security appeal tribunals (SSATs) under the auspices of the Office of the President of Social Security Appeal Tribunals (OPSSAT, later the Independent Tribunal Service).[28] Under the same legislation there was also merger at the officer level where original decisions are taken, insurance, benefit and supplement officers being replaced by adjudication officers; in practice, however, integration was more semantic than real in that staff still worked in separate sections, specialising in particular benefits. The post of Chief Adjudication Officer was established to provide independent advice for and monitoring of adjudication officers.[29] SSATs lost a substantial part of their caseload when the supplementary benefits single payments scheme was abolished in 1988.[30] The government took the controversial step of denying any right of appeal from decisions relating to its replacement, the discretionary social fund. The Council on Tribunals described this as 'the most substantial abolition of a right of appeal to an independent tribunal' since its institution in 1958.[31] There is a right of appeal to an appeal tribunal from decisions relating to payments from the regulated social fund,[32] but decisions on applications to the discretionary social fund

---

24 N 6, above, para 182.
25 Bell *Research Study of Supplementary Benefit Appeal Tribunals, Review of Main Findings: Conclusions: Recommendations* (1975) pp 5–10; this report, commissioned by the DHSS, strongly influenced the changes made in 1979–83.
26 The 'presidential system' was not new; it had already been a feature of industrial (now employment) tribunals and pensions appeal tribunals (see pp 211–213, below) for some years.
27 SSA 1980, s 12; see now SSAA 1992, s 52 and Part 3, below for further discussion. With the creation of child support appeal tribunals in 1993 (now subsumed within the generic appeal tribunals), the Commissioners were retitled the Social Security and Child Support Commissioners.
28 Health and Social Services and Social Security Adjudications Act 1983, s 25 and Sch 8 (HSSSSAA 1983); see now Social Security Administration Act 1992, ss 40–41 (SSAA 1992). See further Bradley (1985) 26 *Les Cahiers de Droit* 403; and Brown (1986) 17 Cambrian LR 40.
29 Replacing the former Chief Insurance Officer and Chief Supplementary Benefit Officer.
30 Baldwin, Wikeley and Young *Judging Social Security* (1992) pp 19–20.
31 *Social Security – Abolition of independent appeals under the proposed Social Fund* (1986, Cmnd 9722) para 12.
32 Eg on payments to meet maternity, funeral and cold weather expenses.

may be reviewed only by 'appropriate officers' and social fund inspectors.[33] In 1992 the reform of the non-contributory disability benefits led to the abolition of the Attendance Allowance Board and the creation of a new tribunal, the disability appeal tribunal (DAT). However, there was no automatic right of appeal to a DAT; a dissatisfied claimant had first to invoke an internal review procedure.[34] A similar requirement was made a precondition of access to the child support appeal tribunal. Both new tribunals, along with medical appeal tribunals and vaccine damage tribunals, came within the remit of the Independent Tribunal Service.

In 1996 the then Conservative government launched its DMA programme with a consultation paper on the decision making and appeals systems for social security benefits.[35] This advocated more streamlined adjudication arrangements with a more flexible appeals structure. Some of these changes were introduced by regulations, but the main changes were adopted by the incoming Labour administration and formed the basis of SSA 1998. The 1998 Act abolished the roles of adjudication officer and Chief Adjudication Officer, bringing first-tier decision making and quality assurance control wholly within the control of the then Department of Social Security (DSS) and its various agencies. All decisions became the responsibility of the Secretary of State, but the right of appeal to an independent tribunal was preserved. However, the Independent Tribunal Service was abolished; its judicial arm, still headed by a President, was renamed the Appeals Service, whilst its administrative wing became an executive agency within the DSS. The five tribunals under the Independent Tribunal Service umbrella became the generic 'appeal tribunal', comprised of either one, two or three members, as prescribed by regulations. The role of the Commissioners was left largely untouched by these reforms. The culture of constant change in the social security appeals system was reflected in three further legislative developments. The Social Security Contributions (Transfer of Functions, etc) Act 1999 (SSC(TF)A 1999) moved the Contributions Agency out of the DSS and into the Inland Revenue, with the effect that contributions decisions became the responsibility of officers of the Board. Inland Revenue officers also assumed decision making functions in respect of working families' tax credit and disabled person's tax credit as a result of the Tax Credits Act 1999 (TCA 1999). The prospect of a challenge under the Human Rights Act 1998 then led the government to abolish housing benefit review boards and to replace them with a right of appeal to an appeal tribunal.[36]

Finally, reference must be made to the use of the test case strategy and judicial and governmental responses to such litigation. From the 1970s onwards welfare rights organisations have sought to maximise claimants' entitlement to benefit by pursuing test cases together with publicity campaigns.[37] In such cases the validity of delegated legislation has often been challenged in proceedings before the Commissioners and the higher courts. In 1992 the DSS sought to argue that the Commissioners had no jurisdiction to entertain such challenges. This argument was rejected unanimously by the House of Lords,[38] reversing the decision of the Court of Appeal.[39] In principle it

---

33 Pp 209–211, below. Appropriate officers were formerly known as social fund officers.
34 DATs dealt with appeals relating to attendance, disability living and disability working allowances.
35 DSS *Improving decision making and appeals in Social Security* (1996, Cm 3328).
36 Child Support, Pensions and Social Security Act 2000, s 68 and Sch 7 (CSPSSA 2000).
37 See Prosser *Test Cases for the Poor* CPAG Poverty Pamphlet 60 (1983).
38 *Chief Adjudication Officer v Foster* [1993] 1 All ER 705, HL; see Feldman and Wikeley (1993) 109 LQR 544; and Harris (1993) 56 MLR 710.
39 [1992] QB 31; see Feldman (1992) 108 LQR 45; and Bradley [1992] PL 185.

seems that an appeal tribunal could determine the vires of a provision in a statutory instrument. The practical value of the test case strategy was, however, severely limited by the government's decision in 1990 to minimise the impact of successful appeals. Legislation now provides that where an established interpretation of the law is overturned by a decision of a Commissioner or a higher court, the effect of that decision is retrospective only so far as the individual litigant is concerned.[40] Other claimants only gain the benefit of such a ruling on a review or fresh claim with effect from the date of the new decision. These provisions were carried forward and indeed tightened up further under the DMA changes. The extent to which these complex provisions are consistent with the independence of the judiciary is questionable; eg SSA 1998 empowers the Secretary of State to intervene in the appeals system by staying cases which may be affected by a test case, or requiring a tribunal or Commissioner to determine an appeal on the assumption that the test case had already been resolved 'in the way that was most unfavourable to the appellant'.[41]

Part 2   First-tier adjudication

A   The Secretary of State

i   *General*

Until the DMA changes, introduced by SSA 1998, nearly all claims and questions were initially submitted to an adjudication officer for determination, although some matters were reserved to the Secretary of State.[42] These arrangements were less than satisfactory in a number of ways. For example, the distinction between decisions taken by adjudication officers and decisions taken on behalf of the Secretary of State (both of which might be taken by the same individual working in the Benefits Agency) did not lend itself to ease of comprehension. Yet the status of adjudication officer, with its formal legal independence from line management, was traditionally regarded as one of the strengths of the social security adjudication machinery.[43] The 1998 Act transferred the functions of adjudication officers, child support officers and social fund officers to the Secretary of State.[44] The Secretary of State is thus charged with the task of deciding claims for most benefits and for discretionary social fund payments,[45] as well as with making most other decisions under the social security legislation.[46] In practice civil servants in the Department's agencies are authorised to act as decision makers on behalf of the Secretary of State.

40   SSA 1990, Sch 6, para 7. See later SSAA 1992, ss 68 and 69 and now SSA 1998, s 27.
41   SSA 1998, s 26.
42   See the 4th edition of this book, pp 661–667. Certain medical questions were also subject to a special procedure. The other main exceptions related to claims for housing benefit and for payments from the discretionary social fund.
43   See Baldwin, Wikeley and Young n 30, above, ch 2; and Lynes 'The End of Independent Adjudication?' in Adler and Sainsbury (eds) *Adjudication Matters* (1998).
44   SSA 1998, s 1.
45   In practice the decision making arrangements for the social fund were little changed by SSA 1998; see further pp 209–211, below.
46   SSA 1998, s 8(1). The relevant benefits are listed in s 8(3). First-tier decisions relating to housing benefit and council tax benefit remain excluded, as do matters now determined by officers of the Inland Revenue: s 8(4) and (5).

ii Procedure for determining claims

The decision maker decides a claim entirely on the documents submitted by the claimant and generated within the Department for Work and Pensions (DWP) and does not interview the claimant or witnesses.[47] There are relatively few statutory provisions governing the functions and role of decision makers[48] and to date no relevant case law. Given that the retitling of adjudication officers as decision makers is in large part a semantic rather than substantive change, the case law concerning adjudication officers should continue to apply. The duties of adjudication officers were characterised as 'administrative' in that they were not adjudicating between the contentions of the claimant and those of the DWP or any other party.[49] Thus information supplied by a claimant to an adjudication officer in connection with a claim for benefit was not covered by absolute privilege and could therefore give rise to an action for libel.[50] Adjudication officers were under a duty to act fairly and to obtain any necessary information relevant to a particular claim, but were not obliged to investigate the full financial position of the claimant.[51] Nor are officers liable in negligence for a wrong decision, even if it has been reversed on appeal by a tribunal. The Court of Appeal has held that an officer owes no common law duty of care to a claimant and that the latter has only public law remedies, that is the statutory right of appeal or judicial review.[52]

Adjudication officers were under a statutory duty to decide claims, so far as practicable, within 14 days of their submission; in practice this duty was unenforceable.[53] There is now no statutory injunction on decision makers to determine claims swiftly, but in any event the previous duty had no discernible impact in DSS offices, where management performance indicators (which often set tighter targets) carried much greater weight.[54] Claimants are encouraged by the DWP to ask for an explanation of any decision maker's decision. Whether or not this course is taken, a claimant with a right of appeal against any decision of the Secretary of State must be told in writing of the decision and of their right to appeal to a tribunal. Furthermore, if the written decision does not include a statement of reasons for that decision, a written statement of reasons may be sought within one month.[55] The Secretary of State is obliged to provide such a statement within 14 days of the request.[56]

iii Medical and disability questions

Until SSA 1998, separate procedures were in place to determine medical questions. These principally involved disablement questions and 'diagnosis' or 'recrudescence'

---

47 Contrast the procedure for social fund reviews, p 210, below.
48 SSA 1998, s 11(2) empowers the Secretary of State to refer matters of special expertise to experts for advice. See also SI 1999/991, regs 11–15.
49 See Diplock LJ in *R v Deputy Industrial Injuries Comr, ex p Moore* [1965] 1 QB 456 at 486; and *Jones v Department of Employment* [1988] 1 All ER 725, [1988] 2 WLR 493 at 502–503.
50 *Purdew v Seress-Smith* [1993] IRLR 77 (allegation against former employer).
51 *Duggan v Chief Adjudication Officer*, reported as Appendix to *R(SB) 13/89*.
52 *Jones v Department of Employment* [1988] 1 All ER 725, [1988] 2 WLR 493 (see Swadling [1988] PL 328) and *Onifade v Secretary of State for Social Security* 1999 SCLR 836. It was also held that an estoppel could not arise against an officer in the exercise of his or her statutory responsibilities: *R(SB) 14/88*; *Davies v Social Security Comr*, reported as Appendix to *R(SB) 4/91*.
53 *R v Secretary of State for Social Services, ex p Child Poverty Action Group* [1990] 2 QB 540, [1989] 1 All ER 1047. See Wikeley [1989] JSWL 183; Webb (1990) 53 MLR 116; and the 4th edition of this book, p 662.
54 *Baldwin, Wikeley and Young* n 30, above, p 44.
55 SI 1999/991, reg 28(1).
56 SI 1999/991, reg 28(2).

questions in relation to industrial diseases. Such issues were decided by adjudicating medical practitioners – doctors vested with decision making powers – with a right of appeal to a medical appeal tribunal. The division of functions between the lay and medical adjudicating authorities led to complex legal problems, which twice came before the House of Lords at a time when social security cases reached the highest court even more rarely than they do today.[57] Special procedures also used to operate for attendance allowance and mobility allowance. However, the previous system of mandatory medical examinations for these benefits was criticised for its intrusiveness and its inability to present more than a 'snap-shot' of the claimant's disability. Thus, a fundamental feature of the reform of disability benefits in 1992 was the 'demedicalisation' of decision making,[58] with greater emphasis being given to 'self-assessment' in the completion of benefit claim forms. Thereafter claims for attendance allowance and disability living allowance were determined in the normal way by adjudication officers, who could seek advice and guidance from full-time doctors employed by the Benefits Agency Medical Service. This approach became the model with regard to all medical and disability questions under SSA 1998, with the Secretary of State assuming responsibility for first-tier decision making. Although doctors are no longer appointed to perform adjudication functions, their advice may still prove influential.[59] As we shall see below, the medical appeal tribunal was also formally abolished by the 1998 Act but there remains provision for specialist tribunals to hear appeals in such matters.

iv Quality assurance

Before the 1998 reforms, the Chief Adjudication Officer (CAO) was charged with the duty of providing adjudication officers with independent advice and with keeping their work under review. The CAO was required to report annually to the Secretary of State on adjudication standards; these reports were particularly critical of the standard of monitoring by senior officers.[60] In practice the CAO also decided whether an officer should appeal from a tribunal to the Commissioner, and whether the latter's decision should be appealed to the Court of Appeal. The post of the CAO was abolished by SSA 1998. The government argued that the most effective means of ensuring quality decision making was to make Agency chief executives accountable to the Secretary of State for adjudication standards. The Secretary of State is also required to report annually on the standards of first-tier decision making.[61] There are, in addition, two external safeguards: the National Audit Office (NAO) periodically monitors the accuracy of decision making and the President of the Appeals Service is under a duty to provide an annual report on the standards achieved in those first-tier decisions which go to appeal. It is questionable whether these are an adequate replacement for the previous arrangements. There are obvious dangers in relying on in-house monitoring of adjudication standards, the NAO has neither the specialist experience or expertise of the CAO's staff and the President's report is, by definition, based on a highly unrepresentative sample of cases.

---

57   *Ministry of Social Security v Amalgamated Engineering Union* [1967] 1 AC 725, [1967] 1 All ER 210; and *Jones v Secretary of State for Social Services* [1972] AC 944. See the 4th edition of this book, p 331.
58   See Wikeley (1992) 11 CJQ 227.
59   See SSA 1998, s 19, providing for the Secretary of State to require a medical examination and report. For concern over the standards of examining doctors in incapacity cases, see HC Select Committee on Social Security *Third Report* (1999–2000, HC 183) and Government Reply (2000, Cm 4780).
60   On the work of the CAO, see Sainsbury [1989] PL 323. The CAO's Office was retitled Central Adjudication Services (CAS) in 1992.
61   SSA 1998, s 81. It remains to be seen how these reports compare with those of the CAO.

v Revisions

One of the central goals of the DMA reforms contained in SSA 1998 was to 'produce a less complex, more accurate and cost-effective system for making *and changing* decisions'.[62] The outcome was the replacement of the previous provision for the review of social security decisions[63] with new (but no less elaborate) legislation enabling decisions either to be revised or superseded. In broad terms, revision is appropriate where the initial decision was erroneous when it was made, whilst a supersession is more apt to accommodate a subsequent change in circumstances. There are important differences between revisions and supersessions in terms of the effective date of the new decision.

A decision of the Secretary of State may be revised on his or her initiative or following an application made by the claimant.[64] The most straightforward is the 'any grounds' revision: providing action is taken (eg the claimant makes a request) within the 'dispute period' of 'one month', the initial decision may be revised on 'any grounds'.[65] An 'any grounds' revision may also be sought outside the one-month time-limit, but within an absolute time-limit of 13 months. Reconsideration beyond the initial month will only take place if it is reasonable to grant the application, the application for revision itself has merit and there are 'special circumstances' that made it impracticable to comply with the one-month time-limit.[66] The regulations also provide for a number of situations in which an 'any time' revision may take place. For example, a decision which arose from an official error may be revised at any time.[67] Similarly, the Secretary of State may at any time revise a decision which was more advantageous to the claimant than would otherwise be the case because it was made in ignorance of, or based upon a mistake as to, some material fact.[68] There is considerable overlap between the grounds for 'any time' revisions and those for supersessions, discussed below. The decision maker need not consider any issue that is not raised by the application.[69] The normal rule is that a revised decision takes effect from the date of the original decision.[70] The Secretary of State may treat an application for a revision or a notification of a change in circumstances as an application for a supersession.[71] A decision on a revision application gives rise to a fresh right of appeal.

vi Supersessions

The decision maker may supersede an earlier Secretary of State decision (either an original decision or a revised decision) on his or her own initiative or following an application by the claimant.[72] This facility is especially appropriate where the initial

---

62 DSS *Improving decision making and appeals in Social Security* (Cm 3328, 1996) para 1.2 (emphasis added).

63 See the 4th edition of this book, pp 681–683.

64 SSA 1998, s 9(1). Secretary of State decisions in connection with the discretionary social fund are subject to separate rules: see p 209, below.

65 SI 1999/991, reg 3(1). This one month is extended by 14 days if a written statement of reasons is requested.

66 SI 1999/991, reg 4(3). But note that the decision maker must disregard ignorance of the law or indeed a change in the case law: reg 4(6).

67 SI 1999/991, reg 3(5)(a). 'Official error' excludes 'any error which is shown to have been an error by virtue of a subsequent decision of a Commissioner or the court': reg 1(2).

68 SI 1999/991, reg 3(5)(b). See also reg 3(4) and (6)–(8). For discussion of the meaning of this phrase in the context of the pre-DMA provisions, see *Chief Adjudication Officer v Combe* [1997] SC 299.

69 SSA 1998, s 9(2).

70 SSA 1998, s 9(3). For an exception, see SI 1999/991, reg 5.

71 SI 1999/991, reg 3(10).

72 SSA 1998, s 10(1)(a). Secretary of State decisions in connection with the discretionary social fund are subject to separate rules: see p 209, below.

decision requires altering as a result of a change in circumstances. It may also be suitable in cases where the original decision was wrong but the application falls outside the 'dispute period' of one month and there are no grounds on which it can be revised under the procedures discussed above.[73] A decision may only be superseded if one of a number of specified grounds is made out.[74] A common basis for supersession of an existing award is that there has been a 'relevant change of circumstances', ie something which causes for serious consideration by the decision maker and may (but not necessarily will) lead to a different decision.[75] This may be brought about in a variety of ways: eg by a change in the claimant's condition, evidenced perhaps by a fresh medical report,[76] or by a change in the legislation.[77] But supersession on the basis of a change in circumstances is not available where a claim is correctly disallowed in the first instance and the claimant's situation later changes.[78] The remedy in such a case is to make a fresh claim. A decision may also be superseded if it was based in ignorance of, or upon a mistake as to, any material fact.[79] A decision of an appeal tribunal or a Commissioner may also be superseded on either of the grounds above.[80]

Decisions made by the Secretary of State may be superseded if they are erroneous in law. This enables simple mistakes of law to be corrected without resort by the claimant to the formal appeal process. Obviously it would be inappropriate to extend this particular power of supersession by the Secretary of State to decisions made by tribunals or the Commissioner, when the appellant has already embarked on this process. There are a number of narrower circumstances in which a decision may be superseded. These include cases where jobseeker's allowance is in payment but it is subsequently decided that a sanction applies. Similarly, a new medical report following a personal capability assessment justifies a supersession of a decision that a person is incapable of work.[81] More advantageously for claimants, if a claimant becomes entitled to another qualifying benefit (or to an increase in a qualifying benefit), an award of an existing benefit can be superseded and the higher rate paid from the start of the existing award or the start of the award of the qualifying benefit, if later.[82]

Whereas a revised decision usually takes effect from the date of the original decision, the general rule is that a supersession is effective from the date it is made or from the date when the application was made.[83] This principle is subject to a number of exceptions set out in the complex regulations.[84]

---

73   An application for a revision may be treated as an application for a supersession, but as a general rule revision should take place in preference to supersession where both are available: SI 1999/991, reg 6(3) and (5).
74   SI 1999/991, reg 6(2).
75   *R(A) 2/90*, para 4. In reaching this decision, the Commissioner adopted the approach of the Court of Appeal in interpreting the meaning of a 'material fact' in the context of the previous arrangements for review of medical decisions: see *Saker v Secretary of State for Social Services*, reported as an Appendix to *R(I) 2/88*.
76   *R(S) 6/78; R(M) 5/86*. A new medical report in itself is not a change in circumstances for this purpose: *R(S) 4/86*.
77   *R(G) 3/58 (T); R(A) 4/81*.
78   SSA 1998, s 8(2).
79   On the meaning of 'material fact', see n 75, above.
80   SSA 1998, s 10(1)(b).
81   This reverses the effect of *CIB/3899/97*; but note that a new medical report is not in itself a ground for superseding a decision relating to disability living allowance (see n 76, above).
82   Eg the claimant may have an existing award of income support. She then claims disability living allowance (a qualifying benefit for the disability premium in income support). If, as is usual, there is a delay in awarding disability living allowance, the income support award can be superseded so that the disability premium becomes payable from the start date for disability living allowance.
83   SSA 1998, s 10(5).
84   SI 1999/991, reg 7.

vii   The anti-test case rule

Reference has already been made to the introduction of the first version of the anti-test case rule in 1990.[85] This rule has been progressively tightened over the last decade.[86] If a claimant asks for a decision to be revised or superseded, but entitlement may depend upon the outcome of a test case involving the same issue (but not necessarily the same benefit), then the decision maker has two options in the so-called 'look-alike' case. First, if the outcome of the test case might result in no entitlement, a decision on the application for revision or supersession may be postponed,[87] so denying the claimant a right of appeal until the test case is resolved. Following the decision in the test case, the application can then be determined. In the event that it is favourable, arrears of benefit are then payable.[88] Secondly, if it is considered that the claimant would still be entitled to benefit but that the test case might affect the outcome in some other way (eg as to the rate of benefit), the decision maker may either postpone a decision or proceed to make a decision. However, if the latter course of action is adopted, statute requires that this proceeds on the assumption that the test case has already been decided in a way 'which is the most unfavourable to the claimant'.[89] In this event, if the outcome of the test case is favourable, the decision in the look-alike case must be revised but the claimant is caught by the full rigour of the anti-test case rule.

The anti-test case rule applies where a Commissioner or court decides that an error of law was made in the test case. It means that the decision maker dealing with the look-alike case must determine entitlement for any period before the date of the test case decision as if the initial decision in that litigation 'had been found by the Commissioner or court *not* to have been erroneous in point of law'.[90] This principle applies even where the decision in the test case is that regulations purporting to govern (and, more specifically, to restrict) entitlement to benefit are ultra vires.[91] This rule represents a startling interference with the traditional approach of the courts that case law is retrospective in its effects.

viii   Appealable and non-appealable decisions

Before SSA 1998 the fundamental principle was that decisions made by an adjudication officer could be appealed to an independent tribunal, whereas no such route was available for decisions taken in the name of the Secretary of State. Where such decisions related to relatively minor, technical or procedural issues (eg which day of the week a benefit should be paid), the absence of any means to challenge decisions was relatively unproblematic.[92] However, some Secretary of State decisions involved much more significant issues. Certain contributions questions were subject

---

85   P 181, above.
86   But note that whereas it used to apply to family credit and disability working allowance, it no longer applies to their replacement tax credits: TCA 1999, Sch 2, para 19.
87   SSA 1998, s 25(2). S 25 also applies to initial decisions as well as applications for revision or supersessions.
88   SSA 1998, s 27(2).
89   SSA 1998, s 25(3) and SI 1999/991, reg 21.
90   SSA 1998, s 27(3) (emphasis added).
91   SSA 1998, s 27(5).
92   Obviously the matter could be taken up with the relevant office with a request for the decision to be reconsidered, and judicial review remained an option (in theory at least) in appropriate cases.

to a special procedure under which a member of the DSS Solicitor's Office would hold an inquiry. The Secretary of State's subsequent decision could be appealed on a point of law to a judge of the High Court.[93] Such appeals as were brought mostly concerned whether a person was properly to be regarded as employed or self-employed for the purpose of liability to pay National Insurance contributions, and judicial decisions substantially shaped the development of this area of law. In one of the last cases to be dealt with under this procedure, the issue was whether employers were liable to pay secondary Class 1 contributions on substantial bonuses paid via life policies: some £350 million was at stake. Unusually there was no right of further appeal. [94]

There was never any substantial argument for allocating these more weighty decisions to the Secretary of State, rather than the ordinary adjudicating authorities (and then the courts in the normal way). The Labour government in 1969-70 proposed that 'Minister's questions' should be determined by a new 'special tribunal' with a right of appeal to the High Court on a point of law.[95] The Council on Tribunals argued that such matters should be decided by the existing statutory authorities, with a final appeal to the Commissioner, but this was rejected, apparently on the ground that the matters were too complicated for local tribunals.[96] The Bill lapsed when the 1970 general election was called. A report commissioned by the DSS in 1987 recommended that the Secretary of State's adjudicatory functions should be brought within the mainstream of social security adjudication.[97] This proposal received the support of the Council on Tribunals,[98] but no reform took place for a number of years.

Reform finally came with the advent of SSA 1998. This provides for a right of appeal to an appeal tribunal against any Secretary of State decision 'made on a claim for, or on an award of, a relevant benefit',[99] subject to prescribed exceptions.[100] The 1998 Act also specifies certain decisions 'made otherwise than on such a claim or award' which also give rise to a right of appeal to an appeal tribunal.[101] As first enacted, these included a wide range of contributions questions, which would previously have been handled under the special procedure. However, before these provisions were brought into force, they were repealed by the SSC(TF)A 1999,[102] which transferred initial decision making on such matters to the Inland Revenue with the concomitant right of appeal to the tax appeal commissioners. This has served only to add to the confusing jungle of the social security appeals system.

93   See the 4th edition of this book, pp 665–667.
94   SSAA 1992, s 18(6), precluding any further appeal, was described by Collins J as 'an unfortunate provision since the point to be decided ... is one with which no court has hitherto had to grapple and a very large sum of money depends upon my decision': *Tullett & Tokyo Forex International Ltd, SGW Ltd, Barclays de Zoete Wedd Services Ltd v Secretary of State for Social Security* (2000) Independent, July 10.
95   National Superannuation and Social Insurance Bill 1969, cl 78.
96   See the *Annual Report of the Council on Tribunals for 1969–1970* (1970) para 47 and Appendix B. The complexity argument hardly seemed very persuasive after 1984 with the increasing professionalism of social security appeal tribunals.
97   Partington *The Secretary of State's Powers of Adjudication in Social Security Law* SAUS Working Paper 96 (1991).
98   See the *Annual Report of the Council on Tribunals 1988–89* (1989) para 2.75.
99   SSA 1998, s 12(1)(a).
100   The prescribed exceptions are contained in SSA 1998, Sch 2, SI 1999/991, reg 27 and Sch 2.
101   SSA 1998, s 12(1)(b) and Sch 3.
102   SSC(TF)A 1999, s 18 and Sch 7, para 36. Thus the only surviving provisions in SSA 1998, Sch 3, Pt II ('Contributions conditions') relate to decisions on home responsibilities protection and credits.

B   Board of the Inland Revenue

i   General

In 1999 the Inland Revenue subsumed the Contributions Agency, previously part of the DSS, and also took over the functions of the Benefits Agency in relation to working families' tax credit and disabled person's tax credit.[103] Consequently, officers of the Inland Revenue now have responsibility for making decisions with regard to a range of social security matters. These include the following:

(a) whether a person is an earner and, if so, in which category of earners (employed or self-employed) he or she is to be included;

(b) whether a person is, or was, employed in employed earner's employment for the purposes of industrial injuries benefits;

(c) whether a person is liable, or entitled, to pay National Insurance contributions of any Class and whether the contribution conditions for any benefit have been satisfied;

(d) whether a person was under the relevant regulations precluded from regular employment by home responsibilities;

(e) claims for working families' tax credit and disabled person's tax credit; and

(f) claims for statutory sick pay and statutory maternity pay.

ii   Revisions and supersessions

Officers of the Board of the Inland Revenue have the same powers as their counterparts working in the DWP on behalf of the Secretary of State both to revise decisions and to supersede them.[104] Thus typically a revision is appropriate where the decision was wrong at the time it was made, whilst a supersession may occur where the original decision requires changing, eg because of a change in circumstances. For no immediately apparent reason, the primary legislation refers to the former procedure as resulting in a decision being 'varied' rather than 'revised', but nothing appears to turn on the distinction.[105] It should be noted that the anti-test case rule does not apply to decisions relating to tax credits.[106]

iii   Appeals

Such clarity as was introduced by SSA 1998 was rapidly dissipated by the 1999 changes. Thus the route for appealing against a decision of an officer of the Inland Revenue depends on the question at issue. Most contributions questions and decisions on entitlement to statutory sick pay or statutory maternity appeal are subject to the normal procedures for challenging decisions made by officers of the Board. There is, accordingly, a right of appeal to the tax appeal commissioners.[107] However, appeals against decisions relating to contributions credits or home responsibilities protection

---

103   SSC(TF)A 1999 and TCA 1999.
104   SSC(TF)A 1999, s 10 and SI 1999/991, regs 3–8.
105   SSC(TF)A 1999, s 10(1)(a); the secondary legislation simply refers to 'revision' throughout.
106   N 86, above.
107   See p 200, below.

remain a matter for appeal tribunals constituted under SSA 1998.[108] Likewise, appeals concerning entitlement to working families' tax credit and disabled person's tax credit are currently heard by the same appeal tribunals as hear ordinary social security appeals, although the government has indicated that in the long term it intends to transfer this jurisdiction to the tax appeal commissioners. This seems undesirable so long as there remains a considerable degree of common ground in the principles underlying income-related benefits and the tax credits. Somewhat confusingly, different appeal routes apply to decisions to apply penalties (eg in respect of false claims or failures to provide information). In very broad terms, appeals by claimants lie to the mainstream appeal tribunals whilst appeals by employers against sanctions imposed on them are heard by the tax appeal commissioners.[109]

C Other first-tier decision making arrangements

i Housing benefit and council tax benefit

Although local authorities have had a decision making function in relation to social security since the inception of rent rebates in the 1930s,[110] there has never been a tradition of independent adjudication in this area. Such determinations were seen as no different from other aspects of local government administration and gave rise to no formal rights of appeal. The introduction of housing benefit in 1982 saw the advent of a wholly inadequate system of internal reviews,[111] as well as the promulgation of detailed rules governing decision making procedures. Yet in terms of the actual locus of decision making the legislation remains remarkably vague to this day: decisions are to be made by the 'appropriate authority'.[112] In practice the responsibility for housing benefit and council tax benefit decision making in most local authorities rests with either the finance or housing department. Some authorities, however, have contracted out much of their benefit-related work in the wake of compulsory competitive tendering. The quality of housing benefit and council tax benefit administration remains very uneven, leading to suggestions that such functions should be transferred to the Benefits Agency.[113]

ii Social fund

As part of the reforms instituted by SSA 1998, the functions of social fund officers were transferred to the Secretary of State.[114] Yet in other respects the unique structure of decision making and reviews that governs the discretionary social fund remained largely unchanged by the 1998 Act. These latter arrangements are considered in Part 7, below.

---

108   N 102, above.
109   TCA 1999, Sch 4, para 3.
110   See p 406, below.
111   P 55, above.
112   SSA 1998, s 34 and SI 1987/1971, reg 76.
113   See HC Social Security Committee *Sixth Report* (1999–2000, HC 385) paras 143–146. It should be noted that the former DHSS had responsibility for providing assistance with rent for tenants in receipt of supplementary benefit before the introduction of housing benefit.
114   SSA 1998, s 1. See also SSA 1998, s 36 and p 468, below on initial decision making.

Part 3   The Tribunals

A   The Appeals Service

i   History

The roots of the Appeals Service can be traced back to the highly influential report by Professor Kathleen Bell on SBATs.[115] Bell made a series of recommendations designed to improve the quality of justice in these tribunals, including the appointment of legally qualified Senior Chairmen in each region with responsibility for training and improving the quality of decision making. In 1984 the SBATs were merged with their older and more respected cousins, the National Insurance Local Tribunals, into the social security appeal tribunals (SSATs).[116] In order to establish the independence of the new tribunals, they were brought within the administrative control of a new organisation, the Office of the President of Social Security Appeal Tribunals (OPSSAT), headed by a judge. In 1991 OPSSAT itself was renamed the Independent Tribunal Service (ITS). Initially ITS included within its scope SSATs, medical appeal tribunals and vaccine damage tribunals. Disability appeal tribunals were added in 1992 following the introduction of disability living allowance. A year later these were followed by child support appeal tribunals, constituted to hear appeals in connection with child maintenance decisions made under the Child Support Act 1991 (CSA 1991).[117] Unlike the other ITS tribunals, which adjudicated upon disputes between the individual and the state, these tribunals were equally concerned with disputes between citizens. Although their jurisdiction (and that of the new appeal tribunal) is therefore largely outside the scope of this book, they do hear appeals against reduced benefit decisions.[118]

SSA 1998 amalgamated these five tribunals into unified appeal tribunals.[119] As part of the DMA reforms, ITS itself was bifurcated into its judicial and administrative wings. The Appeals Service comprises the President and tribunal panel members and has sole responsibility for judicial matters relating to social security appeals. The key administrative tasks to support this function – clerking tribunals, calling up members, etc – became the responsibility of the Appeals Service Agency, an agency located within the DSS (and now the DWP), answerable via its chief executive to the Secretary of State. The rationale for this structural reorganisation of ITS was the need to improve efficiency and accountability in the face of increasing delays in hearing appeals, although the arguments advanced were less then compelling. At best the loss of the nomenclature 'independent' in the title of the appeals body is unfortunate; at worst, it reflects serious questions about the extent to which the new arrangements comply with the Human Rights Act 1998.[120]

Paradoxically the advent of the human rights legislation led to the further enlargement of the jurisdiction of the Appeals Service with effect from April 2001 by the addition of appeals relating to housing benefit and council tax benefit.[121] When housing benefit was introduced in 1982, the then government's original plan was to have no form of

---

115   Bell *Research Study on Supplementary Benefit Appeal Tribunals, Review of Main Findings: Conclusions: Recommendations* (1975).
116   See Harris [1983] JSWL 212.
117   On their background, see the *Annual Report of the Council on Tribunals 1990–91* (1991) paras 3.2–3.16.
118   CSA 1991, s 46 and p 320, above.
119   SSA 1998, s 4. For argument that this change was largely semantic, see Wikeley (1999) 6 JSSL 155.
120   *Wikeley* n 119, above and n 4, above.
121   CSPSSA 2000, s 68 and Sch 7. See Rahilly (2001) 8 JSSL 57.

redress for unsuccessful claimants. At a late stage in the Parliamentary process, the government undertook to establish an internal review mechanism under delegated legislation.[122] A dissatisfied claimant could request the authority to conduct a review of its decision and thereafter could request a further review by a housing benefit review board.[123] The review board consisted of at least three councillors from the authority in question.[124] Disputes concerning council tax benefit, introduced in 1993, were subject to the same procedure. There was no statutory right of appeal or further review, although judicial review remained a fruitful option for the determined and well-advised claimant.[125] Research demonstrated that housing benefit review boards compared poorly with social security appeal tribunals in terms of their procedures.[126]

ii Organisation and philosophy

The President of the Appeals Service is by convention a county court judge,[127] appointed by the Lord Chancellor, who is responsible for the organisation and training of tribunal panel members, as well as reporting to the Secretary of State on the quality of first-tier decision making in cases which come to appeal.[128] Although statute makes provision simply for the Lord Chancellor to appoint a President and panel members, in practice the President is assisted by seven Regional Chairmen[129] and some 60 other full-time chairmen, known as District Chairmen.[130] Many of the President's functions are delegated to the Regional Chairmen.

A key feature of the ITS was the inquisitorial and enabling philosophy developed by the first President, Judge Byrt, and continued by his successors. This means that the tribunals are expected to take an active role in eliciting the material facts and identifying the relevant law, rather than merely relying upon points made by either the appellant or the department. This approach obviously contrasts with the adversarial traditions of the ordinary courts. According to Judge Byrt:

> The underlying principle is that the tribunal should in all things conduct itself so as to enable the appellant to maximise his performance and himself to feel that he has done so.[131]

---

122 See Partington and Bolderson *Housing Benefits Review Procedure* Brunel University Law Faculty Working Paper (1984) pp 12–21.
123 For a discussion of how authorities could frustrate claimants' access to the board, see Eardley and Sainsbury (1993) 22 J Soc Pol 461.
124 See the 4th edition of this book, p 684 and p 55 above.
125 See Sainsbury and Eardley [1993] PL 551.
126 See Sainsbury and Eardley *Housing Benefit Reviews* DSS Research Report No 3 (1991) and [1992] PL 551. The Council on Tribunals had consistently argued for the transfer of this jurisdiction to the mainstream social security tribunal system.
127 Statute merely demands a 10-year general qualification: SSA 1998, s 5. This means an advocacy qualification of at least 10 years' standing based on rights of audience granted by an authorised body (eg the Law Society or the Bar Council): see SSA 1998, s 39(2); SSAA 1992, s 191; and the Courts and Legal Services Act 1990, ss 27 and 71.
128 SSA 1998, s 5 and Sch 1. The first OPSSAT President was HH Judge Byrt QC (1984–90). His successors in ITS were HH Judge Holden (1990–92), HH Judge Thorpe (1992–94), HH Judge Bassingthwaighte (1994–98) and HH Judge Harris (1998–), who became the first President of the Appeals Service.
129 The seven Regions are South East, Central, Eastern, Wales and the South West, North West, North East and Scotland.
130 District chairmen sit regularly as chairs of individual tribunals as well as dealing with interlocutory work and the monitoring and training of panel members.
131 House of Commons Social Services Committee *Ninth Report – Social Security: Changes Implemented in April 1988* (1988–89, HC 437-I) p 37.

The extent to which tribunals succeed in this task necessarily varies according to the skills and aptitude of those involved.[132] In addition, the DMA reforms have arguably made this goal still more difficult to achieve within the legislative framework for the Appeals Service.[133]

B Appeal Tribunals[134]

i Panel members

Primary legislation is silent as to the types of members to be appointed to appeal tribunals. It merely provides that the Lord Chancellor shall constitute a panel of persons to act as members of appeal tribunals, 'composed of such persons as the Lord Chancellor thinks fit' and 'possessing such qualifications as may be prescribed'.[135] Prior to SSA 1998, social security appeal tribunals were constituted by a lawyer chair sitting with two lay members, an arrangement dating back to the inception of the National Insurance scheme in 1911.[136] Yet regulations made under the Act make no provision for lay members, to the regret of the Council on Tribunals.[137] Instead, panel members must fall into one of four categories.[138] Lawyer members must have a general qualification under the Courts and Legal Services Act 1990.[139] Every appeal tribunal must include a lawyer member;[140] although there is no statutory requirement that he or she act as chair, this is the invariable practice. This custom – a statutory requirement until 1998 – stems from the Bell report, which identified the use of lay chairs as the main reason for the poor quality of adjudication in SBATs. In addition to presiding over the hearing, the chair has a number of specific duties under the Social Security and Child Support (Decisions and Appeals Regulations) 1999, in particular recording the reasons for the tribunal's decision and deciding whether to grant leave to appeal to a Commissioner.[141] Part-time legally qualified members are expected to sit more often than the other members, at least once every two or three weeks, and thus have the opportunity to develop considerable expertise in social security law and practice. The remaining panel members must have either a medical or accounting qualification, or the rather inelegantly entitled 'disability qualification'. This last category means persons (other than doctors) who are experienced in dealing with the needs of disabled persons, either in a professional or voluntary capacity (eg a nurse, occupational therapist or carer) or because they themselves are disabled. All members are paid a fee for sitting, but these are differentiated according to category of membership.[142]

---

132 See *Baldwin, Wikeley and Young* n 30, above, chs 4 and 5.
133 See *Wikeley* n 4, above.
134 See *Wikeley* n 4, above; and Partington in Harlow (ed) *Public Law and Politics* (1986) ch 9. For an analysis in terms of legitimation, see Dean *Social Security and Social Control* (1991).
135 SSA 1998, s 6.
136 See the 4th edition of this book, p 669.
137 *Annual Report of the Council on Tribunals for 1997/98* (1998–99, HC 45) para 1.3.
138 SI 1999/991, reg 35 and Sch 3.
139 The previous requirement to be of at least five years' standing has been removed, but in practice the Lord Chancellor's Department operates a non-statutory convention that candidates should be at least 35 years of age.
140 SSA 1998, s 7(2).
141 SI 1999/991, regs 53(1) and 58.
142 The former lay members could claim only a very limited loss of earnings allowance and their expenses.

ii   Tribunal composition

The former ITS tribunals always comprised a chair and two other members, unless one member was unable to attend on the day and the appellant consented to a 'short tribunal'. A major thrust of the DMA reforms was the creation of more 'flexible' arrangements for hearing appeals. SSA 1998 provides that appeal tribunals may consist of one, two or three members, but that in any event at least one member must be legally qualified.[143] Subject to this overriding requirement, the precise rules governing tribunal composition are now laid down in secondary legislation.[144] The default position is that an appeal tribunal is constituted by a single legally qualified member sitting alone. The regulations then provide that a lawyer and doctor member should sit together to hear appeals relating to the personal capability assessment (ie for incapacity for work cases) or against certificates of recoverable benefits under the recoupment scheme. A lawyer and two doctor members are assigned to hear industrial injuries appeals (excluding industrial accident declarations) and vaccine damage payment cases, as with the former medical appeal and vaccine damage tribunals.[145] A two-person tribunal composed of a lawyer and an accountant may be convened to hear benefit or child support appeals that involve difficult issues relating to, eg profit and loss accounts or trust fund accounts.[146] Any one, two or three-person tribunal constituted under any of the above provisions may, on the President's direction, be supplemented by an additional panel member. This may only be for the purpose either of providing that member with further experience or for assisting the President in monitoring panel members' decision making standards.[147] Finally, appeals relating to attendance allowance, disability living allowance and disabled person's tax credit must be heard by a three-person tribunal comprised of a lawyer, a doctor and a third member with a disability qualification. This effectively means the continuance of the disability appeal tribunal under a different guise.

Listing arrangements for individual appeal tribunal hearings are the responsibility of clerks, employed by the Secretary of State, who also summon panel members to serve on tribunals.[148] Although much of this process is computerised and there has been no suggestion that this procedure is abused, these arrangements do nothing to assist in asserting the tribunals' independence.

iii   Jurisdiction and powers

SSA 1998 transferred the functions of all five of the former ITS tribunals to the new appeal tribunals.[149] Thus the primary role of appeal tribunals is to hear appeals against the refusal of a benefit by the Secretary of State. They also have an important appellate jurisdiction to determine whether overpaid benefit is recoverable. Although, as we have seen, social security tribunals have traditionally sought to exercise an inquisitorial

---

143   SSA 1998, s 7(1) and (2).
144   SI 1999/991, reg 36. See Wikeley (2000) 8 JSSL 88.
145   Alternatively such tribunals may comprise a lawyer, a doctor and an additional panel member (see n 147, below): SI 1999/991, reg 36(2).
146   In the unlikely event that a tribunal could be constituted in either of the two immediately preceding ways, it must consist of a lawyer, a doctor and an accountant: SI 1999/991, reg 36(3) and (4).
147   SI 1999/991, reg 36(5). This power is used as part of the induction programme for newly appointed members to sit with more experienced members.
148   SI 1999/991, reg 37.
149   SSA 1998, s 4 (ie social security appeal tribunals, disability appeal tribunals, medical appeal tribunals, child support appeal tribunals and vaccine damage tribunals).

jurisdiction, their power to do so was curtailed by several of the amendments made by the 1998 Act.[150]

The right of appeal itself is enjoyed by the claimant and such other persons as may be prescribed; these include appointees and those claiming attendance allowance or disability living allowance on behalf of a terminally ill person.[151] Any person other than the claimant from whom the Secretary of State has decided that an overpayment is recoverable also has the right of appeal.[152]

iv Notice of appeal and pre-hearing procedure

Under the Social Security and Child Support (Decisions and Appeals) Regulations 1999 notice of appeal to an appeal tribunal must be given in writing to the relevant office within one month of the date when notice of the Secretary of State's decision was given.[153] The tight time-limit of one month effectively marks a return to the 28-day rule for appealing that operated before the more generous period of three months, which applied between 1986 and 1999.[154] The chair has the power to admit a late appeal, providing that it is lodged within the absolute time-limit of one year from the expiry of the original month.[155] However, the chair must also be satisfied that the appeal has reasonable prospects of success or that it is in the interests of justice (as defined by the regulations) for the application to be granted.[156] There is no appeal against this decision, although judicial review remains a faint possibility.[157]

The appeal must contain 'particulars of the ground on which it is made' as well as sufficient particulars of the decision itself to enable the latter to be identified.[158] An appeal that fails to satisfy these formalities may be returned by the Secretary of State for completion by the appellant within 14 days; if the appellant fails to comply, the papers are passed to a chair of the Appeals Service to determine whether the appeal should be admitted.[159] Once the appeal has been lodged, the relevant benefit office produces the decision maker's submission, ie an explanation of the decision, along with accompanying papers pertinent to the appeal. The benefits office then sends copies of these appeal papers to the appellant and to the Appeals Service. At the same time the appellant is sent a questionnaire asking whether an oral hearing is sought and, if so, seeking information on the availability of the appellant and any representative to attend.

150   Unlike SSAA 1992, s 36, SSA 1998 does not empower a tribunal to deal with a matter first arising on appeal; in addition s 12(8) precludes the tribunal from taking into account circumstances 'not obtaining at the time when the decision appealed against was made'.
151   SSA 1998, s 12(2) and SI 1999/991, reg 25.
152   See SSA 1998, s 12(4). For decisions which are appealable, see SSA 1998, s 12 and Sch 3 and SI 1999/991, reg 26; for exclusions see SSA 1998, Sch 2 and SI 1999/991, Sch 2. The absence of a single list is regrettable.
153   SI 1999/991, regs 31(1) and 33(1). If the claimant has requested a written statement of reasons, this period is extended by 14 days. Although there is a standard form for lodging an appeal, this does not have to be used: a letter is sufficient.
154   The 28-day time-limit applied to child support appeal tribunals from their inception in 1993 until 1999.
155   Or six weeks where the claimant applies for a statement of reasons.
156   This in turn requires some 'special circumstances', ie the death or serious illness of the applicant, spouse or dependant, the applicant's non-residence in the UK, disruption to normal postal services or 'some other special circumstances exist which are wholly exceptional and relevant to the application': SI 1999/991, reg 32. A decision maker may also admit a late appeal 'in the interests of justice'.
157   SI 1999/991, reg 32(9). (See also *R(I) 44/59*, under a much earlier set of procedural regulations, for a ruling that there is no appeal against the chairman's decision.)
158   SI 1999/991, reg 33(1).
159   SI 1999/991, reg 33(3)–(10).

The inquiry form must be returned within 14 days, or the appeal may be struck out.[160] The requirement to 'opt in' for an oral hearing was introduced by regulations in October 1996 as a precursor to the main DMA reforms under SSA 1998. It is difficult to reconcile the imposition of this further procedural hurdle with the inquisitorial philosophy of social security tribunals. If no express request is made for an oral hearing, the appeal is determined at a paper hearing.

Indeed, the DMA changes significantly extended the powers to strike out appeals. Before SSA 1998 only a legally qualified chair had the power to strike out an appeal, and then only for want of prosecution. Under the new regime a tribunal clerk may strike out an appeal for want of prosecution, for want of jurisdiction or for failure to comply with a direction (this includes a failure to return the inquiry form).[161] In the latter two cases the appellant must have been notified in advance of the possibility of striking out. This raises obvious natural justice concerns, given that the clerk works for the Appeals Service Agency and is hence an employee of the Secretary of State, one of the parties to the appeal. However, the prospect of a successful human rights challenge may be stymied by the fact that an appellant whose appeal is struck out has the right to apply to a legally qualified chair for reinstatement.[162] A chair, as well as having the power to strike out an appeal on any of the above grounds, has the additional power to discontinue an appeal which is 'misconceived', ie is 'frivolous or vexatious' or 'obviously unsustainable and has no prospect of success'.[163]

At least 14 days' notice of the hearing must be given; otherwise it can only take place if the appellant consents.[164] The appeal tribunal may proceed with the case in the appellant's absence and will generally do this, unless there is some good explanation for non-attendance.[165] A tribunal clerk is empowered to determine a request for a postponement of a hearing or to refer it to a chair; if the clerk refuses such an application, the request and the notification of the refusal must be placed before the appeal tribunal.[166] The tribunal also has the power to adjourn an oral hearing.[167]

v   The oral hearing

Oral hearings are held in tribunal rooms rented by the Appeals Service on either a permanent or sessional basis. It has not proved possible to find independent premises for all appeal tribunals, and a few continue to sit in DWP buildings, though the tribunal rooms are segregated from the local office. Nor are all tribunals readily accessible by people with disabilities.[168]

The Social Security and Child Support (Decisions and Appeals Regulations) 1999 set out some basic procedural rules for oral hearings. One important rule is that the hearing must be in public, except where the chairman decides that it should be held in

---

160   SI 1999/991, reg 39.
161   SI 1999/991, reg 46. The clerk has the power to reinstate such an appeal: SI 1999/991, reg 47(1).
162   SI 1999/991, reg 47(2).
163   SI 1999/991, regs 1(3) and 48.
164   SI 1999/991, reg 49(2). This is one of very few respects in which the time-limits were relaxed by the DMA changes, albeit marginally; the previous requirement was for 10 days' notice. Any party can expressly waive the right to receive at least 14 days' notice: SI 1999/991, reg 49(3).
165   SI 1999/991, reg 49(4) and (5). If the clerk cannot show that the appellant has been notified, eg where the papers have been returned with a note that he or she was not known at the address, the SSAT should adjourn: *R(SB) 19/83*.
166   SI 1999/991, reg 51(1)–(3). On withdrawals, see SI 1999/991, reg 40.
167   SI 1999/991, reg 51(4). On the principles, see Harris (1996) 3 JSSL 11.
168   In exceptional cases tribunals may hold a domiciliary hearing.

private in order to protect private or family life or, in special circumstances, because publicity would prejudice the interests of justice.[169] Any parties to the proceedings, and their representatives, have a right to attend and be heard, which may be by live television link.[170] They may also address the tribunal, give evidence, call witnesses and put questions direct to other witnesses.[171] Other persons, in particular the President, any person (typically a District Chairman) acting on behalf of the President in the training, supervision or monitoring of panel members, and any trainee panel member or clerk, are entitled to be present at the hearing, whether or not it is otherwise conducted in private.[172]

Subject to these provisions, the procedure is for the chair to determine.[173] Naturally this will vary from one tribunal to another, but the Appeals Service induction and training programmes and its guide to procedure set out some general principles.[174] It is crucial for the appellant to be put at ease, and so the chair should first introduce him or herself and any other members of the tribunal and emphasise its independence from the government department concerned. Some chairs prefer to identify the point that appears to be at issue and then invite the appellant to open, but many appellants are equally happy for the presenting officer to start (assuming one is actually present), so giving themselves time to settle down and see what are the pertinent points in the appeal. The Court of Appeal and the Commissioner have stressed that a tribunal has investigatory functions, so the chair and any other members are expected to determine the facts themselves through questioning the officer and the appellant;[175] they are not restricted to the precise contentions made by the parties. The presenting officer, whose role has been characterised as that of an amicus curiae, is expected to bring out those points favourable to the claimant.[176] How far presenting officers succeed in fulfilling this function has been questioned.[177] It is normal to conclude proceedings by giving the appellant the last word, and then asking the parties to withdraw while the tribunal deliberates.[178]

Appeal tribunals are not bound by the law of evidence. Thus hearsay evidence is admissible, though it should be considered with caution.[179] Nor is there any requirement that the claimant's own evidence must be corroborated for it to be accepted.[180] But natural justice requires that tribunal decisions be based on probative material.[181] Thus the Secretary of State should produce evidence to support contentions if necessary, eg by calling a visiting officer as a witness.[182] Sometimes the tribunal should consider adjourning the case where a party wishes to have more time to produce evidence or to call witnesses, though this course should not be taken if there has been ample opportunity to do this before the hearing. Generally, tribunals should be reluctant to adjourn in

---

169 Or, presumably very unusually, there are considerations of national security: SI 1999/991, reg 49(6).
170 SI 1999/991, regs 49(7) and (8).
171 SI 1999/991, reg 49(11).
172 SI 1999/991, reg 49(9). Council of Tribunal members also fall into this category, as does 'any other person' who has the leave of the tribunal chair.
173 SI 1999/991, reg 49(1).
174 This is now incorporated in the internal *TAS Benchbook* (2001).
175 *R v Deputy Industrial Injuries Comr, ex p Moore* [1965] 1 QB 456 at 486; *R(S) 4/82(T)*, *R(S) 1/87*, *R(IS) 5/93*. See p 192, above.
176 *R v Deputy Industrial Injuries Comr, ex p Moore* [1965] 1 QB 456 at 486.
177 See *Baldwin, Wikeley and Young* n 30, above, ch 7; and Wikeley and Young (1991) 18 JLS 464.
178 See also SI 1999/991, reg 49(12).
179 *R(SB) 5/82*. For a discussion of the rules of evidence in social security tribunals, see Yates [1980] JSWL 273; Logie and Watchman (1989) 8 CJQ 109; and Rowe [1994] 1 JSSL 9. A refusal to listen to hearsay evidence is itself a breach of natural justice: *R(IS) 5/93*.
180 *R(SB) 33/85*; *R(SB) 12/89*.
181 *R(S) 1/87*.
182 *R(SB) 10/86*; *R(IS) 6/91*.

view of the expense and delay that will result; one factor is that where the tribunal is differently constituted after an adjournment (as will normally be the case), there should usually be a complete rehearing of the appeal.[183] Finally, if the appeal involves a question of fact of special difficulty, an appeal tribunal has a rarely used power to request the assistance of an expert, who must in turn also be a panel member.[184]

The hearings of appeals involving medical or disability issues are subject to a number of special rules. A doctor who has at any time advised, prepared a report on or regularly attended the appellant may not serve on a tribunal considering that person's appeal.[185] Moreover, an appeal tribunal may not carry out a physical examination of the appellant unless the assessment of disablement or diagnosis in an industrial injuries case is in issue.[186] In this way the specialist character of the former medical appeal tribunals lives on under the new arrangements.[187] Tribunals are also specifically precluded from requiring appellants to undergo a physical test for the purpose of determining whether they satisfy the criteria for the higher rate mobility component of disability living allowance.[188]

Official statistics show that about half of all appellants attend the hearing of their appeals.[189] There are a variety of explanations for the low attendance rate, including practical reasons (ill health, other commitments, etc) as well as other factors such as nervousness and inability to find a representative.[190] Although the official figures suggest that about one in six appellants are represented, this probably includes many who are accompanied by a friend or relative.[191] It is clear that appellants who do attend, and still more those who are represented, have a higher rate of success.[192] This is not surprising, for an appellant who attends is able to challenge the decision maker's summary of the facts or the evidence on which he or she has relied. Community legal service funding, of course, is not available for representation before social security tribunals.[193] Although there are now many local welfare rights centres and Citizens' Advice Bureaux who are willing to assist claimants, national coverage remains patchy and their resources are stretched. It remains doubtful how far an inquisitorial approach on the part of the tribunal can adequately compensate for the lack of competent representation.[194] Furthermore, empirical research has also shown that the identity of the individual chair may have a significant influence on success rates.[195]

---

183   But note the repeal of SI 1999/991, reg 51(5) by SI 2002/1379, reg 15, and *R(U) 3/88(T)*, where the Commissioners gave guidance on the procedure to be followed at the rehearing. On adjournments, see also *Harris* n 167, above.

184   SSA 1998, s 7(4) and (5) and SI 1999/991, reg 50. Tribunals no longer have the power to sit with an assessor (on whose role see *R(I) 14/51* and *R(I) 14/57*).

185   SI 1999/991, reg 36(8).

186   SI 1999/991, reg 52. The tribunal may refer the appellant to a medical practitioner for examination and report: SSA 1998, s 20(2) and SI 1999/991, reg 41.

187   Although it is usual for the medical members to examine the appellant in such cases, this is not required *(R(I) 35/61)*. Research on medical appeal tribunals demonstrated that medical examinations gave rise to the largest number of complaints from claimants: Sainsbury *Survey and Report into the Workings of the MATs* (1992).

188   SSA 1998, s 20(3).

189   DWP *Work and Pension Statistics 2001* (2001) p 222, Table 4.

190   *Baldwin, Wikeley and Young* n 30, above, pp 160–162.

191   Genn and Genn *The Effectiveness of Representation at Tribunals* (1989) found that only 12 per cent of appellants were represented by specialist advisors.

192   *Genn and Genn* n 191, above, p 68

193   But note that the Lord Chancellor may direct the Legal Services Commission to fund representation before the Social Security Commissioners in special cases: Access to Justice Act 1999, s 6(8); see Haley *Legal Action* (2000) p 17.

194   *Baldwin, Wikeley and Young* n 30, above; and *Genn and Genn* n 191, above.

195   *Genn and Genn* n 191, above, pp 71–76.

vi The decision

When the hearing is over, everyone (except the clerk and certain other special categories of observer) must withdraw during the tribunal's deliberations.[196] If the tribunal comprises two panel members, the chair has a casting vote if that proves necessary. A three-person panel may reach their decision by a majority; in practice such decisions are very rare.[197] It is the chair's responsibility to record the tribunal's decision but this need be only in summary form. Since SSA 1998 there has been no requirement for the tribunal's reasons to be recorded in its decision. Instead, any party to the proceedings has one month in which to request a 'full statement', which includes the tribunal's reasons.[198] Typically the appellants are handed (or sent, should they fail to attend) a stencilled copy of the tribunal's handwritten decision on the day, together with a proforma document giving advice as to the procedure for seeking a full statement, setting aside and appealing to the Commissioner.[199] A tribunal chair may, on application, set aside a tribunal's decision if it appears just to do so, either because it subsequently emerges that the appellant did not in fact receive the papers, or that a party to the proceedings was not present at the hearing. If the appellant did not opt in for an oral hearing, the decision may be set aside on the latter ground only if 'the interests of justice manifestly so require'.[200]

SSA 1998 introduced two measures which were designed to reduce the number of cases going on appeal to the Commissioner by making provision for a rehearing by an appeal tribunal without the full panoply (and delay) of an appeal proper.[201] First, an appeal tribunal chair considering an application for leave to appeal, if of the opinion that a tribunal decision is erroneous in law, may set it aside and direct that it be listed for rehearing. Secondly, and more controversially, if both the appellant and the Secretary of State express the view that the decision was erroneous in law, it must be set aside and referred for rehearing. This may have the effect of only postponing inevitable appeals to the Commissioner where the parties are not agreed on the reason why the decision is wrong in law.

vii Suspension of benefit and the anti-test case rule

Where the appeal tribunal makes an award of benefit to an appellant, the Secretary of State has the power to suspend payment of benefit pending appeal to the Commissioner. This power also arises where the outcome of a claim may be affected by the result of an appeal by the Secretary of State against a tribunal's decision in another case.[202] In other cases a claimant may already have lodged an appeal, but its outcome may equally be affected by the result in a test case before the courts. In such circumstances the Secretary of State may serve a notice on the tribunal requiring it to refer the case to him or her or alternatively to decide the look-alike appeal as though the test case had already been

---

196 See SI 1999/991, reg 49(12) on those who may remain during the deliberations.
197 SSA 1998, s 7(3). The decision must record the fact of any dissent: SI 1999/991, reg 53(5). In the study by *Baldwin, Wikeley and Young* n 30, above, which concerned 3-member SSATs, only 6 out of 337 decisions were by a majority: p 147.
198 SI 1999/991, reg 53(4); see reg 54 on late applications for full statements.
199 SI 1999/991, reg 53(3). Increasingly word-processing facilities for decisions are being made available.
200 SI 1999/991, reg 57. Accidental errors in a decision may be corrected under reg 56.
201 SSA 1998, s 13.
202 SSA 1998, s 21 and SI 1999/991, regs 16 and 20, which prescribe the procedure to be followed.

determined in the way 'most unfavourable to the appellant'.[203] Thus the executive has the power to intervene in the workings of the Appeals Service to stay cases.

C   Tax appeal commissioners

The transfer of initial decision making functions in certain social security matters to the Inland Revenue means that the tax appeal commissioners now hear some appeals. The tax appeal commissioners are either General Commissioners (part-time and unpaid lay people, assisted by a clerk who is usually a solicitor) or Special Commissioners (lawyers of at least 10 years' standing). Whereas General Commissioners usually sit in panels of three, Special Commissioners normally sit alone.[204] At present, in the social security field, the tax appeal commissioners only have jurisdiction to hear appeals relating to contributions issues, statutory sick pay and statutory maternity pay, along with certain penalties under the tax credits legislation.[205] The Council on Tribunals has expressed its unease over aspects of the decision making processes of the General Commissioners on a number of occasions,[206] which makes the government's stated intention of transferring all tax credits appeals to their jurisdiction all the more unsatisfactory. Reform of the tax appeals machinery appears to be long overdue.[207]

Part 4   Social Security Commissioners

A   The Commissioners and their jurisdiction

At the apex of the social security tribunal system sit the Social Security Commissioners,[208] of whom there are currently 21 full-timers, including the Chief Social Security Commissioner, currently HH Judge Michael Harris, who is also President of the Appeals Service. They must have a professional legal qualification of 10 years' standing, and are appointed by the Crown.[209] There are also some 20 part-time Deputy Commissioners, appointed by the Lord Chancellor, in consultation with the Lord Advocate. Since 1985 the Lord Chancellor has been responsible for the payment and administrative requirements of the Commissioners and for the procedural regulations governing their proceedings.[210] This change, perhaps more of form than real substance, denotes the Commissioners' status and independence.[211] The Chief Social Security

---

203   SSA 1998, s 26. If the latter course is adopted, then once the lead case is determined the decision in the instant case must be superseded where appropriate.
204   For a general introduction, see Whitehouse *Revenue Law Principles and Practice* (19th edn, 2001) pp 26–31.
205   SSA 1998, s 8(5), SSC(TF)A 1999, ss 11 and 12 and SI 1999/1027.
206   Council on Tribunals *Annual Report 1999/2000* (2000–01, HC 23) pp 48–52.
207   See LCD Consultation Paper *Tax Appeals Tribunals* (March 2000).
208   See further Bonner, Buck and Sainsbury (2001) 8 JSSL 9; and Bonner (2002) 9 JSSL 11.
209   SSA 1998, s 14(12) and Sch 4. For information and statistics on the Commissioners, see HC Social Security Committee *Fourth Report* (1999–2000, HC 263), esp the appendices to the Minutes of Evidence.
210   SI 1984/1818.
211   The Select Committee (n 209, above, para 42) criticised what it viewed as a 'too cosy' relationship between the Commissioners and the DSS. However, evidence from welfare rights organisations to the Committee testified to the respect in which the Commissioners are held.

Commissioner has statutory responsibility for convening a tribunal of three or more Commissioners to hear an application for leave or appeal which involves a legal question of special difficulty.[212] This course was adopted more frequently in the 1980s and 1990s than it had been previously, reflecting both the growing complexity of the cases and the increasing number of Commissioners, with the consequent risk of disagreement between them. It remains, however, the exception rather than the rule. The Chief Commissioner has a number of additional duties, of which the most important is selecting which cases should be reported.[213] Subject to the higher status of tribunal decisions, the authority of each Commissioner is the same. They are appointed to hear appeals in Great Britain, and not for particular areas of the country. However, three of them sit in Edinburgh and hear appeals largely from Scottish tribunals, while the others sit in London, although sometimes they travel to a number of provincial venues to hear cases.

Commissioners exercise an appellate jurisdiction from all tribunals within the Appeals Service with the exception of vaccine damage tribunals.[214] (They also exercise original jurisdiction to determine whether a person who has unlawfully killed another should forfeit entitlement to benefit.[215]) In 1993 the Commissioners acquired a new jurisdiction, albeit in their capacity as Child Support Commissioners, to hear appeals from what were then child support appeal tribunals. The statutory provisions governing their appointment and procedures are the same in all material respects as those relating to the main social security system.[216] The Commissioners' jurisdiction was further extended to include housing benefit and council tax benefit appeals with effect from July 2001.[217]

Historically there used to be significant differences in the extent of rights of appeal,[218] but the position today is that the appellant must always obtain leave either from the chair of the tribunal or the Commissioner.[219] Both the claimant and the Secretary of State (as well as other interested parties) may appeal against a tribunal's decision,[220] but in practice the great majority of appeals are brought by claimants.[221] The requirement for leave is presumably designed to ensure that only appeals involving real points of substance reach the Commissioner. Further, whatever the nature of the benefit, the only ground of an appeal from a tribunal to the Commissioner is on a point of law. The distinction between fact and law is notoriously hard to draw with precision, but in their appellate jurisdiction the Commissioners have laid down some relevant principles. It has been ruled that an appeal will be allowed on a point of law if there has been a breach of the natural justice rules, if the tribunal failed to state the facts and reasons for its decision adequately, if the ruling contained an ex facie false proposition of law or if the findings of fact were unsupported by any evidence.[222] In practice, in recent years, much the most common ground of appeal has been the alleged failure by a tribunal to state the reasons for its decision adequately.

---

212 SSA 1998, s 16(7). See *R(U) 4/88(T)*. This power dates back to NIA 1946, s 43(3)(c), at which time three represented a majority of Commissioners. Its re-enactment in SSA 1998 included applications for leave to appeal and raised the prospect of a bench of *more than* three Commissioners for the first time.
213 In reaching his decision, the Chief Commissioner is advised by a committee of Commissioners.
214 They have no power of judicial review: *R(G) 2/93*.
215 Forfeiture Act 1982, s 4, amended by SSA 1986, s 76; see pp 241–243, below.
216 CSA 1991, ss 22–25 and Sch 4; see also SI 1999/1305.
217 CSPSSA 2000, s 68 and Sch 7, para 8.
218 See the 3rd edition of this book, p 580.
219 SSA 1998, s 14(10).
220 See generally SSA 1998, s 14(2)–(6).
221 Since 1998 fewer than 5 per cent of appeals have been initiated by the adjudication officer or Secretary of State: n 209, above, *Minutes of Evidence* p 34.
222 *R(I) 14/75*. See also *R(A) 1/73*; *R(SB) 6/81*; *R(SB) 11/83*.

B   Procedure for appeals to the Commissioner

i   Pre-hearing procedure

The first step is for the appellant to seek leave to appeal from the chair of the tribunal.[223] This must be sought within one month of receiving the tribunal's 'full statement'.[224] A chair has power to grant leave outside the one-month period providing that the application is made within one year of the expiry of the normal time limit and there are 'special reasons'.[225] Where the tribunal chair has refused leave or rejected the application (eg because no full statement had been obtained), the appellant may then apply to the Commissioner within one month of that refusal or rejection.[226] The Commissioner also has a discretion to consider an application for leave made outside this period if he or she considers there are special reasons.[227] The appellant must then state the grounds for acceptance of the application, despite the delay, etc, in addition to the substantive grounds of appeal.[228]

The Commissioner must make a written decision on the application for leave.[229] Although the Court of Appeal once rejected the view that in some special cases natural justice required the Commissioner to give reasons for refusing leave,[230] since 1999 the Commissioners have been giving reasons when denying leave.[231] The Lord Chancellor's decision not to make a further Order under the Tribunals and Inquiries (Social Security Commissioners) Order 1980[232] means that they are now under a duty to do so. There is no appeal against a refusal of leave, though there may in exceptional circumstances be a judicial review.[233] If leave is granted by the Commissioner, notice of appeal is then deemed to be given by the appellant; but where leave has been granted by the tribunal chair, notice of appeal must be served within one month.[234] The Commissioners' office then notifies the respondent (usually the Secretary of State but sometimes the claimant), who may submit written observations within one month. Observations may be sent in reply. The Commissioner may direct further particulars to be supplied by any party.[235] The Commissioners are assisted in their interlocutory work by a team of legal officers. If both parties agree the decision was wrong in law, the Commissioner has a discretion to make what is effectively a form of consent order, setting aside the decision and remitting the case for rehearing with directions.[236] The rules governing suspension of benefit and test cases that apply to appeal tribunals also affect proceedings before the Commissioners.[237]

---

223   SSA 1998, s 14(10) and SI 1999/1495, reg 9(1).
224   SI 1999/991, reg 58.
225   Statute provides no definition of what amount to 'special reasons'; contrast SI 1999/991, reg 32 on 'special circumstances' in the context of late appeals to tribunals.
226   See SI 1999/1495, reg 9(2).
227   Again, these are not defined in the regulations, but see *R(M) 1/87*; *R(U) 3/89*; *R(I) 5/91*.
228   SI 1999/1495, reg 10. For case law on earlier regulations, see *R(I) 15/53* and *R(F) 1/70*.
229   SI 1999/1495, reg 28.
230   *R v Secretary of State for Social Services, ex p Connolly* [1986] 1 All ER 998, [1986] 1 WLR 421, rejecting the view of Woolf J in *R v Social Security Comr, ex p Sewell* (1985) Times, 2 January.
231   Practice Memorandum *Tribunals and Inquiries (Social Security Commissioners) Order 1980 and the Social Security Act 1998* (1999).
232   SI 1980/1637.
233   *Bland v Chief Supplementary Benefit Officer* [1983] 1 All ER 537, [1983] 1 WLR 262. See also *R v Social Security Comr, ex p Pattni* [1993] Fam Law 214.
234   SI 1999/1495, regs 11(2) and 13(1). Again, the Commissioner may for 'special reasons' accept a late notice of appeal.
235   SI 1999/1495, regs 18–20.
236   SSA 1998, s 14(7). See Chief Commissioner's Practice Memorandum, 11 August 1998.
237   SSA 1998, ss 21 and 26.

Most appeals are determined on the basis of the papers alone; fewer than ten per cent of cases are subject to an oral hearing. But if one is requested by any party in any proceedings (including, it would seem, an application for leave) it will be granted, unless the Commissioner is satisfied that the case can be determined on the papers.[238] The Commissioner can at any stage decide to hold an oral hearing, whether it has been requested or not. At least 14 days' notice of a hearing must be granted, and the Commissioner has the same power to proceed in the absence of a party as a tribunal.[239] It seems likely with the advent of the Human Rights Act 1998 that oral hearings will become more common.

One factor that has troubled the Council on Tribunals over the years, and more recently the Select Committee on Social Security, is the length of time before appeals are heard. The reasons for this vary and cannot simply be attributed to a shortage of Commissioners and a lack of resources. Although the Select Committee criticised what it found to be a 'culture of delay',[240] this is contributed to by delays in the Appeals Service and the DWP in providing papers and written submissions respectively. The complex nature of some cases may also provide a partial explanation. In June 2001 the average length of time for an appeal to be processed by the Commissioners' Office had been reduced to 36 weeks,[241] with a target of 26 weeks for 2002.

ii   The hearing

A number of persons have a right to attend and be heard at an oral hearing, including the appellant, the claimant (if not the appellant) and the Secretary of State.[242] The hearing is in public, unless the Commissioner for special reasons directs otherwise.[243] The Commissioner's permission is necessary for a party to give evidence or call or question witnesses, a rule which bears out the point that appeals at this stage are not primarily concerned with reviewing the facts.[244] The Commissioners have the power to summon a person to attend as a witness to answer questions or produce documents.[245] Apart from these few specific rules, they are free to adopt the procedure they think fit, subject to the rules of natural justice.[246] The hearsay rule does not apply,[247] and the Commissioners have no power to award costs.[248]

Like tribunals, the Commissioners exercise an inquisitorial jurisdiction.[249] They have a statutory power to seek the assistance of an expert where an appeal 'involves a question of fact of special difficulty'.[250] This facility has not been extensively used, and presumably is of relatively little importance, now that the Commissioners hear appeals only on points of law.[251]

---

238   SI 1999/1495, reg 23(2).
239   SI 1999/1495, reg 24.
240   HC Social Security Committee *Fourth Report* (1999–2000, HC 263) paras 10–30.
241   Council on Tribunals *Annual Report 2000–2001* (2001–02, HC 343) p 27.
242   SI 1999/1495, reg 24(6). For a general discussion, see *Micklethwait* n 17, above, pp 48–53.
243   SI 1999/1495, reg 24(5).
244   SI 1999/1495, reg 24(7).
245   SI 1999/1495, reg 25.
246   SI 1999/1495, reg 5 and see *R(M) 1/89(T)*.
247   *R(G) 1/91*.
248   *R(FC) 2/90*.
249   *R(I) 4/75*.
250   SSA 1998, s 16(6); see eg *R(G) 4/93*.
251   It may, however, be valuable if advice on a question of foreign law is needed: see eg polygamy cases.

iii   The decision

The decision must be reasoned and sent to the parties but is sometimes announced at the conclusion of the hearing, should one take place.[252] Where Commissioners hold a decision of an appeal tribunal to be wrong in law, they may decide the case themselves, if necessary after finding fresh or further facts, or send the case back to a tribunal, which will usually be differently constituted from the one which took the original decision.[253] In practice the Commissioners are reluctant to resolve issues of fact,[254] and so, unless the tribunal's error was purely one of law and there is no doubt about the facts, they are inclined to refer the case back. This course sometimes appears circuitous and productive of delay.

In principle the Commissioner's decision is final,[255] but this is subject to three provisos. First, there is a right of appeal to the ordinary courts. Secondly, the decision may be superseded by the Secretary of State on certain grounds.[256] Thirdly, the Commissioner may set aside his or her own earlier decision in circumstances set out in regulations: that relevant documents were not received in time, or that a party was absent from an oral hearing, or that there has been some other 'procedural irregularity or mishap'.[257]

C   Precedent and the reporting of decisions

The Commissioners decide about 4,000 appeals a year.[258] The vast majority do not raise any points of legal principle or importance, and therefore are not reported, the decisions being circulated only to the parties. But if a Commissioner thinks a decision should be reported, it is circulated amongst the Commissioners generally for consideration. In the light of their comments and any representations made, the Chief Commissioner decides whether it should be reported. These decisions must deal with questions of legal principle and command the assent of the majority of Commissioners. The current system of reporting dates from the Chief Commissioner's Practice Direction of 1982.[259] During the 1990s there were considerable delays in reporting cases, leading to the Select Committee expressing its alarm at the 'chaotic and almost laughable situation', redolent of 'typically British, amateur, worst practice'.[260] One Commissioner established an unofficial and much-praised website to increase the availability of decisions, but it appeared to need the impetus of the Select Committee investigation to galvanise the Lord Chancellor's Department and DSS into more concerted action.[261]

Reporting is important not least because of the system of precedent.[262] In the leading case, *R(I) 12/75*, a tribunal of Commissioners set out a number of rules: Commissioners' decisions must be followed by tribunals and decision makers, and where they conflict

252   SI 1999/1495, reg 28.
253   SSA 1998, s 14(8) and (9).
254   Cf *R(SB) 6/88*.
255   SSA 1998, s 17(1).
256   P 186, above.
257   SI 1999/1495, reg 31. See *R(S) 3/89*; *R(U) 3/89* on the previous variant of this rule.
258   They also dispose of a similar number of applications for leave to appeal.
259   The Practice Direction is set out in the bound volume of Social Security Commissioner decisions 1980–82, published by HMSO.
260   N 209, above, paras 31–41.
261   See now www.osscsc.gov.uk.
262   See Harris (1984) 13 ILJ 181; and Prestataire (1990) 87 LS Gaz 28, March, p 20.

a decision of a tribunal must be followed in preference to the ruling of a single Commissioner and reported decisions given more weight than unreported ones. (Unreported decisions are binding on tribunals, and therefore when the Secretary of State relies on one, a copy should be given the claimant.[263]) Commissioners themselves should follow a tribunal decision unless there are compelling reasons for not doing this, and generally should follow the previous decision of another Commissioner. Nor is a tribunal absolutely bound to follow a previous tribunal ruling.[264] So the strict doctrine of stare decisis has not been adopted by the Commissioners.[265]

Part 5 Control by the courts

A History

Historically disputes concerning social security benefits have been kept away from the ordinary courts. Thus, there was no provision in NIA 1946 legislation or in the national assistance (later supplementary benefits) scheme for an appeal to the courts from decisions of the Commissioners and other adjudicating authorities. The position was approved by the Franks Committee, who regarded it as important that final decisions be reached quickly.[266] However, it became clear in the 1950s and 1960s that medical appeal tribunals (before the institution of an appeal to the Commissioner) and the Commissioners were subject to judicial review by the prerogative orders.[267] Judicial review also came to be used to challenge the decisions of SBATs.[268]

The courts were, however, reluctant to exercise their powers of review, deferring on occasion to the expertise of the Commissioners.[269] Further, the Court of Appeal expressed reluctance to question SBAT decisions, a cautious approach that was hard to support in view of the lack of legal expertise in these tribunals.[270] Dissatisfaction with this position led to the institution in 1980 of a right of appeal from SBATs on points of law to the renamed Social Security Commissioners.[271] At the same time provision was made for a right of appeal on a point of law from any decision of a Social Security Commissioner on any benefit to the Court of Appeal, or in Scotland the Court of Session.[272] The Divisional Court, which had heard applications for judicial review, was therefore bypassed altogether. Consequently, whilst recent years have seen a considerable expansion of judicial review litigation in many other fields of government activity, its use remains limited in the arena of social security law.[273]

---

263   For the status of unreported decisions, see *R(SB) 22/86*.
264   *R(U) 4/88(T)*.
265   See *Micklethwait* n 17, above, pp 74 and 129. Decisions of the Northern Ireland Commissioners are of only persuasive authority in Britain, though they may be followed in preference to decisions of the British Commissioner: *R(I) 14/63*. Northern Ireland decisions can be located at www.dsdni.gov.uk/benefitlaw.
266   Franks Committee on Administrative Tribunals and Enquiries (1957, Cmnd 218) para 108.
267   The leading case was *R v Medical Appeal Tribunal, ex p Gilmore* [1957] 1 QB 574, [1957] 1 All ER 796. For a full discussion of these developments, see the 1st edition of this book, pp 644–646.
268   See Robson in Buck (ed) *Judicial Review and Social Welfare* (1998) ch 4.
269   See eg *R v Industrial Injuries Comr, ex p Amalgamated Engineering Union (No 2)* [1966] 2 QB 31, [1966] 1 All ER 97; *R v National Insurance Comr, ex p Michael* [1977] 2 All ER 420, [1977] 1 WLR 109, CA.
270   *R v Preston Supplementary Benefits Appeal Tribunal, ex p Moore* [1975] 2 All ER 807, [1975] 1 WLR 624.
271   This had been preceded in 1978, as a temporary step, by a right of appeal to the High Court.
272   SSA 1980, s 14. See now SSA 1998, s 15.
273   See *Robson* n 268, above.

B   Appeal to the Court of Appeal

Leave of the Commissioner or the Court of Appeal (or Court of Session) is necessary; an application should be made to the Commissioner who took the decision within three months of its notification.[274] The time-limit of three months may be extended at the discretion of the Commissioner;[275] there is no right of appeal to the Court of Appeal against a refusal to extend time, though it is conceivable that a perverse refusal might be the subject of an application for judicial review.[276] An appellant who is refused leave, on grounds other than being out of time, may apply direct to the Court of Appeal for leave to appeal.[277] However, the Court of Appeal has recently held that such an application should be approached with caution, since the Commissioners were best placed to take decisions regarding technical issues of social security law.[278]

C   The contribution of the courts to social security jurisprudence

Now that appeal has replaced judicial review as the means of control, there is in principle more room for intervention by the courts. They are not confined to the narrow grounds available on judicial review and may in principle reverse any error of law, no matter how trivial or technical. Initially there was no fundamental change to the judicial approach. In three leading unemployment benefit cases,[279] the courts approved the cautious stance adopted by Lord Denning MR in a judicial review case:[280] that the courts should treat as binding a Commissioner's decision that has not been challenged and should only intervene in exceptional circumstances, such as where there is a division of opinion between the Commissioners. The House of Lords, in particular, was unwilling to probe deeply into the subtleties of social security law.[281] While there is something to be said for weight being given to the Commissioners' expertise, too great a deference on the courts' part would render pointless the existence of the right of appeal. Whilst it is true that intervention by the ordinary courts has not always been particularly helpful,[282] the last decade has witnessed a number of landmark decisions in test cases by both the Court of Appeal and the House of Lords.[283]

Decisions of the Court of Appeal or the Court of Session are binding on the Commissioners, appeal tribunals and decision makers.[284] A Tribunal of Commissioners

---

274   SSA 1998, s 15(2)(a) and SI 1999/1495, reg 33(1).

275   SI 1999/1495, reg 5(2).

276   *White v Chief Adjudication Officer* [1986] 2 All ER 905; and *Kuganathan v Chief Adjudication Officer* (1995) Times, 1 March.

277   SSA 1998, s 15(2)(b). The time limit is six weeks in England and Wales but only 14 days in Scotland.

278   *Cooke v Secretary of State for Social Security* [2001] EWCA Civ 734 (*R(DLA) 6/01*), where it was held that the court should adopt a 'robust' attitude in deciding whether to grant leave.

279   *Crewe v Social Security Comr* [1982] 2 All ER 745, [1982] 1 WLR 1209; *Presho v Department of Health and Social Security* [1984] AC 310, [1984] 1 All ER 97; *Cartlidge v Chief Adjudication Officer* [1986] QB 360, [1986] 2 All ER 1.

280   *R v National Insurance Comr, ex p Stratton* [1979] QB 361, [1979] 2 All ER 278, CA.

281   Eg *Presho v Insurance Officer* [1984] AC 310, [1984] 1 All ER 9; and *Chief Adjudication Officer v Brunt* [1988] AC 711, [1988] 1 All ER 754, HL.

282   See in particular *Nancollas v Insurance Officer* [1985] 1 All ER 833, CA discussed at p 733, above, and *Jones and Sharples v Chief Adjudication Officer* [1994] 1 All ER 225.

283   See eg *Mallinson v Secretary of State for Social Security* [1994] 2 All ER 295. But see Robertson *Judicial Discretion in the House of Lords* (1998), esp pp 92–97.

284   On the status of decisions of the Divisional Court on applications for judicial review from SBATs (pre-1978), and of the High Court on appeal from SBATs (1978–80), see the 4th edition of this book, p 687.

has held that decisions of the Court of Appeal in Northern Ireland are not binding but as a matter of comity should be preferred to decisions of Commissioner status where identically worded provisions are in issue.[285]

Part 6 Reference to the European Court of Justice

The significance of EU law for particular social security benefits is fully discussed in chapters 2 and 3. The EC regulations governing migrant workers[286] are directly applicable; they must, therefore, be implemented by the British courts and adjudicating authorities.[287] In most cases it will be for the national courts to interpret EC regulations but, in order that there may be uniformity of application in the member states, there is a procedure under which a point of difficulty may be referred to the European Court of Justice (ECJ) in Luxembourg for it to give a preliminary ruling.[288] The EC Treaty, article 234 (formerly the Treaty of Rome, article 177) provides that the ECJ has jurisdiction to give preliminary rulings on the interpretation of the Treaty and the validity and interpretation of EU legal acts, eg regulations and directives. It further provides in paras 2 and 3:

> Where such a question is raised before any court of tribunal of a Member State, that court or tribunal may, if it considers that a decision on the question is necessary to enable it to give judgment, request the Court of Justice to give a ruling thereon.
> Where any such question is raised in a case pending before a court or a tribunal of a Member State, against whose decisions there is no judicial remedy under national law, that court or tribunal shall bring the matter before the Court of Justice.

A The discretion to refer

i 'Court or tribunal'

Under the EC Treaty, article 234, para 2 a question may be referred for a preliminary ruling by a 'court or tribunal'. This enables any part of the Supreme Court of Judicature to ask for a preliminary ruling in a suitable case. A Social Security Commissioner is clearly entitled to refer,[289] and in principle an appeal tribunal could do so.[290] The fact that there is an existing precedent of a domestic superior court on the point is no bar to a reference.[291] It seems unlikely that the Secretary of State could make such a reference,

---

285 *R(SB) 1/90(T)*.
286 Council Regulation (EEC) 1408/71, as amended, now consolidated in Council Regulation (EEC) 2001/83.
287 For the direct applicability of EU law, see Craig and De Bûrca *EC Law: Text, Cases and Materials* (2nd edn, 1998) ch 4.
288 For an overview see Lenaerts and Arts *Procedural law of the European Union* (1999) ch 2 and for a detailed treatment Anderson *References to the European Court* (1995).
289 See eg Case 384/85 *Clarke v Chief Adjudication Officer* [1987] ECR 2865, [1987] 3 CMLR 277; and Case 377/85 *Burchell v Adjudication Officer* [1987] ECR 3329, [1987] CMLR 757.
290 In practice a tribunal may prefer to decide the appeal and leave the relevant party to appeal to the Commissioner, who is better placed to judge whether a reference is appropriate.
291 Case 146/73, Case 166/73 *Rheinmühlen-Düsseldorf v Einfuhr- und Vorratsstelle für Getreide und Futtermittel* [1974] ECR 139, [1974] ECR 33.

since the referring body must be independent of the parties to the action in order to constitute a 'tribunal' for the purpose of article 234.[292]

ii   The decision must be 'necessary'

A question may only be referred to the ECJ if a decision on it is 'necessary' for the national court or tribunal to give judgment. Since the early reluctance on the part of Lord Denning MR to embrace the possibility of referral,[293] the British courts have adopted a more positive approach to the use of the EC Treaty, article 234. According to Sir Thomas Bingham MR, 'if the facts have been found and the Community law issue is critical to the court's final decision, the appropriate course is ordinarily to refer the issue to the Court of Justice unless the national court can with complete confidence resolve the issue itself'.[294]

iii   Factors relevant to the exercise of the discretion

The English judiciary have emphasised that the ECJ is better placed to determine issues of EU law than domestic courts, given the composition of the ECJ and the nature of its proceedings.[295] The desirability of ensuring uniform interpretation of EU law is also an important factor. The delay and costs entailed by a reference might seem to be a consideration weighing against referral, but a reference may save time and money if it is likely to be made at some later point in the proceedings. In the past the Commissioners have generally decided questions of European law themselves, although this may change now that the Court of Appeal has encouraged lower courts to be more active in using the EC Treaty, article 234 procedure.

In only a few reported cases have the Commissioners discussed at length whether to request a preliminary ruling. In one, *Re an Illness in France*,[296] the Commissioner decided to refer a question on the invitation of the DHSS. It was emphasised that the claimant welcomed this step. The issue – the meaning of 'worker' for the purposes of the EU regulation – was one which had been previously ruled on by the Commissioner, and it was clear that an authoritative interpretation from the ECJ was desirable.[297] In *Re a Visit to Italy*,[298] however, the Commissioner refused to refer, largely because of the delay involved and the fact that the claimant might not be paid benefit for the interim period. A reference is unlikely to be made if the sum in question is very small.[299]

---

292   Case C-24/92 *Corbiau v Administration des Contributions* [1993] ECR I-1277. In other respects, however, the ECJ, which may give a preliminary ruling on the interpretation of art 234 itself, has interpreted 'tribunal' broadly: see *Anderson* n 288, above, ch 2.
293   *H P Bulmer Ltd v J Bollinger SA* [1974] Ch 401, [1974] 2 All ER 1226, CA. A less restrictive approach was adopted by the Commissioners in *Re an Illness in France* [1976] 1 CMLR 243; and *Kenny v Insurance Officer* [1978] 1 CMLR 181. Lord Denning's guidelines 'must be regarded, with the greatest respect, as binding on nobody': Kapteyn and VerLoren van Themaat *Introduction to the Law of the European Communities* (2nd edn, 1990) p 315.
294   *R v International Stock Exchange of the United Kingdom and the Republic of Ireland Ltd, ex p Else (1982) Ltd* [1993] 1 All ER 420 at 426.
295   *R v International Stock Exchange of the United Kingdom and the Republic of Ireland Ltd, ex p Else (1982) Ltd* [1993] 1 All ER 420 at 426; and *Customs and Excise Comrs v Samex ApS* [1983] 3 CMLR 194. See Anderson n 288, above, ch 5.
296   *Re an Illness in France* [1976] 1 CMLR 243.
297   The earlier decision of the Commissioner in *Re an Ex-Civil Servant* [1976] 1 CMLR 257 did not satisfy the DHSS.
298   [1976] 1 CMLR 506, *(R(I) 1/75)*.
299   *Re Search for Work in Ireland* [1978] 2 CMLR 174.

B The duty to refer

In the circumstances covered by its third paragraph quoted above, EC Treaty, article 234 imposes a duty to refer.[300] Which British courts or tribunals deciding issues of social security law are under this duty, because 'there is no judicial remedy' against their decision? In *Re a Holiday in Italy*,[301] the Commissioner, J G Monroe, decided that he was not bound to refer, as the prerogative order of certiorari was then available to quash his decision for an error of law, including a wrong interpretation of the EU regulation; it did not matter that leave had to be obtained from the Divisional Court before the order could be applied for. This decision was criticised on the ground that it assumed that leave to apply for certiorari is granted as a matter of course, where a point of EU law is involved.[302] Now that there is an appeal to the Court of Appeal, admittedly only with leave, there is a somewhat stronger argument for holding that the Social Security Commissioner is never bound to refer to the ECJ.[303] However, if the Commissioner declines to make a reference, it is arguable that the Court of Appeal is bound to grant leave to appeal so that the effect of EC Treaty, article 234 (3) can be considered. A more difficult question is whether the Court of Appeal is similarly bound, on the argument that leave of either the Court of Appeal or the House of Lords is required for an appeal to the latter. There are early dicta to the effect that the Court of Appeal is never bound to refer,[304] but the weight of later authorities support the view that a reference should be made if leave to appeal cannot be obtained.[305] There is no authority on this point in a social security case.

Part 7   Social fund reviews

A   Internal review

Decisions relating to social fund maternity, funeral, cold weather and winter fuel payments are dealt with according to the normal mechanisms of revision, supersession and appeal. These procedures do not apply to discretionary social fund payments; in the absence of any right of appeal to a tribunal, the procedure for internal review therefore assumes great importance.[306] Reviews can arise in any one of three ways. First, an appropriate officer[307] must review a discretionary social fund decision following an application from the claimant (or anyone acting on his or her behalf, with written consent) within 28 days of notification of the decision.[308] Specific grounds must be given for the application.

---

300   This duty is not absolute: see Case 283/81 *CILFIT v Italian Ministry of Health* [1982] ECR 3415.
301   [1975] 1 CMLR 184 (*R(S) 4/74*, para 8).
302   See Bridge (1975–76) 1 EL Rev 13 at 19; Jacobs (1977) 2 EL Rev 119.
303   But note that there is an obligation to make a reference if the question raised in the proceedings concerns the validity of an EU measure, as only the ECJ has jurisdiction to determine the validity of EU acts: see Case 314/85 *Foto-Frost v Hauptzollant Lübeck-Ost* [1987] ECR 4199.
304   *HP Bulmer Ltd v J Bollinger SA* [1974] Ch 401 at 420, per Lord Denning MR; and *Pickstone v Freemans* [1989] AC 66 at 96, [1987] 2 CMLR 572 at 591, per Purchas LJ.
305   *Hagen v Fratelli D and G Moretti SNC and Molnar Machinery Ltd* [1980] 3 CMLR 253 at 255; and *R v Pharmaceutical Society of Great Britain, ex p the Association of Pharmaceutical Importers* [1987] 3 CMLR 951.
306   See generally Bolderson (1988) 15 JLS 279; Dalley and Berthoud *Challenging Discretion* (1992); and the Annual Reports of the Social Fund Commissioner.
307   The new nomenclature given to social fund officers by SSA 1998, s 36.
308   SSA 1998, s 38(1). The time-limit (which can be extended where there are 'special reasons') and other requirements are imposed by SI 1988/34.

Secondly, an officer may review a decision on the basis that the claimant misrepresented or failed to disclose a material fact.[309] Thirdly, an officer may review a decision 'in such other circumstances as he thinks fit'. There are no time limits for reviews in the second or third categories.

The scope of reviews differs depending on the type of the original application. In conducting reviews of decisions on community care grants and crisis loans, officers must consider all the circumstances of the case. These include the statutory criteria governing awards and the Secretary of State's directions; likewise they must take into account the Secretary of State's general guidance.[310] In doing so, the need and priority of an application should be assessed before budgetary constraints are considered.[311] Officers must also decide whether the decision was consistent with the evidence, that all relevant and no irrelevant considerations were taken into account, and that the law and directions were properly interpreted. They are also supposed to ensure that the officer making the original decision acted fairly and exercised their discretion reasonably, and to consider any new evidence or relevant changes of circumstances.[312] Some but not all of these considerations apply to reviews of decisions made on applications for budgeting loans. In particular, reviewing officers are governed by the same factors as initial decision makers and thus have no scope for the exercise of individual discretion. Whichever procedure applies, if the decision is not wholly revised in the applicant's favour, there is a right to attend an interview, with a friend or representative, before a final determination is made, and reasons must be given for the original decision.[313]

B Review by social fund inspectors

A claimant dissatisfied with the review may then apply for a further review by a social fund inspector.[314] This application is subject to the same time-limit and other jurisdictional and procedural requirements as the initial review.[315] The inspector's review is a two-stage process, and is almost always dealt with on the papers alone. The first stage is similar to that performed on an application for judicial review, but the inspector must then go on to consider any new evidence and any changes in circumstances.[316] An inspector may confirm the original decision, make any decision which the appropriate officer could have made or remit the matter to the officer for him or her to decide.[317] This is not a fully independent review in institutional terms in that the inspectors are appointed and their training directed by the Social Fund Commissioner, who is an appointee of the Secretary of State.[318] Moreover, the inspectors, like the officers, are

---

309   This may result in recovery of the overpayment: SSAA 1992, ss 71 and 71ZA. This ground for review was introduced by SSA 1998. See also DSS *Social Fund Guide* (1999) Directions 43–48.
310   SSA 1998, s 38(7).
311   *R v Social Fund Inspector, ex p Taylor* [1998] COD 152; see Buck (1998) 5 JSSL 89.
312   *Social Fund Guide* n 309, above, Directions 32 and 39.
313   *Social Fund Guide* n 309, above, Directions 33 and 34.
314   SSA 1998, s 38(3).
315   SSA 1998, s 38(7) and (12).
316   The constraints governing reviews of budgeting loan decisions means that over 90 per cent of decisions in this category are confirmed by inspectors, as against 45 per cent of community care grant decisions: DWP *Annual Report by the Secretary of State on the Social Fund 2000/2001*(2001, Cm 5238) p 25.
317   SSA 1998, s 38(4).
318   See p 466, below. In a deliberate echo of the (then) Independent Tribunal Service (ITS), the inspectorate was restyled as the Independent Review Service (IRS) in 1992. Ironically, IRS has retained this nomenclature whilst ITS has transmuted into the Appeals Service. IRS decisions are usefully reported in IRS *The Journal and Digest of Decisions*, available on its website at www.irssf.gov.uk.

subject to the guidance and directions issued by the Secretary of State.[319] Notwithstanding these reservations, research findings suggest that inspectors approach their work in an independent manner.[320]

C Judicial review of social fund decisions

Although the clear intention of the government was to insulate the social fund scheme from control outside the DWP, the courts have intervened in appropriate cases. Buck has identified three phases in the development of judicial review by the courts in social fund cases.[321] The first phase involved fundamental challenges to the vires of the Secretary of State's directions and guidance.[322] In the second phase the focus was on the construction of individual directions, especially those concerning exclusions and the qualifying criteria for community care grants. The Court of Appeal has expressed its surprise and concern at the exceptionally wide powers granted to the Secretary of State to define the categories of need which qualify for assistance.[323] The third phase was more procedural in nature and concerned various challenges to the priority stage of decision making.

Part 8 Pensions appeal tribunals

A Composition and structure

Pensions appeal tribunals (PATs) were first set up in 1919.[324] Their composition and procedures are governed by the Pensions Appeal Tribunals Act 1943. The consultation paper that led to SSA 1998 raised the possibility of incorporating PATs within the mainstream social security appellate machinery,[325] but this idea was quietly dropped.[326] Persistent concerns about the extensive delays experienced in appeals lodged with PATs prompted the government to commission a management consultants' report on the system.[327] This in turn led to amending legislation in CSPSSA 2000, which introduced time-limits for appeals and modified the rules governing the composition of PATs.

The PATs are organised on the presidential model, which was subsequently adopted for SSATs,[328] with three Presidents covering the main jurisdictions in the UK. Members are appointed by the Lord Chancellor, who is also responsible for providing the tribunals' staff. There are four categories of member: those who are legally or medically qualified,

---

319 SSAA 1992, s 66(7) and (10).
320 *Dalley and Berthoud* n 306, above.
321 Buck *The Social Fund: Law and Practice* (2nd edn, 2000) para 4.12.
322 *R v Social Fund Inspector and Secretary of State for Social Security, ex p Stitt* [1990] COD 288.
323 *R v Secretary of State for Social Security, ex p Stitt Sherwin and Roberts* [1991] COD 68; this might be seen as 'an unwelcome feature of a dominating executive in a basically two-party democracy', per Purchas LJ.
324 See ch 21, Pt 1, below for the history of war pensions.
325 DSS *Improving decision making and appeals in Social Security* (Cm 3328, 1996) pp 38–39.
326 This reflects the enduring and universal disinclination of governments to introduce significant change in the field of war pensions appellate systems. Thus in Australia the Veterans' Review Tribunal was not included in plans for an Administrative Review Tribunal (unlike the SSAT).
327 Ernst & Young *War Pension Agency: Review of Decision Making and Appeals* (1999).
328 See *Wraith and Hutchesson* n 11, above, pp 85–86. For the presidential system for SSATs, see Pt 3 of this chapter, above.

service members and 'other members'. Until CSPSSA 2000, the service member on a PAT had to be a retired or demobilised officer or serviceman of the same sex and rank as the person in respect of whose disability the claim is made. The Pensions Appeal Tribunals Act 1943 now provides merely that the Lord Chancellor must appoint to the tribunals 'persons with knowledge or experience of service' in HM Forces.[329] 'Other members' will typically be those with knowledge or experience of disability issues.[330] The 2000 Act also introduced a requirement that a legally qualified member sit on all appeals.[331] The actual composition of PATs is not prescribed by legislation – in contrast to appeal tribunals for social security cases – but is a matter to be dealt with by the President in directions. In addition to issuing such directions and sitting as a chairman, the President has general administrative responsibilities for the tribunals. These include a number of specific procedural powers: eg ordering the disclosure to the claimant of official documents and making arrangements where an infirm appellant is unable to attend the hearing.[332] Although the tribunals are national in terms of their administration and jurisdiction, they sit in regional centres as well as in London.

B   Rights of appeal and procedure[333]

The Pensions Appeal Tribunals Act 1943 provided for a right of appeal against most decisions on entitlement and assessment of disablement.[334] However, there was no right of appeal in relation to decisions on some of the supplementary allowances or in respect of service between the two World Wars. These lacunae were remedied by CSPSSA 2000.[335]

The detailed procedural rules governing appeals to PATs, compared with the provisions concerning other social security tribunals, are often favourable to the appellant. In appeals concerning issues of entitlement, where the issue is whether the Secretary of State was right to reject the claim, the hearing is de novo and there is no onus on the appellant to show that the decision was wrong.[336] Similarly, the time-limits for appeals, although tightened by CSPSSA 2000, remain significantly more generous than in the rest of the social security system.[337] An appellant has six months in which to appeal against a decision on entitlement or a final assessment, or three months in the case of an interim assessment.[338] Furthermore, on receipt of the notice of appeal (which need not state its grounds), it is for the Secretary of State to prepare a Statement of Case, containing the relevant facts and the reasons for the decision, to which the claimant may submit an answer; the Statement of Case, the claimant's answer

---

329   Pensions Appeal Tribunals Act 1943, Sch, para 2A(1). The original Bill preceding CSPSSA 2000 had omitted any reference to a *duty* to appoint such members, as opposed to the *desirability* of so doing.
330   Pensions Appeal Tribunals Act 1943, Sch, para 2A(4).
331   Before CSPSSA 2000, PATs hearing appeals relating to the assessment of disabilities consisted of an ex-services member and two medical members, one of whom was appointed to act as chairman of the tribunal.
332   SI 1980/1120, rr 6 and 10. (These rules govern PATs in England and Wales; the comparable rules for Scotland are to be found in SI 1981/500.)
333   For further details, see the 3rd edition of this book, pp 589–590.
334   Pensions Appeal Tribunals Act 1943, ss 1 and 5.
335   CSPSSA 2000, s 57, inserting Pensions Appeal Tribunals Act 1943, s 5A, and SI 2001/1031.
336   *Barratt v Minister of Pensions* (1946) 1 WPAR 1225. The rules concerning the burden of proof discussed at pp 778–780, below, therefore apply.
337   On the background, see DSS *War Pensions Appeals: Proposals for Regulations Discussion Paper 1* (2000).
338   Pensions Appeal Tribunals Act 1943, s 8; the period is 12 months for assessment and entitlement decisions made before 9 April 2001. There is also provision for late appeals: SI 2001/1032.

and the Secretary of State's comments on this (if any) are then sent to the Pensions Appeal Office.[339] In addition, the appellant may apply to the President of the PATs for disclosure of official documents that are likely to be relevant to the case.[340] The interests of appellants are also safeguarded by the provision that the appeal is not to be heard in their absence, without their request; even then the tribunal has a discretion not to hear the case.[341] If for some reason an appeal is not prosecuted, eg the appellant simply fails to attend without explanation, it may be put on the deferred list.[342] An application may then be made within the next year for the case to be heard,[343] and this will be granted unless the President is satisfied 'that the appellant's failure to prosecute the appeal was due to his wilful default'.[344] After the lapse of a year, an appeal still on the deferred list will be struck out and may not be brought again without the President's leave.[345]

C Appeal to the nominated judge

From decisions on entitlement (but not on assessment) there is a further right of appeal on a point of law to a High Court judge nominated by the Lord Chancellor to hear such appeals (hence the phrase, 'the nominated judge').[346] Leave of either the tribunal or the judge must first be obtained; this should be granted whenever there is any reasonable doubt as to the correctness of the tribunal decision.[347] Quite exceptionally in the social security system, a claimant's legal expenses may be paid where a successful application for leave is made, either by the individual or by the Secretary of State, or where the latter makes an unsuccessful application for leave.[348] There is no further appeal to the Court of Appeal,[349] which may afford some justification for the view expressed in two cases by Denning J, that the doctrine of stare decisis does not apply in its full rigour in war pension cases.[350] There are now very few appeals to the nominated judge, partly because since 1970 the claimant and the Secretary of State may present a joint application to the President of the PATs requesting the setting aside of the tribunal's decision and the rehearing of the case.[351]

---

339   SI 1980/1120, r 5.
340   SI 1980/1120, r 6.
341   SI 1980/1120, r 20.
342   SI 1980/1120, r 10.
343   SI 1980/1120, r 26(3).
344   SI 1980/1120, r 26(4).
345   SI 1980/1120, r 26(5)(b). In practice the prime cause of delay is the failure of the Benefits Agency to prepare the Statement of Case promptly. In 2001 the average time taken was over 82 weeks: *Council on Tribunals* n 241, above, p 28.
346   Pensions Appeal Tribunals Act 1943, s 6(2); for the distinction between an appeal to the High Court and to a nominated judge, see *Wraith and Hutchesson* n 11, above, p 160. In Scotland appeal lies to the Court of Session. There is now power to suspend benefit pending an appeal: SI 1983/883, arts 67A–67C, inserted by SI 1994/772.
347   *Atkinson v Minister of Pensions* (1947) 1 WPAR 981.
348   SI 1980/1120, r 28. For grounds of appeal, see *Armstrong v Minister of Pensions* (1948) 16 WPAR 1449.
349   Pensions Appeal Tribunals Act 1943, s 6(2). Nor is there a right of appeal to the Court of Appeal from a decision of the nominated judge refusing leave to appeal: see *Ex p Aronsohn* [1946] 2 All ER 544, CA.
350   *James v Minister of Pensions* [1947] KB 867, [1947] 2 All ER 432; *Minister of Pensions v Higham* [1948] 2 KB 153 at 155.
351   Pensions Appeal Tribunals Act 1943, s 6(2A), added by the Chronically Sick and Disabled Persons Act 1970, s 23. Setting aside may be sought either on the ground that additional evidence is available or because of some error of law. For the position where the Secretary of State refuses to accede to a rehearing, see *Rivett v Secretary of State for Social Security* [1990] COD 479.

Chapter 7

General provisions

In this chapter we consider a number of issues and concepts which are common to several or all of the contributory and non-contributory benefits payable under Parts II, III and V of the Social Security Contributions and Benefits Act 1992 (SSCBA 1992) (namely those discussed in chapters 14 to 17, 19 and 20). The principles to be described are themselves primarily drawn from Part IV of SSCBA 1992 and, as a matter of law, do not govern the income-related benefits (chapters 8 to 13), child benefit (chapter 18) or war pensions (chapter 21), unless, and to the extent that, they are specifically adopted in the legislation concerned with the latter schemes. In practice, however, where there is no reason to adopt a different interpretation, the provisions governing the contributory and non-contributory benefits, as developed by the Commissioners' decisions, may properly act as guidelines for the administration of these other social security benefits. This applies particularly to the meaning attributed to such concepts as 'marriage', 'living together as husband and wife', 'residence', 'presence', 'imprisonment' and 'detention in legal custody'. For that reason these generic issues are dealt with first in this chapter, along with the general provisions relating to persons subject to immigration control (Parts 1 to 6). The remaining Parts deal with a miscellany of rules relating to contributory and non-contributory benefits: forfeiture, the calculation of earnings, dependency increases, overlapping benefits, up-rating rules[1] and the Christmas bonus (Parts 7 to 12). The nature of the income-related benefits is such that they necessarily have a more detailed common set of rules concerning the assessment of both needs and means; these issues are addressed in chapter 12, below.

Part 1   Marriage

A   General

While it may be the case that a significant proportion of social welfare provision is concerned with remedying the lack of a traditional family structure, nevertheless much social security legislation, particularly that part concerned with contributory benefits,

---

1   For convenience the rules on up-rating all benefits are dealt with in Pt 11, below.

focuses on the unit of the family as defined by the general law. References in the legislation to 'marriage', 'wife', 'husband', 'widow' and 'widower' have all been construed to require the existence of a marriage which is recognised in the UK,[2] and which was subsisting at the time of the claim or the event which gave rise to entitlement.[3] What is legally recognised as a valid marriage is determined according to the general law of England (or Scotland), including as it does the principles of private international law when eg the validity of foreign marriages or divorces is in question. There is no space here to describe such rules in detail.[4] Instead, a brief outline will be provided, together with such principles as have developed within the framework of the social security legislation.

B Marriages celebrated in the UK

A marriage celebrated in England and Wales must have satisfied the rules regarding formalities, which include the necessary preliminaries as well as due solemnisation, whether by civil or religious proceedings.[5] Production of the marriage certificate[6] will constitute prima facie evidence that the marriage has been duly celebrated,[7] but the absence of such a certificate will not be fatal. Provided that the parties can establish with sufficient reliability that a ceremony in due form took place[8] and that it was followed by prolonged cohabitation as husband and wife, a valid marriage will be presumed.[9] The strength of this presumption is evident from the decision of the Court of Appeal in *Chief Adjudication Officer v Bath*:[10]

> In 1956 Mrs B and her husband went through a ceremony of marriage in a Sikh temple in London. The building was not at the time registered for the celebration of marriages, nor were other formalities satisfied. No other ceremony took place. The parties lived in a monogamous relationship until the husband's death in 1994. The Court of Appeal held that the marriage was not void as the parties had not 'knowingly and wilfully' intermarried contrary to the provisions of the Marriage Act 1949. Moreover, the failure to comply with the necessary formalities was cured by the subsequent long cohabitation. Mrs B was accordingly a 'widow' for the purpose of SSCBA 1992, s 38.

The presumption will be rebutted by proof as to the invalidity of the marriage[11] but the standard of proof required is uncertain. One authority suggests that 'clear proof' will be sufficient,[12] but perhaps the better view is that the invalidity must be proved beyond

2 *CG 3/49; R(S) 4/59.* Thus under Scots law if the claim is made in Scotland.
3 *R(G) 1/52; R(P) 14/56; R(G) 2/73.*
4 For English family law see Lowe and Douglas *Bromley's Family Law* (9th edn, 1998) ch 2; and Cretney and Masson *Principles of Family Law* (6th edn, 1997) chs 1–2; for Scots family law see Clive *The Law of Husband and Wife in Scotland* (4th edn, 1997) chs 3–4; and for the relevant principles of private international law, Dicey and Morris *The Conflict of Laws* (13th edn, 2000) chs 6 and 17.
5 *Lowe and Douglas* n 4, above, pp 34–57; *Cretney and Masson* n 4, above, pp 8–30.
6 The Social Security Administration Act 1992, s 124 (SSAA 1992) makes provision for the obtaining of copies of the certificate for this purpose.
7 *CG 203/49.*
8 See *38/49 (P); R(P) 4/60; R(G) 2/70.*
9 *CG 53/50.*
10 *CG/11331/1995* (see Wikeley (1999) 21 JSWFL 63) and [2000] 1 FLR 8 (see Wikeley (2000) 22 JSWFL 313).
11 *R(G) 1/51.*
12 Per Harman LJ, *Re Taylor* [1961] 1 All ER 55 at 63.

reasonable doubt.[13] It follows that an English 'common law' marriage is not sufficient.[14] Scots law, in contrast, recognises a marriage 'by habit and repute', but the doctrine is narrowly confined.[15] There must have been a substantial period of cohabitation,[16] the bulk of which was in Scotland,[17] and the parties must have been free to marry[18] and consented, as between themselves, to a state of marriage.[19] Moreover, the parties must hold themselves out as being married and not merely act as though they were.[20]

C   Marriages celebrated abroad

In general a foreign marriage will be recognised as valid by English and Scots law if it satisfied the formalities of the law of that jurisdiction where the marriage took place,[21] and if each party had capacity according to the law of their domicile at the time of the alleged marriage.[22] Where one is concerned with marriages contracted overseas by immigrants, particularly those from India and Pakistan, considerable problems may arise. The difficulties may be even more acute where the validity of such a marriage may turn in part on whether a previous marriage has been validly terminated by divorce under the local law.[23] The problem is that sometimes expert evidence on the foreign law in question is required but it will not always be readily available to a decision maker or appeal tribunal.[24] Decisions on the domicile of individuals, at different stages of their lives, are also fraught with practical difficulties, depending as they do on a considerable amount of background information on family circumstances at some remote time or place.[25]

D   Effects of marriages void or voidable or terminated by divorce

A marriage which is void[26] because eg it is bigamous[27] or within the prohibited degrees[28] has no effect at law and cannot be relied on for the purposes of entitlement to benefit.

13 Per Sir Jocelyn Simon P, *Mahadervan v Mahadervan* [1964] P 233 at 244–246, adopted (obiter) by R J A Temple, Comr, in *R(G) 2/70*, para 17. See also *Chief Adjudication Officer v Bath* [2000] 1 FLR 8 at 18, per Evans LJ, holding that 'positive', not merely 'clear', evidence is required.
14 *R(S) 6/89*; cf in relation to income tax *Rignell v Andrews* [1991] 1 FLR 332.
15 See *Low v Gorman* 1970 SLT 356; Thomson *Family Law in Scotland* (3rd edn, 1996) pp 14–20; and generally Clive n 4, above. The law appears not to have been affected by the Marriage (Scotland) Act 1977.
16 'Years' rather than 'months': *R(G) 8/56*, para 11. In *Vosilius v Vosilius* 2000 SCLR 679 the period of cohabitation was at least 15 years. But see *Kamperman and MacIver* 1994 SLT 763, suggesting that six months' cohabitation might suffice where the 'quality' of the habit and repute is sufficient. See also *CSG/7/95* and *CSG/7/96*, discussed in Bonner, Hooker and White *Social Security Legislation 2001* (2001) vol I, para 1.89.
17 *R(G) 1/71*.
18 *R(P) 1/51*; *R(I) 37/61*; *R(G) 2/82*; *R(G) 7/56* which regarded an impediment to marry as fatal only if known to the parties. The period during which the parties are free to marry need only be short relative to their period of cohabitation: *R(G) 5/83(T)*. See also *CSG/4/92*.
19 *R(G) 8/56*; *R(P) 1/58*; *R(G) 1/71*; *R(G) 2/82*. A deliberate rejection of the institution of marriage is sufficient to rebut a presumption, arising from prolonged cohabitation, that there has been tacit consent: *R(G) 4/84*. Cf in the context of the Rent Acts *Helby v Rafferty* [1978] 3 All ER 1016, [1979] 1 WLR 13.
20 *Ackerman v Blackman* [2000] Fam LR 35 and 2002 SLT 37.
21 *R(U) 1/68* and see *Dicey and Morris* n 4, above, pp 651–671.
22 *R(G) 3/75*, *R(G) 1/93* and *R(G) 4/93*: see Dicey and Morris n 4, above, pp 671–688.
23 See eg *CG/13358/1996* ((2000) 7 JSSL D46).
24 See the remarks of R S Lazarus, Comr, in *R(G) 2/71*, paras 4 and 8, and now the guidance contained in DMG, vol 3, ch 10.
25 See eg *R(P) 1/57*; *R(G) 2/71*; *R(G) 3/75* and *R(G) 1/95*.
26 See generally *Lowe and Douglas* n 4, above, pp 82–87.
27 *R(G) 2/63*.
28 *R(G) 10/53*.

On the other hand, the fact that a marriage is void may revive an entitlement to widow's benefit from a 'previous' marriage if it had ceased to be payable on the alleged remarriage.[29] The widow may not, of course, claim for any period during which she was cohabiting with the second 'husband' and she will in any event be subject to the rules on time-limits.[30] A marriage which is terminated by divorce is treated as valid until the decree is made absolute, but from that date it is no longer effective to ground entitlement. Though there is no direct decision on the point, it is assumed that a previous entitlement to widow's benefit is not revived by dissolution of a subsequent marriage[31] – in this respect it is different from a marriage held to be void. The problems to which marriages subject to divorce give rise are concerned mainly with whether a foreign decree should be recognised; this is determined by the rules of private international law.[32]

Between void marriages and those terminated by divorce comes the third and problematic category of voidable marriages[33] (eg those which have not been consummated). Prior to 1971, for most legal purposes, such a marriage was regarded as valid and subsisting until the time of the decree of nullity, but the securing of such a decree would operate to invalidate the marriage retrospectively.[34] Under a legislative reform of 1956,[35] power was given to the minister to provide by regulations that, for specified purposes, a voidable marriage was to be treated as a marriage terminated by divorce. This power was exercised as regards questions of entitlement to guardian's allowance and the now obsolete child's special allowance.[36] The principles governing other benefits under social security legislation were unclear. In particular, there were conflicting decisions on whether a widow who lost benefit on entering a voidable marriage was entitled to claim for all periods except those during which she was cohabiting with the second 'husband'.[37] The process of retrospectively invalidating a marriage caused grave problems in other areas of the law and in 1971, following the recommendations of the Law Commission,[38] the Nullity of Marriage Act was passed. As re-enacted by the Matrimonial Causes Act 1973, s 16 (MCA 1973), this provides that:

---

29 *CG 28/53*, cited in *R(G) 1/73(T)*. The same principle is unlikely to apply in practice to bereavement allowance as this benefit is time-limited to one year.

30 P 150, above.

31 See *R(G) 1/73*, para 14 (tribunal majority).

32 The law on recognition of foreign divorces is now governed exclusively by the Family Law Act 1986, ss 45–54 (FLA 1896). See, in general, Cheshire and North *Private International Law* (13th edn, 1999) pp 791–825. The Commissioner has in several instances been faced with the problem of customary divorces by 'talaq'. In *R(G) 2/71* and *R(G) 4/74* such a divorce was recognised because, on the expert evidence available, it was found that on the balance of probabilities the divorce would have been recognised by the law of domicile even though there was no direct judicial authority in the particular jurisdiction (cf *R(G) 1/70*), though it was important to ascertain whether the correct procedure had been adopted (see *R(G) 5/74*). FLA 1986, s 46 draws a distinction between divorces obtained through 'judicial or other proceedings' and divorces obtained otherwise than by means of such proceedings. This suggests that recognition may be granted to a 'full talaq' but not to a 'bare talaq'. Cf *Quazi v Quazi* [1980] AC 744; *Chaudhary v Chaudhary* [1985] Fam 19; *Re Fatima* [1986] AC 527 and; *R(G) 1/94*. It should not be assumed that Islamic divorces monopolise the case law on FLA 1986, ss 45–54: on the non-recognition of a Jewish *get*, see *Berkovits v Grinberg, A-G intervening* [1995] 1 FLR 477.

33 See generally *Lowe and Douglas* n 4, above, pp 87–102.

34 *Lowe and Douglas* n 4, above, p 101.

35 National Insurance Act 1957, s 9(1)(c) (NIA 1957).

36 SI 1957/1835. See now SI 1975/497, reg 3 and SI 1975/515, reg 4(3).

37 In *R(G) 3/72*, following unreported decisions in *CG 2/70*, *CG 1/71* and *CG 2/71*, J S Watson, Comr, held that a widow was not so entitled. In *R(G) 1/53* it had been held that she was entitled.

38 Report No 33 (1970–71, HC 164).

a decree of nullity granted ... on the ground that a marriage is voidable shall operate to annul the marriage only as respects any time after the decree had been made absolute, and the marriage shall, notwithstanding the decree, be treated as if it had existed up to that time.

Some consequences of this provision are undisputed. For the purpose of claiming benefit based on the marriage, it is, during its subsistence to the time of the decree of nullity, to be regarded as valid. It is also clear that a widow cannot claim benefit on a previous marriage for any period before the decree.[39] The problem is, however, whether such a claim is valid for the period after the decree: in other words, is the woman's status as a widow revived by the annulment of the second marriage? The arguments are evenly balanced. If attention is focused on the first part of s 16 (down to the words 'after the decree had been made absolute'), it might be said that, for the period after the decree, the marriage is annulled and therefore to be regarded as if it had never existed. If, conversely, attention is focused on the last limb of s 16 ('and the marriage shall, notwithstanding the decree, be treated as if it had existed up to that time'), it might be said that even for purposes subsequent to the decree the marriage is to be treated as having existed at some time, and thus the woman's status as a widow is forever lost. A Tribunal of Commissioners, having taken into account the Law Commission's report on which proposals the measure was passed, preferred the second interpretation.[40] The same conclusion has been reached by the Divisional Court in connection with the war pension scheme.[41]

E Polygamous marriages

The extent to which a polygamous marriage should be recognised in this country has always been a difficult issue,[42] and entitlement to social security benefits features not least among the problems to which it has given rise.[43] Originally, only marriages celebrated in a monogamous form were recognised as valid for the purpose of entitlement to benefits under the National Insurance legislation – a harsh interpretation since it excluded not only an actual polygamous marriage but also any marriage celebrated under a law which permitted polygamy, whether or not it had at all times been in fact monogamous.[44] There is no apparent policy justification for denying social security entitlement to parties to a marriage which is in fact monogamous and, following reforms enacted in 1956[45] and 1971,[46] the position is now that:

a polygamous marriage shall ... be treated as having the same consequences as a monogamous marriage for any day, but only for any day, throughout which the polygamous marriage is in fact monogamous.[47]

---

39   *R(G) 1/73(T)*, para 14.
40   *R(G) 1/73*, paras 18–20 and 25; *R(G) 2/73*. Cf the discussions in *Lowe and Douglas* n 4, above, pp 101–102; and Cretney and Masson *Principles of Family Law* (6th edn, 1997) pp 72–75.
41   *Ward v Secretary of State for Social Services* [1990] 1 FLR 119.
42   See Law Commission Reports Nos 42 (1970–71, HC 227) and 146 (1985, Cmnd 9595).
43   Pearl [1978–79] JSWL 24.
44   *R(G) 6/51; R(G) 18/52(T); R(G) 11/53; R(G) 3/55; R(G) 7/55*; and see Webb (1956) 19 MLR 687.
45   Family Allowances and National Insurance Act 1956, s 3 (FANIA 1956), implementing proposals in National Insurance Advisory Committee (NIAC) *Report on the Question of Widow's Benefit* (1955, Cmd 9684).
46   NIA 1971, s 16(3).
47   SI 1975/561, reg 2(1). For equivalent provisions for child benefit, see SI 1976/965, reg 12.

There are also special rules enabling a woman to claim retirement pension on her husband's contributions as from any date on which the marriage was in fact monogamous, and in such cases the rate of pension payable is that which would have been payable in the case of a monogamous marriage whether or not, prior to the date in question, the marriage had been polygamous.[48]

It should be noted, however, that these provisions only apply to a polygamous marriage which 'was celebrated under a law which, as it applies to the particular ceremony and to the parties thereto, permits polygamy'.[49] As regards English law, marriages celebrated after 31 July 1971[50] in a polygamous form are void if at the time either party was domiciled in England.[51] There seems to be no obvious reason why contributory benefits should be denied to a party of such a marriage when it in fact remains monogamous.[52]

The position of persons who at the time of the claim (or in the case of widow's benefit at the time of the contributor's death) are actually polygamously married is more problematic. The fact that there are relatively few actual polygamous families (ie where a man has two or more dependent wives) present in this country no doubt helps to explain why the decision to grant them entitlement under the income-related benefit schemes, the conditions for which include presence in Great Britain, has not been controversial.[53] The position as regards contributory benefits is different since payments can be made for persons, particularly pensioners, abroad. Actual polygamous marriages are not recognised for the purpose of these benefits, as reaffirmed by the Court of Appeal as recently as 1997,[54] notwithstanding the objection that it is unfair on a party to such a marriage who has duly paid contributions.[55]

In 1968 the Law Commission studied the problem in depth but felt unable to recommend on grounds of administrative feasibility or acceptability by the general public a number of proposed solutions.[56] These included: full entitlement for each wife (with or without increased contributions); a sharing of normal benefit by the wives; nomination by the husband (or the Secretary of State) of one wife for full benefit; full benefit for a wife living in Britain. Previous editions of this work have argued that the last suggestion would seem to be the most attractive and that the objection raised to it, that it would be inequitable to the wife (or wives) living abroad, does not seem very persuasive.[57] Yet such an approach, involving the treatment of one spouse as in some way inferior, seems difficult to justify under the Human Rights Act 1998.[58] However unsatisfactory this option for reform may be, there seems to be considerable scope for arguing that the current state of the domestic law on the point is not itself human rights compliant. Perhaps the optimum solution is to divide the pension equally between the

---

48 SI 1975/561, reg 3.
49 SI 1975/561, reg 1(2).
50 For marriages before this date see the controversial decision in *Radwan v Radwan (No 2)* [1973] Fam 35, [1972] 3 All ER 1026, where it was held that the common law permitted a person presently domiciled in England to contract a valid potentially polygamous marriage if the intention of the parties at the time of celebration was to set up a home in a country permitting polygamy.
51 MCA 1973, s 11(d).
52 A view taken by the Law Commission in *Report No 146* n 42, above.
53 Cf p 295, n 233, below.
54 *Bibi v Chief Adjudication Officer* (reported as *R(G) 1/97*); see Wikeley (1998) 5 JSSL 83.
55 Poulter *English Law and Ethnic Minority Customs* (1986) para 3.09.
56 Law Commission Working Paper No 21 (1968) paras 61–66. The Report which followed (No 42) took the matter no further: n 42, above.
57 See also *Pearl* n 43, above, at 29.
58 P 58, above.

surviving spouses. This approach is already taken under the National Health Service (NHS) superannuation scheme.[59]

Part 2   Living together as husband and wife

A   General

For certain purposes social security legislation treats an unmarried couple living together as husband and wife as if they were married. One important consequence is that a widow or widower in this situation may lose entitlement to a bereavement benefit;[60] another is that the couple are treated as a family unit for the purposes of the income-related benefits.[61] The 'cohabitation rule', as it is often referred to, was included in the National Insurance widow's scheme introduced in 1925[62] but, perhaps surprisingly, was not expressly contained in the National Assistance Act 1948. If a woman cohabiting with a man claimed assistance, the National Assistance Board was compelled to use its discretionary powers to refuse an award. In 1966, when supplementary benefits replaced national assistance, the rule was embodied in the legislation and has remained a constant, if controversial, feature of both the contributory and the means-tested schemes.

In the 1970s and 1980s there was a lively debate on the legal consequences of cohabitation in general and the merits of the social security rule in particular.[63] The main justification for the latter is that:

> ... it would be wrong in principle to treat the women who have the support of a partner both as if they had not such support and better than if they were married. It would not be right, and we believe public opinion would not accept, that the unmarried 'wife' should be able to claim benefit denied to a married woman.[64]

To counter this, notions of individual autonomy are urged. It is said that, in deciding not to marry, the parties are, by implication at least, declaring an intention that the legal consequences of marriage should not apply to them.[65] Thus since an unmarried woman is not legally entitled to support from the man with whom she is living, it is wrong for the state to assume that such support is provided.[66] The argument may be persuasive

---

59   SI 1980/362, reg 14A, inserted by SI 1989/804, reg 4 and see *R v Department of Health, ex p Misra* [1996] 2 FCR 464. The German social insurance system also adopts this approach: §§91(3) SGB VI, 34(2) SGB I.

60   SSCBA 1992, ss 36(2), 39A(5)(b) and 39B(5)(b).

61   P 443, below. This has become all the more significant since the introduction of joint claim jobseeker's allowance (pp 357–358, below).

62   Widows', Orphans' and Old Age Contributory Pensions Act 1925, s 2(1).

63   Lister *As Man and Wife* (1970); Supplementary Benefits Commission (SBC) Report *Cohabitation* (1971); SBC Report *Living Together as Husband and Wife* (1976); Deech (1980) 29 ICLQ 480; Pearl in Eekelaar and Katz *Marriage and Cohabitation in Contemporary Societies* (1980) p 335; Freeman and Lyon *Cohabitation Without Marriage* (1983); Fairbairns and Donnison in Ungerson *Women and Social Policy* (1985). For a more contemporary analysis, see Harris (1996) 18 JSWFL 123.

64   *Cohabitation* n 63 above, para 7; and see *Report of the Committee on One-Parent Families* (1974, Cmnd 5629) para 5.269.

65   *Deech* n 63, above.

66   The argument was regarded as crucial by the US Supreme Court in holding invalid a cohabitation regulation introduced in Alabama: *Smith v King* 88 S Ct 2128 (1968); see also *Van Lare v Hurley* 95 S Ct 1741 (1975).

more for private law than public law consequences and (because of the analogy with private insurance) more for contributory than for income-related benefits. For if state assistance is invoked to meet actual need, it can hardly be right to ignore the de facto meeting of that need by another party.[67]

So long as married couples are treated as one unit,[68] it may be inevitable that the same principles will continue to apply to the unmarried. It has nevertheless been contended that the problems of applying the rule, in particular the intrusion of privacy necessarily involved, on balance impair its legitimacy.[69] There is no obvious answer to this contention since much depends on departmental practice. The level of complaints against the Department's inquiry agents seems to have dropped since the late 1960s and 1970s. It should also be noted that income support decisions under the rule are now taken at a more senior level within local offices rather than in the normal way by decision makers.

B The meaning of 'living together'

The term 'cohabiting' has never been defined in social security legislation. This was criticised by the Fisher Committee Report on Abuse of Social Security Benefits,[70] arguing that individuals should not be left in such uncertainty as to what will lead to forfeiture of benefit. But the view has always been taken that precise statutory definition is impossible.[71] Indeed, in one case Lord Widgery CJ said that the phrase 'cohabiting as man and wife', then in force, was 'so well known that nothing I could say about it could possibly assist in its interpretation'.[72] In 1977 the term 'cohabiting' was replaced by 'living together',[73] largely on the ground that the former had acquired a pejorative meaning,[74] but it is clear that no different interpretation was intended.[75]

'Living together as husband and wife' is a ground for forfeiture from both contributory and income-related benefits. The intention is clearly that a uniform interpretation should govern these various provisions.[76] It is therefore proposed to consider together such guidelines on the meaning as emerge from Commissioners' and court decisions, and also statements of Departmental policy which were formulated for the supplementary benefit scheme[77] and which have been described judicially as 'admirable signposts'.[78] Most of these authorities point to a number of factors whose absence or presence may assist in deciding the issue; but none is to be regarded as conclusive.[79] What is clear is that the rule presupposes a heterosexual relationship,

---

67 Cf *Living Together as Man and Wife* n 63, above, para 22.
68 See generally Duncan, Giles and Webb *Social Security Reform and Women's Independent Incomes* (1994).
69 *Lister* n 63, above.
70 Para 330(b).
71 N 67 above, paras 49–51.
72 *R v South West London Supplementary Benefits Appeals Tribunal, ex p Barnett* (1973) SB Dec 28 (Decision SB4).
73 Social Security (Miscellaneous Provisions) Act 1977, ss 14(7) and 22(2)–(4) (SS(MP)A 1977).
74 N 67 above, para 52.
75 *R(SB) 17/81*, para 9, D G Rice, Comr.
76 *R(SB) 17/81*, para 4; and see *R(G) 3/81* and *R v Penwith District Council Housing Benefit Review Board, ex p Menear* (1991) 24 HLR 115.
77 In a revised form, they are summarised in DSS *A Guide to Income Support* IS20 (2002) pp 73–76.
78 Woolf J, *Crake v Supplementary Benefits Commission* [1982] 1 All ER 498 at 505. See also *Campbell v Secretary of State for Social Services* (1983) 4 FLR 138.
79 *Crake v Supplementary Benefits Commission* [1982] 1 All ER 498; *Re J (income support: cohabitation)* [1995] 1 FLR 660 (see Harris (1995) 2 JSSL 49, sub nom *CIS/087/1993*). See also *R(G) 3/71*, para 5; *R(G) 1/79*, para 8; *R(SB) 17/81*, para 11. On tactics, see Crasnow (1996) Legal Action, June, at 15.

and so should not apply to partners of the same gender.[80] Harris has argued that consideration should be given to adopting the Australian approach, under which the various court-sanctioned guidelines have been codified in legislation, as a means of curtailing the discretion currently granted to decision makers.[81]

i   Members of same household

It is a necessary condition for the application of the rule to the income-related benefits,[82] and an obvious assumption for its application to the contributory benefits,[83] that the man and woman should be members of the same household, ie residing together under the same roof.[84] If eg the man spends much of his time at another house, it will be difficult to infer that the two parties are living together.[85] A finding that they live in the same household is not by itself sufficient: the relationship might be commercial (eg landlady and lodger)[86] or to provide mutual aid and support in relation to disability.[87] In *Butterworth v Supplementary Benefits Commission*,[88] Woolf J said that the crucial issue was why they did so; it was thus a question of whether they intended to establish a marriage-like relationship.[89] If the intentions of the parties are clear, this is no doubt an appropriate test,[90] but in many cases a subjective inquiry of this kind will prove to be elusive and some authorities have preferred an objective approach which has regard primarily to the conduct of the parties.[91]

ii   Duration and stability

The duration and stability of the cohabitation (as opposed eg to a long-term landlady-lodger relationship) is clearly an important factor.[92] Where there is no evidence as to continuity of co-residence or where its existence remains uncertain, benefit should not be refused, though once it has been established that the required relationship exists, it is much easier to show that it continues.[93] The suggestion that a couple should be allowed to live together for a number of months without entitlement being affected has, however, been rejected.[94]

80   Cf the decisions of the House of Lords in *Harrogate Borough Council v Simpson* [1986] 2 FLR 91 (Housing Act 1985) and in *Fitzpatrick v Sterling Housing Association Ltd* [1999] 4 All ER 705 (Rent Act 1977).
81   Harris (1996) 18 JSWFL 123; see further SSA 1991 (Cth), s 4(3), detailing considerations also considered relevant in the UK case law; and Carney *The Laws of Australia* (2000) subtitle 22.3, para 58.
82   SSCBA 1992, s 137(1).
83   See eg *R(G) 11/55*.
84   On 'residing together', see pp 252–255, below. The parties may be residing together although temporarily apart: see SI 1977/956, reg 2(4); SI 1987/1967, reg 16; *R(SB) 30/83*; and *R(SB) 19/85*.
85   A person can be a member of only one household at a time: *R(SB) 8/85*. See also *G v F (Non-molestation Order: Jurisdiction)* [2000] 3 WLR 1202 at 1210, per Wall J.
86   *R(G) 3/71*.
87   *Robson v Secretary of Social Services* (1981) 3 FLR 232; *R(SB) 35/85*.
88   [1982] 1 All ER 498 at 502.
89   An intention to *marry* need not be shown: *R(SB) 17/81*.
90   *Robson v Secretary of Social Services* (1981) 3 FLR 232, per Webster J, who, however, suggested that 'purpose' was more apposite than 'intention'.
91   *R(G) 3/81*, para 8, D G Rice, Comr.
92   *R(P) 6/52*.
93   *Crake v Supplementary Benefits Commission* [1982] 1 All ER 498 at 502.
94   SBC Report *Living Together as Husband and Wife* (1976) para 55(2).

iii Financial support

While the financial support by one party of the other would seem to be an important factor – it is the existence of that support which primarily explains why public funds should not be used – it is less reliable than might be supposed. In the first place, financial payments might be attributed to a commercial relationship;[95] secondly, evidence of regular financial support might be difficult to obtain; and thirdly, undue emphasis on this factor might encourage one party not to support the other, in order to improve the latter's chance of receiving benefit.[96] Financial support is, therefore, not required for a finding of cohabitation[97] but where there is evidence that the parties do pool their resources, this will be taken into account as one relevant factor.[98]

iv Sexual relationship

In the light of criticisms of intrusions of privacy and of forming judgments on the basis of sexual morals, the Department for Work and Pensions (DWP) now places much less emphasis on this factor and indeed has instructed its staff not to question claimants about their sexual relationships but to consider any information volunteered.[99] Thus where claimants choose to make statements about this matter, they may help to determine whether a marriage-like relationship exists. In particular, if a couple have never had a sexual relationship, it is most unlikely that the cohabitation rule will apply. Thus in an unreported case the Commissioner held that an unmarried Mormon couple who refrained on principle from any sexual relationship could not be regarded as living together as husband and wife.[100]

v Children

There will be a strong presumption that a man and woman are living together as husband and wife if they are looking after their own children.[101]

vi Public acknowledgement

A public acknowledgement by a woman that she is living with someone as his wife by taking his surname is compelling evidence of cohabitation.[102] On the other hand, little significance is to be attached to a refusal to acknowledge the relationship in public.[103]

In finely balanced cases the burden of proof may be decisive. Where an initial claim for benefit has been denied on the grounds of 'living together', it is for the claimant to establish title to benefit. If, however, evidence of cohabitation appears after an award has been made, the onus is on the Secretary of State to justify grounds for revision or supersession.

---

95 *R(G) 3/71*, para 7.
96 N 94, above, para 55(3).
97 *R(G) 2/64*, para 7.
98 *R(G) 2/72; R(G) 1/79; Kaur v Secretary of State for Social Services* (1981) 3 FLR 237, criticised by Poulter *English Law and Ethnic Minority Customs* (1986) para 3.24.
99 DSS *Decision Makers Guide* (DMG) (2000) vol 3, para 11046. But see *Re J (Income Support: Cohabitation)* [1995] 1 FLR 660.
100 *CSB/150/1985*; see also *R(SB) 35/85*, para 9(3).
101 *CG 214/50; R(G) 3/64; R(G) 3/71; R(G) 2/72*.
102 *R(G) 5/68; R(G) 1/79*.
103 *CP 97/49; R(P) 6/52*.

Part 3   Residence and presence

A   General

At first sight the geographical boundaries of the social security system may not seem to raise complex policy issues, yet this area has provided a fruitful supply of problems for lawyers. Under the poor law, perhaps the question giving rise to most litigation was that concerned with the 'settlement' of paupers, the condition of residence on which the responsibility of parishes was based.[104] Happily, the centralisation of social security obviated the need to distinguish between parts of the country, but the increased facilities for foreign travel, the growth of multinational enterprises and the emergence of the 'migrant worker' all underline the continued importance and difficulty of the topic. To some extent the problems have been solved by reciprocal agreements with other national systems and by the 'co-ordinating' regulations of the EU. These instruments are described in chapter 3. The discussion in the present chapter is concerned with the limits imposed by the British social security legislation independently of the provisions contained in those instruments. The rules emerging will thus indicate the circumstances in which an individual must resort to the additional facilities described in chapter 3.

B   The framework

In general, the relationship with Great Britain, as expressed in such concepts as 'residence', 'presence', or (in a very few instances) 'nationality', is relevant for four different purposes. Part 4 of this chapter deals with the separate rule precluding any 'person subject to immigration control' from entitlement to means-tested and non-contributory benefits.

i   Participation in the contributory scheme

There are rules to determine who is compelled (or in the case of non-employed persons and certain self-employed persons who is entitled) to contribute to the scheme. These have been set out in chapter 4.[105]

ii   Alternatives to contribution conditions

For contributory benefits there is no *positive* requirement as to residence. Participation in the National Insurance scheme for the requisite number of years is prima facie sufficient to justify the conferring of benefit. Indeed, to a limited extent, the system is prepared to make concessions to those whose work abroad has prevented them from making the requisite contributions. The rules designed to implement this policy were also mentioned in chapter 4.[106]

---

104   Blackstone *Commentaries*, vol 1, p 362, refers to the 'infinity of expensive law suits between contending neighbourhoods'. See, generally, Holdsworth *History of English Law* (1938) vol X, pp 257–269. See also pp 272–273, below.
105   Pp 105, 113, 115 and 116, above.
106   P 120, above.

iii Disqualifications for absence

SSCBA 1992 lays down as a general ground for disqualification for contributory benefits absence (whether of the claimant himself or a dependant for whom an increase is claimed) from Great Britain.[107] This principle, as elaborated and modified in the Regulations, is described in this Part.

iv Requirements for non-contributory benefits

For non-contributory benefits, the need to impose limits on the scheme, according to an individual's connection with Great Britain, is more obvious and important. For each such benefit there is, therefore, a combination of rules generally requiring 'residence', 'ordinary residence', or at least 'presence' in Great Britain. The rules are stated in the appropriate chapters; here it will be necessary only to give an account of the interpretation of the general concepts employed.

C Absence as a ground of disqualification from contributory benefits

The principles applicable proceed according to consistent but sometimes controversial policy dictates.[108] Except for EU instruments,[109] there is no relief for absent persons claiming contribution-based jobseeker's allowance, it being felt desirable to maintain unequivocally the claimant's attachment to the labour market in this country (or the rest of the EU). Those entitled by reason of their incapacity or confinement are given some concessions, notably for temporary absences. The most generous provision is for those whose entitlement in no way rests on their inability to work, because eg they have reached pensionable age or are caring for dependent children. Here the disqualification is often removed altogether. The general rule is then that a person is disqualified from receiving benefit (or an increase in benefit for a dependant) for a period during which the person (or the dependant) is absent from Great Britain.[110] The modifications to the rule are as follows.

i Benefits for incapacity

For the purposes of any benefit in respect of incapacity,[111] a temporary absence of up to 26 weeks is disregarded if the Secretary of State has certified that it is consistent with the proper administration of SSCBA 1992 that the disqualification should not apply, *and either*:
(a) the absence is for the specific purpose of being treated for incapacity which commenced before the claimant left Great Britain, *or*

---

107 SSCBA 1992, s 113(1)(a). This does not discriminate, either directly or indirectly, on grounds of nationality: *R(S) 2/93*.
108 See Bolderson [1991] JSWFL 243.
109 Pp 81–83, above.
110 N 107, above.
111 Incapacity benefit, severe disablement allowance, unemployability supplement and maternity allowance: SI 1975/563, reg 2(5)(a).

(b) in the case of incapacity benefit, the absence is for the specific purpose of being treated for an industrial injury, *or*
(c) when the absence began the person was, and had for six months continuously been, incapable of work and when benefit is claimed has remained continuously so incapable since the absence began.[112]

A   THE 26-WEEK RULE

In the past, payment of such benefits abroad has generally been allowed for up to 12 months,[113] although there was no fixed statutory limit. The 26-week rule was introduced by regulations in 1994,[114] against the advice of the Social Security Advisory Committee (SSAC), which could find no 'overwhelming reason' for changing the customary 52-week period.[115] The 26-week rule does not apply to recipients of attendance allowance or disability living allowance who satisfy any of conditions (a) to (c) above.[116]

B   TEMPORARY ABSENCE

The claimant must in any event establish that the absence is only temporary. No guidance is given for the interpretation of this and the Commissioner has held that there is no universal period to which reference may be made in determining whether an absence is temporary or not: the particular circumstances of the case are crucial.[117] It was further held that a finding that the absence is 'permanent' or 'indefinite' precludes it being 'temporary', but 'temporary' should not be regarded as synonymous with 'not permanent'.[118] The stated intentions of the claimant are not decisive[119] but are clearly relevant. A vague hope to return to Great Britain sometime in the future, or when health permits, will not normally render the absence temporary.[120] If there is an unequivocal intention to return when the claimant is fit to do so, the issue will turn on the duration of the absence.

C   CERTIFICATION BY THE SECRETARY OF STATE

This requirement was originally introduced in 1975 to solve some of the difficulties, described below, arising from the other conditions. It conferred a discretion on the Secretary of State to determine what was 'reasonable in all the circumstances of the

112   SI 1975/563, reg 2(1). See *R(S) 2/94*.
113   In *R(S) 9/55* an absence of nearly four years was disregarded, although this decision was doubted in *R(S) 1/85*.
114   SI 1994/268.
115   SSAC Report (1994, Cm 2450) p 6.
116   SI 1975/563, reg 2(1A). Special provision is also made for recipients of incapacity-related benefits who are family members of those serving in the forces abroad: reg 2(1B).
117   *R(S) 1/85*, para 19. In the event of an appeal, account may be taken of events occurring since the initial decision: *R(S) 10/83*, para 9.
118   *R(S) 1/85*, para 20 and *R(S) 1/96* (sub nom *Chief Adjudication Officer v Ahmed* (1994) Times, 6 April).
119   *R(S) 1/85*; *R(S) 1/96*; and *R(S) 10/83*.
120   *R(S) 3/58*; *R(S) 5/59*; *R(S) 9/59*. Thus an expressed wish to return that is a 'remote hope rather than a realistic intention' is not sufficient: *R(S) 1/93*, para 5.

case, having regard in particular ... to the nature of the person's incapacity and to his location'.[121] In 1976 the Commissioner held that the regulation was ultra vires.[122] The concept of consistency with the proper administration of what is now the SSCBA 1992 was inserted by an amendment in 1977 and the Court of Appeal has held that the present form of the regulation is valid.[123] It is to be anticipated, however, that the Secretary of State will continue to have regard to the considerations mentioned under the 1975 regulation. Decisions on certification by the Secretary of State are not subject to a right of appeal.[124]

D   ABSENCE ABROAD FOR PURPOSE OF BEING TREATED

According to two decisions by Tribunals of Commissioners, there are three conditions to be satisfied under this head:[125]

(1) Immediately prior to departure, the claimant must have been incapable of work, as that expression is interpreted in relation to entitlement to benefit,[126] namely, some specific disease or bodily or mental disablement, and hence not including pregnancy.[127]

(2) The absence abroad is for the specific purpose of having treatment for that condition. The treatment need not be the sole objective of the absence – it may rank alongside social or pleasurable purposes[128] – but the intention to be treated must be formed before the claimant leaves this country.[129] As regards the meaning of 'treatment', there is general agreement that some activity by a person other than the claimant must be involved,[130] but there is little uniformity on what form is envisaged. Some decisions imply that medical supervision or care is required;[131] others do not regard this as necessary.[132] It is not necessary for the treatment to effect a cure.[133] In cases of mental illness, the authorities scrutinise the nature of the 'treatment' with particular care,[134] but in one case a claimant with psychological problems avoided disqualification when he was assisted in the solving of his spiritual problems by a Doctor of Divinity.[135] On one major issue there is, however, no disagreement: it has repeatedly been held that to go abroad merely to convalesce, for a change of environment, air or food, or to obtain freedom from anxiety, even if undertaken according to medical advice, does not amount to 'being treated'.[136]

---

121   SI 1975/563, reg 2(1).
122   *CS 5/76.*
123   *Bhatia v Birmingham (Insurance Officer)* (1985), reported as Appendix to *R(S) 8/83*.
124   SI 1999/991, reg 27 and Sch 2, para 21.
125   *R(S) 2/86(T); R(S) 1/90.*
126   Pp 538–555, below.
127   *R(G) 5/53; R(S) 1/75.*
128   *R(S) 6/61.*
129   *R(S) 1/90*(T), paras 29–30. The Commissioners therefore overruled a series of earlier cases to the contrary, as an 'over-liberal and erroneous interpretation' of the regulation (see *CS 317/49; R(S) 1/57; R(S) 1/75; R(S)1/77*).
130   *CSS 71/49; CS 474/50; R(S) 10/51.*
131   *R(S) 16/51; R(S) 5/61; R(S) 2/69.*
132   *R(S) 10/51; R(S) 2/51.*
133   *Chief Adjudication Officer v Ahmed* (1994) Times, 6 April.
134   See *R(S) 5/61.*
135   *R(S) 1/65.*
136   *R v National Insurance Comr, ex p McMenemy* (1966), reported as Appendix to *R(S) 2/69; R(S) 16/51; R(S) 10/52; R(S) 25/52; R(S) 5/61; R(S) 3/68; R(S) 1/69; R(S) 4/80; R(S) 6/81.*

(3) The condition for which treatment abroad is sought can be identified with the incapacity from which the claimant was suffering immediately prior to departure. The question as to whether the latter incapacity must continue without interruption from the date of departure to the date of the claim has been left open. However, the majority (albeit obiter) view of one Tribunal of Commissioners considered that this was not necessary.[137]

E   THE REMAINING GROUNDS

Condition (b) above was introduced in 1983 to accommodate the slightly more generous rule previously applied to recipients of industrial injury benefit, which was abolished in that year. Condition (c) dates from 1967 and is designed to assist the long-term incapacitated. In these cases, proximity to the labour market is obviously of less importance. On the other hand, the absence must still be temporary, and therefore the number likely to succeed on this ground must be relatively small.

ii Long-term benefits immune from disqualification

When the benefit in question is paid irrespective of the individual's working capacity, supervision of the claim is less important and, arguably, claimants should receive the return on the contributions paid, irrespective of where they choose to live.[138] The disqualification does not, therefore, apply to retirement pensions, bereavement[139] and industrial disablement benefits, attendance, disability living, guardian's and carer's allowances.[140] On the other hand, those claiming bereavement allowance or retirement pension[141] may not be entitled to an increase resulting from an up-rating of benefit unless they satisfy certain residence conditions.[142] The disqualification is not, however, automatic and it is for the Secretary of State to determine, when issuing the up-rating order, whether or not these special conditions are to apply.[143] The discretion has invariably been exercised to exclude beneficiaries living abroad from the increases. The justifications for this are that the contributions on which entitlement to the benefits was based were not actuarially related to the increases and that it would be inequitable for the other contributors to the fund, effectively paying for the increases, to assist those living abroad.[144] In practice, however, not all beneficiaries are disadvantaged as some are entitled to the increases under EU law and reciprocal arrangements with other countries.[145]

---

137   *R(S) 2/86*; J N B Penny, Comr, dissented on this point.
138   Bolderson [1991] JSWFL 243.
139   In the case of a bereavement payment, however, either the surviving spouse or the deceased spouse must have been in Great Britain at the time of the latter's death, or the survivor must have returned to Britain within four weeks of that death, or the contribution conditions for widowed parent's allowance or bereavement allowance must have been satisfied: SI 1975/563, reg 4(2B).
140   SI 1975/563, regs 4(1), 9(3), 10 and 10B.
141   This includes the guaranteed minimum pension, payable as part of an occupational pension.
142   Normally 'ordinary residence' in Great Britain: SI 1975/563, reg 5. See p 231, below; and *R(P) 1/78*.
143   SI 1975/563, reg 5(1).
144   But see HC Social Security Committee *Third Report* (1996–97, HC 143) and *Seventh Report* (1999–2000, HC 606) Appendix 16.
145   Cf ch 3, above. See the unsuccessful human rights challenge in *R (Carson) v Secretary of State for Work and Pensions* [2002] EWHC Admin 978.

iii Dependants

It is part of the general rule that a claimant may not receive an increase for an absent dependant. In some cases, this caused hardship, for a person resident in Great Britain might, while abroad, have married a person who had never set foot in this country. The foreign spouse would not, as a result of the marriage, 'acquire' the residence of the claimant (as eg under the old rules whereby a woman on marriage acquired the domicile of her husband) and the increase would not be payable.[146] The general rule is therefore modified so that:

> a husband or wife shall not be disqualified for receiving any increase (where payable) of benefit in respect of his or her spouse by reason of the spouse's being absent from Great Britain, provided that the spouse is residing with the husband or wife, as the case may be.[147]

As regards increases for child dependants, these are generally linked to entitlement to child benefit. The residence and presence requirements of the latter are generally stricter than those applied previously to child dependency increases and so regulations exist to preserve the broader base of entitlement: in general, the increase is payable if the claimant or the child is only temporarily absent from Great Britain.[148]

D Some common concepts

It remains to provide an account of the meaning of concepts which are common to the various rules on residence and absence. The notion of 'habitual residence' is considered separately in chapter 8 as this applies only to the income-related benefits.[149]

i 'United Kingdom' and 'Great Britain'

For some purposes the geographical unit is the 'United Kingdom', but for the majority it is 'Great Britain'. The former means 'Great Britain and Northern Ireland',[150] the latter, England, Wales and Scotland.[151] Territorial waters are included[152] but, notwithstanding the fact that British courts may exercise criminal jurisdiction over British ships, aircraft and embassies, they are not regarded as part of the territory for purposes of the residence requirements.[153] The same is true of the Continental Shelf but special provisions render persons employed there immune from disqualification.[154]

---

146 See eg *CG 32/49* and *55/50 (MB)*.
147 SI 1975/563, reg 13.
148 SI 1975/563, reg 13A.
149 Pp 280, below.
150 Royal and Parliamentary Titles Act 1927, s 2(2).
151 Union with Scotland Act 1706, Preamble, art 1; and Wales and Berwick Act 1746, s 3. Northern Ireland, the Isle of Man and the Channel Islands are thus excluded. However, as a result of the relevant reciprocal agreements, the various schemes are almost wholly integrated.
152 SSCBA 1992, s 172 (formerly Social Security and Housing Benefits Act 1982, s 44, rendered necessary by the decision in *Earl of Lonsdale v A-G* [1982] 3 All ER 579, [1982] 1 WLR 887).
153 *CSG 2/48*; *CP 93/49*; *R(S) 8/59*; *R(I) 44/61*; *R(P) 8/61*. Cf *Bradford Metropolitan City Council v Anderton* [1991] RA 45 (merchant seaman's ship not a residence for community charge purposes).
154 SI 1975/563, reg 11.

ii   Presence and absence

The two concepts are mutually exclusive.[155] To be 'absent' from Great Britain does not necessarily imply that the person concerned must have been present at some time in the past – it simply means not present.[156] Both presence and absence are questions of fact dependent on physical circumstances and concerned in no way with intention, or external events. Thus in a case where a claimant would have arrived in England but for technical problems in the mode of transport, it was to no avail for her to argue that she would but for another's fault have been present in Great Britain.[157]

iii   'Residence'

This is the term most widely used to represent the necessary connection with Great Britain. Its use has not of course been confined to social security legislation. There are many other areas, notably taxation,[158] insolvency[159] and matrimonial causes,[160] where it features prominently. Although the Commissioners have pointed out the danger of relying on decisions made in quite a different context,[161] nevertheless they have drawn freely from them for ideas in elucidating the term.[162]

The burden of proof is normally on the claimant to show that he or she is 'resident' in Great Britain at the relevant time.[163] The question is one of fact and degree[164] and does not lend itself easily to definition but reference has been made to the word's ordinary meaning, formulated in the *Oxford English Dictionary* as 'to dwell permanently or for a considerable time, to have one's settled or usual abode'.[165] Though the claimant need not be physically present at any one particular time, there must be a sufficient amount of physical presence in the place on which the residence may be grounded: a theory of 'constructive residence' is not recognised.[166] Conversely, the degree of permanence necessary need not be such as to render the place in question the claimant's domicile.[167] A claimant may, consequently, be resident in more than one place or country at any one time.[168] But a person who has their matrimonial home in one country is not normally to be treated as resident in another while residing at the matrimonial home.[169]

---

155   *R(U) 18/60.*
156   *R(U) 16/62.*
157   *R(S) 8/59.* See also *R(S) 6/81.*
158   Eg Income and Corporation Taxes Act 1988, ss 334–336.
159   Eg Insolvency Act 1986, s 265(1)(c).
160   Eg Matrimonial Causes Act 1973, s 35(1).
161   Eg *R(G) 2/51; R(P) 4/54; R(P) 1/72; R(P) 1/78.*
162   A prime example is *R(F) 1/62(T).*
163   *R(G) 2/51(T).*
164   *R 5/62 (UB); R(P) 2/67.* See also *Levene v IRC* [1928] AC 217 at 222; *IRC v Lysaght* [1928] AC 234 at 241, 243; and *Hipperson v Newbury District Electoral Registration Officer* [1985] QB 1060, [1985] 2 All ER 456.
165   Quoted in *Levene v IRC* [1928] AC 217 at 222; *Fox v Stirk and Bristol Electoral Registration Officer* [1970] 2 QB 463 at 475, 477; and *CG 32/49.*
166   *CG 32/49; 55/50 (MB); R 5/62 (UB); R(P) 1/72.* For the theory as applied to the poor law see *R v Glossop* (1866) LR 1 QB 227; and *West Ham Union v Cardiff Union* [1895] 1 QB 766.
167   *R(F) 1/62(T); R 1/71 (P).* For the concept of domicile generally, see Dicey and Morris *The Conflict of Laws* (13th edn, 2000) ch 6.
168   *R(G) 2/51; R(P) 2/67.* See also *Re Norris, ex p Reynolds* (1888) 4 TLR 452; *Levene v IRC* [1928] AC 217; *IRC v Lysaght* [1928] AC 234; and *Fox v Stirk and Bristol Electoral Registration Officer* [1970] 2 QB 463.
169   *R(P) 1/78,* para 7, H Magnus, Comr.

Within these broad outlines there are a number of factors to be taken into account. Perhaps the most important is the intention of claimants themselves. If they intend to settle in one place, they are likely to reside there.[170] In *R(P) 6/58*:

Mr C returned from Rhodesia (now Zimbabwe) where he had been living for nine years in the hope that he would benefit under the will of a relative. 11 months later, when his expectations were not fully realised, he went back to Rhodesia. It was held that during these 11 months he was 'resident' in Great Britain, as it had been, at the time, his intention permanently to stay there.

Conversely, a person taking a job abroad may still be resident in Britain if he or she intends to return immediately on its completion.[171] But in this situation the authorities are likely to have regard to the nature of the employment: if it is of a finite nature, eg a fixed term contract, the intention to return will prevail;[172] if, however, it is of indeterminate length, the mere expression of hope to return at some time in the future will generally be insufficient.[173] Of course, the amount of time actually spent in Britain (or abroad) may be significant – in *Fox v Stirk*,[174] Lord Denning MR spoke of a stay amounting to residence when it involves 'a considerable degree of permanence' – but if the intention is unequivocal, even a short time may be sufficient.[175] Another very important factor in practice is the nature of arrangements made for living while the individual is in Britain. It is not necessary that claimants should own or rent their own accommodation, but if they stay throughout in a hotel or with relatives, they must be able to show that they made their 'home' there.[176] If furniture and other personal effects are left in one place, this will help to show that the claimant is still resident there even if he or she has lived for a considerable period elsewhere.[177] In any event, it is easier to prove a continued residence in one place than a change to another country.[178]

iv 'Ordinarily resident'

Social security law employs the term 'ordinarily resident' less frequently than 'resident'. Where it is used it connotes the idea of residence with 'some degree of continuity'.[179] Its object is to exclude from entitlement persons who live mostly abroad but who come to reside in Great Britain intermittently without wishing to settle here.[180] According to the House of Lords, interpreting the same expression in relation to eligibility for an education grant, it means 'that the person must be habitually and normally resident

---

170   See esp the dictum of Somervell LJ in *Macrae v Macrae* [1949] P 397 at 403.
171   *CG 204/49*.
172   *R(G) 2/51*.
173   *CG 165/50; R(G) 5/52*. See also *Lewis v Lewis* [1956] 1 All ER 375, [1956] 1 WLR 200.
174   [1970] 2 QB 463 at 475.
175   *R(F) 1/62*; and see *Macrae v Macrae* [1949] P 397.
176   *R(P) 4/54; R(F) 1/62; R(P) 1/72*; and see *Re Norris, ex p Reynolds* (1888) 4 TLR 452; *Re Erskine, ex p Erskine* (1893) 10 TLR 32; *Levene v IRC* [1928] AC 217; and *Re Brauch, ex p Britannic Securities and Investments Ltd* [1978] Ch 316, [1978] 1 All ER 1004.
177   *R(G) 2/51; R(F) 1/62; R(P) 2/67*. See also *Hopkins v Hopkins* [1951] P 116, [1950] 2 All ER 1035; *Stransky v Stransky* [1954] P 428; *Lewis v Lewis* [1956] 1 All ER 375, [1956] 1 WLR 200; and *Brickfield Properties Ltd v Hughes* (1987) 20 HLR 108.
178   *R(F) 1/62; Macrae v Macrae* [1949] P 397.
179   *R(P) 1/78*, paras 7–8, adopting a dictum of Viscount Cave LC in *Levene v IRC* [1928] AC 217 at 225. See also *Stransky v Stransky* [1954] P 428 at 437, per Karminski J.
180   *R(P) 1/78*, para 9.

here, apart from temporary occasional absences of long or short duration'.[181] 'Habitually' implies that the residence should be adopted both voluntarily and for settled purposes, eg education, business employment or health, but it does not require an intention to live in a place permanently or indefinitely.[182]

v   Days of residence and absence

A person bearing the burden of proving that he or she was resident, or absent, on a day or period, must establish residence or absence throughout that day or period.[183]

Part 4   Persons subject to immigration control

A   General

One of the most politically controversial issues in social security law is the extent to which immigrants – especially those who have recently arrived and asylum seekers – should be entitled to social security benefits. For many years the response of the legislature was piecemeal. No particular provision was made in respect of contributory benefits, the assumption being that recent immigrants would have failed to build up an insurance record. In principle, once they had done so, they should be entitled to contributory benefits on the same basis as other contributors.[184] Non-contributory benefits have traditionally been subject to residence and presence conditions as a means of limiting entitlement to those claimants with a sufficient link with Great Britain, irrespective of their nationality or citizenship. Means-tested benefits, as the safety net of the welfare state, were originally not subject to any residence and presence conditions. However, some categories of immigrants were not able to claim, eg supplementary benefit and later income support for their normal living expenses, but were sometimes eligible for reduced rates of urgent cases payments.

The law governing the entitlement of persons from abroad to income support and the other means-tested benefits was made increasingly more restrictive during the 1990s. In 1994 the 'habitual residence' test was introduced to the income support scheme.[185] In February 1996 the Conservative government introduced regulations designed to remove the residual entitlement of most persons from abroad to income support, housing benefit and council tax benefit, with savings provisions for certain categories of asylum seekers. These provisions were ruled to be ultra vires by the Court of Appeal in *R v Secretary of State for Social Security, ex p Joint Council for the Welfare of Immigrants (JCWI)*,[186] only to be re-enacted shortly afterwards in primary legislation.[187] The

---

181   Per Lord Scarman, *Shah v Barnet London Borough Council* [1983] 2 AC 309 at 342, adopting a dictum of Lord Denning MR in the same case: [1982] QB 688 at 720.
182   Per Lord Scarman *Shah v Barnet London Borough Council* [1983] 2 AC 309 at 343–344. See *R(P) 2/90*.
183   *R(S) 1/66* and *Re a Farm Manager* [1979] 1 CMLR 445 at 446, in preference to an earlier interpretation that the state of affairs at the beginning of a day should be treated as persisting throughout that day: *CU 54/48.*
184   The more pressing issue was the extent to which entitlement to contributory benefits could be retained by those moving abroad: pp 225–229, above.
185   P 280, below.
186   [1996] 4 All ER 385.
187   IAA 1996, s 11 and Sch 1.

subsequent development of these rules as regards the principal means-tested benefits is considered further in chapter 8, below. The 1996 regulations also introduced restrictions on the eligibility of persons coming from abroad to a range of non-contributory disability benefits.[188] Essentially claimants had to have a right to reside in Great Britain that was not subject to any limitation or condition.[189] This effectively excluded asylum seekers and sponsored immigrants who had been given permission to stay in Great Britain so long as they did not have recourse to public funds. This requirement was additional to the traditional residence and presence conditions and was not invalidated by the decision of the Court of Appeal in *Ex p JCWI*.

In 1999 the Labour government introduced legislation which brought together these various exclusions from benefits (whether contributory, non-contributory or means-tested in nature), as well as making further radical changes to the arrangements for supporting asylum seekers, involving assistance in kind.[190] Section 115 of the Immigration and Asylum Act 1999 (IAA 1999) precludes persons who are 'subject to immigration control' (with certain exceptions) from a range of social security benefits. The official justification for these measures was that 'direct cash benefits provided under the social security system have proved to be a magnet, drawing economic migrants to the United Kingdom and undermining the integrity of the asylum system'.[191]

B   The exclusion of persons subject to immigration control

Section 115 of IAA 1999 excludes any 'person subject to immigration control' from entitlement to any of the following benefits:
- attendance allowance;
- carer's allowance;
- child benefit;
- council tax benefit;
- disability living allowance;
- disabled person's tax credit;
- housing benefit;
- income support;
- income-based jobseeker's allowance;
- severe disablement allowance;
- social fund payments; and
- working families' tax credit.[192]

Thus all of the means-tested benefits and tax credits are caught by the rule; conversely, none of the contributory benefits are listed, as the contributions conditions themselves debar claims from persons other than those settled and previously employed in Great Britain. The only non-contributory benefits to be omitted from this exclusionary rule will normally be unavailable to immigrants for other reasons. These are guardian's allowance (for which entitlement to child benefit is a precondition[193]), industrial injuries benefits (which presupposes the person has suffered an injury or contracted a disease

188   Attendance allowance, disability living allowance, carer's allowance and severe disablement allowance.
189   Family credit and disability working allowance (now working families' tax credit and disabled person's tax credit respectively) were made subject to the same rule.
190   Pp 313–316, below.
191   Mr M O'Brien MP, Special Standing Committee, col 1435,11 May 1999.
192   IAA 1999, s 115(1).
193   P 586, below.

as a result of working as an employed earner[194]) and war pensions (which presume service in the armed forces).

A 'person subject to immigration control' means:

a person who is not a national of an EEA State and who—
(a)   requires leave to enter or remain in the United Kingdom but does not have it;
(b)   has leave to enter or remain in the United Kingdom which is subject to a condition that he does not have recourse to public funds;
(c)   has leave to enter or remain in the United Kingdom given as a result of a maintenance undertaking; or
(d)   has leave to enter or remain in the United Kingdom [only as a result of appealing a decision as to their immigration status].[195]

The primary legislation itself contains no exceptions to this rule, but provision is made for regulations to provide for such special cases.[196] Those categories of persons from abroad who are exempt from this rule for the purposes of means-tested benefits are discussed in chapter 8, below. So far as attendance allowance, child benefit, disability living allowance, carer's allowance, severe disablement allowance and social fund payments are concerned, the following categories of person are *not* excluded from entitlement by virtue of section 115 of IAA 1999:
(1)   a member of a family of an EEA national;
(2)   a person who is lawfully working in Great Britain and is a national of a state with which the EEA has an agreement on equal treatment in social security (Algeria, Morocco, Slovenia, Tunisia and Turkey);
(3)   a person who is a member of a family of and living with a person under (2) above; and
(4)   a person admitted to the United Kingdom as a sponsored immigrant.[197]
The regulations merely lift the exclusionary effect of section 115; the individual concerned will still have to satisfy the residence and presence conditions applying to the benefit in question, discussed in Part 3, above.

Part 5   Hospital in-patients

A   General

Where the claimant, or a dependant for whom he or she is entitled to an increase, is a long-term hospital in-patient, enjoying free maintenance there under the NHS, the amount payable is reduced. The policy is an obvious one, and may be seen as part of the provisions for overlapping benefits.[198] Thus to the extent that a person's primary

---

194   SSCBA 1992, Pt V is silent on the position of those with no leave to remain. It follows that, in principle at least, such an immigrant who suffers an injury whilst (illegally) working would be eligible to claim industrial disablement benefit. The reality, however, is that any such claim would jeopardise the person's immigration status: Cox et al *Migration and Social Security* (2nd edn, 1997) p 217. In any event, any such claim must be supported by a national insurance number: SSAA 1992, s 1(1A)–(1B).
195   IAA 1999, s 115(9). On the definition of a 'maintenance undertaking', see s 115(10).
196   IAA 1999, s 115(3)–(6).
197   SI 2000/636, reg 2(2) and Sch, Pt II. See also reg 2(3) and (4)(b).
198   Cf pp 259–265, below.

living needs are being supplied by services financed by public funds, full benefit is inappropriate.[199] Notwithstanding opposition from the SSAC,[200] some major amendments to the rules were made in 1987, the majority of which further reduced the entitlement of claimants.[201] The government justified the reforms on the grounds that the rules needed to be simplified[202] and to be brought into line with what it assumed to be changing patterns in hospitalisation practices and domestic expenditure.[203] The rules discussed below apply principally to the retirement pension, incapacity benefit, bereavement allowance and the widowed parent's allowance.[204] It should be noted that special provisions apply to income support, housing benefit, attendance allowance and disability living allowance.[205]

B Adjustments to personal benefit

No adjustment is made for the first six weeks of free in-patient treatment. It is assumed that expenditure will continue to be incurred during short stays: in particular, it is very unlikely that claimants will give up occupation of their homes, and thus they will remain liable for rent or mortgage repayments. Once, however, this period has elapsed, it is assumed that their living expenses will be significantly reduced, though if they have dependants the family home will still have to be maintained. The rules are classified, therefore, according to the length of stay in hospital, and the existence or non-existence of dependants; they incorporate references to the current standard rate of a Category A retirement pension.[206]

i   *From 7 – 52 weeks* Where claimants have a dependant for whom an increase is, or would but for the rules to be described in the next paragraph be, payable, benefit is reduced by 20 per cent of the standard rate; if they have no such dependant it is reduced by 40 per cent; but the reduction in any case is not to leave them with less than 20 per cent of the standard rate.[207]

ii *After 52 weeks* After a year, the principle is modified so that claimants themselves, while in receipt of treatment, never receive more than 20 per cent of the standard rate – often referred to as 'pocket-money' benefit. The next 40 per cent is not payable, but if they have a dependant, and have made an appropriate application to the Secretary of State, any excess remaining is paid to that dependant.[208] A spouse

---

199 See NIAC Reports on *Draft Hospital In-Patient Regulations* (1948–49, HC 241), on the *Question of Long-Term Hospital Patients* (1960, Cmnd 464) and SSAC *Report on Draft Hospital In-Patient Amendment Regulations 1987* (1987, Cm 215).
200 See the Reports cited at n 199, above.
201 SI 1987/1883. For a critical study see Age Concern *Penalised for being ill* (2001). The government has announced its intention to extend the six week period before downrating applies, discussed below, to 13 weeks: 380 HC Official Report (6th series) cols 501 and 529.
202 More specifically to integrate the contributory benefit rules with the income support rules – on the latter, see pp 328–329, below.
203 See the Secretary of State's statement which precedes the *SSAC Report* n 199, above.
204 For the full list, see SI 1975/555, Sch 2. It follows that industrial injuries benefits (with the exception of constant attendance allowance and unemployability supplement), statutory sick pay, statutory maternity pay and state maternity allowance are unaffected by a stay as an in-patient. For child benefit and guardian's allowance, see p 665, below.
205 See p 328 (income support); p 427 (housing benefit); and pp 703–705 (attendance allowance and disability living allowance) respectively.
206 SI 1975/555, Pt II.
207 For the meaning of 'dependant' see SI 1975/555, reg 2(3).
208 The excess may, alternatively, be paid to another person who satisfies the Secretary of State that he or she will apply the sum for the benefit of the dependant.

who has also received free in-patient treatment for a year or more is not regarded as a dependant for this purpose.[209]

C Adjustment to increases for dependants

There are analogous rules governing the adjustment of increases for dependants.[210]

i   *Dependent spouse in-patient* Where a dependent spouse has been an in-patient for a period of six weeks, the increase payable for that person is reduced by 20 per cent of the standard pension rate, though not so as to reduce it to less than 20 per cent of that rate. After 52 weeks, if the dependent in-patient is a spouse and is still regarded as 'residing with' the claimant,[211] the reduced increase is not payable at all unless the latter is regularly incurring expenditure, or causing some payments to be made, on the spouse's behalf.

ii   *Both claimant and dependent spouse in-patients* Where both have been in-patients for a period of six weeks, the increase is reduced by 20 per cent of the standard pension rate (though not so as to reduce it to less than 20 per cent of that rate). After 52 weeks, the increase can never exceed 20 per cent of the standard pension rate; the next 20 per cent is not payable, and any part of the remaining increase exceeding 40 per cent of the standard pension rate is payable for the benefit of a child of the claimant's family to some other person undertaking to use it for that purpose or to the dependant (if he or she leaves hospital).

iii *Child dependant in-patient* Where a child dependant has been an in-patient for a period of 12 weeks the increase is payable only if the claimant is regularly incurring expenditure on the child's behalf, or causing some such payment to be made for his or her benefit.

D Incapacity to enjoy proceeds

The condition of some long-term patients is such that there is little personal use to which the 'pocket-money' benefit (20 per cent of the standard pension rate) can be put. The regulations therefore provide that where a single claimant has been an in-patient for over a year and a medical officer treating him or her issues a certificate to the effect that no sum, or only a specified weekly sum (less than that to which he or she could otherwise be entitled) can be applied for the 'personal comfort or enjoyment' of the patient, the weekly entitlement is reduced to that sum (if any).[212]

E Free in-patient treatment

Adjustments are made only for periods of 'free in-patient treatment'. The regulations provide that 'a person shall be regarded as receiving or having received free in-patient

---

209 The provisions which enabled a claimant without a dependant to accumulate the excess and receive it in the form of a 'resettlement benefit' on discharge from hospital have been abrogated. The policy is to target resources on those in need at this time through the social fund: *SSAC Report* n 199, above, p 2; and see pp 481–486, below.
210 SI 1975/555, Pt III.
211 Cf pp 252–255, below.
212 SI 1975/555, reg 16.

treatment for any period for which he is or has been maintained free of charge while undergoing medical or other treatment as an in-patient' in a 'hospital or similar institution' maintained or administered under the NHS (or by the Defence Council).[213] It is clear, in the first place, that the word 'treatment' is a misnomer. The object of these regulations is to avoid overpayments to persons being maintained free of charge in hospitals and similar state-financed institutions, and the nature of the treatment offered there is not crucial. Hence the Chief Commissioner ruled in 1967 that the phrase should not be the subject of refined distinctions: the mere fact that a person is an in-patient in a hospital is strong prima facie evidence that he or she is undergoing 'medical or other treatment'.[214] In any event, the receipt of nursing services will be sufficient.[215] It is questionable whether this broad approach is still appropriate today, given the radical changes in the delivery of community care. The underlying issue in the recent case law has been whether the health authority or the DWP should bear the cost of maintaining vulnerable individuals in the community.[216]

In the light of these policy objectives, the finding that the person is an 'in-patient' is obviously very important; and the phrase has been consistently interpreted to mean 'housed overnight' at the relevant institution.[217] Thus a person living at home because there are insufficient beds available at hospital, even though in all other respects he or she is treated as an in-patient, is not an 'in-patient' for the purposes of these regulations.[218] Conversely, a long-term hospital patient whose wife brings in all his meals because of his special dietary requirements is regarded as an 'in-patient'.[219] These principles are now subject to the 1999 amendment to the regulations to the effect that a period as an in-patient is deemed to start on the day after the individual enters the hospital (or other similar institution) and to end on the day of departure.[220]

While private patients in a hospital or equivalent institution are not subject to the reduction rules, the onus is on them[221] to show that they (or a third party, but not a public fund[222]) are paying charges designed to cover the whole cost of accommodation and services other than treatment.[223]

F Calculation of periods

The periods of in-patient treatment referred to must in principle be continuous, but this is modified by the regulations to take account of the possibilities both of time spent in other accommodation maintained at public expense, and of short interruptions to the free treatment.

213 SI 1975/555, reg 2(2). For the institutions covered, see *R(S) 4/53* and *R(S) 2/54*.
214 *R(P) 1/67*, para 14, R G Micklethwait, Comr.
215 *R(P) 1/67*, para 13; and see *Minister of Health v General Committee of Royal Midland Counties Home for Incurables at Leamington Spa* [1954] Ch 530 at 541, 547, 549–550.
216 *Chief Adjudication Officer v White (R(IS) 18/94)*; and *Botchett v Chief Adjudication Officer (R(IS) 10/96)*; see Ashton (1996) 3 JSSL 185.
217 *CS 65/49*; *R(S) 8/51*; *R(I) 14/56*. But where patients only sleep in the institution and are responsible for their own maintenance during the day, they are not covered by the rules: *R(S) 4/84*.
218 *R(I) 27/59*.
219 *CS 249/1989*.
220 SI 1975/555, reg 2(2A), inserted by SI 1999/1326, reg 2.
221 *CS 59/49*.
222 *R(S) 4/53*.
223 SI 1975/555, reg 2(2), now incorporating a reference to National Health Service Act 1977, s 65 and analogous provisions. See also *R(P) 13/52*.

i   Residence in other accommodation

The period of in-patient treatment is deemed to include any period of prior residence in 'prescribed accommodation' which, broadly speaking, covers publicly financed caring or residential accommodation.[224] If it has been decided by the appropriate authority that residence in such accommodation is not temporary, it is deemed, for purposes of the rules on adjustment, to have lasted for 52 weeks.[225]

ii   Linking of periods

Any two or more periods of free in-patient treatment (or residence in prescribed accommodation) separated by intervals not exceeding 28 days may be linked,[226] though the aggregate period thus taken into account does not include the intervals themselves.[227]

G   Benefit to be adjusted

The benefit to be reduced is, with one exception,[228] that which is payable after the Overlapping Regulations have taken effect.[229] The age addition is not affected, however, unless the claimant has been an in-patient for more than 52 weeks and there is no spouse or child 'residing' with him or her.[230]

Part 6   Imprisonment and detention in legal custody

A   General

The disqualification from benefit (or a dependant's increase) during periods when a person is 'undergoing imprisonment or detention in legal custody'[231] has always existed in social security law,[232] and yet its policy basis remains ambiguous. It may be seen simply as a penal provision to apply to persons who have forfeited their natural rights as citizens.[233] If this were so, it would be appropriate to confine the disqualification to those imprisoned or detained in connection with a criminal offence. As will appear, this is in practice how the provision has been interpreted, though its wording is not so limited. The alternative policy basis is identical to that encountered in relation to hospital in-patients: the detainee is being maintained at public expense and thus has no need of income maintenance. This may indeed be the case but it is to be observed that in

---

224   SI 1975/555, reg 17(6) and see: *R(S) 26/54*; *R(S) 15/55*; and *R(S) 6/58*.
225   SI 1975/555, reg 17(2). For the meaning of 'residence' see *R(P) 17/55*; *R(P) 1/67* and pp 230–232, above.
226   SI 1975/555, reg 17(4).
227   See *R(S) 8/51*. On parts of a day see *CS 131/49*; *R(S) 8/51, R(S) 9/52* and *R(S) 4/84*. But see now SI 1975/555, reg 2(2A).
228   SI 1975/555, reg 18(2).
229   SI 1975/555, reg 18.
230   SI 1975/555, reg 19.
231   SSCBA 1992, s 113(1)(b).
232   Cf NIA 1911, s 87(3).
233   *Per* Widgery, arguendo, *R v National Insurance Comr, ex p Timmis* [1955] 1 QB 139 at 145.

comparison with the hospital in-patients rules, those on detention are much stricter: there is no period of six weeks to adapt to new circumstances; and there is no provision for 'pocket-money' benefit.

B Scope of disqualification

A person shall be disqualified for receiving any benefit, and an increase of benefit shall not be payable in respect of any person as the claimant's wife or husband, for any period during which that person is undergoing imprisonment or detention in legal custody.[234]

i Benefits affected

This disqualification applies to most non-means tested benefits except for child benefit,[235] guardian's allowance[236] and industrial disablement benefit.[237] There are special rules relating to income support and housing benefit.[238]

ii Connection with criminal offence

A literal reading of the regulation quoted above indicates that it should cover all cases where the claimant is lawfully detained in custody, in other words, where a court would legitimately refuse an order of habeas corpus. This was, indeed, the interpretation suggested by the Divisional Court in 1955,[239] notwithstanding a stream of earlier Commissioners' decisions which held that the detention must be connected with criminal proceedings or a criminal act.[240] The NIAC, when it examined the matter in 1960, manifestly preferred the narrower interpretation.[241] But the amending regulations, consequential on its Report, failed fully to implement this view.[242] They provided that there will be no disqualification for a period of imprisonment or detention in legal custody which arises from criminal proceedings unless a penalty is imposed at the conclusion of the proceedings.[243] This does not make criminal proceedings a condition of the disqualification; it only adds a further condition – that of a penalty – where the detention is connected with criminal proceedings.

Thus in strict law the position is that someone, for example, remanded in custody in respect of a criminal charge from which he or she is later acquitted does not lose benefit, but those detained for civil contempt are disqualified. However, the adjudicating

---

234 SI 1982/1408, reg 2(1).
235 SSCBA 1992, s 113(1)(b) does not apply to Pt IX of that Act.
236 SI 1982/1408, reg 2(5). The allowance is payable to a person appointed by the Secretary of State to receive and deal with it on behalf of the claimant: reg 3(3).
237 SI 1982/1408, reg 2(6). Payment of the disablement benefit is, however, suspended: p 241, below, and the disqualification applies to the additions and increases to the disablement benefit.
238 See p 331 (income support) and p 417 (housing benefit) respectively.
239 Per Lord Goddard CJ, *R v National Insurance Comr, ex p Timmis* [1955] 1 QB 139 at 149.
240 *R(S) 20/53; R(S) 21/52; R(P) 10/54; R(S) 3/55; R(S) 4/55; 1/55 (SB)*.
241 *Report on the Question of Long-Term Hospital Patients* (1960, Cmnd 964).
242 SI 1960/1283, now SI 1982/1408, reg 2(2).
243 For the definition of 'penalty', see SI 1960/1283, reg 2(8)(c).

authorities are not, it seems, prepared to tolerate such a result. In 1974 the High Court of Northern Ireland reiterated the traditional view that the detention had to be connected with a criminal offence,[244] and in *R(S) 8/79* the British Commissioner held that a claimant who was committed to prison for failing to comply with a maintenance order was not to be disqualified. He admitted that if the point has been raised for the first time, he would have preferred the literal interpretation suggested by the Divisional Court, but he considered himself bound by the authorities adopting the narrower view.[245]

iii   Mentally abnormal offenders

If this narrower view be maintained, those detained under the mental health legislation but who have not been the subject of criminal proceedings escape disqualification. Understandably, the NIAC considered that it was, however, appropriate to disqualify an individual who was transferred from a prison (or analogous institution) to a mental hospital during the currency of a penal sentence.[246] The regulations thus provide[247] that a person shall not be disqualified for a period of:

> detention in legal custody after the conclusion of criminal proceedings[248] if it is a period during which he is liable to be detained in a hospital or a similar institution[249] in Great Britain as a person suffering from mental disorder[250] unless
>
> (a)   pursuant to any sentence or order for detention made by the court at the conclusion of those proceedings, he has undergone detention by way of penalty in a prison, a detention centre, a borstal institution or a young offenders' institution; and
>
> (b)   he was removed to the hospital or similar institution while liable to be detained as a result of that sentence or order, and, in the case of a person who is liable to be detained [under the Mental Health Act 1983] ... a direction restricting his discharge has been given [under such legislation] and is still in force.

Thus, a person transferred from a prison, detention centre, borstal or young offenders' institution may be disqualified but only for the period of his or her original sentence[251] and for this purpose the Home Secretary, or Secretary of State for Scotland, will issue a certificate stating the earliest date on which the person would have been expected to be discharged.[252] Of course, any other period of detention may well be subject to the rule on hospital in-patients.

---

244   *R (O'Neill) v National Insurance Comrs* [1974] NI 76, approving *R 1/76 (P)(T)*.
245   See also *R(S) 1/81*, para 4. In considering an application to quash this decision, the Divisional Court refers without comment to the fact that the narrower view has been 'accepted by all concerned': *R v National Insurance Comr, ex p Warry* [1981] 1 All ER 229 at 231.
246   NIAC n 241, above, para 19.
247   SI 1982/1402, reg 2(3).
248   'Criminal proceedings against any person shall be deemed to be concluded upon his being found insane in those proceedings so that he cannot be tried or his trial cannot proceed': SI 1960/1283, reg 2(8)(g).
249   This means any place (other than prison or analogous institution) in which 'persons suffering from mental disorder are or may be received for care or treatment': SI 1960/1283, reg 2(8)(b). For 'mental disorder' see n 10 below.
250   The reference to 'mental disorder' is to be construed as including references to any mental disorder within the meaning of the Mental Health Act 1983: SI 1982/1402, reg 2(8)(f), as amended.
251   See eg *R(P) 2/57*.
252   SI 1982/1408, reg 2(4).

iv Detention abroad

As a matter of construction, it has been held, after protracted litigation, that the provisions apply to periods of detention abroad.[253] To meet the objection that they are in consequence discriminatory under EU law, because the exceptions considered in the previous paragraphs have reference only to British legislation,[254] the regulations have been amended, so that claimants are not disqualified if they are detained in circumstances similar to those which if they had existed in Great Britain would have excepted them from the disqualification.[255] A final problem, as yet unresolved, is whether a criminal conviction abroad is to be treated as conclusive for British social security purposes. A conviction in Britain is certainly conclusive; but the Commissioner and the courts have left it open whether they might go behind a foreign conviction on the ground that it offends British notions of justice.[256]

C Suspension of benefit

It follows from the previous discussion that there are circumstances in which persons undergoing imprisonment or detention in legal custody are not disqualified from benefit. Those transferred to mental hospitals are entitled to receive the benefit themselves,[257] in other cases payment is suspended until their release.[258] The European Commission on Human Rights has concluded that the suspension of industrial disablement benefit that would otherwise be payable to a prisoner is not a breach of either article 14 or article 1 of the First Protocol of the European Convention on Human Rights.[259]

Part 7 Forfeiture

A General

The social security legislation contains a number of provisions which deny benefit to a claimant on grounds which to a greater or lesser extent include considerations of public policy: eg a person is disqualified from incapacity benefit and jobseeker's allowance if the contingency occurred through his or her own misconduct. In *R v National Insurance Comr, ex p Connor*,[260] the question arose, apparently for the first time in this context, whether there are general principles of public policy not incorporated in the legislation but which might be invoked by the authorities to deny benefit in appropriate circumstances.

---

253 *R(S) 2/81*, following *R v National Insurance Comr, ex p Warry* [1981] 1 All ER 229; and Case 1/78 *Kenny v Insurance Officer* [1978] ECR 1489.

254 *R v National Insurance Comr, ex p Warry* [1981] 1 All ER 229 ; and p 76, above.

255 SI 1982/1408, reg 2(9)–(10).

256 *R(S) 1/81*, para 5, J G Monroe, Comr, referring to *R v Brixton Prison Governor, ex p Caborn-Waterfield* [1960] 2 QB 498, [1960] 2 All ER 178. The Divisional Court in *R v National Insurance Comr, ex p Warry* [1981] 1 All ER 229 did not consider this suggestion.

257 SI 1982/1408, reg 3(2).

258 SI 1982/1408, reg 3(1); for guardian's allowance, however, see n 236, above.

259 *Carlin v United Kingdom* (1998) 25 EHRR CD75.

260 [1981] QB 758, [1981] 1 All ER 769, upholding *R(G) 2/79*, R J A Temple, Chief Comr. The decision was followed in Scotland: *R(G) 1/83*, upheld by the Court of Session in *Burns v Secretary of State for Social Services* 1985 SLT 351.

In the instant case a woman had been convicted of the manslaughter of her husband. The Chief Commissioner decided that since her status as a widow directly resulted from the unlawful act of manslaughter she had properly been denied benefit; and the Divisional Court upheld this decision.[261] Although the social security legislation was, in effect, a code, it was not exhaustive of the principles to be applied and it was to be assumed that those drafting it formulated its content against the background of the general law.

B Adjudication

Shortly after the *Connor* case, the Forfeiture Act 1982 was passed.[262] In the context of social security, it is mainly concerned to determine which authorities are to decide questions of forfeiture and not how they are to exercise their discretion in that regard. Section 4 provides that the question whether benefit has been forfeited as the result of any unlawful killing is to be determined by a Commissioner.[263] Unusually the Commissioners' jurisdiction is one of first instance, the justification presumably being that, given the rarity of the issue and the probability that each case will have its own individual aspects, it is thought desirable to concentrate the discretionary decision in the hands of a single authority at a senior level. The jurisdiction originally differed from that given by section 2 to the courts in relation to property cases in that there was no power to modify the effects of the forfeiture rule when the justice of the case so required.[264] In 1986 the Act was amended so that there is now power under section 4(1A) to modify the effect of the rule in cases of unlawful killing where:

> having regard to the conduct of the offender and of the deceased and to such other circumstances as appear to the Commissioner to be material, the justice of the case requires the effect of the rule to be so modified.[265]

Once it is decided as a matter of policy that the forfeiture rule applies, total relief from the operation of the rule is not possible under the terms of the Act.[266] This discretion to modify the impact of the rule does not apply in cases of murder.[267]

C Application of rule

The scope of the rule is still somewhat uncertain. So far, it seems only to have been applied in cases of unlawful killing,[268] though arguably it could be extended to assaults giving rise to a disability as a result of which the assailant receives some benefit, for

261   Applying by analogy the principles developed in the law of succession (eg *Re Giles, Giles v Giles* [1972] Ch 544, [1971] 3 All ER 1141) and private insurance (eg *Beresford v Royal Insurance Co Ltd* [1938] AC 586, [1938] 2 All ER 602; *Gray v Barr* [1970] 2 QB 626, [1970] 2 All ER 702).
262   See generally Matthews [1983] JSWL 141 and Cretney *Law, Law Reform and the Family* (1998) ch 3.
263   The onus is on the decision maker to justify a reference to the Commissioner and to prove that there has been an 'unlawful killing': *R(G) 2/90(T)*. For rules of procedure, see SI 1999/1495, regs 14 and 15. In *R(G) 2/84(T)* the Commissioners considered that it made no difference whether the rule disentitled the claimant or merely prevented enforcement of entitlement; cf *R(G) 1/83*, para 10.
264   *R(G) 1/84(T)*; *R(G) 2/84(T)*.
265   Forfeiture Act 1982, s 4(1B), inserted by SSA 1986, s 76.
266   *R(G) 3/90(T)*, agreeing with *Cross, Petitioner* 1987 SLT 384 and disagreeing with *Re K* [1985] 1 Ch 85.
267   *R(G) 1/90*.
268   This includes aiding and abetting suicide: *Dunbar v Plant* [1997] 4 All ER 289.

example a dependant's increase. In any event, receipt of the relevant benefit (most obviously a widow's or bereavement benefit but also, for example, retirement pension where the claimant bases entitlement on a deceased spouse's contributions[269]) must directly result from the unlawful act.

There is no requirement that the claimant be convicted of any offence: it is the unlawful action itself which gives rise to the application of the rule.[270] A conviction of murder will nonetheless invariably lead to forfeiture.[271] But lesser degrees of homicide will not always have this consequence. According to Lord Lane CJ in the *Connor* case, 'it is not the label which the law applies to the crime which has been committed but the nature of the crime itself which in the end will dictate whether public policy demands the court to drive the applicant from the seat of justice'.[272] In subsequent cases, the Court of Session in Scotland[273] and the Commissioners[274] have invoked judicial dicta from other contexts which suggest that the requisite moral culpability must be established by acts which are deliberate or intentional.[275] As such, the rule has been applied to disentitle a widow convicted of manslaughter (or the Scottish equivalent, culpable homicide) where a killing by poisoning was premeditated but a verdict of manslaughter substituted on appeal because of a technical error by the trial judge.[276] Where a history of abuse and provocation by the deceased has been shown, although the killing itself was deliberate, partial disentitlement has been applied.[277] The rule has been held to be inapplicable where the killing resulted from a mental disorder.[278]

The Commissioner is bound under the terms of the legislation to investigate the possible application of the forfeiture rule. The fact that the claimant was acquitted in a criminal court does not therefore preclude the operation of the rule, although an acquittal on the merits will be accorded 'substantial' weight.[279] As yet, there has been little discussion of wider policy considerations; eg the problem of double penalties, the protection of the public purse (or social security contributors) and financial hardship to the claimant.[280]

Part 8 Earnings

A General

There are a number of rules arising under SSCBA 1992 in connection with entitlement to, or assessment of, contributory and non-contributory benefits which refer to the

---

269 *R(P) 1/84.*
270 *R(G) 1/84(T)*, para 14; and *R(G) 2/90(T)*, para 20.
271 See Forfeiture Act 1982, s 5 and *R(G) 1/90.*
272 [1981] QB 758 at 765.
273 *Burns v Secretary of State for Social Services* 1985 SLT 351.
274 *R(G) 1/83; R(G) 2/84(T); R(G) 3/84.*
275 Notably, *Hardy v Motor Insurers' Bureau* [1964] 2 QB 745 at 760, 762, 766–767; *Gray v Barr* [1970] 2 QB 626 at 640, on appeal [1971] 2 QB 554 at 568; see also *Re H* [1990] 1 FLR 441. There is no need for acts or threats of violence per se for the rule to operate: see *Dunbar v Plant* [1997] 4 All ER 289.
276 *R(G) 1/91.*
277 *R(G) 3/90(T). R(G) 2/84(T)* and *Burns v Secretary of State for Social Services* 1985 SLT 351, where full disentitlement was applied in cases of provocation, were both decided before the power to modify the effect of the rule was inserted.
278 *R(G) 3/84.*
279 *R(G) 2/90(T).* The standard of proof is approaching that in criminal cases: para 22.
280 Cf Robilliard (1981) 44 MLR 718 at 720. These issues were raised during parliamentary discussions of the 1982 Bill: see *Matthews* n 262, above, at 147.

weekly earnings of a person either before benefit was payable or during a period of entitlement. They are for the following purposes:[281]
(1) to disregard casual or subsidiary work, the earnings from which are below a specified level, where entitlement to benefit is based on incapacity for work or unemployment – such rules apply to incapacity benefit,[282] severe disablement[283] and carer's allowance[284] and contribution-based jobseeker's allowance[285];
(2) to determine whether the earnings of a spouse or child carer disentitle a claimant to a dependant's increase for such a person.[286]

The law governing the calculation of earnings for these purposes is primarily to be found in the Computation of Earnings Regulations 1996.[287] These regulations replaced more general provisions that had been in force since 1978.[288] The new rules make separate and detailed provision for employed and self-employed earners, as well as providing for the determination of notional earnings, borrowing certain concepts from the law governing income-related benefits. There are special rules for contribution-based jobseeker's allowance and, inevitably, further provisions governing income-related benefits.[289]

The basic rule is that an individual's earnings for any period are the whole of that person's earnings, including any notional income, except in so far as any allowances or deductions are permissible under the regulations.[290] While payments under occupational or personal pension schemes do not, in general, count as earnings, they are treated as such for the purpose of all rules governing increases for dependants.[291]

B 'Earnings' of employed earners

SSCBA 1992 provides that '"earnings" includes any remuneration or profit derived from an employment', the latter term being defined to include 'any trade, business, profession, office or vocation'.[292] These definitions show that a line is to be drawn between earnings, including profits, which are derived from an occupation, and payments vesting in the recipient in some other capacity, eg as shareholder.[293] The primary legislation also provides that both statutory maternity pay and statutory sick pay are to be treated as earnings.[294] The former regulations were phrased rather more narrowly in that 'earnings' (whether for employed or self-employed earners) were defined as 'earnings derived from a gainful employment',[295] but further elucidation was left to the

---

281 Earnings are also relevant for those claims under the industrial injuries scheme for which reduced earnings allowance remains payable. They were formerly important for assessing the amount to be deducted from retirement pension for earnings received during the period of entitlement.
282 P 549, below.
283 P 549, below.
284 P 711, below.
285 P 502, below.
286 P 249, below.
287 SI 1996/ 2745. These rules apply for the purposes of Pts II to V (other than Sch 8) of SSCBA 1992: SI 1996/2745, reg 3(1).
288 SI 1978/1698, on which see the 4th edition of this book, pp 412–418.
289 P 502 (contribution-based jobseeker's allowance) and pp 449–453 (income-related benefits), below.
290 SI 1996/2745, reg 3(2).
291 SSCBA 1992, s 89.
292 SSCBA 1992, ss 3(1)(a) and 122(1).
293 *R(P) 22/64.*
294 SSCBA 1992, s 4(1)(a).
295 SI 1978/1698, reg 1(2).

case law.[296] The 'earnings' of an employed earner are now defined to mean 'any remuneration or profit derived from that employment'.[297] The regulations list various types of payments which are specifically included within the ambit of this definition. These are exactly the same as the definition of an employee's earnings under the income support scheme,[298] with two minor exceptions.[299] As with the income support rules, any payment in respect of expenses that are wholly, exclusively and necessarily incurred in the performance of the duties of the employment do not count as earnings.[300] Net earnings are now arrived at, as with means-tested benefits, by deducting income tax, primary Class 1 National Insurance contributions and half of any occupational or private pension contributions.[301] The resulting figure is then adjusted if any of the specified disregards or deductions apply, which are discussed further below.[302] The normal rule is that a person is treated as having received earnings on the first day of the benefit week in which they are due to be paid.[303] The earnings, as so assessed, are then regarded as applying to a future period of equal length to the period for which they were paid.[304]

C 'Earnings' of self-employed earners

The 'earnings' of a self-employed earner are defined as the 'gross receipts of the employment' in the same terms as under the income support scheme. These are then adjusted in accordance with the regulations to arrive at the net profit derived from the self-employment, which in turn is subject to designated disregards or deductions.[305] The usual rule is for such earnings to be calculated over a period of one year. However if the work has only recently started, or 'there has been a change which is likely to affect the normal pattern of business', such other period may be adopted as may enable 'the weekly amount of earnings to be determined more accurately'.[306]

296　See further the 4th edition of this book, pp 412–418. This National Insurance case law will now only be of limited relevance given the comprehensive overhaul of the regulations in 1996 and the incorporation of many concepts from the income-related benefits schemes.

297　SI 1996/2745, reg 9(1).

298　SI 1987/1967, reg 35(1); see p 450, below.

299　The income support regulations include non-cash vouchers, not mentioned in SI 1996/2745, whilst the latter specifically lists employer's payments of maternity or sick pay as a type of earnings. The latter count as other income for income support purposes: p 451, below.

300　SI 1996/2745, reg 9(3). Contrast the more generous provision under the former SI 1978/1698, reg 4(c), permitting the deduction of 'any other expenses ... reasonably incurred by him without reimbursement in connection with and for the purposes of that employment'.

301　SI 1996/2745, reg 10(4). See also reg 8 on calculation.

302　SI 1996/2745, reg 10(1)–(3).

303　SI 1996/2745, reg 7(b); there are certain exceptions where increases for adult dependants are being claimed, in which case earnings are treated as having been paid on the first day of the benefit week after the week in which they are due to be paid: reg 7(a).

304　SI 1996/2745, reg 6(2)(a). For the attribution of payments which are not expressed to cover a specific period, see reg 6(2)(b).

305　SI 1996/2745, regs 12–14. The net profit excludes expenses wholly and exclusively defrayed for the purposes of the self-employment as well as tax, self-employed National Insurance contributions and half of any private pension payments.

306　SI 1996/2745, reg 11(1). This reflects the income support rule: SI 1987/1967, reg 30. There is likewise a special rule for royalties: SI 1996/2745, reg 11(2).

D   Disregarded earnings and deductions from earnings

The regulations set out a number of types of payments which are to be disregarded when calculating the earnings of both employed and self-employed earners.[307] These include:

- the first £4 a week of any contractual payments received for renting out a room (currently £13.40 if heating is included);
- the first £20 a week and 50 per cent of any excess over such sum of any payments received from a lodger; any other payment (in full) received as a contribution towards living and accommodation costs from another person on a non-contractual basis;
- earnings payable abroad which cannot be brought into the country and bank charges payable on earnings in currencies other than sterling; payments from local authorities or voluntary organisations for fostering or accommodating children;
- payments by such bodies or health authorities for providing respite care;
- bounties paid to part-time members of various emergency services; refunds of income tax; and
- any advance on earnings or loans made by an employer.

In addition, child care costs may be deducted from weekly earnings, whether as an employed or self-employed earner, up to a ceiling of £60 per week.[308] These rules were based on the child care allowance originally introduced into the family credit scheme but have not been revised to take into account the more generous provision now made for working families' tax credit. Thus for present purposes deductions may only be made for child care charges incurred in respect of children under the age of 11, rather than the new limit of 15 (or 16 for disabled children) for the tax credits.[309]

E   Notional earnings

As has been mentioned above, the code contained in the 1996 regulations makes specific provision for notional earnings, borrowing this concept from the income-related benefits schemes. However, the regulations only specify two types of notional income for inclusion in a person's earnings.[310] The first situation is where the claimant's earnings are not ascertainable at the date of the Secretary of State's decision. If so, the claimant is to be treated 'as possessing such earnings as is reasonable in the circumstances of the case having regard to the number of hours worked and the earnings paid for comparable employment in the area'.[311] The second type of case is where a claimant undertakes a service either for no payment or for less remuneration than is normal in the area; again, the individual is deemed to be in receipt of reasonable earnings for such work.[312]

---

307   SI 1996/2745, Sch 1.
308   SI 1996/2745, regs 10(2) and 13(2) and Sch 2. Special provisions apply where the claimant is entitled to carer's allowance and incurring child care costs: regs 10(3) and 13(3) and Sch 3.
309   P 394, below.
310   These mirror SI 1987/1967, reg 42(5) and (6).
311   SI 1996/2745, reg 4(1).
312   SI 1996/2745, reg 4(2). On the calculation of tax etc from notional earnings, see reg 4(3).

Part 9   Increases for dependants

A   General

The principle that special allowance should be made for persons dependent on the claimant was, of course, recognised from the beginning as regards benefits which were means-tested. Family support is without doubt the most significant differential in assessing an individual's need. For those benefits governed wholly or partly by the contributory principle such provision is not so obvious but is readily acceptable. If the benefit is intended to provide a minimum standard of living for the claimant, then regard should be had to the person's family needs, even though, in the absence of a family-weighted contribution, this will mean that those without family obligations will be subsidising those with them.

The history of dependency provision for non means-tested benefits has been far from consistent. Before the Second World War, it was incorporated in various benefit schemes only gradually and somewhat haphazardly. It was added to the unemployment insurance scheme in 1921 on a temporary basis to relieve 'winter hardships',[313] but in the next year was made permanent.[314] Remarkably, additions for dependants were never included in the National Health insurance scheme, and the reasons for the distinction remain far from obvious. They were belatedly added to workmen's compensation in 1940.[315] Beveridge, in his restatement of the social insurance principle, based as it was on a system of flat-rate benefit, was content to see the increase payable to all recipients of insurance benefit.[316]

By the time earnings-related supplements were introduced for short-term benefits in 1966, the principle of increases for dependants was already firmly entrenched, and there was at that time no serious attempt to argue that it should be discontinued.[317] But the reform prompted the decision to pay the increase on a higher scale to long-term beneficiaries who were not entitled to the supplement. Paradoxically, this more favourable treatment of pensioners was not affected by the introduction of the earnings-related component under the 1975 scheme, nor by the abolition of the earnings-related supplements for short-term beneficiaries. Indeed, the position of the latter has deteriorated further as a result of later reforms. First, statutory sick pay which replaced sickness benefit[318] for most employed claimants does not include an allowance for dependants.[319] Secondly, the consolidation of child endowment through the child benefit scheme was rationalised as the first step of a new policy to reduce differences in the level of family support between short-term beneficiaries and those in employment.[320] As a result, the value of the child dependency increases payable with short-term benefits was frozen and subsequently they were abolished altogether.[321]

---

313   Unemployed Workers Dependants' (Temporary Provisions) Act 1921.
314   Unemployment Insurance Act 1922 (UIA 1922).
315   Workmen's Compensation (Supplementary Allowances) Act 1940. This was as a result of continuous complaints that the ceiling to earnings-related compensation was too low for those with heavy family responsibilities
316   Beveridge Report *Social Insurance and Allied Services* (1942, Cmd 6404) paras 311 and 325. The contemporaneous introduction of family allowances necessitated a technical modification of the rules, though in no fundamental way interfered with them.
317   Cf Walley *Social Security: Another British Failure?* (1972) p 206.
318   Now the lower rate of short-term incapacity benefit.
319   Cf p 530, below.
320   See Brown *Children in Social Security* (1984) pp 116–121.
321   Health and Social Security Act 1984, s 13.

While concern for work disincentives may have motivated these changes, it does not explain a later decision not to up-rate, in line with inflation, the child dependency increases paid to long-term beneficiaries (and those over pensionable age).[322] Thirdly, the changes associated with the introduction of incapacity benefit in 1995 and jobseeker's allowance in 1996 saw a further reduction in the level of support provided for dependents within the contributory scheme. Child additions for incapacity benefit mirror those previously available with sickness and invalidity benefit, but the rules governing adult dependants were made significantly more restrictive.[323] This process was taken still further with contribution-based jobseeker's allowance, which carries with it no dependency additions at all.

The traditional rules on dependency allowances assumed stereotyped family relationships in which the husband/father is the primary or only breadwinner, while the wife/mother assumes domestic responsibilities and her earnings, if any, are inessential additions to the family income. The Council Directive on Equal Treatment for Men and Women in Social Security[324] prompted the government to make fundamental changes so that eg the rules governing a husband's entitlement to claim for a wife and a wife's entitlement to claim for a husband have been largely harmonised.[325] For the future, the child dependency allowances are to be abolished as part of the government's plans to introduce a child tax credit under the Tax Credits Act 2002.

B   Persons for whom increase payable

i   Children

Increases for child dependants may, at present, be added to the following benefits:
- short-term incapacity benefit at the higher rate or where the claimant is over pensionable age;
- long-term incapacity benefit;
- Category A, B or C retirement pensions; and
- widowed parent's, carer's and severe disablement allowances.[326]

To qualify for the increase, claimants must satisfy three conditions, the first referring to their relationship with the child, the second to the state of the latter's dependence on them and the third to the earnings (if any) of their spouse or unmarried partner. The rate for a child dependant is reduced where child benefit is in payment at the highest rate for that child.[327]

322   In 1990 the weekly rate of invalidity benefit was £46.90 and the child dependency addition £9.65. In 2002 the comparable rates for long-term incapacity benefit and the child addition were £70.95 and £11.35, increases of 51 per cent and 18 per cent respectively.

323   SI 1994/2945; this is a self-contained code for dependency additions for incapacity benefit, whilst other relevant benefits remain covered by SI 1977/343: see reg 1(3A).

324   Council Directive (EEC) 79/7.

325   SSA 1980, Sch 1, Pt I, on which see Atkins [1980] JSWL 16.

326   SSCBA 1992, ss 80(2), (5) and 90. The Conservative government's intention was that child dependency increases would be payable only the long-term incapacity benefit (ie after 52 weeks); a defeat in the House of Lords during the passage of the Social Security (Incapacity for Work) Act 1994 restored the additions to the higher rate of short-term incapacity benefit (ie from 29 weeks), as with the former invalidity benefit: 554 HL Official Report (5th series) cols 1451–1463.

327   Using powers under SSAA 1992, s 154. The current reduction is £1.70 in the weekly rate of the child dependency addition.

A SUFFICIENT RELATIONSHIP

The first general rule for the increase simply incorporates the law on child benefit: it is payable where the claimant is 'entitled to child benefit in respect of a child or children'.[328] On this test, therefore, reference should be made to the discussion in chapter 18, below.

In certain respects, however, the traditional rules on increases covered a wider range of relationships than those acknowledged under the child benefit scheme. To ensure that the entitlement of this broader group is preserved, a regulation sets out circumstances in which for the purpose of the increase a person is treated as if he or she were entitled to child benefit.[329]

(1) The claimant is *either* a parent of the child *or* is wholly or mainly maintaining the child, *and* the claimant resides with a parent of the child to whom child benefit has been awarded and with whom the child is living; or

(2) the claimant (or spouse) would have been entitled to child benefit for the child if the latter had been born at the end of the week before that in which the birth in fact occurred;[330] or

(3) the claimant is entitled to a family benefit in respect of that child payable by the government of a country outside the UK.

Conversely, there is a situation where child benefit is payable but the increase is excluded.[331] This applies where the claimant of the increase (who is entitled to child benefit) is not a parent of the child and someone who is his or her parent is treated, under section 143(1)(a) of SSCBA 1992,[332] as responsible for the child. Nevertheless, claimants remain entitled to the increase if, under the same provision, they are also treated as responsible for children and are wholly or mainly maintaining them.

B DEPENDENCE

The second condition is that the claimant must prove either that the child in question is living with him or her or that he or she is contributing to the cost of providing for the child at a weekly rate of not less than the amount of the increase, over and above the amount (if any) received by way of child benefit.[333]

C EARNINGS OF SPOUSE OR PARTNER

The 'equal treatment' reform of 1983 abolished the discriminatory rule that a married woman residing with her husband could be paid a child dependency increase only if the husband was 'incapable of self support'. The current provisions nevertheless reflect a similar policy, that the earnings of a partner should affect entitlement to the increase. So, where the claimant is a member of a married or unmarried couple residing together, and the partner earns £155 or more per week, no increase is payable for a first or only

---

328 SSAA 1992, s 80. It is sufficient if a claim for child benefit has been made for the relevant period: *R(S) 3/80*.

329 SI 1977/343, reg 4A and SI 1994/2495, reg 6. For the meaning of 'parent' in these rules, see SSCBA 1992, s 147(3); *R(S) 4/81*; and *R(S) 9/83*.

330 This reflects the rule that child benefit entitlement is determined weekly by reference to facts existing at the end of the previous week.

331 SI 1977/343, reg 4B and SI 1994/2495, reg 7.

332 See p 664, below.

333 SSCBA 1992, s 81(1)–(2).

child; each complete £20 in excess of £155 precludes an increase for a further child.[334] Where the partner's earnings fluctuate, an award continues in force but is not payable in a week for which the earnings exceed the appropriate level.[335]

ii Husband or wife

An increase for a spouse may supplement short-term, as well as long-term, benefits, and hence may be claimed in respect of the following:

- incapacity benefit;
- Category A or C retirement pensions; and
- maternity, carer's and severe disablement allowances.[336]

A dependency addition was previously available for spouses where the claimant was in receipt of unemployment benefit. This was abolished with the transition to contribution-based jobseeker's allowance, on the argument that the latter is a personal benefit based on an individual's work record and the addition duplicated assistance provided under the then income support scheme.[337] Precisely the same argument could be used in respect of additions to incapacity benefit. Although dependency additions for spouses were retained for incapacity benefit, further conditions have to be satisfied for this benefit. These are that either the spouse must be 60 or over, or, if the spouse is aged under 60, the claimant must be residing with him or her and receiving a dependency addition for a child.[338]

Where a dependency addition is payable, the marriage must be one recognised by law and sufficiently proved.[339] The usual test of dependency applies: the claimant must either be residing with the spouse[340] or contributing to his or her maintenance at not less than the amount of the increase.[341] While much of the sex discrimination previously existing in this area[342] has been eliminated, nevertheless a woman claiming a dependency increase to a Category A retirement pension for a husband has to satisfy an additional condition: immediately prior to entitlement to that pension she was in receipt of a dependency increase for him as an addition to incapacity benefit.[343] It has been held that this requirement, though clearly discriminatory, is not in breach of the Council Directive on Equal Treatment,[344] since the latter explicitly excluded from its provisions increases to an old age benefit for a dependent spouse.[345]

The possibility of the claimant's spouse being an earner raises an important policy question: presumably, the increase should be paid if its object is to provide

---

334   SSCBA 1992, s 80(4). Earnings include occupational and personal pension payments: s 89. These figures are reviewed annually but up-rated at the discretion of the Secretary of State: see SSAA 1992, s 150(1)(f),(2) and (3).

335   See the unhappily worded SSCBA 1992, s 92.

336   SSCBA 1992, ss 82–84 and 90.

337   Lord Mackay of Ardbrecknish, 563 HL Official Report (5th series) col 688.

338   SSCBA 1992, s 86A and SI 1994/2945, reg 9. Given that child additions are not available with the lower rate of short-term incapacity benefit, a deeming rule applies to ensure qualification for the adult dependency addition: reg 9(2).

339   Pp 214–220, above.

340   Pp 252–255, below.

341   SSCBA 1992, ss 82(1), 83(2) and 84(2). But for carer's allowance, the claimant must prove residence – there is no maintenance alternative: SI 1977/343, Sch 2, para 7.

342   See the 2nd edition of this book, pp 367–369.

343   SSCBA 1992, s 84(1).

344   Council Directive (EEC) 79/7, art 7(1)(d).

345   *R(P) 3/88* and Case C-420/92 *Bramhill v Chief Adjudication Officer* [1994] ECR I-3191.

compensation for the loss of actual support but not if it is instead to satisfy the need for support. Quite apart from this, there is the question of incentives: should claimants' partners be encouraged to work, assuming they are capable of it? While previous governments have appeared unequivocally to adopt the 'needs' approach,[346] the various statutory provisions are not uniformly consistent with it. Certainly it is adopted in the case of the relevant short-term benefits, maternity allowance and short-term incapacity benefit; the increase is not payable if the spouse's weekly earnings exceed the amount of that increase.[347] The same also applies to long-term benefits (long-term incapacity benefit and retirement pensions) where the spouse is not residing with the claimant, ie where the alternative maintenance test has to be satisfied.[348] If the spouses do reside together, no increase to the long-term benefits is payable if the dependent spouse's earnings exceed the standard adult rate of contribution-based jobseeker's allowance.[349]

Just as the earnings rule differs according to the nature of the benefit, so also does the amount of increase which is payable for adult dependants. Broadly speaking, the highest increase is paid with the contributory long-term incapacity benefit and retirement pension, the lowest increase with non-contributory benefits and there is a middle rate for increases to the short-term contributory benefits.

iii Other adult dependants

The British social security system has never been generous in its support of dependants who are not members of the nuclear family. Provisions allowing for increases for certain adult relatives were abolished in 1980.[350] While unmarried partners are treated as spouses for the purposes of the income-related benefits,[351] their position with regard to contributory and non-contributory benefits payable is less favourable. Except for a short period of 'entitlement' under the Unemployment Insurance Acts,[352] dependency increases have not been payable for cohabitants as such. They are, however, payable for a dependant who cares for a child of the claimant and, since 1983, following the 'equal treatment' reforms, such a person can be male or female.[353]

The claimant must be entitled to child benefit[354] – or treated as so entitled[355] – for the child who is the subject of the care. As regards the latter, the Commissioner has held that the necessary care will be shown if the alleged carer 'to a substantial extent ... performs those duties for a child, with which a child needs assistance because he or she is a child, or exercises that supervision over a child which is one of the needs of

---

346 Report of Secretary of State on the Earnings Rule for Retirement Pensioners and the Wives of Retirement and Invalidity Pensioners (1977–78, HC 697) para 5.6.
347 SSCBA 1992, s 82(2) and SI 1994/2945, reg 10.
348 SSCBA 1992, ss 83(2)(b) and 84(2)(b).
349 SI 1977/343, reg 8(2). For this purpose, 'earnings' include occupational and personal pension payments: SSCBA 1992, s 89.
350 SSA 1980, Sch 1, para 3. On the repealed provisions, see the NIAC *Report on the Question of Dependency Provisions* (1956, Cmd 9855).
351 P 443, below.
352 UIA 1922, s 1(1), repealed by UIA 1927, s 4(2).
353 The requirement in the case of Category A and C retirement pensions that the carer must be a woman was abolished later: SI 1989/523, reg 7, revoking SI 1977/343, reg 10(f).
354 SSCBA 1992, ss 82(4) and 85(2); SI 1977/343, regs 10, 12 and Sch 2. For incapacity benefit the test is whether the claimant is entitled to a child dependency addition for that child: SI 1994/2945, reg 9(1)(c) and (d).
355 SI 1977/343, reg 4A and SI 1994/2495, reg 6.

childhood'.[356] It does not connote exclusive care[357] or even a greater amount of care than that provided by the claimant.[358] But the mere distant supervision of a child's needs while he or she is at boarding school does not qualify.[359]

This firm emphasis on the care of a child carries no necessary implication of a sexual relationship with the claimant. The carer can be of the same sex as, and need not reside with, the claimant.[360] Indeed, the increase may be paid for a carer where the claimant is living with a spouse, provided that the latter is in full-time work and is not substantially involved in the care of the child.[361] The short-term benefits which may be supplemented by the increase are those for maternity and incapacity.[362] The long-term benefits are long-term incapacity benefit, Category A and C retirement pensions, carer's and severe disablement allowance.[363]

To qualify for any of these increases the child carer must either be residing with the claimant or be maintained by him or her at not less than the standard rate of the increase, or employed for consideration of not less than that amount.[364] No increase is payable where the carer earns more than the amount of the increase but the amounts (if any) which the claimant pays the child carer are, of course, ignored, and the exclusion does not apply at all to those employed by the claimant and not residing with that person.[365] There are, moreover, some further limitations which do not apply to spouses. Thus the child carer must not be imprisoned or detained in legal custody[366] or absent from Great Britain.[367] Finally, an increase to incapacity benefit is not payable if the claimant has a wife who is entitled to a Category B or C retirement pension.[368]

C 'Residing with' or 'living with' the claimant

The principle that a claimant should be either maintaining the dependant or residing (or living) with him or her is not difficult to rationalise. If the claimant shares a home with another, and is an earner, it is reasonable to infer a contribution to that other's maintenance. The different formulation for adult dependants ('residing with') and children ('living with') is deliberate. The latter concept was that used in the family allowances, and subsequently the child benefit, legislation and was explicitly incorporated into the National Insurance scheme in 1957.[369] As the Commissioner has consistently held, 'living with' does not carry the same meaning as 'residing with'.[370] It seems clear, therefore, that the intention of Parliament was to apply to child dependency

---

356 *CS 726/49*, para 11.
357 *UD 10914/31*.
358 *CS 726/49*, paras 9, 10.
359 *R(S) 17/54*.
360 *CS 726/49*, unless an increase is claimed for carer's allowance: n 341, above. A non-residing child carer must, however, be maintained by the claimant.
361 *R(S) 20/54*.
362 SSCBA 1992, s 82(2)–(3) and SI 1994/2945, reg 9.
363 SSCBA 1992, s 85(1); SI 1994/2945, reg 9; SI 1977/343, reg 1(3).
364 SI 1994/2945, reg 10(2)(b) and SI 1994/2945, reg 9(1)(d) and 9(3). For carer's allowance, residence must be proved: n 341, above.
365 SI 1977/343, reg 10(2)(e).
366 SI 1977/343, reg 10(2)(d) and SI 1994/2945, reg 14.
367 Unless residing with the claimant who is not disqualified: SI 1977/343, reg 10(2)(c) and (3).
368 SSCBA 1992, s 85(3), presumably because this is analogous to an increase for a wife, and a claimant may not claim increases for both a wife and a resident child carer.
369 NIA 1957, s 6(4).
370 *R(I) 10/51*; *R(U) 11/62*; *R(F) 2/79*.

increases the interpretation given to the phrase in child benefit law; this is fully discussed in chapter 18.[371] It thus remains to consider the concept of 'residing with' which qualifies the relationship with adult dependants.

The term is not defined in SSCBA 1992 and guidance is to be had only from the case law.[372] The basic idea is that the two people concerned should be living under the same roof.[373] This does not mean either that one of them should be the owner or tenant of the property[374] or that, in the case of spouses, they are sleeping in the same bed or otherwise maintaining the normal relationship of husband and wife.[375] But there must be an element of continuity and permanence in the co-residence.[376] In some cases, it will be necessary for the claimant to prove that he or she has acquired a new 'co-resident'. It will be more difficult to establish that living in a hotel, lodgings or the home of relatives constitutes co-residence than the entering into a tenancy agreement or setting up home as man and wife.[377] More often, the question is whether an admitted co-residence has in fact ceased. On this the legislation is more helpful. Regulations lay down three rules.

i Temporary absence

Under the first rule:

> two persons shall not be treated as having ceased to reside together by reason of any temporary absence the one from the other.[378]

This reinforces the notion that 'residing with' implies a permanent rather than a temporary condition, but it is naturally difficult to draw the line between the two. Some authorities, applying an equivalent rule under regulations previously in force, held that the test depends primarily on the parties' state of mind: did they intend to resume co-residence when the period of separation had ceased? Or has the separation been so long that, on reasonable inference, it was likely to be permanent?[379] On this view, the purpose of the absence becomes important. Thus the acquisition of accommodation removed from the family but near the claimant's employment will not generally be regarded as indicative of 'temporary' absence,[380] but it may be so categorised if the claimant is merely looking for a job and intends that the family should join him or her when one is found,[381] or lodges near the work but returns home at weekends and for holidays.[382] Other authorities have regarded the claimant's intention as too elusive a criterion and

---

371 Pp 664–666, below.
372 The expression also has been used in the Rent Acts (see eg *Swanbrae Ltd v Elliot* (1986) 19 HLR 86 and Hill [1987] Conv 349); the Housing Acts (see eg *Waltham Forest London Borough Council v Thomas* [1992] 2 AC 198); and in the law of family maintenance (see eg *Curtin v Curtin* [1952] 2 QB 552).
373 Per Lord Goddard CJ, *Curtin v Curtin* [1952] 2 QB 552 at 556; *R(P) 15/56*.
374 *CU 201/50.*
375 *Curtin v Curtin* [1952] 2 QB 552; *R(S) 14/52*, though cp *Hopes v Hopes* [1949] P 227, [1948] 2 All ER 920 and the child benefit decision *R(F) 3/81*.
376 *CS 3/48*. See also SI 1977/956, reg 2(3); p 255, below.
377 *R(P) 4/54; R(F) 1/62.*
378 SI 1977/956, reg 2(4).
379 See eg *CS 3/48; CS 6/48; R(S) 1/51*.
380 *UD 4053/28; UD 5131/29; R(S) 10/55; R(I) 37/55.*
381 *R(S) 14/58.*
382 *UD 6702/29; UD 15405/32.*

have concentrated more on the duration of the absence. In the early 1950s the Commissioner devised a rule of thumb that:

> a period of absence which has lasted for more than a year, and of which there is no reasonable prospect of its coming to an end, cannot ... be spoken of as 'temporary'.[383]

This was then combined with another rule of thumb that the 'reasonable prospect of its coming to an end' should be judged within a period of six months from the date of application.[384] The two tests were regularly applied[385] but they were not regarded as hard and fast rules, and might be ousted by special circumstances.[386] In 1962 a Tribunal of Commissioners reported on a tendency to take a 'much shorter term view of residence', and implied that it would be better to regard the matter as one of degree in each case, rather than argue it in terms of legal presumption.[387] More recently, it has been confirmed that the claimant's intention, the purpose of the absence and its duration (actual and prospective) are all relevant factors.[388]

ii   Hospital in-patients

The application of the 'residing with' criterion to cases where the claimant or the dependant is in hospital has been equally problematical. The NIAC reviewed the matter in 1955 and concluded that special provision should be made for spouses.[389] Under the current rule:

> two spouses shall not be treated as having ceased to reside together by reason only of the fact that either of them is, or they both are, undergoing medical or other treatment as an in-patient in a hospital or similar institution, whether such absence is temporary or not.[390]

Where the treatment of a dependant is free under the NHS, the need of the claimant to provide support is obviously reduced. For this reason, as has been seen earlier in this chapter, there are rules for adjusting the rates of the increases.[391] In that context, too, the meaning of 'medical or other treatment as an in-patient in a hospital or similar institution' was also considered.

iii   Widows

In relation to widow's benefit, the position of persons under 19 who may be engaged in full-time education or training away from home caused some difficulties in the past.[392] The regulations thus prescribe that:

---

383   *CP 84/50*, unreported, but cited in *R(P) 7/53*, para 8.
384   *R(P) 7/53*.
385   See eg *R(U) 15/54*; *R(S) 7/55*; *R(U) 14/58*.
386   See eg *R(S) 14/55*.
387   *R(U) 11/62*.
388   *R(P) 1/90*.
389   *Report on the Question of Dependency Provisions* (1955, Cmd 9855).
390   SI 1977/956, reg 2(2).
391   Pp 234–238, below.
392   Cf *Fox v Stirk and Bristol Electoral Registration Officer* [1970] 2 QB 463, [1970] 3 All ER 7 (on franchise qualifications).

in the case of a woman who has been widowed, she shall not be treated as having ceased to reside with a child or person under the age of 19 by reason of any absence the one from the other which is not likely to be permanent.[393]

No equivalent provision has been made for the new bereavement benefits.

D Maintenance by claimant

In some cases, beneficiaries may prove as an alternative to 'residence' that they are 'maintaining' the dependant. In others, they must prove both 'residence' and 'maintenance'. To establish the required degree of maintenance, the claimant must contribute to the cost of providing for the dependant at a weekly rate of not less than the amount of the increase claimed.[394]

i Mode and time of payments

The maintenance question is one of fact and not of legal liability. The mere existence of an obligation to maintain, even if the result of a court order, will not be sufficient to establish title to the increase.[395] The test of maintenance is to be determined according to the circumstances prevailing immediately before the event giving rise to the claim.[396] Claimants must therefore prove that they have actually been making the appropriate payments during the relevant period, though in the case of an increase for a child the condition is satisfied if an undertaking in writing is given to make such payment and the payment is made on receipt of the increase.[397] In no case does it have to be shown that the maintenance payments were actually received or consumed by the dependant.[398] The fact that the prescribed amount of maintenance is expressed in terms of weekly payments does not, of course, mean that the actual payments must be made weekly. They must be, however, regular payments and hence a payment of an occasional lump sum cannot be treated as regular maintenance and apportioned to weekly payments.[399] Interruptions in payments cannot be ignored,[400] so that if claimants fall in arrears, they may not count against current payments any payments made to clear arrears.[401] To hold otherwise would unduly benefit those who accumulated arrears.[402]

---

393   SI 1977/956, reg 2(3).
394   SSCBA 1992, s 81(3)(a); SI 1977/343, reg 11; SI 1994/2495, reg 12.
395   *R(U) 25/59; R(U) 1/77.*
396   *R(S) 7/89(T).*
397   SI 1977/343, reg 5(1). For the origins of this regulation, see NIAC Report (1966, Cmnd 2959). It cannot be invoked to support entitlement for a period longer than a week before the undertaking was made: *R(U) 3/78;* cf *R(U) 6/79,* where the undertaking confirmed one that had been made earlier.
398   Eg the money might be held by the clerk of a court: *CS 638/49;* presumably the same would apply now where payment of child support is made to the Child Support Agency.
399   *R(U) 14/62.*
400   Compare child benefit, p 666, below, where the rule is perhaps more generous.
401   *R(U) 11/62.*
402   *R(U) 25/58,* para 7. In *R(S) 3/74* R G Micklethwait, Chief Comr, refused to apply the 'allocation' regulation, (p 256, below) to assist in cases of regular but inadequate payments.

ii Payment in kind

It has long been recognised that maintenance need not necessarily take the form of a monetary payment. Account may be taken of the regular provision of food, clothing, fuel and other items necessary for sustenance and welfare.[403] So also if the claimant conveys to the dependant a beneficial interest in the matrimonial home.[404] The calculation of maintenance will then proceed on the basis of the rateable value, or interest on the capital value, of the property transferred.[405] In another case, the same principle was applied to the transfer of a business share: the interest obtained on the purchase-money of the share sold was deemed to be a regular contribution to maintenance.[406]

iii Joint maintenors

A regulation deals with the situation, presumably not of frequent occurrence, where a dependant is being maintained by two or more claimants. If the aggregate amount of such maintenance equals or exceeds the rate necessary for any one of them to claim the increase, such increase is payable notwithstanding that no one individual is able to satisfy the criterion.[407] The recipient will be the person who makes the largest contributions, or, if there is no such person, then either the eldest member of the group or one designated by the majority in a written notice sent to the Secretary of State.[408]

iv Allocation principle

Sometimes maintenance payments are explicitly allocated as between spouse (or ex-spouse) and children; sometimes they are not. It would be invidious if the exact classification of the payments were to be decisive in determining whether one or other dependant would qualify for the increase. So long as a marriage is subsisting,[409] the system assumes a principle of non-discrimination between a claimant's spouse and the children. Where a payment is made to a spouse or children or both, the authorities are given discretion to apportion the maintenance in such a way as will entitle the claimant to the largest payment by way of increase.[410] A typical exercise of this power would be as follows:

Mr C, in receipt of incapacity benefit, is paying by way of maintenance every week £40.00 for his wife and £10.00 for each of two children. If the apparent apportionment were to be binding, Mr C could claim no increase since the currently prescribed amount of maintenance is for an adult dependant £42.45, and for a child £11.35.[411] By notionally apportioning the

---

403 *CI 111/50*; *R(I) 10/51*.
404 *R(U) 3/66*, though J S Watson, Dep Comr, reserved his opinion on whether the position would have been the same if the dependant had sold or let the property in question. In *R(S) 6/52* it was held that such a sale would not affect the claimant's rights.
405 *R(U) 3/66*.
406 *R(I) 37/54*.
407 SI 1977/343, reg 2(2) and SI 1994/2945, reg 2(2).
408 SI 1977/343, reg 2(2)(b) and SI 1994/2945, reg 2(2)(b).
409 Cf *R(S) 9/61*.
410 SI 1977/343, reg 3 and SI 1994/2945, reg 3.
411 SSCBA 1992, Sch 4, Pt IV. These figures are subject to mandatory annual review and up-rating: SSAA 1992, s 150(1)–(3).

aggregate of £60.00 into £43.00 for the wife, £12.00 for the first child and £5.00 for the second child, the authorities will be able to confer on Mr C title to an increase for the wife and for the first child.

v Family fund [412]

The technique used for calculating individual dependency in the typical situation where money from various sources is used to support a number of individuals is a judicial creation and owes nothing to legislative prescription. It was originally conceived by judges deciding dependency issues under the Workmen's Compensation Acts,[413] and subsequently adopted by the Umpire adjudicating unemployment insurance claims.[414] There being nothing in the post-war legislation to discourage its continued application, it has been accepted by Commissioners as part of modern social security law.[415]

The fundamental principle is that the authorities should have regard to the normal phenomena of family support rather than to strict legal obligations to maintain.[416] Thus if a woman is in fact supported by her brother, a cousin or a son, it is irrelevant that she is in law wholly dependent on her husband. The technique proceeds by calculating the 'unit cost' of each family member. For this, the total family income[417] is divided by the number of individuals (counting two children under 14 as one adult).

In a family group of three adults (H, the husband, W, his wife and B, his brother) and two children (K and L) there will be four units. If the total family income is £240.00 (H contributing £140.00, W £20.00 and B £80.00) per week, the unit cost of one adult is £240 ÷ 4 = £60.00 and of one child £30.00.

Each individual then has a surplus or deficit of contribution over cost.

H has a surplus of £80.00, B a surplus of £20.00, W a deficit of £40.00, and K and L each a deficit of £30.00.

To assess the degree of dependency of an individual with a deficit on an individual with a surplus, one divides the amount of the deficit proportionally between those providing a surplus.

H is providing 4/5 of the total surplus and B 1/5. Thus the extent of W's dependency on H is 4/5 x 40 = £32.00, and the extent of K's (or L's) dependency on H is 4/5 x 30 = £24.00.

The calculation is to be applied to the family circumstances existing at the time immediately prior to the event (eg incapacity or retirement) for which the benefit is

---

412 See generally, Kahn-Freund (1953) 16 MLR 148, 164–173.
413 See esp *Main Colliery Co v Davies* [1900] AC 358; and *Hodgson v West Stanley Colliery* [1910] AC 229.
414 See esp *UD 1838/31*.
415 *CSI 59/49*, affirmed in *R(I) 1/57(T)* and *R(I) 20/60(T)*. For a valuable exposition of the principles, see *R(S) 12/83*. For a detailed treatment, see *DMG* n 99, above, vol 3 para 16550ff, esp paras 16604–16607.
416 See particularly the speech of Lord Loreburn LC in *Hodgson v West Stanley Colliery* [1910] AC 229 at 232.
417 Typically, earnings after deductions for tax and social security, plus any social security benefits and/or maintenance payments: *R(S) 12/83*, para 10(a).

payable: subsequent changes in the composition of the group or financial contributions are to be ignored,[418] and the average or normal contributions of individuals are to be assessed as at that date.[419]

If the method is one of simple arithmetic, it nevertheless raises some delicate issues when applied to actual family situations. It is sometimes argued that the method does not accord with the reality of how a particular family organises its household budget. The answer to this is that it is a convenient and less expensive method of calculating typical expenditure. Complete accuracy is neither obtainable nor (presumably) desirable. The method should be departed from only in wholly exceptional cases where there is clear evidence that it substantially conflicts with the actual circumstances, or where the relevant facts cannot be determined.[420] It may be that an individual member consumes more or less than the attributed 'unit cost', eg because of age or disability, but it has always been held that no account is to be taken of the actual way in which money is spent.[421] Forms of income other than earnings, eg social security benefits, raise greater difficulties: (1) are they to be regarded as contributions by one or more family members, or are they provided by an 'outsider'?; (2) should they be regarded as part of the aggregate household resources, or rather earmarked for a particular person, or persons? As regards (1), a contributory benefit is regarded as a resource provided by the person on whose contributions the benefit is payable.[422] Similarly, supplementary benefit (and so now income support or income-based jobseeker's allowance) has been seen as a contribution by the claimant. However, non-contributory benefits are normally treated as income from an 'outsider'.[423] The possibility of earmarking some income, for the purposes of (2), and thus excluding it from the calculations, has been admitted by some authorities (eg where there are maintenance payments for children[424] or an attendance allowance has been used to pay a non-family carer[425]), but some have regarded this as an unnecessary complication.[426] In any event, child benefit and the income-related benefits are normally integrated into the household fund.[427]

E Trade disputes

As part of its general programme to limit the social security entitlement of strikers and their families,[428] the government in 1986 introduced a provision to disentitle a claimant from receiving an increase for any dependant who has been disqualified from what is now contribution-based jobseeker's allowance under section 14 of the Jobseekers Act 1995,[429] or would have been so disqualified if he or she had claimed that benefit.[430]

418   *CS 52/50.*
419   *R(I) 10/51; R(S) 12/83.*
420   *R(I) 46/52; R(U) 37/52; R(I) 20/60; R(S) 12/83.*
421   *CS 52/50; R(I) 1/57; R(I)20/60.*
422   *CP 96/50; R(S) 12/83.*
423   *R(S) 2/85; R(S) 12/83*, though J G Monroe, Comr, left open the question whether child benefit might not be treated as a contribution by the person entitled to it: *R(S) 12/83*, para 14.
424   *CU 544/50.*
425   *R(I) 1/57(T)*, para 19, obiter.
426   *UD 12616/31; R(S) 12/83.*
427   *R(I) 8/65; R(S) 12/83.*
428   Cf pp 332–334 and pp 379–381, below.
429   See pp 505–514, below.
430   SSCBA 1992, s 91 (formerly SSA 1975, s 49A, inserted by SSA 1986, s 44); see *R(S) 6/94.*

Part 10   Overlapping benefits

A   General

Any broadly based system of social welfare encounters the problem arising from the availability of two or more benefits to cover the same, or an essentially similar, risk. The problem has two dimensions. The first is concerned with overlaps in the social security system itself; an obvious example is contribution-based jobseeker's allowance and carer's allowance, both of which are earnings replacement benefits. The general principle to be applied has never been in doubt: 'double provision should not be made for the same contingency.'[431] The principle may be stated easily but its implementation is more difficult as it begs the question of which benefits are intended to cover the same contingency: eg does a war pension deal with the same risk as incapacity benefit? Moreover, even where it is conceded that two benefits are concerned with the same risk, the intention may be to allow the claimant to accumulate them: one obvious example is child benefit and increases to a personal benefit for dependent children. Finally, there is the problem of deciding what are the limits of the social welfare system for the purpose of applying the principle: are local authority benefits included? Most of these questions receive a solution, explicit or implicit, within the social security legislation itself. An account of these rules forms the subject matter of sections B and C, below. The second dimension poses even greater difficulties. In many cases there is an overlap between public welfare benefits and private provision, eg occupational schemes. There is no consistent policy on this issue, partly because there has never been an overall view of the relationship between the public and private sector, partly because the policy issues themselves are so difficult.[432] They include deciding whether benefits are payable 'as of right' as under a private insurance contract, or are payable rather 'according to need'. In section D a brief summary will be given of the various measures taken, most of them discussed in detail in other parts of the book.

B   Recipients of benefits payable under SSCBA 1992

i   Income-maintenance benefits

The principle that double payments should not be made for the same contingency finds its first and most obvious application with regard to benefit intended as basic income maintenance. Thus adjustment is made to those in receipt of two or more of the following non-industrial, personal benefits:[433] contribution-based jobseekers' allowance, incapacity benefit, retirement pension, maternity, bereavement, widowed parent's, carer's and severe disablement allowance. Entitlement to benefits not intended for income maintenance (attendance and disability living allowance) is not affected, nor, of course, is entitlement to any earnings-related additional component in pensions, or the graduated retirement benefit.[434] The latter are treated as part of the principal benefit which they supplement.[435]

---

431   NIAC *Report on Draft Overlapping Regulations* (1948–49, HC 36) para 9. The principle had been stated both by the *Beveridge Report* n 316, above, para 321 and in *Social Insurance* (1944, Cmd 6550), Pt I, para 147.
432   For an invaluable discussion, see Lewis *Deducting Benefits from Damages for Personal Injury* (1999) chs 1–5.
433   SI 1979/597, reg 4(1).
434   SI 1979/597, reg 4(2).
435   SI 1979/597, reg 4(4).

Any adjustment is made according to the following rules.[436]
(1) A non-contributory benefit is deducted from a contributory benefit.
(2) Unless an alternative arrangement has been made, a proportionate part of a benefit paid weekly is deducted from one paid on a daily basis.
(3) In all other cases, the claimant receives the higher or highest of the benefits to which he or she is entitled.
There are analogous rules for adjustment where entitlement to a personal income maintenance benefit under SSCBA 1992 overlaps with entitlement to a similar benefit under other publicly-financed schemes, notably a training allowance[437] or an unemployability supplement payable under the war pensions scheme.[438] However, entitlement to the basic pensions awarded for disablement under the war pension and industrial injury schemes is not affected since these are available irrespective of working capacity and are intended more as 'compensation' for the injury itself.[439] The adjustment rules do not apply to the receipt of statutory sick pay or statutory maternity pay for the simple reason that statute precludes any overlap of entitlement with the corresponding national insurance benefits (incapacity benefit and maternity allowance).[440]

ii Benefits for special needs

The case for adjusting benefits intended to remedy specific needs arises only as regards overlap between the different schemes for disability. Thus the attendance allowance, the care component of disability living allowance and the age allowance in incapacity benefit may not be accumulated with their equivalents in other schemes.[441]

iii Dependency benefits

Dependency benefits payable under the general social security provisions, the industrial injury and war pension schemes and government training allowance schemes for the same dependant for the same period may not be accumulated.[442] There are two exceptions to this: both a war pension allowance for a child's education and a dependency benefit which is part of a war disablement pension (not being payable as an increase to unemployability supplement) are disregarded.[443] The former may be rationalised on the ground that it covers a special need, and the latter in that it is really part of the 'compensation' for the injury.

436 SI 1979/597, reg 4(5).
437 Grants for full-time education and teacher training, and training bonuses paid under the Employment and Training Act 1973 are not, however, treated as 'training allowances' for this purpose: SI 1979/597, reg 2(1); and see *R(U) 38/56* and *R 1/68(P)*.
438 SI 1979/597, reg 6 and Sch 1.
439 Cf pp 750 and 781, below. This does not apply to a war widow's pension which cannot be accumulated with a corresponding benefit under the general scheme: SI 1979/597, reg 6 and Sch 1.
440 SSCBA 1992, Sch 12, para 1 and Sch 13, para 1.
441 SI 1979/597, Sch 1, paras 5 and 6.
442 SI 1979/597, regs 7, 9 and 10. The Court of Appeal has held that reg 10 is not in breach of Council Directive (EEC) 79/7: *Jones v Chief Adjudication Officer* [1990] IRLR 533.
443 SI 1979/597, reg 7(3).

iv Child benefit

The traditional view has been that child benefit, which is payable to all families as a general redistributive device, is distinguishable from child dependency increases which are primarily intended to cope with the additional financial problems arising when the main source of income is lost. The legal position remains that in general they may be aggregated but this principle has been undermined by government policy in recent years: the increase payable with long-term benefits has diminished in value and that payable with short-term benefits abolished altogether.[444] In addition, there is a rule that dependency increases may not be aggregated with the increases to child benefit paid for the first or only child.[445]

v Income-related benefits

The income-related benefits are designed to raise the income of an individual or family to specified levels. In the light of this aim, the general principle is that all other social security benefits are treated as 'income' and thus, effectively, deducted from the amount otherwise payable.[446] There are, nevertheless, some exceptions: in particular, child benefit may be accumulated with working families' tax credit. Furthermore, any amounts received by way of attendance allowance or disability living allowance (or their equivalents under other schemes) are disregarded in computing entitlement both for the tax credits and the other income-related benefit schemes.[447]

C Recipients of NHS facilities

To the extent that a social security claimant is being maintained free of charge at a hospital or other institution his or her need for financial support is reduced, and if the maintenance is financed from public funds, there is a strong argument for reducing the amount of benefit. There are special rules governing this subject which have been fully discussed in Part 5, above, of this chapter.

D Social security benefits and private rights

In many situations, a person subject to a hazard covered by the contributory or non-contributory schemes will be entitled to benefit from another source directed towards the same hazard but arising by way of private law, eg through an occupational scheme. Indeed, in the Beveridge scheme such arrangements were to form an important part of the general welfare system: while the state was to provide the minimum security for each kind of hazard, 'it should leave room and encouragement for voluntary action by each individual to provide more than that minimum for himself and his family'.[448] The

---

444   P 247, above.
445   SSAA 1992, s 154 and SI 1979/597, reg 8.
446   There is a special rule to cover the contingency where income support is not so reduced (often because it is paid earlier than the other social security benefit): the authority administering the other social security benefit is given power to deduct the amount of overpayment of income support (SSAA 1992, s 74).
447   P 453, below.
448   *Beveridge Report* n 316, above, para 9.

argument logically leads to a principle that those prudent enough to avail themselves of facilities elsewhere should be entitled to reap the reward of their prescience and aggregate the public with the private benefit. Increasingly, however, the very existence of private sector provision (typically through occupational pensions) has been used by government as an argument for reducing or withdrawing entitlement to social security benefits. For example, Conservative government ministers deployed this argument in the debates on the abolition of invalidity benefit and the introduction of the more 'focused' incapacity benefit.[449] Their Labour successors in office used the same argument in respect of the changes to incapacity benefit under the Welfare Reform and Pensions Act 1999.[450]

In the light of these considerations, we may briefly survey the position reached in the most important areas of overlap between public and private provision. Because no general principle exists, different rules prevail in different areas, and these have generally been described in the sections of the book devoted to the specific benefits in question. The purpose here is to provide, by way of summary, an outline of the various approaches adopted.[451]

i Private insurance

Life insurance is very common; accident or sickness insurance is comparatively rare and, for practical purposes, private insurance against unemployment (as opposed to redundancy schemes) is virtually non-existent.[452] Where private insurance does exist, it fits neatly into Beveridge's prototype and it has never been doubted that the income so obtained might be fully accumulated with the non-means tested benefits.

ii Redundancy payments and compensation for wrongful or unfair dismissal

The state redundancy payments scheme is intended to provide compensation for the loss of a job, the employee having been deprived of his or her proprietary interest in the employment; the social security benefit is intended as a partial replacement of income lost as the result of the redundancy. Entitlement to one benefit is not affected by receipt of another. Other categories of redundancy payments are similarly treated to the extent that they are regarded as compensation for the loss of a job; but if intended as a substitute for the wages which would otherwise be paid, their receipt disentitles the claimant from jobseeker's allowance.[453]

On general common law principles, income support or jobseeker's allowance are deductible from an award of damages for wrongful dismissal.[454] The same principle in effect applies to awards of compensation for unfair dismissal[455] but in this case the employee receives the net award and the amount of income support or jobseeker's allowance is recouped from the liable employer.[456]

---

449   P 524, below.
450   P 525, below.
451   See further *Lewis* n 432, above.
452   See SSAC *State Benefits and Private Provision* The Review of Social Security, Paper 2 (1994).
453   P 450, above.
454   *Parsons v BNM Laboratories* [1964] 1 QB 95, [1963] 2 All ER 658.
455   But not to settlements of unfair dismissal claims.
456   SI 1996/2349.

iii Guarantee payments

In some circumstances employers will agree, or be bound, to maintain a certain degree of remuneration for periods when an employee is laid-off or put on short-time. The guarantee payments are treated as earnings for the purposes of contributory, non-contributory and means-tested benefits.[457]

iv Sick pay and maternity pay

Short-term income maintenance for those incapable of work through sickness or maternity is now provided primarily by an employer under the statutory sick pay and statutory maternity pay schemes.[458] Since, where payable, these replace entitlement to short-term incapacity benefit and maternity allowance, respectively, no overlap arises. However, the employer may be contractually bound to make payments which exceed in length or amount those prescribed under the statutory schemes. Such additional payments will not affect any social security entitlement (other than that to an income-related benefit) and the question whether the employee should account to the employer for the value of a social security benefit (eg long-term incapacity benefit) is a matter which is left to the contract of employment.[459]

v Occupational and personal pension schemes

The relationship between state and occupational or personal pensions is complex and is discussed in chapter 17, below. Broadly speaking, all claimants who satisfy the relevant conditions are entitled to the basic state pension to which may be added *either* a state earnings-related pension (and/or a state second pension) *or* an equivalent under an approved occupational or personal scheme.[460] Apart from this, private pension payments may, in general, be accumulated with social security benefits. There are, however, three important exceptions. First, and most obviously, such payments are treated as 'income' for the purpose of the income-related benefits and are thus, in effect, deducted from the amounts otherwise payable. Secondly, and more controversially, since 1980 there has been a pound for pound reduction of contribution-based jobseeker's allowance (formerly unemployment benefit) in respect of proceeds of an occupational pension in excess of a prescribed sum. As will be seen,[461] this was to deal with an alleged anomaly whereby those in receipt of such a pension had claimed unemployment benefit without any real expectation that suitable work would be available for them. Thirdly, and even more controversially, the same principle was extended to incapacity benefit (with modifications) as a result of changes made by the Welfare Reform and Pensions Act 1999.[462]

---

457 SI 1987/1967, reg 35(1)(e); SI 1996/207, reg 98(1)(d); and SI 1996/2745, reg 9(1)(e). See also *R(IS) 9/95.*
458 Pp 527–531 and 560–564, below.
459 See also Employment Rights Act 1996, ss 86–88.
460 Though, for inflation-proofing purposes, some entitlement to SERPS remains: p 631, below.
461 P 516, below.
462 P 538, below.

vi   Tort damages

The overlap between tort claims for personal injury or death and social security provision has been an area of great difficulty and much discussion.[463] Beveridge had assumed that some adjustment was necessary.[464] The Monckton Committee, examining the question in 1946, agreed but sensibly concluded that it would be wrong to disturb full entitlement to the social security benefit.[465] The latter was payable almost immediately and was not subject to problems of proof of fault, or quantum of damages. It recommended instead that the damages award should take account of the benefit paid or payable,[466] a proposal which in its entirety proved to be politically unacceptable, and resulted in an unsatisfactory compromise: a deduction of one-half of any sums paid or payable within five years from the time when the cause of action accrued for sickness or invalidity,[467] industrial disablement benefit and severe disablement allowance.[468] No deduction is made from a damages award under the Fatal Accidents Act 1976 for any social security benefit.[469] The legislation was silent on the effect of other social security benefits on personal injury claims, and it was left to judges to apply general common law principles, with the trend being towards full deduction for benefits.[470]

The Pearson Royal Commission on Civil Liability and Compensation for Personal Injuries made proposals for substantial reform of these matters; they argued that the full value of social security benefits payable to an injured person or the dependants of a deceased person should be deducted.[471] A scheme for recoupment of benefits from awards in tort was finally introduced by the Social Security Act 1989 (SSA 1989) amid much controversy.[472] The fundamental premise of the recoupment scheme – that claimants are compensated twice over by the receipt of both damages and benefits – seems highly questionable in the light of research into the levels of damages awarded in personal injuries actions.[473] The original recoupment scheme applied to all court awards and settlements from September 1990 where the claimant suffered an accident or injury on or after 1 January 1989 or first claimed benefit in respect of a disease on or after that earlier date.[474] The Secretary of State was empowered to recover from tortfeasors and others making compensation payments in relation to personal injury actions a sum representing specified benefits paid during a period of five years, or the period until the making of the compensation payment (if shorter).[475] The recoupment scheme did not apply to small payments (defined as those for £2,500 or less), resulting in a significant bunching of settlements at or below this threshold.[476] The original scheme

---

463   See esp Report of the Royal Commission on Civil Liability and Compensation for Personal Injury (the Pearson Report) (1978, Cmnd 7054-I) ch 13; Cane *Atiyah's Accidents, Compensation and the Law* (6th edn, 1999) ch 15; Lewis *Deducting Benefits from Damages for Personal Injury* (1999) ch 12.

464   *Beveridge Report* n 316, above, para 260.

465   Final Report of Departmental Committee on Alternative Remedies (1946, Cmd 6860) paras 41–43.

466   *Departmental Committee on Alternative Remedies* n 465, above, paras 48, 92, 96, 98.

467   Now known as incapacity benefit.

468   Law Reform (Personal Injuries) Act 1948, s 2(1), as amended.

469   Fatal Accidents Act 1976, s 4(1).

470   *Hodgson v Trapp* [1989] AC 807, [1988] 3 All ER 870.

471   *Pearson Report* n 463, above, paras 467–498.

472   SSA 1989, s 22 and Sch 4. See Wikeley (1991) 10 CJQ 10 and *Compensation for Industrial Disease* (1993) pp 66–71.

473   See Harris et al *Compensation and Support for Illness and Injury* (1984); and Law Commission *Personal Injury Compensation: How Much is Enough?* Report No 225 (1994).

474   SSAA 1992, s 81(7) (now repealed).

475   SSAA 1992, s 82 (now repealed).

476   *Lewis* n 432, above, p 123. Small payments were still (in principle) subject to offsetting under the Law Reform (Personal Injuries) Act 1948, s 2, as amended by SSA 1989, s 22 and Sch 4.

attracted considerable criticism because all components of damages awards were subject to recoupment, including compensation for non-pecuniary losses which were not paid for the same purposes as social security benefits.[477] This sometimes had the effect of leaving the claimant with no damages at all.

A revised scheme was launched with effect from October 1997 by the Social Security (Recovery of Benefits) Act 1997 (SS(RB)A 1997). This legislation largely re-enacted the existing framework for recoupment but introduced two particularly important reforms. First, damages may only be reduced if benefits equivalent to particular heads of damage have been paid. A Schedule to the Act sets out the various benefits that are treated as equivalent to compensation for the three heads of loss of earnings, the cost of care and loss of mobility respectively during the relevant period.[478] Several benefits do not appear in the Schedule and therefore are not liable to recovery under any circumstances.[479] Secondly, no benefits are identified as being associated with non-pecuniary losses. Consequently damages for pain, suffering and loss of amenity are effectively ringfenced.[480] The small payment exemption has been abolished, so potentially benefit payments can be recovered from any level of damages awarded.[481]

Part 11   Up-rating of benefits

A   General

The problem of maintaining the value of benefits in relation to rising prices and wages and the various solutions available were considered in chapter 1, above.[482] It remains here to describe the methods currently adopted under the social security legislation. Prior to 1973 there were no legislative obligations to ensure that benefits kept pace with inflation, and the real value of some, notably family allowances, declined considerably. The sharp increase in the rates of inflation in the early 1970s and the desire to confer on contributors the security that benefits would retain their value prompted the Conservative government in 1973 to introduce for the most important contributory benefits a mechanism for annual 'up-rating'[483] – a word which one judge has described as 'a recruit to the English language which does not notably enrich it'.[484] As a result of a later amendment, the annual review of long-term benefits was to take account of rises in prices or earnings whichever would be more advantageous to claimants.[485]

In retrospect, 1975 may be regarded as the year in which the legal obligations to maintain the value of social security benefits were at their most powerful. In the subsequent period there has been an almost continual tendency to impair their efficacy, a consequence predominantly of the aim of successive Conservative governments in

---

477   HC Social Security Committee *Fourth Report* (1994–95, HC 196).
478   SS(RB)A 1997, Sch 2.
479   Eg child benefit, housing benefit and retirement pensions.
480   *Lewis* n 432, above, p 136.
481   SS(RB)A 1997, Sch 1, paras 1 and 9 contains a power to reintroduce the lower limit, but this has not been exercised: *Lewis* n 432, above, p 162.
482   P 24, above.
483   SSA 1973, ss 7–8.
484   Per Megarry VC, *Metzger v Department of Health and Social Security* [1977] 3 All ER 444 at 445.
485   NIA 1974, s 5; SSBA 1975, ss 3–4.

the 1980s and 1990s to reduce public expenditure.[486] The relevant measures included an up-rating of short-term benefits for 1980–81 at 5 per cent *less* than the increase in prices[487] and the release from the obligation to maintain the value of the earnings limits placed on the dependants of beneficiaries. The most important measure was the 1980 decision to link the up-rating of benefits to increases in prices (rather than prices *or* earnings, whichever was more favourable to claimants). This has resulted in a substantial erosion in the value of the basic retirement pension. Whilst in Opposition the Labour party had been committed to restoring the link between the state pension and increases in earnings, but following the 1997 election the new government adopted other strategies in an attempt to tackle poverty amongst pensioners. The restoration of the link with earnings remains a highly emotive issue in Labour party ranks.[488]

To analyse the current principles, it is necessary to distinguish between the Secretary of State's duty to review the value of benefits, a consequential duty to up-rate certain benefits in the light of that review, and a power to up-rate others.

B   Duty to review value of benefits

The Secretary of State is under a legislative duty to review annually almost all benefits, but not the income-related benefits, to determine whether 'they have retained their value in relation to the general level of prices obtaining in Great Britain estimated in such manner as the Secretary of State thinks fit'.[489]

C   Duty to up-rate certain benefits

Where, as a result of the review, the Secretary of State finds that there has been an increase in the general level of prices, a draft order up-rating the amounts payable for certain benefits by the same percentage increase must be laid before Parliament.[490] It follows that the value of these benefits must keep pace with price inflation only on an historical basis; the Secretary of State is not required to predict the future rate of inflation, something which understandably created great difficulties under previous legislation.[491] The benefits protected by these provisions are, broadly speaking, all contributory and non-contributory benefits payable under SSCBA 1992 (as well as statutory sick pay and statutory maternity pay) except the age addition.[492] It will be noted that, significantly, the duty to up-rate does not apply to child benefit or to the income-related benefits. In

---

486   See generally Lynes *Maintaining the Value of Benefits* (1985).
487   However, the cut was later restored when the relevant benefits became taxable.
488   See Child Support, Pensions and Social Security Act 2000, s 36, an amendment pressed upon the government by Lady Castle, requiring a report to be laid on the effect on the National Insurance Fund of restoring the link. See further Government Actuary *Report on the cost of uprating the basic retirement pension* (2000, Cm 4920).
489   SSAA 1992, s 150(1). The further provision in respect of child benefit, requiring account to be taken of 'increases in the Retail Price Index and other relevant external factors' (s 153, formerly SSA 1988, s 5), has never been brought into force: see Wikeley [1989] JSWL 285–287.
490   SSAA 1992, s 150(2)(a). The duty does not apply where the amount of the increase would be 'inconsiderable': s 150(4). The draft order must be accompanied by a report of the Government Actuary on the likely impact of the increases on the National Insurance Fund: s 150(8). Errors can be rectified later: s 152.
491   See the 2nd edition of this book, p 412; and *Lynes* n 486, above, pp 17–19.
492   SSAA 1992, s 150(2)–(3). The earnings rule for carer's allowance (p 711, below) is now linked to the lower earnings limit, which has the effect of introducing mandatory up-rating.

addition, the duty as applied to certain payments made for children, for example a dependency increase or guardian's allowance, is in effect weakened by the power conferred on the Secretary of State to reduce those payments in the light of the rate of child benefit currently payable.[493]

D Power to up-rate other benefits

The Secretary of State has a broad discretion as regards benefits subject to the duty of review but not to the duty to up-rate (notably child benefit). If 'he considers it appropriate, having regard to the national economic situation and any other matters which he considers relevant' he may increase the relevant payments 'by such percentages or percentages as he thinks fit'.[494] Finally, there is a power, the exercise of which is not constrained in any way, to include in the draft of any up-rating order provision for increases to the income-related benefits.[495]

Part 12   Christmas bonus

A   General

The origin of this curious, and far from commendable, feature of British social security is to be located in the political and economic circumstances of 1972. The Conservative government was, at the time, planning a major offensive against inflation, mainly through centralised controls on wages and prices. It was acknowledged that certain groups within the community, notably pensioners, were particularly in need of protection against rising prices. The government decided to make a single lump-sum payment of £10 at Christmas time to long-term social security claimants,[496] while considering the possibility of introducing statutory obligations for up-rating benefits, as an 'earnest of their good intentions'.[497] Apart from one minor hitch – under the original Act it was not paid to those deprived of a pension by the earnings rule and a new Act had to be swiftly passed to remedy this defect[498] – the measure proved to be politically popular. It was therefore repeated in 1973 and 1974. The Labour government was not initially enthusiastic, preferring to concentrate attention on the major reforms of 1975 but the practice was renewed in 1977 and 1978. The Conservative Party Manifesto for the general election of 1979 included a commitment that the Christmas bonus would continue. Consequently the Pensioners' Payments and Social Security Act 1979 established the payment as a permanent feature of the social security system. In social policy terms, it serves little obvious purpose except that of courting political popularity, but its importance is no doubt sufficient to justify a short description of the principles governing payment, as re-enacted in SSCBA 1992.

---

493   SSAA 1992, ss 150(6) and 154.
494   SSAA 1992, s 150(2)(b).
495   SSAA 1992, s 150(7).
496   Pensioners and Family Income Supplement Payments Act 1972.
497   Sir K Joseph MP, Secretary of State, 846 HC Official Report (5th series) col 971.
498   Pensioners' Payments and National Insurance Contributions Act 1972.

B   Persons entitled

To receive payment, an individual must be entitled (or treated as entitled) to one of the following benefits for a period which includes a day in a prescribed week in December:[499]
- retirement pension;
- incapacity benefit;
- bereavement, widowed parent's, severe disablement, attendance, disability living or carer's allowance;
- war pension; or
- income support (if over pensionable age).

Claimants are treated as being so entitled if the non-receipt is the result of some other payment from public funds or from an employer, or the operation of the earnings rule; so also if their earnings or those of any spouse render them ineligible for income support.[500]

C   Residence

The claimant must be present or ordinarily resident in the UK or any other EU member state at any time during the prescribed week.[501]

D   Amount

The amount payable (£10) has remained the same since 1972, although the Secretary of State has the power to increase this by an appropriate order.[502] Claimants may receive a second payment for their spouses if they are both over pensionable age and they are entitled (or treated as entitled) to an increase to the qualifying benefit for that person.[503] The same applies in relation to an unmarried couple, living together as husband and wife, one of whom is entitled to income support. These payments are tax free, and are disregarded for the purposes of any income-related benefit.[504]

E   Adjudication

Questions of entitlement are determined by the Secretary of State, from whose decision no appeal lies.[505] This would hardly seem consistent with the Human Rights Act 1998, but given the fact that entitlement is contingent upon the receipt of other named benefits it is difficult to see that this bonus is likely to give rise to many disputes.

---

499   SSCBA 1992, ss 148(1) and 150(1). The prescribed list also includes unemployability supplement and industrial death benefit (both only payable for old cases).
500   SSCBA 1992, s 149(2)–(3).
501   SSCBA 1992, s 148(1)(a).
502   SSCBA 1992, s 148(3)(b).
503   SSCBA 1992, s 148(2).
504   SSCBA 1992, s 149(6).
505   SSA 1998, s 33 and Sch 2, para 2.

Chapter 8

Income support

Part 1　Introduction

A　General

i　The role of income support

Most social security systems provide some form of public assistance for people in need who are not, for one reason or another, able to maintain themselves from other resources. In Great Britain there are now two means-tested (or, as they are now referred to legislatively, 'income-related') benefits which are designed to guarantee a sufficient income to meet regular needs, other than housing. The first is income support, which was introduced by the Social Security Act 1986 (SSA 1986) and came into force in April 1988, replacing supplementary benefit which itself had succeeded national assistance as the principal means-tested benefit. Income support is paid to individuals or families in prescribed categories without an income from full-time employment.[1] The other is income-based jobseeker's allowance, introduced in October 1996, which replaced income support for unemployed people; the rules governing the two benefits are, in nearly all respects, identical, with the fundamental difference that claimants of income-based jobseeker's allowance must fulfil the labour market conditions.[2] Until October 1999 there were also two 'in work' means-tested benefits: family credit and disability working allowance. These have now transmuted into tax credits.[3]

On the assumption that the coverage and level of National Insurance benefits would be adequate, Beveridge had envisaged only a residual role for national assistance.[4] However, his expectations were to be disappointed: the level of insurance benefits never exceeded the minimum income guaranteed by the means-tested benefits and so the latter became in practice the primary instrument of welfare for the large numbers of individuals and families who had no other resources. Indeed, there has been a steady growth in the number of recipients. At the end of 1979, supplementary benefit was paid to nearly three million claimants, compared with approximately one million in receipt

---

1 Claimants in part-time work (less than 16 hours a week) may be entitled to income support: p 285, below.
2 Pp 340–353, below.
3 See ch 10.
4 Beveridge Report *Social Insurance and Allied Services* (1942, Cmd 6404) para 369.

of national assistance in 1948.[5] By May 2001, 3.9 million people were receiving income support, a figure that does not include members of the claimant's family also dependent on the benefit.[6] A further 701,000 claimants (and their dependants) were reliant on income-based jobseeker's allowance.[7] Although these figures are highly sensitive to changes in the levels of unemployment and the rates of other benefits, it may safely be assumed that income support (and its companion income-based jobseeker's allowance) will continue to serve as the primary instrument for maintaining the incomes of the poorest sections of the community for the foreseeable future.

ii   Benefits and poverty

Definitions of 'poverty' and therefore also the principles for determining the levels of income maintenance have always given rise to debate and controversy.[8] It seems that in 1948 the assistance rates were fixed at a level just above the subsistence standard set by Beveridge for single adults and married couples, but a little below that for a family with children.[9] This standard was itself lower than that arrived at by Rowntree in his studies shortly before the Second World War.[10] Both calculations had proceeded on the assumption that it was possible to measure 'poverty' by reference to absolute standards: a certain amount of money is needed for food, housing and clothing, and then a margin may be added for other expenditure and to allow for inefficiency.[11] There is no reason why weekly payments of public assistance could not be calculated in this way. It is very likely that initially such assessments played some part in the determination of weekly benefit rates but, on this 'absolute standards' approach, it would be plausible to expect poverty to disappear over the years with continued economic growth, and that correspondingly the numbers of people relying on assistance would decline.[12] In fact, as has just been mentioned, the opposite has occurred.

It is now more common to measure poverty not by the absolute approach of a minimum standard of living, but as relative to the general or average quality of life in the country.[13] In his major study, Townsend defined the 'poverty line' as the point at which a person's or family's withdrawal from participation in social activities increases disproportionately in relation to declining resources.[14] On this approach those with an income below, say, 40 per cent of the average industrial wage may be characterised as poor, even though they may have adequate resources to feed and house themselves, and so would not fall beneath the poverty line on the more traditional 'subsistence' definition. The difficulty with the concept of 'relative poverty' is arguably that it confuses poverty with inequality.[15]

5   SBC Annual Report 1979 (1980, Cmnd 8033) paras 8.1–8.33.
6   Department for Work and Pensions (DWP) *Social Security Statistics 2001* (2001) p 124.
7   *Social Security Statistics 2001* n 6, above, p 77.
8   Parker (ed) *Low Cost but Acceptable* (1998); and Veit-Wilson *Setting Adequacy Standards* (1998).
9   Fiegehen, Lansley and Smith *Poverty and Progress in Britain 1953–1973* (1977) p 13; Townsend *Poverty in the United Kingdom* (1979) pp 242–243. See further Veit-Wilson (1992) 21 J Soc Pol 269.
10 Rowntree *Human Needs of Labour* (1937).
11 It is this further margin which identified people living in what Rowntree described as 'secondary poverty': 'primary poverty' refers to the situation where the people, however carefully they marshal their resources, cannot afford the necessities of life. See Harris *William Beveridge* (1997) p 382.
12 *Fiegehen et al* n 9, above, pp 13–14.
13 *Fiegehen et al* n 9, above, pp 14–15. See also pp 22–24, above.
14 *Townsend* n 9, above, pp 57, 248–262. This approach won the support of the Supplementary Benefits Commission: SBC *Annual Report 1978* (Cmnd 7725) paras 1.4 and 3.13; see also Donnison *The Politics of Poverty* (1982) pp 148–151.
15 Robson *Welfare State and Welfare Society* (1976) pp 142–143; but see *Townsend* n 9, above, p 57.

The policy of successive governments has traditionally been ambivalent with regard to the relative poverty criterion. A White Paper published in 1959 acknowledged that those in receipt of assistance should have a 'share in increasing national prosperity'[16] and for some time the scale rates of benefits rose more than increases in the Retail Prices Index and indeed improved relative to the average net earnings of manual workers.[17] The policy of the Conservative administrations from 1979 to 1997 was to prioritise economic growth as a precondition of social security spending. One consequence was that benefits were up-rated by reference to prices, rather than earnings. However, Labour governments since 1997 have adopted a very different approach, emphasising the need to reform the welfare state in order to tackle growing inequality and social exclusion.[18] Once in office, the Blair administration also made an ambitious commitment to eradicate child poverty within a generation.[19]

Income support rates may be said, therefore, to reflect an uncertain compromise between the absolute and relative concepts of poverty. The standards of eligibility for benefit are also sometimes used to measure the extent of poverty in British society.[20] It is obviously outside the scope of this book to pursue these questions in detail,[21] but some reservations to this test should be stated. First, if income support rates are increased relative to earnings and other income, so more people are defined as having a standard of living below the official 'poverty' line. This odd consequence – the more the government attempts to help the poor, the more 'poor' there are – is perhaps inevitable if this relative concept of poverty is adopted. Secondly, the number of recipients of benefit is an unreliable guide to the extent of poverty in so far as otherwise eligible people are disentitled to assistance by the legislation. Persons in full-time work, however low their earnings, may not claim income support or jobseeker's allowance, though if responsible for a family with at least one child, they may be entitled to working families' tax credit. Claimants of jobseeker's allowance may also be sanctioned because they are not genuinely looking for work or because of their participation in a trade dispute.[22] Finally, an important group, living below the official poverty line but not receiving benefit, are those who for one reason or another do not make a claim. It has been officially estimated that the take-up rate for income support in 1999–2000 was between 87 per cent and 94 per cent by expenditure and between 77 per cent and 87 per cent by caseload.[23] These global estimates disguise significant differentials in take-up rates amongst client groups: eg take-up by caseload is between 95 per cent and 100 per cent for lone parents but only 64 per cent to 78 per cent amongst pensioners. To sum up, 'definitions of poverty lines in terms of social security scales, or in terms of what the taxpayer is willing to pay, are statements about the maximum which those who have power over resources are willing to pay the poor, and both are flawed as statements about the nature of poverty as such'.[24]

16 *Improvements in National Assistance* (1959, Cmnd 782) para 3.
17 See eg SBC *Annual Report for 1976* (Cmnd 6910) paras 9.14–9.20; but see Veit-Wilson in Fawcett and Lowe (eds) *Welfare Policy in Britain* (1999) on an unpublished NAB study of the adequacy of benefit rates.
18 DSS *New ambitions for our country: A New Contract for Welfare* (1998, Cm 3805). See also DSS *Opportunity for All* (2000, Cm 4865) and *UK National Action Plan on Social Inclusion 2001–2003* (2001).
19 HM Treasury *Tackling Child Poverty* (2001). See further Sutherland and Piachaud (2001) 111 Econ J F85.
20 Atkinson *Poverty in Britain and the Reform of Social Security* (1969) and in Wedderburn (ed) *Poverty, Inequality and Class Structure* (1974) p 48. *Townsend* n 9, above, pp 241–247, is very critical of this approach.
21 See Barr and Coulter in Hills (ed) *The State of Welfare* (1990) and *Veit-Wilson* n 8, above.
22 Pp 348 and 379, below.
23 DWP *Income Related Benefits Estimates of Take Up in 1999/2000* (2001).
24 Veit-Wilson (1987) J Soc Pol 183 at 187.

B   History of public assistance

i   Early history of the poor law[25]

The first statutes encouraging parishes to assist the deserving poor (the old, sick and infirm) were passed in 1531 and 1536. The Acts, and subsequent legislation, were consolidated in the famous Poor Relief Act 1601. Under this, overseers were appointed in each parish under the general supervision of the Justices of the Peace to give relief to the deserving poor and to raise local taxes for this purpose. The able-bodied were to be given work. Section 6 imposed a duty on a person's father, grandfather, mother, grandmother and child to maintain him or her, an assertion of family responsibility which was not repealed until 1948. Although the parish might provide relief to those neglected by their relatives, it could recover this from the defaulters. Thus, two important features of the poor law regime were established from the outset: local administration, which led to inconsistent provision in different parts of the country,[26] and the emphasis on family responsibility.

Inevitably, there were many changes in the administration of the poor law in the two centuries before the major reform of 1834. The most important resulted from the Act of Settlement 1662, the object of which was to prevent paupers wandering from their home to impose themselves as charges on other parishes. People without property or other means of support could be removed to their parish 'of settlement', generally their place of birth. In effect paupers had to look to their own parish for relief, a restriction that naturally hindered freedom of movement.

The eighteenth century saw the first workhouses which the able-bodied were required to enter as a condition of securing relief.[27] But the experiment was halted towards the end of the century. The poverty of agricultural workers at this time led to the use of poor law relief to supplement wages in the famous 'Speenhamland system'.[28] This, in its turn, became one of the reasons for the disquiet responsible for the setting up of the Poor Law Commission in 1832. Many felt that relief for the employed merely subsidised low wages, an argument since deployed against family income supplement, family credit and now working families' tax credit.[29]

ii   Poor law reform: 1834-1930[30]

The Poor Law Commission found that provision for those able to work was corrupting for the recipients; in future, they were only to be given relief in the workhouses. Under the notorious principle of 'less eligibility', conditions there were to be less attractive than those of the poorest worker outside. Thus, the familiar distinction was drawn between the deserving poor, who might benefit from allowances paid outside the workhouse ('outdoor relief') and the less deserving, who in practice would be able to

---

25   De Schweinitz *England's Road to Social Security* (1949) ch 1; Bruce *The Coming of the Welfare State* (4th edn, 1968) ch 2; Checkland (ed) *The Poor Law Report of 1834* (1974) editors' introduction; Cranston *Legal Foundations of the Welfare State* (1985) ch 2; Quigley (1996) 30 Akron LR 73; Slack *From Reformation to Improvement* (1999).
26   See further King *Poverty and welfare in England 1700–1850* (2000).
27   *Bruce* n 25, above, pp 54–55.
28   Cf p 383, below.
29   P 386, below.
30   Rose *The English Poor Law 1780–1930* (1971); Rose *The Relief of Poverty 1834–1914* (1972); *Bruce* n 25, above, chs 4, 5; Englander *Poverty and Poor Law Reform in 19th Century Britain 1834–1914* (1998).

secure relief only in conditions of destitution. The objective of more efficient administration was achieved, first, by the merging for poor law purposes of parishes into unions, with elected Boards of Guardians, and, secondly, by the institution of a central Board of three Commissioners, responsible for the making of regulations and the national administration of the poor law.

Though well intentioned, the remedy was perhaps worse than the disease. The horrors of the workhouse, with their degrading treatment of the inmates and enforced separation of husband and wife, are well-known from the novels of Dickens.[31] The sick and the old were often, for reasons of economy, housed with the unemployed. Eventually a Royal Commission was appointed in 1905. All its members were agreed that the 1834 reforms had been misconceived, that the workhouses should be abolished and the administrative structure changed.[32] But it was divided in its proposals for specific solutions; partly because of this and partly because other events dominated political discussion, there was no immediate attempt at reform.

During the 1920s unemployment increased, exposing the weaknesses of the poor laws. With the workhouses quite unable to cope, many unions used their power to afford outdoor relief for the able-bodied in cases of 'urgent necessity'. But they were not all so generous, with the result that provision varied widely from area to area. Naturally those with the heaviest unemployment were the least able to afford the costs of relief. The inherent weakness of local administration and financing became widely recognised. But, even then, the solution of national administration was not immediately adopted. Instead, the functions of the poor law guardians and unions were transferred by the Local Government Act 1929 to the local authorities, to be discharged largely by their public assistance committees. In the following year, the last Poor Law Act, a consolidation measure, was passed.[33] A more significant event was the repeal of the regulation which had made entry into the workhouse a condition of relief to the able-bodied.[34]

iii   Unemployment assistance and the end of the poor law 1930-1948[35]

Governments in this period were troubled by the problems of the unemployed who were unable to claim contributory benefit.[36] In 1931 the national government introduced means-tested transitional allowances for people out of work for more than 26 weeks. These were funded nationally, but administered by the local authority public assistance committees. When it became clear that there was inconsistency in their administration of the allowances, the demand for a national scheme could no longer be resisted. The Unemployment Assistance Act 1934 instituted a Board to administer public assistance for the unemployed.[37]

Assistance was calculated by reference to the applicant's requirements, based on weekly scale rates, with a deduction for any resources. Extra lump sum payments could be made for exceptional needs and the regular weekly payments could be increased in special circumstances. An important feature of the scheme was the 'household means' test: the resources of all members of the applicant's household were taken into account

---

31   Most notably *Oliver Twist* (1838).
32   *Report of the Royal Commission on the Poor Law* (1909, Cd 4499).
33   The Act is exhaustively analysed in Jennings *The Poor Law Code* (2nd edn, 1936).
34   SR & O 1930/186, art 6.
35   Deacon and Bradshaw *Reserved for the Poor* (1983) chs 2–3.
36   Cf p 490, below.
37   Millett *The Unemployment Assistance Board* (1940).

before determining whether there was a need for assistance. During the Second World War, the functions of the Unemployment Assistance Board were extended to cover administration of the means-tested supplementary pensions payable to widows and the elderly under the Old Age and Widows' Pensions Act 1940.[38] A further significant development was the virtual abolition of the 'household means' test by the Determination of Needs Act 1941. In future, where the applicant was a householder, only the resources of any spouse and dependants were to be taken into account in assessing need.[39]

It was the Beveridge Report which heralded the final demise of the poor law. He pointed to the anomalies necessarily entailed by the co-existence of a number of tests for different groups, administered by different authorities.[40] The 'existing poor law' was repealed by the National Assistance Act 1948. The provision of public financial assistance became exclusively the function of central government, acting through the National Assistance Board (NAB), as it was now called. Many of the features of the poor law went: there was no law of settlement, so that it no longer mattered where the applicant resided; the requirement that able-bodied applicants be set to work was replaced by a discretionary requirement to register for employment; and relief by way of loan, a common provision under the poor law, was abolished as a normal form of assistance.[41]

iv   The reforms of 1966[42]

In 1948 it was thought right to keep the administration of means-tested assistance entirely separate from that of the insurance benefits; the NAB was, therefore, an independent government department.[43] However, it gradually became apparent that national assistance was playing a more important role than had been envisaged and that some potential applicants were discouraged from applying because of the wide area of discretion accorded to officials under the National Assistance Act 1948 and the residual connotations of the poor law inherent in the scheme. The Labour government decided, therefore, in 1966 to make some changes to the scheme, from that time to be known as supplementary benefit.[44] The major alteration was to confer a *right* to benefit in the circumstances set out in the legislation; another was the automatic provision of higher benefit rates for pensioners and those who had been in receipt of the benefit for two years – both reduced the amount of discretion in the system. The principal administrative change was that the NAB was dissolved and its functions transferred to the Ministry of Social Security[45] and to the Supplementary Benefits Commission (SBC), though the latter was not a separate department.[46] The object of these changes was to merge the administration of contributory and means-tested benefits and thereby remove the stigma associated with claiming the latter.[47]

38   Cf p 591, above.
39   The 'household means' test survived in vestigial form for non-householders until 1948.
40   *Beveridge Report* n 4, above, para 372.
41   This last concept has of course now resurfaced in the social fund: see ch 15, below.
42   Webb in Hall et al *Change, Choice and Conflict in Social Policy* (1975) ch 14.
43   Cf p 131, below.
44   The changes were made by the Ministry of Social Security Act 1966, later renamed the Supplementary Benefit Act 1966: SSA 1971, s 11(1)(c).
45   Its functions were later transferred to the Secretary of State for Social Services: p 132, below.
46   P 132, below.
47   Miss M Herbison, Minister of Pensions and National Insurance, 729 HC Official Report (5th series) cols 355ff.

v *The reforms of 1980*[48]

Mrs Thatcher's first administration instituted major changes to the supplementary benefits scheme in 1980, implementing many (but not all) of the recommendations contained in a report undertaken by a team of Department of Health and Social Security (DHSS) officials between 1976 and 1978.[49] Their report broadly recommended that the scheme should be simplified to make it more intelligible and less costly. In particular, awards of discretionary additions to benefit had radically increased in the 1970s and these were making the scheme both expensive to administer and unfair in its application, since it was difficult to ensure equal and uniform allocation of such payments throughout the country. The main reform was to incorporate in a voluminous set of regulations detailed rules of entitlement, most of which had previously existed only as internal instructions to officials for the exercise of discretion. The balance between regulation-based rights and discretion in the supplementary benefits scheme had been a subject of much debate in the 1970s.[50] Thus the primary effect of the 1980 reforms was to increase 'legalisation' and reduce the role of discretion: the discretionary weekly 'exceptional circumstances additions' and lump-sum 'exceptional needs payments' were replaced by detailed regulations on, respectively, 'additional requirements' and 'single payments'.[51] In principle the claimant had only to meet the prescribed criteria in the regulations to gain entitlement to these additions to the basic benefit, though some residual discretion was retained. In practice the reforms enabled the government to exert greater fiscal control over the supplementary benefits system.[52]

The revised legal structure was reflected in changes made to administrative and adjudicative institutions. There was no longer any need for the SBC to formulate informal rules and policies for the exercise of discretion. Its advisory role was, therefore, transferred to the new Social Security Advisory Committee (SSAC), which was concerned with advice on almost all social security matters.[53] The adjudicative arrangements were also, by stages, integrated: first, a right of appeal on questions of law was introduced from decisions of supplementary benefits appeal tribunals (SBATs) to the Commissioner; subsequently, adjudication officers (AOs) became responsible for first instance decisions on almost all social security claims (including those for supplementary benefit) and SBATs were merged with national insurance local tribunals to form the social security appeal tribunals (SSATs).[54] These reforms were to survive only until SSA 1998.[55]

---

48 Walker in Jones and Stevenson (eds) *The Yearbook of Social Policy in Britain 1982* (1983) ch 8.
49 DHSS *Social Assistance* (1978). See also White Paper *Reform of the Supplementary Benefits Scheme* (1979, Cmnd 7773) and SSA 1980. There were, however, some key differences, such as the government's rejection of the recommendation that long-term recipients of supplementary benefit receive a lump sum every six months. For the background to, and comments on, the report, see Donnison *The Politics of Poverty* (1982) chs 5–6; and Lister [1978–79] JSWL 133.
50 See, esp: Titmuss (1971) 42 Political Q 113; Adler and Bradley *Justice, Discretion and Poverty* (1975); Bull [1980] JSWL 65.
51 For details, see the 2nd edition of this book, pp 477–480, 487–493. See also Beltram *Testing the Safety-Net* (1984).
52 See McKenna [1985] PL 455 and, for an historical assessment of the 1948–1980 period, Silburn in Bean and MacPherson (eds) *Approaches to Welfare* (1983).
53 Pp 137–139, above.
54 Pp 180–181, above.
55 Ch 6, above.

vi   The Fowler Reviews and income support

In 1984, Norman Fowler, then Secretary of State for Social Services, announced four parallel reviews of aspects of social security policy and provision, one of which focused on the supplementary benefits scheme. The primary purpose of the reviews was to examine whether the benefits system could be made simpler and whether resources could be targeted more effectively on those in need. In June 1985 the reviews were published in a Green Paper;[56] a White Paper followed in December 1985,[57] the main proposals of which were implemented in SSA 1986.[58]

The review team identified complexity as the main defect in the supplementary benefits scheme.[59] The detail of the regulations, subject to a substantial body of case law, was intimidating.[60] For the purpose of determining the basic weekly rates, difficult distinctions were drawn between 'householders' and 'non-householders' and a further set of complex rules were used to define categories of claimants entitled to the 'long-term' rate. The regular weekly additions to cover such items as heating, diet, and laundry had become an integral part of the scheme[61] but many applications required considerable investigation of the claimant's circumstances, which could be unduly intrusive.[62] The most stringent criticism was, however, reserved for the system of 'single payments' designed to meet one-off needs. The 'labyrinth' of rules and the very large number of appeals to which their application gave rise involved a disproportionately heavy administrative burden and cost and was a significant cause of friction between claimants and staff.[63] Further problems arose from the relationship between supplementary benefit and the other means-tested schemes, family income supplement and housing benefit. The various schemes operated different criteria of need and different methods of assessing income and capital. This both confused claimants and hindered the development of a coherent strategy to deal with the problems of work incentives and the 'poverty trap' – the situation in which efforts to increase income result in a withdrawal of benefit and thus to a net loss.[64]

The Green and White Papers in 1995 characterised the core problem as being structural.[65] The supplementary benefit system was being over-extended in attempting to fulfil two separate roles: the provision of weekly income, its basic purpose; and help with special needs, a complementary function which was designed to take account of particular exceptional pressures faced by a minority of claimants but which had grown to unmanageable proportions. 'The result is that the efficient delivery of a regular weekly income for claimants is prejudiced by the attempt to incorporate in the main structure the detailed consideration of special needs.'[66] It was necessary to separate the two roles.

56   Green Paper *Reform of Social Security* (1985, Cmnd 9517).
57   White Paper *Reform of Social Security* (1985, Cmnd 9691).
58   See Harris in Harris (ed) *Social Security Law in Context* (2000) ch 5 on the Fowler Reviews.
59   *Green Paper 1985* n 56, above, vol 2, para 2.27ff and vol 3, para 4.49. See also Berthoud *The Reform of Supplementary Benefit* Research Paper 84/5.1 (1984).
60   The rules on single payments alone ran to over 1,000 printed lines and one regulation contained 20 separate categories of essential furniture and household equipment: SI 1981/1528, reg 9.
61   Over 90 per cent of pensioners received at least one such addition: *Green Paper 1985* n 56, above, vol 2, para 2.55.
62   The age-related heating addition did not require investigation of the claimant's circumstances but for this reason was criticised for being poorly targeted: *Green Paper 1985* n 56, above, vol 2, para 2.57.
63   *Green Paper 1985* n 56, above, vol 2, para 2.63.
64   *White Paper 1985* n 57, above, para 3.3.
65   *Green Paper 1985* n 56, above, vol 2, para 2.30.
66   *Green Paper 1985* n 56, above, vol 2, para 2.30.

'Income support' would replace weekly supplementary benefit by fulfilling its basic purpose of providing regular income. While need would obviously vary according to the situation of each claimant, individual circumstances should not be investigated in detail; rather, in addition to standard personal allowances, there would be 'premiums' for different 'client' groups, eg families, the elderly, people with disabilities and lone parents.[67] The system of single payments and urgent needs would be replaced by the new 'social fund' which would operate quite independently of income support and would be administered on a discretionary basis and subject to budgetary limits.[68]

The consultation period following the Green Paper was only three months, and responses from pressure groups were predominantly hostile to the proposals. While the SSAC in general approved the structural changes *within* the income support system (personal allowances plus premiums for particular client groups), there was some concern that an appropriate balance between a 'broad brush' approach and an investigation of individual needs had not been struck.[69] The SSAC predicted that unless the new benefit was set at levels adequate to meet the everyday expenses of most claimants there would be an 'intolerable pressure' on the social fund, which would threaten the viability of the reform.[70]

Some important recommendations were brought into force under the existing supplementary benefit legislation; eg a significant reduction in entitlement both to single payments[71] and to the meeting of mortgage interest payments.[72] The main reforms were effected by SSA 1986, which provided for the new income support scheme to be introduced in April 1988.[73]

vii Further reform by Conservative governments after 1988

The income support scheme was subject to frequent amendments in the following decade. These changes were principally aimed at removing certain groups from reliance on income support or otherwise limiting the scope of the benefit.[74] As a consequence of the Conservative government's new policy towards the employment training of young people, SSA 1988 restricted the entitlement of this group to income support.[75] Two measures introduced in 1993 were similarly designed to make savings in expenditure on income support: the child support scheme and the community care reforms.[76] In 1994 the habitual residence test was introduced and in the following year the rules governing the scope of assistance with housing costs were made significantly more restrictive.[77] From October 1996, as a result of the Jobseekers Act 1995 (JA 1995),

---

67 Thus the complexities of the 'householder' and 'non-householder' categories, the 'long-term' rates and the weekly additional requirements were abolished.
68 For further details, see ch 13, below.
69 SSAC *Fourth Report* (1985) para 1.4.
70 *SSAC* n 69, above, para 3.5. See also SSAC *Seventh Report* (1990) paras 3.2–3.9 and *The Social Fund – A New Structure* (1992).
71 SI 1986/1961 and 1987/38; see Rowell [1987] JSWL 137.
72 SI 1987/17.
73 Complex transitional arrangements were made to protect existing supplementary benefit claimants against losses that might otherwise result from the changes: SI 1987/1969. See also *Chief Adjudication Officer v Dommett*, reported as an Appendix to *R(IS) 6/93*. An ingenious argument that the single payments scheme survived these reforms was dismissed in *R(SB) 1/94*.
74 There are, obviously exceptions, such as the introduction of a carer's premium: p 301, below.
75 P 284, below.
76 Pp 318–324 and 330, below.
77 Pp 280–283 and 302–313 respectively, below.

income support for the unemployed was redesignated as income-based jobseeker's allowance. Consequently, income support has become the residual safety net benefit for those who are not required to fulfil the labour market conditions.

viii   New Labour and reform of income support

The new Labour government was elected in 1997 on a manifesto which included a commitment to adhere to the previous administration's public expenditure targets.[78] This resulted in the first significant backbench rebellion for the new government, as it proceeded to implement the Conservatives' plans to abolish the lone parent premium in the means-tested benefits schemes, along with one-parent benefit itself.[79] However, the publication of its Green Paper on welfare reform led to the development of a series of more positive initiatives for those on the lowest incomes.[80] These included significant increases in the value of personal allowances for children under the income support scheme and the introduction of the Minimum Income Guarantee (MIG), effectively an enhanced rate of income support for pensioners.[81] Other developments, most notably the various New Deals, sought to provide opportunities for those outside the labour market to improve their prospects of finding work. Indeed, the new administration emphasised the importance of 'welfare to work' measures as the primary means of combating poverty and social exclusion. This was most evident in the development of tax credits, which led to a significant recasting of the social assistance scheme under the Tax Credits Act 2002. With effect from April 2003, income support allowances for children are to be amalgamated with the child credits in working families' tax credit and the child dependency additions to National Insurance benefits to form the new integrated child tax credit. The State Pension Credit Act 2002 will involve a radical restructuring of means-tested benefits and credits for pensioners with effect from October 2003, with the result that the role of income support will become much less significant than had been the case at its inception in 1988.

Part 2   General conditions of entitlement to income support

The principal conditions of entitlement to income support are set out in the Social Security Contributions and Benefits Act 1992 (SSCBA 1992).[82] Broadly speaking, the claimant:

(1)   must fall within one of the prescribed categories of persons;
(2)   must be present and habitually resident in Great Britain;
(3)   must be over the age of 16;
(4)   must not be engaged in remunerative work or full-time (non-advanced) education;
(5)   must not be entitled to jobseeker's allowance (and, if a member of a couple, his or her partner must not be entitled to income-based jobseeker's allowance);
(6)   must not have income exceeding the 'applicable amount'; and
(7)   must not have more than a prescribed amount of capital.

---

78   See Toynbee and Walker *Did Things Get Better?* (2001).
79   See p 658, below.
80   DSS *New ambitions for our country: A new contract for welfare* (1998, Cm 3805).
81   P 596, below.
82   SSCBA 1992, ss 124(1) and 134(1).

Most of these conditions of entitlement apply not only to the claimant but also to the partner (if any) and the income and capital of other members of the family unit may also be relevant. Conditions (1) to (5) will be discussed in this Part, while the rules for determining the membership of the family unit are described in Part 3. The mode of assessing the 'applicable' amount (condition (6)) will be dealt with in Part 4 but the principles governing the determination of income and capital (condition (7)) are considered in chapter 12, as they are to a substantial degree common for the various means-tested benefits and tax credits.

A The prescribed categories of persons

Until October 1996 it was a condition of entitlement to income support that claimants be both available for and actively seeking employment.[83] Some categories of claimants – eg pensioners – could not reasonably be expected to demonstrate an attachment to the labour market as a precondition of receiving benefit and were accordingly relieved by regulations of the obligation to 'sign on'.[84] JA 1995 transferred unemployed claimants to the new regime of income-based jobseeker's allowance, with the result that the labour market conditions were removed from the income support scheme. A new gateway to entitlement to income support was then needed. The course adopted was to require all income support claimants to fall within 'a prescribed category of person'[85] as listed in a Schedule to the regulations.[86] In most respects these prescribed groups mirror the categories of claimants who were previously exempt from the requirement to be available for and actively seeking employment.[87] Schedule 1B thus specifies the following groups as eligible for income support:
(1) lone parents, single persons looking after foster children,[88] persons responsible for a child while their partner is temporarily not present in the UK, persons temporarily caring for a child whose parent or carer is ill or temporarily absent from home or for a relative who is ill, persons taking parental leave,[89] pregnant women,[90] and those engaged full-time in caring for a seriously disabled person;
(2) persons who are incapable of work[91] or are appealing against a decision that they are not incapable of work, persons whose earning capacity has been reduced by 25 per cent, or are working while living in a residential care or nursing home; disabled or deaf students and persons who are registered as blind;
(3) persons under 24 undertaking training provided under the auspices of the Learning and Skills Council or similar agencies, and those 16 and 17-year-olds in full-time

83 See the 4th edition of this book, pp 467–470.
84 See the 4th edition of this book, p 469.
85 SSCBA 1992, s 124(1)(e).
86 SI 1987/1967, reg 4ZA and Sch 1B.
87 There are some differences: eg there is no provision in SI 1987/1967, Sch 1B for persons taking a child or young person abroad temporarily for medical treatment, discharged prisoners or Open University students attending a residential course; but see SI 1996/207, reg 14(1)(c), (f) and (j) as regards entitlement to jobseeker's allowance.
88 'Child' in the context of SI 1987/1967, Sch 1B means a person under the age of 16: SSCBA 1992, s 137(1).
89 See SI 1999/3312; this only covers those who do not receive any payment from their employer and who were receiving working families' tax credit, disabled persons tax credit, housing benefit or council tax benefit immediately before such leave.
90 But only during the period from 11 weeks before the expected week of confinement to seven weeks after the end of the pregnancy.
91 See p 538, below.

education who are parents, seriously handicapped, orphans or estranged from their parents;[92]

(4) persons over 60, or not less than 50 and who were not required to be available for work under the pre-1996 scheme because they had been out of work for ten years, and those bereaved persons claiming as a single person and aged between 55 and 60;

(5) persons treated as not being in remunerative work as they are entitled to a mortgage interest run-on;

(6) certain refugees, persons from abroad entitled to an urgent cases payment,[93] persons in custody, persons required to attend court and those subject to a trade disputes disqualification.[94]

The exclusion of most students from the income support scheme was also carried forward in the 1996 amendments.[95] The status of students is discussed further below in the context of the rules governing the limited entitlement to benefit for those in full-time education.[96]

This restructuring is more fundamental than may appear at first sight. A person cannot claim income support unless he or she falls within one of the categories set out in Schedule 1B. The statutory list is therefore exhaustive, and there is no equivalent to the residual category under the pre-1996 scheme, whereby a reduced rate of benefit was available at the discretion of the adjudication officer in cases of hardship.[97]

B Presence and habitual residence in Great Britain

i Immigration controls and income support

As a result of the Immigration and Asylum Act 1999 (IAA 1999), any individual who is a 'person subject to immigration control' is now precluded from entitlement to income support.[98] Previously, secondary legislation excluded certain categories of immigrant from the income support scheme, through the concept of a 'person from abroad' – an individual who is effectively barred from receiving income support by being ascribed an applicable amount of nil.[99] These categories included a variety of individuals whose status was in some way controlled by immigration law,[100] such as overstayers, those subject to a deportation order, illegal entrants, those granted only temporary admission to the UK or who were awaiting a decision on immigration status and EU nationals who had been required by the Secretary of State to leave the UK.[101] It remains the case that an immigrant may be allowed into this country under a sponsorship agreement, whereby the sponsor, generally a relative, undertakes to maintain him or her. In such a

92   See p 288, below.
93   P 313, below.
94   Pp 332–334, below.
95   SI 1987/1967, reg 4ZA(2).
96   P 287, below.
97   See the 4th edition of this book, p 469, n 11. See also the restrictive rules governing urgent cases payments (p 313) and jobseeker's allowance hardship payments (p 377).
98   IAA 1999, s 115(1)(e). See p 232, above.
99   SI 1987/1967, reg 21(3) and Sch 7, para 17.
100 These categories were primarily defined by reference to the Immigration Act 1971, on which see Macdonald and Webber *Immigration law and practice in the United Kingdom* (5th edn, 2001).
101 See *R v Secretary of State for Home Department, ex p Vitale and Do Amarol* [1995] All ER (EC) 946; and *Secretary of State for Social Security v Remelien; Chief Adjudication Officer v Wolke* [1998] 1 All ER 129, reported as an Appendix to *R(IS) 13/98*.

case, the immigrant is normally able to obtain income support if the sponsor is unable, or refuses, to meet the undertaking.[102]

ii Presence and habitual residence

Until August 1994 it was sufficient simply for the claimant to be present in Great Britain.[103] Since then there has been an added requirement of 'habitual residence'. This controversial test was introduced by the then Conservative government, ostensibly to tackle the problem of 'benefit tourism', a phenomenon which is premised on the assumption that the generosity of the British social security system attracts potential claimants from other EEA states. No evidence was produced to suggest that this was a significant problem.[104] In practice the requirement, which was imposed contrary to the recommendations of the SSAC,[105] tended to impact most on UK citizens returning from living and working abroad for several years and on UK residents from ethnic minority backgrounds who spent prolonged periods abroad visiting their families.[106]

The new condition was not introduced by primary legislation.[107] Instead, regulations further extended the definition of a 'person from abroad'; individuals falling into this category are ascribed an 'applicable amount' (ie the weekly amount of benefit which is deemed to be sufficient in their circumstances)[108] of nil.[109] Under the amending regulations,[110] a 'person from abroad' also includes 'a claimant who is not habitually resident in the United Kingdom, the Channel Islands, the Isle of Man or the Republic of Ireland'.[111] In principle the requirement is non-discriminatory in that it applies to UK nationals, other EU nationals and non-EU citizens alike. However, the regulations, in a phrase with an ugly and unfortunate double negative, expressly provide that 'no claimant shall be treated as not habitually resident' if they fall into one of three categories. In numerical terms the first of these is the most important: any person who is a 'worker' for the purposes of Council Regulation (EEC) 1408/71.[112] A person who moves to the UK seeking employment, having worked in another member state but not in the UK, is not apparently a worker for these purposes.[113] The other two categories comprise refugees

---

102   P 327, below and see 147 HC Official Report (6th series) written answer col 231. This exclusion now only applies for five years from the date of entry into the UK or the undertaking, whichever is the later, or until the person becomes a British citizen.
103   For the meaning of 'presence', see p 230, above. The *Green Paper 1985* n 56, above, proposed that claimants would need to be present in Great Britain for a set (unspecified) period: vol 2, para 2.87, but the idea was dropped in the *White Paper 1985* n 57, above, para 3.30.
104   See Adler (1995) 2 JSSL 179.
105   SSAC *Report on the Income-Related Benefit Schemes (Miscellaneous Amendments) (No 2) Regulations 1994* (Cm 2609, 1994).
106   NACAB *Failing the Test* (1996).
107   A challenge against the rule on the ground that it was ultra vires SSCBA 1992, s 124(1) failed in *R v Secretary of State for Social Security, ex p Sarwar, Getachew and Urbanek* [1997] 3 CMLR 647; a parallel challenge on the basis that the rule was in breach of art 48 of the Treaty of Rome also failed. However, the habitual residence test has been found to be in breach of the European Social Charter: p 41, above.
108   Pp 293–302, below.
109   SI 1987/1967, Sch 7, para 17.
110   SI 1994/1807.
111   SI 1987/1967, reg 21(3). This geographical area is known as the Common Travel Area for immigration purposes.
112   Pp 66–68, above; this group also includes those with a right to reside in the UK under Council Directive (EEC) 68/360 or 73/148.
113   R(IS) 3/97. But see the discussion in Wood, Poynter, Wikeley et al *Social Security Legislation 2001* (2001) vol II, para 2.103.

under the Geneva Convention and individuals granted exceptional leave to enter or remain in the UK. Assuming the claimant does not fall within one of these three groups, he or she must be habitually resident in the Common Travel Area.[114]

The test of habitual residence itself, which is deployed in a number of other legal contexts,[115] is notoriously opaque. Early Commissioners' decisions emphasised that it was impossible to provide a comprehensive definition of the term; all the circumstances had to be taken into account, but especially the length, continuity and general nature of the residence. In particular, residence for an 'appreciable period of time' was required, along with a settled intention to do so.[116] The potential conflict between this requirement and the right to freedom of movement enjoyed by EU nationals came to the fore in *Swaddling*[117] but was not satisfactorily resolved:

> Mr S, a British national, had lived and worked in the UK until the age of 23. For 14 years he then lived and worked mostly in France. In 1994 he was made redundant in France and was unable to find further work there. He returned to the UK in 1995 and claimed income support. The Commissioner referred to the European Court of Justice the question whether the habitual residence test was in breach of Article 48 of the Treaty. The court declined to answer this question; the case could be dealt with under Council Regulation (EEC) 1408/71, article 10a(1), entitling those covered to non-contributory benefits in the member state in which they resided. In this context, the court held that the length of residence in the member state where benefit was sought could not be seen as an integral part of the concept of residence.

This meant, at the very least, that individuals coming back to the UK after a period in another member state had to be treated as habitually resident immediately upon their return. Following the European Court of Justice's decision, the new Labour administration issued a Department of Social Security (DSS) press release which announced that this interpretation would also apply (effectively by executive fiat, rather than any change to the legislation) to claimants returning from any country overseas and re-establishing their ties here.[118] The confusion as to the meaning of habitual residence was compounded by the decision of the House of Lords in *Nessa*:[119]

> Mrs N came to the UK in 1994 at the age of 55 from Bangladesh, where she had lived all her life. Her late husband had lived and worked in the UK from 1962 until his death in 1975. Accordingly, Mrs N enjoyed a right of abode in the UK, and came to live with her brother-in-law's family. She brought most of her belongings with her and came on a one-way ticket. She claimed income support but was found to be not habitually resident.

The House of Lords concluded that 'a person is not habitually resident in any country unless he has taken up residence and lived there for a period'.[120] The requisite period is not a fixed period, but a question of fact and degree, taking into account all the circumstances.[121] Notwithstanding the fact that income support is a safety-net benefit,

114   As this is a bar on benefit, the onus of proof is on the Secretary of State: *R(IS) 6/96*.
115   Eg in revenue law and in relation to child abduction.
116   *R(IS) 6/96*.
117   C-90/97 *Swaddling v Adjudication Officer* [1999] All ER (EC) 217, reported as an Appendix to *R(IS) 6/99*.
118   DSS Press Release, 14 June 1999.
119   [1999] 4 All ER 677; see Harris (2000) 7 JSSL 54.
120   [1999] 4 All ER 677 at 682, per Lord Slynn.
121   'Bringing possessions, doing everything necessary to establish residence before coming, having a right of abode, seeking to bring family, "durable ties" with the country of residence or intended residence, and many other factors have to be taken into account', per Lord Slynn, [1999] 4 All ER 677 at 683.

the House of Lords suggested that there could be a 'gap' in habitual residence, with the result that an individual may have no habitual residence at a given point in time.[122] The test of habitual residence thus appears to operate in two different ways, depending upon the jurisdictional context.[123] In cases with a European dimension, an individual covered by Council Regulation (EEC) 1408/71 can be habitually resident as from the day of arrival. As a result of the government's concession, this also applies to those *returning* to the UK from outside the EU (regardless of their nationality). Other claimants, however, can only become habitually resident after an appreciable but indeterminate period of time.

Given the general rule in IAA 1999, discussed in the section above, it is arguable that the habitual residence test is otiose. If individuals have been permitted entry to the UK free of the state's restrictive immigration controls, then in principle they should be entitled to income support, assuming they meet the other criteria for entitlement. In this context it is noteworthy that the US Supreme Court has ruled residency requirements for benefit claimants in state laws to be unconstitutional.[124]

iii Temporary absence from Great Britain

Assuming that the claimant does not fall foul of any of the exclusions discussed above, regulations also provide that a period of up to four weeks' temporary absence[125] may be ignored. This is subject to the proviso that the absence is unlikely to last for a year and during that period the claimant continues to meet the conditions of entitlement to income support. In addition, the claimant must satisfy *one* of the following conditions,[126] namely that he or she:

(1) is in Northern Ireland;
(2) is not within one of the categories in Schedule 1B who are denied this concession;[127]
(3) is incapable of work and the sole purpose of the absence is to receive treatment for that incapacity;[128]
(4) has been continuously incapable of work for 52 weeks (or 28 weeks if either terminally ill or in receipt of the highest rate of the care component of disability living allowance); or
(5) has a partner who is also abroad and for whom a pensioner premium, a higher pensioner premium, a disability premium or a severe disability premium is payable.[129]

Income support can be paid for the first eight weeks of an absence where the claimant is accompanying a child or young person (who must be a member of their family) for the purposes of medical treatment abroad.[130]

---

122 [1999] 4 All ER 677 at 682, per Lord Slynn (obiter). For the contrary view, see the dissenting judgment of Thorpe LJ in the Court of Appeal, [1998] 2 All ER 728 at 737.
123 *Gingi v Secretary of State for Work and Pensions* [2001] EWCA Civ 1685, [2002] 1 CMLR 587.
124 *Shapiro v Thompson* 394 US 618 (1969) (see Bussiere *Disentitling the Poor* (1997) ch 6); and *Saenz v Roe* 526 US 489 (1999).
125 For the meaning of 'temporary absence', see p 226, above.
126 SI 1987/1967, reg 4(1)–(2).
127 Broadly speaking those who are incapable of work – unless they can satisfy condition (3) or (4) above – or appealing against a decision that they are not incapable of work, or in full-time education, or affected by a trade dispute or who are a person from abroad.
128 Cf p 538, below.
129 Cf pp 298–301, below.
130 SI 1987/1967, reg 4(1) and (3). Such treatment must be from 'a person appropriately qualified' within reg 4(4).

C Age

SSA 1986 originally provided that the claimant must be at least 16,[131] a lower age limit which had existed in the public assistance schemes since at least 1948. Young persons above this age could not claim income support in their own right if they remained at school; in these circumstances, parents were paid child benefit and, if they were eligible, could also claim allowances for them in respect of income support. However, in the period immediately following the passing of SSA 1986, the Conservative administration resolved to narrow the entitlement of young persons aged 16–17 who left school and remained unemployed. The aim was to encourage them to participate in employment training schemes and, more generally, to discourage them from leaving home and establishing a dependence on social security.[132] Notwithstanding objections from the Opposition that the measure would lead to compulsory 'workfare',[133] SSA 1988 raised the basic age of entitlement to income support to 18.[134] Claimants aged between 16 and 18 who had left school then had either to satisfy the narrowly defined special conditions prescribed in the regulations[135] or to persuade the Secretary of State to issue a direction that severe hardship would result unless income support was paid.[136] The treatment of those who remained at school after this age was left unchanged. When income-based jobseeker's allowance was introduced in October 1996 for those required to be available for work as a condition of receiving benefit, these rules for young people were carried over, with some modifications, into the new scheme.[137] At the same time the lower age limit for income support was reduced again to 16; this was merely consequential upon the restructuring of the benefit, and involved no change in policy or generosity towards young people. Claimants aged 16 or 17 must, as with other income support claimants, fall into one of the prescribed categories in Schedule 1B.[138] Most of those young people leaving local authority care who fall in this age group are now excluded from income support, as their maintenance is the responsibility of the relevant authority.[139]

D Exclusion of persons engaged in remunerative work

With the exception of the Speenhamland system introduced in 1795,[140] public assistance was not used to supplement low earnings until the introduction of family income supplement in 1970. Supplementary benefit was, therefore, not available if the claimant was engaged in 'remunerative full-time work',[141] which normally denoted work

---

131 S 20(3).
132 The 1987 Conservative party election manifesto had included a pledge that young persons who chose to be unemployed would be denied benefit. See further on the reform: SSAC *Sixth Report* (1988) (ch 2; Harris (1988) 15 JLS 201, (1988) 17 J Soc Pol 501 and [1992] JSWFL 175; and Wikeley [1989] JSWL 277).
133 121 HC Official Report (6th series) col 665.
134 SSA 1988, s 4(1).
135 SSCBA 1992, s 124(1)(a) and SI 1987/1967, reg 13A and Sch 1A.
136 SSCBA 1992, s 125(1) (now repealed).
137 Pp 354–357, below.
138 SI 1987/1967, Sch 1B.
139 Children (Leaving Care) Act 2000, s 6 and SI 2001/3070. Care leavers who would qualify for income support on other grounds, eg as a lone parent, remain eligible. See further the discussion in the context of income-based jobseeker's allowance, p 355, below.
140 P 383, above.
141 Supplementary Benefits Act 1976, s 6(1).

amounting to 30 hours or more a week. In 1988 the term 'full-time' was dropped and the threshold reduced to 24 hours. At the same time it became a requirement of entitlement to income support that the claimant's partner (if any) was not in such work.[142] In April 1992 the limit was lowered again to just 16 hours, thus excluding many part-time workers from entitlement to income support. At the same time, however, eligibility for family credit was extended to those working for 16 hours or more a week. This reflected the government's concern to provide incentives for working families on low incomes. When jobseeker's allowance was introduced in October 1996, the hours threshold for the claimant's partner was raised to 24 but remained at 16 hours for the claimant.[143] There was no change to these rules when working families' tax credit replaced family credit in October 1999.

i Remunerative work

The concept of 'remunerative work',[144] which marks the boundary between income support and working families' tax credit, is defined as:

> work in which a person is engaged, or, where his hours of work fluctuate, he is engaged on average, for not less than 16 hours a week being work for which payment is made or which is done in expectation of payment.[145]

'Work' is evidently a broader notion than 'employment', and so may cover work of a spiritual rather than contractual nature.[146] It must, however, be performed for payment or in the expectation of payment. The Court of Appeal has held that this may include unproductive waiting time: a self-employed minicab driver waiting at the cab office for potential customers to call is working in this sense.[147] This must be distinguished from the mere hope of payment, as where a 'self-employed writer' had sent several manuscripts to publishers but with no realistic prospect of any payment.[148]

ii Calculation of hours

The regulations provide methods to assist in a determination of the average number of hours worked per week.[149] Where no 'recognisable cycle' of work has been established (eg where the claimant has just started work), the test is the number of hours which he or she is expected to work.[150] Where there is a 'recognisable cycle' of work, hours will

---

142 Under the supplementary benefit scheme the claimant's partner could be in work, but obviously that partner's earnings (subject to any disregard) would be taken into account as an income resource.
143 SI 1987/1967, reg 5(1A).
144 SSCBA 1992, s 124(1)(c).
145 SI 1987/1967, reg 5(1).
146 *R(FC) 2/90* (Salvation Army officers), applying *Rogers v Booth* [1937] 2 All ER 751. Given the common ground between the respective tests, family credit (and now working families' tax credit) decisions are equally relevant in the context of income support.
147 *Kazantzis v Chief Adjudication Officer* (1999) CA, reported as *R(IS) 13/99*.
148 *R(IS) 1/93*.
149 SI 1987/1967, reg 5(2). Unfortunately these rules have not been restructured in the same way as those that now govern working families' tax credit (and previously family credit): see p 388, below. Paid lunch or tea breaks are included in the calculation of the claimant's hours: reg 5(7).
150 SI 1987/1967, reg 5(2)(a). This also covers the situation where there has been a change in working hours: see *R(FC) 8/95*.

be averaged over that cycle. The regulations fail to provide any assistance as to the period over which any such cycle is to be determined.[151] Where the hours of work fluctuate but there is no such cycle, the Secretary of State should derive an average from the period of five weeks preceding the date of claim, or such other period as, in the circumstances of the case, may enable the average to be determined more accurately.[152] The difficulties inherent in the application of this rule are perhaps most acute in the case of school ancillary workers, for whom special provision has now been made. Regulations provide that where the claimant is not required to work in the school holidays, such periods are disregarded in calculating the average number of hours for which they are engaged in work.[153] This has the effect of making it easier for such workers to claim working families' tax credit but not income support. Until the new working tax credit is introduced in 2003, this leaves childless low-paid workers at a severe disadvantage:

> B, a single claimant, was employed as a special needs assistant in a junior school. He was not paid during the school vacations. A majority of the House of Lords held that the regulations required B to be treated as engaged in remunerative work during those vacations, even though he did not work and received no pay. Thus weeks in the holidays were to be disregarded in determining the average number of hours worked in the cycle.[154]

iii   Persons deemed as engaged or not engaged in remunerative work

For the purpose of these rules, a person is treated as being engaged in 'remunerative work' during periods of absence from work which in other respects satisfies the definition, if the absence is for holiday or 'without good cause', and the same applies during the first seven days of a stoppage of work due to a trade dispute.[155] The exclusion from benefit also applies to the weeks covered by holiday pay received within four weeks of the termination of employment or by pay in lieu of notice or of wages.[156]

Conversely, there are a number of situations in which claimants (or their partners) are treated as if they were *not* engaged in 'remunerative work', even if they are working for more than 16 hours a week.[157] These are where the person:

(1) has an earning capacity reduced by 25 per cent or more as a result of mental or physical disablement;

(2) is engaged in childminding at home or regularly and substantially engaged in caring for a severely disabled person who is entitled to disability living allowance or attendance allowance;

(3) is engaged in charitable or voluntary work for which the only payment is the reimbursement of expenses or is a carer;

(4) is in receipt of a training allowance;[158]

---

151   See *R(IS) 15/94*.
152   SI 1987/1967, reg 5(2)(b); see also *R(IS) 8/95*.
153   SI 1987/1967, reg 5(3B).
154   *Banks v Chief Adjudication Officer* [2001] UKHL 33, [2001] ICR 877. See Harris (2002) 9 JSSL 94.
155   SI 1987/1967, reg 5(3)–(4). A person is not to be treated as engaged in remunerative work while on maternity or sick leave: reg 5(3A).
156   SI 1987/1967, reg 5(5).
157   SI 1987/1967, reg 6(1) and (4).
158   Paid out of public funds by a government department or by or on behalf of the Secretary of State for Employment for following an approved training scheme, but not for full-time education (except under the Employment and Training Act 1973, s 2) or a teacher training course: SI 1987/1967, reg 2.

(5) is without work as a result of a stoppage due to a trade dispute and that stoppage has lasted for more than seven days;[159]

(6) lives in (or is temporarily absent from) a residential care home, nursing home or residential accommodation;

(7) is a local authority councillor or is engaged in specified volunteer rescue services;

(8) is a foster parent and receives an allowance for such work;

(9) is engaged in an activity in relation to which a sports award has been paid under the National Lottery etc Act 1993;

(10) qualifies for the lone parent benefit run-on or the mortgage interest run-on.

People in these categories may qualify for income support despite working for 16 or more hours a week, but they must still fall within one of the prescribed groups in Schedule 1B[160] and their earnings (subject to the appropriate disregard) will be taken into account as income.

The lone parent benefit run-on and mortgage interest run-on provisions were introduced in October 1999 and April 2001 respectively as work incentive measures. A lone parent who has been on either income support or income-based jobseeker's allowance for at least 26 weeks before starting 'remunerative work' (ie work of 16 hours or more a week) is treated as not in such work for a period of 14 days.[161] The effect is that the lone parent may continue to receive benefit for a fortnight after starting a job, so bridging the gap between leaving benefit and receiving the first wages and working families' tax credit payments. Similarly, where any claimant (or partner) has been on benefit continuously for 26 weeks before starting work, he or she may be able to take advantage of the mortgage interest run-on. This means that for a period of four weeks from starting work the claimant will continue to receive the lower of their income support housing costs or the actual amount of benefit previously in payment.[162]

E Exclusion of persons in, or having recently left, full-time education

The provisions governing the entitlement to benefit of young people – or more commonly the absence of such entitlement – who are involved in or have recently completed their education exemplify the worst features of British social security legislation. The rules in question are tortuous and have been amended on an ad hoc basis with little regard to underlying principles. 'The results ... are distinctions which are often inappropriate and which often hamper the fulfilment of educational aspirations.'[163] Three different categories can be identified: those under 19 in full-time education, those 19 or over in full-time education, and those (regardless of age) studying part-time.

i Young people under 19 in full-time education

The basic principle is that a child or young person who is in receipt of, or who has recently left, 'relevant education' is denied benefit. The intention is to ensure that income

159 See, further, p 332, below.

160 P 279, above. Note that there is no express provision in SI 1987/1967, Sch 1B for childminders to qualify for income support, but they arguably do so under Sch 1B, para 3 (see *Social Security Legislation 2001* n 113, above, vol II, para 2.46).

161 SI 1987/1967, reg 6(2)–(3).

162 SI 1987/1967, reg 6(5)–(8). Lone parents cannot claim the advantage of both the two-week and then the four-week run-on. In both types of case it must be anticipated that the work in question will last for at least five weeks.

163 Harris *Social Security for Young People* (1989) p 140.

support interlocks with child benefit, so that if parents are able to claim child benefit in respect of such young persons (and indeed, where appropriate, include them in the family unit for the purposes of any entitlement to income support), the young persons themselves are not entitled to income support.

Thus, except in prescribed circumstances, a person 'receiving relevant education' is not entitled to income support.[164] For this purpose, children or young persons are treated as 'receiving relevant education' in two alternative situations: first, where they are engaged in full-time non-advanced education, that is GCE 'A' Level or below; or, secondly, where they are treated as 'children' for child benefit purposes.[165] The latter alternative is fully discussed in chapter 18,[166] but it is important to observe here that, following modifications to the arrangements for young persons aged 16 to 17 made in 1988, it now covers the child benefit extension period.[167]

There are, however, exceptional circumstances in which young persons aged between 16 and 18 in receipt of 'relevant education' may nevertheless be entitled to income support.[168] These cover claimants who fall into any of the following categories, namely those who are:

- parents and responsible for a child;
- unlikely to be able to obtain work because of a severe handicap;
- orphaned;
- living away from their parents of necessity and estranged from them, or in physical or moral danger, or subject to a serious risk to their physical or mental health;[169]
- living away from their parents of necessity, having left local authority care;
- living away from their parents because the latter are financially unable to provide support and are in custody, prohibited from entering Great Britain or chronically sick or mentally or physically disabled; and
- certain refugees.

ii   Students in full-time education

Since the mid-1970s the benefit entitlement of full-time students has been significantly eroded.[170] The high administrative costs of paying benefit to this group partly accounts for this trend. From the late 1980s government policy has been that student support is a matter for the education budget, and not the social security system. The starting point now is that those students who are in full-time education are excluded from entitlement to income support from the start of their course right through to its end, including all vacations within it. As a general rule 'a full-time student during the period of study' cannot fall into any of the prescribed categories of persons for the purpose of claiming income support.[171] A 'student' means a person who is 'attending or undertaking a course of study at an educational establishment', other than a person receiving a training

---

164   SSCBA 1992, s 124(1)(d).
165   SI 1987/1967, reg 12.
166   P 660, below.
167   This is a period during which an unemployed school-leaver is registered for work or youth training. The period in question is, for summer school leavers, 16 weeks, and, for those leaving school at Christmas or Easter, 12 weeks: see p 660, below.
168   SI 1987/1967, reg 13.
169   Such danger or risk need not be posed by the parents: *R(IS) 9/94* (Somalian refugee).
170   See the 3rd edition of this book, pp 467–469; and Harris (1991) 54 MLR 258.
171   SI 1987/1967, reg 4ZA(2) (there are exceptions in reg 4ZA(3), discussed further below); see also regs 2(1) and 61(1) for definition of 'course of study' and 'period of study'.

allowance.[172] A 'full-time student' is defined as a person who is *either* aged under 19 and attending or undertaking a full-time course of advanced education[173] *or* is 19 or over (but under pensionable age) and attending or undertaking a full-time course of study at an educational establishment.[174] The concepts of a 'full-time course of advanced education' and a 'full-time course of study' are also partially defined by regulations as including those funded in full or in part by the Learning and Skills Council and involving a minimum of 16 'guided learning hours' per week.[175]

A university degree programme, supported by one of the Higher Education Funding Councils, may also be a 'full-time course of study', but this depends on the circumstances of the case. In practice the institution's own definition has traditionally been decisive.[176] However, the full-time/part-time dichotomy fails to reflect developments in the higher education sector such as the advent of modularity and other more flexible modes of learning.[177] The Court of Appeal has considered the implications of classifying modular degrees for the purposes of social security law on two occasions. The majority view appears to be that the status of the student is determined by the nature of the course at the outset. Thus a claimant who begins a modular degree course that does not require full time attendance cannot later be excluded from income support because he or she is not a 'student' within the statutory definition.[178] On the other hand, an individual who starts a full-time course cannot later escape from the benefit consequences of being a 'student' even if permitted to take a year's break to resit examinations.[179] Amending regulations in July 2000 sought to clarify the rules relating to modular courses, so that a student is treated as a full-time student if taking a part of the modular course which would be regarded as a full-time course.[180]

The definition of 'student' has proven problematic in other respects, most notably the deeming provision that (until the July 2000 amendments) read that:

a person who has started on such a course shall be treated as attending it … until the last day of the course or such earlier date as he abandons it or is dismissed from it.[181]

The original formulation of this rule included the words 'throughout any period of term or vacation within it' after 'attending it' in the definition above. The Court of Appeal, by a majority, held that this meant that two claimants who had been allowed to take time out from their studies (to 'intercalate'), eg because of illness, were not 'students' during their intercalating years.[182] Hoffmann LJ's reasoning was that an individual must

---

172   SI 1987/1967, reg 61(1); see reg 2 for the definition of 'training allowance'.
173   Ie essentially any course of study above GCSE 'A' Level: SI 1987/1967, reg 61(1).
174   SI 1987/1967, reg 61(1). Persons on sandwich courses also count as full-time students. A person attending the Bar Vocational Course is a student but a barrister's pupil is not: *R(SB) 25/87* and *R(IS) 5/97*.
175   SI 1987/1967, reg 61(1). 'Guided learning hours' presumably presupposes the presence of a member of staff and so excludes private study time. Separate definitions apply to Scotland given the different funding arrangements in existence North of the border.
176   *R(SB) 40/83; R(SB) 41/83*.
177   Mullan and McKeown (1999) 6 JSSL 56.
178   *Chief Adjudication Officer v Webber* [1997] 4 All ER 274.
179   *O'Connor v Chief Adjudication Officer* [1999] 1 FLR 1200, reported as an Appendix to *R(IS) 7/99*.
180   SI 2000/1981, inserting SI 1987/1967, reg 61(2)–(4).
181   SI 1987/1967, reg 61(1), prior to amendment in July 2000.
182   *Chief Adjudication Officer and Secretary of State for Social Security v Clarke and Faul* [1995] ELR 259. The Court of Appeal also accepted the argument that 'abandon' in this context means 'abandon permanently'.

either be eligible for a student grant *or* be outside the higher education system and so entitled to claim benefit: 'Otherwise there would be an anomalous class of people who for no obvious reason were left to destitution without State support of any kind.'[183] The original (and contrary) policy intention was reaffirmed by a 1995 amendment deleting the offending words, so that in principle a person classified as a 'student' at the outset of their course retained that status (and so was excluded from income support) throughout, notwithstanding any temporary interruptions. The Court of Appeal subsequently upheld this construction in a further decision, determining that the 1995 amendment, although harsh in its effects, was not ultra vires on the ground of irrationality.[184] These rules were also carried over into the jobseeker's allowance scheme in 1995, subject to some minor differences.[185] The then Conservative government's original proposals for amending regulations were not pursued in the face of strong opposition from the SSAC.[186] In July 2000 the new Labour administration reformulated the deeming rule for both income support and jobseeker's allowance, but with some modifications.[187] The basic exclusionary rule was retained, but full-time students who interrupt their studies owing to illness or caring responsibilities, but who are no longer ill or a carer, may now claim jobseeker's allowance.[188]

Notwithstanding the general exclusion of university students from benefit, certain vulnerable groups continue to be entitled during their period of study.[189] These include: lone parents, single foster parents, students qualifying for the disability or severe disability premiums, deaf or certain other disabled students and some refugees. Students who are persons from abroad and eligible for urgent cases payments because they are temporarily without funds may also qualify. In addition, where a couple are both students and they have a child, they may qualify for income support during the summer vacation subject only to meeting the other criteria for entitlement.

iii   Part-time students

In the past the difficulty for part-time students who wished to claim income support was the need to demonstrate that they were still available for and actively seeking employment. The so-called '21 hour rule' provided only limited scope for combining part-time study with receipt of benefit.[190] In October 1996 this rule was repealed as regards income support and a revised version re-enacted in the provisions governing jobseeker's allowance. There is, therefore, now no impediment to a part-time student claiming income support – providing he or she falls within the prescribed categories and meets the other eligibility criteria.

---

183   *Chief Adjudication Officer and Secretary of State for Social Security v Clarke and Faul* [1995] ELR 259 at 264.
184   *O'Connor v Chief Adjudication Officer* [1999] 1 FLR 1200 at 1214, reported as an Appendix to *R(IS) 7/99*.
185   SI 1996/207, regs 1(3) (definition of 'course of study') and 130. On the differences between the two sets of rules, see *Social Security Legislation 2001* n 113, above, vol II, para 2.318.
186   Cm 4739 (2000).
187   Thus a person is regarded as attending or undertaking a full-time course of study 'throughout the period beginning on the date on which he starts attending or undertaking the course and ending on the last day of the course or on such earlier date (if any) as he finally abandons it or is dismissed from it': SI 1987/1967, reg 61(2)(b). Provision of students on modular courses is made by reg 61(2)(a). As regards jobseeker's allowance, see SI 1996/207 reg 1(3A)–(3C).
188   SI 1996/207, reg 1(3D) and (3E).
189   SI 1987/1967, reg 4ZA(3). There is special provision for care leavers: reg 4ZA(3A).
190   See Harris [1988] JSWL 21 and, for a practical example of the difficulties involved, Smith [1990] JSWL 116.

Part 3 The 'family' for income support purposes

A General

Obviously eligible persons living alone can claim income support for themselves, but only one member of a 'family' can claim benefit at any one time.[191] The scheme, recognising the economies of scale involved in family life, in general treats a heterosexual couple living together (whether married or not) and their children (if any) as one unit for the purposes both of determining whose needs are relevant to the claim and whose resources should be taken into account in determining the amount payable.[192] The statutory definition of a 'family'[193] may be considered under three heads: married couples; unmarried couples; children and young persons. Where both members of a couple qualify for income support, either can make the appropriate claim[194] but care is necessary in exercising the choice since in some circumstances consequences vary according to which member is the 'claimant' and which is the 'partner'.[195] There is no equivalent within the income support scheme to the joint claim required for certain couples claiming jobseeker's allowance.[196]

B Married couples

A married[197] couple who are 'members of the same household' are treated as a family unit. The term 'members of the same household' is not defined by legislation so recourse must be had to general principles.[198] In divorce law, where it is sometimes an issue whether spouses are living separately, the test seems to be whether cohabitation and forms of common life have ceased. If they have not, the courts will generally rule, at least if the parties are under the same roof, that they are still living in the same household.[199] This seems to be the appropriate approach here. The fact that one partner is not giving the other any financial support does not in itself prevent them from being regarded as 'members of the same household'.

Regulations provide that generally a couple will be treated as members of the same household notwithstanding that one of them is temporarily living away from the other.[200] However, this rule does not apply where the absentee has no intention of resuming cohabitation or where the absence is likely to exceed 52 weeks, unless there are exceptional circumstances (eg a stay in hospital) and the absence is unlikely to be

---

191 SSCBA 1992, s 134(2).
192 SSCBA 1992, s 136(1). This provision does not contravene Council Directive (EEC) 79/7: *Blaik v Chief Adjudication Officer*, reported as an Appendix to *R(SB) 6/91*.
193 SSCBA 1992, s 137(1).
194 SI 1987/1968, reg 4(3), a refreshingly simple rule which replaced the 'nominated breadwinner' provisions under the supplementary benefits legislation, on which see Luckhaus [1983] JSWL 325. See also *R(SB) 1/93*.
195 Notably where a disability premium is applicable (p 298, below). If the couple wish to change roles, a new claim must be made: SI 1987/1968, reg 4(4).
196 P 357, below.
197 For 'marriage', see pp 214–220, above. Polygamous marriages are covered but there are special rules applying to them: n 233, below.
198 The supplementary benefit case law (eg *R(SB)13/82* and *R(SB) 4/83*) interpreting this phrase to determine whether the claimant came within the now defunct 'householder' status seems equally applicable here.
199 Eg *Hopes v Hopes* [1949] P 227, [1948] 2 All ER 920.
200 SI 1987/1967, reg 16(1).

substantially more than 52 weeks.[201] Furthermore, a couple will not be treated as sharing the same household where either of them is in custody or on temporary release, is detained in hospital under the mental health legislation, is permanently in residential accommodation[202] or has been abroad for more than four weeks.[203] The position of separated and divorced partners is treated separately in Part 6 of this chapter.

C Unmarried couples

'A man and a woman who are not married to each other but are living together as husband and wife' are treated as if they were married and living in the same household.[204] The concept of 'living together as husband and wife' is used elsewhere in social security legislation and, as such, has been the subject of critical discussion in chapter 7.[205]

D Children and young persons

The general position is that a child (under 16) or a young person (aged 16–18 and in receipt of full-time education) who is a member of the same household as the claimant is treated as part of the family unit for income support purposes, provided that the claimant (or the claimant's partner, in the case of a couple who are members of the same household) is 'responsible' for the child or young person.[206]

i 'Responsible' for child or young person

The basic rule is that a person 'is to be treated as responsible for a child or young person for whom he is receiving child benefit'.[207] Clearly, this cannot apply to those young persons who, exceptionally, can themselves claim income support under rules which have already been considered,[208] nor does it apply to children being fostered under statutory provisions or while awaiting an adoption order.[209] Where one child (eg a young teenage mother) receives child benefit in respect of another child, the person receiving child benefit for the teenager is also regarded as responsible for the second child.[210] If, unusually, no one is receiving child benefit, the responsible person is the one with whom the child or young person usually lives, unless only one claim for that benefit has been made, in which case it is the person making that claim.[211] Where a child regularly stays with one parent for part of the week, and the other parent for the rest of the week, only one parent can claim income support.[212] This rule has the merit of

201   SI 1987/1967, reg 16(2). See *CIS/13805/1996*.
202   Or in a residential care or nursing home; on 'residential accommodation' see SI 1987/1967, reg 21(3).
203   SI 1987/1967, reg 16(3).
204   SSCBA 1992, s 137(1).
205   Pp 220–223, above.
206   SSCBA 1992, s 137(1) and SI 1987/1967, reg 14(1).
207   SI 1987/1967, reg 15(1). Until October 1993 the test was one of 'primary responsibility'. Although this was also determined largely by reference to entitlement to child benefit, it allowed rather more flexibility.
208   SI 1987/1967, reg 14(2)(b); and see p 284, above.
209   SI 1987/1967, reg 16(4).
210   SI 1987/1967, reg 15(1A).
211   SI 1987/1967, reg 15(2).
212   SI 1987/1967, reg 15(4). This rule does not apply where the child falls within either category (3) or (4) in the discussion under heading (ii) below.

administrative convenience but does little to support family life. Where parents have separated and both are on benefit (eg the mother claiming income support and the father income-based jobseeker's allowance), the children's weekly personal allowances will be paid to the holder of the child benefit book (typically the mother). Thus although the children may have staying-over contact with their father, he will receive no assistance with the costs of this from the social security system.[213] In contrast, if he was in work, his child support liability would be reduced if the children stayed with him for more than one night a week on average, in recognition of the costs he then has to bear. Although the income support rule cannot be challenged under the EC Equal Treatment Directive,[214] the Court of Appeal has accepted that the parallel provision in the income-based jobseeker's allowance scheme is potentially indirectly discriminatory under the Directive.[215] It is also arguable that the income support rule is inconsistent with at least the spirit of the European Convention on Human Rights.[216]

ii Member of same household

The second condition is that the child (or young person) should be a member of the same household as the claimant. While the general principles regarding the interpretation of this phrase and the disregard of temporary absences which we have examined in relation to couples apply equally here, there is a special set of rules. A child (or young person) is treated as *not* being a member of the claimant's household where he or she:[217]

(1) has been abroad for more than four weeks;[218]
(2) has been in hospital or residential accommodation for more than 12 weeks and has not been in regular contact with the claimant or members of the claimant's household;
(3) is being looked after by a local authority, or has been placed for (or prior to) adoption; or
(4) is in custody.

Part 4 Assessment of the applicable amount

A General

A claimant's needs might be met in three quite different ways. Assistance in kind might be provided, at least where this was practicable. If there was a need for clothing or toilet articles, these would be provided (or a voucher for their purpose) on proof that the claimant was unable to afford them. This approach is still used in the US, eg by the distribution of 'food stamps', but has been relatively uncommon in this country. However, most controversially, support for certain asylum seekers was provided by way of

---

213 Cf *Vaughan v Adjudication Officer* [1987] 1 FLR 217.
214 Council Directive (EEC) 79/7.
215 *Hockenjos v Secretary of State for Social Security* [2001] EWCA Civ 624, [2001] ICR 966. Income support itself does not fall within the material scope of Council Directive (EEC) 79/7: p 44, above.
216 Art 8 ECHR, guaranteeing the right to family life. See p 57, above.
217 SI 1987/1967, reg 16(5).
218 Or eight weeks in the case of absence abroad for medical treatment: SI 1987/1967, reg 15(5)(aa).

vouchers for a limited period.[219] Secondly, cash payments might be awarded for the purposes of purchasing the specific goods or services required by the applicant. Traditionally this method has been used in British means-tested systems, notably under the supplementary benefit legislation in the form of 'single payments'. While this kind of relief is still available under the social fund, most such payments are made by way of loan.[220] The third method is the one most widely adopted in Great Britain: cash payments are made to cover the applicant's assumed needs, which are calculated according to formulae set out in legislation (or regulations made under it).

The advantage of paying benefit according to a standard scale rate is that it gives the recipient some discretion as to how to spend it. Different claimants have varying needs, particularly with regard to clothes and amenities, and the system of scale rates enables them to exercise a limited degree of choice. There is considerable evidence that long-term benefit claimants necessarily develop budgeting skills in order to manage their limited incomes.[221] Since the late 1950s, it has been generally agreed that those in receipt of assistance should share in increasing national prosperity and in consequence the payments are designed, in theory, to be high enough to cover some amenities as well as the goods necessary to carry on a subsistence existence.[222]

Under the supplementary benefit scheme, a person's needs were assessed by aggregating 'normal', 'additional' and 'housing' requirements. 'Normal' requirements were intended to cover 'items of normal expenditure on day-to-day living apart from housing costs', for example food, household fuel, clothing, normal travel and laundry costs, miscellaneous household expenses and leisure amenities.[223] To reflect an assumed higher cost of living, the scale rates varied according to whether the claimant was a 'householder' or a 'non-householder'; larger payments were also made to pensioners and those in receipt of benefit for over a year who were not required to be available for employment (the 'long-term' rate).[224] 'Additional requirements', which had replaced the discretionary 'exceptional circumstances additions', enabled the weekly payments to be increased to cover regularly occurring expenditures, such as heating, laundry and diet, resulting from the individual circumstances of the claimant or the family unit. Finally, 'housing requirements' were to deal with housing costs though in the latter years of the supplementary benefit scheme, given the introduction of housing benefit, they principally covered only mortgage interest payments, water rates and the maintenance and insurance of property.

The structure of the income support scheme is significantly different. While the 'personal' allowances are, broadly speaking, the equivalent of 'normal requirements', the 'additional requirements', the 'long-term rate' and the distinction between 'householder' and 'non-householder' have all disappeared.[225] Instead, the varying needs of different client groups (families, the disabled and the elderly) are met by a system of premiums. For some claimants (typically those with mortgages) an element of housing costs may still be included, provided that they are not met by housing benefit.

---

219   IAA 1999, ss 95 and 96 and SI 2000/704; see Billings (2002) 9 JSSL 115. In addition, the passported fringe benefits available to income support claimants include, in certain circumstances, milk tokens and free vitamins.

220   See ch 13, below.

221   See eg National Children's Home *Deep in Debt* (1992) ch 6; Cohen et al *Hardship Britain* (1992) ch 3; and Huby and Dix *Evaluating the Social Fund* DSS Research Report No 9 (1992) pp 103–105.

222   The reality can be very different: see *Cohen et al*, n 221, above.

223   DHSS *Supplementary Benefits Handbook* (1984) para 3.13; and see SI 1983/1399, reg 2, which listed the main items included.

224   See the 2nd edition of this book, pp 466–472.

225   The resulting simplification of adjudication procedures is illustrated by Figure 1 in National Audit Office *Support for Low Income Families* (1990–91, HC 153) p 10.

The income support scheme thus attributes to each claimant an 'applicable amount' which is the aggregate of the relevant personal allowances (Section B), premiums (Section C) and housing costs (Section D).[226] Benefit entitlement is then calculated by subtracting the relevant income of the claimant (discussed in chapter 14) from the applicable amount.[227]

B Personal allowances

The White Paper of 1985 promised a simple system of personal allowances varying according to age and whether the claimant was single or living with a partner,[228] but later amendments have introduced similar complexities to those which bedevilled the supplementary benefit scheme. There are three different rates for single claimants, covering five distinct categories.[229] The highest rate applies to those aged 25 and above; the middle rate to those aged 18–24, and those aged 16 or 17 who *either* qualify for the disability premium *or* fall into one of a number of especially vulnerable groups.[230] The lowest rate is paid to any other 16 and 17-year-olds who exceptionally qualify for income support. The same three rates also apply to four separate groups of lone parents: the highest rate to those aged 18 or over, the middle rate to 16 and 17-year-olds in the two special sets of circumstances as individual claimants, and the lowest rate for other lone parents under the age of 18.[231]

The position with couples is even more complex, and has been made more so as a result of amendments consequential upon the introduction of jobseeker's allowance.[232] There are two basic rates payable where both members qualify for income support (one for where both partners are aged 18 or over and a lower rate where both are under 18).[233] If, however, one member of a couple is aged under 18 and would not be eligible for income support or jobseeker's allowance in their own right, the amount payable for the couple is that for a single person at the rate appropriate for the age of the elder partner. Similarly, if both are under 18 but only one partner is eligible for income support, then the personal allowance corresponding to that individual's status is paid. The normal under-18 couple rate nevertheless applies if at least one of the couple is responsible for a child or the claimant's partner is subject to a severe hardship direction or falls into various exceptional circumstances.

The differential treatment of single claimants (without children) aged under and over 25, respectively, has been a matter of some controversy. It is intended to reflect an assumption that most single claimants under 25 do not have full household

226 In addition, groups whose entitlement to benefit would otherwise have been reduced following various changes to the rules are entitled to transitional protection: SI 1987/1967, reg 17(1)(f)–(g). The special rules for boarders were abolished with their integration into the housing benefit scheme. For the difficulties which arose, see Stewart, Lee and Stewart (1986) 13 JLS 371.

227 SSCBA 1992, s 124(4).

228 *White Paper 1985* n 57, above, para 3.14.

229 SI 1987/1967, reg 17(1)(a) and Sch 2, para 1(1).

230 SI 1987/1967, Sch 2, paras 1A and 11(a). The Social Services Committee recommended that these exceptional 16 and 17-year-old cases should be paid at the full adult rate: *Ninth Report* (1988–89, HC 437-I) para 22.

231 SI 1987/ 1967, reg 17(1)(a) and Sch 2, para 1(2).

232 SI 1987/1967, reg 17(1)(a) and Sch 2, para 1(3).

233 In the case of a polygamous marriage (cf p 218, above) the higher couple rate is applicable to the claimant and one partner, and the difference between that rate and the highest rate for a single claimant is applied to each other partner: SI 1987/1967, reg 18.

responsibilities and thus, in effect, replaces the householder/non-householder distinction, the application of which generated considerable administrative difficulties.[234] Originally, the government proposed that the same age split should apply to couples but this was withdrawn in the light of criticism, particularly from the SSAC,[235] that it failed to take account of the trend to establish households at increasingly younger ages.[236] The previous Conservative government refused to act on advice from the SSAC that the full rate should be restored to those living away from home[237] and there has been no indication of a change in policy on the part of the Blair administration. On the contrary, the government successfully resisted a human rights challenge to the parallel lower rate for adults in the contributory jobseeker's allowance scheme.[238]

As we have seen,[239] the 'family' for income support purposes does not include adult dependants (other than partners). Consequently, the only dependants for whom personal allowances are available are children and young persons (under 19). At the time of the Fowler Reviews considerable attention was given to the impact of age differences on the cost of bringing up children.[240] The Green Paper of 1985 sought views on the possible restructuring of the age bands, with the dividing lines at 8 and 13, rather than 11 and 16 as was then the case.[241] The proposal received support but the government eventually concluded that it could not be implemented without making available additional resources.[242] The income support scheme then operated for nearly a decade on four age bands: under 11, 11 to 15, 16 to 17-year-olds and 18-year-olds. In April 1997 the Major government reduced these to three, at the same time providing that increases only took effect from the first Sunday in September following the child's 11th or 16th birthday. This resulted in significant reductions in benefit depending upon the happenstance of when the individual child's birthday fell.[243] As part of its strategy to combat child poverty,[244] the first Blair government phased in equalised personal allowances for children in the two lower bands. In October 1999 the lowest rate was increased substantially above the rate of inflation and in April 2000 a uniform rate for children from birth to the September after their 16th birthday was introduced. Thus there are now just two age bands: one for children aged under 16 (as defined) and another for those aged 16–18.[245]

234   *Green Paper 1985* n 56, above, vol 2, para 2.34.
235   *Fourth Report* (1985) para 3.6.
236   Cf *White Paper 1985* n 57, above, paras 3.10–3.11. On this phenomenon, see Harris *Social Security for Young People* (1989) pp 43–44, 96 and 108. No equivalent protection was offered to the 20 per cent of single supplementary benefit claimants in the 18–24 age group who had been paid at the householder rate. It was argued that the reform released resources for older people: *White Paper 1985*, para 3.13.
237   See eg SSAC *Sixth Report* (1988) ch 2, *Seventh Report* (1990) pp 41–42 and *Eighth Report* (1992) pp 39–40.
238   *Reynolds v Secretary of State for Work and Pensions* [2002] EWHC 426 (Admin).
239   P 291, above.
240   Field *What Price A Child?* (1985). The contrast between the social security rates and those prescribed by the National Foster Care Association, based on the Family Expenditure Survey, was the subject of comment during discussion of the 1986 Bill: Mr M Meacher, Standing Committee B Debates, col 698.
241   *Green Paper* 1985 n 56, above, vol 2, para 2.77.
242   *White Paper 1985* n 57, above, para 3.16.
243   For criticism, see SSAC report (1996, Cm 3393).
244   DSS *Opportunity for All: Tackling poverty and social exclusion* (1999, Cm 4445) ch 3.
245   SI 1987/1967, reg 17(1)(b) and Sch 2, para 2. No allowance is payable where the child in question has capital in excess of £3,000.

C Premiums

The system of premiums for different 'client groups' represented the Thatcher government's attempt to resolve the tension between the concern to simplify the means-testing process and the recognition that there are wide divergences of need according to individual circumstances. The groups originally designated for such premiums were: families, lone parents, pensioners (at two rates), the disabled, the severely disabled and disabled children. Whether this structure adequately compensated claimants for the loss of the 'additional requirements' and 'long-term' rates, previously available under the supplementary benefit scheme, has been much debated.[246] Criticism has focused, in particular, on the provisions for the disabled.[247] The central problem is that, as will be seen, application of the premiums typically requires the claimant (or the disabled member of the family) to satisfy the conditions for other social security disability benefits, whereas under the more flexible supplementary benefit system additions were available for a broader range of health and disability problems.[248] As the House of Commons Social Services Committee observed, 'help can be targeted more accurately or the benefit system can be made simpler to operate but not both at the same time'.[249]

The original structure of premiums has been modified several times since the inception of the income support scheme in 1988. A third rate of premium for pensioners, the enhanced pensioner premium, was added in 1989 and a carer's premium followed in 1990. In 2001 a bereavement premium and an enhanced disability premium were both added. However, the most significant change was the abolition of the lone parent premium in 1997. The scheme originally provided for an additional premium (in addition to the family premium) where the claimant was a member of a family but had no partner.[250] This was payable from the start of a claim in recognition of the extra costs associated with lone parenthood, whereas formerly lone parents only qualified for the 'long-term' rate of supplementary benefit after 52 weeks.[251] This policy was reversed by the Major government in a phased process that was carried through by the following Labour administration and also resulted in the abolition of one-parent benefit.[252] As a first step the lone parent premium was frozen at its April 1995 rate in the 1996 up-rating exercise. In April 1997 the lone parent premium was abolished and replaced by a new higher rate of the family premium incorporating the lone parent premium.[253] From April 1998 lone parents making a new claim and existing claimants who became lone parents qualified only for the ordinary, lower rate of the family premium.[254] The higher rate of the family premium has remained frozen and will shortly be abolished as the standard rate overtakes it in value. The justification advanced by the previous Conservative government was the need to ensure that lone parents were not unduly advantaged by the benefits system in comparison with couples.[255] The Blair government has maintained this rhetoric but, no doubt in part because of the intense political

---

246 See, esp, SSAC *Fourth Report* (1985) paras 3.13–3.21; Select Committee on Social Services *Seventh Report* (1984–85, HC 451) and *Ninth Report* (1988–89, HC 437); and Dalley (ed) *Disability and Social Policy* (1991).
247 See the references cited at n 246, above..
248 See Rowell and Wilton *The Law of Supplementary Benefits* (1982) pp 54–55, 61–63.
249 *Ninth Report* n 246, above, para 24.
250 SI 1987/1967, Sch 2, para 8 (now repealed).
251 *Green Paper 1985* n 56, above, vol 2, para 2.82.
252 P 658, below.
253 See SSAC report Cm 3296 (1996).
254 See SSAC report Cm 3713 (1997).
255 *SSAC report* n 254, above, Appendix 2.

difficulties it encountered in abolishing one-parent benefit, has made improvements elsewhere in the benefit system which provide more assistance for those raising children, whether or not as lone parents.[256] As part of its child support reforms, the government also introduced a 'child maintenance premium' in 2001. This is a misnomer, as in structural terms this involves a disregard on assessable income rather than the creation of a new premium.[257]

i Family premium

This applies where at least one member of the family is a child or young person.[258] The idea is to provide additional help to families which had previously been largely dependent on the ordinary rates of supplementary benefit.[259] Only one such premium is payable, however many children there are in the family.[260] As described above, the special lone parent rate of the family premium has been frozen in cash terms and will be overtaken in a matter of a few years by the ordinary family premium.[261]

ii Disability, severe disability and enhanced disability premiums

As indicated above, the income support provision for disabled persons has given rise to considerable controversy. The approach taken to reform in 1988 included not only the first two premiums discussed here but also, for the purpose of computing the claimant's income, the total disregard of disability living allowance and the partial disregard of earnings.[262] In defence of this strategy, the then government pointed out that the disability and severe disability premiums are applied as soon as the conditions for them are fulfilled, whereas the 'long-term' supplementary benefit rate was in general only paid after one year's incapacity for work.[263] The government suffered a defeat in the House of Lords when this part of the Social Security Bill 1986 was being considered[264] and, to pacify critics, introduced what is now section 135(5) of SSCBA 1992. This stipulates that 'the applicable amount for a severely disabled person shall include an amount in respect of his being a severely disabled person' – a curious provision, since there is no explicit reference in the parliamentary legislation to other 'client groups', or to the premiums applicable to them.

The disability premium applies to persons under 60. Where the claimant is single (or a lone parent) he or she must[265] *either*:

---

256   Most notably in the increases to the value of the personal allowances for children, discussed above.
257   P 455, below.
258   SI 1987/1967, reg 17(1)(c) and Sch 2, para 3. For definitions, see pp 291–293, above. The family premium is payable irrespective of whether any personal allowance is excluded because a child has more than £3,000 in capital.
259   *White Paper 1985* n 57, above, para 3.15.
260   If a child lives with the claimant for part of the week, and for the remainder is being looked after by a local authority, has been placed for (or prior to) adoption, or is in custody, the relevant proportion of the premium is payable: SI 1987/1967, regs 15(3) and 16(6).
261   Since April 1997 the aggregate family premium (lone parent rate) has been frozen at £15.75. By April 2002 the family premium had risen to £14.75.
262   Pp 452–453, below.
263   Though, as the *White Paper 1985* n 57, above, acknowledges, some of the conditions are based on entitlement to disability benefits which require a qualifying period: para 3.23.
264   477 HL Official Report (5th series) cols 12–24.
265   SI 1987/1967, Sch 2, para 11(a).

(1) receive an attendance,[266] disability living,[267] or severe disablement allowance, long-term incapacity benefit,[268] disabled person's tax credit or a mobility supplement;[269] *or*

(2) be provided with an invalid carriage or a DWP grant towards the cost of maintaining a car, or be registered as a blind person; *or*

(3) have been treated as incapable of work[270] for a continuous period of 52 weeks[271] (or 28 weeks in the case of a person who is terminally ill).

In the case of a couple, the claimant must satisfy one of these three conditions or the partner must satisfy (1) or (2).[272]

To qualify for a severe disability premium, single claimants[273] (or lone parents) must satisfy three conditions: they must be in receipt of the care component of disability living allowance at the highest or middle rate (or attendance allowance); there must be no non-dependants aged 18 or over residing with them; and no one must be in receipt of carer's allowance for looking after them.[274] However, where someone comes to the household to care for the claimant, an existing entitlement to a severe disability premium will continue for 12 weeks.[275] If the claimant is one of a couple, the same conditions broadly apply[276] but both partners must be in receipt of disability living or attendance allowance.[277]

The scope of the Secretary of State's powers to prescribe such criteria were challenged in *Chief Adjudication Officer v Foster*.[278] The House of Lords rejected the appellant's argument that these powers were limited to specifying conditions which were connected with the claimant's disability. The intricate definition of 'non-dependant'[279] for the purpose of the second of these three conditions has been the subject of several convoluted amendments[280] and a considerable body of Commissioners' case law. In particular, it was redrafted in order to reverse the effect of the Court of Appeal's judgment in *Bate v Chief Adjudication Officer*.[281] Here the Court of Appeal had held that where a severely disabled young woman resided with her parents, the converse did not hold true. In

---

266 See the extended definition of 'attendance allowance' in SI 1987/1967, reg 2(1). On the meaning of 'in receipt of', see *R(IS) 10/94*.
267 Or would have satisfied the conditions for either disability living allowance or attendance allowance but for the fact that he or she has been in hospital for more than 28 days: see p 704, below.
268 Or did receive long-term incapacity benefit which has ceased because of that benefit's age limit or because a retirement pension became payable, and has since been continuously entitled to income support.
269 An extra-statutory payment made to compensate for an official error counts for these purposes: SI 1987/1967, Sch 2, para 14A.
270 Within the meaning of SI 1987/1967, Sch 1, para 5: see p 538, below.
271 The waiting period of 52 weeks need not be served again if an intervening period of less than 8 weeks occurs between two spells of incapacity for work: SI 1987/1967, Sch 2, para 12(1)(b)(ii). This linking period is 52 weeks in the case of a welfare to work beneficiary, as defined by reg 2: Sch 2, para 12(1A).
272 SI 1987/1967, Sch 2, para 11(b).
273 A member of a couple is deemed to have no partner if their partner is blind or treated as blind.
274 SI 1987/1967, Sch 2, para 13(2)(a).
275 SI 1987/1967, Sch 2, para 13(3)(c) and (4).
276 Except that carer's allowance might be payable in respect of one member of the couple.
277 SI 1987/1967, Sch 2, para 13(2)(b).
278 [1993] 1 All ER 705, HL. See Feldman and Wikeley (1993) 109 LQR 544.
279 See SI 1987/1967, reg 3 and Sch 2, para 13(3). Those who are not treated as 'non-dependants' and so whose presence can be ignored include: partners (but only if in receipt of attendance allowance or the highest or middle rate of the care component of disability living allowance); children; persons caring for, and paid by, the claimant (or partner) under arrangements with a voluntary organisation; joint occupiers of the dwelling, other than close relatives; tenants and lodgers.
280 See SSAC Report (1991, Cm 1694), for the background to these changes, and their *Eighth Report* (1992) ch 4 for a call for a longer-term strategy.
281 [1995] 3 FCR 145; see Ashton [1995] 2 JSSL 155.

other words, her parents did not reside *with her*, as they were the householders and joint tenants. On this construction the parents did not fall within the definition of 'non-dependants' so as to exclude their daughter from receipt of the severe disability premium. The House of Lords subsequently reversed the decision of the Court of Appeal, holding that the 'residing with' was mutual in this type of situation.[282]

The enhanced disability premium was introduced in April 2001. It is payable where the claimant or a member of the claimant's family (in either case aged under 60) receives the highest rate care component of disability living allowance.[283] This represents the mechanism by which the Blair government has implemented its pledge to increase the basic income support allowance for the most disabled people by the creation of a 'Disability Income Guarantee' (DIG).[284]

iii   Pensioner, enhanced pensioner and higher pensioner premiums

Under the original scheme there were just two such premiums, but in 1989 the government announced its intention to target more assistance on the poorest pensioners, resulting in three different pensioner premiums. The 'ordinary' pensioner premium is applicable where the claimant, or partner, is aged 60 to 74 (inclusive).[285] The enhanced pensioner premium is payable where the claimant, or partner, is aged 75 to 79 (inclusive).[286] There is automatic entitlement to the higher pensioner premium if the claimant, or partner, is aged 80 or over; those aged 60 to 79 receive the higher award if one of two conditions relating to disability is fulfilled:[287]

(a)   The claimant or partner is over 60 and either of them satisfies conditions (1) or (2) for the disability premium, specified above.[288]

(b)   The claimant was entitled to income support, including a disability premium, in respect of a benefit week within eight weeks of his or her 60th birthday and has remained continuously entitled to income support since reaching that age.[289]

Under successive Conservative administrations the three pensioner premiums were paid at different rates, with the highest rate premium being paid to the disabled and most elderly pensioners. In 1999 the first Blair government introduced the Minimum Income Guarantee (MIG) for the poorest pensioners.[290] At the outset the MIG was effectively simply a renaming of income support for pensioners, although the levels of the premiums were increased above the rate of inflation and steps taken in an attempt to improve take-up amongst pensioner households. More substantial reform followed in 2001, when the cash distinctions between the three different pensioner premiums were swept

---

282   [1996] 2 All ER 790; see Harris (1996) 3 JSSL 130.

283   SI 1987/1967, Sch 2, para 13A(1). There are exceptions, eg where the claimant has been a hospital patient for more than six weeks or in respect of a child or young person who has £3,000 or more in capital: Sch 2, para 13A(2). On the highest rate care component of disability living allowance, see ch 19, below.

284   DSS *A new contract for welfare: Support for Disabled People* (1998, Cm 4103).

285   SI 1987/1967, Sch 2, para 9. Similarly, the 'long-term' rate of supplementary benefit was automatically awarded where the claimant (or partner) was aged 60 or over.

286   SI 1987/1967, Sch 2, para 9A.

287   SI 1987/1967, Sch 2, para 10.

288   The condition for the disability premium relating to claimants formerly in receipt of certain benefits which have ceased solely because of age limits or going into hospital applies equally here: see nn 267 and 268, above.

289   A gap in entitlement to income support not exceeding eight weeks (or 52 weeks in the case of a welfare to work beneficiary) and which spans the claimant's 60th birthday is disregarded for this purpose.

290   DSS *A new contract for welfare: Partnership in Pensions* (1998, Cm 4179) ch 5. On the extent of pensioner poverty, see p 589, below.

away, creating one higher rate of the MIG. This reflected the government's decision in the April 2001 up-rating exercise to increase the pensioner premiums by more than the Retail Price Index (RPI) or the ROSSI index (or indeed earnings).[291] As a result all three pensioner premiums are now paid at the same rate, one for a single person and a higher rate for a couple. However, the different qualifying criteria have been retained in the regulations and so it remains possible for a future government to make differential provision for pensioners other than on their relationship status. It is clear, however, that there will be further changes in income support provision for pensioners in the near future with the establishment of the Pension Service in 2002 and the introduction of the state pension credit in October 2003 to reward those pensioners on low incomes who have made their own provision for retirement.

iv Disabled child premium

The introduction of this premium constituted a response by the then Conservative government to the criticism that its original proposals took insufficient account of the needs of disabled children.[292] It is applicable for each child or young person who is a member of the family unit[293] *and* is either blind or in receipt of disability living allowance[294] *and* does not have capital exceeding £3,000.[295]

v Carer premium

The carer premium was introduced in 1990 as part of the then government's package of disability benefit reforms.[296] It is payable where the claimant or partner receives carer's allowance, or would do so but for the operation of the overlapping benefit rules.[297] In order to ease the transition when the caring role ends, entitlement to the carer premium continues for eight weeks after the claimant ceases to receive (or is treated as receiving) carer's allowance. A double premium is paid where both partners meet the qualifying criteria.

vi Bereavement premium

Since April 2001 a bereavement premium has been payable where an individual aged between 55 and 60 claims income support as a single person within eight weeks of their entitlement to a bereavement allowance ceasing.[298] This addition to the list of available premiums was consequential upon the changes to widows' benefits introduced by the Welfare Reform and Pensions Act 1999.[299] Its purpose appears to be to provide

---

291   The ROSSI index is based on the RPI less housing costs.
292   *White Paper 1985* n 57, above, para 3.22. See also p 298, above.
293   See pp 291–293, above.
294   Or is no longer receiving disability living allowance because he or she is a patient, provided he or she continues to be a member of the family.
295   SI 1987/1967, Sch 2, para 14. On the capital condition, see pp 463–464, below.
296   See SSAC *Benefits for Disabled People: a Strategy for Change* (1988) p 64 and *The Way Ahead: Benefits for Disabled People* (1990, Cm 917) p 41.
297   SI 1987/1967, Sch 2, para 14ZA.
298   SI 1987/1967, para 8A.
299   See ch 16, below.

some compensation to those newly widowed who would previously have received widow's pension until the age of 65 but who now, as a result of those reforms, receive only bereavement allowance for 52 weeks.[300] As a result this premium, unusually, is time-limited.[301] The statutory provision for the bereavement premium ceases in April 2006 as by that time all those who are entitled to income support as a result of the addition of this premium will qualify for income support as a pensioner (having reached the age of 60). At that point the bereavement premium would be superseded by the pensioner premium, paid at a higher rate, and so the former premium will become otiose.

vii   Accumulation of premiums

The family premium, the severe disability premium, the enhanced disability premium, the disabled child premium and the carer premium may be accumulated with any other premium.[302] For example:

> a single parent with three children, two of whom are disabled, would qualify for a family premium[303] + two disabled child premiums + carer premium.

The general principle is that only one of the other premiums is applicable to a family at any one time and therefore if the claimant satisfies the conditions for more than one of these, the higher or highest applies.[304]

D   Housing costs

i   History and policy

A feature of social assistance schemes since 1935 has been the payment of separate allowances to cover housing costs. Two arguments in particular have been used to justify them.[305] First, there are significant variations in such costs, and these cannot easily be covered by standard scale rates; this is not really the case for any other goods or services. Secondly, while a claimant can, within reason, adjust expenditure on, say, food or clothing, this is impossible with housing costs. They have to be paid regularly and it is unreasonable to expect claimants to move to cheaper accommodation every time they are ill or unemployed, and have to rely on benefit.

Until 1983, housing costs formed a very significant portion of total supplementary benefit expenditure and indeed many claimants only qualified for that benefit because of their expenditure on rent or other housing costs.[306] The system was, however, expensive to administer and the rules added considerably to the overall complexity of the scheme. Another drawback was that there was often overlap between the rent element of

---

300   *Social Security Legislation 2001* n 113, above, vol II, para 2.400.
301   SI 2000/2239, reg 6.
302   SI 2000/2239, reg 17(1)(c) and (d) and Sch 2, para 6(1). But note that the enhanced disability premium cannot be paid in addition to a pensioner or higher pensioner premium: Sch 2, para 6(2).
303   Which might be at the standard or higher rate, depending on when he or she claimed benefit: see p 297, above.
304   SI 1987/1967, Sch 2, para 5.
305   Cf George *Social Security: Beveridge and After* (1968) pp 214ff.
306   In its *Annual Report for 1979* (1980, Cmnd 8033) para 4.2, the Supplementary Benefits Commission estimated that there were 0.3 million such claimants.

supplementary benefit and the rent rebates and allowances, and rate rebates, available from local authorities. The problem was partly resolved by the Social Security and Housing Benefits Act 1982 which introduced the housing benefit scheme, administered by local authorities. Nevertheless, mortgage interest payments, water rates and some other miscellaneous housing costs, such as additions for insurance and maintenance, continued to be administered by the DHSS under the supplementary benefit scheme.

The Fowler Reviews examined afresh the arrangements for dealing with housing costs. While most of the recommendations related to housing benefit and, as such, are noted in chapter 11, the role of income support was not ignored. Indeed, one of the most discussed issues was whether the latter system could adequately cope with the consequences of the controversial proposal that, to ensure political accountability for local authority spending, no household should be able to recover more than 80 per cent of chargeable rates.[307] The prospect of income support not supplying any recompense for the 20 per cent loss in rate rebates was the subject of critical comments by the SSAC,[308] among others, but these did not lead to any significant change in government policy.[309] As regards those housing costs met by the supplementary benefit scheme, the government made two main proposals.

The first was that water rates and certain residual housing costs, such as insurance and minor building repairs, should no longer be separately covered, since the amounts were small and the administrative cost of dealing with them was high; rather, they should be subsumed under the general system of personal allowances.[310] Though widely criticised,[311] this proposal was implemented in SSA 1986.[312]

Secondly, it was suggested that the meeting of mortgage interest payments in full led to work disincentive problems and to unfairness between those in and out of work.[313] The decision was accordingly made to limit the entitlement to 50 per cent of the eligible housing costs for the first 16 weeks of an income support claim. This restriction only applied to those of working age, partly in response to objections that these arguments were hardly applicable to, for example, the elderly and the disabled and a reduction in this form of assistance would discriminate unfairly between tenants and owner-occupiers.[314] This reform was applied to the supplementary benefit legislation and was subsequently carried over into the income support scheme.

After 1988 there was a steady stream of amendments to the rules governing housing costs under the income support scheme, culminating in a major overhaul in 1995. For example, in April 1992, faced with a deepening crisis in the housing market, the government introduced direct payments of income support mortgage interest to recognised lenders.[315] In August 1993 a ceiling was imposed on the maximum amount of a loan which was eligible for assistance under income support,[316] and in May 1994

---

307 *Green Paper 1985* n 56, above vol 1, para 9.20.
308 SSAC *Fourth Report* (1985) para 3.33.
309 Cf *White Paper 1985* n 57, above, para 3.56.
310 *Green Paper 1985* n 56, above, vol 2, para 2.49.
311 The government considered that such criticisms had 'exaggerated the effect on claimants and under-estimated the gains from this simplification for local office staff': *White Paper 1985* n 57, above, para 3.42.
312 The amount transferred to the basic rate of income support quickly proved inadequate as water rates increased at well over the level of the Retail Price Index between 1988 and 1991: SSAC *Eighth Report* (1992) pp 16–18.
313 *Green Paper 1985* n 56, above, vol 2, para 2.48.
314 SSAC *Fourth Report* (1985) para 3.39.
315 Social Security (Mortgage Interest Payments) Act 1992, see now SSAA 1992, s 15A and SI 1987/1968, Sch 9A. Under this scheme direct payments came into operation once the claimant was entitled to 100 per cent of eligible interest.
316 P 311, below.

the rules were further amended to frustrate the possibility of 'upmarketing' (ie trading up while on benefit) at the expense of the benefits system.[317]

Despite these changes, the cost of income support mortgage interest payments rose steadily from £31 million in 1979 to £1.1 billion in 1994. In October 1995 the government instituted a fundamental overhaul of the way in which housing costs are met under the income support scheme.[318] The government's position was that the availability of state aid had undermined the growth of private insurance. The principal changes involved restricting further the level of assistance at the outset of a claim for benefit, imposing a standard rate of interest and narrowing the range of loans for repairs and improvements which qualify for support. These changes, which the government argued would stimulate more comprehensive market coverage, came into force despite intensive lobbying by mortgage lenders, the insurance industry and the poverty lobby, and notwithstanding the strong reservations of the SSAC.[319] Early surveys suggested that take-up amongst home-owners of mortgage payments protection insurance provided by the private sector remained low. Moreover, such policies typically have their own deferral periods and a substantial minority of benefit claimants could not claim on their policy owing to the restrictive coverage of such schemes.[320]

ii Conditions of entitlement

For housing costs to be included in the applicable amount, two conditions must be satisfied.

A   RESPONSIBILITY FOR HOUSING COSTS

The claimant, or any other member of the family unit, must be 'liable to meet housing costs'.[321] This does not necessarily mean 'legal' responsibility in the strict sense and so will arise not only where the claimant or partner is liable to meet the costs[322] but also where a person so liable does not in fact meet them, the claimant has to meet them to stay in the home and it is reasonable to attribute the expenditure to the claimant.[323] This will commonly arise where couples have separated and the partner who has left was legally responsible for the mortgage payments. Another situation is where a person in practice shares the costs with someone other than a partner or a close relative;[324] such a person will be treated as having a shared responsibility, particularly where the expenditure is similarly shared for the purpose of the housing benefit regulations.[325] Where some but not all members of a family are involved in a trade dispute, the housing costs are treated as those of the members not so involved.[326]

---

317   P 312, below.
318   See Wikeley (1995) 2 JSSL 168; and Lundy (1997) Conv 36.
319   Cm 2905 (1995). The amending regulations, SI 1995/1613 substituted an entirely new SI 1987/1967, Sch 3.
320   Ford and England *Data and Literature on Mortgage Interest: State Provision and Private Insurance* DSS In-house Report No 65 (2000) p 24.
321   SI 1987/1967, Sch 3, paras 1(1) and 2.
322   Provided that this is not to a member of the same household.
323   See *R(IS) 12/94* (on the pre-1995 formulation of this provision).
324   For the meaning of 'close relative', see SI 1987/1967, reg 2(1).
325   Cf p 413, below.
326   SI 1987/1967, Sch 3, para 2(2).

B   DWELLING OCCUPIED AS THE HOME

The second condition is that the housing cost for which the relevant person is responsible must be in respect of a dwelling which the claimant, or a member of the family, occupies as their home.[327] This means:

> the dwelling together with any garage, garden and outbuildings, normally occupied by the claimant as his home including any premises not so occupied which it is impracticable or unreasonable to sell separately, in particular, in Scotland, any croft land on which the dwelling is situated.[328]

Generally a person is treated as occupying only the dwelling in which he or she normally lives.[329] But the regulations provide for exceptions to this rule.[330] Costs for two dwellings may be allowed where a person has moved from one house to another through fear of violence[331] or where one member of a couple is a student or on a training course and the occupation of two dwellings is 'unavoidable'.[332] The same applies where the claimant moves to a new dwelling, though the costs of both the old and the new home will be met only for a maximum of four weeks. This provision does not apply where the move is a purely temporary one, undertaken in order that repairs are carried out on the normal home. In some circumstances, a person is treated as occupying a dwelling for a period of up to four weeks before actually moving in (eg because a member of the family is disabled and adaptations have to be made to the house or because the move cannot be undertaken until a decision on a social fund application for removal expenses has been made[333]). Finally, there are provisions allowing for the disregard of temporary absences from the home of up to 13 weeks (or, in exceptional cases, 52 weeks).[334] The conditions are that: the claimant intends to return to occupy the dwelling as a home; the part of the premises which he or she normally occupies is not let (or sub-let); and the period of absence is unlikely to exceed 13 weeks or, in exceptional circumstances (eg where the person is hospitalised), is unlikely substantially to exceed that period.[335] Until April 1995 the general rule allowed temporary absences of up to 52 weeks, subject to the same conditions. This extended period is now only available to specified categories of vulnerable claimants.[336]

iii   Assessable housing costs

Housing costs under the income support scheme primarily comprise mortgage interest payments; depending on when the mortgage was taken out, these may be either 'existing'

---

327   SI 1987/1967, Sch 3, paras 1(1) and 3.
328   SI 1987/1967, reg 2(1). A plot of land by itself cannot be a 'home': *R(IS) 11/94*.
329   SI 1987/1967, Sch 3, para 3(1) and (2).
330   SI 1987/1967, para 3(3)–(12).
331   The fear of violence must be 'in that dwelling or by a former member of his family'. It therefore covers domestic violence generally but racist attacks only in the home.
332   It must also be 'reasonable' for housing costs to be paid for both properties.
333   And a member of the family is aged under 5, 60 or over or disabled.
334   SI 1987/1967, Sch 3, para 3(10).
335   The limited number of students eligible for income support who are absent from their term-time home during the summer vacation cannot invoke this rule: SI 1987/1967, Sch 3, para 3(4).
336   SI 1987/1967, para 3(11). See SSAC Report (1995, Cm 2783). See also the special rule for those entering a residential care or nursing home on a trial basis: SI 1987/1967, Sch 3, para (8) and (9).

or 'new' housing costs. Assistance may also be provided with the interest on loans for repairs and improvements or with other miscellaneous housing costs, but in nearly all cases such support is provided at a standard interest rate, not the actual interest rate incurred by the claimant. Each of these issues must be considered in turn.

A   MORTGAGE INTEREST PAYMENTS

The principal type of housing cost met under the income support scheme is that of mortgage interest payments. Traditionally systems of social assistance have not covered capital repayments. The argument is presumably that public money should not be used to allow individuals to acquire capital assets, though the provision of home improvement grants and generous discounts to council tenants exercising the right to buy their homes is difficult to reconcile with it. A mortgagor who claims income support should therefore attempt to persuade the building society to accept interest payments only and defer repayment of capital. It would also appear possible for a claimant who lets the premises to arrange for the tenant to make payments, reflecting the capital element. Under the regulations, such a payment would not be treated as part of the claimant's resources.[337]

'Housing costs' are defined by regulations[338] as those costs which the claimant (or a member of his or her family) is liable to meet in respect of the dwelling occupied as the home and which arise from a loan on a residential property,[339] a loan for repairs or improvements, or other prescribed housing costs. As will be seen below, there is a fundamental difference in the level of support provided for 'existing' and 'new' housing costs respectively. 'Existing housing costs' are those housing costs arising under an agreement entered into before 2 October 1995, or under an agreement entered into after 1 October 1995 which replaces an existing agreement between the same parties in respect of the same property.[340] 'New housing costs' are simply defined as those arising under an agreement made after 1 October 1995, other than the exceptional type of case which falls within the definition of 'existing housing costs'. As was the case prior to the 1995 changes, claimants who are aged 60 or more (or have a partner of that age) are entitled to housing costs from the start of their claim and so are exempt from the rules discussed below.[341]

B   EXISTING HOUSING COSTS

Before 2 October 1995 claimants were entitled to assistance with 50 per cent of their mortgage interest repayments for the first 16 weeks of their claim.[342] Since that date, if

337   SI 1987/1967, regs 42(4)(a)(ii) and 51(3)(a)(ii). See also Sch 9, paras 18, 19 and 30(b).
338   SI 1987/1967, Sch 3, para 1(1), referring to paras 15–17.
339   This is defined as a loan taken out for the purpose of 'acquiring an interest in the dwelling occupied as the home', or a second loan taken out to pay off a first loan, provided that the latter itself related to acquiring an interest in the home. This does not cover mere recovery of title deeds (*R(IS) 18/93*), but includes a leaseholder taking out a further advance to buy the freehold reversion (*R(IS) 7/93*) and a purchase from a partner's trustee in bankruptcy (*R(IS) 6/94*). Interest payments under a hire purchase agreement to buy the dwelling occupied as the home are also covered: SI 1987/1967, Sch 3, para 15(2).
340   SI 1987/1967, para 1(2). In addition, the existing agreement must have been entered into before 1 October 1995 and the new agreement must be for a loan of the same amount or less than the amount of the loan under the agreement it replaces (for this purpose any amount payable to arrange the new agreement and included in the loan is to be disregarded).
341   SI 1987/1967, para 9; housing costs under a co-ownership agreement, a Crown tenancy or in respect of a tent(!) are also payable from the outset.
342   See the 4th edition of this book, pp 483–484.

the claimant has 'existing housing costs', no income support is payable in respect of that loan for the first eight weeks of a claim. This is then followed by payment of 50 per cent of housing costs for the next 18 weeks. Assistance with the full amount of the loan (subject to the qualifications discussed further below) only begins after a continuous period of 26 weeks on benefit.[343] The need for a continuous period of entitlement to income support means that the rules governing linking periods may be of critical importance in practice as regards both existing and new housing costs. The position since 1995 is that there is, for most purposes, a standard 12-week linking period rather than the eight weeks which applied previously.[344] The SSAC had recommended a 26-week linking period, given that the extended waiting periods might otherwise act as a disincentive to work.[345] However, there is now a 52-week linking rule for welfare to work beneficiaries and for those claimants (or their partners) who either start work or increase their hours such that they no longer qualify for income support.[346] The regulations also provide that entitlement to income-based jobseeker's allowance counts as entitlement to income support and vice versa, so as to ensure that claimants transferring from one benefit to the other are not prejudiced.[347]

It is not simply in terms of the delay before full housing costs are met that the scheme is less generous than previously. Under the old scheme, income support covered the interest which accrued on mortgage arrears during the first 16 weeks. In addition, the previous arrangements provided protection for claimants who, because of the 50 per cent rule, would never actually qualify for income support and so build up entitlement during the necessary 16 waiting weeks. Furthermore, interest on loans that constituted ineligible housing costs were previously met in the case of separated spouses. The current rules omit any assistance with these various costs.[348]

C   NEW HOUSING COSTS

The position is even grimmer for those with 'new housing costs' (ie the great majority of post-2 October 1995 mortgages) who will, with the passage of time, form an increasing proportion of income support claimants. Claimants in this position receive no assistance at all with housing costs for the first 39 weeks (effectively nine months).[349] It is only after that extended period that they will receive help with 100 per cent of their housing costs (again, subject to the further qualifications discussed below). There are, however, four categories of claimants who would otherwise be new borrowers who are deemed to have 'existing housing costs' and so are dealt with under the less restrictive provisions described in the previous section.[350] These groups comprise people who would find it very difficult, if not impossible, to secure adequate mortgage protection insurance. These groups are:

---

343   SI 1987/1967, Sch 3, para 6(1).
344   SI 1987/1967, para 14.
345   SSAC report (1995, Cm 2905).
346   SI 1987/1967, Sch 3, para 14(10)–(13). There is also a 26-week rule for the purposes of the upmarketing rule discussed further below: para 4(4) and (5).
347   SI 1987/1967, para 1A; SI 1996/30, reg 32; SI 1996/207, Sch 2, para 18.
348   Some claimants who would otherwise not qualify during the waiting period may be covered by the new linking rule: SI 1987/1967, para 14(4)–(9).
349   SI 1987/1967, para 8(1). A claimant who has both existing and new housing costs has them calculated separately and then aggregated: para 11(2).
350   SI 1987/1967, para 8(2)–(5).

- carers who fall within the category of prescribed persons so as to qualify for income support (eg those receiving carer's allowance);
- those detained in custody pending trial or sentence upon conviction;
- people who have been refused payments under a mortgage insurance policy, because the claim is the outcome of a pre-existing medical condition which relieves the insurer of any liability or they have been infected by HIV; and
- claimants with children who apply for income support because of the death of a partner or because of being abandoned by a partner.

These exceptional cases are narrowly defined. For example, they do not cover those claimants who were refused insurance cover in the first place because of their medical condition. The final exception, making provision for abandoned partners, has also been restrictively interpreted by the Commissioners. In this context 'abandonment' has a meaning akin to 'desertion' and so involves both physical separation and a deliberate withdrawal of support by the abandoning partner, to which the remaining partner does not consent.[351] It may, however, include constructive abandonment.[352]

D   INTEREST ON LOANS FOR REPAIRS AND IMPROVEMENTS

Assessable housing costs may include interest payable on a loan taken out for the purpose of carrying out repairs or improvements to the home or for repaying a second loan entered into to pay the interest on a first loan taken out for the same purposes.[353] The pre-1995 scheme covered loans taken out to pay for 'major repairs necessary to maintain the fabric of the dwelling' or for one or more of a number of specified measures 'undertaken with a view to improving its fitness for occupation'.[354] The government took the view that it was not reasonable for improvements to the standard of privately owned housing stock to be made at taxpayers' expense and accordingly introduced a number of significant restrictions in October 1995. First, the governing test was made much narrower: a loan qualifies only if the works are 'undertaken with a view to maintaining the fitness of the dwelling for human habitation'.[355] Secondly, the scope of the individual measures was curtailed in a number of significant respects. For example, the regulations now refer only to the *provision* (and not, as before, the *improvement*) of ventilation and natural lighting, drainage facilities and home insulation. The precise ambit of the term 'provision' is unclear: it might be argued that it is not confined to initial installation, but includes repairs to or replacement of an existing facility.[356] Similarly, the former coverage of any 'improvement in the structural condition of the dwelling' was replaced by 'repairs of unsafe structural defects'.[357] The installation of

351   *CIS 5177/1997*; *CIS 2210/1998* (reported as *R(IS)12/99*) and *CIS 2790/1998*: see further Miln [1999] 29 Fam Law 168; and Wikeley [1999] 29 Fam Law 702 and [2001] 31 Fam Law 672.
352   *R(IS) 2/01*.
353   SI 1987/1967, Sch 3, para 16(1), which also covers a loan to pay a service charge imposed to meet such costs. Any loan must be used for the relevant purpose within six months or such further period as is reasonable.
354   See the 4th edition of this book, p 484.
355   SI 1987/1967, Sch 3, para 16(2).
356   *R v Social Fund Inspector, ex p Tuckwood* CO 3807-94 (27 April 1995, unreported) see *Social Security Legislation 2001* n 113, above, vol II, para 2.479. However, the DSS *Decision Makers Guide* (DMG) (2000) vol 4, ch 23, para 23531 cites an unreported Scottish decision to the effect that provision means the installation of items that do not already exist to maintain the fitness of the home for human habitation:*CSJSA/160/98*.
357   The general catch-all category in the former SI 1987/1967, Sch 3, para 8(3)(k) to cover loans for 'other improvements which are reasonable in the circumstances' was also abolished.

new kitchen units, and the provision of heating (including central heating, where none previously existed), both common reasons for home improvement loans, are excluded under the new arrangements.

E MISCELLANEOUS HOUSING COSTS

The scheme covers a number of miscellaneous housing costs which are to some degree analogous to those already considered but which are not covered in the housing benefit scheme. These include ground rents relating to long tenancies (and in Scotland, feu duty), service charges,[358] rent charges, payments under a co-ownership scheme or relating to a Crown tenancy or licence and site charges for tents, but deductions will be made for heating, water and electricity charges if they are included in any such payments.[359] Buildings insurance under a mortgage (as opposed to a liability to the landlord as part of the service charges) is not covered.[360]

F STANDARD RATE OF INTEREST

Under the pre-1995 regime the amount of income support housing costs was based on the actual rate of interest charged on the individual claimant's loan. This undoubtedly caused considerable administrative difficulties, as every individual change in interest rates had to be notified to the Department and the assessment revised.[361] The new system is more streamlined, in that the calculation depends on the prescribed 'standard rate of interest' which is intended to reflect the average rate of interest set by the major lenders.[362] This figure is subject to periodical review and is varied according to movements in interest rates nationally, being triggered by a change in the average rate of 0.25 per cent or more. If, however, the actual rate of interest charged is less than 5 per cent, then that real interest rate is used in calculating income support housing costs.[363] The use of a broad-brush standard rate of interest necessarily means that many claimants do not have their full housing costs met. As the SSAC observed, it is often those on the lowest incomes who have to resort to lenders charging higher than average rates of interest in order to secure a loan.[364] This illustrates the difficulty in reconciling the goals of targeting resources effectively on those who are most in need whilst also simplifying the administrative process of assessing entitlement to benefit.

iv Restrictions and deductions

The standard rate of interest applies to all claimants (except for those with mortgages of less than 5 per cent) and will result in many claimants not receiving assistance with the full cost of their mortgage or other housing costs. In addition, there are a number of further provisions, discussed below, which may restrict the amount of help available.

---

358 See *R(IS) 3/91* (but see now SI 1987/1967, Sch 3, para 17(2)(c)); *R(IS) 4/91*; and *R(IS) 4/92*.
359 SI 1987/1967, Sch 3, para 17.
360 *R(IS) 19/93*; *R 1/93(IS)*; *Secretary of State for Social Security v McSherry* 1995 SLT 371.
361 The obligation was on the claimant to notify in each case, even though annual changes may be in the public domain: *R 5/94(IS)*.
362 SI 1987/1967, Sch 3, paras 10(1) and 12.
363 SI 1987/1967, para 12(2).
364 The SSAC's proposals to protect those most at risk were rejected by the government: (1995, Cm 2905).

A   HOUSING COSTS COVERED ELSEWHERE IN THE BENEFITS SYSTEM

There is an overriding principle that assessable housing costs may not include anything in respect of housing benefit expenditure, to avoid overlap with that scheme.[365] Similarly, the housing costs of a claimant in a residential care or nursing home are excluded because of the special arrangements that apply in such cases.[366]

B   HOUSE PURCHASES BY TENANTS

If, while in receipt of income support, a claimant purchases property from a private landlord, or exercises the 'right to buy' option available to public sector tenants, the assessable housing costs will be limited to the amount of 'eligible rent' – the figure used for calculating housing benefit[367] – immediately before the purchase.[368] This figure can subsequently be raised to take account of any increase in the standard rate of interest or in the other miscellaneous housing costs. The more generous treatment under the pre-1995 rules, which provided for variation if the application of the restriction 'becomes inappropriate by reason of any major change in the circumstances of the family affecting their ability to meet expenditure on housing costs', no longer applies.[369]

C   EXCESSIVE HOUSING COSTS

The Secretary of State may disallow housing costs to the extent that they are 'excessive'.[370] They will be so regarded where the dwelling is 'larger than is required ... having regard, in particular, to suitable alternative accommodation occupied by a household of the same size', where there is suitable accommodation available in a less expensive area,[371] or where the housing costs are higher than the outgoings for suitable alternative accommodation in the same area. Thus if the costs of such accommodation are nil (because a property could be purchased without a mortgage), no housing costs will be allowable.[372] However, the existence of certain 'relevant factors' may make it unreasonable to expect the claimant to seek alternative accommodation, in which case the costs will be allowed in full. The regulations define 'relevant factors' to include the general factors of 'the availability of suitable accommodation and the level of housing costs in the area'. More specifically, decision makers must have regard to 'the circumstances of the family including in particular the age and state of health of its members, the employment prospects of the claimant and, where a change in accommodation is likely to result in a change of school,

365   SI 1987/1967, Sch 3, para 4(1)(a).
366   Pp 329–330, below. A person who is temporarily in such accommodation may still receive help with housing costs on their home under para 3(8)–(12).
367   Pp 420–424, below.
368   SI 1987/1967, Sch 3, para 4(8). Any housing costs already in payment will be included in this figure. See also para 4(11).
369   See the 4th edition of this book, p 485. The separate rule for tenants who buy their own homes was abolished in 1995, and such cases now fall under SI 1987/1967, Sch 3, para 4(8).
370   SI 1987/1967, Sch 3, para 13. Note that this restriction operates in addition to the restriction on loans entered into by claimants in receipt of benefit and the general ceiling on housing costs, discussed further below.
371   An 'area' is 'not capable of precise definition' but is a narrower term than 'a locality or district': *R(IS) 12/91*. But note that SI 1987/1967, Sch 3, para 13(1)(b) refers to 'immediate area' whilst para 13(1)(c) just refers to the 'area'.
372   *R(IS) 9/91* and *R(SB) 6/89*, both on earlier formulations of the same rule.

the effect on the education of any child or young person' in the family.[373] This list is not exhaustive, and so all the relevant circumstances of the family must be considered.[374] It follows that while the test for whether there is suitable accommodation available is objective, the claimant's inability to secure such accommodation must be judged subjectively.[375] If there are no 'relevant factors', the restriction does not apply for the first six months of a claim, and this may be extended by a further period of six months if, and so long as, the claimant 'uses his best endeavours to obtain cheaper accommodation'.[376] These relaxations only apply if the claimant was able to meet the housing costs when the accommodation was first taken on – clearly an anti-abuse provision, to prevent claimants using the social security system to 'move up' the housing market.[377] However, although the test of ability is objective, it is confined to the point at which the mortgage was entered into; the test is not one of financial prudence.[378]

D MORTGAGE INTEREST CEILING

In the early 1990s a small number of well-publicised cases in which claimants received income support for very high mortgages[379] prompted the then government to introduce a new restriction. A ceiling of £150,000 was imposed from August 1993 on the size of a loan eligible for income support housing costs, reducing to £125,000 from April 1994 and to £100,000 since April 1995.[380] The Secretary of State, noting that the previous open-ended commitment was unusual by international standards, stated that the original limits were chosen to 'reflect a suitable balance between the interests of the taxpayer and those of mortgage holders and lenders'.[381] All eligible loans (eg for purchase and/ or repairs and improvements) are aggregated for the purposes of this rule. Following the SSAC's recommendation, loans taken out for the purpose of adapting a dwelling for the special needs of a disabled person are disregarded in such a calculation.[382] Although this capping rule affects only a limited number of claimants,[383] its significance is more in that it is consistent with increasing government emphasis on private welfare provision (eg mortgage protection insurance).

373 SI 1987/1967, Sch 3, para 13(5).
374 *R(SB) 6/89*; *R(SB) 7/89*. An official assurance that the full mortgage would be met on moving house, whilst not capable of creating an estoppel, is a relevant factor to consider: *R(SB) 14/89*.
375 *R(IS) 10/93*.
376 SI 1987/1967, Sch 3, para 13(6). The deferment period only operates on a further claim to income support where the break in entitlement is at least 12 weeks.
377 Cf the next two heads of restrictions and the comparable provisions in the housing benefit scheme, p 432, below, and Housing Benefit Review *Report of the Review Team* (1985, Cmnd 9520) paras 3.7–3.9.
378 *Secretary of State for Social Security v Julien*, CA, reported as an Appendix to *R(IS) 13/92*. But see the next section on the mortgage interest ceiling. See also *Town and Country Building Society v Julien* (1991) 24 HLR 312.
379 Eg *Secretary of State for Social Security v Julien*, CA, reported as an Appendix to *R(IS) 13/92* (£630,000 mortgage); and the case of a Mr Deaves (£832,500 mortgage): (1992) *Independent*, 21 December.
380 SI 1987/1967, Sch 3, para 11(4)–(11).
381 See SSAC Report (1993, Cm 2272) Appendix 2, para 12. A more cynical view would be that the limits represented a compromise between the reported opening bids of the Treasury and the DSS (£100,000 and £200,000 respectively): (1993) *Independent*, 31 January.
382 See *SSAC Report* n 381, above, paras 21–22 and SI 1987/1967, Sch 3, para 11(9). The SSAC's other recommended safeguards were not followed.
383 Initially these were estimated to number approximately 2,000, most of whom lived in Greater London and the South East (there is no adjustment to take account of the regional disparities in property values): *SSAC Report* n 381, above, Appendix 2, para 11. With rising house prices, this figure will obviously have increased.

E   ADDITIONAL LOANS INCURRED BY INCOME SUPPORT CLAIMANTS

In 1994 the government introduced further measures to frustrate what was portrayed as the phenomenon of 'upmarketing' by income support claimants.[384] Under these provisions, assistance is no longer available to meet the additional interest on an increase in loan commitments for home purchase taken out while the borrower or a member of his or her family is on income support. For this purpose periods of entitlement separated by gaps of 26 weeks or less are treated as continuous.[385] Thus a claimant who leaves benefit on finding work and three months later purchases a house, only to become unemployed again after a further two months will receive no assistance with those housing costs. There are a number of exceptions to this draconian rule, such as special loans taken out to meet the special needs of a disabled person, but these exemptions are not as generous as those urged on the government by the SSAC.[386]

F   APPORTIONMENT OF HOUSING COSTS

There are provisions to reduce the amount of assessable housing costs where part of them are met, or deemed to be met, by other persons. We have already seen[387] that there are situations in which the costs are shared between the claimant and someone other than a partner or a close relative. In such a case, it is the proportionate part of those costs for which the claimant is responsible which are allowed.[388] Analogously, where the claimant's premises is a 'mixed hereditament', in the sense that it is used for both domestic and business purposes, the allowable amount is the proportion of the mortgage interest attributable to that part of the premises in which the claimant (and family, if any) lives.[389] A reduction is also made where a non-dependant normally resides with the claimant, because that person is deemed to contribute to housing expenditure.[390] 'Resides with' here means sharing any room (eg kitchen) except a bathroom, toilet or common access area, but not where each person is separately liable to make payments to the landlord.[391] The most common example of a 'non-dependant' is an adult son or daughter still living at home, but a member of the claimant's family unit[392] is not covered. The expression 'non-dependant' also excludes:[393]

(1)   any other child or young person living with the claimant, or
(2)   a joint occupier[394] who is a co-owner or joint tenant with the claimant (or partner), since that will be treated as a case of shared responsibility (above), or

384   SI 1987/1967, Sch 3, para 4(2)–(12).
385   This contrasts with the eight-week linking rule which previously applied to the 50 per cent provisions and the 12-week linking rule which applies in other contexts in SI 1987/1967, Sch 3, para 14(1).
386   SSAC Report (1994, Cm 2537).
387   P 304, above.
388   SI 1987/1967, Sch 3, para 5(5).
389   SI 1987/1967, para 5(1). The apportionment follows the rateable value or (for a composite hereditament built since the abolition of rates) the current market value of the relevant parts of the premises.
390   SI 1987/1967, para 18.
391   SI 1987/1967, reg 3(1) and (3), but not rooms of common use in sheltered accommodation: reg 3(4).
392   P 291, above.
393   SI 1987/1967, reg 3(2)–(2B). This test is also relevant to the criteria for the award of the severe disability premium: p 298, above. See further the discussion in *Social Security Legislation 2001* n 113, above, vol II, paras 2.10–2.16.
394   Close relatives who meet this condition are nonetheless treated as non-dependants unless they shared joint liability before 11 April 1988.

(3) any person, other than a close relative, who is liable to make payments (ie as a tenant, licensee or boarder) to the claimant (or partner), or, conversely, to whom the claimant (or partner) is liable to make such payments (since the rent payable will normally be treated as part of the claimant's income),[395] or

(4) any person engaged by a charitable or voluntary organisation to care for the claimant (or partner) and who is paid by the claimant (or partner).

There are currently six rates of deduction:[396] the lowest rate (currently £7.40) is for non-dependants who are not in remunerative work or are in such work but have a gross income of less than £88 per week. The other five rates, all of which are subject to annual adjustment, are £17.00 (for gross incomes between £88 and £130.99 per week), £23.35 (for gross incomes between £131 and £169.99 per week), £38.20 (for gross incomes between £170 and £224.99), £43.50 (for gross incomes between £225 and up to £280.99) and £47.75 (for gross incomes of £281 or more per week).[397] The number of bands was increased from four to six in 1998; at the same time the levels of deductions made were substantially increased. The effect of these non-dependant deductions is to wipe out, or at least significantly reduce, any entitlement to income support housing costs in some cases.

Only one deduction (the higher one) can be made in respect of a couple.[398] Where the claimant is a joint occupier, the deduction will be apportioned in accordance with the proportion of housing costs attributed to him or her.[399] Finally, no deduction is made if the claimant (or partner) is blind or in receipt of attendance allowance or the care component of disability living allowance, or where a deduction is already being made under the housing benefit scheme. Deductions are also not made if the non-dependant is aged 16 or 17, aged 18 to 24 and in receipt of income support or income-based jobseeker's allowance, a full time student, or receiving a youth training allowance. Similarly, non-dependants do not give rise to a deduction where they are joint tenants or co-owners (even if they are close relatives) or are not living with the claimant because they have been a patient for more than six weeks or are in prison.[400]

Part 5   Urgent cases

A Background

Until 1980, the now defunct Supplementary Benefits Commission had a discretion to make urgent needs payments to persons not entitled to ordinary supplementary benefit in circumstances where the need was 'urgent, sudden and unforeseeable'.[401] In that year, as part of the general retreat from discretion, many of the circumstances in which such payments could be made (and these included some cases where ordinary benefit was payable) were prescribed by regulations,[402] but a residual discretion was retained

---

395   P 459, below.
396   Before April 1992 there were just two; the extra rates were introduced to permit greater differentiation between levels of earnings. On the background to this reform, see SSAC *Ninth Report* (1993) pp 23–25.
397   SI 1987/1967, Sch 3, para 18(1)–(2).
398   SI 1987/1967, para 18(3)–(4).
399   SI 1987/1967, para 18(5).
400   SI 1987/1967, para 18(6)–(7).
401   Supplementary Benefits Act 1976, s 4.
402   Subsequently consolidated in SI 1981/1529.

for cases where the payment was 'the only means by which serious damage or serious risk to the health or safety' of the family could be prevented.[403] The Urgent Cases Regulations were aptly described as the 'long-stop' of the supplementary benefit scheme;[404] as such, and not surprisingly, the Fowler review team recommended return to the discretionary approach which was to be adopted more generally for one-off needs.[405] The proposal was implemented in the 1986 reforms and much of the function of the Urgent Cases Regulations was taken over by the social fund. As will be seen in chapter 13, the latter makes provision for emergency relief in the form of 'crisis loans'[406] and several principles of the Urgent Cases Regulations have been adopted, eg that a need should be regarded as urgent only if it cannot be met from other sources. Nevertheless, the overriding discretionary character of the social fund means that some claimants who would have obtained an urgent needs payment under the old law may now receive nothing or else only a reduced amount.

Until February 1996 asylum seekers were entitled to urgent cases payments from the submission of their claim for asylum until its final determination (including any appeal process). The government then introduced severe restrictions on the rights of asylum seekers to claim benefit, arguing that the previous arrangements encouraged abuse of the system.[407] The amending regulations were subsequently struck down as ultra vires by the Court of Appeal.[408] The government responded by inserting amendments into primary legislation then passing through Parliament in order to restore the original policy intent.[409] From that point, asylum seekers were only eligible for urgent cases payments if they submitted a claim for asylum *either* 'on arrival' in the UK *or* within three months of the Secretary of State making an 'upheaval declaration' in relation to that individual's home state.[410] The requirement to have submitted a claim for asylum on arrival was strictly construed by the Commissioners: essentially such a claim must have been made before leaving the port of entry. Thus an asylum seeker who was smuggled into the UK, sedated in the back of a lorry, and made a claim for asylum a matter of days later did not do so 'on arrival'.[411] The arrangements for support of asylum seekers were radically changed in April 2000. Since that date, new asylum seekers have been denied access to urgent cases payments; instead applications must be made to the National Asylum Support Service (NASS). NASS then determines eligibility for emergency support, which was originally paid in the form of vouchers rather than cash.[412]

There remains within the income support system two very narrow categories of urgent cases, where the circumstances are such that claimants cannot meet the ordinary conditions for benefit, but have a need for recurrent payments which are not available from the social fund.

403   SI 1987/1967, reg 24.
404   Mesher CPAG's Supplementary Benefit and Family Income Supplement: The Legislation (4th edn, 1987) p 386.
405   *Green Paper 1985* n 56, above, vol 2, para 2.67.
406   P 475, below.
407   See DSS Explanatory Memorandum in SSAC Report (1996, Cm 3062).
408   *R v Secretary of State for Social Security, ex p Joint Council for the Welfare of Immigrants* [1996] 4 All ER 385. See Scouler (1997) 4 JSSL 86.
409   Asylum and Immigration Act 1996, s 11 and Sch 1, with effect from July 1996.
410   Ie that it 'is subject to such a fundamental change in circumstances that he would not normally order the return of a person to that country': SI 1987/1967, reg 70(3A)(aa) (now repealed). These declarations were made only infrequently (eg for three months in respect of Zaire in May 1997 and Sierra Leone in May 1997, and not in respect of the former Yugoslavia).
411   *CIS 3231/1997.*
412   See Willman, Knafler and Pierce *Support for Asylum Seekers* (2001); and Billings (2002) 9 JSSL 115; see SI 2000/704 and SI 2002/782.

B The categories of urgent cases

The first of the categories to which the urgent cases regulations apply covers certain very narrowly defined persons from abroad. It will be recalled from an earlier section of this chapter[413] that some foreign visitors are not entitled to the standard amounts of income support. Of these, only the following may claim an urgent cases payment:[414]

(1) any person whose leave to stay was conditional on having no recourse to public funds but whose support from abroad has been temporarily interrupted; and

(2) a sponsored immigrant who has been in the UK for less than five years and whose sponsor has died.

The other category comprises cases where notional income is attributed to persons who are due to receive certain payments.[415] An urgent cases payment may be paid in such cases if the notional income is not in fact available *and* the amount of such a payment (see below) is higher than what would be paid under the ordinary income support rules *and* the Secretary of State is satisfied that the claimant (or family) will 'suffer hardship' if such a payment is not awarded.[416]

C Applicable amounts

In general, the applicable amount in urgent cases is the aggregate of 90 per cent[417] of the personal allowances for the claimant and partner (if any), the full personal allowance for any children, all relevant premiums and any assessable housing costs. For persons in residential accommodation, the applicable amount is 90 per cent of their personal allowance, the full personal allowance for any children and the amount normally allowed for accommodation.[418]

D Assessment of income and capital

The means test applied to applicants for urgent cases payments is more severe than that to which ordinary income support claimants are subjected. All income, except housing benefit and 'tariff' income from capital,[419] is deducted from the applicable amount and, apart from payments from the Macfarlane Trusts, Independent Living Fund, etc, social fund payments and concessionary payments for the non-payment of income support, there are no disregards.[420] The treatment of capital is even more different. No 'tariff' income is deemed to arise from it; rather, available capital is itself deducted from the applicable amount. In other words, claimants are expected to use up all available capital

---

413 P 280, above.

414 SI 1987/1967, reg 70(2) and (2A). In some of the cases there is a prescribed maximum period of entitlement to an urgent cases payment. There is also transitional protection for certain groups.

415 P 456, below.

416 SI 1987/1967, reg 70(2), (4). Hardship is not defined, but official guidance suggests it should be given its normal everyday meaning of 'severe suffering or privation': *DMG* n 356, above, vol 6, para 31173, citing *R(SB) 19/82*.

417 Where the '40 per cent deduction rule' applies (cases of voluntary unemployment, pp 359–377, below), the 90 per cent formula is applied after the relevant deduction has been made.

418 SI 1987/1967, reg 71(1)(b). For those in local authority accommodation, 98 per cent of the personal allowance is paid, but in such cases no accommodation allowance is payable: reg 71(1)(c).

419 Notional income attributed where a claimant is due to receive payments is also excluded.

420 SI 1987/1967, reg 72(1).

before relying on an urgent cases payment. For this purpose, capital is assessed in accordance with the rules described in chapter 12, below, but with various modifications. The most notable are that the liquid assets of a business, arrears of certain benefits and the proceeds of the sale of a home which are intended to be used for the purchase of another home are all taken into account.[421] Most importantly, there is no disregard of the first £3,000 of capital.

Part 6   Income support and maintenance

A   Introduction

This Part is concerned with the benefit implications of the breakdown of family relationships. The central policy issue here is the extent to which one partner should be expected to exhaust any remedies for maintenance against the other before relying on benefit. The primacy of the private law obligation of financial support was reinforced by the Child Support Act 1991 (CSA 1991), albeit that this duty is now enforced by a public agency. To facilitate exposition, it will be assumed in the discussion that follows that the claimant is female.[422] Section B outlines the evolution of the law; Sections C and D consider the position as regards maintenance for children and separated wives respectively while Section E considers the analogous situation where a sponsor is liable to maintain an immigrant.

B   Evolution of the present law[423]

The position of deserted wives and children was not specifically covered by the Poor Law Amendment Act 1834. The practice of poor law guardians varied widely; some refused relief on the ground that payment of assistance might encourage collusive desertion and fraudulent claims.[424] Those who did provide outdoor relief could, after the Poor Law Amendment Act 1868, apply to a summary court requiring the woman's husband to reimburse them.

The antecedents of the present law with regard to unmarried mothers can be seen even earlier in the nineteenth century.[425] The 1834 Act enabled parishes to recover from the putative father any money spent on the relief of illegitimate children. Amending legislation in 1844 temporarily took matters out of the hands of the poor law guardians, and introduced a direct civil action by the mother against the putative father.[426] But in 1868 the poor law authorities regained their power to recover from him when a mother and her child became a charge on the parish. These principles

---

421   SI 1987/1967, reg 72(2).
422   While there are reciprocal duties of maintenance between spouses, this assumption accords with the reality in the large majority of cases and is reflected in the terminology of the 1991 Act itself: see CSA 1991, s 6(1).
423   See Report of the Committee on One-Parent Families (1974, Cmnd 5629) Appendix 5, s 5; Brown (1955) 18 MLR 113; and the judgment of Lord Goddard CJ in *National Assistance Board v Wilkinson* [1952] 2 QB 648, [1952] 2 All ER 255.
424   *Committee on One-Parent Families* n 423, above, Appendix 5, para 69.
425   *Committee on One-Parent Families* n 423, above, Appendix 5, paras 55–65.
426   This was the precursor of affiliation proceedings, abolished in 1989 by the Family Law Reform Act 1987, s 17.

were substantially reflected in the National Assistance Act 1948. This removed the obligation of grandparents and children to maintain destitute relatives, which had existed since 1601; but spouses remained under a duty to maintain each other and parents, including the putative father, owed the same obligation to their children. These 'liable relative' provisions, as they are known, have been re-enacted in the present legislation and the Secretary of State (referred to subsequently for convenience as the Department) has a right to recover sums paid in benefit from those with obligations of maintenance.[427]

In 1974 the Finer Committee criticised the existence of three separate systems for providing support for lone parent families: financial provision on divorce (principally through the county court), the magistrates' domestic jurisdiction[428] and social security. The Committee recommended a new, non-contributory benefit for single parent families, the 'guaranteed maintenance allowance', payable after three months of separation.[429] In addition, a lone mother would receive benefit in the normal way and no advice (or encouragement) would be given to her on possible proceedings against the husband, or father.[430] Instead the Department would determine what he should pay as a contribution and this would be enforced by the issue of an 'administrative order'. There would be an appeal to a tribunal on questions of quantum, while on legal issues (eg the paternity of a child) the husband/father could appeal to a court. The woman would only be motivated to take proceedings herself if she thought there was a real chance of obtaining more by such means than she would in benefit. The then Labour administration showed little enthusiasm for these proposals, and any realistic prospect of their implementation disappeared with the return of a Conservative government in 1979. The Finer philosophy was however recognised in part by the introduction of a special rate of child benefit for lone parents, but this was abolished in 1998.[431]

Between 1981 and 1988 the number of lone parent families receiving supplementary benefit and later income support increased by 86 per cent from 388,000 to 722,000. Over the same period, the proportion of these families in receipt of regular maintenance fell from 50 per cent to 23 per cent.[432] This meant that by 1988 only 7 per cent of the cost of providing benefits was collected from liable relatives.[433] The reasons for the decline in the amount recovered included the DSS's own failure to make liable relative work a priority and the effect of increasing unemployment among liable relatives.[434] In October 1990 the government published its White Paper, *Children Come First*, on the future of maintenance for children.[435] This drew attention to the inconsistency in the levels of such maintenance paid to lone parents, which arose from the high degree of discretion vested in both the courts and the Department. The existing arrangements were seen as leading inevitably to both out-of-date awards and arrears of maintenance. The White Paper proposed the creation of an administrative machinery for assessing, collecting and enforcing child maintenance which would place the responsibility for supporting children firmly with their parents. In doing so,

---

427   SSAA 1992, s 106.
428   In Scotland, the sheriffs' jurisdiction.
429   *Committee on One-Parent Families* n 423, above, Pt 5, ss 5–7.
430   *Committee on One-Parent Families* n 423, above, Pt 4, ss 11–12; and see Eekelaar [1976] PL 64.
431   P 658, below.
432   National Audit Office *Department of Social Security: Support for Lone Parent Families* (1989–90, HC 328) p 22.
433   Bradshaw and Millar *Lone Parent Families in the UK* DSS Research Report No 6 (1991) p 79.
434   *Bradshaw and Millar* n 433, above; and *National Audit Office* n 432, above.
435   Cm 1264. See also *Bradshaw and Millar* n 433, above.

the cost to the taxpayer and the risks of benefit dependency would be reduced.[436] In the same month that the White Paper appeared the liable relative rules were amended by SSA 1990.[437] Further immediate reforms on the private law side were implemented by the Maintenance Enforcement Act 1991.[438] The White Paper's proposals were embodied in CSA 1991, which came fully into force in April 1993.

The debacle of the early years of the Child Support Agency has been fully analysed elsewhere.[439] At the legislative level there were frequent complex changes to the regulations governing the assessment of child support liabilities. In addition, CSA 1995 introduced a system of departures from the formula for special cases.[440] The incoming Labour government in 1997 identified the reform of child support as one of its key priorities in the field of social policy. Its proposals were published in a Green Paper[441] and White Paper[442] and subsequently embodied in the Child Support, Pensions and Social Security Act 2000 (CSPSSA 2000). The main feature of the 2000 Act, which was scheduled to come into force in April 2002 but was then postponed, is that the previous highly complex formula is replaced by a simple slice of the non-resident parent's income, depending upon the number of children involved in the assessment.[443]

C Children

i General

CSA 1991 radically changed the law governing maintenance for children. The Act applies irrespective of whether the child is living with a lone parent or with a married or unmarried couple. It also applies regardless of whether the child's parents are on benefit. It is, therefore, primarily a matter of family law, but the assessment and enforcement of child maintenance now rests with an executive agency of the DWP, the Child Support Agency.[444] It follows that this is not the place for a comprehensive account of the child support system.[445] Instead, this section will provide a brief overview of the scheme and then concentrate on those aspects which interact directly with the social security scheme, namely the obligation imposed on certain claimants to co-operate with the Agency and the extent of the financial contribution required of absent parents who are themselves on benefit.

Section 1 of CSA 1991 lays down the principle that 'each parent of a qualifying child is responsible for maintaining him'.[446] A child is defined as a person aged under 16, or aged between 16 and 18 and in prescribed education.[447] This follows the definition

---

436 For a more sophisticated analysis, see Brown *In Search of a Policy: the rationale for social security provision for one parent families* (1988) and *Why don't they go to work? Mothers on benefit* SSAC Research Paper 2 (1989).
437 See Wikeley [1990] Fam Law 458.
438 See Wikeley [1991] Fam Law 353.
439 Davis, Wikeley and Young *Child Support in Action* (1998).
440 Priest (1998) 5 JSSL 118.
441 DSS *Children First: a new approach to child support* (1998, Cm 3992).
442 DSS *A new contract for welfare: Children's Rights and Parents' Responsibilities* (1999, Cm 4349), on which see HC Social Security Committee *Tenth Report* (1998–99, HC 798).
443 See Wikeley [2000] 30 Fam Law 820 at 888 and [2001] 31 Fam Law 35 at 125.
444 On the executive agencies, see p 134, below.
445 See further Bird *Child Support: The New Law* (5th edn, 2002).
446 CSA 1991, s 1(1).
447 CSA 1991, s 55(1).

used for the purposes of the child benefit legislation.[448] A 'qualifying child' is one for whom one or both parents are 'absent parents', that is where the child and absent parent(s) do not live in the same household and the child has his or her home with a 'person with care'.[449]

The statutory duty to maintain a qualifying child is met by making periodical payments of maintenance in accordance with the provisions of CSA 1991.[450] The maintenance assessment itself is based on the formula, contained in the Act and elaborated upon in the regulations, which leaves very little scope for any discretion to operate. Any person with care (whether or not a parent) of a qualifying child *may* apply for a maintenance assessment by the Child Support Agency.[451] This right was initially subject to complex phasing in rules until 1997, when it was envisaged that the Agency would become fully operational. In fact the administrative disaster which befell the Agency made this target unattainable and there remain some cases which are still subject to the courts' jurisdiction.[452]

ii The application procedure for income support claimants

Section 6(1) of CSA 1991 deems parents with care who are claiming income support or income-based jobseeker's allowance to have made an application for child support maintenance.[453] This obligation rests on parents alone, and so any other relative caring for a child who then claims income support is not required to make an application.[454] However, the duty applies to parents claiming benefit even where they do not receive any such benefit in respect of a qualifying child.[455] The claimant is asked to complete a maintenance assessment form (MAF),[456] a substantial document which deals with the person's circumstances and resources. The claimant is required, so far as she reasonably can, to provide information enabling the absent parent to be traced and the child support maintenance to be assessed and collected.[457] The type of information or evidence which may be required is set out in extensive detail in regulations.[458] The Secretary of State may prescribe circumstances in which this obligation does not apply, or in which it may be waived,[459] but to date no such provision has been made. If the claimant is no longer covered by section 6(1), she can ask the Secretary of State to cease to act, who is then obliged to comply.[460]

448 P 660, below.
449 CSA 1991, s 3(1)–(3).
450 CSA 1991, s 1(2).
451 CSA 1991, s 4(1). Absent parents may also apply, although not surprisingly very few do so. In Scotland, children who are aged at least 12 and habitually resident there may apply in their own right: s 7.
452 See Wikeley [2001] 31 Fam Law 35.
453 Income-based jobseeker's allowance was added in October 1996: JA 1995, Sch 2, para 20(2). This rule also applies to 'any other benefit of a prescribed kind'; this included disability working allowance (now disabled person's tax credit) until October 1999, since when there has been no benefit so prescribed.
454 Such a carer could apply under CSA 1991, s 4 as a person with care.
455 CSA 1991, s 6(6). This might arise where a capital settlement has the effect of taking the child out of the assessment unit for social security purposes: see p 463, below.
456 The MAF comes in two versions, with the shorter one for existing claimants whose means are known to the Benefits Agency, and must be supplied free of charge: SI 1992/1813, reg 2(2).
457 CSA 1991, s 6(7).
458 SI 1992/1812, reg 3(2).
459 CSA 1991, s 6(8).
460 CSA 1991, s 6(9)–(11).

The requirements under section 6 have changed in two important respects since it was first enacted in CSA 1991. First, the duty under section 6 originally also applied to family credit and disability working allowance claimants. However, when these benefits were converted into tax credits in October 1999, this requirement was abolished.[461] As part of the same package of reforms, recipients of tax credits are allowed to keep all their maintenance or child support, without it affecting their entitlement to credits (in contrast to the maximum £15 per week disregard which applied to family credit and disability working allowance).[462] The purported justification for this change of policy was that the tax credits were not social security benefits and so different considerations applied. This reasoning is less than convincing, but one major administrative advantage of the reform is that some of the Agency's caseload might migrate out of the child support system with the abolition of the requirement to co-operate for working families' tax credit cases.[463] Secondly, the original section 6 required claimants to make an application for a maintenance assessment unless they could show good cause for not doing so. CSPSSA 2000, substituting a new section 6,[464] treats claimants as having made such an application, unless they can show good cause for opting out. The circumstances in which a claimant, who is otherwise deemed to have applied for an assessment, may opt out now fall to be considered.

iii The risk of harm or undue distress

The most obvious way to encourage claimants to comply with their obligations under the original CSA 1991 would have been to provide some form of incentive, such as a maintenance disregard for the purposes of income support.[465] This would, however, have had significant public expenditure implications and so would have defeated the goal of securing benefit savings.[466] The then Conservative government therefore chose a different approach, and proposed a penalty for non-compliance. Considerable concern was expressed during the debates on the 1991 Act that some parents with care, for very good reasons, might not wish to apply for child support maintenance.[467] The government's approach was defeated in the House of Lords, only for the relevant provision to be reinserted by the House of Commons.[468] The provisions governing the good cause exemption, as it has become commonly known, were modified by CSPSSA 2000.[469] That Act also changed the formal title for the sanction from a 'reduced benefit direction' to a 'reduced benefit decision'. As part of its reforms, the Labour government also introduced a disregard of £10 a week, known as the 'child maintenance premium', where child support maintenance is in payment.[470]

461   Tax Credits Act 1999, s 2(3) and Sch 2, para 17(a) and s 19(4) and Sch 6.
462   P 456, below.
463   There is little evidence to date of this happening. In November 1999 23 per cent of parents with care with full maintenance assessments were either family credit or working families' tax credit claimants; two years later 25 per cent were in receipt of working families' tax credit: Child Support Agency *Quarterly Summary Statistics* (2002).
464   CSPSSA 2000, s 3.
465   There was quite separate provision for claimants of family credit and disability working allowance to have the first £15 per week of any maintenance received disregarded: see p 456, below.
466   It would also raise questions of equity with lone parents who did not receive maintenance: Burghes *One-Parent Families: Policy Options for the 1990s* (1993) p 13.
467   Standing Committee A, cols 37–64 (13 June 1991).
468   See 527 HL Official Report (5th series) cols 526–545; and Standing Committee A, cols 208–236.
469   CSPSSA 2000, ss 3 and 19, the latter substituting a new CSA 1991, s 46.
470   SI 2000/3176. At the time of writing this provision had not been brought into force.

A   HARM OR UNDUE DISTRESS

Good cause applies to a claimant where 'there would be a risk to her, or of any child living with her, suffering harm or undue distress as a result'.[471] Two points are clear on the scope of this exemption. First, there need not be any actual harm or undue distress; it is the *risk* of such damage that matters. Secondly, risk of harm or undue distress to *any* children living with the claimant suffices; they need not be the children of the absent parent. The term 'harm or undue distress' itself is not without difficulty and has been the subject of case law from the Child Support Commissioners.[472] The ordinary dictionary definition of 'harm' means injury or damage while 'undue distress' implies unreasonable or excessive strain, stress or pain. There is official guidance on the situations which might warrant a finding of harm or undue distress,[473] but such guidance is not binding. Clearly, where there is a history of rape or violence, a finding of harm or undue distress may be almost inevitable. The diversity of human nature is such that there will be many other circumstances in which the caring parent will be reluctant to co-operate. Such unwillingness may commonly arise where there are concerns over contact with the absent parent. Official guidance stresses that contact is a matter for the courts.[474] Whilst this is undoubtedly correct, the reality is that non-resident parents see a connection between the contact and child maintenance.[475]

A reduced benefit decision may only be issued after the appropriate procedures have been followed, and in the meantime the substantive claim for benefit should be dealt with normally.

B   PROCEDURE

The parent with care who is on benefit may ask the Secretary of State not to act under section 6 of CSA 1991.[476] In that event, the Secretary if State may require her to give her reasons for such a request.[477] A parallel procedure applies where the parent with care fails to comply with the information requirements or refuses to take a scientific test to determine paternity.[478] Such reasons must be provided within a 'specified period', which is set by regulations at four weeks.[479] The Secretary of State is then required to consider, in the light of any such reasons provided, whether, if he were to take action to pursue maintenance, 'there would be a risk to her, or of any child living with her, suffering harm or undue distress as a result'.[480] The normal procedure is for a claimant to be asked to attend an interview with an officer of the Child Support Agency at which she will be asked for the reason for the non-compliance. This procedure may be repeated 'from time to time' with a view to establishing whether circumstances have changed.[481]

471   CSA 1991, s 46(3).
472   Effectively the Social Security Commissioners in another guise: see p 200, above. See *CCS 7559/99*.
473   Child Support Agency *Decision Makers Guide* (2000) Pt 2, paras 2550–2555.
474   *Child Support Agency* n 473, above, para 2555 (Table, para 1).
475   Bradshaw et al *Absent fathers?* (1999); and Wikeley et al *National Survey of Child Support Agency Clients* DWP Research Report No 152 (2001) p 153.
476   Such a request need not be in writing: CSA 1991, s 6(5).
477   CSA 1991, s 46(2)(a). The Secretary of State must serve a written notice requesting reasons.
478   CSA 1991, ss 6(7) and 46(1)(b) and (c).
479   SI 2001/157, reg 9; previously this 'period of grace' was six weeks.
480   CSA 1991, s 46(3).
481   CSA 1991, s 46(6).

If the claimant's explanation is regarded as satisfactory, no further action is taken in respect of the possible reduced benefit decision and the claimant is informed accordingly.[482] If the Secretary of State's representative considers that 'no reasonable grounds' have been shown for the belief that there is a risk of harm or undue distress, then a reduced benefit decision *may* be made. However, such a decision cannot be given if the claimant's income support includes a disability premium, disabled child premium or higher pensioner premium.[483] In other cases, the officer making the decision must have regard 'to the welfare of any child likely to be affected by his decision'.[484] This is, of course, not the same as requiring that the child's welfare is paramount, the principle enshrined in section 1 of the Children Act 1989. However, it might be considered inappropriate to issue a notice or direction where a child is disabled or seriously ill. Furthermore, the welfare of any children of the absent parent's second family can be taken into account at this stage.

The Department's decision makers must implement reduced benefit decisions issued by the their counterparts in the Child Support Agency.[485] This is done by way of a revision or supersession of the existing award of benefit.[486] The sanction operates as a reduction in the level of benefit payable, and is not simply another deduction from benefit. Thus where income support is payable the reduction operates before deductions are made for items such as fuel costs.[487] There is a right of appeal against a reduced benefit decision to an appeal tribunal.[488]

C   THE LENGTH AND AMOUNT OF THE PENALTY

The reduced benefit decision lasts for three years, the reduction itself being 40 per cent of the income support personal allowance for a person aged 25 or over.[489] Until October 1996 the sanction only lasted for 18 months, consisting of a reduction of 20 per cent in the first 26 weeks and then 10 per cent for a further 52 weeks. The length and amount of the penalty were increased owing to government concerns that separated parents were colluding over 'good cause' in order to avoid the imposition of maintenance assessments.[490] In contrast to the labour market sanctions in the jobseeker's allowance scheme, there is no discretion to impose a reduction for a shorter period.[491] If the decision would have the effect of reducing the claimant's entitlement to nil or to less than the minimum amount of weekly benefit payable,[492] then a lower reduction is made leaving the claimant with at least the minimum amount.[493] The amount of any reduction is increased in line with the annual up-rating exercise.[494]

---

482   CSA 1991, s 6(4).
483   SI 1992/1813, reg 35A.
484   CSA 1991, s 2.
485   See the definition in CSA 1991, s 46(11).
486   There would appear to be nothing to stop a claimant eligible for housing benefit or council tax benefit to apply for a review of their entitlement, as the penalty does not apply to either benefit.
487   Pp 334–335, below.
488   CSA 1991, s 20(1)(c) and (6).
489   SI 1992/1813, reg 36(2). The reduction is based on the income support adult personal allowance regardless of the age of the parent with care, and so has a particularly harsh effect on younger claimants.
490   HC Social Security Committee *Fourth Report* (1995–96, HC 440).
491   P 373, below.
492   Currently 10 pence a week for income support (SI 1987/1968, reg 26(4)) and for jobseeker's allowance (SI 1996/207, reg 87A).
493   SI 1992/1813, reg 37.
494   SI 1992/1813, reg 36(7).

The reduced benefit decision will end early if the parent with care subsequently co-operates with the Child Support Agency or if the non-resident parent applies for a maintenance calculation.[495] A decision can be cancelled if it has been made, or not lifted, as a result of an official error.[496] A decision may also be suspended for up to 52 weeks if the parent with care ceases to claim income support.[497] If she later reclaims within this period, the balance of the penalty can be reimposed on 14 days' notice. After a year the original sanction is invalid, but a new reduced benefit decision can be made in respect of the same failure to comply. This new decision can again run only for the balance of the original reduction period.[498] A penalty may be suspended on similar terms where the child concerned is no longer covered by CSA 1991[499] or where the claimant ceases to live with and care for the child.[500]

D   SUCCESSIVE REDUCED BENEFIT DECISIONS

Only one reduced benefit decision can be in force against a parent at any one time.[501] Originally, once a sanction had been applied and run its course, no further penalty could be imposed with regard to any continuing failure to comply concerning that child. This safeguard was removed in October 1996, raising the prospect of successive penalties in respect of the same case. A further decision can also be imposed where a new qualifying child joins the claimant's household.[502] Where a second reduced benefit decision is issued against a claimant who is already subject to an existing reduction in respect of another child, the original order ceases to have effect.[503] The new order then lasts for a further three years, subject to the possibility of suspension or termination for the reasons indicated above. Special rules govern the position where the second decision would otherwise cease, eg following compliance, and where the first sanction would not have been withdrawn but for the imposition of the new order.[504] In such a case the second direction continues in existence for an extended period, being the difference between three years and the aggregate of the number of weeks served under both sanctions.

iv   Non-resident parents on benefit

Under the original child support scheme, non-resident parents claiming benefit were required to pay a minimum weekly contribution in lieu of child support unless they fell into one of a range of exceptional categories.[505] In particular, non-resident parents with second families and in receipt of income support or income-based jobseeker's allowance

495   SI 1992/1813, reg 41. The latter of these eventualities will be a very remote prospect in practice. The Secretary of State must notify the claimant of any such termination or suspension: reg 49.
496   SI 1992/1813, reg 46.
497   SI 1992/1813, reg 38. A similar provision operates where the claimant goes into hospital, a residential care or nursing home or local authority residential accommodation: reg 40.
498   SI 1992/1813, reg 38(7).
499   Eg because he or she is 16 or over and has left school or is aged 19 or over.
500   SI 1992/1813, reg 48.
501   SI 1992/1813, reg 36(8).
502   Eg if a new child is born or a child not previously subject to a decision moves in with the claimant.
503   SI 1992/1813, reg 47.
504   SI 1992/1813, reg 47.
505   See the 4th edition of this book, pp 506–507.

were exempted from making these contributions. The Labour government, as part of its package of reforms implemented from 2002, made the minimum payment payable in nearly all such cases. Under the new formula there are four rates payable: the basic and reduced rates for employed non-resident parents, the flat rate (initially fixed at £5 a week, replacing the minimum contribution) and the nil rate. The nil rate applies only if the non-resident's weekly income is less than £5 or he falls within various narrowly prescribed categories (prisoners, students, young people aged 16 or 17 and people who have been in hospital for more than a year).[506] The great majority of benefit claimants are, accordingly, liable to pay the flat rate.[507] The symbolic honouring of the child support commitment was seen as important in terms of setting a pattern of regular payments. However, this necessarily results in claimants on some of the lowest incomes receiving a sum in benefit which is below the weekly threshold set for their family composition. There is provision for such minimum payments and arrears of child support maintenance to be deducted from benefit.[508]

D   Separated wives

i   General

The discussion that follows is concerned with the situation where a childless married couple separate. If the couple are both childless and unmarried, then of course neither party is liable to support the other. If they have children, then the question of maintenance, irrespective of whether they are married, is seen predominantly in terms of the child support scheme. It follows that in practice the rules discussed below are unlikely to be applied where there are children involved.

A separated wife has an autonomous entitlement to income support (ie the aggregation provisions do not apply), provided that she and her husband are no longer considered to be members of the same household.[509] The husband's income and capital are irrelevant to the assessment of her benefit but, as a general rule, maintenance paid to her is fully taken into account when assessing her income.[510] A separated wife will be asked about the circumstances of the separation and her husband's whereabouts.[511] This is to enable the DWP to contact him as soon as possible in order to induce him to pay maintenance and reduce the burden on the state. However, the Department will not usually approach him if maintenance is being paid regularly under a court order, or if she has already started proceedings.[512] If the amount paid or offered by the husband equals (or exceeds) the wife's benefit entitlement, this is accepted and, provided payments are made, that is the end of the matter. However, much more often than not, the husband will have taken on other commitments since the separation, eg by living with a new partner, and he will be unable, or unwilling, to pay very much. The question of a liable relative's contribution then arises.

506   CSA 1991, Sch 1, para 5 and SI 2001/155, reg 5.
507   CSA 1991, Sch 1, para 4.
508   CSA 1991, s 43(2) and p 334, below.
509   On which, see p 291, above.
510   Pp 454–455, below.
511   Unlike under CSA 1991, there is no sanction where a woman declines to co-operate.
512   This, of course, again stands in stark contrast to the position under CSA 1991.

ii The liable relative's contribution

We have already seen that there is a reciprocal liability between spouses to support each other so long as income support is in payment.[513] In contrast to the child support scheme, there is no rigid statutory formula in operation for calculating the level of the liable relative's contribution. However, a non-statutory formula, originally devised under the supplementary benefit scheme, allows an assessment to be made based on his needs and those of his new dependants.[514] In this way, it is recognised that priority will be given to the family actually living with, and dependent on, the husband.[515] Thus a weekly 'protected' income is calculated by reference to what would have been the applicable amount, if he had claimed income support, including any premiums and eligible housing costs, plus one-quarter of his net earnings[516] (that is, after deducting tax and social security contributions). It is only the sum left after deducting this protected income from his resources which is to be regarded as available for meeting his wife's needs. Even then, this figure is seen only as a starting point for negotiations and it is hardly surprising, given the discretion available within the guidelines, that Departmental practice varies considerably between offices. These variations may also be caused by different approaches among officers engaged on this work, or simply the staffing levels in liable relative sections of local offices.

The absence of a satisfactory 'fit' between social security law and the private law of maintenance has long been evident in this area. Traditionally the courts have relied on two principles in assessing maintenance where both parties are on low incomes. These are, first, that the availability of income support should in principle be ignored[517] and, secondly, that where the husband is in work, an order should not be made which would have the effect of depressing his income below a subsistence level. As regards the latter, the courts have never adopted the more generous Departmental formula for assessing the husband's subsistence level.[518] So far as the former is concerned, the reality is that state benefits are not excluded from the court's calculation. It is probably true to say that, while the availability of benefit is not in itself a persuasive factor against an award of maintenance, the financial impact of benefit entitlement will be considered in determining what level of award should be made. Indeed, modern appellate decisions have tended to recognise the underlying financial realities in cases where both parties are of limited means, often imposing a 'clean break'.[519] Such an arrangement effectively transferred the responsibility for supporting the dependent partner to the state, given the moribund nature of DSS liable relatives sections in the 1980s and early 1990s. This phenomenon provided part of the impetus for the creation of the Child Support Agency.[520]

---

513 P 317, above.
514 See DSS *Residual Liable Relative and Proceedings Guide* cited in CPAG *Welfare benefits handbook 2002–2003* (4th edn, 2002) p 800.
515 The CSA 1991 operates on the converse presumption, ie that a person's primary liability is to the first family.
516 This is intended to cover expenses, such as fares to work and hire purchase payments. These are not deductible under CSA 1991.
517 *Barnes v Barnes* [1972] 3 All ER 872.
518 *Shallow v Shallow* [1979] Fam 1. The later decision in *Allen v Allen* [1986] 2 FLR 265 suggests that account will be taken of the husband's applicable amount if he were entitled to income support. For judicial criticism of this dual system, see Finer J in *Williams v Williams* [1974] Fam 55 at 61.
519 *Ashley v Blackman* [1988] Fam 85 and *Delaney v Delaney* [1990] 2 FLR 457; see Lowe and Douglas *Bromley's Family Law* (9th edn, 1998) pp 826–828.
520 Davis, Wikeley and Young *Child Support in Action* (1998) ch 1.

iii   The DWP and private law maintenance applications

If the husband is not paying any maintenance when his wife claims benefit and is not persuaded to make a contribution when contacted by the DWP, the question arises whether she should be encouraged in any way to make a maintenance application. Official policy is to discuss the possibility with the wife but to make it clear that the choice is entirely hers;[521] full entitlement to income support is preserved, whatever she decides.[522] In principle this policy seems reasonable. But it is questionable whether there are often substantial advantages to the initiation of maintenance proceedings. It is very rare for the sum awarded on such an application to be larger than benefit. It is true that a maintenance award will not lapse when benefit is no longer payable, but this may only be of academic interest in the case where a woman is left to look after young children and there is no realistic prospect of her finding work. Conservative government initiatives in this area included the introduction of a maintenance disregard and child care allowance for the in-work means-tested benefits and the extension of family credit eligibility to those working for as little as 16 hours a week.[523] In addition, the DSS was given wider powers under SSA 1990 to intervene in private law proceedings.[524] The subsequent Labour administration placed greater emphasis on incentives by introducing working families' tax credit and the income support child maintenance premium.

iv   Enforcement by the DWP

A   CIVIL PROCEEDINGS

There are three options available to the DWP in civil proceedings. First, the DWP has an independent right under section 106 of SSAA 1990 to apply to the magistrates' court for an order, but only where income support has been claimed or paid for the person liable to be maintained. Where an application is made, the court 'shall have regard to all the circumstances and, in particular, to the income of the liable person'.[525] It is clear that a husband may be liable to make payments to the DWP even though a condition of the separation from his wife was that she would not claim maintenance.[526] It has also been held that the husband's statutory obligation is not discharged by the making of a consent order under which he transferred the former matrimonial home to his ex-spouse.[527] Furthermore, although there is no express legal duty to support a former spouse or unmarried partner, the financial contribution expected from the liable relative may reflect the fact that the former partner is engaged in caring for the children of the relationship.[528] The court, in assessing the appropriate amount payable under section 106, may include a sum corresponding to the income support paid to the caring parent. Under regulations, this amount consists of the personal allowance for the joint children

---

521   This follows the recommendations of the Report of the Committee on One-Parent Families (1974, Cmnd 5629) paras 4.199–4.202.
522   Cf the position under the CSA 1991, p 320, above.
523   See pp 388, 450 and 456, below.
524   Now consolidated in SSAA 1992, ss 106–108 and discussed in the context of enforcement below.
525   SSAA 1992, s 106(2).
526   *National Assistance Board v Parkes* [1955] 2 QB 506, [1955] 3 All ER 1.
527   *Hulley v Thompson* [1981] 1 All ER 1128, [1981] 1 WLR 159. This is, however, a factor to be taken into account by the court, unlike under CSA 1991. Similarly, adultery or desertion on the part of the wife are not a defence, although they can be considered in the court's exercise of its discretion.
528   SSAA 1992, s 107(1)–(2), consolidating amendments made by SSA 1990 to SSA 1986.

plus various premiums.[529] In addition, if the court is satisfied that the liable parent has the means to pay, the sum ordered may include part or all of the personal allowance paid to the ex-partner.[530] This was designed very much as an interim reform pending the introduction of the child support scheme and so is unlikely to be invoked now if there are children involved.

Secondly, the DWP may now transfer an order which it has obtained in its own right to the wife when she comes off benefit, so avoiding the need for her to apply for her own order.[531] This is only possible where there are children under the age of 16 and there are no existing maintenance orders. The Department must also give notice to the court which made the original order and to both parties. Any element in the order representing the income support personal allowance for the caring parent is not transferable.

Thirdly, the DWP has the power to enforce existing private law maintenance orders made in favour of a lone parent claiming income support.[532] This applies only where that benefit is claimed for children and the liable person defaults on any terms of the order. The DWP may bring enforcement proceedings without the consent of the payee under the order, but any sums recovered are payable to her.[533]

B CRIMINAL PROCEEDINGS

The DWP may take criminal proceedings under section 105 of SSAA 1992 for a persistent failure to maintain a spouse or dependant. The Finer Committee was not in favour of this method of enforcement[534] and, in fact, it now appears to have fallen into disuse.[535]

v *Divorced wives*

For income support purposes, the position of a divorced wife is very similar to that of woman separated from her husband. Thus she may claim benefit in her own right and the amount of maintenance paid by her former husband is included in her income.[536] The only significant difference is that a former spouse is not a 'liable relative' under the legislation.[537] This does not, of course, affect either party's liability to maintain their children under CSA 1991.

E Sponsored immigrants

Until 1975 the Supplementary Benefits Commission used to withhold benefit from immigrants if their sponsor was able to support them. The practice was ruled illegal by the

---

529 SI 1990/1777, reg 2(1).
530 SI 1990/1777, reg 2(2).
531 SSAA 1992, s 107(3)–(15).
532 SSAA 1992, s 108. Lump sum orders are excluded: s 108(8).
533 SSAA 1992, s 108(3).
534 N 521, above, para 4.211.
535 *Bradshaw and Millar* n 433, above, p 79.
536 P 454, below.
537 However, the DWP has power to recover payments from one spouse for benefit paid to the other under CSA 1991, s 107, discussed above.

Divisional Court, as it was improper to take into account an undertaking to support, rather than actual support, in assessing the claimant's resources.[538] The position now, of course, is that most persons from abroad who are subject to immigration control are denied access to income support and other benefits.[539] A person who has been resident in the UK for less than five years and is subject to a mandatory sponsorship undertaking under the Immigration Act 1971[540] is thus precluded from claiming income support, unless their sponsor dies within that period.[541] In the latter case an urgent cases payment may be made.[542] Sponsored immigrants who were entitled to income support before February 1996, when this rule was first introduced, continue to qualify under transitional protection provisions.[543] In such cases an immigrant's sponsor remains liable to maintain that person,[544] and this duty may be enforced by the Department in the same way as it enforces the obligations of liable relatives.[545]

Part 7   Special cases

In this Part there is a short summary of the principal rules governing the award of benefit to some special categories of claimant.[546] These mostly entail modifications to the normal rules for assessing the applicable amount.

A Hospital patients[547]

The amount of benefit paid to patients in hospital depends on a number of factors, principally whether the claimant is a member of a couple or single and the duration of the stay. The general aim of the provisions is to ensure that claimants (and their families) have enough to meet continuing commitments while they are in hospital and to pay for some personal expenses during that period. On the other hand, there will generally be a reduction in the benefit payable to take account of diminished costs.[548]

During the first six weeks of a stay in hospital, benefit is generally unaffected.[549] The position thereafter may be summarised in outline under the following heads.[550]

---

538 *R v West London Supplementary Benefits Appeal Tribunal, ex p Clarke* [1975] 3 All ER 513, [1975] 1 WLR 1396.
539 Pp 280–281, above. See the invaluable historical survey by Hale LJ in *R v Wandsworth London Borough Council, ex p O* [2000] 1 WLR 2539 at 2553–2558.
540 IAA, s115(10) provides a definition of such an undertaking.
541 SI 2000/636, Sch, paras 2 and 3. See also *Shah v Secretary of State for Social Security* [2002] EWCA Civ 285. After five years' residence, a sponsored immigrant may apply for income support in the usual way.
542 P 313, below.
543 SI 1996/30, reg 12(2).
544 SSAA 1992, ss 78(6)(c) and 105(3).
545 SSAA 1992, s 106(2)–(4). The DWP may recover sums which it has paid in benefit.
546 Other special rules apply to members of religious orders and claimants without accommodation: SI 1987/1967, Sch 7, paras 6 and 7.
547 For the similar rules for contributory benefits, see pp 234–238, above.
548 For policy discussion, see SSAC *Report on Draft Hospital In-Patient Amendment Regulations 1987* (1987, Cm 215).
549 But if the claimant was previously in residential accommodation, only if he or she continues to pay the relevant accommodation charge: SI 1987/1967, Sch 7, para 18. In addition, attendance allowance and the care component of disability living allowance are normally not payable after four weeks as an in patient, which in turn will usually result in the withdrawal of the severe disability premium. The six week period is due to be extended to 13 weeks: p 235, above.
550 SI 1987/1967, paras 1–3, 18.

(1) *Adults in hospital 6-52 weeks* For each adult in hospital there is a special rate known as the higher hospital personal allowance (HHPA),[551] to which may be added (where appropriate) the ordinary personal allowances for other members of the family, and the family and disabled child premiums, and housing costs. The calculation is different where one member of a couple is in hospital: the normal benefit is then payable minus the standard hospital personal allowance (SHPA).[552]

(2) *Children in hospital for a period exceeding 12 weeks* The personal allowance for the child is reduced to the SHPA but any premium in respect of the child remains payable.

(3) *Adults in hospital over 52 weeks* Adults remaining in hospital for a period exceeding 52 weeks are treated as single claimants, whatever their family circumstances,[553] and will be entitled only to the SHPA.[554] The SHPA can be reduced to such figure 'as is reasonable having regard to the views of hospital staff and the patient's relatives if available as to the amount necessary for his personal use'.[555] This applies only to patients who are unable to act for themselves and are certified by a doctor as being unable to make personal use of all or any of the SHPA. Lone parents, even if they have been in hospital for 52 weeks, can continue to claim for dependent children. If the patient is a member of a couple, the other partner (if not also in hospital) becomes entitled to income support as a single person or lone parent (as appropriate) and the standard rules for assessing the applicable amount, including premiums and housing costs, as appropriate, prevail.

(4) *People in residential care or nursing homes* There is a set of complex rules which determine the entitlement of those who prior to being a hospital patient were living in residential care or nursing homes. In general, after six weeks in hospital, such individuals are entitled to the HHPA plus any part of the accommodation charge for which they remain liable.

For the purpose of these rules, periods in hospital which are not separated by more than 28 days are aggregated and treated as continuous.[556] In deciding whether a person is indeed an in-patient, the circumstances existing at the beginning of the day are to be treated as continuing throughout the day – so a day on which a person is admitted or re-admitted is not a day in hospital, whilst a day on which an individual is discharged remains a day in hospital.[557]

B Persons in residential accommodation

The statutory provisions governing claimants living in residential accommodation have undergone two major reforms in the last decade. Before April 1993 claimants residing in local authority homes[558] received income support at the rate of the basic state retirement pension. Claimants living in independent residential or nursing homes were eligible for enhanced rates of income support to meet their fees. The 1980s saw a rapid expansion

---

551 This is equivalent to about 25 per cent of the standard retirement pension.
552 This is equivalent to about 20 per cent of the standard retirement pension.
553 Because they are treated under the regulations as no longer being a member of the same household as, eg, a partner: SI 1987/1967, reg 16(2).
554 It is assumed that such persons are no longer liable for housing costs.
555 SI 1987/1967, Sch 7, para 2(a).
556 SI 1987/1967, reg 21(2).
557 *R(IS) 8/96*.
558 This is conventionally known as 'Part III accommodation'. See National Assistance Act 1948, s 21 and *R v Sefton Metropolitan Borough Council, ex p Help the Aged* [1997] 4 All ER 532.

of private sector residential care and nursing homes, partly encouraged by changes in the social security entitlement of those in long-term care.[559] The introduction of upper limits to the allowable accommodation charges in 1985[560] failed to halt this trend.

As part of the implementation in April 1993 of the community care reforms in the National Health Service and Community Care Act 1990,[561] the bulk of the responsibility for such claimants was transferred to local authorities. Under these arrangements, the income support entitlement of claimants in residential care or nursing homes depended on whether or not they had entered such accommodation before 1 April 1993.[562] Those already resident had 'preserved rights' to income support calculated on the 'old' basis, giving them a small personal expenses allowance, a weekly accommodation charge (subject to the national ceilings) and the cost of meals not included in that charge.[563] Since April 1993, local authorities have been responsible for assessing the needs of persons wishing to enter such accommodation at public expense.[564] 'New' claimants were entitled only to the normal income support personal allowances, together with any premiums and a contribution to the accommodation charges known as the residential allowance.[565] The local authority is also responsible for meeting those charges and assessing the amount due from the claimant.[566] There is considerable scope for disagreement between the local authority and the claimant (or, more often, the claimant's family) as to what is appropriate for that individual. Income support claimants living in local authority homes received a residential accommodation rate and, if they were only temporary residents, their housing costs. In 1996 the upper capital limit for claimants living permanently in either independent or local authority homes was raised to £16,000, with the tariff income rule applying only to income in the band between £10,000 and £16,000.[567]

These arrangements were radically altered in April 2002 by the Health and Social Care Act 2001 (HSCA 2001).[568] The 2001 Act completes the process of making local authorities responsible for arranging and meeting the care needs of people in long-term care. The higher capital limits for income support were retained, but the system of preserved rights and residential allowances abolished.[569] Consequently today most income support claimants who live in residential care or nursing homes (whether operated independently or by the local authority) are entitled to benefit on the normal basis, calculated according to an applicable amount comprised of the standard personal allowances and premiums.

C Temporary separation of couples

As we have seen, where a couple is temporarily separated because one partner is in residential accommodation, the partner who remains at home is treated as a single

---

559   See Evandrou et al in Hills (ed) *The State of Welfare* (1990) pp 252–254. In 1979 there were 12,000 residents in such accommodation reliant on supplementary benefit at a cost of £10 million; by 1993 there were 265,000 income support claimants being supported at a cost of £2,530 million: DSS *The Government's expenditure plans 1993–94 to 1995–96* (1993, Cm 2213) p 18.

560   See the 3rd edition of this book, pp 466–467.

561   On the background to the benefit changes, see Fimister in Carter, Jeffs and Smiths (eds) *Social Work and Social Welfare Yearbook 3* (1991) ch 11.

562   See SSAC report (1992, Cm 2115).

563   SI 1987/1967, reg 19 (now repealed).

564   National Health Service and Community Care Act 1990, s 47.

565   SI 1987/1967, Sch 2, para 2A.

566   SI 1992/2977.

567   SI 1987/1967, regs 45(b) and 53.

568   HSCA 2001, ss 49–58.

569   SI 2001/3767; see further Simmons (2002) Welfare Rights Bulletin 167, p 6.

claimant (or lone parent). Analogously, where the temporary separation is the result of one partner being in a nursing or residential care home, a rehabilitation unit (for drug or alcohol addiction), a probation or bail hostel or is attending a residential employment rehabilitation course, each partner is treated as a single claimant (or lone parent) if the aggregate of the two claims exceeds what would have been paid to them as a couple.[570] Finally, where one partner is temporarily absent abroad, the standard rules for assessment apply during the first four weeks of such absence; thereafter the applicable amount of the remaining partner is assessed as if he or she were a single claimant (or lone parent).[571]

D Prisoners

Income support is not payable to a prisoner, defined as a person who is *either* detained in custody pending trial or sentence or under a sentence imposed by a court *or* is on temporary release.[572] The single exception to this is that housing costs such as mortgage interest payments will be covered during periods of custody on remand pending trial or sentence.[573] The aggregation rules do not apply to a prisoner's family, since a prisoner is not treated as a member of the same household as their partner.[574] The latter may, therefore, make an independent claim for income support. On final discharge, the prisoner is entitled to income support in the usual way, assuming he or she falls within one of the prescribed categories, and any discharge grant will be treated as capital rather than income.[575]

E Students

The general rule now is that students are not eligible for income support, although certain vulnerable groups remain entitled.[576] There are, however, special provisions governing the assessment of their income. Subject to certain disregards, educational grants including any parental contribution (whether or not it is actually paid[577]) are fully taken into account as income for the period they are intended to cover,[578] normally the whole of the academic year but not the summer vacation.[579] The list of disregards includes tuition and examination fees, book and equipment grants and travelling

---

570 SI 2001/3767, Sch 7, para 9. The other partner need not be at home; the rule also applies where he or she is a patient or in residential accommodation, a residential care or nursing home.
571 SI 2001/3767, Sch 7, para 11. Or eight weeks where a child or young person is taken abroad for treatment: para 11A.
572 SI 2001/3767, reg 21(3). The Court of Appeal had earlier held, by a majority, that a prisoner on home leave was not a prisoner for these purposes (*Chief Adjudication Officer v Carr (R(IS) 20/95)*; see Rowe (1994) 1 JSSL 133), which prompted an amendment to the statutory definition. Persons detained under the Mental Health Act 1983 and parallel legislation in Scotland are specifically excluded from the definition. A person required to reside in a bail hostel is also not a prisoner (*R(IS) 17/93*) as are, by implication, those released on parole or licence or under the electronic tagging scheme.
573 SI 1987/1967, Sch 7, para 8(b).
574 SI 1987/1967, reg 16(3)(b). Similarly where a dependent child or young person is detained in custody: reg 16(5)(f).
575 SI 1987/1967, reg 48(7).
576 Pp 288–290, above.
577 Though if the claimant is a lone parent or disabled only if it is paid: SI 1987/1967, reg 61(1).
578 SI 1987/1967, reg 62(1), (3).
579 For some, eg postgraduate students, it may cover the summer vacation. The same applies to maintenance allowances for dependants and mature students: SI 1987/1967, reg 62(3A). For sandwich courses, see reg 62(4).

expenses.[580] There are detailed provisions concerning the treatment of other forms of students' income;[581] for these purposes the maximum student loan which the student is eligible for counts as income whether or not he or she has applied for it.[582]

F Strikers

i Strikers without families

The policy issues relating to the treatment of strikers are considered in more detail in the context of both income-based and contribution-based jobseeker's allowance.[583] A claimant without a family who is involved in a trade dispute is not entitled to income support and the same applies where both members of a couple are so involved and have no children.[584] So far as income support is concerned, the rules apply to a person:

> other than a child or young person ...
> (a)   who is prevented from being entitled to a jobseeker's allowance by section 14 of the Jobseekers Act 1995 (trade disputes);
> (b)   who would be so prevented if otherwise entitled to that benefit,
> except during any period shown by the person to be a period of incapacity for work ... or to be within the maternity period.[585]

For the purposes of the first exception, 'incapacity for work' has the meaning attributed to it in the context of incapacity benefit.[586] The second exception relates to a period beginning six weeks before the expected week of confinement and ending seven weeks after confinement.[587] If these excepting circumstances fall within the period of a trade dispute, income support will be paid for as long as those circumstances last.

ii Strikers' families

The family of a striker or someone otherwise involved in a trade dispute may claim income support but only after a period of seven days following the start of the stoppage or the withdrawal of labour.[588] After that period has elapsed, the applicable amount will be as follows:[589]
(1)   for a couple without children, where only one partner is involved in the dispute, one half of the personal allowance for a couple, plus one half of the couple rate of any premium for the partner not on strike;
(2)   for a couple with a child or children, where only one partner is involved, as (1) plus the personal allowance(s) for the child(ren), the family premium and any disabled child premium;

---

580   SI 1987/1967, reg 62(2), (2A).
581   SI 1987/1967, regs 63–69.
582   SI 1987/1967, reg 66A.
583   Pp 379–381 and 505–514, below. See also Lundy [1995] 2 JSSL 129.
584   SSCBA 1992, s 126(3)(a) and (d)(i).
585   SSCBA 1992, s 126(1).
586   Pp 538–555, below.
587   SSCBA 1992, s 126(2).
588   During this period, strikers are treated as being in full-time work: SI 1987/1967, reg 5(4).
589   SSCBA 1992, s 126(3).

(3) for a couple with a child or children, where both partners are involved, the personal allowance(s) for the child(ren), the family premium and any disabled child premium;

(4) for a single parent, the personal allowance(s) for the child(ren), plus the family premium, and any disabled child premium;

and assessable housing costs may be added in any of these cases.[590]

Some important modifications are made to the rules on assessment of income and capital which therefore significantly affect the amount of income support payable. Tax refunds and any advance of earnings or a loan made by an employer are treated as income, rather than capital.[591] The usual disregards for payments in kind, payments under sections 17 or 24 of the Children Act 1989 and charitable or voluntary payments do not apply (unless they are from the Macfarlane Trusts, the Independent Living Fund, etc) and thus are fully taken into account as income.[592]

The regulations also provide that any payment (up to a specified maximum – currently £29.00[593]) which the striker receives, or is entitled to receive, from a trade union because of the dispute is to be *disregarded* in assessing income.[594] This disregard can only be understood in the light of the requirement[595] that any income support payable for the family of a striker is subject to a deduction of a prescribed amount equal to the specified maximum disregard (£29.00), referred to above.[596] The combined purpose of the deduction rule and the disregard is to encourage trade unions to assume responsibility for providing for the needs of families affected by labour disputes. This can be illustrated by the following example:

> Suppose the applicable amount for a family affected by a dispute is £89.00 and the striker receives £29.00 in strike pay. This latter sum is disregarded but, because of the deduction rule, the family is only entitled to £60.00 weekly benefit. This in effect tops up the basic provision made by the union. If, however, no strike pay was received, the family would still be entitled to only £60.00.

As revealed in this example, an obvious consequence of the rule is that where a union cannot make the appropriate payment, hardship may be suffered by the family.[597] Such a situation arose during the Miners' Strike of 1984–85 when the sequestration of the NUM's funds precluded any possibility of strike pay.[598]

iii   The position after return to work

Claimants who resume work after a trade dispute are entitled to claim benefit for the first 15 days after their return, subject to the condition that, in the case of a couple, the

---

590   They are attributed to a member of the family not involved in the trade dispute: SI 1987/1967, Sch 3, para 3(2).

591   SSCBA 1992, s 126(5)(a)(ii) and SI 1987/1967, regs 41(4) and 48(6).

592   SI 1987/1967, reg 41(3) and Sch 9, paras 15, 21, 28, 39.

593   This figure must be increased in line with the percentage increases to benefit made by up-rating orders: SSCBA 1992, s 126(8) and SSAA 1992, s 150.

594   SI 1987/1967, Sch 9, para 34 and SSCBA 1992, s 126(7).

595   This controversial and bitterly opposed measure was made by SSA (No 2) 1980, s 6(1). Previously, only the claimant's actual income, subject to a £4 disregard, was taken into account: see generally on this Gennard and Lasko [1974] Br J Industrial Relations 1.

596   SSCBA 1992, s 126(5)(b)–(7).

597   All the more so where an individual is not a member of a union or is not even on strike.

598   See Mesher (1985) 14 ILJ 191; Booth and Smith (1985) 12 JLS 365.

person's partner is not engaged in remunerative, full-time work.[599] The benefit payable includes amounts in respect of the person resuming work after the strike but in most cases is effectively a loan as certain sums are recoverable from the employer (or, where this is not practicable, from the claimant) by the Secretary of State.[600] The decision maker determines a level of 'protected earnings' below which no recovery may be made. This is assessed as the claimant's applicable amount, excluding housing costs, *plus* a prescribed sum (which is reduced in the case of a person in a hostel and is thus effectively a fixed-rate for housing costs), *less* any child benefit payable.[601] A notice is then served on the employer to deduct one-half of any excess of the beneficiary's 'available earnings'[602] over the 'protected earnings'.[603]

Part 8   Deductions and payment to third parties

There is provision for certain deductions to be made from the weekly amount of income support. This may occur where claimants have received an overpayment of this, or any other social security benefit,[604] or where they are required to repay a social fund loan.[605] Here we are concerned with the powers under the Claims and Payments Regulations[606] to withhold certain sums in order that payment may be made directly to a third party to whom the claimant is in debt.[607] The underlying policy is to help those claimants who have shown themselves, perhaps only temporarily, incapable of budgeting for their own needs. The number of cases involved is considerable. In 1999 there were 606,000 deductions for social fund repayments and 131,000 for overpayment recoveries in a typical week. In all some 29 per cent of income support recipients have deductions from benefit made at source.[608] While a prudent use of these powers can prevent a crisis of eviction or fuel disconnection which might otherwise arise, this type of intervention in a claimant's financial affairs arguably undermines individual responsibility and self-reliance. In addition, the SSAC has drawn attention to the dangers of the proliferation of such deductions, which 'is likely to lead to a large number of items competing for a finite amount or the possibility that creditors' bills are met at the expense of food and other essential items of day to day living'.[609] Research suggests that claimants are broadly satisfied with the arrangements, although they would welcome more detailed and regular information about deductions.[610]

For present purposes, there are two distinct sets of arrangements under the income support system for making payments to third parties. The first is where debts have been

599   SSCBA 1992, s 127.
600   SI 1988/664, Pt VIII.
601   SI 1988/664, reg 19.
602   For definition, see SI 1988/664, reg 18(2).
603   SI 1988/664, reg 22.
604   See generally pp 163–167, below.
605   Pp 479–481, below.
606   SI 1987/1968.
607   The power applies to income support (either alone or where it is paid together with incapacity benefit, retirement pension or severe disablement allowance) and jobseeker's allowance: see definition of 'specified benefit' in SI 1988/664, Sch 9, para 1.
608   DSS *Social Security Statistics 1999* (1999) Table A2.27. These data are omitted from more recent editions.
609   SSAC *Eighth Report* (1992) p 13.
610   Mannion, Hutton and Sainsbury *Direct Payments from Income Support* DSS Research Report No 33 (1994). See also Rahilly in *Harris* (ed) n 58, above, pp 431–439.

incurred by the claimant (or partner) in relation to housing costs,[611] miscellaneous accommodation charges, gas, electricity and water charges, council tax, child support maintenance and court fines costs or compensation orders.[612] The decision to make a direct payment can normally only be made if it is in the 'interests' or the 'overriding interests' of the claimant's family.[613] Unlike the equivalent provisions in the supplementary benefit legislation, it is not generally a condition for the exercise of these powers that the claimant should have failed to budget for the item in question.[614] The payments to the third party creditor are made at intervals determined by the Secretary of State and they may continue even after the initial debt has been discharged.[615]

The regulations prescribe the normal sum which may be deducted from the benefit paid to the claimant and made over to the third party: this is typically the sum of a weekly amount equal to 5 per cent (in the case of fuel debts, 10 per cent) of the personal allowance for a single claimant over 25 and the weekly cost (actual or estimated) of the items in question.[616] But a complex set of rules then sets out various maximum limits to the sums which may be deducted in this way, and other qualifications to the formula.[617] There are two provisions relevant to the maximum amounts that can be deducted. The total amount for arrears must not exceed a sum representing 15 per cent of the personal allowance for a single claimant aged over 25.[618] Where the arrears are for housing costs, rent, fuel costs or water charges, the deductions can be made only with the claimant's consent if the aggregate sum for arrears and current usage exceeds 25 per cent of the family's applicable amount.[619] It may well be that a claimant has accumulated debts under more than one of the relevant heads, so there are rules for determining priority between them.[620] Debts are to be met in the following order: mortgage interest payments, other housing costs, fuel charges, water costs, arrears of council tax, unpaid fines, costs and compensation orders and payments of child support maintenance.

The second situation in which direct payments may be made to third parties is confined to payments of mortgage interest. In response to the growing number of repossessions in the early 1990s, the government introduced arrangements whereby income support housing costs may be paid direct to building societies and other mortgagees.[621] This is only possible where the claimant has 100 per cent of their eligible mortgage interest included in their applicable amount.[622] Payments are made in arrears at four-weekly intervals. When the scheme was introduced it was widely thought that building societies would refrain from seeking repossession where direct payments were being made, but they are under no obligation to do so.

611 Defined principally in the same terms as under SI 1987/1967, Sch 3, para 1: see p 304, above.
612 SI 1987/1968, reg 35 and Sch 9, para 2. See also on housing benefit, p 436, below. For court fines see SI 1992/2182; and for council tax deductions see SI 1993/494.
613 Neither expression is defined in the legislation, but there is guidance in *DMG* n 356, above, vol 6, ch 33.
614 The exceptions are miscellaneous accommodation costs and water charges: SI 1987/1968, Sch 9, paras 4(1) and 7(2).
615 See eg SI 1987/1968, Sch 9, para 6(4).
616 SI 1987/1968, Sch 9, paras 3(2), 6(2) and 7(3).
617 SI 1987/1968, Sch 9, paras 6(5) and 8.
618 SI 1987/1968, Sch 9, para 8(1).
619 SI 1987/1968, Sch 9, para 8(2). Housing costs are not included when calculating the applicable amount for this purpose.
620 SI 1987/1968, Sch 9, para 9.
621 Social Security (Mortgage Interest Payments) Act 1992; see now SSAA 1992, s 15A and SI 1987/1968, reg 34A and Sch 9A.
622 SI 1987/1968, Sch 9A para 2.

Chapter 9

Income-based jobseeker's allowance

Part 1   Introduction

A   Scope of chapter

This chapter is concerned with means-tested assistance for unemployed people. Throughout the greater part of the twentieth century the British social security system operated a twin-track system of benefits for the unemployed: one scheme for the insured population, supported by a parallel means-tested scheme for those who had exhausted (or had never attained) any entitlement under the contributory scheme.[1] From April 1988 until October 1996 the latter was provided through the income support scheme. Since the implementation of the Jobseekers Act 1995 (JA 1995), as we have seen in the previous chapter, income support claimants have not been required to be available for and actively seeking work. Instead, jobseeker's allowance (JSA) superseded the functions of both means-tested income support and the contributory unemployment benefit for this group of claimants. Although formally a unified benefit,[2] JSA is in fact an umbrella designation for two variants: income-based JSA and contribution-based JSA. In this chapter we examine the common rules which govern both forms of this benefit as well as those provisions which apply solely to income-based JSA. Later, in chapter 14, we consider the further conditions that must be satisfied to establish entitlement to contribution-based JSA. The justification for treating the benefit in this way is simple: contribution-based JSA remains a contributory benefit, notwithstanding the encroachment of means-testing into certain of its provisions, and so properly belongs in Part III of this book. The reality, however, is that the insurance-based benefit is only available to a small minority of unemployed claimants. In May 2001, 683,000 unemployed people received only income-based JSA, 147,000 qualified solely for contribution-based JSA whilst just 18,000 received both components.[3] Thus, as most unemployed people are reliant upon income-based JSA, it is logical to deal with the common provisions in this chapter.

Accordingly, Part 2 below deals with the general conditions of entitlement to JSA; these include the labour market conditions of availability, actively seeking employment

---

1   Or indeed whose needs were not fully met by the insurance benefit. These developments, culminating in JA 1995, are charted in chapter 14, below.
2   *CJSA/1920/1999*.
3   Department for Work and Pensions (DWP) *Work and Pension Statistics 2001* (2001) p 75.

and entry into a jobseeker's agreement, which are explored in more depth in Parts 3 to 5. Part 6 concerns the extra conditions of entitlement to income-based JSA while Part 7 summaries the rules as regards joint-claim JSA, effectively a sub-species of income-based JSA introduced by the Welfare Reform and Pensions Act 1999 (WRPA 1999). Part 8 deals with the amount and duration of income-based JSA. Parts 9, 10 and 11 consider sanctions, hardship payments and the rules relating to trade disputes.

Part 2   General conditions of entitlement to jobseeker's allowance

A   General

The principal conditions of entitlement to JSA are set out in sections 1 to 4 of JA 1995. Section 1 lays down the core conditions of eligibility whilst sections 2 and 3 make specific provision for contribution-based and income-based JSA respectively.[4] Section 4 then prescribes how the amount of JSA is to be calculated. The core conditions of entitlement to JSA, which apply to both variants of the benefit, mean that the claimant must:
(1) be available for employment;
(2) be actively seeking employment;
(3) have entered into a valid jobseeker's agreement;
(4) satisfy the conditions set out in *either* section 2 *or* section 3;
(5) not be engaged in remunerative work;
(6) be capable of work;
(7) not be receiving relevant education;
(8) be under pensionable age; and
(9) be in Great Britain.
The first four of these conditions are unique to JSA and therefore require separate analysis in the following Parts of this chapter.[5] The final five requirements draw on concepts which are considered elsewhere in this book (particularly with regard to income support) and so can be dealt with more succinctly in this Part.

B   Exclusion of persons engaged in remunerative work

We have already seen that a person engaged in remunerative work, defined as being for 16 or more hours a week (or 24 hours or more in the case of their partner), is precluded from claiming income support.[6] A parallel rule applies to JSA,[7] but with one fundamental difference. Although the 16 and 24 hours rules apply to income-based JSA, entitlement to contribution-based JSA is unaffected by the hours (or indeed earnings) of the claimant's partner.

More generally, as with income support, there are provisions which treat various categories of claimant as either engaged or not engaged in remunerative work, with the consequential effect that such individuals are respectively excluded from or included

---

4   Joint-claim JSA is governed by JA 1995, ss 1(2B) and 3A–3B.
5   Or, in the case of the conditions under JA 1995, s 2, in ch 14.
6   Pp 284–287, above. 'Partner' here, as elsewhere in social security law, is used in the heterosexual sense: see pp 220–223.
7   JA 1995, s 1(2)(e) and SI 1996/207, reg 51.

within the scope of JSA. These rules are broadly the same as for income support,[8] but with some limited exceptions. Under the income support rules a childminder is treated as not engaged in remunerative work, regardless of the number of hours worked. Thus a childminder working 16 hours or more a week may be able to claim either income support (assuming she falls within one of the prescribed categories of claimant) or working families' tax credit. There is no parallel provision for JSA and so presumably a childminder working 16 hours or more a week will be in remunerative work and so excluded from JSA. Such differences, however, are at the margins. Moreover, the definition of 'remunerative work' is the same for both variants of JSA so far as single claimants are concerned.[9] One welcome effect of this rationalisation is that the tortuous regulations and complex body of case law concerning the eligibility of part-time workers for unemployment benefit – such as the normal idle day and full extent normal rules – have now been swept away.[10]

C   Capacity for work

The line between capacity and incapacity for work represents one of the key demarcation lines in the social security system.[11] The underlying policy premise is easy to grasp: a claimant who is capable of work should be searching for employment and so falls within the ambit of JSA. Those who are incapable of work qualify as one of the prescribed groups eligible to claim income support.[12] A claimant who is incapable of work may also be entitled to incapacity benefit, which may or may not be supplemented by income support, depending on the operation of the means test. Capacity for work for the purposes of JSA is judged according to the own occupation test and the personal capability assessment, which are applied in the context of incapacity benefit.[13] It follows that where, on a claim for incapacity benefit, a claimant is found by the Secretary of State to be *not* incapable of work, the condition of capacity for work for the purpose of JSA should be treated as satisfied. There is evidence, however, that in the past some JobCentre staff made it difficult to claim JSA where the claimant's health or disability made them question the individual's capability for work.[14] Claimants in this position could find themselves in a Kafkaesque 'Catch 22' as they shuttled between different benefit offices. This phenomenon should no longer be possible under the regulations[15] and, theoretically at least, should in any event disappear with the advent of the new 'joined up' Jobcentre Plus arrangements.

Finally, there is a useful provision in the regulations which enables a claimant to remain in receipt of JSA for up to two weeks whilst actually incapable of work.[16] This avoids the claimant having to transfer from one benefit to another during a period of short-term illness.

---

8   JA 1995, regs 52 and 53; see p 286, above.
9   The fact that a claimant's partner is working is irrelevant for contribution-based JSA, but a claimant is not entitled to income-based JSA where his or her partner works for 24 hours a week or more.
10   See the 4th edition of this book, pp 89–99.
11   See further pp 525–526, below.
12   P 279, above.
13   JA 1995, Sch 1, para 2. See pp 538–555, below.
14   NACAB *An Unfit Test* (1997) pp 57–59.
15   JA 1995, Sch 1, para 2 and SI 2001/991, reg 10.
16   SI 1996/217, reg 55; there is a limit of two such periods in any 12 months.

D Exclusion of claimants in relevant education

Children and young persons who are in full-time education are excluded from entitlement to JSA.[17] The definition of full-time education is the same as for the purposes of income support.[18] We have already seen that a limited number of 16 and 17-year-olds may qualify for income support despite being in relevant education, assuming that they fall within one of the prescribed categories of claimants for that benefit.[19] Alternatively, such young people may claim income-based JSA, but this would expose them to risk of being sanctioned for failing to comply with the labour market conditions that apply to JSA.[20]

Part-time students in the 16 to 18 age range are treated as not being in relevant education (and so remain eligible for JSA) providing that that one of two further conditions is met:

(1) for three months before starting the course the claimant was in receipt of JSA, incapacity benefit or income support while sick or was on a course of training; or

(2) for six months before starting the course the claimant satisfied (1) above and was thereafter in remunerative work for the other three months or earning too much to be entitled to benefit.[21]

Similarly a young person taking part in the Full-Time Education and Training Option of the New Deal is not treated as being in relevant education.[22]

E Exclusion of claimants over pensionable age

Before the inception of JSA it was possible (albeit very rare) for claimants over pensionable age to claim unemployment benefit.[23] This anomaly was abolished by JA 1995. Pensionable age means 65 for both men and women born after 5 April 1955, and 60 for women born before 6 April 1950.[24]

F Presence (and habitual residence) in Great Britain

The general rule for JSA is simply that the claimant must be 'in Great Britain'.[25] A person who is claiming income-based JSA must also be habitually resident in the Common Travel Area.[26] The regulations make provision for claimants who are temporarily absent from Britain for periods of up to four or eight weeks, depending on the circumstances, to be treated as being still present in Britain.[27]

---

17 JA 1995, s 1(2)(g) and SI 1996/207, reg 54.
18 P 287, above. Thus a 'course of advanced education' (SI 1996/207, reg 1(3)) does not fall within this definition.
19 P 288, above.
20 SI 1996/207, regs 57 and 61; see Wood, Poynter, Wikeley et al *Social Security Legislation 2001* (2001) Vol II, para 3.134.
21 SI 1996/207, regs 11(2) and 54(3) and (4).
22 SI 1996/207, reg 54(5).
23 See the 4th edition of this book, p 147.
24 SI 1996/207, reg 3, applying the Social Security Contributions and Benefits Act 1992, s 122(1) (SSCBA 1992) which in turn applies the Pensions Act 1995, s 126 and Sch 4, Pt I. Women born between 6 April 1950 and 5 April 1955 reach pensionable age at a date between their 60th and 65th birthdays: see p 601, below.
25 JA 1995, s 1(2)(i).
26 Pp 281–283, above.
27 SI 1996/207, reg 50. The rules mirror those for income support (SI 1987/1967, reg 4; see p 283, above) with the addition of an extra deeming provision where a claimant is abroad for seven days or less in order to attend a job interview, having previously notified the authorities of such a trip.

These conditions are necessarily subject to the provisions of EU law. It is clear that, subject to the fulfilment of various conditions, a worker can 'export' contribution-based JSA to another member state for a period of up to three months.[28] The position as regards income-based JSA is much less clear. Income support (when available to unemployed people) was construed as a form of social assistance outwith the scope of Council Regulation (EEC) 1408/71.[29] Subsequently, the UK government added income-based JSA to the list of 'special non-contributory benefits' to which Council Regulation (EEC) 1408/71 applies; it may therefore not be exported to another member state.[30] This classification is at best doubtful, as it assumes that income-based JSA remains on all fours with income support. There is a strong argument that both forms of JSA now fall within article 4(1) of Council Regulation (EEC) 1408/71[31] and so claimants should be able to export either form of the benefit for up to three months, subject to the strict conditions laid down by EU law.

Part 3   Availability for employment

A   History

The requirement that claimants of income-based JSA be available for employment reflects the traditional concern of policy makers that benefit be paid only to those who are involuntarily unemployed. The difficulty has been to formulate a test which provides sufficiently precise guidelines for officials and yet is flexible enough to allow for consideration of all the relevant factors, including the claimant's age, qualifications, working capacity and intentions, as well as the general level of unemployment and characteristics of the labour market particular to the locality.[32] Under the National Insurance Act 1911 (NIA 1911), claimants had to prove that they were 'capable of work but unable to obtain suitable employment'.[33] Faced with a sudden and dangerous rise in unemployment in the 1920s, the government decided that the conditions of eligibility had to be strengthened and introduced the notorious requirement that claimants must prove that they were 'genuinely seeking whole-time employment but unable to obtain such employment'.[34] Although regarded by employers as an essential feature of unemployment insurance,[35] it had a serious impact on the workings of the scheme,[36] and was bitterly attacked by the trade union movement.[37] As it was interpreted, the new

---

28   P 82, above; and see Wikeley [1988] JSWFL 300 at 310–312.
29   *CIS 863/1994* and *CIS 564/1994*. See also *Jackson and Cresswell v Chief Adjudication Officer* C-63, 64/91 [1993] 3 All ER 265.
30   Council Regulation (EEC) 1408/71, art 10a and Annex IIa; see p 79, above.
31   See by analogy *Hockenjos v Secretary of State for Social Security* [2001] EWCA Civ 624, [2001] 2 CMLR 1379.
32   *Report of the Committee on Abuse of Social Security Benefits* (1973, Cmnd 5228) para 237; and for economic considerations see Worswick (ed) *The Concept and Measurement of Involuntary Unemployment* (1976).
33   S 86(3).
34   It was applied to claims for uncovenanted benefit by Unemployment Insurance Act 1921, s 3(3)(b) (UIA 1921), and extended to covenanted benefit by UIA (No 2) 1924, s 3(1).
35   *Report of the Committee on the Procedure and Evidence for the Determination of Claims for Unemployment Insurance Benefit* (the Morris Report) (1929, Cmd 3415) para 37.
36   In 1928–29 of approximately 10 million claims, 340,000 were denied benefit for not genuinely seeking work: *Morris Report* n 35, above, para 36.
37   *Morris Report* n 35, above, para 38. See the essay by Deacon in Briggs and Saville (eds) *Essays in Labour History* (1977).

condition seemed to require that a claimant look around for work where there might be none available. An adverse decision left a stigma which was difficult to remove. On the recommendations of a committee,[38] the condition was repealed in 1930.[39]

Under NIA 1946, the question was simply whether claimants were 'available for employment',[40] and this was construed to mean whether there was a reasonable prospect of their obtaining the work for which they held themselves out to be available.[41] This resulted in the anomaly that some claimants might place such restrictions on their availability that for all practical purposes they were not available. On the recommendations of the National Insurance Advisory Committee (NIAC),[42] a regulation was therefore introduced which limited the restrictions which an unemployed person might place on his or her availability.[43] In 1980 the working of this area of law was critically examined by a joint Department of Employment and Department of Health and Social Security (DHSS) team.[44] In its view, the 'availability' condition, as then administered, was inefficient and too imprecise. The vagueness of the statutory criteria led, in the team's view, to too much discretion and it was suggested that more specific rules should be formulated.[45] In response, the government decided to tighten the administrative arrangements rather than the law, in particular by the completion of questionnaires, both at the time of the claim and after every six months of unemployment, which would serve to clarify the terms on which the claimant was prepared to accept work.[46]

JA 1995 paved the way for more extensive definitions in the regulations of the requirement of availability. In addition to the tests governing actual availability in both primary and secondary legislation (discussed in Section B), there are also regulations deeming the test to be satisfied (or not, as the case may be) in defined circumstances (Section C).

B Statutory test

i The meaning of availability

The basic principle of availability is now enshrined in the primary legislation:

> a person is available for employment if he is willing and able to take up immediately any employed earner's employment.[47]

In itself, this formulation essentially codifies principles established in the earlier case law.[48] Thus a claimant will not be available if he or she is going to move abroad within a matter of days.[49] Nor can claimants be available if, during the relevant period, they

---

38 *Morris Report* n 35, above, para 43.
39 UIA 1930, s 6.
40 NIA 1946, s 11(2)(a)(i).
41 See esp, *R(U) 12/52(T)*.
42 NIAC *Report on the Availability Question* (1953, Cmd 8894).
43 SI 1955/143.
44 Report of Joint DE/DHSS Rayner Scrutiny *Payment of Benefits to Unemployed People* (1980).
45 *Joint DE/DHSS Rayner Scrutiny* n 44, above, paras 4.54–4.55. See the 4th edition of the book, p 105.
46 White Paper *Training for Employment* (1988, Cm 316) para 7.13ff. See Brown *Victims or Villains?* (1990) pp 188–201.
47 JA 1995, s 6(1).
48 See *R(U) 1/53*; and the 4th edition of this book, pp 105–109.
49 *R(U) 1/90(T)*.

cannot lawfully accept an offer of employment, eg if they are contractually bound to be at the disposal of another employer[50] or are immigrants without an appropriate work permit.[51] Although it is customary to refer to the test as one of availability for work, the availability must relate to employed earner's employment.[52] A claimant does not meet the requirement by being solely available to work in a self-employed capacity; conversely, refusing to work as self-employed does not make a claimant unavailable for work.[53]

As a general rule, and subject to the possibility (discussed further below) that some claimants may be able to restrict their hours of availability, those who only hold themselves out as ready to take on part-time work are not available for employment. The starting point is that claimants must be able and willing to take up employment both of 'at least 40 hours a week' and also 'of less than 40 hours a week', subject to any such restrictions.[54] Thus in principle claimants must be ready to take on full-time employment but must not refuse offers of part-time work. However, a claimant has automatic good cause for refusing to take up a part-time job of less than 24 hours and hence may escape the imposition of any benefit sanction, so presumably the same lower limit should apply in this context.[55]

The insistence on availability for full-time work stands in contrast to the position under the former unemployment benefit scheme, where availability solely for part-time work did not necessarily disentitle a claimant. The new scheme is harsher too in that whereas unemployment benefit was a daily benefit, JSA is weekly in nature.[56] It follows that a single day of non-availability, which is not subject to any dispensation under the regulations, means that the claimant loses benefit for the entire week in question.

> D was held in police custody for two days but released without charge. An adjudication officer decided he was not available for work, and so not entitled to JSA, for the whole week. The Court of Appeal held this decision to be correct, observing that there was a lacuna in the statutory scheme.[57]

There is, however, some recognition that the demanding nature of the statutory requirement may not always be appropriate. Thus regulations provide for some leeway on the requirement to take up an offer of employment 'immediately', enabling claimants to impose restrictions on their availability in certain cases and in other narrowly defined situations deeming them to be available for employment.

---

50   *R(U) 11/51; R(U) 1/53; R(U) 1/69.* See also *R(SB) 25/87.*
51   *R(U) 13/57; R(U) 1/82(T); Shaukat Ali v Chief Adjudication Officer,* reported as Appendix to *R(U) 1/85.*
52   The usual meaning in SSCBA 1992, ss 2(1) and 122(1) applies: JA 1995, s 6(9).
53   A claimant may, however, be actively seeking employment by confining jobsearch activities to self-employment: SI 1996/207, reg 20(2).
54   SI 1996/207, reg 6.
55   SI 1996/207, reg 72(5A). The lower limit is 16 hours in a case where the claimant has been allowed to restrict availability to less than 24 hours a week, eg on account of caring responsibilities.
56   JA 1995, s 1(3) and SI 1996/207, reg 7(3).
57   *Secretary of State for Social Security v David (R(JSA) 3/01).* Per Simon Brown LJ: 'The claimant might have been kidnapped and detained by a criminal gang. Or stuck in a train for 8 hours. These things happen. Yet under the scheme as it stands the allowance for the week would be forfeit.' The court encouraged the Secretary of State to consider amending the scheme to provide some discretion to mitigate the rigour of the rule in cases where claimants are unavailable for work 'through unforeseen and excusable circumstances'. No such action has yet been taken.

ii Exceptions to immediate availability

The requirement that the claimant be 'immediately' available to take up employment 'means within a very short space of time indeed'.[58] Regulations provide for a number of exceptions. Any persons who have caring responsibilities, or are engaged in voluntary work, may satisfy the condition so long as they are willing and able to take up employment on 48 hours' notice.[59] If the claimant is a carer, the person being cared for must be in the household or be a close relative.[60] Voluntary work is defined as work for a not-for-profit organisation, or work other than for a member of the family, for which no payment is received (other than for expenses reasonably incurred).[61] Claimants who are providing services other than as a carer or in voluntary work, whether or not for remuneration or under a contract, are entitled to a period of 24 hours' grace.[62] In addition, claimants who are in part-time work of less than 16 hours a week may qualify so long as they are willing and able to take up other employment immediately after the expiry of any statutory notice period.[63] Finally, those claimants who are permitted to restrict their availability to certain times, under various of the provisions discussed below, need not be available at other times.[64]

iii Restrictions on availability

The general rule is that claimants may not restrict their availability for employment to less than 40 hours a week.[65] In principle they must also be willing and able to work on any day of the week and at any time of day. That said, claimants are allowed to limit their availability to a fixed number of hours, being 40 hours (or more) in a week, providing that the pattern of availability affords them 'reasonable prospects of securing employment'.[66] In deciding this issue, the regulations stipulate that regard must be had to the person's skills, qualifications and experience, the type and number of vacancies within daily travelling distance from home, the duration of the individual's unemployment, the outcome of job applications already made and (if the claimant wishes to place restrictions on the *nature* of employment being sought) whether he or she is willing to relocate to take up employment.[67] In addition, there is a further requirement that the prospects of securing employment must not be 'considerably reduced' by the restricted pattern of availability. Any such pattern of availability must also be recorded (as must any variations) in the claimant's jobseeker's agreement. Availability for 40 hours or more in a week is not in itself sufficient: if the claimant has

---

58 'No doubt the requirement for immediate availability allows the claimant time to wash, dress and have his breakfast, but strictly it would seem inconsistent with, say, a claimant's stay overnight with a friend or relative, or attendance at a weekday cricket match, or even an evening at the cinema (unless perhaps he had left a contact number and had not travelled far)': *Secretary of State for Social Security v David (R(JSA) 3/01)*, per Simon Brown LJ.
59 SI 1996/207, reg 5(1).
60 See the definitions in SI 1996/207, reg 4.
61 SI 1996/207, reg 4. See also reg 12 where a person undertaking voluntary work has restricted their availability in certain respects.
62 SI 1996/207, reg 5(2).
63 SI 1996/207, reg 5(3).
64 SI 1996/207, reg 5(4).
65 SI 1996/207, reg 7(1).
66 SI 1996/207, reg 7(2).
67 SI 1996/207, reg 10(1).

imposed a restriction on the pattern of their availability, but is unavailable for employment on just one of such days, the entire week's benefit is lost.[68]

The primary legislation also provides that claimants may restrict their availability for such employment in such ways and/or in such circumstances as may be prescribed.[69] These restrictions may apply to the type of work for which a person is available, their periods of availability, the terms or conditions of employment and the locality or localities concerned.[70] Restrictions on the level of pay sought are permitted for a maximum of six months only.[71] Whatever restrictions are imposed, the claimant must be able to show that 'he has reasonable prospects of securing employment notwithstanding those restrictions'.[72] Clearly, given the criteria applied in applying this concept, the longer the duration of the unemployment, the more difficult it will be for claimants to demonstrate that there is a reasonable prospect of securing employment despite the restrictions imposed.

Regulations also provide for specific restrictions to be attached to claimant's availability for those with religious or conscientious objections, physical or mental disabilities, or caring responsibilities.[73]

A   PERSONS WITH RELIGIOUS OR CONSCIENTIOUS OBJECTIONS

Regulations provide that:

> a person may impose restrictions on the nature of the employment for which he is available by reasons of a sincerely held religious belief, or a sincerely held conscientious objection providing he can show that he has reasonable prospects of employment notwithstanding those restrictions [and any other permitted restrictions].[74]

On one reading such restrictions must therefore relate to the *type* of employment and not the hours of work, pay or other conditions of employment. Clearly, therefore, a peace campaigner could refuse to work in the armaments industry and a vegetarian could decline to be available for work in an abattoir.[75] It is less clear that eg an Orthodox Jew could restrict his availability under this head to exclude any job which involved working Saturday shifts: strictly this relates to the 'terms or conditions of employment' rather than the 'nature of the employment'. An individual in this situation could none the less rely on the general rule on restrictions of availability in regulation 8.

---

68   SI 1996/207, reg 7(3). See *Secretary of State for Social Security v David (R(JSA) 3/01)*.
69   JA 1995, s 6(2).
70   JA 1995, s 6(3).
71   SI 1996/207, reg 9. This must, presumably, be subject to the relevant minimum wage prescribed under the National Minimum Wage Act 1988, although the regulations are not explicit on the point.
72   SI 1996/207, reg 8. Such restrictions may also include those permitted under the various special cases listed below, but are subject to the overriding 40 hour a week rule and the six month rule on minimum pay levels. The onus is generally on the claimant: reg 10(2).
73   See also the special provision for part-time students who restrict their availability in certain respects; in general terms their part-time course of study will be disregarded so long as they are willing and able to re-arrange their hours of study in order to take up employment: SI 1996/207, reg 11. A similar provision applies to volunteers: reg 12.
74   SI 1996/207, reg 13(2).
75   See, on a related point, *R(U) 32/56* and *CU/14/68*.

B PERSONS WITH PHYSICAL OR MENTAL DISABILITIES

The regulations also state that:

> a person may restrict his availability in any way providing the restrictions are reasonable in the light of his physical or mental condition.[76]

This is a very widely drawn formulation. The use of the phrase 'physical or mental condition' means that such restrictions must relate to the claimant's disability.[77] With that proviso, the restrictions may relate to *any* aspect of availability and there is no required lower threshold of hours of availability, unlike with the position for carers, discussed below. The criterion is one of reasonableness in the light of the individual's condition. Restrictions on pay which are reasonably imposed under this head may last beyond the normal maximum of six months.[78] In addition, if the claimant's restrictions relate solely to their physical or mental condition, there is no requirement to demonstrate that there are reasonable prospects of employment notwithstanding the qualified nature of the availability. However, this justification will have to be made out if other non-disability related conditions are attached.[79] The point is illustrated by *R(U) 6/72*, a case decided under the old unemployment benefit law:

> A technical manager, suffering from a heart condition, retired on medical advice at the age of 62. He claimed benefit but restricted his availability to offers of employment at a minimum salary of £5,500 a year in his home town or its close environs. There was no reasonable prospect of finding such employment and it was held that in the light of his physical condition, the restriction to the locality (but not that as to remuneration) was reasonable.

C CARERS

Carers are entitled to reduce their availability to less than 40 hours a week so long as they are available for at least 16 hours in any week but in any event for as many hours as their caring responsibilities permit.[80] In determining the latter point regard must be had to the particular hours and days spent in caring, whether the care is shared with another individual and the age and physical and mental condition of the person being cared for.[81] Carers must also be able to show that, despite the restriction on hours, they have reasonable prospects of securing employment.

C Deemed availability or unavailability

i Deemed availability

There are several circumstances in which a person may be deemed to be available for employment, notwithstanding the fact that they are not able to take up 'immediately

---

76   SI 1996/207, reg 13(3).
77   *Secretary of State for Social Security v David (R(JSA) 3/01)*.
78   Unlike SI 1996/207, reg 13(2), discussed above, reg 13(3) is not made expressly subject to reg 9.
79   Eg under SI 1996/207, regs 7, 8 or 13(2).
80   SI 1996/207, reg 13(4). 'Caring responsibilities' are defined in reg 4.
81   SI 1996/207, reg 13(5).

any employed earner's requirement', as required by section 6(1) of JA 1995. The first, which narrows the scope of 'any' in this context, is the 'permitted period', a concept designed to provide some limited protection for claimants' job skills and normal pay levels. The permitted period thus allows claimants to limit their availability to their 'usual occupation' or to 'a level of remuneration not lower than that which [they are] accustomed to receive' or in both respects.[82] Any such permitted period must be for a minimum of one week and a maximum of 13 weeks from the date of claim; after this point, claimants must be prepared to accept an offer of a less appropriate kind. In determining whether a permitted period applies and the length of any such period, regard must be had to the claimant's usual occupation (and any relevant skills or qualifications), the length of any relevant training, the length of the last employment in the usual occupation and the period since such employment, and the availability and location of employment in that occupation.[83] This provision reflects earlier case law to the effect that claimants may be able to argue that to accept an offer of employment of a lower status than that to which they are accustomed would prejudice their future chances of returning to their usual occupation.[84] After the expiry of the permitted period, claimants are expected both to widen the range of employments they will consider and to lower their expectations about wage levels, subject always to the criteria of 'good cause', discussed below.[85]

Secondly, recent governments of both main political persuasions have adopted a general policy of encouraging the unemployed to engage in activities which do not constitute ordinary, remunerated employment. A strict application of the 'availability' requirement might disentitle those so engaged because they might not be able to take up 'immediately' an offer of suitable employment.[86] The regulations thus treat the availability condition as having been satisfied in appropriate, albeit narrowly defined, circumstances.[87] The categories include claimants who are:

•   persons attending residential work camps or full-time students (but only where an employment officer has given prior approval) who are participating in an employment-related course, but in both cases only for two weeks in any year;[88]
•   persons temporarily absent from Great Britain because they are accompanying their child going abroad for treatment[89] (for up to eight weeks), or a partner who is disabled or over 60 (for up to four weeks), or attending a job interview (maximum absence of one week);
•   persons looking after their child as their partner is temporarily absent from Great Britain, or looking after a child as the child's usual carer is ill or absent from home (in either case for no more than eight weeks);

---

82   JA 1995, s 6(4), (5) and (7) and SI 1996/207, reg 16. There is special provision for laid off and short-time workers in reg 17. The permitted period, if any, should be noted in the jobseeker's agreement: reg 31(f).

83   SI 1996/207, reg 16(2). The concept of the claimant's 'usual occupation' is not defined in the regulations and so must be a question of fact. For early case law see the 4th edition of this book, p 125, n 6, but see now DSS *Decision Makers Guide* (DMG) (2000) vol 4, para 21397ff.

84   Accepted in *R 21/60 (UB)*, but not in *R(U) 35/52* where the offer was only for two weeks' employment.

85   The rationale for the changes made by SSA 1989 was said to be 'not to penalise the unemployed but to encourage them to be more realistic about their labour market potential': Mr N Scott, Standing Committee F, col 505.

86   Cf *R(U) 1/53*.

87   See generally the SSAC Report on the Draft Amendment Regulations (1982, Cmnd 8486) on an earlier version of these regulations.

88   Or attending a Venture Trust residential training programme (for up to four weeks in any year).

89   Defined by SI 1996/207, reg 14(4).

- persons engaged in crewing or launching lifeboats, as part-time firefighters or otherwise acting in emergency[90] duties for the benefit of others;[91]
- those attending a one week Open University residential course;
- prisoners in their first week after release; or
- persons suffering from short-term sickness.[92]

In addition, a claimant may be treated as available for work for up to one week (and on up to four occasions in any period of 12 months) in any for the following circumstances:

- where he or she, or a close relative or close friend, is affected by a domestic emergency; a close relative or close friend is seriously ill or dies;
- there is a funeral of such a person; or
- he or she has caring responsibilities and the person being cared for has died.[93]

Thirdly, as part of the New Deal arrangements, a claimant who is a full-time student following an employment-related course lasting for no more than 12 months is to be treated as available for employment, notwithstanding their usual deemed *un*availability. In order to qualify, the claimant must be 25 or over, have made a claim for JSA and been receiving one of a number of specified benefits for two years within one jobseeking period. The claimant must also have the agreement of an employment officer to participate in the course.[94]

Finally, a person who is laid off[95] is regarded as available for work for the first 13 weeks of their period of lay-off, so long as he or she is willing and able to resume their employment immediately and to take up any casual employment[96] which falls within reasonable travelling distance of home.[97] An analogous rule applies to those who are subject to short-time working.[98] In addition, the aggregate number of hours that a short-time worker is in employment and their hours of availability for casual work must be at least 40 hours, unless this figure can be reduced because of their physical or mental condition or caring responsibilities.[99] For both categories of worker the 13 week limit is absolute.[100]

---

90 This includes '(a) a fire, a flood or an explosion; (b) a natural catastrophe; (c) a railway or other accident; (d) a cave or mountain accident; (e) an accident at sea; (f) a person being reported missing and the organisation of a search for that purpose': SI 1996/207, reg 14(5)(b).

91 This covers: '(a) providing assistance to any person whose life may be endangered or who may be exposed to the risk of seriously bodily injury or whose health may be seriously impaired; (b) protecting property of substantial value from imminent risk of serious damage or destruction; or (c) assisting in measures being taken to prevent a serious threat to the health of the people; [and in any one such case] as a member of a group of persons organised wholly or partly for the purpose of providing such assistance or, as the case may be, protection': SI 1996/207, reg 14(5)(a).

92 SI 1996/207, reg 14(1). Provision is made for part weeks by reg 14(1)(i) and (3).

93 SI 1996/207, reg 14(2).

94 SI 1996/207, reg 17A.

95 Defined as 'a person whose employment has been suspended owing to temporary adverse industrial conditions': SI 1996/207, reg 4. This would appear to exclude normal seasonal fluctuations, such as those which prevail in seaside resorts out of season: see *R(U) 3/59*; and the 4th edition of this book, pp 94 and 107 on the old law.

96 Defined as 'employment from which the employee can be released without notice': SI 1996/207, reg 4.

97 SI 1996/207, reg 17(1). This is subject to the special cases in reg 5, where availability on 24 or 48 hours' notice is permitted.

98 Defined as 'a person whose hours of employment have been reduced owing to temporary adverse industrial conditions': SI 1996/207, reg 4.

99 SI 1996/207, reg 17(2).

100 SI 1996/207, reg 17(3). A 'week' means any period of seven consecutive days (reg 17(5)) rather than the usual JSA week which starts on a Sunday: JA 1995, s 35(1). Once 13 weeks have elapsed, the claimant cannot then take advantage of the 'permitted period' of 13 weeks discussed below: SI 1996/207, reg 17(4).

ii Deemed unavailability

As well as deeming certain preferred categories of claimants as being available for employment, the regulations also deem other groups as not being so available. Those concerned are full-time students during their period of study,[101] prisoners on temporary release, women in receipt of maternity allowance or statutory maternity pay and any claimants in respect of part weeks at the beginning of their claim, unless they fall within one of the categories of deemed availability described in the preceding section.[102]

Part 4   Actively seeking employment

A   General

Notwithstanding the tightening up of the administration of the requirement that claimants be available for work in the course of the 1980s, the then Conservative government declared its dissatisfaction with the rule in 1988. One White Paper argued that the availability for work test was an insufficient safeguard against fraud and abuse,[103] whilst a second concluded that inadequate job-search activity by unemployed people was itself a significant reason for continuing high levels of unemployment.[104] The government's solution was to introduce a new requirement that claimants 'actively seek employment', reminiscent of the test applied between 1921 and 1930 that claimants be 'genuinely seeking employment'.[105] This rule was carried over into, and tightened further in, the JSA scheme. Accordingly, section 7(1) of JA 1995 declares that:

> a person is actively seeking employment in any week if he takes in that week such steps as he can reasonably be expected to take in order to have the best prospects of securing employment.

This represents a subtle semantic shift in emphasis from the previous formulation, which referred to the 'best prospects of *receiving offers* of employment', so further emphasising the onus on the claimant to take positive action. In this context actively seeking employment can include steps to secure self-employment.[106] A week is defined as a 'benefit week',[107] which means in practice that that the test must be satisfied in respect of each of the two periods of seven days (including Sundays) ending on the day in the fortnight on which the claimant signs on. Regulations provide guidance as to the

---

101 Subject to one narrowly drawn exception where the claimant has a partner and both are full-time students and one of them is responsible for a child or young person (and even then only during the summer vacation and providing the claimant is available for work). Those undertaking specified employment-related courses are not caught by the rule: ibid, reg 17A.
102 SI 1996/207, reg 14.
103 White Paper *Training for Employment* (1988, Cm 316) para 7.7.
104 White Paper *Employment for the 1990s* (1988, Cm 540) para 7.17.
105 See p 340, above. For critiques see Wikeley (1989) 16 JLS 291 at 298–300; and Buck (1989) 18 ILJ 258. For a detailed comparative study of the UK and the US, see King *Actively Seeking Work?* (1995). Research suggests that awareness of this rule among claimants has increased since the introduction of JSA: Smith et al *Understanding the Impact of Jobseeker's Allowance* DSS Research Report No 111 (2000).
106 JA 1995, s 7(8) and SI 1996/207, regs 18(3)(i), 19(1)(r) and 20(2), (3).
107 SI 1996/207, regs 1(3) and 4. On part weeks at the start of a claim, see reg 18A.

steps that a person may reasonably be required to take in any week (section B) and the circumstances in which claimants are deemed to satisfy this test (section C).

B Steps in actively seeking employment

i Reasonable steps

Regulations define reasonable 'steps' to include[108] oral and/or written applications to persons who have advertised vacancies or 'who appear to be in a position to offer employment'; seeking information on the availability of employment from advertisements, employers, employment agencies, employment businesses and other appropriate sources; and registration with an employment agency or business. The appointment of a third party to assist the person in question in finding employment may constitute a reasonable step.[109] These steps were all included in the pre-JSA version of the regulations.[110] The current list also gives as examples seeking specialist advice on improving job prospects following referral by an employment officer, drawing up a CV, seeking references or testimonials from former employers, drawing up a list of and seeking information about employers who may be able to offer employment and seeking information on an occupation with a view to securing such employment.

The regulations stipulate that claimants are expected 'to have to take more than one step on one occasion in any week unless taking one step on one occasion is all that is reasonable for that person to do in that week'.[111] This is pre-eminently a question of fact, but taking one step might well suffice in the period between Christmas and New Year when all factories are closed.[112] Whether the steps taken are reasonable and offer the claimant the best prospects of securing employment is likewise a question of fact to be decided in the light of the individual's circumstances. Decision makers are directed to have regard to all the circumstances of the case,[113] including, in particular, such factors as: the claimant's skills, qualifications, abilities and physical or mental limitations; the person's work experience and the duration of their unemployment; any steps taken in previous weeks to seek employment (and their effectiveness); the availability and location of vacancies; and engagement in activities or training of the kind which may enable the claimant to be deemed to be available for employment. The special problems faced by homeless people are recognised inasmuch as the fact that they are homeless and the steps they take to secure accommodation are relevant factors.[114]

ii Disregarded steps

JA 1995 introduced a new provision enabling regulations to be made allowing steps taken by a claimant, which would otherwise count for the purposes of actively seeking employment, 'to be disregarded in such circumstances (including circumstances

108 SI 1996/207, reg 18(2). The list is therefore non-exhaustive.
109 Eg a 'resting' actor who employs an agent.
110 SI 1983/1598, reg 12B(4).
111 SI 1996/207, reg 18(1).
112 *Social Security Legislation 2001* n 20, above, vol II, para 3.69.
113 SI 1996/207, reg 18(3).
114 SI 1996/207, reg 18(3)(j).

constituted by, or connected with, his behaviour or appearance) as may be prescribed'.[115] The relevant regulation provides in more detail that any step may be disregarded:

(a)   where, in taking the act, [the claimant] acted in a violent or abusive manner,
(b)   where the act comprised the completion of an application for employment and he spoiled the application,
(c)   where by his behaviour or appearance he otherwise undermined his prospects of securing the employment in question

unless those circumstances were due to reasons beyond his control.[116]

No such provision existed in the previous unemployment benefit regime.[117] The justification for this remarkable provision was the perceived need to tackle the problem of 'workshy' unemployed claimants who deliberately make a poor impression on prospective employers. The proviso relating to circumstances beyond the claimant's control provides some protection to illiterate claimants who might otherwise have jobseeking steps disregarded under heading (b). However, there is clearly potential for heading (c) to be applied in a discriminatory fashion, eg against men with their hair in a pony-tail or Rastafarians with dreadlocks.[118] These provisions have yet to be the subject of interpretation by the Social Security Commissioners and there is no evidence that the powers to disregard such steps are applied in practice.

C   Persons deemed to be actively seeking employment

As with the availability condition, regulations provide that claimants are deemed to satisfy this requirement in certain situations.[119] These circumstances include, for purely practical reasons, the first or last week of unemployment. Other cases are also included as much for administrative convenience as out of consideration for claimants. Thus a claimant who is sick and so incapable of work for at least three days in any week is treated as actively seeking employment in that week.[120] In addition, claimants are deemed to be actively seeking employment for certain periods of absence from home. During any 12-month period, claimants are deemed to meet the requirement for a maximum of two weeks in relation to which they have given written notice that they do *not* intend to be actively seeking employment but that they do intend 'to reside at a place other than [their] usual place of residence for at least one day'.[121] In typically convoluted fashion, this provision effectively allows claimants up to two weeks' holiday a year during which they are not required to be actively seeking employment.[122] The regulation also covers any week in which the claimant is deemed, by virtue of volunteering to assist in dealing within an emergency, to be available for employment for at least three days. Furthermore,

---

115   JA 1995, s 7(3).
116   SI 1996/207, reg 18(4).
117   Although, as now, a claimant could be sanctioned for neglecting to avail oneself of a reasonable (and specific) opportunity of employment: *R(U) 28/55*.
118   *Social Security Legislation 2001* n 20, above, vol II, para 3.69. See further Wikeley (1996) 25 ILJ 71. There is now clearly scope for a human rights challenge under certain circumstances.
119   SI 1996/207, reg 19(1).
120   SI 1996/207, reg 19(1)(l); this is subject to a limit of two weeks in any 12 months: reg 55.
121   SI 1996/207, reg 19(10(p) and (2). On the meaning of 'residence', see *R(F) 1/62(T)* and *R(S) 7/83*. This exemption is extended to three weeks for Outward Bound courses and six weeks for guide dog training courses (in both cases involving a minimum attendance of three days a week).
122   They must, however, still be available for employment. See p 341, above.

claimants are deemed to be actively seeking employment for any week in which, although not receiving a training allowance, they are participating in an employment or training programme for at least three days. Similarly, in order to encourage the entrepreneurial spirit, the deeming rule can apply for up to eight weeks during which the claimant 'is taking active steps to establish himself in self-employed earner's employment' under any scheme established under section 2 of the Employment and Training Act 1973.[123] The other instances in which claimants may be treated as actively seeking employment reflect, with some modifications, those that apply under the deeming rules for availability. Further special provision is made for claimants entitled to a 'permitted period', laid-off and short time workers and full-time students participating in employment-related courses under the New Deal.[124]

Part 5   Jobseeker's agreement

A   General

The requirements that claimants be both available for work and (since 1989) actively seeking work, discussed in the two previous Parts, had been part of the unemployment benefit scheme and were simply reincorporated in the arrangements for JSA, albeit that those two concepts were subject to more detailed definition in the new regulations. In contrast, the requirement that claimants sign a jobseeker's agreement as a condition of entitlement was an innovation of JA 1995. Previously, as a matter of departmental practice, claimants had been asked to agree a 'Back to Work Plan', a pro forma document setting out the steps they were going to take to look for employment.[125] JA 1995 effectively elevated this document into a mandatory requirement, given that JSA is not payable unless the claimant 'has entered into a jobseeker's agreement which remains in force'.[126] This suggests that the 'agreement' in question may not necessarily be entirely voluntary, in the sense that the claimant lacks both bargaining power and knowledge when settling its terms.[127] The justification for this element of compulsion was the importance of identifying the most appropriate steps for a person to take to find work and of ensuring adequate monitoring of the claimant's jobsearch activity.[128] It may be significant that the 'jobseeker's agreement' only has effect for the purposes of entitlement to the benefit.[129] Accordingly, a breach of the agreement (by either party) cannot give rise to a private law remedy, eg in contract. More importantly in practice, the existence of an agreement is without prejudice to the Secretary of State's duty to suspend the claimant's benefit if a doubt arises as to whether the conditions relating to availability and actively seeking work are satisfied.[130]

---

123   SI 1996/207, reg 19(1)(r).
124   SI 1996/207, regs 20–22.
125   Although not a condition of entitlement, the Back to Work Plan carried some evidential value if the claimant was sanctioned for not actively seeking employment.
126   JA 1995, s 1(2)(b).
127   The label 'agreement' was described by the then Conservative backbencher, Mr A Howarth MP, as 'an abuse of language in an abuse of power': 262 HC Official Report (6th Series) col 600.
128   DSS/DE *Jobseeker's Allowance* (1994, Cm 2687) para 4.16.
129   JA 1995, s 9(2). It ceases when the award of benefit expires: s 9(12), but see SI 1996/207, reg 36.
130   SI 1999/991, reg 16(2).

B The requirement for and contents of a jobseeker's agreement

The requirement for a valid jobseeker's agreement as a precondition for the payment of benefit is subject to a number of narrowly circumscribed exceptions so that claimants are not disadvantaged if they are subject to specified administrative delays. Thus a jobseeker's agreement is treated as having been made where eg the claimant is allowed to make a claim by post and is awaiting an interview with an employment officer or 'there are circumstances not peculiar to the claimant which make impracticable or unduly difficult the normal operation' of the JSA scheme (eg a strike by departmental staff or a major computer failure).[131] In all other cases a jobseeker's agreement, which must be signed and in writing, must be in place before benefit is paid.[132] Moreover, employment officers must not enter into such an agreement unless, in their opinion, the claimant would satisfy the availability and actively seeking work requirements if he or she were to comply with the terms of the proposed agreement.[133] This stipulation emphasises the role of employment officers in policing claimants' compliance with the eligibility criteria.

The contents of a jobseeker's agreement are prescribed by regulations. Any such agreement must include:
- the claimant's name;
- their hours of availability and any pattern of availability (where their hours are restricted);
- any other restrictions on their availability;
- a description of the type of work sought;
- action that the claimant will take to seek employment and to improve their prospects of finding work;
- the duration of any permitted period;
- a statement of the claimant's right to challenge the agreement; and
- the date of the agreement.[134]

Assuming that there is no dispute over the contents of the agreement, it is automatically backdated to the date of claim, if earlier.[135]

C Disputes over and variations of a jobseeker's agreement

An employment officer may refer a proposed jobseeker's agreement to a decision maker acting on behalf of the Secretary of State to determine both whether its terms would satisfy the availability and actively seeking work requirements and whether it is reasonable to expect the claimant to comply with it.[136] Although phrased in permissive terms, such a reference will take place if there is any doubt, given the stipulation that an employment officer must be of the opinion that the former requirements would be met if there were compliance. The employment officer must make such a reference if the claimant so requests. The Secretary of State, who is required to dispose of the reference within 14 days, so far as is practicable, may make directions as to the terms on which the employment officer should enter into an agreement.[137] A proposed agreement referred

---

131   SI 1996/207, reg 34.
132   JA 1995, s 9(3). The claimant must be provided with a copy: s 9(4).
133   JA 1995, s 9(5).
134   SI 1996/207, reg 31.
135   SI 1996/207, reg 35.
136   JA 1995, s 9(6).
137   JA 1995, s 9(7). On the flexibility of this time limit, see *R v Secretary of State for Social Services, ex p Child Poverty Action Group* [1990] 2 QB 540.

to the Secretary of State will not automatically be backdated, but directions may provide for this in certain circumstances, depending on the reasonableness of the claimant's conduct.[138] The Secretary of State's decision may be appealed to a tribunal.[139]

A jobseeker's agreement may subsequently be varied, but as with the original document this must be by 'agreement', in writing, signed by both parties and a copy provided for the claimant.[140] The same restrictions on the employment officer's freedom to sign the agreement and the facility for a reference to the Secretary of State, with a right of appeal to a tribunal, also apply.[141] Either party may suggest a variation; in practice an employment officer is more likely to do so in the context of one of the periodic interviews held with unemployed claimants, whereas a claimant may be prompted to ask for a change in the light of a change in personal circumstances (eg the assumption of caring responsibilities).

Part 6 Extra conditions of entitlement to income-based jobseeker's allowance

A General

A claimant who meets the core conditions for JSA must also meet further conditions in order to qualify for income-based JSA.[142] There are six such requirements specified in section 3 of JA 1995, namely that the claimant must:
(1) either have no income or an income which does not exceed the applicable amount;
(2) not be entitled to income support;
(3) not be a member of a family one of whose members is entitled to income support;
(4) not be a member of a family one of whose members is entitled to JSA;
(5) not have a partner engaged in remunerative work; and
(6) either have reached the age of 18, or be subject to a direction under section 16 of the Act, or fall within one of the exceptional prescribed circumstances which enable 16 or 17-year olds to qualify for benefit.

Finally, although it unhelpfully appears elsewhere in the JA 1995, the claimant must not have capital in excess of the prescribed maximum of £8,000.[143] The rules governing the assessment of capital are identical in virtually all respects to those that operate under the income support scheme.[144]

The extra conditions laid down by section 3 fall to be considered under four heads.

B Income not in excess of the applicable amount

This requirement mirrors the similar provision under the income support regime, with necessary modifications. Thus the income of the claimant's family – as defined in the

138   SI 1996/207, reg 32.
139   SSA 1998, Sch 3, para 8.
140   JA 1995, s 10(1)–(3).
141   JA 1995, s 10(4)–(6). See further SI 1996/207, regs 37–40 and SSA 1998, Sch 3, para 8.
142   JA 1995, s 1(2A).
143   JA 1995, s 13(1); see also SI 1996/207, regs 107–116 and Sch 8.
144   Pp 459–463, below; the only exception appears to be the absence of an equivalent provision in the JSA rules to the income support provision concerning the treatment of some elements of payments on the termination of employment: SI 1987/1967, reg 48(11). This is because there are special rules governing compensation payments for the purpose of JSA: SI 1996/207, reg 94.

usual way by social security law[145] – is aggregated with that of the claimant, in the same way as for income support.[146] The regulations governing the assessment of income also follow the equivalent provisions for income support, subject to a number of relatively minor differences.[147] The claimant's income is then compared with the relevant applicable amount.[148] The calculation of the applicable amount itself is likewise based on the model of income support, being the sum of the appropriate personal allowances, premiums and housing costs.[149]

C The mutual exclusivity of income-based jobseeker's allowance and income support

The conditions set out in section 3(1)(b) and (c) of JA 1995 (ie requirements (2) and (3) above) are designed to ensure that entitlement to income-based JSA and income support are mutually exclusive. The legislation governing income support contains a parallel exclusion where the claimant or partner is entitled to income-based JSA.[150] By the same token, a person is not entitled to the latter benefit if another member of the family is already so entitled (requirement (4) above).[151] There is, of course, no difficulty with the claimant (or partner) being simultaneously entitled to *contribution*-based JSA; the rules governing the amount payable in situations where a claimant is eligible for both forms of JSA are discussed below.[152]

D   Exclusion of claimants with partners in remunerative work

As with income support, a claimant is debarred from qualifying for income-based JSA if his or her partner is in remunerative work. Whilst this is defined as 16 hours or more a week for the claimant, the threshold is 24 hours per week for any partner.[153]

E   Special rules for 16 and 17-year-olds

The background to the raising of the minimum age for entitlement to income support to 18 and its subsequent lowering to 16, following the introduction of JSA, has already been discussed.[154] The restrictive rules governing the entitlement of unemployed 16 and 17-year-olds, originally introduced in the context of income support, were incorporated within the new arrangements for JSA. Thus the presumptive rule is that entitlement to

---

145   JA 1995, s 35(1).
146   JA 1995, s 13(2) and SI 1996/207, regs 88, 106 and 109 (and reg 88ZA for joint-claim JSA). See pp 291–293, above.
147   SI 1996/207, regs 93–106; see also, governing special forms of income, regs 117–124 (liable relatives), regs 125–129 (child support) and regs 130–139 (students). See further ch 12, below, on the common provisions.
148   JA 1995, s 4(3).
149   JA 1995, s 4(5) and SI 1996/207, regs 83–86, 87 and Sch 1 (see regs 86A–86D on joint-claim JSA). On the income support rules, see pp 293–313, above.
150   SSCBA 1992, s 124(1)(f).
151   See to similar effect JA 1995, s 134(2) as regards income-related benefits under that Act.
152   P 517, below.
153   SI 1996/207, reg 51(1)(b).
154   P 284, above.

income-based JSA cannot commence until a person is 18.[155] There are two exceptions to this principle: those young people who either fall within one of various prescribed circumstances[156] or are subject to a severe hardship direction. These rules in turn are now subject to the arrangements made under the Children (Leaving Care) Act 2000 for young people leaving care. The 2000 Act requires local authorities to provide maintenance (including regular cash support) to young people aged 16 or 17 who have been in local authority care for at least 13 weeks since the age of 14 but have now left such care.[157] Such young people are excluded from entitlement to income-based JSA (as well as income support and housing benefit).[158]

i Prescribed circumstances

Regulations provide for three types of prescribed circumstances in which 16 and 17-year-olds may be entitled to income-based JSA, albeit for varying periods.[159] The first group of young persons covered by the regulations may claim JSA for the child benefit extension period.[160] This group includes the following sub-categories, namely claimants who are:

(1) married and whose partner is 18 or over, or is a 16 or 17-year-old registered for work and training, or who falls within certain of the prescribed categories for income support or other special cases;[161]
(2) without a parent or anyone acting in their place;
(3) not living with their parents (or anyone acting in their place) and who, immediately before reaching 16, were being looked after by a local authority (and placed otherwise than with a close relative)[162] or were in custody;
(4) in accommodation other than the parental home (or that of someone acting in their place) under the supervision of the probation service or a local authority for purposes of rehabilitation or resettlement, or to avoid physical or sexual abuse, or because special accommodation is needed because of illness or handicap; or
(5) living away from home because their parents (etc) are financially unable to provide support and are in custody, prohibited from entering Great Britain or chronically sick or mentally or physically disabled; or
(6) living away from home of necessity because they are estranged from their parents (etc), or in physical or moral danger, or there is a serious risk to their physical or mental health.

The second group of young people may claim after the expiry of the child benefit extension period for a further period of eight weeks or until the individual reaches 18,

---

155 JA 1995, s 3(1)(f)(i). There is no minimum age in respect of contribution-based JSA, but the contribution conditions are such that it is unlikely that any young people would qualify for that version of the benefit.

156 A similar (but by no means identical) set of prescribed circumstances is used in Australia to determine whether a person is independent for the purposes of qualifying for the higher rate of the youth allowance for those under 25 (Social Security Act 1991 (Cth), s 1067A).

157 Children (Leaving Care) Act 2000 (C(LC)A 2000), inserting Children Act 1989, s 23B(8) and (9).

158 C(LC)A 2000, s 6 (but there are exceptions, set out in s 6(3), for those care leavers who would qualify in any event for income-based JSA or income support); see also SI 2001/3070.

159 SI 1996/207, reg 58.

160 SI 1996/207, reg 57(2) and 59. On the child benefit extension period, see p 660, below. See also the special cases in SI 1996/207, reg 61(1)(d) and (e).

161 On which see SI 1996/207, reg 57(4).

162 However, the definition of 'young person' now excludes those covered by the C(LC)A 2000: see above.

if sooner. This category covers claimants who have ceased to live in local authority care and are of necessity living away from their parents or who are prisoners discharged after the end of the child benefit extension period and who fall within any of sub-categories (1) to (6) above.[163]

The third and final group comprises a number of miscellaneous groups who, because of their circumstances, cannot reasonably be expected to undergo training, namely, young people who are:

- laid off or on short time and available for employment;
- members of a couple with a child;
- not claiming income support but fall within one of the prescribed categories;
- within one of various vulnerable categories but unable to register at the Careers Service owing to an emergency affecting that organisation, or would suffer hardship because of the extra time it would take to register there, and register instead with the Employment Service; or
- enlisting with the armed forces (following an offer made when he was not employed or in training) within eight weeks and have not been sanctioned.[164]

In several of such cases the claimant may potentially be entitled to JSA until reaching the age of 18.[165]

If a young person falls within any one of the three prescribed groups above, they are relieved merely of meeting the usual minimum age requirement for income-based JSA. The claimant must still comply with the other eligibility requirements. In particular, young people claiming this benefit must register with the Careers Service for both employment and training,[166] must be available for and actively seeking employment and must have entered into a jobseeker's agreement.[167]

ii Severe hardship direction

JA 1995 provides for a residual category of 'severe hardship' cases where a young person is 16 or 17, is not entitled to JSA or income support, and is registered for training but is not being provided with any training. In such cases, if 'it appears to the Secretary of State ... that severe hardship will result to him unless a JSA is paid to him', then the Secretary of State may make a direction to that effect.[168] The expression 'severe hardship' is not itself defined in the legislation.[169] Directions are usually made for a fixed period of eight weeks, after which they may be renewed; but they are also subject to revocation on prescribed grounds.[170] Moreover, there is no right of appeal to an appeal tribunal

---

163 SI 1996/207, reg 60.
164 SI 1996/207, reg 61(1).
165 The precise cut-off dates are determined in accordance with SI 1996/207, reg 61(2).
166 There are exemptions for those laid off or on short-time, or about to enlist with the armed forces; in certain exceptional circumstances a young person must register with the Employment Service: SI 1996/207, reg 62.
167 SI 1996/207, regs 64–66. Young people may restrict their availability to employment where suitable training is provided (reg 64(2) and (3)) and are required to seek training as well as employment (reg 65).
168 JA 1995, s 16(1) (replacing the former SSCBA 1992, s 125).
169 Official guidance lists the following factors as relevant: health and vulnerability; the threat of homelessness; income or savings, or the prospect of either; the prospect of finding a Youth Training place; assistance from others; and financial commitments: Employment Service *JSA for 16/17 Year Olds* (1996).
170 JA 1995, s 16(2) and (3). The grounds are changes of circumstances, failing to pursue or rejecting a training opportunity without good cause, and ignorance of, or mistake as to, some material fact.

from any such decision;[171] the only recourse available at law is to apply for judicial review.[172] Special provisions apply where a young person who is subject to a severe hardship direction fails to take up or complete a training course without good cause.[173]

Applications by young people for severe hardship payments are inextricably linked with the state of the job market for school leavers and the availability of training places. Concern has been expressed that, despite its complexity and limited publicity, a scheme designed as a stop-gap measure has become a form of mainstream provision for many young people.[174]

Part 7   Joint-claim jobseeker's allowance

As we have seen, JSA under JA 1995 originally comprised two forms: the insurance version, contribution-based JSA, and the means-tested type, income-based JSA. The former is an individual benefit; thus both partners in a couple may each independently qualify, assuming that they both satisfy the eligibility criteria (including the contribution conditions), but there are no dependency additions payable. Typically, however, where couples are concerned, one partner claims income-based JSA on behalf of himself (or, less commonly, herself) and any dependants. Thus the traditional benefit rules reinforced the stereotype of female dependency on men, at a time when labour market participation rates amongst women were higher than ever before.[175] Social research in the late 1990s also demonstrated the growing divide between 'work-rich' couples (where both partners are in employment) and 'work-less' couples (where both are unemployed).[176] The government was hence keen to ensure that the partners of unemployed claimants (at least so far as childless couples were concerned) explored opportunities to find work. WRPA 1999 introduced joint-claim JSA, as a variant of income-based JSA, to address this phenomenon.[177]

A 'joint-claim couple' is defined as a married or unmarried couple who do *not* have a child in their family in respect of whom either are entitled to child benefit and who are of a 'prescribed description'.[178] The latter concept is explained by regulations: one of the members must have been born after 19 March 1976 but must also be aged at least 18.[179] A joint-claim couple are entitled to joint-claim JSA if they make a joint claim for the allowance, they each individually satisfy the core conditions of entitlement to JSA and, as a couple, they also meet the conditions set out in section 3A of JA 1995.[180]

---

171   SSA 1998, Sch 2, para 1.
172   Not surprisingly, there are to date no reported cases of this avenue being pursued. A slightly more realistic alternative is to take the matter up with a Member of Parliament.
173   P 375, below.
174   Maclagan *Four Years' Severe Hardship* (1993). See also SSAC *Eighth Report* (1992) pp 34–39.
175   See Morris (2000) 7 JSSL 228.
176   See generally Howard et al *Poverty: the facts* (4th edn, 2001).
177   WRPA 1999, s 59 and Sch 7. See also SSAA 1992, s 2AA (inserted by the Employment Act 2002, s 48) on work-focused interviews for partners.
178   JA 1995, s 1(4).
179   SI 1996/207, reg 3A(1) (subject to certain exclusions). This rule came into force on 19 March 2001, thus meaning (at that time) that a childless couple qualified as a joint-claim couple if one member was aged between 18 and 25. From 28 October 2002 the scope of this rule will be extended to include all those aged between 18 and 45: SI 2002/1701. Remarkably, JA 1995, s 1(2D) and SI 1996/207, reg 3A(2) make provision for the Secretary of State to allocate an individual to a specific joint-claim couple if he or she would otherwise be a member of more than one such couple!
180   JA 1995, s 1(2B). Thus both partners must 'sign on': SI 1996/207, reg 23A.

These last requirements are modelled on the additional conditions for income-based JSA, with the necessary modifications to reflect their status as a joint-claim couple. Thus the following conditions must all be met:

(1) the joint-claim couple has no income or their income does not exceed the relevant applicable amount;[181]
(2) no member of their family is entitled to income support;
(3) no member of their family (other than the couple) is entitled to income-based JSA;
(4) at least one member of the couple has reached the age of 18; and
(5) if only one member of the couple has attained that age, the other member is subject to a severe hardship direction or is in one of the prescribed groups of 16 to 17-year olds.

Lastly, the couple must, of course, not have capital above the prescribed limit, which is the same as for income-based JSA.[182]

A joint-claim couple may nominate the partner to whom the joint-claim JSA is payable, in default of which the Secretary of State may decide.[183] Regulations make provision for those who cease to be a joint-claim couple because they become responsible (or are treated as responsible) for a child. In such cases the joint award of benefit is terminated and substituted by a 'replacement award', with the existing joint claim being treated as a claim by either member of the couple.[184] Regulations also provide for cases in which a couple become a joint-claim couple, because they are no longer responsible for a child.[185] There are also certain special cases in which joint-claim JSA is payable to a couple, even though one of them is exempt from the requirement to satisfy the labour market conditions (typically where that partner falls into one of those categories of claimant who would otherwise be eligible for income support).[186] Finally, there are various special circumstances in which one partner in a joint-claim couple can qualify for income-based JSA in his or her own right without making a joint claim. This is possible where the partner claiming benefit satisfies both the core conditions for JSA and the supplementary conditions for income-based JSA and the other partner both fails to meet the latter criteria and falls within various prescribed exceptional categories.[187]

Part 8   Amount and duration of income-based jobseeker's allowance

A   Amount of income-based jobseeker's allowance

The amount of an income-based JSA is calculated in the same way as for income support: claimants who have no assessable income receive their applicable amount and in other cases a sum representing the figure by which the applicable amount exceeds their income.[188] As with income support, there is a minimum weekly allowance of

---

181   SI 1996/207, regs 86A–86D.
182   JA 1995, s 13(2A)–(2B) and SI 1996/207, reg 88ZA.
183   JA 1995, s 3B. The Secretary of State may supply information relating to the claim to either or both partners: SI 1996/207, reg 3G. See also reg 24(1A) and (5A) on the obligation to provide information.
184   JA 1995, Sch 1, para 9A and SI 1996/207, reg 3B.
185   JA 1995, Sch 1, Para 9C and SI 1996/207, reg 3C.
186   JA 1995, Sch 1, para 8A and SI 1996/207, reg 3D and Sch A1.
187   SI 1996/207, reg 3E.
188   JA 1995, s 4(3). A parallel rule applies to joint-claim JSA: s 4(3A). For calculation of the contribution-based JSA, see p 515, below.

10 pence.[189] The fact that there are two principal variants of JSA means that there is a series of complex provisions governing the position where a claimant qualifies for both contribution-based and income-based JSA.[190] The basic rule is that the claimant receives the personal rate under the contribution-based scheme or, if it is higher, the applicable amount (or the difference between any income and the applicable amount) under the income-based scheme. In the latter case this is then deemed to be subdivided into an amount representing the contribution-based personal rate and a 'top-up' income-based element reflecting the difference between the applicable amount (or the excess of the applicable amount over the income) and the personal rate. These rules are necessary both because of the six-month limit on the contributory element and for accounting reasons as the two allowances are paid for from the National Insurance Fund and general taxation respectively.

B Duration of income-based jobseeker's allowance

Contribution-based JSA is available only for six months; thereafter the claimant will have to find work again in order to build up a contributions record for a subsequent claim.[191] There is, at present, no time limit for income-based JSA, just as with income support. It follows that, so long as the claimant satisfies the relevant eligibility criteria, benefit potentially continues in payment until reaching pensionable age.[192] Given the increasing emphasis on the obligation to find work, it is questionable whether the open-ended nature of benefit entitlement will continue. To date no British government has publicly considered the possibility of time-limiting payments of either income-based JSA or income support. The position is very different in the US, where the Personal Responsibility and Work Opportunity Reconciliation Act 1996 replaced the former Aid to Families with Dependent Children (AFDC) programme with Temporary Assistance for Needy Families (TANF). In the first instance a claimant must leave welfare within two years, regardless of whether the individual finds employment. There is also a five-year cumulative lifetime limit on receipt of TANF support.[193]

Part 9 Sanctions for voluntary unemployment

A Introduction

One of the fundamental principles of the former unemployment benefit scheme was that a claimant was only eligible for benefit if his or her unemployment was involuntary. This was reflected in the requirement that claimants be both available for and (from 1989) actively seeking employment. It also explained the provisions for the disqualification of claimants from benefit in circumstances where they were adjudged

---

189 JA 1995, s 4(4) and SI 1996/207, reg 87A.
190 JA 1995, s 4(6)–(11). There are parallel rules for joint-claim JSA: s 4A.
191 P 514, below.
192 JA 1995, s 1(2)(h). Entitlement may lapse, for example, if the claimant falls ill or becomes disabled and qualifies for incapacity benefit at a rate that excludes entitlement to income support.
193 Personal Responsibility and Work Opportunity Reconciliation Act 1996 (US), § 103(a)(1). See Handler (1998) 50 Admin LR 635 (the time limit is subject to exceptions).

to be in some way responsible for losing their employment. Some of these grounds for disqualification date back to the original scheme under NIA 1911, most notably those in relation to loss of employment owing to misconduct or voluntarily leaving a job without just cause. These grounds were the subject of a considerable body of case law emanating from the Commissioners, but there were few statutory developments during the greater part of the last century. In the 1980s, however, the then Conservative government twice extended the maximum length of the potential disqualification and also introduced new grounds that specifically applied to training programmes (as opposed to actual jobs). The framework for disqualifications, now renamed sanctions, was radically altered by JA 1995, although much of the terminology previously in use was reincorporated under the new scheme. The 1995 Act drew a fundamental distinction between employment-related sanctions, where breach may result in disentitlement for a period of up to 26 weeks, at the discretion of the decision maker, and sanctions related to jobseeker's directions or training programmes, which result in disentitlement for a fixed period of two or four weeks. There are parallel provisions to those discussed below for joint-claim JSA.[194] It should be borne in mind that some of the Commissioners' decisions cited in this Part may reflect the social attitudes of their time, and accordingly the principles to be derived from such authorities may need modification before being applied to modern circumstances.[195]

B   Employment-related sanctions

i   Misconduct

The first ground for imposing an employment-related sanction arises where the claimant has 'lost his employment as an employed earner through his misconduct'.[196] The rule was to be found in NIA 1911,[197] and has existed effectively in the same form ever since. However, the exact policy considerations on which it is based have never been made entirely explicit,[198] and as a result its interpretation and evolution have not been wholly consistent.[199] Three alternative theories may be invoked to support the sanction.

(1) *Punishment* From a moral or social point of view, a worker who has been dismissed for misconduct is unworthy of support: he or she has transgressed the ethical standards of the community.

(2) *Suitability* Claimants should be disqualified where their own actions reveal them as unsuitable for the job. Benefit is intended to cover only those who lose employment through external circumstances, and not those whose lack of skill results in dismissal.

(3) *Voluntary unemployment* The purpose of the sanction is to protect against claims caused by voluntary unemployment. Benefit is therefore to be denied to claimants who knew or should have known that their conduct was reasonably likely to incur dismissal.

---

194   JA 1995, ss 20A and 20B; SI 1996/207, reg 74B.
195   See eg *R(U) 20/60*, discussed at n 315, below.
196   JA 1995, s 19(6)(a).
197   NIA 1911, s 87(2).
198   For an economic appraisal, see Fenn in Burrows and Veljanovski (eds) *The Economic Approach to Law* (1981) ch 13.
199   Lewis [1985] JSWL 145.

The first theory has been most explicitly rejected in the UK.[200] The third theory is more consistent with the general purpose of the legislation,[201] and its influence can be seen in certain decisions,[202] but like most doctrines dependent on mental states, it creates grave problems of proof. The suitability theory, though less attractive on policy grounds, can explain most of the law on this subject. Account is rarely taken of whether the claimant appreciated, or might reasonably have appreciated, that the conduct in question would lead to dismissal. While, in theory, an objective test of suitability is adopted – whether a reasonable employer would dismiss the employee[203] – it has been alleged that in practice the authorities rely on the managerial standards adopted by individual employers.[204] If this is the case and the standards vary according to the economic circumstances (eg a stricter standard when there is reduced demand for the firm's output),[205] the employee may be unfairly prejudiced: such circumstances should be irrelevant to the disqualification issue.

Traditionally all such theories have been phrased in terms of protecting the National Insurance Fund, although strictly this is of much less significance today given the limited role for contribution-based JSA. However, that consideration would be thwarted if claimants could receive an equivalent amount of means-tested benefit. Under the previous arrangements a disqualification from unemployment benefit resulted in a knock-on sanction involving a reduction in the relevant award of supplementary benefit and later income support.[206] The same applies for the purposes of JSA, although with the substantial qualification that the sanction applies to either component of the benefit, and there is no automatic entitlement to a reduced rate of benefit following its imposition; instead, the claimant must demonstrate a case of hardship.[207]

A DISMISSAL CAUSED BY MISCONDUCT

In principle the Secretary of State must prove that the claimant was dismissed for an act or omission which constituted 'misconduct'.[208] But the requirement of 'dismissal' and its causal relationship with the alleged misconduct have been broadly construed. The contract of employment need not have been terminated by the employer: it will suffice if, as a result of the misconduct, the contract has been suspended[209] or both parties regard the employment as ended.[210] Nor need the 'dismissal' follow as an immediate consequence of the misconduct. In one case, a lorry driver was convicted of a driving offence committed out of working hours. He was disqualified even though the immediate cause of his dismissal was the loss of his licence rather than the commission of the offence.[211]

---

200 *CU 190/50*; *R(U) 27/52*; *R(U) 8/74(T)*.
201 Cf *Fenn* n 198, above.
202 *CU 190/50*; *R(U) 35/53*; *R(U) 24/55*.
203 *R(U) 2/77*.
204 *Lewis* n 199, above. See generally Collins *Justice in Dismissal* (1992).
205 *Fenn* n 198, above, p 317.
206 See the 4th edition of this book, pp 490–494.
207 See Part 10, below.
208 *R(U) 2/77*, R J A Temple, Chief Comr, and see *R(U) 2/81*, para 9.
209 *R(U) 10/71*.
210 *R(U) 17/64*; *R(U) 2/76*.
211 *R(U) 7/57*.

B   MISCONDUCT CONNECTED WITH EMPLOYMENT

If an employee were to be disqualified for misconduct committed in any circumstance, in effect the system would be regarding the employer's attitude to the misconduct as conclusive, and would be adopting a punitive approach to the claimant's entitlement. If, however, it requires that the misconduct be related to the employment, it may still question whether the dismissal warrants disqualification, as viewed from the policy dictate of protecting the insurance fund and more generally the taxpayer. The Commissioners have adopted this latter stance and ruled that the conduct must be 'causally but not necessarily directly connected with the employment'.[212] The test is whether the misconduct, whenever and wherever it occurred, was such that it would induce a reasonable employer to dispense with the services of the claimant on the ground that he or she was not fit to hold the particular situation.[213] Of course, this will generally depend on the nature both of the misconduct and of the employment. What individuals do outside working hours may be totally irrelevant to their work or their employer's interests. A railway worker who was dismissed for fighting in a railway carriage on his return from work was not disqualified.[214] But the misconduct may so closely affect the individual's suitability for the job that it will justify disqualification no matter where and when it occurs. Such was said to be the case where a park keeper was convicted of gross indecency with another man.[215]

C   TYPES OF CONDUCT

The use of the unqualified term 'misconduct' is unhelpful in determining the standard of conduct which is to be applied. Indeed, in the early years of the scheme it caused some embarrassment as it had to be explained to many women claimants that it was not intended to refer to their moral behaviour.[216] A Royal Commission, reporting in 1932, felt that the choice of language was unfortunate but was unable to suggest any positive improvement.[217] According to a former Chief Commissioner, the conduct must be such that it renders the claimant an unfit person to hold the job[218] and will include:

> industrial shortcomings, disobedience, faulty workmanship, idleness, unauthorised absence, some types of carelessness, and conduct ... connected with the employment adversely affecting the claimant's proper discharge of his duties.[219]

But the refusal to leave[220] or to join a trade union[221] does not constitute misconduct.

---

212   *R(U) 2/77*, para 15, R J A Temple, Chief Comr. See also *R(U) 1/71*.
213   *R(U) 2/77*.
214   *UD 4120*.
215   *R(U) 1/71*, R G Micklethwait, Chief Comr, although the period of disqualification was reduced to one week.
216   Tillyard *Unemployment Insurance in Great Britain 1911–48* (1949) pp 24–25.
217   Final Report (1932, Cmd 4185) para 443. To meet the objection, the ground for disqualification has in practice frequently been called 'industrial misconduct': see esp *R(U) 24/55* and *R(U) 1/71*.
218   *R(U) 24/55; R(U) 7/57*.
219   *R(U) 2/77*, para 15.
220   *UD 1528/26*.
221   *R(U) 2/77*.

D   BLAMEWORTHINESS

It is generally said that there must be blameworthiness,[222] but exactly what must be proved in terms of mental attitude is far from clear. On occasions, Commissioners have tended towards a test appropriate to the 'voluntary unemployment' theory and spoken of the necessity of showing 'deliberate' or 'wilful negligence'.[223] The view most popularly held, however, is that a wilful or reckless breach of the appropriate standard is not required. A valuable illustration is provided by *R(U) 8/57*.

> C, the manager of a branch pharmacy, was dismissed when cash was found to be missing in the shop. He was prosecuted for, but acquitted of, embezzlement. It was held that this was not sufficient to bar disqualification. 'Serious carelessness' only was required, and this might legitimately be inferred from the evidence.

The Commissioner observed, more generally:

> Misconduct ... may be constituted by mere carelessness; but in considering whether a person has been guilty of misconduct it is necessary to discriminate between that type and degree of carelessness which may have to be put up with in human affairs, and the more deliberate or more serious type of carelessness which justifies withholding unemployment benefit because the employee has lost his employment through his own avoidable fault.[224]

E   RELEVANCE OF OTHER LEGAL PROCEEDINGS

The situation in which an employee is dismissed for misconduct may have important repercussions in other areas of law. The conduct may constitute a criminal offence. The employee may allege that he or she has a valid claim for unfair dismissal (the statutory remedy) or wrongful dismissal (the common law remedy for breach of contract). The dispute may have been the subject of a court hearing or of a decision by an employment or disciplinary tribunal. In all such situations, the question arises as to the significance for the sanctioning issue of the findings of such court or tribunal.

It is evident that in many instances the concept of 'misconduct' will be wider than a criminal offence with which the claimant was charged. In such a case an acquittal by a criminal court will in no sense be conclusive of the sanctioning point.[225] Where the claimant has been convicted, there is no question of double jeopardy since the object of the sanction is not punishment,[226] but there is nevertheless some difficulty as to the weight to be given to the conviction. It clearly has evidentiary value,[227] but despite an earlier Commissioner's decision to the contrary,[228] it now seems clear that it will not be regarded as conclusive proof that the facts which were the basis of the criminal charge and also constituted the alleged misconduct actually occurred. In a sickness benefit

222   Eg *R(U) 2/77*, para 15.
223   *R(U) 34/52*, cp 'culpable negligence' (*R(U) 35/53*).
224   *R(U) 8/57*, para 6.
225   *R(U) 10/54; R(U) 8/57*.
226   *CU 190/50; R(U) 27/52*; R(U) 7/75.
227   *R(U) 10/54*.
228   *R(U) 24/55*.

case,[229] the Commissioner adopted a compromise position whereby the initial onus lies on the officer making the decision to show that a conviction relates to the benefit issue involved. The onus then passes to the claimant to show that, notwithstanding the conviction, he or she is nevertheless entitled to the benefit in question.

The position is far from clear as regards the decisions of disciplinary bodies. It would seem to depend on how 'judicial' in character is the tribunal and the nature of the information emanating from its findings. So, in one case, confirmation of dismissal, without detailed reasons, by a hospital management committee afforded little assistance to the Commissioner,[230] but, in another, the more formal 'quasi-judicial' proceedings of a police disciplinary committee, while not 'absolutely conclusive' for social security purposes, were nevertheless treated as 'very cogent evidence'.[231]

One would have thought that a finding by an employment (formerly industrial) tribunal that an employee was entitled to compensation for an unfair dismissal would be almost conclusive that the same employee was not guilty of such misconduct as to be disqualified from JSA. Certainly it is appropriate for the authorities to take full cognisance of any *evidence* given to the employment tribunal,[232] but its finding as to whether or not an employee has been unfairly dismissed is in no sense conclusive of the social security issue whether the claimant has been guilty of misconduct.[233] There are different questions of law involved: whether a person has been unfairly dismissed in the main depends on the conduct of the employer, whereas for benefit purposes the main emphasis is on the behaviour of the employee.[234] The onus and standard of proof applicable may also differ between the two tribunals.[235]

ii Voluntarily leaving without just cause

The second employment-related ground for sanctioning is that the claimant:

has voluntarily left such employment [as an employed earner] without just cause.[236]

Such a provision is a typical feature of all unemployment insurance schemes, and has existed in the British system since its inception in 1911.[237] On the traditional theory, it may be justified on the ground that here unemployment is caused not by external circumstances but by claimants themselves.[238] In recent times, however, some forms of voluntary redundancy are actively encouraged to promote mobility in the labour market and, in 1985, the legislation was amended to take account of this policy goal.[239] For disqualification to be imposed, three conditions must be satisfied: (a) the claimant *left*

---

229 *R(S) 2/80*, J S Watson, Comr. He applied the principle of the Civil Evidence Act 1968, s 11(2)(a) (on which see *Stupple v Royal Insurance Co Ltd* [1971] 1 QB 50, [1970] 3 All ER 230) even though that Act does not apply to social security tribunals.
230 *R(U) 7/61*.
231 *R(U) 10/67*.
232 *R(U) 2/74*, para 15, R G Micklethwait, Chief Comr; and see *R(U) 4/78*, para 6, H A Shewan, Comr.
233 *R(U) 2/74*; *R(U) 4/78*; *R(U) 3/79*.
234 *R(U) 2/74*, para 14.
235 *R(U) 4/78*, para 6.
236 JA 1995, s 19(6)(b).
237 NIA 1911, s 87(2). The disqualification was based on analogous rules in trade unions' private unemployment insurance schemes. See Harris *Unemployment and Politics* (1972) pp 312–314.
238 Cf *R(U) 20/64(T)*, para 8; *Crewe v Social Security Comr* [1982] 2 All ER 745, [1982] 1 WLR 1209, per Donaldson LJ at 750, per Slade LJ at 751.
239 SSA 1985, s 10. See now JA 1995, s 19(7) and SI 1996/207, reg 71; see further p 367, below.

the employment; (b) the leaving was *voluntary*; (c) it was *without just cause*. Following that amendment, the disqualification will be avoided if (d) the claimant was dismissed *by reason of redundancy*. In addition, the disqualification does not operate (e) for certain categories of claimant who try out a job for a *trial period* and then leave within 6 to 12 weeks of starting such employment.[240]

A LEAVING

The onus is on the Secretary of State to show that the claimant left his or her employment.[241] 'Leaving' is not confined to terminating the contract of employment, but includes any temporary severing of the employment relationship, including absenteeism.[242]

B VOLUNTARY

The onus is also on the Secretary of State to show that such leaving was voluntary.[243] It is this condition which distinguishes the case from dismissal for misconduct,[244] but in some cases it will be of no great significance which of the two is adopted,[245] and the word 'voluntarily' has been broadly construed so that it might extend to cases of termination by the employer which are instigated by the employee but which do not amount to misconduct.[246] In *R(U) 16/52*:

> C was engaged as a canteen assistant subject to passing a medical examination. She refused to undergo an X-ray test and was dismissed. She was disqualified for leaving her employment voluntarily without just cause. 'It is an established principle of unemployment insurance', said the Commissioner, 'that, if a person deliberately and knowingly acts in a way which makes it necessary for the employer to dismiss him, he may be regarded as leaving his employment voluntarily.'[247]

But if the dismissal is not the 'natural consequence' of the claimant's actions, the leaving will not be voluntary. Thus in *R(U) 9/59*:

> C was dismissed when he refused to join the employer's superannuation scheme. He did not know at the time he entered the contract that he would be expected to join, and therefore his conduct did not 'invite' dismissal.[248]

Subject to the 1985 saving provisions for redundancy, a decision to take early retirement will normally constitute voluntarily leaving and thus attract disqualification,[249] but it

---

240 P 368, below.
241 *R(U) 20/64(T)*.
242 *R(U) 20/64(T)*, para 7.
243 *UD 10841/30*; *R(U) 20/64(T)*.
244 *R(U) 9/59*.
245 Cf p 361, above.
246 *R(U) 5/71*, but see *R(U) 2/77*, para 26, where R J A Temple, Chief Comr, suggests that as the principle is not to be found in the legislation itself it should be applied with restraint.
247 *R(U) 16/52*, para 8; and see *R(U) 7/74*.
248 See also *R(U) 2/77* (refusal to join trade union).
249 *R(U) 20/64(T)*; *R(U) 4/70*; *R(U) 2/81*, affirmed without discussion of the point in *Crewe v Social Security Comr* [1982] 2 All ER 745, [1982] 1 WLR 1209; *R(U) 3/81*.

has been held that an employee who acceded to a request from his employer to retire did not act 'voluntarily'.[250]

C   WITHOUT JUST CAUSE

Once it has been established that the case is one of voluntarily leaving, the onus passes to the claimant to show that he or she did so for 'just cause'.[251] The phrase is broad and flexible. The primary legislation enables regulations to be made prescribing factors that may or may not be relevant to the consideration of 'just cause', but no such regulations have been made.[252] The only statutory constraint is that, in determining any issue of 'just cause', 'any matter relating to the level of remuneration in the employment in question shall be disregarded'.[253] Traditionally a reduction in wages imposed by an employer would be an obvious example of 'just cause'.[254] The policy intention behind the new rule was apparently to deter workers from leaving a job because they consider their pay too low, rather than to exclude a cut in pay as a relevant factor in determining 'just cause'.[255] That policy intent appears to have been lost in the breadth of the wording of the statutory provision. Even so, it must surely be a material consideration if an employer seeks to reduce a worker's wages below the national minimum wage, as social security law should not be seen to undermine employment protection measures.[256]

   In all other respects the definition of 'just cause' is at large. The leading case remains the decision of the Court of Appeal in *Crewe v Social Security Comr*. The fact that this case concerned unemployment benefit led the court to hold that the expression has to be interpreted by reference to the insurance character of the scheme: 'the justice which the legislature had in mind was justice as between the employee and the general body of persons underwriting the fund'.[257] The interest of contributors to the National Insurance Fund is to be distinguished from the general public interest. In the instant case, a school teacher who had taken early retirement unsuccessfully argued that the 'public interest' of savings in the education budget or of making way for younger members of the profession constituted 'just cause'.[258] Examples of situations in which the interest of the claimant has been allowed to prevail over that of contributors are:

- non-compliance by the employer with the contract of employment,[259]
- lack of confidence in mental or physical ability to perform duties,[260]
- pressing domestic or personal circumstances,[261]

---

250   *R(U) 1/83*. But see now JA 1995, s 19(7) and SI 1996/207, reg 71.
251   *R(U) 20/64(T)*, para 7.
252   JA 1995, s 19(8)(a)(ii) and (b)(ii). Contrast the detailed definition of 'good cause' in SI 1996/207, regs 72 and 73.
253   JA 1995, s 19(9).
254   *R(U) 15/53*.
255   CPAG *Welfare benefits handbook* (2nd edn, 2000–01) p 355.
256   Workers are protected against suffering any detriment by any act or omission of their employer if they take action to enforce their right to the minimum wage: National Minimum Wage Act 1998, s 23 (see also s 25 inserting Employment Relations Act 1999, s 104A as regards protection against unfair dismissal).
257   Per Slade LJ, *Crewe v Social Security Comr* [1982] 2 All ER 745, [1982] 1 WLR 1209. To similar effect, see Lord Denning MR at 749 and Donaldson LJ at 750. See further, *R(U) 4/87*, para 9.
258   See also *R(U) 4/87*. The impact of the 1985 legislative amendment, discussed at p 367, below, must now be considered in such cases.
259   *CU 248/49*.
260   *R(U) 3/73*.
261   *R(U) 31/59*. For the position in the US, see Rosettenstein (1986) XX Family Law Q 393.

- difficulty of travel to work,[262]
- reluctance to join a trade union,[263] and
- general grievances about working conditions.[264]

But though such circumstances may constitute a good reason for leaving the employment, they may not be sufficient in themselves to avoid the imposition of a sanction. It is a general principle that dissatisfied employees should look for an alternative situation before leaving their present job.[265] They need not actually have secured a vacant post,[266] but the prospects of finding one must be good.[267] The principle has not been rigidly applied. For example, it was not invoked where a wife left her job to join her husband who had been posted elsewhere,[268] nor to a spouse who was not the principal breadwinner and who left to look after a child who would otherwise have remained unattended.[269] Nor was it applied where the current employment did not provide any opportunities for looking for another job,[270] or where the relations between the claimant and his employer or his fellow employees had become so strained that it was in the interest of all that he should leave immediately.[271] As regards grievances about working conditions and other disputes with an employer, there is a further general principle, which is again subject to the undue friction exception. This is that, before tendering notice, a claimant should seek to redress the grievances by making representations to the employer through the proper channels, usually, if appropriate, with the assistance of a trade union.[272]

D   LOSS OF EMPLOYMENT BY REASON OF REDUNDANCY

Since 1985 the legislation has provided that:

> In such circumstances as may be prescribed, including in particular where he has been dismissed by his employer by reason of redundancy within the meaning of section 139(1) of the Employment Rights Act 1996 after volunteering or agreeing to be so dismissed, a person who might otherwise be regarded as having left his employment voluntarily is to be treated as not having left voluntarily.[273]

The regulations further provide that a claimant is to be treated as not having voluntarily left any employment where he or she: (i) has been dismissed for redundancy after volunteering or agreeing to be so dismissed; (ii) has left the employment without being dismissed but 'in pursuance of an agreement relating to voluntary redundancy'; or (iii) has been laid off or kept on short-time, subject to the relevant statutory criteria.[274]

262   *R(U) 20/69.*
263   *R(U) 38/53.*
264   *R(U) 33/51.* There may be an overlap here with the criteria applied in deciding whether the claimant had, without good cause, unreasonably refused an offer of employment: pp 369–372, below.
265   *CU 96/48; R(U) 14/55; R(U) 20/64(T).*
266   *R(U) 4/73.*
267   *R(U) 20/64(T); R(U) 4/70.*
268   *R(U) 19/52;* cf *R(U) 2/90(T).*
269   *R(U) 6/59.*
270   *R(U) 25/52.*
271   *UD 5287.*
272   *R(U) 33/51; R 3/65 (UB).* Contrast *R(U) 18/57:* the Commissioner held that such steps were not necessary where the *employer* issued an ultimatum to do additional work, or withdraw.
273   JA 1995, s 19(7). The original and less than happily drafted provision was in SSCBA 1992, s 28(4); see the 4th edition of this book, p 119.
274   SI 1996/207, reg 71.

Originally the legislation as introduced in 1985 was confined to the first situation. The Commissioner held that for social security purposes the term 'dismissal' should not be confined to its technical meaning; thus 'dismissal' also covered situations where employers and employees, in anticipation of future redundancies, agree when and on what terms the employees will leave their employment.[275] This interpretation was consistent with the policy underlying the introduction of this safeguard, but is now effectively superseded by the second set of circumstances prescribed in the regulations.

Notwithstanding this liberal approach, it must still be established that the dismissal or departure is the result of a 'redundancy', an expression which covers only cases where the loss of employment:

> is attributable wholly or mainly to (a) the fact that [the] employer has ceased, or intends to cease, to carry on [the] business in the place where the employee was … employed, or (b) the fact that the requirements of that business for employees to carry out work of a particular kind, or for employees to carry out work of a particular kind in the place where he was so employed, have ceased or diminished or are expected to cease or diminish.[276]

It follows that employees who leave under an early retirement scheme, which is not in fact a disguised redundancy, cannot avail themselves of this exemption, and are subject to the general principles relating to 'just cause', as laid down in *Crewe v Social Security Comr*.[277]

E   TRIAL PERIODS

A provision first enacted in 1989 enables certain claimants to try out an opportunity of employment without risking disqualification for leaving voluntarily should they subsequently decide that the position is unsuitable for them.[278] This amendment was designed to encourage individuals who have been out of work for some time to re-enter the labour market. A claimant can only take advantage of this provision if he or she has been neither employed (nor self-employed) nor been in full-time education in the period of 13 weeks before the trial job.[279] The trial period means that a claimant can leave a new job at any point during the eight-week period from the start of the fifth week to the end of the twelfth week after starting without risking a sanction for having voluntarily left that employment without 'just cause'.[280] Of course, claimants who fail to come within the precise scope of this provision[281] may still be able to establish 'just cause' on the ordinary principles.[282]

---

275   *R(U) 3/91*.
276   Employment Rights Act 1996, s 139. For these purposes, the business of 'associated employers' is treated as the same business as that of the principal employer.
277   *Crewe v Social Security Comr* [1982] 2 All ER 745, [1982] 1 WLR 1209.
278   JA 1995, s 20(3). There is no requirement that the job itself be a trial position.
279   SI 1996/207, reg 74(1); this represents a relaxation of the original 26-week qualifying period. Claimants engaged in various part-time emergency services are not regarded as having been in employment, etc for these purposes.
280   SI 1996/207, reg 74(4). Weeks in which the claimant works for less than 16 hours are disregarded.
281   For a technical failure to meet the original version of these complex rules, see *R(U) 1/92*.
282   *R(U) 1/92*, in which just one day's disqualification was imposed.

iii Refusal or failure to apply for or accept a job vacancy

The third ground for sanctioning is where the claimant:

> has, without good cause, after a situation in any employment has been notified to him by
> an employment officer as vacant or about to become vacant, refused or failed to apply for
> it or to accept it when offered to him.[283]

Of course, this complements the condition that the claimant is available for employment,[284] and there is inevitably some overlap between the two areas of law[285] – most obviously on the question whether the restrictions the claimant places on his or her availability are reasonable. But there is an important difference. The availability test is a *general* one: it is concerned with the claimant's attitude to the labour market. The ground for sanctioning is concerned with the claimant's refusal or failure to follow a *particular* course of conduct, or to accept a *particular* offer of employment.[286]

A ONUS OF PROOF

The burden is first on the Secretary of State to show that a situation has been offered or notified to the claimant. It is then for the latter to prove that he or she had good cause for refusing it, or failing to apply for it.[287]

B NOTIFICATION AND REFUSAL

The job in question must be notified to the claimant by an employment officer or a person designated by the Secretary of State.[288] The claimant cannot complain that the information provided was insufficiently detailed. So long as the broad nature of the situation is clear, it is incumbent upon the claimant to find out further particulars.[289] 'Refusal', too, has been widely construed. An explicit rejection of the offer is unnecessary: it is sufficient if the claimant's conduct was such as positively to discourage the employer from offering him the situation.[290]

C GOOD CAUSE

The imposition of this sanction is subject to the proviso that the claimant may be able to establish 'good cause'.[291] The concept of 'good cause', which had previously been

283 JA 1995, s 19(6)(c).
284 Pp 340–348, above. The disqualification provisions were introduced (UIA 1930, s 4) because failure to satisfy the availability condition entailed disentitlement, a less flexible sanction than disqualification: see *Report of the Committee on Procedure and Evidence for Determination of Claims for Unemployment Insurance Benefit* (1929, Cmd 3415) paras 43–44.
285 See eg *R(U) 2/59*.
286 For policy discussion, see Layard *How to Beat Unemployment* (1986) pp 50–52.
287 *R(U) 26/52*.
288 JA 1995, s 19(6)(c) and (10)(a).
289 *R(U) 32/52*.
290 *R(U) 28/55* (claimant presented himself for interview with the prospective employer in a dirty and unshaven state). See also *R(U) 23/51*.
291 The further statutory requirement that the employment in question be 'suitable' was abolished in 1989: see the 3rd edition of this book, pp 105–108.

elaborated upon in the case law,[292] is now subject to the Secretary of State's wide power to make regulations defining the scope of the 'good cause' escape route.[293] This enabling power has been exercised so as to deem claimants either to have or not to have 'good cause' in specified situations and to lay down certain factors to be taken into account in determining whether 'good cause' has been established.

(i) Circumstances deemed to be 'good cause'

Regulations provide for claimants to be treated as having 'good cause' in a number of situations. First, a claimant has automatic good cause for declining to apply for or to accept a job involving less than 24 hours' work a week.[294] Secondly, a person who has undergone at least two months'[295] training for a particular kind of employment is to be regarded as having 'good cause' for refusing or failing to apply for any other kind of employment for a period of four weeks after the training ends.[296] After the expiry of the four-week period, the claimant may still be able to show 'good cause' on the basis of the general principles discussed below. Thirdly, a claimant who has the benefit of a 'permitted period' (a maximum of 13 weeks) is protected from being sanctioned if he or she fails to take up a job offer other than one in the person's usual occupation and for at least their usual remuneration.[297] Fourthly, claimants who are exempt from the requirement to be available for work immediately have 'good cause' if they decline work for which they would have to be so available.[298] Finally, primary legislation provides that a claimant cannot be sanctioned for refusing 'to seek or accept employment in a situation which is vacant in consequence of a stoppage of work due to a trade dispute'.[299] This provision originally formed part of the test of 'suitable' employment and was designed to prevent employers from using the threat of disqualification to force individuals to be employed as strike-breakers.[300]

(ii) Circumstances deemed not to be 'good cause'

There are three matters that cannot constitute 'good cause'. First, as with the concept of 'just cause', primary legislation stipulates that in determining any issue of 'good cause', 'any matter relating to the level of remuneration in the employment in question shall be disregarded'.[301] This is in marked contrast to the law before 1989 on the definition

---

292   In practice the Commissioners did not distinguish between 'suitability' and 'good cause', regarding them as alternative formulations of the same principle, between them: see eg *R(U) 20/60*. According to Slade LJ in *Crewe v Social Security Comr* [1982] 2 All ER 745 at 751, 'without good cause' perhaps means no more than 'without reasonable cause' and, as such, should be distinguished from 'without just cause', which imposes a heavier burden on those seeking to avoid disqualification for 'voluntary leaving'.

293   JA 1995, s 19(8) and (9).

294   SI 1996/207, reg 72(5A). For those who have been allowed to restrict their availability, automatic good cause applies to jobs for less than 16 hours a week.

295   Meaning two calendar months: *CG 66/49*.

296   SI 1996/207, reg 72(4). In this context training is not defined. See also the special protection available where an employment officer has decided for availability for work purposes that the claimant can pursue a qualifying course: reg 72(3A).

297   SI 1996/207, reg 72(5)(a). This provision also protects those who are laid off or on short time and refuse work outside the scope of their availability.

298   SI 1996/207, reg 72(5)(b).

299   JA 1995, s 20(1).

300   The rule has not caused any difficulty, and consistently with its purpose it has been held not to extend to a situation in which a tool maker, himself laid off as a result of a trade dispute, was offered work by another employer: *R(U) 1/52*.

301   JA 1995, s 19(9).

of 'suitable employment'. Previously, even after a reasonable lapse of time, claimants were not expected to accept jobs which paid less or were on less favourable conditions 'than those generally observed by agreement between associations of employers and of employees or, failing any such agreement, than those generally recognised by good employers'.[302] The corporatist flavour of this provision clearly could not stand with changes that were meant to ease perceived rigidities in the labour market.[303]

The second matter to be disregarded in assessing 'good cause' is intimately related to the first. But whereas the first matter relates to the 'rate for the job', the focus of the second deeming rule concerns the claimant's own financial circumstances. A claimant does not have good cause where the refusal relates to:

> his income or outgoings or the income or outgoings of any other member of his household, or the income or outgoings which he or any other member of his household would have if he were to become employed ...[304]

This provision puts on a statutory footing the principle derived from case law that a refusal of an opportunity of employment is not justified merely because it would make the claimant financially worse off.[305] The only exceptions to this principle are where the claimant has been allowed to impose restrictions on the rate of pay sought, in the light of either the 'permitted period' exemption or his physical or mental condition, or where the employment is paid solely by commission.[306]

Thirdly, as a general rule claimants are expected to accept a travelling time of up to one hour each way to and from work. Thus a person is not to be regarded as having 'good cause' where their refusal is based on:

> the time it took, or would normally take, for the person to travel from his home to the place of employment ... and back to his home where that time was or is normally less than one hour either way by a route and means appropriate to his circumstances and to the employment ... unless, in view of the health of the person or any caring responsibilities of his, that time was or is unreasonable.[307]

The way in which this regulation is formulated means that even where a claimant faces a journey time of more than one hour each way, he or she may still not be able to establish 'good cause'.

(iii) Factors relevant to 'good cause'

Regulations prescribe a number of relevant considerations in determining whether 'good cause' has been shown in relation to a refusal of employment:[308] where the claimant is or is likely to be subject to 'significant harm to his health'[309] or to 'excessive physical or mental stress'; any disparity between the requirements of the job and the claimant's

---

302 SSA 1975, s 20(4), proviso (now repealed).
303 See Wikeley (1989) 16 JLS 291.
304 SI 1996/207, reg 72(6)(a). 'Outgoings' do not include reasonable expenses taken into account under reg 72(2)(f).
305 *R(U) 10/61(T)*.
306 SI 1996/207, reg 72(7).
307 SI 1996/207, reg 72(6)(b).
308 SI 1996/207, reg 72(2).
309 Cf *R(U) 32/56* (claimant who refused to apply for a job at a munitions factory where there had been a recent explosion held not to have 'good cause'). The pre-1995 formulation referred to 'serious harm to his health'; it is unclear whether any change in emphasis was intended.

permitted restrictions on availability; any sincerely held religious or conscientious objection;[310] any caring responsibilities which would make it unreasonable to take on the job;[311] and travelling time (subject to the one hour rule). Expenses necessarily and exclusively incurred for the purposes of the employment[312] and travelling expenses may also constitute 'good cause' if they represent 'an unreasonably high proportion' of the reasonably expected earnings.[313] In determining this issue, 'the principle shall apply that the greater the level of remuneration or income the higher the proportion thereof which it is reasonable should be represented by expenses'. Much of this regulation reflects previous case law,[314] which is still relevant in so far as it is not reversed by these specific statutory provisions.[315] Furthermore, the regulation does not purport to be exhaustive of matters which may be germane to the issue of 'good cause'. Other Commissioners' decisions may therefore still be of assistance in determining whether 'good cause' has been established.[316]

iv Neglect to avail oneself of reasonable opportunity of re-employment

A person may be sanctioned if he (or she):

> has, without good cause, neglected to avail himself of a reasonable opportunity of employment.[317]

In the past this provision has been rarely used and consequently there is relatively little by way of case law to provide guidance on its meaning; it has been employed in the exceptional situation when a claimant so behaves at or before an interview that he effectively deters a prospective employer from offering him a vacancy.[318] The effect of the regulations made under JA 1995 is that this sanction can now only apply in situations where the job vacancy in question is in 'a qualifying former employment of that person'; otherwise the claimant has 'good cause'.[319] This refers to employment with the claimant's former employer (or their successor) on terms and conditions no less favourable than when he or she was last employed by that employer. In addition, the period between the last employment and the date that the question of sanctioning arises must be less than a year.[320] Most of those who might fall within this provision are either women who fail to exercise their statutory right to return to work after maternity leave[321] or employees

---

310   *CU 14/68* (vegetarian refusing job as secretary with sausage and pie company held to have 'good cause'; cited in Mesher *Compensation for Unemployment* (1976)).
311   On the definition of 'caring responsibilities, see SI 1996/207, reg 4. Traditionally 'ordinary domestic duties' (a wife preparing a midday meal!) did not constitute 'good cause': *CU 365/49*; *CU 542/49*.
312   The language is similar to that of the income tax legislation (Income and Corporation Taxes Act 1988, s 198(1)) and so presumably the same principles should apply: see Whitehouse *Revenue Law – Principles and Practice* (19th edn, 2001) para 5.171.
313   SI 1996/207, reg 72(3).
314   See cases cited in nn 309–311, above; and *R(U) 41/52*.
315   However, considerable caution must be exercised in relation to some of the old authorities which reflect different societal norms (see eg *R(U) 20/60*, where it was held unreasonable to expect a married woman with a young baby to be required to be available for work starting at 07.15 as opposed to 09.00).
316   See the examples discussed in *DMG* n 83, above, vol 6, paras 34526–34558.
317   JA 1995, s 19(6)(d).
318   *R(U) 28/55*. See now SI 1996/207, reg 18(4), discussed above, p 350.
319   SI 1996/207, reg 72(8), deeming a person to have 'good cause' in all other situations.
320   SI 1996/207, reg 72(9).
321   Employment Rights Act 1996, s 71.

who fail to return to work after being temporarily laid off.[322] The issue of 'good cause' in all other respects is determined according to the same principles as apply to refusals or failures to apply for or accept job vacancies.[323]

v Period of disqualification

The traditional maximum period, dating from NIA 1911,[324] was six weeks. The concern of the Conservative governments in the 1980s to reduce the level of voluntary unemployment and more generally to discourage abuse of social security provision resulted in radical changes in the duration of disqualification. SSA 1986 extended the maximum period to 13 weeks and, at the same time, enabled the Secretary of State to make further amendments to the period by an order to that effect.[325] Such an order was issued in 1988, extending the maximum period to 26 weeks.[326] In 1989 the Secretary of State's delegated power was limited with the effect that he or she may now only substitute a period shorter than 26 weeks as the maximum period of disqualification.[327]

JA 1995 made three principal changes to the provisions relating to the period of disqualification. First, the minimum period for a sanction to operate became one week, as opposed to one day applicable to unemployment benefit.[328] Secondly, a claimant who is sanctioned retains an underlying entitlement to JSA but the benefit is not payable. This means that any period covered by a sanction erodes rather than merely delays receipt of contribution-based JSA, with the result that payment of that component may be completely precluded.[329] Finally, the Secretary of State has the power to prescribe factors to be taken into account in fixing the appropriate length of the sanction.[330] The relevant considerations are: where the employment would have lasted less then 26 weeks, the length of time which it was likely to have lasted; in misconduct cases only, where the employer has indicated an intention to re-engage the claimant (eg after a period of suspension), the likely date of re-engagement; in cases of voluntary leaving where the job was for 16 hours or less a week, the rate of pay and hours of work involved in that job; and, in cases of voluntary leaving or neglect to avail oneself of an opportunity of re-employment, 'any mitigating circumstances of physical or mental stress connected with his employment'.[331]

These considerations, however, are merely specific factors to which decision makers must have regard. They must also 'take into account all the circumstances of the case',[332] and so the principle governing the determination of the appropriate period of disqualification, as formulated by a Tribunal of Commissioners in 1974, remains relevant. Rejecting a previously expressed view that the maximum period should be imposed unless special circumstances dictated otherwise,[333] they considered that:

322 *DMG* n 83, above, vol 6, para 34597.
323 SI 1996/206, reg 72: see above.
324 NIA 1911, s 87(2), which, however, imposed a mandatory period of six weeks. Following UIA 1920, s 8(2), the period became discretionary, subject to the statutory maximum.
325 SSA 1986, s 43(2)–(3).
326 SI 1988/487.
327 SSA 1989, s 12(2); see now JA 1995, s 19(3).
328 SSA 1989. This was consequential upon the abolition of the 'day of unemployment' as the basic building block for entitlement to unemployment benefit, as JSA is paid weekly.
329 SSA 1989, ss 5 and 19; on the different rule for unemployment benefit, see the 4th edition of this book, p 130.
330 JA 1995, s 19(4).
331 SI 1996/207, reg 70.
332 SI 1996/207, reg 70.
333 *R(U) 17/54.*

the correct approach is to adhere firmly to the statutory language, regarding each case as one in which a sensible discretion has to be exercised in such manner as the justice of the case requires.[334]

The increase of the length of the sanction in the 1980s led one Commissioner to observe that it is 'essential that adjudication officers should abandon their old habit of virtually automatically imposing the maximum'.[335] Decision makers should reveal, on the face of the decision, active consideration of the discretion;[336] a failure to do so may constitute an error of law.[337] In particular, it is wrong to start with the maximum period of disqualification and work down, or vice versa.[338] Furthermore, there is no burden of proof on the claimant to show any reasons justifying a reduction in the period of disqualification.[339] As the official guidance to decision makers observes, 'it is difficult to administer this provision consistently'.[340]

In the early case law the situations which were regarded as justifying a period of disqualification less than the maximum seemed to fall within three main categories:

(1) where the maximum causes hardship, because of the claimant's domestic circumstances[341] or because any misconduct is only indirectly linked with the employment;[342]

(2) where the claimant has come close to justifying the loss of employment (through just or good cause) but has just failed;[343] and

(3) where the insurance fund is already sufficiently protected (eg because the claimant is no longer unemployed).[344]

In the light of the Tribunal of Commissioners' decision in *R(U) 8/74* and the exhortation in the regulations, these circumstances should not be regarded in any way as exhaustive of the circumstances in which a lesser sanction period should be imposed. In cases where the claimant is only technically at fault it may be appropriate to impose the minimum sanction of one week.[345] Where the ground for disqualification is misconduct or leaving voluntarily the period will run, in general, from the date of discharge;[346] in other cases it will commence on the date when the claimant refused or failed to apply for or accept an offer of employment.[347]

---

334   *R(U) 8/74(T)*, para 20.
335   *R(U) 4/87*, para 11. For evidence, see Byrne and Jacobs *Disqualified from Benefit* (1988).
336   *R(U) 3/79*, para 5.
337   *R(U) 4/87*.
338   *R(U) 8/74(T)*, para 16.
339   *R(U) 8/74(T)*, para 20.
340   *DMG* n 83, above, vol 6, para 34029. An unsuccessful attempt was made to amend SSA 1989 during its passage through Parliament which would have allowed the then Chief Adjudication Officer to issue more detailed guidance: 151 HC Official Report (6th series) col 1020.
341   *R(U) 27/52*.
342   *R(U) 1/71*.
343   *R(U) 35/52*; *R(U) 20/64(T)*.
344   Eg *R(U) 20/64(T)*; *R(U) 10/71*.
345   Eg *R(U) 1/92*, when the minimum was one day, concerning a genuine mistake as to the length of the trial period under what is now JA 1995, s 20(3).
346   *CU 155/50*. If, however, the claimant continues to receive remuneration (eg by payment in lieu of notice) it will run from the date when it is no longer payable: *R(U) 35/52*.
347   See further *Social Security Legislation 2001* n 20, above, vol II, para 1.184.

C Jobseeker's directions and training-related sanctions

i Refusal or failure to carry out a jobseeker's direction

The former legislation provided for a disqualification to be imposed where the claimant 'without good cause refused or failed to carry out any official recommendations given to him with a view to assisting him to find employment'.[348] The provision appeared to be rarely used and there were no reported decisions of the Commissioners on the point. JA 1995 reformulated this ground to cover a claimant who:

> has, without good cause, refused or failed to carry out any jobseeker's direction which was reasonable, having regard to his circumstances.[349]

A 'jobseeker's direction' means a written direction given by an employment officer with a view to assisting the claimant to find employment and/or improving the claimant's prospects of being employed.[350] It was envisaged that employment officers might issue directions requiring claimants to attend courses to improve their jobseeking skills or motivation, or to take steps 'to present themselves acceptably to employers'.[351] There is no right of appeal against the direction itself; it is only if the consequential sanction is applied that this arises. The concept of 'good cause' is construed in the same way as for the employment-related sanctions discussed above.[352]

Whereas the duration of the employment-related sanctions is a discretionary matter,[353] a sanction imposed for breach of a jobseeker's direction is for a fixed period of two weeks or, in the event of a further breach within 12 months, four weeks.[354]

ii Training-related sanctions

Dating back to 1946 the social security legislation has provided that a claimant could be disqualified if 'he has without good cause refused or failed to avail himself of a reasonable opportunity of receiving [approved] training'.[355] This provision was repealed in 1988 and replaced by three separate grounds mirroring more fully the sanctions available in respect of loss or refusal of employment.[356] These grounds were further expanded by JA 1995 and now apply to prescribed training schemes and employment programmes. These are defined by regulations, which are themselves regularly amended, and include a range of 'options' available under the New Deal.[357] The sanctions therefore introduce a compulsory element to some of these 'options'.

---

348   SSCBA 1992, s 28(1)(d), now repealed. The recommendations had to be reasonable having regard to the claimant's circumstances and to the means of obtaining that employment usually adopted in the district.
349   JA 1995, s 19(5)(a).
350   JA 1995, s 19(1)(b). On 'employment officer', see s 19(10)(a).
351   DSS/DE *Jobseeker's Allowance* (1994, Cm 2687) para 4.18.
352   SI 1996/207, reg 71.
353   As indeed was the case with the former ground of refusing or failing to carry out official recommendations.
354   JA 1995, s 19(2) and SI 1996/207, reg 69(1)(a) and (b).
355   See eg SSA 1975, s 20(1)(e), now repealed.
356   Employment Act 1988, s 27.
357   SI 1996/207, reg 75(1).

The first situation in which a claimant may be sanctioned is where he (or she) 'has lost his place on such scheme or programme through misconduct'.[358] As a matter of principle this ground for sanctioning should presumably be interpreted in the same way as the equivalent head relating to voluntary unemployment. A claimant may also be sanctioned if he (or she) has, without good cause:

(i)   neglected to avail himself of a reasonable opportunity of a place on a training scheme or employment programme;

(ii)   after a place on such a scheme or programme has been notified to him by an employment officer as vacant or as about to become vacant, refused or failed to apply for it or to accept it when offered to him;

(iii) given up a place on such a scheme or programme;

(iv)   failed to attend such a scheme or programme on which he has been given a place.[359]

The first two heads for sanctioning are derived from the 1988 amendments, whereas the latter two only date from 1995.[360] There is a saving for 'good cause' in respect of any of these four grounds for sanctioning. In this context 'good cause' is again partly defined by regulations, but in different terms to the provision relating to sanctions which are employment-related or for breaches of jobseeker's directions. First, the instances of deemed good cause are more widely drawn, given the limited duration of such courses and the potential hardship caused by imposing the 'failure to attend' sanction without due regard to the circumstances. The claimant has automatic good cause where he or she:

• was suffering from a disease or disability that prevented attendance or attendance would have put the health of the claimant or others at risk;

• gave up a place where continued participation would have (or would have been likely to) put the claimant's health and safety at risk;

• had a sincerely held religious or conscientious objection;

• had more than one hour's travelling time;

• had caring responsibilities which could not be otherwise met;

• was attending court as a juror, party or witness;

• was arranging or attending the funeral of a close relative or close friend;

• was engaged in part-time emergency services;

• was required to deal with some domestic emergency; or

• was engaged during an emergency on duties for others.[361]

This list, however, is not exhaustive. The regulation specifically provides that it is 'without prejudice to any other circumstances in which a person may be regarded as having good cause'.

The standard length of the sanction, as with breaches of jobseeker's directions, is a fixed period of two or four weeks for a second breach. However, where there is a third breach relating to one of the New Deal 'options' within 12 months of a second such breach, there is a mandatory and draconian sanction for a fixed period of 26 weeks.[362]

---

358   JA 1995, s19(5)(c).
359   SSCBA 1992, s 28(1)(e)–(g).
360   Head (iii) is similar to the voluntary leaving provision in the 1988 amendments.
361   SI 1996/207, reg 73(2).
362   SI 1996/207, reg 69(1)(c). See further SSAC Report (2000, Cm 4549).

Part 10 Hardship payments

A General

JA 1995 inaugurated a much harsher regime for claimants who face sanctions as a result of being found to be voluntarily unemployed. Under the previous arrangements a claimant who was adjudged to have lost employment through misconduct or to have voluntarily left a job without just cause would be disqualified for up to 26 weeks from unemployment benefit.[363] During this period the claimant could still qualify for income support; if eligible, benefit was paid subject to a 40 per cent (or, in exceptional circumstances, a 20 per cent) reduction in the personal allowance.[364] This sanction was also imposed whilst a decision on whether the claimant had become voluntarily suspended was awaited.[365] The only improvement under the current scheme, from the claimant's point of view, is that the previous practice of automatically suspending payment of benefit pending the outcome of such a determination has been abandoned. In all other respects the new system is significantly less favourable; in particular, there is no automatic entitlement to hardship payments once a sanction is applied. The regulations draw a fundamental distinction between two categories of persons in hardship – those who may be characterised as 'vulnerable' and 'non-vulnerable' persons respectively – which affects whether hardship payments are available with or without a waiting period. Irrespective of this distinction, hardship payments are only available in any one of the following circumstances:[366]

(1) where a section 19 sanction is imposed on the claimant;
(2) where, at the outset of a claim, a claimant is awaiting a decision on whether he or she fulfils the labour market conditions;
(3) where, in the course of a claim, benefit has been suspended because of a doubt as to whether the claimant satisfies those conditions; or
(4) (for vulnerable persons in hardship only) where the Secretary of State has decided that the claimant does not meet those conditions.

A claimant who is not entitled to JSA and is outwith these four categories has no entitlement to a hardship payment (eg a 'non-vulnerable' person in hardship who has been found not to satisfy the labour market conditions).[367]

B Vulnerable persons in hardship

The regulations list a number of vulnerable types of claimant in this preferential category of persons in hardship.[368] These are:

- single pregnant women, couples where the woman is pregnant,[369] single persons responsible for a young person (ie a 16 to 18-year-old),[370] couples where one or both members are responsible for a child or young person, persons eligible for a disability premium;

---

363 See the 4th edition of this book, pp 113–131.
364 See the 4th edition of this book, pp 490–494.
365 In the event of the decision being favourable to the claimant, arrears of benefit were then paid.
366 SI 1996/207, regs 141 and 142. See regs 146C and 146D for parallel provision for joint-claim JSA.
367 There is the possibility of making a claim for a crisis loan in such circumstances.
368 SI 1996/207, reg 140(1). See regs 146A(1) for parallel provision for joint-claim JSA.
369 Separate provision is made for polygamous marriages to similar effect.
370 There is no need for lone parents with children under 16 to be included, as they will be eligible for income support.

- persons who suffer from (or whose partner suffers from) a chronic medical condition resulting in the limitation or restriction of functional capacity by physical impairment;
- carers or their partners;
- persons who are subject to severe hardship directions (or whose partner is) and who meet the labour market conditions;
- those who are under 18 (or whose partner is) but are eligible for JSA; and
- those under 21 who have been looked after by a local authority within the last three years.

In addition, in each of the above cases the Secretary of State must also be satisfied that the person concerned *will* suffer hardship if JSA was not paid. The term 'hardship' is not itself defined, but official guidance suggests that it should be given its 'normal everyday meaning of "severe suffering or privation"'.[371] Moreover, the following three factors (along with any other relevant circumstances) are to be taken into account in determining whether a person will indeed suffer hardship:[372]

(1) whether there is a family member who meets the conditions for the disability or disabled child premium;
(2) the resources which are likely to be available to the claimant's family in the absence of an award of JSA (including resources 'which may be available to members of the claimant's family' from household members who are not family members); and
(3) whether there is a 'substantial risk that essential items ... will cease to be available' to the claimant's family 'or will be available at considerably reduced levels'.[373]

The second of these factors carries echoes of the household means-test which was so controversial under the old unemployment assistance scheme before the Second World War.

Providing these criteria are met, the claimant may be paid a hardship payment from the outset of the claim. In practice, however, this still means a two-week delay as JSA is paid fortnightly in arrears.[374]

C Non-vulnerable persons in hardship

A claimant who is subject to a sanction but who does not fall within any of the vulnerable categories discussed above may still qualify as a person in hardship. In order to do so, the Secretary of State must be satisfied that the claimant or their partner will suffer hardship.[375] In assessing this prospect, the same three considerations as set out above also apply. Claimants who are found to be non-vulnerable persons in hardship have to serve a two-week waiting period before they become eligible for hardship payments.[376] In practice, given the payment of benefit fortnightly in arrears, this means that no JSA will be payable until the end of the first month.

---

371   *DMG* n 83, above, vol 6, para 35155.
372   SI 1996/207, reg 140(5).
373   'Essential items' are defined to include food, clothing, heating and accommodation: SI 1996/207, reg 140(5)(c).
374   SI 1987/1968, reg 26A.
375   SI 1996/207, reg 140(2).
376   SI 1996/207, reg 142.

D Terms of hardship payments

A claimant seeking a hardship payment must complete and sign the appropriate form detailing the circumstances relied upon and provide any other information required.[377] The amount payable under a hardship payment is calculated on the same basis as before the 1995 Act came into force. In the case of single claimants, the effect of the rule is that 40 per cent is deducted from their personal allowance (being the ordinary rate for a person of their age or the special rate for those 16 or 17-year-olds entitled to a higher rate). In the case of couples, the amount deducted depends on their age and status. If both are under 18, the deduction is 40 per cent of the rate of the appropriate personal allowance for a single claimant aged under 18. Where one partner is aged 18–24 and the other partner is aged under 18, but is not eligible for income-based JSA on the basis of prescribed circumstances or a severe hardship direction, the deduction is based on the personal allowance for a single claimant aged 18–24. In all other cases the deduction is 40 per cent of the personal allowance for single claimants aged 25 or over.[378] The 40 per cent deduction is reduced to 20 per cent where the claimant or a member of the claimant's family is pregnant or seriously ill.[379]

Part 11 Persons affected by trade disputes

A General

The extent to which a social assistance scheme should support strikers and their families has always been a highly controversial question and was the subject of much public attention during the Miners' Strike of 1984–85.[380] Many of the issues on which views sharply differ – eg whether the availability of benefit encourages strikes and whether it is legitimate to deter them by withdrawing benefit – are to some extent peripheral to the principal concerns of a social assistance scheme. It may be for this reason that there has been relatively little discussion of these questions in the major policy documents, such as the Fowler Reviews. Nevertheless, the legal position has remained remarkably constant. Under the poor law, strikers themselves could not lawfully be maintained out of rates, unless completely destitute, though their spouses and children could be so supported.[381] Later strikers were denied unemployment benefit but their families could receive means-tested assistance. This distinction survives under SSCBA 1992 and JA 1995: those involved in trade disputes are not entitled to JSA, though they may be able to claim social fund payments, whilst their dependants may receive income support or indeed income-based JSA, subject to some special rules discussed below.[382]

The arguments[383] against supporting strikers and their dependants are first, that it is wrong for people withholding their labour, usually to 'induce' their employers to pay

---

377 SI 1996/207, regs 143 and 144; see regs 146E and 146F as regards joint-claim JSA.
378 SI 1996/207, reg 145 (and reg 146G for joint-claim JSA).
379 For the meaning of this term, see *R(SB) 14/83*; and on the history of this provision, see the 4th edition of this book, p 493.
380 See generally Mesher (1985) 14 ILJ 191; Booth and Smith (1985) 12 JLS 365.
381 *A-G v Merthyr Tydfil Union* [1900] 1 Ch 516. See Ewing *The Right to Strike* (1991) pp 91–94 and Appendix 2.
382 On the rules governing the trade dispute disqualification, see pp 505–514, below in the context of contribution-based JSA.
383 See also discussion of the analogous arguments used in relation to contribution-based JSA: pp 505–506, above.

them higher wages, to be supported by the general taxpaying public, an argument which is perhaps reinforced by the point that some low-income taxpayers could be said to be subsidising the bargaining strength of groups with more industrial weight than they themselves can command. Secondly, the existence of welfare payments is widely believed to encourage a larger number, and the longer duration, of disputes. The first argument may have some merit with regard to the strikers themselves: they are not the 'deserving poor' and should not expect militancy to be subsidised.[384] It is less attractive when applied to their dependants; the further proposition must then be argued that it is for the strikers themselves, and their unions, to support their families. In any case, it can be replied that for the state not to support people in need because of the particular cause of their privation is to depart from the principle of neutrality, and in the context to take sides in an industrial dispute.[385] Furthermore, the disqualification provision, as will be seen below, applies to persons who would not conventionally be defined as 'strikers', although this term is used throughout for reasons of convenience. It applies to persons locked out of work, or laid off because of a dispute at their place of work. It is difficult to reconcile the denial of benefit to 'the innocent victim of someone else's dispute'[386] with the treatment accorded to claimants found to be voluntarily unemployed, who suffer only a partial loss in benefit. The second argument was strongly voiced, particularly by members of the Conservative Party in the 1970s, and led to the 1980 reform which, effectively, reduced the payments which could be made for a striker's family.[387] But the view that the availability of benefit encourages industrial unrest has been strongly challenged by commentators.[388] Certainly the existing regime did not prevent protracted and bitter disputes in the mining industry and at News International's Wapping plant in the mid-1980s.[389]

B Strikers without families

Single people who are not employed because of a stoppage of work at their place of employment due to a trade dispute (unless they are not 'directly interested' in the dispute) and those who have withdrawn their labour in furtherance of a trade dispute are not entitled to JSA.[390] There is a considerable body of case law on this provision and reference should be made to chapter 14, below, for a full discussion of the relevant legal principles.[391]

C Strikers' families

Income-based JSA may be paid to the partner of an individual caught by the trade dispute disqualification. No benefit is payable for the first seven days following the

---

384 For a particularly robust assertion of this view, see Page in Boyson (ed) *Down with the Poor* (1971).
385 On the fiction of state neutrality, see *Ewing* n 381, above, pp 157–163; and *Lascaris v Wyman* 292 NE 2d 667 (1972) and *Lyng v International Union, United Automobile, Aerospace and Agricultural Implement Workers of America* UAW 99 LEd 380 (1988).
386 *Ewing* n 381, above, p 117.
387 Davies and Freedland *Labour Legislation and Public Policy* (1993) pp 467–469.
388 Eg Duncan and McCarthy [1974] Br J Industrial Relations 26. A more cautious view is expressed by Hunter [1974] Br J Industrial Relations at 438. The incentive argument was implicitly rejected by the Supplementary Benefits Commission in its last Annual Report (1979, Cmnd 8033) para 10.46.
389 *Ewing* n 381, above, p 162.
390 JA 1995, s 14.
391 Pp 505–514, below.

start of the stoppage or the withdrawal of labour.[392] After that period has elapsed, the applicable amount will be as for income support, thus excluding any element for the partner involved in the strike.[393] The same rules governing the treatment of capital and income, including deemed strike pay, also apply.[394] There are, however, no comparable rules in the income-based JSA scheme to those that allow payment of benefit for the first 15 days after a return to work where income support has been claimed during a strike.

There are parallel rules for joint-claim JSA. Where both members of a couple would, as individuals, be precluded from claiming JSA, they cannot claim joint-claim JSA.[395] If only one is ineligible, the other member may qualify for the joint-claim version of the benefit, but their entitlement is calculated without regard to the partner involved in the trade dispute.[396]

---

392 During this period, strikers are treated as in full-time work: SI 1996/207, reg 52(2).
393 JA 1995, s 15(2)(a) and (b) and Sch 2 para 2(2); and see p 332, above.
394 JA 1995, s 15(2)(c) and (d).
395 JA 1995, s 15A(2).
396 JA 1995, s 15A(3)–(5).

Chapter 10

Working families' tax credit and disabled person's tax credit

Part 1 Introduction

A General

Working families' tax credit, which replaced family credit in October 1999 (which in turn had replaced family income supplement, or FIS, in April 1988), is primarily designed to provide financial help for low-paid working individuals or couples who have responsibilities for children. Unlike FIS, which was introduced in 1970 as a temporary measure, family credit had been conceived as a permanent part of the benefit systems developed by the Fowler Reviews. It was also both more generous and more extensive than its predecessor.[1] However, in 1997 the incoming Labour government adopted the concept of tax credits, rather than further improving in-work social security benefits, as part of its overall 'welfare-to-work' policies. As we shall see, the shift to tax credits was essentially both semantic and ideological in nature; in substance both tax credits follow the same structure as their predecessor social security benefits, and retain in common many of the same characteristics as the other income-related benefits. To this extent these tax credits have been described as 'old wine in new bottles'.[2] However, the two tax credits discussed in this chapter are designed to demonstrate the rewards of the world of work and represent the first stage in a more ambitious strategy to engineer a greater integration of the tax and benefit systems, as evidenced by the Tax Credits Act 2002.

The conditions of eligibility for working families' tax credit are considered in Part 2 and the method of calculating entitlement in Part 3, whilst Part 4 concerns the administration of tax credits. Part 5 covers the same ground for disabled person's tax credit, which was also introduced in October 1999, replacing disability working allowance, a partial incapacity benefit for disabled people in work. Disability working allowance was first introduced in 1992 and was itself modelled closely on family credit.

---

1 In 1987–88 there were 220,000 recipients of FIS (DSS *Social Security Departmental Report* (1994, Cm 2513) p 82); by August 1999 there were 784,000 family credit claimants (DSS *Family Credit Quarterly Statistical Tables* (January 2000)).
2 Field *The State of Dependency* (2000) p 145.

B Background to family credit

i The 'Speenhamland' system

Clearly, a wage that is sufficient to support a single person may be totally inadequate for a family. When William Pitt first proposed income tax in 1798 it was recognised that the system should take account of the wage earner's family commitments. A few years before this, the magistrates at Speenhamland in Berkshire declared that the parish could supplement the wages of local farm workers. They conducted a survey into the price of bread as a basis of setting 'out-door' relief, to bring the income of workers up to a prescribed level.[3] There were always legal doubts about this system of wage supplementation and it was swept away by the Poor Law Amendment Act 1834. Since then, British policy-makers have historically shown a marked preference for dealing with the problem of low wages by means of the social security system rather than by the direct regulation of wages.[4] Although there was discussion of the desirability of introducing a minimum wage[5] in the 1960s, the option had receded into the background as a realistic policy choice by the time the Conservative party was returned to office in 1970.

ii Family income supplement

The Conservative government's commitment to raising family allowances as a means of tackling family poverty was abandoned on grounds of both cost[6] and efficiency.[7] Instead the means-tested FIS scheme was introduced.[8] The merit of FIS, it was claimed, was that it directed help where it was most needed and, for the first time, conferred assistance on a family with a wage-earner and only one child.[9] Those in receipt of FIS could also be 'passported' to a number of other welfare benefits, most notably free school meals.[10] In the form in which FIS stood immediately prior to its replacement by family credit, it could be claimed by any person engaged in 'remunerative full-time work', defined as 30 hours per week (or 24 hours in the case of a lone parent[11]) and responsible for at least one child. The calculation was a simple set-off between the family's normal gross income and a 'prescribed amount'. The shortfall of earnings below this amount was halved and, subject to appropriate maximum limits for different sized families, this figure was the claimant's entitlement. The maximum limits were thought necessary both to preserve the work-incentives of employees and to deal with the risks that employers might pay artificially low wages, knowing that any shortfall

---

3 Bruce *The Coming of the Welfare State* (4th edn, 1968) pp 55–56, 91–92; Fraser *The Evolution of the British Welfare State* (1975) pp 34–39; Neuman *The Speenhamland County* (1982).
4 Brown *Family Income Supplement* (1983) p 48. See now, however, the National Minimum Wage Act 1998 (on which see Simpson (1999) 28 ILJ 1 and 171).
5 Eg Department of Employment and Productivity *A National Minimum Wage: An Inquiry* (1969).
6 Sir Keith Joseph MP explained that the extension of family allowances to cover families with only one child would have been too costly: 806 HC Official Report (5th series) col 217ff. This was accomplished some years later by the introduction of child benefit: ch 18, below.
7 The lowering of the tax threshold in the late 1960s made the raising of the allowances, with their 'claw-back' through the reduction in child tax allowance, a less efficient way of helping the poor. Cf *Brown* n 4, above, pp 52–55.
8 Family Income Supplements Act 1970 (FISA 1970).
9 Family allowances only catered for second and subsequent children.
10 For details see the 3rd edition of this book, p 474.
11 This change was made in 1979, following a recommendation of the *Report of the Committee on One-Parent Families* (1974, Cmnd 5629) para 5.279.

below the market rate would be met in full by the government, and that self-employed persons might falsify their incomes.[12]

Conceived as a temporary measure, FIS was broad-brush in its assessment of needs. Thus the scheme contained very few discretionary elements and, in particular, unlike the supplementary benefit scheme, there was no account taken of housing costs.[13] FIS, as with any means-tested benefit, was bedevilled by three inherent weaknesses: the 'poverty trap',[14] the 'unemployment trap'[15] and low take-up. In the first years of the FIS scheme take-up was only about 50 per cent,[16] and the take-up rate did not appear to improve significantly in subsequent years.[17] A number of explanations have been offered for this – stigma, difficulties attaching to the claiming process, lack of incentive to claim small amounts and instability of circumstances – but it would seem that absence of knowledge was still a major factor.

C   Family credit

i   The Fowler Reviews

For the Thatcher governments of the 1980s, neither the minimum wage nor a radical increase in the value of child benefit[18] was a credible policy option to tackle the problem of family poverty. The former represented a distortion of the free market,[19] whilst the latter was 'unsupportable' on economic grounds[20] and inconsistent with the overall policy of targeting resources on those in need. In retrospect, the increase in the real value of FIS in the early 1980s, in contrast to that of child benefit which did not keep pace with inflation, may be seen as paving the way for the introduction of family credit.

The Green Paper of 1985 proposed the replacement of FIS by family credit.[21] Some of the most important features of the new scheme were designed to combat the poverty trap. The family credit rules assessed the claimant's income net of tax and social security contributions and involved no withdrawal of benefit until an income threshold was reached; both factors reduced work disincentives for low earners. However, the poverty trap could not be totally eliminated, since the very nature of means-testing assumes that benefit will be taken away as income rises.[22] Indeed, the fact that the withdrawal rate on income above the threshold was 70 per cent, compared with 50 per cent under

---

12   For criticism, see *Brown* n 4, above, pp 119, 135.
13   Similarly, there was no provision initially for varying the amount according to the age (as distinct from the *number*) of children. From 1985, however, the flat-rate allowances for children gave way to three age bands (under 11, 11–15, and 16 and over) which mirrored the variables used in the supplementary benefit scheme.
14   P 276, above, and see the 3rd edition of this book, p 473.
15   See the 3rd edition of this book, p 474.
16   DHSS *Social Security Statistics 1976* (1976) Table 32.15.
17   Corden *Taking Up a Means-Tested Benefit* (1983); Stanton (1977) 5(4) Policy and Politics 27.
18   Eg as advocated in the SBC Annual Report for 1979 (1980, Cmnd 8033) para 17.16.
19   The Conservative government's aversion to a minimum wage was later demonstrated in its opposition to the EU Social Chapter and the abolition of Wages Councils by the Trade Union Reform and Employment Rights Act 1993.
20   The government estimated the cost at some £4 billion.
21   *Reform of Social Security* (1985, Cmnd 9518) vol 2, para 4.46. See further the 3rd edition of this book, pp 473–474.
22   In 1985 there were 290,000 households facing marginal tax rates of 70 per cent or more while in 1994 there were 545,000: DSS *Social Security Departmental Report* (1994, Cm 2513) p 15. However, the numbers facing marginal tax rates of 90 per cent or more fell from 130,000 to 100,000 over the same period, and no claimants faced a rate of 100 per cent or more, as was possible under FIS.

FIS, to some extent offset the effect of basing the calculation on net, instead of gross, income. The unemployment trap was tackled by setting the prescribed amounts for children at a significantly higher level than the equivalent rates under the income support system.[23]

The family credit scheme, which came into force in April 1988, was essentially the same as that envisaged by both the Green and White Papers of 1985 with one key difference. The original plan was that family credit should be paid by employers in the claimant's pay packet as an offset of tax and social security contributions or, if appropriate, as an addition to gross pay.[24] This proposal was motivated by a desire to reduce administrative costs and to achieve a greater integration between the tax and social security systems but it encountered some fierce resistance, principally on the ground that a benefit intended to relieve family or child poverty should go into the 'handbag' rather than the 'wallet'.[25] Opposition from the poverty lobby was joined by groups representing small businesses, for employers were reluctant to assume an additional administrative burden. By the time the Social Security Bill reached the House of Lords, the government had announced that this aspect of the proposals was to be abandoned. This nettle was not grasped again until the introduction of tax credits in 1999.

ii Family credit in the 1990s

Family credit was the 'jewel in the crown' of the Fowler Reviews. Its favoured status was reflected in a series of modifications to the family credit scheme throughout the 1990s, which were designed to target assistance on low-income families with children, and particularly at encouraging lone parents to enter or rejoin the labour market. Most significantly, the definition of 'remunerative work', and hence the threshold for entitlement to family credit, was reduced from 24 to 16 hours a week in April 1992. At the same time a disregard of £15 per week for maintenance payments was introduced (no such disregard operated under the income support scheme at that time). As part of the same strategy a child care disregard, initially of £40 per week, was introduced for family credit claimants with children under the age of 11 as from October 1994.[26] From July 1995 the maximum available family credit was increased by £10 for those who worked at least 30 hours a week in an attempt to mitigate the effects of the high marginal withdrawal rates, which were caused by an increase in the claimant's hours and earnings.[27] The level of take-up for family credit, at 66 to 70 per cent by case load and 73 to 79 per cent by expenditure, was undoubtedly better than for FIS.[28] However, research demonstrated that take-up varied according to family status and housing tenure.[29] Thus the benefit made 'an important contribution to the labour market participation of lone parents',[30] but provided couples with much weaker

---

23 The decision to incorporate the age-related bands used in the supplementary benefit system in the FIS scheme in 1985 was an early response to this problem.
24 The reimbursement of employers was to be modelled on the statutory sick pay scheme.
25 Cf Sir B Rhys Williams MP, Standing Committee B Debates on Social Security Bill 1986, col 936.
26 This was increased to £60 p w from April 1996 and to £100 p w from June 1998 where the claimant had more than one child.
27 See Duncan and Giles (1996) 155 Econ J 142.
28 DSS *Social Security Statistics 2000* (2000) p 189, Table 2 (figures relate to 1998–99).
29 Marsh and McKay *Families, Work and Benefits* (1993) ch 4.
30 *Marsh and McKay* n 29, above, p 194.

work incentives. Claiming family credit was also strongly associated with being a tenant in social housing; owner-occupiers often perceived themselves as ineligible for benefit.[31] Above all, however, family credit was shown to have little impact in actively facilitating the transition from unemployment back into work.[32]

D Tax credits

i The introduction of tax credits

In May 1997 the incoming Labour government appointed a leading City banker, Martin Taylor, to chair a Task Force to examine the options for integration of the tax and benefits systems. The government swiftly announced its intention to introduce a tax credits scheme to replace the existing family credit. The Taylor report identified four main advantages in a tax credits scheme: it would reduce the stigma in claiming in-work support, be more acceptable to the general public, reinforce the rewards of work as opposed to remaining on benefit and would reduce the highest marginal tax rates as benefits were withdrawn.[33] Initial work on the new scheme was undertaken under the authority of paving legislation.[34] The transition from family credit to working families' tax credit itself was engineered by the Tax Credits Act 1999 (TCA 1999). This transferred responsibility for assessing entitlement to the prototype tax credit from the Department of Social Security (DSS) to the Inland Revenue but also provided for employers to be primarily responsible for actually paying out the tax credit, thus externalising much of the associated administrative cost. The value of the tax credit was made substantially more generous than family credit in a number of respects, but the underlying rules of entitlement were not changed at all. The introduction of tax credits was thus essentially a re-branding. All the changes that were made could equally have been brought forward under the existing family credit scheme.

At the outset, therefore, working families' tax credit was a tax credit in name only. Entitlement bears no relation to a person's income as assessed for tax purposes, but rather depends on the traditional social security means-test. In particular, working families' tax credit operates on the principle of aggregating the needs and resources of married (and indeed unmarried) couples, with no pretence at mirroring the principle of independent taxation that operates for income tax purposes. The tax credit, as with family credit, is also prospective rather than retrospective, with no attempt to effect an end-of-year reconciliation against actual income.[35] Despite these features, the government is clearly wedded to the notion that a tax credit is different in kind from a social security benefit. Thus recipients of working families' tax credit are relieved of the need to co-operate with the Child Support Agency (whereas parents with care in receipt of family credit, as with claimants of income support, were required so to do).[36] In addition, the government has signalled its intention in the longer term to transfer responsibility for hearing tax credits appeals from the Appeals Service to the tax appeal commissioners.

---

31 *Marsh and McKay* n 29, above, p 194.
32 See also Marsh (1997) Social Policy J of NZ 111.
33 HM Treasury Report No 2 *The Modernisation of Britain's Tax and Benefit System* (1998) para 3.19.
34 Tax Credits (Initial Expenditure) Act 1998 (TC(IE)A 1998).
35 See generally Lee (2000) 7 JSSL 159.
36 P 319, above.

ii The child tax credit and working tax credit

The next phase of tax credits reform is more ambitious. The Tax Credits Act 2002, when implemented, will see the abolition of both working families' tax credit and the disabled person's tax credit, together with a reconfiguration of various elements of social security benefits for children. The 2002 Act, which will be brought into force during 2003 and 2004, establishes two new tax credits, a child tax credit and a working tax credit.

The child tax credit, which will be paid on top of child benefit, is intended to provide a 'single seamless system of support for families with children'.[37] It will bring together the support currently provided for children through the child credits in working families' and disabled person's tax credits, the child personal allowances in the income support and income-based jobseeker's allowance schemes and the Inland Revenue's current children's tax credit. The child tax credit will comprise a basic family element (replicating the children's tax credit) with an extra child element for each child in the family, with special allowances for disabled children. As with child benefit, the credit will be payable in respect of children under 16 and young people up to the age of 19 who remain in non-advanced, full-time education. Unlike child benefit, the value of the credit will be reduced as the claimant's income increases. Thus the government has described this reform as based on the principle of 'progressive universalism'.[38] The structure of the new child tax credit includes two significant reforms. First, the new credit is not contingent upon the claimant's working status (and should therefore, in theory at least, assist the transition from welfare to work). Secondly, the child tax credit will be payable, as with child benefit, to the primary carer, thereby meeting one of the principal criticisms of working families' tax credit.

The working tax credit will extend in-work support to low-income households without children for the first time on a national basis. The working tax credit will replace the adult elements of working families' tax credit and disabled person's tax credit. As at present, workers with families or who have a disability will need to work for at least 16 hours a week to qualify. Childless low-paid workers who are aged at least 25 and who do not have a disability will also qualify for the working tax credit, but only if they work for at least 30 hours a week. The basic structure of this credit will be modelled on the current working families' tax credit, shorn of the child credits.

Part 2   Entitlement to working families' tax credit

The underlying conditions of entitlement to working families' tax credit are the same as they were for family credit and may be considered under six heads: (i) presence and residence in Great Britain; (ii) remunerative work; (iii) responsibility for a child; (iv) capital; (v) income; and (vi) non-receipt of disabled person's tax credit.

---

37   HM Treasury *The Modernisation of Britain's Tax and Benefit System – Child and Working Tax Credits* Report No 10 (2002) p 31.
38   *HM Treasury* n 37, above, p 4.

A   Presence and residence in Great Britain

Any person who is 'subject to immigration control', as that expression is defined in social security legislation, is not entitled to working families' tax credit.[39] In addition, the claimant must be in Great Britain,[40] but regulations deem persons to be present (or not present) in given circumstances.[41] These presence and residence conditions distinguish between different members of the family:[42]

(1)   the claimant must be present and ordinarily resident in Great Britain[43] and the right to reside must not be subject to any limitation or condition[44] *and*
(2)   the partner (if any) must be ordinarily resident in the UK;[45] *and*
(3)   at least part of the earnings of the claimant and part of those (if any) of the partner must derive from remunerative work in the UK.

These conditions must be satisfied on the date of the claim;[46] it would not seem to matter if, shortly after an award, the claimant leaves the country. There are no presence or residence conditions for the children of the family but since, as will be seen,[47] a child is treated for working families' tax credit purposes as being a member of the family only if he or she 'is normally living' with the claimant (or partner),[48] it would be rare in practice for an adult member of the family to be ordinarily resident without the relevant children also satisfying that condition.

B   Engaged in remunerative work

i   The 16-hour rule

The claimant (or any partner) must be 'engaged and normally engaged in remunerative work'.[49] The limit for remunerative work, originally set at 24 hours a week in 1988, was reduced to 16 hours in 1992.[50] At the same time the definition of full-time work for the purposes of income support was reduced to the same threshold. In principle, therefore, claimants working for less than 16 hours a week can claim income support, while those working 16 hours or more (providing they have a family) may claim working families' tax credit. However, entitlement to the two benefits is not entirely mutually exclusive in that a child-minder working for 16 hours or more a week is not treated as in full-time work for the purposes of income support,[51] and so could claim either benefit.

---

39   Immigration and Asylum Act 1999, s 115(1) and (9) (IAA 1999). See pp 232–234, above.
40   Social Security Contributions and Benefits Act 1992, s 128(1) (SSCBA 1992).
41   This is a comprehensive deeming provision: *R(FC) 2/93*. Although the European Court of Justice in *Hughes v Chief Adjudication Officer* C-78/91 [1992] 3 CMLR 490 held that family credit fell within the remit of Council Regulation (EEC) 1408/71, art 4(1)(h), the effect of this decision was reversed by the UK government entering a derogation under art 10: see p 79, above.
42   SI 1987/1973, reg 3(1).
43   On these concepts, see pp 230–232, above.
44   This rule, first introduced in February 1996, is subject to certain exceptions: SI 1987/1973, reg 3(1A).
45   But if the claimant's partner lives abroad and is not a member of the claimant's household, he or she cannot be a 'partner' for working families' tax credit purposes: see SI 1987/1973, reg 3(1); SSCBA 1992, s 137(1); and *CFC/11/1992*.
46   SSCBA 1992, s 128(1).
47   P 390, below.
48   SI 1987/1973, reg 7(1).
49   SSCBA 1992, s 128(1)(b).
50   P 285, above.
51   SI 1987/1967, reg 6(b).

In addition, some claimants will fail to qualify for either benefit because they are working for 16 hours or more in a given week but do not 'normally' do so, as required for the purposes of working families' tax credit.

ii Remunerative work

A person is deemed to be engaged in 'remunerative work' where:
(a) the work he undertakes is for not less than 16 hours a week;
(b) the work is done for payment or in expectation of payment; and
(c) he is employed at the date of claim and [works for at least 16 hours in a specified week].[52]

All three conditions must be satisfied,[53] but a person doing charitable or voluntary work for which only expenses are paid is explicitly excluded, as are certain carers and people engaged on a scheme for which a training allowance or employment zone subsistence allowance is paid.[54] Absence from work by reason of jury service does not affect entitlement.[55] Assuming claimants are engaged in remunerative work according to these tests, as amplified below, they are also deemed to be normally so engaged.[56]

A THE WORK HE UNDERTAKES ...

This is expressed very broadly in terms of 'work' rather than 'employment'.[57] Thus the emphasis is on the hours actually worked, rather than those stipulated in the contract.[58] In calculating the numbers of hours worked, meals and refreshment breaks count only if they are paid.[59] Where the claimant is self-employed, the hours of work constitute the time spent in activities which are 'essential' to the employment, that is, were carried out with the desire, hope and intention of deriving some reward or profit, even though the time is not 'costed' for accounting purposes.[60] Thus the Court of Appeal has held that the time spent by a self-employed minicab driver waiting at the minicab office for calls from potential customers was working time.[61]

A complex provision governs the assessment of the period over which the 16-hour requirement is measured. In the normal case, where a recognisable cycle of work has been established by the date of claim, the number of hours worked is reckoned over one complete cycle.[62] If no such cycle has been identified, the test is:

> the average number of hours worked over the five weeks immediately preceding the week of claim, or such other longer time preceding that week as may, in the particular case, enable the person's weekly hours to be determined more accurately ...[63]

---

52 SI 1987/1973, reg 4(1). This formulation, replacing the original regs 4 and 5, was introduced in April 1992.
53 SI 1987/1973, reg 4(2).
54 SI 1987/1973, reg 4(3).
55 SI 1987/1973, reg 4(4B); see also reg 4(5)(d).
56 SI 1987/1973, reg 4(7).
57 See p 285, above on the equivalent provision for income support.
58 *CFC/20/1989.*
59 SI 1987/1973, reg 4(4)(a).
60 *R(FIS) 6/85.*
61 *Kazantzis v Chief Adjudication Officer (R(IS) 13/99).*
62 SI 1987/1973, reg 4(4)(c)(i). Periods in which the person does not normally work are to be included in such a computation, but not other absences (eg sickness).
63 SI 1987/1973, reg 4(4)(c)(ii). Cf *R(FIS) 1/81* and *R(FIS) 2/83.*

If the claimant has an annual cycle of work which includes periods of no work (eg a school dinners assistant during the school holidays), then such periods are ignored in averaging hours of work.[64] The same rule applies to income support and income-based jobseeker's allowance, but whereas it works in favour of tax credit recipients it disadvantages benefit claimants, especially those who are childless.[65] Where the claimant has only just started or restarted work, the hours worked are calculated by reference to the average number of hours which his employer expects him to work in a week.[66]

B   THE WORK IS DONE FOR PAYMENT OR IN EXPECTATION OF PAYMENT

The definition of this concept mirrors that applying to income support.[67]

C   HE IS EMPLOYED AT THE DATE OF CLAIM ...

In addition to being employed at the date of claim, the claimant must satisfy further tests that relate to the 'normality' of the 16 hours work per week. In the usual case it is enough that 16 hours were worked in the week of claim or in either of the two weeks immediately before that week.[68] Alternatively the requirement may be met on the basis of the employer's expectations of the hours of work in the week after the week of claim or in the week following an absence on holiday.[69] In any case the work must be the work the claimant normally does and which is likely to last for at least five weeks.[70] The concept of normality is not defined, leaving the adjudicating authorities with a considerable discretion. Applying the now dated FIS case law, normality should not be judged by reference to some arbitrary period (eg six months preceding the claim). Rather, regard should be had to the circumstances of each individual case as they appear at the time of the claim, including future prospects as well as the past employment record.[71] Further, the standard of normality is personal to the claimant (or partner); what is 'normal' for other persons in that occupation or similarly so employed is irrelevant.

C   Responsibility for child or young person in same household

The family unit for the purpose of entitlement to working families' tax credit comprises: *either*
(1) a single person responsible for at least one child (or young person) living in the same household as that child or those children; *or*
(2) a couple (married or unmarried), one member of which is responsible for at least one child (or young person) living in the same household.[72]

---

64   SI 1987/1973, reg 4(4A).
65   *Stafford v Chief Adjudication Officer* [2001] UKHL 33, [2001] 4 All ER 62: see p 286, above.
66   SI 1987/1973, reg 4(1)(b) and (5). An analogous provision applies to the self-employed: see reg 4(4)(bb).
67   P 285, above.
68   SI 1987/1973, reg 4(5)(a).
69   SI 1987/1973, reg 4(5)(b)–(c). A person is not on holiday when on sick or maternity leave: reg 4(6)(b).
70   SI 1987/1973, reg 4(6)(a).
71   *R(FIS) 1/83(T); R(FIS) 6/83; R(FIS) 1/84.*
72   SSCBA 1992, s 128(1)(d).

In this context, a 'child' must be under 16 and a 'young person' must be aged between 16 and 19 and receiving full-time education.[73]

The concepts of 'responsibility' for a child (or young person)[74] and 'membership of the same household' are to some extent common to the income-related benefits and are explained in chapter 12.[75]

D Capital

Where the relevant capital exceeds a prescribed threshold, currently £8,000, working families' tax credit is not payable.[76] The rules for calculating relevant capital follow almost completely those used for the purposes of income support[77] and are discussed in chapter 14.[78] This degree of harmonisation stands in stark contrast to the position under FIS, where no account was taken of the capital resources of the claimant (and/or partner). It is difficult conceptually to reconcile the imposition of a capital rule with the notion of a tax credit which, in principle at least, should be concerned solely with income. This inconsistency appears to have been recognised by policy makers, as the capital rules will be abolished for the new working tax credit; instead, income from investments will be treated in the same way as other forms of income.

E Income

The fifth condition of entitlement relates to the income of the family, which includes the 'tariff' income that is assumed to be derived from capital holdings between the £3,000 lower level and the £8,000 threshold. The statutory provision is, unfortunately, complex as it incorporates references to the principles governing assessment of working families' tax credit entitlement and cannot, therefore, be fully comprehended until those principles have been explained (see Part 3). Suffice it, at this stage, to indicate that the claimant must establish that the relevant income of the family[79] *either*:

(1) does not exceed the 'applicable amount', a uniform figure prescribed by regulations every year; *or*

(2) exceeds the 'applicable amount' by no more than an amount which will leave some entitlement to working families' tax credit.[80]

F Non-receipt of disabled person's tax credit

As a general rule receipt of working families' tax credit and disabled person's tax credit are mutually exclusive.[81] The one exception to this rule is where an award of disabled

---

73 SSCBA 1992, s 137(1) and SI 1987/1973, reg 6(1). For 'full-time education', see p 287, above, but note the slight difference as regards children who have left school highlighted in *CFC/21/1990*.
74 There is no requirement that the claimant be the parent.
75 Pp 443–444, below.
76 SSCBA 1992, s 134(1) and SI 1987/1973, reg 28.
77 There are some minor differences, eg as regards forms of income treated as capital (compare SI 1987/1967, reg 48 with SI 1987/1973, reg 31). The disregards are almost entirely the same (but SI 1987/1973, Sch 3, para 7 – limited disregard for proceeds of sale of business which are to be reinvested – has no parallel under income support).
78 Pp 459–464, below.
79 See pp 448–449, above.
80 SSCBA 1992, s 128(1)(a)(i)–(ii).
81 SSCBA 1992, ss 128(1)(c) and 129(1)(d). See also s 134(2).

person's tax credit is due to expire within 42 days of a claim for working families' tax credit, the person is otherwise entitled to the latter credit and the claim for that credit is for the period immediately after the expiry of the disabled person's tax credit award.[82]

Part 3   Calculating entitlement to working families' tax credit

A   General

The starting point in any calculation of entitlement is the 'maximum working families' tax credit'. This reflects the number of children in the family as well as giving extra credit for those working 30 hours or more and/or bearing certain childcare costs. The claimant receives in full the maximum working families' tax credit appropriate for those family circumstances until the claimant's income reaches a certain threshold (known as the 'applicable amount'). It is only when the income exceeds the threshold that deductions are made from the maximum credit; such deductions are calculated by applying a prescribed percentage 'taper' to the excess income.

i   Maximum working families' tax credit

Only one adult credit may be awarded, whether the claimant is single or a member of a couple,[83] the original intention being to offer a high degree of assistance to lone parents. The adult credit is then aggregated with credits for each child (or young person) for whom the claimant (or partner) is responsible. There are now only two principal rates of credits for children or young persons, categorised according to whether they are under 16 or aged 16 to 18.[84] Since October 1999 a disabled child credit has also been payable, adopting the same definition as applies in the disabled person's tax credit scheme. Credits are not allowed for children (or young persons) who have capital exceeding £3,000 or an income which is higher than the appropriate credit (excluding disregarded income and maintenance). Nor are credits payable for such dependants who are in hospital or residential accommodation for 52 weeks before the date of claim.[85]

ii   Applicable amount

The lower threshold, the 'applicable amount', is a standard figure whatever the composition of the family.[86] It was originally pegged to the adult rate in the income support scheme for a couple. However, this did not mean that both schemes aimed at the same level of protection: under the family credit scheme, child benefit (along with any disregarded maintenance) and family credit topped up income below the applicable

---

82   See also p 403, below.
83   In the case of a polygamous marriage, the credit for a second or subsequent spouse is equivalent to the highest young person credit or that for ages 16 to 17 if the age of the spouse comes within that band: SI 1987/1973, reg 46(2).
84   SI 1987/1973, reg 46(1) and Sch 4. Until April 2000 there were four age-bands: under 11, 11 to 15, 16 to 17, and 18 to 19.
85   SI 1987/1973, reg 46(4)–(6).
86   SI 1987/1973, reg 47.

amount. For the purposes of income support, the applicable amount included personal allowances for children, as well as a family premium, but child benefit and family credit were taken fully into account as an income resource. The disparity has widened with the introduction of working families' tax credit, for which the applicable amount was initially set at nearly £10 per week above the income support rate for a couple.

iii Prescribed percentage taper

The legislation provides that the percentage of any excess of income over the applicable amount to be deducted from maximum working families' tax credit is to be prescribed by regulation.[87] This enables the government to retain some flexibility in determining levels of marginal tax rates in the light of fiscal and other policies.[88] The prescribed percentage for family credit was kept at 70 per cent[89] but was reduced to 55 per cent with the advent of working families' tax credit. This has simultaneously had the effect of extending the scope of the tax credit, as compared with family credit, and increasing the number of recipients facing relatively high marginal tax rates.

B Amounts payable

On the basis of the principles outlined above, the methods of calculating the amounts payable may now be restated, together with arithmetical examples.

i Income below applicable amount

Where the income to be taken into account falls below the applicable amount, the claimant is entitled to the maximum working families' tax credit appropriate to the composition and circumstances of the family unit.[90] A simple example, using 2002–03 figures, would be as follows:

> H & W, a married couple, live with their children L (aged 17) and M (aged 12), both of whom are at school. The net relevant income is £90, which is less than the applicable amount (£94.50). The working families' tax credit entitlement is:

1 adult credit	60.00
1 child credit (16-18)	27.20
1 child credit (under 11)	26.45
Total payable	£113.65

---

87 SSCBA 1992, s 128(1)(a) and (2).
88 In contrast FIS had a statutory (and uniform) 50 per cent deduction rule. For the purposes of comparison with the FIS withdrawal rate, it should be recalled that the relevant family credit amounts were net of income tax and social security contributions.
89 SI 1987/1973, reg 48.
90 SSCBA 1992, s 128(2)(a). But note the increase in the adult credit (to £62.50) from June 2002: SI 2002/133.

The maximum tax credit can be increased in either or both of two ways. First, where the claimant (or partner) works at least 30 hours a week, an extra credit is payable.[91] Secondly, the claimant may qualify for a childcare tax credit worth 70 per cent of eligible childcare costs, subject to an overall limit of £135 a week for one child or £200 per week for two or more children. This is significantly more generous than the treatment accorded to childcare costs under the family credit scheme.[92] Both the rules governing the financial ceiling on assistance[93] and the age of eligible children[94] have been relaxed. But, more fundamentally still, the mechanism for providing an allowance for childcare costs has been changed. Under the family credit scheme, assistance took the form of a limited disregard against assessable income: accordingly, it could never assist the poorest claimants, whose entitlement was limited in any event by the maximum family credit for their family circumstances.[95] The new scheme has transformed this income disregard into a component element of the maximum working families' tax credit. The TCA 1999 also empowers the Secretary of State to establish a scheme for the accreditation of childcare providers for tax credits purposes.[96]

ii   Income above applicable amount

Where the relevant income exceeds the applicable amount, the claimant is entitled to a tax credit calculated in accordance with this formula:

$$\text{MAX WFTC} - 0.55 \times (I - AA)$$

where MAX WFTC is the maximum working families' tax credit, aggregated as above, I is the net relevant income and AA is the applicable amount.[97] Assuming the facts are as in the above example, but the net relevant income of the family is £144.50, the working families' tax credit entitlement is:

$$£113.65 - 0.55 \times (144.50 - 94.50)$$
$$£113.65 - 0.55 \times £50.00$$
$$£113.65 - £27.50$$
$$= £86.15$$

---

91   This is worth £11.65 at 2002–03 rates. There is a disregard of a corresponding amount for the purposes of housing benefit and council tax benefit, so as to avoid claw back. On the calculation of the 30 hours, see SI 1987/1973, reg 4A.

92   For an ultimately unsuccessful challenge to the family credit childcare disregard, see Case C-116/94 *Meyers v Adjudication Officer* [1995] All ER (EC) 705 and *R(FC)2/98.*

93   For family credit purposes, the disregards were £60 and £100 per week, but the net gain was only in the order of £40 and £70 respectively because of the operation of the 70 per cent taper.

94   The family credit scheme applied to children under the age of 11. For working families' tax credit purposes, childcare costs for children up to the age of 15 (or 16 in the case of a disabled child) are eligible.

95   By August 1999 only 45,000 (6 per cent) of family credit recipients were receiving help with childcare costs: DSS *Family Credit Quarterly Statistics* (January 2000).

96   TCA 1999, s 15 and SI 1999/3110.

97   SSCBA 1992, s 128(2)(b).

C Duration of award

Section 128(3) of SSCBA 1992 provides that working families' tax credit:

> shall be payable for a period of 26 weeks ... and, subject to regulations, an award of working families' tax credit and the rate at which it is payable shall not be affected by any change of circumstances.

The fixed-term nature of working families' tax credit reflects the policy that administrative costs should be minimised by avoiding frequent changes to the amount payable. An award of working families' tax credit can be reviewed in five situations:[98]

(1) on the death of the claimant (though if he or she is survived by a partner, the award is transferred to the latter);

(2) where a new award of working families' tax credit is made on a review or appeal;

(3) where a child or young person, for whom working families' tax credit is payable, leaves the claimant's household, becomes a member of a different household and income support or either of the tax credits is payable in respect of him or her there;

(4) where the last or only young person in the family becomes 16 or leaves full-time, non-advanced education;[99] or

(5) a new baby is born.

The last of these exceptions was introduced in May 2001 and represents a markedly more generous rule than operated under the family credit scheme. An award is, however, still not reviewable simply because the annual up-rating occurs during the relevant six months; any such increases can take effect only on renewal. The omission of the tax credits scheme to provide for revision in the event of a change in earnings during the period of an award will work to the benefit of some claimants but to the disadvantage of others. As noted above, there is no provision for the retrospective reconciliation of the tax credits awarded with actual income during the period in question, as would be expected under any tax system. This is likely to change with the arrival of the new generation of tax credits.[100]

Part 4 Administration of working families' tax credit

A General

This chapter is principally concerned with analysing the rules of entitlement which are peculiar to the tax credit rather than shared in common with other means-tested benefits. Thus the provisions governing the assessment of the family unit, income and capital are dealt within in common with those benefits in chapter 12, below. General matters relating to administration (including making claims) and appeals are similarly considered in the context of chapters 5 and 6, above.

---

98   SI 1987/1973, Pt VI.

99   Pp 390–391, above. This last exception was introduced in July 1996, contrary to the advice of the SSAC (1996, Cm 3297).

100 'We propose that entitlement to the new tax credits should be set on the basis of annual income for the previous tax year, but that they should be adjusted to reflect significant changes in income levels in the current year': Inland Revenue *New Tax Credits: A consultative document* (July 2001) para 126.

In this chapter, however, it is also appropriate to consider the central role of the employer in the administration of working families' tax credit. In the mid-1980s it had been the then government's intention to pay family credit through the wage packet, but this proposal was dropped following pressure both from the small business lobby and welfare rights organisations.[101] TCA 1999 introduced this change, apparently with little effective resistance; the former lobby presumably had very limited political influence on a Labour government with a commanding majority, and groups representing claimants were unlikely to jeopardise a package that promised to deliver substantial benefits to many low-paid workers. However, not all claimants are paid tax credits by employers. Self-employed recipients of tax credits are paid by the Inland Revenue direct, as are some employees who do not fall within the scheme for payment via employers. Finally, where a couple are claiming tax credits they may elect for the non-working partner to receive the tax credit (eg by automatic credit transfer to a bank account).[102]

B The role of employers

TCA 1999 transferred responsibility for policy making in respect of working families' tax credit to the Treasury and for operational matters to the Inland Revenue.[103] The Board of the Inland Revenue is also vested with the 'care and management' of both new tax credits.[104] Employers are charged with the duty of paying out tax credits in any case where they make payments to their employees in respect of income assessable to income tax under Schedule E.[105] Although family credit was relaunched as working families' tax credit with effect from October 1999, this particular provision was not brought into force until April 2000, so as to provide employers with more time in which to ensure that their payroll systems were modified in the necessary respects. For major employers, the imposition of the responsibility for the payment of tax credits may have represented one more irritating example of the state externalising the costs of administering schemes of social protection (eg as for statutory sick pay). Yet this burden doubtless weighs heaviest on smaller firms, especially those least able to bear the associated overhead costs. The extent to which all employers are complying with their obligations under the tax credits legislation remains uncertain.[106]

The detailed provisions governing the payment of tax credits are contained in the Payment by Employers Regulations.[107] The Inland Revenue must issue a 'start notification' to the 'relevant employer' when an employee receives an award or renewal of an award of tax credits. The 'start notification' must include certain details such as the employee's name and National Insurance number, along with the commencement and termination dates for payment, the total amount of tax credit to be paid and the pro rata daily rate.[108] A 'relevant employer' is any employer who is liable to deduct PAYE income tax or National Insurance contributions; if the employee has more than one employer, the employer paying the larger amount in net earnings is responsible.[109] Employers are entitled to be given 14 days' notice of their liability to pay tax credits for

101   P 385, above.
102   SI 1987/1968, reg 4(2), (2A) and (8A).
103   TCA 1999, s 2.
104   TCA 1999, s 5.
105   TCA 1999, s 6(1).
106   NACAB *Work in progress: CAB clients' experiences of WFTC* (2001).
107   SI 1999/3219.
108   SI 1999/3219, reg 4.
109   SI 1999/3219, reg 3(1).

weekly paid employees and 42 days for those paid at longer intervals.[110] The Inland Revenue must also send employees a parallel notification, which must also specify the periods during which the Board and the employer are respectively responsible for the payment of tax credits.[111]

On receipt of the start notification, the employer is responsible for calculating the tax credit due for each pay period and for making such payments. This duty applies only if the employer expects the employee in question to remain in post for at least three consecutive pay periods.[112] The employer is required to record the tax credit as a separate item on the employee's payslip, and the tax credit cannot be subject to set-off or attachment (eg for court orders).[113] There is a rather alarming and apparently unlimited power for employers to recover any overpayments of tax credits from an employee.[114] The employer's responsibility for paying tax credits ceases when the employee dies or leaves that employment, or where the Inland Revenue issue a 'stop notice', which again must include prescribed information and satisfy certain time limits.[115]

Awards of working families' tax credit last for 26 weeks at a time, and many employees will change jobs during the currency of an award. If so, they are required to report the relevant details to the Inland Revenue.[116] The regulations then impose the duty to pay tax credits on the 'relevant subsequent employer', meaning any further employer who is liable to make deductions in respect of PAYE income tax or National Insurance contributions.[117] If an employee leaves a job but there is no such subsequent employer, the responsibility for paying tax credits reverts to the Inland Revenue.[118]

Employers are not expected to fund the payment of tax credits from their own resources. They are entitled to meet the cost of such payments from deductions from wages that would otherwise have to be paid over to the Inland Revenue. The regulations provide for an order of priority: tax credits should be met from PAYE deductions in the first instance; failing that from student loan repayments; and finally from payments of National Insurance contributions.[119] If these sources are insufficient to put the employer in funds, an application may be made to the Inland Revenue for advance funding from the Board.[120]

The Payment by Employers Regulations[121] are supported by a number of further measures in the primary legislation. Employees have a right not to be subject to any detriment in connection with the operation of the tax credits scheme. In particular, a dismissal is automatically unfair if any of the employee's rights in this regard are breached.[122] The Inland Revenue's extensive information-gathering powers under the tax legislation apply also to tax credits[123] and there are a range of sanctions for fraud and non-compliance.[124]

---

110   SI 1999/3219, reg 4(4).
111   SI 1999/3219, reg 5.
112   SI 1999/3219, reg 6(1) and (2).
113   SI 1999/3219, reg 6(4) and (9).
114   SI 1999/3219, reg 6(8); in principle this would permit recovery of a substantial overpayment of tax
      credits in just one pay period.
115   SI 1999/3219, reg 9.
116   SI 1999/3219, reg 10(4) and (5).
117   SI 1999/3219, reg 3(3).
118   SI 1999/3219, reg 11(1).
119   SI 1999/3219, reg 7.
120   SI 1999/3219, regs 8, 12 and 13.
121   SI 1999/3219.
122   TCA 1999, s 7 and Sch 3, adding the Employment Rights Act 1996, s 104B.
123   TCA 1999, s 8, applying the Taxes Management Act 1970, s 20.
124   TCA 1999, ss 9 and 10.

Part 5　Disabled person's tax credit

A　General

Until 1992, there was no financial support from the social security system for people without children who were able to work but whose earning capacity was reduced by disability. The absence of any such partial incapacity benefit had long been recognised as a weakness of the British social security scheme.[125] This gap in provision was highlighted by the Social Security Advisory Committee's (SSAC) report on disability benefits.[126] The SSAC argued that a benefit which raised the incomes of working disabled people to a reasonable level could be justified on grounds both of equity and improving incentives to work.[127] The government's subsequent White Paper[128] set out as one of its main objectives the importance of promoting independence for disabled people. In particular, it stressed the need to help those who wish to work to enter and remain in the labour market. It therefore proposed a new means-tested benefit, disability employment credit, designed for people who were partially rather than fully incapable of work. This benefit, explicitly modelled on family credit, was subsequently retitled disability working allowance.[129] The SSAC welcomed disability working allowance 'as an advance which has the potential for enhancement as time and resources permit'.[130]

Disability working allowance was launched in April 1992[131] with the government estimating that some 50,000 claimants would be claiming the benefit in due course.[132] Notwithstanding a number of measures designed to make the benefit attractive,[133] take-up of disability working allowance remained disappointing throughout its short life span. By July 1999 there were still fewer than 18,000 claimants.[134] Many disabled people are excluded by the strict criteria for entitlement, with the two most common grounds for disallowance being that the claimant was not in receipt of a qualifying benefit or was not in remunerative work.[135] Research demonstrated that awareness of disability working allowance amongst potential claimants was low and that the benefit had generally not acted as a work incentive even amongst those aware of its existence. Claimants with disabilities who had found work were prompted by a range of financial, social and psychological reasons and were driven by a desire to be independent of state help.[136]

Disability working allowance was relaunched as disabled person's tax credit in October 1999 as part of the changes introduced by TCA 1999. There is little evidence that this reform represented a considered response to the particular take-up problems associated with the predecessor benefit. Rather, the government had already decided that family credit would be transformed into working families' tax credit, and so a parallel change for disability working allowance was inevitable. Nevertheless, the opportunity was taken

---

125　Royal Commission on Civil Liability and Compensation for Personal Injury (the Pearson Report) (1978, Cmnd 7054-I) vol I, paras 814–821; Economist Intelligence Unit *Benefits for Partial Incapacity* (1982).
126　SSAC *Benefits for Disabled People: a Strategy for Change* (1988).
127　*SSAC* n 126, above, pp 56–59.
128　*The Way Ahead – Benefits for Disabled People* (1990, Cm 917).
129　Disability working allowance was brought into effect by the Disability Living Allowance and Disability Working Allowance Act 1991, which was itself quickly superseded by the consolidating provisions in SSCBA 1992.
130　SSAC *DWA: Response to a Consultation Document* (1991) p 1.
131　See Luckhaus (1992) 21 ILJ 237.
132　*The Way Ahead* n 128, above, para 5.17.
133　On which see the 4th edition of this book, p 530.
134　DSS *DWA Statistics Quarterly Enquiry* (November 1999).
135　*DSS* n 134, above.
136　Rowlingson and Berthoud (1997) 26 ILJ 198.

to introduce a modest relaxation to the conditions of entitlement in two respects as part of these reforms. First, the period within which one of a number of specified incapacity benefits must have been in payment prior to the date of claim was extended from eight weeks to six months. Secondly, provision was made for a so-called 'fast-track gateway' to disabled person's tax credit to enable those still in work to make a claim when they fall ill or become disabled. Both these changes are discussed further below.

Allied with the higher rates for the individual credits and the lower taper, these changes undoubtedly make disabled person's tax credit a more generous benefit than disability working allowance. Yet these improvements are only at the margins. The government has estimated that only some 6,000 extra awards are likely to be made each year.[137] The UK remains relatively unusual amongst other advanced welfare states in that unemployed disabled people who are insufficiently incapacitated to qualify for incapacity benefit do not have access to a form of income maintenance which recognises their partial incapacity. A major comparative study suggests that the existence of a single benefit which can be held whilst both in and out of work may play a part in facilitating work and sustaining income for disabled workers.[138]

B Entitlement to disabled person's tax credit

The conditions of entitlement to disabled person's tax credit may be considered under eight heads:
(1) presence and residence in Great Britain (for which the rules are the same as those for working families' tax credit[139]);
(2) remunerative work;
(3) capital;
(4) income;
(5) age;
(6) physical or mental disability;
(7) receipt of a relevant incapacity or disability benefit; and
(8) non-receipt of working families' tax credit.
The definition of 'remunerative work' is almost identical to that for working families' tax credit.[140] The only differences in determining whether the claimant meets the 16-hour threshold reflect the particular problems faced by disabled person's tax credit claimants.[141] Thus paid time off to visit a hospital or clinic is included in this calculation, in addition to paid meal breaks. Similarly, hours are estimated not just where the claimant starts a new job, but also where he or she resumes work after a break of at least 13 weeks or changes working hours. The provisions governing capital and income similarly follow in nearly all respects those for working families' tax credit,[142] with one important exception. Disabled person's tax credit has a higher capital limit of £16,000,[143] as against

---

137 HC Standing Committee D, col 188 (11 February 1999), per Mrs B Roche, Financial Secretary to the Treasury.
138 Thornton, Sainsbury and Barnes *Helping Disabled People to Work* SSAC Research Paper 8 (1997).
139 SI 1991/2887, reg 5. See also the Immigration and Asylum Act 1999, s 115(1) on the exclusion of any 'person subject to immigration control'.
140 SI 1991/2887, reg 6.
141 Disabled people employed for less than 16 hours a week may claim income support with the higher rate of disregard (£20 per week), and some, if in receipt of incapacity benefit, may be able to take advantage of the permitted work rule: p 549, below.
142 Pp 448–464, below.
143 SI 1991/2887, reg 31.

£8,000 for working families' tax credit. This difference dates from the introduction of disability working allowance in 1992 and followed pressure from the SSAC[144] and criticisms made during the House of Lords debates on the Bill.[145] The justification is that disabled people may have extra savings to pay for adaptations to their homes, special equipment or services. Here we concentrate on those conditions of entitlement which are unique to disabled person's tax credit.

i Age

Disabled person's tax credit has a minimum age entitlement of 16 (there is no maximum specified).[146] This is presumably because this tax credit may be claimed by single childless people, whereas it is a precondition of working families' tax credit that the claimant is both in work and responsible for a child, so making a minimum age condition superfluous.

ii A physical or mental disability which puts the claimant at a disadvantage in getting a job

Disabled person's tax credit is a benefit for people who are *partially* but not *wholly* incapable of work. Claimants must therefore have a physical or mental disability that puts them 'at a disadvantage in getting a job'.[147] It would have been possible to give decision makers a very broad discretion in deciding this issue, similar to the former test for assessing incapacity for work for the purposes of invalidity benefit.[148] Such an approach, however, would not lend itself easily to routinisation of decision making, and would have made it difficult to contain the overall costs of the benefit. Instead, an alternative strategy was adopted, under which the claimant can only show such 'a disadvantage in getting a job' by reference to prescribed criteria.[149] Regulations provide that such disadvantage is established where the person's disability corresponds to one of those conditions listed in Parts I to III of Schedule 1 to the Disability Working Allowance (General) Regulations 1991.[150]

Part I of the Schedule consists of a list of 20 conditions covering a wide variety of physical and mental disabilities, including the following:
* when standing he cannot keep his balance unless he continually holds onto something;
* he can extend neither of his arms in front of him so as to shake hands with another person without difficulty;
* due to lack of manual dexterity he cannot, with one hand, pick up a coin which is not more than 2.5 centimetres in diameter;[151]
* he can turn neither of his hands sideways through 180°;
* people who know him well have difficulty in understanding what he says;

144 *SSAC* n 130, above, p 3.
145 527 HL Official Report (5th series) cols 49 and 936.
146 SSCBA 1992, s 129(1).
147 SSCBA 1992, s 129(1)(b).
148 At least until its replacement by incapacity benefit in April 1995.
149 SSCBA 1992, s 129(3).
150 SI 1991/2887, reg 3.
151 Eg a ten pence coin. This test is to be performed in the usual way using pinch grip between thumb and fingers, and not by some unusual or awkward manoeuvre: *CDWA/3123/1997*.

- when a person he knows well speaks to him, he has difficulty in understanding what that person says;
- due to mental disability he is often confused or forgetful; and
- he cannot do the simplest addition and subtraction.

The drafting of some of these conditions requires sensitive judgment; eg the expression 'without difficulty' appears in several places but is left undefined. Experience suggests that these broad formulations assist claimants: only six per cent of unsuccessful claims fail on account of the application of the disability test.[152]

Part II of the Schedule essentially defines 'disadvantage in getting a job' by receipt of one of a number of listed benefits. These include the highest or middle rate of the care component, or the highest rate of the mobility component, of disability living allowance, and an industrial disablement or war pension where the disablement is assessed as at least 80 per cent. Part III comprises one condition only: 'As a result of an illness or injury he is undergoing a period of habilitation or rehabilitation.' Where an 'initial claim' is made,[153] the existence of any disability drawn from Parts I, II or III is sufficient.[154] Indeed, claimants' declarations that they have a relevant physical or mental disability are conclusive in establishing that they are at a disadvantage in getting a job.[155] The only exceptions are where the claim itself contains contrary indications or there is other evidence that contradicts the declaration.[156] On repeat claims, claimants must rely on one of the conditions specified in Parts I or II (but not III) of the Schedule.[157]

iii Receipt of a relevant incapacity or disability benefit

It is not sufficient that claimants have a disability that puts them at a disadvantage in getting a job. In addition, they must satisfy the qualifying benefit test.[158] This can be done in any one of five ways.[159]

A RECEIPT OF AN INCAPACITY BENEFIT

For at least one day in the 182 days (effectively six months) immediately before the date of claim,[160] one of the following benefits must have been payable to the claimant: the higher rate of short-term incapacity benefit; long-term incapacity benefit; severe disablement allowance; income support; income-based jobseeker's allowance; housing

---

152 Inland Revenue *DPTC Quarterly Enquiry October 2001* (2002) p 18. The main reasons for disallowances are failing the qualifying benefit test (25 per cent), the employment test (22 per cent) or the means test (22 per cent).
153 Meaning a claim made by a person never previously entitled to disability working allowance, or by someone whose entitlement ceased at least two years prior to the claim being made: Social Security Administration Act 1992, s 11 (SSAA 1992).
154 SI 1991/2887, reg 3(1)(a).
155 SSCBA 1992, s 11(2).
156 SI 1991/2887, reg 4.
157 SI 1991/2887, reg 3(1)(b).
158 SSCBA 1992, s 129(2)–(2F).
159 Receipt of an equivalent benefit from Northern Ireland counts as an alternative in all cases.
160 SSCBA 1992, s 129(2)(a) originally limited this period to 56 days (eight weeks) for disability working allowance, but this was relaxed by TCA 1999, s 14(3) for the purposes of disabled person's tax credit. In practice this route applies to initial claims, but it can be treated as still satisfied on renewal claims: SSAA 1992, s 11(3).

benefit; or council tax benefit. The latter four means-tested benefits only qualify for this purpose if the claimant's applicable amount included a disability or higher pensioner (on grounds of disability) premium.[161]

B   RECEIPT OF A DISABILITY BENEFIT

At the date of the disabled person's tax credit claim, one of the following benefits must have been payable to the claimant: attendance or disability living allowance; constant attendance allowance; or an analogous pension increase under a war pension or industrial injuries scheme.

C   ENTITLEMENT TO INVALID CARRIAGE

At the date of the disabled person's tax credit claim, the claimant must have an invalid carriage provided by the Secretary of State under one of the various statutory powers.

D   PARTICIPATION IN TRAINING FOR WORK

For at least one day in the 56 days (eight weeks) before the date of claim, the claimant was undertaking training for work and had also been in receipt of the higher rate of short-term incapacity benefit, long-term incapacity benefit or severe disablement allowance in the 56 days before such training started.[162]

E   FAST TRACK GATEWAY TO DISABLED PERSON'S TAX CREDIT

The fast track gateway to disabled person's tax credit was introduced in October 2000 as a means of providing access to the tax credit for people still in employment who contract an illness or disability.[163] It is intended to enable such an individual to receive the tax credit in order to cushion the impact of their loss of earning capacity, so avoiding the necessity of leaving work and then subsequently seeking to re-enter the labour market. In order for the claimant to qualify, three conditions must be satisfied:
(1) the claimant must have received statutory sick pay, lower rate short term incapacity benefit, income support on the ground of incapacity, National Insurance credits or occupational sick pay for at least 140 days (the last being within eight weeks of the claim for tax credit);
(2) a doctor must certify that the illness or disability will last for at least six months and that in consequence the person's expected earnings will be lower than would be the case otherwise; and
(3) those expected earnings will be at least 20 per cent lower than would be the case if there were no disability.
It is unclear whether doctors are well placed to certify as to the requisite drop in earning capacity, except in the relatively straightforward case where eg an employee used to be

161   SI 1991/2887, reg 7.
162   Certain days can be disregarded: SI 1991/2887, reg 7B.
163   TCA 1999, s 14(4).

able to work a 35-hour week but can now only manage a 25-hour week. There is also an apparent inconsistency with the income support rules, which provide that a person whose earnings or hours are reduced to 75 per cent (rather than 80 per cent) or less than would otherwise be the case is not to be treated as engaged in remunerative work.[164]

The advantage of the qualifying benefit condition, requiring pre-existing benefit entitlement, is that it makes the standard medical examination for incapacity benefits unnecessary. In addition, a claimant who satisfies the qualifying benefit test should almost always pass the disability test for initial claims. This requirement also acts as an effective device for rationing access to disabled person's tax credit. Thus the principal disadvantage is that disabled people who are in work but are not receiving a qualifying benefit, for whatever reason, will not be eligible for a disabled person's tax credit (unless they fall within the new fast track gateway). According to statistics, a quarter of all unsuccessful claims fail because of the absence of a qualifying benefit.[165]

iv Non-receipt of working families' tax credit

Claimants are not entitled to disabled person's tax credit if they or any member of their family are entitled to working families' tax credit.[166] The one exception to this rule is where a working families' tax credit award is due to expire within 28 days of a claim for disabled person's tax credit, the person is otherwise entitled to that latter tax credit and that latter claim is for the period immediately after the expiry of the working families' tax credit award.[167]

C Calculating entitlement to disabled person's tax credit

i General

The assessment process for disabled person's tax credit is based on the same principles as for working families' tax credit. Thus disabled person's tax credit is based on a comparison of the claimant's income[168] with a set figure known as the applicable amount. A necessary difference is that there are two levels for this threshold, a lower rate for single claimants and a higher rate (the same as that for working families' tax credit) for lone parents or couples. There are also two levels for the adult credit, the disabled person's tax credit single person rate being marginally more than the uniform working families' tax credit adult credit, while the disabled person's tax credit rate for lone parents or couples is substantially more generous. The child credits (and the situations in which they are not allowable) are identical to those applied to working families' tax credit. The disabled child credit was first introduced in the disability working allowance scheme in 1995 and became available to working families' tax credit claimants from 2000. It is payable where a child or young person living in the claimant's household is entitled to disability living allowance or is blind.[169] The taper also operates in the same fashion as for working families' tax credit, so that a claimant with an income at or

---

164 SI 1987/1967, reg 6(a), p 286, above.
165 N 152, above.
166 SSCBA 1992, s 129(1)(d).
167 SI 1991/2887, reg 57.
168 See pp 447–459, below.
169 SI 1991/2887, reg 51(1A).

below the relevant applicable amount is awarded the maximum disabled person's tax credit permissible.[170] Where a claimant's income exceeds the applicable amount, benefit is computed on the basis of maximum disabled person's tax credit less 55 per cent of the difference between the person's income and applicable amount.[171]

ii   Duration of award

As with working families' tax credit, an award of disabled person's tax credit runs for a standard period of 26 weeks,[172] and so is unaffected by changes in hours worked or income or any up-rating order. The exceptions to this rule are the same as for the working families' tax credit.[173]

D   Administration of disabled person's tax credit

The provisions governing the administration of disabled person's tax credit are in nearly all respects identical to those that apply to working families' tax credit. The principal difference is that where couples are concerned the partner with the disability must make the application for disabled person's tax credit.[174] Moreover, there is no provision in such cases for the couple to elect for payment of the tax credit to be made to the non-working partner.

---

170   SSCBA 1992, s 129(5)(a).
171   SSCBA 1992, s 129(5)(b) and SI 1991/2887, reg 53.
172   SSCBA 1992, s 129(6).
173   P 395, above.
174   If both partners have a relevant disability and they cannot agree who should make the application, the Inland Revenue can decide: SI 1987/1968, reg 4(3A).

Chapter 11

Housing benefit and council tax benefit

Part 1   Introduction

A   General

The fundamental importance of good housing to social welfare has long been reflected in government economic and social policy.[1] In general, such policy has two main aims: to secure an adequate supply of good quality homes; and to ensure an equitable distribution of that supply.[2] The cost of housing is relevant to both objectives and it has been a feature of government intervention since at least 1915 to provide some form of assistance with such costs. Initially, at a time when the large majority lived in privately rented accommodation, the assistance took the form of controls on rent.[3] The original system of rent controls was eventually superseded in 1968 by the fair rent system of rent regulation which in turn, following the Housing Act 1988 (HA 1988), came to be confined for the most part to regulated tenancies granted before 15 January 1989. The rents of most residential tenancies created on or after that date are subject only to minimal intervention and then simply to confine them to market rent levels.[4] Indeed, the private rented sector now constitutes only a minor part of the housing market.[5] During the latter half of the twentieth century, two other forms of intervention assumed central importance. First, the supply side was aided by the development of a complex system of public housing finance for local authority and other public sector tenants alongside tax relief for owner-occupiers. In more recent years the scale of such subsidies has been radically reduced. Secondly, pursuit of the distributional objective led to the development of a means-tested benefit system to meet housing costs, so that those on low incomes can afford housing which the market would otherwise place beyond their means. It is this second phenomenon which forms the subject matter of this chapter.

---

1   See DETR *Quality and Choice: A Decent Home for All* (2000).
2   Lansley *Housing and Public Policy* (1979) p 18; Ermisch *Housing Finance: Who Gains?* (1984) p 9.
3   Increase of Rent and Mortgage Interest (War Restrictions) Act 1915.
4   See *Bankway Properties Ltd v Pensfold-Dunsford* [2001] EWCA Civ 528, [2001] 1 WLR 1369.
5   In 1910, 89 per cent of housing stock in the UK was privately rented accommodation. By 2001 only 9 per cent was rented privately; 70 per cent of properties were owner-occupied and 21 per cent were let by social landlords: ONS *Social Trends 2002* (2002) p 167.

B   The evolution of housing benefit

i   Rent rebates

The early history of housing benefit may be located in the introduction of rent rebates for local authority tenants in the 1930s, as part of a programme to encourage slum clearance and public sector rehousing.[6] The need for the rebates occurred because, not surprisingly, the rehoused slum dwellers could not often afford the rent for their new homes. In 1930 local authorities were given financial incentives in connection with slum clearance and encouraged to adopt localised rent rebate schemes for those displaced.[7] Six years later the arrangements were extended to allow rebates schemes covering all tenants.[8] The schemes were not popular, apparently because tenants objected to the resulting differentials in rents.[9] The permissive rather than mandatory nature of these schemes, together with their strictly local application, was an enduring aspect of rent rebate legislation.

Changes in 1956 to reduce the subsidy of local authority housing had the long-term effect of raising rent levels and the Conservative government encouraged the use of rebates, leading to a large rise in the number of schemes.[10] This encouragement was sustained by a subsequent Labour administration which issued a circular containing a model local scheme. By 1970, over 60 per cent of local authorities operated some kind of scheme[11] but, since no compulsory standards applied, there was a wide divergence between them.

In the early 1970s, in order to reduce public expenditure, the Conservative government cut subsidies to local authorities and extended 'fair rent' controls to public sector tenancies. The introduction in 1972 of the first national system of rent rebates for council tenants[12] was, in part, intended to mitigate the impact of this new 'fair rents' policy. Reflecting a concern for the equitable distribution of assistance with rents, the scheme also provided for rent allowances for private and housing association tenants. In partnership with family income supplement (FIS), it was seen as an 'important new weapon against family poverty'.[13] Again, for reasons of equity, assistance was deliberately made available to some tenants who were not entitled to supplementary benefit. This was considered to be necessary in view of the projected increases in public sector rents[14] but in consequence there now existed, alongside supplementary benefit and FIS, a third major means-tested system, with different rules of assessment.

ii   Rate rebates

The expansion of local authority services in the 1960s resulted in significant increases in local rates and there was concern about the impact of this growing burden on

---

6   See generally Deacon and Bradshaw *Reserved for the Poor* (1983) pp 11–14.
7   HA 1930.
8   HA 1936.
9   Ravetz *Model Estate* (1974) pp 37–38.
10   From 1956 to 1965 the proportion of local authorities with schemes rose from 15 per cent to 39 per cent: Parker *The Rents of Council Houses* (1967) p 47.
11   *Deacon and Bradshaw* n 6, above, p 70.
12   Housing Finance Act 1972.
13   White Paper *Fair Deal for Housing* (1971, Cmnd 4728) para 42.
14   *White Paper* n 13, above, para 5.

ratepayers with low incomes.[15] The Rating Act 1966 introduced a national rate rebate scheme as a temporary measure, pending attempts to devise a more radical reform of the rating system in the light of the findings of a Royal Commission on Local Government.[16] The rebate scheme involved a comparison of 'reckonable rates', broadly those in respect of the dwelling in which the applicant lived less a deduction for non-dependants, with 'reckonable income', determined under the Act and set at about the supplementary benefit level. The scheme suffered from low take-up and at certain income levels the tapering of assistance worked unfairly.[17] In 1975 a new scheme, modelled on the rent rebate scheme, was introduced with dramatically improved results in terms of both coverage and the level of assistance offered.[18]

iii General schemes for income maintenance and housing costs

Quite apart from the specific programmes designed to assist with rent and rates, the role of general income maintenance benefits should not be overlooked. Although the poor law made no allowance for, and indeed normally prohibited, relief payments to meet rent,[19] this item was an established component in determining needs under the unemployment assistance scheme, and was retained in the national assistance scheme proposed by Beveridge.[20] Regulations made under the National Assistance Act 1948 defined 'net rent' as including not only the actual rent but also rates, an allowance towards repairs and insurance and, where appropriate, mortgage interest payments.[21] This definition was retained when supplementary benefit replaced national assistance in 1966 and continued to apply until the first stage of housing benefit reform in 1983.

iv The 1983 reform

The picture emerging from the historical survey to this point is of a complex, fragmented approach to the payment of benefit for housing costs. By 1975, the national rent and rebate schemes were fully operative and were administered by local authorities which were, in turn, subject to regulation by the Department of the Environment. At the same time, the Supplementary Benefits Commission (SBC) was making payments for rent and rates to those entitled under its scheme. The Labour government's Green Paper on Housing Policy in 1977 included an undertaking to review the overlap,[22] but the main impetus to reform was given by the SBC in its Annual Reports from 1976 to 1979.[23]

The Commission took as its focus the 'better off' problem, described as the confusion of, and actual loss to, some householders caused by the overlap. Because of the different means-tests and allowances, it was difficult to estimate whether a person not in full-

---

15 See *Report of the Committee of Inquiry into the Impact of Rates on Households* (1965, Cmnd 2582).
16 (1966, Cmnd 2923.)
17 Meacher *Rate Rebates: A Study of the Effectiveness of Means Tests* (1973) pp 1–4.
18 The scheme was set out in the Rate Rebate Act 1973. The reform more than doubled the number of households receiving assistance and by 1976 take-up had reached an estimated 65–70 per cent: *Deacon and Bradshaw* n 6, above, p 91.
19 General Outdoor Relief Regulation Order 1852.
20 Beveridge Report *Socal Insurance and Allied Services* (1942, Cmd 6404) para 206.
21 SI 1948/1344, Sch 1.
22 *Housing Policy Review* (1977, Cmnd 6851) para 12.09.
23 See esp SBC *Annual Report for 1977* (1978, Cmnd 7392) ch 8; and SBC *Annual Report for 1979* (1980, Cmnd 8033) ch 4. See also Donnison *The Politics of Poverty* (1982) pp 184–193.

time work should claim supplementary benefit or rebates. The SBC proposed a single housing benefit to replace rent and rates rebates, rent allowances and the rent and mortgage interest element of supplementary benefit. In addition to clarifying the entitlement issue, it was argued that since the new benefit would be available to those with low earnings, as well as the unemployed, it would not involve work disincentives. The Commission proposed that income tax relief on mortgage interest payments should also be rationalised within the framework of a unified scheme; this would allow a reallocation of resources which would help both to simplify the scheme and to redress inequities in the prevailing systems of housing support. Finally, there would be manifest administrative advantages if responsibility for the unified scheme were to be conferred on the local authorities. The new Conservative administration of 1979 was attracted by the prospect of savings in the civil service establishment but concerned at the cost of a comprehensive scheme for all low-income households.[24] Moreover, it was clear that radical reform extending eg to the system of tax relief on mortgage interest was not on the government's agenda.

The housing benefit reform which was enacted in 1982[25] and brought into force in 1983 proceeded on a 'nil-cost' basis and effectively achieved the unification of the existing means-tested schemes for assisting tenants with their housing costs. Owner-occupiers were included in the new system only so far as general rates were concerned. Thus mortgage interest payments continued to be met by the supplementary benefit scheme alone[26] and the system of tax relief on such interest was, for the time being, unaffected.[27] The legislation followed the pattern set by the existing rent and rebate schemes and, accordingly, administrative responsibility was placed on the local authorities. Those in receipt of supplementary benefit (except boarders) generally qualified for full assistance with rent and rebates (subject to deductions for non-dependants living in the premises). These were referred to as 'certificated cases' since, if the householder was entitled to supplementary benefit, the Department of Health and Social Security (DHSS) would issue a certificate to the local authority which would then meet the eligible housing costs. In cases where there was no entitlement to supplementary benefit (known as 'standard cases'), a 'needs allowance' for the household was compared with gross income. If that income was less than or equal to the allowance, 60 per cent of the rent and rates were met. Income exceeding the allowance gave rise to deductions from the 60 per cent amount, according to a complex system of six tapers which varied as between rent rebates (or allowances) and rate rebates and as between pensioners and non-pensioners. The partial simplification of the previous schemes, together with the 'nil-cost' policy, resulted in a large number of householders sustaining a net loss in benefit,[28] a number reduced by the awkward device of a housing benefit supplement (HBS).[29]

---

24 Consultative Document *Assistance with Housing Costs* (1981); and see *Donnison* n 23, above, ch 7.
25 Social Security and Housing Benefits Act 1982.
26 P 303, above.
27 For comment, see *Donnison* n 23, above, p 188. Mortgage interest tax relief was abolished with effect from April 2000: Finance Act 1999, s 38.
28 Cf Hill (1984) 13 J Soc Pol 297.
29 The need for this arose in cases where householders could not claim supplementary benefit because their income exceeded the relevant threshold by a small amount. In respect of the housing benefit claim, the application of the tapers might result in the householder's unmet housing costs exceeding that small amount; in consequence such a person would be worse off overall than an applicant categorised as a 'certificated case'. HBS was available to make up this difference but, to compound the complexity of the arrangements, though it was added to the housing benefit paid by the local authority, it was formally part of supplementary benefit: SI 1983/1399, reg 19(1). Identifying those entitled to HBS was a major difficulty because of the divided responsibility between the local authorities and the DHSS: *Hill* n 28, above, p 314.

Additional dimensions to the 1983 housing benefit system could be provided by individual local authorities. An authority could seek the approval of the Secretary of State to operate a high rent scheme where the average rents in the area exceeded the national average by 30 per cent or more. If such approval was given, the figure of 60 per cent of eligible rent used in the initial calculation could be raised to 80 or 90 per cent. A local authority could in addition, and at its own cost, increase expenditure on standard cases by up to 10 per cent by paying more to individuals subject to 'exceptional circumstances' or to classes of individuals (such as war pensioners) under so-called 'local schemes'.

Subject to this last qualification, local authorities were subsidised by central government in relation both to housing benefit and to the cost of its administration. Some authorities raised rent by various stratagems and, in so doing, used the subsidy arrangements to increase their own income.[30] Various amendments to the subsidy orders had to be made to halt manipulation of this kind.[31]

v *The 1988 reform*

Shortly after the implementation of the 1983 reforms, the government announced a programme of economies in housing benefit which were to be achieved by adjusting the tapers for both rents and rates. This reflected concern at the substantial rise in expenditure due, at least in part, to growth in unemployment coinciding with increases in local authority rent and rates.[32] Even more important was the decision to set up an independent review of the scheme, the findings of which were published in 1985,[33] at the same time as the Green Paper on the reform of social security generally. Three main problems were identified.[34] First, the housing benefit scheme had not succeeded in removing inequities as between households with similar needs and income; in particular between those entitled and those not entitled to supplementary benefit – the advantages obtained by those in the former category might substantially weaken work incentives. Secondly, the scheme was far too complex, the provision of HBS being an obvious example. Thirdly, and perhaps most significantly, the view was formed that, in comparison with other countries with similar economies and social security systems, housing benefit (which reached about one-third of all households) was too widely available.

The suggested restructuring of the other means-tested benefits[35] created the opportunity to address these problems and, at the same time, to achieve some degree of integration with those systems. Thus, the White Paper of 1985 proposed that the rules for the new income support scheme should be used to assess entitlement to housing benefit.[36] This would considerably simplify the law and would provide uniform support for all claimants with income at or below the appropriate 'poverty' level, whether or not they were in work. It would also avoid the complexities of the HBS and the 'high rent' schemes. There would be just two tapers (for rent and rates, respectively) and these would be set against net, rather than gross income, which would help to deal with the 'poverty trap' problem arising from the withdrawal of benefit as income increased.[37]

---

30 See eg *R v Secretary of State for Health and Social Security, ex p City of Sheffield* (1985) 18 HLR 6.
31 See further pp 433–435, below.
32 Social Security Advisory Committee (SSAC) *Fifth Report* (1986–87) para 2.4.4.
33 Housing Benefit Review *Report of the Review Team* (1985, Cmnd 9520).
34 Cf Green Paper *Reform of Social Security* (1985, Cmnd 9517) vol 1, paras 9.14–9.16.
35 Pp 276–277 and 384–385, above.
36 White Paper *Reform of Social Security* (1985, Cmnd 9691) para 3.45.
37 Cf p 276, above.

In fact this strategy proved to be somewhat too bold. Housing benefit had never taken account of the householder's capital. Harmonisation with income support assessment, as effected in the Social Security Act 1986, meant that there would be no entitlement to housing benefit if the claimant's relevant capital exceeded £6,000 and capital between £3,000 and £6,000 would be treated as generating assessable income. It was estimated that these changes would cause substantial losses and disentitle some 375,000 households from housing benefit.[38] Considerable political pressure at the time that the new scheme came into effect[39] led to a 'thirteenth hour' modification: the upper capital threshold was raised to £8,000.[40] In contrast, no compromise was made to another controversial aspect of the scheme, that in order to enhance the accountability of local authorities, all households, whatever their resources, should make a minimum contribution of 20 per cent to domestic rates.[41] Furthermore, because the new system was coupled with public expenditure reductions on housing benefit of the order of £740 million, many households stood to lose by the changes. The DHSS estimated that over five million households would sustain housing benefit reductions, including one million who would lose all entitlement to benefit, and many pensioners. In response to the consequent political pressure, the government introduced an extra-statutory scheme of transitional payments with the aim of limiting the loss of housing benefit experienced by certain groups.[42]

vi The Housing Acts 1988 and 1996[43]

The legal framework for the private rented sector has been radically transformed by HA 1988 and HA 1996. The 1988 Act provided that most private sector residential lettings created on or after 15 January 1989 would no longer be subject to the rent regulation provisions of the Rent Act 1977 (in particular the registration of a fair rent). The 1988 Act provided for two new types of tenancies. The first was the assured tenancy under which the rent is determined by agreement between landlord and tenant. Only in limited circumstances, where a landlord seeks to increase the rent periodically in accordance with the statutory procedure laid down in the Act, is the tenant able to challenge the (proposed) rent level before a rent assessment committee. Even then the committee's function is limited to determining a market rent for the property. The second type of tenancy created by the 1988 Act was the assured shorthold tenancy (or AST, a sub-species of the assured tenancy, providing no long-term security of tenure and at that time requiring the issue of a prior notice to the tenant). In the case of an AST the rent is again determined by agreement between the parties. However, there is a further procedure whereby the tenant, once only, during the initial fixed term, may refer the rent agreed to a rent assessment committee. Provided the committee consider that there is a sufficient local market of similar dwelling-houses let on assured tenancies which indicates that the rent payable under the tenancy in question is significantly higher than that which the landlord might reasonably expect to obtain, the committee must then

---

38   SHAC *Housing Benefit: is this the promised end?* (1985) p 6.
39   131 HC Official Report (6th series) cols 173–216; 132 HC Official Report (6th series) cols 351–394.
40   SI 1988/909. SSAC in its *Fourth Report* (1985) para 4.16 had recommended that it be raised to £12,000. An ex gratia scheme was devised somewhat later than the '13th hour' for Scotland.
41   *Green Paper* n 34 above, vol 1, para 9.20; *White Paper* n 36, above, para 3.56.
42   See the 4th edition of this book, pp 540–541.
43   On the 1988 Act see Rodgers *Housing – The New Law* (1989); and Davey *Residential Rents* (1990). On the 1996 Act see Cowan (ed) *The Housing Act 1996 – A Practical Guide* (1996).

determine the rent which they consider the landlord might reasonably expect to obtain. The presumption under the 1988 Act that private sector tenancies were assured tenancies unless the parties contracted into an AST was reversed by HA 1996.[44] Thus the requirement for a prior notice was abolished and so private sector tenancies entered into on or after 20 April 1997 are ASTs unless the parties specifically enter into an assured tenancy.

It follows that within the landlord-tenant private law relationship the potential to control rents is limited to the possible reduction of 'excessive rents' to a reasonable market level. There is little evidence that these provisions are widely used. In contrast, in the public law sphere there is a high level of intervention in private sector rents, but solely for the purposes of determining entitlement to housing benefit. In order to prevent potential exploitation of the housing benefit system under the regime of market rents, the government gave rent officers an entirely new housing benefit function.[45] This is dealt with later in this chapter.[46]

vii Reform of the rating system[47]

Domestic rates, for which, as we have seen,[48] assistance was provided through housing benefit, were abolished in Scotland as from 1 April 1989 and replaced by the community charge.[49] The community charge (or poll tax as it was popularly known) was extended to England and Wales a year later.[50] Under that scheme most adults had to pay a personal community charge to the authority responsible for the area in which their only or main home was located.[51] The prime form of assistance with paying the community charge was community charge benefit, which essentially replaced the rates component of housing benefit.[52] Community charge benefit was only payable in respect of a personal community charge or a collective community charge contribution.[53] The community charge was highly controversial. It proved to be short-lived and was replaced, as from 1 April 1993, by the council tax.[54] Thus personal charges were abolished and in their place a bill is sent by the local authority to the owner or resident of each dwelling in the area of that authority. Assistance with paying council tax is available by way of council tax benefit.[55]

---

44 HA 1996, s 96, inserting HA 1988, s 19A.
45 See generally the Consultation Paper *Deregulation of the Private Rented Sector: Implications for Housing Benefit* (1987).
46 See p 421, below.
47 See *Paying for Local Government* (1986, Cmnd 9714).
48 P 408, above.
49 Abolition of Domestic Rates (Etc) Scotland Act 1987. For the year 1989–90 the housing benefit system was extended to provide community charge rebates for eligible individual charge payers on low incomes.
50 Local Government Finance Act 1988 (LGFA 1988), which also amended the Scottish legislation.
51 People with second homes usually had to pay a standard community charge to the authority in whose area that property was located. Landlords of hostels and other short-stay accommodation were responsible for paying a collective community charge and collecting individual contributions from residents.
52 There was also transitional relief, deducted automatically from community charge bills.
53 Students in full-time advanced education normally paid only 20 per cent of the personal community charge and were not eligible for community charge benefit. Registered students were also exempt from the collective community charge contribution. Details of community charge benefit were contained in SI 1989/1321.
54 LGFA 1992. The tax also applies to Scotland but this text is confined to the scheme applicable in England and Wales. For a detailed examination see Ward and Murdie *Council Tax Handbook* (4th edn, 2000).
55 See SI 1992/1814: transitional rules dealt with the change-over from community charge benefit to council tax benefit and with back-payment on the receipt of certain delayed claims: SI 1992/1909. Council tax benefit is dealt with at p 437, below.

viii Further reform

Following the 1988 restructuring of housing benefit, and apart from the reform of the rating system, there has been a host of further amendments to the scheme.[56] The most significant change in recent years was the introduction of a new regime for restricting eligible rent (for housing benefit rather than contractual purposes) from January 1996. There have been several anti-fraud initiatives, primarily targeted at improving local authority performance in identifying fraudulent claims.[57] Despite these changes, the housing benefit budget has continued to grow remorselessly.[58] This reflects the deregulation of the private rented sector and the transition to market rents brought about by HA 1988[59] as well as the changes to local government and housing association finance which has forced rents up sharply from earlier levels. The consequence in housing policy terms has been a massive shift from 'bricks and mortar' subsidy (ie underwriting the cost of new local authority building programmes) to personal subsidy in the form of housing benefit.[60]

Although the Labour government elected in 1997 placed welfare reform at the centre of its strategy, reform of housing benefit proved particularly intractable. At the heart of the problem is the fragmentation caused by the fact that what is a national benefit is administered by 409 local authorities, many of whom appear unable to provide a proper service.[61] In some cases this maladministration leads to tenants losing their homes.[62] The government's first tentative ideas for reform were set out in the Housing Green Paper in April 2000,[63] which was followed by the Housing Policy Statement.[64] These documents focused on process issues rather than the substantive rules governing eligibility to housing benefit.[65] Thus the latter document expressed the government's two main priorities to be raising standards in administration of housing benefit and simplification of the claims system.[66] The House of Commons Social Security Committee has advocated more far-reaching reforms.[67] These include setting housing benefit entitlement for fixed periods (regardless of changes in circumstances), reducing the number of non-dependant deductions and both easing and simplifying the rules

---

56 For a summary of the key changes in the early 1990s, see the 4th edition of this book, pp 542–543.
57 See eg the Social Security Administration (Fraud) Act 1997.
58 From £2.3 billion in 1978–79 to £11.12 billion in 1998–99 at constant prices: DETR *Quality and Choice: A Decent Home for All* (2000) para 11.2. This amounts to 12 per cent of all social security spending and about 1 per cent of GNP: House of Commons Social Security Committee *Sixth Report* (1999–2000, HC 385) para 4. The introduction of the 1996 rent restriction rules and lower unemployment has led to a slight decrease in the late 1990s: *Sixth Report*, para 16.
59 See p 410, above.
60 In 1978–79 public expenditure on housing support was 84 per cent bricks and mortar subsidy and 16 per cent personal subsidy. By 1998–99 the position was reversed: 23 per cent bricks and mortar subsidy and 73 per cent personal subsidy (*DETR* n 58, above, para 11.2).
61 In 1999 it was estimated that 44 per cent of local authorities were providing a poor service: *Audit Commission Update: Fraud and Lodging* (1999) para 16. The Local Government Ombudsman reported that 21 per cent of all complaints received related to the administration of housing benefit, and noted 'systemic defects' in a 'small number of councils', especially in London: *Annual Report 2000/01*, pp 3–4 and ch 7.
62 *Local Government Ombudsman* n 61, above, p 4; and see Heppinstall (2000) NLJ 1332.
63 *DETR* n 58, above; see Cowan and Marsh (2001) 64 MLR 260.
64 DETR *The way forward for housing* (2000).
65 Reflected also in the decision to transfer responsibility for hearing appeals to the Appeals Service: see p 181, above.
66 *DETR* n 63, above, para 10.5.
67 *DETR* n 58, above, and see DSS *Reply by the Government* (2001). See also Kemp *'Shopping Incentives' and Housing Benefit Reform* (2001).

restricting the level of housing benefit paid in respect of private sector rents. The Committee also repeated the call for a fundamental review of state help with housing costs so as to ensure such provision is neutral between tenures. In the immediate future, the interaction between the evolving system of tax credits and housing benefit is likely to be a key focus of developments.

Part 2   Entitlement to housing benefit

There are three basic conditions of entitlement for housing benefit: the claimant must (i) be liable to make payments in respect of a dwelling in Great Britain; (ii) occupy that dwelling as a home; and (iii) not have capital and income in excess of prescribed amounts.[68] The discussion will be divided accordingly.[69]

A   Liability to make payments in respect of a dwelling

i   Dwelling

'Dwelling' for the purposes of housing benefit means:

> any residential accommodation, whether or not consisting of the whole or part of a building and whether or not comprising separate or self-contained premises[70] and which is located in Great Britain.[71]

It follows that accommodation used for business purposes is excluded and the same would seem to apply to holiday accommodation.

ii   Payments

Broadly speaking, housing benefit may consist of a rent allowance or a rent rebate, payable to private sector and public sector tenants respectively. A number of periodical payments, in addition to rent payments themselves, are covered by housing benefit. They include[72]
- payments under a licence or permission to occupy the dwelling;[73]
- informal payments for the occupation of a dwelling;
- mesne profits;
- mooring charges for a houseboat or site payments for a caravan or mobile home;
- rental purchase agreement payments;
- contributions by the resident of an almshouse to the relevant housing association or charity; and
- service charge payments (provided that occupation is conditional on them).

68   Social Security Contributions and Benefits Act 1992, s 130 (SSCBA 1992).
69   See further Findlay, Poynter, Stagg et al *Housing Benefit and Council Tax Benefit Legislation 2001/2002* (14th edn, 2002) and Tonge and Jenkins *Tolley's Housing and Housing Benefit Law: A Practical Guide* (2001).
70   SSCBA 1992, s 137(1).
71   SSCBA 1992, s 130(1)(a).
72   SI 1987/1971, reg 10(1).
73   Eg boarders, including hostel dwellers.

However, certain periodical payments even if included in the above list are not covered by housing benefit. They include payments under a long tenancy (except a shared-ownership tenancy granted by a housing association or a housing authority); payments under a hire purchase, credit sale or conditional sale agreement (eg for the purchase of a mobile home); payments under a co-ownership scheme;[74] payments by a Crown tenant; and payments by owners.[75] Finally, where rent includes an amount attributable to outstanding arrears from the tenancy or a former tenancy, that amount will not be eligible for housing benefit.[76]

iii   Liability for payments

In most cases, the claimant will be the person who is legally liable[77] to make the rent payment in respect of the dwelling. However, the regulations also treat as 'liable':[78]

(1) the partner of the person liable;
(2) a person who has to make payments to continue to live in the home because the liable person has failed to do so (provided that the former was the latter's partner or the authority considers it reasonable to treat the former as liable);
(3) a person whose landlord has waived liability as compensation for repair or redecoration work carried out by the occupier which the landlord would otherwise have had to do (to a maximum of eight weeks in respect of any one waiver);
(4) the partner of a student excluded from the scheme;
(5) a person who has actually made payments wholly or partly in advance of when they were due. (Where rent is varied during a period the variation is treated as effective for the whole of that period.)

Conversely, there are situations (outlined below) in which certain persons are treated as if they were *not* liable for the payments and so cannot themselves claim housing benefit. These categories, known generically as 'contrived lettings', were both amended and extended in their scope with effect from January 1999.[79] The cases referred to are where:[80]

(1) the tenancy (or other agreement under which the claimant occupies the dwelling) is not on a commercial basis;[81]

---

74   Including members of a co-operative housing association: *R v Birmingham Housing Benefit Review Board, ex p Ellery* (1989) 21 HLR 398. But rents payable to a housing co-operative may be eligible.
75   SI 1987/1971, reg 10(2). For the exclusion of mortgage payments from the scheme see SSCBA 1992, s 130(2)(b). Crown tenants on income support or income-based jobseeker's allowance can claim housing costs for their rent; a separate scheme operates for others on low incomes.
76   SI 1987/1971, reg 8(2A); an attempt to have the amending regulation, SI 1992/201, quashed as ultra vires, failed in *R v Secretary of State for Social Security, ex p Association of Metropolitan Authorities* (1992) 25 HLR 131, despite the fact that Tucker J declared that the Secretary of State was in breach of the requirement in s 61(7) of the Social Security Act 1986 that the AMA be consulted before such regulations were laid.
77   See *R v Rugby Borough Council Housing Benefit Review Board, ex p Harrison* (1994) 28 HLR 36; *R v Stratford-upon-Avon District Council Housing Benefit Review Board, ex p White* (1998) 31 HLR 126; and *R v Milton Keynes Housing Benefit Review Board, ex p Saxby* [2001] EWCA Civ 456, (2001) 33 HLR 930.
78   SI 1987/1971, reg 6(1)–(2).
79   SI 1998/3257, increasing the number of situations in which a claimant is deemed not to be liable from 5 to 12. See further Rahilly (2002) 9 JSSL 61.
80   SI 1987/1971, reg 7.
81   Since January 1999 there has been no requirement that the claimant reside with the landlord so as to fall within this deeming rule. The mere fact that the landlord is a relative does not necessarily render the agreement non-commercial: *R v Poole Borough Council, ex p Ross* (1995) 28 HLR 351. See further SI 1987/1971, reg 7(1A).

(2) the liability is to a person who also resides in[82] the dwelling and who is a close relative[83] of the claimant (or partner);

(3) the liability is either to a former partner and relates to the former shared home or is to the claimant's partner's former partner and relates to their former matrimonial home;[84]

(4) the claimant (or partner) is responsible for the landlord's child;[85]

(5) the liability is to a company or to a trustee of a trust and the claimant (or partner, partner's former partner or close relative residing with the claimant) is a director or employee (of the company) or a trustee or beneficiary (of the trust);

(6) before the liability was created, the claimant was a non-dependant of a person who resided, and continues to reside, in the dwelling;

(7) the liability is to a trustee of a trust which the claimant's (or partner's) child is a beneficiary;

(8) the claimant (or partner) previously owned, within the previous five years, the dwelling in respect of which the liability arises (unless the claimant can satisfy the authority that he or she could not have continued in occupation without relinquishing ownership);

(9) the claimant's occupation (or that of his or her partner) of the dwelling is a condition of their employment by the landlord;[86]

(10) the claimant is a member of and is fully maintainable by a religious order;

(11) the claimant is in residential accommodation;[87]

(12) in any other case the authority is satisfied that the liability was created to take advantage of the housing benefit scheme.

In most of these categories of claimants (with the exceptions of (9), (10) and (11)), the rules are clearly intended to deal with cases of collusive agreement and abuse. The deeming rules in (5) and (6) do not apply where the claimant satisfies the authority 'that the liability was not intended to be a means of taking advantage of the housing benefit scheme'.[88] This specific exception does not apply to the other categories. The final category, (12), a general catch-all provision to cover 'contrived lettings' which do not fall within any of the preceding situations, has, with its predecessor, been the subject of most of the case law on cases of deemed non-liability.[89]

---

82 The previous formulation referred to the claimant residing *with* the landlord, as opposed to both parties residing *in* the same dwelling. Arguably the new wording excludes reference to the explanatory provision in SI 1987/1971, reg 3(4), although this is almost certainly accidental. There is a clear distinction in the Rent Act case law as between 'residing with' and living at the same address ('residing in'?): *Foreman v Beagley* [1969] 1 WLR 1387; *Swanbrae Ltd v Elliott* (1986) 19 HLR 86 (see p 252, above).

83 Ie parent, parent-in-law, stepparent, stepson, stepdaughter, brother, sister, or the spouse or partner of any of these: SI 1987/1971, reg 2(1). It would appear that siblings necessarily include half-siblings (*R(SB) 22/87*) although not step-siblings.

84 This provision is not in breach of arts 8 and 14 of the ECHR: *R v Carmarthenshire County Council Housing Benefit Review Board, ex p Painter* [2001] EWHC Admin 308.

85 'Responsible for' means more than simply 'caring for': see SI 1987/1971, reg 14. This provision is also not in breach of arts 8 and 14 of the ECHR: *Tucker v Secretary of State for Social Security* [2001] EWHC Admin 260.

86 Occupation must be a *condition* (rather than a fringe benefit) in such tied accommodation (eg publican).

87 There is transitional protection for certain older cases: SI 1987/1971, reg 7(2)–(12).

88 SI 1987/1971, reg 7(1B).

89 See eg *R v Solihull Metropolitan Borough Council Housing Benefits Review Board, ex p Simpson* [1995] 1 FLR 140; and *R v London Borough of Barking and Dagenham Housing and Council Tax Review Board, ex p Mackay* [2001] EWHC Admin 234. A contrived letting may be found even where the tenant is not party to the abuse of the housing benefit scheme: *R v Manchester City Council, ex p Baragrove Properties Ltd* (1991) 23 HLR 337.

B   Occupation of dwelling as a home

i   The general rule

As a general rule it is only the housing costs of a single dwelling 'normally' occupied by the claimant (and his or her family) as their home which are covered by housing benefit.[90] Thus if a claimant is liable for payments in respect of two homes, benefit is only payable on that which he or she normally occupies. However, if, because of the large size of the claimant's family, it has been necessary for a local authority to accommodate them in two separate dwellings, the claimant is treated as occupying both as a home and is eligible for benefit on both.[91]

ii   The general rule qualified

There are a number of other qualifications to the general rule above. The first two are both cases where the claimant is liable to make payments in respect of one of two homes. They are as follows:
(1) where a single claimant or a lone parent is an eligible student,[92] or is on a training course, and is liable to make payments in respect of either (but not both), the dwelling which is occupied for the purpose of attending the relevant course, or the dwelling which the claimant occupies when not attending the course;[93] and
(2) where a claimant has had to move temporarily from his or her normal residence into another to enable essential repairs to be carried out on the former.[94]
In both of these cases the claimant is treated as occupying as a home that dwelling in respect of which he or she is liable to make payments.
   In three other exceptional cases a person who is liable to make payments in respect of two (but no more than two) dwellings can be treated as occupying both as a home, namely:
•   if the claimant who formerly occupied a dwelling as a home has left that dwelling through fear of violence in the dwelling, or by a former member of the claimant's family, and it is reasonable that housing benefit should be paid in respect of that home and the dwelling presently occupied as a home by the claimant. This exception only applies for a period of absence not exceeding 52 weeks and only while the claimant intends to return to occupy the former dwelling as a home;[95]
•   if one member of a couple is an eligible student, or is on a training course, and it is unavoidable that they should occupy two separate dwellings and it is reasonable that housing benefit should be paid in respect of both dwellings;[96]
•   if a claimant, who has moved home, is unavoidably liable to make payments in respect of two dwellings then benefit may be paid for a maximum of four weeks.[97]
In some cases a person can be treated as occupying a dwelling as a home while not actually living there. The cases are:

90   SI 1987/1971, reg 5(1).
91   SI 1987/1971, reg 5(5)(c).
92   For eligibility of students see p 428, below.
93   SI 1987/1971, reg 5(3).
94   SI 1987/1971, reg 5(4).
95   SI 1987/1971, reg 5(5)(a).
96   SI 1987/1971, reg 5(5)(b).
97   SI 1987/1971, reg 5(5)(d).

- where a claimant who has moved into a new home was liable for payments in respect of the home for a period before that date and a claim for housing benefit has been made, but not decided, before the claimant moved in (or has been refused and a second claim has been made, or treated as having been made, within four weeks of the claimant moving in). In such a case benefit may be paid retrospectively after the claimant has moved in. This provision only applies if the delay in moving is reasonable and either:
  (i) the delay was necessary in order to adapt the dwelling to the disability needs of the claimant or a member of that person's family; or
  (ii) a member of the claimant's family is aged five or under or the claimant's applicable amount includes a pensioner or disability premium (and the delay was caused by awaiting the outcome of an application for a social fund payment for a need connected with the move); or
  (iii) the liability arose at a time the claimant was a hospital patient or in a residential home owned or managed by a local authority.[98]
  In cases where the claimant has occupied another dwelling as a home on any day within a period of four weeks before moving home and where condition (i) above applies the claimant may receive benefit in respect of the former home for a period not exceeding four weeks immediately before the date of the move;[99]
- where a claimant who occupied a dwelling as a home has left that dwelling through fear of violence either in that dwelling or by somebody who was formerly a member of the claimant's family and the claimant has a liability to make payments in respect of the dwelling that are unavoidable. In this case the claimant is to be treated as occupying the dwelling as a home for a period not exceeding four benefit weeks.[100]

iii Temporary absences from home

In certain circumstances a claimant can be treated as occupying a dwelling as a home despite being temporarily absent from that dwelling for a period not exceeding 13 (or, in exceptional cases, 52) weeks. This will be the case provided the claimant intends to return to the home which has not in the meantime been let or sub-let and the period of absence does not exceed 13 (or, as appropriate, 52) weeks or is unlikely to exceed that period.[101] This regulation only applies where the period of absence is continuous and unbroken.[102] The normal maximum permitted period of temporary absence was reduced from 52 weeks to 13 weeks in 1995.[103] The longer period of 52 weeks applies only in the following exceptional circumstances, namely where the claimant is:

- detained in custody on remand pending trial or pending sentence on conviction;
- resident as a hospital in-patient;
- undergoing medical treatment or receiving medically approved care or treatment otherwise than in residential accommodation;
- following a training course;
- undertaking medically approved care of a third party;

---

98 SI 1987/1971, reg 5(6).
99 SI 1987/1971, reg 5(5)(e).
100 SI 1987/1971, reg 5(7A). This provision is not confined to domestic violence; it could encompass violence from neighbours and racist attacks on the home.
101 SI 1987/1971, reg 5(8)–(8C).
102 *R v Penwith District Council Housing Benefit Review Board, ex p Burt* (1990) 22 HLR 292. Thus a short return home should result in a new period of temporarily permitted absence.
103 SI 1995/625.

- undertaking the care of a child whose parent or guardian is receiving medically approved care or treatment;
- a non-excluded student (in certain circumstances);
- in residential accommodation, otherwise than on a trial basis; or
- in fear of violence and not liable for rent at the temporary address.[104]

There is a further proviso in such cases in that the period of absence must either be unlikely to exceed 52 weeks or, in exceptional circumstances (which are left undefined), 'is unlikely substantially to exceed that period'.[105] Official guidance suggests that in such exceptional cases absences up to 15 months would qualify.[106]

C   Capital and income

Where the relevant capital (see Part 4 of chapter 12) exceeds a prescribed threshold, housing benefit is not payable.[107] The prescribed threshold is £16,000.[108] It must also be established that the claimant's relevant income, which includes 'tariff income' assumed to be derived from capital between £3,000 and £16,000, does not exceed the 'applicable amount', a figure prescribed by regulations every year, or by no more than remains after applying the 'tapers'.[109] This condition can best be understood in the context of the method of calculating benefit and will therefore be explained in Part 3.

The income of claimants already entitled to income support will have been assessed in accordance with the rules prescribed for that system and, in their case, no further assessment is required. In other cases, the assessment is carried out by the local authority under the rules contained in the Housing Benefit (General) Regulations 1987.[110] These have been largely harmonised with the equivalent income support rules and are dealt with in detail in Part 3 of chapter 12.[111]

Part 3   Calculating entitlement

A   Applicable amount

The major defect under the original 1983 housing benefit scheme was the use of two different means tests, which resulted in different entitlements for similar households with similar income, depending upon whether or not supplementary benefit was in payment. The current scheme, as introduced in 1988, was designed to avoid these problems. Under this scheme the applicable amount is, subject to certain modifications, the same as that used for income support, so aligning the 'poverty' thresholds in the

---

104   SI 1987/1971, reg 5(8B)(c).
105   SI 1987/1971, reg 5(8B)(d).
106   DSS *Housing Benefit Guidance Manual* (1993) para A3.31.
107   SSCBA 1992, s 134(1). This represented a major departure from the principles governing the pre-1983 housing benefit scheme, which took no account of the capital resources of the claimant (and/or partner).
108   SI 1987/1971, reg 37.
109   SSCBA 1992, s 130(1)(c) and 130(3)(b). The lower threshold for the tariff income rule is £6,000 for claimants aged 60 or over.
110   SI 1987/1971, Pt VI.
111   Pp 447–459.

two schemes. If the claimant's income exceeds the applicable amount, a deduction is made from the maximum housing benefit, calculated by applying a percentage taper to the excess income.

The applicable amount is therefore made up of the same structure of personal allowances and premiums applied to different client groups (eg pensioners and disabled people) as that used in relation to income support and which is fully discussed in chapter 12.[112] There are, nevertheless, two important differences between the schemes. First, and most obviously, housing costs are not included in the applicable amount for housing benefit purposes – those included in the income support system comprise costs (notably mortgage interest payments) which are not covered by housing benefit. Secondly, the premium applied to lone parents is considerably higher under the housing benefit scheme. The explanation for the difference lies in the contrasting functions of the two schemes.[113] Income support is designed to meet the claimant's non-housing needs for food, clothing, fuel and so on; a lone parent would not expect to pay as much on these as a couple. However, to some degree at least, housing costs are independent of the size of the family and the housing needs of lone parents resemble those of a two-parent family, rather than those of a childless single person. The higher premium in the housing benefit scheme represents a compromise between the situation that would have prevailed if the income support level had been adopted and the more favourable treatment accorded to couples.[114]

B Deductions for income and the prescribed percentage tapers

The method devised for taking account of income, in relation to the applicable amount, is identical to that used for working families' tax credit[115] and, as with that scheme, is concerned to preserve work incentives, particularly for persons with low incomes.[116] Until income reaches the level of the applicable amount, or if the claimant is entitled to income support, there is no withdrawal of housing benefit and the claimant is entitled to the appropriate maximum housing benefit (subject to a deduction for non-dependants, as discussed further below). When income exceeds the applicable amount, a prescribed percentage of the excess is deducted from the maximum housing benefit.[117] The prescribed percentage has been 65 per cent since 1988.[118]

C Maximum housing benefit

The claimant's maximum housing benefit is a weekly amount comprising 100 per cent of that person's eligible rent less any deductions for non-dependants who share, or are deemed to share, these costs.[119]

---

112   Pp 444–445, above.
113   Cf SSAC *Fourth Report* (1985) para 4.21.
114   See HC Standing Committee B Debates on the Social Security Bill 1986, cols 692–695.
115   Pp 393–394, above.
116   Cf *White Paper 1985* n 34, above, para 9.25.
117   SSCBA 1992, s 130(3)(b).
118   SI 1987/1971, reg 62.
119   SI 1987/1971, reg 61(1).

i Eligible rent

Prima facie, the eligible rent comprises those payments covered by housing benefit which have been described in Part 2 of this chapter.[120] However, in many cases the whole of such payments will not be met, because either (a) they include components not covered by the scheme, or (b) the rent is restricted because eg the amount paid or the size of the accommodation in question is regarded as unreasonable.

A APPORTIONMENT OF PAYMENTS

As we have seen, only residential accommodation comes within the scheme. Hence if rent payments are for premises which consist partly of business accommodation a proportion of the payments referable to the latter will be deducted.[121] There will be analogous apportionments where more than one person is liable for the payments[122] and where the payments include ineligible service, fuel, or water and sewerage charges.[123] An ineligible service charge is one which does not have to be paid as a condition of occupying the dwelling,[124] or is excessive in relation to the service provided (in which case there is power to substitute a lower figure) or is specified as ineligible in the regulations, notably charges in respect of:[125]

- meals;
- personal laundry services;[126]
- leisure items such as sports facilities (but not a children's play area);
- cleaning of rooms and windows (other than of communal areas) except where no member of the household is able to do this;
- transport;
- furniture and household equipment which will become the claimant's property;
- an emergency alarm system unless the claimant is in supported accommodation;
- medical, nursing or other personal care;
- general counselling or support services;[127] and
- any other services 'not connected with the provision of adequate accommodation'.

Where a person's housing costs include an amount for board (whether by way of meals for the claimant or some other person) the local authority will make standard deductions

---

120 Pp 413–418, above.
121 SI 1987/1971, reg 10(4).
122 SI 1987/1971, reg 10(5). See *R v Camden London Borough Council, ex p Naghshbandi* [2001] EWHC Admin 813.
123 SI 1987/1971, reg 10(3) and Sch 1. Discretionary housing payments are not available to make good the shortfall: SI 2001/1167, reg 3(1)(b).
124 SI 1987/1971, reg 10(1)(e). In such cases where the amount of the charge is separately identified from other payments made in respect of occupation of the dwelling there is power for the appropriate authority to substitute a higher figure for an unreasonably low charge: SI 1987/1971, reg 10(3)(b)(iii) and Sch 1, para 2(1A). Again, discretionary housing payments are not available to make good the shortfall: SI 2001/1167, reg 3(1)(a).
125 SI 1987/1971, Sch 1, Pt I.
126 Charges for communal laundry facilities are eligible costs.
127 The provisions relating to service charges for general counselling and support have been subject to frequent amendment, even by the standards of social security law (see eg Social Security Act 1998, s 69 (SSA 1998)). A transitional scheme now enables payment of such service charges for claimants in supported accommodation from 2000 to 2003. From April 2003, local authorities will assume responsibility for meeting such charges. For the current definition of supported accommodation, see SI 1987/1971, Sch 1, para 7.

for the board element whatever the actual cost might be.[128] Fuel charges (eg for heating, lighting, hot water or cooking) are not eligible unless they are for communal areas.[129]

(i) General

The law relating to the restriction of rents for benefit purposes is contained in regulation 11 of the Housing Benefit (General) Regulations 1987.[130] Unfortunately, at least for the purposes of comprehensible exposition, there are two versions of regulation 11 in operation. Under the current version, which applies to all claimants with post-1996 private sector lettings, the rent officer decides the 'local reference rent', which effectively determines the eligible rent payable under the housing benefit scheme. This 'new regulation 11' was introduced with effect from 2 January 1996 and represents the then governmental response to the rapid increases in private sector rents following deregulation of the sector by HA 1988. For those exempt from these arrangements, the 'old regulation 11' continues to apply. In this latter category of cases the rent officer's determination is merely one factor that must be taken into account, giving the local authority a broader discretion.

(ii) The 'new regulation 11'

Where a local authority has received an application for housing benefit in respect of a tenancy, the authority is required to refer that tenancy to the rent officer.[131] Regulated tenancies[132] are excluded from this procedure, as are lettings by public sector landlords or registered housing associations, unless the local authority considers the accommodation to be either too large or too expensive. Upon receipt of the reference, the rent officer is required to decide whether the rent is 'significantly higher' than the landlord might reasonably be expected to obtain under the tenancy in an open market at the time of the application.[133] If the rent officer decides that the property is too expensive he or she must decide what would be an appropriate market rent for the property, making a 'significantly high rent determination'.[134] If the rent officer takes the view that the rent is *exceptionally* high (a term left undefined), he or she may also make an 'exceptionally high rent determination'. This is a determination of the highest rent that a landlord might reasonably expect to obtain on a similar property but which is not an exceptionally high rent.[135] The rent officer must also, by reference to prescribed size criteria, decide whether the dwelling is too large for the occupants at that time. If the property is considered too large, then a market rent for a property of an appropriate size must be determined, namely a 'size-related rent determination'.[136] This may cause

---

128 SI 1987/1971, Sch 1, para 1A.
129 SI 1987/1971, Sch 1, para 4. The sum deducted is normally the amount included in the rent for heating, where this is readily identifiable; in other cases a tariff of fixed deduction rates applies: para 5. For definition of fuel and communal areas, see para 7.
130 SI 1987/1971.
131 SI 1987/1971, reg 12A. Referrals are also made where there has been a 'relevant change of circumstances' (as defined in Sch 1A) or a pre-tenancy determination. See also HA 1996, s 122 and SI 1997/1984 and (for Scotland) SI 1997/1995.
132 Ie private sector lettings before 15 January 1989 and so still governed by the Rent Act 1977.
133 In making any of the determinations that follow, the rent officer must work on certain assumptions, eg excluding any ineligible service items: SI 1997/1984, Sch 1, para 7.
134 SI 1987/1971, Sch 1, para 1.
135 SI 1987/1971, Sch 1, para 3.
136 SI 1987/1971, Sch 1, para 2 and Sch 2.

difficulties for non-resident parents: their children will be assumed to be occupying the home of the parent in receipt of child benefit (typically the mother). Non-resident parents will not, therefore, be able to insist that the size-related rent determination should reflect their need for a larger property in order to accommodate their children on staying in contact.[137] The next stage is for the rent officer to specify the 'claim-related rent', which is the lowest of any of the above determinations (or, if no such determination has been made, the contractual rent).[138]

The rent officer is also required to provide the 'local reference rent' if it is exceeded by any of the determinations described above. The local reference rent is the midpoint of reasonable market rents for assured tenancies of an appropriate size for the claimant (taking into account the size criteria used in the size-related determination).[139] The local reference rent is thus closer to the median rather than the average market rent for such properties.[140] In addition, if the claimant is a single young person under the age of 25, the rent officer must determine the 'single room rent'. This represents the midpoint of reasonable market rents for accommodation in which the occupier has exclusive use of one room, but shared use of kitchen, toilet and bathroom facilities, and makes no payment for board or attendance.[141] In 1997 it was the intention of the outgoing Conservative administration to extend the single room rent restrictions to all adults, irrespective of age, but this proposal was dropped by the incoming Labour government.[142] As it stands, it operates inequitably in that it only affects private sector tenants: there is no single room rent restriction for tenants in social housing.[143]

Once the rent officer has notified the local authority of the relevant determinations, the authority must determine whether the claimant is exempt from the local reference rent rules, assuming that they would otherwise apply. (Exempt claimants are subject to the pre-1996 rules, discussed further below.) The authority then determines the 'maximum rent', being the lowest of the claim-related rent, the local reference rent and (for those aged under 25) the single room rent.[144] The maximum rent is then the ceiling on the housing benefit payable.[145] Indeed, the authority has a general discretion to reduce the eligible rent further in appropriate cases.[146] Conversely, whilst the authority has no discretion to increase the maximum rent as such, it may decide to make discretionary housing payments to assist in making up any shortfall between the contractual rent and the housing benefit payable.[147] No restriction applies for the first

---

137   Art 8 of the ECHR provides no relief in this respect: *R v Swale Borough Council, ex p Marchant* [1999] 1 FLR 1087.

138   SI 1997/1984, Sch 1, para 6.

139   SI 1997/1984, Sch 1, para 4.

140   It is not strictly the median as exceptionally high and exceptionally low rents are both excluded from the statutory equation.

141   SI 1997/1984, para 5. This provision does not apply if the young person is a housing association tenant, is aged under 22 and was previously in local authority care, is entitled to the severe disability premium or has a non-dependant living with him or her: SI 1987/1971, reg 11(3B).

142   The House of Commons Social Security Committee has recommended the abolition of the single room rent rule: *Sixth Report* (1999–2000, HC 385) paras 38–58.

143   Kemp *Housing benefit – time for reform* (1998) p 23. This assumes, however, that a single person is able to secure a one-bedroom flat from a local authority or housing association landlord.

144   SI 1987/1971, reg 11(3) and (4).

145   SI 1987/1971, reg 10(6A). Some transitional protection is available to those in continuous receipt of housing benefit (and living in the same property) since October 1997, who are entitled to half of the difference between the claim related rent and the local reference rent: SI 1997/852, reg 4. On changes to rent levels during an award, see SI 1987/1971, reg 11(6)–(6B).

146   SI 1987/1971, reg 10(6B).

147   SI 2001/1167, p 431, below.

13 weeks of an award where the claimant was able to afford the rent when the tenancy was taken on, unless he or she received housing benefit in the previous 52 weeks.[148]

The process by which rent officers make their determinations is very difficult to challenge by way of judicial review, and there is no right of appeal against any such determination.[149] It is at least arguable that these arrangements constitute a breach of article 6 of the European Convention on Human Rights (ECHR).

(iii) The 'old regulation 11'

Claimants who have been in receipt of housing benefit since 1 January 1996 and continue to occupy the same home are exempt, as are those living in exempt accommodation, such as hostels or other supervised accommodation.[150] In the case of a regulated tenancy under the Rent Act 1977, where a 'fair rent' has been set by a rent officer or rent assessment committee, the eligible rent cannot exceed the registered rent.[151] More generally, however, the old regulation 11 invests the local authority with a wide discretion, thus spawning a body of case law by way of judicial review.[152] The authority must consider first whether a claimant occupies a dwelling larger than is reasonably required by that person and others who also occupy that dwelling,[153] having regard in particular to suitable alternative accommodation occupied by a household of the same size.[154] The authority must also consider whether the rent payable is 'unreasonably high' by comparison with the rent payable in respect of suitable alternative accommodation elsewhere.[155] In making either such decision, the authority must exclude any consideration of the amount of subsidy payable.[156] When assessing a reasonable market rent for subsidy purposes,[157] the rent officer makes a comparison with rents under similar tenancies for similar dwellings in the locality, whereas the local authority must have regard to the rent payable elsewhere for suitable alternative accommodation. If, after considering the relevant matters, it appears to the local authority either that the dwelling is larger than reasonably required or that the rent is unreasonably high, it must treat the claimant's eligible rent as reduced by such amount as it considers appropriate.[158] In reaching that decision, the authority must have regard in particular to the cost of suitable alternative accommodation elsewhere.[159]

---

148 SI 1987/1971, reg 11(9)–(12). Note also the 12-month protection for the recently bereaved: reg 11(7).
149 There is, at best, a redetermination procedure.
150 SI 1995/1644, reg 10(1) and (2). Breaks of up to four weeks are disregarded (or 52 weeks for welfare to work beneficiaries). In certain circumstances exempt status can be transferred: reg 10(3)–(5).
151 SI 1987/1971, reg 11(1) before its replacement by SI 1995/1644 ('old reg 11'). Similarly, where a rent assessment committee has determined a rent under Pt I of HA 1988 the claimant's eligible rent during the 12 months immediately following the effective date of that determination is not to exceed the amount determined: old reg 11(1A).
152 The case law, much of which turns on its own facts, is summarised in *Findlay et al* n 69, above, pp 277–287.
153 Including any non-dependants and any person paying rent to the claimant.
154 Old reg 11(2)(a); the size criteria under the new reg 11 are *not* binding in this context.
155 Old reg 11(2)(c).
156 *R v Brent London Borough Council, ex p Connery* [1990] 2 All ER 353: see Partington in Buck (ed) *Judicial Review and Social Welfare* (1998) ch 8, pp 194–197.
157 See p 433, below.
158 This imports a broad discretion: see *R v City of Westminster Housing Benefit Review Board, ex p Mehanne* [2001] UKHL 11, [2001] 2 All ER 690, [2001] 1 WLR 539.
159 When determining the appropriate amount it is permissible, at this stage, to consider the consequence of any determination for housing benefit subsidy purposes: *R v Brent London Borough Council, ex p Connery* [1990] 2 All ER 353.

A common feature of these provisions is the comparison with 'suitable alternative accommodation on the market elsewhere', but this need not actually be available to the applicants.[160] In determining suitability, account must be taken of the nature of such accommodation and the facilities provided, in the light of the age and state of health of the claimant (and family).[161] Moreover, if the claimant enjoys security of tenure, other accommodation will be regarded as suitable only if it affords security which is reasonably equivalent.[162]

The regulations provide relief from the above rules in certain circumstances. Some of these reflect protection that is also available under the new regulation 11.[163] However, the old regulation 11 contains added protection for some vulnerable groups. Thus no deduction can be made in certain cases unless suitable cheaper alternative accommodation is available and the authority considers that, taking into account the relevant factors, it is reasonable to expect the claimant to move from the present accommodation.[164] The cases referred to are where the claimant, or a member of the family, or a relative of the claimant or his or her partner, who also occupies the dwelling (and who does not have a right to occupy independent of that of the claimant) is aged 60 or over or is incapable of work or is a member of the same household as a child or young person (under 19) for whom the claimant (or partner) is responsible. It will be noted that, in contrast to the general rule, the emphasis here is on both the availability of alternative accommodation and whether a move is reasonable. As regards the former, there must be evidence that suitable cheaper accommodation is more probably than not available to these applicants.[165] As to the latter, the 'relevant factors' referred to are the effects of the move on the claimant's prospects of retaining employment and the education of any children in the household.[166]

An eligible rent under the old regulation 11 will normally include any increases made to it. However, the authority has an equivalent power (whether by reference to a rent officer's housing benefit subsidy determination or otherwise) not to meet all or some of such an increase if it is considered unreasonably high compared with the level of increases for suitable alternative accommodation or, when it takes place within a year of the last increase, is 'unreasonable having regard to the length of time since that previous increase'.[167] Official guidance suggests that account should also be taken of any general increase in the level of local rents and of any improvements to the accommodation which may justify the increase.[168]

ii Deductions for non-dependants

The attribution of part of the housing costs to non-dependent members of the household has been an important feature of all the modern housing benefit schemes. The principle

---

160 *R v Housing Benefit Review Board of East Devon District Council, ex p Gibson* (1993) 25 HLR 487, CA.

161 SI 1987/1971, old reg 11(6)(a). This list is not exhaustive.

162 SI 1987/1971, old reg 11(6)(a).

163 There are parallel provisions to those under the new reg 11 to protect the recently bereaved and those cases where the claimant was able to afford the rent when the tenancy was secured: old reg 11(3A)–(5).

164 SI 1987/1971, reg 11(3). The relevant factors are those specified in reg 11(2) above.

165 Cf *R v Housing Benefit Review Board of East Devon District Council, ex p Gibson* (1993) 25 HLR 487, CA.

166 SI 1987/1971, reg 11(6)(b).

167 SI 1987/1971, reg 12(1), which remains in force for those subject to the old reg 11. But no restriction can be made within 12 months of the death of anyone who used to live in the accommodation and whose circumstances would have been taken into account in deciding whether or not to impose a restriction: reg 12(2), (3).

168 *Guidance Manual* n 106, above, para A4.125.

that such persons should help to meet the costs if they are able to do so would seem to be unchallengeable[169] but the problem of determining how much they should contribute is a delicate one. The relevant rate of the non-dependant deduction depends on that individual's circumstances.[170] For some non-dependants there is no deduction or only a modest one. For non-dependants who have a gross weekly income above a certain threshold, there are stepped increases in the rate of deduction according to the income band. Non-dependant deductions at these higher rates may extinguish any entitlement to housing benefit altogether.[171] Indeed, if the amount of contribution is disproportionately high relative to the non-dependant's income and the quality of the accommodation, this will reduce the likelihood that contributions will in fact be paid and indeed may encourage the non-dependant to move to accommodation elsewhere.[172] Moreover, criticism can be made of the fact that the assumed contributions are still not related in any way to the claimant's actual housing costs – the amount of deduction is the same whether the eligible rent is £50 or £100 per week. Not only does this seem to be inequitable on a regional basis and as between non-dependants whose accommodation differs significantly in quality; it also means that in some cases the notional contribution will bear little relation to the actual contribution. The categories of persons who are deemed to contribute to housing costs and for whom a deduction will be made are the subject of a definition common to income support and housing benefit, as are the rules governing cases exempt from deduction. This has been examined in chapter 8.[173]

D Amounts payable

On the basis of the principles discussed above, the methods of calculating the amount payable may now be restated, together with arithmetical examples, using 2002–03 figures. It should be noted that no housing benefit is payable if the amount would be less than 50 pence per week.[174]

i Income below applicable amount

For claimants in receipt of income support, or whose relevant net income is less than the appropriate applicable amount, calculation is simple: they are paid the maximum housing benefit, being 100 per cent of eligible rent less any appropriate deduction for non-dependants.[175]

(1)   C and Mrs C live with their child L aged 10, and a non-dependant M, aged 20 and earning £100 per week. C pays a rent of £80 per week and is in receipt of income support. Housing benefit payable is
£80 (eligible rent) - £17 (non-dependent deduction) = £63.

---

169   Cf *Housing Benefit Review* n 33, above, para 4.12; and SSAC *Fourth Report* (1985) para 4.47.
170   SI 1987/1971, reg 63.
171   House of Commons Social Security Committee *Sixth Report* (1999–2000, HC 385) paras 30–35.
172   *House of Commons Social Security Committee* n 171, above, para 4.52. See also SHAC *Housing Benefit: is this the promised end?* (1985) pp 17–19.
173   P 312, above.
174   SI 1987/1971, reg 64(2).
175   SSCBA 1992, s 130(3)(a) and SI 1987/1971, reg 61.

ii   Income above applicable amount

Where claimants' relevant net income exceeds the appropriate applicable amount, they are paid maximum housing benefit less 65 per cent of the amount by which their income exceeds the applicable amount.[176]

> (2)   As in (1) above but C has net earnings of £187.15 per week and Mrs C receives child benefit for L (£15.75). Thus relevant net income is £202.90 per week. The applicable amount for the family is: personal allowance for C and Mrs C (£84.65) + personal allowance for L (£33.50) + family premium (£14.75) = £132.90.
> Housing benefit is £63 – (0.65 x (£202.90 – 132.90)) = £17.50.

E   Duration of awards and the housing benefit run-on

Awards of the amounts calculated in accordance with the rules described above are payable for the 'benefit period', which is at the discretion of the local authority but which cannot exceed 60 weeks.[177] In exercising that discretion, the authority should take account of when a change of circumstances which will affect entitlement is likely to occur.[178] If, nevertheless, such a change of circumstances occurs during a benefit period, the amount can be modified or entitlement can be terminated, normally as from the date of the change or in the week following.[179] Starting work is one obvious such change in circumstances. However, since 1996 extended payments of housing benefit have been available for long-term unemployed claimants who return to work. Claimants are entitled to payment of housing benefit for a further four weeks after starting work, paid at the same rate as when they were on benefit, if they would otherwise lose their entitlement to income support or income-based jobseeker's allowance because of the new job. In order to qualify, the claimant must have been on benefit for at least 26 weeks.[180] This concession is designed to alleviate the financial pressures associated with making the transition from welfare to work.[181]

Part 4   Special cases

A   Persons from abroad

Primary legislation stipulates that a person who is subject to immigration control, within the special statutory meaning of that term[182] is not entitled to housing benefit.[183] Independently of this, the regulations provide that a 'person from abroad' who in fact

---

176   SSCBA 1992, s 130(3)(b) and SI 1987/1971, regs 61 and 62.
177   SI 1987/1971, reg 66. For proposals to modify these provisions, especially for pensioners, see *House of Commons Social Security Committee* n 171, above, paras 28–29 and DETR *The way forward for housing* (2000) paras 10.46–10.47.
178   SI 1987/1971, reg 66(2).
179   SI 1987/1971, regs 67–68.
180   SI 1987/1971, regs 62A, 69(8) and Sch 5A.
181   See Gardiner *Bridges from benefit to work* (1997).
182   See pp 232–234, above.
183   Immigration and Asylum Act 1999, s 115(1)(j). The same exclusion applies to council tax benefit: s 115(1)(k).

has a liability for rent is to be treated in law (for benefit purposes) as not being so liable (and so not entitled to housing benefit).[184] The typical 'person from abroad' is an individual who is *not* a person subject to immigration control but who fails the test for habitual residence in the UK or the Common Travel Area. The habitual residence test is the same as for income support and there are the same categories of persons who are deemed to be habitually resident (eg EU workers).[185]

B Hospital patients

Periods spent in hospital do not normally affect liability for housing costs unless they are prolonged; on the other hand, if the hospital in question provides free treatment and accommodation, the patient's other needs may be reduced. The rules have been designed accordingly.

Entitlement to housing benefit ceases after the claimant has been in hospital for more than 52 weeks, because the claimant is then not treated as occupying the dwelling as a home.[186] Of course, if the patient has a partner who continues to live in the dwelling, who is liable for the housing costs and who satisfies the other conditions, that person may be entitled to benefit. Benefit is not affected if the period spent in hospital is six weeks or less, though for this purpose (and for the other rules described in this section), two or more periods in hospital not separated by intervals exceeding 28 days are aggregated to form one period.[187]

If the claimant or partner is in hospital for a period between six and 52 weeks, the applicable amount, which represents the assumed income needs other than housing costs, is modified save where the claimant is on income support in which case housing benefit payable is unaffected.[188] The rules are identical to those used for income support and described in chapter 8.[189] However, in contrast to that system, no modifications are made for children in hospital, unless the stay exceeds 52 weeks – after such a period of absence, the child ceases to be a member of the claimant's household and no personal allowance for that child is applicable.[190] The reduction in housing benefit for hospital patients may cause hardship and could give rise to a claim for discretionary housing payments.[191]

C Residents of residential care and nursing homes

Special rules govern payments for independent residential care and nursing homes, which are not usually covered by housing benefit.[192] This exclusion dates from the introduction of the community care reforms in 1993.[193] Until 2002 the cost of

---

184 SI 1987/1971, reg 7A.
185 See pp 280–283, above.
186 SI 1987/1971, reg 5(8B) and (8C). See p 417, above.
187 SI 1987/1971, reg 18(3). However, the severe disability premium may be lost after four weeks, reflecting the rules on attendance allowance and disability living allowance for hospital in-patients.
188 SI 1987/1971, reg 18(1).
189 P 328, above.
190 SI 1987/1971, reg 15(2).
191 SI 2001/1167.
192 SI 1987/1971, regs 7(1)(k) and 8(2)(a).
193 There are, however, varying degrees of transitional protection enshrined in the regulations: SI 1987/1971, reg 7(2)–(12).

accommodation for residents excluded by these rules from housing benefit was normally met by income support for eligible claimants; under the Health and Social Care Act 2001 this is now the responsibility of local authorities.[194] Social services departments have power under Part III of the National Assistance Act of 1948 to provide residential accommodation. Persons living in such local authority homes are not entitled to housing benefit where they pay an inclusive charge for the accommodation and board.[195]

D Students

i General

Claims made by students to housing benefit under the original 1983 scheme created major administrative difficulties. Such claims could be made as many as six times per year – at the beginning and end of each vacation – and the students' circumstances might change frequently. In September 1986, reductions were made to students' entitlement to housing benefit, supplementary benefit and unemployment benefit. Housing benefit was no longer payable during the academic year for accommodation owned by an educational establishment, nor, during the summer vacation, for periods of absence from that or other accommodation exceeding a week.[196] These reforms were incorporated into the 1988 scheme. In September 1990 student grants were frozen and top-up loans were introduced for most full-time students in higher education.[197] Since then most full time-students have been excluded from housing benefit. However, complex rules remain with regard to students not so excluded. The structure of the housing benefit regulations in so far as they apply to students is that the general rules in the housing benefit scheme apply to students subject to important variations.

ii Students subject to the special rules

For the purpose of these rules, a 'student' is 'a person who is attending ... a course of study at an educational establishment'.[198] A 'course of study' covers any full-time, part-time or sandwich course, irrespective of whether a grant is paid for attendance. This should be distinguished from a 'period of study' which, for most students, runs from the beginning of the first term to the end of the final term, and thus includes the Christmas and Easter vacations but not the summer vacation.[199] In the case of students who receive a grant for the whole of the academic year (eg postgraduates and clinical medical students), it covers this period. A 'full-time student' is one following a 'full-time course of study', defined in the same way as for income support, and so retains that status until the end of the course (or the student abandons or is dismissed from the course).[200]

---

194   P 330, above.
195   SI 1987/1971, reg 8(2)(b). For persons who were living in such accommodation on 31 March 1993 the exclusion applies regardless of the position as regards board: reg 8(ZA) and (ZB).
196   See further *Housing Benefit Review* n 33, above, paras 4.6–4.9.
197   See the Education (Student Loans) Act 1990 and Harris (1991) 54 MLR 258.
198   SI 1987/1971, reg 46. The definition was extended in 1998 to include long-term unemployed people on New Deal employment-related qualifying courses. With some exceptions, the special rules also apply to a claimant whose partner is a student: reg 52.
199   SI 1987/1971, reg 46.
200   Pp 288–290.

iii Modifications to general rules of entitlement

As stated above – save in exceptional cases – since September 1990 full-time[201] students have been excluded from housing benefit by virtue of the rule that the student is to be treated as if he or she were not liable to make payments in respect of a dwelling.[202] The general exclusion does not apply to a student who falls within one of the following 'vulnerable' categories:

- a student on income support or income-based jobseeker's allowance;
- a student who is a single parent;
- a single claimant with whom a child has been boarded out by a local authority or voluntary agency;
- a student who is disabled and entitled to the disability or severe disability premium, or has been incapable of work for 28 weeks;
- deaf students who receive a disabled person's allowance as part of an educational award;
- a claimant with a full-time student partner if either is treated as responsible for a child or young person;
- a student under 19 who is not following a course of higher education; or
- a student who is a pensioner entitled to one of the pensioner premiums.

Even if the individual falls into one of these special categories of student, and so is eligible to claim, housing benefit is still not payable in two circumstances. First, outside the 'period of study' full-time students are not entitled to housing benefit for any week of absence from their home.[203] However, this does not apply if the absence was for treatment in hospital or if the main purpose of the occupation during the period of study was not to facilitate attendance at the course – in other words, there were family or other reasons for occupying the dwelling.[204] Secondly, students, whether full-time or part-time, cannot generally count as eligible housing costs payments made to their educational establishment for accommodation during the period of study.[205] Rent payable to a third party is not affected unless the arrangement was made by the educational establishment in order to attract housing benefit payments.[206]

iv Modifications to rules governing income and amounts payable

The amount of housing benefit payable to a student who (or whose partner) is in receipt of income support or income-based jobseeker's allowance remains unaffected by the special housing benefit regulations.[207] In other cases modifications are made to the rules governing eligible rent and the assessment of income.

---

201 Apart from the statement that it includes sandwich courses, this is not defined in the regulations. In cases of doubt, local authorities are expected to consult the relevant educational institution: *Guidance Manual* n 106, above, para C5.03.
202 SI 1987/1971, reg 48A.
203 SI 1987/1971, reg 48.
204 Eg because the student was living there before the course began or needs the accommodation to house children: cf *Guidance Manual* n 106, above, para C5.26. This rule also does not affect a claim made by the student's partner.
205 SI 1987/1971, reg 50(1). This does not apply if the educational establishment itself pays rent to a third party, unless the premises are held under a long tenancy or the third party was an educational authority providing the accommodation in exercise of its functions as such an authority: reg 50(2).
206 SI 1987/1971, reg 50(3).
207 SI 1987/1971, reg 51(2), Sch 3, para 10, Sch 4, para 4, and Sch 5, para 5.

A   REDUCTION OF ELIGIBLE RENT

During the period of study, the eligible rent of a full-time student is normally reduced by an amount which correlates with the 'housing' element in the former maintenance grant.[208] An exemption from the deduction is provided in some cases to avoid hardship. For example, the regulations provide that no deduction should be made where the student's relevant income for housing benefit purposes is less than the aggregate of the applicable amount and the amount of the deduction. This particular exception applies to students who are lone parents or have a partner who is not a full-time student or whose applicable amount includes a disability premium.[209]

B   INCOME

Broadly speaking, the special rules used to assess a student's income follow those adopted under the income support system and which have been described in chapter 8.[210] Special rules apply to the assessment of student loans and grants.[211]

Part 5   Discretion and controls of abuse and expenditure

In this Part we discuss the background to, and rules governing, the discretionary features in the housing benefit system, the anti-abuse provisions and the subsidy arrangements which enable central government to control expenditure.

A   Discretion

i   General

As we have already seen, the incorporation of local discretion into the national housing benefit scheme was a significant feature of its development; indeed, the ability to tailor the national scheme to local needs was part of the original rationale for conferring administrative responsibility on the local authorities. Under the original housing benefit scheme, established in 1983, there were three ways in which the calculation of benefit for standard cases (ie where there was no concurrent entitlement to supplementary benefit) formulated by legislation for the national model housing benefit scheme could be modified. First, a 'local scheme' could increase benefit for all or particular groups of claimants (typically war pensioners), provided that expenditure on such a scheme did not exceed 10 per cent of the total cost of benefit payments for standard cases.[212] Secondly, there was power to confer a higher benefit on individual claimants who were subject to 'exceptional circumstances', a phrase which was left undefined and which

---

208   SI 1987/1971, reg 51(1): but this deduction is to be abolished as from August 2002: SI 2002/1589, reg 6.
209   SI 1987/1971, reg 51(2)(c).
210   P 331, above.
211   SI 1987/1971, regs 53–60.
212   The local authority would have to bear the costs of any local scheme but assistance was available through the rate support grant.

therefore involved a very broad discretion.[213] Thirdly, local authorities might apply to the Secretary of State for permission to establish a 'high rent scheme' by showing that rents in its area were 30 per cent or more above the national average.

The first two discretionary elements were retained following the 1988 changes. The Review team's recommendation to abolish 'local schemes'[214] foundered on concerns expressed by, among others, the SSAC,[215] that this would result in significant losses to war pensioners.[216] There was a broad consensus of opinion that the power to grant extra benefit to individual claimants in exceptional circumstances should be retained and this was extended to cover all cases, including those where the claimant was also entitled to income support. The need to preserve 'high rent schemes' was obviated by changes in the method of housing benefit calculation, in particular the fact that maximum housing benefit (potentially at least) comprises 100 per cent of eligible rent.

The power to award discretionary increases for individuals in exceptional circumstances was extended in 1996 to cover cases where exceptional hardship would be caused by the imposition of the rent restriction rules. Following concerns that local authorities were not exercising their discretion to make payments in appropriate cases of 'exceptional circumstances', a new system of discretionary housing payments was introduced in July 2001.

ii Local schemes: disregard of war pensions

Section 134(8) of the Social Security Administration Act 1992 (SSAA 1992) confers a power on authorities to modify any part of the housing benefit scheme:

(a) so as to provide for disregarding, in determining a person's income ... the whole or part of any war disablement pension or war widow's pension payable to that person;

(b) to such extent in other respects as may be prescribed.

Section 134(8)(a) enables local authorities to provide for a more generous disregard of war pensions than the £10 stipulated in the national scheme.[217] The subsection requires that a discretionary modification should be adopted by a resolution of the authority. Nothing has so far been prescribed under subsection (b).

iii Discretionary housing payments

A new scheme for discretionary housing payments was established by the Child Support, Pensions and Social Security Act 2000 (CSPSSA 2000) and become operational in July 2001.[218] A local authority may make such a discretionary payment to persons who are entitled to housing benefit or council tax benefit (or to both) and who 'appear to such an authority to require some further financial assistance ... in order to meet housing

---

213 See *R v London Borough of Barnet Housing Benefit Review Board, ex p Turner* [2001] EWHC Admin 204.
214 On the grounds that these were inconsistent with the overriding aim of simplification and unification, created inequities between householders in different areas and hindered national initiatives to promote or administer the scheme more effectively: *Housing Benefit Review* n 33, above, para 4.21.
215 SSAC *Fourth Report* (1985) para 4.56.
216 *White Paper 1985* n 34, above, para 3.63.
217 SI 1987/1971, Sch 4, para 14.
218 CSPSSA 2000, ss 69 and 70 and SI 2001/1167.

costs'.[219] Such discretionary payments may not be made in a number of specified circumstances, eg where the claimant's need arises because of a liability for water rates or ineligible service charges, or because he or she has been sanctioned with one of a range of benefit penalties.[220] The most common type of case in which a discretionary payment may be sought is where the claimant's entitlement to housing benefit falls short of the contractual rent liability owing to the operation of the rent restriction rules. Other cases (eg where a claimant suffers non-payment of wages) may also arise. In any event a discretionary housing payment may not exceed the eligible rent (or council tax liability) and may be awarded for such period as the local authority deems appropriate.[221] A decision on an application for a discretionary housing payment is not a 'relevant decision' and so carries with it no right of appeal.[222] There is, however, provision for internal review – 'in such circumstances as the [the local authority] thinks fit'.[223]

B   Abuse

While fraud and other forms of abuse are problems common to most social security benefits,[224] their incidence in relation to housing benefit has been a matter of particular concern to successive governments because of the decentralised administration of the system. The control policy of local authorities varies considerably[225] and, as we have seen, in the early years some authorities sought to exploit the system themselves by eg attempting to use the subsidy arrangements to increase their own income.[226]

The scheme also contains provisions for dealing with collusive arrangements designed to attract benefit, such as a tenancy created between the claimant and a close relative. A more general problem lies in the potential for landlords to set higher rents in the knowledge that their tenants are having their rent met by housing benefit. There have long been powers to reduce or withhold benefit where the accommodation was unreasonably large or expensive[227] but there were few incentives for local authorities to use them.[228] The problem became more acute with the deregulation of tenancies in the private-rented sector by HA 1988 and the consequent increase in rent levels.[229] The then government therefore imposed additional safeguards, by means of the subsidy arrangements (outlined below) in connection with which rent officers were given a new role from April 1989. Subsequently, the Social Security Administration (Fraud) Act 1997 introduced a series of measures designed to combat social security fraud in general but housing benefit fraud in particular.[230] These included powers for the Secretary of State and local authorities to share information[231] as well as making provision for the appointment of local authority

---

219   SI 2001/1167, reg 2(1).
220   SI 2001/1167, reg 3.
221   SI 2001/1167, regs 4 and 5.
222   CSPSSA 2000, Sch 7, paras 1(2) and 6 and SI 2001/1002, reg 1(2).
223   SI 2001/1167, reg 8.
224   Cf pp 163–176, above.
225   Loveland [1987] JSWL 216 at 228.
226   P 409, above; *Housing Benefit Review* n 33, above, para 3.10; and *Green Paper 1985* n 34, above, vol 2, para 3.64.
227   P 421, above.
228   *Green Paper 1985* n 34, above, vol 2, para 3.64.
229   P 410, above.
230   P 170, above.
231   SSAA 1992, ss 122C–122E.

inspectors.[232] In addition, the Secretary of State was given extensive powers to appoint inspectors to examine the administration of housing benefit (and especially the prevention of fraud) by local authorities. The Secretary of State is empowered to issue directions to local authorities and in the last resort may require an authority to put its housing benefit work out to tender by the private sector.[233] In an attempt to tackle the problem of fraud by landlords, provision was made for landlords and their agents to be required to provide information about their property holdings and other matters.[234]

C Subsidy arrangements

i General

The government's objective for the subsidy arrangements is to provide incentives for local authorities to monitor and control costs while providing a fair level of support for expenditure which they properly incur.[235] Subsidy covers both housing benefit expenditure and administrative costs. HA 1996 substituted new powers for the subsidy provisions originally contained in SSAA 1992, bringing together the provisions relating to subsidy for both housing benefit and council tax benefit. The amount of subsidy payable to local authorities is calculated by reference to a subsidy order.[236] The subsidy may be a fixed amount or nil; in addition, the Secretary of State may deduct 'any amount which he considers it unreasonable to meet'.[237]

SSAA 1992 provides for three types of subsidy: a rent allowance subsidy, a rent rebate subsidy and a council tax benefit subsidy.[238] The rent allowance subsidy meets the cost of housing benefit in the private sector while the rent rebate subsidy meets the cost of non-housing revenue account rent rebates. Examples of expenditure met by the latter subsidy are payments made for:

- homeless people housed by the local authority in bed and breakfast accommodation;
- accommodation leased by the local authority from a private landlord; and
- accommodation that has been leased to the local authority for a period not exceeding three years when the Secretary of State has agreed to the accommodation being taken out of the authority's housing revenue account.

A separate subsidy, known as housing revenue account (HRA) subsidy, helps meet the cost of HRA rent rebate expenditure in England and Wales.[239] Local authorities are required to keep a ring-fenced HRA which covers expenditure and income in relation to their own housing stock.[240] Thus the HRA subsidy covers expenditure on rent rebates for dwellings which are accounted for in the local authority's housing revenue account

---

232 These inspectors' powers were subsequently extended by CSPSSA 2000: see now SSAA 1992, ss 109A–110A.
233 SSAA 1992, ss 139A–139H.
234 SSAA 1992, s 126A and SI 1997/2436.
235 100 HC Official Report (6th Series) col 209w. For a study highlighting the conflicts inherent in this objective see Audit Commission *Remote Control: The National Administration of Housing Benefit* (1993).
236 SSAA 1992, s 140B(1).
237 SSAA 1992, s 140B(3) and (4).
238 SSAA 1992, s 140A.
239 SSAA 1992, s 140B(2) and see the Local Government and Housing Act 1989, ss 80 and 87 and the annual Housing Revenue Account Subsidy Determination. In Scotland HRA rent rebates are covered by the SSAA 1992 subsidy.
240 Local Government and Housing Act 1989, ss 74–76. These rules can result in council tenants effectively subsidising council tax payers generally: see House of Commons Library *Research Paper 00/87* (2000).

(ie most council lettings). The subsidies under the SSAA 1992 and the HRA subsidy are both examined below.[241]

ii Housing benefit subsidy under the SSAA 1992

At present housing benefit subsidy is normally 95 per cent of expenditure by way of benefit payments,[242] though this does not cover any discretionary additions for war pensioners or individuals in 'exceptional circumstances'. Subsidies for administrative costs are met by a complex assumed workload formula which takes into account types of cases, case-load, turnover data and tenure.[243] In order to provide incentives for local authorities to tackle housing benefit fraud, full subsidies are payable on identified fraudulent overpayments.[244] As a more general means of encouraging control over excessive expenditure, the subsidy is reduced in certain situations.

iii Reduced housing benefit subsidy

A EXCESSIVE RENTS

The normal 95 per cent subsidy for housing benefit expenditure is reduced in various circumstances where the rent in question is excessive. Where the maximum rent for the purposes of housing benefit is determined under the post-1996 version of regulation 11, the rent officer's determination is also directly used to calculate the 95 per cent subsidy.[245] Thus nil subsidy is payable on any housing benefit above the maximum rent determined for a deregulated tenancy. A different mechanism applies to tenancies subject to the old regulation 11. For example, where a claimant occupies premises under a Rent Act 1977 regulated tenancy without a registered rent, and the claimant's rent exceeds that specified as the local threshold figure, then any amount of housing benefit equal to or less than that excess attracts only a 25 per cent subsidy.[246] In those cases where local authorities are unable to restrict benefit payable in this way, or where in a particular case they consider it inappropriate to reduce a person's eligible rent,[247] then 60 per cent subsidy will be payable for benefit attributable to that part of the eligible rent which is in excess of the rent officer's determination.[248]

B OVERPAYMENTS

Penalties are also incurred in cases of overpayment (except in the case of housing revenue account benefit expenditure).[249] In such cases a nil subsidy is paid if the mistake

---

241   See further Rahilly (1995) 2 JSSL 196.
242   SI 1998/562, art 13.
243   SSAA 1992, s 140B(4A)(a) and SI 1998/562, arts 12, 13 and Schs 1 and 2.
244   SSAA 1992, s 140B(4A)(b) and SI 1998/562, art 21 and Sch 5.
245   SI 1998/562, art 16 and Sch 4, para 7. On the new and old versions of the regulations, see pp 421–424, above.
246   SI 1998/562, art 16, Sch 4, para 1. The threshold is based on the average registered rent (or increase in such rent) in the relevant registration area of the authority. A subsidy of 12.5 per cent on the excess applies to non-HRA rent rebate cases in similar circumstances.
247   See p 420, above.
248   SI 1998/562, art 16 and Sch 4, para 8.
249   For HRA benefit expenditure see p 435, below.

has been made by the local authority; 25 per cent if caused by claimant error; and 95 per cent if caused by error of the Department for Work and Pensions (DWP) and the overpayment is not recovered.[250] As indicated above, the government also operates a system of fraud subsidy incentives.

C BACKDATED AWARDS

Finally, so as to discourage local authorities from accumulating arrears of liability, only a 50 per cent subsidy is payable on backdated awards.[251] Formally the subsidy consequences are irrelevant to the issue of whether good cause has been shown, but their restrictive nature can hardly encourage local authorities to view requests to backdate entitlement with sympathy.

iv Housing revenue account subsidy[252]

A GENERAL

The authority's subsidy equals its government assumed expenditure on a number of reckonable items – one of which is 100 per cent of most qualifying rent rebate expenditure, where the authority has kept to government guidelines about public sector rent increases – minus its government-assumed income (including rental income). The other items of assumed expenditure include a notional amount determined by the Secretary of State to reflect expenditure on the management and maintenance of housing revenue account dwellings and actual charges (up to a certain limit) for capital borrowing. The other items of assumed income include assumed rental income set by the Secretary of State and interest earned on capital receipts. Because qualifying rent rebate expenditure is only one element in the equation, the subsidy received by the authority may be significantly less than that expenditure.

B PENALTIES

In calculating qualifying rent rebate expenditure certain areas of expenditure are penalised, ie overpayments (except those caused by DWP local office error), backdated rent rebates, and cases where the average increase in council tenants' rents covered by housing benefit exceeds that of other council tenants' rents within the local authority's area. These areas are penalised not, as formerly, by way of reduced subsidy but by not counting as qualifying expenditure. It follows that the cost of these items is met from council tenants' rents. Authorities are compensated partially for lost subsidy on these items by a specific cash limited sum which is added to the authority's qualifying rent rebate expenditure before operating the HRA subsidy formula.

---

250   SI 1998/562, art 8.
251   SI 1998/562, art 14. Benefit can be backdated for a period not exceeding 52 weeks but only if there was 'good cause' for failure to claim in time: SI 1987/1971, reg 72(15).
252   For details see the annual Housing Revenue Account Subsidy Determination.

Part 6   Direct payment to the landlord

The amounts awarded by way of rent rebates are deducted from the claimant's liability to the local authority. The presumption is that a rent allowance is paid to the claimant[253] but, as with income support,[254] there are prescribed circumstances in which the local authority may, or must, withhold benefit and make payment directly to the third-party landlord. The original intention was that these provisions would only be used to protect potentially vulnerable people (eg from building up arrears and becoming homeless). In practice housing benefit is paid direct in 70 per cent of cases (including, of course, all public sector tenants).[255] Although convenient for local authorities and other landlords, the government has expressed concern that as a result tenants have no real stake in rent levels.[256] It has also been proposed that the availability of direct payment to private sector landlords should be dependent upon the landlord meeting acceptable standards of provision and management.[257]

Under the current rules, the authority must normally pay the rent allowance directly to the landlord where the DWP is, under equivalent powers, paying some part of the claimant's (or partner's) income support or jobseeker's allowance to that person.[258] The same applies where arrears of eight or more weeks' rent have accumulated, unless the authority decides 'that it is in the overriding interest of the claimant' that this should not be done[259] – if such a decision is made, the authority will nevertheless withhold payment.[260] Even if either of these conditions for mandatory direct payments is satisfied, the local authority must not make such payments to the landlord where it is 'not satisfied that the landlord is a fit and proper person'.[261] There is a discretion to make direct payment to the landlord where (a) the claimant requests or consents to such payment, or (b) it is determined to be 'in the interest of the claimant and his family', or (c) the claimant has moved and there are arrears of rent.[262] If the local authority is not satisfied that the landlord is a fit and proper person, it may elect not to make direct payments or may do so if satisfied that this course of action is still in the best interests of the claimant and their family.[263] Further provision is made for circumstances in which a local authority may withhold payments of housing benefit.[264] For example, where payment direct would have been made but the landlord denies access to a rent officer seeking to investigate the reasonableness of the claimant's rent and/or size of accommodation for the purposes of a subsidy related determination, payment may be withheld until the rent officer is granted access.[265]

253   SI 1987/1971, reg 92.
254   Pp 334–335, above.
255   DETR *Quality and Choice: A Decent Home for All* (2000) para 5.44.
256   *DETR* n 255, above, para 11.77.
257   *DETR* n 255, above, paras 5.44–5.45 and DETR *The way forward for housing* (2000) paras 3.10–3.11.
258   SI 1987/1971, reg 93(1)(a).
259   SI 1987/1971, reg 93(1)(b). See *R v London Borough of Haringey, ex p Ayub* (1992) 25 HLR 566.
260   SI 1987/1971, reg 95(1). Eg the tenant may be in dispute with the landlord over disrepair and be seeking to exercise the right of set-off.
261   SI 1987/1971, reg 93(3). This is an anti-abuse provision, inserted in 1997: see DSS Circular *HB/CTB 48/97*. See further SI 1987/1971, reg 95(1A), (1B), (6A) and (6B).
262   SI 1987/1971, reg 94. Where a decision is made under either reg 93 or 94, the landlord (or their agent) is a 'person affected' who has the right of appeal: CSPSSA 2000, Sch 7, para 6 and SI 2001/1002, reg 3.
263   SI 1987/1971, reg 94(1B).
264   SI 1987/1971, reg 95.
265   SI 1987/1971, reg 95(7).

Part 7   Council tax benefit

A   Council tax

As noted above,[266] the community charge, which replaced domestic rates in England and Wales from 1 April 1990, was in turn soon replaced[267] by another form of local taxation – the council tax, which came into operation on 1 April 1993. Council tax is partly a residential property tax and partly personal in nature. It is fixed each year by the local authority and will vary from authority to authority. The basic elements of the council tax are set out below.[268]

The local authority sends a council tax bill to the owner or resident of each dwelling in the area of that authority.[269] The amount of the bill depends on two factors. The first is the value of the dwelling, which will be placed in one of eight valuation bands according to its estimated market value on 1 April 1991. (The higher the band the higher the tax bill will be.[270]) The second is the number of persons over the age of 18 living in the dwelling.[271] In some cases occupied dwellings are exempt from the council tax.[272] They include halls of residence mainly occupied by students as well as any dwelling where all the residents are students (even if that dwelling is occupied only during term time). An exemption also applies in the case of certain unoccupied dwellings such as where the immediately former occupier is in prison or in detention or is receiving care in hospital, a residential care home or nursing home elsewhere.

Liability for payment of the tax is determined by reference to a rule which creates a liability hierarchy.[273] If a dwelling has only one resident that person is liable for the council tax on it but if there are two or more residents the liable person is the person who falls into the highest of the following five categories:[274]

(1) a freeholder;
(2) a leaseholder (not holding a sub-lease);
(3) a statutory or secure tenant;
(4) a contractual licensee;
(5) a resident not within categories (1) to (4) above (eg a bare licensee).

In the absence of any residents the non-resident owner is liable.[275] Two or more residents in the same category (or two or more owners where there is no resident) may be jointly liable.[276] The partner of a liable person is also jointly liable so long as he or she and the liable person are living together as a married or unmarried heterosexual couple.[277] If one of the jointly liable persons is severely mentally impaired, he or she is treated as not being jointly liable unless all other residents are also severely mentally impaired.[278]

---

266   P 411.
267   See LGFA 1992.
268   For a detailed examination of the tax see Ward and Murdie *Council Tax Handbook* (4th edn, 2000).
269   See LGFA 1992, ss 1–4.
270   Valuation is the responsibility of a listing officer appointed by the Commissioners for Inland Revenue: LGFA 1992, ss 20–25. The eight valuation bands (Bands A–H) are different for England, Wales and Scotland. Separate legislation applies in Scotland.
271   LGFA 1992, s 10.
272   LGFA 1992, s 4 and SI 1992/558.
273   LGFA 1992, s 6.
274   LGFA 1992, s 6(1), (2).
275   LGFA 1992, s 6(1)(f).
276   LGFA 1992, s 6(2).
277   LGFA 1992, s 9.
278   LGFA 1992, s 6(4). But dwellings in which all the occupants are severely mentally impaired are exempt, as now are those occupied by at least one severely mentally impaired person together with one or more students.

Owners are also liable in many cases for residential care and nursing homes as well as hostels and houses in multiple occupation (eg a house made up of bed-sits).[279] In certain circumstances owners may, if their tenancy agreement permits, recover the cost from residents by way of increased rent. In such cases residents will be able to treat the increase as 'rent' for housing benefit purposes.

The standard tax bill is set on the assumption that there are in fact two or more such adults at the dwelling. If there are no adult residents the bill is reduced by 50 per cent.[280] If there is only one adult resident the bill is reduced by 25 per cent.[281] For the purpose of these discounts certain people are disregarded when ascertaining who is a resident.[282] The categories of persons who are so disregarded include:

- people in detention (save for non-payment of council tax);
- severely mentally impaired people;
- people aged 18 in respect of whom child benefit is payable;
- students attending college or university, student nurses, apprentices or youth training trainees;
- hospital patients;
- people living in residential care and nursing homes;
- care workers; and
- residents of hostels or night shelters for the homeless.[283]

If any resident of a dwelling is substantially and permanently disabled, and the home has specially adapted facilities[284] (which are essential or of major importance) for that person, the person liable for the council tax can claim a reduction. The reduction, which has the effect of placing the property in the valuation band below the one to which the property belongs, is applied before the discounts referred to above.[285]

Although students are in principle liable for council tax they will often not have to pay the full amount. As noted above, student halls of residence are usually exempt, as well as properties where all the adults are students. Also many students liable for council tax will qualify for a discount (see above) and some may be able to claim council tax benefit (see below).

B   Council tax benefit

i   Introduction

Assistance with paying council tax is by way of council tax benefit,[286] the details of which are contained in the Council Tax Benefit (General) Regulations 1992.[287] In most respects, the Council Tax Benefit (General) Regulations are closely modelled on those for housing benefit. The benefit operates by way of a reduced liability for tax.[288] Council

---

279   LGFA 1992, s 8 and SI 1992/551.
280   LGFA 1992, s 11. In the case of dwellings in Wales, where there is no resident, a local authority may reduce the discount from 50 per cent to 25 per cent or give no discount at all: s 12.
281   LGFA 1992, s 11.
282   LGFA 1992, s 11(5) and Sch 1.
283   LGFA 1992, Sch 1 and SI 1992/548. See further SI 1992/552 and SI 1992/2942.
284   Eligible adaptations are defined by SI 1992/554, reg 3.
285   See LGFA 1992, s 13 and SI 1992/554. The dwelling must be the sole of main residence of the disabled person. Since April 2000 a discount has been available if the property is already in Band A, the lowest band: SI 1999/1004.
286   SSCBA 1992, s 131.
287   SI 1992/1814.
288   SSAA 1992, s 138(1) and SI 1992/1814, reg 77.

tax benefit comes in two forms.[289] The first, maximum council tax benefit, commonly known as 'main council tax benefit' depends on the taxpayer's own and, (if they have one), his or her partner's income and/or capital. The second, alternative, maximum council tax benefit, known as 'second adult rebate', is available only where one or more adults live in the taxpayer's home and neither share liability nor pay rent to him or her. (Their presence means that the taxpayer does not get a discount.) It is related to the income of that other adult or adults. If a claimant qualifies for both forms of benefit the local authority will award whichever amount is the greater.[290]

As in the case of housing benefit it is possible for a claimant who is in hospital to receive council tax benefit. Regulations were made in 1995 purporting to align the rules governing the effect of temporary absences from home on entitlement to both benefits, but it is far from clear that the amendments have achieved their purpose.[291]

ii Main council tax benefit

The maximum council tax benefit is 100 per cent of the claimant's net council tax liability after any applicable reductions.[292] The method of calculating main council tax benefit entitlement is also the same as for housing benefit, except that the taper is 20 per cent for those whose incomes exceed the appropriate applicable amount.[293]

When determining eligibility for main council tax benefit, the rules relating to membership of a family,[294] applicable amounts[295] and the assessment of income and capital[296] are the same as for housing benefit.[297] The upper capital limit is therefore £16,000. The rules determining the cases in which no deduction is made for a non-dependant are also the same as for housing benefit save that there is no deduction for any non-dependant on income support or income-based jobseeker's allowance regardless of his or her age.[298] (Only those under 25 are covered by the similar housing benefit rule.[299]) The regulations also stipulate that no deduction is made for a non-dependant who is disregarded for discount purposes (see above) except for students. However, a further rule provides that a deduction is never made for a person who is a full-time student for the purposes of council tax benefit law (even if working in the long vacation).[300]

The amount of the deduction for a non-dependant adult who is in full-time work with a gross weekly income of up to £131 is £2.30. The amount then increases on a sliding scale: for a gross weekly income between £131 and £224.99 it is £4.60; between £225 and £280.99 it is £5.80; and for £281 or over it is £6.95. The deduction for all

---

289 SSCBA 1992, s 131 and SI 1992/1814, Pt VI.
290 SSCBA 1992, s 131(9).
291 *Findlay et al* n 69, above, p 655.
292 SSCBA 1992, s 131(7) and SI 1992/1814, reg 51. This is in contrast to community charge benefit where the maximum entitlement was to 80 per cent of the charge liability.
293 SSCBA 1992, s 131 and SI 1992/1841, reg 53. The taper for community charge benefit was 15 per cent.
294 SI 1992/1814, regs 5–7.
295 SI 1992/1814, regs 8–10.
296 SI 1992/1814, Pt IV.
297 P 418, above.
298 SI 1992/1814, regs 3 and 52(8)(a).
299 P 425, above.
300 SI 1992/1814, reg 52(7)(c) and 52(8)(b). The definition of student is narrower in LGFA 1992 than that in the Council Tax Benefit Regulations.

other non-dependant adults is £2.30.[301] (The definitions of full-time work[302] and income are the same as for housing benefit purposes.[303])

If a claimant is jointly liable for the council tax with another person, council tax benefit is assessed on the claimant's equal share of the bill.[304] This rule does not apply in the case of a heterosexual couple because one partner claims for both on the total bill.[305] However, where a couple are jointly liable with a single person, liability is apportioned among all the liable residents but benefit entitlement is apportioned on the basis of the number of liable people – ie two-thirds for the couple and one-third for the other resident.[306] No non-dependant reductions will be made in respect of any joint owners or joint tenants.[307]

As in the case of housing benefit, main council tax benefit cannot be awarded to full-time students, save those who fall into one of the vulnerable categories.[308] The rules on the treatment of student income under council tax benefit are the same as those which apply at present in the case of housing benefit.[309]

iii   Second adult rebate

The second adult rebate is a special form of council tax benefit based on the income of any adults who live with the claimant and who receive means-tested benefits or are low earners. Second adult rebate is assessed on the claimant's total liability for council tax after any disability reduction. The rebate amounts to a reduction in the council tax liability of 25 per cent where the other resident(s) in the dwelling are in receipt of income support or income-based jobseeker's allowance. Otherwise there is a rebate of 15 per cent if the total income of all other residents is less than £131 a week and 7.5 per cent if it is £131 or more but less than £170.[310] When a claim is made for a second adult rebate the claimant's capital is ignored, unless he or she is also entitled to main council tax benefit. There is no full-time work rule for second adult rebate.[311] Second adult rebate cannot be claimed in respect of a person who is disregarded for the purposes of a discount.[312]

---

301   SI 1992/1814, reg 52.
302   SI 1992/1814, reg 4.
303   See ch 12, below.
304   SI 1992/1814, reg 51(3).
305   See p 437, above and SI 1992/1814, reg 51(4).
306   SI 1992/1814, reg 51(3). The same rule applies to second adult rebate below: SI 1992/1814, reg 54(2). There is scope for hardship here as a person who is jointly and severally liable for council tax may be pursued for the full amount due, whereas benefit is payable only in respect of his or her 'share': *Findlay et al* n 69, above, p 700.
307   SI 1992/1814, reg 3(1), (2)(d).
308   Full-time students are not excluded from claiming second adult rebates (SI 1992/1814, reg 40(1)) – as to which see below.
309   SI 1992/1814, Pt V (regs 38–50).
310   For certain disregarded income see SI 1992/1814, reg 54 and Sch 2, paras 2 and 3.
311   SI 1992/1814, Sch 5.
312   Ie in accordance with LGFA 1992, Sch 1. See SSCBA 1992, s 131(6), (7).

iv Overpayments[313]

In the case of overpayment of council tax benefit, recovery is from the claimant or the person to whom the benefit was paid.[314] Overpayments can also be recovered by deductions from a claimant's partner's benefit if the claimant and his or her partner were a couple at the time both of overpayment and of recovery.[315] The overpayment can also be recovered by increasing the claimant's outstanding tax liability.[316] If it is not recoverable by this method, the local authority can ask the DWP to make deductions from any other benefits received by the claimant, apart from guardian's allowance.[317]

v Appeals

Until July 2001 council tax benefit determinations could be challenged only through an internal review process leading to a review board. As with housing benefit, appeals relating to council tax benefit now fall within the jurisdiction of the Appeals Service tribunals.[318]

313   SI 1992/1814, Pt XI.
314   SI 1992/1814, reg 86(1).
315   SI 1992/1814, reg 86(2).
316   SI 1992/1814, reg 87.
317   SI 1992/1814, reg 91.
318   SI 1992/1814, regs 69–76; and see p 181, above.

Chapter 12

Common provisions for means-tested benefits and tax credits

In chapter 7 we considered some general principles and issues relating to the contributory and non-contributory schemes. Some of those concepts are equally relevant to the various income-related benefits and tax credits[1] (eg the notion of 'living together as husband and wife'[2]). In this chapter the focus is on the common provisions for assessing a claimant's needs and resources in the context of these benefits. As regards the assessment of needs, the basic rules have already been considered in relation to income support and income-based jobseeker's allowance in chapters 8 and 9 respectively. The principles governing the classification of individuals into family units are to a considerable extent common to all these benefits. Similarly, there is a marked overlap in the provisions for determining a claimant's applicable amount in the context of income support, income-based jobseeker's allowance, housing benefit and council tax benefit.[3] To ease exposition, however, any significant differences in the calculation of needs are discussed here in Part 1. So far as the assessment of resources, ie income and capital, is concerned, Parts 2 to 4 of this chapter are devoted principally to income support (including, for these purposes, income-based jobseeker's allowance); any significant variations within the other benefits are noted as they arise.

A major objective of the Fowler Reviews[4] was the simplification of the structure of the means-tested benefits. Previous piecemeal development had produced 'a system of bewildering complexity, with different benefit levels, different eligibility rules and different rules of assessment'.[5] The scheme introduced by the Social Security Act 1986 (SSA 1986) and now contained in the Social Security Contributions and Benefits Act 1992 (SSCBA 1992) is undoubtedly simpler in this respect, but it remains far from uncomplicated. Considerable complexities persist within the rules for the assessment of claimants' resources. Moreover, the differences between their treatment for the purposes of the various benefits are sometimes grounded more in reasons of *politics*

---

1   Ie income support, working families' tax credit, disabled person's tax credit, housing benefit and council tax benefit: SSCBA 1992, s 123(1). Properly they are all regarded as 'means-tested benefits' (or tax credits), as capital resources are also relevant, but 'income-related' is the official usage: s 123(1). Throughout this chapter, unless the context clearly indicates otherwise, the term 'benefits' includes tax credits.
2   Pp 220–223, above.
3   The applicable amount for working families' tax credit and disabled person's tax credit is a fixed amount, up-rated annually; see p 444, below.
4   Green Paper *Reform of Social Security* (1985, Cmnd 9517).
5   White Paper *Reform of Social Security* (1985, Cmnd 9691) para 1.27.

than *policy*.[6] In addition, the advent of the new tax credits raises the prospect of a greater divergence in the treatment of both capital and income for the purposes of means-tested benefits and tax credits respectively.

Part 1 General principles relating to need

A The 'family' for other income-related benefit purposes

The definition of the 'family' as the claimant, a partner of the opposite sex and any dependent children who are members of their household is common to all the income-related benefits.[7] The rules governing the meaning of 'household' and 'living together as husband and wife'[8] are likewise common to all the income-related benefits.[9] As a general principle, the entitlement of one member of the family to any one of these benefits precludes any other member being entitled to the same benefit for that period.[10] For income support, income-based jobseeker's allowance, housing benefit and council tax benefit either partner can elect to be the claimant.[11] The position with tax credits is slightly different. Either partner can claim working families' tax credit, but this then determines the method of payment. In the case of disabled person's tax credit, the claim must be made by the disabled partner.[12]

When a couple separate permanently, each may immediately claim as a single person. They will still be regarded as a couple during any temporary absences from each other. As with income support,[13] the other benefit schemes include rules which treat individuals as being, or not being, members of the same household. So for working families' tax credit and disabled person's tax credit, a claimant and his or her partner who are living apart are treated as members of the same household unless they do not intend to resume living together.[14] For both tax credits a claimant is no longer seen as a member of a couple if either partner has been in hospital for over a year, is a compulsory patient in a special hospital or is detained in custody for a sentence of at least 52 weeks.[15] Under the housing benefit scheme,[16] claimants who are temporarily away for a period of less than 13 weeks[17] may only be treated as still part of the same household if they intend to

---

6 Eg the higher capital threshold for housing benefit and council tax benefit as compared with income support and working families' tax credit, reflecting the political difficulties facing the government when the reformed housing benefit scheme was introduced in 1988.

7 SSCBA 1992, s 137.

8 Pp 220–223, above.

9 *R v Penwith District Council Housing Benefit Review Board, ex p Menear* (1991) 24 HLR 115.

10 SSCBA 1992, s 134(2).

11 However, in certain cases it may be advantageous for one partner (eg if he or she is entitled to the disability premium) to be the claimant.

12 SI 1987/1968, reg 4(2) and SSCBA 1992, s 129(1). A family credit claim usually had to be made by the female partner, but this rule was abolished when working families' tax credit was introduced in 1999.

13 Pp 291–293, above; for income-based jobseeker's allowance, see SI 1996/207, reg 78.

14 SI 1987/1973, reg 9(1); SI 1991/2887, reg 11(1).

15 SI 1987/1973, reg 9(2); SI 1991/2887, reg 11(2).

16 SI 1987/1971, reg 5(8). For council tax benefit, see SI 1992/1814, reg 4C.

17 In exceptional cases an absence of up to 52 weeks may be permitted: SI 1987/1971, reg 5(8B) and (8C) and SI 1992/1814, reg 4C(4) and (5). The absence must be continuous in order for this rule to come into operation: *R v Penwith District Council Housing Benefit Review Board, ex p Burt* (1990) 22 HLR 292.

return home, the part of the home where they usually live has not been let or sub-let and the period of absence is unlikely to exceed a year.[18]

Under the income support scheme, the test for determining whether a child or young person is part of the claimant's family turns on entitlement to child benefit.[19] The criterion for the other income-related benefits and tax credits is whether or not the child or young person is 'normally living' with the claimant.[20] In cases of difficulty, the deciding factor is who receives child benefit. As with income support, the child or young person must also be a member of the same household, but, as regards the other benefits and tax credits, the circumstances in which such a dependant is treated as *not* being a member of the claimant's household are not as extensive.[21] For income support, income-based jobseeker's allowance, housing benefit and council tax benefit a person may claim for a child until he or she is 16, or 19 if in relevant education.[22] For working families' tax credit and disabled person's tax credit, entitlement ceases if the child has left full-time non-advanced education at the date of claim.[23]

B Applicable amounts

i General

Entitlement to income support (and income-based jobseeker's allowance) is calculated by setting the claimant's 'applicable amount' against any income: if the income is less than the applicable amount, the benefit entitlement is the difference.[24] The applicable amount itself consists of a personal allowance, any applicable premiums and any relevant housing costs.[25] Housing benefit and council tax benefit use the same concept of an applicable amount, which varies according to the claimant's age and status. With these benefits, however, there is no need for a separate component for housing costs.[26] Working families' tax credit is different in that it employs a fixed applicable amount for all couples, regardless of personal circumstances.[27] Disabled person's tax credit uses two such rates, one for single people and one for couples. An applicant for tax credits whose income is less than the applicable amount receives their maximum tax credit. Claimants whose income exceeds the applicable amount receive a reduced tax credit following the application of the taper to the maximum entitlement.

18 Or, in exceptional circumstances, is unlikely substantially to exceed that period. A decision of a Northern Ireland Commissioner on the parallel provision in the income support scheme (SI 1987/1967, Sch 3, para 4(8)) suggests that the three conditions are cumulative: *R 1/91 (IS)*.
19 SI 1987/1967, reg 15. For income-based jobseeker's allowance, see SI 1996/207, reg 77.
20 SI 1987/1973, reg 7; SI 1987/1971, reg 14(1); SI 1991/2887, reg 9(1); SI 1992/1814, reg 6(1).
21 SI 1987/1967, reg 16; SI 1987/1971, reg 15; SI 1987/1973, reg 8; SI 1991/2887, reg 10; SI 1992/1814, reg 7; SI 1996/207, reg 78.
22 SI 1987/1967, reg 14; SI 1987/1971, reg 13; SI 1992/1814, reg 5; SI 1996/207, reg 76.
23 SI 1987/1973, reg 6(2); SI 1991/2887, reg 8(2). If the youngest child leaves such education, that is a ground for terminating an award of working families' tax credit (but not disabled person's tax credit): SI 1987/1973, reg 49A.
24 SSCBA 1992, s 124(4). For income-based jobseeker's allowance, see the Jobseekers Act 1995, s 4(3).
25 Pp 293–313, above.
26 On the actual assessment of entitlement to these benefits, see pp 425 and 439 respectively.
27 The applicable amount for family credit was always the same as the personal allowance for a couple under income support. This linkage was broken with the introduction of working families' tax credit: p 386, above.

ii Personal allowances and premiums

It follows from the above that personal allowances and premiums are only relevant to income support, income-based jobseeker's allowance, housing benefit and council tax benefit. The personal allowances for housing benefit and council tax benefit are the same as for income support except that single claimants aged under 25 are credited with the higher rate which exists under the income support and income-based jobseeker's allowance schemes for that age group. Single parents under 18 are entitled as of right to that same rate while single parents aged between 18 and 24 receive the full adult rate, as with income support and income-based jobseeker's allowance.[28] The lone parent premium for both housing benefit and council tax benefit is the same and is nearly half as much again as the equivalent premium under the income support and income-based jobseeker's allowance schemes. However, it too has been frozen in cash terms as part of the changes to benefits for single parents.[29] In all other respects the levels of personal allowances are common to all four schemes. The basic rules governing eligibility for these and the other premiums are almost identical for all four benefits.[30] The principal differences relate to the definition of 'non-dependant' for the purposes of entitlement to the severe disability premium.[31]

Part 2   General principles relating to resources

A The effect of income and capital

In order to calculate the weekly rate of income support, a claimant's income is deducted from the applicable amount (the aggregate of personal allowances, premiums and housing costs), as assessed under the rules discussed in chapter 8. Here we are concerned with how resources are assessed for the purposes of income support and income-based jobseeker's allowance; significant variations within the other schemes are noted as and when they occur. Sometimes, of course, claimants will be completely destitute and have no resources of any sort; in that case, benefit is calculated simply by reference to the applicable amount. In other cases, however, they will have some savings[32] and will also, or alternatively, be in receipt of other social security benefits or part-time earnings,[33] some or all of which may be deducted from the applicable amount to arrive at the sum payable.

In principle it might seem right to take account of all the claimant's assets. However, the various social assistance schemes have always wholly or partially ignored some

---

28   See generally SI 1987/1971, Sch 2, Pt I and SI 1992/1814, Sch 1, Pt I.
29   P 297, above.
30   SI 1987/1967, Sch 2; SI 1987/1971, Sch 2; SI 1992/1814, Sch 1; and SI 1996/207, Sch 1. There are slight differences, as with the variations in the rules governing entitlement to the family premium where children being looked after by a local authority come home for part of the week: contrast SI 1987/1967, regs 15(3) and 16(6) with SI 1987/1971, reg 15(5).
31   SI 1987/1967, reg 3; SI 1987/1971, reg 3; SI 1992/1814, reg 3; and SI 1996/207, reg 2.
32   In a typical week in 1995 only 734,000 out of over 5.5 million income support claimants possessed any capital, of whom just 129,000 owned in excess of £3,000 capital: DSS *Social Security Statistics 1996* (1996) Table A2.27 (the Table has been dropped from subsequent editions).
33   In February 1999, only 555,000 income support claimants received other income from outside the benefit system: DSS *Social Security Statistics 1999* (1999) Table A2.25.

resources, or 'disregarded' them, to use the term employed in the regulations. The effect of these 'disregards' is to raise the poverty line, for those people with some capital or income, above the weekly scale rates of benefit, and it is partly for this reason that these rates prove to be a misleading guide to the true extent of poverty in the country.[34] Moreover, the disregards, like the premiums, can be used to discriminate between different categories of claimant. The Department of Health and Social Security (DHSS) review of the supplementary benefits scheme published in 1978 justified the system of disregards on the basis that, in the case of capital, it encouraged saving and, as regards earnings, it encouraged self-help.[35] The review team considered that a balance had to be struck between these principles and the general policy that assistance should be directed to those who needed it most and not to those who enjoyed substantial resources of their own.

Subsequent policy discussions, notably those emanating from the Fowler Reviews, have concentrated on how this balance should best be struck. On capital, the then government concluded that the former absolute rule which deprived a claimant with assets over £3,000 of any entitlement to benefit reduced the incentive to save.[36] The income support scheme therefore ignores capital below £3,000 and has a standard upper threshold of £8,000[37] at which all entitlement ceases. Savings between the two thresholds generate a deemed capital tariff income.[38] More generous capital thresholds were subsequently introduced for income support claimants living in residential care or nursing homes and later still for those aged 60 or more. The current Labour government has announced its intention to dispense with the capital limits altogether for pensioners as part of its pension credit scheme, due to be launched in October 2003.[39]

Concern was also expressed in the Fowler Reviews that the rules under which only a small amount of earnings was disregarded discouraged people, particularly those who had received benefit for some time, from regaining contact with the labour market.[40] The result was a substantial increase in the earnings disregard applied to lone parents, disabled people and some of the long-term unemployed. However, these earnings disregards are not indexed to increases in the cost of living, with the inevitable consequence that their real value declines over time.[41]

Finally, it should be noted that since the National Assistance Act 1948, only the applicant's resources and those of any partner and dependants have been taken into account. The ability of other relatives to maintain the claimant was,[42] and remains,[43] wholly irrelevant to the computation of relevant 'resources' (now 'income').

---

34   Townsend *Poverty in the United Kingdom* (1979) p 244.
35   DHSS *Social Assistance* (1978) paras 8.9–8.10. See also Social Security Advisory Committee (SSAC) *Sixth Report* (1988) ch 3.
36   *Green Paper 1985* n 4, above, vol 2, para 2.41.
37   Originally set at £6,000, this was raised to £8,000 in 1990. Income-based jobseeker's allowance and working families' tax credit use the same limit, whereas the other three benefits have an upper threshold of £16,000.
38   P 459, below.
39   Department of Social Security (DSS) *The pension credit* (2000, Cm 4900).
40   *Green Paper 1985* n 4, above, vol 2, para 2.43; see also Lord Grabiner QC *The Informal Economy* (2000) paras 3.29–3.31.
41   See generally SSAC *In work – out of work: The role of incentives in the benefits system* The Review of Social Security, Paper 1 (1994).
42   See *R v West London Supplementary Benefits Appeal Tribunal, ex p Clarke* [1975] 3 All ER 513, [1975] 1 WLR 1396 where the claimant had been denied benefit on the ground that she had resources calculated by reference to her son-in-law's undertaking to the immigration authorities to support her. The Court of Appeal held that the son-in-law (and her son with whom she subsequently lived) did not have any obligation to look after her and therefore that their resources were irrelevant.
43   See SSCBA 1992, s 136(1).

B The distinction between income and capital

It is important for this distinction to be drawn for, as will be seen, virtually all income payments are taken into account but capital below £3,000 is wholly ignored and different rules apply to more specific disregards. There is a general (and very wide) power in SSCBA 1992 enabling income to be treated as capital and capital to be treated as income in prescribed circumstances[44] and under this a number of specific regulations have been made. But the legislation follows income tax law[45] in not drawing a *general* distinction between the two concepts. In consequence, it is sometimes for decision makers and appeal tribunals (and thereafter the courts) to determine whether a particular resource is to be regarded as income or capital. It has been held that the essence of income is an element of 'periodic recurrence',[46] but the nature of the obligation giving rise to the payment must also be taken into account. Thus a capital payment may be made in instalments and yet, subject to regulations,[47] still be treated as capital.[48]

Part 3   The assessment of the claimant's income

A   Time periods for income

Income, whether from earnings or other sources or that deemed to arise from capital between the relevant lower and upper capital limits, is calculated on a weekly basis. The regulations prescribe methods for converting income received at other intervals to weekly sums.[49]

i   Income support and income-based jobseeker's allowance

Where the amount of income fluctuates, an average is derived from a work cycle, if that exists, and, if not, normally over a period of five weeks.[50] Once a weekly figure has been arrived at, it may be important to determine the week to which it relates; eg if it is attributed to a week before that for which a claim is made, it can normally be ignored. The general rule is that the payment will be taken into account from the date on which it was *due to be paid*, rather than that on which it was actually paid.[51] While undoubtedly this may be justified on grounds of administrative convenience, it can give rise to budgeting problems and sometimes hardship where payments are late.[52] For self-employed claimants, earnings are generally averaged over a period of one year,[53] usually

---

44   SSCBA 1992, s 136(5)(c)–(d).
45   Whitehouse *Revenue Law – Principles and Practice* (19th edn, 2001) pp 46–47.
46   *R v Supplementary Benefits Commission, ex p Singer* [1973] 2 All ER 931, [1973] 1 WLR 713.
47   P 454, below.
48   *Lillystone v Supplementary Benefits Commission* (1981) 3 FLR 52.
49   SI 1987/1967, reg 32. See also SI 1987/1971, reg 25; SI 1987/1973, reg 18; SI 1991/2887, reg 20; SI 1992/1814, reg 17; and SI 1996/207, reg 97.
50   SI 1987/1967, reg 32(6) and SI 1996/207, reg 97(6).
51   SI 1987/1967, reg 31 and SI 1996/207, reg 96; see *R(SB) 33/83* and *R(IS) 3/93*.
52   If, as a result of a late payment, two payments of the same kind are received in the same week, the claimant is entitled to apply a relevant disregard to each: SI 1987/1967, reg 32(5) and SI 1996/207, reg 96(5).
53   SI 1987/1967, reg 30(1) and SI 1996/207, reg 95(1).

the last year for which accounts are available. Where the claimant has only recently set up business, or there has been a change in the normal pattern of business, a more representative period can be used.

ii   *Working families' tax credit and disabled person's tax credit*

A   EMPLOYED EARNERS

Eligibility for both tax credits is assessed on the basis of earnings over an immediate past period.[54] For those claiming working families' tax credit, the assessment period runs back from the date of claim and varies according to the basis on which wages are paid.[55] The standard assessment period is six consecutive weeks (or three fortnights) immediately before the week of claim for those paid weekly (or fortnightly). For those paid four-weekly (or monthly), the assessment period is 12 consecutive weeks (or three months). Where a claimant is paid on the basis of some other unit shorter than a month (eg daily), six such units are used. Where he or she is paid at intervals of more than a month, the whole of the previous year is used for the assessment. Any pay period in which earnings are depressed because of involvement in a trade dispute is ignored and replaced by the nearest preceding 'normal' period.[56] In addition, any periods in which earnings are 20 per cent or more above or below the average for the assessment period are disregarded, and the average must then be recalculated.[57] A special rule applies to claimants who have recently started a job, or changed their contractual hours, or resumed work after a gap of at least four weeks. If the period from that event to the date of claim is less than the relevant assessment period based on the principles above, the employer's estimate of likely earnings is conclusive.[58] These rules, introduced originally for family credit in April 1992, lack the flexibility of the earlier provisions.[59] The price for greater routinisation and reliability in decision making is a degree of rough justice,[60] which may make the precise date of claim critical.

The process for calculating normal earnings for disabled person's tax credit claimants is less mechanical, and largely follows the method used for family credit before April 1992. The basic assessment period is five consecutive weeks in the six before the date of claim for those paid weekly. For those paid monthly, the period is two months.[61] In contrast to working families' tax credit, any period in which the claimant's earnings are 'irregular or unusual' is ignored.[62] If the claimant is involved in a trade dispute, or is subject to short-time working of 13 weeks or less, an earlier assessment period is used.[63] Furthermore, where the claimant's earnings fluctuate or the usual manner of assessing

---

54   No substantive changes were made to these rules when the two tax credits replaced their predecessor benefits in October 1999.
55   SI 1987/1973, reg 14(1) and (2). Directors' earnings are assessed over the preceding year: SI 1987/1973, regs 14A and 20ZA.
56   SI 1987/1973, reg 14(3). There is special provision for commission or bonus payments: reg 14(4).
57   SI 1987/1973, reg 20(5). If this leaves no pay periods, only periods in which the claimant received no pay or pay for a longer period than the pay period are ignored. If this still leaves no pay periods at all, the employer's estimate of likely earnings is accepted.
58   Thus there is no ground for review or appeal once an award is made if the employer over-estimates the claimant's future earnings.
59   See the 3rd edition of this book, p 481.
60   Wood, Poynter, Wikeley et al *Social Security Legislation 2001* (2001) vol II, para 4.126.
61   SI 1991/2887, reg 16(1), (2) and (4).
62   SI 1991/2887, reg 19(a).
63   SI 1991/2887, reg 16(3) and (4).

earnings is unlikely to be representative, there is a residual discretion to use any other period before the date of claim which would enable normal weekly earnings to be determined more accurately.[64]

B   SELF-EMPLOYED EARNERS[65]

The standard method of assessment for both tax credits consists of the claimant's accounts for a period of at least six months (but not more than 15 months) which end within 12 months before the date of claim.[66] Failing this, the calculations are based on the six months immediately prior to the date of claim, or on the six consecutive months up to and including the second last complete month before that date. There is a residual discretion to use any other more representative period. If the claimant has been self-employed for less than seven complete months, the assessment is based on any actual earnings in the first six consecutive months and an estimate of likely earnings for the remainder of that period.[67]

iii   Housing benefit and council tax benefit

Employees' earnings are averaged out over five weeks or two months for those paid weekly and monthly respectively.[68] As with disabled person's tax credit, there is then a discretion to use a different period where a claimant's earnings fluctuate.[69] For claimants who have just started work, any initial wages are used if representative of their likely average weekly earnings; failing that, the employer's estimate is conclusive.[70] So far as the self-employed are concerned, earnings are averaged 'over such period as is appropriate', a concept left undefined except that it must not exceed one year.[71]

B   Earnings

The general principle is that, subject to certain disregards, the net earnings of the claimant and partner (if any) count in full as income.

---

64   SI 1991/2887, reg 16(5). This provision presumably applies to those paid other than weekly or monthly. For those just starting work, etc, there is a similar but not identical rule to that operating under working families' tax credit: SI 1991/2887, reg 16(7).
65   See Boden and Corden *Measuring Low Incomes: Self-employment and family credit* (1994).
66   SI 1987/1973, reg 15; SI 1991/2887, reg 17. Weeks in which no work is carried out are excluded: SI 1987/1973, reg 17 and SI 1991/2887, reg 19(b).
67   SI 1987/1973, reg 15(2). For disabled person's tax credit the assessment is simply on the likely earnings for the 26 weeks following the date of claim: SI 1991/2887, reg 17(3).
68   SI 1987/1971, reg 22(1); SI 1992/1814, reg 14(1).
69   SI 1987/1971, reg 22(1)(b); SI 1992/1814, reg 14(1)(b).
70   SI 1987/1971, reg 22(2); SI 1992/1814, reg 14(2). Both regulations include provision for cases where earnings change during a benefit period.
71   SI 1987/1971, reg 23(1); SI 1992/1814, reg 15(1). It would be usual to use the last year's trading account, but a shorter period may be appropriate, eg for a new business.

i Employed earners

For those working under a contract of employment, regard is had to the amount of 'net earnings', that is gross earnings less income tax, social security contributions and one-half of any contributions to an occupational and/or personal pension scheme.[72] For income support purposes, unlike for supplementary benefit, there is no express provision permitting deductions to be made for work-related expenses, such as travel and child-minding costs. This has been held by the European Court of Justice not to be a breach of the Equal Treatment Directive,[73] on the ground that income support is not directly concerned with any of the risks (eg unemployment) covered by the Directive.[74] The income-based jobseeker's allowance scheme likewise makes no provision for such costs, but the Court of Appeal has held that this benefit is within the scope of the Directive.[75] Quite independently, a Commissioner has held that expenses 'wholly, exclusively and necessarily incurred' in the course of the claimant's employment must be deducted in order to arrive at that person's 'earnings'.[76] Yet this decision has only limited value given the strict test applied by the Inland Revenue in deciding what are work-related expenses.[77] A special provision for housing benefit and council tax benefit enables a claimant to offset up to £94.50 per week of childcare costs for one child and up to £140 for two or more children.[78] An equivalent provision used to apply to family credit and disability working allowance, but this assistance has now been converted into a special child care tax credit for working families' tax credit and disabled person's tax credit.[79]

'Earnings' generally are taken to include:[80] bonuses; commission; retainer payments; holiday pay (unless payable four weeks after the termination of employment); payments in lieu of remuneration or notice; expenses paid by the employer 'not wholly, exclusively and necessarily incurred in the performance of the duties of employment'; awards of compensation for unfair dismissal and analogous payments ordered by an employment tribunal; and payments of compensation on termination of employment (eg ex gratia payments).[81]

The following payments do not count as 'earnings': payments in kind;[82] sick pay; maternity pay; payments for expenses 'wholly, exclusively and necessarily incurred in

---

72 SI 1987/1967, reg 36. See also SI 1987/1971, reg 29; SI 1987/1973, reg 20; SI 1991/2887, reg 22; SI 1992/1814, reg 20; and SI 1996/207, reg 99. One-half of both occupational and personal pension contributions can be deducted: *R(FC) 1/90*.

73 *Jackson v Chief Adjudication Officer* C-63, 64/91 [1993] QB 367, [1993] 3 All ER 265.

74 Council Directive (EEC) 79/7, art 3(1).

75 *Hockenjos v Secretary of State for Social Security* [2001] EWCA Civ 624, [2001] ICR 966. However, any such discrimination may be objectively justifiable, as was found to have been the case in *Meyers* (*R(FC) 2/98*); see p 394, above.

76 *R(IS) 16/93*, following *Parsons v Hogg* [1985] 2 All ER 897.

77 *Whitehouse* n 45, above, pp 141–147.

78 SI 1987/1971, regs 21 and 21A and SI 1992/1814, regs 13 and 13A.

79 P 394, above.

80 SI 1987/1967, reg 35(1) and see *R(SB) 21/86*. See also SI 1987/1971, reg 28; SI 1987/1973, reg 19; SI 1991/2887, reg 21; SI 1992/1814, reg 19; and 1996/207, reg 98. There are some minor differences; thus payments in lieu of notice or of wages count as earnings for income support purposes, but as 'other income' for working families' tax credit.

81 Redundancy payments (except to the extent that they represent loss of income) are usually treated as capital. Statutory redundancy payments are expressly excluded from the definition of earnings for the purposes of jobseeker's allowance: SI 1996/207, reg 98(2)(f).

82 Free coal provided by British Coal to its employees, former employees or their dependants is ignored as income in kind, but cash paid in lieu of coal counts as earnings or other income: *R v Doncaster Metropolitan Borough Council, ex p Boulton* (1992) 25 HLR 195.

the performance of the duties of employment'; and any occupational pension.[83] However, such payments do count as 'other income'.[84] The rules governing statutory sick or maternity pay are different for the other income-related benefits.[85] Finally, there is special provision for working families' tax credit or disabled person's tax credit claimants who receive free or subsidised accommodation from their employers: normally they are deemed to receive £12 per week in income, or the balance between £12 and the actual rent paid, if the latter is less than £12.[86]

ii Self-employed earners

The assessable income of a self-employed earner is the 'net profit' from the employment, calculated in the following way.[87] First, the claimant's gross receipts must be ascertained; these include any enterprise allowance but not, it seems, capital introduced to get a business started or to secure its continuance.[88] From this figure are deducted any expenses 'wholly and exclusively defrayed' for the purpose of the employment,[89] income tax, social security contributions and one-half of a premium in respect of a retirement annuity contract or a personal pension scheme. Expenses which have both a domestic and business use (eg telephone charges, motoring costs) may be apportioned accordingly.[90]

iii Disregards

In the working families' tax credit and disabled person's tax credit schemes the fixed applicable amounts perform the same function as formal disregards. Thus virtually all earnings are taken into account for these tax credits.[91] For the purposes of the other

---

83 SI 1987/1967, reg 35(2). See *R(IS) 6/92* on a local councillor's expenses. See also SI 1987/1971, reg 28(2); SI 1987/1973, reg 19(2); SI 1991/2887, reg 21(2); SI 1992/1814, reg 19(2); and SI 1996/207, reg 99(2).

84 SI 1987/1967, reg 40(4). As these are treated as other income, the claimant does not benefit from any disregard of earnings. However, payments for necessary expenses and income in kind are disregarded: SI 1987/1967, Sch 9, paras 3 and 21. See also SI 1987/1971, reg 33(4); SI 1987/1973, reg 24(5); SI 1991/2887, reg 27(4); SI 1992/1814, reg 24(5); and SI 1996/207, reg 103(6).

85 For working families' tax credit and disabled person's tax credit, statutory sick pay is counted as earnings but statutory maternity pay is disregarded: SI 1987/1967, regs 19(1)(g), 19(2)(d) and Sch 2, para 27; SI 1991/2887, regs 21(1)(g), 22(2)(d) and Sch 3, para 27. Both statutory sick pay and statutory maternity pay count as earnings for housing benefit and council tax benefit: SI 1987/1971, reg 28(1)(i) and SI 1992/1814, reg 19(1)(i).

86 SI 1987/1973, reg 19(3); SI 1991/2887, reg 21(3); see *R(FC) 2/90; R(FC) 1/94*.

87 SI 1987/1967, regs 37–39. See also SI 1987/1971, regs 30–32; SI 1987/1973, regs 21–23; SI 1991/2887, regs 24–26; SI 1992/1814, regs 21–23; and SI 1996/207, regs 100–102. Separate provision is made under the income support and income-based jobseeker's allowance schemes for those taking the self-employment route under the New Deal for 18 to 24-year-olds: SI 1987/1967, regs 39A–39D and SI 1996/207, regs 102A–102D.

88 *R(FC) 1/97* and *R 2/92 (FC)*.

89 This includes interest on a business loan, income spent or the repayment of capital on a loan for repairs to a business asset (unless covered by an insurance policy) and repayment of capital on a loan for replacement of equipment. The repayment of capital on other business loans as well as capital expenditure, depreciation and business entertainment expenses are not allowable: SI 1987/1967, reg 38(5), (6) and (8). In the case of child-minders, two-thirds of gross receipts are effectively attributed to expenses: SI 1987/1967, reg 38(9).

90 *R(IS) 13/91; R(FC) 1/91*. The apportionment would normally follow that accepted by the Inland Revenue: DSS *Decision Makers Guide* (DMG) (2000) vol 5, para 27194.

91 The only disregard of any importance concerns the earnings of a child or young person: SI 1987/1973, Sch 1 and SI 1991/2887, Sch 2.

four benefits, detailed provision is made for the disregard of certain earnings.[92] In the first place, final payments of earnings are disregarded[93] as are initial payments for two or four weeks for those qualifying for the lone parent or mortgage interest 'run-on' of benefit on taking up work.[94] The remaining system of earnings disregards, which applies both to employed and self-employed earners, attempts to strike a balance between the desire to encourage recipients to undertake part-time work and a concern that there should be adequate incentives for those of an appropriate age and capacity to relinquish dependence on benefit by engaging in full-time employment.[95] As such, there are three different weekly amounts for the disregard, depending on the claimant's circumstances.

The highest weekly disregard of £25 is available only to lone parents who receive housing benefit or council tax benefit (but not when also entitled to either income support or income-based jobseeker's allowance).[96] A £20 disregard is applicable where presumptively it will not constitute a disincentive for full-time employment. The situations covered for the purposes of income support include those where:[97]

(1) the claimant is a lone parent;
(2) a disability premium is applicable;[98] or
(3) a higher pensioner premium is applicable[99] *and* the claimant (or partner) has reached 60 and at least one of them is working part-time *and* immediately before reaching that age the claimant or partner was in part-time work and entitled to the £20 disregard on the basis of disability *and* the claimant (or partner) has continued in part-time work;[100] or
(4) in the case of a couple, a disability premium would be payable but for a higher pensioner premium being applicable[101] *and* the claimant (or partner) is under 60 *and* at least one of them is working part-time;[102] or
(5) in the case of a couple, both are under 60 *and* there has been continuous entitlement to income support for two years[103] *and* during that period neither has been in full-time work or full-time education or been a student for more than eight consecutive weeks; or

92 SI 1987/1967, Sch 8; SI 1987/1971, Sch 3; SI 1992/1814, Sch 3; and SI 1996/207, Sch 6.
93 SI 1987/1967, Sch 8, para 1. However, payments in lieu of notice, holiday pay or compensation payments made on termination are spread forward over the relevant number of weeks, precluding entitlement for that period: SI 1987/1967, regs 5(5), 29 and 35. Part-time workers and self-employed persons are subject to special rules: SI 1987/1967, Sch 8, paras 2–3. See similarly SI 1987/1971, Sch 3, paras 1 and 2; SI 1991/2887, Sch 3, paras 1 and 2; and SI 1996/207, Sch 6, paras 1 and 2. On the income-based jobseeker's allowance disregard for late or unpaid payments of compensation payments under the employment protection legislation, see SI 1996/207, Sch 6, para 3. There are no special rules for working families' tax credit and disabled person's tax credit.
94 SI 1987/1967, Sch 8, paras 15B–15C.
95 *White Paper 1985* n 5, above, para 3.39. See also SSAC *In work – out of work: The role of incentives in the benefits system* The Review of Social Security, Paper 1 (1994).
96 SI 1987/1971, Sch 3, para 4; SI 1992/1814, Sch 3, para 4.
97 SI 1987/1967, Sch 8, paras 4–5 and 6A–8; for income-based jobseeker's allowance, see SI 1996/207, Sch 6, paras 5–10. The clearest explanation of these tortuous rules is in *DMG* n 90, above, vol 5, paras 26096–26134. The list in the text is not exhaustive, and there are modifications for the housing benefit and council tax benefit: SI 1987/1971, Sch 3 and SI 1992/1814, Sch 3.
98 Or the premium would apply if the claimant had not been living in a residential care or nursing home or a local authority home. These deeming rules also cover cases in which the disability premium is not payable because the claimant is in hospital.
99 Or would be but for the claimant living in circumstances which prevent a disability premium being applicable.
100 Gaps in entitlement of up to eight consecutive weeks (or 12 weeks where either partner has been in full-time work) are ignored.
101 Subject to the same proviso as in n 98, above.
102 The same linking rule applies as in n 100, above.
103 Gaps in entitlement of up to eight weeks are ignored.

(6)   the claimant (or partner) qualifies for the carer's premium; or

(7)   the claimant is a part-time firefighter, member of a lifeboat crew, belongs to the Territorial Army or is an auxiliary coastguard.[104]

Only one £20 disregard can be claimed by a couple or a single claimant. In all other cases, the first £5 of weekly earnings are disregarded.[105] Where the claimant is a member of a couple, a single £10 disregard operates.[106] These disregards have remained at the same level since 1988, with the exception of the £20 disregard, which was raised from £15 in April 2001.[107]

C   Other income

Subject to disregards, all other income is taken into account.[108] This includes payments specifically excluded from the definition of earnings,[109] charitable or voluntary payments, social security benefits, capital which under the regulations is treated as income, maintenance payments and 'notional income' (eg where claimants have deliberately deprived themselves of income). The last four of these call for special discussion.

i   Social security benefits

The following benefits count in full for the purposes of all the income-related benefits and tax credits: contribution-based jobseeker's allowance, incapacity benefit, severe disablement allowance, carer's allowance, maternity allowance, bereavement benefits, retirement pensions and industrial injuries benefits.[110] Child benefit is disregarded for working families' tax credit and disabled person's tax credit, but is taken into account for the means-tested benefits. Working families' tax credit and disabled person's tax credit are ignored completely for the purposes of each other but count in full for the other benefits.[111] Guardian's allowance is disregarded for all benefits except income support and income-based jobseeker's allowance.[112]

Other benefits are disregarded in the public interest or for administrative reasons.[113] The following are therefore ignored:[114] attendance allowance; both components of disability living allowance;[115] the pensioner's Christmas bonus; social fund payments;

---

104   If the claimant earns less than £20 in one of these occupations, up to £5 of the disregard may be used against other earnings (or up to £10 for recipients of housing benefit or council tax benefit).

105   SI 1987/1967, Sch 8, para 9 and SI 1996/207, Sch 6, para 12. Note foreign earnings which cannot be transferred to the UK are wholly disregarded: see eg SI 1987/1967, Sch 8, para 11.

106   SI 1987/1967, Sch 8, para 6; SI 1987/1971, Sch 3, para 5; SI 1992/1814, Sch 3, para 5; SI 1996/207, para 11.

107   In addition, the £15 disregard for long-term unemployed non-pensioner couples was replaced in 1996 by the standard £10 disregard for all couples.

108   SI 1987/1967, reg 40(1); SI 1987/1971, reg 33; SI 1987/1973, reg 24; SI 1991/2887, reg 27; SI 1992/1814, reg 24; and SI 1996/207, reg 103(1).

109   See eg SI 1987/1967, reg 40(4).

110   Except constant attendance allowance and exceptionally severe disablement allowance. The child's special allowance and war orphan's pension also count in full. For the position as regards statutory sick pay and statutory maternity pay, see n 85, above.

111   SI 1987/1968, Sch 2, para 4; SI 1991/2887, Sch 3, para 46.

112   SI 1987/1967, reg 40; SI 1987/1971, Sch 4, para 50; SI 1987/1973, Sch 2, para 50; SI 1991/2887, Sch 3, para 48; SI 1992/1814, Sch 4, para 49; and SI 1996/207, reg 103.

113   For disregards relating to income other than earnings, see p 457, below.

114   For income support, see SI 1987/1967, Sch 9, paras 5–9, 16, 31, 33, 40–42, 47 and 52.

115   There are special rules for claimants in residential care or nursing homes: see p 703, below.

housing benefit; council tax benefit; extra-statutory payments for non-receipt of specified benefits; and certain special war widow's payments.[116] Income support itself is ignored for the purposes of the other income-related benefits. There is also a weekly disregard of £10 for war disablement and war widow's pensions, a concession now also extended to recipients of widowed mother's or bereaved parent's allowance.[117]

ii Capital treated as income

As will be seen below, most lump sum maintenance payments are considered to be income. The regulations provide for five other situations in which capital is to be treated as income under the income support scheme.[118] The first arises where capital is owed to the claimant in instalments:[119] these are treated as income if one or more outstanding instalments would take the person over the normal £8,000 capital threshold, thereby precluding entitlement to income support. The second situation is where payments are received under an annuity. The third and fourth apply to families affected by a trade dispute who receive either social services payments made under the Children Act 1989 or repayments of income tax.[120] Finally, any earnings to the extent that they are not a payment of income are none the less to be treated as income. All of these provisions apply to income-based jobseeker's allowance with the exception of refunds of income tax to those involved in trade disputes.[121] Only the first two apply to working families' tax credit and disabled person's tax credit.[122] The first two and the final categories apply to housing benefit and council tax benefit.[123]

iii Maintenance payments

A   INCOME SUPPORT AND INCOME-BASED JOBSEEKER'S ALLOWANCE

There are special rules under the income support scheme governing the treatment of payments – other than those under the Child Support Act 1991 – made by liable relatives (usually a parent or former spouse) to claimants.[124] Although of considerable complexity, their general thrust is that most such payments are regarded as income rather than capital. The provisions affect all 'payments', a term defined very widely as including sums that have not been received but would be made on application by the claimant.[125] There are, however, several exclusions from this definition, such as payments 'arising from a disposition of property made in contemplation of, or as a consequence of ... any proceedings for ... divorce',[126] school fees, payments in kind and gifts of up to £250 in

---

116   Similarly, the mobility supplement under the war pensions scheme is ignored.
117   Local authorities have a discretion to increase the level of this disregard for the purposes of housing benefit and council tax benefit: SSCBA 1992, ss 134(8) and 139(6).
118   SI 1987/1967, reg 41.
119   See *Lillystone v Supplementary Benefits Commission* (1981) 3 FLR 52.
120   In the latter instance, the refund must be received during the first 15 days of employment after a trade dispute.
121   SI 1996/207, reg 104.
122   SI 1987/1973, reg 25; SI 1991/2887, reg 28.
123   SI 1987/1971, reg 34; SI 1992/1814, reg 25.
124   SI 1987/1967, regs 25 and 54–60. For the parallel income-based jobseeker's allowance provisions, see SI 1996/207, regs 89 and 117–124.
125   SI 1987/1967, reg 54.
126   *R(SB) 1/89(T)*.

a year. A further exception applies to payments made to a third party for the claimant (or a member of that person's family) where, having regard to the purpose, amount and terms of the payment, it is unreasonable to take it into account.[127]

The treatment of maintenance payments depends on whether they are periodical payments[128] or lump sum payments. Any periodical payment (including arrears paid periodically) made by a liable relative, whether by court order or agreement, is taken into account in full as income.[129] A lump sum payment is also normally treated as income and there is a complex formula to determine the number of weeks it is deemed to cover.[130] Broadly, if the maintenance is paid for the claimant (and not just for the children) the lump sum is divided by a figure consisting of an aggregate of £2 and the amount of income support that would otherwise be paid. The number obtained will then constitute the period of weeks to which the lump sum is attributable. The formula is different for lump sums payable only for children. In such cases the lump sum is divided by the lesser of *either* the amount of income support which would otherwise be payable plus £2 *or* the sum of the claimant's personal allowances, the family premium and (if relevant) the disabled child and carer's premium. If the claimant receives a lump sum in addition to periodical payments, and it is equal to or more than the amount of income support to which otherwise he or she would be entitled, it is treated as capital.[131] Payments to immigrants by their sponsors are treated in the same way as maintenance payments.[132]

In many cases the maintenance beneficiary will elect to have their income support paid 'gross', ie with no deduction from the benefit to reflect the maintenance due. If so, the Secretary of State may collect and retain such maintenance; in addition, any such payments are disregarded in calculating the claimant's income.[133] This provision applies to both spousal and child maintenance, including child support.

Payments of child support maintenance have traditionally been regarded as income and taken fully into account on a weekly basis.[134] An assessment of child support maintenance in itself is insufficient; there must actually be a payment under the assessment before income is taken into account.[135] The cumulative effect of these rules is that claimants have had little incentive to secure maintenance orders for themselves or their children.[136] However, when the new child support scheme comes into operation income support claimants will be entitled to a £10 per week disregard on any maintenance received (somewhat confusingly called a child maintenance premium).[137] This is substantially less generous than the complete disregard of maintenance that operates for the tax credits, discussed below.

---

127   See *R(SB) 6/88*.
128   'Periodical payments' are defined very broadly: SI 1987/1967, reg 54; and see *Bolstridge v Chief Adjudication Officer* [1993] 2 FLR 657.
129   SI 1987/1967, reg 55.
130   SI 1987/1967, reg 57.
131   SI 1987/1967, reg 60.
132   Social Security Administration Act 1992, s 78(6)(c) (SSAA 1992) and SI 1987/1967, reg 54.
133   SSAA 1992, s 74A and SI 1987/1967, reg 55A.
134   SI 1987/1967, regs 25A and 60B. This is subject to the same exception for payments covered by SSAA 1992, s 74A.
135   SI 1987/1967, regs 60C and 60D(b).
136   This was undoubtedly a factor behind the introduction of the child support scheme: pp 318–324, above.
137   P 320, above. See further Wikeley [2000] 30 Fam Law 888.

B   OTHER INCOME-RELATED BENEFITS

The formal position is that regular payments of child support or other maintenance are taken into account on a weekly basis for the purposes of working families' tax credit and disabled person's tax credit.[138] Irregular payments of both child support and other maintenance should normally be assessed on the basis of the average amount paid in the 13 weeks preceding the date of claim.[139] Other maintenance payments are treated as capital.[140] However, this process is now artificial in most respects, as all forms of maintenance are disregarded in their entirety for the purposes of both tax credits.[141] This reform was introduced in October 1999, when the previous benefits were transformed into tax credits. At the same time the requirement to co-operate with the Child Support Agency was abolished for tax credit recipients.

Housing benefit and council tax benefit have no special provisions for maintenance, and so the ordinary principles apply: periodical payments count as income and lump sums as capital.[142] These two benefits retain the limited disregard for the first £15 per week of any maintenance, as was formerly the case with family credit and disability working allowance.[143] This applies whether or not the maintenance is paid under a court order. The disregard, introduced for the first time in 1992, reflects the then Conservative government's policy objectives of encouraging lone parents to combine low-paid work with an in-work benefit rather than rely solely on income support.

iv   Notional income

In certain cases account is taken of notional income in addition to, or instead of, actual income.[144] These rules are designed primarily to deal with problems of abuse or collusive behaviour.

(1)   The claimant is treated as 'possessing income of which he has deprived himself for the purpose of securing entitlement to income support or increasing the amount of that benefit'.[145] The Commissioners have held that the desire to obtain (or increase the amount of) benefit must have been a significant, though not necessarily the sole, motive for disposing of resources; mere carelessness in looking after the resources is insufficient.[146]

(2)   Income which would have been available to the claimant, if he or she had applied for it, is treated as being possessed by that person from the date when it would have been paid.[147] The impact of this provision is somewhat unclear. In theory, it could cover a wide range of public and private sources of funds to which the claimant

---

138   SI 1987/1973, reg 16(2)(a), (2A)(a); SI 1991/2887, reg 18(2)(a), (2A)(a).
139   SI 1987/1973, reg 16(2)(b), (2A)(b); SI 1991/2887, reg 18(2)(b), (2A)(b). The rules for child support are different where a maintenance assessment has been notified during this period.
140   SI 1987/1973, reg 31(6); SI 1991/2887, reg 34(6).
141   P 386, above.
142   SI 1987/1971, reg 33(1); SI 1992/1814, reg 24(1).
143   SI 1987/1971, Sch 4, para 47; SI 1992/1814, Sch 4, para 46. The disregard applies to the first £15 of maintenance received by the claimant's household; it is not £15 per beneficiary.
144   SI 1987/1967, reg 42; SI 1987/1971, reg 35; SI 1987/1973, reg 26; SI 1991/2887, reg 29; SI 1992/1814, reg 26; and SI 1996/207, reg 105. The attribution of notional income is mandatory where the conditions in the regulations are satisfied; this contrasts with the position under supplementary benefit law, where the decision maker had an overriding discretion: eg SI 1981/1527, reg 4.
145   See eg SI 1987/1967, reg 42(1).
146   *R(SB) 35/85; R(SB) 40/85; R(SB) 9/91.*
147   SI 1987/1967, reg 42(2).

potentially has access.[148] However, it does not apply to income which could have been obtained from a discretionary trust, a trust set up to provide compensation for personal injury, a personal pension scheme or retirement annuity contract (where the claimant is aged under 60), or compensation for personal injuries held in court or a rehabilitation allowance. The income support and income-based jobseeker's allowance schemes also exclude from the operation of this rule potential income in the form of jobseeker's allowance, working families' tax credit or disabled person's tax credit.

(3) Where the claimant performs a service for another person and the latter either makes no payment or else pays less remuneration than is typically earned for that work in the locality, he or she is treated as receiving such earnings as are reasonable for that employment.[149] Cases where the 'employer' has insufficient means to pay (or pay more) for the work are excluded, as is work for a voluntary or charitable organisation if it is reasonable for the claimant to provide services free of charge.[150]

(4) Payments made, eg by a relative, to a third party in respect of the food, ordinary clothing or footwear,[151] fuel or housing costs (including council tax and water charges) of the claimant (and family, if any) are treated as the claimant's income.[152]

There are three other rules attributing notional income which operate only within the income support scheme. First, payments by a third party towards the cost of residential care or nursing home fees are treated as the claimant's income.[153] The other two rules exist more for reasons of administrative convenience, where it would be difficult to determine the claimant's actual income or prove actual receipt. Thus payments due but not in fact received are treated as income.[154] This apparently harsh rule is mitigated by the fact that it does not apply to income from a discretionary trust or a trust for personal injury compensation, nor to late payments of certain specified social security benefits.[155] Occupational pensions that are not paid or are underpaid because of a shortfall in the scheme's funds are likewise excluded, as are earnings due but not paid on redundancy.[156] Similarly, claimants whose earnings cannot be ascertained at the time of the claim are deemed to receive 'such earnings as is reasonable in the circumstances of the case having regard to the number of hours worked and the earnings paid for comparable employment in the area'.[157]

v Disregards

The disregards relating to social security benefits have been considered above.[158] Some of the other disregards applied to income other than earnings are designed specifically

---

148 Official guidance suggests social security benefits, occupational pensions or councillor's attendance allowances that are unclaimed: *DMG* n 90, above, vol 5, para 28594.
149 SI 1987/1967, reg 42(6). See *R(IS) 12/92*.
150 SI 1987/1967, reg 42(6A), which also makes a limited exception for those on approved work or New Deal programmes. See *R(SB) 13/86* and *Sharrock v Chief Adjudication Officer*, reported as Appendix to *R(SB) 3/92* on the old formulation of the regulation.
151 See the definition in SI 1987/1967, reg 42(9).
152 SI 1987/1967, reg 42(4). Payments from the Macfarlane Trusts, the Independent Living Fund and analogous sources are excluded from the ambit of this provision, as are (in the case of income support) payments in kind unless the claimant is involved in a trade dispute.
153 SI 1987/1967, reg 42(4A).
154 SI 1987/1967, reg 42(3).
155 These are set out in SI 1987/491, regs 9–10.
156 SI 1987/1967, reg 42(3)–(3C) and (8A) (the pensions provision is part of the Robert Maxwell legacy).
157 SI 1987/1967, reg 42(5).
158 P 453, above.

to confer on the claimant a higher level of support than would otherwise be the case, and thus may be regarded as justified on 'public interest' grounds; others exist predominantly for administrative purposes, eg to avoid double counting. The list below, which is based on those applicable to income support,[159] is divided accordingly.

A   'PUBLIC INTEREST' DISREGARDS

The first group reflects recognition of patriotic or community efforts:
- sums payable to holders of the Victoria or George Cross and analogous payments are wholly disregarded.[160] Expenses paid to those working for charities and other volunteers are also excluded.[161]

Secondly, there are disregards intended to promote child welfare. These include:
- adoption and residence order allowances to the extent that they exceed the personal allowance (and disabled child premium, if any) for the relevant child and fostering allowances paid under the Children Act 1989.[162]

The third group serves to encourage claimants to seek training or further education, thus:
- travelling expenses, 'living away from home' allowances and training premiums received in connection with an employment training scheme are disregarded, as are job start allowances and educational maintenance allowances payable for children staying on at school beyond 16 or studying or pursuing non-advanced courses at colleges of further education.[163] Although previously directed primarily at young persons, similar disregards have now been introduced for career development loans and for various grants and payments made under a range of New Deal, training and related initiatives.[164]

A fourth group exists so that the generosity of third parties should not be nullified:
- any income in kind (unless the claimant is involved in a trade dispute); any payment from the Macfarlane Trusts, Independent Living Fund and similar funds; and the first £10 per week of regular charitable and other voluntary payments (other than a payment made by a person for the maintenance of a member of his or her family, or former family).[165]

Finally, there are a number of disregards which offer some assistance to a miscellaneous group of vulnerable people:
- a proportion of income from certain annuities purchased with a loan by persons over 65; resettlement benefits paid to certain hospital patients; cash payments by local authorities in lieu of community care services;[166] payments to assist disabled people to obtain or retain employment (other than training allowances).[167]

---

159   SI 1987/1967, Sch 9. See also SI 1987/1971, Sch 4; SI 1987/1973, Sch 2; SI 1991/2887, Sch 3; SI 1992/1814, Sch 4; and SI 1996/207, Sch 7.
160   SI 1987/1967, Sch 9, para 10.
161   SI 1987/1967, para 2. The claimant must receive no other remuneration from such work and must not be subject to the notional earnings rule. See also para 43 concerning jurors' allowances.
162   SI 1987/1967, paras 25–26. See also para 28.
163   SI 1987/1967, paras 11–14.
164   SI 1987/1967, Sch 9, paras 59–65.
165   SI 1987/1967, paras 15, 21 and 39. On the meaning of voluntary, see *R v Doncaster Borough Council, ex p Boulton* (1992) 25 HLR 195 (cash payments in lieu of coal under a concessionary scheme set up in the interest of good industrial relations were not voluntary).
166   See Community Care (Direct Payments) Act 1996 and SI 1997/734.
167   SI 1987/1967, Sch 9, paras 17, 38, 51 and 58.

B   ADMINISTRATIVE DISREGARDS

To avoid the double counting of the same amount, or so as not to defeat the effect of concessions made elsewhere, the following are among those disregarded:
*   tax paid on unearned income;
*   expenses paid to employees and volunteers;
*   income from most capital assets;[168]
*   any contribution made by a member of the claimant's household towards living and accommodation costs (where there is no contractual liability for such contribution);
*   the first £4 of equivalent payments made by a joint occupier and any payments made to the claimant which are intended as a contribution to mortgage interest, capital repayment or other housing costs which are not assessable housing costs under the regulations; and
*   income support paid to refugees; discretionary housing payments.[169]

Special rules apply to those who take in boarders, or sub-let premises. Money received in this capacity is regarded as income rather than self-employed earnings and so is not calculated on a 'net profit' basis. To make some allowance for the expenses incurred, the regulations therefore provide for the disregard of the first £20 of any weekly charge paid by boarders plus half of the remaining charge and £4 (and, on current rates, an extra £9.70 if heating costs are included in the charge) of that paid by tenants, sub-tenants or licensees.[170]

Part 4   The assessment of the claimant's capital

A   General

It will be recalled that there is no entitlement to income support if the capital of the claimant (and partner, if any) exceeds an upper threshold. The standard upper threshold is currently £8,000 for income support, income-based jobseeker's allowance and working families' tax credit, and £16,000 for disabled person's tax credit, housing benefit and council tax benefit.[171] Capital below the upper limit but above a lower threshold (currently £3,000) is deemed to give rise to a 'tariff income' of £1 per week for each complete £250 (or part thereof) exceeding that threshold[172] – so eg capital of £5,760 is treated as giving rise to weekly income of £12. The tariff income is then aggregated with assessable earnings and/or other income.

Special rules apply to claimants of income support, income-based jobseeker's allowance and housing benefit who are live permanently in a residential care home or in similar accommodation. In such cases the lower threshold is £10,000 and the upper threshold £16,000.[173] The same tariff income rule applies between these limits. Since

---

168   Though a 'tariff income' is derived from some assets; actual income from such assets is treated as capital: p 460, below. Income from property which the claimant owns but does not live in is only disregarded in some circumstances: see SI 1987/1967, Sch 9, para 22 and Sch 10, paras 1, 2 and 4.
169   SI 1987/1967, Sch 9, paras 1–3, 18–19, 22, 30, 57 and 75.
170   SI 1987/1967, Sch 9, paras 19–20.
171   SSCBA 1992, s 134(1) and SI 1987/1967, reg 45; SI 1987/1973, reg 28; SI 1991/2887, reg 31; SI 1987/1971, reg 37; and SI 1992/1814, reg 28.
172   See eg SI 1987/1967, reg 53.
173   SI 1987/1967, reg 53(1A) and (1B).

2001 special provision, albeit on a slightly less generous basis, has also been made for claimants aged 60 or over in respect of each of these benefits, as well as for council tax benefit. Pensioners claiming any of these benefits are subject to a lower threshold of £8,000 and (for income support and income-based jobseeker's allowance) an upper threshold of £12,000.[174]

There are three potential components in capital: ordinary capital such as savings or property, income which is treated as capital and 'notional capital'; these are subject to important disregards.

B   Capital resources

i   Ordinary capital

All capital[175] that is not disregarded or, under the regulations, is treated as income,[176] is valued at its current market or surrender value, less 10 per cent, if expenses would be incurred on sale, and the amount of any encumbrance (such as a mortgage) secured on the asset.[177] The question of jointly owned property causes particular difficulty. A remarkable provision deems joint owners to have an equitable tenancy in common in their capital in equal shares, irrespective of the actual beneficial ownership.[178] This rule has generated a considerable body of case law and has been redrafted on more than one occasion. The crucial issue is whether this deemed equal share is to be valued simply as the equivalent proportion of the market value of the whole, or whether the notional share has to be separately valued, reflecting the limited market for a minority holding. The decision of the Court of Appeal in *Palfrey*,[179] preferring the latter approach, has now been confirmed following the ruling by a Commissioner that subsequent amending regulations were ultra vires.[180]

ii   Income treated as capital

Under the regulations, certain forms of income are treated as capital:[181]
*   income tax refunds;
*   holiday pay which is not treated as earnings because it is paid more than four weeks after the termination of employment;
*   an advance or loan from an employer;[182]

---

174   SI 1987/1967, reg 53(1ZA). The upper threshold for housing benefit and council tax benefit remains £16,000.
175   For the distinction between 'income' and 'capital', see p 447, above.
176   P 454, above.
177   SI 1987/1967, reg 49. For the valuation of land, see *R(SB) 6/84*; of shares, *R(SB) 18/83*, *R(SB) 57/83*, *R(SB) 12/89*, *R(IS) 2/90*, *R(IS) 8/92* and *R(IS) 13/93*; and of National Savings Certificates, SI 1987/1967, reg 49(b). Unsecured debts cannot be deducted from the market value: *R(SB) 2/83*. See also SI 1987/1971, reg 41; SI 1987/1973, reg 32; SI 1991/2887, reg 35; and SI 1992/1814, reg 32.
178   SI 1987/1967, reg 52.
179   *Chief Adjudication Officer v Palfrey* (R(IS) 26/95).
180   *CIS/15936/1996*; see Wikeley [2001] 8 JSSL 95.
181   SI 1987/1967, reg 48. See also SI 1987/1971, reg 40; SI 1987/1973, reg 31; SI 1991/2887, reg 34; and SI 1992/1814, reg 31. There are some differences; thus irregular maintenance payments count as capital for the purposes of working families' tax credit and disabled person's tax credit.
182   These three provisions do not apply for the purposes of income support while the claimant is involved in a trade dispute and for the first 15 days of employment thereafter.

- irregular charitable payments;[183]
- arrears of residence order payments from a local authority;
- discharge payments received on release from prison;
- any bounty paid at intervals of at least one year in relation to certain employments (eg part-time firefighting) which attract the higher earnings disregard;[184] and
- actual income derived from savings or investments.[185]

It follows that all these types of payments are disregarded for the purposes of assessing income.[186]

iii Notional capital[187]

There are provisions analogous to those on 'notional income'[188] to deal with possible abuse or collusive behaviour.[189] In practice the most common ground relied upon is where claimants have allegedly deprived themselves of property for the purpose of obtaining benefit.[190] The word 'deprive' carries no special legal meaning here; so there is a 'deprivation' where the claimant ceases to possess the property, irrespective of the reason for so doing or whether anything has been received in return.[191] If a claimant is shown to have owned the property at some time, the onus is on that individual to show that it is no longer part of his or her actual capital. The Secretary of State must then establish that the claimant so acted 'for the purpose of securing entitlement to income support or increasing the amount of that benefit'.[192] Obtaining benefit need not be the sole or predominant motive, providing it is a 'significant operative purpose'.[193] However, it must be shown that the claimant knew of the capital limit.[194] The underlying test seems to be whether the claimant would have carried out the transaction at the time in question if there had been no effect on eligibility for benefit.[195]

The regulations also treat claimants as possessing capital representing assets which would have been available on application and capital payments to a third party used for purchasing food, clothing, fuel or housing expenditure.[196] In addition, if the claimant does not work for, but is effectively the sole owner of, or partner in, a company, whatever the value of the actual holding in the company he or she is treated as possessing the capital of the company, or (if a partner) the relevant share in the capital.[197]

---

183   The same exception as in n 182, above, applies. Payments under the Macfarlane Trusts and analogous funds are excluded for this purpose.
184   P 452, above.
185   This does not apply to income from certain disregarded property, business assets and personal injury compensation trusts.
186   See eg SI 1987/1967, Sch 9, para 32.
187   See [1994] Conv 173.
188   P 456, above.
189   SI 1987/1967, reg 51; SI 1987/1971, reg 43; SI 1987/1973, reg 34; SI 1991/2887, reg 37; and SI 1992/1814, reg 34.
190   See eg SI 1987/1967, reg 51(1) and *R(IS) 14/93*.
191   *R(SB) 38/85*; *R(SB) 40/85*.
192   SI 1987/1967, reg 51(1). This does not apply to money received for a personal injury which is put into a trust fund. Deprivation of assets under the supplementary benefit system does not count: *R(IS) 14/93*.
193   *R(SB) 40/85*, para 10; *R(SB) 9/91*.
194   *R(SB) 12/91*.
195   *Social Security Legislation 2001* n 60, above vol II, para 2.265.
196   See eg SI 1987/1967, reg 51(2)–(3). An example of the former could be money held in court which is available on application. As regards the latter, there are slight differences as between the different benefit schemes on the coverage of this provision.
197   SI 1987/1967, reg 51(4)–(5).

It would clearly be inequitable 'to fix a claimant with an amount of notional capital for eternity'.[198] The Commissioners therefore developed a diminishing capital rule whereby a claimant was assumed to draw on his or her capital for reasonable living expenses.[199] In 1990 a specific regulation was introduced to deal with this problem. It provides for the reduction of the claimant's notional capital over time by reference to the amount of benefit which would otherwise have been payable,[200] and is less generous than the approach adopted by the Commissioners.

iv Disregards

As with income, these may be categorised into public interest and administrative disregards.

A PUBLIC INTEREST DISREGARDS

The most important group of disregards protects personal possessions (unless they have been acquired to gain entitlement to, or increase the amount of, benefit)[201] and the claimant's home.[202] In addition to the value of one dwelling occupied as a home, this covers:
*   other premises acquired which the claimant intends to occupy;
*   the proceeds of the sale of a home which are intended to be used for the purchase of another home;
*   sums received, and intended to be used, for repairs, replacements, or improvements to the home (in all such cases, the relevant intention must relate to the period of six months following the receipt of the capital or such longer period as is reasonable in the circumstances);
*   sums deposited with a housing association as a condition of occupying premises as a home; and
*   refunds of tax deductions for mortgage interest repayments.
A number of disregards are intended to protect vulnerable groups or promote the welfare of children:[203]
*   arrears of certain benefits which are disregarded in calculating income (for a maximum of 12 months after their payment);
*   the value of premises wholly or partly occupied by a dependant or relative who is over 60 or incapacitated;[204]
*   rights under a trust set up to compensate for personal injury, payments under sections 17 or 24 of the Children Act 1989 (unless the claimant is involved in a trade dispute); and

---

198   *Social Security Legislation 2001* n 60, above, vol II, para 2.266.
199   *R(SB) 38/85; R(SB) 40/85; R(IS) 1/91.*
200   SI 1987/1967, reg 51A. See *R(IS) 9/92.*
201   SI 1987/1967, Sch 10, para 10. This refers only to supplementary benefit and income support; the parallel provisions for the other schemes similarly apply only to property acquired with the intention of obtaining or increasing entitlement to the particular benefit in question.
202   SI 1987/1967, paras 1–3, 5, 8–9.
203   SI 1987/1967, paras 4, 7(a), 12, 17, 22.
204   For the purposes of working families' tax credit and disabled person's tax credit the relative must have been incapacitated for at least 13 weeks: SI 1987/1973, Sch 3, para 4 and SI 1991/2887, Sch 4, para 4.

- payments from the Macfarlane Trusts, the Independent Living Fund or other specified analogous sources.

A third group serves to encourage thrift:[205]
- the surrender value of a life insurance policy;
- an occupational pension or annuity;
- reversionary or life interests in property[206]; and
- the value of a right to receive rent.

Fourthly, so as not to hinder movement in business assets, after the claimant has ceased to work as a self-employed person in a business, the value of any interest in the business is disregarded but only for such time as is reasonable to dispose of those assets.[207] Finally, the long shadow still cast by the Second World War is reflected in the special provision made to disregard payments to those who suffered as a result of enemy action.[208]

B ADMINISTRATIVE DISREGARDS

For administrative convenience or to provide coherence and/or equity between income support and other systems, the following are disregarded:[209]
- social fund payments and arrears of income-related benefits (for a maximum of 12 months after their payment);
- the capital value of the right to receive income of a kind which is disregarded; and
- capital which is treated as income (including, where the claimant's capital exceeds £8,000, outstanding instalments of capital).

Part 5   The income and capital of children and young persons

For the purpose of the rules described above, the income and capital of the claimant and partner are aggregated. One important modification to this arises in the case of a couple, where one or both members are under 18 and, because one of them is ineligible for income support under the special rules for young persons,[210] the personal allowance for the couple is that normally applicable to a single claimant.[211] In this situation, it is only the amount (if any) by which the income of the partner exceeds the difference between the relevant personal allowance for a single person and a couple, respectively, which is taken into account.[212] The treatment of resources belonging to members of the

---

205 SI 1987/1967, paras 5–6, 13–16, 23–24.
206 In *R(IS) 26/95* it was held that an interest in a freehold property which was subject to a tenancy constituted a 'reversionary interest'.
207 SI 1987/1967, para 6. There is an extra disregard for working families' tax credit and disabled person's tax credit covering proceeds of sale of business assets which are due to be reinvested within 13 weeks: SI 1987/1973, Sch 3, para 7 and SI 1991/2887, Sch 4, para 7.
208 SI 1987/1967, paras 61 (ex gratia payments to those imprisoned by the Japanese during the Second World War) and 65 (payments, other than war pensions for those who were slave labourers, etc).
209 SI 1987/1967, Sch 10, paras 7(b), 16, 18, 20–21. See also the disregard in respect of payments from the government-funded trust for those suffering from variant Creutzfeldt-Jakob disease: para 64.
210 P 284, above.
211 P 295, above.
212 SI 1987/1967, reg 23(4).

family unit[213] who are dependent children or young persons (in the discussion that follows 'child' includes 'young person') is even more complex.

A Income

The general principle is that the income of a child is aggregated with that of the claimant.[214] Thus maintenance or child support maintenance which is paid to, or for, a child counts as the claimant's income.[215] School fees paid direct to a school by a third party do not affect the claimant's income,[216] but where the child attends a residential school, payments to the school for living expenses are treated as the child's income.[217] The general principle is modified in the following circumstances. First, the earnings of a child still at school are wholly disregarded.[218] Secondly, if the child has left school but is treated as still in relevant education,[219] any earnings from his or her work[220] are taken into account subject to a £5 disregard.[221] Thirdly, if any such earnings and/or income exceed the personal allowance applied to that child (as part of the claimant's applicable amount), the excess is ignored.[222] Finally, if the child's *capital* exceeds £3,000, as will be seen, income support cannot be claimed for him or her; as a corollary, any such child's income is not aggregated with that of the claimant.[223]

B Capital

Capital belonging to a child is *not* aggregated with that of the claimant.[224] Nevertheless, if the child's capital exceeds the lower threshold (currently £3,000 where the parent is not a pensioner) no personal allowance for that child can form part of the claimant's applicable amount.[225] If the child's capital is payable in instalments, any outstanding instalments (at the date of application for income support) which, when added to the child's capital, exceed £3,000 are treated as the child's *income*.[226]

---

213 Cf p 443, above.
214 SSCBA 1992, s 136(1).
215 SI 1987/1967, regs 25 and 25A.
216 SI 1987/1967, reg 42(4)(a)(ii).
217 But only for periods when the child is present at the school: SI 1987/1967, reg 44(2). Where he or she is maintained there by a local authority, the income is calculated by a special formula: see reg 44(3). There are no special provisions for school fees in the working families' tax credit or disabled person's tax credit schemes.
218 SI 1987/1967, Sch 8, para 14.
219 Ie until the relevant terminal date: see p 660, above.
220 This must be for at least 16 hours a week: cf the definition of 'remunerative work', p 285, above.
221 SI 1987/1967, Sch 8, paras 14–15. The disregard is £20 for disabled children.
222 SI 1987/1967, reg 44(4).
223 SI 1987/1967, reg 44(5).
224 SI 1987/1967, reg 47. Any attempt by well-informed claimants to exploit this rule by transferring their own capital to their children would be thwarted by the 'notional capital' regulation, p 461, above.
225 SI 1987/1967, reg 17(1)(b). Similarly, no child credit is payable for working families' tax credit purposes: SI 1987/1973, reg 46(4).
226 SI 1987/1967, reg 44(1).

Chapter 13

The social fund

Part 1   Introduction

A   General

In the context of overall public expenditure on benefits, the social fund is of no practical significance. Net expenditure on the fund, excluding winter fuel payments, accounts for just 0.27 per cent of all social security spending, and is equivalent to only 2 per cent of the income support budget.[1] Yet its importance is that it 'places resource allocation decisions right at the centre of a policy area which has hitherto primarily been demand-led'.[2] The main part of the social fund provides discretionary grants and loans to income support claimants for one-off needs. Loans may also be made to anyone facing an immediate financial crisis. All these payments are subject to budgetary control. In addition, there are payments from the regulated social fund, which is not subject to direct financial capping, for Sure Start Maternity Grants, funeral payments, cold weather payments and winter fuel payments.

The history of provision for those one-off needs which cannot be met out of weekly benefit has suffered over the last 25 years from 'the windscreen wiper approach to social policy'.[3] Before 1980, exceptional needs payments (in the form of grants) were made under the former supplementary benefits scheme at the discretion of local office staff in an entirely demand-led system. Between 1980 and 1988 discretion was abandoned and claimants were entitled to single payments providing that they satisfied complex criteria laid down in regulations. Some of the most forthright criticisms of the supplementary benefit scheme made in the Fowler Reviews[4] were directed against this system of single payments.[5] For example, the highly detailed rules were little understood by claimants and led to undue legalism. Similar criticisms were levelled against the system of urgent needs payments which provided emergency relief for some claimants, including those otherwise not entitled to supplementary benefit.[6]

---

1   Calculated on the basis of statistics in Department for Work and Pensions (DWP) *DWP Departmental Report* (2002, Cm 5424) p 103.
2   Walker and Lawton (1989) 67 Public Administration 295 at 312.
3   Berthoud (1991) 12 Policy Studies 4 at 16. See further Buck *The Social Fund – Law and Practice* (2nd edn, 2000) ch 1.
4   Green Paper *Reform of Social Security* (1985, Cmnd 9517).
5   Pp 276–277, above.
6   *Green Paper 1985* n 4, above, vol 2, para 2.67, and see p 313 above.

The Green Paper of 1985 argued that the high degree of 'fine-tuning' required for single (and urgent needs) payments obscured and hindered the main purpose of supplementary benefit, which was the provision of regular weekly income.[7] While there would always be some people who would face particular difficulties and special needs which could not be met by normal weekly payments, a new system should be devised to cope with them. Through employing specialist officers to make discretionary decisions with the minimum of formality, and co-ordinating with social services, health authorities and voluntary agencies, this would offer greater flexibility in responding to individual financial problems and adapting to changes in need.[8] The new fund was to be subject to a fixed budget so that spending might be monitored and decisions taken on priorities within available resources.[9] Financial constraint would be further facilitated by the fact that, apart from the meeting of maternity and funeral expenses and grants to support community care, payments would normally take the form of repayable loans.[10] Finally, concern that the system should operate quickly and effectively on the basis of knowledge and experience of local circumstances, combined with a desire to avoid legalism, led to a further proposal that the formal system of external adjudication and review used for other areas of social security should not apply.[11]

Not surprisingly, these proposals generated a considerable amount of criticism from both pressure groups[12] and academic commentators.[13] In addition, 'official' bodies, such as the Social Security Advisory Committee[14] (SSAC) and the Council on Tribunals[15] protested vigorously against the plan to dispense with the independent review of decisions.[16] Prior to, and during, the passage of the Social Security Bill 1986, the government attempted to meet some of these criticisms. A draft Social Fund Manual was published, indicating in detail how the system would work.[17] There would be a system of internal review by social fund inspectors who would be appointed by an independent Social Fund Commissioner. The function of the latter would be in no way equivalent to that of the Social Security Commissioners since he or she would be confined to general guidance on decision-making and the training of inspectors and would have no power to alter individual decisions.[18] Subsequently, the operation of the budgetary system was clarified:[19] it would be based partly on previous expenditure on single payments in the area and partly on other estimates of need;[20] and information on each office's budget would be made publicly

---

7   *Green Paper 1985* n 4, above, vol 1, para 9.3; and see White Paper *Reform of Social Security* (1985, Cmnd 9691) paras 4.4–4.5.

8   *White Paper 1985* n 7, above, paras 4.9–4.11. For an early criticism that this goal was illusory, see Drabble and Lynes [1989] PL 297.

9   *White Paper 1985* n 7, above, para 4.38. The idea of a ceiling on spending had been suggested by the Supplementary Benefits Commission but had been rejected as impracticable by the subsequent departmental review: see *Report of the SBC for 1976* (1977, Cmnd 6910) p 116; and DHSS *Social Assistance* (1978) pp 82–85.

10   *White Paper 1985* n 7, above, para 4.25. Under the supplementary benefit system, this method of assistance had normally been used only for urgent needs cases: see the 2nd edition of this book, p 497.

11   *Green Paper 1985* n 4, above, vol 2, para 2.110; *White Paper 1985* n 7, above, para 4.50.

12   See eg CPAG *Burying Beveridge* (1985).

13   See Bradshaw in Brenton and Ungerson (eds) *Yearbook of Social Policy 1986–87* (1987); Mullen (1989) 52 MLR 64; Mesher in Freeman (ed) *Critical Issues in Welfare Law* (1990); Berthoud (1991) 12 Policy Studies 4. See further the 4th edition of this book, p 595.

14   SSAC *Fourth Report* (1985) p 83.

15   *Social Security: Abolition of Independent Appeals under the proposed Social Fund* (1986, Cmnd 9722).

16   See generally Bolderson (1988) 15 JLS 279.

17   Cf Lister and Lakhani *A Great Retreat in Fairness: a critique of the draft social fund manual* (1987).

18   'The Commissioner is no more than fig-leaf, inserted into the Bill at the last minute to present the inspectors as in some sense independent and thereby head off demands for a proper independent right of appeal': Social Security Consortium *Of Little Benefit* (1986) p 14; and see pp 180–181, above.

19   122 HC Official Report (6th series) written answer col 443.

20   See Walker and Lawton (1988) 17 J Soc Pol 437; and Huby and Walker (1991) 19 Policy and Politics 87.

available. Further, there would be a reserve fund to meet exceptional circumstances, such as a local emergency. Finally, a regulation-based system and the traditional social security adjudication arrangements would be preserved for maternity and funeral expenses.

Since its inception the social fund has been the subject of a considerable research effort.[21] If the purpose of the social fund was to reduce and control spending, then it has undoubtedly been a success.[22] In other respects, however, many of the early criticisms have proven to be well-founded. The most comprehensive empirical study to date concluded that there is no evidence that successful applicants are in greater general need than those who are refused.[23] It also demonstrated that staff often reach different conclusions on the same applications when working in isolation from each other,[24] and that the removal of budget constraints would increase spending on both loans and grants.[25] Moreover, the discretionary nature of the social fund, combined with the effect of the budget and recovery work, make the scheme highly labour intensive: in 1998–99, social fund administration costs accounted for 19.3 per cent of benefit expenditure, nearly twice that of any other benefit.[26] Ten years ago the SSAC put forward detailed proposals for reform, including the relaxation of the strict budgetary criteria and the provision of mandatory non-repayable grants in limited circumstances, based on the currently discretionary community care grants.[27] These recommendations were not implemented. More recently, the Social Security Select Committee has published a highly critical report on the operation of the social fund, arguing that it needs 'urgent overhaul and an injection of funds' if it is to achieve its social policy objectives.[28]

From the outset, the element of discretion in the discretionary social fund has always been constrained by the operation of the budgetary controls. However, in recent years two major developments have marked a fundamental move away from the deployment of discretion as part of the conceptual underpinning of the scheme. First, in 1997 the new Labour government introduced winter fuel payments as part of the social fund. Today these effectively constitute a universal benefit for pensioners, irrespective of their means.[29] Consequently, expenditure on winter fuel payments dwarfs the net outlay on other social fund payments. In 2002–03 it was projected that the net cost of the former would be £1.7 *billion*, equivalent to 12 per cent of the total income support budget, as compared with just £351 *million* on the rest of the social fund.[30] Secondly, changes made by the Social Security Act 1998 (SSA 1998) have reduced such flexibility as previously existed under the discretionary social fund. Applicants must now specify in advance the type of payment for which they are applying. In addition, decision making on applications for budgetary loans is now automated, based on point-scoring applications according to pre-determined objective criteria.[31] The scope for the use of discretion, in the sense of the exercise of individual judgment, is hence severely curtailed.

---

21 See esp Walker, Dix and Huby *Working the Social Fund* Department of Social Security (DSS) Research Report No 8 (1992); and Huby and Dix *Evaluating the Social Fund* DSS Research Report No 9 (1992). See further *Buck* n 3, above, ch 7.
22 Berthoud (1991) Policy Studies 4 at 9; and *Drabble and Lynes* n 8, above, at 322.
23 *Huby and Dix*, n 21, above, p 127 and also pp 76–85 and 110–123.
24 *Huby and Dix*, n 21, above, pp 89–92. See also Dalley and Berthoud *Challenging Discretion* (1992) pp 111–116.
25 *Huby and Dix*, n 21, above, pp 94–95.
26 DSS *Social Security Departmental Report* (2000, Cm 4614) p 88. The true figure is arguably higher: the total expenditure figure cited includes both net expenditure and loan recoveries.
27 SSAC *The Social Fund – A New Structure* (1992) paras 28 and 35.
28 HC Social Security Committee *Third Report* (2000–01, HC 232) para 118; see also the government's reply (2001, Cm 5237).
29 Pp 493–494, below.
30 *DWP* n 1, above, p 102.
31 See Thompson (2000) 7 JSSL 35.

B   The structure of the social fund

The legislative framework for the social fund is now to be found in the Social Security Contributions and Benefits Act 1992 (SSCBA 1992),[32] the Social Security Administration Act 1992 (SSAA 1992)[33] and SSA 1998.[34] Here we outline the main features of the two sharply contrasting parts of the social fund, the discretionary and non-discretionary elements (examined in detail in Parts 2 and 3 respectively) and consider the role of the budget.

i   The discretionary social fund

The discretionary part of the social fund became operative in April 1988. Decisions whether to make an award and, if so, how much, are made by 'appropriate officers'[35] and are subject only to an internal administrative review by the same officer and his or her immediate superior and, following a further application by the claimant, a social fund inspector.[36] Apart from the prospect of any such review, there are three principal constraints on the officer's exercise of discretion in relation to all such 'discretionary decisions'. First, the legislation specifies certain factors to which regard must be had; secondly, determinations must be in accordance with any general directions issued by the Secretary of State; and, thirdly, they must take account of any general guidance issued by the minister or guidance for a particular area issued by a nominated appropriate officer in the local office.[37] These local office lists add to the highly rule-bound nature of what is supposedly a discretionary scheme.[38] The theory, however, is that *directions* of the Secretary of State are legally binding on officers (and inspectors) but *guidance* 'cannot be expected to cover every contingency that will arise and the absence of guidance on a particular situation does not mean that help must be refused'.[39] In practice, however, the discretion of officers in making decisions has been highly circumscribed by these considerations from the outset. Furthermore, the arrangements for determining eligibility for budgeting loans were radically transformed by SSA 1998. This has facilitated the introduction of automated decision making based on proxy indicators of need for this type of loan, thus further marginalising the role of discretion in purportedly discretionary social fund determinations.

The concept of legally binding directions was a novel feature of the social fund,[40] and the Court of Appeal has expressed its surprise at the extent of the powers granted to the Secretary of State.[41] The courts have none the less held in a series of decisions[42]

---

32   SSCBA 1992, ss 138–140 (eligibility), as amended by SSA 1998, ss 70 and 71.
33   SSAA 1992, ss 167–169 (finance).
34   SSA 1998, ss 36–38 (decision making).
35   SSCBA 1992, s 139 and SSA 1998, s 36 (formerly known as social fund officers).
36   SSA 1998, s 37. The only route thereafter is to apply to the courts for judicial review: see p 211, above.
37   SSCBA 1992, s 140 and SSA 1998, s 36.
38   *Walker, Dix and Huby* n 21, above, pp 17 and 25.
39   DSS *Social Fund Officer's Guide* (1999) para 1051.
40   As Drabble and Lynes remark, n 8, above, at 304–309, there was no reason in principle why directions could not have been drafted as regulations.
41   'It may be an unwelcome feature of a dominating executive in a basically two-party democracy': per Purchas LJ in *R v Secretary of State for Social Services and the Social Fund Inspectors, ex p Stitt, Sherwin and Roberts* [1991] COD 68. See Feldman (1991) 107 LQR 39.
42   *R v Social Fund Inspector, ex p Sherwin* [1991] COD 68; *R v Secretary of State for Social Security, ex p Healey, Stitt (No 2) and Ellison* [1992] COD 335, CA.

that the directions should be interpreted in a 'commonsense' manner, which, as shall be seen, is a decidedly problematic concept. The Secretary of State's directions and guidance are both contained in the Social Fund Guide (referred to as 'the Guide').[43]

Initially the types of payment to be made were specified by the Secretary of State in directions, but they are now set out in the primary legislation as budgeting loans, crisis loans and community care grants.[44] Since SSA 1998 it has been necessary for an applicant to make an application for a specified type of payment, rather than to the fund as a whole. It is therefore possible that an individual may apply for a repayable budgeting loan when he or she might be eligible for a non-repayable community care grant.[45]

ii The social fund budget

Payments into the social fund are determined by the Secretary of State with the approval of the Treasury from money voted by Parliament.[46] Each local office receives an allocation from the annual national budget for, respectively, community care grants and loans.[47] In addition, there are contingency arrangements which allow for totally unexpected increases in expenditure, such as a local disaster.[48] In April 2000 the discretionary social fund stood at £596 million, of which £494 million was for loans, £100 million for community care grants and the balance for contingencies.[49] The recovery of loans now provides over 90 per cent of the gross loans budget,[50] so applicants are themselves effectively providing the funds for further loans to other claimants.

At first the legislation simply provided for the budget to be one of the factors to which officers were to have regard,[51] although the guidance originally stipulated that payments must not exceed the annual budget allocations.[52] The Divisional Court held that this advice was too prescriptive to qualify as guidance and so was ultra vires.[53] Amending legislation subsequently empowered the Secretary of State to issue directions requiring officers to keep within the local budget.[54] It is the responsibility of appropriate officers, in processing claims, to determine priority as between budgeting loans and crisis loans (the latter should normally take priority), to maintain consistency with other decisions made in the local office in the same year, as well, of course, as to ensure that the claim can be met from the budget.

---

43 DSS (1999), originally known as *Social Fund Manual* and later as *Social Fund Officer's Guide*.
44 SSCBA 1992, s 138(1)(b) and (5). Loans are, of course, repayable: s 139(4).
45 There is only limited scope for applications to be treated as claims against another part of the fund: SSCBA 1992, s140(4)(aa) and Direction 49. For criticism of this rule, see HC Social Security Committee *Third Report* (2000–01, HC 232) paras 77–78.
46 SSAA 1992, ss 163(2)(e) and 167(2)–(4).
47 SSAA 1992, s 168. In total, the allocations are greater than the voted national budget, as they are expressed as 'gross amounts', which allow for the repayment of loans.
48 *Buck* n 3, above, p 43.
49 Department for Work and Pensions (DWP) *Annual Report by the Secretary of State for Work and Pensions on the Social Fund 2000/01* (2001) para 5.3. In contrast, winter fuel payments cost some £1.2 billion: para 2.16.
50 *DWP* n 49, above, para 6.4.
51 SSA 1986, s 33(9)(e); now SSCBA 1992, s 140(1)(e).
52 *Social Fund Guide* n 43, above, para 2016.
53 *R v Social Fund Inspector and Secretary of State for Social Security, ex p Roberts* [1991] COD 68.
54 SSA 1990, s 10(3), inserting SSA 1986, s 33(10ZA); see now SSCBA 1992, s 140(3) and Directions 40–42.

iii   The non-discretionary social fund

The non-discretionary, regulation-based part, which today governs maternity, funeral, cold weather and winter fuel payments, follows the pattern of provision for single payments under the supplementary benefit system.[55] This part was brought into force in April 1987, a year ahead of the main discretionary scheme, and confers entitlement on those who satisfy the conditions laid down in the detailed regulations. Expenditure thus remains demand-led and is not subject to budgetary control. Decision makers determine claims on behalf of the Secretary of State with a right of appeal to an appeal tribunal and thereafter to the Social Security Commissioner.[56]

Part 2   The discretionary social fund

A   General

The discretionary social fund has been described by the Social Security Select Committee as 'the forgotten end of the social security system'.[57] As we have seen, payments may be made out of the discretionary social fund for budgeting loans, crisis loans and community care grants 'in accordance with directions given or guidance issued by the Secretary of State'.[58] Interpreting the original version of this provision, which did not specify the particular types of payments, the Court of Appeal held that this was a very wide power to make directions defining those needs which are covered by or excluded from the scheme.[59] Indeed, needs may be excluded even if they cannot be met from other sources; the sole constraint is that the Secretary of State must not act irrationally, in the narrow sense that the term is used in administrative law, in exercising this power.[60]

At the time of writing, there are 48 current Directions which are contained in the Guide.[61] Somewhat anomalously, the procedure for making an application is dealt with by regulations.[62] Directions 31 to 39 are concerned with the system of reviewing appropriate officers' decisions, which is considered in chapter 6.[63] The remaining directions specify the needs which may be met by discretionary social fund payments, the conditions which must be satisfied by applicants, the maximum and minimum awards which may be made and deal with the procedure for the recovery of overpayments.[64]

Primary legislation also sets out certain 'principles of determination' to be followed by appropriate officers in making discretionary social fund awards. Until SSA 1998,

55   SSCBA 1992, s 138(1)(a) and (2). SSA 1988 conferred a power to add cold weather payments to the non-discretionary provisions. This was later extended to cover winter fuel payments.
56   See ch 6, above.
57   HC Social Security Committee *Third Report* (2000–01, HC 232) para 118.
58   SSCBA 1992, s 138(1)(b); and see s 140(2).
59   *R v Social Fund Officer and Secretary of State for Social Security, ex p Stitt* [1991] COD 68, CA.
60   *R v Social Fund Inspector and Secretary of State for Social Security, ex p Healey, Stitt (No 2) and Ellison* [1992] COD 335, CA. On irrationality in the sense of Wednesbury unreasonableness, see Wade and Forsyth *Administrative Law* (8th edn, 2000) ch 12 and esp p 356.
61   They are included with detailed commentary in *Buck* n 3, above, Appendix 1. Some directions have been withdrawn.
62   Buck reports that 'it was thought more appropriate to accommodate such rules within a statutory instrument rather than by a direction' (*Buck* n 3, above, para A1-153) but the basis for this is less than obvious, given the scope of other directions. See SI 1988/524.
63   Pp 209–211, above.
64   See SSAA 1992, s 71ZA.

these principles applied uniformly to each category of payment. The original provisions have been retained for crisis loans and community care grants but revised provisions apply to decisions on budgeting loans.

So far as the two former types of payment are concerned, in determining whether to make an award and the amount or value of any such award, the officer is under a legislative duty to have regard:

to all the circumstances of the case and, in particular—
(a) the nature, extent and urgency of the need;
(b) the existence of resources from which the need may be met;
(c) the possibility that some other person or body may wholly or partly meet it;
(d) where the payment is repayable, the likelihood of repayment and the time within which repayment is likely;
(e) any relevant allocation under section 168(1) to (4) of the Administration Act.[65]

The reference in (e) is to allocations made by the Secretary of State to local offices and thus effectively means that cash limits directly impinge on the exercise of discretion. This is reinforced by a legally binding Direction specifically requiring officers to keep within their budgets.[66] It is not made clear whose 'resources' are relevant for the purposes of (b), but since the fund itself is covered by (e), and third parties by (c), the expression should be taken as referring to the income and capital of the applicant and (subject to some exceptions) of any partner or children. Consideration (d), which has been underlined by the Direction that 'no budgeting loan may be awarded in excess of the amount which the applicant is likely to be able to repay',[67] has been much criticised[68] since it appears to lead to the paradoxical result that some requests for loans will be rejected on the ground that the applicants are too poor to repay them. This hardly seems consistent with a system of public assistance of last resort.[69]

The provisions governing the determination of applications for budgeting loans are now very different; in particular, and paradoxically, 'the nature, extent and urgency of the need' is excluded from the principles of determination. The framework of principles for deciding upon budgeting loans is considered in more detail below.

In this Part consideration is given to budgeting loans (section B), crisis loans (section C) and community care grants (section E).[70] Discretion, subject to guidance rather than directions, governs the repayment and rescheduling of loans (section D).

B Budgeting loans

i General

The purpose of a budgeting loan is to assist an applicant 'for the purpose of defraying an intermittent expense'.[71] The underlying principle is that most needs are capable of

65 SSCBA 1992, s 140(1).
66 Direction 42; see p 468, above. On the impact of the budget and strategies adopted to control spending, see *Walker, Dix and Huby* n 21, above, pp 18–20.
67 Direction 11.
68 Eg Lister and Lakhani *A Great Retreat in Fairness: A Critique of the Draft Social Fund Manual* (1987).
69 Inability to repay accounts for less than 1 per cent of refusals: *DWP* n 49, above, Annex 9.
70 The success rate for applications, ie awards as a proportion of decisions, are: budgeting loans 66 per cent; crisis loans 72 per cent; and community care grants 38 per cent: *DWP* n 49, above, Annex 1.
71 SSCBA 1992, s 138(5).

being met from the applicant's normal weekly income support or income-based jobseeker's allowance. Budgeting loans, therefore, are intended to help applicants spread large one-off expenses over a longer period and hence take the form of a loan, rather than a grant.[72] Following the amendments made to the primary legislation by SSA 1998, the relevant direction was reissued to itemise the qualifying expenses:

(a) furniture and household equipment;
(b) clothing and footwear;
(c) rent in advance and/or removal expenses to secure fresh accommodation;
(d) improvement, maintenance and security of the home;
(e) travelling expenses;
(f) expenses associated with seeking or re-entering work;
(g) HP and other debts (for expenses associated with paragraphs (a) to (f) above).[73]

The application form for a budgeting loan simply invites applicants to tick the relevant box(es); they are not required to specify the particular items required under each head and staff make no attempt to evaluate their 'need' for such items.[74]

ii Persons eligible

Under Direction 8, applicants are eligible for a budgeting loan if, at the date of the award, they are in receipt of income support or income-based jobseeker's allowance and they (or their partner) have received that benefit throughout the last 26 weeks (breaks in entitlement of up to 28 days are ignored).[75] Payments cannot, however, be made during periods when the applicant (or partner) is disentitled from receiving jobseeker's allowance because of a trade dispute,[76] or would have been so disentitled if otherwise entitled to that benefit. Persons subject to immigration control are excluded from eligibility.[77]

iii Principles of determination

The formal position is that, in deciding whether to award a budgeting loan, as with crisis loans and community care grants, the appropriate officer must follow the Secretary of State's directions and have regard to any relevant national or local guidance. The officer must also have regard to the criteria set out in section 140(1)(b) to (e) of SSCBA 1992, discussed above, which apply equally to the other two types of discretionary social fund payments. However, the criteria for the award of budgeting loans expressly exclude any reference to section 140(1)(a) ('the nature, extent and urgency of the need'). Moreover, the stipulation that officers have regard 'to all the circumstances of the case', which applies to the other payments, is also omitted with regard to budgeting loans.[78]

---

72 Any award must include a determination that it is repayable: Direction 5.
73 Direction 2; the relevant need must occur in the UK.
74 Furthermore, unlike crisis loans and community care grants, there is now no list of exclusions for budgetary loans.
75 Thus an applicant can rely on a partner's entitlement during the previous 26 weeks but at the date of application must be the claimant: *R v Social Fund Inspector, ex p Davey* (19 October 1998, unreported): see *Buck* n 3, above, para A2-68.
76 Cf pp 379–381, above.
77 Immigration and Asylum Act 1999, s 115(1)(h) (IAA 1999).
78 SSCBA 1992, s 140(1A).

Thus discretion has no place whatsoever in the determination of eligibility for budgeting loans. Instead, appropriate officers are required to have regard to 'such of the applicant's personal circumstances as are of a description specified in directions issued by the Secretary of State'.[79] This has facilitated the introduction of a 'fact-based' approach using automated decision making.[80]

Directions 50 to 53 make detailed provision for prioritising budgeting loan applications and making awards, so much so that the statutory requirement to have regard to the factors set out in section 140(1)(b) to (e) of SSCBA 1992 is of little practical significance. The first stage is to determine whether an award can be made, applying the weightings associated to specified personal circumstances under the 'initial test'; if these do not result in an award of a budgeting loan, wider personal circumstances are considered. Only two personal circumstances are relevant under the initial test: the length of time that the applicant (or partner) has been on income support or income-based jobseeker's allowance at the time of the determination and the number of people in the applicant's household for benefit purposes.[81] These operate as surrogate measures of need.[82]

Each of these factors is then given a weighting which increases according to the length of time on benefit and the number of people in the household. The weighting attributed to the period on benefit is subject to a minimum of six months and a maximum of three years: thus an applicant who has been on benefit for six months receives a weighting of '1', whereas after three years (or any longer period) the weighting is '1.5'. An applicant in receipt of benefit for between six months and three years receives a pro rata rating between '1' and '1.5' according to the nearest full month.[83] A single applicant is given a further weighting of '1', so a single person on benefit for exactly six months receives an aggregate weighting of '2'. Additional household members result in extra weightings: a partner qualifies for a weighting of '0.33', a first child '0.66' and any further child '0.33'. Hence a couple with two children who have been on benefit for three (or more) years will be allotted a total weighting of 3.83 (time on benefit = '1.5' and number in household = '2.33').

The aggregate weighting is then applied to a cash figure representing the value to be attributed to a weighting of '1' for the office in question. The relevant figure is specified in local guidance for appropriate officers but may vary from district to district, depending on the overall budgetary allocation, and may vary over the course of the year. If the relevant local maximum award for a weighting of '1' is £400, that will be the maximum award for a single person in that area who has been in receipt of a qualifying benefit for six months. Applying the equation to a couple with two children, who have been on benefit for three years, would result in a maximum figure of £1,533 (£400 multiplied by 3.83). However, such a family would be restricted to the overall maximum award of £1,000 under Direction 10, arguably penalising larger families.[84] The maximum awards arrived at by this calculation are then subject to further adjustment by Direction 53, which limits awards by reference to the amount applied for and according to whether or not there is an existing social fund debt (see further below).

---

79 SSCBA 1992, s 140(1A)(a).
80 See also SSA 1998, s 2, authorising the use of computers to make decisions and generally *Thompson* n 31, above.
81 Direction 50.
82 *Buck* n 3, above, para A1-253.
83 Direction 52. Gaps of 28 days or less are disregarded.
84 See *Thompson* n 31, above, who also makes the point that the weightings used do not correspond to the differentials in personal allowances or premiums for different family units.

In the event that this initial test results in no award, or an award of less than £30, regard must be had to certain wider personal circumstances.[85] The 'wider test' provides for additional weighting, supplementary to that determined under the initial test, in order to provide for awards at the margins of eligibility. The weighting for the amount of time on income support or income-based jobseeker's allowance can be increased under the wider test to reflect time spent in receipt of specified 'secondary benefits' (working families' tax credit, housing benefit or council tax benefit) in the last three years.[86] Furthermore, the weighting for household size may be increased so as to recognise any other person sharing the applicant's private residence, but not part of the latter's household, who is in turn receiving income support or income-based jobseeker's allowance. In addition, if the applicant or partner is pregnant, any unborn child may be included in the calculation. The enhanced weighting,[87] taking account of any such additional factors, is then applied to the relevant maximum award under the principles described below.

iv Amount

From the outset of the scheme, directions have included a number of controls on the amount of a budgeting loan. As we have seen, the appropriate officer is not permitted to award a sum which exceeds what the applicant is likely to be able to repay.[88] Under Direction 10 the maximum that can be awarded is the difference between £1,000 and any sum already repayable to the social fund by the applicant and any partner; for reasons of administrative cost, it also imposes a minimum limit of £30 per application. The appropriate officer is also bound to set off against the amount of a budgeting loan any capital possessed by the applicant (or partner) exceeding £500.[89] The income support (and income-based jobseeker's allowance) rules for assessing capital[90] are used for this purpose.[91]

Following the amendments made by SSA 1998, a new Direction 53 was issued to make more detailed provision for the calculation of the amount of budgeting loans. The first step is for the maximum amount that the individual applicant may borrow to be determined, according to the weighting values identified above. If the applicant (or partner) has no existing social fund debt, the appropriate officer will offer the maximum amount allowable according to that weighting or the amount actually requested, if that is lower.[92] Where the individual already has a social fund liability, the maximum that can be borrowed is reduced by *twice* the amount of the outstanding debt. Thus if the relevant maximum for an area is £400, an applicant will not be able to obtain a further loan until the current debt falls below £200. Accordingly, the higher the applicant's existing debt, the less likely it is that they will be able to obtain a further loan.[93]

If the appropriate calculation, as described above, results in no award, or an award for less than £30, and there are no relevant 'personal circumstances' which warrant resort to

---

85 Direction 51. An award of less than £30 may well result where the applicant has an existing social fund debt; see further Direction 53.
86 Time on a secondary benefit only qualifies for such enhancement if it precedes the entitlement to the qualifying benefit under the initial test (again, breaks of 28 days or less are disregarded).
87 Calculated in accordance with Direction 52(2).
88 Direction 11; and see SSCBA 1992, s 140(1)(d) and 140(1A).
89 Direction 9(1).
90 Pp 459–464, above.
91 Except that payments from the Family Fund are disregarded: Direction 9(4). In practice these rules have no impact on claimants: *Huby and Dix* n 21, above, p 122.
92 Direction 53(2)(a).
93 Direction 53(2)(b); see *Buck* n 3, above, para A1-264, noting that the self-regulating nature of this rule has resulted in the repeal of the bar on repeat applications for budgeting loans.

the wider criteria, then no award is made.[94] Where wider criteria do apply, the appropriate calculation is recalibrated according to the new weightings; if this second assessment still results in no award or an award for less than £30, the application fails again.[95]

C Crisis loans

i General

Broadly speaking, crisis loans replaced the provision under supplementary benefit law for urgent cases payments.[96] As under that system, they are intended to help those who have encountered a financial crisis but who are not necessarily dependent on public funds for their basic needs and thus may not be in receipt of income support or income-based jobseeker's allowance.

The primary legislation provides that a crisis loan is payable 'in circumstances so specified for the purpose of meeting an immediate short term need'.[97] Direction 3 further specifies that the object of the loan is 'to assist an eligible person to meet expenses ... in an emergency, or as a consequence of a disaster'. Further, the provision of such assistance must be:

> the only means by which serious damage or serious risk to the health or safety of that person, or to a member of his family, may be prevented.

The one exception to this latter condition is where the applicant's need is for rent in advance. A crisis loan may be available for this purpose for applicants leaving institutional or residential care and who receive a community care grant to enable them to return to the community.[98]

The concepts of 'emergency', 'disaster' and 'serious damage or serious risk to health or safety' appeared in the urgent cases regulations governing supplementary benefit payments[99] and were the subject of important case law, emanating from the Social Security Commissioners.[100] However, as is evident from the Guide, the intention is that these expressions should not be given a precise objective meaning; rather, they should be interpreted broadly to take account of the applicant's personal circumstances, because 'individual people may be affected differently by the same situation'.[101]

The reference to 'expenses' in Direction 3 implies that assistance is to be provided for immediate short-term needs and not longer-term financial consequences. Official guidance suggests that such needs will generally be for a specific item or service or for

---

94 Direction 53(3).
95 Direction 53(4) and (5). See further the worked examples in *Buck* n 3, above, para A1-265. Note that under the wider test an existing loan may be disregarded if it was taken out when the applicant had a partner and the new application directly relates to a subsequent separation: Direction 51(2).
96 See the 2nd edition of this book, pp 493–497. The provision for urgent cases in the income support system is to cover the basic needs of two categories of claimant, not otherwise entitled to the weekly benefit: pp 313–316, above.
97 SSCBA 1992, s 138(5).
98 Direction 3(1)(b) and on the community care grant, see p 481, below. The landlord must not be a local authority.
99 SI 1981/1529.
100 On the difficulties in applying this case law in the context of the social fund, see *Buck* n 3, above, paras 4.38–4.46.
101 *Social Fund Guide* n 43, above, para 4650.

immediate living expenses for a short period not exceeding 14 days.[102] Indeed, many crisis loans are made precisely because benefits are typically paid fortnightly in arrears.[103]

ii   Persons eligible

In contrast to budgeting loans, crisis loans are, in general, available to persons not in receipt of income support or income-based jobseeker's allowance.[104] However, just as those benefits deny or reduce benefit for certain groups of individuals whose needs are met in whole or in part by others, so the conditions of eligibility for crisis loans have been formulated to exclude or limit claims from those who will not have to cope with financial crises. Thus, an applicant must be aged 16 or over[105] and Direction 15 specifies that crisis loans cannot be paid to:
(1)   a hospital in-patient, or someone in 'Part III' accommodation, a nursing home or a residential care home, unless it is planned that the person will be discharged within the following two weeks;
(2)   a prisoner or a person lawfully detained;
(3)   a member of a religious order who is fully maintained by that order; or
(4)   a person engaged in relevant education[106] who for that reason cannot claim income support or income-based jobseeker's allowance.

Further, a full-time student (unless in receipt of either of the specified benefits) is only eligible for a loan 'to alleviate the consequences of a disaster'[107] and so the existence of an 'emergency' will not suffice. The same applies to persons from abroad not entitled to the prescribed benefits and those involved in a trade dispute (or subject to various disallowances or sanctions), though in the latter cases the loan may extend to items required for cooking or space heating.[108]

iii   Resources

Given the availability of crisis loans to persons who are not entitled to income support or income-based jobseeker's allowance, some means test is evidently required. Direction 14 imposes a condition that the applicant must be 'without sufficient resources to meet the immediate short-term needs of himself or his family, or both himself and his family'[109] at the date when the application is determined. The Secretary of State has not, however, issued a direction on how resources are to be assessed. Rather, by way of guidance, it is suggested that regard should be had to all income and capital of the family, except those resources which the officer considers it reasonable to disregard in the circumstances.[110] This vague advice is nevertheless complemented by a list of items,

---

102   *Social Fund Guide* n 43, above, paras 4000 and 4002.
103   This represents the largest single category (38 per cent) of crisis loans awarded (including awards made pending first payment of wages): *DWP* n 49, above, Annex 9.
104   Persons subject to immigration control are excluded from eligibility: IAA 1999, s 115(1)(h).
105   Direction 14.
106   This means a young person who is not receiving advanced (eg university) education, but is in full-time education and treated as a child for child benefit purposes: SI 1987/1967, reg 12.
107   Direction 16.
108   Direction 17.
109   'Family' is construed in a broader sense that the meaning attributed to it by SSCBA 1992, s 137(1) for the purpose of the income-related benefits (on which see pp 443–444, above): *Social Fund Guide* n 43, above, para 2758.
110   *Social Fund Guide* n 43, above, paras 4100 and 4120.

largely following those disregarded in the income support and income-based jobseeker's allowance schemes, which might normally be ignored. In addition, legislation specifically stipulates that the mobility component of disability living allowance is to be disregarded.[111]

Capital assets which could be realised in time to meet the need will normally be taken into account.[112] But it is also suggested that resources available on credit should only be taken into account if the applicant is not in receipt of income support or income-based jobseeker's allowance and is likely to be able to afford the required repayments.[113]

As with other discretionary social fund payments, regard must be had to 'the possibility that some other person or body may wholly or partly meet' the need.[114] But the Guide indicates that there should be a realistic expectation that such assistance would be available when the applicant needs it; moreover, appropriate officers should 'not routinely refer applicants to employers, relatives or close friends unless there is reason to believe that an offer of help will be forthcoming'.[115]

iv Situations and needs

As has been observed above, the policy inherent in the arrangements for the social fund is purportedly to avoid 'legalistic' definitions and so the appropriate officer has a very broad discretion in determining what constitutes an 'emergency' or the more serious phenomenon of a 'disaster'. The Guide stresses that the officer must consider the individual circumstances of each case[116] but also lists examples of situations where a crisis loan would normally be appropriate.[117] A fire or flood resulting in significant damage, loss or destruction will typically constitute a 'disaster'. Examples of 'emergencies' are: being stranded away from home without access to means of support; loss of money; the inability to meet living expenses from normal income because of misfortune or mismanagement;[118] hardship due to the payment of benefit in arrears; employers imposing compulsory unpaid holidays; fuel reconnection charges.[119]

v Exclusions

Direction 23 contains a long list of items and services for which a crisis loan cannot be made:

- needs arising abroad;
- educational or training needs (including clothes and tools), distinctive school uniform or sports clothes or equipment, travelling expenses to or from school, school meals;
- expenses in connection with court proceedings;

---

111 SSCBA 1992, s 73(14). See also IRS Advice Note Number 10 (in *Buck* n 3, above, paras A3.13–A3.19).
112 *Social Fund Guide* n 43, above, paras 4101 and 4180.
113 *Social Fund Guide* n 43, above, para 4102.
114 SSCBA 1992, s 140(1)(c) and (1A)(b).
115 *Social Fund Guide* n 43, above, para 4201.
116 *Social Fund Guide* n 43, above, paras 4020, 4023 and 4700.
117 *Social Fund Guide* n 43, above, para 4763.
118 It is suggested that normally payment should cover only two weeks' expenses: *Social Fund Guide* n 43, above, para 4710.
119 SFI Decision 'C', 1993 ([1993] JSWFL 284) suggests that an 'emergency' involves some element of the unforeseen which leads to an urgent predicament; a set of worsening circumstances which gradually lead to a desperate situation would not suffice.

- removal charges where the applicant is permanently rehoused and for which assistance is normally available from another agency (eg local authority);
- domestic assistance or respite care (ie when someone caring for another needs a break or a disabled or elderly person requires some relief from household duties);[120]
- repairs to public sector housing;
- medical (or analogous) items or services;
- work-related expenses;
- debts to government departments;[121]
- investments;
- telephone charges;
- television or radio costs;
- mobility needs;
- holidays;
- the costs of running a motor vehicle (except in relation to an application for emergency travelling expenses);
- housing costs[122] (apart from rent in advance to a non-local authority landlord or for board and lodging and intermittent housing costs not met by the housing benefit and income support systems); and
- council tax.[123]

The list also includes, by way of a 'belt and braces' approach to drafting, expenses already excluded by Direction 17, relating to those involved in a trade dispute or subject to a disallowance or sanction.

Many of these items and services are excluded because relief or assistance is provided by another agency, a consideration which ought to influence the interpretation of the Direction.[124] Thus eg the Guide notes that payment is 'not specifically excluded' for everyday items needed for medical reasons which may be unobtainable through the NHS or the social services (such as cotton sheets for someone with an allergy).[125] In a not entirely helpful judgment, the Divisional Court has held that items in ordinary everyday use are not to be regarded as within the excluded category of 'medical items'.[126] The regulations governing the award of single payments under the supplementary benefit system contained a similar list of exclusions.[127] There were a number of reported Commissioners' decisions interpreting those provisions but the precise status of that body of case law remains uncertain, given the aim of 'delegalising' this area of social security law.[128] Much of the early phase of the judicial review activity in relation to the social fund centred on the proper interpretation of a parallel list of exclusions for the purpose of budgeting loans.[129]

---

120   Cf *R v Social Fund Officer and Secretary of State for Social Security, ex p Stitt* [1991] COD 68, CA.
121   This may include arrears on national insurance contributions and income tax liabilities: *Social Fund Guide* n 43, above, para 4574.
122   Cf *R v Social Fund Inspector, ex p Smith* (1991) Times, 22 April (claim for community care grant to buy caravan).
123   In addition, for Northern Ireland only, specialist home or personal security measures are also excluded.
124   The Guide advises officers to refer the applicant to such other agency: *Social Fund Guide* n 43, above, para 4577.
125   *Social Fund Guide* n 43, above, para 4570.
126   See *R v Social Fund Inspector, ex p Connick* [1994] COD 75; see further Buck [1993] JSWFL 424 and IRS Advice Note No 7 (*Buck* n 3, above, para A3-02–A3-09)
127   SI 1981/1528.
128   See generally *Buck* n 3, above, paras A1-179–A1-192.
129   The budgeting loans exclusions (Direction 12) were deleted with the advent of the new scheme introduced by SSA 1998.

Once a loan has been refused, a second application in relation to the same item or service made within 26 weeks of the refusal will not be entertained unless there has been a change in the applicant's circumstances.[130]

vi Determining priorities

Although the appropriate officer is bound to have regard to budgetary considerations before authorising payment of a crisis loan, the Guide indicates that the majority of crisis loans will have highest priority.[131] This is inevitable given the criteria for awarding such a loan. In 2000–01 some 72 per cent of applications resulted in awards.[132]

vii Amount

There is some overlap with the principles and practice governing the amount of a budgeting loan, although this has reduced with the changes discussed above. Thus there are directions to the effect that no award may exceed what the applicant is likely to be able to repay or the difference between any sum already repayable to the social fund and £1,000.[133] Guidance for crisis loans suggests that the amount awarded will be the smallest sum necessary to tide the applicant over the period of need or remove the crisis.[134]

There are a number of more specific rules. Direction 21 stipulates that the maximum to be awarded for an item or service is, where the item can be repaired, the cost of repair (or cost of replacement, if that is lower) or the reasonable cost of purchasing the item (or service). As regards loans for living expenses, there is a standard maximum amount of 75 per cent of the appropriate personal allowance applicable under the income support (or income-based jobseeker's allowance) system for the applicant and partner, plus for each child, of whatever age, 100 per cent of the personal allowance applicable to children under 16.[135] Those who are sanctioned and receiving hardship payments of jobseeker's allowance cannot be paid more than the applicable amount which would apply to them in relation to such a claim.[136] This restriction reflects the policy considerations applying to benefit claims arising in similar circumstances.

D Repayment and rescheduling of loans

i General[137]

An award of a budgeting or crisis loan must include a determination that it is repayable,[138] and the terms and conditions of repayment must be notified to the applicant before the

---

130 Direction 7 and see IRS Advice Note No 7 (*Buck* n 3, above, paras A3-20–A3-36). The ability to satisfy the 26-week rule may constitute such a change. Note that an earlier award may be extinguished under SI 1990/1788, reg 3.
131 *Social Fund Guide* n 43, above, para 4803.
132 *DWP* n 49, above, Annex 1.
133 Directions 21–22.
134 *Social Fund Guide* n 43, above, para 4851.
135 Direction 18. See pp 295–296, above for discussion of income support personal allowances.
136 Direction 20. See pp 377–379, above for the relevant jobseeker's allowance rules.
137 On the impact of repayments on claimants, see *Huby and Dix* n 21, above, pp 100–109.
138 Direction 5.

award is paid.[139] These terms and conditions are a matter for decision by an officer acting on behalf of the Secretary of State and so are not appealable.[140] The Secretary of State has a statutory power to recover the award from the person to, or for the benefit of whom, the payment was made, that person's partner, and someone liable to maintain[141] that person.[142] The official practice is to seek recovery from the applicant in the first instance; only if this cannot be done is resort had to another party. There is a concomitant power to make appropriate deductions from prescribed social security benefits.[143] These include income support, income-based jobseeker's allowance, the contributory benefits, industrial injury benefits, war pensions and carer's allowance, but not child benefit, disability living allowance or attendance allowance.[144] Before 1999 deductions could be made from family credit, but working families' tax credit is also now exempt.[145] Deductions will normally be made from income support or income-based jobseeker's allowance if that is being paid to the relevant person.

ii   Terms of repayment

The period and rate of repayment are matters for the Secretary of State's discretion. As regards the period of repayment, official guidance suggests that loans should be repaid 'as efficiently as possible, but at a rate that the customer can afford'.[146] The maximum period is 78 weeks or in exceptional cases (for crisis loans only) 104 weeks.[147] In the typical case where deduction is made from the applicant's income support, the rate of repayment should take account of the applicable amount (excluding any housing costs) assessed for that benefit, any continuing commitments at the time of application and the possibility of further commitments during the repayment period.[148] Three normal rates of repayment are suggested accordingly:[149] if there are no existing commitments, 15 per cent of the relevant applicable amount (excluding housing costs); if there are existing commitments, 10 per cent or 5 per cent of that amount, depending on the size of the commitments. However, the rate may be varied up to a maximum of 25 per cent, eg where the applicant is already repaying one loan at 15 per cent and seeks a further loan of high priority. In the case of budgeting loans, applicants are given a range of repayment options depending on whether or not they have an existing social fund debt, eg a lower loan at the standard rate of repayment or a larger loan with higher repayments.[150] These deductions affect a significant number of people: about 16 per cent of all income support claimants are subject to a weekly reduction in their benefit owing to their social fund debt.[151]

---

139   SSCBA 1992, s 139(4).
140   SI 1999/991, Sch 2, para 23.
141   As determined by SSAA 1992, s 78(6)–(9), thus a 'liable relative' or a sponsor, on which see pp 324–328, above.
142   SSAA 1992, s 78(3).
143   SSAA 1992, s 78(2).
144   SI 1988/35, reg 3.
145   Nor is recovery possible from other benefits not administered by the Department, ie housing benefit, council tax benefit, statutory sick pay and statutory maternity pay.
146   DSS *Social Fund Decision and Review Guide* (1993) para 4010. For the sake of convenience, the person liable to repay is referred to here as the applicant.
147   *Social Fund Guide* n 43, above, para 6756. The SSAC had recommended that the repayment period be longer: *The Social Fund – A New Structure* (1992) para 69.
148   *Social Fund Decision and Review Guide* n 146, above, para 4011.
149   *Social Fund Decision and Review Guide* n 146, above, paras 4013–4016.
150   *Social Fund Guide* n 43, above, paras 6752 and 6756.
151   Figure calculated from DSS *Social Security Statistics 1999* (1999) p 57, Table A2.27. More recent editions do not include the relevant data.

iii   Rescheduling loans

Rescheduling a loan is possible if the applicant can show that the loan might be repaid more quickly or that hardship could result if repayment continues at the original rate because eg other deductions from benefit are increased to a high level.

E   Community care grants

i   General[152]

Community care grants (CCGs) constituted a novel feature of the social fund. Their origin lies in the health and social services policy developed by Conservative governments in the 1980s to encourage people to enter or remain in the community rather than be taken into institutional care.[153] The Green Paper of 1985 contained the observation that:

> [a]t present, the social security system can either be seen as an automatic paymaster, as in the case of residential care, or as a barrier to the most sensible mix of cash and services. What we should be aiming for is a more effective and responsive system which can bring social security resources and those of local authority personal social services and health authorities together in a cost-effective way to meet social and financial needs.[154]

The idea of linking a cash grant to health and social service provision was welcomed by the SSAC, though they cautioned that 'it would require a great deal of careful development'.[155] Other commentators expressed concern at proposed changes to the boundaries between the social security system and the traditional domain of the social work professions, particularly when there had been inadequate consultation of the latter.[156]

The primary legislation merely states that a CCG is payable in such circumstances as are specified 'for the purpose of meeting a need for community care'.[157] Direction 4 further specifies that a CCG may be awarded:

> to promote community care—
> (a)   by assisting an applicant with expenses ... where such assistance will—
>   (i)   help the applicant, a member of his family [or a person for whom they will be providing care] to establish himself in the community following a stay in institutional or residential accommodation in which he received care; or
>   (ii)   help [any such person as in (i) above] to remain in the community rather than enter institutional or residential accommodation in which he will receive care; or
>   (iii)   ease exceptional pressures on the applicant and his family; or
>   (iv)   allow the applicant or his partner to care for a prisoner or young offender on release under temporary licence ...; or

---

152   For reform proposals see Berthoud (1991) 12 Policy Studies 4 at 2 and *SSAC* n 27 above.
153   Culminating in the National Health Service and Community Care Act 1990; see further Clements *Community Care and the Law* (2nd edn, 2000).
154   *Green Paper 1985* n 4, above, vol 1, para 9.9.
155   SSAC *Fourth Report* (1985) paras 3.61–3.62.
156   Stewart and Stewart *Boundary Changes: Social Work and Social Security* (1986).
157   SSCBA 1992, s 138(5).

      (v) help the applicant to set up home in the community as part of a planned resettlement programme following a period in which he has been without a settled way of life; or

  (b) by assisting an applicant, and one or more members of his family … with expenses of travel including any reasonable charges for overnight accommodation within the United Kingdom in order to⁻
      (i)   visit someone who is ill; or
      (ii) attend a relative's funeral; or
      (iii) ease a domestic crisis; or
      (iv) visit a child who is with the other parent pending a court decision; or
      (v)   move to suitable accommodation.

In interpreting this Direction, a 'commonsense' approach has been commended by the courts.[158] This may, however, lead to inconsistency in awards, as different officers will interpret Direction 4 in divergent ways.[159] In principle the questions of need and priority must be determined before the state of the budget is taken into account.[160] For several years the overall success rate of CCG applications was about 20 per cent but this increased to 34 per cent in 1999–2000 following the introduction of the requirement to make an application for a specified type of payment, rather than to apply to the social fund as a whole.[161] The great majority of refusals are because the applicant fails to meet any of the criteria under Direction 4.

ii   Persons eligible

The basic rule is that applicants must be in receipt of income support or income-based jobseeker's allowance at the date of their application.[162] However, if the grant sought is to help them establish themselves in the community, under Direction 4(a)(i), it is sufficient if it is planned that they will be discharged from the relevant institution within six weeks and are likely to receive a qualifying benefit on such discharge. Persons involved in a trade dispute can only apply for a CCG under Direction 4(b) and then only in limited circumstances.[163]

iii   Situations and expenses for which CCGs may be awarded

The general guidance on how appropriate officers should exercise discretion in the award of CCGs emphasises that such payments are primarily intended to help people

---

158 See the authorities cited at n 42, above and *R v Social Fund Inspector, ex p Ali* [1993] COD 263.
159 See *Huby and Dix* n 21, above, pp 90–92; and *Dalley and Berthoud* n 24, above, pp 32–35.
160 *R v Social Fund Inspector, ex p Taylor* [1998] COD 152; see Buck (1998) 5 JSSL 89. Earlier research showed that in practice a decision on whether an applicant falls within the direction was inevitably affected by the state of the budget: *Huby and Dix* n 21, above, p 98 and *Dalley and Berthoud* n 24, above, p 35.
161 *Buck* n 3, above, para 2-51 and DSS *Annual Report by the Secretary of State for Social Security on the Social Fund 1999/00* (2000) pp 10–11. However, the number of applications for CCGs fell by 45 per cent: *DSS* p 17.
162 Direction 25. In certain situations an application made on one of the three waiting days is excluded. As with other social fund payments, persons subject to immigration control are excluded from eligibility: IAA 1999, s 115(1)(h).
163 For details, see Direction 26.

to live as independent a life as possible in the community.[164] The role of CCGs is to complement provision for community care by local authorities and other government agencies; the aim should not be to take over the role of other agencies. Thus the guidance stresses the desirability of liaison with, for example, social service departments and health authorities over the closure of a long-term institution.[165] Given this policy context, suggested priority groups for CCGs are: the elderly (especially those with care or mobility needs); the physically disabled and chronically sick; people with learning difficulties or mental health problems; victims of alcohol or drug abuse; ex-prisoners and others requiring resettlement; and young people who are leaving local authority care.[166] This list is neither exhaustive nor in any order of priority. Within this broad framework, the Guide provides specific advice in some detail. It is proposed here to consider this in outline, under the heads specified in Direction 4.[167] Most of the CCG budget is devoted towards grants for families under exceptional pressure (48 per cent) or helping people stay in the community (35 per cent).[168] The reality is that only applications classed as the highest priority have any prospect of success, given the severe budgetary constraints on the fund.[169]

A   ESTABLISHMENT IN THE COMMUNITY

To qualify under this head, the applicant must normally have been in an institution for at least three months[170] and intend, on leaving it, to set up home in the community. The boundary between 'institutional care' and 'community care' is by no means self-evident, and a CCG has been denied where the applicant moved to a 'half-way house' following a stay in care.[171] Payment may, however, be made if the intention is to live permanently with friends or relatives.[172] Those who move house to look after persons discharged from an institution may also be paid a CCG.[173] An eligible applicant leaving an institution is typically paid a 'start-up grant' to cover items of furniture and household equipment, though the amount will be reduced if accommodation is shared or the items are already available.[174] In addition, awards may be made for clothing, removal and travel expenses, and connection charges.[175]

B   REMAINING IN THE COMMUNITY

Applications under this head will typically be for expenses incurred in moving to more suitable accommodation or in making improvements to existing living conditions. In

---

164   *Social Fund Guide* n 43, above, para 2000.
165   *Social Fund Guide* n 43, above, paras 2350–2356.
166   *Social Fund Guide* n 43, above, para 2402.
167   See further the discussion in *Buck* n 3, above, ch 4.
168   *DSS* n 161, above, Annex 4.
169   HC Social Security Committee *Third Report* (2000–01, HC 232) para 37; see also the Committee's comments on the 'postcode' and 'calendar' lottery: paras 39–44.
170   *Social Fund Guide* n 43, above, para 2403. This should not be regarded as a strict requirement: *R v Social Fund Inspector, ex p Sherwin* [1991] COD 68.
171   *R v Secretary of State for Social Security, ex p Healey* [1992] COD 335. See also SFI Decision 'H', 1993 [1994] JSWFL 109.
172   *Social Fund Guide* n 43, above, para 2412.
173   *Social Fund Guide* n 43, above, paras 2540–2543.
174   *Social Fund Guide* n 43, above, para 2423.
175   *Social Fund Guide* n 43, above, paras 2422–2430.

either case there need not be an immediate threat of being taken into care for a payment to be made; rather, the question is whether a CCG would improve the applicant's independent life in the community and so lessen the risk of admission into residential care.[176] Grants made to those moving cover items similar to those for which payment is made to applicants setting up home after leaving an institution, though obviously account will be taken of furniture and household equipment which can be transferred from the previous home.[177] As regards improvements to the existing home, CCGs may provide help with minor structural repairs and maintenance, internal redecoration, reconnection of fuel supply, laundry equipment and clothing.[178]

C   EXCEPTIONAL PRESSURES ON FAMILIES

The guidance states that there is no standard definition of 'family'. The term will generally mean couples (with or without children), people caring for children (including lone parents) and women who are more than 24-weeks pregnant.[179] However, all the circumstances must be considered and officers 'are at liberty to be flexible in their interpretation, bearing in mind the overall intention of CCGs'. Thus a same-sex couple may qualify.[180] The Guide observes that 'all families, especially those on low incomes, face pressure at various times, so that in itself is not a reason to award a CCG'.[181] Accordingly, CCGs are only payable to ease *exceptional* pressures on a family. A number of examples are given: the breakdown of a relationship; a family needing to move house;[182] minor structural repairs to keep the house habitable or safe for children; the high costs of washing or extra clothing associated with a disabled child; the repair or replacement of items damaged by children with behavioural problems; fuel board charges; and short-term boarding-out fees pending adoption.

D   PRISONERS OR YOUNG OFFENDERS ON HOME LEAVE

Some prisoners and young offenders are granted home leave, usually for two to five days at a time, to enable them to re-adjust to life in the community on release. Neither income support nor jobseeker's allowance is payable in these circumstances,[183] but a CCG may be paid to assist with living expenses. Prisoners do not need to be in one of the priority groups.[184]

E   PLANNED RESETTLEMENT

This provision was introduced in 1998 and represents the only significant extension in the scope of CCGs since the start of the social fund scheme. People without a settled

---

176   *Social Fund Guide* n 43, above, paras 2601–2604.
177   *Social Fund Guide* n 43, above, para 2668.
178   *Social Fund Guide* n 43, above, paras 2620–2641.
179   *Social Fund Guide* n 43, above, para 2757.
180   See SFI Decision 'F', 1993 [1993] JSWFL 428.
181   *Social Fund Guide* n 43, above, para 2750.
182   If the family needs to move and the housing authority is not under a duty to rehouse it, a grant for removal expenses, essential items of furniture and connection charges may be made: *Social Fund Guide* n 43, above, paras 2843–2845.
183   P 331, above.
184   *Social Fund Guide* n 43, above, para 3001.

way of life include those who may have been living in hostels and night shelters as well as those sleeping rough.[185] However, an applicant may only qualify if he or she is setting up home in the community as part of a planned resettlement programme, which implies an element of control and progression in the plan.[186]

F   TRAVELLING EXPENSES

While not obviously related directly to community care, help with travelling expenses is conveniently accommodated in this part of the social fund arrangements, since it would be impracticable to treat the sums awarded as loans. As we have seen, in accordance with Direction 4 CCGs are only available to enable the applicant to 'visit someone who is ill ... attend a relative's funeral ... ease a domestic crisis ... visit a child who is with the other parent pending a court decision ... or ... move to suitable accommodation'. The Guide elaborates on these situations. Thus, a visit to a person who is ill would typically be to see a partner, relative or close relative, or a close friend who has no relatives or whose relatives have lost contact.[187] The patient may be in hospital, in institutional care or at home. A CCG may also be awarded to attend a relative's funeral.[188] An example of a journey rendered necessary by the consequences of a family crisis would be where a friend or close relative is looking after a dependent child.[189] A grant to visit 'a child who is with the other parent pending a court decision' illustrates at least the potential flexibility of this aspect of the social fund scheme when compared with the previous arrangements.[190]

G   EXCLUDED ITEMS

The list of items for which, in accordance with Direction 29, a CCG may not be awarded is based on those excluded from crisis loans, with some minor differences.[191] In addition, it may not cover fuel costs, daily living expenses such as food and groceries, nor any expenses which a local authority has a statutory duty to meet.

iv Amount

The amount to be awarded is largely a matter of discretion, particularly in relation to what is reasonable in the circumstances. Thus the Guide states that the amount asked for should be allowed unless that sum is unreasonable.[192] In this context, of course, account need not be taken of what the applicant will be able to repay. But the £500

---

185 *Social Fund Guide* n 43, above, para 3070.
186 See Best Practice Note Direction 4(a)(v) in *Buck* n 3, above, paras A3-65–A3-75.
187 *Social Fund Guide* n 43, above, paras 3151 and 3170.
188 If the applicant is responsible for arranging the funeral, he or she should apply for a non-discretionary social fund funeral payment: pp 489–493, below.
189 *Social Fund Guide* n 43, above, para 3210.
190 See *Vaughan v Adjudication Officer* [1987] 1 FLR 217 (single payment not payable to claimant unable to afford fares to see children living with ex-partner). But note that a CCG is not payable once a residence application has been determined. See SFI Decision 'D', 1993 [1993] JSWFL 341.
191 P 477, above.
192 *Social Fund Guide* n 43, above, para 3500.

capital rule which governs the award of budgeting loans applies also to CCGs.[193] There is a minimum limit of £30 which applies to all applications other than those for travel expenses or for the living expenses of prisoners or young offenders on home leave.[194]

Part 3   The non-discretionary social fund

A   General

The provisions governing the award of maternity expenses, funeral expenses, cold weather payments and winter fuel payments contrast markedly with the arrangements for other parts of the social fund. Regulations made in statutory instruments[195] confer entitlement on claimants who satisfy the prescribed conditions and discretion is reduced to a minimum. Further, claims are determined by decision makers, not appropriate officers, and appeals against such decisions may be made to an appeal tribunal and then to a Social Security Commissioner. The reasons for preserving a more 'legalistic' approach are partly historical and partly pragmatic. Until 1987, non-means-tested grants for maternity and funeral expenses used to be widely available to those able to satisfy lenient contribution conditions. As is explained in chapter 16,[196] the value of these grants declined substantially in the 1960s and 1970s and could be used to reimburse only a small proportion of the actual expenses incurred. In consequence, those with inadequate resources had to claim single payments under the supplementary benefit scheme. The administrative cost of paying the grants was very high. As part of its targeting policy, the government therefore resolved to abolish them and to make available more generous assistance to low-income families under the social fund arrangements. The fact that the replaced benefits had not been means-tested, combined with the certainty of the event giving rise to the need and concern that, at least in the case of death, intrusive questioning would be insensitive,[197] no doubt influenced the decision that, unlike other social fund payments, they should not be made the subject of discretionary determinations.[198] The relevant provisions of SSA 1986 were brought into force in April 1987, one year in advance of the discretionary social fund. Since then the provisions relating to funeral payments have been amended several times, and the social fund maternity payment was renamed the Sure Start Maternity Grant in 2000.

Assistance with heating costs during spells of particularly cold weather falls into another category. Since severe climatic conditions cannot be planned for, it is impracticable to expect that the ordinary weekly amounts of the income-related benefits should cover these costs.[199] Moreover, since the same increased need affects all recipients of those benefits experiencing the conditions it is clearly inappropriate

---

193   Direction 27.
194   Direction 28.
195   SI 1987/481; SI 1988/1724; and SI 2000/729.
196   Pp 557 and 567, below.
197   Cf SSAC *Fourth Report* (1985) para 3.79.
198   The proposals to this effect in the *White Paper 1985* n 7, above, paras 4.18 and 4.20, should be contrasted with those in the *Green Paper 1985* n 4, above, vol 1, para 10.6.
199   See the SSAC *Report on the Draft Supplementary Benefit (Single Payments) Amendment Regulations 1986* (1986, Cm 18). On the impact of cold weather on mortality, see Wilkinson et al *Cold comfort* (2001).

to require them to provide evidence of need in the way usually required for discretionary decisions. Cold weather payments were added to the non-discretionary social fund by SSA 1988. The conditions of eligibility have been revised on several occasions since, most notably in November 1991. Further assistance was introduced in the winter of 1997–98 in the form of one-off annual winter fuel payments.

B Sure Start Maternity Grants

i Conditions of entitlement

The regulations lay down four principal conditions of entitlement:[200]

(1) at the date of claim, the claimant (or partner) has been awarded income support, income-based jobseeker's allowance, working families' tax credit or disabled person's tax credit; *and*

(2) the claimant (or a member of the claimant's family) is pregnant or has given birth to a child or the claimant (or partner) has adopted a child who is not older than 12 months at the date of claim;[201] *and*

(3) the claimant (or partner) has received advice on the child's health and welfare from a health professional;[202] *and*

(4) the claim is made within a period beginning 11 weeks before the expected week of confinement and ending three months after the actual date of confinement[203] (or the date of the adoption order).[204]

As regards condition (1), the more generous nature of the tax credits as compared with their predecessor social security benefits means that more people are able to claim maternity grants than was previously the case. Condition (2) enables a maternity payment to be claimed for a member of the family other than the claimant (or partner) and 'family' for this purpose is defined to include young persons aged 16 or over.[205] It should be noted that a single woman expecting her first child and in receipt of the state maternity allowance[206] is unlikely to be eligible for the social fund payment before confinement, because receipt of the allowance will normally take her above the income threshold for income support.[207] However, once the baby is born, her applicable amount for income support purposes will include a personal allowance

---

200 SI 1987/481, reg 5. Persons subject to immigration control are excluded from entitlement: IAA 1999, s 115(1)(h).

201 The claim can be made by the adoptive parent even though the natural parent received a payment on the birth of the child: SI 1987/481, reg 4(2)(c). Parallel provisions apply in cases of surrogacy (although there is no 12 month rule in such cases): reg 4(1)(b)(iii) and 4(2)(d).

202 Defined as a doctor, midwife, nurse or health visitor: SI 1987/481, reg 3(1). Obviously this requirement does not apply in the case of a still-born child: reg 3(3). If the claim is made before the child's birth, the health professional's advice must have been in relation to maternal health.

203 'Confinement' here includes not only labour resulting in the issue of a living child but also labour after 24 weeks' pregnancy resulting in the birth of a stillborn child: SI 1987/481, reg 3(1).

204 Incorporating a reference to SI 1987/1968, reg 19 and Sch 4, para 8. There is no provision for claims outside these time limits. Cases involving surrogacy orders are also covered.

205 Originally a pregnant member of a family aged above 16 was only able to receive the payment if she was entitled to income support or family credit in her own right.

206 Cf pp 564–566, below.

207 This assumes she has no income support housing costs (eg she lives with her parents or in rented accommodation). She will not qualify for working families' tax credit as at this point she has no children.

for the baby and the family premium[208] which should be sufficient for her to establish entitlement to income support, and hence also to the Sure Start Maternity Grant.

Condition (3) was introduced in June 2000, when social fund maternity payments were renamed Sure Start Maternity Grants. The grant is thus conditional upon parents keeping appointments for child health advice and check-ups.[209] This reflects the government's concern to ensure that greater emphasis is placed upon child health as part of its wider strategy of addressing disadvantage and poverty amongst children.[210] The SSAC has expressed its concern that this involves using the social security system as a driver for the policy of other government departments in a 'somewhat coercive manner'.[211] However, as Buck notes, there appears to be no administrative integration between the maternity grant and the broader government programme on child health issues.[212] In practice this requirement may involve little more than 'ticking the box', with no significant impact on the advice actually sought by mothers.

The impact of a trade dispute disqualification[213] on entitlement depends on whether the claimant (or partner) is in receipt of a means-tested benefit or tax credit. If income support or income-based jobseeker's allowance is in payment, the maternity payment cannot be made during the first six weeks of the dispute; if either of the latter two tax credits, it can only be made if benefit was claimed before the beginning of the dispute.[214]

ii   Amount payable

In the past the level of the social fund maternity grant has been a subject of frequent criticism. The original social fund payment (£85) was approximately equivalent to the aggregate of the former contributory maternity grant and the average single payment made under the supplementary benefit system for maternity needs. Thus even at its inception its value was well below typical maternity costs.[215] It was raised to £100 per child in 1990, but remained at this level for a decade until the introduction of the Sure Start Maternity Grant. It was then rapidly increased to £200 in June 2000, to £300 in December 2000 and then to £500 in June 2002.[216] It is not possible to 'top up' such an award with a payment from the discretionary fund, since SSCBA 1992 provides for payments for maternity expenses to be made in prescribed circumstances and that payments from the discretionary fund are for 'other needs'.[217] The rule requiring any capital over £500 possessed by the claimant or partner to be set off against the award was abolished in October 2001.[218]

---

208   Cf p 298, above.
209   See *Buck* n 3, above, para A1-106 on the type of evidence required.
210   Home Office *Supporting Families; a consultation document* (1998). 'The benefits system should actively address social and health problems rather than simply provide cash': DSS *Annual Report by the Secretary of State for Social Security on the Social Fund 1999/00* (2000) p 5.
211   SSAC *Fourteenth Report* (2001) p 1.
212   *Buck* n 3, above, para 6-32.
213   P 332, above.
214   SI 1987/481, reg 6.
215   For a first child, estimated in 1985 at £250: Brown and Small *Maternity Benefits* (1985) p 135.
216   SI 2000/528, SI 2000/2229 and SI 2002/79.
217   S 138(1)(a)–(b). See *R v Social Fund Inspector, ex p Harper* [1997] COD 221.
218   SI 2001/3023.

C Funeral expenses[219]

i Conditions of entitlement

The rules governing eligibility for a funeral payment were made significantly more restrictive in 1997, notwithstanding the strong reservations of the SSAC.[220] There are now five conditions of entitlement:[221]

(1) at the date of claim, the claimant or partner (known as the 'responsible person') has been awarded income support, income-based jobseeker's allowance, working families' tax credit, disabled person's tax credit, housing benefit or council tax benefit;[222] *and*

(2) the funeral[223] takes place in the UK or, if the responsible person is an EC worker or falls into an analogous category, in an EEA state; *and*

(3) the deceased was ordinarily resident in the UK at the date of death; *and*

(4) the claim is made within three months of the date of the funeral; *and*

(5) the claimant or partner accepts responsibility for the funeral expenses and satisfies the 'immediate family test'.

Condition (1) is markedly more generous than the criterion applying to maternity grants, and enables many elderly people on low incomes to qualify.[224] As regards condition (2), it was originally a requirement that the funeral take place in the UK. Although this condition survived a challenge under the Race Relations Act 1976,[225] it did not withstand scrutiny under EC law in *O'Flynn v Adjudication Officer*:[226]

> Mr O'F was an Irish national resident in the UK. Following his son's death, a service was held in a London parish church but the body was flown back to the Republic of Ireland for burial. Mr O'F's claim for a social fund funeral payment was rejected as the funeral had not taken place in the UK. The European Court of Justice held that this requirement discriminated against migrant workers from other member states and so was in breach of article 7(2) of Council Regulation (EEC) 1612/68. A claim for the travel expenses incurred within the UK was subsequently allowed by the Commissioner.[227]

The regulation now states that a payment may be made in respect of a funeral in another EEA state, so long as the responsible person is a 'worker' for the purposes of EC law or falls into one of the other protected categories (eg a family member of such a worker).[228] These rules fail to reflect the ethnic diversity of the UK today. Thus a burial in Bangladesh is outside the scope of the scheme, even though some funeral costs are incurred in this

---

219 See SSAC *Fourteenth Report* (2001) Annex D.
220 SSAC Report (1997, Cm 3585). Comr Howell QC has described them as a 'dispiriting set of means-testing regulations': *CIS/3150/99*, para 3.
221 SI 1987/481, reg 7. In addition, persons subject to immigration control are disentitled: IAA 1999, s 115(1)(h). The existence of a trade dispute does not affect entitlement to a funeral payment.
222 Since housing benefit and council tax benefit are not administered by the DWP, evidence of entitlement is normally required.
223 Ie burial or cremation: SI 1987/481, reg 3(1). Other, eg family, ceremonies are not included. Cf *R(SB) 23/86*.
224 But if an unemployed or retired husband and a working wife qualify for housing benefit on the basis of the wife's low earnings, and the husband then dies, the wife may no longer qualify for housing benefit (and so for a funeral payment): *R(G) 2/93*.
225 *R v Secretary of State for Social Security, ex p Nessa* [1995] COD 226.
226 Case C-237/94 [1996] All ER (EC) 541.
227 *R(IS) 4/98*.
228 SI 1987/481, reg 7(1A).

country.[229] The Social Security Select Committee has recommended that the scheme should include funeral costs incurred in the UK prior to burial overseas,[230] a proposal which is under consideration by government.[231]

Condition (3) was introduced as part of the 1997 amendments.[232] The time limit under condition (4), as with maternity grants, is now absolute following the abolition of the good cause proviso for late claims.[233] This is especially unfortunate given the impact of bereavement on close family members.[234]

The SSAC expressed its doubts as to whether the eligibility rules were either understandable or workable following the 1997 amendments.[235] This is particularly evident in relation to condition (5), which arguably represents the zenith of tortuous legislative complexity in the social fund. First, and in all cases, the claimant or partner must have accepted responsibility for the funeral expenses. This is a factual question and acceptance of responsibility is not necessarily synonymous with the person who makes the arrangements for the funeral or in whose name the funeral account is in.[236] Secondly, the responsible person must fall within a priority list of four specified relationships. The purpose of this 'immediate family test' was clearly to tighten the eligibility criteria by creating a hierarchy of entitlement.

The first possibility is that the claimant is the partner of the deceased at the time of death.[237] The second, which only applies in the case of a child's death, is that the claimant is the parent (or partner) who is responsible for the child for child benefit purposes.[238] If neither of these scenarios applies, the claimant must be an 'immediate family member of the deceased'[239] and it must be 'reasonable' to accept responsibility for the funeral expenses, bearing in mind the nature and extent of the person's contact with the deceased.[240] Even if these conditions are satisfied, a responsible person will not be entitled to a funeral payment under this third category where there is at least one other immediate family member who is not in receipt of a qualifying benefit and was not estranged from the deceased at the date of his death.[241] Finally, if neither of the above three situations apply, a person may qualify where he or she is either a close relative[242] or close friend of the deceased and it is reasonable to accept responsibility,[243] again

229   *CIS/3150/99.*
230   HC Social Security Committee *Third Report* (2000–01, HC 232) para 14.
231   Cm 5237 (2001) para 3.
232   On 'ordinary residence', see pp 231–232, above.
233   See pp 150–157, above.
234   There is a very limited exception to this time limit where a claim for a qualifying benefit is awaiting determination: 1987/1968, reg 6(24) and (25).
235   N 220, above. See also SSAC *Fourteenth Report* (2001) Annex D.
236   *R(IS) 6/98.* This condition has the potential to raise difficult questions of agency or novation in respect of contracts with funeral directors.
237   SI 1987/481, reg 7(1)(e)(i).
238   If there is an absent parent (defined by SI 1987/481, reg 3(1)) who is not in receipt of a qualifying benefit, he will instead be treated as responsible: SI 1987/481, reg 7(1)(e)(ii). There is special provision for still-born children.
239   Defined as a parent, son or daughter: SI 1987/481, reg 3(1).
240   SI 1987/481, reg 7(5). See *R(IS) 3/98* (lack of contact for 24 years does not necessarily erase contact in the preceding 30 years).
241   SI 1987/481, reg 7(3); note that immediate family members who are under 18, students, recipients of asylum support, prisoners, long-term hospital patients or members of religious orders (and therefore assumed to have no resources) do not count for this purpose: SI 1987/481, reg 7(4). On estrangement, see *R(SB) 2/87.*
242   Defined to cover parents, sons and daughters, including step- and in-law relationships: SI 1987/481, reg 3(1).
243   SI 1987/481, reg 7(1)(e)(iv).

taking into account the nature and extent of the parties' contact. The concept of 'close friend' is not defined, but could include a cohabitant (either heterosexual or same-sex) or a relative of the deceased who falls outside the definition of 'immediate family member' or 'close relative' (eg grandchild or niece). A person who might otherwise qualify for a payment on this basis is likewise precluded from entitlement if responsibility for the funeral can be affixed to an immediate family member not in receipt of a relevant benefit and who was not estranged from the deceased.

The complexity does not end there. A person who would otherwise qualify under either the third or fourth categories described in the paragraph above is also excluded if he or she fails a comparative contact test with any close relative of the deceased.[244] Thus the claimant will fail if there is a surviving close relative who was in closer contact with the deceased. The claimant will also fail even if he or she was in equally close contact but the surviving close relative (or their partner) had not been awarded a qualifying benefit or has capital in excess of £500 (or £1,000 where the close relative or their partner is aged 60 or over).

The 'immediate family test' is not only exceedingly complex to apply, but it also involves potentially highly intrusive questioning of those concerned as well as reflecting a 'narrow and inflexible view of family responsibilities which ignores the diversity of present day society'.[245] The relegation of the deceased's cohabitant to the fourth and final qualifying relationship is particularly regrettable. As a result, wider family members may find themselves suddenly held responsible for the funeral of a relation without any forewarning or expectation.[246]

ii Amount payable

Originally, the amount payable was not specified in the regulations; rather, subject to certain deductions, the claimant was entitled to a payment to cover the cost of any prescribed funeral expenses for which he or she was responsible.[247] In 1995 amendments were made which retained such a list but introduced a cap of £500 on the funeral director's fees. The current formulation, following further changes made in 1997, builds on this restriction.[248] In principle the funeral payment is 'an amount sufficient to meet any of the costs which fall to be met or have been met by the claimant'.[249] Such costs are immediately qualified by the requirement that they relate to fees for the cremation or burial (including the purchase of a burial plot[250]), the cost of necessary documentation, certain transport costs and 'any other funeral expenses' that do not exceed £600.[251]

Express provision is made for transport costs in three situations.[252] First, the reasonable cost of transport in excess of 50 miles is allowable where it is necessary to transport the

244 SI 1987/481, reg 7(6). This exclusion does not apply if the close relative concerned was aged under 18 and was the only close relative whose contact was closer or equal to that of the claimant: reg 7(7).
245 SSAC Report (1997, Cm 3585) para 46.
246 Drakeford (1998) 27 J Soc Pol 507 at 521.
247 See the 4th edition of this book, p 617.
248 SI 1987/481, reg 7A. The revised cap of £600 was not a real increase as at the same time the range of permissible items, which were not subject to this limit, was narrowed.
249 SI 1987/481, reg 7A(1). 'Claimant' includes a partner or 'a person acting on their behalf'. The allowable sum is inclusive of any discount allowed by the funeral director.
250 On the meaning of 'necessary costs' in this context, see *R(IS) 18/98* (decided under a previous formulation of the rules).
251 The cap is £100 in the event that payments have been made under a pre-paid funeral plan, and no payment may be made for specified items provided under such a plan: SI 1987/481, reg 7A(5).
252 SI 1987/481, reg 7A(2)(d)–(f).

deceased within the UK in excess of that distance to the funeral director's premises or to the place of rest. This applies whether the deceased died at home or away from home.[253] Secondly, the reasonable cost of transport in excess of 50 miles is also permitted to transport the coffin and bearers, along with one additional vehicle (ie for mourners), from the funeral director's premises or place of rest to the funeral.[254] Thirdly, the necessary[255] travelling costs for one return journey incurred by the responsible person in connection with arrangement of, or attendance at, the funeral are covered. The requirement that this be limited to a return journey within the UK was repealed following the decision in *O'Flynn v Adjudication Officer*.[256]

The head of 'other funeral expenses', which is subject to a cap of £600, is left undefined but will include items such as fees for a funeral director, a religious minister or organist, as well as disbursements such as flowers.[257] In principle any expense that is a funeral expense could be claimed under this head. In addition, it could also cover costs which are not fully met by other provisions in the regulation (eg travel costs). In practice, however, a funeral director's fee for a modest funeral will leave no excess out of the £600 allowance to be applied to other expenses. Indeed, the cumulative effect of these various restrictions is that the deceased's family, however poor they may be, is required to shoulder an increasing burden of the cost of a funeral.[258]

The following amounts are then deducted from the expenses:[259]

(1) the value of any of the deceased's assets available to the responsible person (or any other member of his or her family) without probate or letters of administration having been granted;[260]

(2) lump sums due to the responsible person (or his or her family) on the death of the deceased under an insurance policy, an occupational pension scheme, a burial club or analogous arrangement;

(3) any surplus remaining from payments by a charity or relative to meet expenses other than those listed above;

(4) a war pensioner's funeral grant; and

(5) any payment under a pre-paid funeral plan or analogous arrangement.[261]

The rule requiring any capital in excess of £500 possessed by the claimant (or partner) to be taken into account was repealed in October 2001.[262] Even so, the increasingly restrictive nature of the principal rules governing eligibility to funeral payments resulted in a reduction in expenditure on such grants from £63 million in 1994–95 to £36 million in 2000–01.[263]

253   'Home' means the place where the deceased lived prior to death (*R(IS) 11/91*), and so is not synonymous with 'home town'.
254   The costs of such transport and of burial in an existing plot must not exceed the costs of such transport and of the purchase and of burial in a new plot: SI 1987/481, reg 7(4A). This appears to be designed to ensure parity between a local burial in a new plot and burial in an existing (family) grave some distance from home: *Buck* n 3, above, para A1-99.
255   As opposed to 'reasonable' under the original formulation.
256   [1996] All ER (EC) 541. However, this allowance is subject to SI 1987/481, reg 7(4B), an obscurely drafted provision that appears to confine such costs to those which would have been incurred had the funeral taken place in the UK.
257   The original version of the regulations separately itemised 'the reasonable cost of flowers'.
258   See *Drakeford* n 246, above.
259   SI 1987/481, reg 8. There is a disregard for any payments under the Macfarlane Trust or other similar schemes: reg 8(2).
260   See *R(IS) 14/91* and *R(IS) 12/93*.
261   This applies whether or not the plan was fully paid for.
262   SI 2001/3023.
263   DWP *Work and Pension Statistics 2001* (2001) p 155, Table 2.

iii Recovery

The Secretary of State has power to recover funeral payments from the estate of the deceased.[264] This takes priority over other liabilities,[265] but in practice personal possessions left to relatives and the value of a home occupied by a surviving partner are disregarded.

D Cold weather payments

i Conditions of entitlement

There are three conditions of entitlement:[266]
(1) a 'period of cold weather' has been forecast or recorded for the area in which the claimant's home is situated; *and*
(2) the claimant has been awarded income support or income-based jobseeker's allowance for at least one day during that period; *and*
(3) that income support includes a pensioner, higher pensioner, disability, severe disability or disabled child premium *or* the family includes a child aged under five.[267]
A 'period of cold weather' means a period of seven consecutive days during which the average of the mean daily temperature was recorded as equal to or below 0° Celsius.[268] Three significant changes in these arrangements were made in 1991. First, a period of cold weather can be based on a forecast from the relevant weather station. This avoids the weakness in the former approach that claimants did not know until after the event whether the temperature was cold enough to trigger entitlement, and thus might be disinclined to incur additional heating costs. Secondly, the requirement to lodge a claim was abandoned; payments should be made automatically to those who qualify. Thirdly, the country is now divided into 72 areas, each covered by a weather station, to which claimants' addresses are allocated by postcode.[269] Although more sophisticated than the old single payments system, based on local office regions, this still has the potential to produce anomalies where claimants living on one side of the street are entitled to a payment but not their neighbours across the road.

ii Amount payable

The amount currently payable is £8.50 per week of cold weather.[270] Since 1991 the claimant's capital has had no effect on entitlement.

E Winter fuel payments

i Conditions of entitlement

In 1997 the new Labour government announced that all pensioner households would receive a one-off payment each winter to help with fuel costs, in addition to any payments

264   SSAA 1992, s 78(4).
265   *R(IS) 12/93*.
266   SI 1988/1724, regs 1A and 2.
267   A person whose applicable amount includes a residential allowance is not entitled to a cold weather payment.
268   SI 1988/1724, reg 1(2). This condition is modelled on the provisions used in the supplementary benefit system: SI 1981/1528 reg 26A, on which see *SSAC* n 199, above.
269   SI 1988/1724, Sch 1.
270   1988/1724, reg 3.

made under the cold weather payments scheme.[271] There are only two conditions of entitlement for a lump sum winter fuel payment:[272]
(1) the claimant must be ordinarily resident[273] in Great Britain; and
(2) he or she must have reached the age of 60 before the 'qualifying week', which is defined as the week beginning on the third Monday in September each year.[274]
At the outset of the scheme payments were made only to those aged 60 or over who were in receipt of income support or income-based jobseeker's allowance or who were over 65 and in receipt of other specified benefits. The European Court of Justice subsequently held that the exclusion of men aged between 60 and 65 on other benefits constituted unlawful discrimination.[275] The government's response was to equalise the age for entitlement at 60 for both sexes and to abandon the means test, with the result that expenditure on winter fuel payments now exceeds the aggregate total of all other social fund spending under both the discretionary and regulated elements. This constitutes a curious sense of priorities, given that the rationale of the social fund is to target support on those who need it most. Buck has characterised the scheme as a high-profile, 'stop-gap' measure, pending a more comprehensive review of welfare reform, utilities regulation and energy conservation measures.[276] Yet such purportedly temporary initiatives, however ill thought out, have a habit of becoming permanent fixtures in the social security landscape (eg the Christmas bonus[277]).

The regulations exclude certain categories of individual from entitlement to a winter fuel payment, namely partners of those entitled to income support or income-based jobseeker's allowance (to avoid double payment), those who have been hospital in-patients for more than 52 weeks, those serving custodial sentences and those who do not automatically receive a payment and who fail to make a claim within the requisite time (see below).[278]

ii Amount payable

The amount currently payable each winter is £100 for claimants who are not receiving income support or income-based jobseeker's allowance and who either live with another person who is entitled to such a payment or live in residential care.[279] Other claimants (typically single pensioners receiving income support) qualify for a payment of £200. Benefit claimants should receive their winter fuel payments automatically by virtue of the Secretary of State exercising the power to make payments in the absence of a claim having been made.[280] Other potential recipients must make a claim before 31 March in the relevant winter.[281]

271   301 HC Official Report (6th series) cols 779–780.
272   SI 2000/729, reg 2.
273   See pp 231–232, above.
274   SI 2000/729, reg 1(2).
275   *R v Secretary of State for Social Security, ex p Taylor* C-382/98 [2000] All ER (EC) 80; see Johnson (2000) 7 JSSL 242.
276   *Buck* n 3, above, para 6-85.
277   Pp 267–268, above.
278   SI 2000/729, reg 3.
279   SI 2000/729, reg 2, as amended by SI 2000/2997.
280   SI 2000/729, reg 4.
281   SI 2000/729, reg 3(1)(b).

Chapter 14

Contribution-based jobseeker's allowance

Part 1 Introduction

A General

Unemployment, as a major cause of earnings loss and financial hardship, has from the beginning been an object for protection under social security legislation. Yet it differs from other social hazards similarly so protected in one important respect: unlike the natural phenomena of sickness, old age, birth and death, it results in a large degree from the interplay of economic forces. As such, the level of unemployment to be tolerated, the means of combating it and the extent of financial support granted to those rendered jobless, can be influenced by a government as part of its overall economic policy.[1] The extent to which the form and level of financial benefits payable to the unemployed affect their willingness to accept redundancies, to remain unemployed, or to seek employment elsewhere, is a much-disputed question.[2] Neo-classical economists have argued that the ratio of benefits for unemployment (along with other social security payments) to post-tax earnings is too high and creates strong work disincentives – and have thus recommended that benefit be 'capped'.[3] Empirical support for this hypothesis is difficult to find, not the least because of the complexities involved in the analysis.[4]

During the 1980s and 1990s successive governments introduced a bewildering variety of arrangements designed to reduce the numbers on the employment register.[5] The most significant of these schemes were demand side measures, intended to stimulate industry's labour requirements, involving typically the subsidising of the cost of employing young people. The two largest programmes during the 1990s were Youth

---

1 For a comparative analysis, see Storey and Neisner (1998) 19 Comp Labor Law & Policy J 585.
2 Barr *Economics of the Welfare State* (3rd edn, 1998) pp 196–198, contains a very helpful survey of the considerable literature. See also OECD *Benefit Systems and Work Incentives* (1999).
3 Minford *Unemployment: Cause and Cure* (2nd edn, 1985); see also Snower (1995) 134 International Labour Review 625. For a neo-classical perspective on the actuarial issues, see Beenstock and Brasse *Insurance for Unemployment* (1986). See also Rappaport (1992) 61 Wis LR 61, arguing for private rather than public unemployment insurance.
4 Cf *Barr* n 2, above; Atkinson et al in Atkinson *Poverty and Social Security* (1989) ch 9; and Atkinson and Micklewright (1991) J Econ Lit 1679. The arguments are reviewed in Harris (ed) *Social Security Law in Context* (2000) pp 57–61.
5 See generally Metcalf *Alternatives to Unemployment* (1982); and Renga (1991) 20 Anglo-Am LR 149.

Training (YT)[6] and, for adults, Training for Work (TFW).[7] Both these schemes were administered by Training and Enterprise Councils (TECs) on behalf of the then Department for Education and Employment (now the Department for Education and Skills). In addition to schemes of this kind, there were, of course, the conventional arrangements to encourage mobility of labour, through the provision of information, guidance and retraining.

The election of a Labour government in 1997 saw a further period of rapid change. Initially existing programmes were repackaged. Thus YT and other programmes for unemployed young people were brought together to provide a guaranteed training place through Work-Based Training for Young People (WBTYP), while TFW became Work-Based Training for Adults and later Work-Based Learning for Adults. However, the government's manifesto commitments included a much more ambitious New Deal programme as part of its 'welfare to work' programme, funded by a one-off windfall tax on private sector profits. The scale of these changes has now overshadowed the traditional employment programmes. In its first term of office, the Labour government introduced the New Deal for Young People (18 to 24-year olds), the New Deal for long-term unemployed people over 25, the New Deal for Lone Parents, the New Deal 50plus, the New Deal for Partners of Unemployed People and the New Deal for Disabled People. The two largest programmes are the New Deals for Young People and for unemployed people aged 25 or more. The former is compulsory for young people who have been unemployed for six months or more,[8] whilst the latter is compulsory for those aged 25 or over and who have been unemployed and claiming jobseeker's allowance for 18 months or more.[9] Participation in the other programmes is voluntary, subject to the condition that many of those affected are required to attend a work-focused interview as part of the process of claiming benefit.[10] The precise details of each scheme vary, but typically the New Deals involve a short initial 'gateway' period, during which guidance and counselling is offered, followed by a placement in one of a number of options (eg subsidised job, self-employed work, full-time education or voluntary sector work) for a longer period of time.[11] The New Deal initiatives reflect the government's philosophy that receipt of benefit is not unconditional. The programmes have, however, been cautiously welcomed by voluntary sector groups working with unemployed people, not least because of the emphasis in the New Deal on individual support and training and on safeguards against exploitation by unscrupulous employers.[12]

B   History of unemployment benefit[13]

Prior to the twentieth century, relief from the consequences of unemployment took one of two forms: private schemes of insurance administered by trade unions and friendly

---

6   YT replaced the Youth Training Scheme (or YTS) in May 1990. Under YT a grant was made to approved employers to cover overheads associated with the training and an allowance was paid to the trainee.
7   TFW replaced Employment Training and Employment Action in April 1993.
8   Jobseeker's Act 1995, s 19(5) (JA 1995) and SI 1996/207, reg 75(1)(a)(ii) and (b)(ii).
9   SI 2000/3134.
10   P 148, above.
11   For details see CPAG *Welfare benefits handbook 2002/2003* (4th edn, 2002) Appendix 10; and Unemployment Unit *New Deal Handbook* (4th edn, 2001).
12   See Lundy in *Harris* n 4, above, pp 305–307.
13   Tillyard *Unemployment Insurance in Great Britain 1911–1948* (1949); Cohen *Unemployment Insurance and Assistance in Britain* (1938) chs 1–3; Harris *Unemployment and Politics, 1886–1914* (1972); Morris *Social Security Provision for the Unemployed* SSAC Research Paper 3 (1991); Clasen *Paying the Jobless* (1994).

societies, or resort to the antiquated and degrading poor law. Once it became widely recognised that unemployment was not, in the great majority of cases, the result of personal moral failing but rather the product of economic forces, there was an obvious case for some form of state protection outside the poor law. The Royal Commission on the Poor Law, reporting in 1909,[14] placed great reliance on the system of labour exchanges (established on a national basis some four years previously), and the redeployment of labour and industry. The majority recommended the extension of unemployment insurance but felt that it should continue to exist on a voluntary basis and should be administered independently for each trade group.

The most penetrating analysis of unemployment in the early years of the last century came from Beveridge.[15] For him, the creation of labour exchanges was only part of a broader approach to unemployment which, though influenced by economic policy, required residual support in an insurance scheme: the unemployed must be able 'to subsist without demoralisation till they can be reabsorbed again after industrial transformations'.[16] The philosophy was reflected in Part II of the National Insurance Act 1911 which established the first compulsory system of unemployment insurance in a major industrialised country,[17] with the employee and the employer contributing in equal proportion and the Treasury providing a supplement. However, its experimental nature should not be overlooked. It was restricted to certain industries (notably engineering and shipbuilding) which were liable mainly to seasonal fluctuations and fell midway between those which had a relatively stable employment record, and for which the need was therefore less pressing, and those liable to chronic unemployment and which were therefore difficult to handle. It covered only 2.25 million of a 10 million working population. Moreover, the benefits payable were not generous; they were not intended to provide a substitute for wages but rather a supplement to personal savings to avoid resort to charity or the poor law. In short, it was conceived of as a temporary lifebelt.[18]

Soldiers returning to civilian life after the First World War but unable to find employment were not insured, and were granted a donation or 'dole'.[19] This led to the feeling that those unemployed through no fault of their own were entitled to relief as of right, which, in turn, induced the government to promise a universal insurance scheme. A reform of 1920 went a long way in fulfilling the promise.[20] The scheme now covered all workers except those in agriculture, domestic service and the civil service, the numbers insured rising from 4 to 11 millions.

Unfortunately the burden placed on the scheme became, in times of great economic depression, too heavy to bear. The actuaries in computing the level of contributions and benefits had assumed an unemployment level of 5.32 per cent. Between 1920 and 1940 the figure never fell below 10 per cent, and during some periods was much higher. The result was a debt of £59 million in the insurance fund and, as a concession to extreme political and economic pressure both at home and abroad, in 1932 the government made its notorious cut in benefit of 10 per cent.[21] But there was a second

---

14 Cd 4499.
15 Beveridge *Unemployment: A Problem of Industry* (1909). See also Harris *William Beveridge* (1997) ch 7.
16 *Beveridge* n 15, above, p 236.
17 On the 'Ghent system' established in Belgium in 1900, see Vanthemsche (1990) XXXV International Review of Social History 349.
18 Royal Commission on Unemployment Insurance, Final Report (1932, Cmd 4185) para 198.
19 Paid under powers conferred on the Board of Trade by the NI (Part II) (Munition Workers) Act 1916, s 3(1).
20 UIA 1920.
21 See Gilbert *British Social Policy 1914–39* (1972) pp 162–175.

problem, even graver. In the 1920s it became evident that a large proportion of unemployment in Britain was confined to certain industries which were situated in narrow geographical areas. In consequence, in these areas there was chronic and long-term unemployment, against which the scheme gave no protection, for benefit was given only for a limited period. The only method of saving the persons affected from the poor law was to establish an uncovenanted benefit scheme which would run alongside standard insurance. Throughout the inter-war years some such system continued to operate, though under different guises. Under the Unemployment Insurance Act 1920 (UIA 1020), eg, benefit might be paid in advance of contributions on the assumption that in the long run such contributions would be made.[22] An 'uncovenanted benefit' was introduced in 1921[23] (later known as 'extended' or 'transitional' benefit). This was payable at the discretion of the minister[24] in the exercise of which the personal and financial circumstances of the claimant might be investigated, a practice, of course, impossible under the standard insurance scheme. The Blanesburgh Committee, reporting in 1927,[25] found this dual system to be unsatisfactory and recommended that all benefits should be paid as of right. The proposal was enacted but the onset of extreme economic difficulties meant that the aim of abolishing uncovenanted benefit was never realised. The 'transitional arrangements' which were intended to be superseded were several times extended. Indeed, in 1933 the number of claimants in receipt of transitional benefit exceeded those on insurance benefit.

A major review of the system was undertaken by the Royal Commission on Unemployment Insurance in 1930–32.[26] As implemented by the Unemployment Act 1934, its recommendations established a pattern which, subject to certain modifications, has remained in force ever since. The basis was a distinction, hitherto only partially recognised, between insurance and relief. The former should continue (and indeed be extended to certain industries as yet excluded, notably agriculture) along traditional lines of covenanted benefit, limited in duration. When the right to benefit had been exhausted special assistance, based on a means test, would be provided and administered by the Unemployment Assistance Board.[27]

Under Beveridge's plan and the subsequent legislation, unemployment was integrated into the general scheme of social insurance and was made compulsory for all employed earners. It was, in fact, Beveridge's intention that the benefit should be of unlimited duration.[28] But the recommendation was not found acceptable: there were fears that it would be an inducement to abuse, and his suggested safeguard – a requirement that an individual undergo training after six months' unemployment – was regarded as impracticable.[29] The only major modification to the scheme subsequent to 1946 was the introduction of the earnings-related supplement in 1966.[30] This was, however, abolished by the Conservative government in 1982, as part of its programme of economies in the public sector. Ironically, the latter reform took place at a time when unemployment had attained a level not experienced since the 1930s. The consequence

---

22   UIA 1920, s 8(4).
23   UIA 1921, s 3.
24   For a short period in 1924–25 the claimant had a right to such benefit (UIA (No 2) 1924, s 1(1)) but this was soon repealed by UIA 1925, s 1.
25   Report of the Unemployment Insurance Committee (1927).
26   Interim Report (1931, Cmd 3872); Final Report (1932, Cmd 4185).
27   See Millett The Unemployment Assistance Board (1940).
28   Beveridge Report *Social Insurance and Allied Services* (1942, Cmd 6404) paras 129–130.
29   White Paper *Social Insurance* (1944, Cmd 6550) Pt I, para 67.
30   For details, see the 1st edition of this book, pp 424–426.

was an ever-growing reliance on means-tested benefits.[31] Moreover, other reforms initiated by Conservative administrations were directed towards further reducing entitlement to unemployment benefit.[32] Thus the contribution conditions became more restrictive;[33] the arrangements for ensuring that the claimants were available for employment were tightened;[34] a new requirement that claimants be actively seeking employment was added;[35] the period of disqualification from benefit for voluntary unemployment and related reasons was extended;[36] and the rights of students and occupational pensioners were curtailed.[37] These changes, however, paled into insignificance with the introduction of jobseeker's allowance in October 1996.

C The advent of jobseeker's allowance

In the November 1993 Budget Statement the Chancellor of the Exchequer announced the planned integration of unemployment benefit and income support for unemployed claimants.[38] Details of the proposed jobseeker's allowance were set out in a White Paper in October 1994[39] and were subsequently embodied in JA 1995.[40] The original intention was that the new arrangements would be in place by April 1996, but concerns over the ability of computer systems to cope with the introduction of the new benefit led to its launch being delayed until October 1996.

Under the new arrangements, income support remains the benefit for those groups of claimants who are not expected to meet the labour market conditions.[41] Those unemployed claimants aged under 60 who are required to sign on may be eligible for jobseeker's allowance. Claimants who meet the contributions conditions receive contribution-based jobseeker's allowance for six months (rather than one year as was the case with unemployment benefit). This element of the benefit is paid at different age-related rates, on the model of income support.[42] Moreover, although the White Paper had stated that it would be paid 'irrespective of their means',[43] the contributory component is reduced (or even extinguished) by the claimant's earnings or pension payments. The contributory element is also paid at a personal rate without any adult dependant additions, and so unemployed couples are reliant in part on income-based jobseeker's allowance from the outset. This means-tested jobseeker's allowance is the only form available after six months

---

31 In 1992–93, of those registered for employment 24 per cent received unemployment benefit without income support, 72 per cent income support without unemployment benefit and 4 per cent both benefits: DSS *Social Security Departmental Report* (1994, Cm 2513) p 83. For comparison with the position in Germany, see *Clasen* n 13, above.
32 For a discussion of these changes, see Atkinson and Micklewright in Dilnot and Walker (eds) *The Economics of Social Security* (1989) ch 1; Wikeley (1989) 16 JLS 291; and *Clasen* n 13, above.
33 P 501, below.
34 P 340, above.
35 P 348, above.
36 P 359, above.
37 P 516, below.
38 Mr K Clarke MP, 233 HC Official Report (6th series) col 927.
39 White Paper *Jobseeker's Allowance* (1994, Cm 2687).
40 See Fulbrook (1995) 24 ILJ 395; Buck (1996) 3 JSSL 149; and Bonner (1996) 3 JSSL 165. As usual, JA 1995 is a skeleton measure; see further SI 1996/207.
41 See ch 9. Claimants who are incapable of work and satisfy the contribution conditions may qualify for incapacity benefit: see ch 15.
42 Jobseeker's allowance is also a weekly benefit, as with income support, rather than the outmoded daily format of unemployment benefit. However, the three waiting days from unemployment benefit apply to both forms of jobseeker's allowance: SI 1996/207, reg 46.
43 *White Paper 1994* n 39, above, para 4.21.

on benefit, thus excluding from that point claimants with a working partner or with savings (eg from a redundancy payment) of more than £8,000.

Jobseeker's allowance is thus a less generous benefit than its predecessor in a number of key respects. The eligibility criteria were also made tighter. As well as being both available for and actively seeking employment, unemployed claimants are now required to enter into a jobseeker's agreement with the benefits office.[44] This can be seen as a further measure designed to characterise unemployment as a function of claimants' attitudes rather than market failure.[45] The jobseeker's allowance scheme has also involved the introduction of a harsher sanctions regime.[46]

Jobseeker's allowance is still not a genuinely integrated benefit, in that contribution-based and income-based jobseeker's allowance remain recognisably based on unemployment benefit and income support respectively. There has, however, been a considerable degree of alignment in some of the eligibility criteria (eg the common rules of entitlement, especially the labour market conditions). In practical terms, the contribution-based component of the benefit is very much in the shadow of income-related jobseeker's allowance. In May 2001 there were over 700,000 claimants of income-based jobseeker's allowance as compared with just 165,000 recipients of the contributory element.[47]

D   Scope and structure

The contracted role of contribution-based jobseeker's allowance within the wider framework of social security is reflected in the brevity of this chapter as compared with its immediate forerunner in the previous edition, relating to unemployment benefit.[48] The core conditions of entitlement to jobseeker's allowance, whether in its contribution-based or income-based form, are discussed in detail in chapter 9, above. This chapter merely examines the extra conditions of entitlement that attach to contribution-based jobseeker's allowance (Part 2), various special cases (Part 3, representing hangovers from the unemployment benefit scheme), the trade dispute disqualification (Part 4) and the duration and amount of the insurance-based element (Part 5).

Part 2   Contribution-based jobseeker's allowance

A   General

Persons claiming contribution-based jobseeker's allowance must meet the same core conditions of entitlement as claimants of the income-based component of the same benefit.[49] They must therefore satisfy the labour market conditions: they must be available for employment, be actively seeking employment and have entered into an extant jobseeker's agreement. In addition, they be must be capable of work and be under

---

44   Pp 351–353, above
45   *Wikeley* n 32, above, at 299.
46   Pp 359–379, above.
47   DWP *Work and Pension Statistics 2001* (2001) p 77, Table 2 (18,000 claimants were in receipt of both types of jobseeker's allowance).
48   See the 4th edition of this book, ch 3.
49   JA 1995, s 1(2).

pensionable age, as well as not being engaged in remunerative work or receiving relevant education. They must also be in Great Britain.[50] As these various conditions apply equally to income-based jobseeker's allowance, they are discussed in chapter 9, above. The common requirement that any claimant of jobseeker's allowance must not be engaged in remunerative work means that the highly technical concept of a 'day of unemployment' under the unemployment benefit scheme has disappeared. Consequently, the obscure regulations governing such peculiarly British concepts as the 'full extent normal rule' and the 'normal idle day' have been abrogated.[51]

There are just three supplementary requirements governing entitlement to contribution-based jobseeker's allowance.[52] These are the contribution requirements, the absence of earnings in excess of the prescribed amount and the condition that the claimant is not entitled to income support.

B   Special conditions of entitlement for contribution-based jobseeker's allowance

i   Contribution conditions

Only persons who have paid Class 1 National Insurance contributions can qualify for contribution-based jobseeker's allowance.[53] The exclusion of the self-employed has not been controversial:[54] it has generally been regarded as too difficult to ascertain when they are not actually working. In the words of Beveridge: 'the income of a farmer, a shopkeeper or a business manager may come at any time; how busy or how active he is on a particular day is largely within his own control. It is not practicable to have a general system of maintaining earnings of persons gainfully occupied otherwise than by way of employment, by benefits conditional upon not working or appearing to work on a particular day.'[55]

The contribution conditions for Class 1 contributors were made significantly more onerous in 1988,[56] but were not affected by the transition to jobseeker's allowance. They are:[57]

(1)   the claimant must have paid contributions of that class for either of the two tax years preceding the year in which benefit is claimed, and the earnings factor derived from such contributions must be not less than that year's lower earnings limit multiplied by 25;[58] and

50   This is, of course, subject to Council Regulation (EEC) 1408/71. The further requirement of habitual residence applies to income-based jobseeker's allowance but not contribution-based jobseeker's allowance.
51   See the 4th edition of this book, pp 92–99.
52   JA 1995, s 2.
53   Social Security Contributions and Benefits Act 1992, s 21(2) (SSCBA 1992). The two exceptions are share fishermen and volunteer development workers: p 504, below.
54   But see Brown *A Policy Vacuum: Social Security for the Unemployed* (1992). Technically the issue is whether the claimant was self-employed throughout the relevant tax and benefit years; an individual who was an employed earner during the period for contributions but then changes to self-employed status before becoming unemployed may well be eligible for contribution-based jobseeker's allowance.
55   *Beveridge* n 28, above, para 122. See also DHSS Discussion Document *The Self-Employed and National Insurance* (1980) paras 44–45.
56   They can still be met fairly quickly by a person on average earnings, when compared with other national schemes: OECD *Economic Outlook 1991* (1991) p 202.
57   JA 1995, s 2(1)(a),(b), (2) and (3). For an explanation of how these rules operate in practice, see Wood, Poynter, Wikeley et al *Social Security Legislation 2001* (2001) vol II, para 1.101.
58   Before the 1988 reform, this condition could be satisfied for any year before the benefit year.

(2)   in each of the last two complete tax years preceding the year in which benefit is claimed, the claimant must have paid, or been credited with, contributions of that class, the earnings factor from which must be not less than the relevant year's lower earnings limit multiplied by 50.[59]

As well as the self-employed, a number of other groups either face difficulty or are unable to meet these contribution conditions. These necessarily include those who have never been employed, as well as others with insufficient contributions records: the low-paid; persons aged under 18; those who have recently been in work but who were unemployed or incapable of work during the relevant tax years; and married women or widows still paying reduced rate contributions.[60] The contributions conditions thus represent a very real barrier to social inclusion. The Social Security Select Committee has recommended that all those earning at least £30 a week should be eligible for contribution-based jobseeker's allowance.[61]

ii   No earnings in excess of the prescribed amount

Claimants are not entitled to contribution-based jobseeker's allowance for any week in which their earnings exceed a prescribed amount.[62] The prescribed amount is not a uniform figure for all; it is calculated by applying the formula:

$$(A + D) - £0.01$$

where A is the age-related person rate of contribution-based jobseeker's allowance for the individual concerned and D is the appropriate earnings disregard for that person.[63] In practice the age-related personal rate (A) will be either the lower rate for 18 to 24-year olds or the standard rate for those aged 25 or over.[64] The usual disregard on earnings for contribution-based jobseeker's allowance (D) is £5 a week; a higher rate of £20 applies to part-time members of certain emergency services, members of the territorial or reserve forces and share fishermen.[65] Any earnings received over and above the disregard result in a pound-for-pound deduction from the individual's contribution-based jobseeker's allowance. The deduction of one penny from the aggregate of A and D ensures that benefit is denied only to those whose earnings exceed their entitlement to contribution-based jobseeker's allowance, once account is taken of the earnings disregard. Thus the effect of the prescribed amount formula is that entitlement may be lost altogether.[66]

> C, aged 24, is entitled to contribution-based jobseeker's allowance of £42.70 a week. He works part-time and is entitled to the standard £5 earnings disregard. C's prescribed amount under the formula is (£42.70 + £5) - £0.01 = £47.69. If C earns more than this amount in a week, he will not be entitled to contribution-based jobseeker's allowance.

---

59   Before the 1988 reform, this condition was applied only to the last year before the benefit year.
60   *Social Security Legislation 2001* n 57, above, vol II, para 1.101.
61   HC Social Security Committee *Fifth Report* (HC 56, 2000) para 145. This rule has been introduced for maternity allowance, effectively converting it from a contributory benefit to a non-contributory benefit with an earnings rule.
62   JA 1995, s 2(1)(c).
63   SI 1996/207, reg 56(1).
64   There is a third rate for those aged under 18, but very few will qualify given the contribution conditions.
65   SI 1996/207, reg 99(2), (3) and Sch 6.
66   If there is no entitlement, weeks so affected do not count for the purpose of the 182-day rule in JA 1995, s 5.

This rule is even harsher than the closest equivalent provision in the unemployment benefit scheme. That rule, introduced in 1989, meant that a claimant with earnings in a seven-day period that were equal to or more than the lower earnings limit for the purposes of National Insurance contributions lost entitlement to benefit for the whole week.[67] That rule had been introduced against the advice of the Social Security Advisory Committee (SSAC),[68] which had argued that the lower earnings limit could not be regarded as a high enough level of income at which to exclude part-time employees from unemployment benefit altogether. The threshold is now even lower with contribution-based jobseeker's allowance.

This further incursion of means-testing into a contributory benefit led one commentator to describe jobseeker's allowance as 'an uneasy hybrid combining in an apparently unified benefit a partly means-tested, insurance based contributory component' with a fully means-tested component based on income support.[69] Yet, as the same writer notes, the element of means-testing in contribution-based jobseeker's allowance remains partial. Thus it is only the claimant's earnings and pension income that can affect entitlement.[70] Somewhat inconsistently, a claimant's investment income is not taken into account. More importantly, as it is a personal benefit, any income received by the claimant's partner or a member of the family is irrelevant.[71]

iii No entitlement to income support

Jobseeker's allowance and income support are mutually exclusive benefits.[72] Only prescribed categories of persons are eligible for income support, and these exclude the unemployed.[73] It is, of course, entirely possible to be entitled to both contribution-based and income-based jobseeker's allowance simultaneously, depending on the operation of the means test, just as the unemployed used to be eligible for both unemployment benefit and the former income support before the 1996 changes.

Part 3 Special cases

The nature of certain occupations made it difficult to accommodate them within the framework of the ordinary law of unemployment benefit. For such cases, specific provision was made. In the past the most important of the special rules applied to seasonal workers. These rules were repealed by the Conservative government in 1989 as being 'outmoded and complicated'.[74] In the following year students were completely excluded from unemployment benefit.[75] With the advent of jobseeker's allowance, the

---

67 See the 4th edition of this book, p 92.
68 SSAC *Report on the Social Security Benefit (Computation of Earnings) Amendment Regulations 1989, etc* (1989, Cm 923).
69 Bonner (1996) 3 JSSL 165 at 183.
70 On the effect of pension payments, see p 516, below.
71 SI 1996/207, regs 56(2) and 80(2).
72 SSCBA 1992, s 124(1)(f) and JA 1995, ss 2(1)(d) and 3(1)(b).
73 P 279, above.
74 143 HC Official Report (6th series) col 754W; see SI 1989/1324, reg 8. See further the 4th edition of this book, pp 142–143.
75 See the 4th edition of this book, p 143. The Court of Appeal upheld the vires of the amending regulation: *R v Secretary of State for Social Security, ex p Moore* (1993) Times, March 9.

rules governing the treatment of occupational pensions was incorporated into the general rule disentitling those with earnings in excess of the prescribed amount.[76] The remaining provisions for special cases were carried forward unaltered and are dealt with below. The particular rules governing those involved in trade disputes are covered in Part 4.

A Armed Forces

Members of the armed forces may not receive benefit while serving.[77] They may become entitled on leaving, and will not be sanctioned under the 'voluntarily leaving' rule if they do so at their own request,[78] though they will be treated as having lost their employment through misconduct if they are dismissed for disciplinary reasons.[79]

B Mariners

Mariners pose problems both because they enjoy substantial periods of paid leave and because when not employed they are sometimes absent from Great Britain. Regulations thus provide that they are deemed not to be available for employment during any period of paid leave[80] and they are deemed to be available for and actively seeking employment during days of absence from Great Britain.[81]

C Share fishermen

Share fishermen hold a somewhat anomalous position under the social security system. Their remuneration takes the form of a share in the profits of the fishing boat and they are not employed under contracts of service.[82] As such they pay Class 2 National Insurance contributions and yet for the purposes of entitlement to contribution-based jobseeker's allowance these are treated as Class 1 contributions.[83] These circumstances necessitate two special conditions.
*   First, a condition is added to the ordinary rule of availability requiring the claimant to prove that in respect of any period of a week in which he did no work as a share fisherman,[84] he did not neglect to avail himself of a reasonable opportunity of employment in that capacity.[85]
*   Secondly, if the claimant is the master or member of the crew of a fishing boat, and either the master or member of the crew of that boat (though not necessarily the claimant himself)[86] is owner or part-owner, he must show that the failure to fish on

---

76　P 502, above.
77　SI 1975/493, reg 2.
78　SI 1975/493, reg 3(2) and SI 1996/207, reg 168.
79　SI 1975/493, reg 3(1) and SI 1996/207, reg 168.
80　SI 1975/529, reg 2.
81　SI 1975/529, reg 6(1). See also regs 4 and 4A, lifting the usual disqualification that applies when the claimant is outside Great Britain.
82　See the definition in SI 1975/529, reg 1(2) and SI 1996/207, reg 156. For a detailed account of this esoteric area of the law, see DSS Decision Makers Guide (DMG) (2000) vol 5, paras 27500–27975.
83　SI 1996/207, reg 158.
84　On which, see *R(U) 9/52*; *R(U) 9/53*; *R(U) 1/81*.
85　SI 1996/207, reg 161(1) and (2).
86　*R(U) 6/63*.

that day resulted from either (1) the state of the weather;[87] or (2) repairs or maintenance of the boat; or (3) absence of fish in the normal fishing grounds; or (4) 'any other good cause'.[88]

D Volunteer development workers

Volunteer development workers[89] are in an analogous position to share fishermen. Since 1986 they have been entitled to pay Class 2 National Insurance contributions providing that the Secretary of State has certified that 'it is consistent with the proper administration of the Act'.[90] Such payments are then deemed to be equivalent to Class 1 contributions for the purpose of satisfying the contribution conditions for contribution-based jobseeker's allowance.[91]

Part 4   Trade disputes disqualification

A   Introduction

The trade disputes disqualification has historically been a highly controversial area. The benefits system must here grapple with problems of industrial relations,[92] and, needless to say, political opinions are well to the fore in discussions of the substantive law. The general position is that unemployment resulting directly from trade disputes in which the claimant is 'involved' should not give him or her a title to benefit. There is a widespread assumption that such a limitation must exist, and the principle finds a place in almost every system of unemployment insurance.[93] But the theoretical or policy justifications of the principle are not so obvious as may appear and require some consideration.[94]

In the first place, it is said that this is but another instance of *voluntary* unemployment (such as misconduct, leaving, refusal, etc),[95] and, as such, does not come within the risk of unemployment for which the insurance fund was established. However, at least by itself, this is not a complete justification, for if applied consistently, it would compel the law to distinguish between *strikes* and *lockouts*, and, in general,[96] the distinction is irrelevant. Moreover, the other grounds of disqualification based on voluntary

---

87   *R(U) 1/81*.
88   SI 1996/207, reg 161(3). For the interpretation of 'good cause', see eg *R(U) 7/55*; *R(U) 17/55*; *R(U) 3/64*.
89   Such persons must be ordinarily resident in Great Britain but employed outside Great Britain: SI 1979/591, reg 123A(2).
90   SI 1979/591, reg 123A(1).
91   SI 1975/563, reg 13B.
92   This was the one area of unemployment benefit law to be considered in detail by the Royal Commission on Trade Unions and Employers Associations (the Donovan Commission). See its Report (1968, Cmnd 3623) paras 953–993.
93   Schindler (1938) 38 Col LR 858; Hickling *Labour Disputes and Unemployment Insurance in Canada and England* (1975).
94   Cf Lesser (1945) 55 Yale LJ 167; Shadur (1950) 17 U Chi LR 294; 2nd Memo of Ministry of Social Security to the *Donovan Commission*, Minutes of Evidence (1968) pp 2310–2318; Gennard *Financing Strikers* (1977); Ewing *The Right to Strike* (1991) ch 5. See also on income support, pp 332–334, above.
95   Given the inter-relationship with hardship payments, these sanctions are discussed in the context of income-based jobseeker's allowance in ch 9, above.
96   JA 1995, s 14(2), first introduced by the Social Security Act 1986, s 44 (SSA 1986), does apply this distinction but broadens rather than limits the scope of the disqualification rule. Cf p 512, below.

unemployment recognise that in certain circumstances the leaving or refusal of employment may be excused on grounds of 'just' or 'good cause'. Here there are no such qualifications. There is, indeed, a fundamental rule that the authorities should not enter into the merits of the dispute.[97]

Secondly, resort is had to the idea of industrial neutrality:

> the National Insurance Fund, to which both employers and employees contribute, should not become involved in industrial disputes ... the scheme should not be open to the criticism that it is supporting one side or the other.[98]

While this is, on the face of it, an appealing argument, it leaves open the question as to what constitutes 'neutrality'. It may not be neutral for payments to be made to strikers (and, as has been seen, the same may be said of income support which is paid to the families of strikers[99]), but it is arguable that it is equally not neutral if workers with a legitimate grievance are deterred from taking industrial action because of the refusal to pay benefit.

The neutrality argument appears often to be a gloss on the less compromising stance taken by others, that on economic and political grounds, contributors to the fund should not financially support those who withdraw their labour, particularly as this may encourage industrial stoppages, and therefore losses in productivity.[100] Finally, removal of the disqualification would arouse the hostility of those contributors who are not able effectively to express their grievances by withdrawing their labour. Whether or not such arguments are found acceptable depends, in the last resort, on political attitudes.[101]

Section 14 of JA 1995 provides that an unemployed person is not entitled to jobseeker's allowance in two situations. The first is where:

(a) there is a stoppage of work which causes a person not to be employed on any day, and

(b) the stoppage is due to a trade dispute at his place of work,

in which case the claimant loses title to benefit for any week so affected 'unless he proves that he is not directly interested in the dispute'.[102] This is discussed under section B below. The second, and much rarer situation, is where a person is not caught by the first rule but 'withdraws his labour in furtherance of a trade dispute' (see section C below).[103] The statutory terminology used in the 1995 Act is slightly different to the formulation previously consolidated in the SSCBA 1992 but this is not thought to change the meaning of the key terms.[104]

B   Loss of employment due to stoppage of work

The onus is on the Secretary of State[105] to prove that: (i) there was a trade dispute; (ii) it was at the claimant's place of work; (iii) it resulted in a stoppage; (iv) the stoppage

---

97   For the experience of the Social Welfare Tribunal in Ireland, which is directed to consider the employer's conduct, see *Ewing* n 94, above, ch 7.

98   *Ministry of Social Security* n 94, above, p 2310.

99   Pp 332–334, above.

100   Conservative Political Centre *Financing Strikers* (1974).

101   Cf Ralph Gibson LJ in *Cartlidge v Chief Adjudication Officer* [1986] QB 360 at 376.

102   JA 1995, s 14(1).

103   JA 1995, s 14(2).

104   Eg JA 1995, s 14 refers to 'place of work' whereas SSCBA 1992, s 27 referred to 'place of employment': see *Social Security Legislation 2001* n 57, above, vol II, para 1.156.

105   *R(U) 17/52(T)*.

caused the claimant not to be employed on any day. To avoid disqualification, it is then for the claimant to show that (v) he or she was not directly interested in the dispute.[106] The discussion is divided accordingly.

i Trade dispute

This is statutorily defined as:

> any dispute between employers and employees, or between employees and employees, which is connected with the employment or non-employment or the terms of employment or the conditions of employment of any persons, whether employees in the employment of the employer with whom the dispute arises, or not.[107]

This is an interesting example of a statutory definition being lifted from another context in which it served a completely different purpose. It was based on that in the Trade Disputes Act 1906[108] the object of which was to create an immunity from certain actions in tort.[109] It is not surprising, therefore, that the definition has given rise to some strange decisions. No one would question the application of the term 'trade dispute' to strikes (official or unofficial),[110] lockouts[111] and demarcation disputes,[112] at least where the dispute arose between a group of employees and their employer or another group of employees.[113] But in *R(U) 1/74:*

> in pursuance of a national pay claim, building labourers withdrew their labour on a number of building sites. The site on which C worked was unaffected until pickets from a nearby site came and persuaded C and his fellow employees not to work. R S Lazarus, Commissioner, relying on certain decisions concerned with common law immunities,[114] held that there was a trade dispute between C's employer and the pickets who arrived from other sites, notwithstanding that he was not their employer.[115]

The necessary connection between the dispute and 'the employment or non-employment or the terms of employment or the conditions of employment' has caused some difficulty.[116] In *R(U) 26/59* it was held that a dispute as to whether an employee was entitled to an income tax rebate under his contract of employment was not a trade dispute, since it was concerned with the existence of a term, not with whether there

---

106 Per Lord Brandon, *Presho v Insurance Officer* [1984] AC 310 at 315.
107 JA 1995, s 35(1).
108 S 5(3). Cf *Ewing* n 94, above, pp 78–80.
109 See the historical survey in *R(U) 1/74*, paras 12–15, R S Lazarus, Comr.
110 *R(U) 5/59; R(U) 5/87.*
111 *R(U) 17/52(T).*
112 *R(U) 14/64.* Demarcation disputes are no longer included in the definition of trade dispute for the purposes of immunity in tort: Trade Union and Labour Relations (Consolidation) Act 1992, s 244.
113 The claimant need not be a party to the dispute: *R(U) 3/69.*
114 Eg *Huntley v Thornton* [1957] 1 All ER 234, [1957] 1 WLR 321.
115 See also *R(U) 2/53* (distinguished in *R(U) 3/69*) where it was held that a claimant, who had been prevented from working by pickets who had threatened him with violence, had lost his employment as a result of the trade dispute between himself and the pickets.
116 This phrase covers disputes as to the manner in which the employment is carried out: *R(U) 5/87.* It may even start as a personal dispute between employer and employee: *R(U) 12/62.*

should be such a term. The distinction is an elusive one and was ignored by the Commissioner in a later case.[117]

Apart from a short period during the 1920s when claimants could escape disqualification if they could show that the stoppage was due to the employer contravening an agreement,[118] the tradition has been that the authorities should not attempt to adjudicate on the merits of the dispute,[119] and so it is of no avail to claim that there was 'just cause' for the withdrawal of labour. There are persuasive arguments for this approach: it would be very difficult for the Secretary of State to reach an objective decision on the merits of a particular dispute, and it would be very costly in terms of time and money.[120] But as a consequence it may penalise employees who have undisputedly legitimate grounds for grievance. So, in one case, a disqualification was imposed on those who had been dismissed by an employer when they had objected to a reduction in wages.[121] Similarly, the Divisional Court has held that complaints that the employer was in contravention of the health and safety legislation may quite properly be characterised as a 'trade dispute'.[122]

It is not entirely clear when a difference of opinion becomes a dispute but 'a question ... must reach a certain stage of contention before it may properly be termed a dispute'.[123] While it will usually end by some form of agreement, it will no longer operate to disqualify from benefit if it results in one party totally severing relations with the other.[124]

ii Place of work

The general rule does not require that claimants themselves be involved in the trade dispute. Subject to the exception on lack of direct interest considered below,[125] it is sufficient if the dispute was located at their place of work. The traditional justification for what is effectively a presumption of participation or interest in the dispute is that there is 'a common bond of mutual interest and loyalty ... between workers at one place of employment which enables them to be distinguished from other workers'.[126] In the days of the small family firm this rationalisation may have been attractive, but in a modern economy its appeal is less obvious.

If, in theory, the identification of the dispute with the place of work is not easy to justify, in practice the application of the test is even more elusive. Section 14(4) of JA 1995 defines a claimant's place of work as 'the premises or place at which he was employed'. This leaves open what is to be considered as a 'premises or place'. It is clear that each case must be decided on its facts, and that some fairly arbitrary lines must be drawn. In one case, it was held that 'the place of employment' (using the

---

117 *R(U) 3/71*, J S Watson, Comr, and see Calvert *Social Security Law* (2nd edn, 1978) p 157.

118 UIA (No 2) 1924, s 4(1). It was repealed by UIA 1927, s 6. See generally Gennard *Financing Strikers* (1977) pp 16–19.

119 Sir J Simon S-G, introducing the trade disputes clause in the 1911 Bill, 31 HC Official Report (5th series) col 1729; Report of the Committee on Unemployment Insurance (Blanesborough Committee) (1927); *Donovan Commission* n 92, above, para 994; *Ewing* n 94, above, pp 67–69.

120 *Donovan Commission* n 92, above, para 994.

121 *R(U) 27/56*. The Donovan Commission assumed that the same result would ensue where the substance of the dispute was that the employer had been in breach of contract: n 92, above.

122 *R v National Insurance Comr, ex p Thompson* (1977), published as Appendix to *R(U) 5/77*.

123 *R(U) 21/59*, para 6.

124 *R(U) 17/52*; *R(U) 1/87*.

125 Pp 511–512, below.

126 Memo of Ministry of Social Security to Donovan Commission, Minutes of Evidence (1968) p 2312.

previous statutory formulation) of someone loading ships was the whole of the docks.[127] In another case, the place of employment of a man working in an engineering shop attached to a group of collieries, but physically separated from them, was not the colliery.[128] To cope with this, section 14(5) provides:

> where separate branches of work which are commonly carried on as separate businesses in separate premises or at separate places are in any case carried on in separate departments on the same premises or at the same place, each of these departments shall ... be deemed to be separate premises or (as the case may be) a separate place.

The onus of proving certain premises are the claimant's place of work is on the Secretary of State. The onus of proving that they constitute a separate business is on the claimant.[129] It is a formidable obstacle, for he or she must satisfy the authorities (i) that there are 'separate branches' of work at the place of work; and (ii) that typically elsewhere such branches are carried on as 'separate businesses in separate premises or at a separate place', and (iii) that at the claimant's place of work the branches are carried on 'in separate departments'. The claim will not succeed on (i) if the branch of work in question is 'a step in an integrated process of production'.[130] As regards (ii), much will depend on evidence of the practices of other firms that the claimant is able to adduce.[131] The concepts of 'branches', 'businesses' and 'departments' are none of them terms of art, and all involve questions of degree. Determination by the authorities may be based on somewhat arbitrary classifications of industrial processes,[132] totally unrelated to the policy behind the rule which is based on the alleged mutual interest and loyalty of those working on the same enterprise.[133]

iii Stoppage due to trade dispute

There may be a disqualification only where there has been a cessation of work by a significant number of employees[134] arising from an unwillingness on their part to work or from a refusal by the employer to provide work until the dispute is settled.[135] The stoppage must constitute a move, by either side, in the contest, the intention of both parties being eventually to resume normal working.[136] If an employer or the whole group of employees decide categorically that they do not wish the employment relationship to continue on *any* terms, the cessation of work no longer forms part of the

---

127 *R(U) 4/58*; cf *UD 5568* where it was held that a person employed on a barge was not employed in the same place as the dockers at the dock where the barge happened to be.
128 *UD 5145/26*. See on the current provision *CU/66/1986(T)*, discussed in *Social Security Legislation 2001* n 57, above, vol II, para 1.159.
129 *R(U) 1/70*, R G Micklethwait, Chief Comr.
130 *R(U) 4/62*, para 7.
131 *R(U) 4/62*, and see *R(U) 6/51*; *R(U) 24/57*; *R(U) 1/70*.
132 See *R(U) 5/61* and *R(U) 3/62*, divergent decisions concerning the same workplace.
133 Suggestions to modify the provision have, however, as yet gone unheeded. The Donovan Commission rejected, on the 'community of interest' argument, the proposal of the CBI that the (then) definition of 'place of employment' should be extended; and, on the grounds that it would encourage selective strikes, that of the TUC that it should be narrowed: *Donovan Commission* n 92, above, paras 970–972.
134 *R(U) 7/58*. 'A situation in which operations are being stopped or hindered otherwise than to a negligible extent': *R(U) 1/87*, para 7, J J Skinner, Comr.
135 *R(U) 19/51*.
136 *R(U) 17/52*; *R(U) 11/63*; *R(U) 1/87*.

trade dispute.[137] The question is then whether persons unemployed as a result should be disqualified on the grounds either of voluntarily leaving or of misconduct. To determine whether an allegedly absolute discharge or withdrawal was intended to be taken seriously may obviously create an acute problem of interpretation for the authorities. A series of Commissioners' decisions shows that many such statements, though formulated in the most categorical terms, are not to be taken at their face value.[138]

The stoppage of work must be 'due to' the trade dispute, but the nature of the causal link involved has given rise to some difficulty where it has been impracticable or impossible to restart work immediately after the settlement of the dispute. For example, in *R v Chief National Insurance Comr, ex p Dawber*:[139]

> the stoppage had created a risk of damage to the industrial plant. Notwithstanding attempts by the employer to forestall damage, it did in fact occur, and he laid off all employees while repairs were carried out. Both the Chief Commissioner and the Divisional Court held that the employees were disqualified from benefit during the lay-off, as the continued stoppage was due to the original dispute.

For the requisite causal connection to exist, it did not have to be shown that the continuance of the stoppage was an 'inevitable' consequence of the dispute; it is sufficient if it was 'reasonably foreseeable'.[140] Moreover, the fact that the employer might not have adopted the most appropriate method of forestalling damage to the plant did not break the chain of causation. It may have been an error of judgment but it was:

> something done not unreasonably or otherwise objectionable. And ... it does not lie in the mouth of those who put the employers in a position of emergency where they had to take a decision to say that, because that was the wrong decision, it breaks the chain of causation.[141]

iv   The stoppage causes the claimant not to be employed on any day

The stoppage of work, which was itself due to the trade dispute at the person's place of work, must cause the claimant not to be employed on any day. If the loss of employment results from a fresh, supervening cause, such as the closure of the employer's business when that closure is attributable not to the trade dispute but to other financial pressures, there is no disqualification from benefit.[142] The principles determining this causal relationship should, mutatis mutandis, be those described above. The motives or attitudes of those losing employment are irrelevant: 'if enough people stay away for a stoppage of work to result then ... all those who are caused to lose employment by the event, whether by their own choice or by the actions of others taking part in the event, must be regarded as losing employment by reason of the stoppage.'[143] It follows that a claimant

---

137   *R(U) 1/65*.
138   *R(U) 17/52*; *R(U) 19/53*; *R(U) 36/53*; *R(U) 27/56*; *R(U) 11/63*; *R(U) 1/65*.
139   (1980), published as Appendix to *R(U) 9/80*.
140   *R(U) 4/62*, para 10, J G Monroe, Comr; per Forbes J, Appendix, p 10. See also *R(U) 19/51*, para 11.
141   Per Forbes J, Appendix to *R(U) 9/80*, p 8.
142   *R(U) 15/80*, R J A Temple, Chief Comr. The question whether, and when, a particular business has closed down is not easy to determine. For guidance, see *R(U) 15/80*, para 17.
143   Per Ralph Gibson LJ, *Cartlidge v Chief Adjudication Officer* [1986] QB 360 at 369.

cannot argue that he or she lost employment because of intimidatory picketing, rather than by reason of a stoppage of work.[144]

Perhaps because of a fear that some unworthy claimants should not be allowed to succeed, the Commissioners have been prepared to find that the causal test has been satisfied in situations where such a result was less than obvious. First, if the period of unemployment begins before the stoppage takes place, it has been held that the stoppage may still have caused the loss of employment, since the claimant may have anticipated what was going to happen and may have attempted to avoid disqualification by this means.[145] Indeed, there was, at one time, a presumption that the employment was lost by reason of the stoppage if the claimant was discharged within 12 working days of the beginning of the stoppage;[146] a harsh approach, the validity of which was deliberately left open by the Commissioner in one authority on the point[147] and which is, apparently, rarely used in practice.[148]

Secondly, the authorities have not taken the reference to 'loss' of employment entirely literally. The claimant need not have been employed on the day immediately prior to the date of unemployment in question.[149] The effect of the stoppage may have been to obstruct an employer's intention to re-engage a worker who had been off work for a period.[150]

Thirdly, it has been consistently held that claimants, who have lost their employment during a stoppage, cannot avoid the disqualification by arguing that they would *in any event* have been unemployed for part or all of that period for reasons of redundancy or short-time.[151] In 1985 the Court of Appeal upheld this approach and, albeit with some reluctance, considered it appropriate in a case where the claimant had resumed the employment before it was terminated on grounds of redundancy, rejecting the argument that the resumption had broken the chain of causation between the loss of employment and the stoppage.[152] As will be seen, legislative amendments in 1986 reversed this decision in part: disentitlement now ceases if either the claimant bona fide resumes the employment and subsequently leaves for reason other than the trade dispute or the employment is terminated by reasons of 'redundancy'.[153] However, 'redundancy' is, for this purpose, given a narrow meaning and the provision does not extend to those claiming that, but for the stoppage, they would have been 'laid-off' or subject to short-time working. It follows that the interpretation upheld by the Court of Appeal continues to apply to some cases.

v Proviso: not directly interested in dispute

The breadth of the general rule is evident. There may be a stoppage at the claimant's place of employment with which his or her connection is remote and yet benefit is denied. Since 1924 there has existed an escape clause to provide relief for some so affected, but over the years its content has undergone several fundamental changes. Originally, the claimant had to show that he or she was neither participating in, financing,

144 *Cartlidge v Chief Adjudication Officer* [1986] QB 360 at 368–369.
145 *R(U) 30/55.*
146 *R(U) 20/57(T)*; *R(U) 31/57*. The rule was originally formulated in *UD 18901/31*.
147 Per H A Shewan, Comr, *R(U) 6/71*, para 8.
148 The 12-day rule is none the less discussed in *DMG* n 82, above, vol 6, paras 32176–32184.
149 *R(U) 12/72(T)*, para 12 and *R(U) 13/72*.
150 Eg *R(U) 19/56*.
151 *R(U) 11/52*; *R(U) 32/55*; *R(U) 17/56*; *R(U) 29/59*; *R(U) 12/61*; all affirmed in *R(U) 12/72(T)*.
152 *Cartlidge v Chief Adjudication Officer* [1986] QB 360.
153 JA 1995, s 14(3)(b) and (c); originally inserted by SSA 1986, s 44; see p 514, below.

or directly interested in the dispute, nor belonged to a grade or class the members of which were participating in, financing or directly interested in the dispute.[154] The position since 1986 is that the claimant need only establish that 'he is not directly interested in the dispute'.[155] The phrase is not defined in the legislation but a decision of the House of Lords[156] has done much to clarify its operation. The proviso comes into play where the stoppage results from a dispute in which one group of employees are involved and leads to loss of employment for others employed at the same place. In the words of Lord Brandon, for the latter to be disqualified on the ground that they are 'directly interested' in the dispute, two conditions must be satisfied.

> The first condition is that, whatever may be the outcome of the trade dispute, it will be applied by the common employers not only to the group of workers belonging to the one union participating in the dispute, but also to the other groups of workers belonging to the other unions concerned. The second condition is that this application of the outcome 'across the board' ... should come about automatically as a result of one or other of three things: first, a collective agreement which is legally binding; or, secondly, a collective agreement which is not legally binding; or, thirdly, established industrial custom at the place (or possibly places) of work concerned.[157]

The 'across the board' outcome is not necessarily confined to remuneration but may include anything relating to the terms and conditions of employment.[158] The fact that the dispute which caused the stoppage also involved another issue in which the claimant had no direct interest will be of no assistance, unless he or she can show that such other issue was the cause of the stoppage, in the sense that without that issue there would not in all probability have been that stoppage at that particular time.[159] It is not necessary that the claimant's remuneration or terms of employment should actually have changed as a result of the dispute[160] – of course, the outcome may be such that no concessions are won from the employer. On the other hand, the outcome must potentially affect the claimant and normally it cannot have this effect once the employment relationship is terminated. In such a case, the direct interest (if any) ends at the date of termination.[161]

C   Withdrawal of labour

The alternative road to disqualification arises under section 14(2) of JA 1995:

> A person who withdraws his labour on any day in furtherance of a trade dispute ... is not entitled to a jobseeker's allowance for any week which includes that day.

---

154   UIA (No 2) 1924, s 4(1). For the history of this provision, see the 4th edition of this book, pp 138–139, 1st Memo of Ministry of Social Security to Donovan Commission: Minutes of Evidence (1968) pp 2298–2304 and *Ewing* n 94, above pp 66–76.
155   JA 1995, s 14(1).
156   *Presho v Insurance Officer* [1984] AC 310, [1984] 1 All ER 97.
157   *Presho v Insurance Officer* [1984] AC 310 at 318. To similar effect, see Lord Emslie P in *Watt v Lord Advocate* 1979 SLT 137, 141; *R(U) 13/71*, para 8; *R(U) 8/80*, para 17. The view of the Court of Appeal in the *Presho* case ([1983] ICR 595) that there was a crucial distinction between being interested in a trade dispute (which alone would warrant disqualification) and being interested in its *outcome* was discredited. See generally Wilton [1984] JSWL 186.
158   *R(U) 5/79*, para 12. Thus eg safety standards: *R(U) 3/71*; *R(U) 5/77*.
159   *Cartlidge v Chief Adjudication Officer* [1986] QB 360 at 372, per Ralph Gibson LJ.
160   *R(U) 5/59*, para 13.
161   *R(U) 5/86(T)*; *R(U) 1/87*. See Lundy (1991) 42 NILQ 150.

The original version of this provision was introduced in 1986 to plug a gap left by the predecessor of section 14(1). Disqualification under that provision can, of course, only arise if there has been a 'stoppage of work', which, as we have seen, must involve a significant number of employees,[162] and which must have resulted from a trade dispute at the claimant's place of employment. While the new ground for disqualification retains the requirement that there has been a trade dispute,[163] this need not have been at the place of employment. More importantly, by dispensing with the condition that there be a stoppage of work, the subsection catches those whose withdrawal of labour is personal or, at least, is not combined with industrial action by many others.

'Withdrawal of labour' is a novel concept in social security law and is bound to give rise to difficult questions of interpretation.[164] Traditionally, in the application of (what is now) section 14(1), the authorities have not had to distinguish between cases of withdrawal of labour and of 'lockouts': it has been sufficient if the employment has been lost as a result of a stoppage of work, whether that stoppage resulted predominantly from action by the employer or the employees. For the purposes of section 14(2), that distinction must now be made and in so doing it is not easy to see how the authorities will be able to avoid being drawn into a consideration of the merits of the dispute.

D Period of disentitlement

Unlike the disqualifications for voluntary unemployment, no maximum period is stipulated for the disentitlement that applies to those involved in trade disputes: under both limbs of section 14 of JA 1995 it applies to any week in which at least one day is so affected. In the case of section 14(1), however, there are circumstances in which the disentitlement will terminate before the stoppage itself ceases. As has been seen, this will occur if the stoppage no longer forms part of the trade dispute,[165] or if the claimant's direct interest in the dispute ends because the relationship with the relevant employer has been terminated, thus allowing the proviso to be invoked.[166] In addition, there are three further statutory grounds for bringing the disqualification under section 14(1) to an end – where the claimant proves that during the stoppage:
(a) he has become bona fide employed elsewhere; or
(b) his employment has been terminated by reason of redundancy within the meaning of section 139 of the Employment Rights Act 1996; or
(c) he has bona fide resumed employment with his employer but has subsequently left for a reason other than the trade dispute.[167]

i Bona fide employment elsewhere

Engagement in other employment normally removes the claimant from the ambit of the dispute. But this will not be the case if a temporary job is taken for a very short time solely to requalify for benefit. The onus is then on the claimant to show that the new

---

162 P 509, above.
163 On which, see p 507, above.
164 The DMG suggests that 'withdrawal of labour' does not extend to a refusal to work overtime: *DMG* n 82, above, vol 6, para 32312.
165 *R(U) 1/65*; p 510, above.
166 *R(U) 5/86(T)*; *R(U) 1/87*.
167 JA 1995, s 14(3).

employment was 'bona fide'.[168] This means both that the employment was genuine and that it was taken up for an honest motive.[169] The mere fact that the employment was of short duration does not, by itself, justify an inference that the employment was not bona fide; but such an inference may be drawn where it is clear from the evidence that the claimant did not intend permanently to sever relations with his or her original employer.[170]

ii   Redundancy

The remaining two statutory grounds were introduced in 1986 to deal with the injustices arising from the *Cartlidge* decision.[171] For the purposes of the first of these, the definition of 'redundancy' is the same as that adopted in the provision conferring relief from disqualification for voluntarily leaving and has been discussed in that context.[172]

iii   Bona fide resumption of employment

The aim of this new provision is clear: an employee who breaks the link with the dispute by resuming work and then loses employment for reasons unconnected with the dispute is not to be disqualified during the latter period of employment. 'Bona fide' carries the meaning attributed to it by the Commissioners in interpreting the first of the statutory grounds.[173] In other respects, however, there is some uncertainty as to the scope of the provision. Interpreted literally, it does not cover an employee who at no point during the stoppage ceases to work, but there is no obvious reason why such a person should not enjoy the same protection. In addition, the phrase 'has subsequently left for a reason other than the trade dispute' is undefined and vague.[174]

Part 5   Duration and amount of benefit

A   Duration

Jobseeker's allowance is not payable for the first three 'waiting days'.[175] Contribution-based jobseeker's allowance is then payable for a maximum of 182 days (ie six months) in any one spell of claiming. Any period for which a person is sanctioned under section 19 of JA 1995 counts for the purposes of the maximum of 26 weeks' entitlement.[176] In

---

168   *R(U) 39/56*.
169   *R(U) 6/74*, H A Shewan, Comr.
170   *R(U) 6/74*, para 10.
171   *Cartlidge v Chief Adjudication Officer* [1986] QB 360, p 143, above.
172   JA 1995, s 19(7), p 367, above.
173   *R(U) 39/56; R(U) 6/74*.
174   The DMG suggests that 'the main reason for leaving' must not be the trade dispute: *DMG* n 82, above, vol 6, para 32272.
175   JA 1995, Sch 1, para 4 and SI 1996/207, reg 46, which details certain exceptions. Jobseeking periods may be linked if they are not more than 12 weeks apart and in the other circumstances set out in SI 1996/207, reg 48. If the linking rules apply, the three waiting days do not need to be served again but only the residue of the 26 weeks' entitlement on the original claim is payable.
176   JA 1995, s 5(3) and SI 1996/207, reg 47(4).

contrast, entitlement to unemployment benefit continued for 312 days (ie one year, as the old benefit worked on the basis of a six-day week) in one period of interruption of employment.[177] Furthermore, under the former rules, the effect of a disqualification was to delay receipt of the potentially full period of entitlement to benefit rather than, as now, eroding that period.

The rules governing requalification for benefit once the maximum period of entitlement has expired also changed with the introduction of jobseeker's allowance. A further period of 182 days' entitlement follows where the claimant satisfies the contribution conditions and the two years which are used to do so include at least one year which is later than the second of the two years used when the first award was made.[178]

C qualified for contribution-based jobseeker's allowance in January 2002 on the basis of contributions paid during the tax years 1999–00 and 2000–01. Once the 182 days' entitlement is reached in June 2002, and assuming the new claim does not fall within a linked jobseeking period, C may requalify if the contribution conditions are met for 2000–01 and 2001–02.

B Amount

After 1982, when the earnings-related supplement was abolished, unemployment benefit was a flat-rate sum, to which could be added an increase for a dependent spouse.[179] The introduction of jobseeker's allowance saw the transformation of unemployment benefit into a personal benefit but modelled on income support in terms of its rates. There are no dependency additions payable with contribution-based jobseeker's allowance. Instead, benefit is payable at a 'personal rate', which is calculated in two stages.

The first step is to determine the appropriate age-related rate, according to whether the claimant is aged under 18, under 25 or 25 and over.[180] This was a major departure for a contributory benefit: indeed, it is not immediately obvious why claimants who have paid the same proportion of contributions into the scheme should receive lower benefits if they are aged under 25. No case was advanced for the introduction of differential age-related rates other than the desirability of alignment with income support, where the assumption is that young adults do not live independently and have fewer financial commitments.[181] These arguments, along with others of a similar nature – eg that younger adults generally earn less – were later successfully advanced in order to resist a human rights challenge to the differential in rates.[182] These rates are hence identical to the standard income support and income-based jobseeker's allowance personal allowances for these age bands. An unemployed single person with an adequate contributions record, no dependents and no mortgage costs, and who has no

---

177 SSCBA 1992, s 26(1) (now repealed). Until 1966 entitlement was only for 180 days: National Insurance Act 1965, s 21(1) and National Insurance Act 1966, s 3(2).
178 JA 1995, s 5(2). On the former rule, see the 4th edition of this book, p 146.
179 Pp 247–258, below.
180 JA 1995, s 4(1) and (2) and SI 1996/207, reg 79.
181 On which see p 295, above.
182 *R v Secretary of State for Work and Pensions, ex p Reynolds* [2002] EWHC 426 (Admin). On the face of it some of these arguments were less than convincing: eg that housing benefit and council tax benefit were available in appropriate cases (but younger adults' housing benefit entitlement may be capped by the single room rent rule) and that the efficient administration of the social security system requires the application of clear and simple rules (but what could be simpler than one rate for all contributors?).

circumstances giving rise to eligibility for one or more of the premiums in the income-related benefit schemes, will therefore be eligible only for contribution-based jobseeker's allowance and not its income-based equivalent.

The second stage in calculating the claimant's 'personal rate' is to make 'prescribed deductions in respect of earnings and pension payments' from the relevant age-related amount. The provisions governing the assessment of earnings for the purposes of contribution-based jobseeker's allowance are in nearly all respects identical to those relating to the income-based component.[183] However, as the insurance-based element is a personal benefit, the earnings disregards are different, as is the impact of any earnings on the contribution-based component.[184] Thus there is no place for a couple rate to the disregard: the standard disregard is £5 a week, with a more generous £20 a week disregard for those involved as part-time members of various emergency services.[185] Any earnings above this count pound-for-pound against contribution-based jobseeker's allowance, as with the income-based component, but where the earnings exceed the relevant 'prescribed amount' entitlement ceases altogether.[186]

Special provision is also made for pension payments, carrying forward in a modified form the rules previously contained in the unemployment benefit scheme. The entitlement to unemployment benefit of those who retired early had long been a controversial issue.[187] Many of those who retire early receive an occupational pension and thus have a reduced need for income maintenance. The policy of previous Conservative administrations was, on the one hand, to preserve entitlement to unemployment benefit without disqualifying early retirers for 'voluntarily leaving',[188] but, on the other hand, to take account of the receipt of occupational pensions in determining the amount payable. Two legislative proposals to introduce abatement of benefit failed to secure parliamentary approval but the principle was finally endorsed for those aged 60 to 65 by the Social Security (No 2) Act 1980 and in 1988 was extended to those aged 55 to 60.[189] Accordingly, there was a weekly reduction from unemployment benefit of 10 pence for each 10 pence of any occupational or personal pension above a prescribed amount, which remained at £35 per week from 1980 until the transition to jobseeker's allowance in 1996.[190]

The scope of the abatement rule was adjusted for the purposes of the new scheme. The weekly pension threshold was raised to £50; any weekly pension payment not exceeding £50 a week is disregarded in calculating entitlement to contribution-based jobseeker's allowance, whilst any amount in excess of that sum is deducted from the individual's age-related amount.[191] At the same time, and to the disadvantage of claimants, the age limit was removed. Pension payments are defined as periodical payments made either under a personal pension scheme or in connection with the coming to an end of the person's employment, under an occupational or public service pension

---

183   Pp 447–453, above. They thus differ from those relating to other contributory benefits, on which see pp 243–246, above.
184   P 502, above.
185   SI 1996/207, regs 80, 99(3) and Sch 6.
186   See pp 502–503, above.
187   NIAC *Report on the Question of Conditions for Unemployment Benefit and Contribution Conditions for Occupational Pensioners* (1968, Cmnd 3545). See also the report on Draft Regulations (1969–70, HC 211).
188   Pp 367–368, above.
189   SSA 1988, s 7. See Wikeley [1989] JSWL 277 at 283–284. Claimants between these ages and already in receipt of unemployment benefit had no accrued right to benefit: *R(U) 1/91(T)*. On the equal treatment implications, see *R(U) 10/88(T)* and *R(U) 3/92*.
190   SSCBA 1992, s 30 (now repealed).
191   SI 1996/207, reg 81(1).

scheme.[192] A lump sum paid solely as compensation for redundancy and not provided for in a pension scheme is disregarded.[193] Any payments made to the claimant as the result of the death of a person who was a member of a pension scheme (eg their late partner) are also ignored.[194] There are rules for calculating the weekly value of a pension when it is not paid on a weekly basis,[195] but if a pension is commuted into a lump sum entitlement to benefit is unaffected[196] – a somewhat anomalous result.[197] It should also be noted that where, as a consequence of these rules, the occupational pensioner receives nothing by way of contribution-based jobseeker's allowance, nevertheless the period in which, but for the reduction, he or she would have been paid benefit still counts towards the maximum duration of 182 days.

Claimants may be eligible to claim income-based jobseeker's allowance from the outset in order to top up their contribution-based component. The rules governing the composition of the amount of an individual's jobseeker's allowance are laid down in primary legislation. Where a claimant is entitled to both components, and has no income, the applicable amount of income-based jobseeker's allowance is payable, assuming this is more than the ordinary personal rate of contribution-based jobseeker's allowance; if not, the latter is payable.[198] Where a claimant is entitled to both components, and has some income, the benefit payable is the sum by which the applicable amount exceeds the individual's income, again assuming this is more than the ordinary personal rate of contribution-based jobseeker's allowance.[199] However the amount of benefit is arrived at when both components are payable, the jobseeker's allowance is deemed to comprise the personal rate of contribution-based jobseeker's allowance with a top-up of the income-based element, so as to give priority and recognition to the insurance part of the benefit.[200]

192   JA 1995, s 35(1). This differs from the definition in SSCBA 1992, s 122(1), on which see *R(U) 8/83*; *R(U) 2/84*; and *R(U) 1/89*.
193   See *R(U) 5/82* and *R(U) 4/85* under the previous provisions.
194   SI 1996/207, reg 81(2)(c).
195   SI 1996/207, reg 81(3).
196   *R(U) 5/85*.
197   *R(U) 5/85*, para 10, R F M Heggs, Comr.
198   JA 1995, s 4(6). Normally, for the reasons discussed above, the applicable amount will be more than the personal rate if there is entitlement to both components. However, if there is a non-dependant deduction to be made from the applicable amount, the personal rate may be higher.
199   JA 1995, s 4(8).
200   JA 1995, s 4(7), (9) and (10).

Chapter 15

Statutory sick pay and incapacity benefit

Part 1 General

A Introduction

The system of benefits for sick and disabled people was described in 1978 as 'a ragbag of provisions based on differing, sometimes conflicting and anachronistic principles'.[1] As will be seen in this chapter, this description remains valid today, despite (or, more accurately, owing to) the changes to incapacity and disability benefits since then.[2] Previous editions of this book have covered both types of benefit within the same chapter.[3] This has not been possible within the organisational framework of this edition, but the new treatment reflects one of the fundamental distinctions within the social security system. In broad terms, benefits for sickness and incapacity are insurance-based earnings-replacement benefits, whilst disability benefits are non-contributory in nature and are designed, in one way or another, to provide financial assistance towards the extra costs associated with disability. The same individual, depending on his or her particular circumstances, may qualify for either or both forms of benefit.

Furthermore, not all forms of assistance for sick and disabled people are properly to be described as 'social security', and some appropriately so termed are also dealt with elsewhere in the book. Excluded from the present chapter, in addition to disability benefits,[4] are the following.

i Disabled person's tax credit

Disabled person's tax credit, the successor to disability working allowance, is a form of means-tested in-work cash assistance for people with disabilities with low earnings. This has already been considered in chapter 10 in the context of tax credits.

---

1 Simkins and Tickner *Whose Benefit?* (1978) p 17. Cf '[t]his dreadful mess is a tribute to the havoc which politicians' over-zealous response to interest group pressures can create': Dilnot, Kay and Morris *The Reform of Social Security* (1984) p 100.
2 Large in Dalley (ed) *Disability and Social Policy* (1991) p 116.
3 See eg the 4th edition of this book, ch 4.
4 On which see ch 19, below.

ii Schemes for disability resulting from specific causes

For historical and policy reasons, there are special social security schemes for those disabled as the result of industrial accident or disease or because of service in the armed forces. These will be described in chapters 20 and 21 respectively. In 1979 two new schemes were introduced to remedy deficiencies in the private law. These are administered by the Department for Work and Pensions (DWP) and the Department of the Environment, Transport and the Regions respectively and are not primarily seen as social security measures. The Vaccine Damage Payments Act 1979 provides for compensation where severe disablement results from vaccination against certain diseases or contact from persons so vaccinated.[5] The Pneumoconiosis etc (Workers Compensation) Act 1979 confers lump sum benefits on those who have suffered from specific lung diseases as a result of their employment but have received no tort compensation because their employer ceased business before the manifestation of the symptoms.[6] Since 1964 a criminal injury compensation scheme has existed under which payments are made to those sustaining personal injury directly attributable to a crime of violence. The payments were originally ex gratia in character but since the Criminal Justice Act 1988, which placed the scheme on a statutory basis, they have been the subject of legal entitlement. The scheme is financed from general taxation, but is not administered by the DWP.[7]

iii Special funds

Over the past 30 years a number of special funds have been established, administered by charities, to provide assistance to people facing particular problems.[8] The first such fund, the Family Fund, was set up in 1973 as an immediate response to the thalidomide disaster.[9] It originally conferred benefits in cash and kind on families having the care of a child with a severe congenital disability, but subsequently all children with severe disabilities became eligible. It is financed by government but is administered by the Joseph Rowntree Memorial Trust. Since 1988 the Macfarlane Trust has administered three government funds established to help people with haemophilia and HIV infection. Payments are made by way of grants or regular payments for living expenses. The Independent Living Fund (ILF) was set up in 1988 for very severely physically or mentally disabled people on low incomes whose needs were not adequately catered for under the income support scheme. The aim of the ILF was to provide extra cash help to enable such individuals to pay for personal care or domestic assistance in order to live in the community. The ILF closed in November 1992 in anticipation of the introduction of the government's community care reforms in April 1993. People assisted by the ILF continue to be helped under a successor fund, the ILF (Extension) Fund. A less generous scheme, the Independent Living (1993) Fund, was created to deal with new cases.

5   See Dworkin [1978–79] JSWL 330; Goldberg (1996) 3 JSSL 100; Pywell (2002) 9 JSSL 73. The 1979 Act has been amended by SI 2002/1592.
6   See Wikeley *Compensation for Industrial Disease* (1993) pp 48–50.
7   See Miers *State Compensation for Criminal Injuries* (1997); and Foster *Claiming Compensation for Criminal Injuries* (2nd edn, 1997).
8   This approach has been criticised for reinforcing dependency and stereotyping disabled people as burdens on charity. See Oliver *The Politics of Disablement* (1990) p 98.
9   See Bradshaw *The Family Fund* (1980); and Lawton (1990) 16 Child: care, health and development 35.

iv   Benefits in kind

There is a wide variety of facilities provided for sick and disabled people under the National Health Service, and local authorities are under a duty to make an assessment where it appears that a person may be in need of community care services.[10] Such services are normally provided in kind, although there is now a limited power for local authorities to make direct cash payments in lieu of such services.[11]

B   History[12]

i   National health insurance

State involvement in provision for the sick and disabled effectively dates from the National Insurance Act 1911 (NIA 1911). Prior to that date, there was no 'system' of medical care outside the rudimentary facilities provided by the poor law. Those who could not afford treatment had to rely on charitable assistance or membership of a friendly society. The latter had existed for several centuries but, with nineteenth-century industrialisation, had come into their own in providing support, particularly in cases of sickness and death, for the more prosperous workman or artisan.[13] In 1905, their total membership amounted to no less than 6 million. Nevertheless, over one half of the working population had no form of sickness insurance.[14] In the words of Lloyd George, the chief architect of national health insurance, there was a perceived need for the state to assist in making 'provisions against the accidents of life which bring so much undeserved poverty to hundreds of thousands of homes, accidents which are quite inevitable such as the death of the breadwinner or his premature breakdown in health'.[15] The conviction was strengthened by the study which he initiated of the German insurance system.[16]

While the case for a national health insurance scheme was a powerful one, the proposal had to face considerable opposition from the friendly societies and the insurance companies, who had vested interests in the existing systems, and from the medical profession who resisted the notion of a national salaried service and bureaucratic control.[17] The result was a compromise. The provision of medical services was administered by specially created bodies, the Insurance Committees, on which insured persons, medical practitioners, local authorities and central government were represented. But the administration of cash benefits was in the hands of 'approved societies', such friendly societies, trade unions, insurance and collecting societies as satisfied two conditions: they were not carried on for profit and they were subject to the absolute control of their members. Individuals would enrol with the society of their

---

10   National Health Service and Community Care Act 1990, s 47. See Clements *Community Care and the Law* (2000).

11   Community Care (Direct Payments) Act 1996 and SI 1997/734.

12   Harris *National Health Insurance 1911–1946* (1946); Levy *National Health Insurance: a Critical Study* (1944); Eder *National Health Insurance and the Medical Profession in Britain, 1913–1939* (1982).

13   Gosden *The Friendly Societies in England, 1815–1875* (1961) and *Self-Help: Voluntary Associations in the 19th Century* (1973).

14   Bruce *The Coming of the Welfare State* (4th edn, 1968) p 214.

15   Quoted in Fraser *The Evolution of the British Welfare State* (2nd edn, 1984) p 161.

16   In 1911 the government issued a Memorandum on Sickness and Invalidity Insurance in Germany (Cd 5678). See further Hennock *British Social Reform and German Precedents* (1987).

17   *Eder* n 12, above, pp 31–45.

choice but, within certain statutory limits, the society had power to make rules and regulations governing the payment of benefit, and might decline to accept a person as member (except on the ground of age). The scheme covered initially all manual workers, and non-manual workers earning less than £160 per year. In return for weekly contributions (4d for men, 3d for women) the insured person would, on proof of incapacity for work, be entitled to 10s per week (7s 6d for women) from the fourth day of incapacity for a maximum of 26 weeks. After that period had elapsed, 'disablement benefit' was payable so long as the member remained incapable of work, though the amounts in question were half those for sickness benefit. The individual society could, however, pay additional benefits at its discretion and in the manner it thought fit from any surplus in its funds. The result was that benefits varied widely according to the membership and geographical location of the society. No doubt the intention was to preserve the 'private' nature of friendly society insurance, but it seemed hardly to be compatible with a compulsory scheme.[18]

In contrast to unemployment insurance, which underwent many changes between 1911 and 1946, the structure of health insurance, at least as regards sickness and disablement benefits, remained more or less intact until the fundamental revision at the end of the Second World War. The number of persons insured was gradually increased. The Royal Commission on Health Insurance, reporting in 1926,[19] recommended certain minor changes in contribution requirements and these were effected two years later. Its most substantial criticisms, however, went largely unheeded until Beveridge's Report in 1942. The scheme, it was said, was too little concerned with health improvement – 'sickness insurance' would have been a more appropriate title than 'health insurance'. The intended democratic nature of the approved societies had become a fiction – they were ordinary commercial undertakings in a different guise.[20] Perhaps most important of all, benefit was inadequate in that, unlike unemployment benefit, it did not provide for dependants' allowances. The 1926 Report, then, in some ways looked forward to the substantial reforms proposed by Beveridge and implemented by the government after the Second World War.

ii Beveridge and the National Insurance Act 1946

The fundamental achievement of this period was, of course, the establishment of the National Health Service.[21] The provision of medical services and of medicaments was extricated from the insurance scheme and they were made freely available to all. Sickness benefit was brought more into line with unemployment benefit: the rates were assimilated and for the first time sick claimants were paid an allowance for dependants. At the same time, though remaining ineligible for unemployment benefit, the self-employed became entitled to sickness benefit.[22] This was, however, a controversial measure and the self-employed were required to pay an extra 3d a week in contributions. The approved societies were abolished and their functions transferred to the newly created Ministry of National Insurance. Disablement benefit also disappeared and sickness benefit became

---

18 *Harris* n 12, above, pp 88–93.
19 Cmnd 2591.
20 The minority recommended the abolition of the approved societies and the transfer of their functions to local authorities.
21 National Health Service Act 1946, implementing proposals in the White Paper (1944, Cmd 6502).
22 See Brown *A Policy Vacuum* (1992) pp 19–22. At first this reform was thought to be too impracticable to administer and the original 1946 Bill had a waiting-period of 24 days for such persons.

payable for an unlimited duration provided that the contribution requirements had been satisfied. But the distinction between short-term and long-term incapacity was not entirely eradicated: the contribution conditions became much more stringent after a year's entitlement to benefit.[23] Indeed, the distinction was broadened in 1966 when an earnings-related supplement was introduced, albeit only for the first 26 weeks of incapacity.[24]

iii New provision in the 1970s for people incapable of work

In the late 1960s the government sponsored a major survey of disabled people in Great Britain, conducted by the Office of Population Censuses and Surveys (OPCS), the findings of which revealed both the significant numbers of people affected and the inadequacy of national insurance in meeting their needs.[25] In response to the problem, the strategy of successive governments was to make piecemeal improvements by identifying and satisfying specific needs.[26] The OPCS Survey had revealed that poverty was particularly prevalent among the long-term disabled. Paradoxically, as we have seen, the national insurance system conferred less generous support on this group than on those whose incapacity for work lasted for less than six months. In 1971 the Conservative government introduced invalidity benefit,[27] comprising a pension (in effect the standard flat-rate sickness benefit) plus a small allowance which varied according to the claimant's age at the onset of incapacity. This allowance was based on the assumed greater loss of those giving up work at an earlier stage in their working life. The emphasis on satisfying needs, rather than providing earnings replacement, was taken further by various complementary measures. These reforms favoured the recipients of invalidity benefit relative to sickness benefit claimants: there was no reduction for contribution deficiencies; higher increases were paid for dependent children; and there was an easier test of dependency for a working wife. The trend was reinforced when, in 1979, an earnings-related component was added to the invalidity pension, though only on the basis of contributions made to the new pension scheme;[28] and in 1982 the earnings-related supplement to sickness benefit was abolished.[29]

Of course, these reforms could not assist those unable to satisfy the conditions for the contributory benefits, the majority of whom had been disabled from birth. There was also a substantial number who had not worked sufficiently to pay the requisite number of contributions.[30] In 1975 the non-contributory invalidity pension was introduced to cater for this group.[31] It became payable in circumstances similar to those of the contributory invalidity pension but without contribution conditions and (to achieve equity as compared with those who had contributed to the National Insurance Fund) at a lower rate.

---

23 NIA 1946, s 12(2).
24 NIA 1966, s 2. This was abolished in 1982: see n 29, below.
25 P 676, below.
26 Report on Social Security Provision for Chronically Sick and Disabled People (1973–74, HC 276) paras 52–53.
27 NIA 1971, s 3. The previous Labour administration had proposed an earnings-related pension for those incapable of work for more than six months: see White Paper *National Superannuation and Social Insurance* (1969, Cmnd 3883) para 88, and the Bill of the same name, cl 12.
28 Social Security Pensions Act 1975, s 14 (SSPA 1975). This has since been phased out: see p 532, below.
29 Social Security Act (No 2) 1980, s 4 (SSA (No 2) 1980).
30 *Report on Social Security Provision* n 26, above, para 24.
31 SSBA 1975, s 6.

In addition, there were two categories of disabled persons who were excluded from the contributory scheme: women not normally engaged in remunerative employment and children. Consideration of the so-called 'disabled housewife' featured prominently in the campaign conducted by the pressure groups.[32] The OPCS Survey revealed that there were some 225,000 married women prevented by their disability from doing housework,[33] though of these only about one-fifth were under pensionable age without entitlement to any personal benefit.[34] Those not engaged in remunerative employment were not, of course, entitled to sickness or invalidity benefit. The solution adopted in 1977 was to extend to this group entitlement to the non-contributory invalidity pension if they were able to show that they were 'incapable of performing normal household duties'.[35] This reform suffered from the obvious and serious objection that it was discriminatory:[36] it assumed that only married women were primarily responsible for housework, and to receive benefit they had to satisfy not only the 'household duties' test but also the condition applied to all claimants, that they were incapable of paid work.

iv Developments in the 1980s

The further reforms carried out by the Conservative governments of the 1980s were explicable in terms of two policy goals: a reduction in administrative costs and the elimination of sex discrimination. So far as the former was concerned, a large majority of employees have a contractual right to sick pay from their employers during short spells off work, independently of social security entitlement. The overlap with sickness benefit suggested that there would be substantial administrative savings if the burden of income replacement were to be borne exclusively by employers for such periods.[37] In 1983, therefore, a statutory obligation on employers to pay prescribed amounts replaced sickness benefit for the first eight weeks of incapacity but the financial burden remained with the National Insurance Fund, as employers deducted the cost of such payments from their contributions liability.[38] In 1986 the period of statutory sick pay was extended to 28 weeks,[39] with the consequence that sickness benefit remained relevant only for the self-employed and the relatively few employees not entitled to statutory sick pay.

Sex discrimination was implicit in two of the non-contributory benefits introduced in the 1970s: women who were married or cohabiting had to satisfy the additional household duties test to gain entitlement to the non-contributory invalidity pension and were excluded altogether from the invalid care allowance (now carer's allowance). The latter provision was held by the European Court of Justice[40] to be in breach of the Council Directive on Equal Treatment[41] and was repealed in 1986.[42] After a prolonged

---

32 Eg Disablement Income Group *Creating a National Disability Income* (1972) pp 19–20.
33 Harris *Handicapped and Impaired in Great Britain* (1971) pp 63–89.
34 *Report on Social Security Provision* n 26, above, para 43.
35 SSBA 1975, s 6.
36 See the NIAC *Report on the Household Duties Test for Married Women* (1980, Cmnd 7955).
37 Green Paper *Income During Initial Sickness* (1980, Cmnd 7864).
38 Social Security and Housing Benefits Act 1982, Pt I. But see now p 527, below.
39 SSA 1985, s 18.
40 *Drake v Chief Adjudication Officer* 150/85 [1987] QB 166, [1986] 3 All ER 65.
41 Council Directive (EEC) 79/7, on which see ch 2, above.
42 SSA 1986, s 37.

review of the former,[43] the government decided to abolish the non-contributory invalidity pension altogether and to replace it by a new benefit, the severe disablement allowance, payable to a narrower range of claimants but without sex discrimination. The favoured groups were those incapable of work since childhood and those who satisfied certain functional tests of severe disablement.[44]

v Change in the 1990s

In the early 1990s the Conservative government, pursuing its relentless quest to find savings in the social security budget, turned its attention to invalidity benefit. In 1993 a Department of Social Security (DSS) report identified three areas in which benefit expenditure was increasing fastest: invalidity benefit, housing benefit and lone parents on income support.[45] This report noted that the number of invalidity benefit recipients had increased from 600,000 in 1978–79 to almost 1.5 million in 1992–93, at a time when the nation's health had improved. The cost of this benefit had doubled since 1982–83.[46] The implication was that at best the existing test for incapacity for work was being incorrectly applied,[47] and at worst the system was encouraging absenteeism and abuse. Yet it is important to explore the reasons for the growth in the numbers of invalidity benefit claimants during this period.[48] One possible explanation is that as the rules governing entitlement to unemployment benefit (as it then was) were both made stricter and enforced more rigorously, so more of those claimants on the borderline between incapacity and unemployment will have moved towards the former. Independent research has also demonstrated that more than half of this increase was attributable to three demographic factors. These were: people over pensionable age drawing invalidity benefit, rather than the retirement pension, for tax reasons; the increased participation of women in the labour market; and a gradual increase in the number of disabled people in the relevant age groups.[49] The impact of a tightening labour market was also highlighted as a contributory factor: 'What is perceived as a problem for the government (increased costs) may actually be a problem for the claimants (inability to find appropriate work).'[50] This is consistent with earlier studies which suggested that, when jobs are scarce, medical certification may be a convenient way of reducing the number of marginal and elderly workers on the employment register, especially in areas of high unemployment.[51]

The government nevertheless argued that invalidity benefit, being non-means-tested and taking no account of occupational pension provision, was poorly targeted. It was also the last pre-pension benefit to contain an earnings-related element, and anomalously could be paid for five years beyond pensionable age. The government also took the view that the test for incapacity for work had been diluted by case law to include too

43 See *NIAC* n 36, above; Equal Opportunities Commission *Behind Closed Doors* (1981); and DHSS *Review of the Household Duties Test* (1983).
44 Health and Social Security Act 1984, s 11.
45 DSS *The Growth of Social Security* (1993).
46 *DSS* n 45, above, paras 4.5–4.6.
47 For some evidence of GPs' misunderstandings of the criteria for the award of invalidity benefit, see Ritchie *GPs and IVB* DSS Research Report No 18 (1993).
48 See also Esping-Andersen *The Three Worlds of Welfare Capitalism* (1990) p 154.
49 Berthoud *Invalidity Benefit: Where will the savings come from?* (1993) p 5.
50 *Berthoud* n 49, above, p 6.
51 Stone *The Disabled State* (1984) p 11. See also Disney and Webb (1991) 101 Econ J 252; and Holmes, Lynch and Molho (1991) 20 J Soc Pol 87.

many non-medical factors, so progressively widening the claimant population beyond those who were 'genuinely' incapable of all work.[52] In order to tackle these perceived defects, the Social Security (Incapacity for Work) Act 1994 was enacted.[53] The legislation came into force in April 1995. Sickness benefit and invalidity benefit were replaced by incapacity benefit, which is less generous than its predecessors in a number of key respects, discussed further below. The most fundamental change, however, was the introduction of the 'all work test', purportedly designed to provide a more objective assessment of a person's capacity or incapacity for work.

The Labour government, elected in 1997, had no intention of reverting to the more generous long-term provision of invalidity benefit. Instead, the new incapacity benefit was adapted so as to ensure that it was consistent with the incoming government's objectives for welfare reform.[54] Thus the Welfare Reform and Pensions Act 1999 (WRPA 1999) renamed the all work test as the 'personal capability assessment':[55] rather than being confined to an assessment of incapacity for work for benefit purposes, it was modified so as to elicit information designed to assist in the process of getting claimants back to work. The legislation also revised the criteria for eligibility for incapacity benefit in key respects, with the dual aim of restricting entitlement to those with close links to the labour market and to those most in need. Accordingly, the contribution conditions are now tighter than before and benefit entitlement is reduced where an occupational or personal pension is in payment.[56] The only way in which the 1999 Act expanded the rules on entitlement was in making incapacity benefit available to persons incapacitated in youth, who were not required to meet the contribution conditions.[57] Yet this reform reflects the fact that the 1999 Act also abolished severe disablement allowance, except for existing claimants.[58] New claimants who are incapacitated later in life, and who fail to meet the tighter contribution conditions for incapacity benefit (typically women), now have no access to any non-contributory incapacity benefit. In the last resort, their only recourse is to income support.

C The concept of incapacity

Incapacity and disability are clearly interrelated concepts. If disability is defined as a reduction or loss of functional ability that results from an anatomic or functional abnormality or loss, then incapacity is the loss of capacity to earn money from working that arises from the disability.[59] On one interpretation, throughout the history of social security there has been a tension between balancing the need to maintain industrial discipline with that of relieving poverty. Thus the question of 'who is excused from work' has been described as 'the heart of poverty policy'.[60] The prevailing definition of incapacity for work thus represents an important economic and social boundary, which reflects and reinforces 'a series of normative values about the nature and extent of the social obligation to work'.[61] Those who are adjudged to be incapable of work

---

52 See eg Mr P Lilley MP, 236 HC Official Report (6th series) col 35.
53 See Berthoud (1995) 2 JSSL 61; Bonner (1995) 2 JSSL 86; and Wikeley (1995) 58 MLR 523.
54 McKeever (2000) 29 ILJ 145.
55 WRPA 1999, s 61.
56 WRPA 1999, ss 62 and 63.
57 WRPA 1999, s 64.
58 WRPA 1999, ss 65 and 85.
59 See Keeler (1994) 44 UTLJ 275.
60 Handler (1990) 56 Brooklyn LR 897. See also Liebman (1976) 89 Harv LR 833.
61 Diller (1996) 44 UCLA LR 361.

accordingly have a socially acceptable reason for their absence from the labour force and are seen as 'deserving' claimants. Claimants who are found capable of work are expected to join the ranks of jobseekers, although they may have disabilities that put them at a distinct disadvantage in the labour market. The 'deserving' status of those who are incapable of work is also reflected in the more generous rate of benefit paid under the incapacity benefit scheme than for those claimants subject to long-term unemployment, a distinction questioned by the Social Security Advisory Committee (SSAC).[62]

D Scope and structure

The income maintenance of those who are unable to work because they are sick remains one of the cardinal purposes of social security. Its importance may be gauged from the fact that studies consistently show that some four to five per cent of the population are absent from work due to sickness for at least one day in the previous week.[63] Under the 1946 legislation there was a single benefit payable, whatever the duration of the incapacity. This approach proved to be inappropriate as it masked fundamental differences between two sections of the population. The majority (some 90 per cent) of those off work experienced a period of incapacity of no more than six weeks; their needs were limited to income maintenance during this short period. However, the remaining 10 per cent evidently required a greater degree of financial assistance for much longer periods.[64] The 1971 reforms adopted a period of six months as the dividing line between the short-term and long-term sick. Hence sickness benefit (and later statutory sick pay) were payable for the first six months of incapacity for work, and invalidity benefit thereafter. The April 1995 changes retained the distinction between these two groups, but effectively extended the definition of short-term illness to cover periods of up to one year. Thus the principal effect of these changes was that, although claimants are now required to satisfy the all work test (now personal capability assessment) after 28 weeks, they have to wait 12 months before qualifying for the top rate of incapacity benefit. The government offered no clear rationale for this distinction during the debates on the Social Security (Incapacity for Work) Act 1994.[65] This downgrading of entitlement to a key contributory benefit necessarily means that more claimants have to supplement their incapacity benefit with means-tested assistance.

In order to aid exposition, the incapacity provisions are dealt with as follows. The principal benefit for those suffering temporary absence from work due to illness is statutory sick pay, or SSP (Part 2). The structure and rules of entitlement for incapacity benefit are considered in Part 3. Finally, Part 4 deals with the assessment of incapacity for work itself and related matters.

---

62 SSAC *Social Security Provision for Disability: A Case for Change?* (1997).
63 ONS *Social Trends 2000* (2000) p 75.
64 Creedy and Disney *Social Insurance in Transition* (1985) p 125.
65 'We decided to replace [invalidity benefit] with a new benefit and it was up to us to make a judgment about both the scope and the levels payable. The figures for the introduction of the new benefit were arrived at using that element of judgment. I cannot say that there is any justification for it besides that simple assertion' (Mr N Scott MP, Standing Committee E, col 195). An amendment to restrict payment of the lower rate of benefit to 196 days was lost by just two votes at the Report stage in the House of Lords: 554 HL Official Report (5th series) cols 1436–1451.

Part 2 Statutory sick pay

A General

Since the Second World War there has been a considerable growth in contractual provision for occupational sick pay; in 1981 it was estimated that some 90 per cent of employees benefited from some such scheme.[66] Entitlement to the state sickness benefit was unaffected, although the employer might, and usually did, take account of social security provision in calculating the amount of sick pay. The processing of two claims for payment seemed wasteful and it was mainly to reduce administrative expenditure that a government Green Paper in 1980 proposed that employers should be bound to pay sick pay, at a minimum level, for the first eight weeks of incapacity, during which period sickness benefit would not be payable.[67] The proposal provoked considerable opposition from different quarters;[68] first, from trade unions and poverty pressure groups, who argued that it would involve a radical departure from the notion of comprehensive state welfare established since Beveridge and less rhetorically that the suggested flat-rate payment, without dependency additions, would disadvantage families in comparison with sickness benefit.[69] Secondly, the CBI felt that the additional burden on the employer would not be sufficiently compensated by the simple reduction of 0.5–0.6 per cent in social security contributions proposed by the government. This latter point was eventually conceded by the government and the Social Security and Housing Benefits Act 1982, which implemented the scheme, made provision for a 100 per cent reimbursement by the National Insurance Fund of statutory sick pay (SSP). Later, in 1985, the Fund also became responsible for paying social security contributions during periods of SSP, notwithstanding the argument that this would leave employers without any financial incentive for verifying the validity of employees' claims. The same legislation extended the scheme to cover 28 weeks of incapacity.

The early 1990s saw a series of further changes. The Statutory Sick Pay Act 1991[70] limited employers to recouping 80 per cent of the cost of SSP payments by way of set-off against National Insurance contributions. However, small employers whose contributions liability in the relevant year did not exceed a prescribed threshold still recovered the full cost of SSP.[71] The 1991 Act also effected substantial cuts in the amount of benefit payable.[72] Three years later the Statutory Sick Pay Act 1994 abolished the right of employers to reimbursement of the costs of SSP altogether.[73] The exception for small employers was maintained, albeit on a different basis.[74] However, the 1994 Act also contained powers enabling the Secretary of State to introduce a new form of reimbursement scheme. This power was exercised so that now all employers, regardless of size, can recover SSP costs, but only where expenditure exceeds 13 per cent of their

---

66 13 HC Official Report (6th series) cols 642–643.
67 *Income During Initial Sickness* (Cmnd 7864).
68 See Appendix 2 to the *Second Report* of the Committee on Social Services (1980–81, HC 113) for a summary of the published responses to the Green Paper.
69 The dependency additions to sickness (and unemployment) benefit were themselves abolished in 1984: p 247, above.
70 See Lewis (1991) 20 ILJ 159.
71 Social Security Contributions and Benefits Act 1992, s 158 (SSCBA 1992) (since repealed by SI 1995/512).
72 See *Lewis* n 70, above. The 1991 Act also abolished the arrangements whereby employers were compensated for the cost of the national insurance contributions which they paid on SSP itself.
73 Statutory Sick Pay Act 1994, s 1 (SSPA 1994).
74 Originally small employers received a refund of 80 per cent for SSP costs for the first six weeks of an employee's illness, followed by 100 per cent thereafter. Then they received no compensation for four weeks, but thereafter qualified for 100 per cent relief. Now they are only eligible under the Percentage Threshold Scheme discussed at n 75, below.

gross National Insurance liability.[75] The main thrust of the 1994 Act was to transfer to industry and business a significant social cost previously borne by the state. The principal justification for this change was the need to improve incentives for employers to tackle high rates of sick leave.[76] The same argument has been deployed as an argument for transferring the cost of the industrial injuries scheme to employers.[77]

B   Entitlement to statutory sick pay

i   Persons covered

The scheme broadly covers all those who are treated as employed earners for social security purposes and thus pay Class 1 National Insurance contributions.[78] Married women with reduced contributions liability are included and there are analogous provisions governing airmen, mariners and workers on the continental shelf.[79] However, the following are not entitled to SSP:[80]

- employees over the age of 65;
- those employed for a period of less than three months;[81]
- those earning less than the lower earnings limit currently in force;[82]
- those who were entitled to incapacity benefit or severe disablement allowance in the 57 days immediately preceding their current period of entitlement;[83]
- those who have not yet started work under their contract of employment;
- those affected by a stoppage of work due to a trade dispute at their place of employment;
- women employees who are pregnant or have just given birth and are within the disqualifying period for statutory maternity pay or maternity allowance;
- and those working for certain foreign employers or international agencies.

Moreover, by definition, self-employed workers are excluded from entitlement, but they may qualify for the lower rate of short-term incapacity benefit.

ii   Period of incapacity for work

The first condition of entitlement is that the day for which SSP is claimed forms part of a period of incapacity for work, that is, a period of four or more consecutive days of incapacity, whether the latter days are normally working days or not.[84] Benefit is not

---

75   SSPA 1994, s 3 and SI 1995/512. This Percentage Threshold Scheme effectively requires a positive epidemic of sickness in the workforce before reimbursement becomes available.
76   234 HC Official Report (6th series) col 1109.
77   Field *The State of Dependency* (2000) pp 21–22.
78   SSCBA 1992, s 151(1). Any attempt to contract out of SSP entitlement is void: s 151(2).
79   SI 1982/1349.
80   SSCBA 1992, Sch 11, para 2 and SI 1982/894, reg 16.
81   Except where the contract has become one for a longer period, or it was preceded by another contract with the same employer and the period linking the two contracts was less than eight weeks: SSCBA 1992, Sch 11, para 4.
82   On the assessment of earnings, see SSCBA 1992, s 163(2); SI 1982/894, reg 19(3); and *R(SSP) 1/89* (school dinner-lady ineligible as unable to include holiday retainer in earnings). On the lower earnings limit, see p 106, above.
83   There are special rules for welfare to work beneficiaries.
84   SSCBA 1992, s 152. Sundays therefore count for this purpose: *R(S) 3/88*. Incapacity during a night-shift is attributed to the day when the shift began: SI 1982/894, reg 2.

paid for the first three 'waiting' days of any period of incapacity for work.[85] Two spells of incapacity may be linked if not separated by more than eight weeks, thus obviating the need to serve again the three 'waiting days'. A day of incapacity is a day on which the employee is (or is deemed to be) 'incapable by reason of some specific disease or bodily or mental disablement of doing work which he can reasonably be expected to do' under the contract of service.[86]

iii Period of entitlement

Secondly, the employee must show that the day in question also falls within a 'period of entitlement'.[87] Most importantly, this limits the employer's liability to 28 weeks of incapacity of work.[88] The period of entitlement may end earlier if, as a result of linking periods of incapacity, SSP has been paid over a period of three years by the same employer[89] or the employee is placed in legal custody or leaves the EU.[90] The period of entitlement also ceases if the employee receiving SSP then falls under one of the various exclusionary heads of 'persons covered' (see above). This might apply if no work has been done by the employee under the contract of employment, or it has expired.[91] However, a series of consecutive daily contracts will be treated as giving rise to continuity of employment.[92] An exclusion also applies where there is a stoppage of work due to a trade dispute at the place of employment.[93] Moreover, SSP is superseded by statutory maternity pay or maternity allowance when the conditions for those benefits are satisfied.[94] Finally, title to incapacity benefit is preserved (and SSP is not payable) if the day of incapacity is separated from a prior period of entitlement to either of those benefits by less than eight weeks.[95]

iv Qualifying days

The final condition is that the day of claim is a 'qualifying day'.[96] This is, effectively, a day on which the employee is required to be available for work. Thus employees working a four-day week may only be paid SSP for absence on the four specified days, but for each such day they will be entitled to one-fourth of the weekly rate. In some cases, there will be evidence of an agreement as between employer and employee as to

85 SSCBA 1992, s 30A(3).
86 SSCBA 1992, s 151(4). On the meaning of 'some specific disease or bodily or mental disablement' see p 539, below.
87 SSCBA 1992, s 153 and Sch 11.
88 SSCBA 1992, s 155(4).
89 SI 1982/894, reg 3(3). Where a contract of service begins between two such linked periods, the period of entitlement begins with the first day of the second of those periods: SSCBA 1992, s 153(8).
90 SI 1982/1349, regs 3 and 5 and SSCBA 1992, s 162.
91 SSCBA 1992, ss 153(2)(c), and Sch 11, para 2(f), though a period of entitlement in relation to one contract of service may form part of a period of entitlement in relation to another such contract: s 153(4). Further, the employer's liability continues if a contract has been brought to an end solely, or mainly, for the purpose of avoiding SSP liability: SI 1982/894, reg 4.
92 *Brown v Chief Adjudication Officer* [1997] ICR 266.
93 SSCBA 1992, Sch 11, para 2(g). The employee is disentitled for the whole of the period of incapacity of work even if the stoppage is terminated: *R(SSP) 1/86*. But SSP is payable if he or she can show that they did not participate, or have a direct interest, in the trade dispute: SSCBA 1992, Sch 11, para 7. The law governing the equivalent disqualification from jobseeker's allowance applies: pp 505–514, above.
94 SSCBA 1992, ss 153(2)(d) and 153(11)–(12), and SI 1982/894, reg 3(4).
95 SSCBA 1992, Sch 11, para 2(d).
96 SSCBA 1992, s 154.

qualifying days, but the authorities will not have regard to such agreements made retrospectively or to those which identify 'qualifying days' by reference to actual days of incapacity,[97] practices which have led to abuse.[98] If there is no appropriate agreement on qualifying days, regard is had to those days when the employee is required to work.[99] If, in a particular week, the employee is not expected to work, Wednesday will nevertheless be a qualifying day; if no pattern of normal work can be established, all days of the week except recognised rest days are qualifying days.[100]

v Amount

Occupational sick pay rarely takes account of family size and, in transferring responsibility for short-term income maintenance to the employer, the government considered it appropriate to follow that model, rather than sickness benefit which included additions for dependants. It follows that those with adult dependants receive less under SSP than under what is now the lower rate of short-term incapacity benefit.[101] There is now just one rate of SSP; between 1983 and 1987 there were three rates of SSP, depending on the claimant's earnings, and between 1987 and 1995 there were two rates, but the lower rate was then abolished as part of the incapacity benefit reforms.[102]

vi Notification and evidence of incapacity

In general, employers are entitled to lay down their own rules as regards both the time and manner of notifying periods of sickness. Thus employers may require their staff to provide such information 'as may reasonably be required' for determining entitlement to SSP.[103] They must take reasonable steps to ensure that such rules are known to their workforce.[104] However, employers cannot require notification in advance of the first qualifying day in the period of incapacity for work.[105] Self-certification applies for the first week of sickness; an employee cannot be required to provide medical evidence for the first seven days in any period of incapacity.[106] In addition, employers cannot require the initial notification to be given personally, in the form of medical evidence or on an employer's document or other printed form, or more than once every seven days in a period of entitlement.[107] Conversely, the question of whether a doctor's certificate is required for periods of incapacity longer than a week is determined solely by the relevant employer. Now that employers generally receive no reimbursement from the National Insurance Fund for SSP, there is a considerable financial incentive for firms to verify the validity of employees' claims.[108]

97   SI 1982/894, reg 3.
98   Harvey *Industrial Relations and Employment Law* H [155–160].
99   SI 1982/894, reg 5(2)(a), thus not days when the employee is merely 'asked' to work overtime: *R(SSP) 1/85.*
100 SI 1982/894, reg 5(2)(b)–(c).
101 SSP involves considerably less redistribution than the state sickness scheme: Creedy and Disney *Social Insurance in Transition* (1985) p 140.
102 Social Security (Incapacity for Work) Act 1994, s 8 (SS(IW)A 1994).
103 Social Security Administration Act 1992, s 14(1) (SSAA 1992).
104 SI 1982/894, reg 7(1) and (4).
105 SI 1982/894, reg 7(1).
106 SI 1985/1604, reg 2(2). See Sch for the proforma medical certificate.
107 SI 1982/894, reg 7(4).
108 For an early analysis see Dean and Taylor-Gooby (1990) 19 J Soc Pol 47.

vii Adjudication and enforcement

SSP involves a mixture of private and public law, the state having a major supervisory role primarily to protect the National Insurance Fund. This is reflected in the arrangements for adjudication and enforcement. Originally employees, employers or DSS inspectors could refer questions to the Secretary of State on the scope of the scheme, following the procedure established for social security questions. As regards entitlement, either an employee or the Secretary of State could refer a question to the adjudicating authorities (adjudication officer, appeal tribunals, Commissioner). As a result of the Social Security Contributions (Transfer of Functions etc) Act 1999 (SS(TF)A 1999), these decision making functions all now fall within the remit of officers of the Board of the Inland Revenue, with rights of appeal to the tax appeal commissioners.[109] Where an employer fails to comply with a court order for payment, or in cases of insolvency, liability for payment is transferred to the Secretary of State.[110]

Part 3   Incapacity benefit

A The structure of incapacity benefit

i General

There are two types of incapacity benefit, described as short-term and long-term, and three different levels of benefit. Where persons who are incapable of work are ineligible for SSP, but satisfy the contribution conditions for what used to be sickness benefit,[111] they receive the lower rate of short-term incapacity benefit for the first 28 weeks of their illness.[112] After the expiry of this period, and providing that they satisfy the new and stricter personal capability assessment (previously the 'all work' test) for incapacity for work,[113] claimants move on to the so-called higher rate of the short-term incapacity benefit.[114] A claimant whose entitlement to SSP has expired makes the same transition.[115] It is only after 52 weeks that the long-term rate of incapacity benefit becomes payable.[116] In contrast, the invalidity pension (the predecessor of the long-term rate) was payable after 28 weeks of incapacity. Long-term incapacity benefit ceases when the claimant reaches pensionable age, although short-term incapacity benefit continues to be paid so long as the incapacity arose before attaining that age.[117]

The former invalidity pension could be supplemented by certain special additions.[118] The availability of these increases was restricted in various ways with the coming into force of incapacity benefit. Child dependency additions remain payable to incapacity

---

109   SSC(TF)A 1999, s 8(1)(f) and (g) and SI 1999/776.
110   SSCBA 1992, s 151(6); SI 1982/894, regs 9A–9C.
111   P 535, below.
112   SSCBA 1992, s 30B(2).
113   P 541, below.
114   SSCBA 1992, ss 30A(4) and 30B(2). 'So-called' as the higher rate of short-term incapacity benefit is the cash equivalent of SSP.
115   Days of entitlement to SSP are treated as days of entitlement to the lower rate of short-term incapacity benefit: SSCBA 1992, s 30D(3) and SI 1994/2946, reg 7.
116   SSCBA 1992, s 30A(5). This will be paid at a level equivalent to the current invalidity pension.
117   SSCBA 1992, s 30A(2).
118   See the 4th edition of this book, pp 165–167.

benefit claimants from the outset of their claim and to claimants who transfer over from SSP as from 28 weeks.[119] Additions for adult dependants remain available from 28 weeks, as previously, but are payable only if the dependant is aged over 60 or caring for children.[120] The age allowances were reduced in number from three to two and withdrawn from claimants aged over 45. Furthermore, there is no equivalent to the earnings-related additional pension for the purposes of incapacity benefit, and existing recipients have had that component of their benefit frozen in cash terms.[121] The net result of these changes is that incapacity benefit is markedly less generous than invalidity benefit.

The structure of incapacity benefit is built upon the foundations of three key concepts: a 'day of incapacity', a 'period of incapacity' and a 'day of entitlement'. These are therefore examined before we consider the conditions of entitlement to the benefit itself.

ii Day of incapacity

A 'day of incapacity' means any day on which a person is incapable of work.[122] The decision on whether a person is incapable of work is governed by Part XIIA of SSCBA 1992, which sets out the 'own occupation test' and the 'personal capability assessment' (previously the 'all work test'), considered in detail under section E, below. Any day falling within the maternity allowance period is treated as being a day of incapacity for work, unless the woman is disqualified for the day in question.[123] In addition, regulations provide for certain days either to be treated as days of incapacity or not to be treated as such days.[124] As regards the former, there are special rules for night-workers whose shifts span midnight, and who might otherwise suffer hardship if a 'day' were always regarded as running from midnight to midnight.[125] Days which are precluded from counting as days of incapacity include days for which no claim has been made (or a claim has been made but good cause has not been shown for a late claim). Days of disqualification during a period of absence from Great Britain or imprisonment in detention or legal custody (where the disqualification exceeds six weeks) and days of attendance at certain training courses for which a training allowance is paid are also excluded.[126]

iii Period of incapacity

A 'period of incapacity' means a period of four or more consecutive days, each of which is a day of incapacity for work.[127] An exception is provided for claimants who receive treatment for certain medical conditions (such as dialysis for chronic renal

---

119   SSCBA 1992, s 80(b) and (c). As originally drafted, the Bill provided for the latter group to qualify for child dependency additions only after 52 weeks, but the 28-week rule was reinstated by the House of Lords during the debates on SS(IW)A 1994: 554 HL Official Report (5th series) col 1452–1463 and 555 HL Official Report (5th series) col 377.
120   SSCBA 1992, s 86A and SI 1994/2945, reg 9.
121   See p 524, above.
122   SSCBA 1992, s 30C(1)(a).
123   SSCBA 1992, s 30C(2).
124   SSCBA 1992, s 30C(3).
125   SI 1994/2946, reg 5.
126   SI 1994/2946, reg 4.
127   SSCBA 1992, s 30C(1)(b). See for similar effect to SSP, SSCBA 1992, s 152(2).

failure); in such cases any two days of incapacity, whether or not consecutive, within a period of seven consecutive days are treated as a period of incapacity for work.[128]

Two periods of incapacity may be linked if not separated by more than eight weeks.[129] It follows that a single period of incapacity may be either one unbroken spell of incapacity or a series of seemingly discrete periods of incapacity which are joined together. There is no entitlement to incapacity benefit during any periods of non-incapacity which are interspersed between linked periods of incapacity.[130] The linking rule has two principal functions. First, it enables claimants who experience repeated bouts of incapacity to aggregate those periods in order to establish entitlement to the long-term rate of incapacity benefit (and so also avoid having to be subject to the three waiting days each time they fall ill). Secondly, it provides some incentive for claimants to try to return to work, knowing that they will be able to return to their previous rate of benefit should the work only last a short period. The Secretary of State is empowered to increase the length of the linking rule from eight weeks.[131]

To date the linking rule has been made more generous in two types of case. In both instances the underlying purpose is primarily to encourage sick or disabled people to take up employment. First, in the exercise of the enabling power to extend the linking rule, a 'welfare to work beneficiary' may link together two periods of incapacity for work providing they are separated by no more than 52 weeks. A 'welfare to work beneficiary' is a person who has been receiving a benefit on the basis of incapacity for work[132] for a period of more than 196 days (ie 28 weeks), but whose benefit has now stopped.[133] In addition, the person concerned, within a week of such entitlement stopping, must have either started a training course (for which an allowance is paid) or have entered paid employment. Such individuals must also have notified the DWP, within a month of their benefit stopping, that they have started training or work (alternatively, they must have appealed successfully against a decision that they were capable of work). Any persons who meet these criteria have the benefit of a fixed 52-week linking period (irrespective of how many periods of incapacity fall within the 52 weeks), enabling them to return to the same level of benefit as they received before the training or work started. Once the 52-week period has expired, claimants may not enjoy the benefit of a further extended linking period until another 28 weeks have elapsed and they again meet the conditions set out above.

Secondly, primary legislation provides for a two-year linking period for individuals who are engaged (and normally so engaged) in remunerative work but then cease to be so engaged, providing that they were entitled to disabled person's tax credit in the week in which they stopped. In addition, the claimant must have qualified for disabled person's tax credit in the first instance by virtue of either the higher rate of short-term incapacity benefit or the long-term rate of that benefit being payable.[134] A parallel provision applies to claimants who have moved from either of those rates of incapacity benefit into training for work.[135]

128 SSCBA 1992, s 30C(4)(a) and SI 1994/2946, reg 6.
129 SSCBA 1992, s 30(1)(c). See for similar effect to SSP, SSCBA 1992, s 152(3). In the context of s 30C a 'week' means any period of seven days (contra the standard definition of a week as seven days starting on a Sunday: SSCBA 1992, s 122(1)).
130 *Chief Adjudication Officer v Astle* (17 March 1999, unreported), CA, Lawtel doc C8400404; see Bonner (1999) 6 JSSL 203.
131 SSCBA 1992, s 30C(4)(b).
132 This need not be incapacity benefit; it might be eg income support paid on the basis of incapacity. SSP is excluded.
133 SI 1995/311, reg 13A.
134 SSCBA 1992, s 30C(5).
135 SSCBA 1992, s 30C(6).

iv   Day of entitlement

In addition to identifying days of incapacity which form periods of incapacity, it is important to be clear as to which are days of entitlement to incapacity benefit. In particular, the number of days on which a person has been entitled to short-term incapacity benefit are crucial for determining the length of entitlement to that benefit and the period for which it is paid at the higher rate. It is also fundamental for identifying the point at which the long-term rate is payable, especially in cases of terminal illness.[136] Legislation provides that the first three waiting days and any days of entitlement to maternity allowance count towards days of entitlement to the short-term incapacity benefit.[137] Days of entitlement to SSP also qualify for this purpose.[138] Predictably, any day for which the claimant is disqualified from incapacity benefit is excluded from consideration.[139]

B   Entitlement to short-term incapacity benefit

i   General

Short-term incapacity benefit is paid for a maximum of 364 days (ie a year) in any period of incapacity for work.[140] It is paid at the lower rate for the first 196 days (ie 28 weeks) of entitlement and at the higher rate thereafter.[141] The introduction of SSP and its extension in 1986 to cover the first 28 weeks of incapacity means that today the lower rate of short-term incapacity benefit (formerly sickness benefit) plays only a residual role in the social security system.[142] It is available to those self-employed and unemployed people who become incapable of work and satisfy the contribution conditions. It is also available to those who are employed but not entitled to SSP, because of one of the various exclusionary rules, for example, where the contract of employment is for less than three months. The lower rate of short-term incapacity benefit is a flat-rate sum, slightly less than the full adult rate of contribution-based jobseeker's allowance to reflect the fact that, unlike the latter, it is not taxable.[143] It may be supplemented by an adult dependant's addition.[144]

The higher rate of short-term incapacity benefit is payable after 28 weeks. Claimants who have previously been entitled to the lower-rate will be required to satisfy the personal capability assessment at this stage, if they have not done so already. The same applies to those previously in receipt of SSP. For most claimants, however, the transition to a 'higher' rate of short-term incapacity benefit after 28 weeks is not as generous as it might sound: the higher rate is actually paid at the same rate as SSP. Unlike SSP, however, it may be supplemented by additions for an adult dependant and any children.[145]

---

136   SSCBA 1992, s 30D(1).
137   SSCBA 1992, s 30D(2).
138   SSCBA 1992, s 30D(3) and SI 1994/2946, reg 7.
139   SSCBA 1992, s 30D(4).
140   SSCBA 1992, s 30A(4). An amendment to restrict payment of short-term incapacity benefit to 196 days was lost by just two votes at the Report stage in the passage of the SS(IW)A 1994 in the House of Lords: 554 HL Official Report (5th series) cols 1436–1451.
141   SSCBA 1992, s 30B(2). But see s 30B(3) for claimants over pensionable age.
142   In 2001 there were on average just 97,000 recipients of the lower rate of short-term incapacity benefit: DWP *Work and Pension Statistics 2001* (2001) p 84, Table 2.
143   See Income and Corporation Taxes Act 1988, s 617.
144   SSCBA 1992, s 86A: see pp 250–251, below.
145   SSCBA 1992, ss 80 and 86A.

Claimants may qualify for short-term incapacity benefit on the basis of either the standard rules or the special rules for those incapacitated in their youth.

ii The standard case

There are two basic rules of entitlement for short-term incapacity benefit in the standard case. First, claimants must satisfy the following contribution conditions:[146]

(1) during one of the last three tax years they must have paid National Insurance contributions of Class 1 and/or Class 2, the earnings factor from which is at least 25 times the lower earnings limit for that year; and

(2) for each of the two tax years immediately preceding the year in which the claim is made, they must have paid, or been credited with, contributions of Class 1 and/or Class 2, the earnings factor for which is at least 50 times the lower earnings limit for that year.

The first of these two contribution conditions was tightened by WRPA 1999. Previously, actual payment of contributions in *any* tax year was sufficient; the change to payment in any one of the three previous tax years was purportedly designed to reinforce the link between entitlement to benefit and recent labour market activity.[147] There is an alternative condition applicable to claimants over pensionable age (but within five years of that age) whose period of incapacity for work began before they reached that age.[148]

Secondly, the day for which benefit is claimed must be a day of incapacity for work forming part of a period of incapacity for work.[149]

iii Persons incapacitated in youth

As a result of amendments made by WRPA 1999, there is now an alternative route by which claimants who are incapacitated in their youth may qualify for short-term incapacity benefit.[150] This applies where the claimant:

(a) is aged 16 or over on the relevant day;

(b) is under the age of 20 or, in prescribed cases, 25 on a day which forms part of the period of incapacity for work;

(c) was incapable of work throughout a period of 196 consecutive days immediately preceding the relevant day (or an earlier day in the period of incapacity for work on which the claimant was aged 16 or over);

(d) satisfies the prescribed conditions as to presence and residence in Great Britain;[151] and

(e) is not receiving full-time education.[152]

A claimant who meets these conditions qualifies for incapacity benefit without having to satisfy the contribution conditions that normally apply. Previously, such claimants would only have been eligible for severe disablement allowance, paid at a lower rate

---

146 SSCBA 1992, s 30A(2)(a) and Sch 3, para 2. The previous dispensation for those whose incapacity resulted from an industrial accident or a prescribed disease, deeming these conditions to have been satisfied, was abolished in 1995 with the repeal of SSCBA 1992, s 102.
147 WRPA 1999, s 62(1); see p 525, above.
148 SSCBA 1992, s 30A(2)(b).
149 SSCBA 1992, s 30A(1).
150 SSCBA 1992, s 30(2A).
151 SI 1994/2496, reg 16.
152 SI 1994/2496, reg 17.

than the contributory benefit. The conditions set out above replicate those for severe disablement allowance, at least so far as access to that benefit for young people was concerned. The normal upper age limit of 20, the 196-day qualifying rule, the presence and residence requirements and the exclusion of those engaged in full-time education have all been transferred over into the new route to qualify for incapacity benefit. The key difference is that claimants could only qualify under this route for severe disablement allowance if their incapacity for work started before their twentieth birthday. For the new route for incapacity benefit, a claim may be made if the claimant had registered on a course of full-time education or of vocational or work-based training at least three months before attaining the age of 20 and the incapacity started before the age of 25.[153]

This special route for establishing entitlement was necessitated by the decision to abolish severe disablement allowance for new claimants.[154] Severe disablement allowance was the non-contributory equivalent of incapacity benefit and the successor to the non-contributory invalidity pension, first introduced in 1975. The existence of severe disablement allowance reflected the fact that social insurance cannot provide a comprehensive system of income maintenance for disabled people for the obvious reason that the congenitally disabled and others outside the labour market for considerable periods will have an inadequate contribution record. The decision to exempt those incapacitated in youth from the normal requirement of meeting the contributions conditions may have important longer term ramifications for National Insurance benefits. In particular, it raises questions about the exclusion of other groups from contributory benefits schemes. In this context it should be noted that the Social Security Select Committee has recommended that all those earning less than the lower earnings limit but more than £30 a week during the relevant qualifying years should have access to incapacity benefit.[155]

The SSAC had previously recommended that severe disablement allowance rates be raised progressively until they equal those for invalidity benefit.[156] The creation of this new route to qualifying for incapacity benefit has achieved that aim by another means, but only for those incapacitated in their youth. Although this group was favoured by the changes effected by WRPA 1999, many potential severe disablement allowance claimants were disadvantaged by the changes. Severe disablement allowance was predominantly a benefit claimed by those women who were unable to work but failed to satisfy the contribution conditions for incapacity benefit.[157] This was the group of claimants for whom the non-contributory invalidity pension was so important. The entitlement of existing severe disablement allowance recipients at the point of transition was preserved, but the benefit was withdrawn so far as new claimants were concerned. An adult (typically a woman) who would formerly have been eligible for severe disablement allowance now has no alternative but to claim income support, assuming she qualifies under the means test. Thus the impact of the abolition of severe disablement allowance will inevitably have a disproportionate effect on women.[158]

153   SI 1994/2496, reg 15 (which also sets out attendance requirements).
154   WRPA 1999, s 65 and SI 1994/2946, reg 19.
155   HC Social Security Committee *Fifth Report* (1999–2000, HC 56) para 145.
156   SSAC *Benefits for Disabled People: a Strategy for Change* (1989) p 63.
157   In 1999 women accounted for 60 per cent of severe disablement allowance claimants but just 32 per cent of recipients of long-term incapacity benefit: DSS *Social Security Statistics 1999* (1999) pp 182 and 193, Tables D1.10 and D2.01.
158   See Wikeley in Harris (ed) *Social Security Law in Context* (2000) pp 376–377.

C Entitlement to long-term incapacity benefit

Following the expiry of an award of short-term incapacity benefit (ie after 364 days), a claimant becomes entitled to the long-term rate of incapacity benefit for any subsequent day of incapacity for work in the same period of incapacity for work.[159] A person over pensionable age cannot receive the long-term rate. It follows that, as a general rule, a person cannot qualify for long-term incapacity benefit without first receiving short-term incapacity benefit. In addition, claimants must, of course, still be found to be incapable of work under the personal capability assessment. However, two exceptionally vulnerable groups of claimants qualify for long-term incapacity benefit after 28 weeks rather than the normal 52 weeks. These are the terminally ill and claimants in receipt of the highest rate of the care component of disability living allowance.[160] In such cases receipt of SSP for 28 weeks is regarded as receipt of short-term incapacity benefit.

The long-term rate of incapacity benefit may be supplemented by additions for an adult dependant and children on the same terms as the higher rate of short-term incapacity benefit (although the adult dependant addition is paid at a slightly higher rate). The long-term rate may also be increased by an age allowance. However, age allowances are only payable at two rates: a higher rate for those incapacitated before the age of 35 and a lower one for those incapacitated between 35 and 45.[161] No age additions are payable where the incapacity for work starts after the age of 45. In contrast, there were three rates of age allowance for invalidity benefit. The highest rate was paid to those under 40 on the first day of their incapacity; the middle rate to those aged 40–49 and the lowest rate to those aged 50–59 (or 50–54 if female). Although the new rules avoid the discrimination against women claimants inherent in the previous scheme, this represented a significant reduction in the value of incapacity benefit when compared with its predecessor, given that the majority of new claimants of invalidity benefit were aged 50 or over.[162]

D Abatement of incapacity benefit

There are two situations in which a claimant's entitlement to incapacity benefit is reduced (or in some cases extinguished) to take account of specified forms of other income. The first form of abatement is relatively uncontested; since 1989, local authority councillors who are in receipt of incapacity benefit have seen their benefit reduced by the extent to which their councillor's attendance allowance exceeds a prescribed earnings limit. This is currently £66.00 a week, the same level as the therapeutic earnings limit. This measure was introduced as a concession; previously councillors who were unable to work had to rely on the therapeutic earnings rule and were unable to retain benefit simply by failing to claim their local government allowance.[163]

---

159 SSCBA 1992, s 30A(5).
160 SSCBA 1992, s 30B(4). On the meaning of 'terminally ill', see p 706, below. These exceptions did not appear in the original Bill, but were inserted during its passage through Parliament in response to pressure from members of both Houses: 554 HL Official Report (5th series) cols 107–108; 555 HL Official Report (5th series) cols 355–364; and 245 HC Official Report (6th series) col 134.
161 SSCBA 1992, s 30B(7) and SI 1994/2946, reg 10.
162 Erens and Ghate *Invalidity Benefit: a longitudinal survey of new recipients* DSS Research Report No 20 (1993) ch 1.
163 SSA 1989, Sch 8, para 2; see *R(S) 3/86* and *R(S) 6/86*.

The second form of abatement, in respect of occupational pensions, provoked intense controversy during the passage of WRPA 1999. SSCBA 1992 now provides that, where a person is entitled to incapacity benefit and a pension is payable to him or her which exceeds the current threshold of £85 a week, that individual's benefit entitlement is reduced by 50 pence in the pound for every pound over the threshold.[164] In this context pension payments include periodical payments made under an occupational or public service pension scheme in connection with the 'coming to an end' of the individual's employment.[165] Periodical payments under personal pension schemes and certain payments under permanent health insurance policies are also included. The government's primary justification for the introduction of this abatement rule was to ensure a 'fairer balance between State and private provision'.[166] The government's original intention was that the rule should apply to pensions in excess of £50 a week, drawing on the parallel with contribution-based jobseeker's allowance.[167] In the event, the threshold was raised to £85 a week as a concession to head off a Parliamentary revolt. In particular, peers and Labour backbenchers were concerned at the further intrusion of means-testing into a contributory benefit. The purported analogy with contribution-based jobseeker's allowance is unsound, as the latter is a short-term benefit whereas incapacity benefit is paid as a long-term benefit.

E   The definition and assessment of incapacity for work

Notwithstanding its title, there was no comprehensive definition of incapacity for work on the face of the Social Security (Incapacity for Work) Act 1994. The 1994 Act[168] inserted a new Part XIIA into SSCBA 1992, giving the Secretary of State extensive regulation-making powers in order to establish a system for determining questions of capacity or incapacity for work. In essence Part XIIA provides for two tests for assessing capacity or incapacity for work: the 'own occupation' test and the 'personal capability assessment', the latter known as the 'all work' test before WRPA 1999. These tests apply to the assessment of incapacity for the purposes of all social security benefits, with the exception of SSP and those under the industrial injuries scheme.[169] This section is divided into five parts; the first and second deal with the own occupation test and the personal capability assessment respectively. The third and fourth parts concern cases of deemed incapacity or capacity for work whilst the final part sets out the disqualifications which may apply.

i   Own occupation test

A   APPLICATION AND SCOPE OF THE OWN OCCUPATION TEST

The 'own occupation' test applies for the first 28 weeks of incapacity for claimants with a regular occupation, defined as one in which they have been engaged in

---

164   SSCBA 1992, s 30DD(1).
165   SSCBA 1992, s 30DD(5).
166   DSS *A new contract for welfare: Support for Disabled People* (1998, Cm 4103) p 21.
167   P 516, above. The previous Conservative administration had rejected a similar proposal to introduce such a claw-back: Timmins *The Five Giants* (rev edn, 2001) pp 571–572.
168   SS(IW)A 1994, ss 5 and 6.
169   SSCBA 1992, ss 171A(1) and 171G(1). Thus entitlement to the income support disability premium on the grounds of incapacity is subject to the new regime.

remunerative work for more than eight weeks in the previous 21 weeks.[170] Remunerative work in turn is defined (in the case of an individual with one occupation) as involving 16 hours work a week, for those eight weeks, for which payment was made or which was done in expectation of payment.[171] If the individual has more than one occupation, the relevant occupation is usually the last such occupation in which the person was engaged.[172] A 'day of incapacity for work' for the purpose of calculating the 28 weeks means a day in respect of which either the individual has been found incapable of work or is entitled to SSP. The statutory definition also includes days of incapacity and days falling within the maternity allowance period.[173] If the criteria for applying the own occupation test are not met, then the claimant is subject to the personal capability assessment from the outset of the period of incapacity.

The own occupation test itself is whether the claimant:

is incapable by reason of some specific disease or bodily or mental disablement of doing work which he could reasonably be expected to do in the course of the occupation in which he was so engaged.[174]

The requirement that the incapacity for work must result from 'some specific disease or bodily or mental disablement' is a formulation carried forward from the previous legislation. Whether the claimant's condition may be so determined is a question of fact[175] for which resort must be had to expert medical opinion. A 'disease' has been defined as 'a departure from health capable of identification by its signs and symptoms, an abnormality of some sort'[176] and 'specific' implies that it is of a kind identified by medical science.[177] 'Disablement' involves a state of deprivation or incapacitation of ability measured against the abilities of a 'normal' person.[178] The ordinary condition of pregnancy does not come within these definitions and is, in any event, the subject of specific provision, namely maternity allowance and (in most cases) statutory maternity pay.[179] During periods of entitlements to either of these, a woman is precluded from claiming an income-maintenance incapacity benefit.[180] But there is no reason why she should not qualify for the latter outside of such periods on proof of a physical or mental disablement resulting from, but going beyond, the ordinary incidents of pregnancy.[181] In addition, however, in certain special cases a pregnant woman is now treated as being incapable of work.[182]

---

170 SSCBA 1992, s 171B(1) and (3).
171 SI 1995/311, reg 4. Such weeks count irrespective of whether the person was on paid or unpaid leave: reg 4(2)(b).
172 SI 1995/311, reg 5. If the person was engaged in both such occupations in the last week, the test must be satisfied in respect of each.
173 SSCBA 1992, s 171(4).
174 SSCBA 1992, s 171B(2).
175 *R(S) 7/53*.
176 *CS 221/49*, para 3.
177 *CS 7/82*, noted at [1982] JSWL 306.
178 There is no reported decision on the question whether damage to a prosthesis, such as an artificial limb, can constitute 'bodily disablement', but for analogous purposes under the industrial injuries scheme it has been held that such damage is to be treated as 'personal injury' where the prosthesis concerned is so intimately linked with the claimant's body as to form part of that body: *R(I) 8/81*.
179 Ch 16, below.
180 SSCBA 1992, ss 153(2)(d), 153(12) and Sch 13, para 1.
181 *CS 221/49*.
182 SI 1995/311, reg 14; see below p 547.

As medical science has shown greater awareness of different types of psychological disorder, so there has been a natural tendency to extend the certification for 'mental disablement'. Case law, however, has focused on the word 'specific' in the statutory definition, which, it is said, qualifies both 'disease' and 'bodily or mental disablement'; so if the alleged condition cannot be identified in the state of current medical knowledge, the claimant may not succeed.[183] This appears to reflect a concern that otherwise the 'work-shy' individual might receive benefit on the basis of incapacity for work. In 1959 a Commissioner characterised Munchausen's syndrome, a rare condition in which the person habitually attends hospital for treatment of a disease from which he or she does not, in fact, suffer as a 'defect of personality', resulting in a denial of benefit.[184] In a later case the Commissioner drew a distinction between a mental disability, as a result of which the claimant could not work, and a voluntary attitude in which the claimant could, but would not, work; however, he went on to suggest that a 'personality disorder' might come within the former category.[185] Given the modern understanding of mental health issues, this would seem to be the better view.

B   MEDICAL EVIDENCE

The onus of satisfying the incapacity for work test is on the claimant.[186] Where a spell of incapacity lasts for seven days or less, or for the first seven days of a longer spell, the claimant is entitled to rely on self-certification, that is a declaration in writing that he or she is unfit for work.[187] The provision of medical evidence is obligatory following the first seven days of incapacity. The regulations provide that evidence of incapacity shall be furnished by the claimant 'by means of a certificate in the form of a statement in writing given by a doctor' in the prescribed manner.[188] Where it would be 'unreasonable' for claimants to provide a statement in the standard form, they may provide 'such other evidence as may be sufficient' to show that they should refrain from work. The alternative, unprescribed method is designed to cater for those, particularly Christian Scientists, who on grounds of conscience prefer not to attend for medical treatment,[189] but it is far from clear what sort of evidence will in such circumstances satisfy the authorities.[190]

183   *CS 1/81*, noted at [1982] JSWL 48.
184   *R(S) 6/59*.
185   *CS 7/82*, n 177, above.
186   *R(S) 13/52*.
187   SI 1976/615, reg 5. The system of self-certification for short periods was introduced in 1982 (SI 1982/699) mainly to reduce costs and the burden on general practitioners who have always regarded the work as interfering with the doctor-patient relationship. See SSAC *Report on the Draft 1982 Regulations* (1982, Cmnd 8560) and more generally *Report of the Committee on Abuse of Social Security Benefits* (1973, Cmnd 5228).
188   SI 1976/615, reg 2(1)(a). For the standard form (the 'MED 4'), see SI 1976/615, Sch 1, Pt II. Provision is made for a special statement where the doctor is not issuing the statement on the day of examination, or is relying on a report by another doctor: reg 2(1)(b) and Sch 1A, Pt II. See also SI 1995/311, reg 6(1) and SI 1999/991, reg 17.
189   See Report of the National Insurance Advisory Committee on the draft regulations (1975–76, HC 349) para 32.
190   In one case an acknowledgment by an employer of the claimant's incapacity was regarded as insufficient: *R(S) 13/51*. On the other hand, the fact of hospitalisation will raise a presumption of incapacity and this remains true even where after investigation the claimant is found not to be suffering from the suspected disease: *R(S) 1/58*.

ii Personal capability assessment

A GENERAL

The all work test originally came into operation in April 1995. The test is designed to measure claimants' ability or inability to perform certain prescribed physical and mental functions as a means of assessing their capacity or incapacity for work. This represents a fundamental shift from the test of incapacity under the former invalidity benefit regime. The previous test was whether there was 'work which the person can reasonably be expected to do'.[191] This required consideration of the claimant's age, educational background and work experience as well as the state of their health.[192] The all work test excluded such broader considerations, focusing solely on the specified physical and mental functions.[193] As well as representing a redrawing of the boundary between capacity and incapacity for work, this has had fundamental repercussions for the social security appeals system. Initially the traditional three-person tribunal of a lawyer chair and two lay members heard incapacity benefit appeals, assisted by a medical assessor. The 'medicalisation' of the assessment process undermined the case for lay participation in the appeals process, with the result that since SSA 1998 incapacity appeals have been heard by a lawyer and a medical member sitting as a two-person tribunal.[194]

The all work test was relaunched by WRPA 1999 as the personal capability assessment with effect from April 2000. At one level this was merely a semantic change, as the criteria for assessing incapacity for work under the personal capability assessment are identical to those under the all work test. At another level, however, the changes reflect the government's concern that the previous test focused solely on what people *cannot*, rather than *can*, do. They are also indicative of a greater emphasis on counselling and advice for claimants rather than simply laying down rules of entitlement. Accordingly, SSCBA 1992 was amended so as to provide for the gathering of information or evidence 'capable of being used for assisting or encouraging the person in question to obtain work or to enhance his prospects of obtaining it'.[195] The doctor carrying out a medical assessment for a personal capability assessment should prepare two reports: an incapacity report and a capability report. The former replicates the report prepared under the all work test procedure. The latter is designed to explore the claimant's capabilities and limitations over a range of work-related activities in order to assist with the provision of advice and guidance in relation to work prospects. Thus the incapacity report is sent to the decision maker, but not the capability report. The latter is sent to the claimant's personal adviser and indeed cannot be used in making a decision on incapacity for work for benefit purposes.[196] Initially the new report was not used on a nationwide basis; between 2000 and 2002 it was piloted in ONE areas.

B APPLICATION OF THE PERSONAL CAPABILITY ASSESSMENT

The personal capability assessment applies from the outset of a period of incapacity unless the individual concerned is initially subject to the own occupation test. In the

191   SSCBA 1992, s 57(1)(a), now repealed.
192   See the 4th edition of this book, pp 176–177.
193   See generally Berthoud (1995) 2 JSSL 61.
194   P 194, below.
195   SSCBA 1992, s 171A(2A).
196   SI 1995/311, reg 6(4).

latter case, the personal capability assessment applies after 28 weeks of incapacity have elapsed.[197] The personal capability assessment may be carried out before the expiry of this period and still be effective.[198] A person who has already experienced 28 weeks of incapacity is treated as incapable of work whilst awaiting a personal capability assessment, providing that he or she continues to provide medical certificates and has not been found capable of work within the last six months.[199] There is also express statutory authority for claimants to be subject to periodic reassessments to determine whether they remain incapable of work.[200] Claimants with certain severe medical conditions are treated as incapable of work and so are exempt from the personal capability assessment.[201]

C   SCOPE OF THE PERSONAL CAPABILITY ASSESSMENT

The personal capability assessment, as with its predecessor the all work test, is not itself defined in the primary legislation. SSCBA 1992 merely provides for regulations to define the assessment:

> by reference to the extent to which a person who has some specific disease or bodily or mental disablement is capable or incapable of performing such activities as may be prescribed.[202]

In addition, regulations may provide for the manner of assessing whether a person is incapable of work under such an assessment.[203] Accordingly, secondary legislation sets out both the framework and the details of the personal capability assessment. The assessment is defined as 'a test of a person's incapacity, by reasons of some specific disease or bodily or mental disablement' to perform various prescribed activities.[204] These activities are listed in the Schedule to the Social Security (Incapacity for Work) (General) Regulations,[205] which makes a rigid distinction between 'physical' and 'mental' disabilities.

(i) Physical disabilities

Part I to the Schedule lists 14 functional areas of activity in which a physical disability may make a person incapable of work.[206] In summary, these are:

* walking on level ground;
* walking up and down stairs;
* sitting in an upright chair;
* standing;

197   SSCBA 1992, s 171C(1).
198   SSCBA 1992, s 171C(4). This provision was introduced by WRPA 1999 in order to speed up the system and avoid unnecessary delay: *DSS* n 166, above, p 17.
199   SSCBA 1992, s 171C(3) and SI 1995/311, reg 28. There are exceptions to the six-month rule in reg 28(2)(b).
200   SSCBA 1992, s 171C(5). This provision was added by WRPA 1999, s 61, but was assumed to be implicit in the original s 171C.
201   SI 1995/311, reg 10; see p 546, below. Some further exemptions for transitional purposes are listed in SI 1995/310, reg 31.
202   SSCBA 1992, s 171C(2)(a). On the meaning of 'some specific disease or bodily or mental disablement', see p 539, above.
203   SSCBA 1992, s 171C(2)(b).
204   SI 1995/311, reg 24.
205   SI 1995/311.
206   SI 1995/311, Sch, Pt I.

- rising from sitting;
- bending and kneeling;
- manual dexterity;
- lifting and carrying;
- reaching, speech;
- hearing;
- vision;
- continence; and
- remaining conscious.

Several of these activities are defined rather more precisely by the Schedule; thus 'standing' is described as 'standing without the support of another person or the use of an aid except a walking stick'. Each of the 14 activities is then subdivided into a series of at least four (and up to eight) descriptors, each of which specifies a level of incapacity for that particular activity and attributes a score to it.[207] Each descriptor qualifies for a score of between 0 and 15. The threshold for incapacity for work for physical functions is 15 points, from any one or more activities.[208] This represents 'the level in each functional area at, or above which, the effect of the medical condition is such that the person should not be expected to work'.[209] By way of example, the descriptors for walking up and down stairs (activity 2) are as follows:

2(a) Cannot walk up and down one stair.	15
(b) Cannot walk up and down a flight of 12 stairs.	15
(c) Cannot walk up and down a flight of 12 stairs without holding on and taking a rest.	7
(d) Cannot walk up and down a flight of 12 stairs without holding on.	3
(e) Can only walk up and down a flight of 12 stairs if he goes sideways or one step at a time.	3
(f) No problem in walking up and down stairs.	0

A considerable body of case law, which cannot be considered within the confines of this book, has been generated in relation to the meaning of the individual descriptors.[210] The proper construction of those descriptors which involve a finding that the claimant 'cannot' perform some activity is important in the case of variable and intermittent conditions. A Tribunal of Commissioners has held that the personal capability assessment should not be applied to each day in isolation; rather, decision makers must apply a broader approach that considers the claimant's abilities 'most of the time'. Thus the frequency of 'bad' days, the length of periods of both 'bad' days and intervening periods and the severity of the disablement on both 'good' and 'bad' days are all relevant.[211]

Claimants who are not exempt from the personal capability assessment are sent a questionnaire (the IB 50) which they are required to complete and return to the relevant office. The questionnaire is subdivided into the same functional areas, and claimants are asked to tick the box that matches most closely the difficulty (if any) which they

---

207 The descriptors are designed to be 'clearly worded statements of disability ranked according to their incapacitating effect in each functional area': DSS *The medical assessment for Incapacity Benefit* (1994) para 1.2.
208 SI 1995/311, reg 25(1)(a).
209 *DSS* n 207, above, para 1.2.
210 See eg *R(IB) 1/99* on the meaning of to 'walk up and down a flight of 12 stairs ... one step at a time'. The fullest account of the case law is in Bonner, Hooker and White *Social Security Legislation 2001* (2001) vol I .
211 *R(IB) 2/99 (T)*, applying the principle of 'averaging' in *R(A) 2/74*.

have with each particular activity.[212] The claimant is also asked to submit a current medical certificate.[213] Such a certificate merely sets out the diagnosis; it does not determine the question of capacity for work under the Schedule. The role of the claimant's doctor as 'gatekeeper' to benefit entitlement, as it existed under the former invalidity benefit scheme, has disappeared. The claimant has six weeks in which to return the questionnaire and must be sent a reminder after four weeks.[214] If the questionnaire is not returned within this timescale, the individual will be treated as capable of work unless good cause can be shown.[215]

The completed questionnaire is referred to a doctor employed on behalf of the DWP to provide advice on incapacity benefit claims. If the doctor is able to confirm that the claimant's self-assessment is consistent with the medical evidence and scores sufficient points to be found to be incapable of work, the case is referred back to the decision maker without the need for a medical examination. If this is not self-evident, the claimant is called in for a medical examination on at least seven days' notice.[216] The doctor interviews the claimant and carries out an examination, completing a parallel questionnaire (the IB 85) to that submitted by the individual concerned.[217] Failure to attend without good cause results in the claimant being treated as capable of work.[218]

The examining doctor's report is then considered by the decision maker alongside the claimant's questionnaire. The doctor's report is advisory only,[219] although in practice it is rare, where there is conflicting evidence, for the decision maker to prefer the claimant's assessment of the relevant descriptor for each activity as opposed to that of the doctor. The claimant's ability to perform any of the various physical activities is assessed taking into account any prosthesis fitted or any 'aid or appliance' which the individual normally wears or uses.[220] The claimant can only qualify for one descriptor in relation to each activity; whichever is the higher is the applicable score.[221] Thus a person who cannot walk up and down a flight of 12 stairs without holding on and taking a rest will receive 7 points in relation to that activity. Any such score may be aggregated with the score from any other functional area to arrive at an overall score, with the one exception that scores from 'walking on level ground' and 'walking up and down stairs' may *not* be combined; only the highest applies.[222]

A claimant who receives a total score in relation to the physical descriptors of 15 points or more 'passes' the personal capability assessment and is therefore incapable of work for most benefit purposes.[223] Such individuals are not required to send in further medical certificates. However, the examining doctor may suggest a period after which

---

212   The questionnaire itself does not provide any indication of the points score for each descriptor.
213   SI 1995/311, reg 6(1)(a) and (b).
214   SI 1995/311, reg 7(2).
215   SI 1995/311, reg 7(1); on 'good cause', see reg 9.
216   SI 1995/311, reg 8.
217   There has been considerable criticism of the way in which these medical examinations are carried out: see House of Commons Social Security Committee *Third Report* (Session 1999–2000, HC 183) and government reply, DSS *Report on Medical Services* (2000, Cm 4780). See also NAO *The Medical Assessment of Incapacity and Disability Benefits* (2000–2001, HC 280). Welfare rights organisations provide detailed advice both on completing the questionnaire and on the medical examination: see eg CPAG *Welfare benefits handbook 2002–03* (4th edn, 2002) ch 30.
218   SI 1995/311, reg 8(2). On 'good cause', see reg 9.
219   SI 1999/991, reg 11.
220   SI 1995/311, reg 25(2). A prosthesis is an 'artifical substitute for a body part' and does not include a colostomy bag: *Perry v Adjudication Officer* [1999] NI 338.
221   SI 1995/311, reg 26(3).
222   SI 1995/311, reg 26(2). The reason for this is that both activities are testing the same physical function (walking); in the draft scheme, prior to enactment, the two activities were combined into a single functional area: DSS *A consultation on the medical assessment for Incapacity Benefit* (1993) p 24.
223   SSCBA 1992, s 171G(1).

the individual's incapacity should be reviewed (eg six months or a year) and, as we have seen, claimants may be called back for periodic reassessments.[224]

(ii) Mental disabilities

There are a number of key differences, especially as regards the scoring system, for claimants with mental disabilities. Part II to the Schedule lists four broad areas of activity in which a mental disability may render a person incapable of work.[225] These are completion of tasks, daily living, coping with pressure and interaction with other people. Each activity is subdivided into individual descriptors and allotted a score. Each activity has seven or eight descriptors except for 'daily living' (activity 16), which lists just five and is used here by way of illustration:

16(a)	Needs encouragement to get up and dress.	2
(b)	Needs alcohol before midday.	2
(c)	Is frequently distressed at some time of day due to fluctuation of mood.	1
(d)	Does not care about his appearance and living conditions.	1
(e)	Sleep problems interfere with his daytime activities.	1

Unlike with the physical activities, these descriptors are cumulative, so a claimant might score 7 points in relation to daily living. The threshold for incapacity for work based solely on mental disabilities is 10 points, which may hence be reached by aggregating the points for any descriptors in relation to any of the four general areas of activity.[226]

The procedure for dealing with claimants with mental disabilities is also different. The 'tick box' approach on the questionnaire for claimants in relation to the physical areas of activity is not replicated for the mental health descriptors. Instead, claimants are simply invited to state if they have any mental health problems. In appropriate cases, examining doctors should then ask claimants how such problems affect their daily life (rather than going through the mental health descriptors one by one) with a view to forming an opinion as to which apply.[227]

(iii) Physical and mental disabilities

Many claimants will present with both physical and mental disabilities. The threshold for incapacity in such cases is 15,[228] but a special aggregation rule operates when combining physical and mental health scores. Any aggregate score between 6 and 9 points on the mental health descriptors is treated as a score of 9 points, whereas an aggregate score of less than 6 in relation to the Part II descriptors is disregarded.[229] Thus 7 points on physical descriptors added to 6 points (deemed to be nine) on the mental health factors results in an aggregate score of 16 (and hence above the threshold for incapacity), not 13. Conversely, 10 points under Part I but just 5 points (which must be disregarded) from Part II results in a score of just 10 points (below the threshold). The justification for this approach is that the 'weighting takes account of the particular aggravating impact of mental health problems on the ability to work, when in

224   SSCBA 1992, s 171C(5).
225   SI 1995/311, Sch, Pt II.
226   SI 1995/311, regs 25(1)(b) and 26(4). Again, there is a wealth of case law; eg on 'needs alcohol before midday' see *R1/00(IB)*.
227   On the difficulties faced by those with mental health problems, see Zarb (ed) *Social Security and Mental Health: Report on the SSAC Workshop* SSAC Research Paper 7 (1996).
228   SI 1995/311, reg 25(1)(c).
229   SI 1995/311, reg 26(1).

combination with physical and/or sensory disabilities'.[230] The extent to which this balance has been struck at the appropriate point remains untested empirically.

Despite the special scoring rule, the Schedule fails fully to reflect the interrelationship between physical and mental disabilities. Indeed, the initial scoring process seeks to keep the two sets of factors entirely distinct. Thus in assessing scores for the physical activities, the person's incapacity must arise 'from a specific bodily disease or disablement', whereas mental health scores must be attributable to 'some specific mental illness or disablement'.[231] This can result in an extremely difficult fact-finding exercise on sometimes limited evidence (eg where a combination of back pain and depression renders a person's walking ability substantially more limited than it would be by back pain alone).

A claimant who is subjected to the personal capability assessment and fails to meet the relevant points threshold (and so would normally be regarded as being capable of work) may nevertheless be treated as incapable of work. This exceptional course of action is only possible in three circumstances, namely where:
(1) the claimant suffers from a severe life-threatening disease that is uncontrollable by a recognised therapeutic procedure or is uncontrolled and there is reasonable cause for it to be not so controlled;
(2) the claimant suffers from a previously undiagnosed potentially life-threatening condition that is only discovered in the course of the medical examination; or
(3) the claimant requires a major surgical operation or other major therapeutic procedure, which is likely to be carried out within three months of the medical examination.[232]
These very restrictively drawn exceptions represent the sole recognition within the scheme that a minority of conditions do not lend themselves to a functional assessment.[233]

iii   Persons treated as incapable of work

As we have seen above, special provision is made for certain exceptional cases in which a person may be found to be capable of work under the personal capability assessment but is to be treated as incapable of work. SSCBA 1992 also contains a general power enabling persons to be treated as incapable of work in prescribed circumstances.[234] Regulations now detail a further eight sets of circumstances in which a claimant is to be so treated (and therefore eligible for incapacity benefit).

A   PERSONS WITH SEVERE CONDITIONS

A claimant who falls into any of the following categories is treated as incapable of work:
• claimants who receive the highest rate care component of disability living allowance (or its equivalent under other statutory schemes);
• those entitled to industrial disablement benefit or severe disablement allowance with a disability assessed as not less than 80 per cent;

---

230   *DSS* n 207, above, para 2.12.
231   SI 1995/311, reg 24(3).
232   SI 1995/311, reg 27. See *R v Secretary of State for Social Security, ex p Moule* (12 September 1996, unreported), transcript CO-934-96 on an earlier ultra vires formulation of this rule.
233   *DSS* n 207, above, paras 1.12–1.13 and 5.19–5.24. Note, however, that the current categories are narrower than those under the original all work test. Cases in which the doctor considers that there would be a substantial risk to others in the workplace if the claimant were found capable of work were excluded by amendments effective in 1997 (SI 1996/3207).
234   SSCBA 1992, s 171D(1).

- the terminally ill;
- the registered blind;
- persons suffering from tetraplegia, persistent vegetative state, dementia or paraplegia or related conditions;
- persons suffering from one of a range of further specified conditions eg a severe learning disability, a severe and progressive neurological or muscle wasting disease or a severe mental illness.[235]

In the final category of cases, involving certain further specified conditions, there must be supporting medical evidence from a departmental doctor or other appropriate medical source.[236]

B CARRIERS OF INFECTIOUS OR CONTAGIOUS DISEASE

This covers the case where claimants, though capable of work, represent a risk to others at their place of employment in that they either are a carrier or have been in contact with a case of infectious or contagious disease. In these rare cases the individual must be excluded from work 'on the certificate of a Medical Officer for Environmental Health'.[237] This provision differs from its predecessor under the pre-April 1995 regime in that the deeming rule is mandatory, rather than discretionary, and covers contagious as well as infectious diseases.

C HOSPITAL IN-PATIENTS

Claimants are treated as incapable of work on any day on which they are undergoing 'medical or other treatment in a hospital or similar institution'.[238] However, a stay in hospital of more than six weeks will result in a reduction of benefit on other grounds.[239]

D PERSONS RECEIVING CERTAIN FORMS OF REGULAR TREATMENT

A claimant who receives regular types of specified treatment (eg dialysis for chronic renal failure or chemotherapy) is treated as incapable of work on any day on which he or she is undergoing such treatment.[240]

E PREGNANT WOMEN

It should be self-evident that pregnancy itself is not a 'specific disease or bodily or mental disablement' for the purposes of incapacity benefit.[241] However, pregnancy may give rise to certain medical conditions which may render the woman incapable

---

235 SI 1995/311, reg 10.
236 See the definition of 'medical evidence' in SI 1995/311, reg 2(1).
237 SI 1995/311, reg 11 and see *R(S) 1/72*.
238 SI 1995/311, reg 12.
239 See p 234, above.
240 SI 1995/311, reg 13, which includes further special provision as regards SSCBA 1992, s 171B(3) and SI 1995/311, reg 16 in such cases.
241 See *R(S) 4/93* in the context of SSP.

of work. The pre-April 1995 scheme made no special provision for such cases. Under the current rules,[242] a woman is to be treated as incapable of work if there is a serious risk of damage either to her health or that of her unborn child if she does not refrain from work. The same deeming rule applies for any days falling in the period from six weeks before the expected or actual date of confinement (whichever is the earlier) to 14 days after the actual date of confinement.[243] This second provision only applies if the claimant would have no entitlement to either statutory maternity pay or maternity allowance during the same period.

F   INCAPACITY FOR PART OF DAY

Where claimants are incapable of work for only a part of the day, they are nevertheless deemed to have been incapable for the whole of the day.[244] The old rule included a qualification that no work was done on the day in question; although now omitted, such a person may still be treated as capable of work under another provision.[245]

G   WELFARE TO WORK BENEFICIARIES

Since October 1998 special provision has been made for welfare to work beneficiaries. A claimant who falls within this description is treated as incapable of work, without having to satisfy either the own occupation test or the personal capability assessment, for a maximum of 91 days which fall within the extended 52-week linking period or the first 13 weeks thereafter.[246] This deeming rule applies only where the claimant submits a medical certificate confirming their current incapacity for work and where in the previous period of incapacity either the personal capability assessment was satisfied or the individual was exempt as suffering from one of the prescribed severe conditions.

H   WORK TRIAL PILOTS

The various categories set out above apply on a national basis. However, further provision is made on a pilot basis in some areas to treat certain claimants as incapable of work. This is part of the strategy of experimenting with incentives to encourage claimants to try out work, where they would otherwise be receiving benefit on the basis of their incapacity. In the pilot areas a claimant may earn a maximum of £15 a week and still be treated as incapable of work.[247] Claimants may also undertake work trials of periods of up to 15 days without losing benefit.[248]

---

242   SI 1995/311, reg 14.
243   This could therefore apply a woman who has recently given birth, as well as to one who is pregnant.
244   SI 1995/311, reg 15.
245   SI 1995/311, reg 16: see further below.
246   SI 1995/311, reg 13A. There is also a deeming rule for claimants engaged in unpaid approved work on a trial basis: reg 10A.
247   SI 1999/1088, reg 4.
248   SI 1999/1088, reg 5.

iv   Persons treated as capable of work

A   THE GENERAL RULE

The primary legislation also contains a general power enabling persons to be treated as capable of work in prescribed circumstances.[249] Regulations accordingly provide that, as a general principle:

> a person shall be treated as capable of work on each day of any week commencing on a Sunday during which he does work to which this regulation applies.[250]

As a starting point, this provision applies to *any* work that a claimant performs, whether or not the individual undertakes it in expectation of payment.[251] Moreover, this deeming rule applies irrespective of whether a person has been found to be incapable of work under the personal capability assessment or whether a person has been treated as incapable of work under the provisions discussed in the section above.

B   EXCEPTIONS TO THE GENERAL RULE

There are also a number of exceptions to the general rule. The rule does not apply where the work involves care of a relative or domestic tasks carried out in the claimant's own home.[252] There are also several public policy exceptions in that any work undertaken by a claimant in their capacity as a local government councillor is to be ignored,[253] as is any activity undertaken as a rescuer in an emergency.[254] The general rule is also disapplied in those pilot areas where claimants are permitted to earn no more than £15 a week whilst still being treated as incapable of work.[255]

There are, additionally, three other categories of 'exempt work': certain forms of 'permitted work', work done as a volunteer and duties undertaken as a member of an appeal tribunal or the Disability Living Allowance Advisory Board (DLAAB).[256] The concept of permitted work was introduced in April 2002 as part of the government's welfare-to-work strategy, replacing the former therapeutic work rules which had required that such work be undertaken on the advice of a doctor. Following these reforms, there are three forms of exempt permitted work. The first is where the claimant earns less than £20 a week, for which there are no restrictions in terms of the number of hours per week or weeks worked. The sole requirement is that the DWP is informed of such work

249   SSCBA 1992, s 171D(1). See also the special rule relating to jobseeker's allowance in SI 1995/311, reg 17A.
250   SI 1995/311, reg 16(1). For weeks at the beginning and end of a period of incapacity, only the days of working are affected: reg 16(3). The rule is also subject to the special provision governing those undergoing regular treatment such as chemotherapy: reg 13(3).
251   SI 1995/311, reg 16(2).
252   SI 1995/311, reg 16(2). For the definition of 'relative', see reg 2(1).
253   SSCBA 1992, s 171F. On the effect of councillors' allowances on incapacity benefit, see SSCBA 1992, s 30E and SI 1994/2496, regs 8 and 9.
254   Such activity must be 'to protect another person or to prevent serious damage to property or livestock': SI 1995/311, reg 16(4).
255   SI 1999/1088, reg 4.
256   SI 1995/311, reg 17. On the DLAAB, see p 140, above.

before the claimant *ceases* so working.[257] The second is where the claimant's work falls within either of the following two categories, namely work:

(a) which is part of a treatment programme and is done under medical supervision while the person doing it is an in-patient, or is regularly attending as an out-patient, of a hospital or similar institution;[258] or

(b) which is supervised by a person employed by a public or local authority or voluntary organisation engaged in the provision or procurement of work for persons who have disabilities.[259]

In either situation, as with the first type of permitted work, the DWP must be informed of such work before it ceases and there are no restrictions as to the duration of such work. Such supported permitted work, however, is subject to a higher weekly earnings limit, currently £66.00.[260] Finally, any claimant may work for up to 16 hours a week in any type of work,[261] so long as earnings do not exceed £66.00 a week and the DWP is notified within 42 days of *starting* work.[262] A claimant can take advantage of this rule for up to 26 weeks; an appropriate official may authorise an extension of a further six months if satisfied that by continuing in such work the claimant 'is likely to improve his capacity to engage in full-time work'.[263]

As regards the other forms of exempt work, there is no hours limit applicable to voluntary work,[264] reflecting the government's welfare to work strategy of encouraging those in receipt of incapacity benefit to try out such work without fear of losing benefit.[265] The last type of exempt work is as a disability member of an appeal tribunal or as a member of the DLAAB, subject to a ceiling of one day a week.[266]

C   FAILURE WITHOUT GOOD CAUSE TO ATTEND A DEPARTMENTAL MEDICAL EXAMINATION

As we have seen, claimants of sickness or invalidity benefit were not necessarily subject to an examination by a departmental doctor. However, an adjudication officer could require the claimant to attend such a medical examination. The sanction for non-compliance was disqualification for up to six weeks, under an analogous provision to those discussed below.[267] Under the new regime, in most cases a medical examination is a central part of the personal capability assessment. Rather than disqualifying a claimant who fails to attend for such an examination, the regulations now deem the

---

257   SI 1995/311, reg 17(1)(a)(i). Earlier notification would be advisable to avoid the risk of overpayments of benefit.

258   SI 1995/311, reg 17(1)(a)(ii). This provision also appeared in the pre-2002 formulation of the rule and avoids the artificiality of the older version of the rule which required hospitalisation (see *R(S) 5/52*).

259   SI 1995/311, reg 17(1)(a)(iii), replacing the former sheltered work rule.

260   SI 1995/311, reg 17(2)(a).

261   SI 1995/311, reg 17(2)(b). This is subject to an averaging rule: reg 17(3).

262   SI 1995/311, reg 17(1)(a)(iv) and (1A).

263   SI 1995/311, reg 17(1C)(a)(ii). Once this extension period has elapsed, the claimant must wait 52 weeks before securing exemption under these provisions again (although work up to the £20 limit is permitted during the intervening year): reg 17(1D).

264   A 'volunteer' means a person engaged in voluntary work, other than for a close relative, where the only payment is for reasonably incurred expenses: SI 1995/311, reg 2(1).

265   *R(S) 4/79*, para 11, V G H Hallett, Comr. An intention merely to earn some money was insufficient: *CS 8/79*, noted [1978–79] JSWL 443. See further the 4th edition of this book, p 182.

266   SI 1995/311, reg 17(2)(c). The rule does not exempt holders of other judicial offices, eg magistrates and members of employment tribunals.

267   See the 4th edition of this book, pp 183–184.

individual to be capable of work in such circumstances.[268] A claimant can only be so regarded if sent at least seven days' written notice of the time and place for the examination.[269] There is a defence of 'good cause', which includes (but is not limited to) taking into account whether the claimant was in Great Britain at the relevant time and their state of health and any disability.[270]

v Disqualification

A GENERAL

There are certain grounds on which the claimant may be disqualified from benefit for a maximum period of six weeks.[271] The underlying purposes of these provisions are threefold: to protect the fund against fraudulent claims; to exclude from benefit those who are incapacitated or remain incapacitated as a result of their own deliberate conduct; and to reinforce the machinery for the control and administration of the system. As the former legislative code governing the grounds for disqualification was largely re-enacted in SS(IW)A 1994, the early case law remains relevant in this context. The main difference between the previous and current regimes is that disqualification upon the grounds set out below applies to all benefits governed by the incapacity provisions enshrined in Part XII of SSCBA 1992. For example, a disqualification may in principle apply to income support paid on the basis of incapacity. Part XXII does not apply to SSP or industrial injuries benefits.[272] As regards the former, control is left in the hands of the individual employer, though the Secretary of State and the Inland Revenue have a residual power to ensure that the system for controlling sickness absence is adequate.[273] The current heads of disqualification were also amended in a number of minor respects at the same time as the introduction of incapacity benefit, as discussed below. The specific basis of disqualification for failing to attend a departmental medical examination was also dropped at the same time, but such a failure may lead to the claimant being treated as capable of work.[274] All the provisions discussed below appear to be little used today.

B MISCONDUCT

The first ground is where the claimant has 'become incapable of work through his own misconduct'.[275] This provision does not limit the misconduct to 'serious' or 'wilful' behaviour,[276] and it is possible to argue that it extends to reckless disregard of precautions ordered or recommended by eg an employer or a doctor.[277] The only reported decision,

268 SI 1995/311, reg 8(2).
269 SI 1995/311, reg 8(3). The old rule provided for only three days' notice.
270 SI 1995/311, reg 9.
271 SSCBA 1992, ss 171A(3)(b) and 171E.
272 SSCBA 1992, s 171G(1).
273 SSAA 1992, s 130. On industrial injuries benefits, see SSAA 1992, s 10.
274 P 550, above.
275 SSCBA 1992, s 171E(1)(a); SI 1995/311, reg 18(1)(a).
276 In contrast to the position under the workmen's compensation scheme. On the history to this provision, see the 4th edition of this book, p 183.
277 Potter and Stansfield *National Insurance* (2nd edn, 1949) p 111.

however, carries the implication that the conduct must be wilful.[278] The incapacity was due to alcoholism and it was held that the claimant could only rebut the inference of misconduct if he could show that his will-power had been so impaired that he was unable to moderate his drinking. There are two explicit situations in which disqualification is not to be imposed: where the incapacity is due to pregnancy or a sexually transmitted disease.[279]

C   TREATMENT

The third ground of disqualification arises where the claimant:

> fails without good cause to attend for or to submit himself to medical or other treatment (excluding vaccination, inoculation or major surgery) recommended by a doctor with whom, or a hospital or similar institution with which, he is undergoing medical treatment and which would be likely to render him capable of work.[280]

The rationale here is similar to that justifying the misconduct rule. The incapacity must not be voluntarily incurred. Consequently, the claimant must take reasonable steps to regain the capacity to work. Difficult questions arise as to the steps in recovery that might reasonably be required of an individual. Should a claimant be compelled to undergo an operation for which he or she has a morbid fear? The matter was very fully discussed at the Committee stage of the 1911 Bill.[281] On the one hand, it was argued that to compel a person to be vaccinated or to undergo an operation interfered with a fundamental liberty, and in many cases would involve a risk greater than that inherent in avoiding the treatment.[282] The opposing view was that the contributors to the fund ought not to support for a number of years a person who refused to undergo on wholly inadequate grounds an operation which was necessary for health reasons and which could not possibly be life-endangering.[283] A compromise solution was reached, and the amendment so formulated has been incorporated in the legislation ever since, subject to two modifications made on the introduction of incapacity benefit.

 .   First, the previous formulation of the rule provided that the disqualification applied if the claimant's conduct involved 'a failure to attend for or submit to a surgical operation of a minor character, and was unreasonable'.[284] As with the other grounds of disqualification, little guidance was to be found in the Commissioners' decisions on what might be regarded as an 'unreasonable' failure and how a distinction was to be drawn between 'major' and 'minor' operations. On the latter point, however, both the policy inherent in the provision, and the currency of medical usage,[285] suggested that a 'minor' operation was one which, in ordinary circumstances, did not involve a risk to life. The current provision adopts an alternative approach by excluding from the ambit of disqualification any refusal by a claimant to undergo 'major' surgery, without reference

278   *R(S) 2/53.*
279   SI 1995/311, reg 18(1)(a). The previous statutory exception was confined to incapacity due to pregnancy or venereal disease: SI 1983/1598, reg 17(1)(a) (now repealed).
280   SSCBA 1992, s 171F(1)(b) and SI 1994/311, reg 18(1)(b).
281   29 HC Official Report (5th series) cols 330–342.
282   See eg Mr D Lloyd-George MP, 29 HC Official Report (5th series) col 333.
283   See eg Mr A Chamberlain MP, 29 HC Official Report (5th series) cols 334–335.
284   SI 1983/1598, reg 17(1)(c).
285   See Dorland *Medical Dictionary* (28th edn, 1994) at p 1182.

to the reasonableness or otherwise of such a decision. It is doubtful whether any change in the law was intended; moreover, 'good cause' remains undefined by regulations in this context and so the issue is at large. Of course, illness or physical disability preventing the claimant attending for treatment would constitute good cause.[286] What of those who on grounds of religious conviction or otherwise object to medical treatment? The question was considered in *R(S) 9/51*. It was held that a Christian Scientist who satisfied the authorities on the conviction of her beliefs should not be disqualified. The onus of proof was on her, and it was not sufficient to show that she was a member of a church whose tenets forbade her submission to treatment or examination. The crux of the matter was her *personal* attitude, and this must be based on a firm conviction that her religious beliefs required her to refuse.

Secondly, the current statutory provision now expressly links the disqualification to failures to submit to appropriate forms of treatment 'which would be likely to render him capable of work'. This has the effect of reversing *R(S) 3/57*, in which a blind claimant abandoned a vocational training course when she became pregnant and later refused to resume it. Under the previous regulations it was held that she had not declined treatment for her disablement as the course could have no effect on her blindness. This technical amendment reflects in a modest way the modern welfare philosophy of 'work for those who can; security for those who cannot'.

D   RULES OF BEHAVIOUR

Under the old National Health Insurance Acts an approved society might, subject to the approval of the minister, make rules governing the behaviour of the insured person during sickness or disability. The Model Rules prepared by the minister, and in practice adopted by most societies,[287] prescribed certain standards of conduct, and after 1946 these were incorporated in the regulations.[288] Under the regulations now in force, disqualification may be imposed if the claimant fails without good cause to observe either of two rules.[289]

(1) To refrain from behaviour calculated to retard his recovery.[290]
     This, as with the 'misconduct' provision, constitutes a statutory safeguard against voluntary disability. The latter ground governs cases where the voluntary conduct causes the incapacity; the behaviour provision applies throughout the period of disability. The word 'calculated' is not to be taken too literally. The test is an objective one: was the behaviour likely to retard recovery?[291] There are few reported instances

---

286   But case law on the former head of failure to attend a departmental medical examination suggests that the test is an objective one: it will be insufficient if the claimant merely 'thinks' that he is not well enough to attend: Reported Decisions on Appeals and Applications under NHIA 1936, Decision XXXVIII.
287   The 1938 version of the Rules are set out in Lesser *The Law of National Health Insurance* (1939) pp 1108–1109.
288   The draft regulations were significantly amended before they were brought into effect following the recommendations of the NIAC (1947–48, HC 162) para 26.
289   SSCBA 1992, s 171F(1)(c) contains the enabling power. A further rule of behaviour, disqualifying a claimant involved in 'work for which remuneration is, or would ordinarily be, payable' (see the 4th edition of this book, p 186) was dropped in the 1995 reforms. This situation is now covered by the provision deeming a person who works as capable of work.
290   SI 1995/311, reg 18(1)(c)(i).
291   *R(S) 21/52*.

of this ground for disqualification.[292] The former and potentially intrusive statutory requirement as to the answering of inquiries by the Secretary of State or departmental officers, directed to ascertaining whether the claimant was acting in such a way, has been abolished.[293]

(2) Not to be absent from his place of residence without leaving word where he may be found.[294]

The purpose of this rule is to provide a safeguard against deliberate and persistent avoidance of DWP visiting officers.[295] The pre-war rules tended to be more rigorous, not only stipulating certain times when claimants must be at home, but also restraining them from leaving their locality at any time without either just cause or the consent of the relevant society. The provision is subject to a defence of good cause.[296]

E   GOOD CAUSE

The claimant may avoid disqualification by showing 'good cause'. Mere ignorance of rules of conduct will not suffice.[297] The following of medical advice, if unambiguous and specific, that the claimant should do a little work,[298] or should leave home for a few days, has been held to constitute good cause.[299]

F   RELEVANCE OF OTHER LEGAL PROCEEDINGS

The circumstances relied on to justify disqualification may also have been the subject of other legal proceedings, for example a criminal prosecution for making false representations to obtain benefit. A finding of fact made in such proceedings is not regarded as conclusive for social security purposes, but may nevertheless be used as evidence by decision makers.[300] The Commissioners have held that a conviction for an offence relating to the same benefit for the same period as is in issue should shift the onus of proof onto the claimant to show that, notwithstanding the conviction, there is entitlement to benefit.[301]

---

292   *R(S) 21/52*: disqualification rightly imposed on a claimant who, suffering from influenzal bronchitis, nevertheless undertook a motoring expedition 60 miles away and was there taken ill.
293   See the 4th edition of this book, p 185.
294   SI 1983/1598, reg 17(1)(d)(ii).
295   But see *R(S) 7/83*.
296   Cf *R(S) 6/55*.
297   *R(S) 21/52*.
298   *R(S) 10/60*.
299   *R(S) 6/55*.
300   See also, on misconduct and jobseeker's allowance, pp 360–364, above.
301   *R(S) 2/80*, J S Watson, Comr, applying by analogy the principle contained in the Civil Evidence Act 1968, s 11(2)(a) – on which see *Stupple v Royal Insurance Co Ltd* [1971] 1 QB 50 – even though that Act does not apply to social security determinations. Cf *R(S) 10/79* where it was held that when the evidence on which the conviction was based is not made available to the adjudicating authorities and the evidence that if available it is plainly inconsistent with any grounds upon which the conviction could have been based, the fact of criminal conviction should be ignored.

G   PERIOD OF DISQUALIFICATION

The maximum period of disqualification under the legislation is six weeks.[302] As with contribution-based jobseeker's allowance, decision makers have a discretion as to the appropriate period for the particular case and the factors considered in that context apply equally here.

---

302   SI 1995/311, reg 18(2). Contrast the maximum period of 26 weeks' disqualification for jobseeker's allowance (p 373, above).

Chapter 16

Benefits for birth and death

Part 1   Maternity benefits

A   General

Social security provision in Great Britain for maternity has a long, if also unstable, history.[1] There are two principal explanations for the lack of continuity in the legislative arrangements. In the first place, different weight has been attributed at different times to two independent policy objectives: on the one hand, the need to protect the health of the mother and child by alleviating financial hardship; and, on the other, to provide a measure of income maintenance for women who, temporarily or permanently, give up paid employment to have children, thus indirectly advancing the social and economic status of women, in particular by consolidating their participation in the labour market. Secondly, there have been major shifts of opinion on the appropriate method of financing and targeting the benefits, themselves reflecting changes in the social and economic structure. Maternity may be perceived as a risk appropriate for inclusion in a social insurance scheme. As such, does the risk attach to the mother who, therefore, must satisfy contribution conditions, or to the family, in which case the father's contribution record will be relevant? The public interest in the healthy production of children might suggest that benefits should be financed from general taxation. If so, should those benefits be universal (and non-contributory) or rather targeted on those who can demonstrate financial need? Finally, at least as regards the income-maintenance goal, there are arguments for employers assuming responsibility and the question then arises whether protection should be mandatory or optional. As will be seen, at various times, each of these solutions, or more typically a combination of them, has been adopted.

B   Assistance with maternity expenses

Under the National Health Insurance scheme of 1911, a lump sum benefit was payable to a mother if she was either insured herself or the wife of an insured person.[2] In practice

---

1   Brown and Small *Maternity Benefits* (1985).
2   National Insurance Act 1911, s 8(1)(e) (NIA 1911).

it was used to pay for medical and nursing care.[3] After the Second World War these were available free of charge under the National Health Service. The inclusion of the maternity grant in the 1946 National Insurance scheme was then rationalised on the need to cover non-medical expenses[4] even though, according to Beveridge, it was not 'intended to cover the whole cost of maternity, which has a reasonable and natural claim upon the husband's earnings'.[5] Nevertheless, following a review of the provision in 1952, the National Insurance Advisory Committee (NIAC) found that the sums paid were inadequate, particularly in relation to the expenses arising on home confinement.[6] A home confinement grant was introduced in 1953 to supplement the existing grant but was abolished in 1964 on the ground that mothers were being discharged from hospital more rapidly and so the difference in costs of a hospital and home birth was no longer substantial.

Although there was no explicit acknowledgement of this, it is clear that from the end of the 1960s the policymakers' concern to assist with maternity expenses diminished.[7] Throughout the period of high inflation in the 1970s, the grant remained at £25, the sum payable in 1969. Faced with increasing criticism,[8] the Conservative government responded by reclassifying the grant as a non-contributory benefit, thereby enabling some additional 60,000 mothers a year to qualify. Enacted in 1980,[9] this was only an interim measure, pending a resolution of the major policy questions thrown up by a review of all of the social security provisions for maternity.[10] In the 1985 Green Paper, the government recognised that, at its current value, the grant was 'hopelessly inadequate' for the job of meeting the immediate costs associated with birth.[11] Given the high cost of restoring it to its 1969 value,[12] the preferred solution was to abolish the grant as a universal benefit and to provide help with maternity costs on a more realistic basis for those in genuine need. This was to be effected through the social fund and, indeed, in 1987 was (with funeral expenses) the first part of that system to be brought into operation.[13] This emphasis on targeting was continued with the Sure Start scheme that came into force in 2001. These arrangements are fully discussed in chapter 13.[14]

C Income maintenance: general

Social security provision for income maintenance was introduced by the National Insurance Act 1946 (NIA 1946). The maternity allowance was payable for 13 weeks spanning the period of confinement. Unlike the grant, entitlement to the allowance was

---

3 *Brown and Small* n 1, above, pp 7–9.
4 Mothers not in receipt of maternity allowance, the income-replacement benefit, were also entitled to an 'attendance allowance', designed to pay for domestic help. In 1953 the allowance was subsumed in the maternity grant, the amount payable being increased accordingly.
5 Beveridge Report *Social Insurance and Allied Services* (1942, Cmd 6404) para 341.
6 NIAC *Report on Maternity Benefits* (1952, Cmd 8446).
7 Cf *Brown and Small* n 1, above, pp 33–36.
8 See eg Social Security Advisory Committee (SSAC) *Report on Draft Maternity Grant Regulations* (1981, Cmnd 8336) para 10.
9 Social Security Act 1980, s 5 (SSA 1980).
10 DHSS Discussion Document *A Fresh Look at Maternity Benefits* (1980).
11 Green Paper *Reform of Social Security* (1985, Cmnd 9517) vol 1, para 10.6.
12 Estimated at over £70 million: *Green Paper 1985* n 11, above, vol 2, para 5.17.
13 SI 1986/2173.
14 Pp 487–488, above.

based on the woman's own contributions[15] – those of her husband did not count for this purpose. The explicit aim of the benefit, to remove from the mother the economic pressure to continue at work for as long as possible,[16] was reconcilable with traditional concerns for the health of the mother. In time, this was complemented by the notion that, in the light of the increasing number of mothers in paid employment, it was necessary to enable them to *maintain* a role within the labour market.[17] As such, it was to rank alongside other measures such as the right to resume work with a particular employer and the provision of child care facilities.[18]

The movement towards equal opportunities in employment also stimulated the growth of occupational maternity pay, especially in the public sector.[19] Developments in the private sector were slower but the position was radically altered by the Employment Protection Act 1975, which introduced a statutory right to maternity pay for women employees who had been continuously employed with the same employer for two years. For the period of six weeks' entitlement, the mother received nine-tenths of her gross weekly pay, less the amount of the maternity allowance, whether or not she actually received the latter benefit. The employer was entitled to a rebate from the Maternity Pay Fund (later merged with the National Insurance Fund), financed by a levy on all employers. The Employment Protection Act 1975 also indirectly strengthened the contractual rights of pregnant employees by restricting the employer's right to dismiss on grounds of pregnancy and by providing the mother with the right to return to work within 29 weeks of confinement. This constituted, in effect, a right to 40 weeks' leave beginning with the eleventh week prior to confinement. Only employees with two years' continuous employment qualified, however, and the protection was further limited by the provision of numerous specific defences to claims for unfair dismissal.[20]

The coincidence of different sources of income maintenance – the maternity allowance, statutory maternity pay and, in some cases, contractual provision – was thought to create confusion and unnecessary administrative expense. A consultative document issued in 1980 put forward several alternative proposals for rationalisation,[21] but it was not until the 1985 White Paper[22] that the government settled on reform along the lines of statutory sick pay which had been introduced three years previously.[23] Under the new scheme of statutory maternity pay (SMP) introduced by SSA 1986,[24] the responsibility for administering payments was, in the large majority of cases, shifted to the employer, although the cost of payments continued to be met from the Maternity Fund. SMP became payable at two rates. Those with two years' qualifying service were entitled to six weeks of payment at the higher rate of nine-tenths of normal weekly earnings and up to a further 12 weeks at a lower rate, roughly aligned with the lower rate of SSP. Those with less than two years but with 26 weeks or more of qualifying

---

15 Until 1953, married women who had exercised the option not to contribute were credited with the appropriate number of contributions: SI 1948/1470.
16 *Beveridge Report* n 5, above, para 341.
17 See generally Creighton *Working Women and the Law* (1979), esp pp 37–51.
18 See generally Terry [1978–79] JSWL 329.
19 *Brown and Small*, n 1, above, pp 39–43.
20 See Conaghan and Chudleigh (1987) 14 JLS 133.
21 *DHSS* n 10, above, and for commentary see Dalley [1981] JSWL 329.
22 White Paper *Reform of Social Security* (1985, Cmnd 9691) paras 5.20–5.22.
23 Though not in the Green Paper which contained less radical proposals: *Green Paper 1985* n 11, above, vol 1, paras 10.4–10.5.
24 The relevant provisions were consolidated in the Social Security Contributions and Benefits Act 1992, Pt XII (SSCBA 1992).

service received the lower rate of SMP for up to 18 weeks.[25] The maternity allowance – now referred to as the state maternity allowance (SMA) – remained available only for some women not entitled to SMP.[26]

Further impetus for change came about with the adoption of Council Directive (EEC) 92/85 on Pregnant Workers. Primarily a health and safety measure,[27] this provided for a 14-week minimum period of maternity leave during which the mother's employment rights, other than pay, must be preserved. This right to maternity leave applies to all pregnant workers, irrespective of their length of service.[28] Legislation must also ensure the 'maintenance of payment to, and/or entitlement to an adequate allowance for' her.[29] The pay or allowance is deemed adequate 'if it guarantees income at least equivalent to that which the worker concerned would receive in the event of a break in her activities on grounds connected with her state of health, subject to any ceiling laid down under national legislation'.[30] The Directive also prohibits dismissal of a pregnant worker other than in 'exceptional cases not connected with her condition' during the period of pregnancy and maternity leave.[31] The leave and dismissal provisions were incorporated into UK employment protection legislation by the Trade Union Reform and Employment Rights Act 1993.[32]

In relation to maternity pay, the Department of Social Security (DSS) published a consultation document aligning the lower rate of SMP with the higher rate of SSP and outlining two possible routes to reform of the rules governing qualifying service and the maternity pay period. The first, a minimal option, confined changes to the 14-week leave period mandated by the Directive but at the cost of numerous complications. The alternative and more generous but administratively simpler scheme involved the abolition of the qualifying period for the lower rate of SMP and reducing that for the higher rate from two years to 26 weeks.[33] Following consultation this second option was largely adopted, but with the retention of a 26-week period of qualifying service for *all* claims. The qualifying rules for SMA were liberalised at the same time and rate of payment for employees receiving SMA raised in line with that for the lower rate of SMP.[34]

The election of the Labour government in 1997 with a commitment to 'family friendly' employment policies led to further reform, in large part driven by the need to apply Council Directive (EC) 96/34 on Parental Leave.[35] The Employment Relations Act 1999 (ERA 1999) set out new provisions on maternity and parental leave. In

25 Altogether, in 1993 around 245,000 women were in receipt of SMP: DSS *Changes in Maternity Pay: Proposals for Implementing the EC Pregnant Workers Directive* (1993) para 2.
26 SSCBA 1992, s 35 (around 55,000 in 1993: *DSS* n 25, above, para 5).
27 See Muffat-Jeandet (1991) 20 ILJ 76; Conaghan (1991) 20 ILJ 314; Ellis (1993) 22 ILJ 63; Nielsen and Szyszczak *The Social Dimension of the European Community* (2nd edn, 1993), p 261.
28 Council Directive (EEC) 92/85, art 8.
29 Council Directive (EEC) 92/85, art 11(2).
30 Council Directive (EEC) 92/85, art 11(3). See *Gillespie v Northern Health and Social Services Board (No 2)* [1997] IRLR 410, in which the Court of Appeal (NI) held that contractual maternity pay cannot be said to be inadequate if it is at least equivalent to statutory sick pay.
31 Council Directive (EEC) 92/85, art 10. This reinforces rights under Council Directive (EEC) 76/207 (as interpreted in C-177/88 *Dekker* [1990] ECR I-3941; 179/88 *Hertz* [1990] ECR I-3979; and C-32/93 *Webb v EMO Air Cargo (UK) Ltd* [1994] All ER 115) and under the Sex Discrimination Act 1975. See further Wintemute (1998) 27 ILJ 23; and Honeyball (2000) 29 ILJ 43 on whether discrimination against pregnant women is best viewed as direct or indirect discrimination.
32 Ss 23–25, amending Employment Protection (Consolidation) Act 1978, Pt III and s 60. These provisions were subsequently superseded by Pt VIII of the Employment Rights Act 1996 (ERA 1996).
33 *DSS* n 25, above, paras 9–10; on the proposals for changes to SMA, see paras 11–13.
34 239 HC Official Report (6th series) cols 139–140; SI 1994/1230, amending SSCBA 1992: see below, p 565.
35 OJ L145 19.6.96 p 4.

particular, pregnant women employees have the right to 18 weeks of ordinary maternity leave, thus aligning the period with that for entitlement to SMP.[36] The previous 'right to return' is replaced by a right – but only for those women employed for at least one year (as against two years previously) at the start of the eleventh week before their expected week of confinement – to take an additional extended period of maternity leave.[37] The upper limit for this period of additional leave remains 29 weeks from the week of childbirth. In addition, ERA 1999 introduced for the first time a right to three months' unpaid parental leave for parents with children aged under five.[38] This was a modest and faltering step forward which of itself achieves little more than the minimum necessary for compliance with the Directive: the UK is one of a minority of EU member states in which parental leave is unpaid.[39] The Welfare Reform and Pensions Act 1999 (WRPA 1999) also broadened eligibility for SMA with effect from 2000. For the first time, women earning below the lower earnings limit became entitled to the benefit, providing that they earned at least £30 a week. The Employment Act 2002 (EA 2002) enacted a series of further reforms which are expected to come into force in 2003. These include the simplification of arrangements for maternity leave and maternity pay and the introduction of statutory adoption pay (for up to 26 weeks) and statutory paternity pay (for up to 2 weeks).[40] The right to ordinary maternity leave is to be extended to 26 weeks, followed by the possibility of additional maternity leave for a further 26 weeks, making one year in total.[41] The new statutory paternity pay and statutory adoption pay are discussed further below.

D Income maintenance: SMP

i Persons entitled

SMP is payable to an employee who satisfies four conditions:[42]
(1) She has been continuously employed in an employed earner's employment[43] for 26 weeks up to the fifteenth week – the 'qualifying week' (QW) – before the expected week of confinement (EWC). The regulations provide for certain periods of absence from work, eg for sickness, to be disregarded in establishing the continuity of employment.[44] Since 1997 a woman who is abroad for any reason is none the less treated as being an employee so long as she remains gainfully employed by an employer who is liable to pay secondary Class 1 National Insurance contributions in respect of her.[45]

---

36 ERA 1996, s 71, as inserted by ERA 1999, s 7 and Sch 4, Pt I. The compulsory minimum period of maternity leave of two weeks is retained: ERA 1996, s 72, as amended. See further SI 1999/3312, regs 4 and 7.
37 ERA 1996, s 73, as amended, and SI 1999/3312, regs 5 and 7(4).
38 ERA 1996, ss 76–80, as amended. See also SI 1999/3312, regs 13–16.
39 See McColgan (2000) 29 ILJ 125.
40 DTI *Work and Parents: Competitiveness and Choice* (2000, Cm 5005).
41 These changes will be made via regulations.
42 SSCBA 1992, s 164(1)–(2). Note the modification to s 164(2)(a) by SI 2000/2883 to deal with the case of women dismissed before they have had an opportunity to start their maternity leave. See also the amendment made by EA 2002, s 20.
43 The maximum period of service envisaged by Council Directive (EEC) 92/85 is 12 months: art 11(4). For 'employed earner's employment', see pp 98–103, above, and SI 1986/1960, reg 17. For the exceptional cases where a change of such employment will not affect entitlement, see SI 1986/1960, reg 14.
44 SI 1986/1960, regs 11–13.
45 SI 1987/418, reg 2A.

(2) Her average weekly earnings in the eight weeks before the QW exceeded the lower earnings limit[46] used for contribution purposes.[47] No contribution conditions are, however, exacted.[48]

(3) She is pregnant at the eleventh week before the EWC or has been confined by that time.[49]

(4) She has ceased to work 'wholly or partly because of pregnancy or confinement'.

Employers may not contract out of their liability for SMP.[50] Similarly, an employer who has terminated a contract of employment 'solely or mainly' to avoid SMP liability cannot rely on a failure by the claimant to fulfil these conditions, provided that the claimant had been continuously employed by that employer for eight weeks.[51]

ii Meaning of 'confinement' and 'pregnancy'

For the purpose of these rules, 'confinement' means 'labour resulting in the issue of a living child, or labour after 24[52] weeks of pregnancy resulting in the issue of a child whether alive or dead'; and where labour begins on one day and birth takes place the following day, the latter is the day of confinement.[53] Difficulties may arise where there is a miscarriage following a number of weeks' pregnancy, for it then has to be determined whether the period of pregnancy amounted to 24 weeks.[54] The approach of the Commissioner, confronted with this question under the maternity allowance provisions, has been to estimate the period by counting back from the expected date of confinement, using 273 days as the conventional gestation period,[55] or, where this is not possible, to take expert medical opinion.[56]

The term 'pregnancy' is not defined in the legislation, giving rise to some flexibility of interpretation. In a Northern Ireland case a woman was held to have been 'confined' when she produced, two months before the expected date of confinement, a foetus which had ceased developing three months after conception.[57]

iii Liability for SMP

SMP is payable by the employer or employers liable to pay secondary Class 1 contributions for the employee;[58] in the case of two or more employers, liability is apportioned as they may agree, or failing such agreement, proportionately according to

---

46 Cf p 106, above.
47 SSCBA 1992, s 164(2)(b). On the calculation of average weekly earnings, see SI 1986/1690, regs 20–21.
48 Thus a married woman who (prior to 1977) had opted for reduced liability may qualify even though she would not be entitled to the maternity allowance: cf p 118, above.
49 An early confinement will affect the application of conditions (1) and (2): see SI 1986/1960, reg 4(2). If the interpretation of the equivalent SMA provisions is relied on, reference to the EWC is not affected by the fact that confinement actually takes place in another week: *R(G) 8/55*; *R(G) 2/61*.
50 SSCBA 1992, s 164(6) and (7).
51 SSCBA 1992, s 164(8) and SI 1986/1960, reg 3.
52 Reduced from 28 weeks by the Still-Birth (Definition) Act 1992, s 2.
53 SSCBA 1992, s 171(1).
54 See *CWG 1/49*, arising under the old maternity allowance legislation, when the statutory definition referred to pregnancy of 28 weeks' duration.
55 *R(G) 4/56*.
56 *R(G) 12/59*.
57 *R 1/64 (MB)*.
58 SSCBA 1992, s 171(1) and SI 1986/1960, reg 17.

earnings paid by them to the employee.[59] Between 1988 and 1994 all SMP payments and employers' National Insurance contributions payable on SMP were reimbursed in full by appropriate deductions being made from the employer's secondary Class 1 contributions. Following the changes introduced in 1994, only 92 per cent of SMP payments are recoverable in this way, a reduction designed to meet the additional cost of implementing Council Directive (EEC) 92/85.[60] An exception relates to small employers (defined as those whose employer's contributions do not exceed £40,000 a year[61]), who recover the cost of SMP payments in full together with an additional amount representing the cost of their secondary Class 1 contributions payable on SMP.[62]

iv   Medical evidence and notice

The employee must produce medical evidence, usually in the form of a maternity certificate, showing the EWC.[63] This must be signed by a doctor or midwife not earlier than 20 weeks before the baby is due.[64] It must normally be given to the employer by the end of the third week of the maternity pay period.[65] The employee must also give notice of her absence for pregnancy or confinement to the liable employer at least 21 days before such absence or, if that is not reasonably practicable, as soon as is reasonably practicable.[66] The latter alternative covers cases of premature labour[67] but may also apply where the employee was unaware of the notice requirement.[68] The employer is entitled to require notice in writing.[69] The notification period will be increased to 28 days under EA 2002, so as to 'increase certainty for employers and allow them more time to plan how to manage the absence'.[70]

v   Duration of SMP

SMP is payable during a 'maternity pay period', the maximum duration of which is currently 18 consecutive weeks, although this will increase to 26 weeks when EA 2002

---

59   SI 1986/1960, reg 18(2).
60   SSCBA 1992, s 167(1), as amended by SI 1994/1230: the amendments affected payments of SMP due on or after 4 September 1994. At the time it was argued that the reduction in SMP reimbursement was more than offset by a contemporaneous reduction in employers' secondary Class 1 National Insurance contributions: per Mr P Lilley MP, 239 HC Official Report (6th series) cols 139–140. By referring to 'pay' and an 'allowance' as alternatives, the Directive fails to clarify whether the principal responsibility for meeting the financial costs of maintenance should rest on employers or the state, although it is arguable that the Directive envisages an element of state subsidy: Conaghan (1991) 20 ILJ 314.
61   SI 1994/1882, reg 2.
62   SSCBA 1992, s 167(1A). The additional amount is currently 4.5 per cent of the employer's total SMP payments: SI 1994/1882, regs 3, 4.
63   SSAA 1992, s 15(1).
64   SI 1987/235, reg 2. This was increased from 14 weeks by SI 2001/2931.
65   SI 1986/1960, reg 22(3). If good cause is shown, it can be submitted late, but not later than the end of the thirteenth week of the maternity pay period (on which see the next section).
66   SSCBA 1992, s 164(4). Obviously this does not apply where the woman is dismissed or her employment is otherwise terminated without her consent: SI 1986/1960, reg 23(4).
67   SI 1986/1960, reg 23(1) and (2).
68   See *Nu-Swift International Ltd v Mallison* [1979] ICR 157, interpreting an equivalent provision under the employment protection legislation.
69   SSCBA 1992, s 164(5).
70   DTI *Government Response on Simplification of Maternity Leave, Paternity Leave and Adoption Leave* (2001) p 8.

comes into force. Within this period no liability arises in respect of any week during which the woman works for her employer.[71] Before 1994, regulations provided that the maternity pay period could begin not later than the sixth week before the EWC and could not extend beyond the eleventh week after that week. When coupled with the rule preventing the receipt of SMP in any week when the employee was working, this had the effect of automatically reducing entitlement if the woman remained in employment after the sixth week before the EWC. The 1993 Consultation Document explained that this disqualification 'stemmed from the view that it was better for the health of the women and her child to stay away from work within six weeks of the birth' and proposed its repeal on the grounds of 'recent medical advice that the woman herself is the best judge of when she should start her maternity option' as well as its incompatibility with Council Directive (EEC) 92/85.[72] The regulations were accordingly amended[73] to provide a greater degree of flexibility as to when the maternity pay period begins.

The period may not begin earlier than the start of the eleventh week before the EWC, unless the woman is confined before that week in which case it will begin in the week following her confinement. Where confinement takes place after the eleventh week before the EWC it will begin in the week following that in which the woman stops work, having given the requisite notice to her employer, or in the week following her confinement if that is earlier.[74]

Complex rules govern the position from the start of the sixth week before the EWC. From that point on, any absence from work on account of pregnancy or confinement will automatically trigger the start of the maternity pay period, unless the woman subsequently returns to work or is entitled to SSP, in which case SMP entitlement may be postponed further; but in any event it cannot begin later than the week following her confinement.[75] The regulations have the effect that a woman who is absent on account of an illness which is unrelated to her pregnancy may retain any entitlement she might have to SSP and postpone the start of the maternity pay period to the week following the birth.[76]

No SMP is payable for periods when the employee works (after confinement) for another employer or is detained in legal custody, and the occurrence of one of these events will bring the maternity pay period to an end.[77]

vi Rates of SMP

SMP is paid at two rates. The higher rate, equivalent to 90 per cent of the woman's average weekly earnings in the eight weeks preceding the QW,[78] is payable for the first six weeks of the maternity pay period.[79] After that she becomes entitled to payment at

---

71 SSCBA 1992, s 165(1), (4); SI 1986/1960, reg 2(2).
72 *DSS* n 25, above, para 14.
73 See SI 1994/1367.
74 SSCBA 1992, s 165(2)–(3); SI 1986/1960, reg 2(1), (3). For cases where a woman is dismissed or her employment otherwise terminated without her consent, see SI 1986/1960, reg 2(6).
75 SI 1986/1960, reg 2(4), (5).
76 See 239 HC Official Report (6th series) cols 139–140; *DSS* n 25, above, para 15. Where the woman is absent from work on account of pregnancy but is *not* entitled to SMP, she may not claim SSP for that period or for a period of 18 weeks from the start of the sixth week before confinement: SI 1982/894, reg 3.
77 SSCBA 1992, s 165(4), (6); SI 1986/1960, regs 8, 9; and SI 1987/418.
78 SSCBA 1992, s 166(2), and for details governing this calculation, see SI 1986/1960, regs 20–21.
79 SSCBA 1992, s 166(4)(a).

the lower rate, which is a flat-rate sum equivalent to the weekly rate of statutory sick pay.[80] Once EA 2002 is in force, the basic rate will increase to £100 per week (for 2003–04).

vii   Adjudication and enforcement

The arrangements are identical to those adopted for statutory sick pay, an account of which is given in chapter 15.[81] Thus although the regulations governing SMP are made by the Secretary of State, decision making functions now lie with the Inland Revenue.[82]

E   Income maintenance: SMA

i   Persons entitled

SMA is payable to a woman who satisfies the following four conditions.
(1) She must be pregnant at the eleventh week before the EWC or have been confined by that time.
(2) She has worked, either as an employee or in a self-employed capacity, for at least 26 out of the 66 weeks immediately before the EWC.[83]
(3) Her average weekly earnings are not less than the maternity allowance threshold (currently £30 per week).
(4) She is not entitled to SMP for the same week and in respect of the same pregnancy.
At the outset SMA, which replaced the former maternity allowance, was, like its predecessor, a contributory benefit payable under the SSCBA 1992. It primarily catered for those women who were not entitled to SMP, typically because they were self-employed or unable to satisfy the test of continuous employment with their current employer. To facilitate entitlement for this group, the contribution condition was significantly relaxed.[84] WRPA 1999 marked a fundamental departure from the contributory principle, abolishing the contributions condition and replacing it with an earnings threshold with effect for births from August 2000.[85] The level of the woman's earnings then determines the amount of benefit payable. Given these reformed conditions, it seems somewhat anomalous that the primary legislation governing entitlement to SMA remains in Part II of SSCBA 1992, which deals with contributory benefits.

In normal circumstances SMA will be claimed before confinement when the woman gives up work, in which case the period of payment is the same as that for SMP.[86]

---

80   SSCBA 1992, s 166(3), (4)(b). If there is a higher rate of SSP in force under SSCBA 1992, s 157(1), that will apply for this purpose.
81   P 531, above.
82   Social Security Contributions (Transfer of Functions, etc) Act 1999, ss 1(2), 8(1)(f) and Sch 2 (SSC(TF)A 1999).
83   Part of a week counts for these purposes as a whole week; this was clarified in the amendments made by WRPA 1999, s 53.
84   The claimant must have had actually paid Class 1 or Class 2 contributions for 26 of the 66 weeks ending in the QW.
85   The new provisions applied to cases in which the EWC began on or after 20 August 2000: SSCBA 1992, s 35A(4). Given that SMA may be payable for premature births up to 19 weeks before the EWC, the first payments could have been as early as April 2000.
86   SSCBA 1992, s 35(2),(3).

However, there is in addition provision for a claim for SMA to be made upon or after the commencement of confinement. The period of entitlement, in such a case, is 18 weeks, if the woman was confined more than 11 weeks before the EWC.[87]

ii Amount

SMA is payable at two rates.[88] The standard rate of SMA, which is set at the same level as the lower rate of SMP, is paid to women whose earnings are, on average, at or above the lower earnings limit.[89] There are complex provisions governing the calculation of 'average weekly earnings'. The starting point is the 'test period', which is the 66-week period prior to the EWC.[90] A woman's earnings are then averaged over the 'specified period', which is normally the 13 consecutive weeks during the test period in which her earnings are the greatest.[91] In making this calculation, earnings from different employers may be aggregated.[92] If, however, the woman's average earnings on this basis would not qualify her for the standard rate of SMA, and her earnings are equal to or exceed the lower earnings limit in *any* 13 weeks, then the specified period is the test period.[93] Under this scenario aggregation of earnings from different employers in the same week is not permitted.[94] In either event 'earnings' include sums payable by way of statutory sick pay and various awards under the employment protection legislation.[95]A backdated pay award received after the end of the specified period is treated as if it had been paid in the week to which it refers.[96] Special provision is made for self-employed women. They are treated as being paid a sum equivalent to the lower earnings limit for weeks in which they have paid a Class 2 contribution, or a sum equivalent to the earnings threshold for weeks in respect of which they hold a certificate of small earnings exception.[97]

Until the changes introduced by WRPA 1999, the self-employed and recently employed women received a somewhat lower weekly payment.[98] The position now is that women who on average earn less than the lower earnings limit, but more than the qualifying earnings threshold, receive SMA at the rate of 90 per cent of their average earnings.[99] In this context the woman's average earnings must exceed the earnings threshold over 13 consecutive weeks.[100]

---

87 SI 1987/416, reg 3(2). See also reg 3(2A). Reg 3(3)–(6) (on which see the 4th edition of this book, pp 274–275) was repealed by SI 1997/793 as part of the process of simplifying the date of claim rules and restricting the scope of the application of the concept of 'good cause'.
88 SSCBA 1992, s 35A(1).
89 SSCBA 1992, s 35A(2). The relevant lower earnings limit is that which applies in the tax year in which the start of the 66-week period falls (ie under s 35(1)(b)).
90 SI 2000/688, reg 1(2).
91 SI 2000/688, regs 5(1) and 6(1)(a).
92 SI 2000/688, reg 4(1).
93 SI 2000/688, regs 5(2) and 6(1)(b).
94 SI 2000/688, reg 4(2).
95 SI 2000/688, reg 2.
96 SI 2000/688, reg 6(2).
97 SI 2000/688, reg 3.
98 The distinction in rates derived from Council Directive (EEC) 92/85 which applies to 'pregnant workers', but it was not clear whether this phrase was truly synonymous with the category of 'employed earner' under UK social security legislation, on which see pp 98–103, above.
99 SSCBA 1992, s 35A(3). If the variable rate is more than the standard weekly rate, the standard rate is payable.
100 SI 2000/688, reg 5(1).

Increases for dependent children are no longer payable, but where a husband is being maintained by the claimant and he earns less than the amount of such maintenance, she may claim an addition for him.[101]

iii   Disqualification

There are three grounds of disqualification from SMA.[102]
(1) A woman doing any work in employment, whether as an employee or self-employed, during the SMA period may be disqualified for such part of that period (not less than the number of days worked) as is reasonable. The reference to 'work in employment' is to make it clear that a woman who does housework cannot be disqualified. In contrast to equivalent provisions governing incapacity benefit,[103] there is no saving for 'good cause'.
(2) If, during the SMA period, the claimant fails without good cause to take due care of her health and answer reasonable inquiries concerning it, she may similarly be disqualified for a reasonable period.
(3) If she fails without good cause to attend a medical examination, she may be disqualified for a reasonable period. But if the confinement occurs after the failure to attend, she cannot be disqualified for the days of, and after, confinement.

F   Income maintenance: statutory paternity pay

EA 2002 amended ERA 1996 to provide for paternity leave and SSCBA 1992 to introduce statutory paternity pay. As we have seen, ERA 1999 established the right to 13 weeks' unpaid parental leave.[104] The new provisions, which are expected to come into force in 2003, create for the first time a statutory right for fathers to two weeks' paid paternity leave.[105] This right will be in addition to the right to 13 weeks' unpaid parental leave. In order to qualify, the father will need to establish 26 weeks' continuous service with the same employer by the fifteenth week before the child is born. Such leave must be taken within 56 days beginning with the date of the child's birth.[106] Fathers will also have the right to statutory paternity pay, which will be modelled on SMP. The qualifying period of service will be the same as for paternity leave; fathers will have to meet conditions to be prescribed in regulations as to their relationship with the child and the mother and will also have to satisfy the notification requirements.[107] They will also be required to have normal average earnings for the previous eight weeks which are equal to or above the lower earnings limit for national insurance purposes. Statutory paternity pay will be paid at the same rate as SMP (the lesser of £100 or 90 per cent of the claimant's average weekly earnings) and employers will be responsible for administering the new benefit in the same way as for SMP.[108] The fundamental difference is that statutory paternity pay will only be paid for two weeks, as against 26 weeks for the improved SMP.

101   Pp 250–251, above.
102   SI 1987/416, reg 2.
103   Pp 551–555, above.
104   P 560, above.
105   ERA 1996, ss 80A–80E, inserted by EA 2002, s 1.
106   ERA 1996, s 80A(4).
107   SSCBA 1992, s 171ZA, inserted by EA 2002, s 2.
108   SSCBA 1992, s 171ZE.

G Income maintenance: statutory adoption pay

EA 2002 also introduced a statutory right to 26 weeks' paid adoption leave and to statutory adoption pay for the same period. As with statutory paternity leave, the right to adoption leave is in addition to the right to unpaid parental leave. The relevant statutory provisions are modelled on those for maternity leave.[109] Employees will have the right to paid adoption leave after 26 weeks' continuous service with the same employer. Although ordinary adoption leave will be for 26 weeks, as with maternity leave employees may qualify for a further 26 weeks' additional adoption leave, making one year in total.[110] Where the adopters are a married couple, only one spouse will be entitled to take adoption leave. Statutory adoption pay will be available to the adoptive parent of a child who is newly placed for adoption. The qualifying conditions and rates are based on those for statutory paternity pay, but statutory adoption pay will last for 26 weeks rather than just two weeks.[111] Again, the new benefit will be administered by employers in the same way as for SMP.

Part 2   Benefits on death

A   Introduction

i General

While, sadly, death is a contingency to which all must succumb, nevertheless its occurrence generates social and economic consequences which have always been thought to justify some form of social protection. A 'rational' social welfare policy in relation to death has not been easy to formulate, primarily because emotional responses, and the political considerations to which they give rise, play a significant role. A pure needs-based approach to social security would, for example, find it difficult to explain why, at least until recently, the meeting of funeral expenses should assume such priority or why a widow should be treated so generously in comparison to a woman whose marriage has been ended for another reason, such as divorce.[112] It is not surprising, therefore, that the law and policy on death benefits have been subject to frequent change and that it is not easy to locate coherent principles.

ii Funeral expenses

The desire to avoid imposing on relatives the humiliation of a pauper's funeral was an important cultural phenomenon of the industrial revolution and accounts in part for the rapid expansion of friendly and burial societies, but particularly industrial assurance companies, in the nineteenth century.[113] Fierce competition between the companies resulted in much sharp practice and exploitation. A series of committees investigated

---

109   ERA 1996, ss 75A–75D, inserted by EA 2002, s 3.
110   ERA 1996, s 75B.
111   SSCBA 2002, ss 171ZL–171ZT, inserted by EA 2002, s 4.
112   Cf Richardson *Widows Benefits* (1984) pp 107–108; Masson [1986] JSWL 343.
113   Wilson and Levy *Industrial Assurance* (1937); Gosden *Self-Help: Voluntary Associations in Nineteenth-Century Britain* (1973) pp 115–132.

the matter and their recommendations, as implemented by legislation, did much to control abuse;[114] but when Beveridge again surveyed the problem[115] he found that there was a strong case for drastic reform, not least because the cost of funeral insurance constituted a substantial drain on the resources of lower-income groups.[116]

As a result of his proposals, a lump sum death grant was included in the 1946 National Insurance scheme, payable on the death of a contributor, or member of his or her family. The rates set varied according to the age of the deceased but were based on pre-war funeral costs. Like the maternity grant,[117] the death grant was neglected by successive governments and the maximum rate remained at £30 from 1967 onwards. By 1982, when the government reviewed the grant, it covered only about 10 per cent of the cost of a simple funeral and the administrative costs consumed about one-half of the amount paid out.[118] The government's proposal to target assistance on those with demonstrated need was reinforced by a survey which showed that very few families had difficulty in meeting funeral costs from their own resources.[119] The grant was abolished in 1986, leaving those with inadequate resources to claim from the newly-established social fund.[120]

iii Income maintenance: widows

It has been written of the history of British provision for widowhood that 'no part of our social security has shown such a consistent pattern of political failure as this',[121] and the phenomenon is not peculiar to this country. The author of a comparative survey has observed that:

> the variety of responses [to the problems of widowhood] is due to historical circumstances and the unequal strength of the pressure groups influencing public opinion and the public authorities. It seldom follows any logical pattern.[122]

The major problem has been to find a satisfactory compromise between two conflicting principles: that of providing universal income maintenance for a widow irrespective of age, family circumstances and attachment to the labour market, and that of guaranteeing an income to a widow only when she is deemed to be unlikely to obtain the necessary income by her own efforts.[123] Overlaying the problem has been an awareness of the public sympathy aroused by widowhood with its important political implications.

These difficulties were manifest from the very beginning. In the early 1920s there was a vigorous campaign, particularly by women's associations, to extend National Insurance to widowed mothers and orphans, following Lloyd George's earlier failure, as a result of pressure from the insurance lobby, to carry through this idea.[124] Yet what

---

114 See *Wilson and Levy* n 113, above, for an historical survey.
115 *Beveridge Report* n 5, above, paras 157–160 and Appendix D.
116 *Beveridge Report* n 5, above, paras 79–80.
117 Cf p 557, above.
118 DHSS Consultative Document *The Death Grant* (1982) paras 5–6.
119 Hennessy *Families, Funerals and Finances* (1980).
120 Pp 489–493, above.
121 Walley *Social Security: Another British Failure?* (1972) p 249.
122 Laroque (1972) 106 Int Lab Rev 1 at 7. See also Tamburi in (1973) 5 ISSA Studies and Research *Women and Social Security* at 128ff.
123 Cf *Richardson* n 112, above, ch 8.
124 Gilbert *The Evolution of National Insurance in Great Britain* (1966) pp 326–343.

emerged in the Baldwin government's proposal was the surprising notion of a pension of 10 shillings per week payable for life or until remarriage to all widows, regardless of means or family commitments. Payment to childless widows was by no means a popular move[125] but Churchill, influenced by the difficulties of providing a more selective scheme and by the naive assumption that, if the husband had paid his contributions, the insurance principle required that benefit could not be refused to the widow, steered the measure through Parliament as part of the Widows', Orphans' and Old Age Contributory Pensions Act 1925.

The rashness of this decision had long-term harmful effects on the future of widows' benefits. For a widow with a family, the flat-rate universal scheme was not always adequate, while for childless recipients it was relatively generous and created a vested interest which it was subsequently difficult to remove. The hostility of Beveridge to the scheme is evident from the incisive terms in which he criticised it:

> there is no reason why a childless widow should get a pension for life; if she is able to work, she should work.[126]

Under his plan, the abolition of long-term entitlement of childless widows or those able to work was to be accompanied by more generous treatment of widows with children. He proposed a short-term benefit payable to all widows for 13 weeks, to allow them to adjust to the new circumstances, and a pension payable only for so long as there were dependent children.[127] The government, while accepting these two basic principles, was also impressed by an argument which he had rejected, that a pension equal to a retirement pension should be paid to a widow who, at her husband's death or when her youngest child ceased to be dependent on her, had reached an age at which she would find it hard to take up paid work.[128] Under NIA 1946, therefore, there was payable a widow's allowance, for the first 13 weeks, a widowed mother's allowance, if there were dependent children, and a widow's pension, if the claimant was widowed over the age of 50 or was over 40 when entitlement to the widowed mother's allowance ceased.[129]

The policy inherent in this approach has been maintained throughout much of the post-war period[130] but the legislative arrangements have been subject to frequent amendments. Some of these reflected the increased participation of married women in the labour market and thus changes in expectations of a widow's earning potential. For example, in 1956 the qualifying age for widow's pension for those previously entitled to widowed mother's allowance was raised to 50 (though since 1970 a reduced widow's pension has been payable to those widowed or ceasing to receive widowed mother's allowance between the ages of 40 and 49). In 1964 the rule which provided for the reduction in benefit if earnings exceeded a certain amount was abolished. Other reforms were aimed at more generous protection for those assumed to be in need: in 1956 additions became available for all dependent children whilst in 1966 the period of widow's allowance was extended to 26 weeks and could be supplemented by an allowance based on the husband's recent earnings. Finally, under the 1975 pension scheme, earnings-

---

125 *Walley* n 121, above, pp 63–64.
126 *Beveridge Report* n 5, above, para 153. Beveridge's approach finally came to pass with the changes instituted by WRPA 1999: see p 578, below.
127 *Beveridge Report* n 5, above, para 346.
128 White Paper *Social Insurance* (1944, Cmd 6550) Pt I, para 121.
129 If the husband had died before 1948 the entitlement of childless widows to the 'ten shillings' pension was preserved.
130 See esp NIAC Report on Question of Widow's Benefits (1956, Cmd 9684).

related components, derived from the husband's contributions, became payable to those entitled to widowed mother's allowance or widow's pension.

A change of direction was evident in the Fowler reforms. Abolition of the earnings-related supplement to widow's allowance and substantial reductions in increases payable for dependent children fell in line with other, general social security economising measures.[131] More specifically, the then Conservative government argued that the situation of widows has altered substantially since 1946.[132] This arose not only from increased participation in the labour market[133] but also from more extensive protection by occupational pension schemes.[134] The aim was to 'give greater emphasis to providing for widows of working age who have children to support, and for older widows less able to establish themselves in work'.[135] In pursuance of this aim, SSA 1986 implemented three reform proposals: widow's allowance was abolished and replaced by the 'widow's payment', a tax-free lump sum of £1,000, payable immediately after the husband's death. Widowed mother's allowance or widow's pension, if the widow was so entitled, was made payable from the same date, instead of 26 weeks later, as previously. At the same time the age threshold for full entitlement to widow's pension was increased to 55, with reduced rates for widows aged between 45 and 55 when their husband died or when entitlement to widowed mother's allowance ceased.

In 1998 the Labour government published its proposals for reform of widow's benefits as part of its overall strategy designed to 'modernise' the welfare state.[136] These proposals were enacted, with some modifications, in WRPA 1999, and were driven by the need to ensure parity of treatment between widows and widowers, whilst ensuring that work incentives were maintained and costs kept under control.[137] In summary, widow's benefits were renamed bereavement benefits and made available to widowers. The bereavement allowance is paid at twice the level of the widow's payment; widowed mother's allowance became widowed parent's allowance and the widow's pension was converted into a time-limited bereavement allowance.

iv   Income maintenance: widowers and the price of equality

In marked contrast to the situation in most other European countries,[138] the general British social security scheme has traditionally conferred income maintenance only on widows. The absence of a widower's pension was a clear example of sex discrimination[139]

---

131   Cf p 275, above.
132   *Green Paper 1985* n 11, above, vol 1, paras 10.8–10.13; vol 2, paras 5.38–5.55. For a study of the working patterns of widows, see Brown *Why Don't They Go to Work?* SSAC Research paper No 2 (1989).
133   In 1985 it was estimated that two-thirds of all married women with children over school age and over 50 per cent of widows between 40 and 60 were in active employment, if only part-time: *Green Paper 1985* n 11, above, vol 1, para 10.9.
134   By 1983, 93 per cent of occupational schemes covered widows, compared with 60 per cent in 1975: *Green Paper 1985* n 11, above, vol 2, para 5.47. The National Association of Pension Funds Annual Survey for 1991 reported that 78 per cent of schemes paid a widow's or widower's pension equal to half the member's pension: see Nobles *Pensions, Employment and the Law* (1993) p 17.
135   *Green Paper 1985* n 11, above, vol 1, para 10.9.
136   DSS *A new contract for welfare: Support in Bereavement* (1998, Cm 4104).
137   A new bereavement premium and disregard of bereavement benefits for the purposes of income support and the other means-tested benefits was also introduced: see pp 301–302, above.
138   See eg MISSOC (Mutual Information System on Social Protection) (2001) Table VII *Survivors – entitled persons*.
139   Survivors' pensions are excluded from Council Directive (EEC) 79/7 on Equal Treatment in Social Security (art 3(a)).

and not simply against men: especially in the light of their increasing role in relation to family incomes, women could legitimately complain that the law provided them with an unfairly reduced return on their contributions. This inability to provide through the state scheme may have discouraged decisions on role reversal within the family or have involved extra expenditure on life assurance.[140] In both the US[141] and Germany[142] there were important judicial decisions declaring unconstitutional social security legislation that conferred death benefits only on the widow. In Great Britain, reform was initially confined to occupational pensions. For such a pension scheme to be 'contracted-out', with consequential reduced contributions to the state scheme, it must provide for a widower's pension payable broadly where the widower receives child benefit for a dependent child, or is over 45 when the wife dies or when entitlement to the relevant child benefit ceases.[143] In addition, regulations concerning the preservation of benefits of early leavers in occupational pension schemes confer rights upon widowers as well as widows.[144]

Equality between widows and widowers finally arrived with WRPA 1999. The immediate impetus for this was the anticipated decision of the European Court of Human Rights on the exclusion of widowers from the state scheme.[145] The 1999 Act renamed the widow's benefits in gender neutral terms and extended entitlement to widowers.[146] Although the value of the lump sum bereavement payment (previously widow's payment) was doubled, the attainment of parity came at a price. Widowers are now entitled to the newly retitled widowed parent's allowance on the same terms as for widowed mother's allowance, but the new bereavement allowance, replacing the widow's pension, is available only to widows and widowers who are aged 45 and over and is time-limited to one year.

v Income maintenance: other adult dependants

Social security provision for divorced spouses, unmarried partners and other surviving dependent adults has always been very limited.[147] Until the 1999 reforms, the single concession granted to widowers for the purposes of the state scheme enabled a husband to rely, in certain circumstances, on his deceased wife's contributions for the purposes of his invalidity or retirement pension.[148] A similar facility applies to a divorced person[149] who otherwise gains no benefit on the death of a former spouse who was contributing to their maintenance. War pensions for parents and other adults were abolished in 1993.[150] Equivalent provisions in the industrial injury scheme were abolished in 1986.[151]

---

140 Masson [1985] JSWL 319 at 331.
141 *Weinberger v Wiesenfeld* 95 S Ct 1225 (1975), noted in 44 Ford LR 170 (1975).
142 Decision of Federal Constitutional Court 12 March 1975 BVerfGE 39, 169; the relevant law (Sozialgesetzbuch VI § 46, 97) now provides for a survivor's pension, but income above an indexed threshold is deducted.
143 Pension Schemes Act 1993, s 17(6) (PAS 1993) and SI 1996/1172, reg 57.
144 SI 1991/167, reg 19.
145 *Willis v United Kingdom* (No 36042/97, judgment issued 11 June 2002); and *Cornwall v United Kingdom* (2000) 29 EHRR CD 30; (2001) 29 EHRR CD 62 (a friendly settlement was reached in the latter case).
146 SSCBA 1992, s 36A, inserted by WRPA 1999, s 55(1), provides that the pre-amendment provisions relating to widow's benefits still apply where death occurred before the new measures came into force (but see also new SSCBA 1992, s 39A(1)(b)).
147 For an unsuccessful application under the ECHR by an unmarried cohabitant, see *Shackell v United Kingdom* (No 45851/99) (2000) 7 JSSL D164.
148 SSCBA 1992, ss 41 and 51 respectively: see p 605, below.
149 SSCBA 1992, ss 41 and 51 respectively.
150 P 788, below.
151 P 765, below.

vi   Income maintenance: children

In the typical case where the dependent children of the deceased live with the surviving parent who is the contributor's widow or widower, provision for them takes the form of a dependency increase to the benefits payable to that parent. Today it is only in the war pension scheme that allowances for surviving children are independent of the widow's benefits.[152] In the past, to deal with cases where the person caring for the child is not the deceased's widow, two special benefits were made available.

The first, the child's special allowance, was introduced in 1957 following a recommendation of the Royal Commission on Marriage and Divorce that the death of a man who had been making payments to a former spouse for the maintenance of their child or children should entitle her to some allowance to compensate for the loss of that maintenance[153] – of course, because of the divorce, she had no entitlement to a widow's benefit. Notwithstanding a substantial increase in the divorce rate, the number of claims to this allowance was always small and it was abolished by SSA 1986.[154] The government's argument was that there was no case for continuing with the allowance, given the additional help available for single parents, as regards both the one-parent benefit and the means-tested benefits.[155] In 1985 there were only about 1,000 families receiving child special allowance; their entitlement was protected by savings provisions, but the last claims lapsed in September 2001.[156]

The guardian's allowance, broadly payable to a person looking after a child, both of whose parents are dead, was introduced in 1946 to replace the orphan's pension for which provision had been made in the Widows', Orphans' and Old Age Contributory Pensions Act 1925. The allowance differs in two significant respects from the pension: first, it is a non-contributory benefit (entitlement to the pension depended on one of the deceased parents having satisfied contribution conditions); secondly, the death of both parents need not be established – it is sufficient if the whereabouts of one of them is unknown. The relaxation of the requirement that the child be an orphan, in the strict sense of that term, raises a difficult question as to the rationale or principle justifying payment of the allowance. Is it designed primarily to 'compensate' the child for the loss of his or her parents or, on the other hand, to provide some state assistance to encourage a person to look after a child who for some reason lacks parental support? As will be seen, the question is not a purely theoretical one, since those, notably the Commissioners, responsible for interpreting the statutory conditions have found it difficult to do so in the absence of a clearly perceived policy goal.[157] The present compromise position appears to be that while the allowance has departed from a principle of orphanhood, it still falls short of providing assistance merely because a parent cannot be found or, if found, cannot be induced to contribute towards the child's maintenance.[158]

---

152   P 788, below. The same applied to the industrial injuries scheme before such allowances were abolished by SSA 1986, s 39.

153   (1956, Cmd 9678) paras 714–716. See also NIAC *Report on Question of Dependency Provisions* (1956, Cmd 9855) paras 72–73.

154   For details see the 2nd edition of this book, pp 236–239.

155   *Green Paper 1985* n 11, above, vol 2, para 4.52.

156   DWP Analytical Services Division, personal communication.

157   See especially *R(G) 2/83*; *R(G) 4/83(T)*; and *Secretary of State for Social Services v S* [1983] 3 All ER 173, [1983] 1 WLR 1110.

158   *R(G) 2/83*, para 16, J G Monroe, Comr, declining to follow the more generous approach taken by Commissioners in Northern Ireland: *R 3/74 (P)*; *R 3/75(P)(T)*. See also NIAC Report 1948, HC 165, paras 8–13.

The uncertainties regarding the function of guardian's allowance have not been resolved by the major reviews and reforms of social security in the 1980s and 1990s. The main thrust of government policy has been to concentrate assistance through means-tested benefits (and now tax credits) and, to a lesser extent, child benefit. Thus the child special allowance and the increases to short-term contributory benefits for children have been abolished. Entitlement to guardian's allowance, however, has been preserved, although the allowance is reduced by a small sum (currently £1.70 per week) where the higher rate of child benefit is paid.

B Bereavement benefits

i Bereavement

A person claiming a bereavement benefit must, of course, prove that his or her spouse has died. This involves two elements: he or she was lawfully married to the person whose contributions are relied upon and, while so married, that other person died. The first has already been considered in chapter 7;[159] the second calls for treatment here.[160]

The primary method of proof is by a certificate issued by the Registrar General for social security purposes only.[161] But other less formal means will suffice, it being necessary to demonstrate on the balance of probabilities that the other spouse is dead.[162] In cases where death is difficult to establish the time-limit for claims may be extended.[163] The real problem arises where the other spouse has gone missing and death cannot be established at all. In Scotland since 1977 legislation has provided that if, on the balance of probabilities, it is determined that a missing person has not been known to be alive for a period of at least seven years, a decree may be granted declaring that that person died seven years after the date on which he was last known to be alive.[164] It has been decided that the social security authorities are competent to apply this criterion for benefit purposes.[165] In England, on the other hand, while a similar presumption exists for several specific areas of law,[166] social security is not one of them, and efforts have consequently been made to find something equivalent in the common law. The reported decisions of the Commissioner on the point suggest that no such general presumption exists. In *R(G) 1/62* it was held that at common law a man is presumed to live his normal span, and that the onus is on the claimant to rebut the presumption by evidence that eg the husband was last seen setting out on a dangerous mission, or was known to be at the site of a calamity. Such evidence had been available in an earlier case when a claim succeeded ten months after the hat and jacket of the missing spouse had been found at the landing stage of a port.[167] In the 1962 case no equivalent circumstances could be invoked and, despite the fact that nothing had been heard of the husband for

---

159 Pp 214–220, below.
160 It should also be noted that a person will forfeit any claim to a bereavement benefit if convicted of the murder of their spouse, and may do so if found guilty of manslaughter. On forfeiture generally, see pp 241–243, above.
161 Social Security Administration Act 1992, s 124 (SSAA 1992) and SI 1987/250.
162 *R(G) 4/57.*
163 SSAA 1992, s 3; p 150, above.
164 Presumption of Death (Scotland) Act 1977, s 2(1)(b).
165 *R(G) 1/80.*
166 Eg Offences against the Person Act 1861, s 57 (as a defence to bigamy); Matrimonial Causes Act 1973, s 19(3) (dissolution of marriage).
167 *R(G) 4/57.*

25 years, the claim failed. It may be, however, that it is open to decision makers and tribunals to take a different approach. The 1962 decision purported only to apply pre-1977 Scots law and the English decision of *Chard v Chard*[168] was not cited. In that case Sachs J, having carefully reviewed the relevant authorities, advanced a proposition to cover the situation where legislation had not intervened and where there was no acceptable affirmative evidence that the missing person was alive at some time during a continuous period of seven years or more. It was to the effect that:

> if it can be proved first, that there are persons who would be likely to have heard of him over that period, secondly that those persons have not heard of him, and thirdly that all due inquiries have been made appropriate to the circumstances,

the missing person will be presumed to have died at some time within that period.[169] Whether this dictum should be applied to social security law remains an open question. *Chard v Chard* was concerned with the validity of a subsequent marriage. The policy considerations relevant to a benefit intended as a replacement for the husband's maintenance which, ex hypothesi, is not paid in cases of prolonged absence, may point to a different conclusion. But it does seem undesirable that English and Scots law should differ, a situation which is hardly compatible with the British basis of social security law.

ii   Remarriage and cohabitation

Entitlement to both widowed parent's allowance and bereavement allowance is lost on remarriage and payment is suspended during a period in which the claimant is living together with a person of the opposite sex as husband and wife[170] (the latter concept is discussed in chapter 7[171]). Remarriage cannot affect entitlement to the lump sum bereavement payment, but it is not payable for claimants cohabiting with a third party in a heterosexual relationship at the time of their spouse's death.[172] Although the amendments made by WRPA 1999 in this respect do no more than preserve the existing principle, the new statutory wording highlights the fact that bereavement benefits are not lost or suspended if the survivor is in a long-term and stable same-sex relationship.[173] So whilst social security law is clearly prepared to assume financial dependency in the context of both married and unmarried heterosexual couples, a widowed person who is supported by a same-sex partner still qualifies for bereavement benefits. As the rights of those in same-sex relationships are increasingly, albeit slowly, recognised in other areas of law,[174] this distinction begins to look somewhat anomalous.

iii   Bereavement payment

SSA 1986 introduced the widow's payment, a lump sum of £1,000, which replaced the widow's allowance, a weekly benefit period paid for the first six months following the

---

168   [1956] P 259, [1955] 3 All ER 721.
169   [1956] P 259 at 272.
170   SSCBA 1992, ss 39A(4) and 39B(5)(b) respectively.
171   Pp 220–223, above.
172   SSCBA 1992, s 36(2), as substituted by WRPA 1999, s 54.
173   The relevant sections all confine the bar on payment to cases where a claimant is living together with 'a person of the opposite sex'.
174   See eg *Fitzpatrick v Sterling Housing Association* [1999] 4 All ER 705.

death. This payment was increased to £2,000, extended to widowers and renamed the bereavement payment by WRPA 1999. The provision is independent of income maintenance, the need for which is met either by the other bereavement benefits (widowed parent's allowance or bereavement allowance) or by the bereaved person's earnings (or benefit in default of such earnings, such as jobseeker's allowance or incapacity benefit). As such, it may be rationalised as compensation for the non-pecuniary losses involved in bereavement, or as providing immediate assistance with the financial adjustments necessitated by the death.[175] However, it is not payable if the bereaved person was over pensionable age at the date of death (unless the deceased was not then entitled to a Category A retirement pension)[176] and presumably bereavement in these circumstances is not significantly different in its impact.

The contribution condition is easily satisfied:

> in any one year before the date on which he attained pensionable age or died, the deceased spouse must have paid Class 1 contributions on earnings amounting to at least 25 times the weekly lower earnings limit for that year, or 25 Class 2 or 3 contributions.[177]

iv Widowed parent's allowance

Widowed parent's allowance replaced widowed mother's allowance as a result of the 1999 reforms. For Beveridge, care of a family constituted the principal reason for making long-term provision for widows.[178] To determine the circumstances in which such care might be presumed, the legislation imposes conditions similar to those employed where an increase to a personal benefit for a child dependant is claimed.[179] It may, however, be questioned whether the two situations are entirely analogous: widowed mother's allowance was based on the idea that family responsibilities prevented a widow working, which implies that the child or children should be living with the widow. The increases to personal benefit, on the other hand, are meant to assist the claimant with financial obligations. The necessary relationship between the widow and child or children was, for the most part, governed by the principles of child benefit.

WRPA 1999 extended entitlement to widowers but made no other changes to the eligibility criteria. Widowed parent's allowance is payable to a surviving spouse who is under pensionable age at the time of the other spouse's death. It is also available to a man whose wife died before the 1999 Act came into force and who has neither remarried nor reached pensionable age by that date.[180] This latter provision was presumably designed to provide a degree of retrospectivity for the benefit of widowers with a view to avoiding further human rights challenges. There are then two substantive grounds upon which a person whose spouse has died may qualify: a gender-neutral criterion and a special provision which is open only to widows.

---

175 Cf *Green Paper 1985* n 11, above, vol 2, para 5.51. In any event, it would not have been politically viable in 1986 to have abolished the allowance without any kind of substitute.
176 SSCBA 1992, s 36(1)(a). Before the 1986 reform, a widow over pensionable age would not have received both a retirement pension and widow's allowance because of the overlapping benefit rules.
177 SSCBA 1992, Sch 3, Pt I, para 4.
178 *Beveridge Report* n 5, above, para 153, where he uses the term 'guardian's allowance'.
179 Cf pp 248–250, above.
180 SSCBA 1992, s 39A(1).

First, the claimant must prove that he or she is entitled to child benefit[181] in respect of a child who is either:[182]

(a) a son or daughter of the claimant and the deceased spouse; *or*

(b) a child in respect of whom the deceased spouse was immediately before his or her death entitled to child benefit;[183] *or*

(c) if the parties were residing together immediately before the death of one spouse, a child in respect of whom the surviving spouse was then entitled to child benefit.

As will be seen, child benefit is generally payable only for children present in Great Britain and, if aged between 16 and 19, are engaged in full-time education. The traditional test of dependency for widowed mother's allowance was not so limited. To preserve the broader base for the allowance, those 'entitled to child benefit' in the rules cited above are deemed to include those who would have been so entitled if the child in question had been present in Britain.[184] However, the equivalent regulation conferring entitlement in relation to children not engaged in full-time education was revoked in 1987.[185]

Secondly, a widow may also qualify for widowed parent's allowance if either she is pregnant by her late husband or they were residing together before he died and she is pregnant as a result of donor insemination or one of various other forms of assisted reproduction.[186] The general position is that the husband of a woman who is pregnant as a result of such treatment is presumptively the child's father, unless it can be shown that he did not consent to his wife's treatment.[187] However, any absence of consent does not affect the claim to widowed parent's allowance. The most likely explanation for the absence of the caveat as to the husband's consent in the social security legislation is that this is hardly an issue that can be sensitively explored in the aftermath of a bereavement, not least as the principal witness will be deceased.[188] It is therefore possible, in theory at least, for a woman who undergoes assisted reproduction treatment without her husband's consent to qualify for widowed parent's allowance should he then die, whereas a woman who becomes pregnant by such means with her unmarried partner's agreement will not qualify for such assistance, should her partner also die. The opportunity was not taken in WRPA 1999 to extend this benefit to cohabitants, although the law recognises the male partner of an unmarried woman who receives assisted reproduction treatment as the father of the child.[189] The European Court of Human Rights has since declared inadmissible a complaint from the surviving female partner in a long-term heterosexual relationship whose claim for widow's benefits after the death of her male cohabitant was refused.[190]

The contribution conditions[191] are different from those applicable to the bereavement payment, resembling instead those imposed for retirement pensions:

181   See ch 18, below.
182   SSCBA 1992, s 39A(2)(a).
183   This is deemed to include a child of the bereaved person's previous marriage if the deceased partner to that marriage was immediately before his or her death entitled to child benefit for that child and the claimant was entitled to child benefit at the time of the death giving rise to the present entitlement to widowed parent's allowance: SI 1979/642, reg 16ZA(2).
184   SI 1979/642, reg 16ZA(1).
185   SI 1987/1854, reg 2(6).
186   SSCBA 1992, s 39A(2)(b). See *R(G) 1/92* as to the presumption of legitimacy.
187   Human Fertilisation and Embryology Act 1990, s 28(2). See Lowe and Douglas *Bromley's Family Law* (9th edn, 1998) pp 265–267.
188   See *R(G) 1/92* for the problems that arose where there was doubt as to whether the late husband was the father of his widow's child.
189   Human Fertilisation and Embryology Act 1990, s 28(3).
190   *Shackell v United Kingdom* (No 45851/99) (2000) 7 JSSL D164.
191   SSCBA 1992, Sch 3, para 5.

(1) In any year before that in which the deceased spouse died or reached pensionable age, he or she must have paid Class 1 National Insurance contributions on earnings amounting to at least 52 times the weekly lower earnings limit for that year, or 52 Class 2 or Class 3 contributions. The condition is deemed to be satisfied if that person was entitled to long-term incapacity benefit at any time during the year in which he or she attained pensionable age or died, or the year immediately preceding that year.

(2) For each year of their working life, less one year for each 10 years' working life, the deceased person must have paid, or been credited with, Class 1 contributions on earnings amounting to at least 52 times the weekly lower earnings limit for that year, or 52 Class 2 or Class 3 contributions. This condition is deemed to be satisfied if the deceased spouse had fulfilled the condition for at least half the number of years (or 20 of them if that is less than half) and in the remaining years was precluded from regular employment by responsibilities at home.

If the second condition is not satisfied, widowed parent's allowance is payable at a reduced rate provided the condition is satisfied in at least 25 per cent of the requisite number of years.[192]

The amount of widowed parent's allowance, payable from the date of the deceased spouse's death, is equivalent to the basic component in the retirement pension and is increased by an amount for each child dependant.[193] Entitlement to widowed parent's allowance ceases on remarriage but otherwise continues so long as child benefit remains in payment and the claimant is under pensionable age.[194] Payment is suspended during any period of heterosexual cohabitation.[195] Originally, widowed mother's allowance was reduced for earnings above a prescribed level but this was an extremely unpopular rule and was abolished in 1964.[196]

v Bereavement allowance

Provision for widows without dependent children has been the subject of greatest dispute and the most frequent changes. Under NIA 1946, a widow's pension was payable to those aged 50 or over when the husband died, or 40 or over when entitlement to widowed mother's allowance ceased. In either case, it was felt necessary to establish evidence of prolonged dependence on the husband by requiring proof that they had been married for at least 10 years, though if the widow was incapable of self-support, the pension was payable irrespective of the duration of the marriage or her age at her husband's death or when widowed mother's allowance ceased. In 1956, this concession was revoked but at the same time the duration of the marriage test for all widows was reduced to three years[197] and subsequently, in 1970, was abolished altogether.[198]

---

192 SSCBA 1992, s 60(1)(aa). The rate of the basic payment, together with any increases for adult dependants, is reduced according to the proportion of qualifying years in the contributor's working life, but any additional pension and any child dependency increases are payable in full: SI 1979/642, reg 6.
193 Pp 248–250, above. See SSCBA 1992, s 39C(1).
194 SSCBA 1992, s 39A(4).
195 SSCBA 1992, s 39A(5)(b).
196 NIA 1964, s 1(5). See NIAC *Report on the Earnings Rule* (1955, Cmd 9752); *Richardson* n 112, above, pp 28–29.
197 Family Allowances and National Insurance Act 1956, s 2 (FANIA 1956), following a NIAC recommendation: *Report on the Question of Widows Benefits* (1956, Cmd 9684).
198 NIA 1970, s 3, which, however, conferred a power by regulations to exclude or reduce the pension where the husband had attained pensionable age before marriage and had died within a year. The power was never exercised and was abolished by SSA 1973, Sch 28.

As regards the age condition, the distinction between those who had, and those who had not, been entitled to widowed mother's allowance was an eleventh-hour political concession made before the 1946 Bill was passed, and was difficult to justify except on sentimental grounds. In 1956, following the NIAC's recommendations,[199] the preferential treatment for widowed mothers was removed and henceforth the '50 year' age test was to apply to all. This, in turn, proved to be politically unacceptable: the main objection was the 'all-or-nothing' distinction which depended on the widow's exact age when her husband died or when entitlement to widowed mother's allowance ceased. Accordingly, as part of its National Superannuation plan, the Labour government proposed to introduce a sliding scale of pensions for those aged between 40 and 50 at the relevant date. The proposal was resurrected by the succeeding Conservative government and was implemented in 1970.[200]

The next modification was enacted in 1986, following the conclusion reached in the Fowler Review that, given the greater involvement of women (and widows in particular) in the labour market, as well as the expansion of occupational schemes, the state system should concentrate on older widows.[201] Thus, in order to receive a pension following SSA 1986, a widow must have been over 45 at the date of her husband's death, or when she ceased to be entitled to widowed mother's allowance.[202] If, at that date, she was under 55, the weekly rate of pension was reduced by 7 per cent for each year of age less than 55 (any fractions of a year counting as one whole year).[203] (For example, the pension payable to a widow aged 52 at her husband's death was reduced by 21 per cent and if aged 46 by 63 per cent).[204] Widow's pension was then payable until the widow reached pensionable age. The contribution conditions were the same as those for widowed mother's allowance,[205] and, as with that benefit, no earnings rule was applied.

The nature of this pension was radically altered by WRPA 1999. Although both widows and widowers can qualify for the new bereavement allowance, it is only payable for a maximum of 52 weeks.[206] The assumption thereafter is that bereaved spouses do not merit any special treatment within the social security system; thus either they must become self-reliant or they have to depend on another (and often less generous) benefit. The period of 52 weeks' entitlement represents a political compromise on the part of government in the face of resistance in the House of Lords to the concept of bereavement benefit being time-limited at all; the original Consultation Paper had proposed a cut-off of six months. As with widowed parent's allowance, the bereavement allowance ceases on remarriage and is not payable during any period of heterosexual cohabitation or beyond pensionable age.[207] The rules governing the calculation of widow's pension, including the sliding scale for those aged 45 to 55, have likewise been carried forward into bereavement allowance.[208]

---

199   *NIAC* n 197, above, para 45.
200   NIA 1970, s 2.
201   *Green Paper 1985* n 11, above, vol 1, para 10.9; *White Paper 1985* n 22, above, para 5.14.
202   SSCBA 1992, s 38(1).
203   SSCBA 1992, s 39(4)–(5).
204   A gap in the transitional provisions protecting the entitlement and rates of pension of those who qualified under the age rules operative before the 1986 reform (see *R(G) 2/89*) had to be remedied by primary legislation which included the power to make retrospective payments in some circumstances: SSA 1989, s 6; SSCBA 1992, ss 38(4), 39(6).
205   SSCBA 1992, Sch 3, para 5.
206   SSCBA 1992, s 39B(3).
207   SSCBA 1992, s 39B(4) and (5). The 52-week limit means that the pensionable age bar will rarely apply in practice.
208   SSCBA 1992, s 39C.

vi Earnings-related additions

The 1975 pensions scheme, described in detail in chapter 17, may have been primarily directed at providing an adequate income during old age but it was also designed to have a considerable impact on widows' rights.[209] Under section 39 of SSCBA 1992, those widowed after 5 April 1979 and entitled to widowed mother's allowance or widow's pension could augment those benefits with an additional pension, calculated on the basis of the earnings-related contributions made by the deceased husband. As originally formulated, the entitlement under the SERPS scheme was to what the husband himself would have received, as an addition to the Category A retirement pension, if he had reached pensionable age and had retired on the day he died.[210]

The additional pension was payable even if, because of deficiencies in the contribution record, the widow was not in receipt of the full basic rate of widowed mother's allowance or widow's pension or the husband, at the time of his death, was not paid the full basic rate of retirement pension.[211] On the other hand, and perhaps inconsistently, the rule which provided for a reduction in the amount of widow's pension where entitlement to this commenced between the age of 45 and 55 operated also to reduce the amount of additional pension payable by 7 per cent for each year of age less than 55.[212]

If the husband had been a member of a contracted-out scheme, the arrangements were analogous to those which applied to retirement pensions and which are discussed in detail in chapter 17.[213] The entitlement of the widow under the scheme varied but during periods when she received a widowed mother's allowance or widow's pension the scheme had to provide a guaranteed minimum pension (GMP) equal to one half of what the husband would have received if he had survived and had retired.[214] The widow was also entitled under the SERPS scheme to the difference between the additional pension, payable if the husband had not contracted out, and her GMP. As with retirement pensions, the object of this provision was for the state to provide some protection against inflation. The GMP had to be revised to cover annual inflation rates of up to 3 per cent.[215] A widower was not so well protected: his GMP was half of that attributable to the deceased spouse for earnings but only from tax year 1988–89 onwards.[216] The GMP requirement for contracted-out pensions has since been replaced by limited price indexation under the Pensions Act 1995 (PA 1995).[217]

Before then, however, the review of the scheme published in 1985 suggested that the original provision for surviving spouses under SERPS was over-generous in the light of the anticipated future burden on contributors and in comparison to what was required for contracted-out occupational schemes.[218] In consequence, the 1986 legislation prospectively reduced the rights of those widowed after 5 April 2000: they were to be entitled to one-half of what would have been paid to the deceased as an addition to his Category A retirement pension.[219] However, this change was not properly publicised, being omitted from departmental leaflets for ten years. Moreover, many people were

209 See White Paper *Better Pensions* (1974, Cmnd 5713) pp iii–iv.
210 SSCBA 1992, s 39(1), and see pp 615–620, below.
211 SI 1979/642, reg 6(1).
212 SSCBA 1992, s 39(4).
213 Pp 631–639, below.
214 Pension Schemes Act 1993, s 17(3) (PSA 1993).
215 PSA 1993, s 109.
216 PSA 1993, s 17(4); SI 1996/1172, regs 57 and 58.
217 PA 1995, s 51; see p 648, below.
218 *White Paper 1985* n 5, above, para 2.15.
219 SSCBA 1992, s 39(3).

advised, incorrectly, that they or their surviving partner could expect to receive the full amount under the SERPS scheme.[220] This was described by the Committee on Public Accounts as 'an appalling administrative blunder'[221] and by the Committee on Public Administration as the result of a 'systemic failure of the Department'.[222] As April 2000 drew nearer, the latent political difficulties created by the 1986 decision and the DSS's subsequent mishandling of the issue began to manifest themselves. Accordingly, WRPA 1999 enabled the Secretary of State to postpone, modify or disapply the 50 per cent reduction in the amount of additional pension which the surviving spouse might receive.[223] The government subsequently decided initially to postpone the operation of the 50 per cent reduction until 6 October 2002 and to establish an Inherited SERPS scheme.[224] The government's proposals envisaged a compensation scheme under which those disadvantaged by the DWP's actions would have been able to claim redress unless the Department could prove that they had not been misled.[225] Following consultations, this plan was abandoned. Instead, the government adopted the advice of the SSAC[226] and introduced an Inherited SERPS scheme which involved phasing in the operation of the 50 per cent reduction in additional pension rights over a period of a further eight years. Thus the surviving spouse of a person who attained (or would have attained, but for their death) pensionable age before 6 October 2002 will receive their full inherited SERPS entitlement.[227] For cases falling between 6 October 2002 and 6 October 2004, the surviving spouse will inherit 90 per cent of their partner's additional pension.[228] The percentage of the late spouse's SERPS entitlement which may be inherited by the survivor then decreases by 10 per cent for every two years until the 50 per cent reduction is reached for cases where the contributor reaches (or would have reached) pensionable age after 6 October 2010. The total cost of this scheme is expected to be in the order of £12 billion up to 2050.[229]

vii   Old cases

In order to protect those now very few individuals with vested interests under pre-Second World War legislation, an equivalent to the flat-rate bereavement allowance is payable to widows of persons over pensionable age on 5 June 1948.[230]

---

220   Parliamentary Commissioner for Administration *3rd Report for session 1999–2000* (1999–2000, HC 305); National Audit Office *SERPS: The failure to inform the public of reduced pension rights for widows and widowers* (1999–2000, HC 320); and HC Committee on Public Accounts *Thirty-Fourth Report* (1999–2000, HC 401).
221   *HC Committee on Public Accounts* n 220, above, para 28.
222   HC Committee on Public Administration *Fifth Report* (1999–2000, HC 433) para 31.
223   WRPA 1999, s 52.
224   Child Support, Pensions and Social Security Act 2000, s 39.
225   346 HC Official Report (6th series) col 307, per Mr A Darling MP.
226   See SSAC *Fourteenth Report* (2001) pp 16–17 and Annex C.
227   SI 2001/1085, reg 2(1).
228   SI 2001/1085, reg 2(2) and Sch. The Sch only makes sense if one bears in mind that the starting point under the primary legislation is now an entitlement of 50 per cent. Hence cases in the 2002–04 period receive that 50 per cent entitlement plus an increase under the Sch of 80 per cent thereon, making 90 per cent in total.
229   HC Committee on Public Accounts *Fifth Report* (2000–01, HC 243) para 21. This fiasco was a major factor in the decision to establish the Pension Service within the DWP to take 'end to end' responsibility for pensions matters (see p 134, above) and the introduction of new audit systems controlling DWP communications to the public.
230   SI 1979/642, regs 13–15.

viii Other benefits

Widow's benefits (and in particular the widow's pension) were paid until the age of 60. When the widow attained that age, she would normally be entitled to a retirement pension, and the same applied if she was over pensionable age when her husband died. The special provisions facilitating entitlement in these circumstances are described in chapter 17.[231] A widow under 60 might have had difficulty in qualifying for other contributory benefits because of an incomplete contribution record, and two special rules dealt with this situation:

(1) As regards short-term incapacity benefit and maternity allowance, once entitlement to widowed parent's allowance has ceased, the claimant is deemed to satisfy the first contribution condition and is granted credits sufficient to satisfy the second condition.[232] This concession does not appear to have been made gender-neutral so far as incapacity benefit is concerned.

(2) A widow may claim long-term incapacity benefit after 364 days of incapacity even though she does not satisfy the normal requirement that short-term incapacity benefit or statutory sick pay has been received during this period.[233] The same applies mutatis mutandis to widowers,[234] one of the few concessions made to this category of social security claimant prior to the changes instituted by WRPA 1999.

C Guardian's allowance

i Orphanhood

Guardian's allowance, as has already been seen,[235] has the character of a compromise – somewhere between a benefit for orphans and a benefit for children who lack parental support. This is reflected in the three possible conditions which form the basis of entitlement.

A BOTH PARENTS DEAD

The first scenario relates to the conventional meaning of orphanhood: both of the child's parents are dead.[236] Proof of death is governed by the same principles as have been considered in relation to widowhood.[237]

---

231 Pp 607–609, below.
232 SI 1974/2010, reg 3(1). This concession also applied to unemployment benefit but this was not carried through into the jobseeker's allowance scheme: SI 1996/1345, reg 13.
233 SSCBA 1992, s 40(3).
234 SSCBA 1992, s 41.
235 P 572, above.
236 SSCBA 1992, s 77(2)(a).
237 Pp 573–574, above and see *R(G) 11/52(T)* (presumption of death after seven years' absence can be relied on for guardian's allowance claims).

B   ONE PARENT DEAD AND THE OTHER MISSING

The second possibility is:

> that one of the child's parents is dead and the person claiming a guardian's allowance shows that he was at the date of the death unaware of, and has failed after all reasonable efforts to discover, the whereabouts of the other parent.[238]

The claimant must show that *one* of the child's parents is dead by the normal means of proof.[239] Claimants will not succeed if they can merely show that they are unaware of (or have failed after all reasonable efforts to discover) the whereabouts of both parents. Although it can be argued that the normal parent-child relationship is as much absent here as it is if one is dead and the other's whereabouts cannot be discovered, for the claim so to succeed would involve a total departure from the orphanhood principle.

Under NIA 1946 the rule was that guardian's allowance could be paid if one parent was dead and the other 'cannot be traced'.[240] Perhaps surprisingly,[241] a Tribunal of Commissioners interpreted this as requiring the claimant to demonstrate that there was no evidence indicating whether the second parent was alive or dead;[242] the claim would thus be defeated if there was *any* evidence that the second parent was still alive. On the recommendation of the NIAC,[243] the rule was changed to the present formulation.[244] Its interpretation has, however, given rise to some conflict of opinion. Influenced by the orphanhood principle, the Commissioner in *R(G) 3/68*[245] was not prepared to give the new formulation a wide ambit. He held that 'whereabouts' does not imply a specific place of residence: since the basis of guardian's allowance remained the entire non-existence of the parent-child relationship (the orphanhood principle), it is not payable if the second parent is known to be alive. This has been regarded, both in Northern Ireland, by a single Commissioner and a Tribunal of Commissioners,[246] and by a British Commissioner,[247] as unduly restrictive; it involves reading the statutory words '... to discover the whereabouts' as if they had been drafted '... to discover whether he is still alive'. On this view, 'whereabouts' means 'a place identifiable with some particularity'[248] and hence mere knowledge that the second parent is still alive somewhere will not suffice to defeat a claim.

Other points emerging from the Commissioners' decisions are less contentious. It seems clear that, in applying the statutory test, decision makers and tribunals should take account of facts which have come to light since the date of the claim, notably that the whereabouts of the second parent have been discovered.[249] Once the whereabouts have been discovered, the condition cannot be met and the claim will not be assisted by

---

238   SSCBA 1992, s 77(2)(b).
239   See n 237, above.
240   NIA 1946, s 19(1).
241   Cf the criticism of J G Monroe, Comr, in *R(G) 2/83*, para 10.
242   *R(G) 11/52(T)*.
243   NIAC *Report on Question of Dependency Provisions* (1956, Cmd 9855) para 88.
244   SSCBA 1992, s 77(2)(b). The revised test was originally in regulations; it was incorporated in parliamentary legislation by SSA 1973, s 22(2). In the opinion of J G Monroe, Comr, this latter step was of significance since it revealed that the statutory principles themselves were no longer exclusively concerned with orphanhood: *R(G) 2/83*, para 16.
245   See also the decision of the same Comr (R S Lazarus) in *CG 1/75*.
246   *R 3/74 (P); R 3/75 (P)(T)*.
247   *R(G) 2/83*.
248   *R 3/74 (P)*, para 7, F A Reid, Comr.
249   *R(G) 3/68; R 3/75 (P)(T)*. See now also SSA 1998, s 12(8)(b) regarding events coming to light *after* the decision.

the subsequent disappearance of that parent.[250] Further, to defeat a claim to guardian's allowance, knowledge of the whereabouts of the second parent need not result from the claimant's own efforts but might be gleaned from another source.[251] Indeed, if exhaustive inquiries have already been made by another source, eg the DWP, it may be reasonable for the claimant not to repeat them; but the mere fact that the Department has been unable to trace the missing person will not by itself suffice.[252] The onus is on the claimant to show that he or she has made 'all reasonable efforts'[253] to discover the whereabouts of the second parent (including during the period after the death of the first parent[254]) and this means 'efforts that would be reasonably expected to be made by a person who wanted to find [the missing] person'.[255] It is irrelevant that it is thought not to be in the interests of the child that the parent be found because eg it is assumed that the latter would be unable or unwilling to contribute to the child's maintenance.[256] This last principle may create a dilemma for the claimant who fears that contacting the missing parent might result in a contest over the child's residence but who knows that a failure to attempt such contact will disentitle him or her to the allowance.[257]

C   ONE PARENT DEAD AND THE OTHER IN PRISON

The third situation giving rise to entitlement is where 'one of the child's parents is dead and the other is in prison'.[258] A person is to be treated as being in prison if he is serving a custodial sentence of at least two years or is subject to a hospital order made under the Mental Health Act 1983 or various other statutory provisions.[259] In assessing the two years for this purpose, no account is taken of any period of the sentence served before the first parent's death.[260] Amending regulations in 2002 reduced the minimum limit for the length of the relevant sentence from five years' to two and included hospital orders within the scope of the provision.[261] Where the condition is satisfied, the amount of guardian's allowance is reduced by any contribution made by the parent in prison or custody to the cost of providing for the child.[262] This suggests that, in this case at least, the rationale for payment of the allowance is 'compensation' not for loss of the normal parent-child relationship but for loss of the financial support usually provided by parents.

ii   Meaning of 'parents'

There are a number of rules governing who are to be treated as 'parents' for the purpose of the statutory provisions considered above and also the stipulation in section 77(10)

---

250 *R(G) 2/83*.
251 *R(G) 3/68*; *R 3/74 (P)*.
252 *R(G) 2/83*, para 21.
253 *R 2/61 (P)*.
254 *R(G) 10/55*; *R 1/73 (P)*.
255 *R(G) 2/83*, para 21, J G Monroe, Comr.
256 *R(G) 2/83*, thus rejecting the so-called 'maintenance principle'.
257 *R(G) 2/83*, para 20.
258 SSCBA 1992, s 77(2)(c).
259 SI 1975/515, reg 5(1). This includes orders for an accused to be detained following a finding that he or she is unfit to plead or not guilty of a criminal charge on the ground of insanity: *R(G) 4/65* and *R(G) 2/80*, para 12.
260 SI 1975/515, reg 5(2)(a).
261 SI 2002/492.
262 SI 1975/515, reg 5(6).

of SSCBA 1992 that 'no person shall be entitled to a guardian's allowance in respect of a child of which he or she is the parent'.

A   STEP-PARENTS

Following a legislative change in 1957,[263] a step-parent is not considered to be equivalent to a natural parent, so the fact that one step-parent is alive does not disentitle the person looking after the child from guardian's allowance. It follows too that a step-parent may claim the allowance, since he or she is not the child's parent within the meaning of section 77(10) of SSCBA 1992.

B   ADOPTIVE PARENTS

Where a valid adoption order has been made in favour of two spouses jointly, they (and not the natural parents) are treated as the child's parents for guardian's allowance purposes.[264] Therefore, for the allowance to be awarded, either both adoptive parents must be dead, or one of them must be dead and the other's whereabouts cannot be discovered, etc. An exception was created by SSA 1986:[265] an adoptive parent may retain the allowance where he or she was entitled to it immediately before the adoption. Where a child has been adopted by one person, guardian's allowance is payable on his or her death.[266] The Court of Appeal has held that on the death of the adoptive parent(s) a natural parent may become entitled, notwithstanding section 77(10) of SSCBA 1992.[267] It did so on the ground that the latter subsection must be interpreted in the light of the relevant legislation on adoption[268] which provides that, subject to any contrary intention in other enactments or instruments, an adopted child is in law treated as if he or she were not the child of any person other than the adopter. Contrary to the view taken by the majority of a Tribunal of Commissioners,[269] the Court of Appeal decided that the forerunner of section 77(10) did not display a 'contrary intention'; the general intention of section 77 was to confer title to guardian's allowance on an individual who assumes care of the child after the death of the person previously caring for the child, whether such person was the natural or adoptive parent of the child.

C   PARENTS OF ILLEGITIMATE CHILDREN

In the case of an illegitimate child, where:

(a)   a person has been found by a court of competent jurisdiction to be the father of the child, or

(b)   ... in the opinion of the determining authority the paternity of the child has been admitted or established,

---

263   NIA 1957, s 6.
264   SI 1975/515, reg 2(2)(a).
265   SSA 1986, s 45, now SSCBA 1992, s 77(11), and, to similar effect, SI 1975/515, reg 2(3).
266   SI 1975/515, reg 2(2)(b).
267   *Secretary of State for Social Services v S* [1983] 3 All ER 173, [1983] 1 WLR 1110.
268   Now the Adoption Act 1976, s 39(2).
269   *R(G) 4/83(T)*.

the mother and father (so determined) of the child are regarded as its parents for guardian's allowance purposes.[270] For the allowance to be payable, therefore, unless the child has been adopted *either* both the natural father and mother must have died, *or* one of them must be dead and the other missing, or in prison. Moreover, for the provision to be invoked there must be determinations as to both the illegitimacy of the child and his or her paternity. As regards the first of these conditions, there is a common law presumption that a child born during the subsistence of a marriage is legitimate.[271] The Commissioner has held that the Family Law Reform Act 1969, section 26, applies to determinations under social security legislation,[272] so that the presumption may be rebutted 'by evidence which shows that it is more probable than not' that the child is illegitimate. As regards paternity, this is deemed to be 'admitted' by the entry of the father's name on the birth certificate.[273] But an order by a district judge under section 41 of the Matrimonial Causes Act 1973 is not regarded as a finding of paternity by a 'court of competent jurisdiction' and is therefore not conclusive of the issue.[274]

D   DIVORCED PARENTS

If the child's parents have been divorced and one of the parents then dies, prior to which the child was neither in the custody of nor being maintained by the other parent, entitlement may arise on the death of the first parent.[275] This applies only where there has been no court order granting custody[276] of the child to that other parent or imposing any liability on him for the child's maintenance, or any child support maintenance assessment in force in respect of that other parent and the child. In such cases the parent-child relationship has already been severed with the other parent, so there is every justification for modifying the usual requirement for both parents to have died. However, the fact that a court order has been made against the surviving spouse means that the parent-child relationship has not been destroyed and guardian's allowance is not payable; it is irrelevant that no money has actually been paid under the order.[277]

E   PARENT CONNECTED WITH GREAT BRITAIN

As with all non-contributory benefits, there is a need to show a sufficient connection with Great Britain. In relation to guardian's allowance, this is met, as will be seen, by the requirement that the *claimant* be entitled to child benefit (which is subject to conditions of residence). It is also enough if one of the child's parents was born in the UK. Alternatively, the requirement is satisfied if, at the time of the death giving rise to the guardian's allowance claim, either parent had been present in Britain for at least 52 weeks in any period of two years after they had attained the age of 16.[278]

270   SI 1975/515, reg 3(1).
271   *Banbury Peerage Case* (1811) 1 Sm & St 153; *R(G) 1/92*.
272   *R(G) 2/81*, paras 16–17, M J Goodman, Comr.
273   *R(G) 15/52*; *R(G) 4/59*. See now in the child support context, Child Support Act 1991, s 26(2), Case A2.
274   *R(G) 2/81*. This is because s 41 uses the broad concept of 'child of the family', which extends beyond a parent's biological children.
275   SI 1975/515, reg 4. This applies also to the annulment of a void marriage: reg 4(3).
276   The regulation still refers solely to custody orders and not residence orders, the appropriate terminology under the Children Act 1989, notwithstanding amendments made by SI 1998/1811.
277   *R(G) 10/52*.
278   SI 1975/515, reg 6, as amended. For the meaning of 'present', see p 230. Periods spent abroad serving in the armed forces or working on the continental shelf are treated as periods of presence in Great Britain.

iii   Conditions imposed on claimant

The conditions of entitlement already described relate primarily to the circumstances of the child's parents or previous maintainors. There are, in addition, two conditions which have to be satisfied by the claimant, designed to ensure that an equivalent to a parent-child relationship exists. It should be noted, however, that the claimant need not have the legal status of 'guardian', as that expression is formally used in family law.[279]

(1)   The claimant must be entitled (or treated under regulations as entitled) to child benefit for the child for whom guardian's allowance is claimed.[280]

(2)   The claimant (or his or her spouse) must *either* be contributing to the cost of maintaining the child[281] by an amount at least equivalent to the rate of guardian's allowance currently payable *or* be treated for the purposes of child benefit legislation[282] as having the child living with him or her.[283]

iv   Payment and amount

Guardian's allowance is a weekly allowance, equivalent in amount to the child dependency addition paid to pensioners and, of course, may be aggregated with child benefit (although not with one-parent benefit[284]). Where a husband and wife are residing together and both satisfy the conditions specified in the previous paragraph, title to guardian's allowance is conferred on the wife, but payment may be made to either, unless she elects that it is not to be made to her husband.[285]

279   *Lowe and Douglas* n 187, above, ch 11.
280   SSCBA 1992, s 77(1)(a). See ch 10, below.
281   On which, see pp 666–667, below.
282   On which, see p 664, below.
283   SSCBA 1992, s 77(5)(a).
284   *R(F) 1/89*, interpreting SI 1976/1267, reg 2(4)–(5) to this effect. Note that one-parent benefit was abolished except for existing claimants in 1998: p 658, below.
285   SSCBA 1992, s 77(9); SI 1975/515, reg 6A.

Chapter 17

Retirement pensions

Part 1   Introduction

A   General

Retirement pensions are the most important benefit provided by the British social security system in terms both of the number of recipients and of total expenditure. In March 2001 over 11 million persons were in receipt of a retirement pension;[1] expenditure amounted to around £33 billion on the basic pension and £4.2 billion on the earnings-related pension, out of total social security benefit expenditure of some £99 billion.[2] The true level of public support for pensions provision is higher still when contracted-out National Insurance rebates and other benefits under the tax system are included. For example, National Insurance rebates and the tax expenditure on relief for approved pension schemes amounted to nearly £10 billion and over £14 billion respectively in 2001–02.[3] In all, direct and indirect public spending on pensions amounts to over 8 per cent of GDP.[4]

The number of persons of pensionable age (currently 60 for women and 65 for men) is set to increase considerably in the first half of the twenty-first century, rising from about 10.5 million in 2000 to over 12.7 million in 2025 and to 14.3 million by 2050.[5] The number of people of working age per person of pension age (the pensioner support ratio) is expected to drop from 3.4 in 2000 to 2.5 in 2050.[6] Both the rising numbers of elderly people and the resulting increase in the cost of pensions are expected to be less substantial in Britain than in most other OECD countries during the same period.[7]

---

1   Department for Work and Pensions (DWP) *Work and Pension Statistics 2001* (2001) p 138.
2   Department of Social Security (DSS) *Social Security Departmental Report* (2000, Cm 4614) Tables 1 and 6. The basic retirement pension thus accounts for more than 80 per cent of expenditure from the National Insurance Fund: HC Social Security Committee *Seventh Report* (1999–2000, HC 606) para 1.
3   For Inland Revenue statistics, see www.inlandrevenue.gov.uk/stats.
4   HC Social Security Committee *Second Report* (Session 2001–02, HC 638-II) Ev 70–71.
5   DSS *A new contract for welfare: partnership in pensions* (1998, Cm 4179) pp 13–14.
6   *DSS* n 5, above, p 13. For an invaluable discussion of the economic issues, see Barr *The Economics of the Welfare State* (3rd edn, 1998) ch 9 and *The Welfare State as Piggy Bank* (2001) chs 6–9.
7   See further the European Commission Communication COM(2001)362 and also Daykin and Lewis (1999) 5 British Actuarial J 55. But see also Concialdi in Hughes and Stewart (eds) *Pensions in the European Union* (2000).

However, their influence on legislative policy has already been felt in the decision to equalise the state pension age at 65 for both men and women.[8]

The state does not have a monopoly in pension provision. Today's pension system is three-tiered.[9] The first tier is the contributory state retirement pension. Pensioners who have no other or insufficient other income to reach the poverty line are entitled to income support, now relaunched for pensioners as the Minimum Income Guarantee (to transmute into the guarantee credit under the State Pension Credit Act 2002, which is due to come into force in October 2003). The second tier is provided by the state earnings-related pension scheme (SERPS) (in relation to employment between 1978 and 2002) and/or the State Second Pension (S2P, in respect of employment after April 2002). These schemes supplement the basic retirement pension for low earners who are not members of occupational or personal pension schemes (including the stakeholder pension schemes launched in 2001). Those who are contracted-out of SERPS or S2P receive a rebate from the National Insurance Fund that goes towards their own occupational or private pension. The third tier consists of voluntary private provision above the compulsory minimum, in the form of occupational or personal pensions.

In the years after the Second World War there was a rapid growth in occupational, employer-based pension schemes.[10] Providing certain conditions are satisfied, members of such schemes can 'contract out' of state pension provision over and above the basic retirement pension. Contracting out is essentially a means whereby the state can fund 'part of its own obligations through the private sector: it gives up contribution income now in return for future savings on pensions expenditure'.[11] In 1998 about one third of all private sector firms offered some sort of occupational pension provision, but coverage remained concentrated in large firms.[12] In the late 1980s, however, there had been a rapid rise in personal pension provision, stimulated by the Social Security Act 1986 (SSA 1986). By 1996 over five million individuals had chosen to opt out of the then state earnings-related pension scheme (SERPS) in favour of a personal pension scheme,[13] a development with major repercussions for the nature and funding of the social insurance system as a whole. The combined effect of these developments was that by 1998, 72 per cent of men and 64 per cent of women in full-time work had either occupational or personal pension coverage or both[14] and 60 per cent of current pensioners receive income from an occupational pension.[15] The market value of the financial assets of all funded occupational pensions schemes and personal pensions was estimated at £830 billion in 1998,[16] making pensions fund investment a key factor in today's economy.[17]

---

8   *Equality in State Pension Age* (1993, Cm 2420); see pp 599–603, below.
9   The World Bank uses the analogy of 'three pillars' (World Bank *Averting the Old Age Crisis* (1994)), but the notion of three tiers is conceptually neater: Barr *The Welfare State as Piggy Bank* (2001) p 133.
10   Membership of occupational pension schemes peaked at more than 12 million in 1967: DSS n 5, above, p 16.
11   Dilnot et al *Pensions Policy in the UK* (1994) p 187.
12   Thus 98 per cent of firms with 1000 or more employees operated occupational pension schemes but only 25 per cent of firms with fewer than six employees: Hales and Stratford *Employers' Pension Provision* DSS Research Report No 123 (2000) pp 22–23. Overall approximately half of the working population is covered by such a scheme.
13   *Work and Pension Statistics 2001* n 1, above, p 198.
14   ONS *Living in Britain* (2000) p 72 (but the proportion of part-time workers with pension provision is much lower: 15 per cent of men and 34 per cent of women).
15   *Social Security Committee* n 2 above, para 12.
16   DSS n 5, above, p 22.
17   See generally Clark *Pension Fund Capitalism* (2000).

The current pensions landscape is thus very different from that envisaged by Beveridge, who anticipated that the flat-rate or 'basic' state retirement pension introduced in 1946 would eventually be adequate for subsistence needs in most cases and that supplementation from other sources would not be required. However, despite the fact that the flat-rate pension has generally at least kept pace with the rises in prices and, for much of this period, with average earnings, it has never been high enough to remove the dependence of a minority of pensioners on means-tested assistance.[18] In the early 1980s the formal link with average earnings was broken,[19] leading to a steady deterioration in the real value of the pension which now represents around 15 per cent of average male earnings.[20] If up-rating continues to be linked to increases in prices rather than earnings, the value of the basic pension will fall to just 6 per cent of average male earnings by 2060.[21] The political debate over the past 30 years has been concerned to a large extent with competing proposals for the provision of additional pension rights to close the gap between the basic state pension and the minimum level of income set by social assistance, and thus reduce dependence on means testing. However, the problem has not been solved even with the steady increase in the coverage and generosity of occupational pension provision, in part because occupational pension payments are offset against income support.[22]

These developments have resulted in a situation where many pensioners enjoy a higher standard of living than their predecessors whilst at the same time pensioner poverty is as enduring as ever for those without access to occupational or private pensions.[23] In this context the gender dimension is of considerable significance in relation to both the state and private sector schemes.[24] For example, 91 per cent of men in receipt of a state pension in 1997 qualified for the benefit on the basis of their own contributions, as compared with just 14 per cent of women drawing on their own insurance record.[25] In addition, part-time workers have traditionally been much less likely to be members of occupational pension schemes than full-time employees, with the proportionately greater adverse impact on women.[26]

The main conditions of eligibility for the basic state retirement pension changed little from its inception in 1946 until 1989 when the retirement condition and earnings rule were abolished,[27] making it possible to combine receipt of the pension with continuing regular employment. Part 2 of this chapter examines the structure of the basic state pension scheme in greater detail, including legislation relating to married women, survivors' benefits, increments payable to those claiming pensions after the minimum pensionable age and other increases to the retirement pension. Part 3 analyses the legislation which provides for earnings-related pensions which are payable on top of the state minimum, namely graduated retirement benefit (paid in respect of earnings

---

18 In 2001 more than 1.7 million persons aged 60 or over were in receipt of income support: *Work and Pension Statistics 2001* n 1, above, p 124.
19 SSA 1980, s 1.
20 Government Actuary *National Insurance Fund – Long-term Financial Estimates* (2000, Cm 4406) para 3.4 and Figure 3.4.
21 *Government Actuary* n 20, above, para 3.5.
22 On the growth of the 'occupational pension trap', see Walker, Hardman and Sutton (1989) 18 J Soc Pol 575. See now the forthcoming pension credit (pp 597–598, below).
23 *Social Security Committee*, n 2 above, paras 7–15.
24 See further Luckhaus (1997) 3 Eur Law J 83; Fredman *Women and the Law* (1997) ch 8; and Kingsford Smith (2001) 64 MLR 519.
25 McKay, Heaver and Walker *Building Up Pension Rights* DSS Research Report No 114 (2000) p 21.
26 But see now SI 2000/1551, prohibiting the exclusion of part-time workers from scheme membership unless this can be objectively justified. For a critical analysis, see McColgan (2000) 29 ILJ 260.
27 SSA 1989, s 7 and Sch 1; see the 4th edition of this book, pp 227–230.

between 1961 and 1975)[28] and SERPS (paid in respect of earnings between 1978 and 2002).[29] Part 4 sets out the new arrangements for S2P as from April 2002. Part 5 is concerned with occupational and personal pensions (including stakeholder pensions) and deals with arrangements for contracting-out from state provision, the requirements of equality legislation and the protection of occupational pension entitlements.

B History

i   The Old Age Pensions Act 1908[30]

Pressure for the introduction of state old age pensions began in the 1870s. The pamphlets of an Anglican clergyman, the Rev William Blackley, and of Charles Booth first drew attention to the acute poverty of many old people and the inadequacy of the poor law to deal with it. The call was taken up by the trade union movement and the new Labour Party. It also attracted a few Liberals, notably Joseph Chamberlain.[31] It was resisted, however, by the Charity Organisation Society, which constantly emphasised the virtues of self-help, and by the friendly societies, worried that a contributory scheme such as that introduced in Bismarck's Germany in 1889 would hamper their recruitment of members.

The introduction in 1899 of a non-contributory pensions scheme in New Zealand[32] increased interest in proposals for a state pension. The following year a Parliamentary Select Committee recommended the introduction of a means-tested scheme. Even the friendly societies were gradually won over to support non-contributory pensions financed by taxation; and in 1906 Asquith, then Chancellor of the Exchequer, promised to introduce old age pensions on this basis as soon as there was a budget surplus. The Old Age Pensions Act 1908 provided for a means-tested pension at a maximum of five shillings a week.[33] This was payable to anyone aged 70 on an annual income of less than £21, with a reduced pension on a sliding scale to persons with less than £31 a year. Those in receipt of poor relief at any time in the previous two years were at first not entitled, nor were those recently in prison or who had failed to maintain themselves and their dependants. At a time when it was more common than now to draw a distinction between the deserving and undeserving poor, these qualifications did not seem surprising. Payment was made, as it still is, through local post offices,[34] but the administration was in the hands of local authority committees, assisted, where investigation of facts was necessary, by the Board of Customs and Excise.[35] Although many aspects of the scheme now appear archaic, at least the principle was established that in certain circumstances anyone over 70 was entitled to support from the state.

---

28   National Insurance Act 1959 (NIA 1959).
29   Social Security Pensions Act 1975 (SSPA 1975).
30   See Gilbert *The Evolution of National Insurance in Great Britain* (1966) ch IV; Bruce *The Coming of the Welfare State* (4th edn, 1968) pp 173–181; Fraser *The Evolution of the British Welfare State* (2nd edn, 1984) pp 150–154; the fullest study is now Macnicol *The Politics of Retirement in Britain 1878–1948* (1998). For a comparative analysis, see Orloff *The Politics of Pensions* (1993).
31   In 1895 Chamberlain joined the Conservative government; his interest in pensions waned over the years, but he continued to support a voluntary, contributory scheme. See *Macnicol* n 30, above, ch 3.
32   McClure *A Civilised Community* (2000) ch 1.
33   Ss 1–3, and Schedule. See Harris *William Beveridge* (revd edn, 1997) p 132.
34   Although payment by direct credit to bank accounts is increasingly common: see p 157, above.
35   The Board retained its functions with regard to the administration of non-contributory pensions until 1947: see *Bruce* n 30, above, p 181. For administration of benefits, see ch 5 above.

ii The establishment of contributory pensions[36]

The Old Age Pensions Act 1919 relaxed the means test a little and, more importantly, enabled a person on poor relief to receive a pension.[37] But more radical reform soon followed. The increasing number of pensioners imposed a large burden on the Treasury at a time when the government wished to reduce taxation.[38] Another factor which induced change was the acceptance of the contributory principle after its successful use in the health and unemployment insurance schemes.

The Widows', Orphans' and Old Age Contributory Pensions Act 1925,[39] for which Neville Chamberlain, then Minister of Health, was largely responsible, introduced contributory pensions for those between 65 and 70 who were covered by the health insurance scheme.[40] The additional contributions were shared equally between employer and employee. The old age pension was payable irrespective of means and the other restrictive conditions existing under the Old Age Pensions Act 1908. At 70, the pensioner received his or her pension under the old non-contributory scheme, without the application of a means test, which therefore applied only to those already in receipt of the pension. Criticism from the Labour benches focused on the low level of the Exchequer contribution to the insurance fund.[41] But, generally, the reform was welcomed as completing the structure of insurance benefits started by the pre-war Liberal government.

The first four decades of the twentieth century also saw a steady rise in the importance of occupational pension schemes, although these tended to be confined to larger employers and to better-off groups of employees.[42] Most of these schemes took the legal form of a trust, one which employers favoured both because of its inherent flexibility and because of tax concessions introduced for the trust form by the Finance Act 1921.[43]

iii Pensions reform and the Beveridge Report

Under the Widows', Orphans' and Old Age Contributory Pensions Act 1925 pensions were only payable at the married couple rate when *both* spouses were over 65. Husbands with dependent wives under 65 only received a single person's pension. This created an anomaly if, immediately before he reached 65, the husband had been in receipt of unemployment benefit, because then he would also have received an additional payment for his dependent wife. The couple would thus become worse off when the husband reached pensionable age unless his wife was also 65. In response to pressure, particularly from women's organisations, the Old Age and Widows' Pensions Act 1940 reduced the pensionable age of women from 65 to 60.[44] This applied whether the claim was brought by an insured woman in her own right or for the wife of an insured pensioner. The

36 *Bruce* n 30, above, pp 246–254; Gilbert *British Social Policy 1914–1939* (1970) pp 235–254; *Fraser* n 30, above, p 204.
37 S 3(1).
38 See *Bruce* n 30, above, p 246.
39 Ss 1(1)(c) and 7–8.
40 This had been introduced by NIA 1911; see p 520, above.
41 See *Bruce* n 30, above, pp 252–253.
42 Hannah *Inventing Retirement: The Development of Occupational Pensions in Britain* (1986) ch 2.
43 See Report of the Royal Commission on the Income Tax (1920, Cmd 615).
44 S 1(1). See *Macnicol* n 30, above, ch 14.

change was in accordance with the position in a number of the then Dominions, such as Australia and New Zealand,[45] and it increased from 28 per cent to 63 per cent the proportion of cases in which the married couple pension rate was payable on the husband attaining pensionable age.[46] The discrepancy between the relevant ages for men and women is now widely regarded as indefensible, and is now in the process of being phased out;[47] in an attempt to remove one anomaly, the 1940 Act had created another.

The other change dating from the Second World War was the availability from 1940 of supplementary pensions administered by the Assistance Board.[48] Pensioners whose means did not equal their basic requirements could supplement their pensions from the Board's funds rather than have recourse to the poor law authorities. The numbers applying for the new form of assistance showed how inadequate their pensions were.[49]

But the most important aspect of this period was the discussion in the Beveridge Report[50] and the adoption (for the most part) of its recommendations in NIA 1946. The Report drew attention to the reasons why old age pensions present particular difficulties; first, old age far exceeds in importance all other causes of inability to earn and to maintain a reasonable standard of living; secondly, the economic and social consequences of old age vary considerably from person to person.[51] Thus, although the frequent recourse to supplementary pensions showed that for many the pension was inadequate, the fact that, at the start of the war, about one-third of all persons over 65 did not receive either a state pension or any form of public assistance revealed that some could manage on their own resources.

Beveridge argued that it would be prohibitively expensive for the state to pay everyone on reaching 65 (or 60) a subsistence income sufficient to remove the necessity to apply for assistance. For this reason, he recommended that the payment of pensions should be made conditional on retirement from regular employment. The TUC had suggested the retirement condition as a way of encouraging older workers to leave the labour market, making jobs available for younger people. Beveridge, however, as his biographer José Harris has noted, 'strongly rejected the view that the elderly should be kept out of the labour market, but adopted the retirement condition (in conjunction with higher pensions for deferred retirement) as a means of *keeping them in*'.[52] It was envisaged that more people over 65 would remain at work, though this expectation was not fulfilled.[53] Beveridge also proposed that full pensions should not be payable immediately, but should be phased in gradually over a 20-year period to allow the National Insurance Fund to accumulate.[54] Instead, the new Labour government decided to introduce the full rate immediately and to allow people who had not been insured before 1948 and were then within ten years of pensionable age to receive a full pension from July 1958.[55] These decisions dramatically increased the cost and led to the reforms of the late 1950s.[56]

NIA 1946 adopted the Beveridge scheme of retirement pensions and increments for postponed retirement, supported by an earnings rule designed to prevent evasion of the

---

45   357 HC Official Report (5th series) col 2148.
46   357 HC Official Report (5th series) col 1198.
47   See p 601, below.
48   See ch 8, above, for a discussion of this aspect of the history of means-tested benefits.
49   See *Macnicol* n 30, above, p 293.
50   Beveridge Report *Social Insurance and Allied Services* (1942, Cmd 6404).
51   *Beveridge Report* n 50, above, paras 233–235.
52   *Beveridge Report* n 50, above, para 244; *Harris* n 33 above pp 394, 412.
53   *Beveridge Report* n 50, above, para 255; see the discussion of pensionable age at pp 599–601, below.
54   *Beveridge Report* n 50, above, para 241; *Harris* n 33, above, pp 411–412.
55   *Macnicol* n 30, above, p 390.
56   Shenfield *Social Policies for Old Age* (1957) p 98.

retirement condition.[57] There were two other respects in which the Act was more generous than either the previous law or Beveridge's proposals. First, a pensioner with a wife under 60 was now entitled to claim a dependant's allowance for her; this had the effect of equating his pension to that payable on a husband's insurance to a married couple both of pensionable age, but it greatly weakened one of the arguments put forward for lowering women's pensionable age in 1940. Secondly, the retirement condition was not to be applied to men over 70 or women over 65, who were thus entitled to full pension no matter to what extent they worked, a modification urged by a number of small traders.[58]

iv The move towards earnings-related pensions

Under the Beveridge proposals, retirement pensions, like the other contributory benefits, were to be flat-rate. This principle was maintained until the late 1950s. In 1958 the government proposed a graduated pensions scheme, under which earnings-related contributions and benefit would be paid in addition to the flat-rate provisions.[59] The main purpose of the scheme was to supplement through graduated contributions the National Insurance Fund which was seriously in deficit.[60] To avoid competing with occupational pension schemes, the additional benefits were set at a low level and contracting-out was allowed on condition that the employee (but not necessarily his widow) enjoyed rights under his occupational scheme broadly equivalent to the maximum available under the state graduated scheme. In practice it was mainly higher paid employees who were contracted out.[61] A major disadvantage of the new scheme was that there was no suggestion that the graduated pension would be inflation-proofed. Any such suggestion would have had serious repercussions because it was assumed that the contracting-out provisions would have had to require occupational schemes to provide similar protection against inflation. When earnings-related supplements to short-term benefits were introduced by the Labour government in 1966, there was no demand for contracting-out and the option was not offered. All employees had to pay the additional graduated contributions, which also counted towards their graduated pension entitlement.[62]

The Labour government's subsequent Bill for radical reform of pensions provision, in particular the introduction of earnings-related pensions at 42.5 per cent of earnings for the average single male earner as part of a new superannuation scheme, fell with the government's defeat at the 1970 election.[63] The Conservatives' own plans to reform the system of retirement pensions reached the statute book but were never implemented. The distinctive characteristic of this scheme, embodied in SSA 1973, was the emphasis on the role of occupational pension schemes in supplementing the basic state pension.[64]

---

57 See the 4th edition of this book, pp 227–230.
58 Mr J Griffiths MP, Minister of Pensions and National Insurance, 418 HC Official Report (5th series) cols 1733ff.
59 *Provision for Old Age: The Future Development of the National Insurance Scheme* (1958, Cmnd 638): see ch 4, above, for the history of contributions
60 For a discussion of graduated pensions, see pp 614–615, below.
61 For a criticism of the graduated pension scheme, see Walley *Social Security: Another British Failure?* (1972) ch XI, passim.
62 NIA 1966, ss 1–4.
63 White Paper *National Superannuation and Social Insurance: Proposals for Earnings-Related Social Security* (1969, Cmnd 3883). See 4th edition of this book, p 218.
64 See the White Paper *Strategy for Pensions* (1971, Cmnd 4755), esp paras 23–28. Between 1953 and 1967 occupational pension coverage expanded from 28 per cent to 53 per cent of all employees: Dilnot et al *Pensions Policy in the UK* (1994) p 16.

The basic pension was to be financed by earnings-related contributions from employees (collected through the PAYE system) and employers, the latter being required to pay more than the former.[65] Occupational pension schemes were to be required to satisfy a new administrative body, the Occupational Pensions Board, on various matters. The main conditions related to the level of benefits – a weekly pension of not less than 1 per cent of total earnings in each year of pensionable employment and some protection of its value against inflation.[66] There was also to be a state reserve scheme for employees not covered by a recognised occupational scheme.[67] The Labour government, which took office in 1974, decided not to use these proposals as a model for reform, partly because of concerns over their effectiveness in protecting older contributors and partly because of the absence of guaranteed inflation-proofing.

The Labour SERPS, which replaced the provisions embodied in SSA 1973,[68] was introduced in the White Paper *Better Pensions*,[69] enacted in SSPA 1975, and came into operation in April 1978. SERPS reversed the relationship between the state and occupational schemes in the previous government's legislation. Now occupational schemes had to follow for the most part the standards set by the state scheme for contracting-out to be allowed. But it was still thought to be impracticable to require private schemes to provide inflation-proofing after retirement. Contracting-out was therefore allowed on the basis that the occupational pension, once in payment, would continue at the same rate, any additions required to compensate for inflation being provided by the state scheme at the same level as if the employee had not been contracted out.

Details of the scheme are considered later in this chapter.[70] In its original form, it offered earnings-related pensions of 25 per cent of earnings between the upper and lower earnings limits for payment of contributions, as an addition to the flat-rate basic pension (in this it differed from the previous Labour government's proposals for a wholly earnings-related pension). The pension was to be based on the individual employee's earnings for the best 20 years of his or her working life from 1978–79 onwards. This meant that those retiring from 1998 would get a full pension after only 20 years' contributions to the scheme. In calculating the pension, each year's earnings were to be revalued in line with the increase in average earnings up to the year before pension age, to give a pension related to living standards at the time of retirement.[71]

v   The growth of diversity in pension provision

Although SSPA 1975 was passed with all-party support, it was not long before the 1979 Conservative government was considering ways of reducing the cost of the new scheme or even abolishing it entirely.[72] This was not simply part of that government's

---

65   The employer's contribution was 7.25 per cent of the employee's PAYE earnings, the employee's contribution being 5.25 per cent. The Treasury contribution was to remain at about 18 per cent of the total employee and employer contributions.
66   See Cmnd 4755, paras 57–62, for the conditions of recognition by the Occupational Pensions Board.
67   Cmnd 4755, para 73.
68   The relevant provisions of the SSA 1973 were repealed by the Social Security (Consequential Provisions) Act 1975, s 3.
69   Cmnd 5713, 1974.
70   Pp 615–620, below.
71   In case of invalidity or death before pension age, the earnings-related pension based on earnings up to then was to be added to the flat-rate invalidity or widow's benefit.
72   Green Paper *Reform of Social Security* (1985) vol 1, ch 7. See the insider's perspective in Lawson *The View from No 11* (1992) ch 47; and generally Nesbitt *British Pension Policy Making in the 1980s* (1995).

continuing quest for cuts in social security expenditure. It was also a response to growing concern about the cost of the scheme in the next century, when the rising proportion of elderly people in the population would add to the emerging cost of pensions as the scheme approached maturity. At the same time, reducing the level of benefits offered by the state scheme would make room for the private alternatives favoured by the then government: occupational and personal pension schemes operating on a 'defined-contribution' or 'money purchase' basis.

SSA 1986 accordingly not only modified the earnings-related pension formula in SERPS to provide pensions of 20 instead of 25 per cent of earnings and abolished the 'best 20 years' provision, but also widened the scope for contracting out to include money purchase schemes, whether provided by an employer or negotiated on an individual basis between the employee and an insurance company, bank or other financial institution.[73] The essence of a money purchase scheme is that the pension is not fixed in advance, either in money terms or as a proportion of final or lifetime average earnings as it is in a 'defined benefit' scheme such as SERPS or most occupational schemes; it depends instead on the value of the fund built up by investing the contributions paid into the scheme. The effect of the 1986 Act was to allow contracting out without any guarantee that the employee would get as good a pension as he or she would have received from the state scheme. Nevertheless, encouraged by the provision of a temporary, additional 2 per cent contracting-out rebate on National Insurance contributions, over five million individuals took out personal pension schemes under these arrangements in the five years following their implementation in 1988.

In the short term this contributed to a deficit in the National Insurance Fund as contributions were diverted into private schemes, which had to be remedied by shifting the costs of certain benefits to general taxation and re-introducing a degree of direct Treasury support for the Fund.[74] In the longer term the aim was to reduce outgoings from the National Insurance Fund as fewer pensioners came to depend directly on the state scheme. However, it was not long after the commencement of SSA 1986 that concern began to be expressed about the capacity of many personal pension schemes to match the benefits provided by SERPS, in particular for lower paid and older earners.[75] This problem was compounded by the phenomenon of pensions mis-selling, ie that personal pension schemes were sold in breach of standards set for the conduct of investment business by the self-regulatory organisations under the Financial Services Act 1986.[76] Indeed, one in three of those who take out personal pensions cease making contributions within three years.[77] The long-term outcome of the growth of personal pensions is therefore unclear.[78]

The period since the mid-1980s has seen a number of other far-reaching changes in the legal framework of pension provision. The earnings condition and retirement rule in the state pension scheme were abolished for most purposes by SSA 1989,[79] thereby

73 White Paper *Reform of Social Security* (1985, Cmnd 9691) ch 2.
74 See p 95, above.
75 Younger earners do better in private schemes than they would, proportionately, in SERPS, owing to the high investment returns which can be achieved in the private sector over a longer period of time. From April 1993 the contracted-out rebate for personal pension has been partly age-related, and since April 1997 fully age-related, in an attempt to provide better provision for older earners. See p 629, below.
76 See further HC Treasury Select Committee *Ninth Report* (1997–98, HC 712-I) and *First Special Report* (1998–99, HC 140); also Ward in Hughes and Stewart (eds) *Pensions in the European Union* (2000).
77 *DSS* n 5, above, p 19.
78 For discussion of the possible impact of pensions mis-selling and the Maxwell pension fund fraud on members' confidence in occupational and personal pension schemes, see Mayhew *Pensions 2000* DSS Research Report No 130 (2001) p 64.
79 SSA 1989 s 7 and Sch 1, repealing SSA 1975, s 27(3)–(5), and SI 1989/1642; see 4th edition of this book, pp 227–230.

enabling the receipt of the pension to be combined with regular employment beyond retirement age. As a result the pension ceased to be linked to retirement *as such* and may more properly be considered as age-related. In practice, however, its receipt is likely to continue to be linked to retirement from regular employment, as most employers continue to require employees to retire at the age of 65 or earlier.[80] The influence of the EU has been strongly felt through the European Court of Justice's application to occupational pensions of the principle of equal pay for equal work under article 119 of the Treaty in *Barber v Guardian Royal Exchange Assurance Group*.[81] This required the equalisation of pensionable ages for men and women in occupational schemes and thereby provided a strong impetus for the final implementation of the principle of equality in the state scheme too.[82] The full implications of *Barber* on the question of the 'retroactive' impact of equalisation have only gradually become clear.[83] Finally, the complex body of law concerned with occupational pension protection has continued to grow. SSA 1985 introduced significant protections for early leavers in respect of the preservation and transfer of occupational pension rights. These were extended by SSA 1990 which also introduced automatic indexation of occupational pension payments and put in place a number of measures designed to protect pension funds in the event of the employer's insolvency. Further recommendations for reform were made by the Goode Committee,[84] established after the Maxwell pension fund fraud, and were incorporated in the Pensions Act 1995 (PA 1995).[85]

vi   New Labour and pensions reform

The Blair government's initial proposals for pensions reform were set out in a Green Paper in 1998.[86] The government's underlying premise was that 'those who can, should save for their retirement, and that the State should provide greater security for those who cannot'.[87] The Green Paper was thus based on the principle that state provision should be concentrated on lower earners whilst funded pensions should be made more attractive to those on moderate incomes. The proposed 'new insurance contract' for pensions, as outlined in the Green Paper, comprised three main elements. First, a 'Minimum Income Guarantee' (MIG) was introduced in April 1999 for those on the lowest incomes.[88] This did not require primary legislation, effectively involving both an element of rebadging and an improvement in benefit levels for pensioners on income support.[89] Secondly, a new State Second Pension (S2P), replacing SERPS, would provide substantially better pension provision for those earning less than about £9,000, as well as for carers and disabled people. Provision for the S2P was contained in the Child

---

80   The age limits (usually to start between 55 and 70) are written into occupational pension schemes in part for tax reasons.
81   Case C-262/88 [1991] 1 QB 344; see pp 641–645, below.
82   On the equalisation of the state pension age, see pp 599–601, below; and *Equality in State Pension Age* (1993, Cm 2420).
83   See pp 644–645, below.
84   *Pension Law Reform: Report of the Pension Law Review Committee* (the Goode Report) (1993, Cm 2343-I and II).
85   See DSS *Occupational Pensions: Discussing the Issues* Papers 1–7 (1993).
86   *DSS* n 5, above.
87   *DSS* n 5, above, p 3.
88   Using the relative definition of poverty adopted in *Opportunity for all* (1999, Cm 4445), more than one in four pensioner households were living in poverty in 1997–98: HC Social Security Committee *Seventh Report* (1999–2000, HC 606) para 17.
89   See p 300, above.

Support, Pensions and Social Security Act 2000 (CSPSSA 2000), which came into effect for these purposes in April 2002.[90] Thirdly, the government argued that stakeholder pension schemes, introduced under the Welfare Reform and Pensions Act 1999 (WRPA 1999), would provide a better deal for those on middle incomes.

Stakeholder pensions are money purchase schemes[91] which can be either occupational or personal pensions, provided that they are registered with the Occupational Pensions Regulatory Authority (OPRA)[92] and comply with the statutory requirements. Since April 2001 people have been able to invest up to a maximum of £3,600 a year tax-free in a stakeholder scheme, even if the member has no earnings.[93] 'Partial concurrency' is permitted, in that members of occupational pension schemes earning less than £30,000 a year may also contribute to a stakeholder pension up to the £3,600 limit.[94] Employers have been required since October 2001 to provide access to a registered stakeholder scheme, unless they fall into one of the exempt categories of employer.[95] Stakeholder pensions were specifically designed to be flexible and low-cost schemes, reflected in a maximum annual administrative charge of 1 per cent of the fund value.[96] It remains to be seen whether stakeholder pensions achieve their objective of providing affordable pensions to those on moderate earnings: there is some evidence that the new pensions are proving most attractive to higher paid earners and their dependants for tax planning purposes. It is also uncertain whether stakeholder pensions can shift the ratio of state pension provision to private provision from the current 60-40 to 40-60, as the government intend, in the absence of some element of compulsion.[97]

The next stage of the government's plans for pensions reform, involving the introduction of a new pension credit, were announced in outline in November 2000.[98] Further details followed a year later,[99] with the legislative framework being set by the State Pension Credit Act 2002. The new pension credit scheme will come into operation in October 2003 and will comprise two elements: the 'guarantee credit' and the 'savings credit'. The discussion below provides an overview of the new arrangements as the detailed regulations were not available at the time of writing.

The first component of the pensions credit, the guarantee credit, will provide a minimum income for pensioners aged 60 and over. The guarantee credit will take the place of the Minimum Income Guarantee (or MIG, the current label for income support for pensioners). It will therefore top up the pensioner's weekly income from other sources (eg state retirement pension, any small occupational pension etc) until it reaches the new minimum income level (which will, as with income support, be higher for those who are severely disabled or who are carers). The government has given a commitment that this minimum income level will rise in line with earnings during the *current* Parliament.[100] In addition, the capital rules will be relaxed for the new guarantee credit. The current rule excluding pensioners with capital in excess of £12,000 from such means-tested help will be abolished and the tariff rate of deemed income on capital of £6,000 or more will be halved.[101]

---

90   Pp 620–625, below.
91   On the difference between salary-related and money purchase schemes, see p 626, below.
92   P 650, below.
93   Finance Act 2000, s 61 and Sch 13. Such investments might be made eg by a spouse.
94   Finance Act 2000, inserting the Income and Corporation Taxes Act 1988, s 632B.
95   WRPA 1999, s 3 and SI 2000/1403, regs 22 and 23.
96   SI 2000/1403, reg 14(3).
97   HC Library *Research Paper 01/69* (1969); and see p 625, below.
98   DSS *The Pension Credit: a consultation paper* (2000, Cm 4900).
99   DWP *The Pension Credit: the government's proposals* (2001).
100 *DWP* n 99, above, p 4.
101 *DWP* n 99, above, p 5.

The second element, the savings credit, is a more radical reform in that it seeks to 'reward' pensioners with modest savings, rather than 'penalise' them (as has traditionally been the impact of means-tested benefit rules) – the loaded terminology being the government's. The present gap between the state retirement pension and the MIG is such that under the existing arrangements pensioners who have small second pensions which take their income up to a level which is still below the MIG see no actual benefit from their thrift. Assuming they apply for the MIG, their final incomes will be the same as for pensioners who have made no such saving. In contrast, the savings credit will provide pensioners aged 65 and over with a credit of 60 pence for every £1 of such extra income up to a certain limit.

The effect of the new pension credit can be demonstrated with a simple example. At present, if the basic state retirement pension for a single person is £77 a week, and the MIG for a single pensioner is £100 a week, pensioner A whose only pension is the basic pension will receive £100 a week (£77 retirement pension and £23 MIG). Pensioner B who has a works pension of £10 a week in addition to the state pension will also receive £100 a week (£77 retirement pension, £10 works pension and £13 MIG). From October 2003, pensioner B's position will be improved vis-à-vis pensioner A, in that she will qualify for a final income of £106 a week (£77 retirement pension, £10 works pension, £13 guarantee credit and £6 savings credit).

The House of Commons Social Security Committee has expressed the view that the new pension credit scheme 'has the potential to go some considerable way' to addressing pensioner poverty and increasing incentives to save.[102] But the Committee also identified a number of concerns with the proposed new arrangements. These included its complexity and uncertainty about the take-up and future up-rating of the pension credit, as well as its interaction with the S2P.

Part 2   Entitlement to a retirement pension

In this Part of the chapter the conditions of entitlement to a retirement pension, laid down now in the Social Security Contributions and Benefits Act 1992 (SSCBA 1992),[103] are set out. Most of these conditions apply to eligibility for the flat-rate basic contributory pension and both the earnings-related additional pension and the state second pension. The special rules relating to the latter two elements are set out in Parts 3 and 4 of the chapter.

A   Categories of retirement pension

A contributory retirement pension is made up of all or some of the following components:
(a) basic (flat-rate) pension;
(b) graduated pension, based on earnings-related contributions paid between 1961 and 1975;[104]
(c) additional (earnings-related) pension, based on contributions paid between 1978 and 2002;[105]

---

102   HC Social Security Committee *Second Report* (2000–01, HC 638-I) para 90.
103   Ss 43–55.
104   See pp 614–615, below.
105   See pp 615–620, below.

(d) state second pension, based on actual or deemed contributions paid since April 2002;[106]

(e) increases for dependants;[107]

(f) incapacity addition;[108]

(g) increments for deferred retirement;[109]

(h) age addition (80 or over).[110]

The basic and/or additional pension can be based either on the pensioner's own contribution record (a Category A pension) or on the contributions of the pensioner's husband or wife (a Category B pension). In some circumstances, the husband's or wife's contribution record can be taken into account in calculating a Category A pension, either by substituting it for the pensioner's own contribution record or by combining them to produce a 'composite' pension. For those who do not qualify for a contributory retirement pension, there is provision for non-contributory retirement pensions (Categories C and D).

It will be recalled that pensioners whose income from their state retirement pension and any other sources is insufficient to meet the threshold for income support may be eligible for the means-tested MIG.

B Pensionable age

i Policy

The first condition of eligibility for a Category A or B retirement pension is that the claimant has attained pensionable age.[111] If the object of retirement pensions were simply to provide an income for those no longer able to earn their living because of the effects of old age, there would in principle be no need to specify a particular age from which the pension should be payable. Provided that the basic condition of loss of earning capacity was satisfied, the pension could be paid from any age. In fact, however, retirement pensions serve the wider purpose of enabling people to retire from paid work before they are compelled to do so by failing powers or loss of relevant skills.[112] More controversially, at a time of high unemployment, pensions are used to encourage older workers to retire so that their jobs can be taken by younger people who might otherwise be unemployed. To achieve these wider aims, it is necessary to fix a minimum age at which the pension can be claimed. Occupational schemes frequently provide for a proportion of the final pension to be paid to employees who take early retirement before reaching the pensionable age set by the state scheme.[113]

Whatever pensionable age is chosen must be to some extent arbitrary. An obvious course would be to choose the age at which most people would wish to retire and at which it would generally be considered reasonable that they should do so. In practice, however, views about retirement age are themselves largely determined by the age at

---

106 See pp 620–625, below.

107 See pp 247–258, above.

108 See p 613, below.

109 See pp 610–613, below.

110 See p 613, below.

111 SSCBA 1992, ss 44(1)(a), 48A(1)(a), 48B(1)(b).

112 See *Macnicol* n 30, above, ch 1.

113 Under Inland Revenue rules, occupational schemes qualifying for tax rebates must specify a normal retirement age between 60 and 75, and may provide for early retirement benefits to be paid from the age of 50. See p 641, below.

which a pension is available. This is particularly true where, as in Great Britain, a large proportion of the working population is covered by occupational pension schemes which typically adopt the same pension ages as the state scheme. Once fixed, therefore, pensionable ages become entrenched in retirement practices. It is this fact, more than anything else, which explains why the present pensionable ages have remained unchanged for nearly half a century in the UK.

It should nevertheless be borne in mind that a degree of flexibility was built into the state scheme from its inception, in the form of increments to the basic pension for those deferring their retirement for up to five years from the minimum pensionable age of 60 or 65.[114] Further provisions treat unemployed people approaching pensionable age as effectively retired, including the award of a 'pensioner premium' to income support claimants of either sex from the age of 60[115] and the exemption of such persons from the requirement to be available for employment.[116]

When pensionable ages were changed, it was initially in a downwards direction: first by the provision of pensions at 65 instead of 70 under the Contributory Pensions Act 1925, and then by the reduction of women's pensionable age to 60. The lower age for women dates from 1940, when the war-time government made the change under pressure from women's organisations. The principal object was to enable the typical married couple, where the husband was 65 and the wife a few years younger, to draw the full married couple's pension.[117] Any further reduction, however, would have large cost implications, both for the state scheme and for occupational schemes. Proposals to raise pensionable ages, on the other hand, encounter the objection that established rights, on which people have based their retirement plans, would be removed.

In recent years the debate has principally been concerned with the difference between pensionable ages for men and women. While Council Directive (EEC) 79/7 on equal treatment for men and women in social security has led to the removal of most other forms of discrimination between the sexes, the Directive specifically allows member states to exclude from its scope 'the determination of pensionable age for the purposes of granting old-age and retirement pensions and the possible consequences thereof for other benefits'.[118] Nevertheless, it gradually came to be accepted that the difference was anomalous and that equal pension ages for men and women were a desirable policy aim. Since the early 1980s a number of official reports have addressed the question. The House of Commons Social Services Committee noted in 1982 that the growing trend towards earlier retirement since the mid-1970s but concluded that simply reducing the pensionable age for men to 60 would be 'massively expensive'.[119] Instead, the committee proposed a 'flexible' pension age: both men and women would be allowed to claim an abated pension at 60, the full pension being available at a 'notional common pension age' of 63.[120]

The 1985 Green Paper *Reform of Social Security* did not endorse the Select Committee's proposals, given the implications for public expenditure, but put forward instead the idea of a 'decade of retirement' between 60 and 70. Within these limits, earlier retirement would give entitlement to a reduced pension and later retirement to

---

114   See pp 610–613, below.
115   See p 300, above.
116   In 1992–93 there were 177,000 men aged between 60 and 64 and in receipt of income support: DSS *Social Security Departmental Report* (1994, Cm 2513) Table 6.
117   See pp 591–593, above.
118   Art 7(1)(a).
119   HC Social Services Committee *Third Report* (1981–1982, HC 26-I) para 69.
120   *HC Social Services Committee* n 119, above, paras 91–99.

an enhanced pension. The White Paper that followed six months later took the idea no further, merely recording that, while many of those responding to the Green Paper favoured greater flexibility, none suggested a way of introducing the 'decade of retirement' without substantial initial costs.[121]

There the matter rested until it was revived by the decision of the European Court of Justice in *Barber v Guardian Royal Exchange Assurance Group*,[122] which interpreted article 119 of the EC Treaty as requiring equality of pensionable ages for men and women in occupational schemes. The essence of *Barber* is that pension benefits paid under occupational schemes are 'pay' within article 119, notwithstanding that they are normally paid after the beneficiary's employment has come to an end and that they are, in the case of contracted-out schemes, paid in substitution for state retirement benefits. The state retirement pension was outside the precise scope of this ruling,[123] and the derogation permitting unequal pensionable ages in state schemes which is contained in article 7(1)(a) of Council Directive (EEC) 79/7 therefore remained good law.[124] However, once equality became mandatory in occupational schemes its adoption for the state scheme was inevitable if practical difficulties arising from the inter-dependence of state and occupational provision, in particular in relation to contracting-out, were to be avoided.

In December 1991 the DSS issued a consultation paper laying out a number of options including the flexible 'decade of retirement' between 60 and 70;[125] however, two years later the government announced its intention to proceed to a new common pensionable age of 65. This proposal was implemented in PA 1995, which phases in the change over a 10-year period from July 2010.[126] Section 126(a) and Part I of Schedule 4 to the 1995 Act lay down four rules regarding the attainment of pensionable age. First, a man reaches pensionable age when he is 65. Secondly, a woman born before 6 April 1950 will continue to be eligible for a pension from the age of 60. Thirdly, women born between 6 April 1950 and 5 April 1955 will see their pensionable age gradually raised during the transitional period, with one month being added to the retirement age for every two months that passes. Thus, fourthly, a woman born on or after 6 March 1955 will receive the pension at the age of 65.[127] The process of equalisation will therefore be complete by 6 March 2020.

Whether a uniform pensionable age of 65 is sustainable is quite another matter. There is a strong case for arguing, given increased longevity and other demographic changes (most notably in the pensioner support ratio), that the retirement age should move upwards.[128]

---

121 *White Paper 1985* n 73, above, para 2.59.
122 Case C-262/88, [1991] 1 QB 344.
123 See p 600, above; *R(P) 3/90*; Deakin [1990] CLJ 408.
124 In Case C-9/91 *R v Secretary of State for the Social Services, ex p Equal Opportunities Commission* [1992] ICR 782 [1992] 3 All ER 577 the European Court of Justice held that art 7(1)(a) authorised different contribution arrangements for men and women where they were the consequence of separate pensionable ages, and in Case C-328/91 *Thomas v Chief Adjudication Officer* [1993] QB 747 it held that the derogation could extend to inequality in other social security benefits where that was objectively necessary to avoid disrupting the financial equilibrium of the social security system or to ensure consistency with the state pension.
125 DSS *Options for Equality in State Pension Age* (1992); see also the report of the House of Lords Select Committee on the European Communities *Equal Treatment of Men and Women in Pensions and other Benefits* (1988–89, HL 51).
126 See *Equality in State Pension Age* (1993, Cm 2420).
127 The Table in PA 1995, Sch 4 provides a sliding scale for the equalisation process.
128 Barr *The Welfare State as Piggy Bank* (2001) p 146. See eg IPPR's proposal to raise the pensionable age to 67 by 2030: IPPR *A New Contract for Retirement* (2002).

ii The law

Until 2010, therefore, there are two pensionable ages, one for each sex: 65 for a man and 60 for a woman.[129] With the abolition of the retirement condition, it is no longer a condition of entitlement to a retirement pension that the person has (or is treated as having) retired from regular employment. The age conditions pose few legal problems, at least so far as claimants born in the UK are concerned. Generally claimants will prove their age by reference to their birth certificate, though a population census has been accepted as providing satisfactory evidence.[130] In a case where the claimant was a Pakistani immigrant from a district where there had been at the relevant time no register of births, it was held that documentary evidence is not the only method of proof of age; medical evidence is admissible.[131]

Since pensionable age depends on the sex of the claimant, difficulties can arise where a person claims to have changed his or her sex. Two such cases have been reported. In the first,[132] the claimant argued that, though born a male, she had been issued with a woman's National Insurance card in her adopted female name after medical treatment and had thus been led to believe she would be treated as a woman for pension purposes. The Chief Commissioner, however, concluded that she remained biologically male and that no pension could be paid until the age of 65; the issue of a woman's National Insurance card could not raise an estoppel binding the statutory authorities.[133] In the second case, the claimant contended that under the legislation what was important was the person's social rather than biological role and that since, as a woman, she would be expected to retire at 60, the award of a pension would then be appropriate. This contention was also rejected on the grounds, first, that the relevant sections of the then Act[134] indicated that a 'woman' is someone capable of forming a valid marriage with a husband, and secondly, that there was no evidence that Parliament ever intended to make more favourable provision for women because in practice they retired earlier than men. It is likely to be only a matter of time before there is a human rights challenge on this point.

It might seem that the pension should be payable as soon as the age conditions are satisfied. Section 44(1) of SSCBA 1992, for example, states that a person is entitled to a Category A retirement pension if he or she is over pensionable age and has satisfied the relevant contribution conditions. Moreover, the claimant 'shall become so entitled on the day on which he attains pensionable age and his entitlement shall continue throughout his life'. This is subject, however, to section 44(2) of SSCBA 1992 and to section 5(1)(k) of the Social Security Administration Act 1992 (SSAA 1992), which provide authority for regulations to specify more precisely the point at which benefit entitlements begin and end. The Social Security (Claims and Payments) Regulations provide that a pension or other benefit is to be payable on a specified day of the week – normally Monday in the case of a new retirement pensioner – unless the Secretary of State arranges for it to be payable on a different day, and that benefit is to commence on that day.[135] The result is that entitlement to pension starts on the appropriate pay day

129   SSCBA 1992, s 122(1) and PA, Sch 4, Pt I and Pt III, para 13.
130   *CP 11/49.*
131   *R(P) 1/75*, R J A Temple, Comr.
132   *R(P) 1/80.*
133   The Chief Comr, R J A Temple, doubted the use of the estoppel doctrine in *Robertson v Minister of Pensions* [1949] 1 KB 227, [1948] 2 All ER 767.
134   SSA 1975, ss 28–29, now contained in SSCBA 1992, ss 44, 47 and 122(1). See *R(P) 2/80* and Harris (1998) 5 JSSL 44 for an equal treatment perspective on this issue.
135   SI 1987/1968, regs 16(1) and (3), 22(3) and Sch 6. Payment days are discussed in the chapter on the administration of benefits, p 159, above.

following the claimant's birthday, rather than on the day when the claimant reaches pensionable age, unless the two days coincide. In *R(P) 2/73* it was regarded as far-fetched to argue that the similar regulation then in force was unreasonable and, therefore, ultra vires in that it discriminated against certain claimants in respect of the date of their birth.[136]

C Category A retirement pensions

i General

As we have seen, the first condition of entitlement to a Category A basic retirement pension is that the claimant has reached pensionable age, as defined above.[137] The second requirement is that the relevant contribution conditions are satisfied.[138] The pension is then payable for life.[139] A Category A retirement pension is normally based on the claimant's own contributions, although special provisions may modify the standard rule for married persons, widows, widowers and those who are divorced. A Category B pension (see section D below) is based on a spouse's contributions. The same person cannot receive both a Category A and a Category B pension, even though the contribution conditions for each may be met; he or she is entitled to whichever is the more favourable.[140]

In addition to the basic pension, a person entitled to a Category A retirement pension may also qualify for a number of additions. The basis of entitlement to such extra amounts, including the additional earnings-related pension and the state second pension (which are technically separate pensions), are discussed later in this chapter. Category A pensions may also be increased by additions for adult and child dependants: entitlement to such dependency additions is covered in chapter 7.

ii Contribution conditions

The contribution conditions, as set out in paragraph 5 of Schedule 3 to SSCBA 1992 are as follows:
(a) the claimant must have paid, in at least one year, contributions of the relevant class on earnings of at least 52 times the lower earnings limit;[141] and
(b) the claimant must have paid or been credited with contributions equivalent to that sum for nine-tenths of his or her working life (if that is not a whole number of years, it is rounded down to the nearest whole number).[142]

---

136 Per H A Shewan, Comr. See also *R(P) 16/52*.
137 SSCBA 1992, s 44(1)(a).
138 SSCBA 1992, s 44(1)(b).
139 SSCBA 1992, s 44(1).
140 SSCBA 1992, s 43(1).
141 The condition is expressed in terms of earnings factors (see p 121, above), enabling Class 2 (self-employed) and Class 3 (voluntary) contributions to be taken into account as well as earnings-related Class 1 contributions. This first condition is deemed to be satisfied if the contributor was receiving long-term incapacity benefit in the year he or she reached pensionable age (or at the date of death), or in the preceding year: SSCBA 1992, Sch 3, para 5(6). It can also be satisfied by having paid 50 flat-rate contributions at any time (not necessarily in one year) before 6 April 1975: SI 1979/643, reg 6(1).
142 On the definition of 'working life', see SSCBA 1992, Sch 3, para 5(8). The total number of flat-rate contributions paid or credited before 6 April 1975 is divided by 50 and the result rounded up to the nearest whole number, to arrive at the number of reckonable years for that part of a person's career: SI 1979/643, reg 7(2).

The effect of this second contribution condition – the continuing contributions condition – is that, where the claimant's working life is of 41 years or more, up to five years' contributions may be missed. However, the second contribution condition is modified to provide 'home responsibilities protection' for persons who have been out of the employment field for considerable periods (generally, though not necessarily, married women).[143] It is enough for a claimant to have complied with the condition for half the required years (ie half of nine-tenths of her working life), or at least 20 years if that is less, provided she (or he) can establish that for all the other years she was 'precluded from regular employment by responsibilities at home'.[144] Regulations define the meaning of this phrase. The claimant will be regarded as satisfying the requirement if, throughout any year after April 1978, she (or he): (a) is awarded child benefit for any child under 16; or (b) is awarded income support on the basis of caring for an elderly or incapacitated person; or (c) is regularly engaged for at least 35 hours per week in caring for a person aged 16 or over who, in turn, is in receipt of the care component of disability living allowance or attendance allowance (or an analogous benefit).[145] But a woman who, at the beginning of the tax year, has elected for reduced contribution liability cannot claim home responsibilities protection for that year.[146] Even with home responsibilities protection, many women will not gain entitlement to the full basic state retirement pension in their own right, given that many will have spent large amounts of time outside the labour market.[147] The second contributions condition was also modified in respect of those over 16 when the post-war National Insurance scheme commenced on 5 July 1948.[148]

A Category A retirement pension may be paid at a reduced rate to a person who does not fully satisfy the second contribution condition.[149] This rate is the proportion of those years of contributions liability (nine-tenths of the claimant's working life) in which contributions of the required amount were in fact paid or credited. No benefit is payable unless this proportion is at least 25 per cent.

iii   Married persons

A married woman who has reached pensionable age may be entitled to a Category A pension on the basis of her own contributions in the same way as a man.[150] Alternatively,

143   The reporting requirements to gain the benefit of this facility have been tightened as a result of CSPSSA 2000, s 40: see SI 1994/704, reg 2, as amended by SI 2001/1323, reg 7.
144   SSCBA 1992, Sch 3, para 5(7). The 20-year minimum will not apply to those attaining pensionable age on or after 6 April 2010: PA 1995, Sch 4, para 4. Home responsibilities protection did not apply to the additional, earnings-related component of the pension (SERPS), but special provision is made in the context of the S2P: see pp 620–625, below.
145   Ie constant attendance allowance under the war pensions or industrial injuries scheme: SI 1994/704. The claimant also satisfies the requirement if he or she meets either of the first two conditions for part of the year and the third condition for the remainder of that year: reg 2(1).
146   SI 1994/704, reg 2(5); an exception is made if between 6 April 1975 and 5 April 1980 she had no earnings in respect of which Class 1 primary contributions were payable and was not at any time a self-employed earner: reg 2(6). For reduced contribution liability, see pp 118–119, above.
147   McKay, Heaver and Walker *Building Up Pension Rights* DSS Research Report No 114 (2000) pp 26–28.
148   SI 1979/643, reg 7; see the 4th edition of this book, pp 230–231. No new cases can now arise given the age of such individuals.
149   SI 1979/642, reg 6.
150   Since December 1984 a married woman has had the same rights as a single woman to a Category A pension on the basis of her own contributions. On the previous discriminatory provisions, see the 4th edition of this book, p 232. The position of married women has been further improved by the 'home responsibilities protection' provisions, discussed above.

she may be entitled to a Category B pension on her husband's contributions. She cannot claim both but she may be able to use her Category B entitlement to enhance the value of her Category A pension. In such a case the Category A pension entitlement can be increased by either the whole of the Category B pension derived from the husband's contributions or as much of it as is necessary to raise the Category A basic pension to the level of the lower-rate Category B pension, whichever is less. The resulting 'composite' pension is the claimant's Category A pension, even if most of it is payable by virtue of the husband's contributions. This facility does not apply where both spouses attained pensionable age before 6 April 1979.[151] Although the relevant statutory provision is phrased in gender-neutral terms,[152] in practice it cannot be used by married men as they will not be able to claim a Category B pension on the same basis as married women until 2010.[153]

iv Widows and widowers

Where a widow's own contributions do not satisfy the contribution conditions for a Category A pension for any year up to that of her husband's death, the husband's contribution record can be substituted for hers. This may be either for the period of the marriage or for the whole of her working life up to his death. This provision only applies where the widow's husband died before she reached pensionable age and she did not remarry before that age.[154] This facility was extended to widowers by SSPA 1975.[155] It also applies to a widower who was himself over pensionable age when his wife died, and where she was under pensionable age at the date of her death.[156]

v Divorced persons

It is unusual for the social security system to make special provision for divorcées, but similar provisions also apply for the purpose of calculating a divorced person's Category A basic pension. The former spouse's contribution record can be substituted for the claimant's own record, either for the period of the marriage or for the whole working life up to the termination of the marriage, provided that he or she has not remarried before reaching pensionable age.[157] This provision does not apply to a person who, on 6 April 1979, was over pensionable age and already divorced; but, with that exception, divorced persons, unlike widows and widowers, can take advantage of it regardless of the age of either partner when the marriage ended.[158] A divorced person, on the other hand, cannot add the former spouse's pension rights to his or her own in order to obtain

151 SSCBA 1992, s 51A.
152 PA 1995, Sch 4, para 21(6) repealed SSCBA 1992, s 53, the equivalent previous provision which expressly applied only to married women.
153 P 607, below.
154 SI 1979/642, reg 8(1)(a), (2)–(6) and Sch 1.
155 SSPA 1975, s 20; see now SSCBA 1992, s 48. This provision, which applies to former spouses generally, does not apply to any person who reached pensionable age before 6 April 1979 if the marriage also ended before that date.
156 SI 1979/642, reg 8(1)(b). A woman in the same situation would be able to rely on her entitlement to a Category B retirement pension at the widow's rate.
157 SSCBA 1992, s 48 and SI 1979/642, reg 8(1)(c), (2)–(6) and Sch 1.
158 Where a person has been married more than once, the right to use a former spouse's contributions applies only in respect of the last marriage: SSCBA 1992, s 48(3). This provision, even if it is discriminatory, is permitted by art 7(1)(c) of Council Directive (EEC) 79/7: *R(P) 1/96.*

a composite pension, since the relevant legislation applies only to surviving spouses.[159] This used to mean that a divorced person could not benefit from a former spouse's entitlement to an additional earnings-related pension. However, this has now been made possible by the pension sharing mechanism introduced by WRPA 1999.[160] This pension sharing facility does not apply to the basic retirement pension, given the existing facility for substituting a former spouse's contribution record in the event of divorce, as discussed above.

D   Category B retirement pensions

i   General

Traditionally the Category B retirement pension has been available for a married woman who did not qualify for a Category A pension on the basis of her own contributions or whose own pension would be less than the rate payable on her husband's insurance record. Provision was also made for widows and widowers (the latter being subject to more restrictive conditions) to qualify for a Category B retirement pension. PA 1995 has provided for gender-neutral criteria for entitlement to such pensions.[161] However, as we shall see below, the full effect of these amendments will not come into force until April 2010, unless a prior human rights challenge is successful.

Where a person qualifies for a Category B retirement pension, it is payable for life.[162] It is paid at approximately 60 per cent of the Category A basic pension rate. A Category B pension may also be increased by additions for child dependants: entitlement to such dependency additions is covered in chapter 7.

ii   Married persons

A person who reaches pensionable age and is married (or marries after that age) is entitled to a Category B retirement pension on the basis of the spouse's contributions providing the latter has also attained pensionable age, has become entitled to a Category A retirement pension and meets the contribution conditions.[163] However, at present only women may qualify under this provision. It does not confer a right to a Category B pension on a man by virtue of his marriage to a woman who was born before 6 April 1950.[164] In other words, men will only be able to take advantage of this provision with effect from 2010.

If the claimant's husband has not fully satisfied the second contribution test, the Category B pension is proportionately reduced, in the same way as the Category A pension.[165] The Category B pension is paid at the same rate as the dependant's allowance which a male pensioner will receive in respect of his wife if she is below pensionable age. The treatment of the Category B pension differs, however, from the point of view

159   SSCBA 1992, s 52.
160   P 619, below.
161   PA 1995, s 126 and Sch 4, para 3.
162   SSCBA 1992, s 48C(1).
163   SSCBA 1992, s 48A. The contribution conditions are the same as for a Category A pension: Sch 3, para 5.
164   PA 1995, Sch 4, para 3(2).
165   SI 1979/642, reg 6; see p 604, above.

of the earnings rule. The dependency allowance is an increase of the husband's pension and may be reduced under the earnings rule because of the wife's earnings.[166] However, the Category B pension is paid directly to the wife and is not subject to reduction on account of her earnings: the earnings rule which previously applied to the Category B pension was abolished in 1989.

The UK is the only EU member state in which a separate pension is paid to a wife by virtue of her husband's contributions.[167] The trend of policy in recent years (as in the introduction of 'home responsibilities protection', and the phasing out of the married woman's option to pay reduced contributions[168]) has been towards enabling wives to qualify for a full pension on their own contributions, thus reducing dependence on their husbands' contributions.

Divorced persons are not eligible for Category B retirement pensions, but, as discussed above, they can substitute their former spouse's contribution record for their own for the purposes of a Category A basic retirement pension.

iii Widows and widowers

A GENERAL

As with the provisions governing the entitlement of married persons, the legislation concerning the entitlement of widows and widowers to Category B pensions is ostensibly expressed in gender-neutral terms. However, men will not be able to take advantage of these rules until 2010. Until such date, different provisions apply in practice to widows and widowers respectively. A widow who has reached pensionable age can benefit from her late husband's contribution record in a number of ways, depending in part on whether he died before or after she reached pensionable age.[169]

B WIDOW AGED UNDER 60 ON HUSBAND'S DEATH

The entitlement of women widowed before pensionable age to a Category B pension has been complicated as a result of the changes made to bereavement benefits by WRPA 1999. The new rules apply to women under pensionable age who were widowed on or after 9 April 2001.[170] Such a widow will qualify for a Category B pension on the basis of her late husband's contributions so long as she was receiving widowed parent's allowance immediately before reaching pensionable age and has not remarried.[171] Such a pension is paid at the same rate as the widowed parent's allowance (and so is equivalent to a Category A basic pension). If the widow received a bereavement allowance at any time before reaching pensionable age and has not remarried, then she is also entitled to a Category B pension on the basis of her late husband's contributions. However, in this case it is calculated as if she had been receiving widow's pension under the rules to be

---

166 SI 1977/343, reg 8.
167 133 HC Official Report (6th series) col 593.
168 See pp 118–119, above.
169 A deceased spouse's contributions may also be used to gain entitlement to a Category A pension: see p 605, above.
170 The new rules are gender-neutral; for convenience of exposition, widowers are dealt with separately (see section D, below).
171 SSCBA 1992, s 48BB(1)–(2).

discussed below. The same applies if she had been in receipt of widowed parent's allowance, but not immediately before reaching pensionable age.[172]

Different rules apply to those widowed before 9 April 2001. In such a case, a widow who was under 60 on her husband's death may be entitled to a Category B pension on his contributions, but only if she was entitled to a widow's pension immediately before her 60th birthday.[173] She may retain her Category B pension even if she remarried after that date.[174] The Category B pension is paid at the same rate as the widow's pension.[175] These provisions do not apply, however, to a woman who was widowed under pensionable age and who did not qualify for a widow's pension because she was under 45 on her husband's death or when her widowed mother's allowance ceased.[176] She may be able to use her husband's contribution record to help her qualify for a full basic retirement pension at 60, as explained above, but she cannot inherit any of his additional pension entitlement.

Like a married woman, a widow cannot receive both a Category A and a Category B pension; but if her husband died on or after 6 April 1979 and her own contribution record does not entitle her to a full Category A basic pension she can receive a 'composite' pension, using all or part of her Category B basic pension entitlement to raise the Category A basic pension to the full standard basic pension rate.[177] This is an alternative to the provision explained above, under which a widow can substitute her husband's contribution record for part of her own: she cannot do this and also receive a composite basic pension, thus taking advantage of her husband's contributions twice over.[178] Her Category B additional earnings-related pension entitlement may also be added to her Category A additional pension, but not so as to raise it above the maximum additional pension that she would have earned as a single person.[179]

The effect of these provisions is that a widow aged between 60 and 65 who qualified for a widow's pension before the April 2001 reforms may be faced with a choice between three courses of action. She can claim a retirement pension (receiving Category A or B, whichever is more favourable); retain her widow's pension until she is 65; or give up her widow's pension and go on working and earning increments to the retirement pension payable when she retires or reaches age 65.[180] Which option is best will depend on the circumstances of the individual case.

C   WIDOW AGED 60 OR OVER ON HUSBAND'S DEATH

A widow who was 60 or over when her husband died can claim a Category B pension at the same rate as the Category A pension that he was receiving or (if he was under pensionable age or had not retired) would have received.[181] If the husband's death occurred after 10 April 1988 and resulted from an industrial injury or disease, the Category B basic pension will be calculated as if he had fully satisfied the contribution

---

172   SSCBA, s 48BB(3)–(10).
173   Or, in certain circumstances, was treated as having been so entitled: SI 1979/642, reg 7.
174   A woman widowed on or after 9 April 2001 would not be able to do so.
175   SSCBA 1992, s 48B(4), (5). On the widow's pension and bereavement allowance, see pp 577–578, above.
176   SSCBA 1992, s 38(1).
177   SSCBA 1992, s 52(2).
178   SI 1979/542, reg 8(5).
179   SSCBA 1992, s 52(3).
180   On the rules concerning increments, see pp 610–613, below.
181   SSCBA 1992, s 48B(1) and (2).

conditions, even if he had not.[182] If a widow is entitled to a Category A pension on her own contributions, it can be topped up by her Category B entitlement to the same extent as if she had been widowed before pensionable age: again, the composite additional pension cannot exceed the maximum to which she would have been entitled as a single person on reaching pensionable age.[183] The alternative of substituting her husband's contribution record for her own is not available to a woman who is over pensionable age when her husband dies.

D WIDOWERS

SSPA 1975 extended entitlement to a Category B pension to a widower whose wife died on or after 6 April 1979 when they were both over pensionable age. Indeed, a widower whose wife died on or after 9 April 2001 may qualify for a Category B pension in just the same way as a widow.[184] However, the position of a widower whose wife died before that date differs from that of a widow in that a widower in such a position cannot qualify for a Category B pension if his wife died before he reached pensionable age. The widower inherits his wife's entitlement to both basic and additional pension. Like widows, a widower will receive less than 100 per cent of his partner's additional pension if she dies after 5 October 2002.[185] The rule that a person cannot receive both a Category A pension and a Category B pension applies to widowers in the same way as to widows; and so does the provision enabling the Category B pension entitlement to be used to top up the Category A pension. The provisions regarding 'composite' pensions are exactly the same for widowers as for widows.[186] However, in the case of a widower, as we have just seen, Category B entitlement and, therefore, the possibility of a composite pension arises only if he and his wife were both over pensionable age on her death (assuming that took place before 9 April 2001). As a result the law of retirement pensions still contains an element of discrimination against widowers.[187]

E Categories C and D non-contributory retirement pensions

Category C retirement pensions were introduced by NIA 1970 and Category D pensions a year later by NIA 1971. The relevant provisions are now in section 78 of SSCBA 1992. Category C pensions were a response to political pressure to help those who were uninsured under the pre-1948 schemes and, being over pensionable age when NIA 1946 came into effect, had not had the chance to establish eligibility to a pension under this legislation. They were to receive a non-contributory flat-rate pension of 60 per cent of the basic contributory pension, with the exception of married women who were to get a similar proportion of the contributory pension for a dependent wife. It was considered inappropriate to pay the same amount as to those who had contributed fully to the National Insurance Fund.[188]

---

182 SSCBA 1992, s 60(2), (3), (8).
183 SSCBA 1992, s 52(2), (3).
184 SSCBA 1992, s 48BB.
185 SSCBA 1992, s 51(3), as amended by CSPSSA 2000, s 39.
186 SSCBA 1992, s 52.
187 This is not contrary to the EC Directive on Equal Treatment (Council Directive (EEC) 86/378): see ch 3, above. This discrimination will finally be removed on 6 April 2010 when the rules governing Category B retirement pensions are finally made fully gender-neutral.
188 Mr P Dean MP, Under Secretary of State, 803 HC Official Report (5th series) col 1551.

Contrary to general expectation, the introduction of Category C pensions still left a number of elderly people without pension entitlement, and Category D pensions were therefore introduced to provide for those over 80 who were in this situation or whose basic pension was less than the Category C rate. Originally, Category D pensions were payable at the same rates as Category C, including the lower rate for married women, but the lower Category D rate was abolished by SSA 1985.[189] All Category D pensions, therefore, are now paid at the higher Category C rate. The lower rate remains in operation for the wife of a Category C pensioner who is over pensionable age and retired.

Both Category C and Category D pensions are subject to a residence test. The Category D test, which is easier to satisfy, is that the person was resident in Great Britain for ten years in any period of 20 years ending on his or her 80th birthday or later and was ordinarily resident in Great Britain on his or her 80th birthday or on the date of claim if later.[190]

The Category C pension is of little importance today, since nearly all those entitled to it would otherwise be entitled to a Category D pension. Moreover, given that entitlement depends on the claimant's husband having been over pensionable age in 1948, it is now virtually confined to widows,[191] very few of whom are still under 80 and therefore dependent on Category C. There are currently perhaps as few as one hundred Category C pensions in payment, along with some 23,000 Category D pensions.[192] There will always be some people whose contribution record is deficient, in particular immigrants and British citizens returning from abroad who have not paid contributions throughout their working lives. Category D remains as a residual provision for them when they reach the age of 80.

F   Increments for deferred pensions

Beveridge hoped and expected that those able to continue working past retirement age would do so.[193] However, the retirement condition which was originally incorporated into the state pension undoubtedly encouraged some persons to give up full-time work upon reaching pensionable age.[194] Provision was made for increments to be earned not only by deferring retirement but also by cancelling retirement and temporarily forgoing the pension.[195] Doubts were expressed at an early stage as to the effectiveness of increments. The Phillips Committee in 1953 found no evidence that they encouraged people to stay on at work: 'a small prospective increase in the pension later on, though welcome when it comes, can seldom affect the decision.'[196] Since then, social and economic pressures inducing early retirement have been far more potent than the system of increments as a reward for later retirement. There was a dramatic fall during the 1970s and 1980s in the number of people of pensionable age deferring claiming their pensions. This trend is strikingly confirmed by a comparison of the proportions of

189   SSA 1985, s 12.
190   SI 1979/642, regs 9–10; the residence conditions are discussed in *Re an Italian Widow* [1982] 2 CMLR 128. For the concepts of 'residence' and 'ordinary residence', see pp 230–232, above.
191   Technically an alternative ground of entitlement is that the claimant herself was over pensionable age in 1948, but this would make such a claimant 114 in July 2002!
192   *DWP* n 1, above, p 114. In December 1971 there 132,000 non-contributory pensions in payment: DSS *Social Security Statistics 1993* (1993) Table B1.25.
193   *Beveridge Report* n 50, above paras 244 ff.
194   See the 4th edition of this book, pp 227–229.
195   On cancellation of retirement, see the 3rd edition of this book, p 198.
196   Phillips Committee Report (Cmd 9333) paras 200–201.

pensioners in different age groups who receive increments to their pensions. In September 1998, 19 per cent of pensioners aged 80 and over received increments, but only 5 per cent of those aged 65 to 69. The average increment (across all ages) was then only £6.20 per week.[197] The abolition of the retirement condition in 1989 was in part designed to encourage persons above pensionable age to remain in regular employment, which they can now do while drawing the state pension in full; provision for increments was retained and adapted, however, in order to offer them the option of deferring the receipt of the pension in order to increase its value. In 1993 the then government indicated that it was considering increasing the rate at which increments are paid and abolishing the current ceiling of five years of deferral from the date of pensionable age.[198] These proposals were implemented by PA 1995, but only with effect from 2010.[199]

Entitlement to increments is at present governed by section 55[200] and Schedule 5 to SSCBA 1992. A person who has met the age and contribution conditions for the receipt of a Category A or Category B pension may choose not to claim the pension, thereby deferring his or her entitlement to receive it.[201] A 'period of enhancement' during which increments are earned begins at that point and continues until the person chooses to claim the pension or for a period of five years, whichever is the shorter.[202] This means that, with the present pensionable ages, women may continue to earn increments up to the age of 65 and men up to the age of 70.

Alternatively, a person who has become entitled to a Category A or Category B pension may elect, after a period of receipt, to cancel that entitlement in order to earn increments. Such an election may currently be made by women under the age of 65 and men under the age of 70[203] and may only be made once.[204] Notice of the election must be made in writing to the Secretary of State[205] and a document should not be construed as a notice unless it is clearly intended as such;[206] nor may it take effect before the date on which it is given.[207] Exceptionally, in the case of a widow who has become entitled to a Category B pension on her husband's death after she has reached pensionable age, the right to earn increments is backdated to the date of her widowhood.[208] A husband whose wife is entitled to a Category B pension on his contributions or a 'composite' Category A pension based in part on his contributions[209] may not elect to cancel his entitlement without the wife's consent, unless that consent is 'unreasonably withheld'.[210]

---

197   DSS *Social Security Statistics 1999* (1999) p 135, Table B1.09 (these statistics are omitted from subsequent volumes).
198   *Equality in State Pension Age* (1993, Cm 2420).
199   PA 1995, s 126 and Sch 4, para 6.
200   As substituted by PA 1995, s 134(3).
201   SSCBA 1992, s 55(2). Entitlement to a benefit is normally dependent on a claim to it being made: SSAA 1992, s 1.
202   SSCBA 1992, Sch 5, para 2(2).
203   SSCBA 1992, s 54(1). This provision originated in NIA 1957 and was formerly known as 'deretirement', but now that retirement is no longer a condition of receipt of the Category A or the Category B pension this term is no longer appropriate. The age limits are prospectively repealed with effect from 2010 by PA 1995, s 126 and Sch 4, para 6. In *R(P) 1/95* the Commissioner held that the current differential provision is not contrary to Council Directive (EEC) 79/7, given the European Court of Justice's decision in Case C-243/90 *R v Secretary of State for Social Security, ex p Smithson* [1992] ECR I-467.
204   SI 1979/642, reg 2(2)(a).
205   SI 1979/642, reg 2(3).
206   *R(P) 1/61.*
207   SI 1979/642, reg 2(4).
208   SI 1979/642, reg 2(6).
209   Under SSCBA 1992, s 51A: see p 605, above.
210   SSCBA 1992, s 54(3); SI 1979/642, reg 2(2)(b).

In *R 6/60 (P)* the Northern Ireland Commissioner held that it was not unreasonable for a wife to refuse consent because of the substantial financial detriment she would suffer: it was for the husband to show that the wife had acted unreasonably, eg through pique, spite or a desire to stand in his way.

A person can claim an increment for each 'incremental period', consisting of six consecutive 'days of increment', assessed as 1/7 per cent of the weekly rate of the relevant pension (Category A or B).[211] But the minimum increment is 1 per cent of that rate,[212] so there must be at least 42 days, or seven weeks (Sundays are not counted),[213] of deferment of retirement to earn any increment (42 days, at 1/7 per cent for every six days, equals 1 per cent). In effect, the pension increases at the rate of 7.5 per cent per year if 'incremental periods' continue without interruption.[214] Days of increment do not include days for which the claimant received certain other social security benefits (principally contributory benefits).[215] Increments are calculated as a percentage of the whole of the Category A or B pension except any increase for an adult or child dependant.[216] This includes the earnings-related additional pension, after deducting the guaranteed minimum pension (GMP) in respect of any period for which contributions were paid to a contracted-out or personal scheme.[217] It also includes any pension up-rating that has taken place during the period of deferment.[218] There is separate but similar provision for increments to graduated retirement benefit.[219]

A married woman can earn increments to a Category A pension (based on her own contributions) in the normal way, by deferring her claim to that pension. She can also obtain increments to a Category B pension (on her husband's contributions) by virtue of her husband's decision to defer his claim to a Category A pension, if she also defers her own claim to the Category B pension on reaching pensionable age or otherwise becoming eligible.[220] The effect is that she will earn an increment to the Category B pension for each 'incremental period' from the time when they have both reached pensionable age until such time as either one of them elects to claim their pension or five years from the point at which the latest relevant period of enhancement began.[221] Days for which she herself receives another social security benefit or her husband receives a dependency addition in respect of her do not count as days of increment for this purpose.[222]

A widow can inherit the whole of the increments to which her husband was entitled, or would have been entitled had he retired immediately before his death and a widower can inherit his wife's increments, provided he was over pensionable age on her death; however, for deaths occurring after 5 October 2002 this rule is modified so that the surviving spouse will inherit less than the full increase in the additional, earnings-

---

211   SSCBA 1992, Sch 5, paras 2, 3. This will increase to 1/5 per cent with effect from 6 April 2010: PA 1995, s 126 and Sch 4, para 6(3).
212   SSCBA 1992, Sch 5, para 1.
213   SI 1979/642, reg 4(1).
214   This will increase to 10 per cent from 2010 with the increase in the rate of increments.
215   SI 1979/642, reg 4(1)(b). Graduated retirement benefit was added to the list by SI 1992/1695, reversing *Chief Adjudication Officer v Pearse* [1992] OPLR 77 *(R(P) 2/93)* with effect from 5 August 1992.
216   SSCBA 1992, Sch 5, para 2(5).
217   SSCBA 1992, para 2(8). On the GMP deduction, see p 632, below.
218   SSCBA 1992, Sch 5, para 2(7).
219   SI 1978/393, Sch 2.
220   This appears to follow from SI 1979/642, reg 4(1)(a).
221   SSCBA 1992, Sch 5, para 8. This has been prospectively repealed as from April 2010 by PA 1995, Sch 4, para 6(4) and (5).
222   SI 1979/642, reg 4(1)(b), (c).

related pension.[223] The inherited increments, up-rated as appropriate, will be paid in addition to any that the survivor may have earned through postponing retirement. But a widow loses the inherited increments if she remarries before pensionable age; she must then look to her new husband for any pension rights based on a spouse's contributions. Remarriage after pension age does not affect entitlement to increments inherited from the former spouse.[224] Members of contracted-out occupational pension schemes of the salary-related type can also earn increments.[225]

G Other additions to retirement pension

i Incapacity addition

A person who was receiving incapacity benefit before becoming entitled to a Category A retirement pension and whose incapacity benefit included an age-related addition[226] may qualify for an incapacity addition to the retirement pension, at the same rate as the age-related addition increased by any subsequent up-ratings. The object of the addition is to ensure that the person's benefit income is not reduced on retirement. The basic condition is that he or she was entitled to an age-related addition at some time in the period of eight weeks and one day before reaching pensionable age. The incapacity addition is payable for life as an integral part of the retirement pension and, as such, is included in the rate of pension on which increments for deferred retirement are calculated.[227] The addition is reduced or eliminated by the amount of any additional pension or GMP (excluding increments for deferred retirement).[228]

ii Age addition

NIA 1971 introduced an additional payment of 25 pence per week, known as the 'age addition', for pensioners of all categories over 80.[229] As Sir Keith Joseph MP said during the Second Reading in the House of Commons, 'this age addition recognises, albeit in a small way, the special claims of very elderly people, who on the whole need help rather more than others'.[230] Since its value has not been increased in over thirty years since its introduction, the measure now appears as an insignificant gesture, bordering on the insulting.[231] A person in receipt of certain other prescribed benefits, and who would be entitled to a retirement pension if he or she were to claim it instead, is also entitled to the addition. It need not be claimed, and is therefore paid automatically.[232] The House of Commons Social Security Committee has recommended that the level of

---

223 SSCBA 1992, Sch 5, para 4(3), as amended by CSPSSA 2000, s 39; the normal sliding scale operates (p 580, above).
224 SI 1974/2010, reg 3A.
225 See p 537, below.
226 The conditions of entitlement for this addition were made much narrower in 1995.
227 SSCBA 1992, s 47.
228 SSCBA 1992, s 47(2), (3).
229 SSCBA 1992, s 79.
230 816 HC Official Report (5th series) col 1019.
231 HC Social Security Committee *Seventh Report* (1999–2000, HC 606) para 87, quoting Mr J Rooker MP, Minister of State, who acknowledged that the age addition was 'a festering sore in the system'.
232 SI 1987/1986, reg 3(c).

the retirement pension for those aged 80 or over should be increased so that it is equivalent to the MIG (the income support threshold for that age group).[233]

Part 3   Earnings-related additions

A   Graduated retirement benefit

Graduated retirement benefit[234] was introduced by NIA 1959, marking the first departure from the principle of flat-rate contributions and benefits. Under NIA 1965[235] the benefit is an increase in the weekly rate of retirement pension, originally calculated as 2.5 pence for each unit of graduated contributions paid by an employee (the scheme did not cover the self-employed) between April 1961 and April 1975.[236] A unit is £7.50 for a man and £9 for a woman; and a fraction of a unit, if a half or more, is treated as a complete unit.[237] There was at first no provision for up-rating the 2.5 pence pension 'bricks', a weakness of the scheme which was strongly criticised since it meant that the benefits were not protected against inflation. Regulations now apply the up-rating provisions introduced by SSA 1986[238] both to the graduated pension rights of future pensioners and to graduated pensions already in payment. Accordingly, the amount of graduated pension payable for each unit of contributions has been increased and is currently set at 9.06 pence.[239]

Although described as an increase in the claimant's retirement pension rate, a graduated pension can be paid to a person over pensionable age but who is not otherwise entitled to a retirement pension because he does not satisfy the contribution conditions.[240] A married woman, similarly, can claim a graduated pension on her own contributions at 60, even if she cannot yet claim a Category B pension on her husband's insurance because he is under 65. A widow is entitled to the graduated pension earned by her own contributions *and* half that earned by her husband. A widower can add half his deceased wife's graduated pension to his own provided that they were both of pensionable age at the time of her death.[241]

NIA 1959 broke new ground not only by adding an earnings-related element to the flat-rate retirement pension but also by allowing employers whose occupational pension schemes satisfied certain minimum standards to 'contract out' of the graduated pension scheme. The basic condition for contracting out was that the employer's scheme must offer pensions at least equivalent to the maximum graduated pension, which was itself extremely modest (widows' benefits equivalent to those of the graduated scheme were not required). The new graduated contributions were not payable in respect of contracted-out employees; instead, they were required to pay a higher flat-rate contribution, in

---

233   HC Social Security Committee *Fifth Report* (Session 1999–2000, HC 56) para 143.

234   The legislation uses the word 'benefit', though Departmental leaflets have referred to graduated pension, and the two words are used interchangeably here.

235   Ss 36, 37: the sections are kept in force in a modified form by SI 1978/393.

236   NIA 1965, s 36(1).

237   NIA 1965, s 36(2), (3).

238   See p 266, above.

239   NIA 1965, s 36(1), kept in force, as amended (notably by SI 1989/1642) by SI 1978/393, Sch 1; for the annual rate, see the relevant up-rating Order, eg SI 2002/668, reg 11(1). See also SSCBA 1992, s 62.

240   NIA 1965, s 36(7).

241   NIA 1965, s 37.

recognition of the first of the scheme's declared aims, which was 'to place the National Insurance Scheme on a sound financial basis'.[242]

Contributions payable since April 1975 have not earned entitlement to graduated retirement benefit, even though entitlement to SERPS, which replaced the graduated retirement benefit, did not begin to accrue until April 1978. Payment of graduated retirement benefits will, however, continue for many years to come. In 1998, 78 per cent of all pensioners were receiving graduated pensions, but the average amount was only £2.47 a week.[243]

B SERPS

A brief account of the main provisions of SSPA 1975, introducing SERPS, and the modifications introduced by SSA 1986, has been given in the introductory section of this chapter. The main purpose of SSPA 1975 was to add a new earnings-related element to the flat-rate basic pension.[244] The resulting combined weekly benefit was conceived as a single pension, consisting of a 'basic component' and an 'additional component'.[245] The basic component was regarded as replacing pre-retirement earnings in full up to the level of the basic pension (roughly a fifth of average earnings but now only about 15 per cent),[246] while the additional component was to replace about a quarter of the individual's earnings above that level and up to the higher earnings limit for payment of contributions.[247] SSA 1986, however, substituted the terms 'basic pension' and 'additional pension' for 'basic component' and 'additional component', wherever they occurred in the legislation.[248] This was more than a change in terminology. It reflected a different approach to pension provision, in which only the provision of a basic flat-rate pension was seen as a necessary function of the social security system. Additional pensions might be provided in a variety of ways and through a variety of financial institutions of which social security was only one; alternatives included not just final-salary occupational schemes but also money-purchase schemes of both an occupational and a personal kind.[249] Even before the 1975 legislation was amended, however, the 'additional component' was already commonly referred to as a separate scheme: the state earnings-related pension scheme, or 'SERPS'.

The provisions of SSPA 1975 relating to SERPS were never simple, but their complexity was increased by the 1986 amendments. The reason for this is that the revised pension formula designed to reduce the cost of the scheme is to be phased in over a long period, in order to provide some protection for pension rights based on contributions payable prior to 6 April 1988 and for employees already near retirement age, and also to avoid dramatic differences in pension rights between people reaching pensionable age on successive days. The method of calculating the additional pension under SERPS will therefore vary according to whether contributions were paid prior to the tax year 1988–89 and whether the contributor reaches pensionable age before 6 April 1999, between then and 5 April 2009, or after the latter date. As a result of the introduction of the S2P by CSPSSA 2000, discussed in Part 4, below, contributors ceased to acquire

---

242   White Paper *Provision for Old Age* (1958, Cmnd 538) p 13.
243   DSS n 197, above, p 138, Table B1.11 (these statistics were omitted from subsequent volumes).
244   See Mesher (1976) 39 MLR 321 for an admirable survey of the Act in its original form.
245   SSPA 1975, s 6(1).
246   P 589, above.
247   But note that the cap imposed by the upper earning limit will be removed in April 2003.
248   SSA 1986, s 18(1). See now SSCBA 1992, s 44(3).
249   See pp 636–640, below; and Nesbitt n 72, above.

new rights to SERPS with effect from April 2002. Indeed, the effect of the various changes to SERPS provision is that only those individuals who retired in 1998–99 will have seen the full benefits promised by the original scheme.[250]

In addition to the basis for calculating the additional pension under SERPS, we also consider briefly the facility for pension sharing, for additional pension rights introduced by WRPA 1999 and the controversy surrounding the payment of SERPS to widows and widowers. It should also be noted that payment of SERPS is suspended if the pensioner is serving a sentence of imprisonment.[251]

i The basis of calculation

In principle the additional pension is calculated as a percentage of a person's earnings above the lower earnings limit, after adjusting each year's earnings to take account of increases in average earnings during the remainder of that person's working life. In this way, the pension, though based on earnings between 1978 and the year before pensionable age or (if earlier) 2002, is related to the general standard of living at the time when it becomes payable.

The method of calculation which is set out in sections 44 and 45 of SSCBA 1992 involves, first, ascertaining the person's earnings factors[252] for each tax year, starting from 1978–79 or the year in which his or her 16th birthday occurred (whichever is later) and ending with the year before he or she reached pensionable age or, if earlier, 2002 – the 'relevant years'.[253] The earnings factor for each year, which represents, in broad terms, the person's earnings between the lower and upper earnings limits (or the difference between, approximately, the basic pension rate for that year and about seven times that level) is revalued in line with the increase in average earnings up to the year before pensionable age. For this purpose, the Secretary of State is required, in each tax year, to review the general level of earnings in Great Britain, estimated in such manner as he or she thinks fit, and to make an order increasing the value of earnings factors from 1978–79 onwards by the amount necessary to restore their value in relation to the general level of earnings.[254]

The next stage in the calculation is to work out the 'surplus' in the earnings factor for each year. There is a surplus for any 'relevant year' if the person's earnings factor exceeds the 'qualifying earnings factor' (52 times the lower earnings limit for the year in question) for that year. The resulting excess is then revalued as above, thus representing the amount of earnings on which the additional pension is calculated as a percentage.[255] This method of calculating SERPS entitlement ('annualisation') applies only to those qualifying after 5 April 2000. For those qualifying before that date, surpluses were arrived at by revaluing the relevant earnings for each year and then deducting the lower earnings limit *for the last complete tax year* from each year's revalued earnings.[256] This

---

250 *Government Actuary* n 20, above, para 6.1.
251 SSCBA 1992, s 113(1)(b); see *Szrabjer v United Kingdom* [1998] PLR 281 (and see (1998) 2 EHRLR 230) for an unsuccessful European Convention on Human Rights challenge.
252 See p 121, above.
253 SSCBA 1992, s 44(6), (7). Note that a different formulation of s 44(6) applies to those who reached pensionable age before 6 April 2000: see the amendments made by PA 1995, s 128.
254 SSAA 1992, s 148. A Revaluation Order is issued annually: see eg SI 2002/519, which specifies that in 2002–03 earnings factors for the 1978–79 tax year are to be increased by 500.7 per cent. Necessarily, lower increases are needed for more recent years, so eg earnings factors relating to the preceding year (2001–02) are subject to an increase of just 4.3 per cent.
255 SSCBA 1992, s 44(5A).
256 SSCBA 1992, s 44(5).

had the effect of increasing SERPS entitlements as the lower earnings limit increased in line with prices. The change over to annualisation will reduce the value of SERPS by some 14 per cent by 2020.[257]

There is no other contribution condition. Provided that there is a surplus for at least one year of a person's working life, this is enough to confer entitlement to an additional pension under SERPS, even if the contribution conditions for a basic pension are not satisfied. The way in which the surpluses are translated into weekly pension entitlement, however, depends on the year in which pensionable age is reached.

A THOSE REACHING PENSIONABLE AGE BEFORE 6 APRIL 1999

In the case of a man reaching age 65 or a woman reaching age 60 before 6 April 1999, the additional pension is calculated by means of the formula originally laid down in section 6 of SSPA 1975[258] in its unamended form. The surpluses in the claimant's earnings factors for the relevant years are added together and the weekly additional pension is 1.25 per cent of the total, divided by 52.

B THOSE REACHING PENSIONABLE AGE BETWEEN 6 APRIL 1999 AND 5 APRIL 2009

Under the original formula described above, the additional pension accrued at the rate of 1.5 per cent of earnings between the lower and upper earnings limits for up to 20 years, producing an additional pension of about 25 per cent of pre-retirement earnings. In a case where there were earnings factor surpluses for more than 20 years, the pension would have been based on the 'best' 20 years, other years being ignored.[259] The effect of the formula enacted by section 18(3) of SSA 1986, which applies only to those reaching retirement age on or after 6 April 1999, is to take into account the surpluses for the whole of a person's working life from 1978 onwards, instead of for a maximum of 20 years. The pension accrual rate is, however, reduced so that the formula will normally produce an additional pension of 20 rather than 25 per cent of pre-retirement earnings. Since no-one reaching pensionable age before 6 April 1999 will have contributed to the scheme for more than 20 years, the change enacted in 1986 means that the 'best 20 years' provision of SSPA 1975 will never take effect.

For those reaching pensionable age during the transitional period from 6 April 1999 to 5 April 2009, the additional pension will be calculated in two parts, the first relating to the part of their working life between 1978–79 and 1987-88 inclusive, and the second to the part falling between 1988–89 and the tax year before they reach pensionable age. The pension based on surpluses for the years up to 1987–88 will be 25 per cent of those surpluses divided by the total number of relevant years, while surpluses for the years from 1988–89 to 2007–08 will produce a pension based on a lower percentage, between 20 and 25, depending on the year in which pensionable age is reached: 25 per cent for those reaching pensionable age in 1999–2000, 24.5 per cent in 2000–01, 24 per cent in 2001–02, and so on, diminishing by a half per cent per year until, for those reaching pensionable age in 2009–10, the 20 per cent rate is reached.[260] For example:

257   See Thomas and Dowrick *Blackstone's Guide to the Pensions Act 1995* (1995) pp 146–147.
258   Now consolidated in SSCBA 1992, s 45(1), (6).
259   SSPA 1975, s 6(2).
260   SSCBA 1992, s 45(3), (4).

A man aged 39 in April 1978 reaches the age of 65 in the tax year 2003–04, with a surplus in his earnings factor for each of the 25 years up to 2002–03 (his last 'relevant year'). If the surplus earnings factors amount to £60,000 for the 10 years up to 1987–88 and £100,000 for the 15 years from 1988–89 to 2002–03, his additional pension will be calculated as follows:

25 per cent of £60,000 ÷ 25   = £600
23 per cent of £100,000 ÷ 25 = £920

$$\text{£1,520} ÷ 52 = \text{£29.23 per week}$$

PA 1995 made special provision to enhance the earnings factors of those on low pay and in receipt of either family credit (now working families' tax credit) or disability working allowance (now disabled person's tax credit). Any amount of either such benefit or tax credit received in the 1995–96 or subsequent tax years may now be used to increase the earnings factor for the year in question.[261]

C   THOSE REACHING PENSIONABLE AGE ON OR AFTER 6 APRIL 2009

For those reaching pensionable age in the tax year 2009–10 or later, a similar two-part calculation will be needed if any of their relevant years were earlier than 1988–89. The percentage to be applied to surpluses for the years from 1988–89 onwards will in these cases always be 20 per cent.[262] However, men reaching age 65 as late as the year 2036–37 will still have part of their pension calculated at the 25 per cent rate, and many such pensions will remain in payment well into the 2060s.

D   PROTECTED YEARS

The 'best 20 years' provision of SSPA 1975 would have been highly advantageous to persons reaching pensionable age in the twenty-first century whose working lives had been interrupted, whether by family responsibilities or by sickness, unemployment or other causes. It would also have helped those whose earnings for part of their working lives were particularly low, such as mothers returning to work part-time and those whose earning capacity was reduced by disabilities. The decision to base the additional pension on a person's earnings averaged over the whole working life (except any years before 1978–79 necessarily disadvantaged such groups. SSA 1986 included a regulation-making power permitting the exclusion of certain years of a person's working life from the number of 'relevant years' over which his or her earnings factor surpluses would be averaged; but not so as to reduce it below 20 years.[263] However, this regulation-making power was never used.[264] Instead, those groups who would have benefited from its exercise are accorded special treatment under the S2P with effect from April 2002.[265]

---

261   SSCBA 1992, s 45A, inserted by PA 1995, s 127(1).
262   SSCBA 1992, s 45(3)(a).
263   SSPA 1975, s 6(2B), inserted by SSA 1986, s 18(3); see now SSCBA 1992, s 45(5).
264   *Government Actuary* n 20, above, para 6.16 and Appendix A, para 11.27. See the 4th edition of this book, p 245, on the government's stated intentions when the power was introduced.
265   See p 621, below.

ii Pension sharing and SERPS

WRPA 1999 introduced the concept of pension sharing on divorce. This enables pension rights to be treated like other assets on divorce and for a proportion (or indeed the entirety) of their value to be transferred from one spouse to the other as part of the overall financial settlement. Any rights created from such a transfer belong to the person for whom they are created, not the (eventual or actual) pensioner. Thus payment of any pension is made direct to the beneficiary and its continuance does not depend on the circumstances of the former spouse. This is primarily of significance in the context of rights under occupational pension schemes, and so is considered further below.[266] Pension sharing does not apply to the basic state retirement pension because of the existing facility allowing a divorced person to substitute a former spouse's contribution record for their own for those purposes.[267]

Under WRPA 1999 pension sharing is applicable to a person's 'shareable state scheme rights', which are defined as his or her entitlement to an additional pension under SERPS or to a shared additional pension (a pension share in respect of a previous divorce or nullity of marriage).[268] The pension sharing procedure can be invoked in the course of any legislation governing the disposition of matrimonial property on divorce or nullity.[269] Its effect is to make the spouse who has a right to a SERPS additional pension (the 'transferor') subject to a 'state scheme pension debit' and his (or her) ex-spouse (the 'transferee') the consequential beneficiary of a pension credit of a corresponding amount.[270] An amendment to SSCBA 1992 provides for the method of calculating the actual reduction in the transferee's SERPS entitlement.[271] If the pension debit applies in or after the tax year immediately before the transferor's pensionable age, the additional pension is reduced by a weekly amount reflecting the actuarially equivalent value of the state scheme pension debit.[272] If, however, the debit applies before the transferor reaches pensionable age, the future additional pension is reduced by the appropriate weekly sum multiplied by the revalued earnings factor percentage for the tax year in which the transferor became subject to the debit.[273] The transferee, in turn, becomes entitled to a 'shared additional pension' assuming he or she is over pensionable age and is entitled to a state scheme pension credit; this shared additional pension entitlement then continues for life.[274] The value of this shared additional pension is expressed in equivalent terms to the provisions governing the calculation of the pension debit and hence varies according to whether the entitlement arose before or after the tax year preceding the transferee's attainment of pensionable age.[275] The shared additional pension may in turn be subject to reduction as a result of pension sharing as part of a financial settlement following a subsequent divorce (or nullity).[276] It may also be increased according to normal principles where entitlement is deferred.[277]

---

266 P 645–646, below.
267 P 605, above.
268 WRPA 1999, s 47.
269 WRPA 1999, s 48.
270 WRPA 1999, s 49. This makes provision for such shares to be expressed in percentage terms or as a cash amount: s 49(2) and (3).
271 WRPA 1999, Sch 6, para 2.
272 SSCBA 1992, s 45B(2).
273 SSCBA 1992, s 45B(3) and (6).
274 SSCBA 1992, s 55A(1) and (2).
275 SSCBA 1992, s 55A(3)–(7).
276 SSCBA 1992, s 55B.
277 SSCBA 1992, s 55C. On deferral, see p 610, above. Note that for incremental periods beginning on or after 6 April 2010, these provisions are made more generous: WRPA 1999, s 50(2).

iii   Payments of SERPS to widows and widowers

The original SERPS scheme provided for a widow who was entitled to a basic state retirement pension on the basis of her husband's contributions also to receive any additional pension based on her late spouse's insurance record.[278] SSA 1986 made provision for this element of 'inherited SERPS' to be reduced to a maximum of 50 per cent of the late spouse's SERPS entitlement in cases where the claimant's spouse died after 5 April 2000.[279] As a result of the government's acknowledgement that the then DSS had failed properly to advise those affected by the change, the implementation of this change was subsequently deferred until 6 October 2002. In addition, the full force of the 50 per cent reduction in inherited SERPS does not take effect until 6 October 2010, being phased in over the interim. Thus the percentage of the late spouse's SERPS entitlement which may be inherited by the surviving spouse reduces on a sliding scale by 10 per cent for every two years during the transitional period from October 2002 until October 2010. Hence if the deceased person reached pensionable age between 6 October 2002 and 6 October 2004, the surviving spouse may inherit 90 per cent of the former's SERPS entitlement.[280]

Part 4   The State Second Pension

The first Blair government's plans for reform of the pensions system were set out in the 1998 Pensions Green Paper.[281] These included the establishment of low-cost and flexible stakeholder pensions, designed for those on middle incomes, which could be either occupational or personal pensions.[282] The framework for stakeholder pensions was enacted in WRPA 1999.[283] The Pensions Green Paper also argued that whilst SERPS had served some pensioners well, it provided least help to those who needed it most. The government accordingly proposed a State Second Pension (known by the acronym S2P to distinguish it from statutory sick pay (SSP)) to replace SERPS. These reforms were enacted in CSPSSA 2000 and involve a phased implementation as stakeholder pensions bed down.[284] In addition, the inevitable long lead-in period for pension reforms is such that any person retiring between 2002 and 2050 who has contributed to both SERPS and S2P will receive a pension based on a mixture of the two schemes.[285] As with SERPS, only employees are covered by S2P. Self-employed workers are thus outside the new scheme, although a government advisory body has recommended that they should be brought into S2P (from its second stage) on a compulsory basis, but with the option of contracting out.[286]

---

278   The same facility was available to widowers entitled to a Category B retirement pension on their late spouse's contribution record but most of those affected were women.
279   SSA 1986, s 19(1).
280   SI 2001/1085; see further pp 579–580, above.
281   *DSS* n 5, above.
282   Described as being between roughly £9,000 and £18,500 a year: *DSS* n 5, above p 3.
283   See p 597, above.
284   See Report by the Government Actuary on the Financial Effects on the National Insurance Fund of the Child Support, Pensions and Social Security Bill (2000, Cm 4573).
285   HC Social Security Committee *Seventh Report* (1999–2000, HC 606) para 59.
286   Pension Provision Group *Pension provision and self-employment* (2001).

A The first stage of the State Second Pension

In the first stage, with effect from April 2002, S2P replaced SERPS. Since that date,[287] an employee paying Class 1 National Insurance contributions has ceased to accrue rights to SERPS, but instead gains rights to S2P.[288] The provisions governing S2P have been integrated into SSCBA 1992, as with those for SERPS, but there are two fundamental differences between SERPS and S2P.

First, the structure of S2P is designed to focus most assistance on those in the lowest income groups, rejecting the earnings-related nature of SERPS. Thus certain categories of claimants are treated as though they had earnings at the low earnings threshold (LET, £10,800 for 2002–03[289]) for any relevant year when in fact they either had no earnings or had lower earnings in that year.[290] The first such group are those who had earnings in the year in question between the National Insurance lower earnings limit (£3,900 for 2002–03) and the LET.[291] On the assumption that their annual earnings are at least 52 times the lower earnings limit, then the year in question qualifies for contributory benefits such as the basic retirement pension. There is, moreover, a significant break point for the purposes of the additional pension: those with earnings below the lower earnings limit, even by a penny, will gain no rights to S2P,[292] whilst those at or just above that limit will accrue S2P rights as if they were earning at the LET.[293]

Additionally, certain carers and disabled people who either have no earnings, or have earnings below the annual lower earnings limit, will be treated as though they have earnings at the LET (and not simply the lower earnings limit) for the year in question.[294] These include carers who had carer's allowance paid to them throughout the year[295] and those who were precluded from regular employment by virtue of their home responsibilities (eg they were paid child benefit for a child under the age of six).[296] The final group comprises those who were paid long-term incapacity benefit throughout the year.[297] However, pensioners can only qualify under this last head if they also meet

---

287 Known as 'the first appointed year': SSCBA 1992, ss 45 and 122(1).
288 SSCBA 1992, ss 22(2A), 44(6)(za) and 45(2)(c) and (3A).
289 SSCBA 1992, s 44A(5) and SI 2002/36. On revaluation of this threshold, see SSAA 1992, s 148A.
290 SSCBA 1992, s 44A(1).
291 SSCBA 1992, s 44A(2)(a). Thus those part-time workers with earnings *below* the lower earnings limit will remain excluded, unless they fall within one of the other preferential categories.
292 SSCBA 1992, s 22(2)(b) and (2A).
293 *Government Actuary* n 20, above, para 2.11. A similar phenomenon occurs in relation to the basic retirement pension given that the lower earnings limit applies on a weekly rather than an annualised basis.
294 The figure of £9,500 (now £10,800) as the LET was initially chosen 'to ensure that someone with a lifetime of employment under the state second pension or periods of caring or disability will retire above the minimum income guarantee' (per Mr J Rooker, Standing Committee F, col 446 (10 February 2000)).
295 SSCBA 1992, s 44A(2)(b). The usual linking rules operate so as to allow short periods of non-entitlement to be disregarded, so eight weeks' respite care in a full year, or four weeks' respite care and four weeks' hospitalisation over 26 weeks, have no effect on the S2P. Carers who would otherwise be entitled to receive carer's allowance but for the operation of the overlapping benefits regulations (SI 1979/597) are also covered.
296 SSCBA 1992, s 44A(2)(c). The age of six was selected to reflect the fact that most children will have started school before their fifth birthday and that the National Insurance accrual system operates on a whole year basis. Thus six years will give a parent with one child five years' crediting into the S2P before the child starts school.
297 SSCBA 1992, s 44A(2)(d). This is extended to include those who would have qualified but for failing to satisfy the contribution conditions for that benefit, or who received an occupational or personal pension which had the effect of reducing their entitlement to incapacity benefit to nil: see s 30DD. See also s 44A(4) on transitional protection for severe disablement allowance claimants.

a labour market attachment condition: they must have either paid, or have been treated as having paid,[298] primary Class 1 National Insurance contributions for at least one-tenth of their working life since 1978 (when the additional pension under SERPS was introduced).[299] In calculating a person's working life since 1978, any year during which the person has been a carer, and so qualifies for the S2P under the preceding provisions, is excluded.[300] Any fractional number of years arrived at in calculating a person's working life is rounded up or down as appropriate.[301]

The second main difference is that under the S2P scheme there are three separate accrual rates on various bands of earnings (these are set out in Tables 1 and 2, below). This contrasts with the uniform rate under SERPS, originally set at 25 per cent but, as we have seen, in the process of reducing to 20 per cent as a result of amendments by the SSA 1986. The manner in which the additional pension is to be calculated under the S2P scheme is set out in Schedule 4A to SSCBA 1992.[302] The S2P is calculated by adding together the amounts for each year since the introduction of the new scheme and then dividing by the number of relevant years.[303] The method of calculating the S2P differs according to whether or not the pensioner is in contracted out employment, as well as whether the retirement date is before or after April 2009.

i Pensioners not in contracted-out employment

The method of calculating the S2P for a person who is *not* contracted-out of the state scheme at any time during the year in question and has a surplus in their earnings factor for that year involves a four-stage calculation.[304] (A surplus exists where the earnings factor for the year exceeds the Qualifying Earnings Factor (QEF), which is the annual equivalent of the weekly lower earnings limit for National Insurance purposes for the year in question.[305]) This method of calculation is more complex than that for SERPS but has the advantage of providing more support for low-earners (and indeed non-earners) than that scheme.

First, the surplus earnings factors for the years in issue are divided into the three income bands shown in Tables 1 and 2 in paragraph 2 of Schedule 4A to SSCBA 1992.[306]

TABLE 1

	Amount of surplus	Percentage
Band 1	Not exceeding LET	$40 + 2N$
Band 2	Exceeding LET but not exceeding 3LET - 2QEF	$10 + N/2$
Band 3	Exceeding 3LET – 2QEF	$20 + N$

---

298 Thus National Insurance credits are not sufficient for this purpose. The reference to being 'treated as having paid' contributions refers to those who had earnings in a given year but did not pay contributions as the earnings were below the primary threshold. Providing that such earnings were above the annual lower earnings limit, the individual is treated as if they had paid contributions by virtue of SSCBA 1992, s 6A.
299 SSCBA 1992, s 44A(3).
300 SSCBA 1992, s 44A(4)(a).
301 SSCBA 1992, s 44A(4)(b).
302 Inserted by CSPSSA 2000, Sch 4.
303 SSCBA 1992, Sch 4A, para 1.
304 SSCBA 1992, para 2.
305 SSCBA 1992, s 122(1).
306 The figure N refers to the adjustment factor used to reflect the changes made by SSA 1986, and is explained further below.

TABLE 2

	Amount of surplus	Percentage
Band 1	Not exceeding LET	40
Band 2	Exceeding LET but not exceeding 3LET - 2QEF	10
Band 3	Exceeding 3LET – 2QEF	20

Table 1 applies where the person reaches pensionable age *before* 6 April 2009 and Table 2 applies to those attaining that age *on or after* that date. Secondly, the surpluses in each of the bands are revalued in order that they retain their value in terms of earnings.[307] Thirdly, the revalued surpluses are then multiplied by the percentage against the relevant band in Table 1 or 2 as appropriate.

Thus those pensioners who will retire after April 2009 (and so will fall within Table 2), whose surplus corresponds to earnings between the QEF and the LET for the year in question (Band 1), will have their revalued surplus multiplied by 40 per cent.[308] This is the highest rate of accrual, twice that which would have applied under SERPS. Band 2 covers surpluses generated from earnings between the lower earnings threshold and up to earnings at a level described by the formula 'not exceeding 3LET-2QEF'. In practice this means that Band 2 covers twice the amount of surplus as falls within Band 1, rounded to the nearest £100.[309]

For example, for 2002–03 the QEF would be £3,900 (52 times the relevant weekly lower earnings limit of £67); as the LET is £10,800, the surplus falling within Band 1 would be £6,900. Thus the amount of surplus in Band 2 would be £13,800, and the upper limit of Band 2 would be £10,800 + £13,800 which is £24,600. The accrual rate for surpluses in Band 2 is 10 per cent, or half that which would have applied under SERPS. The effect of the higher accrual rate on the early part of the surplus in a person's earnings factor is that an individual earning less than £24,600 will receive more from the S2P than from SERPS. A person earning £24,600 would receive the same from the S2P as SERPS, as the 40 per cent in Band 1 is offset by the 10 per cent in Band 2. Band 3 covers surpluses in the earnings factor which correspond to earnings which are above Band 2 but do not exceed the upper earnings limit. The accrual rate for Band 3 is the same as for the revised SERPS rate, ie 20 per cent. Finally, the totals for each band are aggregated to provide the annual total.

The position is more complex still for those retiring before April 2009, and so subject to Table 1. This reflects the staged changes made to the accrual rate for SERPS by SSA 1986. As we have seen earlier, the standard accrual rate on reckonable earnings of 25 per cent was reduced to 20 per cent, but phased in at 0.5 per cent per year over 10 years with effect from April 2000.[310] Consequently, Table 1 accommodates these phased in changes for those retiring before April 2009; thus the percentage to be applied for Band 1 surpluses is not 40 per cent but 40 + 2N per cent, where N represents the adjustment factor of 0.5 per cent a year.[311] The relevant percentages in Table 2 for Bands 2 and 3 are 10 + N/2 per cent and 20 + N per cent respectively. The various banded accrual rates in Table 1 are applicable to all earnings since the start of the S2P scheme in April 2002.

---

307 Applying the percentage specified in the annual Order under SSAA 1992, s 148.
308 This will include those low earners, carers and disabled people with broken work records who benefit from the deeming provisions in SSCBA 1992, s 44A.
309 SSCBA 1992, Sch 4A, para 2(7).
310 Pensioners retiring after April 2009 would in any event have been subject to a uniform SERPS accrual rate of 20 per cent, and so Table 2 is more straightforward (or, rather, less complex).
311 SSCBA 1992, Sch 4A, para 2(6)(a).

ii *Pensioners in contracted out employment*

The rules described above are necessarily modified for those pensioners who were in contracted out employment during the year in question.[312] The amount of additional pension for each year for a person who is in contracted-out employment is described by Schedule 4A to SSCBA 1992 as 'Amount C'. This represents the amount of additional pension they would have received if they had not been contracted-out ('Amount A') less the amount of pension that they are deemed to receive in respect of their contracted-out National Insurance rebate ('Amount B').[313] Amount C is thus the S2P top-up, where appropriate, for the year in question.

The calculation of Amount A for those who were in contracted out employment is the same as that for those in the state scheme in all respects save one. The one exception is that there is no provision requiring a move to a flat-rate scheme as in the second stage of the S2P. Those who are contracted-out will continue to receive contribution rebates and their top-up (if any) will be based on the first stage of the S2P.

The sum known as Amount B is defined in one of two ways. That described as 'Amount B (first case)' concerns those who are contracted-out by an occupational salary-related or money purchase scheme, including an employer's occupational-based stakeholder scheme. It is defined as the amount of contracted-out second pension which a person is treated as receiving by virtue of their National Insurance rebate. This rebate reflects the prevailing accrual rate on earnings under SERPS (and now S2P). Accordingly, the Amount B (first case) is calculated on the basis of 20 per cent of the assumed surplus in their earnings factor for the year.[314] The accrual rate is $20 + N$ per cent for someone retiring before April 2009 and 20 per cent thereafter.[315] The assumed surplus is also revalued to reflect changes in average earnings. This rebate is calculated on the basis of actual rather than deemed earnings where a contracted-out person's earnings fall between the QEF and the LET for the year in question.[316] There should always be a surplus when Amount B (first case) is deducted from Case A as the S2P is more generous than SERPS for those earning less than the upper limit of Band 2. The sum representing Amount C for any given year is then added to the other amounts for each year of the person's working life (whether contracted in or contracted-out), and divided first by the number of years between 1978 (the start of SERPS) and the year before state pension age and then by 52 to find the weekly pension.

The sum known as 'Amount B (second case)' applies to those who are contracted-out by an appropriate personal pension scheme, including a non-occupational stakeholder pension scheme. In this type of case the National Insurance rebate reflects the three-tiered accrual rate for those who are not contracted out. Schedule 4A thus makes equivalent provision for those retiring before and after April 2009 respectively as apply to those in the state scheme.[317] It follows that for people earning at or above the LET, Amount B (second case) and Amount A will be the same, and so Amount C will necessarily be zero. However, there will be a difference when Amount B (second case) is deducted from Amount A for those who earn above the annual lower earnings limit but below the LET. This surplus figure will constitute their Amount C for any given year and will be paid as a top-up to the state pension.

---

312   SSCBA 1992, Sch 4A, para 3.
313   SSCBA 1992, Sch 4A, para 4.
314   The assumed surplus is the surplus there would have been had they not been contracted-out: SSCBA 1992, Sch 4A, para 8(2).
315   SSCBA 1992, Sch 4A, para 6.
316   SSCBA 1992, Sch 4A, para 8(3), disapplying SSCBA 1992, s 44A.
317   SSCBA 1992, Sch 4A, para 7.

iii Pension sharing

As the S2P is an additional pension for the purposes of section 44(3) of SSCBA 1992, it follows that the pension sharing provisions applicable to SERPS in the event of the contributor's divorce apply equally to S2P.[318]

B The second stage of the State Second Pension

The second stage of the S2P scheme will only be introduced when stakeholder pension schemes have established themselves.[319] The government anticipated that this second stage is likely to take place 'for those with a significant part of their working lives still remaining (eg those aged under 45 at the point of change), five years after the introduction of stakeholder pension schemes'.[320] At this point the S2P will become a flat-rate scheme, paying all its members at a single rate on earnings up to the LET (but not above). Thus all those covered by the scheme, regardless of their earnings, will be treated as if they had an earnings factor based on the LET. This means that low earners, carers and disabled people with disrupted working careers will continue to benefit from the deemed earnings factor fixed at the LET. However, all those earning above that threshold will only earn an entitlement to a S2P on the surplus in their earnings factor that falls within Band 1, namely the amount between the relevant QEF and the prevailing LET. Their entitlement accrued in the first stage of S2P (as calculated according to the Tables described above) will be preserved. The S2P scheme will accordingly be primarily for low earners. Those on middle and higher incomes will have an obvious incentive to join occupational or personal pension schemes (including stakeholder schemes), if they have not already done so.[321] In this way the government hope to shift the balance in pension provision from 60 per cent public-40 per cent private to 60 per cent private-40 per cent public.[322] It remains to be seen whether this can be achieved without compulsion on moderate earners to take out private pension provision.[323]

Part 5 Occupational and personal pension schemes

Mention has already been made of the importance of employer-based occupational schemes and of personal or 'individual' pension schemes within the general scheme of pension provision.[324] There is no statutory obligation upon any employer to offer its employees membership of an occupational pension scheme;[325] if, however, the employer operates such a scheme, it must do so subject to legislation designed to achieve a number of objectives. General principles of trust law and employment law will also be relevant.

---

318 P 619, above.
319 The regulation-making power is contained in SSCBA 1992, Sch 4A, para 2(5).
320 *DSS* n 5, above, p 40.
321 *DSS* n 5, above, p 6.
322 *DSS* n 5, above, pp 31–32.
323 Apparently the government very nearly opted for compulsion: Timmins *The Five Giants* (revd edn, 2001) p 573. The HC Social Security Committee has expressed the view that a compulsory rate of saving for pensions 'may be essential': *Fifth Report* (Session 1999–2000, HC 56) para 119.
324 See pp 587–590, above.
325 But employers with five or more employees must facilitate access to a stakeholder pension scheme: WRPA 1999, s 3 and SI 2000/1403, reg 22.

As the non-state sector has grown in size, so has the extent of legal regulation. This comes in a number of forms: of most importance for present purposes is the legislation governing contracting out. This imposes minimum requirements on occupational schemes as a condition of employers and members receiving exemption from participation in the S2P scheme (and previously the earnings-related component of the state scheme). The relevant law is now consolidated in the Pension Schemes Act 1993 (PSA 1993), as substantially amended by PA 1995.[326] PA 1995 additionally introduced reformed regulatory mechanisms for occupational pension schemes, especially as regards controls over the identity and powers of trustees, which are beyond the scope of this work.[327] Brief reference will be made here to the tax regulations which play a similar role in controlling the content of schemes by imposing conditions for tax rebates on contributions and benefits. The chapter concludes with an overview of the requirements of equality legislation, of the provisions governing the treatment of occupational pensions on divorce and of the growing body of legislation in the area of occupational pension protection.

A Contracting out

i *Types of contracted-out schemes*

The legislation on contracting out provides scheme members with certain guaranteed rights in relation to their pensions which may not be avoided by contract or similar transactions.[328] The nature of these rights, however, has differed over time and with respect to the type of scheme adopted. It was a fundamental principle of SSPA 1975 that a person's employment could be contracted out only if he or she were a member of an occupational pension scheme providing pensions of a specified standard and the appropriate consents had been given by the Occupational Pensions Board.[329] Among other conditions, the occupational scheme had to guarantee a minimum pension, the amount of which was to be deducted from the state pension that would otherwise have been payable.[330] Contracted-out employees could thus be confident of receiving at least the same total pension as they would otherwise have received from the state scheme alone. Occupational schemes of this kind are now known as 'defined-benefit' or 'salary-related' schemes. Historically salary-related schemes have constituted the vast majority of employer-based schemes, and of these nearly all are contracted out.[331] It should be noted, however, that since 2001 an increasing number of large companies have closed their salary-related schemes to new employees.[332] The main reason for this trend is a concern about the rising costs of such schemes for employers caused by a range of factors, including depressed stock market performance leading to falling investment returns, longer life expectancy and the withdrawal of tax credits on dividends.[333]

---

326 The government is committed to simplifying pensions legislation; see further Pickering *A simpler way to better pensions* (DWP, July 2002).
327 See *Thomas and Dowrick* n 257, above, ch 3.
328 PSA 1993, s 159; see also SI 1996/1462.
329 SSPA 1975, s 30; see now PSA 1993, ss 7–8. The Occupational Pensions Board has since been abolished. Its functions in this regard were taken over by the Inland Revenue.
330 PSA 1993, ss 14, 46.
331 *Government Actuary* n 20, above, para 7.4.
332 Including Abbey National, Ernst & Young, Marks & Spencer and the Nationwide Building Society. The food retailer Iceland went a step further by closing its salary-related scheme to *existing* employees, and transferring them over to a money-purchase scheme.
333 The introduction of a new accounting standard FRS-17 is also seen by some as a factor.

SSA 1986 extended the contracting out provisions of the 1975 Act to cover occupational schemes providing 'money purchase' benefits: these are 'benefits the rate or amount of which is calculated by reference to a payment or payments made by the member [of the scheme] or by any other person in respect of the member and which are not average salary benefits'.[334] In a money purchase scheme, the pension is not fixed in advance as a percentage of earnings or of contributions paid; instead, its amount depends on the outcome, over the pensioner's working life, of the investment of his or her contributions. It may turn out to be either more or less than the additional pension foregone in the state scheme. There is no 'guaranteed minimum pension' in a money purchase scheme, but the Category A or B pension derived from the contributions of a person who has been contracted out in such a scheme is nevertheless reduced by a 'notional GMP'.[335] The extension of contracting out to money purchase schemes, therefore, represented a radical departure from the principle that no employees should risk losing part of their guaranteed pension as a result of their employer's decision to contract out.

Another innovation made by SSA 1986 was to enable individual employees to contribute to a personal pension scheme providing money purchase benefits[336] in place of their participation in SERPS or in an employer-based scheme. Legislation formally protects the individual's freedom of choice in relation to pension provision by rendering void any term in a contract of employment or in a pension scheme requiring an employee to become or stay a member of a particular personal or occupational scheme.[337] PSA 1993 did not use the term 'contracted out' in this connection, referring instead to an 'appropriate scheme'[338] but the effect is the same: the Category A or B additional pension is reduced by a notional GMP, whether this turns out to be more or less than the pension produced by the personal scheme.[339] PA 1995 introduced new arrangements for contracting out as from 6 April 1997.[340] Since that date the requirement for a guaranteed minimum pension has been removed. Instead, pension schemes must provide benefits which are broadly equivalent to, or better than, those contained in a statutory 'reference scheme'.[341]

ii Contracting out certificates

Under section 8 of PSA 1993 the employment of an earner under pensionable age is 'contracted-out employment' where either the employment qualifies him or her for a pension provided by a contracted-out occupational scheme or the employer makes minimum payments to a money purchase contracted-out scheme.[342] In either case a 'contracting-out certificate' issued by the Inland Revenue must also be in force.[343] The employer must make an application for a contracting-out certificate,[344] first giving at least three months' notice of an application to the other parties concerned. These include

334 PSA 1993, s 181(1).
335 PSA 1993, s 48. This has ceased to have effect with regard to payments made on or after 6 April 1997: PA 1995, s 140(3) and SI 1997/664, reg 10; see now PSA 1993, s 48A, inserted by PA 1995, s 140.
336 PSA 1993, s 31(3)(b).
337 PSA 1993, s 160 (formerly SSA 1986, s 15).
338 PSA 1993, s 7(1)(b).
339 PSA 1993, ss 8 and 46.
340 PA 1995, Pt III and SI 1996/778.
341 PA 1995, s 12A; see p 633, below.
342 Special provision is made for hybrid schemes which pay both salary-related and money purchase benefits: PA 1995, s 149 and SI 1996/1977.
343 PA 1995, s 8(1).
344 PA 1995, s 11(1).

the employees (including any in the employment in question who are not to be contracted out), the trustees (if any) and administrator of the scheme and any independent trade unions (the period of notice can be reduced to one month with the consent of all the unions concerned).[345] The employer is also obliged to consult with the unions on the proposal to contract out.[346] Having done this and given the required notice, it must send a formal election to the Inland Revenue.[347] The Inland Revenue then decides whether the employment should be treated as contracted-out by reference to the scheme and, if so, issues a contracting-out certificate specifying the employments (or the categories of earners in those employments) to which it relates.[348] The Inland Revenue may also cancel or vary a certificate if it has reason to suppose that any employment covered by it should not continue to be contracted out.[349]

iii   The contracted-out contribution rebate

The structure of contracted-out rebates was radically changed by PA 1995, with effect from April 1997.[350] Three categories of earner must be considered[351] (the approximate number of contributors in each group is indicated in parentheses)[352]: (1) those contracted out into a traditional salary-related occupational pension scheme (8.1 million); (2) those contracted out into a money purchase occupational pension scheme (300,000); and (3) those who are members of appropriate personal pension schemes (3.7 million).

A   REDUCED RATES FOR MEMBERS OF SALARY-RELATED OCCUPATIONAL PENSION SCHEMES

Section 41 of PSA 1993 establishes the principle that, where an earner's employment is contracted out into a salary-related occupational pension scheme, the National Insurance contributions payable by employers and employees are reduced. This lower contracted-out contribution rate is payable only on earnings between the lower and upper earnings limits.[353] The Secretary of State is required to lay before Parliament, at intervals of not more than five years, a report by the Government Actuary on the contracted-out contribution rates. The report must also cover any changes affecting the cost to occupational schemes of providing benefits of an actuarial value equivalent to

---

345   SI 1996/1172, reg 3.
346   SI 1996/1172, reg 4.
347   SI 1996/1172, regs 2(1), 5 and 6.
348   SI 1996/1172, reg 8.
349   SI 1996/1172, reg 47.
350   The relevant provisions have also been amended by SSA 1998 and WRPA 1999 to reflect changes to the contributions system.
351   The discussion below assumes, for ease of exposition, that the categories are mutually exclusive. In fact earners may eg be members of a salary-related occupational pension scheme and have their own personal pension arrangements. This necessarily generates complexity in the legislation seeking to accommodate such cases: see SSCBA 1992, Sch 1, para 1(3) and (6), as amended by PA 1995, s 148. On the implications for earnings factors, see PSA 1993, s 48A, as inserted by PA 1995, s 140 and amended by CSPSSA 2000, s 38, and SI 2000/2736.
352   *Government Actuary* n 20, above, para 7.4. The number of people registered with a personal pension scheme is actually more than 5 million, but many have no earnings or earnings below the lower earnings limit and so do not qualify for a contributions rebate. Note that these figures are in the process of change as more companies close their salary-related schemes.
353   PSA 1993, s 41(1)–(1C), as amended by PA 1995, s 137(2) and as substituted and amended by SSA 1998, Sch 7, para 127; WRPA 1999, Sch 9, para 6; and NICA 2002, Sch 1, para 36 (to reflect changes to the structure of National Insurance contributions).

those foregone by members of such schemes.[354] The contracted-out rebate, which is the difference between the normal and contracted-out contribution rates, is fixed on the basis of that report. In 2002–03 the rebate is 5.1 per cent, of which 3.5 per cent is deducted from the normal rate of employers' contributions and 1.6 per cent from employees'.[355] The rebate reflects the estimated cost to salary-related schemes of providing benefits of an equivalent value to those foregone, including an allowance for contingencies. As we shall see in the section below, this rebate used to be available to all earners who contracted out, but now only those who contract out into a traditional contracted-out salary-related occupation pension scheme (COSRS) are eligible for the full flat-rate rebate.

B   REDUCED RATES FOR MEMBERS OF MONEY PURCHASE OCCUPATIONAL PENSION SCHEMES

Section 42A of PSA 1993 makes separate provision for earners who are members of a contracted-out money purchase scheme (COMPS).[356] As with members of salary-related schemes, COMPS members qualify for a reduction in their National Insurance liability in the form of a flat-rate rebate. The flat-rate rebate for this group from April 2002 is 2.6 per cent, of which 1.6 per cent is deducted from the normal rate of employees' contributions and 1 per cent from employers' contributions.[357] The sum paid over to the pension scheme is then the amount by which the appropriate age-related rebate exceeds the flat-rate rebate.[358] The age-related component ranges from 2.6 per cent for someone aged 16 at the start of the relevant tax year to 10.5 per cent for a person aged 63 at that point.[359] As with the rebates for COSRS members, these rates are determined following a review by the Government Actuary[360] and are designed to reflect the sum that would need to be invested to generate a benefit of an actuarial value equivalent to the extra state pension foregone. In order to protect public finances,[361] the combined rebate for COMPS members is subject to an overall cap (now 10.5 per cent of relevant earnings). Age-related rebates first became available to COMPS members under PA 1995; before that legislation was brought into force they applied only to those who contracted out of the state scheme and joined an appropriate personal pension scheme.

C   MEMBERS OF PERSONAL PENSION SCHEMES

Earners who are members of appropriate personal pension schemes do not qualify for any reduction in their National Insurance contributions liabilities; they pay the normal contracted-in rate, as do their employers. However, they do qualify for an age-related rebate, so long as they are over 16 but under pensionable age and have given appropriate notice of their 'chosen scheme'.[362] As with the other rebates, there is provision for the

354   PSA 1993, s 42; see *Occupational and Personal Pension Schemes: Review of Certain Contracting-Out Terms* (2001, Cm 5076).
355   PSA 1993, s 41(1A)–(1B) and SI 2001/1356.
356   On the definition of a COMPS, see p 627, above and p 636, below.
357   PSA 1993, s 42A(1)–(2D) (originally inserted by PA 1995, s 137(5) and then as substituted and amended by SSA 1998, Sch 7, para 128 and WRPA 1999, Sch 9, para 7 to reflect changes to the structure of National Insurance contributions). See also SI 2001/1355, art 2(a).
358   PSA 1993, s 42A(3).
359   SI 2001/1355, art 2(b) and Sch.
360   PSA 1993, s 42B; see *Cm 5076* n 354, above.
361   Eg there would be considerable cost implications if too many older workers were to opt out of the state scheme in order to join money purchase schemes.
362   PSA 1993, ss 43–45 and SI 2001/1354. See p 640, below.

Government Actuary periodically to review the rates at which they are paid.[363] These age-related rebates vary according both to the earner's age (with higher levels of rebates for older workers) and their earnings in a way that reflects the changes to the accrual rates made by the S2P.[364] The purpose of the age-related rebates is to provide a balance between ensuring some incentive for those in the higher age brackets to opt for a personal pension, as opposed to the state scheme, while still limiting the cost to the Exchequer. This is achieved by applying the same 10.5 per cent cap as operates under the arrangements for COMPS. Conversely, this type of rebate makes personal pensions less attractive at younger ages as compared with the previous arrangements.[365]

The provision for rebates for those taking out personal pensions has varied over the years. The White Paper of 1985 announced a controversial proposal to provide an incentive of an 'extra rebate' of 2 per cent of earnings between the lower and upper earnings limits (in addition to the normal contracted-out rebate) in order to encourage employees to contract out of the state scheme and make their own private provision.[366] This was implemented in SSA 1986.[367] This arrangement operated between 1987–88 and 1992–93 for those newly contracting out into an appropriate personal pension scheme.[368] The extent of contracting-out of SERPS in favour of personal schemes turned out to be much greater than expected, resulting in a substantial net loss to the National Insurance Fund of £5.9 billion.[369] Partly as a consequence of this, measures had to be taken to stabilise the Fund by reintroducing a substantial element of Treasury funding to supplement the income from National Insurance contributions.[370] In April 1993 a new rebate scheme was introduced, involving an additional rebate of 1 per cent, but only for people aged 30 and over with appropriate personal pensions.[371] The rationale behind linking the rebate to age was to avoid a situation in which employees in their thirties would find it in their interest to opt back into SERPS owing to the otherwise flat-rate nature of the contracted-out rebate and the better protection the state schemes offers to older workers.[372] This type of extra rebate only operated until April 1997, when the current arrangements were introduced (an age-related rebate without any flat-rate element).

iv   The effect of contracting out on the state pension

Contracting out has no effect on eligibility to the basic state retirement pension. Its impact on rights to the additional state pension varies according to whether one is concerned with accruals before or after April 1997.

---

363   PSA 1993, s 45A.
364   The age-related rebates for personal pensions schemes differ from those for COMPS, reflecting the fact that the former have less scope for securing economies of scale and also lose an investment return on the rebate given the timing of rebate payments at the end of the tax year: *Thomas and Dowrick* n 257, above, p 144.
365   *Government Actuary* n 20, above, paras 7.8–7.9.
366   *White Paper 1985* n 73, above, paras 2.30–2.32.
367   SSA 1986, s 3(2); SI 1987/1115, reg 2. This was paid direct by the DSS to the relevant occupational or personal pension scheme.
368   It was also available between 1988–89 and 1992–93 for those opting into newly contracted-out occupational schemes.
369   National Audit Office *The Elderly: Information Requirements for Supporting the Elderly and the Implications of Personal Pensions for the National Insurance Fund* (1990–91, HC 55). See also 4th edition of this book, p 249.
370   See p 95, above.
371   SSA 1993, s 1; SI 1993/519.
372   *National Audit Office* n 369, above, p 17.

A   THE EFFECT OF CONTRACTING OUT BEFORE APRIL 1997

In respect of periods before April 1997, contracting out does not mean that an employee is totally excluded from SERPS; he or she continues to have a residual right to the state benefit if the guaranteed minimum pension is less.[373] A contracted-out scheme does not have to match the state scheme fully in regard to the inflation-proofing of pensions, protection of the rights of 'early leavers', or provision of widows', widowers' and invalidity pensions. Accordingly, even in a salary-related scheme, which was required to provide a guaranteed minimum pension as a condition of contracting out for periods prior to April 1997,[374] the pension may fall short of the standards of the state scheme.

B   THE EFFECT OF CONTRACTING OUT AFTER APRIL 1997

For periods from April 1997 until SERPS was superseded by the S2P in April 2002, it was possible for earners to contract completely out of the additional pension.[375] This reflects the abolition of the guaranteed minimum pension requirement and its replacement by less onerous conditions for recognising occupational and personal pension schemes for the purposes of contracting out. As a result members of such schemes do not receive their SERPS entitlement less the contracted-out deduction but instead are solely reliant on their non-state provision for any earnings-related component to their pension for this period.[376] There are, however, some circumstances in which a contracted out employee may qualify for an additional pension by way of the S2P.[377]

v   *Contracting out: salary-related schemes*

Occupational schemes of the 'salary-related' type have to comply with a number of conditions in order to qualify for a contracting-out certificate and, once contracted out, are subject to the supervision of the Inland Revenue to a greater extent than the 'money purchase' schemes allowed to contract out since April 1988. This is largely because a salary-related scheme has to provide for the payment of pensions in the distant future, of unpredictable amount but calculated according to a predetermined formula, while money purchase schemes involve no such obligation. As a result of the reforms introduced by PA 1995, the contracting out requirements differ in part according to whether the period of service concerned falls before or after April 1997. Earners who have periods of pensionable service before that date have accrued rights in the form of GMPs; any pensionable service after that date is protected by the new reference scheme rules. As a result, scheme administrators will have to operate two schemes in parallel for many more years until there are no more scheme members in active employment who have any pensionable service before the changeover date.[378]

---

373   PSA 1993, s 46(1). On the complex decision making processes involved, see *CP/4479/2000*.
374   On the conditions for contracting out before and after April 1997, see p 627, above.
375   PSA 1993, s 48A.
376   For criticism, see Nobles (1996) 59 MLR 241 at 247–249.
377   P 624, above.
378   *Thomas and Dowrick* n 257, above, p 138. Unless, of course, the administrators succeed in persuading employees to transfer.

A   PENSIONABLE SERVICE BEFORE APRIL 1997: GUARANTEED MINIMUM PENSION

In relation to any earner's service before 6 April 1997, an occupational pension scheme is only contracted out if it satisfies the certification requirements relating to guaranteed minimum pensions.[379] This means that the scheme must provide a pension, on the earner reaching pensionable age, which is not less than the GMP.[380] The GMP is calculated in broadly the same way as the additional pension in SERPS, by taking the earnings factors derived from primary Class 1 contributions paid on earnings between the lower and upper earnings limits and revaluing each year's earnings factors. The GMP is a percentage of the total revalued earnings factors for the employee's working life.[381] For a person who was within 20 years of pensionable age on 6 April 1978 the GMP is 1.25 per cent in respect of tax years up to and including 1987–88 and 1 per cent for subsequent years. In the case of a younger person, for tax years up to and including 1987–88 the GMP is 25 per cent divided by the number of years of his or her working life from 6 April 1978; for tax years after 1987–88 the GMP rate is 20 per cent divided by the relevant number of years.[382] For a working life of 20 years or more in the same contracted-out employment, therefore, the GMP in respect of years up to 1987–88 will be one-quarter of the person's average revalued earnings between the two earnings limits, and one fifth of average revalued earnings for subsequent tax years. This cut in the value of the GMP for years after 1987–88 mirrors, in general terms, the similar cut in the value of the additional pension introduced by SSA 1986.[383]

The scheme must also provide a GMP for the earner's widow or widower, of half the amount of the earner's GMP.[384] The requirement to provide a widower's GMP, which was added by SSA 1986, applies only where the wife dies on or after 6 April 1989, the widower's GMP being based only on her earnings factors for 1988–89 and subsequent years.[385] The widow or widower's GMP must be payable for those periods when a bereavement allowance, widowed parent's allowance or retirement pension is payable on the late spouse's contributions.[386] The same applies where the survivor's bereavement allowance or widowed parent's allowance has ceased after reaching the age of 45, so long as the survivor does not cohabit in a heterosexual relationship or remarry.[387]

Before SSA 1986 the GMP was fixed at pensionable age and was not raised to take account of subsequent inflation, in contrast to the additional pension in the state scheme which was subject to annual up-rating to take increases in earnings into account. In effect, then, the state scheme bore the risk of post-retirement inflation; if inflation reduced the real value of the GMP, the pensioner would still be able to fall back on his or her residual entitlement to the state additional pension. The 1986 Act introduced partial inflation proofing in the form of annual increases in that part of the GMP derived

---

379   PSA 1993, s 9(2)(a) and (2A). Originally, occupational schemes, as a condition of contracting out, also had to provide a pension of not less than 1.5 per cent of either the employee's average annual salary throughout his or her service in contracted-out employment (after revaluation) or the final salary, multiplied in either case by years of service up to 40: SSPA 1975, ss 33(1)(a) and 34, repealed by SSA 1986, Sch 11.

380   PSA 1993, s 13(1)(b).

381   Even when, before SSA 1986, the state scheme provided for the additional pension to be based on the 'best twenty years', the GMP was based on the full working life of the employee: see the 2nd edition of this book, p 223.

382   PSA 1993, s 14(5). Obviously this applies until the end of the 1996–97 tax year only: s 14(8).

383   See pp 615–618, above.

384   PSA 1993, s 17.

385   PSA 1993, s 17(4).

386   PSA 1993, s 17(4A).

387   See further PSA 1993, s 17(5) and (6) and SI 1996/1172, reg 57.

from earnings factors for 1988–89 and subsequent years until 1996–97. The annual increase in the GMP must be either the percentage increase in prices since the previous review or 3 per cent, whichever is less.[388]

Members of contracted-out occupational pension schemes of the salary-related type can also earn increments for deferring receipt of their pension. The rules of the scheme may provide for payment of the GMP to be postponed if a person continues in employment after pensionable age, but his or her consent is required for any postponement if the employment does not relate to the scheme concerned or if the postponement continues more than five years after pensionable age (ie currently beyond age 65 for a woman or 70 for a man).[389] The GMP must be increased in the same way as the state pension, by 1/7 per cent for each week of deferment, provided that the pension is deferred for at least seven weeks. Unlike the state pension, however, the GMP can be deferred for more than five years after pensionable age, in which case increments continue to accrue at the same rate.[390] There are no similar requirements for COMPS or personal pension schemes to provide increments of any defined amount for deferred retirement (as there is no defined benefit to increment). PSA 1993 requires that the pension should commence at pensionable age or such later date as has been agreed by the member.[391] The value of the member's protected rights will, however, be increased by the investment returns during the period of deferment.

B   PENSIONABLE SERVICE AFTER APRIL 1997: REFERENCE SCHEMES

In relation to any earner's service on or after 6 April 1997, an occupational pension scheme is only contracted out if it satisfies the new requirements laid down by PA 1995.[392] The key condition is that the scheme meets the statutory standard set out in section 12A of PSA 1993, namely that it must provide benefits which are broadly equivalent to, or better than, those contained in a statutory 'reference scheme'.[393] A reference scheme is one that provides for a pension starting at the normal pension age and continuing for life. The annual rate of pension must be 1/80th of average qualifying earnings[394] in the last three tax years of service multiplied by the number of years' service.[395] The number of years' service must not exceed such number as would produce an annual rate equal to half the earnings on which it was calculated.[396] There are also powers to prohibit or restrict the transfer of any liability, the discharge of any liability to provide pensions under a scheme or the payment of lump sums instead of pensions.[397] The other conditions for contracting out in respect of post-April 1997 pensionable service are that the scheme complies with the statutory restrictions on employer-related investments,[398] that it meets

388   PSA 1993, s 109 (limited with effect to April 1997 by PA 1995, s 55; see eg SI 2002/649). Occupational schemes are now subject to 'limited price indexation' of up to 5 per cent under the provisions of PA 1995, s 51: see p 648, below.
389   PSA 1993, s 13(4), (5).
390   PSA 1993, s 15.
391   PSA 1993, s 29(1)(a).
392   PSA 1993, s 9(2)(b) and (2B).
393   PA 1995, s 12A(3).
394   Defined as 90 per cent of earnings between the lower and upper earnings limits in any tax year: PA 1995, s 12B(5).
395   PA 1995, s 12B(3).
396   Pensions for widows and widowers must be one-half of the amount calculated for pensioners: PA 1995, s 12B(4). See further SI 1997/819, reg 2.
397   PA 1995, s 12C and SI 1997/784.
398   PA 1995, s 40: see p 649, below.

other prescribed requirements and that its rules are drafted so as to satisfy the relevant conditions.[399] The post-April 1997 arrangements are unlikely to provide as secure a protection for pensioners as those in place before the abolition of the GMP requirement, not least during periods of high inflation, given the limited indexation under the new arrangements.[400]

C   EARLY LEAVERS

The accrued occupational pension rights of an employee who leaves the employment before pensionable age are protected by the preservation and revaluation requirements of Part IV of PSA 1993; these are discussed below.[401]

At this point it is necessary to consider the ways in which the GMP (in respect of accruals before April 1997) of an early leaver is protected through the conditions for contracting out. There are three possibilities: the scheme can retain the liability for payment of the GMP when the employee reaches pensionable age or dies; the liability can be 'bought out', normally with the member's consent, by means of an insurance policy or annuity contract, or transferred to another contracted-out occupational scheme (including a money purchase scheme) or to a personal pension scheme; or it can be transferred back to the state scheme.

First, if the scheme retains the liability, arrangements must be made to revalue the GMP between the date of leaving and the time when the pension becomes payable. The scheme may continue to revalue the GMP in accordance with the orders for the annual revaluation of earnings factors under section 148 of SSAA 1992 ('full revaluation'),[402] as if the contracted-out employment had not terminated. Alternatively, the scheme's rules may provide for 'limited revaluation' of the GMP at a prescribed rate for each year after the termination of service.[403] Where an employee left contracted-out employment before 1 January 1985, it is possible, in effect, to evade the requirement to revalue the GMP by a practice known as 'franking'. This involves using pension rights in excess of the GMP to offset the GMP revaluation: thus, as GMP rights increase with revaluation, the person's other preserved rights in the scheme diminish. Sections 87 to 92 of PSA 1993 impose restrictions on franking where contracted-out employment ceased on or after 1 January 1985.[404] These provide, in broad terms, that the pension increases resulting from revaluation of the GMP must be paid in addition to the member's pension rights which legislation requires to be preserved, as well as any rights he or she acquires from subsequent employment under that scheme. An alternative methodology to these anti-franking rules, involving the application of a minimum benefits test, may now be used in respect of pensionable service after 6 April 1997.[405]

Secondly, where a person's rights are 'bought out' or transferred to another salary-related occupational scheme, the effect is to preserve entitlement to the GMP automatically.[406] Where the transfer is to a contracted-out money purchase scheme or

399   PSA 1993, s 9(2B).
400   *Nobles* n 376, above; and *Thomas and Dowrick* n 257, above, p 140.
401   Pp 647–648, below.
402   PSA 1993, s 16(1). On revaluation of earnings factors, see p 616, above.
403   PSA 1993, s 16(2), (3). The original requirement for a 5 per cent compound revaluation was repealed by PA 1995, Sch 5, para 28.
404   These measures were first introduced by the Health and Social Security Act 1984, inserting SSPA 1975, ss 41A–41E; further provisions are made by SI 1991/166.
405   CSPSSA 2000, s 56 and Sch 5, Pt II.
406   SI 1996/1462, reg 3.

to a personal pension scheme, a transfer payment must be made, at least equal to the cash value of the GMP rights, calculated on actuarial principles, and the transfer payment must be used to provide money purchase benefits, which may or may not prove as valuable as the GMP would have been.[407] A transfer payment may be made to an overseas occupational scheme if the employee is moving to employment outside the UK, subject to various safeguards being satisfied.[408]

Thirdly, the possibility of transferring GMP liability back to the state scheme arises where the employee leaves or dies after less than two years' pensionable service and does not qualify for preservation of pension rights under Part IV, Chapter I of PSA 1993.[409] If these conditions are satisfied, a 'contributions equivalent premium' can be paid to the state scheme, equivalent to the additional amount of contributions that would have been payable if the employment had not been contracted out.[410] The employee's share can be recovered from any refund of occupational scheme contributions due to him or her.[411] With limited exceptions,[412] in deciding whether to pay contributions equivalent premiums, the trustees of the scheme may not discriminate between members of the scheme on grounds other than length of service.[413]

In addition to these three measures for protecting a vested GMP, a member of an occupational scheme has the right to take the actuarial 'cash equivalent' (generally referred to as the 'transfer value') of his accrued benefits (including the GMP) under the scheme. This right may be exercised at any time one year or more before normal pension age under the rules of the scheme (or before age 60 if normal pension age is earlier).[414] The transfer value must either be transferred to another scheme or invested in an insurance policy or annuity contract on his or her behalf.[415] If the member has left the scheme voluntarily while remaining in the same employment, the scheme may restrict the transfer payment to the cash equivalent of the rights accrued from 6 April 1988 onwards.[416]

D   SCHEME CEASING TO BE CONTRACTED-OUT

A salary-related scheme may cease to be contracted-out either on cancellation or surrender of the contracting-out certificate or because, even though a certificate remains in issue, the scheme no longer provides the benefits required as a condition of contracting out. The Inland Revenue has the power to cancel a certificate under PSA 1993, eg if it considers 'that there are circumstances which make it inexpedient that the employment should be or, as the case may be, continue to be, contracted-out employment by reference to the scheme'.[417]

---

407   SI 1996/1462, reg 5.
408   SI 1996/1462, reg 6.
409   PSA 1993, ss 69–82.
410   PSA 1993, s 55(2) and (2A). S 141 of PA 1995 replaced the former provision for the payment of state scheme premiums with contributions equivalent premiums: see further below.
411   PSA 1993, s 61.
412   SI 1996/1172, reg 51(2).
413   PSA 1993, s 57(2).
414   SI 1996/1847, reg 15. On the meaning of 'normal pension age', see PSA 1993, s 180. This right was originally confined to those whose pensionable service terminated on or after 1 January 1986; this restriction was lifted by PA 1995, s 152, subject to certain exceptions (see SI 1996/1847, reg 2).
415   PSA 1993, ss 93, 94.
416   SI 1996/1847, reg 3.
417   PSA 1993, s 34(4).

On a scheme ceasing to be contracted-out, the Inland Revenue is empowered to approve arrangements for the preservation or transfer of members' pension scheme rights.[418] PSA 1993 originally provided for the option of the payment of a state scheme premium, representing the cost of providing the GMP, as one means of protecting members' rights in such circumstances. The effect of this was to extinguish the accrued rights to a GMP under the scheme, and instead vest the persons concerned with an additional pension under the state scheme as if they had not been contracted out.[419] This arrangement was replaced, under PA 1995, by provision for the payment of contributions equivalent premiums. The trustees of a salary-related occupational pension scheme may elect to pay such premiums to earners with less than two years' service where the scheme ceases to be contracted out or the person's employment (or membership of the scheme) ends.[420] In practice the facility to buy back accrued rights should not be necessary for periods after April 1997 as pension schemes may now discharge their accrued liabilities for COSRS service by enabling employees to transfer to another contracted-out scheme or to buy a personal pension.[421]

vi   Contracting out: money purchase schemes

Before 6 April 1988 employment could only be contracted out where a GMP was provided by an occupational pension scheme. Since that date, the GMP condition does not apply if, instead, the employer makes 'minimum payments' to a 'money purchase contracted-out scheme'.[422] A contracted-out money purchase scheme (generally known as a 'COMPS') is defined as a scheme which is contracted out by virtue of satisfying section 9(3) of PSA 1993, which requires schemes to provide for minimum payments by the employer, to safeguard 'protected rights' and to comply with a number of other conditions concerning benefit payments and treatment of members. The essential distinction between COMPS and salary-related schemes (COSRS) is that the latter must provide a minimum pension while the former must receive minimum contributions but are not required to guarantee a pension of any particular amount.

A   MINIMUM PAYMENTS AND BENEFITS

The minimum payment which the employer is required to make to a COMPS is the amount of the contracted-out contribution rebate.[423] The employer can recover the employee's share of the contracted-out rebate by deduction from earnings, but it is not obliged to do so.[424] Since the value of the benefits produced by a money purchase scheme depends in part on the investment return on the contributions, it is important that contributions should be paid promptly. The employer is therefore required to make minimum payments to the scheme within 14 days of the end of each 'tax month'.[425]

---

418   PSA 1993, s 50(1)(a) and SI 1996/1172, reg 45. On the Board's supervisory role for former contracted-out schemes, see PSA 1993, s 53.
419   See 4th edition of this book, p 253.
420   PSA 1993, s 55(2), (2A).
421   *Thomas and Dowrick* n 257, above, p 140.
422   PSA 1993, s 8(1)(a).
423   PSA 1993, ss 8(2), 10(2)(a).
424   PSA 1993, s 8(3)(b); SI 1996/1172, reg. 31. This power cannot be used if the employee's earnings are below the primary threshold for the purposes of National Insurance contributions: reg 31(3A).
425   SI 1996/1172, reg 32(1).

The minimum payments made to the scheme, together with the age-related rebate, must be used to provide money purchase benefits,[426] except to the extent that they are used for administrative expenses and commission.[427] The Inland Revenue has power to limit by regulations the proportion of the scheme's resources that can be devoted to administration, commission or other non-benefit expenditure.[428] Rights to money purchase benefits derived from minimum payments and age-related rebates are known as 'protected rights' and, unless the scheme's rules provide otherwise, a person's protected rights also include his or her rights to any other money purchase benefits under the scheme.[429] If they do not, the value of the protected rights must be calculated in a way no less favourable than the calculation of the value of other rights under the scheme.[430]

The scheme must give effect to a member's protected rights by payment of a pension, either directly or through an insurance company or friendly society, by a transfer payment to another occupational or personal scheme, or in certain cases by payment of a lump sum.[431] A lump sum must be paid where the member dies before the pension commences and leaves no widow or widower entitled to a pension, or where the widow or widower also dies before effect has been given to the protected rights.[432] An annual pension below an amount prescribed by regulation (currently £260) may be commuted to a lump sum.[433]

In addition, if a pension is provided, it must commence at pensionable age (presently 60 for a woman, 65 for a man) or at a later date agreed by the member and must be payable for life. If the pensioner dies leaving a widow or widower, half the pension must continue in payment to the surviving spouse.[434] If the scheme member dies before receiving a pension, however, and leaves such a widow or widower, the whole of the protected rights must be used to provide their pension.[435] The pension payable by a COMPS, whether directly or by purchase of an annuity, must satisfy a number of other requirements. The rate of the pension or annuity must be determined without regard to the sex or marital status of the scheme member.[436] Thus it is not permissible to pay smaller pensions to women because of their longer expectation of life. It is not clear, on the other hand, whether women's pensions may be reduced under the regulations because of the five years difference in pensionable ages.[437] Once in payment, the pension must be increased annually by at least the percentage prescribed for GMPs under section 109 of PSA 1993: the rate of prices inflation or 3 per cent, whichever is less.[438] The scheme's rules may provide for pension increases of up to, but not more than, 3 per cent to be awarded even when the rate of inflation is less.[439] If the pension is to take the form of a purchased annuity, the member or, where the member dies before receiving a pension, the widow or widower, has the right to choose the insurance company or friendly society which is to provide it. If this right is not exercised by the member at least one month before the pension is due to commence (or by such later date as the rules of the scheme

426 For the definition of 'money purchase benefits', see p 636, above.
427 PSA 1993, s 31(3).
428 PSA 1993, s 31(2).
429 PSA 1993, s 10(2).
430 PSA 1993, s 27(2).
431 PSA 1993, s 28. See further SI 1996/1461. Lump sums may not be paid until the member reaches 60, except in the case of the terminally ill: PSA 1993, s 28(4A) and (4B).
432 PSA 1993, s 28(5); SI 1996/1537, regs 12 and 13.
433 PSA 1993, s 28(4); SI 1996/1537, reg 8 and 12(3).
434 PSA 1993, s 29(1). The requirement that the survivor be a 'qualifying' widow(er) (ie over 45 or with a dependent child) was removed by SI 2002/681.
435 PSA 1993, s 28(5); SI 1996/1537, reg 12(4).
436 SI 1996/1537, reg 4(2).
437 On the European law aspects of this problem, see pp 641–645, below.
438 See p 633, above.
439 SI 1996/1537, regs 4(3), (6), 12(6), (8).

may allow), or by the widow or widower within three months of being notified of the right, the trustees or managers of the scheme can make the choice.[440]

B   EARLY LEAVERS

The range of options available for protecting the pension rights of an employee leaving a money-purchase scheme before pension age is more limited than for those leaving salary-related contracted-out schemes.[441] There is no possibility of 'buying out' the scheme's liability through an insurance policy or annuity contract, or of reinstating the employee's rights in the state scheme by paying a 'contributions equivalent premium'. The protected rights must either be retained in the scheme or transferred to another scheme which is or has been contracted out or to an overseas occupational scheme. The absence of any requirement to provide a GMP, now also removed from salary-related schemes with effect for accrual periods from April 1997, greatly simplifies the protection of early leavers' rights. If the protected rights are retained in the scheme, to provide benefits at pensionable age or on death, all that is required is that the employer should notify the Inland Revenue of the termination of contracted-out employment.[442] There is no need for regulations stipulating the basis on which protected rights should be revalued between the date of leaving and the date of award of a pension, since under the revaluation provisions of PSA 1993 preserved pension rights in a money purchase scheme, whether contracted-out or not, must benefit from the investment yield of the scheme in the same way as the rights of current scheme members.[443]

If protected rights are to be transferred to another scheme, the member's consent must be obtained, and the transfer payment must be at least equal to the value of the protected rights that are being transferred.[444] If the payment is made to a personal pension or COMPS it must be used by the receiving scheme to provide money purchase benefits.[445] It is a condition of making transfer payments from COMPS to salary-related schemes that the receiving scheme makes appropriate provision for both pre-1997 and post-1997 protected rights.[446] A transfer may also be made to a formerly contracted-out occupational pension scheme which the Inland Revenue remains under a duty to supervise.[447] If the member is moving to employment outside the UK, the protected rights can be transferred to an overseas occupational pension scheme which is not contracted out or other overseas arrangement, providing the trustees of the transferring scheme take reasonable steps to satisfy themselves on various requirements.[448]

In addition to the arrangements described above for transferring protected rights in COMPS, any member of a money purchase occupational scheme, whether contracted out or not, can claim a 'transfer value' in the same way as a member of a salary-related scheme.[449]

---

440   PSA 1993, s 29(3), (4); SI 1996/1537, regs 10, 12(12) and (13).
441   See pp 634–635, above.
442   SI 1996/1172, reg 44(1).
443   PSA 1993, s 84(3), (4) and Sch 3.
444   SI 1996/1461, regs 2–4. Amending regulations are expected in 2002 which will extend this facility to deferred members and remove the requirement for consent in such cases.
445   SI 1996/1461, reg 3.
446   Eg for pre-1997 protected rights this means a GMP in respect of the period of employment, equal to the notional GMP deductible from the state pension: SI 1996/1461, reg 4(d).
447   SI 1996/1461, reg 4A.
448   SI 1996/1461, reg 5.
449   PSA 1993, ss 93–101; see p 635, above. See also PA 1995, s 152, giving those with pensionable service ending before 1 January 1986 the right to a cash equivalent.

C SCHEME CEASING TO BE CONTRACTED OUT

Analogously as with occupational pension schemes, where a money-purchase contracted-out scheme ceases to have that status, the Inland Revenue is empowered to approve arrangements for the preservation or transfer of members' protected rights.[450] Typically an earner will transfer to a different COMPS on joining a new employer, or take out a personal pension policy. A further possibility is that a member's protected rights will be secured by making the earner the beneficiary of an appropriate insurance policy.[451]

vii Contracting out: personal pension schemes

SSA 1986 introduced the concept of personal pension schemes as an alternative to full participation in the state scheme.[452] The term 'contracting out' is not, in fact, applied to these schemes in the Act since, unlike contracted-out occupational schemes, they do not depend on a decision by the employer; nor do they affect the rate of National Insurance contributions payable by either the employer or the employee. Both pay the normal contracted-in rate, but the age-related rebate is passed on to the personal scheme by the Inland Revenue,[453] and tax relief on the employee's share,[454] without the employer being involved in the transaction. The rules of the scheme may nonetheless provide for the payment of additional contributions direct to the scheme by employee, employer or both; but very few employers make such additional contributions.[455]

The end result is very similar to that achieved by contracting out through a money purchase scheme, and much of the detailed legislation in this area relates equally to personal pensions and to COMPS too, with only minor modifications.[456] In particular, the payments made by the Inland Revenue to the scheme, known as 'minimum contributions', must be used, after deductions for administrative expenses and commission, to provide money purchase benefits.[457] These benefits and (unless the rules of the scheme provide otherwise) any other money purchase benefits provided by the scheme constitute the member's 'protected rights',[458] to which effect may be given in the same ways as to protected rights in COMPS.[459] With regard to pre-April 1997 pensionable service, the member's state pension is reduced by a notional GMP for any period during which minimum contributions are paid to a personal pension scheme. This operates in the same way as if he or she had been a member of a COMPS; and the effect on a widow's or widower's state pension is also the same.[460]

---

450 PSA 1993, s 50(1)(b) and SI 1996/1172, reg 45.
451 PSA 1993, s 32A. This is particularly useful if the member cannot be traced, as it avoids undue delay in winding up the original scheme: *Thomas and Dowrick* n 257, above, p 151.
452 The first personal pensions were made available in 1955 and in their early years were primarily associated with the self-employed: Nesbitt *British Pensions Policy Making in the 1980s* (1995) p 30.
453 PSA 1993, ss 43 and 45; see p 629, above.
454 Income and Corporation Taxes Act 1988, s 649.
455 Of all male full-time employees in the UK in 1991, 22 per cent had a personal pension without additional employer contributions; 3 per cent had a personal pension with additional contributions from both employer and employee; and 1 per cent had a personal pension with additional contributions from the employer only: CSO *General Household Survey* (1991) p 124. The new ONS *Living in Britain* (2002) does not provide as much detail, but there is no reason to believe that this position has changed.
456 PSA 1993, ss 26–33.
457 PSA 1993, ss 8(2), 31(3).
458 PSA 1993, s 10(3).
459 See p 637, above.
460 PSA 1993, s 48.

In order for the individual to qualify for minimum contributions, the scheme must be an 'appropriate personal scheme' chosen by the earner in question.[461] The earner's choice is revocable: it may be cancelled by notice to the Inland Revenue.[462] The pension can take a number of forms: an arrangement for issuing insurance policies or annuity contracts; an authorised unit trust scheme; or an arrangement for investing in a bank account or building society shares or deposits.[463] An 'appropriate' scheme is one for which an 'appropriate scheme certificate' issued by the Inland Revenue is currently in force[464] and which satisfies the requirements of sections 26 to 32 of PSA 1993 and associated regulations.[465] Even if these requirements are satisfied, the Revenue may withhold or cancel a certificate on the grounds that there are circumstances which make it inexpedient that the scheme should be, or continue to be, an appropriate scheme.[466] Any question as to whether and for what period a scheme is or was 'appropriate' is to be determined by the Revenue.[467] A certificate can have effect from the beginning of the tax year in which the application is received.[468]

When contributions to a personal pension scheme cease before pensionable age, the protected rights can be left in the scheme where they will continue to appreciate, under the revaluation provisions of PSA 1993.[469] Alternatively, the member has a right to a transfer payment on similar terms to a member of a COMPS.[470] It should be noted, however, that one of the advantages of personal pension schemes is their 'portability': an employee who changes jobs can simply continue to have minimum contributions paid to his or her chosen personal scheme.

B Taxation

The tax treatment of occupational schemes lies outside the scope of this book,[471] but some salient features should be noted as tax law is an important influence on the form schemes take and to some extent on their contents too. It also provides a large subsidy to pension provision as compared with other forms of savings.[472] Schemes which are 'approved' for tax purposes gain significant tax advantages: the fund is free from income tax and capital gains tax on its investments, the employer's contributions can be set off against corporation tax as trading expenses and the employee's contributions attract income tax relief. Once in payment, pension benefits are liable to income tax, but a lump sum paid to the member on retirement may be free of tax. To gain the 'exempt approval' needed to benefit from all these advantages, the scheme must be set up in the

---

461 PSA 1993, s 44.
462 PSA 1993, s 44(2); SI 1997/470, reg 11.
463 SI 1997/470, reg 2: those appropriate schemes which do not thereby come under various systems of investor protection set up under the Financial Services Act 1986 must provide separate guarantees of funds to meet protected rights: SI 1988/2238.
464 PSA 1993, s 7(4).
465 PSA 1993, s 9(5).
466 PSA 1993, s 34(5).
467 SI 1997/470, regs 2 and 5.
468 On the notice requirements which must be complied with in relation to appropriate schemes, see PSA 1993, s 44 and SI 1997/470, regs 10 and 11.
469 Ss 83–86: see pp 647–648, below.
470 PSA 1993, ss 93ff; SI 1996/1461. See p 638, above.
471 See Whitehouse *Revenue Law: Principles and Practice* (19th edn, 2001) App II; *Goode Report* n 84, above, para 2.3.2ff.
472 P 587, above.

form of an irrevocable trust[473] and must also provide benefits no greater than limits set by tax regulations. These limits are designed, for the most part, to avoid abuse of the tax exemptions which are provided for occupational schemes. For entrants after 1 June 1989, regulations currently specify a normal pension age between 60 and 75, limit the pension payable to two-thirds of final remuneration after 20 years' service or, for service of less than 20 years, one-thirtieth of remuneration for each year, and place a limit on the tax-free lump sum of 2.25 times the initial pension. Early retirement from the age of 50 is permitted, therefore, with a maximum pension of one-thirtieth of final remuneration for each year of service up to a maximum of two-thirds of the final salary. In addition, employees' contributions are limited to 15 per cent of salary.

A significant change was introduced by the Finance Act 1989.[474] This provided for differences in the tax treatment of occupational and personal pension schemes which had the effect of making personal schemes or unapproved occupational schemes significantly more attractive for higher income earners. For new schemes approved after July 1989 and for employees joining existing schemes from June 1989, an 'earnings cap' limits the level of the final salary on which occupational pensions may be calculated and on which employee contributions may be paid without giving rise to normal tax liability. The 'earnings cap' (£97,200 for 2002–03) rises with annual price inflation rather than with earnings, and so is set to affect increasing numbers of occupational scheme members.[475]

C Equal treatment

i The position before Barber

The application to occupational pension schemes of the principle of equality between male and female employees is part of a wider movement towards the implementation of equal treatment in social security and in employment law. SSA 1989 contained provisions designed to give effect to Council Directive (EEC) 86/378[476] on equal treatment for men and women in occupational pension schemes which were originally due to come into force on 1 January 1993, but which were overtaken by the *Barber* judgment of the European Court of Justice[477] and are still mostly not in force. [478] Schedule 5 to the 1989 Act establishes a general principle of equal treatment which prohibits both direct and indirect sex discrimination in occupational scheme rules and specifically requires schemes to provide for pension rights to continue accruing as normal during periods of paid maternity and family leave. However, the principle of equality is then made subject to a number of exceptions: in particular, it is specified that actuarial calculations may be used to justify different benefit rates in money purchase schemes, although this does not affect the separate rule that a COMP scheme is not permitted to set differential pension rates on the basis of the sex or marital status of members.[479] The 1989 Act also permits the setting of different contribution rates on

---

473 Income and Corporation Taxes Act 1988, s 592.
474 Amending the Income and Corporation Taxes Act 1988, s 590ff.
475 The implications of this and related changes to the taxation of lump sums in personal pension schemes are considered by Dilnot and Disney (1989) 10 Fiscal Studies 34.
476 (1986) OJ L225/40.
477 Case C-262/88 *Barber v Guardian Royal Exchange Assurance Group* [1991] 1 QB 344.
478 SSA 1989, s 23 and Sch 5; Davidson [1990] JSWL 310. The only provisions currently in force are those concerning the accrual of pension rights during periods of maternity and family leave: SI 1994/1661.
479 See p 637, above.

actuarial grounds up to 30 July 1999, and the setting of separate pensionable ages until such time as the state scheme is harmonised or a new Council Directive is passed to make equal pensionable ages mandatory.

ii   The decision in Barber

The European Court of Justice held in *Barber v Guardian Royal Exchange Assurance Group*[480] that the principle of equal treatment was already applicable to employer-based schemes as a result of the direct effect of article 119 of the EC Treaty (now article 141), which requires equality of pay for men and women employed on equal work. A pension paid by an employer is 'pay' within the extended definition in article 119, which refers to the 'wage or salary and any other consideration, whether in cash or in kind, which the worker receives, directly or indirectly, in respect of his employment from his employer'. Article 119 takes priority over both Council Directive (EEC) 86/378 and the SSA 1989, with the result that the exceptions to the principle of equality outlined in the Act – above all, the derogation for separate pensionable ages for men and women – were apparently void.[481] Thus the claimant was entitled to a pension on retirement on the same terms as if he had been a woman.

The major and, as it turned out, practically self-defeating limitation of the *Barber* decision, however, was the ruling that, in so far as it overrode the derogations in Council Directive (EEC) 86/378, it should not apply retroactively. The court limited the effect of article 119 on occupational schemes to claims already initiated and, in other cases, to 'acquisition of entitlement to a pension as from the date of this judgment', 17 May 1990. The reason for this 'non-retroactivity' was that member states and employers had reasonably assumed, by virtue of the derogations in Council Directive (EEC) 86/378, that article 119 was irrelevant to the question of pensions equality; under these circumstances 'overriding considerations of legal certainty preclude legal situations which have exhausted all their effects in the past from being called in question where that might upset retroactively the financial balance' of schemes constructed on this assumption.[482]

iii   Developments in the European Court of Justice case law since Barber

The full implications of the decision in *Barber* were worked through in a series of further references to the European Court of Justice.[483] These other cases led to Council Directive (EC) 96/97,[484] which amended Council Directive (EEC) 86/378 to reflect the court's jurisprudence. This has established that article 119 applies to a wide range of occupational pension benefits, including survivors' pensions (both widows' and widowers'), and to occupational pension schemes which are 'supplementary' or additional to state retirement pensions, as well as to schemes such as the one in *Barber*

---

480   Case C-262/88 [1991] 1 QB 344.
481   Curtin (1987) 24 CML Rev 215 and (1990) 27 CML Rev 475; Ward (1990) 32 EOR 40.
482   Case C-262/88 *Barber v Guardian Royal Exchange Assurance Group* [1991] 1 QB 344, para 44.
483   For detailed analysis see McCrudden *Equality of Treatment between Men and Women in Social Security* (1994); Whiteford (1995) 32 CML Rev 801; Luckhaus and Moffat *Serving the market and people's needs?* (1996); Moffat and Luckhaus (1998) 20 JSWFL 1; and Ellis *EC Sex Equality Law* (2nd edn, 1998) ch 2.
484   (1997) OJ L46/20.

which are 'contracted-out', that is, operate in partial substitution for the state pension.[485] However, the European Court of Justice also held that article 119 only applies to pension benefits arising by reference to service or employment after 17 May 1990.[486] Moreover, article 119 does not prohibit gender-based inequalities in employers' contributions in defined benefit or final salary schemes where these are apparently justified by actuarial factors.[487]

Perhaps the most pressing issue arising from *Barber* was the extent of non-retroactivity, given that the European Court of Justice's decision could have been interpreted in at least four different ways, with very different financial consequences.[488] Such was the concern generated in governmental circles that the member states took 'the unprecedented step of legislating directly on the matter'[489] by annexing the Barber Protocol to the EC Treaty as part of the Treaty of European Union signed at Maastricht. This stipulated that 'For the purposes of Article 119 of this Treaty benefits under occupational social security schemes shall not be considered as remuneration if and so far as they as they are attributable to periods of employment prior to 17 May 1990'. In *Ten Oever*[490] the court adopted the same interpretation, thereby avoiding a clash between the Protocol and the article it purported to clarify. Thus a male employee in a scheme setting a lower pensionable age for women (say, 60) could become entitled to a part of his pension at that age, the part-pension being referable to his service after 17 May 1990.[491]

In *Neath v Hugh Steeper*[492] the court held that unequal employers' contributions could be paid in respect of male and female employees on grounds related to actuarial factors. Because women, on average, live longer than men, some schemes provide for a higher rate of employer contribution to be made in the case of women employees or, alternatively, set a lower pension rate for women pensioners. The court accepted that employees' contributions are 'pay', at least where they are deducted from salary or wages[493], and that so are pension benefits (although subject to 'non-retroactivity' under *Barber*[494]), but then held that the requirement of equality in those two areas 'does not necessarily have to do with the funding arrangements chosen to secure the periodic payment of the pension, which thus remains outside the scope of application of article 119'.[495] Accordingly, 'the use of actuarial factors differing according to sex in funded defined-benefit occupational pension schemes' is not affected by the requirement of equal pay.[496]

In a related context, the European Court of Justice has ruled that article 119 is not infringed by the practice of paying differential rates of 'bridging pensions' to male and

485   Case C-109/91 *Ten Oever v Stichting Bedrijfspensioenfonds* [1993] IRLR 601; Case C-110/91 *Moroni v Firma Collo GmbH* [1993] ECR I-6591; Case C-200/91 *Coloroll Pension Trustees Ltd v Russell* [1995] All ER (EC) 23; Case C-7/93 *Beune* [1994] ECR I-4471.
486   Case C-109/91 *Ten Oever v Stichting Bedrijfspensioenfonds* [1993] IRLR 601; Case C-110/91 *Moroni v Firma Collo GmbH* [1993] ECR I-6591; Case C-152/91 *Neath v Hugh Steeper* [1993] ECR I-6935.
487   Case C-152/91 *Neath v Hugh Steeper* [1993] ECR I-6935.
488   See the 4th edition of this book, p 261.
489   *Ellis* n 483, above, p 78.
490   Case C-109/91 *Ten Oever v Stichting Bedrijfspensioenfonds* [1993] IRLR 601.
491   Nobles *Pensions, Employment and the Law* (1993) p 223.
492   Case C-152/91 [1993] ECR I-6935; applied in Case C-200/91 *Coloroll Pension Trustees Ltd v Russell* [1995] All ER (EC) 23.
493   Case 69/80 *Worringham v Lloyds Bank* [1981] ECR 767.
494   See p 642, above.
495   Case C-152/91 *Neath v Hugh Steeper* [1993] ECR I-6935, para 30.
496   Case C-152/91 *Neath v Hugh Steeper* [1993] ECR I-6935, para 34. By contrast, the use of actuarial factors in this context is contrary to the US Civil Rights Act 1964: *Los Angeles Department of Water and Power v Manhart* 435 US 702 (1978); *Arizona Governing Committee v Norris* 463 US 1073 (1983).

female employees taking early retirement before reaching the state pensionable age. Women normally receive a lower 'bridging pension' from the age of 60, when they become entitled to the state pension, than men aged 60 who do not become entitled to the state pension for a further five years. Because the occupational pension is 'pay' under *Barber* such a practice is arguably contrary to the equality principle, but the court ruled in *Roberts*[497] that since the purpose of the bridging pension was to place the employee in the same financial position once the state entitlement was taken into account, differential rates of payment which were the consequence of the separate pensionable ages for men and women in the state scheme could not be considered discriminatory. However, a court setting aside a discriminatory measure under article 119 can only level up, typically by applying to male employees the same advantageous conditions as applied to female employees.[498]

The European Court of Justice has also confirmed that article 119 applies to the right to join an occupational pension scheme. Moreover, the time limits contained in both the decision in *Barber* and in the Maastricht Protocol do not restrict that right, since equality of access to pension schemes is not one of the derogations allowed by Council Directive (EEC) 86/378.[499] This prompted some 60,000 part-time workers in the UK to bring proceedings in employment tribunals, claiming that they had been unlawfully excluded from membership of the relevant occupational pension schemes.[500]

iv Developments in domestic legislation and case law since Barber

The requirements of the European Court of Justice case law, discussed in the section immediately above, have been incorporated into domestic legislation by virtue of sections 62 to 66 of PA 1995. These provisions are modelled on the Equal Pay Act 1970; thus any 'occupational pension scheme which does not contain an equal treatment rule shall be treated as including one'.[501] An 'equal treatment rule' is one which relates to the terms on which persons become members of schemes and how members are treated.[502] Such a rule requires any discriminatory terms of a scheme to be 'treated as so modified as not to be less favourable'. It applies where women are employed on like work as, or work rated as equivalent with, or work of equal value to, that of men in the same employment.[503] The legislation permits various exceptions, notably where differential actuarial factors apply.[504] The procedural provisions for enforcing rights under the equal treatment rule are contained in regulations,[505] which adopted the same approach as the equal pay legislation. Thus the regulations imposed a two-year limitation on backdating claims, a restriction subsequently held by the European Court of Justice

---

497   Case C-132/92 *Birds Eye Walls Ltd v Roberts* [1993] ECR I-5579.
498   Case C-28/93 *Van den Akker v Stichting Shell Pensioenfonds* [1994] IRLR 616. See also Case C-408/92 *Smith v Avdel Systems Ltd* [1994] IRLR 602.
499   Case C-57/93 *Vroege v NCIV Instituut voor Volkshuisvestig BV* [1995] All ER (EC)193, [1994] ECR I-4541. A worker claiming retroactive membership cannot avoid paying contributions for the relevant period: Case C-128/93 *Fisscher v Voorhuis Hengelo BV* [1995] ICR 635, [1994] ECR I-4583.
500   Case C-78/98 *Preston v Wolverhampton Healthcare NHS Trust* [2000] ICR 961, para 17. See also Case 170/84 *Bilka-Kaufhaus GmbH v Weber von Hartz* [1986] ECR 1607 on part-time workers. See also SI 2000/1551 on part-timers' rights; and the critique by McColgan (2000) 29 ILJ 260.
501   PA 1995, s 62(1). For a critique of this approach, see McCrudden (1996) 25 ILJ 28.
502   PA 1995, s 62(2).
503   PA 1995, s 62(3).
504   PA 1995, s 64(3), thus applying Case C-152/91 *Neath v Hugh Steeper* [1993] ECR I-6935.
505   SI 1995/3183, superseding to similar effect SI 1976/142.

to be contrary to article 119.[506] The House of Lords, following the lead of the European court, subsequently held that the requirement that claims be submitted within six months of leaving a job was not incompatible with EU law as it did not render the enforcement of rights under article 119 impossible or excessively difficult.[507] However, where there was a 'stable employment relationship' characterised by a series of successive contracts of service, the six months period ran from then end of the last such contract. Furthermore, assuming a continuous employment relationship, a claim for retrospective membership on the basis of the equal treatment rule can be backdated to as far back as 8 April 1976, being the date of the landmark decision of the European Court of Justice in *Defrenne v Sabena*.[508]

D Occupational pensions and divorce

The family home and occupational pension rights are the two single assets of greatest value for most married couples.[509] Whilst the courts have demonstrated 'considerable judicial ingenuity' in devising techniques to balance the children's need for a secure home whilst protecting both spouses' investment in the property,[510] they have had less success with regard to pension rights. Yet the gendered reality of child-raising and home-making is that women often have less opportunity to build up their own pension entitlements.[511] Over the last decade there have been a number of legislative initiatives designed to provide a solution to this difficulty.[512]

First, PA 1995 introduced new provisions enabling the courts to reallocate the pension rights of divorcing spouses.[513] These amendments to the Matrimonial Causes Act 1973 require the courts to have regard to the rights under an occupational or personal pensions scheme which a spouse has, or is likely to have, or is likely to lose the chance of acquiring in the event of the dissolution of the marriage.[514] In addition, the court may order those responsible for the pension scheme to make payments for the benefit of a pensioner's spouse at the point when those payments fall due (ie on the pensioner's retirement). These powers are known as 'pension earmarking', but the approach of the higher courts has been cautious as regards their exercise and the provisions are little used in practice.[515]

Secondly, the principle of 'pension splitting' appeared on the face of the Family Law Act 1996, but this section (introduced against the wishes of the then government) was never brought into force, owing not least to technical difficulties.[516] The incoming

---

506 Case C-78/98 *Preston v Wolverhampton Healthcare NHS Trust* [2000] ICR 961.
507 *Preston v Wolverhampton Healthcare NHS Trust (No 2)* [2001] UKHL 5, [2001] ICR 217.
508 Case 43/75 [1976] ECR 455, where the European Court of Justice held that art 119 had direct effect. This assumes, of course, that the applicant pays their share of the relevant pension contributions.
509 Cretney and Masson *Principles of Family Law* (6th edn, 1997) p 490; see also *Brooks v Brooks* [1995] 2 FLR 13 at 15, per Lord Nicholls.
510 *Cretney and Masson* n 509, above, pp 490–491.
511 *Brooks v Brooks* [1995] 2 FLR 13 at 16, per Lord Nicholls. See further Kingsford Smith (2001) 64 MLR 519.
512 The discussion that follows is a summary only; see further Ellison and Rae *Family Breakdown and Pensions* (2nd edn, 2001).
513 PA 1995, s 166. See Dnes (1999) 21 JSWFL 41.
514 See generally the Matrimonial Causes Act 1973, ss 25B–25D.
515 *T v T (Financial Relief: pensions)* [1998] 1 FLR 1072; and *Burrow v Burrow* [1999] 1 FLR 508: see Bird [2000] 30 Fam Law 455.
516 Family Law Act 1996, s 16.

Labour government published its proposals for 'pension sharing' in 1998[517] and these were enacted in WRPA 1999.[518] Under the pension sharing provisions the court may apportion a pension at the time of divorce so that one spouse either becomes a member of the other spouse's pension scheme in her own right or takes a transfer of a designated percentage amount into their own pension scheme.[519] Pension sharing is thus fundamentally different from pension earmarking in that the spouse in question acquires an independent right to the future payment of the pension, rather than one conditional upon the pensioner's circumstances. The new provisions, again involving amendments to the Matrimonial Causes Act 1973, carry with them no presumption of equal sharing; the court is free to determine whatever percentage share it deems appropriate in the circumstances. Courts may thus make a pension sharing order, which has the effect of making the member's pension rights subject to a 'pension debit' at the same time as his or her ex-spouse gains the benefit of a 'pension credit' of a corresponding value.[520] These powers are only available to petitions for divorce (or nullity) issued after 1 December 2000.[521] As well as applying to rights under occupational and personal pension schemes, pension sharing also applies to the additional (but not the basic) state retirement pension.[522]

E   Occupational pension protection

The legal framework of occupational pension provision is essentially derived from trust law. The contracting-out requirements of PSA 1993 impose a minimum floor of benefits which are only partially designed to ensure protection of members' expectations; they are also meant to minimise the burden on SERPS and now the S2P. SERPS bears a residual liability in cases where a contracted-out scheme fails to match the state additional pension, albeit mainly confined to the GMP.[523] The tax regulations are even less concerned with members' vested rights, being aimed largely at avoiding too great a loss of revenue to the Exchequer by limiting employers' use of the various tax exemptions. Trust law is inherently flexible from the employer's point of view, providing the employer with an open-ended discretion in setting the terms of the trust deed which in turn governs the appointment of trustees, determines their powers and establishes levels of funding and the form and extent of benefits (including, most importantly, how to dispose of accrued surpluses in pension funds).[524] Although trust law imposes strict fiduciary duties upon trustees relating to the exercise of their powers once the trust is set up, the content of these duties can be limited by appropriate wording in the trust deed.[525] It is not legislation so much as the scheme rules, the 'balance of power' between

---

517   DSS *Pension sharing on divorce: reforming pensions for a fairer future* (1998, Cm 3345).
518   WRPA 1999, Pts III and IV. For a detailed analysis, see Salter [2000] 30 Fam Law 489 at 543 and 914.
519   The parties may also agree on an apportionment in a 'qualifying agreement' within WRPA 1999, s 28(1)(b) and (c) and (2).
520   WRPA 1999, s 29; and see further SI 2000/1123.
521   WRPA 1999, s 85(3)(a) and SI 2000/1116.
522   P 619, above.
523   See pp 632–636, above. The anti-franking provisions of PSA 1993, ss 87–92 indirectly protect additional benefits by preventing their use to fund increases in the GMP, but they do not stipulate the level at which those additional benefits must be set nor do they provide mechanisms for their preservation or protection in the event of employer insolvency, for example.
524   *Air Jamaica Ltd v Charlton* [1999] 1 WLR 1399; *National Grid plc v Mayes* [2001] UKHL 20, [2001] 1 WLR 864.
525   See *Nobles*, n 490 above, ch 1; and on the relationship between trustees' fiduciary duties and their investment powers, *Cowan v Scargill* [1985] Ch 270.

the employer and the trustees[526] and, to a limited extent, the practices of the actuarial profession, which determine the level of funding of schemes and hence the degree of security which, in the long run, they offer their members.[527] The basic trust law structure of occupational schemes has nevertheless been subject to an incremental but still partial process of protective regulation through statute.

However, even before most of the protective provisions of SSA 1990 could be brought into force, the shortcomings of pension protection were highlighted by the depletion through fraud of the Mirror Group pension funds. This prompted the House of Commons Select Committee on Social Security to put forward a far-reaching programme of reforms, arguing that it is an 'error of major importance' to rely on trust law, with only limited statutory modifications, as the basis for occupational pension provision.[528] The government's response was to set up a Pensions Law Review Committee chaired by Professor Roy Goode, which reported in September 1993. The Report[529] concluded that 'trust law in itself is broadly satisfactory and should continue to provide the foundation for interests, rights and duties arising in relation to pension schemes'.[530] It proposed a limited set of reforms aimed at codifying the relevant principles of trust and employment law as they apply to the pension promise of the employer and adding some new protections for members, including minimum solvency requirements for schemes,[531] the right to appoint a minority of trustees in earnings-related schemes and a majority in money purchase schemes,[532] and the establishment of a compensation fund designed to meet 90 per cent of members' accrued rights in the event of employer dishonesty in dealings with pension scheme assets (the failure of a scheme merely through employer insolvency would not be covered).[533] A stronger monitoring role for scheme actuaries and auditors was envisaged together with an enlarged role for a Pensions Regulator, to replace the Occupational Pensions Board. Although the Report recommended the imposition of some additional restraints on employer withdrawals from scheme surpluses, it upheld the employer's freedom on setting up the scheme to reserve the right to close, freeze or wind it up and to refuse increases and suspend contributions. PA 1995 implemented some of the Report's recommendations; further changes have followed with CSPSSA 2000.

i Early leavers: non-discrimination and revaluation

Protective legislation is designed in part to protect the rights of early leavers, adding to the legislation on contracting-out which seeks to ensure the maintenance of the GMP so far as accrued SERPS rights are concerned.[534] SSA 1973 introduced legislation for the preservation of the deferred pension of employees who leave a scheme before reaching pensionable age and SSA 1985 provided for the revaluation of the deferred pension in line with inflation in respect of benefits accruing after 1 January 1985. SSA 1990 extended revaluation to all benefits in respect of employees changing schemes

---

526 *National Grid plc v Mayes* [2001] UKHL 20, [2001] 1 WLR 864 (see Lord Hoffmann at 869F).
527 *Nobles* n 491, above, p 22.
528 *The Operation of Pension Funds* (1991–92, HC 61-II).
529 *Goode Report* n 84, above; Nobles (1994) 23 ILJ 69.
530 *Goode Report* n 84, above, para 1.2.1.
531 *Goode Report* n 84, above, para 4.4.19.
532 *Goode Report* n 84, above, para 4.5.40.
533 *Goode Report* n 84, above, para 4.11.26.
534 See pp 632–636, above.

after 1 January 1991. This legislation has now been consolidated in PSA 1993.[535] The preserved pension (known as 'short service benefit') must be offered to early leavers, defined as those with at least two years' qualifying service,[536] on the same basis as to those who remain in the scheme.[537] In final salary schemes the deferred pension must be revalued annually by at least the rate of price inflation up to a maximum of 5 per cent from the date of leaving until the member reaches pensionable age under the terms of the scheme;[538] separate provision is made for schemes which offer pensions on an average salary or flat-rate basis,[539] and for money purchase schemes.[540]

ii Protection of accrued rights and pensions in payment

A second area of legislation, originating in SSA 1990,[541] aims to provide protection for the rights of pension scheme members in the event of a scheme winding up following the insolvency of the employer. It also seeks to provide a degree of inflation-proofing for pensions in payment, a particular concern in the context of company mergers and takeovers. Initially the only protection against inflation was that conferred by the legislation concerning the GMP in contracted-out schemes and, indirectly, by the floor of minimum entitlement set by SERPS. 'Limited price indexation' applies only in respect of pensionable service after the coming into force of PSA 1993.[542] The form of this indexation was amended by PA 1995. All pension schemes which are approved by the Inland Revenue (and are not public sector pension schemes[543]) must increase pensions annually at the appropriate percentage.[544] This is defined as the increase in the Retail Price Index up to a maximum of 5 per cent.[545] Money purchase schemes are covered by this requirement, unlike under the original 1993 legislation.[546] Those who take (very) early retirement do not gain the immediate benefit of these provisions. Thus where a member is aged under 55 and in receipt of a pension, the statutory increase is not required. However, once the individual reaches 55, the pension must then be paid at the rate it would have been paid had those annual indexation increases applied.[547] If the pension fund trustees or scheme manager increase pensions over and above the rate required by statute, they may offset any such excess increase from any increase that they would be required to make in the following tax year.[548] Where a scheme is found to be in surplus upon a winding up the return of any such surplus to an employer is conditional upon implementing limited price indexation.[549] These are isolated instances

535   PSA 1993, ss 69–82 (preservation), 83–86 (revaluation); SI 1991/167.
536   PSA 1993, s 71(1)(a); on the meaning of two years' 'qualifying service' in this context, see s 71(7).
537   PSA 1993, s 72(1). This principle is further developed in ss 73–86 of the Act.
538   PSA 1993, s 84(1) and Sch 3, paras 1–2; see eg SI 2001/3690.
539   PSA 1993, s 84(2), Sch 3, paras 3, 4.
540   PSA 1993, s 84(3), Sch 3, para 5.
541   Following the Occupational Pensions Board's report *Protecting Pensions: Safeguarding Benefits in a Changing Environment* (1989, Cm 573).
542   7 February 1994: SI 1994/86.
543   And so covered by the Pensions (Increase) Act 1971.
544   PA 1995, s 51.
545   PA 1995, s 54(3) and PSA 1993, Sch 3 para 2. The indexation requirement does not apply to pension payments derived from voluntary contributions: PA 1995, s 51(6).
546   PA 1995, s 51(2).
547   PA 1995, s 52. There is an exception for disability pensions.
548   PA 1995, s 53. For criticism of this provision, see *Thomas and Dowrick* n 257, above, pp 135–136.
549   PA 1995, ss 76 and 77.

of statutory intervention in the problematic area of rights over scheme surpluses, to which trust law has so far given an unclear answer.[550]

In addition, any deficit upon the winding up of a final salary scheme is deemed a debt due from the employer,[551] and in the event of the employer's insolvency PA 1995 requires the appointment of an independent trustee.[552] The legislation does not specify, however, the manner in which the independent trustee should exercise his or her powers; nor is there a requirement for an independent trustee to be appointed at any time other than insolvency.[553] The Act also sets out to place limits on the practice of 'self-investment' whereby a scheme invests its assets in the employer's own business.[554] These developments are to some extent mirrored in common law decisions which have required employers to take into account the interests of members and employees when exercising fiduciary powers under trust deeds, for example in questions concerning funding and payment, and to provide information to employees about their rights under pension schemes. This notion of the 'duty to act in good faith' is derived from the law of the contract of employment and is based upon the observation that scheme members are not volunteers but provide consideration for their benefits in the form of service.[555]

iii The minimum funding requirement

The Maxwell scandal demonstrated the importance of ensuring that pension schemes are adequately funded and that mechanisms are in place to identify and correct any deficiencies. PA 1995 sought to achieve this by imposing a solvency test, the minimum funding requirement (MFR), on salary-related occupational pension schemes.[556] The MFR is meant to ensure that the value of the assets of the scheme is not less than the amount of the scheme's liabilities. The trustees or managers of an occupational pension scheme must therefore arrange for periodic actuarial valuations in accordance with the methods of valuation stipulated by regulations.[557] If the value of the scheme assets falls below 90 per cent of the scheme's liabilities, steps must be taken to rectify the shortfall.[558] The 'one size fits all' MFR regime was regarded as unhelpful by the pensions industry and in 2001 the government announced its intention to replace the MFR with a long-term scheme-specific funding standard, based on the scheme's own liability structure rather than a purely external benchmark.[559] As an interim measure, a package of amendments was introduced in 2002 (eg removing the requirement for annual re-certification of schemes which are fully funded on the MFR test).[560]

---

550 See Nobles *Pensions, Employment and the Law* (1993) ch 7; Mesher [1993] CLP 96.
551 PA 1995, s 75; SI 1996/3128.
552 PA 1995, ss 22–25 and SI 1997/252.
553 Nobles (1990) 19 ILJ 255.
554 PA 1995, s 40; SI 1992/246.
555 The leading authority is the judgment of Browne-Wilkinson VC in *Imperial Group Pension Trust Ltd v Imperial Tobacco Ltd* [1991] 2 All ER 597, [1991] 1 WLR 589, Nobles (1991) 20 ILJ 130; see also the cases discussed by *Mesher* n 550, above, and *Nobles* n 550, above, ch 4.
556 PA 1995, s 56. By definition COMPS do not require such underpinning.
557 PA 1995, ss 56(3), 57 and SI 1996/1536.
558 PA 1995, s 60. If the necessary steps are not taken, both OPRA and the scheme's members must be informed: s 60(4). If no such notification is made, the scheme's trustees may be liable to prohibition orders and the trustees and managers to civil penalties: s 60(8). Any shortfall is treated as a debt due from the employer: s 60(5).
559 DSS/HM Treasury *Security for Occupational Pensions: The Government's Proposals* (2001) and *The Minimum Funding Requirement: the next stage of reform* (2001).
560 SI 2002/380.

iv   The regulation of occupational pension schemes

A   THE OCCUPATIONAL PENSIONS REGULATORY AUTHORITY

The Occupational Pensions Regulatory Authority (OPRA), established by PA 1995, is based on the concept of a Pensions Regulator advocated by the Goode Report, although its powers are less extensive than those recommended by that Committee. The members of OPRA are appointed by the Secretary of State.[561] OPRA's powers include prohibiting or suspending individuals from acting as trustees of pension schemes and appointing trustees.[562] OPRA has assumed some of the functions of the former Occupational Pensions Board (OPB),[563] eg with regard to winding up schemes[564] and as Registrar of the Register of Occupational and Personal Pension Schemes.[565] The Register is limited in its scope to providing basic information about the companies responsible for such schemes.[566] OPRA has the power to review its own decisions and there is an appeal on a point of law from its decisions to the High Court.[567] The main criticism of OPRA's role is that fundamentally it operates as a long-stop; it has extensive powers to act once called in, but its involvement depends on actuaries, auditors, trustees and others reporting their concerns.[568] There are also limitations on those matters which it can investigate; eg it has no authority to investigate any alleged breach of trusts law.[569]

B   THE PENSIONS OMBUDSMAN[570]

Disputes over pensions schemes have proved fertile ground for litigation in the courts, drawing on and developing the common law principles of the law of trusts. However, it is widely recognised that this may not always be the most cost-effective means of resolving such disputes. A number of alternative mechanisms are available. First, occupational pension schemes must have internal dispute resolution procedures in place.[571] Secondly, complaints may be referred to the Occupational Pensions Advisory Service (OPAS).[572] Thirdly, and most importantly, the Pensions Ombudsman, originally established under SSA 1990, has the authority to investigate and determine complaints arising from both occupational and personal pension schemes.[573] The powers of the

---

561   PA 1995, s 1 and Sch 1. See further *Thomas and Dowrick* n 257, above, pp 7–11.
562   PA 1995, ss 3–15. OPRA must also produce an annual report (s 2). On OPRA's powers as regards both the gathering and disclosure of information, see ss 104–114.
563   The OPB was dissolved by PA 1995, s 150.
564   The PA 1995 vested OPRA with broader powers on winding up than had been enjoyed by the OPB; these have been extended further by CSPSSA 2000, ss 47–50. See also SI 2002/459.
565   PSA 1993, s 6; SI 1997/371.
566   The Act also provides for disclosure of information: PSA 1993, s 113, expanded by CSPSSA 2000, s 52; SI 1996/1655 (occupational schemes); SI 1987/1110 (personal schemes); and SI 2002/1383.
567   PA 1995, ss 96 and 97.
568   *Nobles* n 376, above, at 254–255 and *Thomas and Dowrick* n 257, above, pp 10–11.
569   *Nobles* n 376, above, at 255.
570   See generally DSS *Pensions Ombudsman Quinquennial Review 1999/2000* (2000).
571   PA 1995, s 50 and SI 1996/1270. In practice these resolve over 90 per cent of inquiries: Dundon-Smith et al *Pension Scheme Inquiries and Disputes* DSS Research Report No 66 (1997).
572   OPAS provides information and assistance regarding occupational pensions schemes but has no legal powers, but the Pensions Ombudsman expects individuals to have taken up their complaint with the scheme itself and then with OPAS.
573   PSA 1993, ss 145–152, significantly amended by PA 1995, ss 156–159 and CSPSSA 2000, ss 53 and 54; SI 1995/1053.

Ombudsman are much closer to the model of a tribunal (the recommendation of the former OPB in their report *Protecting Pensions*[574]) than the title would suggest.[575] An appeal on points of law from a determination of the Ombudsman lies to the High Court; the Ombudsman has no jurisdiction in cases where court proceedings have already commenced.[576] Notwithstanding the intention behind establishing the office of the Pensions Ombudsman, there is now an extensive body of case law which has demonstrated 'the clear clash of cultures between the informal nature of the procedures operated by the Ombudsman and the approach of the courts to similar disputes'.[577]

C THE PENSIONS COMPENSATION BOARD

In the wake of the Maxwell scandal, PA 1995 established the Pensions Compensation Board (PCB), the members of which are appointed by the Secretary of State.[578] The PCB has the power to pay compensation to a scheme's trustees where the employer is insolvent, the value of the scheme's assets has been reduced and 'there are reasonable grounds for believing that the reduction was attributable to an act or omission constituting a prescribed offence'.[579] In addition, the value of the scheme's assets must be less than the aggregate of 100 per cent of its liabilities to pensioners and those within ten years of retirement (in the case of a COSRS) and 90 per cent of the liabilities to other active members.[580] It must also be 'reasonable in all the circumstances' that scheme members should be so assisted.[581] The amount of compensation is limited to the amount required to bring the fund's assets back to this level.[582] Compensation payments are funded by a levy on occupational pension schemes generally.[583]

---

574 See p 648, above.
575 See Harris (citing Farrand) in Harris and Partington (eds) *Administrative Justice in the 21st Century* (1999) pp 137–141.
576 PSA 1993, ss 146(6) and 151(4).
577 Harvey *Encylopedia* § [B] 1148; see also Nobles (2000) 29 ILJ 243. See further *Edge v Pensions Ombudsman* [2000] Ch 602, [1999] 4 All ER 546, and the subsequent amendments by CSPSSA 2000, s 54.
578 PA 1995 s 78. The PCB consists of not less than three such members. On information-gathering powers, see ss 110–114.
579 PA, s 81(1)(a)–(c). A 'prescribed offence' is any offence involving dishonesty: SI 1997/665, reg 3.
580 PA 1995, s 81(1)(d). This 'protection level' was amended by WRPA 1999, s 17.
581 PA 1995, s 81(1)(e).
582 PA 1995, s 83. On time limits for applications, see s 82.
583 PSA 1993, s 175(4) and SI 1997/666. For a critique of the PCB provisions, see *Thomas and Dowrick* n 257, ch 4.

Chapter 18

Child benefit

Part 1 Introduction

A General

Family benefits do not fit neatly into the traditional systems and functions of social security.[1] Traditionally the care of children has been seen as a private matter and so outside the usual categories of risk covered by social insurance. Equally, unlike means-tested schemes, family benefits are as much concerned with horizontal equity (between those who care for children and those who do not) as vertical equity (the relief of poverty). As a result, family provision has developed on the periphery of the mainstream social security schemes which are primarily concerned with basic income maintenance. As universal benefits funded by general taxation, family allowances (1945–77) and child benefit (from 1977) also suffered from Treasury neglect for most of the last half century. Thus family allowances were rarely up-rated with rising living standards and did not appear to be regarded as significant benefits. The Child Benefit Act 1975 (CBA 1975) replaced family allowances in a new scheme, integrating them with the more valuable income tax allowances for children. Lower income families, not paying tax, had, of course, not been able to take advantage of the latter. So the change to child benefit was designed to provide a more generous benefit for all families with children, while the tax allowances which had disproportionately benefited higher income groups were withdrawn.[2]

Child benefit performs a number of important functions in the context of the three strategic goals identified by Barr and Coulter for cash benefits generally: income support, the reduction of inequality and social integration.[3] Although not principally concerned with income maintenance, child benefit redistributes income over the life-cycle and, being a non-means tested benefit, avoids the dangers of the poverty trap. It also goes some way to reducing inequality by redistributing resources to those who care for children. Its greatest strength is perhaps in terms of social integration. The criteria for entitlement to child benefit (responsibility for children) are largely unrelated to socio-

---

1   See Bieback (1992) 2 J Eur Soc Pol 239, to which this discussion is indebted. For a recent comparative study, see Battle and Mendelson (eds) *Benefits for Children: A Four Country Study* (2001).
2   On the political background to this reform, see Field *Poverty and Politics* (1982).
3   Barr and Coulter in Hills (ed) *The State of Welfare* (1990) ch 7.

economic status and the claiming process is non-stigmatising, as shown by the very high take-up rate.[4] Yet the very success of child benefit is also its central weakness, as it is open to the criticism that it fails to 'target' assistance where it is most needed. In large part this explains the thinking behind the Tax Credits Act 2002 (TCA 2002), which preserves child benefit as a universal benefit but places greater emphasis on the new means-tested child tax credit.

In this Part of the chapter, there is first a short outline of the history of family allowances, and then an examination of the reasons that led to their replacement by child benefit. The principal policy questions concerning the child benefits scheme are discussed further. In Part 2 of the chapter, the legal conditions for entitlement to the benefit are analysed.

B The history of family allowances[5]

The first proposal to introduce a special allowance for the benefit of children was made in 1796 by William Pitt, then Chancellor of the Exchequer. But the Bill in question never became law, because of the pressure of other business. It seems that the issue was not discussed widely again until after the First World War, when Eleanor Rathbone founded the Family Endowment Society, an important pressure group in the inter-war years. In her book, *The Disinherited Family*, published in 1924, she argued that it was in the interest of society as a whole to ensure that children were well clothed and fed, and that a state allowance should be paid to make this possible. The case for such a payment took on additional strength from the fact that in 1921 and 1922 dependants' allowances were introduced for the unemployed. The absence of any comparable provision for those in work might have been viewed as a disincentive to employment. But, unlike other European countries, there was no move at this time to introduce family allowances in Great Britain.[6]

The introduction of the Family Allowances Bill in 1945, during the last months of the war-time Coalition government, was largely influenced by the Beveridge Report.[7] This adduced three principal arguments for the payment of family allowances. First, the only way of guaranteeing a reasonable subsistence income for all families, whether the head of the family was in work or not, was to pay an allowance for children; this object could not be secured by wages, as they did not take account of family size.[8] Secondly, 'it is dangerous to allow benefit during unemployment or disability to equal or exceed earnings during work. But, without allowances for children, during earning and not earning alike, this danger cannot be avoided'.[9] The third argument seems surprising today: the provision of family allowances was thought conducive to a higher birth rate.[10] The Beveridge Report further argued that payments should be financed by

---

4 Take-up is thought to be close to 100 per cent: Department of Social Security (DSS) *Social Security Departmental Report* (Cm 3213, 1996) p 17.

5 See Walley *Social Security: Another British Failure?* (1972) pp 16–20, 54–55, 70–73; Land in (1966) 2 Poverty 13; Hall, Land, Parker and Webb *Change, Choice and Conflict in Social Policy* (1975) ch 9; Macnicol *The Movement for Family Allowances 1918–45* (1980); Brown *Children in Social Security* (1985) PSI Studies of the Social Security System No 3, pp 27–38.

6 In the inter-war years family allowances were introduced in France, Germany and the Netherlands. New Zealand had been the first country to introduce such a scheme – in 1926.

7 Beveridge Report *Social Insurance and Allied Services* (1942, Cmd 6404).

8 *Beveridge Report* n 7, above, para 411.

9 *Beveridge Report* n 7, above, para 412.

10 *Beveridge Report* n 7, above, paras 15 and 413. Churchill gave particular emphasis to this point when he announced the Coalition government's acceptance of Beveridge's proposals in a broadcast in 1943.

general taxation, so that the whole community should share in the task of maintaining children. But parents were not to be relieved of their entire responsibility, and for this reason it was recommended that nothing should be paid for the first child in a family.[11] Lastly, the Report rejected the argument that the allowance for each child should be reduced as the size of the family increased; there were no real economies of scale when this occurred. A flat rate payment of 8 shillings [40 pence] was proposed, though Beveridge indicated that at some future time consideration should be given to grading allowances according to the children's age.[12]

The government modified the scheme proposed by Beveridge in some minor respects. The most important change was that a substantial part of the allowance was to be paid in kind through the provision of free school meals and milk. This reduced the cash payment to 5 shillings [25 pence] a week, which the government proposed should belong to the father. But on a free vote Miss Rathbone's amendment to make allowances the property of the mother was passed. As the title of the Act and the name of the benefit suggested, the allowance was to be paid to families 'for the benefit of the family as a whole'.[13] The claimant was required to show that the family contained at least two children.

The rate of payment was increased only twice between 1948 and 1967.[14] The Labour government did increase the allowance twice in 1968, but only for the benefit of those too poor to pay any income tax. In order to prevent taxpayers benefiting from the increases, an equivalent sum was 'clawed back' from them by a reduction in the value of their children's tax allowances.[15] The device had originally been suggested in the Beveridge Report, and signalled the new approach which led to CBA 1975.

C The change to child benefit

The change to child benefit cannot be understood without reference to the role of child income tax allowances, because their abolition was a crucial aspect of the new scheme. They were first introduced by William Pitt two years after his unsuccessful attempt to provide a family benefit. But they were abolished in 1806, and were not reintroduced until 1909. From 1957 their value was graduated according to the child's age, a significant difference from family allowances. Unlike the latter, child tax allowances (CTA) could be claimed in respect of the first child. Two further points may be made. First, CTA benefited high earners proportionately more than those on an average income, because they reduced taxable income, and so enabled the former group to pay tax at a lower rate. Secondly, since tax is normally deducted at source through PAYE, CTA typically benefited the male wage-earner rather than the child's mother.

Towards the end of the 1960s a number of schemes were suggested for integrating family allowances and tax allowances.[16] The Labour party put forward proposals in 1969; then the Conservative government, which took office the following year,

---

11 *Beveridge Report* n 7, above, para 417. See Harris *William Beveridge* (rev edn, 1997) pp 403–404.
12 *Beveridge Report* n 7, above, para 421. The argument on the appropriate rates for paying benefit still continues: see pp 657–658, below.
13 Family Allowances Act 1945, s 1 (FAA 1945), repeated in FAA 1965, s 1.
14 Brown *Child Benefit: Investing in the Future* (1988) p 56. On the reasons for the neglect of family allowances throughout this period, see the 3rd edition of this book, p 389. For statistics, see Hemming *Poverty and Incentives* (1984) p 29.
15 For the 'claw-back', see Kincaid *Poverty and Equality in Great Britain* (1973) pp 69–73.
16 See George *Social Security: Beveridge and After* (1968) pp 196–197; *Walley* n 5, above, pp 193–194; *Brown* n 5, above, pp 52–62.

recommended their integration as part of a tax credit system.[17] Although the 1974 Labour government was not in favour of this radical reform, it did support a child endowment scheme which had much in common with the tax credit proposal so far as it applied to children. Thus the Child Benefit Bill, introduced in May 1975, enjoyed all party support, and the opposition was only concerned to amend the measure in detail. Its purpose was well summarised by Mrs Castle, the Secretary of State for Social Services:

> It achieves a long overdue merger between child tax allowances and family allowances into a new universal, non-means tested, tax-free cash benefit for all children, including the first, payable to the mother. In this way it ensures that the nation's provision for family support is concentrated first and foremost where it is needed most – on the poorest families; and that it goes to the person responsible for caring for the children and managing the budget for their food, clothing and other necessities.[18]

The advantages of child benefit over its predecessors are therefore at least twofold. First, it can be paid to all families, whereas families not in receipt of taxable income had not been able to take advantage of CTA. Secondly, unlike the allowance, it is payable for the first child.[19] One important feature is that the benefit is tax free (so far),[20] in this respect differing from the original tax credits for children proposed by the Conservatives and from family allowances. Another is that the benefit is paid to the mother. This had also been the case with the allowance, but some of the early tax credit proposals would have entailed award of the credit to the father.[21]

The actual implementation of the child benefit scheme was by no means trouble-free. In the face of economic and political difficulties, the Labour government appeared to be about to renege on a commitment to introduce child benefit in 1977. Secret Cabinet minutes relating to this volte-face were leaked to the press, and the decision to implement the scheme on schedule was subsequently approved.[22]

D The early years of child benefit

CBA 1975 contained powers for the government to prescribe different rates in relation to different cases, either by reference to the child's age or to other factors.[23] These powers were used immediately to prescribe a higher rate for single-parent families. Child benefit proper became payable from 1977, and the new scheme finally became effective in 1980 with the end of the CTA, which had been phased out gradually over the preceding three years. The level of child benefit has been a matter of intense political controversy ever since. From the start there have been criticisms that the level of benefit is too low, and that there is now less financial support for families with two or more children compared with the previous arrangements. In contrast to many other benefits, there has never been any duty to up-rate child benefit, even when there has been a sharp

---

17 P 34, above.
18 892 HC Official Report (5th series) col 330.
19 Therefore the number of recipients almost doubled with the change to child benefit: *Barr and Coulter*, n 3, above, p 290.
20 See HC Social Security Committee *Fourth Report* (1998–99, HC 114).
21 Eg the Conservative government's Green Paper *Proposals for a Tax-Credit System* (1972, Cmnd 5116).
22 See Field *Poverty and Politics* (1984), esp chs 3, 7 and 10; and McCarthy *Campaigning for the Poor* (1986) ch 11.
23 CBA 1975, s 5; now the Social Security Contributions and Benefits Act 1992, s 145 (SSCBA 1992).

increase in the cost of living.[24] While resisting attempts to link the value of the benefit to price movements, the government did insert an amendment to the 1975 Bill which required the Secretary of State to consider annually whether the rates should be increased.[25] The Conservative government in 1980 also committed itself to maintaining the value of the benefit in line with inflation,[26] but this pledge was not honoured.

The reason for this relative decline in the benefit's value was that during the 1980s the government decided to target financial assistance to help families with low incomes. At first this was brought about by the award of higher amounts of family income supplement for older children and of more generous needs allowances for children under the housing benefits scheme. The 1985 Green Paper[27] then proposed the introduction of family credit, which came into effect in April 1988, as the most effective method of achieving the aim. It rejected the alternative solution of reforming child benefit. Three principal possibilities were canvassed. The first, that favoured by many pressure groups, and in particular CPAG, was a substantial increase in the level of the benefit. This was rejected because of its expense, and further because assistance would also be provided for many families who would not need it. This consequence would not occur under the second alternative: the taxation of child benefit, coupled with its more generous provision. A variant on this proposal would be to abolish the married man's tax allowance and increase radically the level of benefit, a change which would benefit women at the expense of men.[28] These ideas, however, ran counter to the government's general commitment to reducing the level of income tax, and it was not surprising that they were robustly rejected.[29] Finally, the Green Paper considered whether it would be better to adopt a different structure for the benefit, perhaps along the lines followed in some other European countries, where more is paid for older children or larger families. This solution was dismissed as an ineffective and administratively expensive method for steering help where it was most needed.

The then Conservative government's perspective, as revealed in the Green Paper, was that the primary function of child benefit was to recognise, and provide some help towards meeting, the costs of bringing up children. Its purpose was not to assist the needy or, in alliance with the tax system, to act as a general redistributive device. One or two bodies, such as the Institute of Directors and the Institute of Fiscal Studies, have questioned whether the benefit has any place in a social security system which, in their view, should be directed entirely to meet the needs of those with low or no income.[30] This crude perspective ignores the existence of other non means-tested benefits, such as retirement pensions, and other aspects of the child benefit scheme. To a limited extent child benefit does act as a redistributive device: from families without children to those with, and from men to women.[31] For some commentators, eg feminists, these are central features of the scheme.[32] Such arguments were not considered sufficiently

---

24   See pp 265–267, above.
25   CBA 1975, s 5(5).
26   989 HC Official Report (5th series) col 1063.
27   Green Paper *Reform of Social Security* (1985, Cmnd 9518) vol 2, paras 4.28–4.44.
28   See *The Structure of Personal Income Taxation and Income Support* 3rd Special Report of the Treasury and Civil Service Committee for 1982–83 (1983, HC 386) ch 12; Berthoud and Ermisch *Reshaping Benefits: The Political Arithmetic* (1985) PSI Studies of the Social Security System No 10, pp 96–105; *Brown* n 14, above, pp 64–65; Hills *Changing Tax* (1988) pp 30–32 and 52–55.
29   The Labour government elected in 1997 proceeded to abolish the married couple's tax allowance and to increase the rate of child benefit: see p 659, below.
30   (1984–85) 59 Poverty 28 and 39 and (1988) 69 Poverty 14–15; see also Dilnot, Kay and Morris *The Reform of Social Security* (1984) pp 122–123.
31   On the distribution of income within families, see Pahl *Money and Marriage* (1989) and Smith in Smith (ed) *Economic Policy and the Division of Income within the Family* (1991) ch 1.
32   See essay by David and Land *Sex and Social Policy* in Glennester (ed) *The Future of the Welfare State* (1983); *Brown* n 14, above, p 53.

weighty in the 1980s to persuade government to increase the benefit to a level where it even began to meet the real costs of bringing up children. Indeed, in the mid-1980s it appeared as though child benefit might be allowed to 'wither on the vine' before being abolished in the same way as the death grant and maternity grant. Thus in 1986 Parliament repealed the statutory duty to consider an increase in rates. But two years later the government, following the outcry at its failure to increase the rate of benefit, was forced by the House of Lords to accept an obligation to review its level each April, 'taking account of increases in the Retail Price Index and other relevant external factors'.[33] Yet this provision was never brought into force[34] and there was no increase at all to the ordinary rate of child (as distinct from one-parent) benefit between 1988 and 1991, a decision which attracted the fury of the opposition parties and many Conservatives.[35] They argued in particular that the benefit should be up-rated as much as income tax allowances.

E Differential rates of child benefit

A modest improvement in the fortunes of child benefit coincided with the fall from power of Mrs Thatcher. Shortly before her resignation in November 1990, it was announced that a higher rate of child benefit would be payable for the first eligible child. The arguments in favour of differential rates of child benefit have always been finely balanced. There is certainly evidence that the costs of providing for children vary considerably with their age, older children requiring much greater expenditure on food and clothing.[36] The 1975 administration, however, was not persuaded as to the strength of this case[37] and the 1985 Green Paper expressly rejected a higher rate for the first child as being an inefficient means of reaching those families most in need.[38] Further, against the evidence of the higher costs of older children, there is the argument that the poorest families are those with young children below school age where the mother is unable or unwilling to go out to work.[39] However, the practice in many other countries in the EU is often to pay higher allowances for second and third children, etc. Thus in 2001 Germany paid DM 270 a month each for the first and second children, DM 300 for the third, and DM 350 for the fourth and subsequent children. Other countries have more complex provisions under which different payments are made, depending on both the child's age and the number in the family; eg in the Netherlands

---

33 Social Security Act 1998, s 5 (SSA 1988); see Wikeley [1989] JSWL 277 at 285–287. See 129 HC Official Report (6th series) cols 866–962 for the Commons debate on the Lords' amendment imposing the obligation.

34 The successor to SSA 1988, s 10, the Social Security Administration Act 1992, s 153 (SSAA 1992), is likewise omitted by virtue of the Social Security (Consequential Provisions) Act 1992, Sch 4, paras 1 and 16 (SS(CP)A 1992).

35 121 HC Official Report (6th series) cols 179ff. See Field and Raison in Wilson and Wilson (eds) *The State and Social Welfare* (1991) ch 14; Gilmour *Dancing with Dogma* (1992) pp 128–132; and Lawson *The View From No. 11* (1992) pp 725–727.

36 The graduated income tax allowances had recognised this, as did the supplementary benefit scale rates (and now the income support personal allowances). See further Piachaud *The Cost of a Child* (1979) Poverty Pamphlet No 43; Field *What Price a Child?* (1985) PSI Studies of the Social Security System No 8, chs 6 and 7.

37 HC Standing Committee A Debates, cols 99–100 (19 June 1975). But the *Beveridge Report* n 7, above, para 417, and an unpublished DHSS Report by McClements suggested there was no evidence for economies of scale as family size increases: HC Standing Committee A Debates, col 81 (19 June 1975).

38 N 27, above, para 4.36 and accompanying text.

39 See Bradshaw (1980) 45 Poverty 15; and Brown *Child Benefit: Investing in the Future* (1988) ch 4.

a certain amount is paid for a child aged 6 to 11 if there are two children in the family and a little more for a child of the same age if there are three, and so on.[40]

The justification for the 1990 change was said to be the impact on family finances of the arrival of the first child,[41] although the premium in the first year of £1 a week above the ordinary rate seemed little more than a token gesture in this respect. The higher rate, introduced in April 1991, is payable for the only, elder or eldest child of each family.[42] One of the first steps of the Major administration was to give a commitment to up-rating the level of child benefit in line with inflation,[43] a belated recognition that child benefit is well understood and liked, as the government had found in its 1985 review of social security.[44]

F   The rise and fall of one-parent benefit

At the outset of the scheme single parent families were treated more generously. Even before the full introduction of child benefit in 1977, an interim benefit was paid in the preceding year for the children of an unmarried or separated parent, not living with another person as their spouse.[45] When the benefit became payable to all persons responsible for a child, a single parent received an extra 50p a week for the only, or eldest, child, and this differential became £1 in the following year, 1978.[46] This preferential treatment was almost certainly a response to the Finer Committee on One-Parent Families, which had recommended the introduction of a guaranteed maintenance allowance for lone mothers with young children.[47] Their needs have also been recognised in the more generous disregard of earnings for lone parents claiming income support.[48] In order to encourage its take-up, the government renamed 'child benefit increase' in 1980 as 'one-parent benefit', though curiously this nomenclature was found only in government leaflets and not in the regulations. The benefit was a hybrid, sharing the entitlement rules for the principal benefit and enjoying further requirements of its own.[49] The extra amount paid for one-parent children was quite significant, at least in relation to the value of child benefit: by 1994 it was £6.30, three-quarters of the rate of child benefit itself for second and subsequent children. The benefit was unaffected by the changes made in 1986, and indeed its role was scarcely discussed in the preceding Green and White Papers.[50]

This all changed in 1995 with the then Conservative government's announcement of its intention gradually to withdraw the special rates of benefits paid to lone parents. According to the government, there was no empirical evidence of a difference in needs between two-parent and one-parent families; moreover, the changes formed 'part of a wider strategy to encourage lone parents to reduce their benefit dependency and improve

40   MISSOC (Mutual Information System on Social Protection) (2001) Table IX *Benefits* 5.1.
41   178 HC Official Report (6th series) cols 352–353. See SI 1991/502.
42   SI 1976/1267, reg 2(1)(a) and (2ZA). The higher rate is payable only in respect of the older sibling where twins are the first-born: *Walker v Department of Social Security* (29 October 1997, unreported), CA.
43   188 HC Official Report (6th series) col 180.
44   *Green Paper 1985* n 27, above, para 4.44. Also see Walsh and Lister *Mother's Life-line* (1985); and Bradshaw and Stimson *Using Child Benefit in the Family Budget* (1997).
45   CBA 1975, s 16, now repealed.
46   See SI 1976/1267, reg 2 and SI 1977/1328, reg 2.
47   The Finer Committee's recommendations are briefly discussed in ch 8, p 317, above. See Brown *In Search of a Policy* (1988) pp 146–149.
48   See p 452, above.
49   See the 4th edition of this book, p 449.
50   See *Green Paper 1985* n 27, above, vol 1, para 8.9.

living standards for themselves and their children'.[51] As a first step the rate of one-parent benefit was frozen in the April 1996 up-rating exercise. In the following April one-parent benefit was fully reintegrated as a special rate within child benefit and the lone-parent premiums for income-related benefits were likewise consolidated within the family premiums.[52] Early in 1997 the Conservative government proposed to abolish one-parent benefit for new claims with effect from April 1998. This proposal, bitterly attacked by the then opposition, was subsequently introduced by the incoming Labour administration in SSA 1998, notwithstanding a significant backbench rebellion.[53] In an apparent change of strategy, the new government then announced that the rate of child benefit for the first child would be increased by £2.50 a week for the first child, the largest single increase in child benefit since its introduction in 1977.[54]

G Child benefit and tax credits

Child benefit, representing 8 per cent of total social security expenditure and 0.9 per cent of GDP, remains a central part of the welfare state.[55] However, its future role continues to be a matter of political debate. Early in its first term the new Labour government considered whether to replace child benefit for over-16-year-olds with a means-tested educational maintenance allowance. This option was later abandoned, with ministerial assurances that child benefit constitutes a key part of the government's strategy on child poverty.[56] This involves making universal child benefit to be the foundation for the new integrated child tax credit, to be introduced in 2003 by TCA 2002. At the same time, the Department for Work and Pensions' (DWP) policy and operational responsibilities for child benefit were transferred to the Treasury and the Inland Revenue respectively.

Part 2   Entitlement to child benefits

Under section 141 of SSCBA 1992:

> A person who is responsible for one or more children in any week shall be entitled ... to a benefit ... for that week in respect of the child or each of the children for whom he is responsible.

Since 1996 a person who is subject to immigration control has not been entitled to child benefit, with prescribed exceptions.[57]

---

51 See the Secretary of State's Note published in the Social Security Advisory Committee (SSAC) *Report on Draft Child Benefit, Child Support and Social Security (Miscellaneous Amendments) Regulations 1996* (1996, Cm 3296) Appendix 2.
52 See SI 1996/1803 and pp 297–298, above.
53 SSA 1998, s 72; abolition was actually implemented in July 1998: SI 1998/1581. On the political background, see Timmins *The Five Giants* (rev edn, 2001) pp 567–569.
54 This increase (in fact £2.95 by the time of implementation) was paid for by reducing the rate of tax relief in the married couple's allowance from 15 per cent to 10 per cent: House of Commons Research Paper 98/79 *Child Benefit* (1998).
55 DSS *The Changing Welfare State* (2000) p 8.
56 HC Social Security Committee *Second Report* (2000–01, HC 72) paras 18–19.
57 SSCBA 1992, s 146A and SI 1976/965, reg 14B, inserted by SI 1996/2327; see also SI 1996/2530 and *R v Adjudication Officer, ex p Velasquez* (1999) Times, 30 April (see Thomas (1999) 6 JSSL 208). See now the Immigration and Asylum Act 1999, s 115.

There are two major issues in the determination of entitlement to child benefit: first, whether the child is one in respect of whom benefit is payable and, secondly, whether the claimant is to be treated 'as responsible for a child'. Since two or more persons may concurrently be responsible for the same child, difficult questions as to priority of title to the benefit may arise if there is more than one claim; these are discussed at the end of the second section. The third section is concerned with the residence qualifications which have to be satisfied by both the child and the claimant.

A The child

Section 142(1) of SSCBA 1992 provides that:

a person shall be treated as a child for any week in which—
(a) he is under the age of 16; or
(b) he is under the age of 18 and not receiving full-time education and prescribed conditions are satisfied in relation to him; or
(c) he is under the age of 19 and receiving full-time education either by attendance at a recognised educational establishment or, if the education is recognised by the Secretary of State, elsewhere.

There is, therefore, a normal age limit under the 1992 Act of 16, with an upper age limit in some circumstances of 18 or 19.

i The normal age limit

The normal age limit of 16 seems to have been chosen because when CBA 1975 was enacted a young person was entitled to supplementary benefit on attaining that age.[58] In most EU countries the normal age limit is 18.[59] In practice, however, the normal age limit in the UK has since been modified by regulations.[60] The first Thatcher government was anxious to reduce supplementary benefits expenditure on school leavers, so regulations originally made in 1980 provide that school leavers shall continue to be treated as children for benefit purposes from the date they leave school (if then 16) or from their sixteenth birthday until the relevant 'terminal date'. This date, as prescribed in the regulations, is broadly speaking a day at the end of the school holidays following the date on which they left school.[61] Children whose names have been entered as candidates for external examinations before they left school continue to be treated as children for benefit purposes until the first 'terminal date' after the conclusion of their examinations (or after their nineteenth birthday).[62] There is no entitlement to child benefit under these regulations for a young person who is over 19, nor is benefit payable for a child who is in full-time work. Further, a separate regulation provides that no

---

58   HC Standing Committee A Debates, col 10 (17 June 1975).
59   *MISSOC* n 40, above, Table IX *Age Limit* 4.
60   Originally made under CBA 1975, s 2(3), as amended; see now SSCBA 1992, s 142(5).
61   Ie the first Monday in January, the Monday following Easter Monday or the first Monday in September: SI 1976/965, reg 7.
62   SI 1976/965, reg 7(4)–(6), which were amendments inserted following the ruling in *R(F) 2/85(T)*. The Commissioners held that normally a return to sit an examination was not a return to full-time education, so that child benefit would not be payable: see also Report of SSAC (1987, Cm 106) paras 5–28.

benefit is payable for any week in which training is provided for the child under a relevant training scheme and for which an allowance may be paid.[63]

ii The further age limit of 18

SSA 1988 raised the minimum age limit for entitlement to income support from 16 to 18, subject to various exceptions.[64] A consequential amendment provided that child benefit may be paid for a child under 18, who is not receiving full-time education (and does not therefore fall within the third category of beneficiary discussed below).[65] The conditions are set out in the regulations.[66] Young people must be registered for work or for training under a youth training scheme, and must not actually be in employment. Further, they will be treated as eligible for child benefit only for a limited 'extension period' which starts with the Monday after benefit would otherwise cease.[67] The intention was that during this period young people would either find a job or take advantage of the government's guarantee of a youth training place. Initially at least, continued high levels of youth unemployment combined with problems in providing sufficient training places undermined this objective.[68] Young people are ineligible for child benefit during the extension period if they are in receipt of income support or already engaged in training. Finally, the person responsible for the child must have been entitled to benefit immediately before the extension period and must make a written request for payment during the extension period.

iii The further age limit of 19

Under the legislation, benefit may be paid for children under 19 if they are receiving full-time education. The upper limit of 19 is very low in comparison with other EU countries, almost all of which extend the provision of family benefit beyond the normal age limit for children receiving vocational training or further education.[69] Thus in France benefit in either case may be extended for children up to 20, whereas in the Netherlands there is a high upper limit in these circumstances of 24 and in Germany it is 27. The British position also seems difficult to justify as the CTA, abolished when child benefit was introduced, did not have an upper age limit for dependent children. There was some anxiety at the time of the reform that parents with children at college or university would suffer as its result, but changes were then made to the level of student grant to improve their position. The devaluation of the student grant in the 1980s and its subsequent freezing with the introduction of student loans in 1990 meant that such improvement was short-lived.[70] In practice it is difficult to draw satisfactory comparisons between different countries without taking into account the availability

---

63 SI 1976/965, reg 7B.
64 P 284, above.
65 SSA 1988, s 4(3). See Harris (1988) 15 JLS 201; and Wikeley (1989) JSWL 277.
66 SI 1976/965, reg 7D.
67 Thus the extension period runs from the second Monday in September to the last day of the week before the first Monday in January, or for 12 weeks from the second Monday either in January or after Easter Monday, as appropriate: SI 1976/965, reg 7D(2).
68 See Maclagan *A Broken Promise* (1992). Once the extension period has expired, young people can only apply for a severe hardship payment: see p 356, below.
69 *MISSOC* n 40, above, Table IX *Age Limit* 4.
70 See Harris (1991) 54 MLR 258.

and level of student grants, training allowances and other benefits available for young people not fully integrated in the labour market.[71]

At the time of the original reforms there was some criticism of the failure to extend benefit to children over 16 suffering from a physical disability. This is a common provision in other European countries,[72] but, as was mentioned in the Committee proceedings,[73] in Great Britain a young person over 16 may be eligible for non-contributory disablement benefits, and to award child benefit would create an unnecessary overlap.[74]

iv *'Receiving full-time education ...'*

Under the original CBA 1975 benefit could only be paid for children in receipt of full-time education until they were 19, if that education was received 'by attendance at a recognised educational establishment'. By an amendment to that legislation made in 1986, benefit also became payable for a child educated elsewhere, perhaps at home, where this is recognised by the Secretary of State.[75] But in the normal case, the child must be in attendance at a school, college or other institution recognised as comparable.[76] Education is regarded under the regulations as 'full-time' if the time spent receiving instruction and undertaking supervised study, etc, is more than 12 hours a week, no account being taken of meal breaks or unsupervised study.[77] A reasonable interruption of up to six months (or even longer where this is attributable to illness or disability) is allowed. This applies only if the period of interruption is not likely to be followed, or actually followed, by a period in which the child receives financial support under a relevant training scheme or receives education by virtue of any employment.[78] Some of the case law, interpreting the equivalent provisions in the family allowances scheme, may still be of some help in determining what constitutes a reasonable interruption. For example, it was held that school holidays and leaving one school for the purpose of removal to another would be treated as reasonable interruptions to full-time education.[79] Education received by virtue of the child's work, unless it is part of a course for which no financial support is received, does not count as full-time education for benefit purposes; the object of these provisions is clearly to prevent an overlap of benefit and wages or other compensation received from an employer. However, a reimbursement of the cost of books, equipment, examination and travelling expenses does not count as financial support in the context.[80]

No benefit is payable for a child between 16 and 19 who is in receipt of 'advanced education'.[81] This is defined as full-time education for the purposes of a degree, a diploma of higher education, various national diplomas (of a standard above ordinary

---

71 See Harris *Social Security for Young People* (1989) chs 6 and 7.
72 *MISSOC* n 40, above, Table IX *Age Limit* 4.
73 HC Standing Committee A Debates, cols 39–40 (17 June 1975).
74 This would be a reference to non-contributory invalidity pension, later severe disablement allowance, now in turn replaced by a special qualifying route to incapacity benefit: see p 535, above.
75 SSA 1986, s 70(1). See now SSCBA 1992, s 142(1)(c) and (2). No appeal lies from the decision of the Secretary of State: SI 1999/991, Sch 2, paras 1 and 2.
76 See the definition in SSCBA 1992, s 147(1) and *R(F)* 2/95.
77 SI 1976/965, reg 5. 'Supervised study' implies the presence or close proximity of a teacher: *R(F)* 1/93.
78 SI 1976/965, reg 6.
79 *R(F) 4/60, R(F) 1/68.*
80 SI 1976/965, reg 8.
81 SI 1976/965, reg 7A.

national diploma), a teaching qualification or any other course above GCE 'A' level and its Scottish equivalents.[82] The purpose of this rule is clearly to prevent benefit being paid for someone eligible for a student grant or other educational maintenance allowance, though the patchy award of these latter benefits may mean that it sometimes operates harshly.

v Married children

The general rule is that there is no entitlement to child benefit for a married child.[83] In any event this question could normally arise only in respect of a child over 16 for whom benefit is payable under section 142(1)(b) or (c) of SSCBA 1992.[84] Regulations, however, provide an exception in that a person may be entitled to benefit in respect of a married child only if:[85]
(a) that person is not the spouse of that child; and
(b) that child either is not residing with their spouse or, if so, the spouse is receiving full-time education.[86]
Interesting possibilities occur if the married child is herself a mother. She will be entitled to benefit in respect of her infant merely on the ground that the baby is living with her.[87] Further, her own mother (or other person with whom she is living) will also be entitled to benefit in respect of her.

vi Disqualified children

Benefit is not payable in respect of certain children under Schedule 9 to SSCBA 1992. First, there are disqualifications if the child in the particular week is 'undergoing imprisonment or detention in legal custody', or is in the care of a local authority in various prescribed circumstances.[88] Care in this sense includes the situation where a child is being accommodated by a local authority in the absence of a formal order under the Children Act 1989.[89] The disqualification only applies if the child has been in detention, care, etc, for more than eight weeks. It does not apply after that period for a week in which the child lives with a person otherwise entitled, or if that person establishes that as at that week the child ordinarily lives with him or her throughout at least one day in each week.[90] There is no entitlement where a local authority pays a boarding out allowance in respect of a child placed for adoption.[91] Further exclusions apply to apprentices[92] and to those children exceptionally entitled to income support,

---

82   SI 1976/965, reg 1(2). Although benefit is not *payable* during this period, *entitlement* continues.
83   SSCBA 1992, Sch 9, para 3. See HC Standing Committee A Debates, cols 19–22 (17 June 1975).
84   In a few cases a child under 16 will lawfully be married under a foreign legal system and the marriage will be recognised in England if neither spouse is domiciled there: Dicey and Morris *The Conflict of Laws* (13th edn, 2000) vol 2, p 678. See *Mohamed v Knott* [1969] 1 QB 1.
85   SI 1976/965, reg 10.
86   SI 1976/965, reg 11, prescribes the circumstances in which persons are not to be treated as having ceased to reside together: p 669, below.
87   SSCBA 1992, s 143(1)(a).
88   SSCBA 1992, Sch 9, para 1 and SI 1976/965, reg 16(2)–(5A). See also *R(F) 1/91*.
89   *McLavey v Secretary of State for Social Security* [1996] 2 FCR 813. This was the claimant's unsuccessful appeal from *R(F) 1/97*.
90   SI 1976/965, reg 16(6).
91   SI 1976/965, reg 16(8)–(9), as amended by SI 2000/2891.
92   SSCBA 1992, Sch 9, para 2 and SI 1976/965, reg 8.

income-based jobseeker's allowance or incapacity benefit under the special rules for those disabled at a young age.[93] As noted above, a similar exclusion operates where the young person is receiving training for which an allowance may be paid.[94] There is also a disqualification for persons otherwise entitled to benefit if they or their spouse (if they are residing together) are in receipt of any income exempt from UK income tax, eg because they are a member of visiting forces or work in an embassy or consulate.[95] This provision is understandable in view of the connection between the tax and child benefit systems, but it works rather harshly for those whose exempt earnings are considerably lower than their total earnings, the greater part of which is liable to tax here.[96]

B 'Person responsible for the child'

Under section 141 of SSCBA 1992, it is the person responsible for a child who is entitled to the benefit. This term is primarily defined in section 143(1):

> a person shall be treated as responsible for a child in any week if—
> (a) he has the child living with him in that week; or
> (b) he is contributing to the cost of providing for the child at a weekly rate which is not less than the weekly rate of child benefit payable in respect of the child for that week.

The claimant must, therefore, comply with one of these two conditions in order to establish entitlement. In many cases more than one person will satisfy them, and there are, therefore, rules in Schedule 10 to the Act determining which claimant has priority of title to the benefit. These rules are discussed in detail later, but it is perhaps useful to indicate at the outset that generally a person claiming it as 'responsible for a child' under section 143(1)(a) will have priority over a person claiming under section 143(1)(b); in other words, normally the person with whom the child is actually living will be entitled to benefit.[97] The child benefit provisions stand in sharp contrast to the equivalent rules in the former family allowances scheme, under which allowances were paid 'for the benefit of the family as a whole'.[98] Child benefit is paid to the person who prima facie most needs it.[99] No special privileges are conferred on a parent as such, though, of course, in normal circumstances it will be he or she who will receive it.

i 'Child living with him in that week'

A   GENERAL

SSCBA 1992 does not define 'living with', but it would seem generally to mean living in the same place, under the same roof or in the same residence. The term was used in

---

93 SI 1976/965, reg 7C.
94 SI 1976/965, reg 7B. See p 661, above.
95 SSCBA 1992, Sch 9, para 4 and SI 1976/965, reg 9. See *R(F) 3/89*, confirming the interpretation in the text.
96 There used to be an exception for such claimants, but this was removed by SI 1984/337. However, the disqualification itself will be abolished from 2003 by TCA 2002.
97 SSCBA 1992, Sch 10, para 2; see pp 667–671, below, for discussion of the priority rules.
98 FAA 1965, s 1. See further the 3rd edition of this book, p 398.
99 Mrs B Castle MP, Secretary of State, 892 HC Official Report (5th series) col 337.

the family allowances legislation,[100] where it was construed by the Commissioners to mean no more than that the claimant and the child must be living together; it did not necessarily imply a requirement of financial support.[101] On the other hand, in an earlier case it had been ruled that the relationship between a parent and a child might be so tenuous that the former could not be said to be 'living with' the latter, even though they both resided in the same premises.[102]

It seems that the Commissioners in construing the term in the child benefit legislation have adopted a similar, pragmatic approach. In *R(F) 2/79* it was said that the expression 'living with' should bear its ordinary and natural meaning in the context in which it occurs. Moreover, each case should be decided on its own particular facts after taking all the circumstances into account. Rather more helpfully, the Commissioner confirmed that 'living with' is not synonymous with 'residing together' or 'presence under the same roof'. In addition, the term does not necessarily require the exercise of de facto care and control, although where this does exist it will be an important factor in the argument that the child is living with the person concerned.

Under the Children Act 1989 it is possible (although not common) for joint residence orders to be made where parents separate or divorce.[103] In such a situation both parents could claim child benefit in the same week, provided that the child's presence in each household is more than merely transitory.[104] However, only one person can be entitled to benefit in any one week and so entitlement would be determined under the priority rules.[105] In practice if the parties can operate a joint residence arrangement satisfactorily, they should also be able to reach agreement over the use of child benefit.

B TEMPORARY ABSENCE[106]

Entirely different problems occur when a child and the responsible adult (usually the mother) are temporarily apart, perhaps because the former is away at school or is in hospital or for some reason is staying with other relatives. An absence of 56 days or less during the 16 weeks preceding the claim is to be disregarded.[107] Thus where a mother boards her child out with a relative for up to eight weeks, she continues to be entitled to benefit as she is to be treated as having her child living with her for that time. Only then (or after cumulative periods totalling 56 days within 16 weeks) would she lose her entitlement on the basis of section 143(1)(a) of SSCBA 1992, so that the relative with whom the child is physically living would, if a claim was made, become entitled to benefit in priority to the mother.[108]

In some cases, a longer absence is disregarded in determining whether persons are to be treated as having a child living with them in a particular week. A separation which is attributable solely to the child's 'receiving full-time education by attendance at a

100 FAA 1965, s 3. It was also used in the National Insurance legislation for the purposes of dependants' allowances: p 252, above.
101 *R(F) 1/74.* J S Watson, Comr, pointed out that there was a separate provision enabling a person providing for a child to claim benefit, as is the case under the SSCBA 1992.
102 *R(F) 1/71.* This decision was mentioned with approval in *R(F) 2/81*, para 12.
103 See Lowe and Douglas *Bromley's Family Law* (9th edn, 1998) pp 413–415 and Cretney and Masson *Principles of Family Law* (6th edn, 1997) pp 675–676.
104 *R(F) 2/81* (daughter not 'living with' her father when with him from 11.30am to 6.30pm at weekends).
105 SSCBA 1992, s 144(3); on the priority rules, see pp 667–671, below.
106 See pp 253–254, above, for equivalent rules for contributory benefits.
107 SSCBA 1992, s 143(2).
108 Before this period, the relative might claim under s 143(1)(a), but the parent would have the prior entitlement: SSCBA 1992, Sch 10, para 4; p 670, below.

recognised educational establishment' is wholly disregarded.[109] Secondly, absence attributable to the child's 'undergoing medical or other treatment as an in-patient in a hospital or similar institution', or being in residential accommodation under the Children Act 1989 or associated legislation is to be disregarded for up to 84 consecutive days.[110] In these circumstances an unlimited period of absence (beyond the 84 days) may be ignored if 'the person claiming to be responsible for the child regularly incurs expenditure in respect of the child'.[111] Regulations may be made prescribing the circumstances in which this condition is satisfied[112] but none has been issued.

The purpose of these provisions is clearly to enable persons (generally, though not necessarily, parents) to receive benefit for children normally living with them. This is reasonable as a parent will often spend money on clothes and other articles for a child, even when the latter is away at school or in hospital. In the second situation there may also be the expense of paying frequent hospital visits.

C   THE RIGHT TO BENEFIT OF A VOLUNTARY ORGANISATION

A voluntary organisation may be regarded as a person with whom the child is living for any week he or she is residing in premises managed by that body or is boarded out by it.[113] Very similar provisions to those described in the previous section cover the temporary absence of the child from the voluntary organisation, so that the latter may continue to be entitled to receive benefit, even though the child is not in fact living in its premises.[114] The eligibility of an organisation for benefit here seems to be unique in the social security system;[115] there is no clear reason why it was decided to depart from the general rule that only natural persons are entitled. It should be noted, however, that an organisation is not entitled to child benefit on the alternative basis that it is contributing to the cost of providing for the child.[116]

ii   *'Contributing to the cost of providing for the child'*

The second way in which a person may be treated as 'responsible for a child' is when:

> he is contributing to the cost of providing for the child at a weekly rate which is not less than the weekly rate of child benefit payable in respect of the child for that week.[117]

An application on this alternative basis will not succeed, because of the priority rules, if a claim has also been made by a person who has the child living with them. The main

---

109   SSCBA 1992, s 143(3)(a).
110   SSCBA 1992, ss 143(3)(b), (c) (as amended by the Child Support, Pensions and Social Security Act 2000, s 72) and 143(4). See SI 1976/965, regs 3 and 4.
111   SSCBA 1992, s 143(4).
112   SSCBA 1992, s 143(5).
113   SI 1976/965, reg 17(1).
114   SI 1976/965, reg 17(2). Voluntary organisations do not receive the higher rate of child benefit for the first child: SI 1976/1267, reg 2(2ZB), added by SI 1991/502.
115   Cf the refusal by the Commissioner to allow Dr Barnardo's to claim attendance allowance: *R(A) 3/75*, p 703, above. Note that disability living allowance (the successor to attendance allowance) for a child is claimed by the individual rather than the carer.
116   SI 1976/965, reg 17(6).
117   SSCBA 1992, s 143(1)(b).

purpose, therefore, of this second head of eligibility is to cover the case where a parent arranges for a child to be boarded with a relative or friend, and it is agreed that the parent should receive the benefit to cover the costs of the child's maintenance to which he or she is contributing.[118] If, however, the relative or friend claims in this situation, then the latter, and not the parent, would be entitled to the benefit.

Neither the Act nor the regulations define 'providing for' the child. This might seem odd because FAA 1965 had defined this phrase.[119] It was, however, also used in SSA 1975 for the purposes of entitlement to an increase of benefit for a dependent child,[120] and there are a number of Commissioners' decisions interpreting it in this context. In some respects it seems that the 1975 Act was the model for the concepts used in the child benefit scheme and, therefore, the discussion in chapter 7 would appear to be relevant here.[121]

Occasionally problems may arise about how periodic, but not weekly, payments made by the claimant to the person actually maintaining the child are to be treated for the purpose of determining the former's entitlement. The point is important because the claimant must contribute at a weekly rate not less than the weekly rate of benefit payable in respect of the child. The principles of 'spreading', as it is known, were set out in *R(F) 8/61*.[122] The period the payments relate to is a question of fact, the determination of which should take into account the payer's intentions. Regular periodic payments may be intended to cover a future period, and then they will be averaged over the number of weeks in this period. But if the claimant has fallen behind with the payments, and then makes a large payment, this may be attributed to arrears.

The only regulations made for the purposes of child benefit in this context provide that where two or more persons make weekly contributions, which individually do not, but together do, equal the amount of the benefit, the aggregate amount is to be treated as paid by one of them or, if they cannot agree on this, by that person nominated by the Secretary of State.[123] But after the week in which benefit is first paid under this arrangement, the recipient must contribute the full amount to retain entitlement. It is further provided that where two spouses are residing together, a contribution made by one of them shall by their agreement, or (in default of that) at the discretion of the Secretary of State, be treated as contributed by the other.[124] This ability to 'transfer' benefit to the non-contributing spouse may give a sensible measure of flexibility in some cases, although it is less easy to see the justification for the power of the Secretary of State to treat the non-contributing spouse as the contributor.[125]

iii Priority between persons entitled

It has already been mentioned that one of the principal features of the scheme is the priority given to a claimant with whom the child is living, over other claimants, who might include the child's parents. SSCBA 1992 sets out the relevant rules in Schedule 10.

118 HC Standing Committee A Debates, cols 44–45 (17 June 1975).
119 FAA 1965, s 18.
120 SSA 1975, s 43(1)(b); see now SSCBA 1992, s 81(1) and (2).
121 Pp 255–258, above.
122 See also *R(F) 1/73*.
123 SI 1976/965, reg 2.
124 SI 1976/965, reg 2(3).
125 For the rule under the family allowances scheme, see Calvert *Social Security Law* (1st edn, 1974) p 267 and the 3rd edition of this book, p 401, n 19.

The exposition in this section follows the order of priority laid down there – with some examples to make it clearer. Three important preliminary points should be made. First, title to child benefit is important not just in its own right but because of the implications for other benefits: eg entitlement to income support personal allowances for children is dependent upon the position as regards child benefit.[126] Secondly, entitlement to child benefit is dependent on the making of a claim in the prescribed manner,[127] so if a person with a prior right under these rules has not in fact made a valid claim, they do not come into operation. Finally, the right conferred by any of the priority rules (except, of course, the first one) only vests if nobody is entitled under one of the previous provisions.

A   PERSON WITH PRIOR AWARD

A person with an existing award of child benefit for a certain week is entitled to priority over anyone else who claims benefit in respect of the same child for that period. But this rule does not apply where the claim is made for a week later than the third week after that in which it is made.[128] The effect of these provisions is that, whatever the circumstances, a person with an existing award is entitled to priority over all other claimants for up to four weeks.[129] This rule allows payments to continue, while the authorities investigate the facts to determine whether the new claimant should be awarded benefit.

B   PERSONS HAVING THE CHILD LIVING WITH THEM

Any persons entitled to benefit by virtue of having children living with them are entitled to priority over anyone entitled on the alternative basis of contributing to the cost of maintenance.[130] The rationale for this is that generally it is the person with whom the child is living who is the primary carer, and he or she should be entitled to priority.

C   HUSBAND AND WIFE

The principle of the family allowances legislation, under which the benefit went to the mother, was carried over into the child benefit scheme. In the debates on the Child Benefit Bill, there was a move to provide for equal entitlement, where both spouses were in agreement on this course,[131] but this was resisted. There are strong grounds for arguing that the mother should receive the benefit, as it is still usually she who is

---

126   Pp 292–293, above; see *Devoy v Social Security Comr* (28 July 1998, unreported), CA, and for the position as regards housing benefit, see SI 1987/1971, reg 14(2) and *R v Swale Borough Council Housing Benefit Review Board, ex p Marchant* [2000] 1 FLR 246, CA.
127   SSAA 1992, s 13(1).
128   SSCBA 1992, Sch 10, para 1. Claims may be made three months before the claimant is entitled to benefit: SI 1987/1968, reg 13.
129   If it is later decided that the person with the existing award was not entitled to benefit and has been required to repay it, then the second claimant may be awarded it for that week: SI 1976/965, reg 14A, modifying SSAA 1992, s 13(2).
130   SSCBA 1992, Sch 10, para 2.
131   Sir G Young MP, HC Standing Committee A Debates, cols 57ff (19 June 1975), arguing that in some European countries children's benefits are paid to the father.

responsible for the day-to-day care of children.[132] There has subsequently been general agreement on this principle, and indeed it is seen as one of the benefit's chief merits that it steers some money towards the mother. The SSAC considered it as a powerful argument for the universal character of the benefit, for even in well-off families the mother herself might have insufficient funds of her own to look after the children.[133] The criticism which followed the Thatcher government's original intention to pay family credit through the wage packet rather than directly to the mother further shows the support for the principle.[134]

Thus if a husband and wife, who are residing together, both claim child benefit, the wife is entitled in priority to her husband.[135] So:

> where Mr and Mrs A live with their children (and nobody has a prior award under the first rule), Mrs A is entitled to the benefit. On the other hand, where they live together, but the child lives with B, it is B who has the prior entitlement and Mrs A will only secure payment if B does not claim or waives priority.

If the husband does claim he may be awarded the benefit, though he may be required to submit a written statement signed by his wife that she does not wish to claim it.[136] Further, he may receive payment of the benefit on behalf of his wife.[137]

These provisions only apply when the husband and wife are residing together. If they are residing apart, the spouse with whom the child is living has priority under the rule described above. Spouses are treated as residing together for any period of absence from each other until either there is a formal separation or they have been apart for 91 consecutive days, and even after those dates they are to be regarded as residing together where the absence is not likely to be permanent.[138] In *Grove v Haydon (Insurance Officer)*[139] the Court of Appeal held that two spouses may be regarded as 'residing together', even though they have never in fact lived together, as they married when the husband was in prison; the absence was clearly not permanent.[140] They are also to be regarded as residing together if one, or both, of them is receiving treatment in hospital, whether this is temporary or not.[141] The consequence of these provisions may be illustrated by the following example:

> Mrs A leaves her husband and her child, in respect of whom she is in receipt of benefit. Unless there has been a formal separation, the spouses are to be treated under the regulations as residing together until they have been apart for at least 91 days and, therefore (subject to the other priority rules), Mrs A retains her prior entitlement to benefit. It does not seem that Mr A can claim priority over his wife under the previous priority rule for 56 days. This is because under section 143(2) of the SSCBA 1992, Mrs A is still to be treated as

---

132 See Walsh and Lister *Mother's Life-line* (1985).
133 SSAC *Third Report* (1984) para 6.12. See also *Brown* n 14, above, pp 51–53.
134 But see now the position as regards working families' tax credit: pp 396–397, above.
135 SSCBA 1992, Sch 10, para 3.
136 SI 1987/1968, reg 7(2).
137 1987/1968, reg 36: see Mr B O'Malley MP, Minister of State, HC Standing Committee A Debates, col 71 (19 June 1975).
138 SI 1976/965, reg 11. Spouses can be treated as separated if they are living under the same roof, but not living as one household: *R(F)3/81*.
139 Reported as Appendix to *R(F) 4/85*.
140 See also *CF 1/81* on the meaning of 'permanent'.
141 SI 1976/965, reg 11(2). This rule has the harsh effect of denying entitlement to one-parent benefit where one spouse is permanently in a coma in hospital: see Baldwin, Wikeley and Young *Judging Social Security* (1992) p 176.

living with her child, despite their absence from one another for 56 days. Until that period is over, Mr A cannot claim to be entitled on the ground that he is living with the child, and his wife is not.[142]

This result seems difficult to defend, as for a considerable period Mrs A has 'abandoned' her child, for whom Mr A has been caring without any support.

D   PARENTS

The fourth priority rule is that, as between a parent and someone who is not a parent, the former is to have priority.[143] 'Parent' for this purpose includes adoptive parents and step-parents.[144] The priority is, of course, subject to the previous rules: this can be illustrated by the following two examples.

> Ms A lives with her young child and Mr B, who is not the child's father. Each is equally entitled as a person who has the child living with them. Ms A is awarded the benefit because she is a parent, and Mr B is not.
>
> Ms A does not live with her young child, who lives with her brother, Mr A, though Ms A sends him a weekly sum towards the cost of providing for her child. Ms A does not have priority as a parent because Mr A has priority under the earlier rule, which accords entitlement to the person with whom the child is living.

Where two unmarried parents are residing together, the mother enjoys priority;[145] this is comparable to the priority a wife has under the previous rule. Regulations provide that two unmarried parents are to be treated as residing together during a period of 'temporary absence',[146] but there is no specific rule (as there is for husband and wife) explaining the meaning of this phrase. The consequences of the regulations may be illustrated by the following example:

> Ms A who has been residing with Mr B and is in receipt of benefit in respect of their child, leaves that child with Mr B. Under section 143(2) of SSCBA 1992 she is to be treated as having the child living with her for 56 days of absence. During this period, she will continue to have priority over Mr B, provided it is held that she is still residing with Mr B, notwithstanding her departure. But if it is decided that the absence is permanent, the rule conferring priority on her as the mother does not apply. It seems in that event that for the period of 56 days priority is to be determined under the rule discussed below, covering priority in other cases, where no previous rule applies. Under this either Ms A and Mr B may elect which of them is to be entitled or priority is decided by the Secretary of State. After 56 days Mr B enjoys priority because he has the child living with him, and Ms A does not.

---

142   It is possible that before then payment could be made to the husband on the wife's behalf under the Secretary of State's power to divert payments: SI 1987/1968, reg 34. On the 56-day rule, see p 665, above.

143   SSCBA 1992, Sch 10, para 4(1).

144   Adoption Act 1976, s 39 and SSCBA 1992, s 147(3). The status of step-parent continues after the termination of the relevant marriage by death (*R(F) 1/79*) or by divorce (*R(F) 4/81*), and it does not depend on whether the child was the legitimate child of a previous marriage or was illegitimate (*R(F) 9/83*).

145   SSCBA 1992, Sch 10, para 4(2).

146   SI 1976/965, reg 11(3).

E   OTHER CASES

Finally, if none of the other priority rules determines entitlement, benefit is awarded to the person elected jointly by those eligible to claim it, or in default of election, the person chosen by the Secretary of State.[147] An election must be made in writing on the appropriate form; it is not permanently binding, and may subsequently be changed.[148] An example of the possible application of this provision was given in the paragraph above, but a more typical case might be the following:

> Mr A and Ms A (a brother and sister living together) look after the young child of Mrs B (their deceased sister). Neither has priority under any of the earlier rules, so they may elect which of them is to receive child benefit. If it subsequently becomes more appropriate for the other to receive it, another election may be made and entitlement varied.

In *R(F) 2/79*, where the two claimants were parents of the child, but were not married and were not residing together, the Commissioner ruled that the child was 'living with' them both. In this circumstance, none of the previous priority rules applied and, as they were unwilling to make a joint election, the issue was referred to the Secretary of State. He decided the child's mother was entitled for the relevant weeks, and this was binding on the Commissioner.[149]

F   WAIVER OF PRIOR ENTITLEMENT

A person with a prior entitlement under these provisions may waive it in favour of a new claimant. In order to do so the existing claimant[150] must give the Secretary of State notice in writing at a benefit office that he or she does not wish to have priority.[151] In that case the provisions are ousted, and the new claimant is awarded the benefit (provided, of course, that the other conditions of entitlement are met). But the original claimant may subsequently make a further claim, and then the priority provisions in the Schedule to SSCBA 1992 take effect to restore title to benefit.[152]

C   Residence qualifications

SSCBA 1992, as modified by regulations,[153] set out a number of detailed provisions concerning residence qualifications. These concern both the residence, or more accurately, the presence in Great Britain of the child and the claimant.[154] The law is extremely complex, largely because when child benefit was introduced the government attempted to formulate rules which would combine the presence requirements for family

147   SSCBA 1992, Sch 10, para 5. There is no right of appeal: SSA 1998, Sch 2, para 4.
148   SI 1976/965, reg 13.
149   SI 1986/2218, reg 23.
150   The problem only arises when the person with the prior entitlement is actually in receipt of the benefit, since under SSAA 1992, s 13(1), no person is entitled to benefit unless they have made a claim.
151   SI 1976/965, reg. 14.
152   SI 1976/965, reg 14(2).
153   SI 1976/963.
154   The usual requirements in social security law of 'residence' and/or 'ordinary residence', for which see pp 230–232, above, do not apply in this area.

allowances with the more generous conditions for tax allowances. Modifications applying to certain classes of persons were introduced by regulations,[155] but they do not cover immigrants to Britain who are supporting children overseas.[156] Even if there is no entitlement under the rules discussed below, EU law may assist the claimant in certain cases.[157]

This section first discusses the general requirements concerning the presence of the child, secondly, those concerning the presence of the claimant and thirdly, the special relaxing provisions which are applicable to certain categories of persons.

i Presence of child in Great Britain

Section 146(2) of SSCBA 1992 provides that:

> Subject to any regulations ...no child benefit shall be payable in respect of a child for any week unless—
> (a) he is in Great Britain in that week; and
> (b) either he or at least one of his parents has been in Great Britain for more than 182 days in the 52 weeks preceding that week.

Both these requirements have been modified by regulations made under section 146(1).

First, the absence of a child from Britain for a particular week will not be material if three conditions are satisfied:[158]

(1) a person must be entitled to benefit for the week immediately before the first week of the child's absence from Great Britain;

(2) the child's absence is both initially and throughout intended to be temporary;[159] and

(3) the child must not be absent from Great Britain for more than 12 weeks[160] or for more than such extended period as the Secretary of State allows if the absence is for the purpose of treatment for an illness, etc which began before the period of absence. An absence of more than 12 weeks is also disregarded if it is only by reason of the child receiving full-time education in another EEA state or being engaged in an educational exchange or visit made with the written approval of the child's own school or other recognised educational establishment. Other reasons, such as a desire that the child experience at first hand the religion and culture of another country, do not qualify for such dispensation.[161]

Secondly, the second requirement specifies that either the child or one of the parents must have been present for more than half the year preceding the week for which benefit is claimed. This is to ensure that benefit is payable only for those children who have more than a transitory connection with Britain. The requirement is modified in certain ways by the regulations.[162] The principal relaxation is that benefit may be payable

---

155 SI 1976/963, Pt II.
156 See the criticism of the law in Gordon and Newnham *Passport to Benefits* (1985) pp 38–40.
157 See *R(F) 1/98* and also *CF/3532/1997*.
158 SI 1976/963, reg 2(2). It follows that the regulation is of no help where the child has never been in Great Britain: *R(F) 1/88*.
159 For the meaning of 'temporary absence', see p 253, below.
160 Increased from eight weeks by SI 1999/198.
161 See *CF/7146/1995* (1996) 3 JSSL D157, in which the children went to stay in Pakistan for eight months, decided on the wording of SI 1973/963, reg 2(2)(c)(ii) before its amendment by SI 1999/198.
162 SI 1976/963, reg 3.

for children who are in Britain and (though not residing with their parents) are living with another person with whom they are likely to continue to live permanently, and that person satisfies the requirements under section 146(3)(b) of SSCBA 1992, ie has been in Britain for more than 182 days in the year preceding the relevant week. The result is that benefit is payable for a child who has recently been left in Britain with a person who has been resident there for at least half the year preceding the week for which the claim is made.

ii Presence of claimant in Great Britain

There is a general requirement that the claimant is present in Great Britain, and has been present there for some time. Subject to regulations, the claimant must be there for the week for which benefit is claimed, and must have been there for more than 182 days in the 52 preceding weeks.[163] Both these requirements have been modified to cover the cases where the claimant is, or has been, temporarily absent from the country, but still has sufficient connection with it to justify entitlement to benefit.

First, the absence of the claimant from Britain for the relevant week is not material if three conditions are satisfied:[164]
(1) that person must have been entitled to benefit for the week immediately before the first week of the absence from Great Britain;
(2) the claimant's absence is both initially and throughout intended to be temporary; and
(3) the absence must not be longer than eight weeks.

A person's absence for a week is also immaterial with regard to a child born to a mother within eight weeks of her departure for a temporary absence – so that the claimant (usually the mother) may be entitled to benefit for the eight weeks following the mother's departure from Britain.[165] This enables a mother to be entitled in respect of a child born abroad, perhaps because she wished to join her husband for the birth, even though she has been outside Britain for more than 26 weeks, so that she could not otherwise take advantage of the regulations.

Secondly, the general requirement that the claimant must have been present for the six months preceding the week for which benefit is claimed has been modified substantially.[166] In particular, the general condition is not to apply if the person is in fact in Britain and is responsible for a child who satisfies the presence requirements of section 146(2) of SSCBA 1992. This appreciably reduces the significance of the six months' presence requirement.

iii Special relaxing provisions

The general requirements, together with these modifications in the regulations, may be further relaxed with regard to certain categories of persons by the rules in Part II of the Child Benefit (Residence and Persons Abroad) Regulations 1976.[167] These additional provisions were a response to the anxiety that the presence requirements for child benefit

---

163 SSCBA 1992, s 146(3). This rule is subject to repeal by TCA 2002.
164 SI 1976/963, reg 4(2). See *R(F) 2/92*.
165 SI 1976/963, reg 4(3).
166 SI 1976/963, reg 5.
167 SI 1976/963.

appeared from the draft Bill to be more onerous than those applicable to the child tax allowance. Part II applies to civil servants (other than those recruited outside the United Kingdom for service abroad), serving members of the forces,[168] and people temporarily absent from Britain, by reason only of employment abroad, for an income tax year in which at least half the earnings are liable to UK income tax.[169] A payment of income tax in relation to a pension, rather than on earnings from employment, is not sufficient.[170] It also applies to spouses of such people and those living with them as their spouses providing that they were doing so when last in Britain.[171]

Any week in which persons to whom Part II applies are away from Britain in connection with their employment is to be treated for the purposes of the presence requirements as one in which they are present there; moreover, a child's absence is to be disregarded entirely if he or she is living with a person to whom Part II applies, and that person is either a parent or someone who before the week in question was entitled to benefit.[172] Days of separation of a child and such a person, which are attributable to the latter being abroad, are to be wholly disregarded under SSCBA 1992 for the purposes of determining whether the adult has the child living with him or her. Thus, civil servants serving in a foreign embassy may be entitled to child benefit in respect of children for whom they are responsible, even if their children spend the whole year in Britain, both school terms and holidays. It seems that they would also be entitled if their children are being educated in and spend their holidays in another country, not the one in which the civil servant is working.[173]

168   Defined by SI 1975/492, reg 1(2).
169   SI 1976/963, reg 6(1)(a)–(c). The original wording of reg 6(1)(a), referring to a person 'whose employment is by or under the Crown', enabled a claimant seconded to the government of Hong Kong to claim (*R(F) 1/89*). The effect of this decision was reversed, and the policy intention of confining entitlement to home civil servants restored, by SI 1992/2972.
170   *R(F) 1/94*.
171   SI 1976/963, reg 6(1)(d) and (e).
172   SI 1976/963, reg 7(1) and (2).
173   SI 1976/963, reg 7(3). The Secretary of State, however, has a discretion to refuse to apply this disregard of days of absence in any case.

Chapter 19

Benefits for severely disabled people and carers

Part 1 General

A The failure of National Insurance

The architects of the early welfare state recognised that the loss of earnings caused by illness was one of the major causes of poverty. As we saw in chapter 15, the major part of the National Insurance Act 1911 (NIA 1911) was devoted to sickness insurance. The other major source of assistance in the first half of the twentieth century was workmen's compensation. Beveridge's reforms retained that dichotomy with the same basic degree of coverage, notwithstanding his recognition that logically there was a strong case for an integrated disability benefit. Yet a National Insurance scheme premised on providing an alternative source of income to the labour market failed disabled people in at least two respects. First, it was a contributory scheme and thus did not cater for those who, through no fault of their own, had been unable to build up a contributions record. Secondly, the flat-rate insurance benefits were designed to do no more than provide a subsistence means of living and did not purport to accommodate the extra costs associated with long-term disability.

B New provision for disabled people in the 1960s and 1970s

During the 1960s the political background to provision for disabled people altered significantly. On the one hand, there had emerged some powerful pressure groups,[1] concerned to bring to public attention the plight of such people, to conduct inquiries and publish their findings, and to campaign actively for reform. On the other hand, the 'rediscovery' of poverty in the 1960s had brought to light that disability featured prominently among the causes of deprivation and financial hardship.[2] Under the influence of these movements, the government sponsored in 1968–69 a massive survey

---

1　The two most influential have probably been the Disablement Income Group, formed in 1965, and the Disability Alliance. See generally on these movements Whiteley and Winyward (1983) 12 J Soc Pol 1 at 12–13 and Oliver *The Politics of Disablement* (1990) pp 117–118.

2　See particularly Abel-Smith and Townsend *The Poor and the Poorest* (1965) p 62.

of disabled people in Great Britain.[3] The findings largely confirmed the conjectures of those campaigning for more generous financial support. It was estimated that there were about three million 'impaired' persons, that is those lacking part or all of a limb, or having a defective organ or mechanism of the body, and that about 1.1 million were 'handicapped' in the sense that they had difficulty in carrying out the normal functions of daily living.[4] Perhaps the most significant finding was that more than a third of the latter group were in receipt of supplementary benefit, thus demonstrating the inadequacy of National Insurance protection.[5]

Yet income replacement alone constituted insufficient financial support for the severely disabled. Government policy then shifted to targeting help on categories of particular need. The first group to benefit from this approach comprised those who required assistance to cope with the normal functions of living. The Conservative government introduced an attendance allowance for such persons in 1970.[6] Five years later, it was complemented by a measure designed to assist those who sacrificed their own work opportunities: the non-contributory invalid care allowance.[7] Quite apart from the justice of compensating a group who performed a difficult and unpaid task, there was the economic consideration that by so doing they relieved the social services of the burden.

The second category of disabled people to be identified as having a specific financial need was the immobile. Those unable to walk but able to drive had for some time been entitled to invalid carriages or, if they owned a car, to a private car allowance; but the disabled passenger was not assisted and the safety and reliability of the carriage had been subjected to considerable doubt.[8] Rather than switch entitlement to a small car, which would have involved a considerable increase in expenditure, the government decided to introduce, as an alternative to the invalid carriage, a cash allowance payable to adults of working age and children aged five and above who were unable, or virtually unable, to walk.[9]

These reforms were predicated on the assumption that disability was almost exclusively a problem facing adults. The chief difficulty posed by children with disabilities was that the extent of the problem was largely unknown. The OPCS Survey did not cover children under 16, and such estimates as were made of the number involved ranged from 80,000 to 350,000.[10] Moreover, as with those adults with mobility problems, it was not clear whether the main effort should be directed at improving facilities or granting cash allowances.[11] Attendance allowance was payable for children aged two or more,[12] and those aged five and over were to become entitled to the mobility allowance.

3   The Report of the Survey by the Office of Population Censuses and Surveys (OPCS) was published in three volumes: Part One, Harris *Handicapped and Impaired in Great Britain* (1971); Part Two, Buckle *Work and Housing of Impaired Persons in Great Britain* (1971); Part Three, Harris, Smith and Head *Income and Entitlement to Supplementary Benefit of Impaired People in Great Britain* (1972).
4   *Harris* n 3, above, p 18.
5   *Report on Social Security Provision for Chronically Sick and Disabled People* (1973–74, HC 276) paras 8 and 41.
6   NIA 1970, s 4. This proposal was adopted from Labour's ill-fated National Superannuation Bill of 1969.
7   Social Security Benefits Act 1975, s 7 (SSBA 1975).
8   See pp 682–683, below.
9   SSPA 1975, s 22. See pp 682–683, below.
10   See Disability Alliance *Poverty and Disability* (1975) pp 4–5; Pearson Royal Commission on Civil Liability and Compensation for Personal Injury (1978, Cmnd 7054-I), vol I, paras 1514–1520; and Townsend *Poverty in The United Kingdom* (1979) ch 21. A later OPCS study arrived at the figure of 360,000: Bone and Meltzer *The prevalence of disability among children* (1989) p 17.
11   *Report on Social Security Provision* n 5, above, para 45.
12   This age restriction was removed in 1990: SI 1990/581.

But it was the plight of the thalidomide children that prompted immediate government action. Since 1973 a Family Fund established on a non-statutory basis and administered by the Rowntree Memorial Trust had conferred benefits on severely disabled children. The government, which finances the scheme, had indicated that this was not intended as compensation for disablement, but rather to complement services already provided by statutory and voluntary bodies.[13]

C Reform in the 1990s

The Fowler Review of social security provision[14] excluded consideration of disability benefits, in large part because in 1984 the Department of Health and Social Security (DHSS) had commissioned a major new OPCS study of the numbers, circumstances and needs of disabled persons. The OPCS surveys were carried out between 1985 and 1988 and were published as six separate reports.[15] The first of these estimated that there were 6.2 million adults with varying degrees of disability.[16] It also demonstrated a marked correlation between age and disability: 69 per cent of disabled people were over 60, compared with 25 per cent of the general population, and 32 per cent aged 75 or over, compared with 8 per cent of the general population.[17] The second report showed that 31 per cent of disabled adults below pension age were in employment compared with 69 per cent of the general population.[18] Overall two main themes emerged: on average disabled people had lower incomes than the rest of the population, but most incurred extra costs as a direct result of their disability.[19] Critics have argued that the OPCS methodology none the less underestimated the real costs associated with disability.[20]

As the first of the OPCS reports was being published, the Social Security Advisory Committee (SSAC) produced its own special report on disability benefits.[21] The SSAC's most important long-term recommendation was for a unified benefit to help with the costs of disability and to replace the incomes of those disabled people incapable of work.[22] It was envisaged that the first step towards this would be an integrated disablement allowance. Such a benefit would supersede attendance allowance and

---

13 848 HC Official Report (5th series) cols 241–242W. See generally Bradshaw *The Family Fund* (1980); and Lawton (1990) 16 Child: care, health and development 35.

14 Green Paper *Reform of Social Security* (1985, Cmnd 9517).

15 Report 1, Martin, Meltzer and Elliot *The prevalence of disabilities among adults* (1988); Report 2, Martin and White *The financial circumstances of disabled adults living in private households* (1989); Report 3, Bone and Meltzer *The prevalence of disability among children* (1989); Report 4, Martin, White and Meltzer *Disabled adults: services, transport and employment* (1989); Report 5, Smyth and Robus *The financial circumstances of families with disabled children living in private households* (1989); Report 6, Meltzer, Smyth and Robus *Disabled children: services, transport and education* (1989). For criticism of the reports' emphasis on disability as an individual problem rather than a social construct, see Oliver *The Politics of Disablement* (1990) and Abberley (1992) 7 Disability, Handicap and Society 139.

16 *Martin, Meltzer and Elliot* n 15, above, p 16.

17 *Martin, Meltzer and Elliot* n 15, above, p 27 and see HC Social Services Committee *Ninth Report* (1989–90, HC 646) p vi.

18 *Martin and White* n 15, above, pp 12–13.

19 *Martin and White* n 15, above, p xviii.

20 See Thompson, Lavery and Curtice *Short-changed by Disability* (1990); Berthoud in Dalley (ed) *Disability and Social Policy* (1991); and Large in Dalley (ed) *Disability and Social Policy* (1991).

21 SSAC *Benefits for Disabled People: a Strategy for Change* (1988). See further SSAC *Social Security Provision for Disability: a Case for Change?* (1997); and Larkin (1998) 5 JSSL 9.

22 *SSAC (1988)* n 21, above, p 61.

mobility allowance in order to provide assistance with the extra costs of disability. The second step would be the development of an income replacement element.[23] To this end the SSAC recommended the raising of severe disablement allowance to invalidity benefit levels and the extension of the latter benefit to people without contribution records. Other recommendations included the development of a partial incapacity benefit.

The government's subsequent White Paper set out four policy objectives for benefits for disabled people.[24] The first was to improve the balance of benefits available to those unable to work, and especially to do more for those disabled from birth or early in life. The second was to improve the coverage of help with the extra costs of disability for people of working age and below. The third was to help disabled people to enter and remain in the labour market. The fourth was the need to avoid duplication with other sources of help. The White Paper accordingly proposed a programme of action to reflect these priorities. Stage one consisted of relatively minor changes to the benefits system which had already been announced in 1989.[25] Stage two comprised three more far-reaching changes to the existing structure which were enacted in the Social Security Act 1990 (SSA 1990).[26] These were the introduction of an age-related addition to severe disablement allowance, the abolition of reduced earnings allowance for new claimants[27] and the phasing out of the earnings-related element in invalidity benefit. The third stage involved the introduction of two new benefits which went some way to meeting the recommendations of the SSAC. The first benefit was to be created from a merger of attendance allowance and mobility allowance. Initially known as disability allowance, it later became disability living allowance.[28] The second benefit was a partial incapacity benefit, originally called disability employment credit but later retitled disability working allowance.[29] These benefits were introduced in April 1992 by the Disability Living Allowance and Disability Working Allowance Act 1991 (DLADWAA 1991), although the legislation was swiftly consolidated in the Social Security Contributions and Benefits Act 1992 (SSCBA 1992).

The reaction of the disability lobby to this package was generally one of disappointment. Three main criticisms were advanced. First, the OPCS study was based on the benefit system before the 1988 changes and so represented an inadequate basis for future policy development. Secondly, it was argued that in any event the government's response ignored the most important OPCS findings. The government estimated that the total reform package would benefit about 850,000 people (including some carers),[30] yet the OPCS reports found more than 6 million disabled people. Furthermore, there were no improvements for pensioners, despite the clear correlation between age, disability and poverty.[31] Thirdly, there had been no comprehensive review of the whole range of sickness and disability benefits, nor had there been any prior consultation with disabled people or their organisations about these proposals.[32]

23   *SSAC (1998)* n 21, above, p 63.
24   *The Way Ahead: Benefits for Disabled People* (1990, Cm 917) p 5. See Buck (1990) 19 ILJ 125.
25   See *HC Social Services Committee* n 17, above, p viii. Of these changes, only the waiver of the six-month qualifying period for attendance allowance for the terminally ill required primary legislation: SSA 1990, s 1.
26   Ss 2–4.
27   This was part of the industrial injuries scheme: see p 762, below.
28   See pp 682–705, below.
29   This has since transmuted into disabled person's tax credit. See pp 398–404, above.
30   181 HC Official Report (6th series) col 353.
31   Walker and Walker in *Dalley* (ed) n 20, above.
32   Although after DLADWAA 1991 was enacted, the DSS consulted widely on the draft regulations and on the new benefit claim forms.

Since the introduction of disability living allowance (DLA) in 1992 there has been a considerable increase in both the cost of the benefit and the numbers of awards. Expenditure rose from £2.3 billion in 1992–93 to over £5 billion in 1998–99 and the number of claimants increased from 1.3 million in 1994 to 2.2 million in 2001.[33] The reasons for this growth in the caseload include the availability of the new lowest rate care component and lower rate mobility components as well as factors such as a new claims procedure, based on self-assessment, and greater public awareness of the benefit. However, recipients of the lower rate components are scarcely less disabled than other DLA claimants.[34] The eligibility criteria for the benefit are also skewed in favour of those with physical as opposed to mental disabilities.[35] Whilst this might suggest that DLA is failing to reach many potential recipients, concerns about inappropriate awards of the benefit and its potential for fraud led the Department of Social Security (DSS) to launch the ill-fated Benefit Integrity Project (BIP) in 1997. As part of the BIP, claimants who fell into certain categories were visited and their benefit entitlement reassessed, causing considerable distress to many recipients. The Department's handling of the BIP was roundly condemned by the House of Commons Social Security Committee.[36] The Committee has also described DLA as 'an unstable benefit ... The structure of the benefit and its administrative procedure fails in terms of simplicity and workability'.[37]

D Determining priorities and defining disability

The dominant trends, to be perceived from the section above, of a major expansion of benefit programmes in the 1970s and some retrenchment or only limited extension of coverage thereafter has occurred also in other countries.[38] The political dimension is important. Growth in provision for the disabled may be attributed to an increasing public recognition, fostered particularly by pressure group activity, of the moral worthiness of such persons to benefit from redistributive measures.[39] The reluctance to maintain the momentum in the 1980s resulted from a reassertion of more traditional values which gave priority to reward for work over the fulfilment of need, however legitimate. The tension between the rival values is evident not only in the evolution of the current system but also in the prolific debate concerning the future.[40]

As has been observed:

33 DSS *The Changing Welfare State* (2000) pp 72–75; and the Department for Work and Pensions (DWP) *Work and Pension Statistics 2001* (2001) p 165, Table 1.

34 Sainsbury, Hirst and Lawton *Evaluation of Disability Living Allowance and Attendance Allowance* DSS Research Report No 41 (1995). See further Hirst (1997) 31 Soc Pol & Admin 136.

35 Zarb (ed) *Social Security and Mental Health: Report on SSAC Workshop* SSAC Research Paper 7 (1996); and Hirst and Sainsbury *Social Security and Mental Health: the impact of disability living allowance* SPRU Social Policy Report No 6 (1996).

36 HC Social Security Committee *Fourth Report* (1997–98, HC 641) paras 46–73 and *Third Report* (1998–99, HC 63).

37 *Fourth Report* n 36, above para 79. See further *SSAC (1997)* n 21, above; and Wikeley in Harris *Social Security Law in Context* (2000) ch 12.

38 Stone *The Disabled State* (1985); Copeland (1981) 44 Soc Sec Bull 25; DSS *Containing the Cost of Social Security – the international context* (1994).

39 Haber and Smith (1971) 36 Am Soc Rev 87.

40 *Pearson* n 10, above, esp chs 10–11; Walker and Townsend *Disability in Britain: A Manifesto of Rights* (1981); Brown *The Disability Income System* (1984); Harris et al *Compensation and Support for Illness and Injury* (1984); Stapleton *Disease and the Compensation Debate* (1986); Walker and Walker in *Dalley (ed)* n 20, above.

> It would be difficult to find anyone involved in the present disability income system –
> from politicians through officials, voluntary agencies, academics, lobby groups to individual
> disabled people – who is not highly critical of the current arrangements.[41]

It is clear that such dissatisfaction has different sources. In the first place, there is considerable criticism of the complexity of the system.[42] While, in part, this is a consequence of incremental change and a disinclination to engineer radical restructuring, nevertheless, in part, it also results from specific claims of distributional justice. The argument is that different groups of disabled persons deserve to be treated differently, even at the price of complexity and high administrative cost. The more generous protection offered to the victims of war, industrial accidents, crimes of violence and torts is often rationalised on this basis – it is argued that the cause of the disability strengthens the case for compensation[43] – and the notion that social security contributors should be more favourably treated than non-contributors can be similarly justified. Naturally, as policymakers quickly discover, there are those with vested interests in each special scheme who will resist simplification, if it involves some loss to those interests.[44]

Perceptions of distributional justice can generate other complexities. The more diverse the need, the greater the pressure on legal and administrative machinery to evaluate it. For example, it was originally suggested that entitlement to DLA might be based on a 'points index', under which points are related to the costs associated with particular disabilities.[45] This idea has been rejected by the government on the grounds of the complexity and practical problems involved.[46]

Nor is it to be assumed that there is general agreement on how disability should be defined.[47] Other areas of social security entitlement can adopt criteria which are predominantly objective in character: age, joblessness and even 'poverty' in the sense that available resources are below a prescribed level. 'Disability', on the other hand, is 'a socially created category rather than an attribute of individuals',[48] and, as such, depends crucially both on policy goals and on those responsible for assessment. In terms of policy goals, we can observe the primacy within the British system of 'incapacity for work' because the system focuses traditionally on income replacement for those unable to participate in the labour market. This is the test used for statutory sick pay and incapacity benefit, although it was substantially restructured in 1995.[49] The creation of benefits to meet special needs called for criteria tied to those needs; thus, requiring 'attention' and 'supervision' from another person and/or being 'unable or virtually unable to walk'. Pressure groups and others arguing for more comprehensive provision for the disadvantages suffered by physically or mentally disabled people have of necessity to propose criteria which involve assessing the

41   *Harris et al* n 40, above p 313.
42   *Walker and Walker* n 40, above. For some empirical evidence on the difficulties posed for claimants, see *Harris et al* n 40, above, ch 5.
43   Pp 717–718, below.
44   Cane *Atiyah's Accidents, Compensation and the Law* (6th edn, 1999) p 404; *Brown* n 40, above, pp 315–316.
45   *SSAC (1998)* n 21, above, paras 3.17–3.20 and 11.13–11.17.
46   (1990, Cm 917) para 3.15 and DSS *Social Security Benefits for Disabled People* (1991, Cm 1608) para 22 and Annex A. Yet these difficulties have not deterred the government from adopting a similar approach in relation to assessing incapacity for work: p 541, above.
47   Blaxter *The Meaning of Disability* (1967); Duckworth *The Classification and Measurement of Disablement* (1983); *Stone* n 38, above; Oliver *The Politics of Disablement* (1990).
48   *Stone* n 38, above, p 26. See further *Wikeley* n 37, above, p 365.
49   See pp 538–555, above.

degree of such disability.[50] This approach was first adopted in the industrial injury and war pension schemes[51] and was introduced into the general social security programme in 1984 to determine entitlement to severe disablement allowance.

All of these definitions require assessment which, itself, poses practical and theoretical difficulties.[52] Traditionally most reliance has been a placed on clinical assessment: for most purposes the views of the medical profession, in the form either of medical statements by general practitioners or of examination by specialists, have been regarded as decisive. In some respects[53] there has been a recent tendency to reduce the significance of clinical assessment for questions of entitlement and the reasons are not, perhaps, difficult to locate.[54] First, clinical tests cannot themselves determine functional incapacity, eg incapacity for work or an inability to self-care. Quite apart from the fact that such definitions require a decision as to which tasks it is reasonable for the claimant to perform,[55] there is no objective measurement of physical and mental ability. At the last resort, the ultimate obstacle to human functioning lies in the subjective experience of the claimant; pain, fatigue and so on are not susceptible of measurement.[56] Secondly, unlike administrators concerned with cost constraints, doctors have no motivation to restrict entitlement, particularly if they are general practitioners who wish to preserve good relations with their patients. Also, given the sometimes high degree of uncertainty involved in diagnosis, they may wish to err on the side of assisting claimants where serious hardship may result from an adverse determination.[57] The apparent shift away from medical assessment has not been accompanied by a markedly greater involvement of other professionals, such as social workers and psychologists, notwithstanding the views of some that the social and emotional consequences of disability are as important as financial consequences.[58]

The distributional dilemma of deciding who should benefit from financial support, involving, as it does, difficult issues of defining disability, is in practice and for the foreseeable future dominated by cost considerations. This explains the hitherto cool official responses to the far-reaching proposals for a disability income scheme advanced by pressure groups representing the disabled.[59] The basic idea is for a single state scheme for all disabled people with uniform criteria of entitlement. It would comprise: an income replacement benefit, on the lines of the existing long term rate of incapacity benefit, but without contribution conditions and with a reduced rate for those partially incapable of work; and a disablement costs allowance to cover other losses, payable on a scale according to the degree of disablement. The costs of such a scheme[60] make it unlikely that any future government will adopt anything other than an incremental approach to the reform of disability benefits.

---

50 Disablement Income Group *DIG's National Disability Income* (1987) and Disability Alliance *Poverty and Disability: Breaking the Link* (1987). See the discussion in *SSAC (1988)* n 21, above, pp 48–55.

51 Pp 753–754, below.

52 *Duckworth* n 47, above; Mashaw *Bureaucratic Justice: Managing Social Security Disability Claims* (1983).

53 Eg in self-certification for short periods of sickness (see p 530, above) and in the so-called 'demedicalisation' of the claims assessment procedure for disability living allowance (see p 684, below).

54 Cf *Stone* n 38, above, ch 4.

55 Cf pp 542–544, above.

56 *Blaxter* n 47, above, pp 11–13; *Stone* n 38, above, pp 134–139. See also *SSAC (1997)* n 21, above, para 4.6.

57 *Stone* n 38, above, pp 148–152; *Mashaw* n 52, above, pp 26–29. See also Ritchie *GPs and IVB* DSS Research Report No 18 (1993).

58 Townsend *The Disabled In Society* (1967) pp 5–6; *Blaxter* n 47, above, pp 6–7 and ch 8. But note that the claim form for DLA asks a carer or friend to confirm the nature of the claimant's problems, and appeal tribunals hearing DLA or attendance allowance cases must include one member who is either a disabled person or carer.

59 See the references cited in n 50, above.

60 Estimated to be about £3 billion in 1987 terms: *Disability Alliance* n 50, above.

E   Overview of the current disability and carers' benefits

The remainder of this chapter deals with the three non-contributory and non-means tested benefits paid for or in connection with severely disabled people: DLA, attendance allowance for people aged 65 or over and carer's allowance (formerly invalid care allowance, or ICA). DLA, which was introduced in April 1992, consists of two elements: a care component and a mobility component.[61] A person's entitlement to DLA may be to either or both of these components.[62] Thus DLA is essentially an amalgamation of the former attendance and mobility allowances, although new lower levels of benefit exist to cater for less severely disabled people who would not have been eligible for either of the old benefits. The care component is payable at one of three rates, depending upon the criteria satisfied.[63] There are, however, only two rates for the mobility component.[64] The result is that there are in total 11 different levels of DLA payable, depending on the combination of components and rates payable. The decision to model DLA on existing benefits enabled the DSS to build on the practical experience of those schemes. The prime disadvantage of this policy was that it excluded people whose disabilities impose other kinds of costs.[65] The following Parts deal with the mobility component (Part 2), the care component (Part 3), the residual attendance allowance for people who claim after the age of 65 (Part 4) and the rules common to DLA and attendance allowance (Part 5).

Finally, Part 6 concerns carer's allowance. Although this is a benefit for carers, rather than for severely disabled people themselves, entitlement is contingent upon the person being cared for receiving DLA[66] or attendance allowance and so it is conveniently dealt with in this chapter. Carers also receive some limited recognition elsewhere in the social security system. For example, carers constitute one of the prescribed categories of persons who are eligible for income support.[67] In addition, a carer may qualify for a carer's premium as part of their applicable amount for the purposes of income support or income-based jobseeker's allowance.[68] Caring responsibilities may also result in some relief from the full rigours of the labour market conditions that are imposed on jobseeker's allowance claimants.[69]

Part 2   The mobility component of disability living allowance

A   General

Historically assistance for people with mobility needs has been provided primarily in kind rather than money.[70] Invalid vehicles, generally a single-seat three-wheeler, were

---

61   SSCBA 1992, s 71(1).
62   SSCBA 1992, s 71(2). As DLA is a single composite benefit, a claimant appealing against a disallowance of one component may advance a claim for the other component, even if that has previously been disregarded: *R 2/95 (DLA)*.
63   SSCBA 1992, s 72(3) and (4).
64   SSCBA 1992, s 73(10) and (11).
65   Eg people with digestive disorders, which create the greatest need for extra costs: see Berthoud in Dalley (ed) *Disability and Social Policy* (1991) p 92.
66   To be precise, the highest or middle rate of the care component of DLA.
67   SI 1987/1967, Sch 1B, paras 4–6 (this category is wider than recipients of carer's allowance); see p 279, above.
68   P 301, above. Such a premium is also available in the housing benefit and council tax benefit schemes.
69   P 345, above.
70   For further detail see the 3rd edition of this book, pp 171–172 and the government-sponsored report by Lady Sharp *Mobility of Physically Disabled People* (1974).

first supplied to war pensioners in 1921. In the following decades these 'trikes' were gradually made available under the National Health Service legislation to narrowly defined groups amongst the civilian disabled population. War pensioners became entitled after 1945 in certain cases to a small car as an alternative to the trike (the same facility became available in 1964 for non-war pensioners). Alongside these provisions, certain cash allowances were made available such as exemption from road vehicle excise duty and a tax-free sum of £100 per year to help those eligible for a trike to run and maintain their own car. The whole structure of mobility benefits was examined in a report undertaken by Lady Sharp, published in 1974,[71] the findings of which were critical of the prevailing system. First, existing facilities were distributed inequitably – in particular, they were limited to invalids who themselves were able to drive. Secondly, the three-wheeler itself was unsatisfactory – it was dangerous, noisy, uncomfortable, liable to break down and could not carry a passenger. The recommendation was that it should be replaced by a small car as soon as this became economically feasible, but with a narrower range of individuals retaining the right to elect instead for a cash allowance to help maintain and run the car.

The provision of cars would indeed have been too expensive, and the Labour government resisted Lady Sharp's proposal as it would have reduced the range of disabled persons entitled to assistance. Instead it was decided to provide as an alternative to the three-wheeler a flat-rate, non-contributory mobility allowance. This solution, implemented by SSPA 1975, did not, however, prove to be entirely satisfactory. On the one hand, there was continuing concern for the safety of the three-wheeler; on the other hand, the allowance was insufficient for many of those without a vehicle of any kind to finance the necessary means of locomotion.[72] As regards the first of these problems, the government decided to phase out production of the vehicle and to allow those already in possession of one to qualify automatically for the mobility allowance, as and when they gave up use of it.[73] Secondly, the 'Motability' scheme was established to help immobile persons to get maximum value for their resources, and, in particular, to enable them to lease or obtain on hire purchase a car on favourable terms.

Expenditure on mobility allowance increased rapidly following its introduction in 1976. In 1977 there were 62,000 successful claims; by 1992 there were 699,000 current awards.[74] The OPCS surveys conducted between 1985 and 1988 found that locomotion problems were the most common type of disability.[75] This study also revealed that mobility difficulties gave rise to the highest levels of extra expenditure by individuals associated with their disability.[76] However, both the OPCS research and a subsequent study based on the Family Expenditure Survey suggested that such disability-related expenditure was actually less than the current rate of mobility allowance.[77] This conclusion became a central theme of the policy making which led to the introduction of DLA, although its basis is questionable given the doubts over the methodology used to assess disability-related costs.[78]

---

71 *Lady Sharp* n 70, above.
72 Cf DHSS *The Impact of Mobility Allowance* Research Report No 7 (1981).
73 Social Security (Miscellaneous Provisions) Act 1977, s 13.
74 DSS *Social Security Statistics 1993* (1993) Table E2.03.
75 Over 4 million adults were estimated to have mobility problems: Martin, Meltzer and Elliot *The prevalence of disability among adults* (1988) p 25.
76 Martin and White *The financial circumstances of disabled adults living in private households* (1989) p 53.
77 *The Way Ahead: benefits for disabled people* (1990, Cm 917) p 26.
78 See the literature cited at n 20, above.

Despite the apparent success of mobility allowance, three aspects of the benefit became the subject of criticism. The first concerned its scope; the criteria for mobility allowance depended upon proof of inability or virtual inability to walk, resulting from a physical disability. This often excluded claimants with severe learning difficulties or behavioural problems, who might have the ability to walk but be unable to make proper use of that faculty.[79] The introduction of DLA was used to graft on a new basis for entitlement to the higher rate of the mobility component for people in this group,[80] as well as the addition of a new lower rate for those less seriously disabled (whether physically or mentally) who still had mobility problems.[81] The second criticism of mobility allowance centred on the age restrictions. Children under five and adults who satisfied the mobility criteria after reaching 65 were not eligible for benefit.[82] The 1992 reforms made no changes to these rules, but children aged three and four became eligible for the higher rate of the mobility component as a result of the Welfare Reform and Pensions Act 1999 (WRPA 1999).[83] In the case of those who claim after reaching the age of 65, the resource implications of an extension in coverage would be considerable.[84] Finally, pressure groups criticised the adjudication procedure,[85] and especially the invasive nature of the medical examinations involved, including the notorious 'walking test' conducted by medical appeal tribunals.[86] These complaints were addressed by the 'demedicalisation' of decision making for DLA, with the consequential greater reliance on self-assessment by claimants of their disabilities.[87] More recently, however, the Department has again increasingly relied on clinical assessments (either from the claimant's GP or specialist, or from an examining medical practitioner visiting the claimant in their home and preparing a report) when considering claims for DLA and requests to reconsider existing awards.[88]

B   Amount

The mobility component is payable at two rates: a higher rate where the conditions described under section C, below, are satisfied and a lower rate for cases within section D.[89] The general rule is that it is disregarded in the assessment of the income-related benefits.[90] The rationale for this is that the mobility component is not intended to assist with general living costs, but rather with the extra costs associated with mobility problems. It is also exempt from income tax.[91]

79   See p 686, below for a discussion of *Lees v Secretary of State for Social Services* [1985] AC 930.
80   P 689, below.
81   P 691, below.
82   As a result OPCS found that 10 per cent or less of those over pension age in severity categories 8 to 10 received mobility allowance: *Martin and White* n 76, above, p 22.
83   P 692, below.
84   This has not prevented the DLA Advisory Board from advocating consideration of this approach: see p 693.
85   See the 3rd edition of this book, pp 175–176.
86   See NACAB *Assessing the Assessors: medical assessments for disability benefits* (1990).
87   P 184, above.
88   The so-called Safeguarding Project, which led to a marked decline in the number of awards of the higher rate mobility component: DSS *The Changing Welfare State* (2000), p 75.
89   SSCBA 1992, s 73(10)–(11).
90   SSCBA 1992, s 73(14).
91   Income and Corporation Taxes Act 1988, s 617.

C Entitlement to the higher rate

There are four possible ways to qualify for the higher rate of the DLA mobility component. The first, and by far the most common in practice, is where the claimant is either unable to walk or virtually unable to do so. The second group consists of people who are both blind and deaf. The third category comprises people with severe mental impairment and severe behavioural problems. Finally, those who give up use of an invalid vehicle may qualify for the higher rate.

i Inability or virtual inability to walk

The basic statutory test of entitlement is that the claimant is 'suffering from physical disablement such that he is either unable to walk or virtually unable to walk'.[92] The regulations then prescribe more specifically two ways in which this requirement can be satisfied, each of which is subdivided so as to cover a range of different scenarios:

    (a) his physical condition as a whole is such that, without having regard to circumstances peculiar to that person as to place of residence or as to place of, or nature of, employment,—
        (i) he is unable to walk; or
       (ii) his ability to walk out of doors is so limited, as regards the distance over which or the speed at which or the length of time for which or the manner in which he can make progress on foot without severe discomfort, that he is virtually unable to walk; or
      (iii) the exertion required to walk would constitute a danger to his life or would be likely to lead to a serious deterioration in his health.
    (b) he has both legs amputated at levels which are either through or above the ankle, or he has one leg so amputated and is without the other leg, or is without both legs to the same extent as if it, or they, had been so amputated.[93]

So far as the principal condition (a) is concerned, the claimant must fulfil one of the three conditions (i), (ii) or (iii). The alternative condition (b) was first introduced in 1991 and is a deeming provision for people without feet. It covers both double amputees and people born without feet (eg some Thalidomide victims). Before the principal condition is examined, it is necessary to consider the factors that are common to the three separate sub-heads.

ii Factors common to the three sub-heads of the principal condition

A PHYSICAL DISABLEMENT

A controversial feature of the original mobility allowance,[94] and one which distinguished it from other disability benefits, was its restriction to physical disablement, thus excluding cases such as agoraphobia where the inability to walk results solely from mental disablement.[95] Since the introduction of DLA, this requirement applies only to the first

---

92 SSCBA 1992, s 73(1)(a).
93 SI 1991/2890, reg 12(1).
94 Cf *Pearson* n 10, above, para 534.
95 *R(M) 1/80*.

two and the final ways of qualifying for the higher rate of the mobility component.[96] Claimants with a mental disability may satisfy the third criterion for the higher rate, or the single test for the lower rate mobility component.

The distinction drawn by the legislation between the two types of disablement is difficult to justify in medical terms[97] or indeed as a matter of principle.[98] It has certainly been difficult to draw the distinction in practice, so giving rise to a substantial body of not wholly consistent case law.[99] The reference in SI 1991/2890, regulation 12(1)(a) to the claimant's 'physical condition as a whole' was apparently designed to clarify the issue by concentrating on the effect of a disabling condition rather than its causation.[100] Nevertheless, in the leading House of Lords decision of *Lees v Secretary of State for Social Services*, it was held that impairment of the capacity for spatial orientation is not sufficient to render the claimant unable (or virtually unable) to walk unless it results from a physical disablement.[101] So claimants who have the ability physically to control the movement of their feet so as to move in an intended direction do not qualify under this head even though they need the assistance of another to steer them in the right direction.

The application of this principle to the facts in *Lees* itself may have been relatively unproblematic – the claimant was blind but capable of putting one foot in front of the other – but how far it extends to more complex behavioural limitations on mobility is unclear.[102] As one Commissioner has observed:

> It may be that in the last analysis all mental disablement can be ascribed to physical causes. But if so, it is obvious that the Act on drawing the distinction between physical and mental disablement did not mean this last analysis to be resorted to.[103]

In another case, a Tribunal of Commissioners indicated that the criterion was 'whether the claimant *could* not walk, as distinct from *would* not walk'.[104] This is an easier test to state in theory rather than to apply in practice. Manifestly, all such attempts to devise verbal formulae to address what are essentially medical questions are flawed; inevitably, decisions by decision makers, be they officers acting on behalf of the Secretary of State or appeal tribunals,[105] will remain difficult to predict.

B   PERSONAL CIRCUMSTANCES

Circumstances relating to the physical condition of the claimant are, of course, crucial, but the regulations provide that the authorities should ignore where he or she lives and

---

96   Namely SSCBA 1992, s 73(1)(a), under consideration here, and s 73(1)(b) (blind and deaf claimants). This requirement necessarily also applies to the fourth route (prior entitlement to invalid vehicle) which is contingent on having satisfied the old mobility allowance test.

97   See Lord Lloyd of Berwick on categories of personal injury in *Page v Smith* [1995] 2 All ER 736 at 759.

98   See *Wikeley* n 37, above, pp 394–396.

99   For commentary, see Richards [1985] JSWL 16; and Mesher [1986] JSWL 62. Non-binding guidance on the types of mobility requirements associated with various disabilities is to be found in Aylward, Dewis and Henderson (eds) *The Disability Handbook* (2nd edn, 1998).

100   See NIAC *Report on Draft Amendment Regulations* (1979, Cmnd 7491) para 6.

101   [1985] AC 930, [1985] 2 All ER 203, effectively overruling the more generous interpretation suggested in *R(M) 1/83(T)*: see *R(M) 3/86(T)*, para 6. See also, applying *Lees*, *Hewitt v Chief Adjudication Officer; Diment v Chief Adjudication Officer*, CA, reported as *R(DLA) 6/99*.

102   See Blom-Cooper (1986) 57 Political Q 144 at 153 for criticism.

103   *R(M) 1/88*, para 6, J G Monroe, Comr, quoted with approval by O'Connor LJ in *Harrison v Secretary of State for Social Services*, reported as Appendix to *R(M) 1/88*.

104   *R(M) 3/86(T)*, para 8.

105   For the composition of such tribunals (one member of which is a doctor), see p 194, above.

the place and nature of any employment. In other words, the extent of mobility is to be determined by a mechanical test, not by reference to the purpose of the locomotion.[106] In social policy terms this test ignores what is reasonably necessary for the claimant to participate in the minimal essential activities of life, a failure recognised by the introduction of the lower rate of the mobility component for DLA.

C USE OF PROSTHESES ETC

The ability to walk is to be judged having regard to a prosthesis or artificial aid which the claimant habitually wears or uses.[107] So claimants who are able to walk with such an appliance are not entitled to benefit. Of course, a claimant still unable (or virtually unable) to walk with the appliance will succeed.[108]

iii The principal alternative conditions

Subject to these general considerations, the claimant must satisfy one of the following conditions.

A TOTAL INABILITY TO WALK

'Walk' is an ordinary word of the English language and should be interpreted as such; thus it means 'to move by means of a person's legs and feet or a combination of them'[109] in such a way that one foot is always on the ground.[110]

B VIRTUAL INABILITY TO WALK[111]

The present wording of the second, crucial, condition results from amendments made in 1979.[112] As one Commissioner has noted, 'the base point is a total inability to walk, which is extended to take in people who can walk but only to an insignificant extent'.[113] It requires both a qualitative and a quantitative assessment of the limits of the claimant's ability to walk outdoors without severe discomfort, having regard to distance, speed, length of time and of manner. In doing so the adjudicating authorities must ignore 'any extended outdoor walking accomplishment which the claimant could or might attain only with severe discomfort'.[114] In applying this test, reasonable outdoor conditions should be assumed.[115] In considering what the claimant is able to do with, and without, severe discomfort,[116] the authorities are to have regard only to the discomfort which

---

106 *R(M) 3/78*, paras 9–12, J S Watson, Comr.
107 SI 1991/2890, reg 12(4) and see *R(M) 2/89*. This test does not apply to double amputees etc.
108 *NIAC* n 100, above, para 13.
109 *R(M) 3/78*, para 10, J S Watson, Comr; but also an intended direction: *R(M) 2/81*.
110 *R(M) 2/89*, para 8, J J Skinner, Comr.
111 A term described by one medical commentator as 'meaningless clinically': Hunter (1986) 292 BMJ 172.
112 On which see *NIAC* n 100, above.
113 *R(M) 1/91*, para 6, D G Rice, Comr.
114 *R(M) 1/81*, para 9, I Edward-Jones, Comr.
115 *R(M) 1/91*, paras 8–9, D G Rice, Comr (stressing that the test concerns ability to walk, not to climb).
116 This need not amount to severe pain or distress, but could arise through breathlessness: *Cassinelli v Secretary of State for Social Services*, reported as *R(M) 2/92*.

arises from the exertion of moving, not from external factors, such as the risk of encountering obstacles or stepping in front of traffic.[117] Similarly, the Court of Appeal has reluctantly held that a claimant who can physically walk, but who suffers from porphyria, is not entitled to the higher rate mobility component notwithstanding the extreme discomfort suffered by being exposed to daylight.[118] According to Ward LJ: 'If the intention was to confer the benefit on one who suffers from *being* outside, the regulation could easily have said so. Instead, it uses the phrases "his ability to *walk* out of doors" and to "*making progress* on foot".' A need for guidance of a precautionary or reassuring nature may preclude the claimant from qualifying, whereas a need for physical support itself may lead to the statutory test being satisfied.[119]

C   EXERTION CONSTITUTING RISK TO LIFE OR HEALTH

It is important, for this condition, to establish a connection or a relationship between the 'exertion required to walk' and the danger to life or a risk of serious deterioration in health. So, eg a person advised medically not to walk because he or she might, in the process, be subject to an epileptic fit is not entitled on this ground alone, for there is no causal relationship between the exertion of walking and the risk of a fit.[120]

iv   Blind and deaf claimants

The second way in which a person may qualify for the higher rate of the mobility component is if he or she is 'both blind and deaf'.[121] Regulations provide that a person is to be taken to meet this dual requirement only where the degree of disablement amounts to 100 per cent and 80 per cent respectively.[122] So far as blindness is concerned, the regulations provide no indication whatsoever as to how the level of disablement is to be assessed.[123] The Commissioners have sanctioned the practice of decision makers applying the same rules of thumb as under the industrial injuries scheme,[124] and so it suffices that the claimant cannot count fingers beyond one foot or has vision assessed as less than 6/60 using both eyes with glasses. The regulations are a little more helpful with deafness, requiring 80 per cent disablement 'on a scale where 100 per cent represents absolute deafness'.[125] According to the Commissioner the standard test for occupational deafness should be employed[126] and so an audiogram test is used.[127] In addition, the claimant must, by reason of the combined effect of their blindness and

---

117   *R(M) 1/83(T)*.
118   *Hewitt v Chief Adjudication Officer; Diment v Chief Adjudication Officer*, CA, reported as *R(M) 6/99*. Porphyria is a condition causing severe blistering of the skin within minutes of exposure to daylight.
119   *R(M) 1/90*.
120   *R(M) 3/78*.
121   SSCBA 1992, s 73(1)(b) and (2). Entitlement to mobility allowance was first extended to this group in 1990.
122   SI 1991/2890, reg 12(2).
123   Cf SI 1982/1408, Sch 2 and SI 1985/967, Sch 3 under the industrial injuries scheme.
124   *R(DLA) 3/95*.
125   SI 1991/2890, reg 12(2)(b). Regard should be had to any hearing aid which the claimant 'habitually uses or which is suitable in his case': see SI 1994/1779, reg 3(5).
126   *R(DLA) 3/95*, para 9, D G Rice, Comr.
127   For the relevant chart see DSS *Decision Makers Guide* (DMG) (2000) vol 10, paras 61390–61392. When DLA was first introduced, the crude extra-statutory test was whether the claimant was able to hear a shout from beyond one metre away, using any hearing aid.

deafness, 'be unable, without the assistance of another person, to walk to any intended destination while out of doors'.[128]

v Claimants with severe mental impairment and severe behavioural problems

The third means of qualifying for the higher rate mobility component is the most narrowly-drawn. Its introduction in 1992 was a response to the difficulties faced by claimants with severe behavioural problems in meeting the conventional test of entitlement to mobility allowance.[129] The claimant must satisfy a threefold test:[130] he or she must (1) be 'severely mentally impaired'; (2) display 'severe behavioural problems'; and (3) satisfy both the day and the night time conditions for the award of the care component of DLA. None of these three conditions is allowed to stand undefined.

A   SEVERELY MENTALLY IMPAIRED

Regulations provide that a person meets this requirement if:

> he suffers from a state of arrested development or incomplete physical development of the brain, which results in severe impairment of intelligence and social functioning.[131]

(i) A state of arrested development or incomplete physical development of the brain
The original intention behind this formulation was to limit entitlement to claimants who were severely mentally impaired from birth or from early childhood, on the basis that the human brain is not fully developed until the age of about five years old.[132] It was therefore envisaged that it would cover a child aged four who was severely disabled as a result of falling out of a tree or an attack of meningitis, but not a teenager injured as a result of a motorcycle accident. The Commissioners, on the basis of expert medical advice, have taken a somewhat broader approach. A person with Alzheimer's disease does not suffer from 'a state of arrested development or incomplete physical development of the brain' as this degenerative condition only occurs after the brain has fully developed.[133] However, the stage at which the brain reached full development would depend on the individual, albeit it would invariably take place before the age of 30. Thus a person who suffered from schizophrenia from the age of 16 might well meet this component of the statutory test, albeit that he or she also had lucid intervals.[134]

(ii) Severe impairment of intelligence and social functioning
The Court of Appeal has held that this test is only satisfied if a person suffers from severe impairment of both intelligence and of social functioning.[135] Clearly, a particular claimant may suffer from one (severe impairment of social functioning) but not the other (severe

---

128   SI 1991/2890, reg 12(3).
129   See Wikeley (1999) 6 JSSL 10.
130   SSCBA 1992, s 73(1)(c) and (3).
131   SI 1991/2890, reg 12(5).
132   Personal communication, Benefits Agency Medical Service doctor.
133   *R(DLA) 2/96.*
134   *R(DLA) 3/98.* However, schizophrenia is not associated with below normal intelligence, and so a sufferer would fail to meet the second limb of SI 1991/2890, reg 12(5), discussed under section *(ii)*, above.
135   *M (A Child) v Chief Adjudication Officer,* reported as *R(DLA) 1/00.*

impairment of intelligence), as with some sufferers from autism. Equally the converse may be true (as with some people with Down's syndrome). The court expressly rejected the argument that the phrase should be read conjunctively to arrive at a single composite assessment.[136] However, the court also rejected the approach of the Benefits Agency and the Commissioner, which was to equate 'severe impairment of intelligence' with an IQ of 55 or less. This was 'too narrow and mechanistic': IQ assessments were a relevant but not determinative factor; other evidence should be admitted as 'in some cases at least an impairment of social functioning will shade into an impairment of intelligence'.

B   SEVERE BEHAVIOURAL PROBLEMS

This condition likewise is comprehensively defined. The person must display disruptive behaviour which:

(a) is extreme;

(b) regularly requires another person to intervene and physically restrain him in order to prevent him causing physical injury to himself or to another, or damage to property; and

(c) is so unpredictable that he requires another person to be present and watching over him whenever he is awake.[137]

The stringent nature of sub-conditions (a) and (b) arguably makes requirement (c) superfluous.

C   ENTITLEMENT TO THE HIGHEST RATE OF THE DLA CARE COMPONENT

In addition to the conditions above, the claimant must satisfy both the day and night-time tests for the DLA care component.[138] This will exclude some people with severe behavioural problems who can sleep unattended at night. Given that the benefit is directed to those with mobility problems out of doors, the insistence on the satisfaction of the night time care condition is difficult to justify, other than as a crude rationing device. Such individuals may still qualify for the higher rate of the mobility component on the basis that they are virtually unable to walk, or they may satisfy the test for the lower rate of the component, described below.

vi   Prior entitlement to mobility assistance

As indicated above, the government decided to phase out the supply of invalid vehicles with the introduction of mobility allowance. A person entitled to such a vehicle may not in addition receive the mobility component of DLA, but if he or she (1) elects no longer to use it, or (2) has acquired a private car or (3) intends, with the help of the allowance, to acquire one and also to learn to drive it, the higher rate of the mobility component becomes payable. For this purpose, claimants are deemed to satisfy the medical criteria, provided that their physical condition has not improved.[139]

---

136 For criticism of the Commissioner's decision see *Wikeley* n 129, above, pp 18–26, and of the Court of Appeal's judgment, see Wikeley (2000) 7 JSSL 117.

137 SI 1991/2890, reg 12(6).

138 P 696, below.

139 SSCBA 1992, s 74 and SI 1991/2890, reg 13 and Sch 2.

D Entitlement to the lower rate

There is only one way to qualify for the lower rate of the DLA mobility component, namely that the claimant:

> is able to walk but is so severely disabled physically or mentally that, disregarding any ability he may have to use routes which are familiar to him, he cannot take advantage of that faculty out of doors without guidance or supervision from another person most of the time.[140]

This formulation first appeared in DLADWAA 1991[141] in response to the need shown by the OPCS survey for assistance to be directed at those who are able physically to walk but who are not independently mobile. People with learning difficulties or behavioural problems who do not meet the strict conditions laid down for the higher rate of the mobility component may be entitled on this basis. The lower rate may also be available to blind or partially sighted people[142] and agoraphobics.[143]

It is important, however, to appreciate that the lower rate is not some form of 'consolation prize' for claimants who have narrowly failed to qualify for the higher rate mobility component. The eligibility criteria focus on very different factors from those that are relevant to an award of the higher rate mobility component.[144] The crucial issue is whether the claimant 'cannot take advantage of the faculty [of walking] out of doors without guidance or supervision from another person most of the time'. 'Cannot', in this context, means that the claimant is either actually unable to do so or it would be completely unreasonable to expect him to do so.[145] A problematic issue has been the meaning of 'guidance or supervision' in the context of section 73(1)(d) of SSCBA 1992. On one level 'guidance' may be seen as more active than 'supervision'. The former implies physically leading a person or giving oral guidance or encouragement, whilst the latter suggests a precautionary role, but one that may shade into more active assistance. But can 'supervision' which counts for the purpose of qualifying for the care component, discussed further below, also be taken into account in assessing entitlement to the lower rate mobility component? Following a series of conflicting unreported Commissioners' decisions on the point, a Tribunal of Commissioners held that there may be some overlap between 'supervision' in the two contexts.[146]

In response to the decision of the Tribunal of Commissioners, the Department did not seek to change the law relating to the meaning of 'supervision'. The official view, however, was that a further aspect of the Commissioners' decision, dealing with the effects of fear or anxiety, had created confusion and uncertainty for decision makers and unduly extended the scope of entitlement to DLA. The DWP thus brought forward amending regulations in April 2002.[147] These provided that, for the purposes of entitlement to the lower rate of the mobility component:

---

140 SSCBA 1992, s 73(1)(d).
141 S 1(2), inserting SSA 1975, s 37ZC(1)(d).
142 See also *Mallinson v Secretary of State for Social Security* [1994] 2 All ER 295, HL.
143 Agoraphobics were excluded from mobility allowance: *R(M) 1/80*.
144 This may be contrasted with the care component, where the three rates are clearly designed to deal with ascending degrees of care needs, assessed according to their severity.
145 *R 2/99 (DLA)*, but note the Commissioner's caveat that 'this is not to say that everyone suffering from epilepsy is entitled to this component'.
146 *R(DLA) 4/01 (T)*.
147 SI 2002/648. For the SSAC's critical report, see Cm 5469.

a person who is able to walk is to be taken not to satisfy the condition of being so severely disabled physically or mentally that he cannot take advantage of the faculty out of doors without guidance or supervision from another person most of the time if he does not take advantage of the faculty in such circumstances because of fear or anxiety.[148]

Thus pre-lingually deaf persons whose physical condition makes them anxious about going out (eg in terms of their likely communication problems) would not qualify for the lower rate of the mobility component. This exclusionary rule does not apply where the fear or anxiety is both 'a symptom of a mental disability' itself and 'so severe as to prevent the person from taking advantage of the faculty in such circumstances'.[149] Despite this limited concession, the new rule is unsatisfactory in several respects. In particular, its reliance on a rigid demarcation between physical and mental disabilities is artificial and reflects an increasing emphasis on a medical model of disability in establishing entitlement to DLA. Finally, purely as a matter of drafting, the triple negative deployed in the new provision is less than ideal.

E Exclusions

i Age

Mobility allowance was not payable to children aged under five. The same rule was originally carried over into the mobility component of DLA. The justification for the age condition was that children below the age of five are not independently mobile and need constant supervision.[150] This rationale failed to give any weight to the very demanding task of caring for a disabled child.[151] Although arguably a lower age limit of two would be more consistent with this justification,[152] WRPA 1999 lowered the age limit for the higher rate mobility component to three, thus enabling three and four-year-olds to qualify with effect from April 2001.[153] This reform was not retrospective in its effect.[154] To qualify for the lower rate of the component, children aged between 5 and 16 must require substantially more guidance or supervision than children of their age in normal physical and mental health would require. Alternatively, it must be shown that persons of their age in normal physical or mental health would not require such guidance or supervision.[155]

At the other end of the age spectrum, claims for the mobility component must be made before the age of 65.[156] Once a claimant becomes entitled to the mobility

148   SI 1991/2890, reg 12(7).
149   SI 1991/2890, reg 12(8).
150   'A child who is severely or completely unable to walk under the age of five requires supervision, but not much more than a normal child under that age who can walk': Miss A Widdicombe, Standing Committee E, cols 76–77.
151   Eg the OPCS research gave a three-year-old with cerebral palsy (who was unable to get in and out of a chair without help, and unable to walk even when holding on) an overall severity score of 7.8 on a scale of 1–10: Bone and Meltzer *The prevalence of disability among children* (1989) p 15.
152   As recommended by *Pearson* n 101, above, para 1533.
153   SSCBA 1992, s 73(1) and (1A), as amended by WRPA 1999, s 67(3). The three months before the child's third birthday can count as the qualifying period for DLA.
154   WRPA 1999, s 67(4).
155   WRPA 1999, s 73(4).
156   SSCBA 1992, s 75. The former rule enabling claimants who were 65 but who had not yet reached their 66th birthday to claim, providing they could show that their disability started before they attained the age of 65, was repealed in 1997 (SI 1997/349).

component, it is payable for a fixed period or indefinitely, assuming that the person's condition does not improve.[157] The Disability Living Allowance Advisory Board, in a report which is in many respects critical of the perceived overly generous nature of DLA, has argued that this discrimination against elderly disabled people should be removed.[158] The cost implications of such a reform would be substantial.

ii Ability to benefit from locomotion

The mobility component is not available to all severely disabled persons. Legislation provides that it is payable only where the invalid's condition is 'such as permits him from time to time to benefit from enhanced facilities for locomotion'.[159] This excludes patients in a persistent vegetative state, those whom it is unsafe to move and persons so severely mentally deranged that a high degree of supervision and restraint is required to prevent them injuring themselves or other.[160] Only a few of the remainder will not benefit from an occasional sortie and the authorities have been slow to apply the exclusion.

iii Duplication of assistance

The reluctance to apply the exclusion described above resulted in awards accumulating for some hospital patients unable to spend them. This issue was reviewed in 1983[161] and then again in 1996, following which the rules governing the payment of mobility component for hospital patients were aligned with those for the care component. As a result payment of the mobility component ceases after the claimant has spent 28 days (84 days for a child) in a hospital or similar institution.[162] The alignment is not, however, complete; an award of the mobility component, unlike payment of the care component, is unaffected by a stay in a residential or nursing home.

Under a more longstanding provision, the Secretary of State has reduced or excluded the entitlement of those receiving a grant or receiving any payment by way of grant under the National Health Service Act 1977 towards the cost of running a private car. This also covers any payment out of public funds which he or she regards an analogous thereto.[163] The regulation apportions the payments over the various weeks of entitlement, and the weekly amounts so apportioned are deducted from the claimant's DLA.

157 Mobility allowance was originally not payable to persons over pensionable age (SSA 1975, s 37A(5)(a)). The limit was subsequently raised to 75 (SSA 1979) and then 80 (SSA 1989).
158 Disability Living Allowance Advisory Board 'The future of disability living allowance and attendance allowance' in HC Social Security Committee *Fourth Report* Minutes of Evidence (HC 641 1997–98) p 4.
159 SSCBA 1992, s 73(8).
160 *R(M) 2/83*.
161 Oglesby *Review of Attendance Allowance and Mobility Allowance Procedures* (1983) para 161. Oglesby proposed that when the balance standing to a patient's credit exceeds £1,000, the Hospital Management Team might certify that it was not likely to be used for the claimant's benefit and, in consequence, the adjudication officer should be empowered to withdraw the allowance: para 162. This proposal was not implemented at the time.
162 SI 1991/2890, regs 12A–12C. Transitional protection was provided for long-stay patients who had already been in hospital for 12 months or more. The SSAC opposed the changes, arguing that the mobility and care components serve very different purposes: SSAC *Report on Social Security (Disability Living Allowance and Claims and Payments) Amendment Regulations 1996* (1996, Cm 3233).
163 SI 1987/1968, reg 42, made in the exercise of a power conferred under the overlapping benefits provisions.

Part 3　The care component of disability living allowance

A General

The new concern for disabled people manifested in the 1960s was directed in particular to a major group insufficiently protected under existing schemes, comprising those who needed substantial personal assistance from another in matters of self-care. A new benefit, attendance allowance, was proposed in 1969 as part of the Labour government's National Superannuation plan,[164] and was adopted by the Conservative government immediately on assuming power in 1970. Provision was made for a single flat-rate benefit payable to a person requiring either 'frequent attention throughout the day and prolonged or repeated attention during the night; or ... continual supervision from another person in order to avoid substantial danger to himself or others'.[165] The joint test on the first of the alternative conditions excluded many potential claimants, and in 1973 a lower rate of allowance became payable to those who required the necessary attendance either during the day or during the night.[166] The question of what degree of attendance should be required during the night proved to be troublesome. An authoritative interpretation of the statutory provisions by the Court of Appeal in 1987[167] appeared to resolve the matter but the government considered this to be too generous and the criteria of entitlement were narrowed by SSA 1988.[168]

As with mobility allowance, attendance allowance proved to be a highly successful benefit in terms of the number of recipients. In 1973 there were 101,000 recipients at the higher rate and 44,000 at the lower rate. By 1990 there were 342,000 at the higher rate and 493,000 at the lower rate.[169] The OPCS surveys conducted between 1985 and 1988 found that around two-and-a-half million adults experienced personal care disabilities.[170] It was also found that personal care needs gave rise to relatively high levels of extra expenditure when compared with other costs associated with disabilities.[171] However, as with mobility allowance, both the OPCS research and a subsequent study based on the Family Expenditure Survey suggested that such disability-related expenditure was actually less than the then rate of attendance allowance.[172] Furthermore, a clear correlation was identified between the degree of disability and the award of attendance allowance. Some 74 per cent of those in the most severely disabled group (category 10) received attendance allowance, compared with just 8 per cent in categories 1 to 5 inclusive.[173] On the other hand, this means

---

164　See White Paper *National Superannuation and Social Insurance* (1969, Cmnd 3883) paras 90–91.
165　NIA 1970, s 4(2).
166　NIA 1972, s 2(1).
167　*Moran v Secretary of State for Social Services*, reported as an Appendix to *R(A) 1/88*.
168　P 702, below.
169　DSS *Social Security Statistics 1991* (1992) Table E1.05.
170　This amounts to a rate of 57 per 1,000 of the population: Martin, Meltzer and Elliot *The prevalence of disability among adults* (1988) p 25. Only locomotion problems (99 per 1,000) and hearing difficulties (59 per 1,000) were more common.
171　Martin and White *The financial circumstances of disabled adults living in private households* (1989) p 53. It should be noted that there is no need for attendance allowance to be spent on personal care; attendance is merely the criterion for the award of benefit. There continues to be confusion as to whether DLA was designed to help with extra costs or to pay for care: see the discussion in Berthoud *Disability benefits* (1998) pp 47–48.
172　*The Way Ahead: benefits for disabled people* (1990, Cm 917) p 26.
173　*Martin and White* n 76, above, p 22.

that about one-quarter of people with multiple disabilities were not receiving attendance allowance.

The similarities with mobility allowance continued in that, notwithstanding the increasing number of awards, disability pressure groups continued to express reservations about aspects of the scheme. In its 1990 White Paper the government announced two important but relatively minor reforms which were to take place that year: the extension of attendance allowance to severely disabled children under the age of two and the abolition of the six-month qualifying period for the terminally ill.[174] More substantial reform followed with DLADWAA 1991, which merged attendance and mobility allowances into disability living allowance. The care component of DLA now consists of a highest and middle rate (equivalent to the two levels of attendance allowance) and a lowest rate for people who previously failed to qualify for the predecessor benefit. The previous complex and unsatisfactory adjudication arrangements for attendance allowance were abolished at the same time.[175] In keeping with the policies outlined in the White Paper, these changes primarily benefited disabled people of working age. Attendance allowance, without the new lowest rate, was preserved for those who claim after the age of 65.

B Amount

The care component is payable at three rates: the lowest rate where the less demanding day-time attention or cooking test is satisfied, the middle rate where either the ordinary day or night condition applies, and the highest rate where both of the latter criteria are satisfied.[176] These care criteria are discussed in section C, below. Although the care component is disregarded in the assessment of the income-related benefits, it is withdrawn where the claimant is cared for in residential accommodation paid for out of public funds.[177] It is also exempt from income tax.[178]

C Care criteria

The original OPCS Survey in 1968–69 used very detailed criteria to determine the number of persons who required substantial personal assistance from others in matters of self-care.[179] For the purposes of the attendance allowance it was decided not to adopt such precise tools, but rather to allow the decision-making authority (at that time the Attendance Allowance Board) considerable discretion. This approach was carried forward in the 1991 reforms. SSCBA 1992 lays down three sets of criteria, building on the original tests for attendance allowance. The first test, which only gives entitlement to the lowest rate of the DLA care component, is that the claimant:

---

174 N 172, above, p 41.
175 See Cooke, Hirst and Bradshaw (1987) 13 Child: care, health and development 169; SSAC *Benefits for Disabled People: a strategy for change* (1988) p 22. Subsequent research found that the great majority of claimants were satisfied with their medical examination: Chilvers *The Attendance Allowance Medical Examination* DSS Research Report No 5 (1991).
176 SSCBA 1992, s 72(3)–(4).
177 SSCBA 1992, s 72(8); and see p 703, below.
178 Income and Corporation Taxes Act 1988, s 617.
179 These are set out in Appendix D of Harris *Handicapped and Impaired in Great Britain* (1971).

is so severely disabled physically or mentally that—
  (i)   he requires in connection with his bodily functions attention from another person for a
        significant portion of the day (whether during a single period or a number of periods); or
  (ii) he cannot prepare a cooked main meal for himself if he has the ingredients ... [180]

The second or 'day' condition is that the claimant:

is so severely disabled physically or mentally that, by day, he requires from another person—
  (i)   frequent attention throughout the day in connection with his bodily functions, or
  (ii) continual supervision throughout the day in order to avoid substantial danger to himself
        or others. [181]

The third or 'night' condition is that:

he is so severely disabled physically or mentally that, at night,—
  (i)   he requires from another person prolonged or repeated attention in connection with
        his bodily functions, or
  (ii) in order to avoid substantial danger to himself or others he requires another person to
        be awake for a prolonged period or at frequent intervals for the purpose of watching
        over him. [182]

As we have seen, a claimant who satisfies both the day and the night conditions qualifies
for the highest rate of the care component; fulfilment of either alone is sufficient for the
middle rate. [183]

i Nature of tests

The first issue that arises is whether the three tests raise questions of law, and thereby
come within the jurisdiction of the Commissioners (and eventually the ordinary courts),
or are rather questions of fact on which the decision of an appeal tribunal is final. The
issue is part of the general nature of decision making and is treated as such in another
chapter. [184] It is necessary here to see what implications the general principles have for
entitlement to this specific benefit. On the one hand, the tendency has been for the
courts to treat the question as to whether 'the words of the statute do or do not as a
matter of ordinary usage of the English language cover or apply to the facts which have
been proved' as a question not of law but of fact. [185] It follows that the fulfilment of the
above conditions is regarded primarily as a question to be decided by the decision
maker or appeal tribunal. [186] But where a word is capable of different nuances of meaning,

---

180   SSCBA 1992, s 72(1)(a). There is no equivalent provision for attendance allowance.
181   SSCBA 1992, s 72(1)(b).
182   SSCBA 1992, s 72(1)(c).
183   SSCBA 1992, s 72(4).
184   Pp 183–184, below.
185   Per Lord Reid *Brutus v Cozens* [1973] AC 854 at 861: applied by the Divisional Court in *R v National
      Insurance Comr, ex p Secretary of State for Social Services* [1974] 3 All ER 522 at 526; and by
      R G Micklethwait, Chief Comr, in *R(S) 3/74*.
186   Per R G Micklethwait, Chief Comr, *R(S) 1/73*, para 13. Non-binding guidance for decision makers on
      the types of care needs associated with various disabilities is to be found in Aylward, Dewis and
      Henderson (eds) *The Disability Handbook* (2nd edn, 1998).

decisions as to the correct shade of meaning in a given statute are a matter of construction and therefore of law.[187]

ii General factors

A SEVERELY DISABLED

The claimant must be 'severely disabled physically or mentally'. In the first reported decision directly on this point, it was held that the expression refers to a condition of body or mind that can be medically defined. It does not cover antisocial or aggressive behaviour unrelated to serious mental illness.[188] This approach seems to have been confirmed by the Court of Appeal.[189] The difficulty with this construction is that, under the Mental Health Act 1983, mental illness may be defined by reference to a person's behaviour.[190] It would also seem to be no obstacle that the disability is attributable solely to age.[191]

B REQUIRES

It is important to observe that the attention or supervision referred to in the statutory conditions must be 'required' rather than 'provided'. In other words, the test is based on the objective existence of the need rather than on the actual provision of a service.[192] As such it must be 'reasonably required',[193] but that does not necessarily imply for medical reasons: the physical comfort of the claimant may be sufficient.[194]

C NIGHT AND DAY

The second condition applies to day-time attention; the third to night-time.[195] The distinction is crucial, since the claimant seeking the highest rate of benefit must satisfy both conditions, but 'night' is not defined in the SSCBA 1992 or its predecessors. To resolve a conflict of different interpretations of this word, the Divisional Court in 1974 ruled that it meant:

---

187 Per Lord Widgery CJ in *R v National Insurance Comr, ex p Secretary of State for Social Services* [1974] 3 All ER 522 at 526; and Lord Woolf in *Mallinson v Secretary of State for Social Security* [1994] 2 All ER 295 at 304, the latter taking a markedly more interventionist line than Lord Bridge in *Woodling v Secretary of State for Social Services* [1984] 1 All ER 593 at 596 (see Blom-Cooper (1986) 57 Political Q 144 at 152–153).

188 *R(A) 2/92.*

189 *Re H (A Minor)*, reported as an appendix to *R(A) 1/98.*

190 See Mental Health Act 1983, s 1; see also *W v L* [1974] QB 711.

191 See eg *R(A) 2/80* where the claimant was senile (the Court of Appeal in *R v National Insurance Comr, ex p Secretary of State of Social Services* [1981] 2 All ER 738, [1981] 1 WLR 1017 quashed the decision allowing her claim, but on other grounds).

192 *R(A) 1/72; R(A) 1/73; R(A)3/74; R(A) 1/75.* It follows that there is no need for the benefit to be spent on care or attendance.

193 *CA 26/79* quoted with approval by Slade LJ in *R v Secretary of State for Social Services, ex p Connolly* [1986] 1 All ER 998 at 1001.

194 *R(A) 3/86.*

195 The notion of 'day' also appears in the first limb of the first condition.

that period of inactivity, or that principal period of inactivity through which each household goes in the dark hours, and the ... beginning of the night [could be measured] from the time at which the household, as it were, closed down for the night.[196]

This definition was adopted because it had clearly been the intention of Parliament to treat as more onerous on members of the household attention provided during the night as opposed to during the day: this will occur if the carer has to interrupt his or her normal period of sleep to attend to the claimant. It follows that the definition applies equally to children, even though their sleeping hours are more prolonged.[197]

iii   Attention in connection with bodily functions[198]

This is relevant for the purposes of the first alternative head under each of the three conditions. For the lowest rate the attention must be for 'a significant portion of the day (whether during a single period or a number of periods)'. The government envisaged that this would mean about an hour a day, eg in assistance in getting in or out of bed, or in administering injections.[199] This interpretation was subsequently implicitly approved by one Commissioner, whilst in a Scottish decision the Commissioner held that attention for a lesser period than one hour could be significant, depending upon the circumstances.[200] For the day condition the attention must be 'frequent', which means 'several times, not once or twice',[201] while for the night condition it must be 'prolonged', that is, lasting for 'some little time',[202] or 'repeated', which means at least twice.[203]

The common condition of 'attention in connection with bodily functions' has caused considerable difficulty. The notion of 'attention' is broader than that of dealing with a specific health risk[204] but still has its limits. According to Dunn LJ in *R v National Insurance Comr, ex p Secretary of State for Social Services* (the *Packer* case),[205] attention:

indicates something more than personal service, something involving care, consideration and vigilance for the person being attended ... a service of a close and intimate nature.[206]

This formulation was approved by Lord Woolf in *Mallinson v Secretary of State for Social Security*, with the caveat that the 'service' need not involve physical contact.[207] It could therefore extend to include guidance by the spoken word to a blind person.

---

196   *R v National Insurance Comr, ex p Secretary of State for Social Services* [1974] 3 All ER 522 at 527. See also *CA 15/81*, noted at [1983] JSWL 311.

197   *R(A) 1/78*.

198   See Pollard (1998) 5 JSSL 175.

199   Per Lord Henley, 526 HL Official Report (5th series) col 884.

200   See *CDLA/58/93* ((1995) 2 JSSL D2) and *CSDLA/29/94* ((1995) 2 JSSL D117) respectively.

201   Per Lord Denning MR in *R v National Insurance Comr, ex p Secretary of State for Social Services* (the *Packer* case) [1981] 2 All ER 738 at 741.

202   *R v National Insurance Comr, ex p Secretary of State for Social Services* (the *Packer* case) [1981] 2 All ER 738. See also *R 1/72 (AA)*, para 22.

203   Per Lord Denning MR in *R v National Insurance Comr, ex p Secretary of State for Social Services* (the *Packer* case) [1981] 2 All ER 738 at 741.

204   *R(A) 3/78*, R J A Temple, Chief Comr.

205   *R v National Insurance Comr, ex p Secretary of State for Social Services* (the *Packer* case) [1981] 2 All ER 738 at 742.

206   See to similar effect: Lord Denning MR in *R v National Insurance Comr, ex p Secretary of State for Social Services* (the *Packer* case) [1981] 2 All ER 738 at 741; *R(A) 3/74*, para 11; *R(A) 3/80*, para 8.

207   *Mallinson v Secretary of State for Social Security* [1994] 2 All ER 295 at 302.

Subsequently, the House of Lords has reiterated that 'attention' presupposes that the activity takes place in the presence of the disabled person. 'Assistance would cover activities done for the person. Attention implies services done to the person.'[208] An amendment to the regulations in 2000 reinforced this point: the required attention must be such as would be 'given in the physical presence of the severely disabled person'.[209]

But what of 'bodily functions'? This might literally include, as Forbes J in the *Packer* case suggested, 'every mode of action of which the fit body is capable at the dictate of the normal brain'.[210] As such, it would cover functions of which the claimant is capable, and those quite irrelevant to his or her circumstances and needs – which would surely be inconsistent with the purpose of the provision. The most helpful explanation (leaving aside its sexist assumptions) is that of Lord Denning MR, in the *Packer* case, who held that the words:

> include breathing, hearing, seeing, eating, drinking, walking, sleeping, getting in and out of bed, dressing, undressing, eliminating waste products, and the like, all of which an ordinary person, who is not suffering from any disability, does for himself. But they do not include cooking, shopping or any of the other things which a wife or daughter does as part of her domestic duties, or generally which one of the household normally does for the rest of the family.[211]

Finally, the attention must be 'in connection with' the bodily functions. In *Mallinson*[212] the issue was whether a blind person could qualify for the lower rate of attendance allowance on the basis that he needed frequent attention in connection with bathing, cutting up food and walking in unfamiliar surroundings. The House of Lords, by a majority, held that he required attention with the bodily function of *seeing*, not *walking*. There was some doubt as to whether on the facts this constituted 'frequent' attention, and the question of entitlement was therefore remitted to an adjudication officer (now the Secretary of State) to determine. According to Lord Woolf:

> The attention is in connection with the bodily function if it provides a substitute method of providing what the bodily function would provide if it were not totally or partially impaired.[213]

This test also involves a test of remoteness or proximity, as to which there has again been a diversity of opinion.[214] The Court of Appeal held in the *Packer* case that ordinary domestic duties such as shopping and cooking are too remote.[215] These were to be distinguished from:

---

208   *Cockburn v Chief Adjudication Officer* [1997] 1 WLR 799 at 824, per Lord Clyde.
209   SI 1991/2890, reg 10C; see also for attendance allowance SI 1991/2740, reg 8BA.
210   Quoted at [1981] 2 All ER 738 at 740. See also Dunn LJ at 742; and to similar effect *Deme v DSS* (1998) 27 AAR 193 (Federal Court of Australia).
211   [1981] 2 All ER 738 at 741. See also *R(A) 3/78*, para 12. The list of functions is not, of course, exhaustive. In *R v Social Security Comr, ex p Butler* [1984] Legal Action 117, the Divisional Court quashed the decision of a delegated medical practitioner that a claim based solely on the need for a mother to act as interpreter for a profoundly deaf child could not constitute 'attention ... in connection with ... bodily functions'.
212   *Mallinson v Secretary of State for Social Security* [1994] 2 All ER 295.
213   *Mallinson v Secretary of State for Social Security* [1994] 2 All ER 295 at 306.
214   See the authorities reviewed in *R(A) 2/80*, paras 9–17. The latter confirmed a trend which commenced in *CA 2/79*, and included *R(A) 1/80*, that cooking for the claimant was a relevant factor. But the decision in *R(A) 2/80* was quashed by the Court of Appeal, n 191, above.
215   *R v National Insurance Comr, ex p Secretary of State for Social Services* (the *Packer* case) [1981] 2 All ER 738, per Lord Denning MR at 741 and Dunn LJ at 744.

duties that are out of the ordinary, doing for the disabled person what a normal person would do for himself, such as cutting up food, lifting the cup to the mouth, helping to dress and undress or at the toilet.[216]

Subsequently, however, the Commissioners held that in exceptional cases such 'normal duties' can constitute attention 'in connection with [the claimant's] bodily functions'.[217] The problem was revisited, albeit rather unsatisfactorily, in *Cockburn*,[218] in the context of a claim for attendance allowance by an elderly woman suffering from arthritis and incontinence. On the facts the woman received regular visits from her daughter who would wash her mother, strip the bed linen and take the laundry away to be washed. The House of Lords held by a majority that the need to deal with the extra laundry generated could not be taken into account in assessing whether she required 'frequent attention ... in connection with [her] bodily functions'. This was in part because the service in question must be directed primarily to those bodily functions 'which the fit person normally performs for himself'.[219] Yet it seems that the claim might have succeeded, had the daughter performed all the tasks at her mother's house.[220] This fine distinction seems all the more problematic when the outcome in *Cockburn* is contrasted with that in *Secretary of State for Social Security v Fairey*, which was heard at the same time by the House of Lords. In *Fairey* a young deaf woman required the assistance of an interpreter to communicate effectively with hearing people outside her own family. The House of Lords, following *Mallinson*, agreed that signing constituted 'attention' within the meaning of the Act; moreover, decision makers had to take into account such attention as was required in order to enable her to carry out a reasonable level of social activity. These contrasting outcomes reflect both the failure of policy makers to elucidate the underlying purpose of DLA and attendance allowance and the haphazard development of judicial precedents.[221] Consequently, as Commissioner Howell has observed, 'an incontinent old lady who cannot go out may not get the allowance while a healthy blind person who likes going to parties, theatres and restaurants does'.[222]

iv   Cannot prepare a cooked main meal

This is the alternative requirement for the lower rate care component and was introduced by DLADWAA 1991. The government stressed that it is a purely hypothetical test;[223] it was intended to be a relatively simple test amenable to self-assessment and speedy adjudication. Thus the claim form asks whether the claimant needs help in peeling and chopping vegetables, using taps and a cooker safely and coping with hot pans, as well as with the mental task of planning a meal. However, the test becomes wholly artificial when applied to claimants who, for gender or social reasons rather than for those associated with their disability, have never learnt how to

---

216   Per Lord Denning MR in *R v National Insurance Comr, ex p Secretary of State for Social Services* (the *Packer* case) [1981] 2 All ER 738 at 741–742.
217   *R(A) 1/87* (food preparation for special diet) and *R(A) 1/91* (frequent washing of clothes and bedclothes because of skin condition); but see O'Connor LJ in *R v National Insurance Comr, ex p Secretary of State for Social Services* (the *Packer* case) [1981] 2 All ER 738 at 745.
218   *Cockburn v Chief Adjudication Officer* [1997] 1 WLR 799.
219   *Cockburn v Chief Adjudication Officer* [1997] 1 WLR 799 at 802, per Lord Goff.
220   See Wikeley (1998) 61 MLR 551 at 553.
221   *Wikeley* n 220, above, at 560.
222   *CDLA/11652/95*.
223   181 HC Official Report (6th series) col 313, 21 November 1990.

cook. The Court of Appeal has held that it must be assumed that the claimant is 'willing to learn how to cook'.[224] Beyond that, a Commissioner has held that a 'cooked main meal' means 'a labour intensive reasonable main daily meal freshly cooked on a traditional cooker'.[225]

v Continual supervision to avoid substantial danger

This is the alternative requirement for the day condition. According to a Tribunal of Commissioners,[226] it contains four elements. First, 'the claimant's medical condition must be such that it may give rise to a substantial danger either to himself or to someone else'. It has been suggested that the phrase, though incapable of precise definition, should not be narrowly construed – the risk of harm could result not only from a fall but also from exposure, neglect 'and a good many other things'.[227] 'Substantial danger ... to himself or to someone else' includes not only the risk of such an injury created by claimants themselves, but also such risks caused by others.[228] Care must be taken to assess this risk in relation to the individual claimant and not to the general class of persons suffering from the condition or disability.[229] Similarly, claimants suffering from schizophrenia may be a danger to themselves even though they have not been detained on an in-patient basis.[230] If the decision maker considers that the risk can be avoided by the claimant taking precautions, any such practical measures must be identified and be reasonable.[231]

Secondly, 'the substantial danger must not be too remote a possibility'.[232] The fact that it may take the form of an isolated incident does not necessarily make it too remote.[233] In weighing up whether or not a risk is remote, it is important to consider the seriousness of the consequences involved.[234]

Thirdly, supervision by a third party must be necessary to effect a real reduction in the risk of harm, albeit not to eliminate all substantial danger.[235] In comparison with 'attention', 'supervision' is a passive concept, perhaps of only a precautionary or anticipatory nature, being prepared to intervene if necessary in emergencies.[236]

Fourthly, the supervision must be 'continual'. This will generally involve overseeing or watching,[237] as would be expected of a childminder in care of young children. In *R(A) 1/83*, a Tribunal of Commissioners held that epileptics capable of looking after themselves between attacks are unlikely to establish the need for continual supervision unless the attacks are very frequent. This approach was criticised by the Court of Appeal

---

224   *R v Secretary of State for Social Security, ex p Armstrong* (1996) 32 BMLR 32, p 401, per Staughton LJ (also holding that the test is not discriminatory).
225   *R(DLA) 2/95.*
226   *R(A) 1/83(T)*, paras 5–8.
227   *R(A) 1/73*, para 17, R G Micklethwait, Chief Comr.
228   *R(A) 5/81.*
229   *R(A) 2/83.* But for guidance involving claimants prone to falls, see *R(A) 3/89*, para 12 and *R(A) 5/90(T)*, para 6.
230   *R(A) 2/91* and *R(A) 3/92.*
231   *R(A) 3/90(T)* and *R(A) 5/90(T).*
232   On which see also McNeill J in *Morris v Social Security Comr*, reported as Appendix to *R(A) 5/83.*
233   *R(A) 1/83(T)*, para 5. See also *R(A) 5/81*; *R(A) 3/89*; and *R(A) 3/90(T).*
234   *R(A) 6/89(T)*, para 24.
235   *R(A) 3/92.*
236   *Moran v Secretary of State for Social Services*, reported as Appendix to *R(A) 1/88*; *R(A) 2/75*, para 9; *Mallinson v Secretary of State for Social Security* [1994] 2 All ER 295 at 303, per Lord Woolf.
237   *R(A) 2/75.*

in *Moran v Secretary of State for Social Services*;[238] in its view, the need for supervision might arise even between attacks, particularly if they could occur without warning. The position might, however, be different if the sufferer had the opportunity, and was able, to summon help. The requirement that the supervision be continual is not met where a claimant can cope with potentially dangerous situations and needs only periodic supervision.[239]

vi   Another person awake to avoid substantial danger

Originally, the wording of the alternative night condition was identical to that of the alternative day condition. As a consequence of the *Moran* decision, it was considered that 'constant' supervision could be provided while the carer was asleep, so long as he or she could respond when the danger arose. The amended version of the condition, applicable since 1988, eliminates this possibility since, to avoid the danger, the carer must now be required to 'be awake for a prolonged period or at frequent intervals for the purpose of watching over' the disabled person.[240] According to a Northern Ireland Commissioner, the intervals must be more than twice at least.[241] The Court of Appeal has also held, interpreting this provision, that a disabled person did not qualify for benefit on this basis where she was in danger of falling over if required to get up to care for her disabled husband (who was himself already in receipt of attendance allowance).[242] This was seen as 'double recovery' of the husband's needs.

vii   Intermittent needs

The phrases 'a significant portion of the day', 'by day ... throughout the day' and 'at night ... during the night' do not indicate on how many days (or nights) during the week the need must occur. It is clear that the conditions do not have to be satisfied on each and every day (or night),[243] but apart from this ruling the Commissioners have generally left it to the discretion of appeal tribunals to reach a decision on the frequency and pattern of the need.[244] In a surprising decision, however, the Court of Appeal has recently adopted a more interventionist stance. In *Moyna v Secretary of State for Social Security* the appeal tribunal had held that the claimant could prepare a cooked main meal 'on most days' a week and so did not qualify for the lowest rate care component of DLA. Although the Commissioner agreed with this approach, the Court of Appeal held that the regular pattern of inability to cook on at least one day a week brought her within the scope of entitlement.[245]

Special provision is made for patients on dialysis. In 1977 the Attendance Allowance Board, then responsible for decision making, ruled that, subject to each case being

238   *Moran v Secretary of State for Social Services*, reported as Appendix to *R(A) 1/88*. See also *Young v Department of Health and Social Security* (1991) Legal Action, April at 21, Northern Ireland CA.
239   *Devlin v Secretary of State for Social Services* 1991 SLT 815.
240   SSCBA 1992, s 72(1)(c)(ii). Presumably the interpretation of 'for a prolonged period or at frequent intervals' will be influenced by the decisions on the analogous phrases used for 'attention in connection with bodily functions': p 698, above.
241   *R 2/99 (DLA)*, para 9, M F Brown, Comr (obiter).
242   *Miller v Secretary of State for Social Security* (1994) Times, 4 May.
243   See esp *R(A) 3/74* and *R(A) 4/78*.
244   *R(A) 4/78*, para 28.
245   [2002] EWCA Civ 408.

considered individually, a person suffering from renal failure should require at least three sessions a week on a kidney machine if he or she is to qualify. The Chief Commissioner held in *R(A) 4/78* that this did not amount to an error of law. Following that decision, the regulations were amended so that a person receiving dialysis treatment for two or more sessions a week is deemed to satisfy either the day or the night condition, and thus is entitled to the allowance at the middle rate. If, however, that person is an out-patient at an NHS hospital, the treatment must not be provided by a member of the staff of that hospital.[246]

D Exclusions

i Age

It is implicit in the legislation that only individuals are entitled to the care component of DLA.[247] In addition, as with the mobility component of DLA, there are special (although different) rules relating to age. Where children (aged under 16) are concerned, the care component is potentially payable from birth[248] but either the attention or supervision required must be 'substantially in excess of that normally required by a child of the same age and sex' or the child must have 'substantial requirements of any such description which younger persons in normal physical and mental health may also have but which persons of his age and in normal physical and mental health would not have'.[249] However, all children have to satisfy the three-month qualifying period unless they are terminally ill. The hypothetical 'cooking test' for the lowest rate care component does not apply to children as it is clearly inappropriate.[250]

As with the mobility component, the care component is not payable after the claimant's 65th birthday unless he or she has already claimed benefit before that date.[251] There is then no upper limit for entitlement. A person who lodges a claim after attaining the age of 65 is entitled only to attendance allowance. There is no equivalent to the lowest rate of the DLA care component for the latter benefit.[252] Where a person aged over 65 does receive the care component, any changes in their condition are governed by the same rules as for recipients of attendance allowance.[253]

ii Duplication of assistance

There are explicit exclusions from the care component (and from attendance allowance) for those who are already in receipt of state subsidy for their accommodation.[254] More

---

246   SSCBA 1992, s 72(7) and SI 1991/2890, reg 7.
247   The Act stipulates that 'a person' is entitled to DLA: SSCBA 1992, s 71(2). See also *R(A) 3/75* (Dr Barnardo's not eligible for attendance allowance).
248   Children under the age of two were excluded from attendance allowance until 1990. This restriction was subsequently ruled to be ultra vires in *CA/380/1990*.
249   SSCBA 1992, s 72(6)(b). See *CDLA/92/92* and on the equivalent Australian legislation *Re Secretary DSS and Bosworth* (1989) 10 AAR 514 and *Re MacQueen and Secretary, DSS* (1997) 50 ALD 231.
250   SSCBA 1992, s 72(6)(a).
251   SSCBA 1992, s 75(1).
252   Thus the lower rate of attendance allowance actually corresponds to the middle rate of the DLA care component.
253   SI 1992/2890, reg 3 and Sch 1.
254   SSCBA 1992, s 72(8). Similarly, for attendance allowance see s 67.

precisely, the regulations provide that it shall be a condition for receipt of the care component that the claimant is not maintained free of charge while undergoing medical treatment as an in-patient in either an NHS hospital or similar institution.[255] A claimant already in receipt of benefit remains entitled for the first 28 days (84 days in the case of a child) of treatment or accommodation excluded under the rules.[256] The exclusionary rule does not apply to the terminally ill residing in a hospice.[257]

A similar exclusionary rule applies where such a person is living in special accommodation other than hospitals. This is defined as accommodation provided under the National Assistance Act 1948[258] (or equivalent Scottish legislation) or for which the cost is borne wholly or partly out of public funds. If the latter, this must be in pursuance either of those statutes or of any other legislation relating to disabled persons, young persons or education or training.[259] To encourage local authorities in particular to assume the financial burden, the latter exclusion extends to accommodation the costs of which *may* be borne out of public funds, in pursuance of such enactments.[260] The Court of Appeal has construed this provision literally to disentitle a claimant where there existed a relevant power to subsidise the accommodation even though the power had not been exercised.[261] Given the extensive powers contained in the scheduled enactments, this has potentially grave implications for claimants. The rules governing special accommodation are subject to a number of exceptions. First, as with stays in hospital, they do not apply during the first 28 days in such accommodation[262] or to the terminally ill.[263] Secondly, the provisions may not operate to exclude children under 16 who are being 'looked after by a local authority',[264] or who are under 18 and, as children 'in need' within the Children Act 1989, are placed by the local authority in a private house.[265] The final exception applies to persons who are not entitled to income support, income-based jobseeker's allowance or housing benefit and who have met the whole cost of their accommodation either from their own resources (with or without charitable assistance) or from a third party (including a charity). The complex interaction between this provision and the definition of special accommodation has perhaps generated the most difficulty in construing these regulations. This is in the context of a broader political

255   SI 1991/2890, reg 8(1). A person is only to be regarded as 'not being maintained' free of charge if he or she pays charges which are intended to cover the whole cost of accommodation and services (excluding the cost of treatment): reg 8(2) and see *R(A) 3/75*. For identical rules relating to the mobility component of DLA see SI 1991/2890, reg 12A and for attendance allowance see SI 1991/2740, reg 6.

256   SI 1991/2890, reg 10(1) and (2). Periods of less than four weeks may be aggregated provided they are not separated by more than 28 days. The enables arrangement to be made for 'respite care' (ie carer given respite from attendance duties) without loss of benefit.

257   SI 1991/2890, reg 10(6). On the definition of 'hospice' see reg 10(7).

258   On the powers of local authorities under Pt III of the National Assistance Act 1948, see *Chief Adjudication Officer v Quinn* [1996] 4 All ER 72; and *Steane v Chief Adjudication Officer* [1996] 4 All ER 83.

259   SI 1991/2890, reg 9(1)(a)–(b). Where accommodation is so provided it is irrelevant that the claimant himself contributes to the cost: *R(A) 2/79*. SI 1991/2890, reg 9(6) lists ancillary matters which are not to be regarded as 'costs of accommodation' (see *Chief Adjudication Officer v Uprichard* [1999] NI 331). For attendance allowance, see SI 1991/2740, reg 7.

260   SI 1991/2890, reg 9(1)(c). The regulations provide for certain exceptions to this provision, such as where the person living in temporary accommodation provided for the homeless: reg 9(4)(b). Similarly, no exclusion operates where a person has been moved out of publicly funded accommodation into a private residential care home at the instigation of the public body concerned: reg 9(4)(d), (5) and (5A).

261   *Jones v Department of Health and Social Security*, reported as Appendix to *R(A) 3/83*.

262   SI 1991/2890, reg 10(1). This same period of grace also applies to children, who benefit from the 84 day concession for hospital stays under reg 10(2). For the linking rule, see reg 10(5).

263   SI 1991/2890, reg 10(6).

264   On the meaning of this term, see the Children Act 1989, s 22(1).

265   SI 1991/2890, reg 9(2) and (2A).

debate as to how far such costs should be borne by central or local government. In many cases local authorities have provided assistance to severely disabled people in finding a suitable residential home and either funded such accommodation in part or paid the charges pending sale of the person's own home, at which point the claimant has reimbursed the authority. In such cases the DWP has traditionally sought to argue that DLA is not payable for the period when the local authority is providing assistance (albeit it is later reimbursed). However, the Northern Ireland Court of Appeal has held that DLA is payable in such circumstances.[266]

Part 4 Attendance allowance[267]

Since the amendments made by DLADWAA 1991, attendance allowance has been a benefit for people aged over 65 whose care needs arise too late in life for them to be entitled to DLA.[268] Claimants already in receipt of DLA before they reach the age of 65 do not lose their entitlement unless their condition improves to the extent that they would not be eligible for attendance allowance. Attendance allowance is only payable at two rates:[269] a higher rate (equivalent to the highest rate of the DLA care component) where the person satisfies both the day and the night-time attention or supervision conditions and a lower rate (equivalent to the middle rate of the DLA care component) where only one of these conditions is fulfilled. There is therefore no equivalent to the lowest rate of the DLA care component. The other rules of entitlement are the same as for DLA,[270] except that there is a six-month qualifying period.[271] At present the principal rules governing eligibility to attendance allowance, as with those for the care component of DLA, are enshrined in primary legislation. However, WRPA 1999 introduced a regulation-making power for attendance allowance to mirror that which applies to DLA (and is used for the mobility component).[272] This appears to be a response to the success of test cases such as *Mallinson* and *Halliday*.[273]

Part 5 Common rules for disability living allowance and attendance allowance

A Period

In order to claim either component of DLA, the claimant must show that the relevant conditions of entitlement have been satisfied for three months.[274] In addition, the person

---

266 *Chief Adjudication Officer v Creighton* [2000] NI 222 *(R1/00 (AA))*.
267 See Horton and Berthoud *Attendance Allowance and the Costs of Caring* (1990).
268 SSCBA 1992, s 64(1).
269 SSCBA 1992, s 65(3).
270 SI 1991/2740.
271 SSCBA 1992, s 65(1)(b).
272 SSCBA 1992, s 64(4), added by WRPA 1999, s 66(1).
273 The Explanatory Notes to WRPA 1999 state that the power would be used 'if a judicial decision departed significantly from the policy intention' (p 140). It was first used in SI 2000/2313 to reverse the effect of *CDLA/1148/1997*, in which the Commissioner had held that telephone contact could amount to 'attention' for a person with mental health problems.
274 SSCBA 1992, ss 72(2)(a) and 73(9)(a).

must be likely to continue to satisfy these conditions for a further period of six months.[275] This represents a compromise between the previous requirements for attendance allowance and mobility allowance.[276] The period of three months need not be served again if the claimant recovers but subsequently suffers a relapse and again satisfies the requirement within two years.[277] As we have seen, attendance allowance in its attenuated form still requires a six-month qualifying period.[278] Either component of DLA can be awarded for a fixed period or indefinitely, but if both components are awarded they cannot be for different fixed periods.[279] This rule is designed to avoid repeated reassessments. Attendance allowance is payable for the period 'throughout which he has satisfied or is likely to satisfy' the relevant conditions.[280]

B   Residence and presence

DLA and attendance allowance are not payable to a person who is subject to immigration control.[281] The claimant must be ordinarily resident in Great Britain, present in Britain, and have been present in Britain for an aggregate of not less than 26 weeks in the year immediately preceding the date of the claim.[282] For the purpose of the latter two conditions, however, claimants are deemed to be present in Britain: (i) if an absence is for a temporary purpose and has not lasted for more than six months; or (ii) where the absence is temporary and for the specific purpose of being treated for an incapacity from which they suffered before they left Britain, and the Secretary of State certifies that it is consistent with the proper administration of IAA 1999 that they should be treated as though they were present in Britain.[283] There is also relief for airmen, mariners, persons employed on the continental shelf and members of the armed forces and their families.[284] The position as regards claimants resident in other EU countries is considered in chapter 3, above.[285]

C   Terminally ill

Claimants who are terminally ill are subject to special rules so far as the care component of DLA and attendance allowance are concerned. A person is terminally ill:

275   SSCBA 1992, ss 72(2)(b) and 73(9)(b).
276   Attendance allowance had a prior qualifying period of six months but no prospective test (SSA 1975, s 35(2)); mobility allowance had no qualifying period but a prospective test of 12 months (SSA 1975, s 37A(2)). As originally drafted, the DLADWA Bill had a prospective period of nine months.
277   SI 1991/2890, regs 6 and 11.
278   SSCBA 1992, s 65(1)(b). See SI 1991/2740, reg 3 on the two-year rule.
279   SSCBA 1992, s 71(3). The original wording of an award 'for life' was replaced by 'for an indefinite period' by WRPA 1999, s 67(1) to signal that 'life' awards can be superseded should the person's condition improve.
280   SSCBA 1992, s 65(1)(a). In practice this again means awards for a fixed number of years or indefinitely.
281   Immigration and Asylum Act 1999, s 115 (IAA 1999). Earlier restrictions were imposed by SI 1996/30; on the limited nature of the transitional protection see *M (A Minor) v Secretary of State for Social Security* [2001] UKHL 35, [2001] 1 WLR 1453.
282   For DLA see SI 1991/2890, reg 2(1)(a). A further condition of three years' presence out of the last four years must be satisfied where tax-free emoluments are received: reg 2(1)(b). For attendance allowance, see SI 1991/2740, reg 2. The conditions must be satisfied on a continuing basis, throughout the period of entitlement: *Insurance Officer v Hemmant* [1984] 2 All ER 533, [1984] 1 WLR 857.
283   SI 1991/2890, reg 2(2)(d)–(e).
284   SI 1991/2890, reg 2(2)(a)–(c).
285   P 69, above.

at any time if at that time he suffers from a progressive disease and his death is expected in consequence of that disease or can reasonably be expected within six months.[286]

This provision presumably covers (but is not confined to) certain forms of cancer, but it is by no means clear what is required in terms of the likelihood of death following within six months. Is it sufficient if death may well occur within that period, but the patient might equally survive another year? The policy behind the rule – to avoid the position where people died during the qualifying period or before their claim was determined – would suggest that where the claimant has a 50-50 chance of surviving six months he or she may still qualify. Certainly the practice of the DWP is only to reconsider cases if the patient survives beyond 15 months.[287] Amendments made by WRPA 1999 have clarified that entitlement continues only so long as the person remains terminally ill; an improvement in the prognosis can lead to a supersession decision.[288]

Claimants who meet this test are deemed to satisfy the three-month qualifying period for the highest rate care component of DLA and to continue to do so for the rest of their lives.[289] A claim must be made expressly on the basis that the person is terminally ill, but the claim may be made by another person on their behalf without the patient knowing.[290] Similar provision is made for attendance allowance.[291] Terminally ill claimants still have to satisfy the residence and presence conditions[292] and are subject to the exclusions relating to hospital and other similar accommodation considered below. So far as the mobility component of DLA is concerned, the only concession to the terminally ill is that they are deemed to satisfy the three-month retrospective and six-month prospective qualifying periods.[293]

Part 6   Carer's allowance

A   General

A household in which a severely disabled person requires attendance may suffer from financial hardship not only directly through the needs of the invalid, but also from the sacrifices made by other members of the household, typically but not exclusively women,[294] in providing care. In a study carried out in 1970,[295] it emerged that about two-thirds of disabled persons requiring care received it from relatives, and frequently this would involve a complete or partial interference with the relative's own earnings potential. Quite apart from the social justice of compensating such persons, the granting of state financial support also makes economic sense. In many cases, the care supplied voluntarily by the individual involves a substantial saving on public facilities which would otherwise have been

---

286   SSCBA 1992, s 66(2)(a).
287   Personal communication, Benefits Agency Medical Service doctor.
288   WRPA 1999, s 66(2).
289   SSCBA 1992, s 72(5). Note also the clarifying amendment by WRPA 1999, s 67(2).
290   SSAA 1992, s 1(3).
291   SSCBA 1992, s 66(1).
292   *R(A) 1/94*, in which M H Johnson, Comr, suggests that this is a lacuna in the law in so far as those who are born terminally ill are concerned: para 13.
293   SSCBA 1992, s 73(12).
294   It is impossible to ignore the gender dimension to benefits for carers: see Driscoll *Social Policy: A New Feminist Analysis* (1997) ch 3.
295   Sainsbury *Registered as Disabled* (1970) p 135. See further Parker *With due care and attention* (1990).

necessary.[296] In addition, an estimated 11,500 persons were in receipt of supplementary benefit substantially because they had forsaken gainful employment to care for an elderly or disabled relative,[297] and there was pressure to transfer such persons to a non-means tested benefit. The arguments apply not only to the care of severely disabled persons but also to that of small children, those temporarily sick and elderly persons. The government was not, however, prepared to introduce a general 'home care' allowance.[298]

The non-contributory invalid care allowance (ICA) was introduced by legislation in 1975.[299] Initially entitlement was limited to a prescribed category of relatives of the invalid.[300] This had no obvious justification apart from saving on public expenditure and it led to some arbitrary distinctions. The limitation was abolished in 1981,[301] but there was greater government resistance to reform of a more important, and discriminatory, exclusion, that of women living with a husband or a cohabitee. Criticism within Great Britain[302] failed to provoke a response and it required a decision of the European Court of Justice[303] that the exclusion was contrary to the principle of equal treatment enshrined in Council Directive (EEC) 79/7[304] to force a repeal of the provision.[305] This led to a considerable increase in the number of awards: in 1987 there were 91,392 carers receiving ICA compared with just 30,587 in the previous year.[306] Yet despite this reform, many married women carers still found themselves financially no better off because of the operation of the overlapping benefit regulations.[307] The Court of Appeal rejected the argument that the application of these rules constitutes indirect discrimination contrary to Council Directive (EEC) 79/7.[308] The overlapping benefit regulations also meant that carers in receipt of income support received no financial benefit from claiming ICA.[309] In 1988 the SSAC recommended that such carers be entitled to an income support premium,[310] and this proposal was implemented in October 1990. Even with these reforms, ICA still failed to reach the majority of carers: in 1988 there were an estimated 850,000 carers providing at least 50 hours care a week.[311]

A further discriminatory element in the eligibility criteria for ICA disappeared in 1994 with the introduction of a standard upper age limit of 65, rather than one based on differential

---

296   One estimate values the support provided by carers at approximately £34 billion a year: Nuttall *Financing Long-Term Care in Great Britain* (1993).
297   *Report on Social Security Provision for Chronically Sick and Disabled Persons* (1973–74, HC 276) para 61.
298   *HC 276* n 297, above, para 60.
299   SSBA 1975, s 7.
300   See the 1st edition of this book, pp 181–182.
301   SI 1981/655, following NIAC *Report on Extension of Title to Invalid Care Allowance to Non-Relatives* (1980, Cmnd 7905).
302   NIAC, in its *Report on Non-Relatives*, n 301, above, exceeded its terms of reference to attack the provision. See also Equal Opportunities Commission *Behind Closed Doors* (1981) pp 14–23; CPAG *Dear SSAC* CPAG Poverty Pamphlet 49 (1980); and SSAC *First Annual Report* (1983, Cmnd 8993) para 75.
303   *Drake v Chief Adjudication Officer* 150/85 [1987] QB 166, [1986] 3 All ER 65. See Luckhaus [1986] PL 526.
304   In the light of the European Court of Justice ruling, L Bromley, Chief Comr, held that the terms of the Directive were of direct legal effect, enabling an individual to invoke them: *R(G) 2/86*.
305   SSA 1986, s 37.
306   DSS *Social Security Statistics 1991* (1992) Table E3.03. By 1990 the number of current awards had risen to 188,717: DSS *Social Security Statistics 1993* (1993) Table E5.02.
307   SI 1979/597; see p 259–261, above. Eg receipt of a retirement pension will usually preclude payment of ICA. The indignation of carers about this rule is captured well in McLaughlin *Social Security and Community Care* DSS Research Report No 4 (1991) p 41.
308   *Jones v Chief Adjudication Officer* [1990] IRLR 533 (*R(G) 2/91*); see also *Re a Farmer's Widow* [1990] 2 CMLR 399 (*R(S) 2/89*).
309   In 1984 this group amounted to about a third of all ICA recipients: *SSAC 1998* n 21, above, para 4.42.
310   *SSAC 1988* n 21, above.
311   *McLaughlin* n 307, above, p 2. For reform proposals, see HC Social Services Committee *Fifth Report* (1989–90, HC 410).

retirement ages. Such measures have been described as providing a 'veneer of equal treatment' in that the distribution of unpaid work 'continues to have a major impact on women's access to paid work and their treatment in social welfare systems'.[312] One of the difficulties in framing a coherent policy for carers lies in their diversity. There are now an estimated 5.8 million adults who provide unpaid support to a disabled, ill or elderly relative or friend.[313] Other legislative developments in recent years have provided a further modest degree of recognition for the work of carers.[314] In 1999 the government launched a national strategy for carers. It may be telling that a document comprising over 70 pledges promised, so far as cash benefits for carers were concerned, merely to 'keep under review how financial support for carers can best meet their needs'.[315] Meanwhile broader government policies in relation to welfare have continued to emphasise the primacy of paid work over unpaid caring, as in the requirement for new claimants of ICA to attend work-focused interviews. A package of further reforms was introduced under the Regulatory Reform (Carer's Allowance) Order 2002.[316] These included the renaming of ICA as carer's allowance (thus losing the negative connotations associated with the term 'invalid'), the removal of the upper age limit of 65 for entitlement to benefit and the extension of entitlement for up to eight weeks after the death of the person being cared for.

B   Persons for the care of whom carer's allowance is payable

As indicated above, the category of persons for the care of whom the allowance was made payable was not intended to be wide. SSCBA 1992 limits it to 'a severely disabled person',[317] and this is defined as a person in receipt of attendance allowance or the middle or highest rate of the care component of DLA.[318] Regulations extend this definition to the equivalent allowances under the industrial injuries and war pensions schemes.[319] This definition has the merit of avoiding the addition of yet another concept of disability to those already existing in the law. But it does mean that where the conditions of entitlement to the attendance allowance are satisfied, perhaps only marginally, the household will effectively benefit from the two allowances (plus the income support carer's premium where appropriate), while a marginal decision that the conditions have not been satisfied results in neither being payable.[320]

C   Persons entitled to carer's allowance

There are two substantive conditions which the claimant must satisfy:
(a)   he is regularly and substantially engaged in caring for that person; and
(b)   he is not gainfully employed.[321]

---

312   *Driscoll* n 294, above, p 105.
313   Office of National Statistics *Informal Carers* (1998).
314   Carers (Recognition and Services) Act 1995 and Carers and Disabled Children Act 2000.
315   DoH *Caring about Carers: A National Strategy for Carers* (1999).
316   SI 2002/1457. See HC Deregulation and Regulatory Reform Committee *Eighth Report* (2001/02, HC 691).
317   SSCBA 1992, s 70(1).
318   SSCBA 1992, s 70(2). This definition is exclusive: *Pridding v Secretary of State for Work and Pensions* [2002] EWCA Civ 306.
319   SI 1976/409, reg 3.
320   Cf *Brown* n 40, above, p 264.
321   SSCBA 1992, s 70(1). The third condition in s 70(1) (that the severely disabled person is a relative of the carer or falls into such other category as may be prescribed) is effectively disapplied by SI 1976/409, reg 6.

i   Regularly and substantially engaged in caring

The linking of carer's allowance with attendance allowance and DLA is sufficient in itself to establish that the severely disabled person is in substantial need of care, but it was still necessary to provide more guidelines for the requirement of 'regularly and substantially engaged in caring ...'. It was decided that the best approach was to set a minimum number of hours' care which was consistent with the notion of it being a full-time occupation for the claimant, but yet which was not 'so high as to cause the claimant to have to examine in detail what among her activities constituted "caring" and whether the minimum had been met'.[322] The result was the creation of the '35 hours' rule formulated in the following regulation:

> A person shall be treated as engaged and as regularly and substantially engaged in caring for a severely disabled person on every day in a week if, and shall not be treated as engaged or regularly and substantially engaged in caring for a severely disabled person on any day in a week unless, as at that week he is, or is likely to be, engaged and regularly engaged for at least 35 hours a week in caring for that severely disabled person.[323]

The reason for the rather circuitous form of this provision is that the base period of the claim is for 'any day' of care, but the 35-hour criterion of course applies to a calendar week. The regulation has been held not to permit 'averaging', so the claimant must have been engaged in caring for at least 35 hours in the week of claim.[324] The regulation itself gives no guidance on what is meant by 'caring', and so this is an issue for the authorities to determine. In an unreported case the Commissioner held that the link between attendance allowance or DLA and carer's allowance supported the contention that caring 'presupposes the more or less continuous presence of the person cared for'.[325] While temporary absence (eg shopping for such a person) could still be seen as caring, a longer period of absence would not suffice.[326]

The care provided may be temporarily interrupted by eg a short period of respite for the carer or either party's need to enter hospital. To achieve flexibility, and to reduce the administrative expenses of frequent investigation, the '35 hours' rule is relaxed in certain circumstances. The Regulations provide that the rule is deemed to have been satisfied if:

(1)   the claimant has only temporarily ceased to satisfy the conditions; and

(2)   he or she has satisfied them for an aggregate period of 14 or more weeks in the immediately preceding six months; and

(3)   he or she would have satisfied them for at least 22 weeks in such a period but for the fact that he or she (or the disabled person) was undergoing treatment as an in-patient in a hospital or similar institution.[327]

In effect this permits carers up to four weeks' break in every six months, assuming that this is feasible, without loss of benefit. In practice the 35-hour rule poses few problems to carers: 77 per cent of recipients of carer's allowance provide more than 50 hours'

---

322   NIAC *Report on Draft Regulations* (1975–76, HC 271) para 12.
323   SI 1976/409, reg 4(1).
324   *R(G) 3/91*. 'Week' here bears its normal meaning of seven days starting with a Sunday: *R(G) 3/91* and *CG/052/1993* ((1995) 2 JSSL D48). See also SSCBA 1992, s 122(1).
325   *CG/012/91*.
326   Contrast *CG/006/1990* (10 hours of absence spent cooking, cleaning etc constituted 'caring') with *CG/012/91* (one month's separation spent making arrangements for care and being on 'stand-by' not 'caring').
327   SI 1976/409, reg 4(2).

care a week, and only 10 per cent of unsuccessful claimants provide less than 35 hours.[328] However, it is not possible for two carers simultaneously to be awarded benefit in respect of care provided for the same severely disabled person.[329] In addition, there is no entitlement where a carer is looking after two individuals whose care needs together amount to more than 35 hours a week.[330]

ii Gainful employment

The intention being to confer benefit only on those engaged in full-time care, it was thought appropriate to have some form of earnings rule. Indeed, the DWP appears at one stage to have considered the argument that in principle all earnings should be taken into account.[331] However, the fact that the majority of persons benefiting from the new allowance were previously in receipt of supplementary benefit, to which an earnings disregard applied, induced the proposal that a similar disregard should apply. Treatment of the value of the disregard has been erratic. For example, there was no up-rating of the disregard between 1982 and 1990;[332] it was then increased beyond the rate of inflation until 1993, when it stood at £50 per week. It then remained at that level until April 2001, when it was aligned with the current year's lower earnings limit for National Insurance contributions.[333] This limit must not be exceeded in the week immediately preceding that in which carer's allowance is claimed, and all subsequent weeks of entitlement.[334] The ordinary rules for the computation of earnings apply to this provision,[335] but the claimant is entitled to have disregarded any earnings during a week in which he or she temporarily ceases to satisfy the 'caring' provisions, or during any week of absence (with the employer's authority) from employment.[336]

D Age

Carer's allowance is not payable to those under 16 or in receipt of full-time education.[337] The rules relating to the upper age limit have been subject to a series of changes. After October 1994, when the standard upper age limit was introduced, SSCBA 1992 provided that carers over the age of 65 were not entitled to ICA unless they were already entitled to it when reaching that age.[338] This age limit was originally based on pensionable age (65 for men, 60 for women), but the Court of Appeal held that this provision contravened the equal treatment principle in Council Directive (EEC) 79/7.[339] Article 7(1)(a) of the

---

328 *McLaughlin* n 307, above, p 9.
329 SSCBA 1992, s 70(7).
330 SI 1976/409, reg 4(1A).
331 See *NIAC* n 322, above, para 18.
332 It remained at £12 per week until raised to £20 a week by SI 1990/620.
333 SI 2001/538; on the lower earnings limit, see p 106, above.
334 SI 1976/409, reg 8(1).
335 Pp 243–246, above.
336 SI 1976/409, reg 8(2).
337 SSCBA 1992, s 70(3). Full-time education is defined as a course involving attendance of 21 hours or more a week: SI 1976/409, reg 5. See *Flemming v Secretary of State for Work and Pensions* [2002] EWCA Civ 641. Before 1992 the Secretary of State applied a 12-hour rule as a matter of practice.
338 SSCBA 1992, s 70(5), as amended by SI 1994/2556; this covers those who would have been entitled to ICA but for the operation of the overlapping benefit rules: SI 1976/409, reg 10.
339 *Thomas v Chief Adjudication Officer* [1991] 2 QB 164, [1991] 3 All ER 315; see Webb (1992) 55 MLR 393.

Directive, which excludes benefit conditions linked to pensionable age, was inapplicable as the discrimination in relation to the then invalid care allowance was not a necessary consequence of the different pensionable ages. This decision was subsequently confirmed by the European Court of Justice.[340] The regulations were amended to make provision for entitlement for carers who reached the age of 65 before the law changed in 1994.[341] These reforms prompted spin-off test-case litigation on the availability of interest on the arrears of ICA due. The European Court of Justice confirmed that interest on arrears of the allowance was not available under Council Directive (EEC) 79/7 but that it could be available under the *Francovich* principle.[342] The Divisional Court subsequently held that a claimant was entitled to interest on arrears of the backdated carer's premium under the income support scheme, which was itself triggered by the retrospective entitlement to ICA.[343]

Until October 2002, claimants who reached the age of 65 and who were still in receipt of ICA continued to receive benefit thereafter even if they took up gainful employment or were no longer involved in caring.[344] For this group ICA effectively transmuted into a non-contributory pension.[345] This anomaly was removed by the Regulatory Reform (Carer's Allowance) Order 2002, which also abolished the upper age limit on claiming the renamed carer's allowance.[346]

E   Residence and presence

Carer's allowance is not payable to a person who is subject to immigration control.[347] The requirements as to residence and presence[348] are substantially equivalent to those which must be satisfied by a severely disabled person claiming attendance allowance or DLA.[349]

F   Amount

Carer's allowance is a flat-rate benefit, equivalent in amount to the severe disablement allowance and the increases for dependants also follow that benefit.[350] Of course, not more than one person can claim the allowance for the same period,[351] and two or more who satisfy the conditions may elect, by sending an appropriate notice to the Secretary of State, which is to benefit; in default of such election, entitlement is determined at the discretion of the Secretary of State.[352]

---

340   P 48, above.
341   SI 1976/409, reg 10A; see also *CG/5425/95* and *CSG/6/95*, both discussed in Bonner, Hooker and White *Social Security Legislation 2001* (2001) vol I, para 1.195.
342   Case C-66/95 *R v Secretary of State for Social Security, ex p Sutton* [1997] ECR I-2163.
343   *R v Department of Social Security, ex p Scullion* [1999] 3 CMLR 798. In this particular case ICA was not payable because of the overlapping benefit rules.
344   SSCBA 1992, s 70(6). See also SI 1976/409, regs 11 and 11A.
345   *Social Security Legislation 2001* n 341, above, vol I, para 1.195.
346   SI 2002/1457.
347   IAA 1999, s 115.
348   SI 1976/409, reg 9.
349   P 706, above.
350   SI 1976/409, regs 12, 13.
351   SSCBA 1992, s 70(7).
352   SSCAB 1992, s 70(7) and SI 1976/409, reg 7. There is no right of appeal on this point: SSA 1998, Sch 2, para 3.

Chapter 20

Industrial injury

Part 1   Introduction

A   History

Provision for the consequences of industrial accidents and diseases has always taken a prominent position among social welfare systems. Typically it manifests four characteristics:

> It is the oldest branch of social security, it provides the most generous benefits, it is a pace-setter for other social security provisions and it is administered as a separate entity.[1]

The surge of legislation at the end of the nineteenth century in the industrialised countries was quite remarkable in its coincidence.[2] The movement may be attributed to a number of causes:[3] the increasing power of the trades unions; the inadequacies of the tort system as a means of compensation; social concern at the high accident rate in industry; the need for an incentive to industrial safety and the rehabilitation of disabled members of the labour force.

The British Workmen's Compensation Act 1897 (WCA 1897), in certain respects, bore traces of the traditional common law liability, but in more important respects foreshadowed a system of social insurance. Liability was imposed on the employer, but compensation was payable for all accidents 'arising out of and in the course of employment', irrespective of proof of negligence.[4] Loss was effectively shared between employers and employees, for the latter might claim at most only one half of their average earnings,[5] and that subject to a statutory maximum.[6] Short-term claims were

1   Kaim-Caudle *Comparative Social Policy and Social Security* (1973) p 65.
2   1883, Italy; 1884, Germany; 1894, Norway; 1897, UK; 1898, France and Denmark.
3   Köhler and Zacher (eds) *A Century of Social Insurance* (1982) pp 18–19, 112–114, 166–175; Bartrip and Burman *The Wounded Soldiers of Industry* (1983); Wilson and Levy *Workmen's Compensation* (1939) vol 1, ch 1.
4   In 1897 £1.00 per week (WCA 1897, Sch 1, para 1(b)). The WCA 1923, s 4(1) raised the maximum to £1.50.
5   WCA 1897, s 1(1).
6   WCA 1897, Sch 1, para 1(b). Under WCA 1923, s 4(2), for workmen earning less than £2.50 per week, the proportion was fixed on a scale varying from 50 to 75 per cent.

excluded by a waiting period of three weeks.[7] The principle of individual employer's liability led naturally to an adversarial method of adjudicating claims, and, though provision might be made for less formal arbitration, proceedings would typically be taken in the county courts and often, on appeal, to the higher courts.[8] Apart from cases of death, for which a lump sum of three years' annual earnings, to a maximum of £300, was payable to dependants,[9] compensation would normally take the form of weekly payments. However, the concept of a 'private right' was used to support the idea that employees might compromise their claim for a lump sum settlement. Indeed, after six months of payments, an employer had the *right* to redeem the continuing obligation by a lump sum, provided only that it was registered with, and obtained the approval of, a county court judge.[10]

Originally the Act was confined in its scope to certain dangerous trades. In 1906, it was extended to cover all manual occupations, and those non-manual workers earning less than £250 a year.[11] Employment-related illnesses had been a major source of hardship, and in the same year compensation became payable to those suffering from certain specified diseases which were attributable to the nature of the employment.[12] The only other substantial reform before the scheme was abolished in 1946 was the introduction of increases for dependants.[13]

The brevity of this account should not be allowed to disguise the complexity of the scheme's operation, the frequency of government reviews and legislative changes, and the general contention and dissatisfaction which it engendered. The criticism reached its height in the late 1930s with the publication by Wilson and Levy of their massive sociological and comparative treatise on the subject.[14] A Royal Commission established in 1938 curtailed its inquiries on the outbreak of war and its task was assumed by Beveridge as part of his overall survey of social security.[15] His own dislike of the scheme is immediately apparent: 'the pioneer system of social security in Britain was based on a wrong principle and has been dominated by a wrong outlook'.[16] From his exposition of the weaknesses of workmen's compensation the following may be highlighted: the adversarial nature of adjudication which was disruptive of good industrial relations and which created problems of adequate representation for the workman;[17] the lack of any obligation on employers to insure against liability with the consequent lack of security for accident victims;[18] the ability to compromise a claim for a lump sum settlement, which presupposed equality of bargaining power and under which claimants were tempted to accept less than their due;[19] the high administrative costs of the scheme,

---

7   WCA 1897, s 1(2)(a), reduced to one week by WCA 1906, s 1(2)(a) and three days by WCA 1923, s 5.
8   See *Wilson and Levy* n 3, above, vol 3, pp 255–262.
9   WCA 1897, Sch 1, para 1(a)(i).
10 WCA 1897, s 1(3)–(4).
11 WCA 1906, s 13.
12 WCA 1906, s 8.
13 For cases of death by WCA 1923, s 2 and in other cases by the Workmen's Compensation (Supplementary Allowances) Act 1940, s 1(1).
14 *Wilson and Levy* n 3, above.
15 Beveridge Report *Social Insurance and Allied Services* (1942, Cmd 6404).
16 *Beveridge Report* n 15, above, para 80.
17 *Beveridge Report* n 15, above, para 79(i)–(ii); *Wilson and Levy* n 3, above, vol 2, ch 15. The point was also stressed in White Paper *Social Insurance* (1944, Cmd 6551) Pt II, para 23.
18 *Beveridge Report* n 15, above, para 79(iii). If the defendant was insured, the worker's position was more secure. The Employers' Liability Insurance Companies Act 1907 required a deposit of £20,000 with the Board of Trade.
19 *Beveridge Report* n 15, above, para 79(iv); *Wilson and Levy* n 3, above, vol 2, ch 7.

resulting in part from the inefficiencies of the private insurance market[20] and in part from excessive resort to litigation.[21]

Beveridge's plan to unify responsibility and administration of industrial injuries compensation under a national insurance scheme, and at the same time to afford more generous benefits than those available for unemployment and sickness,[22] and without contribution requirements, was accepted. The exact form and level of benefits remained, however, a matter for considerable dispute. The proposal to pay a rate of benefit which would, only after a period of 13 weeks' incapacity, be higher than that for sickness,[23] was rejected: preferential treatment was to be provided throughout.[24] Conversely, the government was not prepared to depart from the general principle of flat-rate benefits in favour of an earnings-related pension,[25] as Beveridge had recommended.[26] It proposed, for long-term cases, the tariff method of compensation, derived from the war pensions scheme and based on the degree of disablement.[27] This idea of basing benefits on need rather than earnings-potential proved to be unacceptable politically. There ensued an unsatisfactory compromise combining the tariff benefit with the so-called 'special hardship allowance' (later renamed reduced earnings allowance) which compensated for impaired earning capacity.

Apart from the introduction in 1966 of a new allowance for the very seriously disabled, the substance of the law governing industrial injury benefits remained largely unaltered until 1982. Administratively, however, there was a gradual process of integrating the scheme within the general structure of social security. In 1973–75 the high point of this process was reached by the abolition of the separate Industrial Injuries Fund,[28] and by the inclusion of both the general National Insurance and the industrial injury schemes in the Social Security Acts (SSAs).

These developments took place against the background of a marked improvement in the general social security provision for the disabled,[29] a decline in the real value of the preferential treatment offered under the industrial injury scheme,[30] and also a reduction in the number of work-related accidents.[31] Not surprisingly, therefore, the scheme was then subject to critical scrutiny and ultimately major reforms took place in the 1980s. The Pearson Royal Commission on Civil Liability and Compensation for Personal Injury concluded that the scheme 'had stood the test of time'[32] and argued for

---

20 *Beveridge Report* n 15, above, para 79(vii). Appendix E of the Report revealed that the proportion of administrative costs to premiums paid was, for some insurance companies, 46 per cent.
21 In 1938 alone 75 appeals had gone to the Court of Appeal: Potter and Stansfield *National Insurance (Industrial Injuries)* (2nd edn, 1950) p 8.
22 *Beveridge Report* n 15, above, paras 97–105. The idea of a state insurance system dates back to the turn of the twentieth century: see *Departmental Committee on Workmen's Compensation* (1904) p 123.
23 *Beveridge Report* n 15, above, para 332.
24 *Social Insurance* n 17, above, Pt II, paras 26–27.
25 *Social Insurance* n 17, above, Pt II, paras 28–29.
26 *Beveridge Report* n 15, above, para 332.
27 *Social Insurance* n 17, above, Pt II, para 29; and see pp 752–759, below.
28 SSA 1973, s 94. It may not have been irrelevant that, at the time, the Industrial Injuries Fund, unlike the non-industrial fund, was showing a healthy surplus; cf Brown *Industrial Injuries* (1982) p 86.
29 Pp 675–677, above.
30 As a result of inflation, in 1982 the short-term injury benefit then provided was only 12 per cent higher than sickness benefit; the death benefit payable to widows was only 55p per week more than that available under the general scheme. See further Lewis *Compensation for Industrial Injury* (1987) pp 16–17.
31 A consequence of improved safety but also of a reduction in the number employed in manual work and dangerous industries: *Brown* n 28, above, p 67.
32 Pearson Royal Commission on Civil Liability and Compensation for Personal Injury (the Pearson Report) (1978, Cmnd 7054-I) para 283.

its extension,[33] though it also found several respects in which it could be improved.[34] A more radical stance was taken by a Department of Health and Social Security (DHSS) team in a study consequential on the Pearson Report and published as a discussion document in 1980.[35] They focused, in particular, on the high cost of administering a system[36] which in practice offered to most of its beneficiaries a relatively small material advantage over the general social security provisions.

The government accepted the force of this criticism and in a White Paper, published in 1981,[37] indicated a general commitment to restructure the scheme so as to concentrate resources on the more seriously disabled. The first step, taken in 1982, was to abolish injury benefit; henceforth, the short-term consequences of an industrial injury or disease were to be met through the standard provisions for statutory sick pay and sickness benefit.[38] Following a further policy document,[39] the government in 1986 abolished industrial death benefit and three of the five special allowances payable with the disablement benefit.[40] The latter was, itself, only to be granted to those with more significant disablements. The withdrawal of entitlement to reduced earnings allowance in 1990 marked the final and most significant cut in the scheme. Although existing entitlements were preserved, the reforms left only one benefit in the scheme. Hence disablement benefit, which always accounted for most of the scheme's expenditure, continues to compensate for 'loss of faculty' (ie the non-pecuniary effects of injury). There are additionally two supplements to disablement benefit which are payable in cases of the utmost severity.[41] A simplified scheme has thus replaced the complex, more sophisticated provision that existed for the first 40 years of the state scheme's existence.

Although these reforms may be rationalised primarily as economy measures, the then government portrayed them as 'a sensible further step towards a more coherent system of benefits for sick and disabled people'.[42] The focus on provision for the more seriously disabled may, indeed, point the way forward for the disability programme as a whole. It is, perhaps, for this reason that, while the reforms met considerable opposition from the trade union movement and the Industrial Injuries Advisory Council (IIAC),[43] criticism by the pressure groups representing disabled people generally was somewhat muted.[44] On the other hand, it is not to be assumed that the industrial scheme will continue to decline in importance. Technological change is creating new risks in the workplace and, at the same time, medical research is uncovering new links between the

---

33   To cover eg the self-employed, commuting accidents and a wider range of industrially-caused diseases: see *Pearson Report* n 32 above ch 17. The proposed scheme for road accidents would be modelled on industrial injuries: *Pearson Report* n 32 above ch 18.

34   Eg increases to short-term benefit and an advanced entitlement to full payment of the earnings-related element in the invalidity pension.

35   DHSS *Industrial Injuries Compensation* (1980): see Lewis [1980] JSWL 330.

36   13.3 per cent of benefit expenditure, compared with 4.2 per cent for the general contributory scheme: *DHSS* n 35, above, para 1.1.

37   *Reform of the Industrial Injuries Scheme* (1981, Cmnd 8402).

38   Social Security and Housing Benefits Act 1982, s 39 (SSHBA 1982) and SI 1983/186; see Lewis (1983) 34 NILQ 44.

39   Consultation Paper *Industrial Injuries Scheme* (1985).

40   SSA 1986, s 39 and Sch 3. Details are provided below, pp 759–766.

41   Below, p 759.

42   Mr T Newton, Minister for Social Security, in the introduction to the Consultation Paper, n 35, above, p 1.

43   IIAC is an independent body responsible for advising the Secretary of State on matters relating to the scheme: see Lewis (1986) 15 ILJ 256 at 258 and pp 139–140, above.

44   Cf Disability Alliance *Reforming the Industrial Injuries Scheme: The Wrong Priorities* (1982). The speed with which the government executed the reform did, however, stifle debate and discussion: *Lewis*, n 30, above, pp 258–259.

working environment and conditions, such as cancer, mental illness and heart disease, which, in the past, have not typically be seen as occupational hazards.[45] The industrial scheme was most recently subject to an internal departmental review in 1999, when civil servants were asked to explore the possibility of reform with a view to improving the links between the compensation, rehabilitation and prevention of occupational injury and ill-health.[46]

B Industrial preference

Fundamental to the debate on the future of the industrial injuries scheme has been the question whether the industrial preference, that is, the more favourable treatment given to the victims of industrial accidents and diseases over those disabled by other causes, can still be justified.[47] The classic arguments for the preference are to be found in a famous passage in the Beveridge Report.[48] Having conceded that, 'a complete solution is to be found only in a completely unified scheme for disability without demarcation by the cause of disability', it nevertheless submitted three grounds for maintaining a differential:

> First, many industries vital to the community are also specially dangerous. It is essential that men should enter them and desirable, therefore, that they should be able to do so with the assurance of special provision against their risks. ... Second, a man disabled during the course of his employment has been disabled while working under orders. This is not true generally of other accidents or of sickness. Third, only if special provision is made for the results of industrial accident and disease, irrespective of negligence, would it appear possible ... to limit the employer's liability at Common Law to the results of actions for which he is responsible morally and in fact, not simply by virtue of some principle of legal liability.

The main difficulty with the first argument is that it confuses the source of the injury – the environmental condition of working – with its consequences. The fact that individuals may be subjected to a greater hazard at work than elsewhere does not mean that their need will be greater if the risks materialise. If there is a case for discrimination between various groups of disabled persons it must surely be made according to the gravity of the consequences to the individual and their family rather than to the cause of the injury. The argument based on the need to pay more compensation to those encountering higher risks in special occupations would carry more force if there were evidence that current wage rates were insufficiently high to attract individuals to the workforce.[49]

Beveridge himself conceded that the second and third arguments were less convincing than the first and they are less persuasive than they were at the time of his report.[50] The notion of working 'under orders' is certainly artificial and arbitrary: why should a risk arising from employment be treated differently from one generated by self-

---

45 *Lewis* n 30, above, pp 19–20; Wikeley *Compensation for Industrial Disease* (1993) pp 3–6. See also Roberts and Lewis (1994) 23 ILJ 80.
46 There are apparently no immediate plans for reform: 345 HC Official Report (6th series) col 351W, 2 March 2000.
47 There is a wealth of literature on the subject. See, especially: Higucha (1970) 102 Int Lab Rev 109; *DHSS* n 35, above, pp 1–12; Walker (1981) 15 Soc Pol & Admin 54; *Brown* n 28, above, pp 277–295.
48 *Beveridge Report* n 15, above, paras 80–86.
49 *DHSS* n 35, above, para 1.10.
50 *DHSS* n 35, above, paras 1.11–1.15; *Pearson Report* n 32, above, para 290.

employment?[51] As regards the third argument, ironically tort liability for industrial injuries has expanded rather than retracted.

In spite of these arguments, the IIAC has continued to support the industrial preference, most notably in its report in 1990.[52] It concluded that, in its view, the state still had a duty to make special provision, and although common law remedies and general social security provision had a part to play, the requirements of a scheme for injured workers could only be met in full through a scheme designed for the purpose. The political fact remains that it is difficult to remove an advantage once it has been conferred on a group with significant voting power.[53] However, the waning influence of trade unions in Great Britain today suggests that the industrial scheme may yet be vulnerable to a further narrowing of its scope.

C   Financing

When workmen's compensation, with its notion of individual employer liability, was replaced by social insurance the question arose whether all risks should be pooled, as for unemployment and sickness, or whether each industry should continue to bear at least a part of its own accident costs, by eg varying the contribution on the basis of the industry's accident record.[54] There are two main arguments for relating the financial responsibility of the industry or firm to the risks created by its activities. The first is that it acts as an incentive to safety and the prevention of injuries.[55] Secondly, it avoids the price distortion which results from a low-risk industry subsidising a high-risk industry. Such distortion, it may be argued, leads to over-employment in dangerous industries and insufficient expenditure on accident prevention. Opponents of the differential approach doubt the force of the incentive argument for which, in any event, there is a lack of compelling empirical evidence. Risk-rating cannot be applied to small firms whose accident record is too limited for statistical purposes.[56] It is always based on past experience which may be unreliable as a guide for future contingencies, particularly in relation to diseases for which there is a long latency period.[57] The price-distortion argument is countered by the principle of social interdependence. No industry works in isolation from others. Finally, even if the differential approach may be more equitable it is certainly much more expensive to administer.

In the light of such considerations, Beveridge formulated a compromise solution: a general pooling of responsibility with a special charge on certain high-risk industries.[58] The proposal did not win the approval of the government[59] and the National Insurance (Industrial Injuries) Act 1946 created a fund based on flat-rate contributions (five-twelfths

---

51 Hence the recommendation in the *Pearson Report* n 32, above, that the scheme should be extended to this group: para 853. See further p 720, below.

52 IIAC *The Industrial Injuries Scheme And The Reform Of Disability Income* (1990).

53 Eg in Australia the National Compensation Bill encountered strong opposition from the trade unions on the ground that it would abolish advantages hitherto enjoyed under the workmen's compensation scheme: *Pearson Report* n 32, above, vol 3, para 812.

54 *Pearson Report* n 32, above, paras 898–904; and Cane *Atiyah's Accidents, Compensation and the Law* (6th edn, 1999) pp 371–374.

55 Calabresi *The Cost of Accidents* (1970).

56 The firm must employ at least 100 workers and it would not be fully rated on its own experience unless it had 500 workers. Only 1 per cent of manufacturing firms are of this size, although they employ half of the total manufacturing workforce: *Cane* n 54, above, p 373. See further Ison (1986) 24 Osgoode Hall LJ 723.

57 Barth (1984) 13 J Legal Stud 569 at 582.

58 *Beveridge Report* n 15, above paras 88–92.

59 *Social Insurance* n 17, above, Pt II, para 31.

each from the employer and employee, the remaining one-sixth being paid by the Exchequer). Despite a recommendation of the Robens Committee on Safety and Health at Work to reopen the issue of risk-rating,[60] and a greater readiness in some foreign systems to apply this method,[61] the principle of uniform contributions remained unchanged. The Pearson Commission, with one dissenter (significantly an economist),[62] reaffirmed the principle, mainly on the ground that risk-relating contributions for each employer, or industry, would involve substantial administrative costs which would outweigh any benefits in terms of increased safety.[63]

In 1975 the Industrial Injuries Fund was abolished, and the scheme was then financed by the general National Insurance Fund. The removal of any risk relationship was completed in 1990 when the funding was transferred to the Consolidated Fund, where it is wholly tax supported. The government justified this by arguing that the scheme could now be regarded as non-contributory. However, it was later learned that the decision was part of a package of measures taken to maintain a prudent balance of the National Insurance Fund following greater than expected costs arising from personal pension rebates and incentives.[64]

D Outline of the chapter

Claims under the industrial injuries scheme must satisfy two conditions:
(a) that the person injured or killed was an employed earner (Part 2); and
(b) that the injury or death was caused by 'accident arising out of and in the course of his employment' (Part 3) or resulted from a disease prescribed in relation to that employment (Part 4).

The principal instrument of compensation is disablement benefit (Part 5), as supplemented by two allowances (Part 6). The chapter concludes with an examination of, firstly, old cases of injury and, secondly, benefits now withdrawn but remaining important because of the preserved rights of existing recipients (Part 7).

Part 2   Persons covered

WCA 1897 covered only specified dangerous employments,[65] but in 1906 it was extended to all persons working under a contract of service or apprenticeship, with a few exceptions, the most important of which were non-manual workers earning more than £250 (subsequently £420) a year.[66] The 1946 state scheme covered the same categories, but included also all non-manual employees irrespective of income, and did not permit contracting-out which had been possible under workmen's compensation. In general, the categories of insured persons were the same as those regarded as 'employed persons' for the purposes of the non-industrial national insurance schemes. However, there were reasons for creating distinctions between the scope of the two schemes. First,

---

60   *Report of the Committee on Health and Safety at Work* (1972, Cmnd 5034) para 447.
61   Most notably in France and Germany.
62   *Pearson Report* n 32, above, paras 940–948.
63   *Pearson Report* n 32, above, paras 898–904.
64   IIAC *Periodic Report 1993* (1993) p 11.
65   WCA 1897, s 7.
66   WCA 1906, ss 1, 13.

'employment' in the non-industrial scheme was confined to those working a minimum number of hours a week, a limitation which had not existed under WCA 1897 and which was therefore considered inappropriate for the industrial scheme. Secondly, the non-industrial benefits were, in general, payable only on the fulfilment of certain contribution conditions, whereas under the industrial scheme, as with its predecessor, the employee was covered as from the first day of employment, irrespective of contributions.

The present position is, then, that the scheme covers those who are 'employed earners', as the term is interpreted for the purposes of paying social security contributions.[67] But the claimant for industrial injury benefit need not have paid, or indeed be liable for, Class 1 National Insurance contributions; he or she may eg be exempt from such contributions on the ground of low earnings,[68] and still be covered by the scheme.[69] Moreover, the Secretary of State has power to extend or exclude, by regulation, categories of employed earners for the purposes of the scheme.[70] The more important categories so regulated may be summarised as follows.

(1) Included are apprentices,[71] special constables, members of fire brigades and other rescue services, mine inspectors and certain ferry operators or taxi drivers.[72]

(2) Excluded is employment (i) by a relative or spouse where not for the purpose of trade or business,[73] and (ii) as a military or civilian member of a visiting force or as a member of an international headquarters or defence organisation unless, in either case, the civilian pays Class 1 contributions.[74]

(3) Those employed abroad are covered if they pay either Class 1 contributions or, as volunteer development workers, Class 2 contributions.[75] They may also be covered if working in the EU or in a country with which Great Britain has a reciprocal agreement.[76]

The minister also has the power to direct that where a contract of service is rendered void or unlawful as a result of non-compliance with any statutory requirement passed for the protection of employed persons, the employment is nevertheless, for the purposes of industrial injury benefits, to be treated as an employed earner's employment.[77] Disputes as to classification were traditionally determined by the Secretary of State rather than by the adjudicating authorities.[78] However, in 1999 this function was transferred, along with contributions matters, to the Board of the Inland Revenue, with a right of appeal to the tax appeal Commissioners.[79]

The most important economically active group outside the scheme is the self-employed.[80] These number nearly three million, about eight per cent of the workforce.[81]

---

67   Social Security Contributions and Benefits Act 1992, ss 2(1)(a), 95(1) (SSCBA 1992) and SI 1975/467.
68   P 106, above.
69   Married women with reduced liability (p 118, above) are also covered.
70   SSCBA 1992, s 95(1), SI 1975/467 and SI 1978/1689.
71   Trainees working under government schemes are not covered but in practice discretionary payments are made under the Analagous Industrial Injuries Scheme operated by the Department for Education and Employment (DfEE). The unsatisfactory nature of these was highlighted by the IIAC in its *Periodic Report 1993* n 64, above, p 14. See also Wikeley (1990) 53 MLR 363.
72   SI 1975/467, Sch 1, Pt I.
73   Where employed by a spouse for the purposes of business, the claimant must also be a Class I contributor.
74   SI 1975/467, Sch 1, Pt II.
75   SI 1975/563, reg 10C, as amended in 1986. For discussion of the reform, see *DHSS* n 35, above, pp 57–60.
76   Lewis *Compensation for Industrial Injury* (1987) pp 35–36.
77   SSCBA 1992, s 97.
78   See *R(I) 2/75*. See generally, pp 187–188, above.
79   Social Security Contributions (Transfer of Functions, etc) Act 1999, ss 8(1) and 11 (SSC(TF)A 1999).
80   For a general critique see Brown *Social Security For The Self Employed* (1992).
81   ONS *Social Trends 2002* (2002) Table 4.3.

A significant proportion work in safety conditions which are little different from those of employees, and they have been seen as equally deserving of compensation. However, the government resisted proposals from both the Pearson Commission[82] and the IIAC[83] that the self-employed be brought within the scheme. The change would have increased the number of new recipients of disablement benefit by about 4 per cent. Arguments against the reform are, firstly, that there has been insufficient demand from the self-employed for such protection; secondly, that coverage would create difficulties in determining the scope of employment;[84] and thirdly, that it would amount to a significant extension of the scheme which, at least in the government's view, is not justified in principle or workable in practice. However, many of these objections can be overcome. They overlook the fact that several European schemes offer protection, apparently without undue problems.[85]

Part 3 Industrial injury

Entitlement to the various industrial benefits is fundamentally based on proof that the 'employed earner suffers personal injury caused ... by accident arising out of and in the course of his employment'.[86] This contains three different elements:[87]
(a) a personal injury;
(b) caused by an accident; and
(c) arising out of and in the course of employment.
The discussion will be divided accordingly.

A Personal injury

This means a 'hurt to body or mind'.[88] Thus it includes a nervous disorder or nervous shock.[89] In principle even a trivial hurt which is ephemeral, like the watering of an eye,[90] will qualify, though, as will be seen, the claimant must establish a loss of faculty resulting in a disablement of 14 per cent in most cases. Real difficulty arises where there is damage to a prosthesis, such as an artificial limb. In *R(I) 7/56* it was ruled that there had to be an injury to the living body of a human being. This was decided at a time when replacement surgery was in its infancy and in *R(I) 8/81* the Commissioner was prepared to give 'personal injury' a broader interpretation. On his view, the test was 'whether or not the prosthesis has become so intimately linked with the body that

---

82 *Pearson Report* n 32, above, paras 851–857.
83 Following a consultation paper in 1991 the Council issued a full report in 1993 (Cm 2177). As a first step it proposed only that the self-employed working in construction and agriculture be brought within the scheme. These workers suffer the majority of major accidents which occur to the self-employed. In 1999 the government announced it had no current plans to extend the scheme to the self-employed: 324 HC Official Report (6th series) col 288W, 27 January 1999.
84 *Reform of the Industrial Injuries Scheme* n 37, above, paras 63–65.
85 Mutual Information System on Social Protection (MISSOC) *MISSOC 2001* (2001) Table VIII *Field of Application* 1.
86 SSCBA 1992, s 94(1). As discussed above, this concept 'is one of some antiquity in the law': per Swinton Thomas LJ in *Chief Adjudication Officer v Rhodes* [1999] ICR 178 at 187.
87 Cf Lord Denning MR in *Re Dowling* [1967] 1 QB 202 at 217.
88 *Jones v Secretary of State for Social Services* [1972] AC 944 at 1020, per Lord Simon.
89 *R(I) 49/52; R(I) 22/59.*
90 *R 5/60 (II).*

on any realistic assessment of the situation it can be said to have become part of that body'.[91] On this definition, there is no doubt that where the prosthesis damaged is a living tissue or synthetic material inserted into the body, the claimant has sustained a 'personal injury'. In cases of external appliances it is a question of fact and degree. The Commissioner suggested that the 'intimate link with the body' might be regarded as broken by the detachability of the appliance. A claimant would succeed where damage is inflicted on an artificial limb permanently attached to the body but not, for example, where the appliance in question is a pair of spectacles,[92] a hearing-aid or a crutch.

B Accident

The personal injury must be caused 'by accident'.[93] This indicates the preference granted by the system – itself, of course, a preferential system – to traumatically caused disability. As will be seen, sickness and disease are covered, but only within carefully prescribed limits. The preference is deeply rooted in most legal systems[94] and it is not difficult to locate the reasons for this. Industrial injury schemes replaced systems of individual responsibility which in practice, if not theory, attached to accidents rather than processes. This reflected an assumption that, while diseases were natural hazards, accidents were typically 'man made'; in its turn, the assumption underpinned the deterrence function of the compensation process. The assumption is manifestly false,[95] but pragmatically it is certainly easier to prove the causal relationship between an accident and working conditions.[96] Although some systems have abandoned the requirement of an 'accident', it is retained in the great majority, not the least because of cost constraints. Paradoxically, there is empirical evidence which suggests that victims of illness are more likely than accident victims to suffer residual incapacity and to incur serious medical needs.[97]

The preference for accidents is also reflected in the special procedure enabling an individual to apply for a declaration that he or she has suffered an industrial accident, irrespective of whether it is their current intention to claim benefit.[98] This is a useful facility that allows an injured worker to protect their position (eg should their condition deteriorate later).

i Meaning of 'accident'

The starting point is still Lord Macnaghten's famous dictum in 1903:[99]

> The expression 'accident' is used in the popular and ordinary sense of the word as denoting an unlooked-for mishap or an untoward event which is not expected or designed.

91   *R(I) 8/81*, para 14, D G Rice, Comr.
92   *R(I) 1/82*.
93   SSCBA 1992, s 94(1).
94   Barta *Kausalität in Sozialrecht* (1983), esp chs 17 and 18.
95   Stapleton *Disease and the Compensation Debate* (1986) ch 1.
96   *Stapleton* n 95, above, ch 3; and see *Report of the Departmental Committee on Disease Provisions of the National Insurance (Industrial Injuries) Act* (1955, Cmd 9548) para 55.
97   Harris et al *Compensation and Support for Illness and Injury* (1984) pp 242, 323.
98   SSA 1998, s 29. See *Lewis* n 30, above, p 202.
99   *Fenton v J Thorley & Co Ltd* [1903] AC 443 at 448.

But 'popular' meanings are notoriously unreliable and, as critics have pointed out,[100] nowhere more so than in this context. It soon became clear that Lord Macnaghten's definition was neither accurate nor sufficient. In the first place, while it was construed to exclude deliberate acts by the injured party himself, it has been held to include a deliberate, even unlawful, act of a third party. The point was decided in *Trim Joint District School v Kelly*,[101] in which pupils assaulted and killed a schoolmaster responsible for discipline. Secondly, the phrase 'not expected' could not be taken seriously. An event need not be unforeseeable or exceptional to constitute an 'accident'.[102] To take a frequently encountered example, claimants who incapacitate themselves by heavy exertions do not have to prove that the strain was violent or exceptional for their job.[103]

As the case law on the statutory principle developed, it became crucial to distinguish an 'event' from a 'process', thereby ensuring that the scheme retained its character as one concerned with traumatic work injuries. However, a generous interpretation initially by the courts and then by the Commissioner of what constituted an 'event' created logical and practical difficulties. First, in 1905, the House of Lords held that unobservable infection of bacteria could constitute an 'injury by accident'.[104] Secondly, it was held, again by the House of Lords, that while an 'accident' does not include the growth of incapacity by a continuous progress, nevertheless the employee would succeed if he or she was able to point to 'an incident *or series of incidents* ... which caused or contributed to the origin or progress of the disease'.[105] The distinction is neither logical nor recognised in medical usage.[106] As a result, decision making in this area has been somewhat arbitrary.[107] Reference to a few of the decisions should be sufficient to illustrate the point.

- Strain to chest muscles caused by the daily lifting of heavy weights is not covered,[108] but a claimant, who, when lifting heavy equipment on a particular day, felt severe pains in the chest and subsequently suffered from coronary thrombosis, was entitled to succeed. He had experienced a physiological change at that particular time.[109]

- A worker who developed a psychoneurotic condition having worked near a machine which produced explosive reports at irregular intervals recovered. Each explosion was 'an accident' and thus the condition was the result of a 'series of accidents'. The interval between each such explosion was not so short that the series was to be regarded as a single continuous process.[110] On the other hand, a claimant who became sick on inhaling gas which leaked from the vehicle he used from time to time did not succeed: the illness was caused by the taking of breath on an infinite

---

100   See *Trim Joint District School Board of Management v Kelly* [1914] AC 667 at 681, per Lord Loreburn; *Re Dowling* [1967] 1 AC 725 at 759, per Lord Wilberforce; *Jones v Secretary of State for Social Services* [1972] AC 944 at 1009, per Lord Diplock. See also Bohlen (1912) 25 Harv LR 328.
101   *Trim Joint District School Board of Management v Kelly* [1914] AC 667. See also *CI 51/49* and *R(I) 30/58*.
102   *Clover Clayton v Hughes* [1910] AC 242; *CWI 6/49*; but the 'abnormality' of an event may be relevant in proving the causal link between the injury and the accident: p 725, below.
103   *CI 5/49*. This passage was cited with approval by the Commissioner in *CI/15589/1996*, referred to by the Inner House of the Court of Session in *Chief Adjudication Officer v Faulds* 1998 SLT 1203 at 1209 (reversed on other grounds by the House of Lords: see n 120, below).
104   *Brinton's Ltd v Turvey* [1905] AC 230.
105   Per Lord Porter in *Roberts v Dorothea Slate Quarries* [1948] 2 All ER 201 at 205–206, adopted by a Tribunal of Commissioners in *CS 257/49(T)*, para 11.
106   *Stapleton* n 95, above, pp 50–51.
107   See the decisions collected in *Lewis* n 30, above, pp 39–42.
108   *R(I) 42/51*.
109   *R(I) 54/53*. See generally Lee (1995) 2 JSSL 9.
110   *R(I) 43/55*.

number of occasions, and these did not constitute separate incidents.[111] This contrasts with the case in which an asthmatic exposed to passive smoking was able to show that she had inhaled considerable quantities of smoke on six separate identifiable occasions.[112]

Apart from the somewhat arbitrary nature of some of these distinctions, it is apparent from other decisions that certain illogicalities may ensue. A claimant will be fortunate if the condition, though developing gradually, manifests itself on a particular occasion. Thus in *R(I) 18/54* the claimant had been using a pad for three months, the buckle of which rubbed against a nerve. One day, he felt a numbness in his leg, and he was allowed to recover on the basis that this constituted a particular incident.[113] Even more anomalously, a person who encounters an employment risk only once will be in a better position than one who is exposed to it regularly. Hence, a nurse who had come into contact with, and was infected by, a child with poliomyelitis succeeded,[114] but a doctor who was attending a large number of patients infected with tuberculosis and subsequently contracted the disease was refused benefit. It was assumed that he must have been infected by the regular penetration of bacteria into his system.[115] It must be noted, however, that once the claimant has succeeded in establishing, on the balance of probabilities, that the injury resulted from an event or a series of events,[116] the claim will not be jeopardised by a failure to identify the specific occasion when the condition began or was aggravated: for procedural purposes the earliest probable date will be taken.[117]

In recent years the definition of 'by accident' has proved most problematic in the context of claims based on post-traumatic stress, particularly by members of the emergency services and others commonly exposed to stressful incidents in the course of their work. A senior prison officer who developed stress following a specific confrontation with a disruptive prisoner, who was known to be violent, was entitled to a declaration of an industrial accident.[118] In *Chief Adjudication Officer v Faulds*[119] a senior fire officer suffering from post-traumatic stress disorder was discharged from the service. The basis of his claim was that his condition had been brought on by his attendance at a series of horrific fatal accidents, including road traffic accidents and aircraft crashes. The House of Lords held that it was essential to identify the relevant incident or incidents which had caused the injury. The event itself was not an 'accident' in the required sense: 'What has to be identified is not the occurrence of some or other accident in general, but an accident to the claimant, an accident suffered by him'.[120] On the available evidence, the majority of the House doubted whether it could be demonstrated that the aetiology of the claimant's disorder could be identified with

---

111   *R(I) 32/60*. See also *Fraser v Secretary of State for Social Services* 1986 SLT 386.
112   *R(I) 6/91*. Contrast *CI/073/1994* ((1996) 3 JSSL D41).
113   The case should be compared with *R(I) 11/74* in which the claimant was unable to rely on a specific date.
114   *CI 159/50*.
115   *CI 83/50*.
116   See *R(I) 8/66*.
117   *CI 49/49; CI 196/50*.
118   *CI/15589/1996*; see Jones (1998) 5 JSSL 139. But see *CI/289/1994* ((1997) 4 JSSL D45) concerning a lorry driver who heard the news of the Zeebrugge ferry disaster while driving on a motorway the day after using the same route. Although his post-traumatic stress disorder developed following an incident in the course of his employment (hearing the news on the radio), it did not arise out of his employment.
119   [2000] 2 All ER 961.
120   *Chief Adjudication Officer v Faulds* [2000] 2 All ER 961 at 977, per Lord Clyde. See further Bonner (2001) 8 JSSL 35; and eg *CI/2414/98*, in which an Employment Service deputy manager experienced shock as a result of a distressing conversation with a senior colleague.

particular incidents that occurred to him.[121] In practice few such claims are likely to succeed.[122]

The IIAC considered three options for reform as a means of reducing the anomalies that may result from the distinction between accident and process.[123] These were a statutory definition of 'accident' to include injury by process, the repeal of the requirement for injury to be caused by such accident and the introduction of a system of individual proof. The IIAC declined to recommend any of these options, concluding that the gap in coverage for injury by process was unclear.[124] Moreover, many of the diseases which might be subject to claims in relation to injurious processes are extremely common in the community and have both occupational and non-occupational causes.

ii   Causal link between accident and injury

The claimant must also prove,[125] on the balance of probabilities, that the accident 'caused' the injury.[126] This does not mean that it has to be the sole cause of the injury; it is sufficient if it is a contributory cause, in combination with eg a condition from which the claimant already suffered.[127] It is irrelevant that the previous condition rendered the claimant more susceptible to the later event.[128] But, at the same time, the accident must have been 'an efficient cause (*causa causans*) and not a mere condition (*causa sine qua non*)' in which the earlier cause operated.[129] Thus in *R(I) 4/58*,

> The claimant suffered from burns when his clothing, which had been soaked in inflammable liquid in a work accident, caught fire when coming into contact with a cigarette which he was lighting at home. It was held that the *causa causans* of the injury was the lighting of the cigarette, and not the accidental soaking.

iii   Critique

It will be apparent from the analysis above that the requirement of an 'accident' has produced severe difficulties and that, quite apart from being an elusive criterion for distinguishing between injuries and sickness, it is not conclusive of the issue. On the one hand, claimants will succeed if it can be shown that an illness (not an injury) was attributable to an event rather than to a process. On the other hand, as will be seen, claimants are entitled to benefit if they suffer from a prescribed disease, provided that it was contracted in the appropriate prescribed employment. One alternative, then, would

---

121   The case was remitted to the Commissioner with the suggestion that a specially commissioned medical report might assist.

122   In 1998 there were just 700 current awards for mental or behavioural disorders following accident assessments (as against 212,000 for all accidents): 341 HC Official Report (6th series) col 330W, 20 December 1999.

123   IIAC *Coverage under the industrial injuries scheme for injury by 'process'* IIAC Position Paper 9 (1995).

124   See Jones in Harris (ed) *Social Security Law in Context* (2000) ch 15, p 476.

125   In contrast to the war pension scheme, where the burden of proof of the causal link between service and the disability generally favours the claimant: p 778, below.

126   For a detailed analysis of the case law, see Lewis n 30, above, pp 45–49.

127   *R(I) 19/63.*

128   *CI 147/50.*

129   *R(I) 14/51,* para 6. See also *R(I) 12/58,* para 5.

be to link the two concepts and allow recovery for any injury or disease that was work-caused. The possibility is considered later in connection with prescribed diseases.[130] An alternative, less radical, is that proposed by Sir Owen Woodhouse as part of his recommendations for new schemes in both New Zealand[131] and Australia.[132] The idea is to incorporate in legislation a list of all possible forms of accident to be made the subject of compensation, and for such a purpose it might be possible to adopt a classification of injuries and external causes of injury prepared by the World Health Organization.[133] Of course, as with all attempts at exhaustive listing, this could not be a perfect solution and would have to be supplemented by some residual general clause. But it might serve to remove some of the doubts and uncertainty generated by the case law on the more traditional approach.

C Employment risk

i General

It is of the essence of an industrial injuries insurance scheme that the accident must be connected with the employment. In 1897, WCA 1897 contained a test which was adopted by English speaking jurisdictions throughout the world, and remains the basis of the current scheme: personal injury by accident 'arising out of and in the course of employment'.[134] This classic formulation, perhaps the most notorious in the whole of social security law, has been responsible for vast amounts of disputed claims and complex litigation. In 1920, Lord Wrenbury was moved to remark that:

> The language of the Act and the decisions upon it are such that I have long since abandoned the hope of deciding any case upon the words 'out of and in the course of' upon grounds satisfactory to myself or convincing to others;[135]

and two years later a Departmental Committee reported that:

> No other form of words has ever given rise to such a body of litigation.[136]

The original Act sought to delimit the connection with the employment more precisely by requiring that the accident should occur, 'on, in or about' the employer's premises,[137] but this condition was soon abandoned.[138] Most obviously it discriminated against employees whose work took them away from the employer's premises. Other common law jurisdictions have attempted to mitigate the rigours of the statutory test by amending

---

130   P 743, below.
131   *Report of Royal Commission of Injury into Compensation for Personal Injuries in New Zealand* (1967) para 289(c).
132   *Report of National Committee of Injury into Compensation and Rehabilitation in Australia* (1974) para 350.
133   The relevant parts are conveniently published in a Schedule to the draft Bill at the end of the Australian report, n 132, above.
134   WCA 1897, s 1.
135   *Armstrong, Whitworth & Co v Redford* [1920] AC 757 at 780.
136   *Departmental Committee Report on Workmen's Compensation* (Holman Gregory Report) (1920, Cmd 816) para 29.
137   WCA 1897, s 7(1).
138   WCA 1906, s 1(1).

the formula. Thus, in some systems, workers need only show that the accident arose '*in the course of employment*',[139] while in others they are given the alternative of proving that it happened '*out of or in the course of employment*'.[140] But no formula adopted (and this includes non-English speaking jurisdictions[141]) has managed to alleviate problems involved in establishing the connection between the work and the accident.[142] As Atiyah has observed:

> The difficulty is inherent in the concept of insurance against 'employment risks' because there is no clear and sound policy reason for distinguishing between employment risks and non-employment risks.[143]

The most significant reforms, therefore, both in Great Britain and elsewhere, have not been through a modification of the basic formula, but rather by specific extensions of the scheme to cover contingencies which might not otherwise have been regarded as employment risks. As will be seen, the most important developments in this respect have been the coverage of certain accidents occurring on a journey to or from work, or caused by a natural event or the conduct of a third party.

ii The statutory test

It has long been a subject of debate whether the formula 'out of and in the course of employment'[144] involves two different principles or only a single test. In the past it has been said that the authorities should treat the phrase as a combined whole.[145] The more generally accepted view is that the 'in the course of' criterion delimits the time, place and activity of the work, while the 'out of' criterion concerns itself with the cause or connection between the accident and the work.[146] In the simple case, the distinction is obvious. A person working at a bench inadvertently sits on a pin which he or she had earlier put in a trouser pocket. The accident arises 'in the course of' the employment but not 'out of' it. The converse may also hold true. In *Chief Adjudication Officer v Rhodes*,[147] the respondent was a Benefits Agency officer, at home on sick leave, who was assaulted in her own driveway by her neighbour. The respondent had earlier reported her neighbour for working whilst claiming income support. The majority of the Court of Appeal held that the assault undoubtedly arose 'out of' her employment, but it could not be said to have taken place 'in the course of' that employment. The latter required a focus on what she was actually doing at the time (returning home after a visit to her doctor), rather than what was done to her.[148]

---

139 Eg in the US: North Dakota, Pennsylvania, Texas and Washington.
140 Eg in Australia, New South Wales.
141 See eg Dupeyroux *Droit de la sécurité sociale* (14th edn, 2001) pp 628–642.
142 Cf *Pearson Report* n 32, above, para 896.
143 *Cane* n 54, above, p 282.
144 It should be noted that since the scheme covers 'office-holders' as well as 'employed earners', the appropriate test for those in the former category would seem to be whether the accident arose out of and in the course of the office: see *CI 6/78*; and Partington (1978) 7 ILJ 251, (1979) 8 ILJ 64. It is not, however, clear whether this test requires any modification to the principles expounded in this section.
145 See eg *CSI 63/49*; *R(I) 62/51*.
146 Eg per Lord Wright in *Dover Navigation v Craig* [1940] AC 190 at 199; *R(I) 10/52*; *R(I) 2/63*.
147 [1999] ICR 178; see also Bonner (1998) 5 JSSL 72 (on the Commissioner's decision) and (1999) 6 JSSL 33 (CA).
148 Thus the outcome may have been different had she been assaulted whilst telephoning the office on her mobile phone to report that her neighbour was defrauding the benefits system. Per Schiemann LJ in *Chief Adjudication Officer v Rhodes* [1999] ICR 178 at 185.

There are, however, other situations where there is an inevitable overlap between the two tests. If eg an employee suffers injury while engaging in horseplay on the employer's premises and during the normal hours of duty, it might be said that the accident did not arise out of the employment because the risk was not caused by the work. Alternatively, it might be argued that it did not arise in the course of employment, because the claimant's activity at the time interfered with and diverged from his or her ordinary working duties. For the sake of clarity of exposition, the traditional distinction has been followed in this work, and the overlap recognised at appropriate points in the discussion.

The exposition of the law which follows is, of course, primarily based on decisions of the courts and Commissioners under the Workmen's Compensation and modern legislation respectively.[149] While such decisions are undoubtedly authoritative, the Court of Appeal has, in *Nancollas v Insurance Officer*,[150] suggested that they should not be treated as binding precedents, in the commonly accepted meaning of that term.

> [T]he reality is that none of the authorities purports to lay down any conclusive test and none propounds any proposition of law which, as such, binds other courts. They do indeed approve an approach which requires the courts to have regard to and weigh in the balance every factor which can be said in any way to point towards or away from a finding that the claimant was in the course of his employment.[151]

On this view decision makers should aim at an aggregate picture from each set of facts and should then approach questions regarding the employment risk as if they were jury questions. Such an impressionistic approach, taken to its limits, would do nothing to improve the quality of decision-making: the traditional approach has the merits of (relative) certainty and consistency, and therefore also of horizontal equity between claimants.[152] It is, perhaps, not without significance that the Pearson Commission rejected a proposed change in the statutory formula precisely because 'a considerable body of case law has been developed around the existing definition and we should be reluctant to change the definition after such a long period of use'.[153] Subsequent decisions have not gone so far as *Nancollas*. The House of Lords in *Smith v Stages*[154] stressed that the factual picture as a whole should be looked at, and any approach which made any one factor conclusive was to be rejected. But Lord Lowry also set out six key propositions on the meaning of 'in the course of' employment.[155] The subsequent decisions of the Court of Appeal in *Faulkner*[156] and *Rhodes*[157] represent a return to legal orthodoxy as contrasted with *Nancollas*. They indicate that an accident arises in the course of employment if it occurred whilst the claimant 'was doing something he or she was employed to do, or something reasonably incidental to those things that the applicant was employed to do'.[158]

---

149 For a more comprehensive analysis, see *Lewis* n 30, above, pp 50–89.
150 [1985] 1 All ER 833.
151 *Nancollas v Insurance Officer* [1985] 1 All ER 833 at 836, per Sir John Donaldson MR.
152 Cf Mesher [1986] JSWL 244.
153 *Pearson Report* n 32, above, para 896.
154 [1989] AC 928.
155 *Smith v Stages* [1989] AC 928 at 955–956.
156 *Faulkner v Chief Adjudication Officer*, reported as *R(I) 8/94*.
157 *Chief Adjudication Officer v Rhodes* [1999] ICR 178.
158 *Chief Adjudication Officer v Rhodes* [1999] ICR 178 at 191, per Roch LJ.

iii In the course of employment

According to the classic formulation of Lord Loreburn:

> An accident befalls a man 'in the course of' his employment if it occurs while he is doing what a man so employed may reasonably do within a time during which he is employed, and at a place where he may reasonably be during that time to do that thing.[159]

From this, it will be seen that the limits to the course of employment are determined by three different criteria: place, time and activity. A claimant will set up a prima facie case if he or she is able to show that the accident occurred at the normal *place* of work during the normal *hours* of work. The *activity* at the time of the accident may be relevant in two different respects. It may serve to defeat a prima facie case by showing that the claimant interrupted the time element in the work or deviated from the spatial element for reasons unconnected with the employment. Or it may serve to extend the 'course of employment' to cover hours or places not normally considered as within its ambit. The discussion will proceed accordingly.

It must also be observed that the notion of employment covers functions and objectives which are regarded as reasonably incidental to the actual work process. The contract of employment is rarely relevant or helpful in determining what is to be so regarded. Obviously this varies enormously according to the nature of the work and the status of the claimant but the case law reveals that resort is usually had to two different but related notions. Under the first (supervision test) the question is whether the accident happened while the claimant was under the authority, supervision or control of the employer.[160] The alternative and complementary criterion (public zone test) is concerned to ascertain whether the claimant's activities at the time of the accident were such as could be distinguished from those of an ordinary member of the public.[161]

Most employees have fixed places and hours of work. The task, here, is to determine what, for the purposes of benefit, are to be regarded as the limits of the employment, though this is not always easy. The mere fact that during a period when not actually working employees must remain available to be summoned by their employer – in other words, when they are 'on call' – is not sufficient by itself to bring that period within the course of employment.[162] Similarly, the fact that the employee is at home on paid sick leave and that under her contract preparation work at home can be credited under a flexitime arrangement is insufficient if she is not actually working at the time of the accident.[163] But if the employees' freedom of movement is limited or their activities controlled by the employer, then, in accordance with the 'supervision test', they may

---

159 *Moore v Manchester Liners Ltd* [1910] AC 498 at 500–501.
160 See particularly *R(I) 84/51*.
161 See particularly *R(I) 61/51*.
162 *R(I) 10/52*, para 8; *R(I) 11/55*, para 6; *R(I) 5/81*.
163 *Chief Adjudication Officer v Rhodes* [1999] ICR 178.

be covered.[164] This seems to be the best explanation of the perhaps surprising decision in *R v National Insurance Comr, ex p Reed*.[165]

A police sergeant was permitted to take lunch at home during his period on duty, but throughout he remained on call. He was injured while travelling back to the police station and the Divisional Court held that he was entitled to benefit. Woolf J stressed that his choice as to where refreshment could be taken was limited and while at home he was still responsible for performing his duties.[166]

The limits of work, as defined by the contract, are not rigidly applied. The law allows the claimant a certain amount of time and space to 'prepare himself for, or to disengage himself from' his employment.[167] As regards time, the course of employment includes a reasonable period at either end of the official hours of duty.[168] What this amounts to may depend on the nature of the job and the character of the claimant. Arriving early the more properly to equip oneself for work will be generously treated,[169] but not if the intention is instead to fit in a game of billiards.[170]

As regards place, the exact area is difficult to locate. It generally includes the premises in which the claimant is about to work, has just worked and the access to them.[171] The 'public zone' test will usually be conclusive in determining the necessary limits. The claimant must be within an area excluded from public access,[172] but this is to be decided according to existing practice rather than legal rights.[173] The question is whether the members of the public make substantial use of that part of the land.[174] Equally, the mere fact that the land on which the accident occurs is owned by the employer is rarely conclusive.[175] Some industrial enterprises own vast areas of land, and the claimant may be on a part of it miles from his or her place of work.[176] Conversely, a social worker injured while descending a staircase common to several households may recover, though her business took her to only one.[177] The authorities must determine the part of the land on which the claimant normally works, and this may be particularly difficult in agricultural cases.[178] It is not possible to reconcile all the decisions.[179] In some cases the authorities are apparently prepared to show some indulgence, and avoid nice distinctions which would have the effect of depriving the claimant of benefit. They may then admit a claim on the vague basis that the claimant had 'so nearly approached the means of

---

164   *R(I) 49/51*; *R(I) 11/55*.
165   (1980) reported as Appendix to *R(I) 7/80*; and see *R(I) 5/81*, paras 11–14.
166   Cf J G Monroe, Comr, who drew a distinction between being employed to stand by, and being given leave of absence on condition that the employee stands by: *R(I) 7/80*, para 8.
167   *Gane v Norton Hill Colliery* [1909] 2 KB 539; *R(I) 61/51*; *R(I) 3/72*.
168   *R v National Insurance Comr, ex p East* [1976] ICR 206.
169   *R v National Insurance Comr, ex p East* [1976] ICR 206; and to similar effect: *R(I) 22/51*; *R(I) 72/54*; and *R(I) 3/62*.
170   *R(I) 1/59*.
171   *R(I) 7/52*; *R(I) 5/67*.
172   Even if the claimant's duties sometimes take him or her into the 'public zone': *R(I) 72/51*; *R(I) 7/62*. See also *R(I) 7/52*; *R(I) 23/55*; *R(I) 70/57*. 'Access' here means qua member of the public – not, of course, for business purposes: *R(I) 41/57*.
173   *R(I) 43/51*; *R(I) 1/68*.
174   Per Lord Macmillan in *Northumbrian Shipping Co Ltd v McCullum* (1932) 25 BWCC 284.
175   *CI 65/49*; *R(I) 67/52*; *R(I) 43/51*.
176   *R(I) 67/52*.
177   *R(I) 3/72*. See also *CI/3579/1995* ((1997) 4 JSSL D45).
178   See *R(I) 7/52* and *R(I) 42/56*.
179   Cf *R(I) 42/56*, para 11.

access as to make it reasonable to hold that he had returned to the sphere in which his employment operated'.[180]

C EXTENSIONS FOR AUTHORISED OR INCIDENTAL PURPOSES

The spatial and temporal boundaries may be extended for purposes which are reasonably necessary for, or incidental to, the employment.[181] In *R v National Insurance Comr, ex p Michael*, the Court of Appeal stressed that the 'reasonably incidental' test is not part of the statutory formula and should not be applied without careful consideration: 'if the injury is not suffered in the actual course of the work which the employee is engaged to do, it must have at least been suffered by reason of some event incidental to *that work*'.[182] Obviously this covers, primarily, situations where employers directly or indirectly authorise employees to perform their duties outside normal hours, or their usual locality.[183] But it seems that 'employer' in this context must be strictly construed. An unauthorised request from an immediate superior will not bring the resulting activity within the scheme.[184] This may operate harshly, for the employee may find it difficult to refuse the request and feel that any prospects of promotion will otherwise suffer. But the test should be a subjective one: if the employee has reasonable grounds to think that the request has the implied authority of the employer, the claim should succeed.[185] Where the claimant is under no obligation to carry out the activity, but is merely permitted to, the case is more difficult. Clearly, mere knowledge of, or acquiescence by, the employer is insufficient. The issue becomes whether or not the activity in question is sufficiently connected with the employment. There are obvious cases, such as working overtime,[186] collecting equipment or clothing necessary for work,[187] or taking a bath after duty in a mine.[188] The receipt of wages comes within the scope of employment but not the cashing of a money order representing them: the processes of employment are complete when the money order is received by the employee.[189] Participants in a trade union meeting are also covered, provided that it is directly concerned with the terms and conditions of employment with the particular employer.[190]

The status of recreational activities is problematic. In the leading case of *R v National Insurance Comr, ex p Michael*, the Court of Appeal held that a police constable injured when playing football for his force was not covered by the statutory formula.[191] The court was not impressed by the argument, which had been regarded as sufficient by

---

180 *R(I) 3/53*, para 4; cf *R(I) 10/81*.
181 *Armstrong, Whitworth & Co v Redford* [1920] AC 757 at 777, 779, 780; *R v Industrial Injuries Comr, ex p Amalgamated Engineering Union (No 2)* [1966] 2 QB 31 at 48, 50, 51.
182 *R v National Insurance Comr, ex p Michael* [1977] 2 All ER 420 at 427, per Roskill J. See also Lord Denning MR at 423–424.
183 Eg *R(I) 21/53* (where a bus conductor was required by her employer to make a cup of tea for herself and the driver at the end of each journey); cf *R(I) 5/77*. See also the cases where the employee is obliged to participate in physical education, competition or other 'outside' activities, eg *CI 228/50*; *R(I) 4/51*; *R(I) 80/52*; *R(I) 66/53*; *R(I) 39/56*.
184 *R(I) 36/55*; *R(I) 8/61*.
185 In *R(I) 36/55*, paras 7, 8, the Commissioner speaks of acting under the 'ostensible' authority of the employer.
186 *R(I) 52/52*.
187 *R(I) 72/54*; *R(I) 20/58*.
188 *CI 22/49*.
189 *R(I) 34/52*.
190 *R(I) 63/51*; *R(I) 9/57*; *R(I) 46/59*; *R(I) 10/80*.
191 *R v National Insurance Comr, ex p Michael* [1977] 2 All ER 420; and followed in *Faulkner v Chief Adjudication Officer*, reported as *R(I) 8/94* (see Jones (1995) 2 JSSL 45). See also *R(I) 2/80* and *R(I) 4/81*.

some Commissioners,[192] that such activity improved the fitness and morale of the force and therefore was in pursuance of the employment. At the same time, the view held by one Commissioner,[193] that recreation can never come within the course of employment, was rejected.[194] Clearly, claimants will succeed if they can show that they were required by their employer to participate in the activity.[195] Moreover, it is doubtful whether the *Michael* ruling has affected the authority of previous decisions entitling a claimant injured while engaged in physical exercises as part of a training course authorised by the employer,[196] or in games which were regarded as therapeutically valuable to patients at the hospital where he was employed.[197]

Injuries incurred while meeting an emergency may be covered even if the incident occurred away from the employee's place of work or outside normal working hours.[198] It is, however, necessary that the action can be construed as being in some way in the employer's interests (eg the protection of property[199]) and was reasonable in the circumstances.[200]

D   ACCIDENTS WHILE TRAVELLING

Accidents to the claimant while travelling have always posed special problems for industrial injury schemes, and they have been the subject of much dispute both general and specific. For the purposes of discussion it is necessary to distinguish between three types of case.[201]
(1) The employee is required to make a journey for purposes necessary or incidental to the employment.
(2) The employee's work is peripatetic: that is, the employment consists of travelling from place to place.
(3) The employee merely travels to and from work.
(1) This is merely an instance of the situation discussed in the preceding section. The employee's place and hours of work are defined but he or she is required by the employer, expressly or impliedly, to make a journey for purposes connected with the employment.[202] Thus an employee instructed to proceed at a specified time from one working place to another is protected.[203] Travel from home to work does not, in general, come within this category even if the claimant is paid for travelling time or for expenses incurred.[204] The traditionally stated distinction is between a journey *to* duty and a journey *on* duty.[205] The latter may, however, be given a liberal construction, as can be observed from a

192   *R(I) 13/66; CI 7/73.*
193   *R(I) 5/75*, para 21, J S Watson, Comr.
194   *R v National Insurance Comr, ex p Michael* [1977] 2 All ER 420, per Roskill LJ at 426, per Lawton LJ at 431.
195   See eg *R(I) 3/81.*
196   *R(I) 31/53; R(I) 66/53; R(I) 2/68*; and see *R v National Insurance Comr, ex p Michael* [1977] 2 All ER 420, per Lawton LJ at 430–431.
197   *R(I) 3/57.*
198   *R(I) 63/54(T).* See also p 742, below.
199   *R(I) 63/54(T)*; cf *R(I) 6/63.*
200   *R(I) 32/54.*
201   See generally Lewis [1986] JSWL 193; and the principles laid down in *Smith v Stages* [1989] AC 928.
202   See generally *R v National Industrial Injury Benefits Tribunal, ex p Fieldhouse* (1974) 17 KIR 63; *Vandyke v Fender* [1970] 2 QB 292, [1970] 2 All ER 335; *R(I) 5/77*; and *R(I) 14/81.*
203   *R(I) 11/57; R(I) 4/59; R(I) 34/59; Smith v Stages* [1989] AC 928; *R(I) 1/88.*
204   *R(I) 9/51; R(I) 34/57; R(I) 3/71.*
205   *R(I) 45/52*, para 3; *R(I) 14/81*, para 7.

Court of Appeal decision[206] which involved an application of the vague, impressionistic test which it had, itself, formulated in the *Nancollas* case.[207] The decision went in favour of a policeman injured while travelling from home to work. The approach, it will be recalled, requires consideration to be taken of all of the facts of the case. It may be inferred that some or all of the special facts here – the destination was not the normal place of work, the claimant had first telephoned his station to report for duty, his travel expenses were reimbursed – were instrumental to the decision. Previous cases allowing recovery can be rationalised on the basis of the supervision principle: an employee obliged by his employer to travel to work by a specific mode of transport;[208] an employee called out from home by his employer for a specific purpose (eg an emergency) and under a duty, expressly or impliedly, to arrive by the shortest practical route and as quickly as possible.[209] The suggestion has also been made that the exclusion of journeys to and from work should be confined to cases involving 'reasonable daily travelling distance or commuter distance', and that different considerations apply where the journey involves longer distances.[210] But the suggestion was rejected by a Commissioner who decided that a civil servant injured during the journey from his home to a temporary place of employment some 100 miles away was not entitled.[211] Nor does it necessarily make any difference if the employee is carrying work tools or other essential equipment.[212] However, a claim is more likely to be allowed if a special journey is required to deliver or collect such equipment.[213] The question whether employees who are injured while staying away from home during the course of their travels may succeed is resolved along similar lines. If the employee is required by the employer to stay at a particular place,[214] or is in some way supervised by the employer there,[215] benefit is more likely to be payable. Employees who are free to stay where they choose are less likely to be covered during the passage to, or while at, the chosen accommodation.[216]

(2) Certain types of employment are peripatetic: they necessarily involve frequent journeys. Obvious examples of such situations are sales representatives,[217] insurance agents,[218] journalists[219] and home helps.[220] In such cases, benefit is payable for accidents occurring during travel for the purposes of the work. But in defining the limits of the course of the employment, an important distinction has to be drawn.[221] A person who has no fixed hours and no precisely definable place of work may be protected against injuries while travelling to or from home.[222] Conversely, persons whose work requires them to be at particular places at particular times are treated no differently from other employees who have fixed places of work. Their employment does not begin until they

---

206 *Ball v Insurance Officer* [1985] 1 All ER 833.
207 *Ball v Insurance Officer* [1985] 1 All ER 833, on which see Mesher [1986] JSWL 244.
208 *R(I) 8/51*; *R(I) 17/51*; *R(I) 3/81*.
209 *R(I) 21/51*; *R(I) 27/56*: the mere fact that the employee is required to report for duty earlier than normal is not sufficient – the employer is not concerned with the mode or speed of the journey.
210 *CI 21/68*.
211 *R(I) 3/71*, J S Watson, Comr.
212 *R(I) 48/52*; *R(I) 78/53*; *R(I) 16/58*.
213 *R(I) 34/59*.
214 *R(I) 30/57*.
215 *CI 347/50*.
216 *R(I) 22/54*; *R(I) 4/81*.
217 *R(I) 38/53*.
218 *CSI 63/49*.
219 *R(I) 55/53*.
220 *R(I) 2/67*.
221 *R(I) 2/67*, para 10.
222 *Nancollas v Insurance Officer* [1985] 1 All ER 833; *R(I) 4/70*.

arrive at their first call, unless the employer specifies a particular route or mode of transport.[223] To decide into which of the two categories a particular case falls involves consideration of the circumstances of the particular job.

(3) If the journey comes within neither category described above, it is difficult to regard it as creating an 'employment risk'. In terms of the 'public zone' principle, the commuting employee is in a position no different from other members of the public, and, as regards the 'supervision' principle, the employer generally exercises no control over the journey. Yet special provision to cover commuting accidents has been made in most other EU jurisdictions,[224] notwithstanding the blurring of the concept of employment risk which is involved, and the practical problems of definition and administration to which it may give rise.[225] The Pearson Commission found the arguments to be very finely balanced but by a bare majority of one recommended that accidents to and from work should be covered.[226] The government, on the other hand, considered the objections, both of principle and of practice, to be significantly greater and therefore rejected the proposal.[227]

The current legislation in Great Britain offers only very limited coverage for commuting accidents, such as would be justifiable on the 'supervision' principle. Section 99(1) of SSCBA 1992 provides that:

An accident happening while an employed earner is, with the express or implied permission of his employer, travelling as a passenger by any vehicle to or from his place of work shall, notwithstanding that he is under no obligation to his employer to travel by that vehicle, be deemed to arise out of and in the course of his employment if—
(a) the accident would have been deemed so to have arisen had he been under such an obligation; and
(b) at the time of the accident, the vehicle—
    (i)   is being operated by or on behalf of his employer or some other person by whom it is provided in pursuance of arrangements made with his employer; and
    (ii) is not being operated in the ordinary course of a public transport service.

The requirement in the opening paragraph that travel in the vehicle be permitted by the employer might seem to be otiose when regard is had to the condition in (b) that the vehicle be operated by the employer (or through some third-party arrangement). But the Commissioner has held that they are independent conditions, both of which must be satisfied.[228] The first envisages permission given prior to the event, though exceptionally subsequent permission may be acceptable provided that it is express.[229] As regards the second condition, the employer need not initiate the arrangement, and need not own or provide the vehicle,[230] but there must be something more than a mere undertaking by a third party to provide a vehicle for the use of the employees. The employer must be involved in some way in the running of the service:[231] an unauthorised

223   *R(I) 19/57; R(I) 2/67; R(I) 12/75.*
224   Only Denmark and Italy do not cover commuting accidents: *MISSOC 2001* n 85, above, Table VIII *Risks Covered* 2. See also International Labour Organisation's Recommendation 121 (1964).
225   Cf *DHSS* n 35, above, paras 6.38–6.43. For the difficulties arising in France, see *Dupeyroux* n 141, above, pp 642–653.
226   *Pearson Report* n 32, above, paras 858–867.
227   *Reform of the Industrial Injuries Scheme* n 37, above, paras 66–67.
228   *R(I) 5/80*, R S Lazarus, Comr.
229   *R(I) 5/80*, para 7.
230   *R(I) 49/53.*
231   *R(I) 5/60.*

conveyance of the employee, even for the employer's purposes, will not suffice.[232] The 'public zone' principle features in the exclusion of vehicles 'operating in the ordinary course of a public transport service'. But the words do not imply that the vehicle must be provided by a private company. The question is whether members of the public may and do habitually use the service.[233] A claimant cannot be a 'passenger' if also driving the vehicle.[234] A 'vehicle' includes 'a ship, vessel, hovercraft, aircraft'[235] and, perhaps surprisingly, need not be designed to carry a passenger (eg a tractor).[236] The accident must happen while the claimant is 'travelling as a passenger', so that walking to meet the vehicle, or between two vehicles, is not included.[237]

E   INTERRUPTIONS AND DEVIATIONS

The 'course of employment' includes not only the objective elements of time and space but also the subjective one of the claimant's activity.[238] The traditional criterion is that of performing a duty for the employer,[239] but the tendency has been to mitigate the rigours of this notion and to concentrate instead on what is 'reasonably incidental to' the employment: 'if the man is doing something for his own purposes which is reasonably incidental to his employment, he is still acting in the course of his employment.'[240] Only *material* interruptions of the working pattern destroy the connection with the employment:[241] trifling or inadvertent departures are disregarded.[242] Of course, what is reasonably incidental to a person's employment is a question very much for individual judgment, but the case law has established a pattern of activities and events which are normally to be regarded as coming within or outside the course of employment.

(i)   Deviation from journey

Most obviously, an employee who deviates from a journey for purposes unconnected with work, eg to visit a public house, will not succeed.[243] But stopping to take a meal en route is covered.[244] The position of an employee whose duties are peripatetic will, of course, be more flexible, as, ex hypothesi, there are no fixed hours or places of work. Thus a salesman returning home after entertaining a business associate succeeded.[245] But a point may be reached in the employee's travels where he or she steps beyond the boundaries of the employment. Generally, the employee will have discretion where an overnight stay is made so the course of employment will be broken from the point at

---

232   *R(I) 5/80.*
233   *R(I) 67/51*: a claim does not fail merely because the public is entitled to use the service (though ordinarily this will be the case) if there is evidence that it rarely does so. On this point, the authorities have regard to such factors as whether the service is advertised in the ordinary timetable, whether it connects directly with the employer's premises, whether it ceases during closure of the factory: *R(I) 15/57.*
234   *CI 49/49; R(I) 9/59.*
235   SSCBA 1992, s 99(2).
236   *R(I) 42/56.*
237   *R(I) 67/52; R(I) 48/54.*
238   See esp Lord Finley LC in *Davidson & Co v M'Robb* [1918] AC 304 at 314–315.
239   See eg *St Helens Colliery Co Ltd v Hewitson* [1924] AC 59.
240   Per Salmon LJ in *R v Industrial Injuries Comr, ex p Amalgamated Engineering Union (No 2)* [1966] 2 QB 31 at 51. See also *R(I) 1/77* (putting up Christmas decorations).
241   *R(I) 4/73*, para 5, per H A Shewan, Comr.
242   Per Salmon LJ in *R v Industrial Injuries Comr, ex p Amalgamated Engineering Union (No 2)* [1966] 2 QB 31; per O'Connor J in *R v National Insurance Comr, ex p East* [1976] ICR 206 at 208.
243   *R(I) 40/55.*
244   *CI 148/49.*
245   *R(I) 38/53.*

which the journey ends.[246] An apparent deviation may, however, be covered where the employee had no reasonable alternative.[247]

(ii)   Breaks between spells of duty
There are many cases involving accidents to employees in breaks between spells of duty, and it is impossible to reconcile all of them. Certainly, as one Commissioner remarked,[248] some fine distinctions are necessary (though undesirable) if decisions are to be based on logical principles. But the 'logical principle' involved is a vague one of the supervision and control of the employer, which does not make the prediction of decisions easy. Lunch and tea breaks, if spent on the employer's premises, are usually protected,[249] but not for employees off the premises and free to do what they like,[250] nor, of course, where the time allocated is exceeded.[251] Quite apart from formal breaks, many occupations involve lulls in the working effort. A distinction is drawn between voluntary idleness which will interrupt the course of employment[252] and a lull imposed by the pattern of work. If, in the latter case, an employee, to fill in time, does something not unreasonable, not prohibited by the employer and which does not interrupt someone else's work, the claim will succeed.[253] But this will not be so if the employee departs completely from the sphere of operations and is then is no longer under the supervision of the employer.[254]

(iii)   Non-working activities
Even though a claimant may have been at the place of work during normal working hours, what was being done at the time of the accident may have been so far removed from the employee's duties that he or she is regarded as having been outside the course of employment. The widow of an employee killed by gas poisoning while taking a nap during night duty could not recover.[255] The interruption of work to achieve something entirely for personal purposes is similarly treated: a level-crossing keeper fetching milk from the garden;[256] a factory worker leaving work without permission to accompany a fellow employee to the work stores.[257] As regards physical activities not incidental to work, later cases suggest a significant change of attitude marked, in particular, by the decision of the Court of Appeal in *R v Industrial Injuries Comr, ex p Amalgamated Engineering Union (No 2).*[258] Lord Denning MR said:

---

246   *R(I) 22/51; R(I) 22/54;* cf where the employee is bound, in practice if not by the terms of his employment, to stay at a particular place: *CI 374/50; R(I) 30/57.*
247   In *R(I) 40/56* the widow of an employee succeeded when her husband, a passenger in his employer's van, had departed from the prescribed route to enable a fellow employee to visit a doctor: it would have been unreasonable to expect the deceased to have left the van during the deviation.
248   *R(I) 11/55,* para 5.
249   *R(I) 11/53,* but not at the beginning or end of a day's work (*CI 120/49; R(I) 11/54*) unless the meal or refreshment is regarded as part of the employee's remuneration (*R(I) 15/55*).
250   *R(I) 84/52; R(I) 24/53; R(I) 4/79; R(I) 10/81.* See also *R(I) 6/76* where the employee was forced to vacate the premises as the result of a bomb scare. If, however, the claimant continues to perform an employment duty during the break he is covered: *R(I) 20/61; R v National Insurance Comr, ex p Reed* (1980), reported as Appendix to *R(I) 7/80.*
251   *R(I) 44/57; R v Industrial Injuries Comr, ex p Amalgamated Engineering Union (No 2)* [1966] 2 QB 31.
252   *R v Industrial Injuries Comr, ex p Amalgamated Engineering Union (No 2)* [1966] 2 QB 31.
253   *R(I) 46/53; R(I) 13/66; R(I) 13/68.*
254   *R(I) 1/58.*
255   *R(I) 68/54;* cf where sleeping is involuntary: *R(I) 36/59.*
256   *R(I) 9/59.*
257   *R(I) 1/58.*
258   [1966] 2 QB 31.

> In the ordinary way, if a man while at his place of work, during his hours of work, is injured by a risk incidental to his employment, then the right conclusion usually is that it is an injury which arises out of and in the course of the employment, even though he may not be doing his actual work but chatting to a friend or smoking or doing something of that kind.[259]

The course of employment is not broken merely because, at the time, the employee was doing something for his or her own purposes. The question is, first, whether the interruption was a natural one and, secondly, whether it was a reasonable use of the employee's time.[260]

iv Out of the employment

A GENERAL CAUSAL TEST

The second element in the statutory test requires that the accident arises '*out* of [the] ... employment'.[261] It is not sufficient that the accident happens within the temporal and spatial limits of the employment: it must be causally linked to it.[262] For example, a claimant may suffer from a heart attack while at work, but benefit is not payable unless, in some way, the condition resulted from the work.[263] The courts and tribunals have been wary of precise formulations on this point.[264] Some have generalised in terms of employment being the 'proximate' cause of the accident;[265] others have stipulated that it be the *causa causans,* rather than the *causa sine qua non,* of the accident.[266] In 1963, a Tribunal of Commissioners argued that the crucial question is whether the claimant's own act (or by implication an 'external cause') creates a risk which is different from that created by the employment.[267] Once the sine qua non test is satisfied, ie it is established that the accident would not have happened but for the employment, then it will generally be held to have arisen out of that employment, unless the claimant (or another) added or created 'a different risk ... and this different risk was the real cause of the accident'.[268] But like all similar tests of causation, it is of limited utility. The authorities will always have to form their own decision on the facts of a given case,[269]

259 *R v Industrial Injuries Comr, ex p Amalgamated Engineering Union (No 2)* [1966] 2 QB 31 at 49.
260 Eg in *R(I) 4/73* the claimant, a factory worker, was acting as agent for a football pools firm. While being handed a coupon by a fellow employee he was injured. It was held that though strictly speaking he was not, at the time, doing something he was employed to do, nevertheless it did not involve a material interruption of his employment
261 SSCBA 1992, s 94(1).
262 *Dover Navigation Co Ltd v Craig* [1940] AC 190, [1939] 4 All ER 558; *R(I) 16/61; R(I) 2/63.*
263 Eg by lifting a heavy weight. But, as has been observed, 'Inclusion of such cases in the scheme seems to be the result of sympathy more than logic. The anomaly in such a case is that the incident may have acted merely as a trigger; the worker may have been prone to a heart attack at any moment from any cause': *Cane* n 54, above, p 284.
264 See eg *Dover Navigation Co Ltd v Craig* [1940] AC 190, [1939] 4 All ER 558, per Viscount Maugham at 193 and Lord Wright at 199; *R(I) 2/63* para 20.
265 Eg *R(I) 8/54; R(I) 75/54; R(I) 27/60.*
266 Eg *R(I) 13/65; R(I) 26/59.* See Lee (1995) 2 JSSL 9.
267 *R(I) 2/63.* This view was based on some prominent House of Lords' decisions under the Workmen's Compensation Acts, notably *Thom v Sinclair* [1917] AC 127; *Upton v Great Central Rly Co* [1924] AC 302; *Harris v Associated Portland Cement Manufacturers Ltd* [1939] AC 71; and *Cadzow Coal Co Ltd v Price* [1944] 1 All ER 54.
268 *R(I) 2/63,* para 26.
269 *R(I) 2/63,* para 16.

guided only by the general orientation of the test, which in this instance implies that the requirement of a causal link should be liberally construed.

B STATUTORY PRESUMPTION

Under the Workmen's Compensation Acts, the onus of proving that the accident arose both out of and in the course of employment lay on the claimant. In 1946, it was felt that some of the difficulties of establishing the causal link might be mitigated if the burden was on the authorities to prove that the accident did not arise out of the employment. The statutory presumption in its present form provides that:

> an accident arising in the course of an employed earner's employment shall be taken, in the absence of evidence to the contrary, also to have arisen out of that employment.[270]

Its introduction was greeted by some as a revolutionary measure which would lead to a great improvement in the claimant's position.[271] They were to be disappointed. No major change resulted and it is not difficult to see why. For the presumption to apply, not only must the claimant prove that the accident occurred in the course of the employment,[272] but also there must be no 'evidence to the contrary'. In fact, in almost every disputed case, there is some evidence to the contrary. The approach taken by the Commissioners is that the presumption applies only if there is nothing in the known circumstances from which it might reasonably be inferred that the accident did not arise out of the employment.[273] Thus an epileptic found injured at the foot of a staircase could not invoke the principle: the fact of his epilepsy was 'evidence to the contrary'.[274] The first sign of a more generous interpretation of the provision came in 1964.[275]

> C, a post office engineer, was repairing a fault in a phone box when a young man opened the door apparently to make a call. C remembered nothing more until he arrived home bleeding from a head wound. The Commissioner discounted the possibly that C might have provoked an assault as being too 'speculative' and thus not constituting contrary evidence. The presumption therefore applied and C was awarded benefit.

C PRE-EXISTING CONDITIONS

A major problem that arises in applying the general causation principles concerns the effect of pre-existing conditions. An employee may have a latent physical disability (eg a heart condition) unconnected with work. Should the disability manifest itself during the course of the employment, the authorities must decide whether the accident arose 'out of' that employment. The problem is resolved on principles analogous to

---

270   SSCBA 1992, s 94(3).
271   See Mr R Prentice, Standing Committee B Debates on the Family Allowances and National Insurance Bill 1961, cols 51–52.
272   *CI 47/49.*
273   *CI 3/49*, approved in *R v National Insurance (Industrial Injuries) Comr, ex p Richardson* [1958] 2 All ER 689, [1958] 1 WLR 851. See also *R(I) 41/55* and *R(I) 30/60.*
274   *CI 68/49.*
275   *R(I) 1/64.*

those already described concerning the causal link between the 'accident' and the 'injury'.[276] If the employment provides merely the background or setting for the event, the claimant will not succeed.[277] The work must contribute in a material degree to the risk.[278] Once that is established, the fact that the prior condition rendered the person more liable to sustain an accident will be irrelevant. So in *R(I) 11/80*:

> C, who suffered from postural hypotension, fell during his course of work at a factory, and was rendered unconscious when his head struck the floor. The Commissioner, J G Monroe, held that he could succeed on the alternative grounds: (i) that he fainted as a result of changing his posture, which he did for the purpose of his employment; or (ii) that, in any event, the fact that he came into physical contact with the employer's premises was sufficient to associate the accident with the employment.[279]

D   COMMON RISKS

The causation test implicit in the requirement that the accident arises out of the employment carries with it the assumption that the employment creates a risk for the claimant which is greater than, or at least different from, that to which he or she would have been subject as a member of the public. Should the assumption not be justified, the employment may not be the substantial cause of the accident. In principle, then, employees who are struck by lightning,[280] or bitten by an animal,[281] while working should not succeed. The employment has not exposed them to a risk greater than that to which an ordinary member of the public is subject. On the other hand, if the 'accident has occurred to the workman by reason of the employment bringing about his presence at the particular spot and so exposing him to a danger ...', he will be entitled.[282] So a seaman suffering from heat exhaustion while working aboard a vessel in the Arabian sea was clearly covered, and it was irrelevant that other persons living in tropical climates are exposed to the same risk.[283] Here the employment took the claimant to a locality to which he would otherwise not have gone. While the theoretical distinction between these cases may be clearly recognised, there is a large shady area between them which cannot easily be divided according to any precise criterion. As a consequence, the authorities tended to approach the problem casuistically, declining to justify their decisions in terms of principle. The resulting unpredictability may be gauged from comparing two, unhappily typical, cases:

> A foreign body struck the eye of a lorry driver while on the road. He was not entitled: 'I do not think that a person driving a lorry is thereby exposed to any greater risk of getting something in his eye than anyone else.'[284]

276   P 725, above.
277   *R(I) 12/52.*
278   *R(I) 73/51.*
279   Applying a dictum of Lord Atkin in *Brooker v Thomas Borthwick & Sons (Australasia) Ltd* [1933] AC 669 at 677. See also *CI 82/49* and *R(I) 6/82.*
280   *R(I) 7/60.*
281   *CI 101/50; R(I) 89/52.*
282   Per Russell LJ in *Lawrence v George Matthews (1924) Ltd* [1929] 1 KB 1 at 20.
283   *R(I) 4/61,* following *Dover Navigation Co Ltd v Craig* [1940] AC 190, [1939] 4 All ER 558.
284   *R(I) 62/53,* para 3.

A piece of grit entered the eye of a police motorcyclist when on patrol duty. He succeeded: 'a man who is employed to drive a motor-bicycle about the streets of a city is exposed by his employment to a greater risk of getting something in his eye than a person not so employed.'[285]

The confusion created by such decisions led to dissatisfaction with the statutory formula. The reaction of some Commissioners was to aid the injured person by broadening the category of 'locality risks'. They were prepared to hold, more often than was perhaps justifiable, that the employment had taken the claimant to the particular spot where the hazard was encountered. It was so decided in the case of a bus driver stung by a wasp[286] and that of an agricultural worker struck by lightning.[287] Another device was to find an intermediate agent which intervened between the original hazard and the injury and so to regard it, rather than the original hazard, as the 'proximate cause' of the injury. Thus when an employee, riding a bicycle on her employer's business, was blown off by a freak gust of wind, the Commissioner felt able to decide in her favour on the somewhat artificial ground that 'the proximate cause was that she fell from her bicycle while travelling on duty, and it does not seem to me to be necessary to consider any remoter cause'.[288]

Such generous approaches were by no means universal. In 1958 the Divisional Court held that a bus conductor, attacked while on duty by a gang of youths, could not succeed because his position was no different from that of any other person on the bus.[289] The decision created consternation among the trade unions, and there was immediate pressure for legislative reform.[290] It was forthcoming in 1961, the method chosen being to extend the coverage of the scheme to certain specified risks.[291] The provision, as re-enacted in 1992, is that:

an accident ... shall be treated ... as arising out of an employed earner's employment if–
(a) the accident arises in the course of the employment; and
(b) the accident either is caused (i) by another person's misconduct, skylarking or negligence, or (ii) by steps taken in consequence of any such misconduct, skylarking or negligence, or (iii) by the behaviour or presence of an animal (including a bird, fish or insect), or is caused by or consists in the employed earner being struck by any object or by lightning; and
(c) the employed earner did not directly or indirectly induce or contribute to the happening of the accident by his conduct outside the employment or by any act not incidental to the employment.[292]

The risks selected for special protection manifestly reflect particular situations in which claimants had previously encountered difficulty in recovering benefit, and there is no obvious common principle to which they all relate.[293] The cumulative effect of this

---

285 *R(I) 67/53*, para 5. See also *R(I) 71/53*.
286 *R(I) 5/56*.
287 *R(I) 23/58*.
288 *R(I) 27/60*, following a similar idea in *R(I) 46/54*.
289 *R v National Insurance (Industrial Injuries) Comr, ex p Richardson* [1958] 2 All ER 689, [1958] 1 WLR 851.
290 See General Council Report of the TUC (1960).
291 Family Allowances and National Insurance Act 1961, s 2 (FANIA 1961).
292 SSCBA 1992, s 101.
293 See the Standing Committee B Debates on the 1961 Bill.

provision, and the Commissioners' decisions previously referred to, reduces the significance of the 'out' requirement, provoking one commentator to the conclusion that:

> we appear to have got very close to a point where an accident arising in the course of employment will almost inevitably fall within the system.[294]

But, so far at least, successive governments have refused to abandon the 'out of' requirement. To do so, it is argued, would make nonsense of the existence of the special scheme for work-caused accidents.[295] The argument is obviously sound, but it seems hard to reconcile with the policy behind the 1961 reform.

E CLAIMANT'S CONDUCT

The third condition of the 1961 provision quoted above, that the claimant should not contribute to the accident by conduct outside the employment, restates a principle existing in the case law prior to the enactment and falls now for consideration. It is clear, in the first place, that the mere negligence or carelessness of the claimant is not by itself sufficient to bar entitlement to benefit:[296] the legislation has not incorporated the common law doctrine of contributory negligence. Rather the conduct of an employee will defeat a claim only if (1) he or she 'added or created a different risk' to or from that arising from the employment and (2) 'this different risk was the real cause of the accident'.[297] In the case in which this test was propounded,

> C, attempting to light a cigarette, as permitted by his employer, ignited gas which was escaping from an unlit blow-pipe. He was awarded benefit. C's act converted a potential risk into an actual explosion. 'It did not make it a different danger or create a fresh one.'[298]

In contrast, in another case:

> In an effort to warm himself, C poured petrol onto a fire and was burned by the conflagration. Fires were prohibited on the site, but in terms of causation C's act had added or created a different risk from that inherent in the circumstances of the employment.[299]

It is convenient here to consider the relevance of the fact that the claimant's conduct was prohibited by the employer or by the law generally. In the early years of the Workmen's Compensation Act, employers were frequently able to rely on the existence of such a prohibition as a defence.[300] The position was altered in 1923, when the legislature provided that an act would be:

> deemed to have arisen out of and in the course of employment, notwithstanding that the workman was ... acting in contravention of any statutory or other regulation ... or of any

294 *Cane* n 54, above, p 283.
295 Mr J Boyd Carpenter, Minister of Pensions and National Insurance, in the Standing Committee B Debates on the 1961 Bill, cols 59–60.
296 *Harris v Associated Portland Cement Manufacturers Ltd* [1939] AC 71; *R(I) 36/59.*
297 *R(I) 2/63*; *R(I) 3/63.*
298 *R(I) 2/63*, para 29.
299 *R(I) 24/51.*
300 See eg *Lowe v Pearson* [1899] 1 QB 261.

orders given by or on behalf of his employer, or that he was acting without instructions from his employer, if such act was done by the workman for the purposes of and in connection with his employer's trade or business.[301]

It was optimistically argued by some that this effectively overruled the 'out' requirement. Such an interpretation, though perhaps feasible on a literal view of the phrase 'acting without instructions', was obviously unintended: it would place disobedient employees in a better position than obedient ones. The argument was quickly denounced by the House of Lords.[302] 'Acting without instructions' was equated with an implied prohibition. More importantly, the provision left open the possibility that the employee was, in any event, acting outside the scope of the employment. If so, the claim failed. The effect of the 1923 reform was merely to prevent a certain class of evidence being sufficient of itself to oust the right to compensation.[303] It did not operate to extend the scope of the employment. The point was confirmed by legislative amendment when the provision was incorporated into the national insurance scheme. A new condition was added. For the fiction to apply, the claimant must now show that:

(a) the accident would have been deemed so to have arisen had the act not been done in contravention of any such regulations or orders, or without such instructions as the case may be; and

(b) the act is done for the purposes of and in connection with the employer's trade or business.[304]

On condition (a), the claimant must show that apart from the contravention the accident arose out of and in the course of employment. Thus, the claimant cannot benefit from the provision of doing something quite different from that which he or she was employed to do.[305] For example, in *R v D'Albuqerque, ex p Bresnahan*:[306]

D, a dock labourer engaged in loading a ship, attempted to move an obstacle with a fork-lift truck which had been left unattended by its driver. He fell into the dock with it and was drowned. His widow's claim failed. It was not within the scope of his employment to use a fork-lift truck and therefore condition (a) was not satisfied.

Whether the act is 'done for the purposes of and in connection with the employer's trade or business' has been given a generous interpretation in later cases. Thus it was held to be in the interests of both the employer and the employee (though prohibited by the former) that a locomotive driver should take a short cut on his way from the railway shed to a station.[307]

F   EMERGENCIES

It is an obvious principle that the causal link with the employment is not broken if the accident occurs through the employee responding to an emergency. To this end, section 100 of SSCBA 1992 provides that:

---

301 WCA 1923, s 7.
302 *Kerr v James Dunlop & Co* [1926] AC 377.
303 Per Viscount Dunedin in *Kerr v James Dunlop & Co* [1926] AC 377 at 386.
304 SSCBA 1992, s 98.
305 *CI 11/49*; *R(I) 77/54*; *R(I) 6/55*; *R(I) 41/56*; *R(I) 12/61*.
306 [1966] 1 Lloyds Rep 69.
307 *R(I) 5/67*.

An accident happening to an employed earner in or about any premises at which he is for the time being employed for the purposes of his employer's trade or business shall be deemed to arise out of and in the course of his employment if it happens while he is taking steps, on an actual or supposed emergency at those premises, to rescue, succour or protect persons who are, or are thought to be or possibly to be, injured or imperilled, or to avert or minimise serious damage to property.

The provision does not cover all possible emergencies; in particular, the emergency must have occurred 'in or about' premises where the employee is working.[308] But it is complemented by a case law doctrine which holds that the act of meeting an emergency arises out of the employment if it can be construed as being in some way in the interests of the employer and was reasonable in the circumstances.[309]

v Special cases

Finally, mention should be made of rules which deem that accidents occurring to special categories of employee arise out of and in the course of employment.
(a) Airmen and mariners are covered if the accident occurs when returning from work abroad at the employer's expense.[310]
(b) An airman travelling to his work in an aircraft is deemed to have the permission of his employer, for the purpose of section 99(1) of SSCBA 1992,[311] and to like effect a mariner travelling to his work in a vessel need not show that this was under an arrangement with his employee.[312]
(c) A mariner employed on a vessel as a pilot is covered for accidents while on board, while embarking or disembarking, or while returning (without undue delay) to a port other than that from which he normally plies his trade.[313]

Part 4   Industrial diseases

A   General

Soon after the passing of the first Workmen's Compensation Act (WCA 1897), it became clear that the 'personal injury by accident' formula was inadequate to cope with sickness or disease resulting from employment. It has already been seen that in principle an incapacity resulting from a 'process' as opposed to an 'event' is not caught by the general provisions. Granted that protection should be afforded in these cases, there would appear to be two basic possibilities:[314] (1) to provide a general definition of occupational disease as an alternative to the 'accident' formula, the claimant having to satisfy the authorities (with or without the aid of a presumption) that the disease was

---

308   On which see *R(I) 6/63*.
309   *CI 280/49; R(I) 63/54; R(I) 46/60*.
310   SI 1975/469, reg 3(a); SI 1975/470, reg 3(a).
311   SI 1975/469, reg 3(c).
312   SI 1975/470, reg 3(b).
313   SI 1975/470, reg 4.
314   Cf Riesenfeld (1964) 52 Calif LR 531 at 542–543.

contracted as a result of the employment; (2) to create a list of specified diseases which experience and medical expertise have shown to be typical risks for certain specified categories of employment. Generally with the aid of a presumption, the claimant would then have to show that he or she contracted a prescribed disease as a result of working in the prescribed occupation. Persuasive arguments can be made out for either policy. Approach (1) has the great advantage that its scope is wider (those suffering from non-prescribed diseases in (2) are without remedy) and it is more flexible: legislatures, it is claimed, cannot keep pace with new and changing industrial risks. The advantages claimed for (2) tend to be more incidental to the policy of providing compensation for those suffering from industrial diseases. Thus it is said that the requirement of prescription encourages more detailed and intensive study of the problems, which in turn contributes to safety and rehabilitation systems. The more general coverage in (1) creates difficulties of proof (particularly of causation) and thereby greater uncertainty and, it is claimed, is thereby more costly and more conducive to false claims and abuse.

Most countries, including Great Britain have adopted the more restrictive approach in (2).[315] But recommendations have been made both by the EU[316] and the International Labour Organisation[317] for a so-called 'mixed system' which effectively combines the two approaches: claimants benefit from a presumption that they incurred a scheduled disease from employment in a relevant occupation; but if they are suffering from a non-scheduled disease, the onus is on them to establish the causal link with the employment. Such a system operates in several other EEA member states[318] and was urged on the British government by the Pearson Commission.[319] The matter was fully considered by the IIAC in a report published in 1981.[320] While acknowledging the merits of the individual proof method, and recommending that in general it should be available, it considered nevertheless that some diseases, such as lung cancer, strokes, coronary diseases and mental diseases, should be excluded because, though often thought to be connected with certain types of employment, they would give rise to considerable difficulty. Medical opinion would differ as to their aetiology, thus leading to a lack of uniformity in decisions on entitlement, and claimants might have inappropriately high expectations of success.[321] Even this limited proposal proved to be unacceptable to the Conservative government in 1984,[322] with the result that the British system remains wedded to protection only against those diseases which are prescribed. However, since the government's rejection of its proposal for a general system of individual proof, the IIAC has adopted a strategy of considering whether individual proof might be used on a case by case basis, as it examines each new disease or potential extension to the prescribed list. As a result it has recommended eg that occupational asthma be prescribed for a list of workplace agents including 'any other sensitising agent inhaled at work', and similarly, that carpal tunnel syndrome – compression of a nerve in the wrist – be prescribed on an individual basis where relevant workplace experience can be shown.[323] To date only the former of these recommendations has been accepted by government and the relevant legislation enacted.[324]

315   See generally IIAC *Report on Industrial Diseases* (1981, Cmnd 8393) paras 6–32.
316   Recommendation EC/90/326 considered by the IIAC in its paper in 1992, and by *Wikeley* n 45, above, p 194. See further COM(96) 454 final of September 20, 1996.
317   Recommendation No 121 (1964).
318   *MISSOC 2001* n 85, above, Table VIII *Risks Covered* 3.
319   *Pearson Report* n 32, above, paras 880–887.
320   *IIAC* n 315, above; and see Wilson (1982) 11 ILJ 141; Lewis [1983] JSWL 10; and *Wikeley* n 45, above.
321   *IIAC* n 315, above, paras 144–149.
322   52 HC Official Report (6th series) written answer col 327.
323   See the respective reports in 1990 (Cm 1244) and 1992 (Cm 1936).
324   See SI 1985/967, as amended by SI 1991/1938 and SI 1993/862. See Larkin (2000) 29 ILJ 88 on carpal tunnel syndrome.

The system of prescribed diseases was introduced by WCA 1906.[325] A Departmental Committee set up shortly after the passing of the Act felt that a new disease should be included only if it were so specific to the prescribed employment that in individual cases the causal link with the employment could be established without difficulty, or, in other words, that the claimant would be unlikely to contract it away from work.[326] Thus bronchitis was not added since 'it would attract endless litigation, as no one knows whether the sufferer has contracted it from dust irritation, or would have contracted it anyway, as hundreds of other people in the locality do'.[327] Notwithstanding severe criticism of the approach by trade unions, on the ground that it was too restrictive,[328] the principle of inclusion is still law. A disease will only be prescribed if:

(a) [the disease] ought to be treated, having regard to its causes and incidence and any other relevant considerations, as a risk of their occupations and not as a risk common to all persons; and

(b) it is such that, in the absence of special circumstances, the attribution of particular cases to the nature of the employment can be established or presumed with reasonable certainty.[329]

Although the principle has remained unaltered, it is clear that its application, now primarily the responsibility of the IIAC,[330] has in practice shifted significantly.[331] In the early days, the emphasis was on showing that the disease was peculiar to the specified employment, and not to others. Later, the crux became whether the employment created a vulnerability to the disease greater than that of the general public, even though other employments were equally susceptible. While proviso (b) remains a serious obstacle to the admission of some diseases, there is apparently a tendency to attach less importance to it. So in 1974 occupational deafness was added, notwithstanding the finding of the IIAC that loss of hearing is a common affliction and has 'a number of different causes'.[332] However, the proviso is still interpreted as meaning 'on the balance of probabilities'.[333] This meant eg that in its 1986 report on occupational lung cancer IIAC was unable to recommend prescription for gas retort workers because, although there was evidence of an increased risk of the disease, the relative risk was insufficiently high.[334] As the House of Lords has recently observed, in noting that post-traumatic stress disorder is not a prescribed disease, IIAC's approach 'is, no doubt for good reasons, a cautious one'.[335]

Naturally the current approach still gives rise to considerable dissatisfaction. The IIAC has made some organisational changes to meet complaints that the prescription

---

325 S 8, following proposals of a Departmental Committee (1904, Cd 2208).

326 *Report of the Departmental Committee on Compensation for Industrial Diseases* (Samuel Committee) (1907, Cd 3495).

327 *Samuel Committee* n 326, above, para 25. Chronic bronchitis was finally prescribed for certain categories of coal miners in 1993.

328 Considered in the *Report of the Departmental Committee on Compensation for Industrial Diseases* (Holman Gregory Committee) (1920, Cmd 816); and the *Report of the Departmental Committee on Compensation for Industrial Diseases* (1932). See *Wikeley* n 45 above, ch 5.

329 SSCBA 1992, s 108(2).

330 *Lewis* n 30, above, pp 95–97; and pp 139–140, above.

331 Young *Industrial Injuries Insurance* (1964) p 29.

332 IIAC Report on Occupational Deafness (1973, Cmnd 5461) para 45. But this prescription is subject to a number of restrictive conditions: see n 359, below.

333 IIAC *Periodic Report 1993* (1993) p 23.

334 Cm 37.

335 *Chief Adjudication Officer v Faulds* [2000] 2 All ER 961 at 969, per Lord Hope.

process was too slow.[336] There remains doubt as to whether these arrangements can cope adequately with the growth of occupational hazards resulting from the introduction of new toxic hazards in the workplace. Certainly, the existing approach cannot meet the more fundamental criticism that the system offers no (or at best very limited) compensation for diseases which occur generally in the community and yet in particular cases may be employment-related. The restrictive manner in which lung cancer is prescribed for workers exposed to asbestos dust is a case in point.[337] So long as the general proposal that compensation be available on the basis of individual proof remains unimplemented, unequal treatment between the victims of occupational disease will, therefore, persist. On the other hand, there are inherent limits to the ability to connect some hazards to working conditions:

> the only conclusion that can be drawn is that no-one knows how much industrial disease exists and whether it is increasing or decreasing.[338]

B   Proof of prescribed disease

Proof that the claimant is suffering from a prescribed disease or injury 'due to the nature of (the) employment' is an alternative basis of entitlement to that provided by 'a personal injury caused by accident arising out of and in the course of employment'.[339] Inconvenient overlaps between the two criteria are prevented by the provision that:

> a person shall not be entitled to benefit in respect of a disease as being an injury by accident arising out of and in the course of any employment if at the time of the accident the disease is in relation to him a prescribed disease by virtue of ... that employment.[340]

Prescribed diseases accounted for only 21 per cent of all the 281,000 pensions in payment in 2000.[341] This reflects the historic preference in favour of traumatically caused disability.[342] The picture, however, in terms of new claims is very different: since the mid-1990s more claims have been submitted each year on the basis of prescribed diseases than accidents (but their success rate is lower). In 1989 pneumoconiosis accounted for 18,000 payments, occupational deafness for 12,000, and the remainder of the prescribed diseases for only 7,000. This changed with the prescription in 1993 of chronic bronchitis and emphysema in coal miners;[343] by 2000 pneumoconiosis accounted for 11,000 payments, occupational deafness for 14,000, and the remainder of the prescribed diseases

---

336   *Lewis* n 30, above, p 132; and see the IIAC's account of its work in its *Periodic Report 1990*. In January 1997 IIAC announced a review of the Schedule of Prescribed Diseases. At the time of writing, this was still ongoing.
337   *Wikeley* n 45, above, ch 7, (1997) 26 ILJ 283 and (2002) 70 Medico-Legal J 17.
338   *Brown* n 28, above, p 145. See also *Wikeley* n 45, above, p 3; and Stapleton *Disease and the Compensation Debate* (1986). The latter refers (p 54) to the 'essential dilemma ... that the more generous the scheduling guidelines and the more available is the device of individual proof, the more non-occupational claims will be admitted to the scheme, calling into doubt its preferential basis itself'.
339   SSCBA 1992, s 94(1).
340   SSCBA 1992, s 108(6).
341   DWP *Work and Pension Statistics 2001* (2001) p 176, Table 1.
342   Ie the emphasis on compensation for accidents: see p 743, above.
343   SI 1993/1985; see Wikeley (1994) 23 ILJ 85 and (1994) JSSL 23. The rules were relaxed somewhat in 1997: see SI 1997/810; and Wikeley (1997) 26 ILJ 283.

for 36,000.[344] Some 45 per cent of all new awards of disablement benefit based on a prescribed disease are now ascribed to vibration white finger, which has been the subject of vigorous take-up campaigns (eg in the shipbuilding industry).[345]

To establish entitlement on the basis of a prescribed disease, the claimant must satisfy three conditions:

(a) he or she suffers from a prescribed disease;
(b) that disease is prescribed in relation to the occupation; and
(c) the disease developed as a result of employment in that occupation.

i Suffering from a prescribed disease

A Schedule to the Social Security (Industrial Injuries) (Prescribed Diseases) Regulations 1985 lists descriptions of conditions covered by the scheme.[346] The claimant must prove that he or she is suffering from or has suffered from[347] one such condition which resulted in loss of faculty on which title to benefit is based. Obviously the claim is more likely to succeed if it is supported by a consultant who specialises in the relevant disease, although not all are necessarily familiar with the specific prescription rules.[348] For example, vibration white finger is prescribed according to the number of fingers on a person's hand which are affected.[349] A decision is then made by the Secretary of State in the light of such evidence as is provided, who may also refer the question for report to a departmental medical practitioner.[350] In practice, the Secretary of State refers claims in respect of prescribed chest diseases to specialist in-house doctors because of the expertise required.[351] There is then a right of appeal to an appeal tribunal.[352]

Prescription is not retrospective in its effect. Thus a coal miner, who had suffered from chronic bronchitis or emphysema since 1970, was only entitled to disablement benefit from the date of prescription in September 1993.[353]

ii Disease prescribed for claimant's occupation

Against the description of each disease, there is listed in the Schedule to the Social Security (Industrial Injuries) (Prescribed Diseases) Regulations 1985[354] the occupation or occupations for which the disease is prescribed. The claimant's task is to prove that

344 *DWP* n 341, above.
345 *DWP* n 341, above, p 178, Table 4.
346 SI 1985/967, Sch 1, Pt I. The conditions are classified according to whether the cause is a physical, biological, chemical or other agent.
347 Thus the condition from which the claimant is currently suffering may be a sequela (after-effect) of a prescribed disease: see SI 1985/967, reg 3.
348 Details of typical symptoms and after-effects of prescribed diseases are given in the DSS booklet *Notes on the Diagnosis of Occupational Diseases* (1991).
349 Three fingers in the case of a person who retains all four fingers and the thumb on the hand in question: SI 1985/967, Sch 1, para A11. See further *CI/520/1992* ((1995) 2 JSSL D38) on an unsuccessful challenge to the vires of this provision.
350 SI 1999/991, reg 12.
351 For the previous statutory special arrangements for adjudication in cases of lung disease see *Wikeley* n 45, above, ch 8.
352 SSA 1998, s 12. Until July 1999 a distinction was drawn between medical and non-medical issues, which determined the respective jurisdictions of the social security and medical appeal tribunals.
353 *R(I) 4/96*. This assumes, of course, that the claim is made in time: see pp 150–157, above.
354 SI 1985/967.

he or she has been employed in the relevant occupation on or after 5 July 1948.[355] It is important to appreciate that the scheduled description is not a legal categorisation of the type of occupation but a factual account of work actually undertaken.[356] Thus the fact that the claimant has succeeded in a claim in tort against the employer is irrelevant if the terms of prescription are not met.[357] It also follows that though a claimant's employment may in theory include work in the prescribed activity, in practice he or she may not be engaged at all on it, or only for a trivial amount of time. In such circumstances there will be no entitlement to benefit.[358] There are additional and stringent requirements in terms of years of employment in a prescribed occupation for claims based on occupational deafness and chronic bronchitis and emphysema.[359] Moreover, claims based on occupational deafness or occupational asthma must also be brought within five or ten years respectively of last working in the relevant employment.[360] These conditions, whilst reflecting the difficulty in attributing causality to the workplace, undoubtedly have the effect of limiting the number of successful claims, even where a tort settlement has been reached. The scheduled descriptions of the occupation vary from the very vague[361] to the highly specific.[362] There is a considerable case law on some of these but consideration of it lies beyond the scope of this work.[363] In some cases the Commissioners have obtained valuable guidance from the IIAC report which led to the prescription of the relevant disease.[364] The Court of Appeal has also approved a purposive reading of the regulations.[365]

iii   Causal link between occupation and disease

Finally, the claimant must establish the causal link between employment in the prescribed occupation and the prescribed disease. In ordinary cases, there is a presumption that the disease was due to the nature of the relevant occupation for workers who were employed in it at any time within one month preceding the date on which they are treated as having developed the disease,[366] normally the date on which they first suffer the relevant loss of faculty.[367] There are, however, special conditions for the presumption

---

355   SI 1985/967, reg 2(a).
356   Therefore it is not sufficient for the claimant to establish that he or she was contractually bound to undertake such work. The question is whether he or she actually *did* the work (*CI 59/49*; *R(I) 3/78*) which depends on the individual circumstances of the case: *R(I) 2/77*.
357   See eg *R(I) 6/85* and *CI/496/1993* ((1995) 2 JSSL D38). If the social security claim is successful and is followed by an award in tort, there will be implications under the recoupment scheme: see pp 264–265, above.
358   Eg *CI 265/49*; *R(I) 40/57*.
359   In cases of occupational deafness the claimant must have been employed for a minimum of ten years in one or more of the prescribed occupations: SI 1985/967, reg 25(2). On the 20-year rule for chronic bronchitis and emphysema, see Sch 1, para D12; and Wikeley (1994) 1 JSSL 23 at 27–29.
360   See SI 1985/967, reg 25 for occupational deafness. Although the imposition of this five-year limit was declared ultra vires in *McKiernon v Secretary of State for Social Security* (1989) Times, 1 November, it was held in *R(I) 1/92* that SSA 1990, Sch 6 retrospectively declared the limitation to be valid. For occupational asthma, see SI 1985/967, reg 36.
361   Eg Prescribed Diseases B4 and A8: 'work in or about a mine'.
362   Eg Prescribed Disease C23. Both *R(I) 3/90* and *R(I) 2/92* reveal a narrowing of the list of occupations where technology overtook the specific terminology used in the regulations.
363   Reference should be made to Bonner, Hooker and White *Social Security Legislation 2001* (2001) vol I.
364   See eg *R(I) 2/01* on the definition of 'hand-held chain saws in forestry' in the context of a claim based on vibration white finger. See also *R(I) 4/98* on the prescription of nasal carcinoma.
365   *R(I) 2/01*.
366   SI 1985/967, reg 4(1).
367   SI 1985/967, reg 6, though earlier if there has been a recrudescence of the disease previously suffered: reg 7(3).

to apply to cases of pneumoconiosis, chronic bronchitis or emphysema, byssinosis, tuberculosis and occupational deafness,[368] and it does not apply at all to two diseases commonly caused by non-occupational factors: carpal tunnel syndrome and non-infective dermatitis.[369]

To rebut the presumption, where it exists, the Secretary of State must prove on the balance of probabilities that the disease was not due to the nature of the relevant occupation.[370] In some cases, the argument will be made that the disease was caused by employment in an occupation not prescribed.[371] In others, the disease may allegedly arise from activities or contacts outside the employment[372] or from a condition pre-existing in the claimant before the commencement of the occupation.[373] In all cases, the question is not whether the employment was the sole cause of the disease: it is sufficient if it was the real and substantial cause.[374]

C Recrudescence and fresh attacks

A claimant may have been awarded disablement benefit for a particular disease and then have recovered wholly or partly. If he or she subsequently suffers a further attack, this may be diagnosed as a 'recrudescence', that is, continuation of the old disease. In such a case, the conditions of entitlement do not have to be satisfied again and the claimant gains immediate entitlement to benefit.[375] Conversely, if it is diagnosed as the contraction of a new disease, the conditions must be satisfied afresh. If the further attack occurs during the period covered by an existing assessment of disablement, there is a rebuttable presumption that it is a recrudescence of the earlier disease, but if it occurs after the end of such a period, it is always treated as the contraction of a new disease.[376]

Part 5   Disablement benefit

A General

From 1948 until 1982, provision was made in the industrial scheme both for short-term incapacity for work – injury benefit, payable for a maximum period of six months – and for residual disability, whether or not accompanied by incapacity for work – disablement benefit, payable when entitlement to injury benefit had expired. The existence of the flat-rate injury benefit had its origin in pressure on the post-war government to offer a higher level of compensation to those off work as the result of an

---

368 SI 1985/967, reg 4(2)–(6). For a critique of the presumption for pneumoconiosis in the context of asbestos-related disease, see *Wikeley* n 45, above, ch 10.
369 Until 1996 this exclusion also applied to allergic rhinitis (inflammation of the nose, throat or mouth): see SI 1996/425.
370 *R(I) 37/52.*
371 Eg *R(I) 9/53.*
372 Eg *R(I) 20/52.*
373 Eg *R(I) 37/52; R(I) 38/52.*
374 *R(I) 10/53.*
375 SI 1985/967, reg 7(1). The regulation does not apply to certain diseases full recovery from which is rarely obtained.
376 SI 1985/967, reg 7(1).

industrial accident or disease than they would obtain under the non-industrial sickness benefit.[377] However, the real value of the difference between the injury and sickness benefits declined over the years as successive governments became sensitive to criticisms of the industrial preference, at least with regard to short-term consequences.[378] The 1980 departmental study of the industrial scheme produced an almost unanswerable argument for rationalisation: 'considerable administrative cost is ... incurred to deal with hundreds of thousands of cases in most of which little extra benefit is at stake.'[379] A suggestion to abolish injury benefit was accepted forthwith by the government[380] and implemented in 1982.[381] The very great majority of those who would have received injury benefit would, of course, be entitled to sickness benefit, or statutory sick pay which, in 1986, became available for the first six months of incapacity. To protect the few who would not be so entitled, the legislation initially provided that a person incapable of work as a result of an industrial accident or prescribed disease should be treated as having satisfied the contribution conditions for sickness benefit. This protection was withdrawn when incapacity benefit superseded sickness and invalidity benefit.[382]

The method of compensating long-term disability was a much disputed question during the Second World War and immediately thereafter.[383] First, should provision be made for those who were only partially disabled, that is, whose earning capacity had been reduced rather than eliminated altogether? Such persons had been covered by the workmen's compensation legislation, and the principle of compensation applicable there, both to totally and to partially disabled, had been that of 50 per cent (and for lower paid workers 75 per cent) of lost earnings, though subject to a statutory maximum.[384] Beveridge preferred to retain this mode of compensation, but on the level of two-thirds of lost earnings, to bring the scheme in line with the more generous protection offered by European and American systems.[385] The post-war government was not, however, prepared to accept this recommendation. It was seen as conflicting with the then generally held dogma of social insurance that any differential in benefit should be based on need, typically according to the extent of family responsibility, rather than on earnings.[386] Further, it was felt that one of the main weaknesses of the workmen's compensation scheme had been the difficulty of calculating the earnings-based award: predictions had to be made not only on claimants' future earnings in the light of their reduced capacity, but also on those which they would have received if they had not been injured. The government proposed what was described as 'an entirely new approach' (though it had formed the basis of the war pensions scheme for some time[387]): benefit payable according to the degree of disablement, irrespective of actual earnings loss. The rates would be assessed on the claimant's assumed needs, and therefore might include increases for family responsibilities and for any additional care and attention necessary.

As the following pages will reveal, the principles of assessment and modes of payment have continued to be the subject of considerable debate and substantial reform.

---

377   *Brown* n 28, above, p 30. Beveridge had recommended that the injured employee should rely on sickness benefit for the first 13 weeks: *Beveridge Report* n 15, above, para 100.
378   P 717, above.
379   *Industrial Injuries Compensation* n 35, above, para 2.7. The difference between injury and sickness benefit was, at the time, £2.73 per week.
380   *Reform of the Industrial Injuries Scheme* n 37, above, ch 2.
381   SSHBA 1982, s 39(1).
382   SSCBA 1992, s 102 (now repealed): see Bonner (1995) 2 JSSL 86 at 93–94.
383   *Brown* n 28, above, pp 213–218.
384   WCA 1925, s 9(2).
385   *Beveridge Report* n 15, above, paras 99–100.
386   *Social Insurance* n 17, above, Pt II, paras 28–29.
387   Cf p 781, below.

Nevertheless, the principle of providing *basic* compensation according to the severity of disablement has remained unaltered and uncontroversial.[388] Indeed, it has served as a model for those arguing for a universal system of disability income, not confined to industrial cases.[389]

B Loss of faculty

To gain title to disablement benefit, the claimant must show that 'he suffers as the result of the relevant accident from loss of physical or mental faculty ...'.[390] The legislation does not define 'loss of faculty'. It is one link in the statutory chain of causation:

$$\left.\begin{array}{l} \text{accident – injury} \\ \text{prescribed disease} \end{array}\right\} \text{– loss of faculty – disablement}$$

and its meaning, therefore, must be understood in the light of those other elements.[391] Whereas 'injury' covers all the adverse physical or mental consequences of the accident,[392] 'loss of faculty' connotes 'impairment of the proper functioning of part of the body or mind',[393] and this is 'a cause of disabilities to do things which in sum constitute the disablement' which is the subject of the assessment.[394] If this seems to be very complicated, its practical importance is small. Though decision makers are expected, in theory, to make separate determinations on loss of faculty and disablement respectively, because of the possibility that either might not exist,[395] in practice this rarely occurs.[396] In any event, SSCBA 1992 provides that 'there shall be taken to be no relevant loss of faculty when the extent of the resulting disablement, if so assessed, would not amount to 1 per cent'.[397]

What amounts to an 'impairment of the proper functioning' may sometimes cause difficulties. In one case, the malfunctioning of one kidney was regarded as a loss of faculty, even though the claimant could survive by using the other kidney.[398] For some time there was doubt as to whether disfigurement constituted a loss of faculty, on the ground that people do not put their appearance to any use. The traditional view that it was covered is confirmed by the legislation which provides that reference to '"loss of physical faculty" includes disfigurement whether or not accompanied by any loss of physical faculty'.[399]

---

388 Cf *Pearson Report*, n 32, above, paras 822–824; *Industrial Injuries Compensation* n 35, above, para 3.11.
389 P 681, above.
390 SSCBA 1992, s 103(1).
391 *Jones v Secretary of State for Social Services* [1972] AC 944, per Lord Diplock at 1009–1010 and Lord Simon at 1019.
392 Per Lord Diplock in *Jones v Secretary of State for Social Services* [1972] AC 944 at 1010; and 'hurt to body or mind', per Lord Simon at 1020.
393 Per Lord Simon in *Jones v Secretary of State for Social Services* [1972] AC 944; cf 'loss of power or function of an organ of the body', per Lord Diplock at 1010.
394 Per Lord Diplock in *Jones v Secretary of State for Social Services* [1972] AC 944.
395 *R(I) 5/84(T)*.
396 *Lewis* n 30, above, pp 138–139. The fact that now the assessment of disablement must, in general, be at least 14 per cent renders the distinction of even less importance.
397 SSCBA 1992, s 103(5).
398 *R(I) 14/66*.
399 SSCBA 1992, s 122(1).

C   Causal link with relevant accident

The next task is to establish that the loss of faculty resulted from the industrial accident or prescribed disease. The onus of proof is on the claimant and the standard is the balance of probabilities.[400] The ordinary principles of causation apply,[401] so the claimant need not show that the accident was the sole or even *the* effective cause – it is sufficient if it was *a* real and effective cause.[402] In the past the major problem here has been the question of the respective competencies of the medical and lay adjudicating authorities to make a binding decision on the point. This issue was tested on more than one occasion before the House of Lords, which held that a decision by the lay adjudicating authorities that the claimant had suffered an injury by accident precluded the medical authorities from making a subsequent decision that a loss of faculty did not result from the accident.[403] This ruling was subsequently reversed by statute.[404] SSA 1998 swept away the distinction between the lay and medical adjudicating authorities, making such provision otiose.[405]

D   Degree of disablement

The 1946 legislation did not confer benefit in all cases of disablement: the claimant had to show that the loss of faculty, resulting from the industrial accident, was likely to be permanent or substantial, the latter meaning an assessment of 20 per cent or more.[406] There was soon pressure to extend entitlement to less serious cases and in 1953 the threshold was reduced to 1 per cent, thus excluding only trivial handicaps.[407] Those benefiting from the reform, because their disablement was assessed between 1 and 20 per cent, received a lump-sum 'gratuity', rather than a pension.[408]

The DHSS team which reviewed the scheme in 1980 saw no reason to question the appropriateness of these arrangements. Indeed, they remarked on the popularity of gratuities with claimants and on the medical opinion that, in comparison with pensions, lump sum awards had a positive effect on rehabilitation.[409] The government White Paper, published 18 months later, took quite a different line. In accordance with the policy that the industrial preference should concentrate on more serious cases, it argued for a threshold similar to that prevailing before 1953: a 10 per cent assessment where the disablement was not likely to be permanent.[410] In the event, the reform effected in 1986 went even further: the threshold, at which point the pension is payable, was raised to 14 per cent; and the gratuity was abolished.[411] An exception was made for three lung

---

400   *R(I) 12/62.*
401   Cf p 725, above.
402   *R(I) 3/66(T).*
403   *Minister of Social Security v Amalgamated Engineering Union* [1967] 1 AC 725, [1967] 1 All ER 210; *Jones v Secretary of State for Social Services*; *Hudson v Secretary of State for Social Services* [1972] AC 944, [1972] 1 All ER 145. The latter two cases were heard *en banc*. See also the 4th edition of this book, p 331.
404   National Insurance Act 1972, s 5 (NIA 1972), against determined opposition: cf Mrs B Castle who characterised the reform as 'designed to establish the victory of unimaginative bureaucracy' (Standing Committee D Debates on the Bill, col 373). The relevant provision was later re-enacted in the Social Security Administration Act 1992, s 60(3) (SSAA 1992).
405   SSA 1998, s 17, the successor to SSAA 1992, s 60, thus omits any comparable provision.
406   National Insurance (Industrial Injuries) Act 1946, s 12(1)(a) (NI(II)A 1946).
407   NI(II)A 1953, s 3.
408   For details, see the 2nd edition of this book, pp 308–309.
409   *Industrial Injuries Compensation* n 35, above, para 3.25.
410   *Reform of the Industrial Injuries Scheme* n 37, above, ch 3.
411   SSA 1986, Sch 3, para 3, following the consultation paper: DHSS *Industrial Injuries Scheme* (1985), paras 2.1–2.4.

diseases – byssinosis, diffuse mesothelioma and pneumoconiosis – for which benefit is still payable on assessments of 1 to 13 per cent.[412] Many other diseases, however, typically attract only low assessments and their continued existence in the schedule of prescribed diseases has become largely symbolic.[413] Moreover, as regards the whole field of industrial accidents and diseases, the abolition of the gratuity eliminated about 90 per cent of all new awards.[414]

E Assessment of disablement

i General

The general principle of assessment is to take into account all disabilities incurred as a result of the loss of faculty:

> to which the claimant may be expected, having regard to his physical and mental condition at the date of the assessment, to be subject during the period taken into account by the assessment as compared with a person of the same age and sex whose physical and mental condition is normal.[415]

With the exception of the factors mentioned in this provision, measurement is objective: 'the assessment shall be made without reference to the particular circumstances of the claimant other than age, sex and physical and mental condition.'[416] It follows that not only is the effect of the disability on the claimant's earning capacity irrelevant,[417] but personal and social circumstances are also ignored,[418] and, unlike the system of common law damages, there is no attempt to compare the claimant's condition before and after the injury.[419] The objective approach, though found to be satisfactory by a departmental committee reporting in 1965,[420] may be criticised on the basis that it ignores the functional, social and psychological aspects of disability. This weakness is all the more apparent now that there is no provision within the scheme for loss of earning capacity caused by injury or disease. A statement in the 1980 discussion document that 'the department ... has no evidence that the present schedule is outmoded'[421] was surprising in the circumstances,[422] but it is characteristic of the generally negative government response to suggestions for reform in this area.

---

412   SI 1985/967, reg 20(1), substituted by SI 1986/1561. Note that from July 2002 cases of mesothelioma are deemed to be 100 per cent assessments: SI 1985/967, reg 20A (inserted by SI 2002/1717).
413   *Lewis* n 43, above, at 259. In 1999 there were 6,250 diagnoses of prescribed diseases, of which 4,250 were assessed at between 1 and 13 per cent disabled: Department for Work and Pensions (DWP) *Industrial Injuries Disablement Benefit Statistics – Dec 2001* (2002) Table 2.1. However, a finding of disablement of less than 14 per cent may lead to a successful claim in tort.
414   *Lewis* n 43, above, at 260.
415   SSCBA 1992, Sch 6, para 1(a).
416   SSCBA 1992, Sch 6, para 1(c).
417   *R(I) 3/61*; *Murrell v Secretary of State for Social Services* (1984), reported as Appendix to *R(I) 3/84*.
418   In *R(I) 6/75* the claimant sought to have his assessment of disability reduced from 20 per cent to 19 per cent on the ground that the consequent award of a lump sum gratuity instead of a pension would enable him to purchase a small business. The reduction was quashed by the Commissioner.
419   A suggestion that the comparison should be attempted was rejected in *Industrial Injuries Compensation* n 35, above, para 3.16.
420   *Report of the Committee on the Assessment of Disablement* (McCorquodale Committee) (1965, Cmnd 2847).
421   *Industrial Injuries Compensation* n 35, above, para 3.19.
422   The document did, admittedly, precede the comprehensive report published by the DHSS: Duckworth *The Classification and Measurement of Disablement* (1982).

ii Assessment for prescribed conditions

Schedule 2 to the Social Security (General Benefit) Regulations 1982[423] contains a tariff of the prescribed degrees of disablement. The first column sets out descriptions of the injury and the second column the degree of disablement, expressed as a percentage of total disablement (eg loss of a hand and a foot, 100 per cent; loss of thumb, 30 per cent etc). For each specified condition, then, the prima facie assessment is the prescribed degree of disablement, but decision makers are not tied to this figure; it is subject:

> to such increase or reduction ... as may be reasonable in the circumstances of the case where, having regard to the [statutory provisions and regulations] ... that degree of disablement does not provide a reasonable assessment of the extent of disablement resulting from the relevant loss of faculty.[424]

The conditions specified in the tariff must, it seems, be construed literally. Thus eg reference to the loss of the phalanx of a finger does not cover loss of *part* of the phalanx of a finger.[425] Although SSCBA 1992 specifically entitles the Secretary of State to make special provision for the difference between injuries to the hand and arm of right- and left-handed persons,[426] this has not been done. But it may be a suitable case for decision makers to increase or reduce the assessment in the exercise of their discretion referred to above.

A problem arises if, as a result of the accident, the claimant suffers from two of the conditions specified in the tariff. The regulations provide that assessment at the prescribed degree of disablement should be made only where the condition in question is 'the sole injury which a claimant suffers as a result of the relevant accident ... whether or not such injury incorporates one or more other injuries' as specified.[427] In other words, if one injury is incorporated into another, the assessment should be made according to the prescribed degree of the more serious disability. Where the accident results in two separate injuries, there is no automatic assessment under the tariff, and the principles next to be described apply.

iii Assessment for non-prescribed conditions

For conditions not specified in the Schedule to the Social Security (General Benefit) Regulations 1982, assessment is at large. It is a question of fact, and the decision of the medical authorities will generally be regarded as conclusive, though they 'may have such regard as may be appropriate to the prescribed degrees of disablement' of the injuries specified in the Schedule.[428] The prescribed degrees of disablement, then, provide a guideline for the appropriate assessment, but no more. In one case,[429] the claimant suffering from a condition of the finger which was more severe than one prescribed finger condition but less severe than another prescribed finger condition sought to argue

---

423   SI 1982/1408.
424   SI 1982/1408, reg 11(6).
425   *R(I) 22/63.*
426   SSCBA 1992, Sch 6, para 2.
427   SI 1982/1408, reg 11(6). The regulation was made in 1970 to deal with uncertainty in the case law, especially *R(I) 39/61* and *R v Industrial Injuries Comr, ex p Cable* [1968] 1 QB 729, [1967] 1 All ER 9.
428   SI 1982/1408, reg 11(7). There are, however, some non-statutory guidelines which are used in practice: see *Lewis* n 30, above, pp 146–147.
429   *R(I) 23/63.*

that as a matter of *law* medical authorities were bound to assess at a figure between the two prescribed degrees of disablement. The argument was rejected. The discretion of the (then) medical authorities was not to be fettered by thus enlarging the Schedule. In cases where the claimant has sustained multiple (and separate) injuries, and there is no composite disability for which the Schedule prescribes an assessment, decision makers must form their own judgment on the total disablement resulting from the various injuries.[430] They may compare this total condition with those giving rise to the prescribed degrees of disablement and select an appropriate figure.

The prescribed degrees of disablement refer only to traumatically caused injuries, with the result that there is no statutory guidance (beyond the general rubric) for disablement induced by disease.[431] There are, however, some special rules which apply to the assessment of disablement in cases of occupational deafness and pneumoconiosis.[432]

iv Successive industrial accidents

Where successive accidents (or diseases) are covered by the scheme and give rise to separate conditions, the claimant is entitled to an assessment based on the aggregate of the respective degrees of disablement.[433] This principle is, however, subject to two qualifications. First, if the condition caused by the first accident gave rise to a lump sum gratuity payment, it cannot count towards the aggregate[434] – the claimant has already been compensated in full for the condition. Secondly, the aggregate cannot exceed 100 per cent.[435]

v Reductions for disability resulting from extraneous causes[436]

The fact that the claimant's condition results in part from an extraneous cause, that is, one not arising from an industrial accident, in principle justifies a reduction in the assessment of the disability. It is felt that the scheme should not be charged with the burden of such disabilities as the claimant would have suffered if he or she had not been injured in the industrial accident. The policy is a simple one to understand, but the provisions implementing it have caused great difficulties. The chief concern has been to see that generous treatment should be given to an employee who sustains two disabilities, only one of which is caused by an industrial accident, but which are in some way connected, so that the total disability resulting is greater than the sum of the two disabilities taken separately. A simple example will illustrate the point:

430 *R v Industrial Injuries Comr, ex p Cable* [1968] 1 QB 729, [1967] 1 All ER 9; and see *Murrell v Secretary of State for Social Services*, reported as Appendix to *R(I) 3/84.*
431 *Wikeley* n 30, above, p 181. 'There are no magic formulae and no secret tables. It is a question of judgement': Ward (1986) 41 Thorax 257.
432 SI 1985/967, regs 20–22, 34 and Sch 3.
433 SSCBA 1992, ss 103(2)–(4) and 109(4)–(6).
434 SSCBA 1992, ss 103(2)–(4) and 109(4)–(6) and SI 1982/1408, reg 38.
435 SSCBA 1992, s 107(1). Regulations made under s 91(1)(b) provide that the principle should not affect entitlement to dependency additions or the allowances for constant attendance and exceptionally severe disablement, though, of course, the claimant cannot receive more than one each of such addition or allowance: SI 1982/1408, reg 39.
436 Lewis (1980) 43 MLR 514.

Under the tariff, the loss of vision in one eye, the other being normal, is 30 per cent, but the loss of sight 'to such an extent as to render the claimant unable to perform any work for which eyesight is essential' is assessed at 100 per cent.[437] Thus a claimant, already blind in one eye, who loses the sight of the other eye in an industrial accident under the ordinary principle unmodified would be entitled to only 30 per cent but the effect of the accident has been to increase disablement from 30 per cent to 100 per cent.[438]

The solution originally adopted was the so-called 'paired-organs' rule. Where the claimant sustained an injury to one of a pair of similar organs, whose functions were interchangeable or complementary, and the other had already been incapacitated – in an industrial accident or otherwise – the total disablement was treated as resulting from an industrial injury.[439] Application of the doctrine, however, produced difficulties and anomalies,[440] and in 1969–70 it was replaced by a new set of rules.

A   TOTAL DISABLEMENT

Decision makers should first assess the total disablement resulting from the relevant loss of faculty, whether or not it was derived in part from another cause.[441] In so doing, they should not merely arbitrate between two opposing views (those of the claimant and those of the DWP) but rather obtain all the information that they regard as relevant, and assess the disablement resulting from the relevant loss of faculty on the balance of probabilities.[442] They may then, for the purpose of making a reduction from the first assessment, only take account of causes other than the relevant accident to the extent allowed by the Social Security (General Benefit) Regulations 1982.[443] These apply to disabilities from other causes suffered, respectively, before and after the industrial accident. But for there to be a 'disability' for this purpose, there must have been some inability to perform a bodily or mental process which manifested itself; a constitutional or latent condition which simply renders the sufferer more prone to such an inability cannot be invoked as a ground for reducing benefit.[444]

B   OTHER DISABILITY PRECEDING INDUSTRIAL ACCIDENT

Regulation 11(3) of the Social Security (General Benefit) Regulations 1982[445] provides that where the disability, defined as above, preceded the industrial accident, the medical authorities must assess what degree of disablement would have resulted from that disability if the industrial accident had not occurred and deduct it from the total disablement. For example:

---

437   SI 1982/1408, Sch 2, items 32 and 4 respectively.
438   Cf *R(I) 1/79*.
439   SI 1964/504, reg 2(4).
440   See *R v Medical Appeal Tribunal, ex p Burpitt* [1957] 2 QB 584; see also *Report of the Industrial Injuries Advisory Council on the Rules Governing the Assessment of Disablement* (1956, Cmd 9827); and Micklethwait (1969) 37 Medico-Legal J 172 at 185.
441   SI 1982/1408, reg 11(2).
442   *R v Industrial Injuries Comr, ex p Cable* [1968] 1 QB 729, [1967] 1 All ER 9; *R v National Insurance Comr, ex p Viscusi* [1974] 2 All ER 724, [1974] 1 WLR 646.
443   SI 1982/1408, reg 11(3) and (4). The individual assessments for the disablement arising from each accident must be stated: *R(I) 1/95*.
444   *R(I) 13/75; R(I) 3/76; R(I) 1/81*.
445   SI 1982/1408.

C has suffered an amputation to one foot. In the industrial accident he suffers an amputation to the other foot. Total disablement is 90 per cent. If there had been no industrial accident he would have been disabled to the extent of 30 per cent. Benefit is then payable on an assessment of 90 per cent - 30 per cent = 60 per cent.

C INDUSTRIAL ACCIDENT PRECEDING OTHER DISABILITY

In the converse case where the industrial accident precedes the other disability, the solution is not so simple. On the ordinary principles of causation, it is arguable that no account should be taken of the fact that the subsequent event has exacerbated the claimant's condition, since it has superseded the effect of the industrial accident. This was indeed the position prevailing before the 1970 reform, and yet it created an apparent inequality of treatment according to the sequence of events.[446] The Committee that reviewed the issue in 1956[447] was divided on the issue. The minority opinion was that the assessment should take account of the greater incapacity caused by the non-industrial accident (as in regulation 11(3) of the Social Security (General Benefit) Regulations 1982), but the majority found no justification for such a 'radical' departure from the ordinary rules of causation. Aware, presumably, of the political repercussions of strict adherence to the ordinary rules, however, they suggested the compromise solution of taking into account 50 per cent of the increase in disability. A compromise solution was in fact adopted by the Department in 1970, but not that proposed by the Committee. It was decided to take into account the *whole* of the increase for those more seriously injured, but to ignore it altogether for those less seriously injured. The dividing line was arbitrarily made at an 11 per cent disablement. Regulation 11(4), which now incorporates the solution, lays down two rules:
(1) The authorities should only take into account the disablement which would have resulted if the non-industrial accident had not occurred. For example:

C loses the whole of a ring finger in an industrial accident. As a result of a later non-industrial accident, the hand containing that finger is rendered useless. The relevant assessment for the disability of the ring finger = 7 per cent.

(2) Where the assessment made under the first rule is 11 per cent or more, a solution analogous to that in regulation 11(3) is adopted. From the assessment of total disablement is deducted the degree of disablement resulting solely from the non-industrial accident (ie if the industrial accident had not occurred). For example:

In an industrial accident, C is amputated through the left foot. He is subsequently amputated through the right foot. Amputation of a foot is 30 per cent, thus the second rule applies. Total disablement is 90 per cent from which is deducted 30 per cent for the right foot. Benefit is payable for 60 per cent.

---

446 Cf at common law *Baker v Willoughby* [1970] AC 467, [1969] 3 All ER 1528; *Jobling v Associated Dairies Ltd* [1982] AC 794.
447 *Report of the Industrial Injuries Advisory Council* n 440, above.

D WHERE 100 PER CENT DISABLEMENT

A special rule operates where the total assessment of disablement is 100 per cent. In such circumstances, the Secretary of State is given power *not* to reduce for the fact that some of the disablement has been caused by a non-industrial event, if satisfied that 'in the circumstances of the case, 100 per cent is a reasonable assessment of the extent of disablement resulting from the loss of faculty'.[448] This is designed to cover cases where the disability caused by the industrial accident itself, without the addition of disability arising from an extraneous event, would amount to 100 per cent. It would obviously be unjust to make a deduction merely because the non-industrial event has made the claimant's condition even worse. The anomaly arises because the tariff knows no degree of assessment higher than 100 per cent.

vi Rounding modifications

When the total assessment of disablement has been reached in accordance with the principles described above, the percentage figure must be expressed in a multiple of 10:[449]

> Assessments of between 14 per cent and 19 per cent inclusive are rounded up to 20 per cent; those which are multiples of 5 are rounded up to the next multiple of 10; others are rounded up or down to the nearest multiple of 10. Thus eg assessments of 25 per cent and 28 per cent become 30 per cent, while 24 per cent becomes 20 per cent.

The most significant consequence of these modifications, effected by SSA 1986, is that those whose disablement is assessed between 14 and 19 per cent, previously entitled only to a gratuity, now receive a pension.

vii Period of assessment

The assessment is made for the period 'during which the claimant has suffered and may be expected to continue to suffer from the relevant loss of faculty', beginning not earlier than 90 days (not counting Sundays, thus 15 weeks) after the accident or onset of the prescribed disease.[450] It will in any event terminate on the claimant's death,[451] but it may be limited to an earlier day, if the disability is expected to end by that date. If the assessment is less than 14 per cent, the period must last for so long as the prognosis suggests that disablement of at least 1 per cent will persist.[452] Determination of the period is either 'provisional' or 'final'.[453] A final assessment is appropriate where the medical authorities are reasonably certain in their prognosis; it may be modified only by a revision or a supersession. An assessment of less than 14 per cent must also be final unless an aggregation with other disablement is likely.[454] A provisional assessment

448 SI 1982/1408, reg 11(6).
449 SSCBA 1992, s 103(3). The rounding modification applies only to the aggregate assessment, not to any component forming part of an aggregate.
450 SSCBA 1992, s 103(6) and SI 1985/967, reg 6.
451 SSCBA 1992, Sch 6, para 6(1).
452 SSCBA 1992, para 6(3).
453 A first assessment for occupational deafness is always provisional for five years: SI 1985/967, reg 29.
454 SSCBA 1992, Sch 6, para 6.

is to be made where 'the condition of the claimant is not such, having regard to the possibility of changes therein (whether predictable or not) as to allow of a final assessment'.[455] The claimant's condition must be examined again before the end of the period for which the assessment was made, and the new assessment (either provisional or final) will apply from that time.[456] A provisional assessment is in no sense binding on a subsequent assessment, and the decision maker determining the latter may come to a different view on whether a condition which was also the subject of the previous assessment resulted from the relevant accident.[457] On the other hand, a subsequent assessment cannot modify the benefit for the earlier period.[458]

The specialist adjudication arrangements for decisions under the industrial injuries scheme were abolished by SSA 1998. This included the separate provisions for reviews on the grounds of 'unforeseen aggravation';[459] decisions are now subject to the standard provisions governing revisions and supersessions.[460]

F Benefit

Since the gratuity was abolished in 1986, disablement benefit is payable only in the form of a pension, a weekly sum proportionate to the degree of disablement (after rounding modifications).[461] For example, in 2002–03, the relevant rates for 100 per cent and 50 per cent are £114.80 and £57.40 respectively. Beneficiaries under 18 and not entitled to an increase for dependants are paid less, about 60 per cent of the general rate.[462] In the 1980s, as part of its policy to confer preferential treatment on more seriously disabled beneficiaries, the then Conservative government proposed some revision of the amounts payable. This would have resulted eg in a 30 per cent assessment giving rise to payment of 25 per cent of the maximum pension, and an 80 per cent assessment would have lead to an 85 per cent pension.[463] However, this reform was never implemented.

Part 6 Supplements to disablement benefit

A General

Although disablement benefit is the only benefit provided by the industrial scheme, until 1986 the pension could be increased by the addition of up to five supplements. Of

455 SSCBA 1992, para 6(2).
456 SSCBA 1992, Sch 6, para 6(1).
457 *R v Industrial Injuries Comr, ex p Howarth* (1968) 4 KIR 621; *R v National Insurance Comr, ex p Viscusi* [1974] 2 All ER 724, [1974] 1 WLR 646; but see *Kitchen v Secretary of State for Social Services* [1993] NLJR 1370.
458 *R(1) 8/69.*
459 See the 4th edition of this book, p 339.
460 Pp 185–186, above.
461 SSCBA 1992, s 103(3). For the rules on calculating the pension for the three diseases for which the threshold remains at 1 per cent, see SI 1986/967, reg 20.
462 SSCBA 1992, Sch 4, Pt V, para 1.
463 *Reform of the Industrial Injuries Scheme* n 37, above, para 22; and DHSS Consultation Paper *Industrial Injuries Scheme* n 39, above, para 7.1.

these only two now survive,[464] and even they are of benefit to but few people.[465] This is because entitlement to them is restricted to those who are 100 per cent disabled, with the result that only about 1 per cent of those entitled to monies from the industrial scheme qualify for the supplements. However, the additional monies are still important to claimants suffering the most severe injuries because they can more than double the amount of pension received.

Although relatively few people qualify, an assessment of 100 per cent disablement is not intended to represent total disablement. It can be attained eg if both hands are lost or if the claimant is made completely deaf. The maximum assessments thus cover a wide range of severe disablement from total helplessness to disablement which, although severe, does not prevent the claimant from carrying out a job. This lack of differentiation between severe disablements means that, in the more serious of the 100 per cent cases, additional assistance will be needed. This can be sought by claiming constant attendance allowance and exceptionally severe disablement allowance.[466]

B   Constant attendance allowance

Section 104(1) of SSCBA 1992 provides that:

> where a disablement pension is payable in respect of an assessment of 100 per cent, then, if as a result of the relevant loss of faculty the beneficiary requires constant attendance, the weekly rate of the pension shall be increased by an amount determined in accordance with regulations by reference to the extent and nature of the attendance required by the beneficiary.

The regulations prescribe four different rates for the allowance and two of these may be further increased by the addition of exceptionally severe disablement allowance. The rates depend upon the extent of both the disablement and the need for attendance, and vary according to whether full or part-time attendance is required. A threshold condition is that a claimant must be 'to a substantial extent dependent on [constant] attendance for the necessities of life and is likely to remain so dependent for a prolonged period.'[467]

Neither these words nor the other conditions of payment of the various rates have received interpretation from either the Commissioners or the courts. This is because historically questions on the allowance were not decided by the usual statutory authorities but by DSS staff on behalf of the Secretary of State. The cases were not reported and there was no effective right of appeal; this omission was not remedied by the reforms in appeal structures initiated by SSA 1998.[468] The result is that in terms of legal principle much concerning this area of the social security system is shrouded in secrecy.[469] Internal

---

464   Apart from the allowances for constant attendance and exceptionally severe disablement, there used to be supplements for unemployability, for receiving hospital treatment and for suffering a reduction in earning capacity, as considered in Part 7 of this chapter.

465   In 1994–95, the last year for which published statistics are available, there were 2,000 recipients of constant attendance allowance and 1,000 for exceptionally severe disablement allowance: DSS *Social Security Statistics 1996* (1996) Table F2.07.

466   In the past there have been government proposals to abolish both allowances: see the 4th edition of this book, pp 341–342.

467   SI 1982/1408, reg 19(1).

468   SI 1999/991, Sch 2, para 14.

469   See the pertinent criticism of Carson (1976) 126 NLJ 59. In Partington *The Secretary of State's Powers of Adjudication in Social Security Law* (1990) the power to determine entitlement to the supplements for industrial injury was described as 'quite anomalous'. The report, commissioned by the DSS, had recommended that the Secretary of State's adjudicatory functions be brought within the mainstream of social security adjudication.

guidelines for interpretation are circulated within the DWP, but their contents have been jealously guarded.[470] They state eg that 'a prolonged period' is one that lasts for at least six months. In addition, 'dependent on ... attendance for the necessities of life' is interpreted in a similar way to the criterion of 'attention ... in connection with ... bodily functions' used for the non-industrial attendance allowance and disability living allowance.[471] This means, according to the internal guidelines, that although 'an applicant can expect to have a reasonable degree of physical or mental comfort ... the allowance is not granted in respect of help in housework or other purely domestic purposes, or for only slight intermittent attendance such as help in dressing or undressing'.

The words of the regulation do not require that the claimant should actually receive attendance, but only that it should be needed. Although the provision of attendance is some evidence of the need for it, severely disabled claimants should not be refused only because they live on their own. Nor will the fact that the attendance is unpaid or provided by a spouse or other relative prejudice a claim, for the attendance need not come from outside.[472] However, after four weeks in hospital the claimant will only be entitled if the treatment being received is not provided free.[473]

C Exceptionally severe disablement allowance

This allowance was introduced in 1966[474] after a committee had reported that constant attendance allowance did not provide 'a wholly adequate recognition of disablement which is extremely severe even within the class of 100 per cent pensioners'.[475] Rather than modify the scale of assessment the committee favoured the introduction of a new flat-rate supplement to disablement pension.

Entitlement arises if a 100 per cent disablement pension is payable and two other conditions are satisfied. These are that the claimant is entitled to a certain rate of constant attendance allowance and that the need for such attendance is of an extent and nature that it is likely to be permanent.[476] As with constant attendance allowance this condition is determined by the Secretary of State, from whose decision there is no right of appeal. No cases have been reported.

Part 7 Old cases and benefits now withdrawn

A Workmen's compensation cases

The industrial injuries scheme applies only to accidents occurring or diseases developing on or after 5 July 1948; earlier cases were governed by the Workmen's Compensation Acts. There is only a very remote chance of any new claim arising under these Acts, for even the most latent and insidious form of disease is now likely to have shown its

---

470   The *Decison Makers Guide* (DMG) (DSS, 2000) merely refers readers to the guidance in the internal Industrial Injuries Disablement Benefit (IIDB) General Topics guide.
471   Pp 698–700, above.
472   Mr J Griffiths, Minister of National Insurance, introducing the 2nd reading of the 1946 Bill in the House of Commons, 414 HC Official Report (5th series) col 278.
473   SI 1982/1408, reg 21.
474   NIA 1966, s 6.
475   The McCorquodale Committee on the Assessment of Disablement (1965, Cmnd 2847).
476   SSCBA 1992, s 105(1)(b).

effects.[477] However, rights which have been established under the earlier legislation are still important. This is because the value of workmen's compensation has been increased in order to bring the benefits more into line with those of the present industrial injuries scheme.

For this to be done no further contributions have been required from the employers or private insurers who originally paid for workmen's compensation. Instead, extra funds have been made available by the state to provide either a supplement to existing benefit, or an entirely new benefit. The supplement increases the value of the workmen's compensation payments still being received by the claimant. By contrast the new benefit is available to those who have contracted certain diseases attributable to employment before 5 July 1948 and who have never received workmen's compensation. These benefits can be claimed under the Industrial Injuries and Diseases (Old Cases) Act 1975 and its regulations.[478] There are few recipients and the number is, of course, declining.[479]

B   Reduced earnings allowance

i   Objective and history

Reduced earnings allowance was a major feature of the industrial scheme until it was withdrawn in respect of any accident or disease occurring after the end of September 1990.[480] Whereas disablement benefit provides compensation for personal injury – a 'loss of faculty' – irrespective of its effect upon earnings, reduced earnings allowance provided for the loss of earning capacity. That is, it compensated for injury to pocket consequent upon injury to person. From the very beginning of the industrial injuries scheme there was confusion about the role and nature of disablement benefit. In the debates on the proposals for the new scheme the government felt that it was, in part, an instrument for income replacement,[481] and it was believed that for most workers it would provide compensation at a higher level than a wage-related benefit.[482] The original Industrial Injuries Bill, therefore, made no provision for lost earnings. However, during its passage, it was criticised because it offered insufficient protection to workers who suffered a relatively minor disablement which, nevertheless, prevented them from pursuing their regular occupation.[483] As a result, at the last minute an allowance was added to compensate for such a loss. In a side heading to the Act it was described as payable 'in case of special hardship', revealing the intention to compensate only where there was a disproportionate loss of income. 'Special hardship' continued to be used to describe the allowance until it was renamed (and technically made a benefit in its own right) in 1986.[484] The old name was quite inappropriate because the original intention

---

477   A case in point might be the asbestos-related cancer mesothelioma, for which latency periods of more than 50 years have been reported: *Wikeley* n 45, above, p 29.
478   SI 1982/1489 and SI 1983/136. See *Lewis* n 30, above, pp 263–266.
479   In 1999 just 488 supplementary allowances were in payment according to the DSS *Social Security Statistics 1999* (1999) Table F4.01. The number had fallen by nearly three-quarters in ten years.
480   SSA 1990, s 3.
481   See the Commons' debate on *Social Insurance Part II* 404 HC Official Report (5th series) cols 1396–1397.
482   *Social Insurance Part II* n 481, above, p 17. For more detail see the 2nd edition of this book, pp 297–298.
483   413 HC Official Report (5th series) cols 1589–1590. The example frequently given was that of a compositor who suffered the loss of an index finger.
484   See *Chief Adjudication Officer v Maguire* [1999] 2 All ER 859, holding that a claim for special hardship allowance survived the repeal of SSA 1975.

was soon forgotten, and the allowance was available for any loss of pre-accident earning capacity, no matter how small; it was never necessary for a disproportionate earnings loss to be suffered.

ii Entitlement

The basic conditions for entitlement[485] are that the relevant accident or disease must pre-date September 1990 and the claimant must be:

(a) ... entitled to a disablement pension or would be so entitled if that pension were payable where disablement is assessed at not less than 1 per cent; and

(b) as a result of the relevant loss of faculty, he is either—
    (i) incapable, and likely to remain permanently incapable, of following his regular occupation; and
    (ii) incapable of following employment of an equivalent standard which is suitable in his case,

or is, and has at all times since the end of the period [of 15 weeks after the accident or onset of the disease] been, incapable of following that occupation or any such employment.

Entitlement to reduced earnings allowance could therefore arise even though the claimant's disablement was assessed as less than 14 per cent and therefore too low to found entitlement to a disablement pension. In addition, it had to be shown that the injury made the claimant incapable of following his or her regular occupation, or any other suitable occupation which offered equivalent pay. For example, a coal face worker injured in an accident, or diagnosed as suffering from pneumoconiosis, might be forced to accept lighter, less well paid work above ground. The allowance could then be claimed based on the difference in remuneration, although in practice there was a maximum amount payable that prevented 90 per cent of recipients from obtaining their full wage loss.[486] The legislation gave rise to many appeals and a very large number of Commissioners' decisions. Reference should be made to other texts if detailed guidance is required either about entitlement to the allowance or about calculating the amount payable.[487]

iii Reform and eventual withdrawal

The allowance generated more criticism and difficulties than any other aspect of the industrial injuries scheme and was the subject of several investigations and reform proposals.[488] The formulation of the law, in terms of different standards of remuneration for categories of occupation or employment, created great complexity and uncertainty. This meant that claimants were disadvantaged because they rarely

---

485 SSCBA 1992, Sch 7, para 11(1).
486 *Industrial Injuries Compensation* n 35, above, para 3.43. The maximum was 40 per cent of the maximum weekly disablement benefit.
487 See *Social Security Legislation 2001* n 363, above, vol I; and also *Lewis* n 30, above, ch 7 for the background.
488 Fourth Report of the Ministry of National Insurance (1953, Cmnd 8882) pp 29–30; *Pearson Report* n 32, above, pp 176–178 and Annex 6; *Industrial Injuries Compensation* pp 29–42; *Reform of the Industrial Injuries Scheme* ch 4; and *Brown* n 28, above, ch 11.

had access to the evidence required for the issues of entitlement and calculation. In addition, high administrative costs were incurred by the DSS in periodically ascertaining not only the claimant's current pattern of earnings but also what would have been earned if employment had continued in the regular occupation – which might no longer exist.

Various reforms and proposals for reform were made following the DSS review in 1980 and the White Paper published two years later. They culminated in the withdrawal of the allowance in 1990. However, important changes were made before that was done. For example, in order to simplify the calculation of the earnings loss on the third and subsequent renewals, wage levels were indexed to inflation.[489] In addition, as discussed below in relation to retirement allowance, entitlement was ended for those reaching retirement age after 9 April 1989. Although entitlement was preserved for life for those who had already retired by that date, the amount of the allowance for such recipients was frozen.[490] Reduced earnings allowance was also withdrawn for injuries occurring after September 1990. The government's main reason for doing so was that the savings could be used to help finance a package of new benefits to improve the position of disabled people as a whole.[491] It also suggested that the allowance overlapped with invalidity benefit.[492] However, there was no overlap where the claimant was still working but had reduced earnings. The IIAC strongly opposed withdrawal, claiming that the allowance had: 'enabled employees in the early stages of the potentially crippling or even fatal occupational disease to move to a safer [less well paid] job. It is vital to retain such a measure which acts to protect the individual from further harm.'[493] There is now no earnings-related element in the industrial scheme for new claims, but, as a result of the protection for existing claimants there continue to be 152,000 recipients of the allowance.[494] However, a single day's gap in entitlement will bring any preserved rights to this allowance to an end.

It is to be regretted that, given the time spent in considering reform, little effort was made to investigate how foreign legal systems deal with the same problems. The typical European scheme combines a scale of disablement with a multiplicand based upon the claimant's earning potential.[495] Thus, for 100 per cent disablement there is an effective indemnity of total earning capacity, subject to a maximum amount. For lesser degrees of disablement the figure is reduced on a proportionate basis, so that eg for 30 per cent disablement, the injured worker receives a pension based on 30 per cent of the pre-accident earning capacity. The failure to consider models of this kind was all the more reprehensible given that the Pearson Commission specifically urged that it be done.[496]

489   SSCBA 1992, Sch 7, para 11(13) and SI 1987/415.
490   SSCBA 1992, Sch 7, para 12.
491   165 HC Official Report (6th series) col 630.
492   *The Way Ahead – Benefits For Disabled People* (1990, Cm 917).
493   *The Industrial Injuries Scheme And Reform Of Disability Income* (1990) p 11.
494   DWP *Work and Pension Statistics 2001* (2001) p 179, Table 5. This figure includes payments of retirement allowance (a condition of eligibility for which is prior entitlement to reduced earnings allowance; see below).
495   *MISSOC 2001* n 85, above, Table VIII *Benefits* 2.5; invariably a more complex formula is used to provide higher rates for the more seriously disabled.
496   *Pearson Report* n 32, above, para 820. The proposal extended beyond the industrial scheme which, perhaps, helps to explain the government's failure to respond.

C Retirement allowance

Reduced earnings allowance was ended for those who retired,[497] or were deemed to retire,[498] after 9 April 1989.[499] This was to end the apparent anomaly whereby compensation for lost earning capacity continued even when work would no longer have been done. However, failure to provide in retirement for those who had suffered earnings losses during their working lives penalised those who would have received a bigger earnings-related pension had it not been for their industrial injury. To compensate for this loss, on their retirement, instead of receiving reduced earnings allowance, claimants were able to obtain a new benefit – retirement allowance.[500] Claimants had to be over pensionable age, have given up regular employment and have been previously entitled to at least £2 a week in reduced earnings allowance.

The allowance cannot exceed 10 per cent of the current maximum weekly rate of disablement benefit or 25 per cent of the rate of reduced earnings allowance previously in payment, whichever is the lower. Although payable for the rest of the claimant's life, it will decline in value because it is frozen at the amount fixed at the date of retirement. No entitlement will arise in respect of accidents or diseases occurring after September 1990 because, as discussed above, there will then be no entitlement to reduced earnings allowance.

D Death benefit

WCA 1897 made provision for those wholly or partly dependent on the victim of a fatal industrial accident. It took the form of a lump sum, based on the deceased's earnings but subject to a statutory maximum,[501] and, after 1923, a children's allowance.[502] In devising the new scheme in 1944, the government accepted the arguments for industrial death benefit but was not attracted by the lump sum method of compensation.[503] It therefore introduced a pension analogous to that payable to non-industrial widows: an initial high flat-rate benefit for the first six months, which would thereafter fall to a lower level.[504] More money was payable if the widow had to care for children or was otherwise deemed incapable of joining the labour market.

Industrial death benefit was more generous than the general National Insurance provisions in a number of respects: the standard widow's pension was paid at a higher rate; a small permanent pension was payable to a childless widow under 40; benefit was paid for children independently of the widow's entitlement (and thus could continue after she had remarried) and also, under highly restrictive conditions,[505] to widowers

---

497 This means that women lose their reduced earnings allowance at the age of 60, five years before men. See Case C-196/98 *Hepple v Adjudication Officer* [2000] All ER (EC) 513, ECJ (also reported as *R(I) 2/00*).
498 The statutory formulation is 'gives up regular employment', a term widened by SI 1996/425. See further *Plummer and Hammond v Chief Adjudication Officer*, reported as an Appendix to *R(I) 2/99*.
499 SSCBA 1992, Sch 7, para 13(1).
500 SSCBA 1992, Sch 7, para 13(2).
501 WCA 1897, Sch 1, para 1(a)(i).
502 WCA 1923, s 2(a).
503 *Social Insurance Part II* n 481, above, para 30; cf *Beveridge Report* n 15, above, para 34 (proposal for a lump sum grant to supplement benefits paid under the non-industrial scheme).
504 NI(II)A 1946, ss 19–24, re-enacted as SSA 1975, ss 67–75, on which see the 2nd edition of this book, pp 331–336.
505 So restrictive that in 1980 only one widower's pension was being paid: *Industrial Injuries Compensation* n 35, above, para 5.26.

and other dependents; and a widow could accumulate her pension with income maintenance benefits (eg sickness or unemployment benefit).

Support for these particular features of the industrial preference was, however, never very strong and successive governments allowed the real value of many of the advantages to be eroded by inflation so that when the Pearson Commission reviewed the matter in 1978, the standard industrial widow's pension was only 55p higher than that payable under the general scheme. The Commission felt that the financial provision for dependants should not vary according to the cause of death and recommended that industrial death benefit be abolished.[506] The government, mindful of the high cost of administering the benefit relative to the marginal advantages it conferred, agreed[507] and implemented the proposal with effect from April 1988.[508] However, the fact that a death after that date resulted from an industrial accident or disease may still be relevant in a few cases since, in that event, a widow may gain entitlement to appropriate benefits under the general scheme in spite of an insufficient contribution record.[509]

E   Unemployability supplement

The purpose of this supplement to a disablement pension was to provide benefit for the few industrial injury victims who lacked sufficient National Insurance contributions to qualify for sickness benefit. The supplement was abolished in 1982 when the contribution requirements were eased to enable industrial injury victims to gain entitlement to sickness benefit.[510]

F   Hospital treatment allowance

The main objective of this supplement to disablement benefit was to encourage workers to obtain in-patient treatment for their industrial injury by providing increased benefit at a time when wages might be lost. It increased the pension to that payable for 100 per cent disablement. However, with the improvement in benefits for sickness and in the coverage provided by occupational schemes, the benefit was no longer thought necessary. It was abolished except for those who began to receive in-patient treatment before 6 April 1987.[511]

---

506   *Pearson Report* n 32, above, paras 835–844. However, somewhat inconsistently, it also suggested that entitlement to the full earnings-related component in the general scheme should be accelerated for industrial widows. For criticism, see Ogus, Corfield and Harris (1978) 7 ILJ 143 at 150–151.

507   *Reform of the Industrial Injuries Scheme* n 37, above, ch 6, following the review in *Industrial Injuries Compensation* n 35, above, ch 5.

508   SSA 1986, Sch 3, paras 8, 11. Protection for those entitled on the date of abolition is maintained by SSCB 1992, Sch 7, Pt VI. In 1999 there were 16,000 industrial widow's pensions in payment, as compared with 30,000 in 1984: DWP *Work and Pension Statistics 2001* (2001) p 183m, Table 1.

509   SSCBA 1992, s 60(2).

510   SSCBA 1992, s 102. For the position of those in receipt of the allowance before 6 April 1987, see Sch 7, Pt 1.

511   SSCBA 1992, Sch 7, Pt III. Before its withdrawal it was of little significance, being received only by about 100 people at any one time and adding only £200,000 a year to the industrial preference.

Chapter 21

War pensions

Part 1   Introduction

A   General

War pensions are almost certainly the most ancient type of state benefit. They existed in classical Greek and Roman times,[1] and in Great Britain their history has been traced back to the days of King Alfred.[2] The first statutory provisions, for payment of benefit to soldiers and sailors from the local rates, can be found in measures at the end of the sixteenth century.[3] The explanation for this rich heritage is not hard to discover: it has generally been thought right to make special provision for those injured, and also for the relatives of those killed, in the service of their country.

In terms of critical analysis and policy discussion, the war pension scheme is the most neglected area of social security law.[4] In the 1980s and 1990s the analogous scheme for industrial injuries was the subject of a major scrutiny and substantial reform but war pensions remained largely unaltered during the latter half of the twentieth century. The unwillingness to disturb the status quo may be due in part to the comparative absence of armed conflict since 1945 and a consequent reduction in the number of pensioners.[5] A second explanation may lie in the peculiarly emotive character of the subject – until recently the special position and privileges of those maimed or killed in the service of their country has not been questioned.[6] Thirdly, it was only in 1978 that the scheme was regulated by statutory instrument and thus became subject to parliamentary scrutiny; traditionally, as part of the Royal Prerogative, it was legally exclusively within the control of the Crown and thus in practice a matter for executive or administrative decision.

1   Cf Schneider *Das Problem der Veteranenversorgung in der späten römischen Republik* (1977).
2   49(1) *Halsbury's Laws* (4th edn, reissue) para 665, n 1.
3   Eg 35 Eliz 1 c 4 (1592–93); 39 Eliz 1 c 21 (1597–98); 43 Eliz 1 c 3 (1601).
4   It was ignored in the Report on Social Security Provision for Chronically Sick and Disabled People (1973–74, HC 276) and the White Paper *The Way Ahead: Benefits for Disabled People* (1990, Cm 917).
5   In 2000, 292,980 pensions were in payment, compared with over one million in 1950: DSS *Social Security Statistics 2000* (2000) p 206, Table 1. This does, however, represent a modest increase on the 252,000 in payment in 1989.
6   Cf Standing Committee B Debates on the Social Security Benefits Bill 1975, col 145. Cp the extensive literature on the 'industrial preference': ch 20, p 717, above.

In this introductory part of the chapter, there is an outline of the modern history of war pensions and an examination of the reasons for their special position in the social security system. Parts 2 and 3 are respectively concerned with the rules regarding entitlement to, and the assessment of, war pensions. Part 4 deals with those payable on the death of a member of the forces, and Part 5 with some miscellaneous rules. Part 6 discusses very shortly other comparable schemes providing pensions for persons outside the regular forces. Administrative and adjudicatory aspects are dealt with in chapters 5 and 6, above, respectively. This chapter is not concerned with pensions paid by the armed forces themselves, or with other compensation schemes for disablement or death available to service personnel and their families.[7]

B History

During the early nineteenth century, the Commissioners of the Chelsea Hospital were responsible for the award of disability pensions to soldiers wounded in combat.[8] From 1846 payment of pensions was made by the Secretary of State for War. Provision for widows and children dates from the institution of the Patriotic Fund in 1854.[9] During the later part of the century entitlement to pensions was regulated by the terms of the Royal Warrants in the case of soldiers, and by Orders in Council in the case of navy personnel and marines. The Boer War was responsible for a further development: for the first time, disease attributable to war service was compensated in the same way as physical injury.

War pensions became a crucial problem in the course of the First World War. Many changes were made in the rules concerning entitlement to pensions, and also, and perhaps more importantly, with regard to their administration. In this latter respect these changes have for the most part survived the last 50 years, so that despite the improvements to the system during the Second World War, the years 1914–18 were perhaps the most influential in the development of war pensions.

In 1914, pensions were administered by four authorities: the Chelsea Commissioners, the War Office, the Admiralty Commissioners (for navy pensions) and the Royal Patriotic Fund Corporation. Considerable disquiet was expressed at this dispersal of authority and there was criticism that decisions on entitlement were not subject to any appeal and that no minister was answerable for them. The mischief suggested its own remedy. Responsibility was transferred to a new Ministry of Pensions.[10] From that time, decisions were taken in the name of the Minister, and shortly afterwards an appeal tribunal was formally constituted.[11] Legislation passed at the end of the First World War established a legal right to receive a war pension, once it had been awarded by the minister.[12] With regard to the conditions of entitlement, the major changes were: a disability aggravated by war service (as distinct from one attributable to service) attracted a full pension instead of the previous four-fifths award; and a claim could be made by a widow in respect of the death of her husband which was not in itself attributable to war service, provided that he was then in receipt of a pension.[13] The principal alteration in the rules

---

7   Eg the Criminal Injuries Compensation (Overseas) Scheme, introduced in 1979: see *R v Ministry of Defence, ex p Walker* [2000] 1 WLR 806.
8   See further Lin (2000) 7 Social Politics 5.
9   The Patriotic Fund was put on a statutory basis by the Patriotic Fund Reorganisation Act 1903.
10   Ministry of Pensions Act 1916, s 2.
11   War Pensions (Administrative Provisions) Act 1919, s 8.
12   War Pensions (Administrative Provisions) Act 1919, s 7; War Pensions Act 1920, s 8. See also Pensions Appeal Tribunals Act 1943, s 11.
13   The changes were introduced by the Royal Warrant 1917.

of assessment made during the same period was that pensions were from then on to be assessed with regard to the degree of *physical disability itself* rather than the loss of earning capacity. Alternative pensions, as they were then known, could be awarded to compensate for the claimant's loss of earning capacity.

Claims for a disability pension in respect of service after 30 September 1921 were transferred back to the Chelsea Commissioners and the other authorities which had administered them in 1914.[14] The outbreak of the Second World War, and the consequent increase in claims, necessitated the retransfer of administration to the Ministry of Pensions which, with its departmental successors (now the Department for Work and Pensions (DWP)), remained responsible for war pensions until June 2001.[15]

From 1939 criticism of the entitlement rules mounted and several changes were made in response. By far the most important was the imposition in some cases of the burden of proof on the Ministry to show that the disablement was neither attributable to, nor aggravated by, service. The claimant was given the benefit of any doubt on this question.[16] Another change enabled claims to be made more than seven years after the termination of the service, though here the claimant has to satisfy an initial evidential burden.[17]

The Royal Warrants issued during this war limited entitlement to injuries due to *war* service. By the Warrant of 1949 pensions could be awarded for disablement occasioned in peace-time service, and, with some qualifications, service in the Territorial and Reserve Forces.[18] Another major development was the provision of additional benefits for seriously injured servicemen and their dependants. For the most part, these mirrored provisions in the industrial injury scheme but the substantial amendments to that scheme enacted in recent years, including the abolition of lump sum payments for minor disabilities,[19] have not been followed by equivalent changes in the war pensions scheme. Nevertheless, in 1993 and 1997 steps were taken to abolish several allowances, eg additions to the basic award reflecting the rank of the disabled serviceman and those paid to non-dependent relatives.[20] These had long been recognised as anachronistic and their value had been allowed to dwindle to relatively trivial amounts.

An important structural reform took place in 1978. The scheme regulating the benefits for the three services was consolidated in a single Order in Council.[21] This (together with any amendment) is now issued as a statutory instrument, which must be laid before Parliament.[22] In April 1994 the War Pensions Agency (WPA) was launched, as an executive agency within the DSS, with responsibility for administering war disablement pensions and for providing support and welfare services.[23] Two years later the WPA also assumed the task of administering war pensions relating to service before the First World War or between September 1921 and September 1939, following the transfer of responsibility for these pensioners from the Ministry of Defence to the DSS.[24]

---

14 War Pensions Act 1920, s 1.
15 The 1939 transfer did not affect war pensions payable in respect of service either before the First World War or between 30 September 1921 and 2 September 1939; responsibility for these was transferred from the Ministry of Defence to the Department of Social Security (DSS) by SI 1996/1638 (but note below the transfer back of responsibilities in 2001).
16 A similar relaxation of the law occurred at much the same time in the US: Fitzgibbons (1945) 31 Iowa LR 1 at 13–16.
17 Royal Warrant 1964 (Cmnd 2467) art 5.
18 Royal Warrant 1949 (Cmd 7699).
19 P 752, above.
20 SI 1993/598 and 1997/286.
21 SI 1978/1525.
22 The current version is SI 1983/883, as amended.
23 The WPA also manages the Ilford Park Polish Home.
24 See SI 1996/1638, amending SI 1983/883.

The war pensions scheme now seems to be at the threshold of a period of major change. Appeal rights were rationalised by the Child Support, Pensions and Social Security Act 2000.[25] In 2001 a Minister of Veterans' Affairs was appointed for the first time and this was followed in June of the same year by the transfer of the WPA from the DWP to the Ministry of Defence (MoD). This appears to be just the prelude to further and more substantial structural reform. In March 2001 the government published a consultation paper following a joint MoD/DSS review of compensation payments, which proposed a new scheme to replace both the DWP war pensions scheme and the MoD's own Armed Forces Pension Scheme. This would include a tariff-based lump sum payment to compensate for pain and suffering and, at higher levels of the tariff, a guaranteed income to cover loss of earnings and pension.[26]

C Policy

Mention has been made of the privileged position of war pensioners. Not only is there the strong presumption in certain cases that a serviceman suffering from a disability is entitled to a pension, but the level and range of awards is wider than that afforded by other benefits for people suffering from similar disabilities. 'The Scheme is deliberately generous to claimants, is loosely worded and relies on a curious mixture of discretion and medical decision taking and aetiology.'[27] The most obvious analogy is industrial disablement benefit, which also compensates for mere disability, not necessarily related to loss of earning capacity. War pensions compare favourably with this benefit, however, in the matters of burden of proof, the absence of any requirement that the injury be attributable to an 'accident' as distinct from a continuous process of events,[28] the concept of 'war' or 'service risk' which is wider than that of 'course of employment',[29] and the range of allowances which supplement the basic disablement benefit in the two cases. While the death benefits paid to widows under the industrial injury scheme have been abolished, they have been retained at a generous level in the war scheme.

War pensioners also enjoy other advantages. War pensions are subject to a disregard for the purposes of assessing entitlement to means-tested benefits.[30] Widow's pensions are exempt from income tax[31] and the estates of those who have died from wounds inflicted during active service are exempt from inheritance tax.[32] Those leaving the service, and those widowed, after 1973 may derive additional benefits under the Armed Forces Pension scheme introduced in that year.[33] As regards those injured or killed in

---

25   See pp 211–213, above.
26   See MoD *Joint Compensation Review: A consultation document* (2001). Existing war pensioners and those whose disablement is the result of injuries sustained before the implementation date for the new scheme would continue to be covered by the present arrangements. On the background to the review, see HC Social Security Committee *Sixth Report* (1998–99, HC 377) paras 25–27.
27   Ernst & Young *War Pension Agency: Review of Decision Making and Appeals Process – Final Report* (1999) p 2. See also *MoD* n 26, above: 'This generosity means that War Pensions are sometimes lawfully awarded for conditions only tenuously linked to service': p 13.
28   Cf for industrial injuries, pp 722–726, above.
29   Cf pp 729–737, above.
30   See p 458, above.
31   Income and Corporation Taxes Act 1988, s 318.
32   Inheritance Tax Act 1984, s 154.
33   Brown *The Disability Income System* (1984) p 65; Richardson *Widows Benefits* (1984) pp 69–70. Since 1990, weekly payments have been made to those widowed before 1973 to compensate for their lack of entitlement under the scheme. See now SI 1994/1906.

the Falklands campaign in 1982, charitable donations are available from the South Atlantic Fund.[34] Moreover, the system of cash benefits is complemented by a welfare service to help war pensioners and widows with problems.[35] This reflects a general policy of care and concern which is not matched elsewhere in the social security system and which is epitomised in the following statement, made in 1950.

> The award of a pension by the Department entitles the individual to more than merely the payment of a sum of money. It gives him a passport to the goodwill of a large Government Service, to the benefit of a sympathetic interest in his affairs and to such help as may be given or obtained for him in the solving of his problems. It entitles him to believe that nothing which should be his is held back ...[36]

Two explanations may be adduced for the traditional preferences given to war pensioners. In the first place, the force of popular sentiment cannot be overestimated. It is this which was responsible for the frequency of parliamentary debates and questions in both wars. In the First World War the facts that the numbers involved were so large, and that frequently the wounded or killed would be conscripts, reinforced the general feeling that those disabled and their families should be generously treated.[37] This political factor has been reinforced by the pressure exerted by the British Legion (now the Royal British Legion) and other ex-servicemen's organisations. The enduring force of this lobby has been reflected in recent years in measures such as the Pensions Act 1995[38] and the Hong Kong (War Wives and Widows) Act 1996.[39]

The second argument is based on the fact that, as a result of the Crown Proceedings Act 1947, servicemen had, in general, no rights of action in tort against the Crown for injuries sustained during the course of that service,[40] and thus their position was distinguishable from that of employees injured in an industrial accident who might have a tort claim against the employer. The provision has now been repealed,[41] though without retrospective effect,[42] so that only a small number of war pensioners will be able to benefit. Nevertheless, the argument does not seem convincing. It is not obvious why greater state provision should be made for those whose common law rights of action are excluded by special defences, whether statutory or common law, than for those who never have any right at all.

---

34 The 138 women widowed as a result of the campaign each received an average of £40,000 in addition to their war pensions: *Richardson* n 33, above, pp 71–72.
35 'The role of the WPA Welfare Service requires clarification. Currently they are acting as something between a pseudo ex-service organisation and a social worker, but they appear to work independently of the WPA': *Ernst & Young* n 27, above, p 36.
36 Annual Report 1949–50 of Ministry of Pensions (1950) p 1, quoted in *Brown* n 33, above, p 48.
37 Cf Mr R Whitney MP, Under-Secretary of State for Heath and Social Security, 80 HC Official Report (6th series) col 1118.
38 Cf p 787, below.
39 The 1996 Act conferred British citizenship on some 50 female residents of Hong Kong who were the wives or widows of men who had fought in defence of Hong Kong during the Second World War. The women were thus able to acquire British citizenship without fulfilling British residency requirements.
40 S 10, on which see *Pearce v Secretary of State for Defence* [1988] AC 755, [1988] 2 All ER 348.
41 Crown Proceedings (Armed Forces) Act 1987, s 1.
42 See further *Matthews v Ministry of Defence* [2002] EWCA (Civ) 773, [2002] 3 All ER 513, CA.

Part 2   Entitlement

A   General

The fundamental principle under the Naval, Military and Air Forces etc (Disablement and Death) Service Pensions Order 1983 (the Service Pensions Order) is that war pension 'awards may be made ... where the disablement or death of a member of the armed forces is due to service'.[43] The use of the permissive '*may*' is deliberate and reflects the origins of the scheme in the Royal Prerogative: strictly speaking, and rather anachronistically, the Secretary of State is under no obligation to carry out the provisions of the Order beyond the duty he owes to the Sovereign.[44] However, once an award has been made the claimant has a statutory right to receive it.[45]

There must be some causal connection between the disablement or death and service; it is not enough that either occurred *during* service. During the Second World War the principle was defended by government on the ground that to treat indiscriminately all disablement arising during service would be to do less than justice to those whose injury or illness was genuinely due to the dangers and risks of service.[46] Given, as we shall see, the more generous criteria of eligibility introduced towards the end of the war and their interpretation by the relevant authorities, the principle is no longer controversial. It should also be noted that the award of a war pension is not dependent upon service in the armed forces during wartime; pensions are also payable in respect of disablement or death arising out of peacetime service. In addition, there are analogous schemes covering civilians, as well as merchant seamen and Polish Forces serving under British command during the Second World War.[47]

Article 4 of the Service Pensions Order sets out the basic conditions for entitlement to a pension on a claim in respect of disablement brought within seven years of the end of the member's service; or when the death of a member occurs within that period, whenever the claim is brought. In such circumstances, the disablement or death is:

> accepted as due to service ... provided it is certified that—
> (a)   the disablement is due to an injury which—
>   (i)   is attributable to service; or
>   (ii) existed before or arose during service and has been and remains aggravated thereby; or
> (b)   the death was due to or hastened by—
>   (i)   an injury which was attributable to service; or
>   (ii) the aggravation by service of an injury which existed before or arose during service.

Article 5 is concerned with entitlement when the claim for disablement is brought, or the death occurs, more than seven years after termination of service. The principles governing the issue of a certificate are the same as those in article 4 except in three important respects. The first relates to the burden of proof: for claims under article 5, the onus of proving that the disablement or death was due to service is initially on the serviceman, while under article 4 it is for the Secretary of State to rebut the presumption

---

43   SI 1983/883, art 3. On making a claim see further arts 3A–3D.
44   *Griffin v Lord Advocate* 1950 SC 448 at 450, per Lord Sorn.
45   Pensions Appeal Tribunals Act 1943, s 11.
46   White Paper *Changes in War Pensions* (1943, Cmd 6459).
47   Pp 790–791, below.

of this causal link.[48] Secondly, for the purposes of article 5 it must be certified that 'the death was due to or *substantially* hastened by' an injury attributable to or aggravated by service.[49] Thirdly, while both articles cover only cases of disablement attributable to, or aggravated by, service since 2 September 1939,[50] article 5 provides that an award may be made in respect of death more than seven years after the end of service, irrespective of the date of that service.

B Disablement

'Disablement' means physical or mental injury or damage, or the loss of physical or mental capacity.[51] A successful claim may, therefore, be made for acute hysteria or neurosis, provided, of course, that it is attributable to, or aggravated by, service.[52] 'Injury' is defined as including 'wound or disease'.[53] There is virtually no limit, therefore, to the quality or type of impairment which may entitle the claimant to a war pension,[54] though many difficult cases naturally concern claims in respect of illness and disease where the causation issue is complex.[55] In the late 1980s and early 1990s there was a flood of claims for deafness alleged to have resulted from service[56] and, to stem the tide, the Service Pensions Order has been amended so that awards can no longer be made for noise-induced sensorineural hearing loss if the degree of disablement is less than 20 per cent.[57] Equally controversial was the change in assessment practice in 1996, as a result of which pensions are no longer increased as overall hearing loss increased with age.[58] Further, awards can no longer be made for an injury resulting from the use of tobacco or the consumption of alcohol, unless as a result of service the claimant suffers from a mental condition, giving rise to a degree of disablement of at least 50 per cent, and the use of tobacco or consumption of alcohol was a consequence of that condition.[59]

Given the broad definition of 'disablement', it has been held that claimants may be entitled in respect of their injuries, even though they have not suffered any loss of capacity for work or the enjoyment of life.[60] In this case, however, a nil assessment will

---

48 Pp 778–780, below.

49 P 780, below.

50 Claims for disablement in the 1914–1918 war, of which there are very few, are brought under the Royal Warrants of 1919 (Cmd 457) and 1920 (Cmd 811).

51 SI 1983/883, Sch 4, Item 22.

52 Cf the more restrictive position under the civilians' scheme, where recovery is limited to personal injuries, p 791, below.

53 SI 1983/883, Sch 4, Item 27.

54 Cf the prescribed list of diseases and occupations under the industrial injuries scheme: pp 743–749, above.

55 There must, however, be some causal connection: thus a serviceman's peptic ulcer and other illnesses could not be attributed to the nutritional deprivation suffered by prisoners of war in the Far East in the absence of some evidence to raise a reasonable doubt to that effect: *Sanderson v Secretary of State for Social Services* (20 July 1995, unreported). Cases involving former service personnel who participated in nuclear test programmes in Australia and the South Pacific and who subsequently contracted eg leukaemia have proved particularly problematic: see 349 HC Official Report (6th series) cols 496W–498W.

56 Approximately 100,000 of 180,000 claims for a disablement award made in 1991–92 related to this condition: Committee of Public Accounts *27th Report* (1992–93, HC 339) para 9. See also *HC Social Security Committee* n 26, above, Minutes of Evidence.

57 SI 1983/883, art 8(2A), inserted by SI 1992/3208.

58 See *HC Social Security Committee* n 26, above, Supplementary memorandum WPA 8, paras 5.1–5.12.

59 SI 1983/883, Sch 4, Item 27. The amendment, effected by SI 1994/772, was designed to reverse a High Court decision awarding a pension to a widow whose husband died of lung cancer: *Hunt v Secretary of State for Social Services* (21 December 1993, unreported).

60 *Harris v Minister of Pensions* [1948] 1 KB 422, [1948] 1 All ER 191.

be made until the time when the injury causes a loss of flexibility or movement in the injured limb, or some other handicap.

Occasionally the question arises whether a particular disease is a separate phenomenon from another injury or illness for which a claim has already been made.[61] If an acute anxiety state is brought about by worry over a disease, in respect of which a pension is already being paid, the appropriate course is to apply for an increase in the assessment for the first disease, not to make an entirely new claim.[62] The test would appear to be whether the further condition is a separate disease rather than part of the accepted illness or injury.

C 'Attributable to service'

i General principles

A war pension will be awarded if it is certified that the disablement or death is due to service in the armed forces. This is a question of fact, but the nominated judge will allow an appeal by either the claimant or the Secretary of State if the appeal tribunal has applied the wrong principles of law in arriving at its decision.[63] A tribunal makes a mistake of law if it holds that a particular injury or type of disease cannot be attributable to war service merely because a previous decision of the judge in another case was to the effect that that injury or disease was not then attributable to service.[64] In each case the Secretary of State (or medical decision maker) and, on appeal the tribunal, must consider all the circumstances, and must not be bound by previous decisions regarding the same type of injury.

The court's attitude on questions of attributability has been shown clearly in the cases dealing with the issue whether it should be held that a disease or neurosis was attributable to service when the soldier's pre-existing temperament or disposition made him especially vulnerable to it. The court has consistently held that where service brought on a disease, which did not exist before, it was attributable to the service; only if the soldier's condition before service actually amounted to the illness in question, albeit a latent illness, could it be held that the service merely aggravated the injury.[65] Denning J stated the principle to be as follows:

> The task of the Minister and of the tribunal is to ascertain what are the causes of the arising of the disease, not to assess their relative potency. If one of the causes is war service the disease is attributable to war service, even though there may be other causes and, it may be, more powerful causes, operating, and to which it is also attributable.[66]

The court's refusal to evaluate the relative weight of service and other factors in bringing about the disablement, coupled with the fact that the onus of proof is on the Secretary of State in those cases where the claim is brought, or the death occurs, within seven

---

61   Eg *Secretary of State for Social Services v Yates* (1969) 5 WPAR 765. (The War Pensions Appeal Reports (WPAR) were available for consultation at the DSS, though they are not published.)
62   *Goodman JA v Minister of Pensions* (1951) 5 WPAR 13. See Parliamentary Commissioner for Administration *5th Report* (1972–73, HC 406) Case No C33/T.
63   *Horsfall v Minister of Pensions* (1944) 1 WPAR 7. Cf pp 211–213, below.
64   See *Freeman v Minister of Pensions and National Insurance* [1966] 2 All ER 40, [1966] 1 WLR 456 (suicide); *Kincaid v Minister of Pensions* (1948) 2 WPAR 1423 (leukaemia).
65   Eg *Baird v Minister of Pensions* (1946) 1 WPAR 169; *O'Neill v Minister of Pensions* (1947) 1 WPAR 839. For the similar principles in industrial injuries cases, see p 725, above.
66   *Marshall v Minister of Pensions* [1948] 1 KB 106 at 109.

years of the end of service, has meant that in practice the criteria for entitlement are generous. On the other hand, the court has been aware that the law does not embody the maxim, 'fit for service, fit for pension', so that in a number of circumstances a pension has been refused although the disability arose during the claimant's period of service. Three types of cases have proved particularly difficult.

ii Anxiety states

In the first, the question has been whether an acute anxiety state was attributable to service. In one decision it was held that the strain of hard training, followed by the worry induced by orders for foreign service, might well be the precipitating cause of the claimant's acute neurosis, although there was medical evidence to the effect that he had an unstable personality.[67] On the other hand, in two cases, the nominated judge, Denning J, held that the claimant's worry about his wife's relations with other men while he was in the army, leading in both cases to acute neurosis, could not be held attributable on the facts to service.[68] The husband's enforced separation from his wife was not the cause, but only the circumstance in which the real cause of the illness, the wife's conduct, operated. It is not easy to reconcile these cases, and the latter two decisions may be thought wrongly decided in the light of Denning J's principle set out earlier.

iii Suicide

The second difficult question is whether suicide can be said to be caused by service in the forces. In *XY v Minister of Pensions*:[69]

> the deceased's fiancée attempted to persuade him to marry her while he was on embarkation leave. He refused, and shortly after his return to service, she wrote calling off the engagement; he then shot himself. Denning J held that the tribunal was right not to attribute the death to service.

However, in another decision,[70] it was held that the suicide was so attributable; the deceased took his life because of the pain and anxiety resulting from a disability which was itself due to service. Edmund Davies J emphasised that each case should be decided on its own facts, and that there is no rule of law prohibiting a suicide's dependants claiming a war pension.

iv Claimant on leave

The third line of cases occurs when the serviceman is injured or killed when on leave, or temporarily away from camp.[71] This has been the topic of political debate as well as

---

67 *Hollorn v Minister of Pensions* [1947] 1 All ER 124.
68 *W v Minister of Pensions* [1946] 2 All ER 501; *R J v Minister of Pensions* (1947) 1 WPAR 351.
69 [1947] 1 All ER 38, followed in *Miers v Minister of Pensions* (1964) 5 WPAR 673. See also *Wedderspoon v Minister of Pensions* [1947] KB 562 and *Monaghan v Minister of Pensions* (1947) 1 WPAR 971.
70 *Freeman v Minister of Pensions and National Insurance* [1966] 2 All ER 40, [1966] 1 WLR 456.
71 There are analogous problems in the industrial injuries scheme, when the accident occurs while the employee is travelling, pp 732–735, above.

legal argument. The 1943 White Paper[72] stated that the Ministry of Pensions would relax its attitude to claims in respect of accidents occasioned outside the serviceman's place of duty; it would in future treat accidents sustained in the soldier's spare time, or while he was travelling to and from home on short leave, or when he was travelling between his place of duty and privately arranged accommodation (if he were allowed to live out) as attributable to war service. But an injury or illness arising during a period of full leave would not be treated as so attributable. The nominated judge, however, has pointed out that question of attributability must be decided solely on the facts in the light of the legal provisions. Thus, a bicycling accident suffered on the claimant's day off,[73] and an accident at the claimant's home where, owing to a lack of room in the barracks, he was billeted,[74] have both been held not to be attributable to service. On the other hand, in two cases the judge held that an injury while on full leave was so attributable. In the first,[75] Denning J held that the injury suffered by a soldier who shot himself in the left foot while cleaning his rifle on embarkation leave was attributable to war service; in the second,[76] Ormerod J decided that the appellant shot in the back with a blank cartridge by some cadets on shooting practice was entitled to a pension, although the incident occurred while he was on leave; the decisive fact was that he was required to wear uniform which may have created the impression in the cadets' minds that he was involved in their exercise!

v   Miscellaneous cases

The court has had less difficulty in other situations. Injuries occasioned by playing a game for the serviceman's own amusement are not attributable to service,[77] nor are injuries resulting from private fights between soldiers[78] or from assaults by third parties entirely unrelated to the military character of the victim.[79] But even if the initial injury is not attributable to service, negligent treatment in hospital will enable the claimant to be considered for a pension, if he went to that particular hospital because he was a serviceman, rather than merely because it was the nearest available.[80]

vi   Critique

It is difficult to detect any clear principle or policy running through these decisions, despite the attempt by the nominated judges, particularly Denning J, to formulate one. On the one hand, they have been concerned to award a pension when the service has any real causal connection with the injury or disease but, on the other hand, they have carefully refrained from holding a claimant entitled merely because the service was a cause (*causa sine qua non*) of the disablement. The case law sometimes resembles in its apparent inconsistency the decisions of the Commissioners interpreting the 'out of and in the course of employment' test for entitlement to industrial injuries benefit.[81]

---

72   *Changes in War Pensions* (Cmd 6459).
73   *Standen v Minister of Pensions* (1947) 1 WPAR 905.
74   *Ridley v Minister of Pensions* [1947] 2 All ER 437.
75   *Williams v Minister of Pensions* [1947] 2 All ER 564.
76   *Giles v Minister of Pensions* (1955) 5 WPAR 445.
77   *Horsfall v Minister of Pensions* (1944) 1 WPAR 7; cf, on industrial injuries, p 731, above.
78   *Richards v Minister of Pensions* (1956) 5 WPAR 631.
79   *Gaffney v Minister of Pensions* (1952) 5 WPAR 97.
80   *Minister of Pensions v Horsey* [1949] 2 KB 526, [1949] 2 All ER 314. See also *Buxton v Minister of Pensions* (1948) 1 WPAR 1121.
81   See pp 726–743, above.

The absence of such a two-limbed test in the war pensions provisions makes the reasoning less complex than in the Commissioners' rulings, but the results are often as hard to understand. In the last resort the decision depends on the court's judgment about how closely related the injury is to the incidents of service life.

D Aggravated by service

The issue as to whether the claimant is entitled to a pension because service has aggravated an injury, which is primarily attributable to other causes, only arises if it is first found that the injury was not attributable to service conditions.[82] The difference between an award on the basis of attributability and an award on the basis of aggravation is that in the former case the pension is paid as long as the disability continues, while in the latter it is payable only so long as the disability remains aggravated by the service conditions.

It must be certified that the disablement is due to an injury which 'has been *and remains aggravated*' by service.[83] The construction of this part of article 4 of the Service Pensions Order was considered in the leading case, *Shipp v Minister of Pensions*.[84] Denning J held that it did not mean that the disablement must be found to be aggravated by service at the time the claim was made, or at the date of the minister's decision. Such a construction would penalise those who made late claims or whose claims were handled slowly by the ministry; the words must be read as meaning, 'and remains aggravated or remained aggravated during the period of disablement'.[85] A claim may, therefore, be made in respect of a past disablement. However, where a claim in respect of a disablement is brought under article 5 more than seven years after the end of service, the aggravation must remain at the time the claim is made, though it need not subsist after that date.[86] In this case it is reasonable to require the aggravation to remain at this time in view of the long period which has passed since discharge from service. In all cases the tribunal is entitled to consider whether the aggravation remains at the date of the hearing before it, provided the claimant has been told that the question will be raised.[87]

The nominated judge has held that the Secretary of State and tribunal should be reluctant to conclude that the injury is no longer aggravated by service unless the evidence is quite clear.[88] The reason is that once an award on this basis has been terminated, it cannot be revived. The award should only be terminated if the claimant is in no worse a condition than before the service, or if the disease has progressed to the same extent as it would have done if there had been no service.[89] The tribunal may take into account the fact that the claimant is working full-time in coming to its conclusion whether the injury remains aggravated by service.[90]

Rather oddly, aggravation by service may occur before the onset of a disease. Thus, where the serviceman was so weakened by his period of service that he was unable to resist typhoid contracted on leave, his widow was awarded a pension.[91] The reasoning

---

82 Eg *Baird v Minister of Pensions* (1946) 1 WPAR 1121.
83 SI 1983/883, art 4(1)(a)(ii).
84 [1946] KB 386.
85 [1946] KB 386 at 390.
86 SI 1983/883, art 5(3).
87 *Ansell v Minister of Pensions* (1948) 2 WPAR 2237.
88 *Sanders v Minister of Pensions* (1948) 4 WPAR 31.
89 *Whitt v Minister of Pensions* (1947) 1 WPAR 343.
90 *Collicott v Minister of Pensions* (1948) 3 WPAR 1715.
91 *Bridge v Minister of Pensions* (1946) 1 WPAR 139.

is that the disease, though not attributable to service, was more acute because of his weakened condition.

As in attributability cases, the problem sometimes arises whether the serviceman's own responsibility for the course of action which leads to the disablement or death precludes a finding that service aggravated the injury. In *Jones v Minister of Pensions*,[92] a hard-working officer with a strong sense of duty refused to report sick. About 18 months later he died from cancer. Denning J held that the officer's conduct was a reasonable response to the pressures of war service, which was, therefore, responsible for aggravating the disease and so hastening his death.

E   Burden of proof

Before 1943 the burden of proof was on the serviceman. The imposition of the burden on the minister in those cases governed by article 4 of the Service Pensions Order,[93] where the claim is brought within seven years of the end of service, so that it is for him to show the absence of any connection between service and the injury, was the most important of the reforms made in that year. However, under article 5 an initial burden of proof is on the applicant, so this provision must be considered separately. One point, however, is common to both articles: it is for the applicant to prove that there is a disablement.[94] It is only after this is shown that the cause of the disablement must be considered. That said, 'in essence the dice are loaded in favour of those who claim pensions'.[95]

i   Claims under article 4

The relevant provisions of article 4 of the Service Pensions Order[96] are:

(2)   ... in no case shall there be an onus on any claimant under this article to prove the fulfilment of the conditions set out in paragraph (1)[97] and the benefit of any reasonable doubt shall be given to the claimant.

(3)   ... where an injury which has led to a member's discharge or death during service was not noted in a medical report made on that member on the commencement of his service, a certificate under paragraph (1) shall be given unless the evidence shows that the conditions set out in that paragraph are not fulfilled.

A   ARTICLE 4(2)

After some vicissitudes of judicial interpretation,[98] it has been held that this article imposes on the Secretary of State the criminal burden of proof – to show beyond reasonable doubt that the injury was not attributable to, nor aggravated by, service in general – rather than the civil burden of proof – to make out the case on the balance of probabilities.[99]

92   [1946] 1 All ER 312.
93   SI 1983/883.
94   *Royston v Minister of Pensions* [1948] 1 All ER 778.
95   *Secretary of State for Social Security v Tait* [1995] COD 440 at 441, per MacPherson J.
96   SI 1983/883.
97   See p 772, above.
98   *Irving v Minister of Pensions* 1945 SC 21; *Starr v Minister of Pensions* [1946] KB 345, [1946] 1 All ER 400; *Rowing v Minister of Pensions* [1946] 1 All ER 664; *Miller v Minister of Pensions* [1947] 2 All ER 372.
99   *Judd v Minister of Pensions* [1966] 2 QB 580.

A perennial problem has been the application of the principles of proof where the aetiology of the disease concerned is unknown, and surmises about the part played by service conditions are necessarily conjectural. During the Second World War the ministry had a list of diseases which, according to the weight of medical opinion, could not be held attributable to war service.[100] It was revised from time to time, and was used as a guide rather than as a determinant of particular applications. Nevertheless, its use was criticised in Parliament, and certainly its employment was outside the legal provisions. The nominated judge has consistently ruled that the evidence must show that it is improbable that the service played any part.[101] In the leading case of *Coe v Minister of Pensions and National Insurance*, Edmund Davies J laid down three rules to assist the Minister and tribunals in determining the issue.[102]

(1) If the medical evidence is that nothing at all is known about the aetiology of the disease, then neither the presumption in article 4(2), nor that in article 4(3), is rebutted.
(2) If there is evidence before the tribunal to the effect that the disease is one which arises and progresses independently of service factors, then the presumption is rebuttable even if the precise origins are not known.
(3) It is not enough for the Ministry to argue that there is no evidence suggesting any connection between the onset of the disease and service conditions.

As attributability is a question of fact, there is nothing to prevent tribunals coming to different conclusions on the attributability to service of a particular disease of unknown origin; but they must apply the correct test with regard to the onus of proof.

B 'THE COMPELLING PRESUMPTION' UNDER ARTICLE 4(3)

The presumption applies whenever the serviceman is discharged, or dies, because of an injury not noted in the medical report which was made on him at the start of his service. Its effect is that the pension will be awarded, unless it is shown beyond reasonable doubt that the injury was not attributable to, or aggravated by, service.[103] The serviceman who is invalided has the advantage that his case is automatically considered by the Department.[104] There is no need for him (or his dependants if he is killed) formally to apply for a pension. In cases under article 4(3) of the Service Pensions Order the nominated judge has held that the tribunal should look at all the facts[105] and it is not bound to accept that the diagnosis which led to the man's discharge was correct.[106]

ii Claims under article 5

Paragraph (2) of article 5 of the Service Pensions Order[107] provides that where a claim is brought, or the death occurs, more than seven years after the end of service, the

---

100 Sir W Wormersley MP, Minister of Pensions, 391 HC Official Report (5th series) cols 796–798.
101 *Smith AS v Minister of Pensions* (1947) 1 WPAR 495; *Donovan v Minister of Pensions* (1947) 1 WPAR 609.
102 [1967] 1 QB 238, [1966] 3 All ER 172.
103 *Birchenough v Minister of Pensions* (1949) 3 WPAR 635.
104 See Ministerial Statement, 401 HC Official Report (5th series) col 970.
105 *Troughear v Minister of Pensions* (1947) 1 WPAR 569.
106 *Hayden v Minister of Pensions* (1947) 1 WPAR 775.
107 SI 1983/883.

disablement or death shall only be certified as due to, or substantially hastened by, service if 'it is shown that the conditions' set out in the article are fulfilled. Paragraph (4) states that where on reliable evidence a reasonable doubt exists whether they are fulfilled, the benefit of that doubt should be given to the claimant. The onus is initially on the claimant to adduce 'reasonable evidence' that a reasonable doubt exists.[108] If such evidence is adduced, the doubt is resolved in favour of the appellant, as is well illustrated by *R v Secretary of State for Social Security, ex p Edwards*.[109]

> A claim for a pension had been rejected in 1957 on the ground that, in the light of the medical opinion then prevailing, the claimant's schizophrenia had not been caused by the ordinary stresses of war service. In 1968 a study was published which challenged that opinion and in 1980 a consensus began to emerge that conditions, like that of the claimant, could be caused by ordinary stress. The Divisional Court held that there must have been a date between 1968 and 1980 when a 'reasonable doubt' existed concerning the causal connection, and that the benefit of the doubt should be given to the claimant from such a date.

F   Serious negligence or misconduct

Article 6 of the Service Pensions Order[110] provides that the Secretary of State may withhold, cancel or reduce an award on the ground that the injury or death 'was caused or contributed to, by the serious negligence or misconduct' of the serviceman. There is surprisingly little case law on this provision, nor is there any indication how the responsible minister has applied his discretionary power. The two leading cases are both decisions of Ormerod J. In the first,[111] 'serious negligence' was defined 'as negligence of a quality that would certainly call for some criminal action if it were done in civil life'. However, shortly afterwards the judge said this remark was only obiter, and should be related to the particular facts of this case, in which the alleged 'serious negligence or misconduct' consisted in the careless riding of a motor-cycle. In the second case,[112] he therefore allowed the minister's appeal and ruled that the applicant was guilty of serious negligence or misconduct in disobeying an order not to handle enemy ammunition.

It is possible to infer from the comparative dearth of reported decisions that article 6 has rarely been invoked; this may be because the view is taken that it should only apply in extreme circumstances. As in the industrial injuries system, it is clear that the common law test of contributory negligence has no place in the war pensions scheme. But the latter differs from industrial injuries in providing that 'serious negligence or misconduct' may as such debar recovery.[113] In both systems wrongful conduct may lead to a ruling that the injury was not due to the employment or service.[114] Outside the situation where there is deliberate disobedience to orders it is hard to think of circumstances where the application of article 6 is necessary or appropriate.

---

108   *Dickinson v Minister of Pensions* [1953] 1 QB 228, [1952] 2 All ER 1031. See also on the civilians' scheme *Cadney v Minister of Pensions and National Insurance* [1965] 3 All ER 809, [1966] 1 WLR 80.
109   [1993] COD 68.
110   SI 1983/883.
111   *Robertson v Minister of Pensions* (1952) 5 WPAR 245 at 266.
112   *Minister of Pensions v Griscti* (1955) 5 WPAR 457.
113   It has been suggested that inclusion of the 'serious negligence or misconduct' rule in the war pensions scheme may reflect the higher value placed on discipline in the armed services: *Brown* n 33, above, p 51.
114   Pp 741–742, above.

Part 3   Awards for disablement

War pensions for disablement are payable only after the termination of service.[115] They consist of a basic award, assessed according to the degree of disablement, and a variety of allowances covering dependants, losses to earning capacity of, and the needs of, the more seriously disabled.

A The basic award

The principles for assessing the basic award are in almost all material respects identical to those adopted by the industrial scheme; these have been fully analysed in chapter 20, above.[116] The degree of disablement is determined by comparing the condition of the disabled person with 'the condition of a normal healthy person of the same age and sex, without taking into account the earning capacity of the member in his disabled condition in his own or any other specific trade or occupation, and without taking into account the effect of any individual factors or extraneous circumstances'.[117] This is then expressed as a percentage, total disablement being represented by 100 per cent. A Schedule to the Service Pensions Order sets out assessments for some particular injuries in the same form as is adopted for the industrial injuries scheme;[118] in other cases, the appropriate percentage is determined by the Secretary of State (in practice a medical officer appointed by him) or on appeal by a pensions appeal tribunal.[119] Where the serviceman's condition has not stabilised, the assessment is made on an interim basis,[120] and may be revised where there is a subsequent change in the degree of disablement due to service.[121] A final assessment may be increased, but not reduced, in similar circumstances.[122]

A pension is payable for degrees of disablement between 20 per cent and 100 per cent inclusive.[123] Awards for disablement of less than 20 per cent are paid as lump sum gratuities.[124] These provisions are different from those now applicable to the industrial injuries scheme under which the gratuity has been abolished and pensions are payable on assessments of 14 per cent and above.[125]

B Increases and additions

A variety of supplementary allowances may be paid with the basic award. Some of these correspond to the allowances which are, or were, available under the industrial injury scheme.

---

115 SI 1983/883, art 8(2). In the case of an officer it is payable when he ceases to be on the Active List.
116 Pp 753–759, above.
117 SI 1983/883, art 9(2)(a).
118 SI 1983/883, Sch 1, Pts III, V. For the special rules relating to hearing loss, see reg 9(2A) and (2B).
119 Pensions Appeal Tribunals Act 1943, Sch, para 3.
120 SI 1983/883, art 9(2)(d).
121 SI 1983/883, art 67.
122 SI 1983/883, art 67.
123 SI 1983/883, art 10.
124 SI 1983/883, art 11.
125 Pp 752–753, above.

i Reduced earning capacity allowances

The first group of supplementary payments is designed to compensate the war pensioner for the reduced opportunities for earning suffered as a result of the disabilities. To some extent, they counterbalance the inflexibility of the basic award, which does not take into account loss of, or reduced, earning capacity.

A   UNEMPLOYABILITY ALLOWANCE

This provides an equivalent to the general social security invalidity pension for a claimant who does not qualify for that benefit but whose disablement is 'so serious as to make him unemployable'.[126] Since 1997 an allowance is not payable to an individual who is aged 65 or over or who has a disablement assessed at less than 60 per cent.[127] The claimant may be deemed unemployable even though he has earnings below a prescribed threshold of therapeutic earnings.[128] If over pensionable age, the claimant must show that, on reaching that age, he was unemployable by reason of pensioned disablement and, in any event, the allowance may not be accumulated with the basic component of a retirement pension.[129] In addition to the personal allowance, increases may also be payable for one adult dependant and any child dependants.[130]

B   INVALIDITY ALLOWANCE

Those entitled to the unemployability allowance may also receive a further payment similar to the age-related addition for incapacity benefit, payable under the general social security scheme.[131] However, the invalidity allowance is paid at three rates, unlike the two rates payable with incapacity benefit.[132]

C   ALLOWANCE FOR LOWERED STANDARD OF OCCUPATION

This allowance is broadly equivalent to the reduced earnings allowance payable under the industrial injuries scheme to those injured before October 1990.[133] Thus the grounds of entitlement are virtually identical,[134] although in the case of a war pensioner the present earning capacity is generally compared with the regular occupation before entry into military service.[135] The allowance, when combined with the pension, may not exceed that payable for 100 per cent disablement,[136] and is in any event subject to a prescribed maximum. In addition, since 1997 the allowance cannot be awarded to a claimant who is aged 65 or over or who has a disablement assessed at less than 40 per cent.[137]

---

126   SI 1983/883, art 18(1).
127   SI 1983/883, art 18(1A); but note the linking rule contained in art 18(1B), inserted by SI 2002/792.
128   SI 1983/883, art 18(2).
129   SI 1983/883, art 18(2A)–(3).
130   SI 1983/883, art 18(5).
131   SI 1983/883, art 19.
132   See the 4th edition of this book, p 167.
133   Pp 762–764, above.
134   SI 1983/883, art 21.
135   SI 1983/883, art 21(2)(c).
136   SI 1983/883, art 21(1).
137   SI 1983/883, art 21(1B).

ii Serious disablement allowances

This second group comprises a variety of further allowances which may be conferred in cases of serious disablement.

A CONSTANT ATTENDANCE ALLOWANCE

This may be awarded in respect of a pensioned disablement, the degree of which is not less than 80 per cent, if it is shown to the Secretary of State's satisfaction that constant attendance is necessary because of the disablement.[138] There are now four rates at which the allowance may be paid under the Service Pensions Order: a part day rate, a full day rate, an intermediate and an exceptional rate.[139] In 2000 there were 4,552 such allowances in payment under the war pensions scheme.[140]

B SEVERE DISABLEMENT OCCUPATIONAL ALLOWANCE

Article 16 of the Service Pensions Order[141] provides that a pensioner in receipt of either the intermediate or exceptional rate of constant attendance allowance may also receive this further allowance, 'for any period during which he is ... ordinarily employed in a gainful occupation'. The object of this provision is to compensate the exceptionally severely disabled pensioner who nevertheless is able to pursue an occupation. There is no parallel benefit in the industrial injuries system. In 2000 there were just 13 such allowances are being paid.[142]

C EXCEPTIONALLY SEVERE DISABLEMENT ALLOWANCE

This was introduced, as was the equivalent provision in the industrial injuries system,[143] following the recommendations of the McCorquodale Committee on Assessment of Disablement.[144] It will be paid when the disablement is, and is in the Secretary of State's view likely to remain, one for which the intermediate or exceptional rate of constant attendance allowance is payable, or would be if the serviceman were not in a hospital or other institution.[145] As with the industrial injuries supplement, entitlement is, therefore, geared to eligibility for the constant attendance allowance; however, it does not appear to depend on the pensioner's receipt of a 100 per cent disablement benefit.[146] In 2000 there were 688 such allowances in payment.[147]

---

138 SI 1983/883, art 14.
139 The part day and intermediate rates were previously paid on a purely discretionary basis: DSS *Proposals for Amendments to War Pensions Legislation* Discussion paper 2 (2000) p 6.
140 *Social Security Statistics 2000* n 5, above, p 207, Table 2.
141 SI 1983/883.
142 *Social Security Statistics 2000* n 5, above.
143 P 761, above.
144 Committee on the Assessment of Disablement (1965, Cmnd 2647) para 9.
145 SI 1983/883, art 15.
146 Cf p 760, above.
147 N 142, above.

D   TREATMENT ALLOWANCES

A pensioner receiving medical treatment, and in consequence sustaining a loss of earnings, may claim an allowance equal to the 100 per cent disablement pension, but in lieu of the pension (at whatever rate) payable to him.[148] 'Treatment' is defined as 'a course of medical, surgical or rehabilitative treatment', which the Secretary of State is satisfied the pensioner should receive.[149] It excludes treatment which involves only an occasional interruption in the pensioner's normal work; in this situation a part-time treatment allowance is payable.[150] The allowance itself may be paid for a discretionary period when treatment as an in-patient at a hospital has been completed but the pensioner is still incapable of work.[151] Finally, the Secretary of State has a broad discretion to indemnify the claimant for 'any necessary expenses in respect of the medical, surgical or rehabilitative treatment ... and of appropriate aids and adaptations for disabled living'. This applies where the expenses wholly or mainly arise as a result of disablement due to service and where there is no equivalent provision on a without charge basis under any other legislative scheme.[152]

E   MOBILITY SUPPLEMENT

The general policy issues regarding assistance for disabled persons with limited mobility have been discussed in chapter 19, above.[153] In 1983 it was decided to introduce a special allowance for war pensioners which might complement that available under general social security provisions.[154] Entitlement is based on proof that the disablement for which the pension is payable satisfies one of four alternative conditions:[155]

(1) it results from amputation of both legs, either through or above the ankle;
    or
(2) it results from another injury which is wholly or mainly responsible for
    (i)   rendering him unable to walk, or
    (ii) restricting his leg movements to such an extent that his ability to walk without severe discomfort is of little or no practical use to him, or
    (iii) restricting by physical pain or breathlessness his ability to walk to such an extent that it is of little or no practical use to him, or
    (iv) rendering the exertion required to walk a danger to his life or a likely cause of serious deterioration in his health;[156]
    or
(3) as a result of being both blind and deaf, he is unable, without the assistance of another person, to walk to any intended or required destination while out of doors;
    or
(4) immediately prior to the date of claim, it had been such as to entitle him to the use of an invalid carriage, a grant towards the cost of running a private car (or analogous payment) or the mobility component of the disability living allowance payable under the social security legislation.

148   SI 1983/883, art 23(1), (2) and (4).
149   SI 1983/883, art 23(6).
150   SI 1983/883, arts 23(6)–(6A) and 25.
151   SI 1983/883, art 24, provided he is not in receipt of an unemployability supplement.
152   SI 1983/883, art 26.
153   Pp 682–684, above.
154   SI 1983/883, art 26A, inserted by SI 1983/1116 and subsequently much amended.
155   SI 1983/883, art 26A(1).
156   These criteria are similar, but not identical, to those used for the higher rate mobility component of disability living allowance: see pp 685–690, above.

New claims since April 1997 are excluded if the level of disablement is assessed at less than 40 per cent. A pensioner may accumulate a mobility supplement with the mobility component payable under the general scheme, but the supplement is not paid during periods when the pensioner makes use of an invalid carriage.[157] Unlike the mobility component of disability living allowance, there is no upper age limit for claiming the mobility supplement.

F   COMFORTS ALLOWANCE

This supplement, like the following two, is without an equivalent in the industrial injuries and general social security schemes. It may be awarded where the claimant is in receipt of a constant attendance allowance, and *either* an unemployability allowance *or* a 100 per cent basic award from multiple injuries which, in the Secretary of State's view, are so serious as to justify the award of a comforts allowance.[158] A lower rate of comforts allowance is payable to a pensioner who is in receipt of either the constant attendance allowance or the unemployability allowance.[159]

G   ALLOWANCE FOR WEAR AND TEAR OF CLOTHING

Since 1997 a single rate for such an allowance has applied, where either the pensioner regularly wears an artificial limb or the Secretary of State is satisfied that the wear and tear on the pensioner's clothing as a result of the disablement is exceptional.[160]

H   AGE ALLOWANCE

A supplement is paid to pensioners over 65 with a disablement assessed at 40 per cent or over.[161] This is paid at four different rates for degrees of pensioned disablement of, respectively, 40 to 50 per cent, 50 to 70 per cent, 70 to 90 per cent, and 90 to 100 per cent.

Part 4   Awards in respect of death

A   General

Awards may be made in respect of a death of a member of the forces which is due to service.[162] As with claims by disabled members of the forces, the conditions of entitlement depend on the date of the material event; in this case, however, they vary according to whether the *death* (rather than the claim in respect of that death) occurs less or more than seven years after the termination of service. If the death occurs not later than seven years after this, the death is to be accepted as due to service, provided

157   SI 1983/883, art 26A(3); but note the exception in art 26A(4).
158   SI 1983/883, art 20(1)(a).
159   SI 1983/883, art 20(1)(b).
160   SI 1983/883, art 17.
161   SI 1983/883, art 22.
162   SI 1983/883, art 27(1).

it is certified that it was 'due to or hastened by *either* an injury attributable to service, *or* the aggravation by service of an injury which existed before or arose during service'.[163] Where the death occurs more than seven years after service, it must be certified that it was due to, or *substantially* hastened by, an injury attributable to, or aggravated by, service.[164]

The general condition that death must be due to service is more restrictive than the approach which obtained in the First World War. Then a widow might receive what was termed a 'modified pension' (half the husband's pension) if he was in receipt of a war pension at the date of his death, even though the death itself was not caused by his war service. This provision seems to have been unique to the British war pensions scheme.[165] Awards of this type were not made after 1921. But there have been three modifications to the general position, though in the first case only for the benefit of widows, and not for all dependants. Since 1966 a temporary allowance has been payable for 26 weeks to the widow, or unmarried dependant who has lived as the wife of a severely disabled pensioner, whatever the cause of his death.[166] It is payable whenever the member of the forces was in receipt of a constant attendance or an unemployability allowance, or in a case where though eligible for the latter, he was in fact in receipt of the lowered standard of occupation allowance.[167] Additional allowances may be paid for this period for the serviceman's children. The second change provides that the death of a member of the forces in receipt of a constant attendance allowance (or one who would have been in receipt of this allowance if he had not been in hospital) is to be treated as due to service for the purposes of awards on his death.[168] The third change, introduced in 1997, provides that the death of a member of the forces in receipt of an unemployability allowance, whose disability was assessed as not less than 80 per cent, is likewise to be treated as due to service.[169]

Finally, in respect of deaths of serving members of the armed forces since April 1997, the Secretary of State 'may defray so much of any reasonable funeral expenses as he may determine'.[170] The only requirements are that the funeral took place in the British Isles or the Republic of Ireland, a claim is made within three months of the funeral, and that death was either due to service or occurred while the member of the services was receiving in-patient treatment in respect of a disablement for which an award had been made.

B Widows, widowers and unmarried dependants

There are two basic rates for war widows' pensions (with small additions reflecting the deceased's rank[171]). The higher rate is paid where the widow is not expected to join or

163 SI 1983/883, art 4(1)(b). See pp 774–778, above, for 'attributable to' and 'aggravated by' service.
164 SI 1983/883, art 5(1)(b).
165 See Comparative Tables of War Pension Rates in Allied Countries and Germany during Great War (1920, Cmd 474).
166 SI 1983/883, art 33.
167 A person in receipt of the allowance for lowered standard of occupation may prefer not to apply for the unemployability allowance because of the loss of concurrent social security benefits.
168 SI 1983/883, art 27(3).
169 SI 1983/883, art 27(4).
170 SI 1983/883, art 42A. Although the components of 'reasonable funeral expenses' have been itemised since 2001 (art 42A(3)), this remains a much broader discretion than exists under the tightly regulated social fund funeral payments scheme: see pp 489–493, above. Thus there is no £600 cap on funeral directors' fees.
171 SI 1983/883, Sch 2, Pt II, Tables 2 and 4. The HC Social Security Committee has expressed its surprise at the 'anachronistic treatment of officers and other ranks' in this respect: *Sixth Report* (1998–99, HC 377) para 26. See further WPA Supplementary memorandum in the Report, WPA 8A, paras 4.1–4.6.

rejoin the labour market: where she is over 40, or is the widow of an officer who served between 1914 and 1921, or is in receipt of an allowance for the child of the deceased, or is incapable of self-support.[172] In other cases, the lower rate is paid.[173] However, the widows of the highest ranking officers (in the army, Lieutenant-Colonel and above) are always paid at the higher rate, whatever their age and family commitments. Presumably it is regarded as inappropriate for such widows to earn their livelihood. A supplementary rent allowance may be paid to a widow provided the household includes a child. A further allowance is paid to some widows at 65, and then at higher levels when they reach 70 and then 80.[174] There is also provision for a supplementary pension where the widow's late husband was discharged from the services before April 1973.[175]

Widow's benefits are effectively suspended on the remarriage or cohabitation of the widow.[176] The Pensions Act 1995 now enables a widow's pension to be restored to a war widow who has remarried but whose subsequent marriage is terminated by death, divorce, annulment or judicial separation.[177] Similarly, the regulations now also provide that where a pension has been withdrawn because of cohabitation, but that relationship subsequently ceases, any claim for the later period 'shall be determined as though the relationship had never existed'.[178] The Secretary of State's power to pay gratuities in connection with remarriage or cohabitation has thus been removed.

Under the original 1983 scheme a widower could only be awarded a pension where he was dependent on a female member of the armed forces, was in pecuniary need and incapable of self-support. The rate was at the discretion of the Secretary of State and subject to a prescribed maximum.[179] In 1984 widowers became eligible for most of the ancillary benefits under the scheme on the same conditions as widows, with the exception of the widow's benefit itself.[180] Widowers thus became eligible for rent, age and dependency allowances. This equality of treatment was also extended to unmarried male partners of women serving in the forces. Thus an unmarried dependant who lived as a spouse of the member of the forces[181] may be awarded a pension on the latter's death, as long as the dependant has in their charge that person's child and is in receipt of a child allowance.[182] The amount of this pension, which has no counterpart elsewhere in the social security system, is at the discretion of the Secretary of State, subject to a prescribed maximum. Such surviving partners are also eligible for age, rent and dependency allowances. They are also subject to the rules relating to remarriage or repartnering. Full equality for widowers, involving entitlement to a widower's pension, finally arrived in April 2002.[183]

---

172   SI 1983/883, art 29(1)(a). Cf the age threshold and reduced rates applied to widow's pensions under the general social security scheme: p 578, above.
173   SI 1983/883, art 29(1)(b).
174   SI 1983/883, art 32.
175   SI 1983/883, art 29(1A).
176   SI 1983/883, art 42(1).
177   Pensions Act 1995, s 168. This reversed the effect of *Ward v Secretary of State for Social Services* [1990] FCR 361, in which it was held that the annulment of a second, voidable, marriage did not revive entitlement to a pension from the first marriage. See SI 1983/883, arts 42, 65A and Sch 3, para 2.
178   SI 1983/883, art 42(1A).
179   SI 1983/883, art 34. In addition, the death had to be due to service after September 1939.
180   SI 1984/1154. The amendments made by SI 1996/2882 to the headings of the relevant regulations appear to be for the purpose of clarification only. For the position as regards army occupational pensions, see *Howard v Ministry of Defence* [1995] ICR 1074. In 1999 there were 54,714 widow's war pensions in payment as against just seven for widowers: 350 HC Official Report (6th series) col 143W.
181   See SI 1983/883, Sch 3, Item 51A.
182   SI 1983/883, art 30.
183   SI 2002/792.

C   Children

Allowances are payable for children of the deceased who are under 16, or, if older, are apprenticed, in full-time education or incapable of self-support by reason of an infirmity which arose before the age of 16.[184] The amount is increased if the child is under 16 and is not under the control of the surviving parent.[185]

D   Parents and other relatives

Allowances for parents were paid as a matter of course for deaths occurring during the First World War. Despite pressure in the House of Commons for equivalent provision,[186] the instruments governing military service during the Second World War and afterwards imposed very restrictive conditions on entitlement to such awards, and the sums payable were frozen at their 1949 level. These allowances, and those payable for other relatives, were abolished in 1993.[187]

Part 5   General miscellaneous provisions

A   Overlap provisions

The object of these provisions is to prevent over-compensation from public funds or from a combination of these funds and a damages award. Article 55 of the Service Pensions Order[188] provides that the Secretary of State may take into account any other compensation which is, or may be, awarded a claimant and may withhold or reduce the pension or gratuity accordingly. Compensation which might have been obtained but for the unreasonable act or omission of the claimant may also be taken into account for this purpose. 'Compensation' means any periodical or lump sum payment in respect of death or disability for which provision is made under any statute, ordinance, regulation or scheme, or any sum recoverable as damages at common law.[189] A similar rule applies to children who are provided for from public funds.[190] Another overlap measure enables a deduction to be made from a pension or gratuity where the claimant is being cared for in an institution which is supported by public funds.[191] The pensions of servicemen entering Chelsea Hospital are terminated, but may be restored on departure from it.[192]

---

184   SI 1983/883, arts 35, 37.
185   SI 1983/883, art 36. The more stringent rules applicable to children of male ex-service members were abolished in 2001.
186   387 HC Official Report (5th series) col 1511; 391 HC Official Report (5th series) col 764; 433 HC Official Report (5th series) col 159.
187   SI 1993/598.
188   SI 1983/883.
189   SI 1983/883, art 55(3).
190   SI 1983/883, art 58. This extends to maintenance which it would be reasonably practicable to obtain from any non-resident parent: art 58(2).
191   SI 1983/883, art 56, as substituted by SI 2001/409.
192   SI 1983/598, art 57.

B Forfeiture and related provisions

The Secretary of State may withhold, or direct the forfeiture of, a pension on the ground that the person to, or in respect of whom, it has been awarded is serving a term of imprisonment or detention after a court order, or is deported from or required to leave the UK.[193] A forfeited pension may be restored upon terms imposed by the Secretary of State.

There are two other provisions analogous to forfeiture rules. Under the first, the Secretary of State may reduce a pension by not more than half, if the claimant refuses unreasonably to undergo medical, surgical or rehabilitative treatment.[194] Secondly, an award may be cancelled if a pension is not drawn for a continuous period of a year or more.[195] In addition, war pensions may not be assigned or made subject to any charge, and do not pass on bankruptcy to the pensioner's trustee.[196]

C Commencing date of awards

The general principle is that awards are payable only from the later of the date of termination of service, the date of death and the date of claim.[197] Thus the date of claim will normally be the earliest date for payment. There is limited provision for back payments in five types of circumstances. First, a claim made within three months of the date of termination of service or the date of death will be treated as effective as from the earlier date.[198] A second exception applies where the Secretary of State is satisfied that a claim would have been made earlier 'but for the fact that [the claimant] was incapable of so doing or of instructing someone to act on his behalf by reason of illness or disability'.[199] In such a case the claim may be backdated for a maximum of three years, assuming good cause is shown throughout. Thirdly, a series of provisions allow backdating, again for up to three years, in cases in which medical evidence has developed,[200] or the decision is revised following a test case, or additional evidence becomes available to the claimant for the first time.[201] Fourthly, if an award is made following a successful appeal to the High Court, payment may be made for a past period representing no more than six years from the date of application for leave to appeal.[202] A similar provision applies where a decision of the Pensions Appeal Tribunal is set aside.[203] Finally, the only situation in which backdating is unlimited is where a

---

193 SI 1983/883, art 62; cf under the Social Security Contributions and Benefits Act 1992, pp 241–243, below.
194 SI 1983/883, art 63.
195 SI 1983/883, art 64.
196 SI 1983/883, art 63A.
197 SI 1983/883, Sch 3, para 1(2). Note that a new Sch 3 was substituted by SI 1997/286, art 10(3) and Sch 7.
198 SI 1983/883, Sch 3, para 1(3) and (4). This appears to be the intent of these provisions but the drafting is less than clear.
199 SI 1983/883, para 5.
200 Otherwise the mere fact that fresh medical evidence casts doubt on an earlier decision does not warrant any further backdating if the original decision was reasonable on the evidence then available: see *R v Secretary of State for Social Security, ex p Muat* (16 February 1999, unreported), CA, decided on the earlier version of Sch 3.
201 SI 1983/883, Sch 3, paras 6–9.
202 SI 1983/883, para 3.
203 SI 1983/883, para 4. These are the only two provisions enabling up to six years' backdating. The previous rule enabling back-dating for a maximum period of six years prior to a successful application for review has been abolished. On the old rule, see the 4th edn of this book, p 370.

claim is not made earlier owing to an administrative error on the part of the authorities. Moreover, it must be the case that the error 'continued to be the dominant cause of the delay' up to the moment the claim was actually made.[204]

Part 6   Other war pension and civilian schemes

There are a number of schemes similar to the war pensions scheme providing pensions for those outside the regular armed forces who are injured in war service. The conditions of entitlement are on the whole more restrictive in these schemes, due to the fact that for members of the forces pensionable disablement can result from any aspect of service, whereas for civilians the disablement must be related specifically to the effects of war. They have been less liberally construed by the nominated judge than the equivalent requirements in the Service Pensions Order.[205] One reason for this was that often the effect of allowing a claim by a merchant mariner or civilian for a pension was to debar him from pursuing his remedy under the workmen's compensation legislation or at common law.[206] In other respects, eg on the questions of causation and burden of proof, authorities on the construction of these schemes have followed cases on the armed forces provisions and in their turn they have been cited in war pensions cases. There are two principal types of scheme, neither of which is of much practical importance now.

A   Schemes for mariners and other seafaring persons

Under the Pensions (Navy, Army, Air Force and Mercantile Marine) Act 1939, as amended by the Pensions (Mercantile Marine) Act 1942, the Secretary of State may make schemes for the benefit of merchant marines and other sea-faring persons who have suffered war injuries, war risk injuries, or have incurred disabilities from certain other specified causes. There are a number of such schemes,[207] administered in much the same way as war pensions; there is a right of appeal from the initial decision to a pensions appeal tribunal.[208] The concepts of 'war injury' and 'war risk injury' have been more narrowly developed than the notion of 'injury attributable to service' in the Service Pensions Order:[209] eg a merchant mariner injured by equipment which was not normally kept on board ship during peace-time was held not to have incurred a 'war risk injury'.[210]

---

204   SI 1983/883, para 10. These various provisions replace the Secretary of State's general discretion under the former rules to direct an earlier payment 'to any particular case or class of case': see the 4th edn of this book, p 370.
205   SI 1983/883.
206   See Tucker J in *Re Kemp* [1945] 1 All ER 571, discussing the Personal Injuries (Emergency Provisions) Act 1939, s 3.
207   Eg the War Pensions (Naval Auxiliary Personnel) Scheme 1946, SI 1964/1985; the War Pensions (Mercantile Marine) Scheme 1964, SI 1964/2058.
208   See the Pensions Appeal Tribunals Act 1943, s 2.
209   SI 1983/883.
210   *Douglass v Minister of Pensions* (1952) 5 WPAR 85; see also *Cook v Minister of Pensions* (1948) 1 WPAR 1223.

B Civilian Injuries' Scheme

Under the Personal Injuries (Civilians) Scheme 1983,[211] made under the Personal Injuries (Emergency Provisions) Act 1939, a civilian may receive a pension for disablement or incapacity due to a 'war injury', or in the case of a civil defence volunteer a 'war service injury', in both cases sustained between 3 September 1939 and 19 March 1946. 'War service injury' and 'war injury' are both defined in the 1939 Act, the latter being accorded the same definition as in the Pensions (Navy, Army, Air Force and Mercantile Marine) Act of 1939. An appeal lies from the Secretary of State's decision to a pensions appeal tribunal.[212] The nominated judge seems to have adopted a restrictive approach when the claimant has suffered mental shock or hysteria at the sight of war damage. The definitions in the 1939 Act of both 'war injury' and 'war service injury' refer to '*physical* injury', and Tucker J has held that this excludes mental shock, in contradistinction to the position under the armed forces' scheme where 'disablement' is defined to mean 'physical or mental injury or damage'.[213] Furthermore, the physical injury must be caused by the discharge of any missile, the use of any weapon or explosive or 'the doing of any other injurious act'. Thus a woman who sustained an injury as a child being carried into an air raid shelter did not suffer a 'war injury' as, although the sirens had been sounded, there was no evidence that the enemy aircraft had actually discharged their bombs.[214] Similarly, an injury suffered by a boy picking up an explosive device left behind after a military training exercise did not constitute a 'war injury'.[215]

A 'war service injury' must have arisen out of and in the course of the performance by the volunteer of civil defence duties and, therefore, an injury sustained while bicycling to his place of duty did not entitle a defence worker to recover a pension.[216] In an important ruling, often followed in cases under the services' scheme, it was held that a 'war injury' was caused by the discharge of a missile, even though it was a few days before it was carelessly picked up and tampered with by a small boy, resulting in injury to the claimant.[217] The discharge of the missile was not too remote for it to be regarded as the cause of the injury and so a pension was awarded.

---

211 SI 1983/686.
212 Pensions Appeal Tribunals Act 1943, s 3.
213 *Young v Minister of Pensions* [1944] 2 All ER 308 ('war injury'); *Ex p Haines* [1945] KB 183, [1945] 1 All ER 349; and *Re Drake* [1945] 1 All ER 576 ('war service injury'): see p 773, above.
214 *Secretary of State for Social Security v Clelland* 1997 SC 40.
215 *Morley v Secretary of State for Social Security* [2001] EWCA Admin 206.
216 *Davis v Minister of Pensions* [1951] 2 All ER 318.
217 *Minister of Pensions v Chennell* [1947] KB 250.

Index